D0182144

THE COMPLETE GUIDE TO
NATIONAL PARKS
OF THE WEST

WELCOME TO THE NATIONAL PARKS OF THE WEST

Awe-inspiring, often remote landscapes and unlimited recreational opportunities make a trip to any western national park a grand adventure. You can raft the raging Colorado River as it pushes through the Grand Canyon, view wildlife in Yosemite while you hike, or watch Yellowstone's Old Faithful geyser in action. Places such as Mesa Verde also preserve the long history of life in the West. Wherever you explore in the parks, these sprawling treasures invite you to discover nature's stunning variety and connect with the great outdoors.

TOP REASONS TO GO

★ **Wildlife:** From bison to bald eagles to bears, the parks shelter amazing species.

★ **Hiking:** Countless scenic trails for all levels inspire and challenge walkers.

★ **Geology:** Unique formations like Oregon's Crater Lake and Utah's Arches astound.

★ **Great Views:** Mountain peaks and scenic overlooks reward climbers and drivers alike.

★ **History:** Monuments and outposts trace the settling of the former Wild West.

★ **Luxury Lodges:** Famous hotels pair old-school grandeur with splendid surroundings.

Fodor's THE COMPLETE GUIDE TO NATIONAL PARKS OF THE WEST

Publisher: Amanda D'Acierno, *Senior Vice President*

Editorial: Arabella Bowen, *Editor in Chief*; Linda Cabasin, *Editorial Director*

Design: Tina Malaney, *Associate Art Director*; Chie Ushio, *Senior Designer*; Erica Cuoco, *Production Designer*

Photography: Jennifer Arnow, *Senior Photo Editor*; Mary Robnett, *Photo Researcher*

Production: Linda Schmidt, *Managing Editor*; Evangelos Vasilakis, *Associate Managing Editor*; Angela L. McLean, *Senior Production Manager*

Maps: Rebecca Baer, *Senior Map Editor*; Mark Stroud (Moon Street Cartography), *Cartographers*

Sales: Jacqueline Lebow, *Sales Director*

Marketing & Publicity: Heather Dalton, *Marketing Director*; Katherine Punia, *Publicity Director*

Business & Operations: Susan Livingston, *Vice President, Strategic Business Planning*; Sue Daulton, *Vice President, Operations*

Fodors.com: Megan Bell, *Executive Director, Revenue & Business Development*; Yasmin Marinaro, *Senior Director, Marketing & Partnerships*

Copyright © 2016 by Fodor's Travel, a division of Penguin Random House LLC

Writers: Sarah Amandolare, Shelley Arenas, Lea Brayton, Whitney Bryen, Lisa Church, Andrew Collins, Martha Connors, Cheryl Crabtree, Lindsey Galloway, Thomas D. Griffith, Melynda Harrison, Aimee Heckel, Deb Hopewell, Kellee Katagi, Mara Levin, Debbie Olsen, Marty Racine, Elise Riley, Stina Sieg, Mike Weatherford

Editors: Luke Epplin, Carol Clurman, Daniel Mangin, Teddy Minford

Production Editor: Carolyn Roth

5th Edition

ISBN 978-1-101-87975-7

ISSN 1941-5419

SPECIAL SALES

This book is available at special discounts for bulk purchases for sales promotions or premiums. For more information, e-mail specialmarkets@penguinrandomhouse.com.

PRINTED IN THE UNITED STATES OF AMERICA

10 9 8 7 6 5 4 3 2 1

CONTENTS

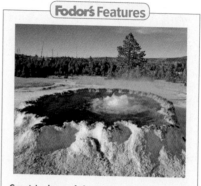

MAPS

ABOUT THIS GUIDE

Fodor's Recommendations

Everything in this guide is worth doing—we don't cover what isn't—but exceptional sights, hotels, and restaurants are recognized with additional accolades. **Fodor'sChoice★** indicates our top recommendations. Care to nominate a new place? Visit ⊕ *Fodors.com/contact-us*.

Trip Costs

Hotel and restaurant price categories from $ to $$$$ are noted alongside each recommendation. For hotels, we include the lowest cost of a standard double room in high season. For restaurants, we cite the average price of a main course at dinner, of if dinner isn't served, at lunch. For attractions, we always give standard adult admission fees; reductions are usually available for children, students, and senior citizens.

Restaurants

Unless we state otherwise, restaurants are open for lunch and dinner daily. We mention dress code only when there's a specific requirement and reservations only when they're essential or not accepted.

Hotels

Our local writers vet every hotel to recommend the best overnights in each price category, from budget to expensive. Unless

Top Picks	Hotels &
★ **Fodor'sChoice**	**Restaurants**
	⌨ Hotel
Listings	↗ Number of
⊠ Address	rooms
⊠ Branch address	⦿ Meal plans
☎ Telephone	✕ Restaurant
🖷 Fax	⟨ Reservations
⊕ Website	⌂ Dress code
✉ E-mail	⊟ No credit cards
🖃 Admission fee	$ Price
⊙ Open/closed	
times	**Other**
Ⓜ Subway	⇨ See also
⊹ Directions or	☞ Take note
Map coordinates	⅄ Golf facilities

otherwise specified, you can expect private bath, phone, and TV in your room. **For expanded hotel reviews, visit Fodors.com.**

Credit Cards

The hotels and restaurants in this guide typically accept credit cards. If not, we'll say so.

EUGENE FODOR

Hungarian-born Eugene Fodor (1905–91) began his travel career as an interpreter on a French cruise ship. The experience inspired him to write *On the Continent* (1936), the first guidebook to receive annual updates and discuss a country's way of life as well as its sights. Fodor later joined the U.S. Army and worked for the OSS in World War II. After the war, he kept up his intelligence work while expanding his guidebook series. During the Cold War, many guides were written by fellow agents who understood the value of insider information. Today's guides continue Fodor's legacy by providing travelers with timely coverage, insider tips, and cultural context.

EXPERIENCE THE NATIONAL PARKS OF THE WEST

NATIONAL PARK SERVICE THEN AND NOW

Go West, Young Man

A romantic image of the West has gripped the American psyche since the nation's birth. As the frontier shifted from the Ohio River Valley to the Great Plains to the Rocky Mountains and finally to the Pacific coast, the land just over the horizon promised freedom, open space, self-sufficiency, and adventure. Manifest Destiny, gold rushes, and the Homestead Act of 1862—which offered 160-acre parcels of land to anyone 21 years or older with $18—spurred settlers, prospectors, soldiers, and laborers to tame the American West.

Vocal Pioneers

During this unprecedented land grab, interest in preserving scenic Western lands and archaeological sites emerged, along with a national sense of responsibility for the wilderness. While exploring the Dakotas in 1832, painter George Catlin noted the potential for loss of wildlife and wilderness. He wrote that they could be preserved "by some great protecting policy of government . . . in a magnificent park."

The tipping point came three decades later. In 1864, in the midst of the Civil War, President Lincoln set aside Yosemite Valley and the Mariposa Grove of giant sequoias as a public trust to preserve the land for future generations. This revolutionary federal preservation concept was just the beginning. When a handful of would-be entrepreneurs explored Yellowstone in 1870, dreaming up the possibilities for development of this fantastic land they'd found, a lawyer, Cornelius Hedges, made the bold suggestion that they preserve this geologically astounding land rather than capitalize on it.

Whatever persuasive prose Hedges used is not certain, but persuade them he did.

A year later, one of these explorers was in the House of Representatives promoting the idea of preserving Yellowstone as a natural place. Also lobbying for the plan were artist Thomas Moran, photographer William Henry Jackson, and U.S. Geological Survey Director Ferdinand Hayden, who'd been appointed by Congress to lead an expedition to Yellowstone to validate the rumors of its otherworldly features. Congress was more than convinced of its merits (and the need to preserve them), and in early 1872, President Ulysses S. Grant signed into law the bill creating Yellowstone National Park.

The 1890s saw the creation of several more national parks, as well as the Forest Reserve Act of 1891, which led to the establishment of our first national forests. In 1906, the Antiquities Act passed, which allowed presidents to name national monuments. That same year, President Theodore Roosevelt established Devils Tower as the first such site, making Wyoming the home of both the first national park and first national monument.

Pioneering conservationists like Robert Underwood Johnson and John Muir advocated for further preservation of Western treasures. Muir, who founded the Sierra Club in 1892 and is often called the father of the National Park System, greatly influenced Theodore Roosevelt, who went on to establish five national parks.

The Birth of the National Park System

By 1916, the Interior Department was handling 14 national parks. In order to streamline the management of the national parks and monuments, President Woodrow Wilson approved legislation creating the National Park Service, or NPS, within the Department of the

Interior. The mission of the new agency was "to conserve the scenery and the natural and historic objects and the wildlife therein and to provide for the enjoyment of the same in such manner and by such means as will leave them unimpaired for the enjoyment of future generations."

While Washington made these lands protected, railroads made them accessible. Thousands traveled west to such national parks as Grand Canyon, Glacier, Yosemite Valley, and Crater Lake, and stayed in the extravagant lodges constructed there by the railroad companies.

Growing Pains
The parks were initially established to ensure land preservation and visitor enjoyment, but by 1932, the park concept had expanded to include educational components with the formation of the NPS's Naturalist Division. The naturalists were assigned to interpret park features to the public through educational outreaches. The park system had also begun to rethink its wildlife management practices.

Between 1933 and 1942, thousands of hardy workers came to the nation's parks and forests through the Civilian Conservation Corps (CCC), part of President Franklin Delano Roosevelt's Works Progress Administration, established during the Great Depression. A total of 70 work camps were set up within the national parks.

As the country's population continued to grow, and society learned more about the environment and the effects of pollution and increasing demands on natural resources, there was a need to take additional steps to maintain pristine wilderness and historic areas. Congress addressed this in the 1960s and early '70s with a host of legislative measures: the Clean Air Act (1963), Wilderness Act (1964), National Historic Preservation Act (1966), Wild and Scenic Rivers Act (1968), National Environmental Policy Act (1969), and the Endangered Species Act (1973).

The NPS Today
The National Park Service now manages more than 400 natural, cultural, and recreational sites on some 84 million acres. These sites include national parks as well as monuments, memorials, historic parks, and national preserves. The NPS defines these lands as follows:

National Park: A natural place, generally large in size, that possesses an array of attributes, such as providing an outstanding example of a particular type of resource and great opportunities for public use and enjoyment (or for scientific study). It may also be historically significant. National parks are protected from hunting, mining, logging, and other consumptive activities.

National Historic Park: A historic site that extends beyond single properties.

National Historic Site: Usually containing a single historic feature directly associated with its subject. Derived from the Historic Sites Act of 1935, a number of historic sites were established by secretaries of the Interior, but most have been authorized by acts of Congress. They appear on the National Register of Historic Places.

National Memorial: A site that is commemorative of a historic person or episode.

National Monument: A landmark, structure, or other object of historic or scientific interest situated on lands owned or controlled by the government.

National Preserve: An area having characteristics associated with national parks, but in which oil and gas exploration and extraction, hunting, and trapping are allowed. Many existing national preserves, without sport hunting, would qualify for national park designation.

National Recreation Area: Places with this designation include reservoirs used for water-based activities and urban parks that combine outdoor recreation with the preservation of significant historic resources and important natural areas.

The NPS Centennial

In 2016, the National Park Service celebrates its 100th anniversary, a defining moment for both the NPS and the millions of people who have visited the parks and enjoyed their natural, historical, and cultural splendor. The NPS is celebrating its centennial with a renewed mission to maintain and promote the parks even while it helps to support environmental recovery and sustainability efforts, foster education and understanding, build local economies, and boost public involvement and attendance so that the parks continue into the next century and beyond.

What does NPS have planned for the next 100 years? Its Centennial 2016 logo states their main goal in a nutshell: "Connect with and create the next generation of park visitors, supporters, and advocates." A cornerstone of centennial initiatives is the Find Your Park program (⊕ *www.findyourpark.com*). NPS has partnered with the National Parks Foundation to offer this extensive public awareness and education effort to help people connect with parks and public lands using social media and other means. It highlights historical, cultural, and urban parks as well as the better-known NPS properties, such as Yellowstone and Yosemite; it also helps increase awareness of the NPS and its work in recreation, conservation, and historical preservation.

NPS is also engaging the next generation of park stewards through various programs. For example, Every Kid in a Park (⊕ *www.everykidinapark.gov*) enables fourth graders nationwide to obtain a pass that provides access to all federally managed lands and water and public lands. The pass is valid for the school year and grants free entry for the student and three accompanying adults (or an entire

NATIONAL PARKS TIMELINE

1872	Yellowstone National Park becomes the world's first national park.
1890	Sequoia, Yosemite, and General Grant (later part of Sequoia and Kings Canyon) become national parks.
1902	President Theodore Roosevelt establishes the first of his five parks, Crater Lake.
1903	Theodore Roosevelt makes Wind Cave the country's seventh national park, and the first dedicated to preserving a cave.
1906	Congress designates Mesa Verde as a national park. It is the first cultural park in the system.
1916	President Woodrow Wilson signs the Organic Act, creating the National Park Service.
1919	The Grand Canyon goes from a national monument to a national park.

car for drive-in parks). The NPS has also partnered with the Student Conservation Association and other groups to introduce more young people to service in national parks and NPS programs.

Also on the Centennial agenda are activities and celebrations at the individual parks throughout 2016. Expect an array of events during the month of August, especially on and around NPS's official birthday, August 25th. Yellowstone, for example, will rededicate its iconic Roosevelt Arch that day. In September 2016, the World Conservation Congress will convene in Hawaii in honor of the NPS Centennial. This is the first time the United States has hosted this event; it's a testament to the NPS's commitment to foster sustainability and reduce damaging environmental impacts.

For more information on the centennial events at each park, go to ⊕ *www. findyourpark.org.*

Hot Issues

More than a century ago, conservationists were instrumental in establishing the national parks as preserved areas; their efforts continue today, as these set-aside areas face a host of challenges, including overcrowding, noise and light pollution, and wildlife management. And, of course, funding is always a concern.

Here are a few of the issues facing the National Park Service today:

Attendance. Although the parks must compete for our attention with an ever-expanding range of entertainment options, attendance has been holding steady for the past several years, with a record 293 million recreational visits in 2014. A major challenge for the coming century is convincing an increasingly busy, plugged-in population to visit the wilderness. Paradoxically, the most popular parks are facing the opposite problem: making sure huge seasonal crowds don't negatively impact the parks.

Funding. Tight budgets are a concern for the NPS, and the service has had to be savvy with its spending and consider alternative revenue sources, including corporate sponsorships. Recently, the NPS has been able to more than double the federal dollars it received through matching donations made by private companies and individuals.

1933	Franklin Delano Roosevelt develops the Civilian Conservation Corps, which plants close to three billion trees in nine years.
1951	The National Park Service adopts its official emblem: the outline of an arrowhead surrounding a mountain, a sequoia tree, a river, and a bison. The arrowhead represents historical and archaeological values, the tree and bison represent vegetation and wildlife, and the mountains and water represent scenic and recreational values.

1967	Congress establishes the National Park Foundation as a separate, fund-raising arm for the parks.
1984	The fossils of one of the oldest dinosaurs ever unearthed, *Chindesaurus bryansmalli* (nicknamed "Gertie"), are found in Petrified Forest National Park.
1987	Annual recreational visitors to the parks hits an all-time high: 287,244,998.
1988	Devastating fires rage through Yellowstone National Park, spreading to 793,000 of the park's 2.2 million acres.

Migration Patterns. Managing wildlife is an increasingly complex responsibility. The parks' animal inhabitants don't recognize political boundaries: for example, elk stray into unprotected areas around Rocky Mountain National Park, where they wreak havoc on the native vegetation, and wolves hunt beyond the confines of Yellowstone, sometimes killing livestock on nearby ranches.

Pollution. Standing in a pristine natural paradise like Yellowstone or the Grand Canyon, you're not likely to think about pollution—but the problem encompasses more than just visible smog. As development encroaches on the parks, it brings the bright lights of the city one step closer to the wilderness. The resulting light pollution causes overly illuminated skies with fewer visible stars, which can be disappointing for visitors and deadly for disoriented birds and other animals.

Meanwhile, noise pollution, much of it from aircraft, threatens to break the silence that many visitors seek in the parks. This is especially troublesome at the Grand Canyon. There are also other factors putting the parks' air, water, and land at risk. High ozone levels in Sequoia and Kings Canyon National Park, for example, can cause respiratory irritation and are damaging the native Jeffrey pines.

Conservation Efforts

The NPS is continuing its efforts to sustain and recover in-park populations of threatened and endangered plant and animal species. More than 200 of the 408 NPS units (including national parks, national monuments, and other designated areas) are home to at least one endangered species. The system as a whole contains more than 400 threatened and endangered species.

The NPS has had several successes in recent years, including the dramatic recovery of endangered island foxes within the Channel Islands National Park. There are now more than 1,800 foxes on the islands, up from fewer than 500 animals in 1999, and the population is on the road to recovery. Meanwhile, a project in Olympic National Park has reintroduced endangered fishers—rare, reclusive mammals related to minks and otters—which were once plentiful in the area but had disappeared due to habitat loss and over-trapping.

1994	Death Valley and Joshua Tree National Monuments become national parks.
2001	The National Parks Legacy Project is established to provide funds to restore and improve park facilities and landscapes, increase park trails, and uphold existing initiatives to protect parkland from fires as well as mining and drilling operatives.
2007	Congress is presented with a record $2.4-billion budget for the parks, plus a $100-million donation match program as part of the Centennial Initiative.
2009	President Barack Obama signs the American Recovery and Reinvestment Act (ARRA), which allocates $3 billion to the Interior Department, including $750 million to restore and protect America's national parks.

Acknowledgments: We thank the Department of the Interior for their helpful resources, including *A Brief History of the National Park Service.*

Resources

National Park Foundation. This is the nonprofit, fundraising arm of the National Park Service, administering grants and programs designed to support the parks. ✉ *1110 Vermont Avenue NW, Ste. 200, Washington* ☎ *202/796–2509* ⊕ *www. nationalparks.org.*

National Park Service (*NPS*). A bureau within the Department of the Interior, the NPS manages 408 sites, including the national parks, as well as battlefields, monuments, seashores, and other important areas. ☎ *202/208–3818* ⊕ *www.nps.gov.*

National Park System: Map and Guide. This two-part map and guide, published by the National Park Service, includes a full-color map and listing of activities at more than 300 parks and other federal lands. You can get it free online (PDF) from the Federal Citizen Information Center (FCIC) website. ☎ *719/295–2675* ⊕ *publications.usa.gov/USAPubs.*

National Parks Conservation Association. The National Parks Conservation Association is a nonpartisan advocacy group that raises awareness of the parks and the issues that face them through public, media, and government education. ✉ *777 6th St. NW, Ste. 700, Washington* ☎ *800/628–7275* ⊕ *www.npca.org.*

Parks Canada. The Canadian equivalent of the U.S. National Park Service, this agency runs Canada's national parks, historic sites, and marine conservation areas. ☎ *888/773–8888, 819/420–9486* ⊕ *www. pc.gc.ca.*

2010	The Department of the Interior spends almost $270 million to enhance the infrastructure, facilities, and overall user experience within the National Parks and Wildlife Refuges under the AARA. At the one-year mark, the DOI had completed more than 80 projects within the NPS and was continuing work on another 243.
2011	The NPS announces its new Call to Action program, aimed at improving the parks without requiring additional federal funding.
2013	Pinnacles National Monument in California gains national park designation, becoming the newest national park.
2016	The National Park Service celebrates its 100-year anniversary.

WILDLIFE IN THE PARKS

(A) Bats: Caves within the national parks teem with bats, the only mammals that can fly. Large bat colonies can be observed whirling and flying out of caves at dusk for feeding time, returning around sunrise. You also can observe bats when they roost in snags—dead, hollowed-out trees left standing in the forest after lightning strikes and wildfires.

(B) Bighorn Sheep: Clambering along rocky ledges, bighorn sheep fascinate with their ability to travel so easily where the rest of us can't. In winter the docile herd animals descend to lower elevations. Like their fellow park residents, the mule deer and elk, bighorns rut in autumn, when antlered males fight each other dramatically over mates. Rams have heavy, curled horns, while ewes' horns are short and slightly bent. From afar it's easy to spot both sexes' white rumps, which stand out brightly against their brown coats.

(C) Bison: The nappy, grouchy bison, also known as the American buffalo, may not be the Western frontier's most charismatic ungulate, but it's certainly the most iconic. Yellowstone is the only place in the country where bison have lived continuously since prehistoric times (between 2,300 and 4,500 animals make up the park's two herds), though you also can see the large creatures in other national parks. A bison can reach 6 feet at the shoulder, and males can weigh a ton (females typically weigh about 1,000 pounds). Bulls and cows alike sport short, curved horns, which they'll use to gore predators (or tourists who invade their space).

(D) Black Bear: These excellent sniffers can smell your freeze-dried dinner from a mile away. Though they naturally forage for acorns and berries, black bears are omnivores and can be aggressive, especially if they're protecting their cubs. The animals measure about 3 feet at the shoulder and weigh up to 300 pounds, depending on their age and sex. They hibernate for about five months in the winter, and at lower elevations that see more moderate winters they may not sleep much at all. Most have inky black fur, but a brown or cinnamon color is not uncommon, especially in the western United States.

(E) Bobcat: Bobcats are solitary, elusive cats with reddish-brown coats, streaked with black or dark brown. They have prominent, pointed ears with a tuft of black hair at the tip and typically weigh between 16 and 30 pounds.

(F) Coyote: Coyotes are highly adaptable, intelligent animals (their name is derived from the Aztec word meaning "trickster") whose indiscriminate diets include carrion, small mammals, insects, and grasses. About the size of a mid-size dog, weighing between 25 and 35 pounds (much less than a wolf), the gray-tan canines thrive throughout the western United States.

They travel most often alone or in pairs, but occasionally form small packs for hunting. Although coyotes generally pose little threat to humans, you should never feed or approach one.

(G) Eagles: With a wingspan of 6 to 8 feet, bald eagles are primarily fish eaters, but they will also take birds or small mammals when the opportunity presents itself. Bald eagles' unmistakable white heads distinguish them from golden eagles, which nest on cliffs and prey on small mammals and birds. With a wingspan of up to 7½ feet, the adult golden eagle has plumage that is entirely dark, except for a golden head.

(H) Elk: A bull's antlers can weigh 40 pounds and, in summer, shed a soft fur known as antler velvet. Elk congregate where forest meets meadows, summering at high elevations before migrating lower in winter. In September and October, bulls attract a "harem" of mating partners by bugling, a loud and surreal whistling.

(I) Gray Wolf: These impressive canines, listed as threatened or endangered in parts of the United States, form family packs, which may range from a few animals to more than 30. They communicate with each other through body language, barks, and howls. Gray wolves tend to be 70 to 120 pounds, much larger than coyotes.

(J) Grizzly Bear: These creatures both fascinate and frighten. A mature male grizzly can weigh 700 pounds and stand about 3½ feet at the shoulder (or reach a height of 8 feet when standing up on its hind legs). Whitish shoulder hairs give grizzlies their name and distinguish them from black bears, as do a distinctive muscle mass on their back and the convex curve of their snout. Grizzlies are also much larger and less common than black bears.

(K) Jackrabbit: Unmistakable for its mule-like ears and swift, bounding gait, the jackrabbit can induce a brief case of heart failure if you happen upon one and startle it into an explosive escape.

(L) Marmot: A few species of marmot like to live high up among granite rock piles of talus slopes and along riverbanks, so if you see them, it's likely to be along high-country trails. The rocky strongholds help protect these furry ground squirrels—one of the largest rodents in North America—from such natural predators as eagles and hawks.

(M) Moose: Feeding on fir, willows, and aspens, the moose is the largest member of the deer family: the largest bulls stand 7 feet tall at the shoulders and weigh up to 1,600 pounds. The moose's distinctive characteristics include its antlers, which lie flat like palmate satellite dishes, and its pendulous (and prehensile) upper lip. The peak of breeding occurs in late September. Females give birth to calves in late May and early June; twins are the norm.

(N) Mountain Goat: Not really goats at all (they're actually related to antelope), these woolly mountaineers live in high elevations throughout the northwestern United States.

(O) Mountain Lion: Although mountain lions live throughout the American West (their range runs from northern Canada through the South American Andes), chances are you won't see them at most of the parks due to their elusive nature. Also called cougars, these enormous carnivores can be 8 feet long and weigh up to 200 pounds. They're capable of taking down a mule deer or elk.

(P) Mule Deer: Often seen grazing in meadows and forests are mule deer, with their black-tipped tails and distinctive mulelike ears. Mule deer can run like other deer or do what's known as stotting—springing gazelle-like with all four feet leaving the ground at once—which allows them to change direction instantly and gives them an advantage over predators.

(Q) Prairie Dog: Called "petit chien" (little dog) by French explorers, the prairie dog is a prolific member of the squirrel family. They get their name from the way they communicate: It sounds like a bark.

Pronghorn: Pronghorns are North America's only native hooved mammals and are one of the fastest land animals in the world, capable of speeds of up to 70 mph. Often called "antelopes," even though they're technically a different species, pronghorns can be spotted in open grassland areas.

Rattlesnake: About a dozen species of rattlesnake live in the American West, where in cooler weather they enjoy sunning on rocks or coiling in other open spaces. A snake will typically strike only when it senses a threat, but when it does bite, it can deliver a lethal dose of venom.

FIELD GUIDE: GEOLOGY AND TERRAIN

Arches and Bridges

(A) An arch is a window in a rock wall that typically forms through erosion, when wind and/or water wear away the rock face to create a hole that extends all the way through the rock. A natural bridge is a type of arch that was created by rushing water. Together, the two types of forms are called windows.

Buttes and Spires

(B) A butte is an isolated hill with very steep sides and a flat top (it's defined as a hill that's higher than it is wide). Buttes are formed in sedimentary (layered) rock by erosion, when wind or water wear away softer layers to leave a section of harder rock behind. As a butte erodes, it may become one or more spires, which look like giant stone columns (with a uniform thickness and smooth profile that tapers slightly at the top).

Canyons

(C) A canyon, also known as a gorge, forms when water (usually a river or glacier) erodes soft layers of Earth's crust. The hardness of the rock determines the shape of the canyon: a narrow, or slot, canyon generally results when the rock is the same composition all the way down and water runs through the crack. A stepped canyon, such as the Grand Canyon, forms when alternating soft and hard layers are eroded by wind and water, with a river cutting a groove at the bottom.

Caves

Caves—or caverns—are natural underground chambers that give you an opportunity to descend below Earth's surface and learn about the forces of heat and water upon rocks and minerals.

Craters and Calderas

(D) A crater is a bowl-shape depression that's left behind when a volcano erupts. A caldera (Spanish for "cooking pot" or "cauldron") is essentially a big, sunken crater in which the volcano's inner magma chamber has also collapsed.

Desert Pavement

(E) High winds can scour away sand, silt, and other small particles of soil, leaving behind a densely packed layer of coarse pebbles and gravel known as desert pavement. This surface acts as a protective crust and is fragile, so you shouldn't walk on it.

Desert Varnish

(F) This reddish-brown or black coating, sometimes called rock varnish, seems to drip down arid canyon walls as if from a spilled can of paint. Windblown dust or rain containing iron and manganese, along with microorganisms living on the rock's surface, create the color. Ancestral Puebloans and other ancient American Indians scratched drawings, called petroglyphs, into it.

Erosion and Weathering

(G) The Earth's surface is mechanically worn away by water, ice, or wind, which use abrasive elements like sand or small rocks to remove the material. Weathering often accompanies and assists erosion by using chemical action (from things like water, air, plants, and bacteria) and temperature changes (freeze/thaw cycles).

Fault Zones

(H) Shifting underground landmasses such as those of California's famous San Andreas Fault have helped create many of the dramatic elevations in the parks, and this same geologic upheaval has shifted and cracked underground rocks, damming up the flow of groundwater and forcing it to the surface, making precious moisture available to wildlife and plants.

Geothermal Features

(I) Hissing geysers, burbling mud pots, and steaming hot springs have fascinated travelers ever since mountain man John Coulter described them to an unbelieving public in 1810. Today, these "freaks of a fiery nature," as Rudyard Kipling described them, are created when superheated water rises to Earth's surface from a magma chamber below. In the case of geysers, the water is trapped under the surface until the pressure is so great that it bursts through. Mud pots, also known as paint pots, are a combination of hot water, hydrogen sulfide gas, and dissolved volcanic rock. The mixture looks like a hot, smelly, burping pudding.

Glaciers and Glacial Features

(J) Heavy snow compacted by centuries of pressure forms the slow-moving river of ice known as a glacier. Although most of the glaciers of North America have retreated, you can still see them in some of the Western parks.

Mesas and Cuestas

(K) A mesa ("table" in Spanish) is an isolated hill with a smooth, flat top and steeply sloping sides. Its topmost layer is comprised of rock that is much harder than the rocks below, which protects the lower layers from erosion. A cuesta is essentially a mesa that dips slightly to one side. A single mesa or cuesta may cover hundreds of square miles.

Monument

(L) This general term applies to two distinct geologic formations: those that are much taller than they are wide, and those that resemble man-made structures.

Peaks

A peak is what most people picture when they think "mountain"—a horn-shape formation created by ancient ice that juts up into the sky, generally surrounded by smaller peaks and gentler foothills.

Playas
(M) Shallow lake beds known as playas ("beaches" in Spanish) commonly lie in the low points of arid Southwestern valleys. These sedimentary basins often fill with rainwater, then dry again as the water evaporates.

Spheroidal Weathering
This unique type of chemical weathering is similar to exfoliation. It typically affects sandstone and intrusive igneous rock (the kind that's created when superheated molten rock seeps up from beneath Earth's crust to reach the surface).

Volcanoes and Volcanism
(N) Volcanoes are openings in Earth's crust where magma reaches the surface. Volcanic activity, or volcanism, can create many geologic formations beyond the lava-spewing, cone-shape mountains most of us think of as volcanoes. For example, volcanic intrusions, which are formed where magma pushes up between sections of existing rock, can create formations such as batholiths (large rounded domes), dikes and sills (banded, sheetlike formations), and laccoliths (domes created when magma pushes up on existing rock layers instead of erupting out). Geothermal features occur when water enters the picture.

THE PRESIDENTS ROOSEVELT

Without Theodore Roosevelt and Franklin Delano Roosevelt, many of America's natural treasures would have ceased to exist. A generation apart, the two men were moved by the dire state of their nation's wilderness areas to make monumental changes in how the country preserved its outdoor wonders.

For Theodore, the impetus was the disappearance of the bison and rampant misuse of the land in the western United States. For Franklin, it was the needs of an unemployed population—and the need to save the country's ravaged forestland. Both men, through sheer force of will, drove their ideals into law.

Theodore, who believed America had an almost divine responsibility for proper stewardship of its ample resources, brought his conservationist leanings to the presidency in 1901. As part of his revolutionary administration, he established the U.S. Forest Service, along with 150 national forests, the first national wildlife refuge, 51 bird preserves, four game preserves, five national parks, and 18 national monuments, including four that became national parks—Grand Canyon, Petrified Forest, Lassen Peak, and Mount Olympus (now Olympic). His efforts accounted for more than half the lands that would be managed by the National Park Service when it was created in 1916—seven years after his presidency ended.

Franklin, who believed the president was called to lead with character and morality (and to rescue the country from the throes of the Great Depression), created millions of jobs on public works projects—including many in the national parks. Almost immediately after his inauguration in 1933, he developed the Civilian Conservation Corps. Over nine years,

> ## DYNAMIC DUO
>
> **THEODORE ROOSEVELT**
> **Lifespan:** 1858–1919
>
> **Regulated:** Railroads
>
> **Unique qualities:** Youngest president (age 42); won Nobel Peace Prize (for mediating the Russo-Japanese War)
>
> **FRANKLIN DELANO ROOSEVELT**
> **Lifespan:** 1882–1945
>
> **Regulated:** Wall Street
>
> **Unique qualities:** Only president with polio; only four-term president; established the WPA (Works Progress Administration)

it employed 5% of American males and planted about 3 billion trees. The corps was instrumental in suppressing forest fires, clearing campgrounds, constructing roads and trails, controlling floods and soil erosion, and eradicating undesirable plants. The CCC also enabled the NPS to improve existing public lands, establish new national parks, and guide the development of a system of state parks. Seven states gained their first state parks through the CCC's efforts, and at the project's end in 1942, a total of 711 state parks had been established. Additionally, Franklin's Hyde Park, New York, home was added to the NPS holdings as a National Historic Site in 1946.

Though the inspiration for each differed, their contributions were similar, as are their legacies. They stand as giants among American presidents and as standard-bearers for government-aided conservation.

GREAT LODGES
OF THE NATIONAL PARKS

"IF YOU BUILD IT, THEY WILL COME" could apply to the railroad barons who laid track in the early 1900s to lure wealthy Easterners westward. But these scrappy companies took the declaration an inspired step further by building luxury hotels at the end of the line.

In 1901 the Atchison, Topeka, and Santa Fe Railway finished a 65-mile railroad spur from Williams, Arizona, to the South Rim of the Grand Canyon, and soon after built the spectacular Arizona lodge El Tovar. Union Pacific helped finance lodges at Bryce and Zion, Northern Pacific was behind the hotels in Yellowstone, and the Great Northern Railway built Glacier Park Lodge, and many other Glacier hotels. Today, the rails don't drive tourism to the parks all that much. But the lodges still do. And you don't have to be wealthy to stay in one.

What makes them great? Unlike previous wilderness accommodations, which were built like city hotels so guests would feel safe, these new lodges incorporated materials from the environment like the lodgepole pines and Rhyolite stone used in building Old Faithful Inn. As long as these nature-inspired structures had creature comforts—which then, and in some cases now, doesn't include in-room televisions—architects felt guests would be happy.

> *Architects felt guests would be happy as long as the lodges had creature comforts.*

Above: The historic El Tovar Hotel sits at the edge of the Grand Canyon's South Rim.

TOP LODGES

EL TOVAR, GRAND CANYON

"In the Grand Canyon, Arizona has a natural wonder, which, so far as I know, is in kind unparalleled throughout the rest of the world," said Teddy Roosevelt in 1903, speaking from the area where the El Tovar would open two years later. "What you can do is to keep it for your children, your children's children, and for all who come after you, as one of the great sights which every American if he can travel at all should see."

Set atop the South Rim of the Grand Canyon, El Tovar so blends into the landscape, with its stone foundation and rugged beams, that it looks almost like another tier of the multilayered, multihued canyon. With the elegance of a European villa and warm atmosphere of a rustic log cabin, it is arguably the most luxurious of the lodges.

Opened in 1905, El Tovar was named for Spanish explorer Don Pedro de Tobar (the "b" was changed to "v" to avoid people saying "to the bar") and was designed by architect Charles Whittlesey. Built for $250,000, it had 95 rooms, electricity, indoor plumbing, steam heat, solariums, and lounges. Originally, Jersey cows and poultry grazed on site, and greenhouses provided fresh herbs and flowers for guests feasting in the dining room. One of its most famous diners and overnight guests was **Teddy Roosevelt**, who came to dinner in muddy boots and dusty riding gear—or so says local lore. In addition to Roosevelt, seven other presidents have stayed here. For its 100th birthday, the hotel received a $4.6 million restoration.

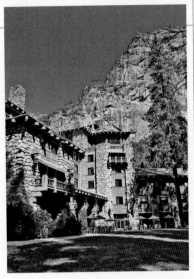

Ahwahnee Hotel

THE AHWAHNEE, YOSEMITE

Blending into a backdrop of granite cliffs, the elegant Ahwahnee hotel, which opened in 1927, is six stories tall with three wings in a "Y" layout. Then-NPS Director Stephen Mather believed that attracting wealthy, influential folks into Yosemite would lend support and congressional funding to the national parks system.

Architect Gilbert Stanley Underwood was commissioned to build a first-class fireproof hotel that blended in with the landscape. In order to resist fire, concrete was formed within timbers and then dyed to resemble redwood. The motifs and patterns found in the basketry of the local Indian tribes were used on the ceiling beams, stained-glass windows, and concrete floors. Luminaries who have signed the lodge guest book include Franklin and Eleanor Roosevelt, John F. Kennedy, Queen Elizabeth, and Clark Gable.

Right, president Teddy Roosevelt.

OLD FAITHFUL INN, YELLOWSTONE

Amazement and awe may best describe the reaction of people entering the lobby of Old Faithful Inn for the first time. Its 76-foot high lobby has four levels of balconies with supports created from a tangle of gnarled branches reaching the ceiling. It was built in 1903–1904 at a cost of $140,000. Wings were added to the hotel in 1915 and 1927—it would be difficult to duplicate the inn's construction today, as cutting down trees, gathering wood, and quarrying rock inside the park are now illegal.

The park's most famous geyser, Old Faithful, is less than 100 yards from the inn. Approximate times for its eruptions are posted in the lobby.

BRYCE CANYON LODGE

Bryce Canyon Lodge was the second structure built in the Union Pacific's Loop Tours building program, which included lodges in Zion and the Grand Canyon National Parks. In a grove of ponderosa pines within walking distance of the rim, the lodge opened in 1925 and expanded throughout the late 1920s. It now has 70 guest rooms, three deluxe suites, one studio room, and 40 log cabins. The property was known for its sing-aways, where employees lined up in front of the lodge and sang a farewell to departing guests. When plans to build a second lodge on the rim didn't materialize, a gift shop, soda fountain, barbershop, and auditorium were added.

WHAT TO EXPECT

Some lodges were built more than 100 years ago, when rooms and beds were smaller. However, the difference in room size is more than offset by the huge amount of public space offered on the properties. The availability of television and Internet access varies from lodge to lodge.

Above, Old Faithful Inn. Top, Bryce Canyon Lodge.

IN FOCUS GREAT LODGES OF THE NATIONAL PARKS

1

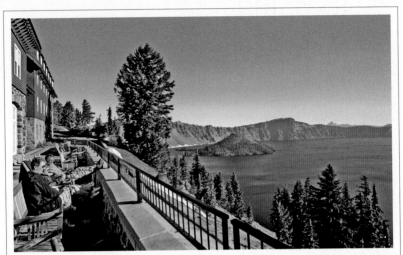

Crater Lake Lodge

CRATER LAKE LODGE

When Crater Lake Lodge opened in 1915, it was anything but grand: the exterior was covered in tarpaper, fiberboard separated the guest rooms, bathrooms were shared, and the electricity seldom worked. But visitors loved it anyway because of the lake view. Due to its structural defects and lack of funding, the building was closed to the public in 1989. Public pressure convinced the National Park Service to spend $15 million for renovations, and the lodge was completely rebuilt and reopened in May 1995. Perched on the rim of a defunct caldera filled with cobalt blue water, the lodge has a fantastic deck, as well as an architectural trademark, a massive stone fireplace.

GLACIER PARK LODGE

An eclectic interior design with towering tree trunks highlights Glacier Park Lodge. Samuel L. Bartlett was the architect of record, but Louis Hill, president of the Great Northern Railway, controlled every aspect of the design. Hill based the lodge, which opened in 1913, on a Christian basilica, creating a rustic, cathedral-like building. He had 60 Douglas firs (averaging 40 feet high and 40 inches in diameter) shipped in from the Pacific Northwest for the construction.

When rail passengers arrived at Glacier Park Station, they saw Indian teepees scattered across the lawn as part of a show presented to visitors, along with colorful banks of flowers surrounding the majestic lodge.

The park and lodge were heavily promoted. On top of the half a million dollars it took to build and furnish Glacier Park Lodge, Hill spent $300,000 on artists, filmmakers, calendars, playing cards, and a special train car with a public exhibit. *The New York Times* said, "Next to Col. Roosevelt, L.W. Hill is about the best advertising man in the United States."

Glacier Park Lodge

FAIRMONT CHATEAU LAKE LOUISE & FAIRMONT BANFF SPRINGS LODGES

In the late 1800s, William Cornelius Van Horne, general manager of the Canadian Pacific Railway, said, "Since we can't export the scenery, we will have to import the tourists." And so they did. The railroad developed Fairmont Banff Springs Hotel and the Fairmont Chateau Lake Louise, both of which opened their doors in 1890.

While the great lodges of America's national parks have a comfortable hunting-lodge aura, Canada's Banff and Lake Louise accommodations have a stately, opulent ambience.

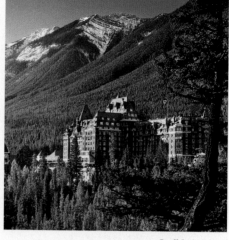

Banff Springs Hotel

Fairmont Banff Springs, a mile walk from downtown Banff, is styled after a Scottish baronial castle. The hotel offers tennis, golf, bowling, horseback rides, indoor and outdoor swimming, and one of the largest spas in Canada.

Surrounded by snow-tipped mountain peaks and the majestic Victorian Glacier, Chateau Lake Louise is on the shore of pristine Lake Louise, where you can hike, downhill or cross-country ski, cycle, and canoe.

TO RESERVE A ROOM

Reservations at historic lodges should be made six months to a year in advance (for Yellowstone, definitely 12 months in advance) directly with the lodge's websites; however, you can always check for last-minute cancellations. Be wary of other Internet reservation services that charge a non-refundable fee of up to 12 percent to book the lodging. ■ TIP→ Dining reservations at lodge restaurants often can be made when you book your room.

OTHER GREAT LODGES

Zion Park Lodge.

GLACIER NATIONAL PARK
Belton Chalet, Lake McDonald Lodge, Many Glacier Hotel, Sperry & Granite Park Chalets

GRAND CANYON NATIONAL PARK
Grand Canyon Lodge—North Rim

MOUNT RAINIER NATIONAL PARK
Paradise Inn

WATERTON LAKES NATIONAL PARK
Prince of Wales Hotel

ZION NATIONAL PARK
Zion Park Lodge

CHOOSING A PARK

WHAT'S WHERE

Parks in this section are organized by state; numbers refer to chapters in the book

Canada

7 Banff. The Canadian Rockies are one of the most beautiful ranges on Earth, and Canada's first national park is nestled among these mountains, glaciers, and forests. It also has some of the world's best skiing. **Best Paired With:** Jasper

23 Jasper. One of the largest protected mountain ecosystems in the world and the largest of the Canadian Rocky Mountain parks, Jasper woos visitors with its lakes, glaciers, waterfalls, and mountains. **Best Paired With:** Banff

Washington

27 Mount Rainier. The fifth-highest mountain in the Lower 48, Mount Rainier is so massive that the summit is rarely visible—but when conditions are right, the image of the entire mountain is unforgettable. Hikes cover temperate rain forest, old-growth forests of hemlock and fir, high meadows, and tundra—not to mention hot springs, glaciers, lakes, and waterfalls. **Best Paired With:** North Cascades and Olympic

28 North Cascades. Hiking on a real glacier is a memorable experience—especially if you add in marmots, golden eagles, and coyotes—and

North Cascades is home to several hundred of them. **Best Paired With:** Mount Rainier and Olympic

29 Olympic. Centered on Mount Olympus and framed on three sides by water, this park is known for its temperate rain forests, rugged coastal expanses, Sol Duc hot springs, and hiking (or skiing) at Hurricane Ridge. **Best Paired With:** North Cascades and Mount Rainier

Oregon

15 Crater Lake. Crater Lake is a geological marvel—the 21-square-mile sapphire-blue lake inside a caldera is the nation's deepest. The park itself includes about 90 miles of trails. **Best Paired With:** Mount Rainier and Olympic or Redwood and Lassen Volcanic

Montana

17 Glacier–Waterton Lakes. The rugged mountains that weave their way through the Continental Divide in northwest Montana are the backbone of Glacier and its sister park in Canada, Waterton Lakes. The park's Going-to-the-Sun Road is a spectacular drive that crosses the crest of the Continental Divide.

North Dakota

36 Theodore Roosevelt. Theodore Roosevelt is known for chunks of badlands on the Little Missouri River and the 26th president's beloved

Elkhorn Ranch. This is one of the most isolated parks in the country.

Wyoming

19 Grand Teton. With no foothills, the unimpeded view of the Teton Range rising out of Jackson Hole is stunning. Wildlife from short-tailed weasels to grizzly bears abound. **Best Paired With:** Yellowstone

38 Yellowstone. Best known for Old Faithful, the world's most famous geyser, flowing hot springs, and mud pots, Yellowstone is the oldest national park in the world. Spotting the abundant wildlife, like bison, elk, moose, and bears is the other main draw. **Best Paired With:** Grand Teton

South Dakota

6 Badlands. The park's eroded buttes and spires cast amazing shades of red and yellow across the South Dakota prairie. In addition to scenery, it has some of the world's richest mammal fossil beds. **Best Paired With:** Wind Cave

37 Wind Cave. One of the largest caves in the world, with beautiful cave formations including boxwork (3-D calcite honeycomb patterns on cave walls and ceilings), Wind Cave is the place to go spelunking. **Best Paired With:** Badlands

WHAT'S WHERE

Nevada

20 Great Basin. It may be one of the nation's least visited national parks, but the stalactites, stalagmites, and popcorn in Lehman Caves and the solitude of backcountry treks are big draws.

Utah

5 Arches. Four hours (235 miles) from Salt Lake City, this park has the world's largest concentration of natural sandstone arches, including that most-famous symbol of Utah, Delicate Arch. Nearby is Moab, an adventure hot spot, with world-class white-water rafting on the Colorado River, rock climbing, four-wheeling, and mountain biking. **Best Paired With:** Canyonlands

10 Bryce Canyon. Exploring the hoodoos (spectacular columns of rock) at this park is like wandering through a giant maze. Bryce is within a few hours of Utah's other national parks and near Kodachrome . Basin State Park and Grand Staircase–Escalante National Monument. **Best Paired With:** Capitol Reef and Zion

11 Canyonlands. Biking on White Rim Road, white-water rafting in Cataract Canyon— plus spires, pinnacles, cliffs, and mesas as far as the eye can see are the top reasons to go. **Best Paired With:** Arches

12 Capitol Reef. Seven times larger than nearby Bryce Canyon and much less crowded, Capitol Reef is known for its 100-mile-long Waterpocket Fold, a monocline (or "wrinkle" in the Earth's crust). It has many options for day hikes as well as backcountry trips into slot canyons, arches, cliffs, domes, and slickrock. **Best Paired With:** Bryce Canyon and Zion

40 Zion. Sheer 2,000-foot cliffs and river-carved canyons are what Zion is all about, and hiking the Narrows and the Subway are on many an adventurer's bucket-list. Zion is right next to hospitable Springdale, which is full of amenities and charm. **Best Paired With:** Bryce Canyon and Grand Canyon

Colorado

9 Black Canyon of the Gunnison. This steep and narrow river gorge has sheer cliffs and a drop twice as high as the Empire State Building.

21 Great Sand Dunes. The roughly 30 square miles of landlocked dune fields are an impressive sight. Aside from the dunes there are eight different life zones to explore, ranging from salty wetlands to alpine peaks.

26 Mesa Verde. Located in the Four Corners region—the junction of Utah, Colorado, New Mexico, and Arizona— this park houses an amazing collection of Ancestral Puebloan dwellings, some carved directly into cliff faces, and ancient artifacts.

33 Rocky Mountain. Alpine lakes, mountain peaks, and wildlife such as elk and bighorn sheep draw visitors to the park. There are more than 350 miles of trails leading to meadows filled with wildflowers and crystal lakes and 14,259-foot Long's Peak to summit.

WHAT'S WHERE

California

14 Channel Islands. You must take a boat or plane to reach the five islands, which are home to 145 species of terrestrial plants and animals found nowhere else on Earth. You're bound to see wildlife such as dolphins, sea lions, island foxes, and pelicans and can kayak, dive, and go whale-watching. **Best Paired With:** Yosemite and Sequoia and Kings Canyon

16 Death Valley. This is a vast, lonely, beautiful place with breathtaking vistas, blasting 120-degree heat, and mysterious moving rocks. The desert landscape is surrounded by majestic mountains, dry lakebeds, spring wildflowers, and Wild West ghost towns. **Best Paired With:** Joshua Tree and Zion

24 Joshua Tree. Large stands of Joshua trees gave the park its name, but it's also a great spot for bouldering and rock climbing. Brilliant wildflower displays and starry nights add to the draw. **Best Paired With:** Death Valley

25 Lassen Volcanic. Lassen Peak, a dormant plug dome volcano that last erupted in 1915, and every other type of known volcano (shield, cinder cone, and composite) are here, as well as roiling mud pots and hissing steam vents. **Best Paired With:** Redwood and Crater Lake or Yosemite

31 Pinnacles. Hiking among rugged volcanic spires is the most popular activity at Pinnacles, and the best chance you'll have at encountering one of the extremely rare California condors that make their home here. **Best Paired With:** Yosemite

32 Redwood. Redwood is home to the world's tallest trees: giant coast redwoods, which grow to more than 300 feet tall. **Best Paired With:** Lassen Volcanic and Crater Lake

35 Sequoia and Kings Canyon. Sequoias are the big trees here, which have monstrously thick trunks and branches. The Generals Highway, which connects the two parks, features many of these natural marvels. The Kings Canyon Scenic Byway offers views into a canyon deeper than the Grand Canyon. **Best Paired With:** Yosemite National Park

39 Yosemite. Dozens of famed features, from the soaring granite monoliths of Half Dome and El Capitan, to shimmering waterfalls like Yosemite Falls and Bridalveil Fall, lie within reach in the Yosemite Valley. **Best Paired With:** Sequoia and Kings Canyon

Arizona

18 Grand Canyon. The Grand Canyon both exalts and humbles the human spirit. You can view the spectacle from the South Rim, the less-traveled North Rim, or hike or take a mule ride into the canyon for a richer experience. For adventure junkies, rafting the Colorado River through the canyon can't be beat. **Best Paired With:** Petrified Forest

30 Petrified Forest. This park is known for fallen and fossilized trees, which look like they are made of colorful stone. **Best Paired With:** Grand Canyon

34 Saguaro. The park takes its name from the saguaro cactus, the largest of its kind in the United States, found here. The park is split into two districts bookending Tucson (about 30 miles apart); the better collection of cacti is found in the west district.

New Mexico

13 Carlsbad Caverns. The park's 113 caves, bizarre underground rock formations, and 400,000 diving, dipping, sonar-blipping bats are the main draws. **Best Paired With:** Guadalupe Mountains

Texas

8 Big Bend. In a remote location, with the Rio Grande River along its southern border, its limitless skies and ample space are two of its strongest selling points.

22 Guadalupe Mountains. This remote park draws thousands of visitors every fall, when the hardwoods of McKittrick Canyon burst into flaming color. The park is home to the Guadalupe Peak, the highest point in the state. **Best Paired With:** Carlsbad Caverns

BRITISH COLUMBIA

Jasper

Banff

ALBERTA

SASKATCHEWAN

Olympic

North Cascades

Seattle

WASHINGTON

5

Mt Rainier

82

Portland

90

Glacier and Waterton

CANADA
UNITED STATES

Theodore Roosevelt

MONTANA

Butte

94

N.D.

84

OREGON

5

Crater Lake

IDAHO

15

90

90

S.D.

32
Redwood

15

Yellowstone

Grand Teton

Badlands

Wind Cave

Lassen Volcanic

25

WYOMING

NE

80

80

25

San Francisco

NEVADA

Great Basin

Great Salt Lake

Salt Lake City

Rocky Mountain

76

39

Yosemite

CALIFORNIA

35

Sequoia/ Kings Canyon

31

Pinnacles

16

Death Valley

Las Vegas

15

UTAH

Arches

15

River

70

Denver

70

Capitol Reef

Bryce Canyon

Zion

Black Canyon of the Gunnison

Canyonlands

Great Sand Dunes

Colorado

Mesa Verde

COLORADO

14

5

Los Angeles

Channel Islands

Joshua Tree

18

Grand Canyon

40

Flagstaff

Santa Fe

25

24

ARIZONA

17

30

Petrified Forest

Albuquerque

40

San Diego

10

8

UNITED STATES
MEXICO

Phoenix

Saguaro

34

NEW MEXICO

25

Carlsbad Caverns

13

El Paso

22

Guadalupe Mountains

20

Rio Grande

TEXAS

10

Big Bend

8

Pacific Ocean

0   200 mi

0   200 km

THE BEST OF THE NATIONAL PARKS

Best Parks for Accessibility

The best way to get an in-depth look at the parks is by exploring them on foot, horseback, or via some other mode of transportation, but sometimes physical condition or time prevents this from happening. The main sites at the following parks aren't too far off the beaten path—many are even visible from the comfort of your car.

Badlands. Drive slowly on the two-lane loop through the park, setting aside plenty of time for stopping at the overlooks. The view changes as you drive, moving from rocky formations to prairie.

Bryce Canyon. The 18-mile road along Plateau Rim has numerous overlooks and a handful of spurs, and provides fabulous views of this park's famous red-orange hoodoos and points beyond. If you want to journey beyond the overlooks, several nearby trailheads offer quick escapes into the park's interior.

Crater Lake. View the lake from various perspectives along the 33-mile loop Rim Drive. Though you can see much without pulling over, take the time to stop at a few overlooks off the road. The drive will take two or more hours.

Mesa Verde. Once the main park road passes the Morefield Campground, it forks, and the two branches lead to the archaeological treasures of the Wetherill and Chapin Mesas, respectively. Most sites are close enough to be viewed from the road, but short trails lead in for a closer look (and a few sites are wheelchair accessible).

Petrified Forest. Whether you enter from the north or the south entrance, the 28-mile park road leads to both visitor centers and a handful of quick and easy trails that meander among petrified trees.

Best Parks for Bear Spotting

One of the parks' greatest attractions is their wildlife, and few animals attract as much attention as black and grizzly bears. Cubs are cute and playful, but they shouldn't be approached—Mama is often close and will view you as a threat to her little ones. Still, when seen from a safe distance, bears serve as great reminders of the wildness that the national parks are meant to preserve and protect.

Glacier. There are so many black and grizzly bears in this part of Montana that they often come onto people's property, getting inside homes and causing general mayhem—though attacks on humans are rare. When hiking, make noise, especially when about to turn a corner or bend in the road.

Waterton Lakes. In this Canadian national park, grasslands sweep up the lower slopes of the mountains providing a unique topography that lends itself to wonderful wildlife viewing. Grizzlies and black bears can be seen from park roads and watched safely from the inside of a vehicle. Bears are plentiful here, so make sure you always hike in groups and make enough noise that you won't surprise one.

Yellowstone. Yellowstone is home to the greatest concentration of grizzly bears in the Lower 48. Black bears are also present here. They can be blond, brown, cinnamon, or black. If you see a bear in the park, keep your distance and don't give it food.

Yosemite. American black bears are the only bruins left in Yosemite (the California grizzly was hunted to extinction in the early 20th century). Today, the park is home to between 300 and 500 black bears; most are brown. If a bear threatens you, make noise and look big.

2

Best Parks for Burning Calories

The national parks are great places for a workout. Whether you walk, run, ski, paddle, or bike, you'll rarely have an excuse not to keep up with your exercise regimen while you're on vacation here. Hard-core fitness junkies should check out the following parks, which are particularly well suited for extreme exertion.

Canyonlands. Three distinct areas, or districts—Island in the Sky, the Maze, and the Needles—comprise this popular but spacious national park; each one offers plenty of opportunities to put boot (or mountain bike) to sandstone and become totally immersed in sun and solitude. The Maze is your best bet for getting away from it all—you can reach it only by driving at least 20 miles on lonely dirt roads.

Channel Islands. Kayakers can explore 175 miles of picturesque coastline around this island park, including one of the world's largest sea caves. Marine mammal sightings are common, and below the waves a kelp forest makes for some of the best scuba diving in the world. On land, take a hike to discover nearly 150 species of plants and animals that exist nowhere else on Earth.

Mount Rainier. This Washington park is encircled by the aptly named Wonderland Trail—a whopping 93-mile trek that takes 10–14 days to complete. It's as rugged as it is long; elevation gains and losses of 3,500 feet in a day are not uncommon. Snow hangs around higher elevations into June and even July, and rain can appear at almost any time. The faint of heart and tender of sole should tramp elsewhere.

Best Parks for Cultural History

When surrounded by such overwhelming natural beauty, and many opportunities to take part in outdoor activities, it's easy to overlook the parks' cultural attractions. But it would be a shame to miss out on a history lesson during your visit, whether it's touring an ancient dwelling, witnessing a historical reenactment, or visiting a great American icon.

Mesa Verde. Established in 1906, Mesa Verde was the first national park to "preserve the works of man," according to President Theodore Roosevelt. The Ancestral Pueblo people lived here from AD 550 to AD 1300, and to date more than 4,000 archaeological sites—including 600 cliff dwellings—have been unearthed. Researchers continue to discover and catalog artifacts at Mesa Verde.

Petrified Forest. The roots at this park aren't just from its ancient trees: the area's human history and culture extend back more than 13,000 years, from prehistoric people to the more modern travelers of Route 66. You can still see petroglyphs scratched and carved into stone, as well as many other artifacts, from the ancestors of the Hopi, Zuni, and Navajo.

Theodore Roosevelt. It's fitting that Theodore Roosevelt—a major proponent of preservation who signed into law five national parks—should have a national park named in his honor. This North Dakota gem contains land that was once part of Roosevelt's Dakota Territory ranch. Visitors can step inside the former president's log cabin or peruse the visitor center's wide selection of books, posters, audio recordings, and videos dedicated to telling his many stories.

Best Parks for Day-Trippers

Some urbanites are fortunate to live just a short drive away from a national park. For those who live elsewhere, these parks have large gateway cities nearby that are served by major airports with plenty of car rental agencies, making a trip to a park a surprisingly quick getaway.

Joshua Tree. A quick two- or three-hour drive east from the urban sprawl of Los Angeles brings you to the junction of the Mojave and Colorado deserts. Joshua Tree National Park, named for extensive stands of the gnarled tree, is home to one of the finest wildflower displays in Southern California each spring.

Mount Rainier. Why just stare at the elusive, majestic mountain from afar? Seattle residents and visitors can easily make their way to Mount Rainier National Park, just 60 miles away. You can pack a lot in a day: gawk at glaciers, hike one of the trails (the park has more than 240 miles of maintained trails), and poke around the Longmire historic district.

Rocky Mountain. It's about a 1½-hour drive from Denver up to one of the most visited national parks in the country, where you can view elk, enjoy alpine scenery, and see myriad flora and fauna. Hiking and picnicking along its lakes make perfect activities for a day retreat.

Saguaro. You'll find the largest concentration of the towering saguaro cactus, famed emblem of the desert Southwest, just minutes outside Tucson. The park is divided into two sections: the Rincon Mountain District to the east and the Tucson Mountain District to the west.

Best Parks for Desert Solitude

America's national parks run the gamut in terms of cultural, geographic, and geological attractions, but the desolate, arid environs offer a unique experience often colored by our nation's romantic notion of the desert. If you're seeking peace and quiet, you'll likely find it here.

Arches. Edward Abbey wrote his seminal *Desert Solitaire,* the book that defined the term, while stationed here as a park ranger in the 1960s. Though most often seen by car these days, Arches has an uncrowded backcountry that Abbey—were he alive—would argue is the best way to experience the place anyhow.

Big Bend. Even in West Texas—a region known for wide-open and silent spaces—Big Bend is quite remote. Among the least visited of the nation's national parks, it was dubbed El Despoblado (The Unpopulated Place), by early Spanish explorers, and has changed little since then. This is a great place to lose yourself among cacti and sprawling mountains.

Death Valley. With its inhospitable environment and forbidding name, Death Valley has come to epitomize the desert of the American Southwest. It attracts only one million visitors a year, mainly outside the scorching summer months—but even in the high season, the park's vast acres of space guarantee peace and solitude.

Joshua Tree. This south-central California park is prime hiking, rock-climbing, and exploring country, where you can have a close-up encounter with coyotes, desert pack rats, golden eagles, and exotic plants like the white yucca, crimson-tipped ocotillo, and spiny cholla cactus.

2

Best Parks for Fun and Funky Activities

All the national parks exist for a reason: to protect something that was deemed worthy of recognition and preservation. Still, a few have such unusual and unique features, or unusual surroundings, that they stand out from the rest.

Badlands. The park and surrounding Black Hills are perfect for family getaways, and you can't get much funkier than Wall Drug on Main Street in nearby Wall, South Dakota. It even has an animated T. rex in the yard. In the park itself, visiting the prairie-dog towns and seeing these creatures' antics can bring laughter to your carload of people.

Carlsbad Caverns. From mid-May to mid-October, watch thousands of bats spiral up into the evening sky from deep within the earth as they set out on their nightly hunt. If possible, get in on the ranger-led discussion beforehand in the nearby amphitheater.

Crater Lake. Take a boat tour on the clearest, deepest lake in the United States (and the seventh deepest in the world). Formed by volcanic activity, Crater Lake's deepest point is 1,943 feet down, and the sapphire-blue water is so clear that sunlight can penetrate to a depth of 400 feet.

Lassen Volcanic. Though dormant since 1921, activity around volcanic Lassen Peak makes it clear that there's still a lot going on beneath the ground. Fumaroles, mud pots, and bubbling hot springs dot the landscape. It's a fun and sometimes-smelly place to explore, but beware of the scalding water.

Best Parks for Getting a Taste of the Wild West

The American West isn't as wild as it once was, but you can find traces of its storied past. From small preserved towns to vast desert spaces, it's still possible to feel like you've stepped into a Western movie.

Badlands. Few words conjure up images of the old Wild West better than the word "Badlands"—except maybe "Deadwood," a town 100 miles northwest of the park. Once an infamous gold camp, the entire town of Deadwood has been named a National Historic Landmark. A nearby cemetery is the final resting place of Wild Bill Hickok and Calamity Jane.

Big Bend. Far from civilization, this West Texas park can easily bring out the John Wayne or Clint Eastwood in you. The desert environs are exactly where a Hollywood cowboy would feel at home. Try a tour by horseback to complete the experience.

Death Valley. Death Valley is not the most hospitable place—at least during certain times of the year—but the climate isn't as horrible as the park's reputation would suggest. Still, the name and the location have long epitomized the very idea of the desert in American literature, film, and television.

Zion. Thirty miles southeast of Zion's east entrance is the small city of Kanab, Utah, famously known as Little Hollywood for all the old Westerns shot in its environs. Downtown hotels still highlight the rooms where John Wayne and other film stars slept. This area of southern Utah has also served as the backdrop for TV shows (including *Gunsmoke*) and many Jeep commercials.

Best Parks for Inspiration

It's hard to not be inspired when you're at a national park. Natural wonders, peace and quiet, and ancient sites will likely leave you awestruck, no matter where you visit. These five parks, however, have left their mark on some famous visitors and influenced their subsequent work.

Glacier. It took a lot to impress pioneering naturalist John Muir, who once called Glacier a "precious reserve" and "the best care-killing scenery on the continent." Take a boat ride on one of the lakes for particularly inspiring views.

Great Basin. Among America's least visited national parks, Great Basin is also one of the most beautiful. Tucked away on Nevada's eastern border, the park is a great place to hide from life and work back home.

North Cascades. Jack Kerouac, Gary Snyder, and Philip Whalen, fixtures of the Beat scene, all worked as National Park Service fire lookouts in the 1950s at Desolation Peak in North Cascades. Portions of Kerouac's *Desolation Angels* and *The Dharma Bums* chronicle his experiences on the mountain.

Rocky Mountain. With more than 60 mountains 12,000 feet or higher, more than 350 miles of hiking trails, 150 lakes, 450 miles of streams, and countless far-reaching vistas, Rocky Mountain has plenty to keep you inspired (and off the phone).

Yosemite. Ansel Adams's repeated visits to Yosemite provided him with the intimate understanding necessary to previsualize many of the famous images he captured here. His exposures of Half Dome are particularly noteworthy and are among his best-known works.

Best Parks to Pitch a Tent in

The national parks offer myriad options for sleeping close to nature, whether on the plush bunks of an RV or beneath a tree separated from the stars by just a thin sheet of nylon. The facilities may vary, but many campers agree that the best way to see the parks is to get out into the undeveloped wilderness.

Banff. You'll be camping in bear country, but Parks Canada takes precautions to separate the humans and the animals—a protective electrical fence with a Texas gate (cattle guard) surrounds the wooded Lake Louise campground, which is open year-round (with restrictions in spring and fall). Many sites are great for families.

Capitol Reef. Remote Cathedral Valley, accessible by crossing the Fremont River in a high-clearance vehicle, is filled with stunning monoliths and silence. First-come, first-served primitive backcountry campsites provide a base for exploration.

Olympic. Don't be deterred by the very real threat of rain at this mossy, misty, and wonderfully undeveloped national park. With the Pacific Ocean and temperate rain forests to the west and craggy peaks scattered throughout its interior, Olympic is a backpacker's delight. Its designated campgrounds are popular, too. Several have water views and kids' activities.

Yosemite. Beyond the Yosemite Valley and iconic sites like Half Dome, this park has a huge, almost secret backcountry perfect for backpackers and horseback riders wishing to embark on extended trips. In fact, more than 90% of the park is undeveloped wilderness. If you choose instead one of the developed campgrounds, book early—at least three months in advance.

2

Best Parks for Romantics

One of the marks of a great relationship is the ability to travel together. And while getting there may induce some stress, once you're at a national park, your spirits should lighten. The beauty and serenity of the parks can help you focus on each other, not your Day-Timer. Each of these national parks is a destination well suited for celebrating your bond with that special someone.

Banff. There is no shortage of escapist lodging at Banff, regardless of your budget or interests. There are more than 100 accommodation options around Lake Louise alone, from cozy little cottages to large historic lodges. And when you're not gazing into each other's eyes, you can stare at the breathtaking mountain scenery. Any one of the scenic drives can also help you relax and unwind.

Channel Islands. The mountains that dot this park off the coast of California are often obscured by mists, and animals found nowhere else on Earth add to the park's otherworldly feel. The Pacific Ocean is the main attraction here: play on its beaches, ply its waters in a kayak, or tour it by boat as you enjoy an island escape for two—albeit one totally different from a typical Caribbean trip.

Grand Canyon. For couples who don't mind sweating a little to get to a romantic destination, the depths of the Grand Canyon offer the quintessential Western camping experience. Sleeping at the base of this massive canyon under a clear black sky blazing with bright stars is something to add to your life's to-do list. (After a long hike—or mule ride—it is also the perfect occasion for a massage!)

Best Parks for Scenic Drives

Sometimes the road to the trailhead is as amazing as the trail itself. For those who want to experience the parks from behind the wheel, these drives are top-notch.

Glacier. Even the hardiest hiker will admit that there's something special about speeding along a road named Going-to-the-Sun. The 50-mile stretch of road crosses the Continental Divide at Logan Pass, and is one of America's most beautiful drives.

Jasper. The Icefields Parkway is one of the world's most spectacular drives, winding its way for 230 km (143 miles) between Banff and Jasper past powerful rugged mountain scenery, massive glaciers, rushing waterfalls, icefalls and wildlife.

Redwood. Keeping your eyes on the road can be a challenge when you're passing 300-foot-tall trees. The 8-mile Coastal Drive is especially wonderful, offering views of the Pacific Ocean, with glimpses of sea lions and pelicans likely, and access to a section of the Coastal Trail, with turnouts for picnicking and gawking in wonder at majestic redwoods.

Rocky Mountain. The 48-mile Trail Ridge Road is the world's highest continuously paved road, with a maximum elevation of 12,183 feet. Connecting the park's east and west entrances, the road crosses the Continental Divide at Milner Pass, and it can take up to two months to clear off snow for its Memorial Day opening. The entire drive can be done in a couple of hours, but allow more time to stop and gaze out from the many turnouts.

Best Parks for Spotting Bald Eagles

It may sound clichéd, but you'll never forget the first time you see a bald eagle in person. The national icon's white head and tail, set against a dark body, are not its only points of distinction—eagles are huge, far larger than even the biggest hawk. You can view these amazing birds at many of the national parks, but visit one of the following for your best chance at a sighting.

North Cascades. Bald eagles are so much a part of this region that an annual festival is held in their honor along the Upper Skagit River. Highlights include American Indian music and dancing and bluegrass workshops. In the park itself, look for them along the Skagit River and various lakes.

Olympic. A coastal section of this park protects a stunning 65-mile stretch of Pacific Ocean coastline, providing an ideal environment for the fish-loving bald eagle. Another fish lover, the osprey, is also commonly found here—and from a distance, these birds can look like bald eagles. You're most likely to spot an eagle on the Shi Shi or Rialto beaches or the Ozette Loop hiking trail.

Yellowstone. As much a part of Yellowstone as the grizzly bear and bison, bald eagles can usually be seen in the vicinity of Yellowstone Lake—though you may see them in the park's interior as well, especially around the Madison River or the Hayden Valley. Greater Yellowstone provides habitat for more than 100 breeding pairs of bald eagles.

Best Parks for Train Travel

Traveling by train to and from a national park is a rare treat, harking back to the days when most visitors arrived by rail. Fortunately, two of the nation's grandest and most historic national parks are still fully accessible via trains coming from a handful of major metropolitan areas.

Glacier. Amtrak's *Empire Builder* stops at the east and west sides of Glacier on its way from Chicago to either Seattle or Portland. Shuttle service is available from either station to lodging in the park (with a prior reservation). The train also stops to the west in Whitefish, Montana, where there are additional lodging options.

Grand Canyon. Grand Canyon Railway offers a variety of daily train services from Williams, Arizona, to the park's South Rim. The adults-only *Sunset Limited* runs during weekends in the fall, allowing passengers to witness one of Grand Canyon's unmatched sunsets while enjoying appetizers and full bar service. From November through January, the *Polar Express* train reenacts the classic children's book (make sure to reserve far in advance). Amtrak's *Southwest Chief* stops in Williams on its Chicago-to-Los Angeles run, making Grand Canyon one of the few national parks fully accessible by rail transportation.

Rocky Mountain. Amtrak's *California Zephyr* line, running from San Francisco to Chicago, covers some of the West's most beautiful terrain, including the Rockies and Sierra Nevada. It stops at Granby, Colorado, the western gateway to Rocky Mountain National Park.

NATIONAL PARKS OF THE WEST BEST BETS

2

BEACHES
Channel Islands
Olympic
Redwood

BIRDS
Big Bend
Carlsbad Caverns
Great Sand Dunes
Guadalupe Mountains
Joshua Tree
Mount Rainier
Pinnacles
Rocky Mountain
Theodore Roosevelt

BISON
Grand Teton
Great Sand Dunes
Theodore Roosevelt
Yellowstone

BOATING
Big Bend
Channel Islands
Glacier-Waterton
Grand Canyon
Grand Teton
Lassen Volcanic
North Cascades
Olympic
Redwood
Theodore Roosevelt
Yellowstone
Yosemite

CAVES AND CAVERNS
Carlsbad Caverns
Channel Islands
Great Basin
Sequoia and Kings Canyon
Wind Cave

FISHING
Big Bend
Black Canyon of the Gunnison
Capitol Reef
Channel Islands
Glacier-Waterton
Grand Canyon
Grand Teton
Great Basin
Mount Rainier
North Cascades
Olympic
Redwood
Rocky Mountain
Sequoia and Kings Canyon
Theodore Roosevelt
Yellowstone
Yosemite

GEOLOGICAL GREATS
Arches
Bryce Canyon
Canyonlands
Carlsbad Caverns
Crater Lake
Grand Canyon
Lassen Volcanic
Petrified Forest
Yellowstone

GEYSERS
Death Valley
Lassen Volcanic
Mount Rainier
Olympic
Yellowstone

GLACIERS AND ICE FIELDS
Banff
Glacier-Waterton
Grand Teton
Jasper
Mount Rainier
North Cascades
Olympic

HORSEBACK RIDING
Banff
Glacier
Jasper
Lassen Volcanic
Mount Rainier
Olympic
Rocky Mountain
Theodore Roosevelt
Yosemite

MOUNTAINS
Big Bend
Capitol Reef
Glacier
Grand Teton
Guadalupe Mountains
Jasper
Lassen Volcanic
North Cascades
Olympic
Rocky Mountain
Sequoia and Kings Canyon
Yosemite

TREES AND FORESTS
Joshua Tree
North Cascades
Olympic
Petrified Forest
Redwood
Sequoia and Kings Canyon
Yosemite

VOLCANOES
Crater Lake
Death Valley
Lassen Volcanic
Mount Rainier
Yellowstone

WATERFALLS
Banff
Crater Lake
Jasper
Great Sand Dunes
Lassen Volcanic
Mount Rainier
Olympic
Rocky Mountain
Yellowstone
Yosemite

WINTER SPORTS
Bryce Canyon
Jasper
Joshua Tree
Mount Rainier
Olympic
Rocky Mountain
Yellowstone
Yosemite
Zion

PLANNING
YOUR VISIT

PARK PASSES

Nationwide Passes

If you're going to visit several American national parks in one vacation or over the course of a year, you can save money by investing in an "America the Beautiful" (or "Interagency") Pass, which admits the cardholder and others in the vehicle (or up to three others at places that charge per person) to more than 2,000 sites managed by the NPS and four other federal agencies, including national parks as well as national wildlife refuges, forests, and grasslands. (Find participating areas at ⊕ *www.store.usgs.gov/pass*).

There are several different passes, including one that's available to members of the U.S. military and their dependents. All can be purchased from the NPS or the U.S. Geological Survey (USGS) online (at ⊕ *www.store.usgs.gov/pass* or ⊕ *www.nps.gov/findapark/passes.htm*), through the mail, in person at participating federal recreation sites (go to ⊕ *www.nps.gov/findapark/passes.htm* for a state-by-state listing), or by phone (☎ *888/275–8747 Ext. 3*). All passes have a $10 processing fee, with the exception of those bought in person.

You must have photo identification with you when presenting your pass at any park entrance. All passes are nontransferable and nonrefundable. If they are lost or stolen, they will need to be repurchased.

Annual Pass. This pass costs $80 and is valid for a year from the date of purchase. It can be shared by two "owners," who need not be related or married (both must sign the back of the pass).

Senior Pass. If you're 62 or older, you can purchase this pass for $10. It is valid for a lifetime.

Access Pass. Those with permanent disabilities may acquire a parks pass that is free and valid for a lifetime.

Canadian Park Passes

Canada also offers annual passes to its parks. In Canada, an individual pass is good only for the pass holder, not for everyone in the vehicle. For a carload of people, you need the family/group pass (covers up to seven people in one vehicle). Passes may be purchased online at ⊕ *www.pc.gc.ca* or in person at one of the participating areas.

The pass must be signed by the cardholder and is nontransferable. Retain your receipt/proof of purchase in case you lose your pass and need to have it replaced.

National Discovery Pass. Good for entrance to Canada's national parks, national marine conservation areas, and national historic sites (close to 100 in all) for a year, this pass costs $68 for individuals, $58 for those 65 and older, and $33 for youths up to age 16. A family/group package pass is $136.

Single-Location Annual Pass. This pass will get you unlimited access to one park for a year. Fees range from $15 for a youth pass to $74 for a family or group.

Other Annual Passes

Most individual national parks also offer an annual pass for unlimited access to that particular park. Prices vary, but hover around $30 to $50. In a few cases these passes include admission to two parks that are near each other, such as Grand Teton and Yellowstone. If you think you might be back to a park within a year, ask the gate attendant how much the annual pass is. In some parks, there's only a small difference between a single day's and a year's admission.

FAMILY FUN

Top 5 Tips

1. Plan ahead. At many parks, rooms and campsites fill up fast, so make your reservations as early as you can. Many parks will have every room and campsite booked several months in advance (weekends are especially popular). We recommend booking at least six months ahead, and more if you plan to visit one of the more popular parks, such as Grand Canyon, Grand Teton, Rocky Mountain, Yellowstone, or Yosemite. If you plan on staying outside the park, check with the hotels you're considering as far ahead as you can, as these places can fill up fast as well. You also can go online. All the national parks have websites—links to all of them are at the National Park Service page, ⊕ *www.nps.gov.*

2. Get the kids involved. It might seem easier to do the planning yourself, but you'll probably have a better time—and your kids definitely will—if you involve them. No matter how old they are, children ought to have a good idea of where you're going and what you're about to experience. It will help get them excited beforehand and will likely make them feel like they have a say and a stake in the trip. Discuss the park's attractions and give your kids a choice of two or three options (that are all amenable to you, of course). Many of the parks' Web pages have a "For Kids" link, with helpful advice and suggestions.

3. Know your children. Consider your child's interests. This will help you plan a vacation that's both safe and memorable (for all the right reasons). For starters, if you have kids under four, be honest with yourself about whether the national park itself is an appropriate destination. Parents are notorious for projecting their awe for majestic scenery and overall enthusiasm for sightseeing on their younger kids, who might be more interested in cataloging the snacks in the hotel room's minibar. Likewise, be realistic about your child's stamina and ability. If your children have never been hiking, don't expect them to be able to do a long hike at a higher altitude than they are used to. Remember: Children's first experience hiking can make them a lover or a hater of the activity, so start off slowly and try some practice hikes near home.

4. Pack wisely. Be sure you're bringing kid-size versions of the necessities you'll pack for yourself. Depending on the park you're visiting (and the activities you're planning), that will probably include sturdy sandals or hiking shoes, sunglasses, sunscreen, and insect repellent. You'll almost certainly need a few layers of clothing and plenty of water and snacks. Kids can be more susceptible to heat stress and dehydration than adults, meaning they need plenty of water when exercising. The American Academy of Pediatrics recommends giving your child about five ounces of water or another beverage every 20 minutes during strenuous exercise.

5. Develop a Plan B. National parks are natural places, meaning they change dramatically with the seasons and the weather, so you should plan on alternate activities if Mother Nature isn't cooperative. And if you've already talked with your kids about your options, you can pick a new plan that appeals to everyone.

SAMPLE BUDGET FOR A FAMILY OF FOUR

Here is an idea of what a family of four might spend on a three-day trip to Grand Canyon National Park, during which they stay and eat all their meals within the park. Depending on your accommodations and dining-out options, the total you spend can vary dramatically.

Admission: $30 per car; admission covers seven days in the park.

Lodging: A standard double room in one of the in-park lodges on the popular South Rim ranges from approximately $90 to $250 a night. Total for three nights: $270 to $750; double that ($540 to $1,500) if you have older children in a separate room. Tent camping in one of the park's campgrounds averages $15 per night. Total: $45. Backpackers must pay $10 for a backcountry permit and $8 per person, per night to camp below the rim (or $8 per group, per night above the rim). Total: $35 to $110.

Meals: Dining options in the park range from no-frills snack bars to upscale restaurants. Per-meal costs run from $10 to $40 or more, per person (you might be able to spend less if you're cooking meals over your campfire or packing bag lunches). Total (three meals per person, per day for three days): $360 to $1,440.

Souvenirs: Budget $5 to $10 per person per day for souvenirs so that everybody can get something small each day, or one or two larger items per trip. Total: $60 to $120.

TOTAL COST: $490 to $3,100

Budgeting Your Trip

Like most vacations, a trip to a national park can be as frugal, or as fancy, as you like. Here are a few things to consider:

Getting in. Individual admission to the national parks ranges from free to $30, depending on the park. You also can buy an America the Beautiful Pass for $80, which will get you and three other adults (kids 15 and under are free) into any national park (as well as other designated federal lands) for one year.

Sleeping. Fewer than half of the parks charge for camping; the cost is typically less than $20 per night. In many parks, you also can stay at a lodge, where prices run from $100 to $500 a night. Most parks have several accommodation options outside the park, as well.

Eating. In each of the parks, all the in-park concessions are run by companies under contract with the National Park Service, meaning their prices are set by the government. Generally speaking, prices are a bit higher than what you'd pay outside the park, but not significantly so. You also can bring in your own food and eat at one of the park's picnic areas.

Entertainment. Just looking at the wonders of the park is entertainment enough for many youngsters, but the many sports and outdoor activities—from hiking and bicycling to horseback riding and cave touring, depending on the park—help children stay active while exploring. Many park visitor centers also have films; some parks, such as Grand Canyon and Zion, even have IMAX movies. Cost for these offerings varies, ranging from free to a couple hundred dollars for more involved programs, such as a white-water rafting trip.

Souvenirs. All the parks have gift shops, and many stock items that are actually useful. For example, you'll find things like kid-size binoculars, fanny packs, and magnifying glasses, all of which can make your child's visit even more enjoyable. Budget $5 or $10 to cover one item (maybe something you might have bought for your child anyway, like a new sun hat).

Kids' Programs

More than half of the 408 U.S. National Park Service areas (national parks as well as historic sites, national monuments, preserves, and other significant places) are part of the Junior Ranger Program, which offers school-age kids the opportunity to learn about individual parks by filling out a short workbook or participating in an activity such as taking a hike with a park ranger. After completing the program, kids get a badge (or a pin or patch, depending on the park). For availability, check with the ranger station or visitor center when you arrive. Kids can also complete Junior Ranger activities online (⊕ *www.nps.gov/kids/jrrangers.cfm*).

In addition to the Junior Ranger Program, kids can find a variety of activities in the parks designed just for them. Some parks, such as Canyonlands, Grand Canyon, and Saguaro, loan "Discovery Packs," backpacks filled with kid-friendly tools like magnifying glasses. Call ahead for availability.

Many parks also have general-interest programs for kids. For example, Rocky Mountain National Park offers "Skins and Skulls," where visitors can touch a bear's fur and a marmot's skull, among other things. It's a safe way to get hands-on with wildlife.

When you're through with the organized activities and are ready to head off on your own, remember that kids often take a shorter view of things than adults do,

WEBSITES FOR KIDS

⊕ www.smokeybear.com

⊕ www.nationalparks.org/connect/npf-kids

⊕ www.nps.gov/kids/jrrangers.cfm

⊕ www.doi.gov/public/teachandlearn_kids.cfm

meaning they may need to be reminded once in a while of why you're there and what lies ahead (especially if it's a cool waterfall or swimming hole). Singing camp songs, playing games like I Spy, or staging scavenger hunts will help kids refocus if they get bored or whiny.

Pets in the Parks

Generally, pets are allowed only in developed areas of the national parks, including drive-in campgrounds and picnic areas. They must be kept on a leash at all times. With the exception of guide dogs, pets are not allowed inside buildings, on most trails, on beaches, or in the backcountry. They also may be prohibited in areas controlled by concessionaires, such as restaurants. Some national parks have kennels; call ahead to learn the details and to see if there's availability. Some of the national forests (⊕ *www.fs.fed.us*) surrounding the parks have camping and are more lenient with pets, although you should not plan to leave your pet unattended at the campsite.

TIPS FOR STARGAZING IN THE NATIONAL PARKS

If your typical view of the night sky consists of a handful of stars dimly twinkling through a hazy, light-polluted sky, get ready for a treat. In most of the national parks, the night sky blazes with starlight—and with a little practice, you can give your family a memorable astronomical tour.

Constellations

Constellations are stories in the sky—many depict animals or figures from Greek mythology. Brush up on a few of these tales before your trip, and you'll be an instant source of nighttime entertainment.

The stars in the Northern Hemisphere appear to rotate around Polaris, the North Star, in fixed positions relative to one another. To get your celestial bearings, first find the bright stars of the Big Dipper. An imaginary line drawn through the two stars that form the outside edge of the cup (away from the handle) will point straight to Polaris (which also serves as the last star in the handle of the Little Dipper). Once you've identified Polaris, you should be able to find the other stars on our chart. Myriad astronomy books and Web sites have additional star charts; *National Geographic* has a cool interactive version with images from the Hubble Space Telescope (www.nationalgeographic.com/stars).

Planets

Stars twinkle, planets don't (because they're so much closer to Earth, the atmosphere doesn't distort their light as much). Planets are also bright, which makes them fairly easy to spot. Unfortunately, we can't show their positions on this star chart, because planets orbit the sun and move in relation to the stars.

The easiest planet to spot is Venus, the brightest object in the night sky besides the moon and the Earth's closest planetary neighbor. Look for it just before sunrise or just after sunset; it'll be near the point where the sun is rising or setting. (Venus and Earth orbit the sun at different speeds; when Venus is moving away from Earth, we see it in the morning, and when it's moving toward us, we see it in the evening.) Like the moon, Venus goes through phases—check it out through a pair of binoculars. You can also spot Mars, Jupiter, Saturn, and Mercury—with or without the aid of binoculars.

Meteors

It's hard to match the magic of a meteor shower, the natural fireworks display that occurs as Earth passes through a cloud of debris called meteoroids. These pieces of space junk—most the size of a pebble—hit our atmosphere at high speeds, and the intense friction produces brief but brilliant streaks of light. Single meteors are often called "shooting stars" or "falling stars."

Because our planet passes through the same patches of interstellar refuse each year, it's easy to roughly predict when the major meteor showers will occur. Notable ones include the Perseids (mid-August), the Orionids (late October), the Leonids (mid-November), and the Geminids (mid-December). Each shower is named after the point in the sky where meteors appear to originate. If you're not visiting during a shower, don't worry—you can spot individual meteors any time of the year.

Satellites

Right now, according to NASA, there are about 3,000 operative man-made satellites (along with 6,000 pieces of space junk) orbiting the Earth—and you can catch a glimpse of one with a little practice. Satellites look like fast-moving, non-blinking points of light; the best way to spot one is to lie on your back and scan the sky for movement. Be on the lookout for satellites an hour or two before or after sunset (though you may see them at other times as well).

You can take the guesswork out of the search with a few cool online tools (⊕ *www.nasa. gov* or *www.heavens-above.com*). Select your location, and these Web sites will help you predict—down to the minute—when certain objects will be streaking overhead. It's especially worthwhile to use these sites to look for the two brightest satellites: the International Space Station and the space shuttle.

WHAT TO PACK

Top 10 Essentials

Packing lists for any trip vary according to the individual and his or her needs, of course, but here are 10 essential things to include in your luggage for a national parks vacation.

1. Binoculars. Many of the parks are a bird- (and animal-) watcher's dream. A pair of binos will help you spot feathered friends as well as larger creatures. Binoculars are sold according to power, or how much the objects you're viewing are magnified (i.e., 7x, 10x, 12x), and the diameter of objective lens, which is the one on the fat end of the binoculars; 10x is a good choice for magnification, field of view, and steadiness.

2. Clothes that layer. In much of the West (especially at higher elevations), days are often warm while nights turn chilly. The weather also can change quickly, with things going from dry and sunny to windy and wet in a matter of minutes. This means you need to pack with both warm and cold (as well as wet and dry) weather in mind. The easiest solution is to dress in layers. Experts suggest synthetics such as polyester (used in Coolmax and other "wicking" fabrics that draw moisture away from your skin, and fleece, which is an insulator) and lightweight merino wool. Look for socks in wicking wool or polyester. Don't forget a waterproof poncho or jacket.

3. Long pants and long-sleeve shirts. It's wise to minimize exposed skin when hiking, especially in areas with poison ivy and/ or ticks and at higher elevations, where the sun's radiation is much stronger. Convertible pants (the bottom portion zips off, leaving you in a pair of shorts) are another good option—they're often made of quick-drying and rugged material and

MAPS

If you plan to do a lot of hiking or mountaineering, especially in the backcountry, invest in detailed maps and a compass. Topographical maps are sold in well-equipped outdoor stores (REI and Cabela's, for example). Maps in different scales are available from the U.S. Geological Survey. To order, go to ⊕ *www.usgs.gov/pubprod/maps.html* or call ☎ *888/275–8747*.

allow you the flexibility of pants or shorts at a moment's notice.

4. Sturdy shoes or sandals. If you plan to do any hiking, be sure your footwear has rugged soles, a necessity on unpaved trails. Be sure to break in your shoes before the trip.

5. Insect repellent. If you're hiking or camping in an area with lots of mosquitoes, a good bug spray can help keep your trip from being a swatting marathon. A repellent also helps deter ticks. Most experts recommend repellents with DEET (N,N-diethyl-m-toluamide); the higher the level of DEET, the longer the product will be effective. Just be sure to use a separate sunscreen, not a single product with both ingredients (this is because you're supposed to reapply sunscreen every few hours, but doing so with DEET could deliver a dangerous dose of the chemical).

6. Skin moisturizer, sunscreen, and lip balm. In the parks, you're likely to be outside for longer—and in higher altitudes and drier climates—than you're used to. All of this can leave your skin and lips parched and burned. Sunscreen should provide both UVA and UVB protection, with an SPF of at least 15; look for a lotion marked "sweatproof" or "sport" and be sure to reapply throughout the day.

3

7. Sunglasses and hat. Higher elevation means more ultraviolet radiation; research shows there's an 8% to 10% increase in UV intensity for every 1,000 feet in elevation gain. Look for sunglasses that provide 100% UV protection.

8. Journal and camera. When your jaw drops at the glorious vistas and your head clears from all the fresh air, you may want to try your hand at sketching what you see or jotting down your thoughts. And of course, you'll want to get photographs.

9. Snacks and water. National parks by their nature are remote, and some are lacking in services. Bring plenty of water and healthy snacks (or meals, depending on how long you plan to be out and what you're likely to find in the park). When hiking in hot weather, experts recommend ½ to 1 quart of water (or another fluid) per person, per hour, to prevent potentially dangerous dehydration. The risk of dehydration is greater at elevations above 8,000 feet. Even if you're not hiking, have water and food in the car for long drives where facilities might be scarce.

10. First-aid kit. A solid kit should contain a first-aid manual, aspirin (or ibuprofen), razor blades, tweezers, a needle, scissors, adhesive bandages, butterfly bandages, sterile gauze pads, 1-inch-wide adhesive tape, an elastic bandage, antibacterial ointment, antiseptic cream or spray, antihistamines, calamine lotion, and moleskin (for blisters).

Hiking Items
For vacations where you'll be hiking for longer than an hour or two at a time, consider investing in the following:

■ **a compass and map**

■ **a daypack** with enough room for everybody's essentials

■ **energy bars** (they may not be five-star dining, but they do give you energy and keep your kids—and you—from getting cranky)

■ **a hiking stick or poles,** especially if you've got bad knees

■ **a water filter** to treat water

■ **bear bells** if you're in bear country

■ **reusable water bottles**

Camping Gear
Planning on roughing it on your national parks vacation? In addition to a working tent (check the zipper before you go!), sleeping bags and pillows, and, of course, the ingredients for s'mores (graham crackers, chocolate bars, and marshmallows), here are some things veteran campers recommend be among your gear:

■ **camping chairs** (folding or collapsible)

■ **camp stove and fuel**

■ **cooking utensils, plates, and cups**

■ **duct tape** (great for covering tears)

■ **flashlight, headlamp, and lantern**

■ **matches**

■ **paper towels, napkins, wet wipes**

■ **a multipurpose knife and cutting board**

■ **a rope** (for laundry or to help tie things down; pack clothespins, too)

■ **a sleeping pad or air mattress**

■ **a tarp** (will help keep the bottom of your tent—and you—dry)

■ **a cooler**

■ **toilet paper**

■ **a shovel** (to bury waste) or **plastic bags** (to haul it out)

OUTDOOR ADVENTURES

HIKING

Hiking in the national parks can mean many things, from a leisurely hour-long stroll along the rim of the Black Canyon of the Gunnison to a half-day scramble over ancient ruins at Mesa Verde to a multiday trek across Yellowstone. No matter what your fitness level, you'll find at least one hike that meets your needs.

Safety

Staying safe while hiking should be your number-one concern. While the vast majority of park visitors head off on hikes and return unscathed, there is a handful each year that get hurt. If your hike involves anything more strenuous than a short walk from the car to an observation area, check with a ranger to learn the special concerns for your planned adventure. Trails might be closed or rerouted, bad weather may be expected, or park wildlife may be causing problems on your route. Check the trail map carefully and pay attention to elevation changes, which make a huge difference in the difficulty of a hike (a steep 1-mile-long trail is much tougher to negotiate than a flat 2- or even 3-mile trail). And before you go, be sure to tell someone where you're going and how long you expect to be gone (if everyone in your group will be taking the hike, that someone should be a park ranger).

Best Hikes

Delicate Arch Trail, Arches National Park. This 3-mile round-trip hike takes you to the park's most famous sight and an iconic image of the American West: Delicate Arch. Hike over open, sun-baked slickrock marked with cairns, then along a 200-yard stretch of rock ledge just before you reach the arch.

Highline Trail, Glacier National Park. The Garden Wall section of this popular trail takes you from Logan Pass to Granite Park Chalet. On the way, it passes over mostly open terrain, much of it just above the tree line, where you're likely to see lots of wildlife—bighorn sheep, mountain goats, ptarmigan, and even grizzly bears—along with mountain vistas. It's a challenging hike, with a few narrow sections only 3 to 5 feet wide.

The Narrows Trail, Zion National Park. Experience the thrill of walking in the Virgin River, peering up at millennia-old rock canyons, hanging gardens, and sandstone grottoes. To see the Narrows you must wade—and occasionally swim—upstream through chilly water and over uneven, slippery rocks, but the views are breathtaking. Unless you've got a wet suit, plan to hike in the summer months, and even if you're hiking on a hot day, the water is likely to be very cold.

Panorama Trail, Yosemite National Park. If you're looking for eye-popping scenery and a heart-pounding hike, it doesn't get better than this. This 8-mile (one-way) trek is a doable, if strenuous, day trip, and delivers views of Yosemite Valley, several waterfalls, and the incomparable Half Dome. Take the hiker's bus ($25 one-way for adults) from Yosemite Lodge to the trailhead at Glacier Point and hike back down.

Widforss Trail, Grand Canyon National Park. Head to the less-crowded North Rim for this 10-mile round-trip hike that takes you along the canyon rim, through forests of aspen and Ponderosa pine, then out to Widforss Point, with incredible views of Haunted Canyon and its distinctive peaks, as well as a 10-mile stretch of the South Rim.

ROCK CLIMBING AND MOUNTAINEERING

Mountaineering can involve heavy traveling in the mountains, usually with the aim of reaching a summit. Mountaineers often employ rock climbing to reach their objectives, and the national parks are prime venues for both sports.

Getting Started

To get started in rock climbing, experts suggest taking an introductory course at an indoor climbing wall, which will give you a basic understanding of the techniques and equipment in a safe and controlled environment. After that, you can head out with a guide to try your skills on the real thing. A good guide will choose climbs that don't have a lot of exposure, so that you'll have time to get used to the sensation of climbing and being off the ground.

If you work with an instructor or go out with experienced friends, you'll only need a few items. Once you learn the basics and are ready to climb on your own, you'll need to invest in a lot more equipment. But getting started is easy and not terribly expensive. You'll need a harness, a helmet, rock shoes (special sticky, tight-fitting shoes), a locking carabiner, and a belay device.

Best Climbs

Angel Wings, Sequoia and Kings Canyon National Park. Climbers flock to the sheer south face of this 1,800-foot granite wall, which offers several stellar climbs. Across the park, the west face of Moro Rock, a 6,725-foot granite monolith, provides another 1,000 vertical feet of cracks and knobs.

Longs Peak, Rocky Mountain National Park. At 14,255 feet, this is the tallest of Colorado's fourteeners. Take the Keyhole Route to the top for classic mountaineering challenges (steep cliffs, narrow ledges, and loose rocks) as well as spectacular views. The round-trip 7½-mile trek takes between 10 and 15 hours, and late-afternoon thunderstorms are fairly common, so you should head out early (rangers recommend a pre-sunrise start).

Mount Olympus, Olympic National Park. This 7,980-foot peak offers all the good parts of mountaineering (crossing snowfields and crevasses, ridges and moraine fields) without the expense of leaving the continental U.S. (or subalpine elevation).

Painted Wall, Black Canyon of the Gunnison National Park. A mecca for serious climbers, Painted Wall, on the north side of the canyon, is a jaw-dropping, 2,250-foot-high sheer cliff that's strictly for experts only.

Tuolumne Meadows, Yosemite National Park. Yosemite Valley has El Capitan and Half Dome, but it's hot (and crowded) enough in the summer to send savvy climbers up to Tuolumne Meadows, a spectacular subalpine playground studded with granite domes and cliffs, with multipitch face, knob, crack, and slab climbing routes for all levels.

RAFTING, KAYAKING, AND CANOEING

The national parks offer plenty of opportunity for aquatic adventures, from high-adrenaline trips through rapids (via raft or kayak) to more relaxing outings over gentler waters.

Getting Your Feet Wet

Unless you're a real pro at rafting or kayaking, with your own equipment and loads of experience under your belt, you're most likely going to hit the river with a guide, who will teach you the basics. Navigable rapids are typically classified from I to V, with V being the roughest. If you're interested in white water, and this is your first time, pick a trip on gentler waters (Class II or III). This will give you the chance to see some whitecaps without overwhelming you. This is also a good strategy if you're traveling with kids who may be frightened on more intense rapids.

Experts advise dressing for the temperature of the water, not the air (meaning you'll be bringing clothes that you wouldn't need if you were staying on dry land). Depending on where you are, you might want a few layers, with a sweatshirt or light jacket on top (fleece or another synthetic). Don't wear cotton or jeans: once they get wet, they stay wet (and will leave you chilled). Wear old tennis shoes, water shoes, or sandals that strap securely to your feet (not flip-flops). If you're wearing glasses or sunglasses, be sure you've got a "Croakie" or leash to keep them attached to you. The same goes for your hat (if yours doesn't have a chin strap, you can use a cord to tie it to your life jacket).

Be sure to apply plenty of water-resistant sunscreen. If yours is not the kind that dries completely, skip the backs of your legs: If your skin is slippery, you'll be sliding all over the place and have more trouble staying in the raft.

Best Places for Paddling

Colorado and Green Rivers, Canyonlands National Park. The Colorado and Green Rivers thread through the park, meeting at a confluence before spilling down Cataract Canyon and creating a 14-mile stretch of world-class white water. Upstream, you can hit the flat waters of either river (most launch locations are north of the park boundaries) in a kayak or canoe.

Colorado River, Grand Canyon National Park. You can tackle the rapids and smoother waters of the Colorado on both professionally guided and self-guided river trips.

East Santa Cruz Island, Channel Islands National Park. You'll find your sea kayaking nirvana here, with clear ocean waters and a spectacular shoreline with beautiful sea caves and cliffs to explore.

Kaweah River, Sequoia and Kings Canyon National Park. The middle fork of this river offers challenging Class IV rapids for expert kayakers.

Merced River, Yosemite National Park. A popular summer destination (and a designated Wild and Scenic River), the Merced offers white-water adventures for rafts and kayaks.

Snake River, Grand Teton National Park. The well-named Snake River winds its way through the southeast corner of Yellowstone before spilling into Jackson Lake in Grand Teton National Park, offering opportunities for both shooting some mild rapids and floating (or paddling) over more tranquil waters.

CAMPING

A night in a tent under the stars is the highlight of many trips to a national park.

Camping Tips

Ensuring a pleasant camping experience takes some preparation. Check the weather forecast—and your equipment—before you go. Test out a new tent to find out if there are any problems to contend with, like a faulty zipper, and be sure you know how to set it up.

If you can reserve your tent site ahead of time, take a look at the campground map and try to choose a site that meets your needs—nearer to a bathroom if you have small children, farther away if you want more privacy. The best sites, like ones with lake views, are often snapped up early, so try to reserve in advance.

Best Campgrounds

Fruita, Capitol Reef National Park. Here, there are cool, shady campsites near the orchards and the Freemont River.

Gold Bluffs Beach, Redwood National Park. Situated in nearby Prairie Creek Redwoods State Park on a stretch of rugged Pacific coastline, this campground has easy access to a beach and 70 miles of hiking and biking trails.

Manzanita Lake, Lassen Volcanic National Park. At Manzanita Lake, there are lots of ranger programs, plus fishing, swimming, and a boat launch. The camp store has food, hot showers, and a laundromat.

Mather, Grand Canyon National Park. These comfortable sites on the South Rim have all the comforts of home, including bathrooms, laundry, a cafeteria, and hot showers in nearby Grand Canyon Village.

Morefield, Mesa Verde National Park. Shady, pleasant campsites are adjacent to Morefield Village, a minicity with a café offering a daily all-you-can-eat pancake breakfast and free Wi-Fi, general store, and coin-operated laundry. They'll even rent you a tent, complete with cots and lanterns.

Sheep Creek, Sequoia and Kings Canyon National Park. This campground is nestled in the canyon near the middle fork of the Kings River, with groceries, showers, and other amenities about ¼ mile away, at Cedar Grove Village.

South Rim, Black Canyon of the Gunnison National Park. This conveniently located, fully loaded campground is open year-round.

Tuolumne Meadows, Yosemite National Park. Large, private sites in a spectacular subalpine campground just south of the Tuolumne Meadows and River have easy access to hiking and climbing and lots of ranger programs around the campfire.

Wheeler Peak, Great Basin National Park. Perched at 10,000 feet on Wheeler Peak Scenic Drive, the campground has spectacular views and a short commute to popular trailheads.

3

NATIONAL PARK TOURS

Whether you want an experienced guide for an active-sport trip or an educational but leisurely program that takes the planning out of your hands, tours can be ideal for all ages and life situations—families, outdoor enthusiasts, and retirees.

Adventure Trips

Many trip organizers specialize in only one type of activity, while a few companies guide several kinds of active trips. (In some cases, these larger companies also act essentially as a clearinghouse or agent for smaller trip outfitters.) Be sure to sign on with a reliable outfitter; getting stuck with a shoddy operator can be disappointing, uncomfortable, and even dangerous. Some sports—white-water rafting and mountaineering, for example—have organizations that license or certify guides, and you should be sure that the guide you're with is properly accredited.

American Alpine Institute (AAI). One of the premier rock-climbing and mountaineering schools in the United States, AAI offers courses all over the world in all types of climbing, from trekking and backpacking to high-altitude ascents. ✉ 1515 12th St., Bellingham ☎ 360/671–1505, 800/424–2249 ⊕ www.alpineinstitute.com.

Backroads. Arguably the best-known adventure travel company in the country, Backroads organizes trips to destinations all around the world—including the national parks of the West, Southwest, and Rocky Mountains. ✉ 801 Cedar St., Berkeley ☎ 510/527–1555, 800/462–2848 ⊕ www.backroads.com.

The Great Canadian Adventure Co. This company organizes trips into Canada's wilds, including those in Banff and Jasper national parks. ✉ 6714 101 Ave., Edmonton ☎ 780/414–1676, 888/285–1676 ⊕ www.adventures.ca ✐ From $140.

Off the Beaten Path. This company organizes trips throughout the U.S. and the world—including the national parks in the Rockies, desert Southwest, and Pacific coast—that combine outdoor activities with learning experiences. Their various National Parks Guided Group Journeys hit Arches, Canyonlands, Big Bend, Yellowstone, Glacier, Grand Canyon, Mount Rainier, and Zion national parks, among others. ✉ 7 E. Beall St., Bozeman ☎ 800/445–2995 ⊕ www.offthebeatenpath.com ✐ From $2,295.

REI Adventures. The outdoor outfitter conducts trips to the national parks, among other destinations. Examples include hiking in Arches, Capitol Reef, or Death Valley; cycling in Zion and Bryce Canyon; kayaking in Yellowstone or Grand Teton; rock climbing in Joshua Tree; and backpacking in the Grand Canyon, Rocky Mountain, or Yosemite National Park. ☎ 253/437–1100, 800/622–2236 ⊕ www.rei.com/adventures.

Sierra Club Outings. The travel arm of the iconic environmental organization, which was founded in 1892 by John Muir, organizes a variety of active trips (some of them service-oriented "volunteer vacations") to the national parks, including Grand Canyon, Guadalupe Mountains, North Cascades, Olympic, Mount Rainier, and Yellowstone. ✉ 85 2nd St., 2nd fl., San Francisco ☎ 415/977–5522 ⊕ www.sierraclub.org/outings.

Timberline Adventures. Through Timberline Adventures, you can book hiking and cycling trips into virtually all of the Western parks, including Arches, Bryce Canyon, Big Bend, Capitol Reef, and Zion. ✉ 505 Stacy Ct., Suite F, Lafayette ☎ 303/664–8388, 800/417–2453 ⊕ www.timbertours.com.

The World Outdoors. This guide company offers hiking and multisport trips in Arches, Banff, Big Bend, Bryce Canyon, Canyonlands, Glacier, Grand Canyon, Grand Teton, Rocky Mountain, Sequoia and Kings Canyon, Yellowstone, Yosemite, and Zion national parks (and other places around the world). ⊠ *2840 Wilderness Pl., Suite D, Boulder* ☎ *303/413–0946, 800/488–8483* ⊕ *www.theworldoutdoors.com.*

Senior Tours

Those in their golden years can join special tours, some of which are quite adventurous.

Road Scholar. This branch of the not-for-profit group Elderhostel, Inc., sends adult travelers on educational and adventurous trips all around the world. They've got offerings in many national parks, including less-visited parks like Big Bend, Channel Islands, and Lassen Volcanic. ⊠ *11 Ave. de Lafayette, Boston* ☎ *800/454–5768* ⊕ *www.roadscholar.org.*

Walking the World. This tour company offers adventure travel for the 50+ crowd to U.S. and international destinations—including Arches, Capitol Reef, and Rocky Mountain national parks. ☎ *970/498–0500* ⊕ *www.walkingtheworld.com.*

Single-Park Tours

If you want to concentrate solely on one park, contact the park directly to learn about organized tours they may have. There is also an array of tour companies that focus on specific parks.

Grand Canyon Tour Company. This operator provides tours of the park—by bus, helicopter, or plane—from nearby Las Vegas. They also offer guided rafting, hiking, and overnight camping trips in the park. ⊠ *795 E. Tropicana Ave., Las Vegas* ☎ *702/655–6060, 800/222–6966* ⊕ *www.grandcanyontourcompany.com* ✉ *From $79.99.*

The Yellowstone Association Institute. The field institute of this nonprofit offers educational seminars and guided one-day and multiday tours and trips for adults and families in Yellowstone, ranging from backcountry expeditions to "Lodging and Learning" experiences. ⊠ *Yellowstone National Park* ☎ *406/848–2400* ⊕ *www.yellowstoneassociation.org.*

Tours with Accessibility

Access Tours. This group leads eight- to 12-day trips into U.S. and Canadian national parks (and other Western destinations) for people who use wheelchairs or have other mobility impairments; trips can be customized for small groups. ⊠ *Driggs* ☎ *208/787–2338* ⊕ *www.accesstours.org.*

PHOTOGRAPHY TIPS

Today's digital cameras make it difficult to take a truly lousy picture, but there are still some things even the best models can't do on their own. The tips here (some of them classic photography techniques) won't turn you into the next Ansel Adams, but they might prevent you from being upstaged by your eight-year-old with her smartphone.

The Golden Hours. The best photos are taken when most of us are either snoozing or eating dinner: about an hour before and after sunrise and sunset. When the light is gentle and golden, your photos are less likely to be overexposed or filled with harsh shadows and squinting people.

Divide to Conquer. You can't go wrong with the Rule of Thirds: When you're setting up a shot, mentally divide your picture area into thirds, horizontally and vertically, which will give you nine squares. Any one of the four places where the lines intersect (the four corners of the center square) represents a good spot to place your primary subject. (If all this talk of imaginary lines makes your head spin, just remember not to automatically plop your primary focal point in the center of your photos.)

Lock Your Focus. To get a properly focused photo using a camera with auto-focus, press the shutter button down halfway and wait a few seconds before pressing down completely. (On most cameras, a light or a beep will indicate that you're good to go.)

Circumvent Auto-Focus. If your camera isn't homing in on your desired focal point, center the primary subject smack in the middle of the frame and depress the shutter button halfway, allowing the camera to focus. Then, without lifting your finger, compose your photo properly (moving your camera so the focal point isn't in the center of the shot), and press the shutter all the way down.

Jettison the Jitters. Shaky hands are among the most common causes of out-of-focus photos. If you're not good at immobility, invest in a tripod or rest the camera on something steady—such as a wall, a bench, or a rock—when you shoot. If all else fails, lean against something sturdy to brace yourself.

Consider the Imagery. Take a moment or two to consider *why* you're shooting what you're shooting. Once you've determined this, start setting up your photo. Look for interesting lines that curve into your image—such as a path, the shoreline, or a fence—and use them to create the impression of depth. You can do the same thing by photographing people with their bodies or faces positioned at an angle to the camera.

Ignore All the Rules. Sure, thoughtful contemplation and careful execution are likely to produce brilliant images, but there are times when you just need to capture the moment. If you see something wonderful, grab your camera and just get the picture. If the photo turns out to be blurry, off-center, or over- or underexposed, you can always Photoshop it later.

Smartphone Tips: When possible, don't use the zoom tool. This reduces the picture's resolution and can lead to fuzzy photos. Instead, it's best to crop your photos manually. Also, it's helpful to turn on the grid feature, which helps you compose your shots.

Special Considerations. If you're going to any Indian reservations (many are near national parks), check the rules before you take photographs. In many cases you must purchase a permit.

STAYING HEALTHY, PLAYING IT SAFE

Altitude Sickness

Altitude sickness can result when you've moved to high elevations without having time to adjust. When you're at a mile (5,280 feet) or more above sea level, and especially when you're higher than 8,500 feet, you may feel symptoms of altitude sickness: shortness of breath, light-headedness, nausea, fatigue, headache, and insomnia. To help your body adjust, drink lots of water, avoid alcohol, and wait a day or two before attempting vigorous activity. If your symptoms are severe, last several days, or worsen, seek medical attention.

Animal Bites

Although animals abound in the national parks, the odds of your meeting one face to face, let alone sustaining a bite, are slim (especially if you follow the rules about not feeding them). But if you are bitten or scratched by any wild animal—even a small one—seek medical attention. You may need stitches and antibiotics, or a rabies or tetanus shot. If that animal is a snake, stay calm (if the snake is venomous, a lot of movement can spread the poison). Have someone else get medical help for you right away.

Dehydration

If your body doesn't have the fluids it needs, you're dehydrated. Symptoms can range from minor (a dull headache) to life-threatening (seizures, coma). Dehydration is often caused by excessive sweating coupled with inadequate fluid intake, and is a real concern in the national parks, where visitors are generally active (hiking, climbing) but not good at carrying and drinking water. Dehydration is a particular problem for children and seniors and for anyone exercising in dry climates; it's also more likely at high altitudes. To counter a mild case, drink water or another beverage. Take small sips over a period of time instead of trying to force down a large amount. A serious case requires immediate medical attention. To prevent dehydration, be sure to bring and consume enough water: ½ to 1 quart per person for each hour of exercise.

Don't Feed the Animals

It's dangerous—and illegal (you'll be fined). Animals in many national parks are used to humans being around and may not flee at your presence. But feeding wild animals habituates them to humans and teaches them to look to us for food. When that happens, they lose the ability to hunt or forage on their own, meaning they might starve to death or be hit by cars when looking for handouts. Feeding animals also causes them to be more aggressive, and thus more dangerous, to future visitors. Aggressive animals are removed from areas where they'll have contact with people; in some cases, they're relocated, but in others, they're put down.

Heat-Related Illness

Typically caused by excessive exertion in high temperatures such as a strenuous hike in the desert, heat exhaustion or more serious heatstroke can cause nausea, headaches, and dizziness—and even seizures, unconsciousness, and death. If you suspect heat-related illness, rest in a cool, shady place and drink water. Dehydration is often a factor in heat exhaustion and heatstroke. Apply cool compresses to the head, forehead, and trunk. If the victim is unconscious or confused, seek medical help immediately.

GREAT ITINERARIES

4

Updated
by Martha
Connors

Due to their grand size and endless recreation opportunities, visitors can easily spend an entire trip exploring just one national park. But adventurous travelers looking to discover more of the West can take on a bigger itinerary involving several parks, plus a couple of other destinations (national monuments, state parks, scenic byways, and the like) that show off some of the most impressive scenery America has to offer. We've put together a collection of these itineraries, aimed at the most popular (and feasible) routes taken by curious explorers.

Most of the national parks are so large you need a vehicle to properly explore, so planning a driving trip to visit them is a no-brainer. Whether you fly into the nearest airport and rent a car or drive all the way in your own vehicle, these itineraries can help you plan your route—and your time in the parks—to give you the best experience possible. Each itinerary is meant to be used for inspiration in planning your own trip, tailored to your interests and your travel style. We suggest you pick the parks that most appeal to you and linger a little longer there. That being said, those who want to see more in less time will prefer the tours just as they are.

We've developed these itineraries based on the idea that you'll be traveling during the summer, when you'll find most roads and facilities open in the parks. If you'll be traveling at another time of year, be sure to check with the park(s) you'll be visiting about road conditions and closures. Many parks are in remote and/or mountainous areas, accessible by roads that are subject to seasonal closures.

You should also note that "summer" can mean something different in different parts of the West; warm weather typically arrives much later in the year in Canada and the northern United States than it does in Arizona and New Mexico. Additionally, we're assuming you'll be traveling in a passenger car. If you're driving an RV (or pulling a trailer), check with the park(s) ahead of time to see if they have any restrictions on these vehicles.

WASHINGTON STATE NATIONAL PARKS ROAD TRIP ITINERARY, 8 DAYS

A trip to Washington's three national parks—plus a visit to Mount St. Helen's National Volcanic Monument—takes you through rugged Pacific coastline and high alpine terrain as well as lush temperate rainforest, glaciers, waterfalls, and some of the largest remnants of ancient forests in the U.S.

4

DAY 1: WELCOME TO WASHINGTON STATE

For those coming from out of state, the nearest airport is ❶ **Seattle-Tacoma International,** where you can start your journey by picking up a rental car. Depending on when your flight gets in, you can rest up at a nearby hotel for the night or make the 85-mile, 1½-hour drive to ❷ **Sedro-Woolley,** Washington, where you can spend the night.

DAY 2: NORTH CASCADES NATIONAL PARK

46 miles or about an hour drive from Sedro-Woolley.

From Sedro-Woolley, drive east for 46 miles along Route 20, also known as the North Cascades Highway, to the entrance of ❸ **North Cascades National Park.** Take your first stroll through an old-growth forest on the Skagit River Loop (1.8 miles), which starts at the visitor center near the town of Newhalem, about 9 miles from the entrance, then devote the rest of the day to driving through the park on Route 20, stopping at various overlooks. Exit the park and continue through the scenic Methow Valley and on to ❹ **Chelan** (about 190 miles from the park's western boundary) to stay the night.

DAYS 3 AND 4: MOUNT RAINIER NATIONAL PARK

205 miles or a 3-hour, 45-minute drive from Chelan; 136 miles or a 2-hour, 45-minute drive from Arlington.

From Chelan, get an early start to drive to Ohanapecosh, the southeastern entrance to ❺ **Mount Rainier National Park.** When you arrive, take a drive on the spectacular Sunrise Road (about 30 miles round-trip), which reveals the "back" (northeast) side of Rainier. Book a room in nearby ❻ **Ashford** (about 19 miles east of the park's Nisqually entrance) and make that your base for the next two nights.

The next day, energetic hikers will want to tackle one of the four- to six-hour trails that scale the park's many peaks. Less ambitious visitors can take one of the shorter hikes in the Paradise Inn area or join a ranger-led walk through wildflower meadows. Another option is to hike to Panorama Point (a strenuous 4-mile round-trip), near the foot of the Muir Snowfield, for breathtaking views of the glaciers and high ridges of Rainier. Finish your day with dinner at the Paradise Inn, where you can watch the sunset on the peak.

DAY 5: MOUNT ST. HELENS AND THE OLYMPIC FOOTHILLS

120 miles or a 2½-hour drive from Mount Rainier.

Today, drive south to spend the day visiting the **❼ Mount St. Helens National Volcanic Monument,** where you can enter from the west side via Route 504 and see the destruction caused by the 1980 eruption. After leaving the monument, follow Route 504 back to Interstate 5 and head north to Olympia, winding through scenic Puget Sound countryside, skirting the Olympic foothills, and periodically dipping down to the waterfront en route to **❽ Port Angeles,** where you'll spend the night.

DAYS 6 AND 7: OLYMPIC NATIONAL PARK

212 miles or a 4-hour drive from Mount St. Helens to Port Angeles.

The next morning, launch into a full day at **❾ Olympic National Park.** From the Port Angeles entrance, drive 17 miles south to Hurricane Ridge, where you'll find several trails taking you through meadows and subalpine forest. The Hurricane Hill Trail (3.2 miles round-trip) delivers panoramic views of the mountains and ocean. Afterward, head back to Port Angeles for the night.

On Day 7, follow U.S. 101 west to ❿ **La Push,** a skinny satellite of coastal land that's part of the national park (69 miles from Port Angeles). From La Push, hike 1.4 miles to Third Beach for a taste of the wild Pacific coastline. Back on U.S. 101, head south to the town of Forks and then east to the ⓫ **Hoh Rain Forest,** also part of Olympic National Park. Explore the moss-covered alders and big-leaf maples, then follow a circular route on U.S. 101 to ⓬ **Lake Quinault,** winding west toward the coast, then back to the lake and the national park. Check into the Lake Quinault Lodge, then drive up the river to access one of several trails—the Graves Creek Trail is a popular choice—through the lush Quinault Valley.

DAY 8: HEADING HOME

Catch your flight back home from Seattle–Tacoma International, about 130 miles (a 2½-hour drive) from Olympic.

CANADIAN ROCKIES NATIONAL PARKS ROAD TRIP ITINERARY, 8 DAYS

A few hundred miles from the U.S. border, the national parks of Jasper and Banff offer spectacular scenery like glaciers, hot springs, and snow-capped peaks, along with the incomparable blue waters of Lake Louise.

DAY 1: WELCOME TO THE CANADIAN ROCKIES

Most visitors will arrive at ❶ **Edmonton International Airport.** You can spend your first night in a hotel close to the airport or make the 4-hour drive to Jasper right away.

DAYS 2 AND 3: JASPER NATIONAL PARK

396 km (246 miles) or a 4-hour drive from Edmonton International.

Begin your trip to ❷ **Jasper National Park** with a tour of the historic Jasper Townsite; be sure to stop at the Jasper Information Centre to get trail maps and information about free park interpretive programs. Then take a drive to ❸ **Disaster Point,** about 40 km (24 miles) east of Jasper on Highway 16 (Yellowhead Highway), while keeping an eye out for bighorn sheep and other wildlife. Stop at nearby ❹ **Miette Hot Springs,** 61 km (37 miles) east of Jasper, to enjoy a swim in the hot mineral pools. Book a room in Jasper for the next two nights.

Spend the next morning exploring ❺ **Mount Edith Cavell,** located off Highway 93 (the Icefields Parkway) and Cavell Road about 28 km (17 miles) south of Jasper. The 1-km (0.6-mile) trail from the parking lot leads to the base of an imposing cliff, where you can see Angel Glacier. A steep 3-km (2-mile) trail climbs up the valley to Cavell Meadows, which are carpeted with wildflowers from mid-July to mid-August. There are many options for the afternoon: hiking in nearby ❻ **Maligne Canyon,** kayaking in Maligne Lake, horseback riding, or mountain biking.

DAY 4: ICEFIELDS PARKWAY TO LAKE LOUISE

230 km (140 miles) or a 3-hour drive to Lake Louise.

From Jasper, head south 31 km (19 miles) on Highway 93, otherwise known as the Icefields Parkway, to ❼ **Athabasca Falls.** The 75-foot falls are some of the most powerful in the Canadian national parks. Continue along the Parkway until you reach the Athabasca Glacier, one of the eight major glaciers making up the ❽ **Columbia Icefield.** This incredible ice field is one of the largest accumulations of ice and snow south of the Arctic Circle.

Enjoy lunch at the Icefield Centre, and then experience an ice explorer bus tour or a guided hike of the Athabasca Glacier. ■ **TIP➜ For safety reasons, do not venture onto the glacier without a guide.** Continue driving along the Icefields Parkway and into Banff National Park, passing the Weeping Wall and stopping to stretch your legs at the Saskatchewan River Crossing and scenic Bow Lake, before stopping for the night at ❾ **Lake Louise.**

DAY 5: LAKE LOUISE

Spend the morning enjoying the scenery at beautiful Lake Louise, snapping a few pictures of the impressive Victoria Glacier flowing off the mountain at the lake's end. You can enjoy afternoon tea at the classy Fairmont Chateau Lake Louise Hotel adjacent to the lake, then ride the Lake Louise Sightseeing Gondola to the Interpretive Centre at the top, where you can participate in a guided hike or presentation (or just have lunch) on an alpine plateau with a view of a dozen-plus glaciers. If time permits, take a drive 40 km (24 miles) west to ❿ **Yoho National Park** and **Emerald Lake,** where you can rent a canoe, have dinner, or just take a stroll. Afterward, head back to Lake Louise for the night.

DAYS 6 AND 7: BANFF NATIONAL PARK

57 km (36 miles) or an hour drive from Lake Louise.

Spend the morning of Day 6 exploring the quaint shops and restaurants crammed together on Banff Avenue in the town of ⓫ **Banff.** Stop at the Fairmont Banff Springs Hotel, a National Historic Site, and stroll the grounds or take a guided horseback ride from the on-site stables. Finish your day with a late-night dip in the Banff Upper Hot Springs. Spend the next two nights at the gorgeous Fairmont Banff Springs (or one of the more affordable lodgings in town).

On your second day in Banff, hike around Vermilion Lakes, off Highway 1. Common wildlife sightings in this wetlands setting include elk, bighorn sheep, muskrats, and the occasional moose. Then hop on the Banff Gondola to enjoy the view from the 7,500-foot summit of Sulfur Mountain. Later on, you can hike the 3-km (1-mile) trail around Johnson Lake or hit the water in a canoe or kayak.

Canadian
Rockies

DAY 8: HEADING HOME

It's 355 km (221 miles), about 3½ hours of driving, from Banff back to Edmonton International Airport.

YELLOWSTONE AND GRAND TETON NATIONAL PARKS ROAD TRIP ITINERARY, 7 DAYS

A visit to these two parks takes you through one of the last remaining natural ecosystems in this region of the world. Here, you'll see wildlife ranging from beavers, bison, and bears to weasels and wolves, plus pristine mountain lakes, bubbling mud pots, and the world's biggest collection of geysers.

DAY 1: WELCOME TO YELLOWSTONE

If you'll be flying, the ❶ **Jackson Hole Airport** in Jackson, Wyoming, is probably the best place to start, as it's only an hour from the southern entrance of Yellowstone. You'll find plenty of lodging options in Jackson

Yellowstone and
Grand Teton

for your first night, or you can book a room at one of the park's nine lodges—the centrally located Lake Hotel or the iconic Old Faithful Inn.

DAYS 2–4: YELLOWSTONE NATIONAL PARK

Dedicate the next three days to ❷ **Yellowstone National Park,** which, because of its sheer size and incredible diversity of wildlife and scenery, could take a lifetime to explore. Spend your first day on the park's 140-mile Grand Loop Road. This road forms a big figure-eight as it passes nearly every major Yellowstone attraction, and offers interpretive displays, overlooks, and short trails along the way.

On your second day in the park, visit ❸ **Old Faithful** and take a short hike (about 2½ miles round-trip) around Mystic Falls, then head up to the Canyon Village section of the park for a look at the Grand Canyon of Yellowstone, with its two separate waterfalls. For a more strenuous option, hike from Dunraven Pass to the summit of Mount Washburn for wildflowers, wildlife, and panoramic views (6.2 miles round-trip).

For your third day, explore the northern part of the park, starting with the ❹ **Mammoth Hot Springs** area, with its terraced limestone formations. From there, head past Tower-Roosevelt to the Lamar Valley in the far northeast corner of the park for gorgeous mountain views, enormous

The largest hot spring in the country, the striking Grand Prismatic Spring, is located in Yellowstone, just north of Old Faithful.

herds of bison, and your best chance to spot wolves. Then check out the Mud Volcano and Sulphur Caldron in the Hayden Valley area, just south of Canyon Village.

DAYS 5 AND 6: GRAND TETON NATIONAL PARK

8 miles from Yellowstone's southern entrance to the northern boundary of Grand Teton.

Leaving Yellowstone, drive south into ❺ **Grand Teton National Park.** The sheer ruggedness of the Tetons makes them seem imposing and unapproachable, but a drive on Teton Park Road, with frequent stops at scenic turnouts, will get you up close and personal with the peaks. The Jenny Lake Scenic Drive delivers fantastic views as well; just north of ❻ **Jenny Lake,** pull over to the Leigh Lake Trailhead for a hike. You can take the 3.7-mile loop around String Lake, or head north, then take the right-hand branch of the trail and follow the eastern shore of the lake (turn around at the campground on Trapper Lake) for a 9-mile hike. Spend your two nights at any of the excellent lodges or cabins in the park.

Your second day in the park, head back to Jenny Lake and catch a ferry across to the western side, where you can take either a short hike along the Cascade Canyon Trail (2 miles round-trip) or hike the Forks of Cascade Canyon, a 9.6-mile trip that's well worth the effort. If you'd rather explore Jenny Lake from the water, rent a canoe or kayak or take a guided tour.

Black Hills
and Badlands

DAY 7: HEAD HOME

When your visit to Grand Teton is complete, getting back to the Jackson Hole Airport couldn't be simpler: it's actually inside the park boundary, about 4 miles from the southern entrance.

BLACK HILLS AND BADLANDS NATIONAL PARKS ROAD TRIP ITINERARY, 6 DAYS

The national parks of southwestern South Dakota—along with the state park and two national memorials nearby—deliver a surprising variety of sights: the swaying grasses and abundant wildlife of one of the country's few remaining intact prairies, the complex labyrinth of passages and unique geologic formations in one of the world's longest caves, and some of the richest fossil beds on Earth.

DAY 1: WIND CAVE NATIONAL PARK

The closest commercial airport is ❶ **Rapid City Regional Airport**, about 70 miles from Wind Cave. Arrive in the morning to pick up your rental car and make the 1½-hour drive to ❷ **Wind Cave National Park**, with more than 33,000 acres of wildlife habitat above ground (home to bison, elk, pronghorn, and coyotes) and one of the world's longest caves below. Take an afternoon cave tour and a short drive through the park. Spend the night in ❸ **Hot Springs**, about 7 miles from the park's southern boundary.

DAY 2: CUSTER STATE PARK

20 miles or a 40-minute drive from Hot Springs.

Spend today at ❹ **Custer State Park,** which is adjacent to Wind Cave, about 20 miles north of Hot Springs. The 71,000-acre park has exceptional drives, lots of wildlife (including a herd of 1,300 bison), and fingerlike granite spires rising from the forest floor (they're the reason this is called the Needles region of South Dakota). While you're in the park, be sure to visit Limber Pine Natural Area, a National Natural Landmark containing spectacular ridges of granite. If you have time, check out the Cathedral Spires trail, 2.5 miles round-trip. Overnight in one of five mountain lodges at the Custer State Park Resort.

DAY 3: JEWEL CAVE NATIONAL MONUMENT AND CRAZY HORSE MEMORIAL

About 16 miles from Custer State Park to Jewel Cave; 19 miles from Jewel Cave to Crazy Horse Memorial.

Today, venture down U.S. 16 to ❺ **Jewel Cave National Monument**, 13 miles west of the town of Custer, an underground wilderness where you can see beautiful nailhead and dogtooth spar crystals lining its more than 168 miles of passageways.

After visiting Jewel Cave, head back to Custer and take U.S. 16/385 to ❻ **Crazy Horse Memorial** (about 5 miles north of Custer), home to a colossal mountain carving of the legendary Lakota leader and the Indian Museum of North America. Afterward, head 10 miles north to the former gold and tin mining town of ❼ **Hill City**, where you'll spend the night.

DAY 4: MOUNT RUSHMORE NATIONAL MEMORIAL

12 miles or about a 30-minute drive from Hill City.

This morning, travel 12 miles to ❽ **Mount Rushmore National Memorial,** where you can view the huge carved renderings of presidents Washington, Jefferson, Theodore Roosevelt, and Lincoln. Afterward, head northwest for 23 miles back to Rapid City, the eastern gateway to the Black Hills. Spend the night here.

DAY 5: BADLANDS NATIONAL PARK

75 miles or a 1-hour, 15-minute drive from Rapid City to the northeast entrance of Badlands.

Begin your day early and drive west (75 miles via Interstate 90) to ❾ **Badlands National Park**, a 244,000-acre geologic wonderland. The Badlands Highway Loop Road (Highway 240) wiggles through the moonlike landscape of the park's north unit for 32 miles. Stop in at the Ben Reifel Visitor Center, at the far eastern edge of the park, to pick up a trail map and head out on a hike. The Notch Trail, 1.5 miles round-trip, offers spectacular views of the White River Valley, but is definitely not for anyone with a fear of heights. The Cliff Shelf trail, 0.5 mile round-trip, is a more mellow option that showcases rock formations and juniper forest as well as occasional wildlife sightings.

After you leave the park, head back to Rapid City to spend the night.

DAY 6: HEADING HOME

The airport in Rapid City is about 10 minutes southeast of town.

CALIFORNIA NATIONAL PARKS ROAD TRIP ITINERARY, 9 DAYS

This trip takes you to California's most popular national parks. Yosemite is a nearly 1,200-square-mile expanse in the western Sierras filled with meadows, waterfalls, and spectacular granite domes and canyons. Nearby Sequoia and Kings Canyon national parks deliver spectacular alpine scenery along with the world's largest trees. And Death Valley is a land of extremes, with its impossibly dry (and hot) below-sea-level basin alongside high mountain peaks and diverse wildlife.

DAY 1: WELCOME TO CALIFORNIA

If you're planning to start this trip with a flight, your best bet would be to arrive at ❶ **Fresno Yosemite International Airport,** which is about 70 miles from the southern entrance to Yosemite (your first stop) and 80 miles from the northern entrance to Sequoia and Kings Canyon (your last).

From the airport, head north toward ❷ **Yosemite National Park** and its ❸ **Mariposa/Wawona Entrance,** following Highway 41. Depending on how much time you've got, either do some exploring (head for the Yosemite Valley Visitor Center, about 32 miles from the Wawona entrance) or look for lodging. You can stay in the park (there are several options, from primitive camping to luxury rooms at The Ahwahnee hotel) or in ❹ **Mariposa,** about 43 miles (1 hour) west of the Wawona Entrance on Route 140.

DAYS 2–4: YOSEMITE NATIONAL PARK

70 miles or about a 1½-hour drive from the airport.

Early in the morning of Day 2, head into Yosemite Valley, near the center of the park, and take a hike on Lower Yosemite Fall Trail, an easy 1.1-mile loop. If you've got more time and ambition, continue on for the first mile of the Upper Fall Trail to Columbia Rock, where you'll be rewarded with spectacular views of both the upper and lower sections of the highest waterfall in North America. Afterward, stop in at the historic The Ahwahnee hotel, then attend one of the ranger programs or a presentation at Yosemite Theater.

Best of California

On your second day in the park, head back to the Yosemite Valley area and take an easy hike around Mirror Lake (5 miles round-trip) or a more strenuous trek to Vernal Fall (2.4 miles round-trip), then drop in at the Yosemite Museum (next to the visitor center) and the nearby reconstructed Indian Village. Drive up to Glacier Point for a valley-wide view, timing your arrival for sunset.

On your last day in the park, head east to Tuolumne Meadows, where you can stretch your legs with a hike (an easy option is the 1.5-mile round-trip trail to Soda Springs and historic Parsons Lodge). Then take a drive on Tioga Road, a 59-mile stretch through the high country that takes you over Tioga Pass (9,941 feet) and along the highest stretch of road in California. Leave the park through the ❺ **Tioga Pass Entrance,** then drive southeast 134 miles (about 2 hours, 15 minutes) to the town of ❻ **Lone Pine,** where you'll spend the night.

DAYS 5 AND 6: DEATH VALLEY NATIONAL PARK

38 miles or a 40-minute drive from Lone Pine to the park's western entrance.

On Day 5, drive to ❼ **Death Valley National Park,** known as the lowest, driest, and hottest place in North America. Covering more than 5,300 square miles, it's also the biggest national park in the lower 48, with vast expanses of desert and mountain ranges extending as far as the eye can see.

Begin in the Furnace Creek area, roughly in the middle of the park. If you're getting an early start, hike into Golden Canyon by taking the 1-mile-long interpretive trail, which starts 2 miles south of Highway 190 on Badwater Road. From there, head to Devil's Golf Course (11 miles south of Furnace Creek) to see millions of tiny salt pinnacles and, if you get up close, a mass of perfectly round holes. Badwater Basin, 8 miles farther south, has expansive saltwater flats and the lowest point in the park, which is 282 feet below sea level. Then go to the highest spot—Dante's View, 5,000 feet above the valley floor—for the best views and blessedly cooler temperatures (the lookout is about 20 miles southeast of Furnace Creek). If you want to hike, there's a trail leading from the parking area onto Dante's Ridge that offers even more spectacular vistas (it's ½ mile to the first summit, then another 4 miles to Mount Perry).

On your second day in Death Valley, explore the northern section of the park, near Grapevine Canyon (about 52 miles north of Furnace Creek). Uhebe Crater is visible from a turnout on the road. From there, if your car has high clearance and good tires, you can drive 27 miles southwest on a rough dirt road to the Racetrack, a phenomenal dry lake bed famous for its mysterious moving rocks (to see the rocks, drive 2 miles past the Grandstand parking area). From there, double back and drive another 3 miles east to Scotty's Castle, a quirky historic mansion.

Leave the park via the western (Panamint) entrance and head southwest toward Sequoia and Kings Canyon. Stop in ❽ **Sanger,** 280 miles (about 4½ hours) from Death Valley, to spend the night.

DAYS 7 AND 8: SEQUOIA AND KINGS CANYON NATIONAL PARKS

41 miles or a 55-minute drive from Sanger.

From Sanger, drive east to the Big Stump Entrance of ❾ **Kings Canyon National Park.** Inside the park, head to Grant Grove Village and stop at the visitor center there, then take the Kings Canyon Scenic Byway (Route 180) along the Kings River and its giant granite canyon that is well over a mile deep at some points. Stop along the way at pull-outs for long vistas of some of the highest mountains in the United States. Hike the Zumwalt Meadow Trail (1.5 miles), which starts just before the end of the road, 4.5 miles from Cedar Grove Village, for gorgeous views of the park's largest meadow, plus high granite walls, talus, and the river below. At the end of the day, follow Route 180 back to Grant Grove Village and take Generals Highway south into Sequoia National Park. Leave through the Ash Mountain Entrance and head to the nearby town of ❿ **Visalia** (35 miles, about 46 minutes away) for the night.

Spend the next day exploring ⓫ **Sequoia National Park,** where some of the world's oldest and largest trees stand. Driving the winding, 40-mile-long Generals Highway takes about two hours. Be sure to stop at the Redwood Mountain Overlook, just outside Cedar Grove Village, for terrific views of the world's largest sequoia grove. Take a hike on the Congress Trail (2 miles), which starts at the General Sherman Tree, the world's largest tree, just off the Generals Highway near Wolverton Road. At the end of the day, head back to Sanger for the night.

DAY 9: HEADING HOME

From Sanger, it's a short 13-mile drive (about 20 minutes) to the Fresno airport.

UTAH AND ARIZONA NATIONAL PARKS ROAD TRIP ITINERARY, 9 DAYS

This itinerary takes you through Zion's massive sandstone cliffs and narrow slot canyons, the hoodoos (odd-shape pillars of rock left by erosion) of Bryce Canyon, and the overwhelming majesty of the Grand Canyon, close to 300 river miles long, 18 miles wide, and a mile deep.

DAY 1: WELCOME TO CANYON COUNTRY

Plan to fly into and out of ❶ **St. George Municipal Airport** in St. George, Utah. It's close to all three parks, with Zion a little more than an hour away.

From the airport, head east toward ❷ **Zion National Park,** about 46 miles. Depending on how much daylight you've got, you can start exploring the park—enter at the south entrance and head to the Zion Canyon Visitor Center—or find a room for the next three nights in ❸ **Springdale,** the bustling town just outside the park (1.1 miles from the south entrance).

DAYS 2 AND 3: ZION NATIONAL PARK

46 miles or about a 1-hour drive from the airport to the south entrance of Zion National Park.

Start your day at the visitor center, just inside the south entrance, south of the junction of the Zion–Mount Carmel Highway and the Zion Canyon Scenic Drive. Then explore the Drive, either in your own vehicle or via the park's free shuttle, which runs during the summer months (a round-trip ride takes about 80 minutes). Intrepid hikers will want to tackle the Narrows, Zion's infamous 16-mile-long gorge cut by the Virgin River, which requires hikers to spend more than half of their time walking, wading, or swimming in the fast-flowing river. For everyone else, Zion offers plenty of other hiking options. The Emerald Pool trails (about 1 mile each) take you on a fairly easy hike from Zion Lodge, about 3 miles from Canyon Junction, to Lower and Upper Emerald Pool and waterfalls.

Spend the next day exploring the Kolob Canyons, in the northwestern corner of the park about 40 miles from Canyon Junction. Take the Kolob Canyons Road 5 miles to its end at the Kolob Canyons Viewpoint, where you'll get fabulous views of the surrounding red rock canyons. For a spectacular 5-mile hike, drive about 2 miles back on the Kolob Canyons Road to the Taylor Creek Trail, which takes you past historic homesteaders' cabins and through a narrow box canyon to the Double Arch Alcove, a large arched grotto.

At the end of the day, leave the park via the beautiful Zion–Mount Carmel Highway and its historic mile-long tunnel. You'll pass through slickrock country, with huge, petrified sandstone dunes etched by ancient waters, and head to Bryce Canyon, where you'll spend the night (you've got a few lodging options, both inside and just outside the park in the town of Bryce Canyon).

DAY 4: BRYCE CANYON NATIONAL PARK

74 miles or about a 1-hour, 25-minute drive from the east entrance of Zion.

Start your tour of ❹ **Bryce Canyon National Park** at the visitor center, about 1 mile past the park entrance. Central to your tour of Bryce Canyon is the 18-mile-long main park road, where numerous scenic turnouts reveal vistas of bright red-orange rock. ■ **TIP→ If you're visiting in the summer, the free Bryce Canyon Shuttle will take you to many of the park's most popular attractions.** Trails worth exploring include the 1-mile Bristlecone Loop Trail and the 1.3-mile Navajo Loop Trail, both of which will get you into the heart of the park.

At the end of the day, leave the park and head toward ❺ **Kanab**, 78 miles (about 1 hour, 25 minutes) away, to spend the night en route to the Grand Canyon.

DAY 5: EN ROUTE TO THE GRAND CANYON

284 miles or a 5-hour, 25-minute drive from Bryce Canyon to the South Rim of the Grand Canyon.

Today, you'll drive from Kanab to ❻ **Grand Canyon National Park**, about 210 miles away. Check into a hotel in Grand Canyon Village on the ❼ **South Rim** or in ❽ **Tusayan**, a few miles to the south, for the next two nights. If you've got time, hike (or take the shuttle) to Yavapai Point, just west of the visitor center in the South Rim Village, to catch the sunset.

DAYS 6–8: GRAND CANYON NATIONAL PARK

If you didn't make it yesterday, begin today's tour with a stop at the Grand Canyon Visitor Center, near Mather Point in the South Rim Village, for the latest maps and information. While you're there, check out the Historic District, with its early-19th-century train depot and other buildings, many built by the Santa Fe Railroad. Get your bearings with a drive (or, if you're visiting early spring–late fall, a free shuttle ride) on the 7-mile-long Hermit Road. Take a hike on the Rim Trail, a nearly flat path (much of which is paved) that hugs the edge of the canyon from the Village to Hermit's Rest, 2.8 miles to the west.

On your second day in the park, tackle the upper section of one of the "Corridor Trails"—South Kaibab or Bright Angel—which start at the South Rim and meet in the Bright Angel Campground at the bottom of the canyon (the third Corridor Trail, North Kaibab, connects the

"Every turn on the Fiery Furnace Trail in Arches brought views of unbelievable natural sculptures, including this double arch." —photo by CarlB9090, Fodors.com member

bottom of the canyon to the North Rim). Bright Angel, the easier of the two, is one of the most scenic paths into the canyon; the trailhead is near Kolb Studio, at the western end of the Village.

For your last day in the park, take an interpretive ranger-led program; they cover a wide variety of subjects, including geology, history, and wildlife so pick up a list at the Grand Canyon Visitor Center. Afterward, you can spend the night in (or near) the park again, or start your drive back toward the airport in St. George. The town of ❾ Fredonia, Arizona (200 miles; 3 hours, 40 minutes from the South Rim) would be a good stopping point for the night.

DAY 9: HEADING HOME

The St. George Municipal Airport is 74 miles (1 hour, 22 minutes) from Fredonia.

UTAH AND COLORADO NATIONAL PARKS ROAD TRIP ITINERARY, 6 DAYS

With this itinerary, you'll get to experience two of Utah's best parks. There's Arches, famous for its spectacular colors and unique land-forms—natural stone arches, soaring pinnacles, plus giant fins and balanced rocks—and Canyonlands, with a wilderness of canyons and buttes carved by the Colorado River and its tributaries. A few hours

away, Colorado's Mesa Verde offers a peek into the lives of the Ancestral Puebloan people, who made it their home from AD 600 to 1300.

DAY 1: WELCOME TO UTAH

The closest airport to your first two destinations is ❶ **Canyonlands Field**,
also known as Moab Airport, where you can get flights to and from
Denver. After you land and get your rental car, head into ❷ **Moab** (18
miles; 25 minutes away), where you'll find plenty of options for food
and lodging. Book yourself a room for the next three nights.

DAYS 2 AND 3: ARCHES NATIONAL PARK

5 miles from Moab.

Your trip begins at ❸ **Arches National Park**, which holds the world's
largest concentration of natural rock windows or "arches." Start with
a guided hike in the Fiery Furnace, a maze of sandstone canyons and
fins that is considered one of the most spectacular hikes in the park. On
your second day, explore the Devil's Garden and Windows sections of
the park. Head back to Moab for the night.

DAYS 4 AND 5: CANYONLANDS

30 miles or about a 35-minute drive from Moab.

From Moab, head to ❹ **Canyonlands National Park.** Start at the park's Island in the Sky District, at the northern end of the park (about 30 miles from Moab). Explore the area from the road, which has many overlooks, or hike the first section of the Upheaval Dome Trail, an 8.3-mile loop that starts at Whale Rock, about 11 miles from the visitor center and spotlights an enormous syncline, or downward fold in the Earth's crust (there are overlooks ½ mile and 1 mile from the trailhead). At the end of the day, on your way back to Moab, take a detour into ❺ **Dead Horse Point State Park**, about 11 miles from the Canyonlands entrance, and head up to the top of the mesa for magnificent views of the Colorado River as it goosenecks through the canyons below.

On Day 5, head to the Needles District, at the southwest corner of the park, and hike the Slickrock Trail (2.4 miles round-trip), keeping an eye out for bighorn sheep. At the end of the day, drive east about 110 miles (2 hours) to ❻ **Cortez,** where you can find a hotel for the night.

DAY 6: MESA VERDE NATIONAL PARK

120 miles or a 2-hour, 12-minute drive from Canyonlands.

From Coretz, drive about 11 miles east to ❼ **Mesa Verde National Park,** with 5,000 archaeological sites (including 600 cliff dwellings) left behind by the Ancestral Puebloan people, who lived here more than 1,000 years ago. Begin your visit at the visitor center, just before the entrance station, to get the latest park information and purchase tour tickets for some of the more popular tours (to get the most out of your visit, plan to take at least one ranger-led tour). Inside the park, stop at the Chapin Mesa Museum, then hike the 0.5-mile Spruce Tree House Trail for a glimpse of the best-preserved cliff dwelling in the park.

After exploring Mesa Verde, you can spend the night at the Far View Lodge inside the park or head back to Cortez. Or, if you've got an early flight in the morning, you can drive back to Moab.

From Mesa Verde, it's a 143-mile (2½-hour) drive to Canyonlands Field airport.

ARCHES
NATIONAL PARK

5

Visit Fodors.com for advice, updates, and bookings

WELCOME TO ARCHES NATIONAL PARK

TOP REASONS TO GO

★ **Arch appeal:** Nowhere in the world has such a large array and quantity of natural arches.

★ **Legendary landscape:** This section of Utah is every photographer's dream. No wonder it's been the chosen backdrop for many Hollywood films.

★ **Treasures hanging in the balance:** Landscape Arch and Balanced Rock look like they might topple tomorrow, and they could! Come quick as the features in this park erode and evolve constantly.

★ **Fins and needles:** Fins are parallel vertical shafts of eroding rock that slowly disintegrate into towerlike "needles." The spaces around and between them will carve their way into your memories like the wind and water that formed them.

★ **Moab:** Known as Utah's "adventure capital," this small town is a great base from which to explore by foot, bicycle, balloon, watercraft, and four-wheeler.

1 Devils Garden. About 18 miles from the visitor center, this is the end of the paved road in Arches. The park's only campground, a picnic area, and access to drinking water can be found just outside the. Trails in Devils Garden lead to a number of picturesque formations including the incomparable Landscape Arch.

2 Fiery Furnace. This forbiddingly named area about 14 miles from the visitor center is so labeled because its orange spires of rock look much like tongues of flame, especially in the late-afternoon sun. Reservations are required weeks in advance to join the twice-daily ranger-guided treks. To visit the Fiery Furnace on your own you'll need a permit and canyoneering savvy.

3 Delicate Arch/Wolfe Ranch. A spur road about 11.7 miles from the visitor center leads to the trail and viewpoint for the park's most famous feature—Delicate Arch. To see the arch from below, follow the road to the viewpoint, park, and take the short walk to one or both easily accessible viewing areas.

4 The Windows. Reached on a spur 9.2 miles from the visitor center, this area of the park is where visitors with little time stop. Here you can see many of the park's natural arches from your car or on an easy rolling trail.

5 Balanced Rock. This is the kind of landmark only nature can conjure up—a giant rock teetering atop a pedestal, creating a 128-foot formation of red rock grandeur right along the roadside, about 9 miles from the visitor center.

6 Petrified Dunes. Just a tiny pull-out about 5 miles from the visitor center, this scenic stop is where you can take pictures of acres and acres of petrified sand dunes.

7 Courthouse Towers. The Three Gossips, Sheep Rock, and Tower of Babel are the rock formations to see here. Enter this section of the park 3 miles past the visitor center. The Park Avenue Trail—named for its steep walls and soaring rocks that look like buildings—winds through the area.

8 Moab. A river-running, mountain-biking, canyoneering hub, unconventional Moab—about 5 miles south of the park—is the can't-miss base for all your adventures and comforts.

UTAH

1 DEVILS
GARDEN   Private Arch

KLONDIKE   Dark Angel
BLUFFS   Double O Arch   Wall Arch
                                (Collapsed)
·Tower Arch   Navajo Arch·   Pine Tree Arch
·   Partition Arch·   Tunnel Arch
Marching   **Landscape Arch**   Devils Garden Trailhead
Men
                    Skyline Arch· ▲ **Amphitheater**
                                    ·· Broken Arch

                                  ·· Sand Dune Arch

                          2 FIERY
                            FURNACE   **3** **Delicate
                                                      Arch**
                              Fiery Furnace
                              Viewpoint
            Salt Valley Overlook   **Wolfe Ranch**·
                                                    Delicate
                                                    Arch Viewpoint
            HERDINA
            PARK   Eye of the
                    Whale Arch·   ·Panorama Point

                      Willow
                      Flats
                              ▲   **5** ·Ham Rock
                          **Balanced   GARDEN OF EDEN
                            Rock**   ·Double Arch
                      Parade of Elephants·   ·North Window Arch
                        Turret Arch· ·· ·South Window Arch

                                    4 THE   128
                                        WINDOWS

                          ·Petrified Dunes Viewpoint

                      6 PETRIFIED
                            DUNES
                          Tower of Babel
            Sheep Rock· ·Courthouse Towers Viewpoint
            Three Gossips· ·The Organ
            7 COURTHOUSE   ·· La Sal Mountains Viewpoint
                    TOWERS
            191   ·· Park Avenue Viewpoint
                    ·Entrance station

                    Visitor Center   128

                    TO
            AIRPORT, GREEN RIVER
            AND CANYONLANDS
            NATIONAL PARK
                                    8 ○ **Moab**

GETTING
ORIENTED

Southeastern Utah's
Arches National Park
boasts some of the
most unimaginable
rock formations in the
world. Off U.S. 191,
Arches is 236 miles
southeast of Salt Lake
City, 27 miles south
of I–70, and 5 miles
north of Moab.

KEY
🏠 Ranger Station
▲ Campground
🎪 Picnic Area
🍴 Restaurant
🏨 Lodge
🥾 Trailhead
🚻 Restrooms
≫ Scenic Viewpoint
⋯⋯ Walking/Hiking Trails
═══ 4-Wheel Drive Dirt Road
═══ 2-Wheel Drive Dirt Road

5

0   1 mi
0   1 km

Updated by
Lisa Church

More than 1 million visitors come to Arches annually, drawn by the red rock landscape and its teasing wind- and water-carved rock formations. The park is named for the 2,000-plus sandstone arches that frame horizons, cast precious shade, and nobly withstand the withering forces of nature and time. Fancifully named attractions like Three Penguins, Queen Nefertiti, and Tower of Babel stir the curiosity, beckoning even the most delicate of travelers from roadside locales. Immerse yourself in this immense park, but don't lose yourself entirely—summer temperatures frequently crack 100°F, and water is hard to come by inside the park boundaries.

ARCHES PLANNER

WHEN TO GO

The busiest times of year are spring and fall. In the spring blooming wildflowers herald the end of winter, and temperatures in the 70s bring the year's largest crowds. The crowds remain steady in summer as the thermostat approaches 100°F and above in July and August. Sudden dramatic cloudbursts create rainfalls over red rock walls in late-summer "monsoon" season.

Fall weather is perfect—clear, warm days and crisp, cool nights. The park is much quieter in winter, and from December through February you can hike many of the trails in relative solitude. Snow seldom falls in the valley beneath the La Sal Mountains, and when it does, Arches is a photographer's paradise, as snow drapes slickrock mounds and natural rock windows.

AVG. HIGH/LOW TEMPS.

Jan.	Feb.	Mar.	Apr.	May	June
44/19	53/25	64/33	76/39	84/49	98/58

July	Aug.	Sept.	Oct.	Nov.	Dec.
100/62	99/61	86/50	77/40	58/32	48/21

Note: Extreme highs often exceed 100°F in July and August.

FESTIVALS AND EVENTS

SPRING **Moab Art Walk.** Moab galleries and shops celebrate the perfect weather of spring and fall with a series of exhibits. Art Walks are held the second Saturday of the month from March through June and September through November. Stroll the streets (6–9 pm) to see and purchase original works by Moab and regional artists. ⊠ *Moab* ☎ *435/259–4912* ⊕ *www.moabartwalk.com.*

FAMILY **Moab Arts Festival.** Every Memorial Day weekend, artists from across the
Fodor's Choice West gather at Moab's Swanny City Park to show their wares, including
★ pottery, photography, and paintings. This fun festival is small enough to be manageable, charges no admission, and offers an array of affordable artwork. There's live music, cultural entertainment, a kids' tent, and lots of food. The arts festival partners with local libation producers to bring a wine and beer festival at the park as part of the event. ⊠ *Moab* ☎ *435/259–2742 Moab Arts Council* ⊕ *www.moabartsfestival.org.*

SUMMER **Canyonlands PRCA Rodeo.** Cowboys come to the Old Spanish Trail
FAMILY Arena (just south of Moab) for three days in late May or early June
Fodor's Choice to try their luck on thrashing bulls and broncs at this annual West-
★ ern tradition. ⊠ *3641 S. Hwy. 191, Moab* ☎ *435/259–4852* ⊕ *www. moabcanyonlandsrodeo.com.*

FALL **Green River Melon Days.** The town claims its melon festival, dating to
FAMILY 1906, is the world's oldest. All the watermelon you can eat, an old-fashioned parade, a 5k run, and other small-town-America activities await you on the third Saturday of September. ⊠ *Green River* ☎ *435/564–3427* ⊕ *melon-days.com.*

Moab Music Festival. Moab's red rocks resonate with world-class music—classical, jazz, and traditional—during this annual festival that takes place in indoor and outdoor venues including the city park, local auditoriums, private homes, and a natural stone grotto along the Colorado River. Musicians from all over the globe perform, and it's one of the West's top music showcases. The festival starts the Thursday before Labor Day and runs about two weeks. ⊠ *Moab* ☎ *435/259–7003* ⊕ *www.moabmusicfest.org.*

PLANNING YOUR TIME

There's no food service within the park, so you'll need to pack snacks, lunch, and plenty of water each day before you head into Arches. You'll also need to plan ahead to get tickets to the daily Fiery Furnace walk with a ranger. It's a highlight for those who are adventurous and in good shape, but during most of the year, you must reserve your spot in advance at ⊕ *www.recreation.gov*. If you don't have a reservation, you can check for spots at the visitor center (make that your very first stop). The one-day itinerary *(below)* is based on what to do if you can't take the walk or what to do on a different day. On the day of your Fiery Furnace walk, you can fill in your spare time with a walk on the Park Avenue trail. And if you have a third day, take a rafting trip on the Colorado River, which runs along the park's boundary.

ARCHES IN ONE DAY

Start as early as sunrise for cool temperatures and some of the best natural light, and head out on the 3-mile round-trip hike on the **Delicate Arch Trail.** The route is strenuous but quite rewarding. Pause for a healthy snack before heading to **Devils Garden,** another great spot for morning photography, where you'll also find the easy, primarily flat trail to **Landscape Arch,** the second of the park's two must-see arches. If you're accustomed to hiking, continue on to **Double O,** but be aware that this portion of the trail is strenuous. Along the way, picnic in the shade of a juniper or in a rock alcove. By the time you return you'll be ready to see the rest of the park by car, with some short strolls on easy paths.

In the mid- to late afternoon, drive to **Balanced Rock** for photos, then on to the **Windows.** Wander around on the easy gravel paths for more great photo ops. Depending on what time the sun is due to set, go into town for dinner before or after you drive out to Delicate Arch or the **Fiery Furnace** and watch the sun set the rocks on fire.

GETTING HERE AND AROUND

AIR TRAVEL

The nearest large airport to southeastern Utah is Walker Field Airport in Grand Junction, Colorado, 110 miles from Moab. Rental cars are available at the Moab Airport, 18 miles north of town, although advance reservations are recommended (☏ 970/244–9100).

CAR TRAVEL

Interstate 70 is the highway that gets you across Utah from Denver. To dip southeast toward Moab, exit the interstate onto U.S. 191, a main artery running all the way south to the Arizona border, skirting Arches' western border, Moab, and the Manti–La Sal National Forest along the way. Alternatively, you can take Route 128, the Colorado River Scenic Byway, traveling just east of Arches. On either road, services can be far apart.

Branching off the main, 18-mile park road are two spurs, one 2½ miles to the Windows section and one 1.6 miles to the Delicate Arch trailhead and viewpoint. There are several four-wheel-drive roads in the park; always check at the visitor center for conditions before attempting to drive them. U.S. 191 tends to back up mid-morning to early afternoon. There's likely to be less traffic at 8 am or sunset.

TRAIN TRAVEL

The *California Zephyr,* operated by Amtrak (☏ 800/872–7245), stops daily in Green River, about 50 miles northwest of Moab.

PARK ESSENTIALS
PARK FEES AND PERMITS

Admission to the park is $25 per vehicle, 15 per motorcycle, and $5 per person entering on foot or bicycle, good for seven days. To encourage visitation to the park during less busy times, Arches also offers an off-peak admission fee of $10 for vehicles and motorcycles; check the Arches website (⊕ *www.nps.gov/arch*) and at the Moab Information Center in town for updated information. You must pay admission to Canyonlands separately. A $50 local park pass grants you admission to both Arches and Canyonlands parks as well as Natural Bridges and Hovenweep national monuments for one year.

Fees are required for the Fiery Furnace ranger-led hike ($16 per adult, $5 per child ages 7–12) and for a permit to hike without a park ranger in the Fiery Furnace ($6 per adult, $3 per child).

PARK HOURS

Arches National Park is open year-round, seven days a week, around the clock. It's in the Mountain time zone.

CELL-PHONE RECEPTION

Cell-phone reception is available intermittently in the park. You can find a public telephone at the park's visitor center.

EDUCATIONAL OFFERINGS
RANGER PROGRAMS

As you explore Arches, look for sandwich boards announcing "Ranger Sightings" and stop for a 3- to 10-minute program led by park staff. Topics range from geology and desert plants to mountain lions and the Colorado River. Most nights, spring through fall, more in-depth campfire programs are available at Devils Garden Campground amphitheater. You may also find guided walks (in addition to the beloved Fiery Furnace walk) during your visit. For information on current schedules and locations of park programs, contact the visitor center (☎ *435/719–2299*) or check the bulletin boards throughout the park.

FAMILY
Fodor'sChoice
★

Fiery Furnace Walk. Join a park ranger on a two- or three-hour walk through a labyrinth of rock fins and narrow sandstone canyons. You'll see arches that can't be viewed from the park road and spend time listening to the desert. You should be relatively fit and not afraid of heights if you plan to take this moderately strenuous walk. Wear sturdy hiking shoes, sunscreen, and a hat, and bring at least a liter of water. Walks into the Fiery Furnace are usually offered twice a day (hours vary) and leave from Fiery Furnace Viewpoint, off the main road, about 15 miles from the park visitor center. Tickets for the morning walks must be reserved up to six months in advance (at *www.recreation.gov*) mid-March–October, or purchased at the visitor center November–February. Tickets for afternoon Fiery Furnace ranger-led walks must be purchased in advance at the park visitor center, ideally as soon as you arrive in Moab and at least a day or two ahead. Children ages 7–12 pay half price; the walk is not recommended for children under 5. Book early as the program usually fills months prior to each walk. ⊹ *Trailhead: on Arches Scenic Dr.* ⊕ *www.nps.gov/arch* ⊑ *$16* ☾ *Mid-Mar.–Oct., daily (hrs vary).*

5

FAMILY **Junior Ranger Program.** Kids 2–12 can pick up a Junior Ranger booklet at the visitor center. It's full of activities, word games, drawings, and thought-provoking material about the park and the wildlife. To earn your Junior Ranger badge, you must complete several activities in the booklet, attend a ranger program, or watch the park film and pick up some trash in the park. For ranger program veterans ages 8 and up, ask about the "extra credit" Red Rock Ranger Program. ⊠ *Arches National Park* ☎ *435/719–2299* 🖥 *Free.*

LEARNING RESOURCES

FAMILY **Red Rock Explorer Pack.** Better than borrowing from a library, families can check out a youth backpack filled with tools for learning about both Arches and Canyonlands national parks. A guide for naturalists, a three-ring binder of activities, hand lens magnifier, and binoculars are just some of the loaner items. Backpacks can be returned to either Arches or Island in the Sky visitor centers. Use of the backpack is free with a credit-card imprint in case of loss or damage to the pack or enclosed items. ⊠ *Arches National Park* ☎ *435/719–2299* 🖥 *Free.*

RESTAURANTS

Because most people come to Arches to play outside, casual trekking-wear rules—sandals, shorts, and T-shirts in the very hot summers. Whether you select an award-winning Continental restaurant in Moab, a nearby resort, or the tavern in Green River, you can dress comfortably in shorts or jeans. But don't let the relaxed attire fool you. There are some wonderful culinary surprises waiting for you, a few with spectacular views as a bonus.

In the park itself, there are no dining facilities and no snack bars. Supermarkets, bakeries, and delis in downtown Moab will be happy to make you food to go. If you bring a packed lunch, there are several picnic areas from which to choose.

HOTELS

Though there are no hotels or cabins in the park itself, in the surrounding area every type of lodging is available, from economy chain motels to B&Bs and high-end, high-adventure resorts. It's important to know when popular events are held, however, as accommodations can, and do, fill up weeks ahead of time. *Hotel reviews have been shortened. For full information, visit Fodors.com.*

WHAT IT COSTS			
	$	$$	$$$	$$$$
Restaurants	under $13	$13–$20	$21–$30	over $30
Hotels	under $101	$101–$150	$151–$200	over $200

Restaurant prices are the average cost of a main course at dinner, or if dinner is not served, at lunch. Hotel prices are the lowest cost of a standard double room in high season.

VISITOR INFORMATION

Park Contact Information Arches National Park. ⊠ *N. U.S. 191* ☎ *435/719–2299* ⊕ *www.nps.gov/arch.*

VISITOR CENTER

FAMILY

Fodor'sChoice

★

Arches Visitor Center. With hands-on exhibits that provide information about the park's geology, wildlife, and history, helpful rangers, and a bookstore, the center is a great way to start any visit to the park. Newcomers will find it especially helpful, but even those who have traveled to the park before often will discover something new. ⊠ *N. U.S. 191* ☎ *435/719–2299* ⊕ *nps.gov/arch* ☉ *Hrs vary but generally daily 9–4, with frequently extended hrs Apr.–Oct.*

EXPLORING

SCENIC DRIVES

Arches Main Park Road. Although they are not formally designated as such, the main park road and its two short spurs are scenic and allow you to enjoy many park sights from your car. The main road leads through Courthouse Towers, where you can see Sheep Rock and the Three Gossips, then alongside the Great Wall, the Petrified Dunes, and Balanced Rock. A drive to the Windows section takes you to attractions like Double Arch, and you can see Skyline Arch along the roadside as you approach the Devils Garden campground. The road to Delicate Arch is not particularly scenic, but it allows hiking access to one of the park's main features. Allow about two hours to drive the 45-mile round-trip, more if you explore the spurs and their features and stop at viewpoints along the way. ⊠ *Arches National Park* ⊕ *www.nps.gov/arch.*

HISTORIC SITES

Wolfe Ranch. Civil War veteran John Wesley Wolfe and his son started a small ranch here in 1888. He added a cabin in 1906 when his daughter Esther and her family came west to live. Built out of Fremont cottonwoods, the rustic one-room cabin still stands on the site, listed on the National Register of Historic Places. Look for remains of a root cellar and a corral as well. Even older than these structures is the nearby Ute rock-art panel by the Delicate Arch trailhead. About 150 feet past the footbridge and before the trail starts to climb, you can see images of bighorn sheep and figures on horseback, as well as some smaller images believed to be dogs. To reach the panel, follow the narrow dirt trail along the rock escarpment until you see the interpretive sign. The cabin is 12.9 miles from park entrance, 1.2 miles off main road. ⊠ *Off Delicate Arch Rd.*

SCENIC STOPS

It's easy to spot some of the arches from your car, but you should really take the time to step outside and walk beneath the spans and giant walls of orange rock. This gives you a much better idea of their proportion. No doubt you will feel as writer Edward Abbey did when he awoke on his first day as a park ranger in Arches: that you're walking in the most beautiful place on Earth.

Plants and Wildlife in Arches

As in any desert environment, the best time to see wildlife in Arches is early morning or evening. Summer temperatures keep most animals tucked away in cool places, though ravens and lizards are exceptions. If you happen to be in the right place at the right time, you may spot one of the beautiful turquoise-necklace-collared lizards. It's more likely you'll see the western whiptail. Mule deer, jackrabbits, and small rodents are usually active in cool morning hours or near dusk. You may spot a lone coyote foraging day or night. The park protects a small herd of desert bighorns, and some of their tribe are sometimes seen early in the morning grazing beside U.S. 191 south of the Arches entrance. If you encounter bighorn sheep, do not approach them. They have been known to charge people who attempt to get too close. The park's ravens, mule deer, and small mammals such as chipmunks are very used to seeing people and may allow you to get close—but don't feed them.

■TIP➜ **Visit as the sun goes down.** At sunset, the rock formations in Arches glow like fire, and you'll often find photographers behind their tripods waiting for magnificent rays to descend on Delicate Arch or other popular park sites. The Fiery Furnace earns its name as its narrow fins glow red just before the sun dips below the horizon. Full-moon nights are particularly dramatic in Arches as the creamy white Navajo sandstone reflects light, and eerie silhouettes are created by towering fins and formations.

Balanced Rock. One of the park's favorite sights, 9¼ miles from the park entrance, this rock is visible for several minutes as you approach—and just gets more impressive and mysterious as you get closer. The formation's total height is 128 feet, with the huge balanced rock rising 55 feet above the pedestal. Be sure to hop out of the car and walk the short (530-yard) loop around the base. ⊠ *Arches Scenic Dr.*

Fodor's Choice ★ **Delicate Arch.** The iconic symbol of the park and the state (it appears on many of Utah's license plates), the Delicate Arch is frankly tall and muscular compared to many of the spans in the park—and it's big enough to shelter a four-story building. The arch is a remnant of an Entrada Sandstone fin; the rest of the rock has eroded and now frames the La Sal Mountains in the background. Drive 2.2 miles off the main road to the viewpoint to see the arch from a distance, or hike right up to it from the trailhead that starts near Wolfe Ranch. The trail, 13 miles from the park entrance and 1.2 miles off the main road, is a moderately strenuous 3-mile round-trip hike. ⊠ *Delicate Arch Rd.*

Double Arch. In the Windows section of the park, 11¾ miles from the park entrance, Double Arch has appeared in several Hollywood movies, including *Indiana Jones and the Last Crusade*. The northern arch is visible from the parking lot, but walk the short trail to see the southern one, as well as Turret Arch. ⊠ *The Windows Rd.*

GOOD READS

Arches Visitor Center Bookstore. Operated by Canyonlands Natural History Association, this bookstore at the park entrance is the place in the park to buy maps, guidebooks, driving tours on CD, and material about the natural and cultural history of Arches National Park. Park souvenirs are also sold here. ⊠ *Off Hwy. 191* ☎ *435/259–6003.*

■ *127 Hours: Between a Rock and a Hard Place* by Aron Ralston. This true story—made into a movie of the same name starring James Franco—took place southeast of Arches and is a modern-day survivor story of solitary man in nature.

■ *A Naturalist's Guide to Canyon Country,* by David Williams and Gloria Brown, is an excellent, compact field guide for both Arches and Canyonlands national parks.

■ *Desert Solitaire.* Eminent naturalist Edward Abbey's first ranger assignment was Arches; this classic is a must-read.

■ *Road Guide to Arches National Park,* by Peter Anderson, has basic information about the geology and natural history in the park.

■ *Moab Classic Hikes,* by Damian Fagan, succinctly gives the skinny on 40 area hikes and includes maps and photos.

Fiery Furnace. Fewer than 10% of the park's visitors ever descend into the chasms and washes of Fiery Furnace (a permit or a ranger-led hike is the only way to go), but you can gain an appreciation for this twisted, unyielding landscape from the Overlook, 14 miles from the park entrance. At sunset, the rocks glow a vibrant flamelike red, which gives the formation its daunting moniker. ⊠ *Off Arches Scenic Dr.*

Skyline Arch. A quick walk from the parking lot at Skyline Arch, 16½ miles from the park entrance, gives you closer views and better photos. The short trail is less than a half mile round-trip and only takes a few minutes to travel. ⊠ *Devil's Garden Rd.*

FAMILY **The Windows.** As you head north from the park entrance, turn right at Balanced Rock to find this concentration of natural windows, caves, and needles 11¾ miles from the park entrance. Stretch your legs on the easy paths that wind between the arches and soak in a variety of geological formations. ⊠ *The Windows Rd.*

SPORTS AND THE OUTDOORS

Arches National Park lies in the middle of one of the adventure capitals of the United States. Deep canyons and towering walls are everywhere you look. Slick sandstone surfaces, known as slickrock, make for some of the world's best mountain biking. Thousand-foot sandstone walls draw rock climbers from across the globe. Hikers can choose from shady canyons or red rock ridges that put you in the company of the West's big sky. The Colorado River forms the southeast boundary of the park and can give you every grade of white-water adventure.

Moab-based outfitters can set you up for any sport you may have a desire to try: mountain biking, ATVs, dirt bikes, four-wheel-drive vehicles, kayaking, climbing, stand-up paddleboarding, and even skydiving. Within the park, it's best to stick with basics such as hiking, sightseeing, and photography. Climbers and other adventure seekers should always inquire at the visitor center about restrictions.

MULTISPORT OUTFITTERS

FAMILY **Adrift Adventures.** This outfitter takes pride in well-trained guides who can take you via foot, raft, kayak, 4X4, jet boat, and more, all over the Moab area, including the Colorado and Green rivers. They also offer history, movie, and rock-art tours. They've been in business since 1977 and have a great reputation around town. ⊠ *378 N. Main St., Moab* ☎ *435/259–8594, 800/874–4483* ⊕ *www.adrift.net* ✑ *From $50.*

Dual Sport Utah. If you're into dirt biking, this is the only outfitter in Moab specializing in street-legal, off-road dirt-bike tours and rentals. Follow the Klondike Bluffs trail to Arches, or negotiate the White Rim Trail in Canyonlands in a fraction of the time you would spend on a mountain bike. ⊠ *197 W. Center. St., Moab* ☎ *435/260–2724* ⊕ *www.dualsportutah.com* ✑ *From $225.*

Moab Adventure Center. At the prominent storefront on Main Street you can schedule most any type of local adventure experience you want, including rafting, 4X4 tours, scenic flights, hikes, balloon rides, and much, much more. You can also purchase clothing and outdoor gear for your visit. ⊠ *225 S. Main St., Moab* ☎ *435/259–7019, 866/904–1163* ⊕ *www.moabadventurecenter.com* ✑ *From $67.*

NAVTEC. Doc Williams was the first doctor in Moab in 1896, and some of his descendants have never left, sharing his love for the area through this rafting, canyoneering, and 4X4 company. Whether you want to explore by boat, boots, or wheels, you'll find a multitude of one-day and multiday options here. ⊠ *321 N. Main St., Moab* ☎ *435/259–7983, 800/833–1278* ⊕ *www.navtec.com.*

BICYCLING

There's world-class biking all around Arches National Park, but the park proper is not the best place to explore on two wheels. Bicycles are allowed only on established roads, and because there are no shoulders cyclists share the roadway with drivers and pedestrians gawking at the scenery. If you do want to take a spin in the park, try the dirt-and-gravel Willow Flats Road, the old entrance to the park. The road is about 6½ miles long one-way and starts directly across from the Balanced Rock parking lot. It's a pretty mountain-bike ride on dirt and sand through slickrock, pinyon, and juniper country. You must stay on the road with your bicycle or you chance steep fines.

TOURS AND OUTFITTERS

Fodor's Choice **Poison Spider Bicycles.** In a town of great bike shops, this fully loaded shop
★ is considered one of the best. Poison Spider serves the thriving road-cycling community as well as mountain bikers. Rent, buy, or service your bike here.

You can also arrange for shuttle and guide services and purchase merchandise. Want to ship your bike to Moab for your adventure? Poison Spider will store it until you arrive and the staff will reassemble it for you and make sure everything is in perfect working order. ✉ *497 N. Main St., Moab* ☎ *435/259–7882, 800/635–1792* ⊕ *www.poisonspiderbicycles.com.*

Rim Tours. Reliable, friendly, and professional, Rim Tours has been taking guests on guided one-day or multiday mountain-bike tours, including Klondike Bluffs (which enters Arches) and the White Rim Trail (inside Canyonlands) since 1985. Road-bike tours as well as bike rentals are also available. Bike skills a little rusty? Rim Tours also offers mountain-bike instructional tours and skill clinics. ✉ *1233 S. U.S. 191, Moab* ☎ *435/259–5223, 800/626–7335* ⊕ *www.rimtours.com* 🖃 *Day tours from $140; multiday from $800.*

Western Spirit Cycling Adventures. Head here for fully supported, go-at-your-own-pace, multiday mountain-bike and road-bike tours throughout the western states, including trips to Canyonlands, Trail of the Ancients, and the 140-mile Kokopelli Trail, which runs from Grand Junction, Colorado, to Moab. Guides versed in the geologic wonders of the area cook up meals worthy of the scenery each night. Ask about family rides, and road bike trips, too. There's also the option to combine a Green River kayak trip with the three-night White Rim Trail ride. ✉ *478 Mill Creek Dr., Moab* ☎ *435/259–8732, 800/845–2453* ⊕ *www.westernspirit.com* 🖃 *From $925.*

BIRD-WATCHING

Within the park you'll definitely see plenty of the big, black, beautiful raven. Look for them perched on top of a picturesque juniper branch or balancing on the bald knob of a rock. The noisy black-billed magpie populates the park, as do the more melodic canyon and rock wrens. Lucky visitors will spot a red-tailed hawk and hear its distinctive call.

Serious birders will have more fun visiting the **Scott M. Matheson Wetlands Preserve** 5 miles south of the park. The wetlands is home to more than 225 species of birds including the wood duck, western screech owl, indigo bunting, and plumbeous vireo.

BOATING AND RIVER EXPEDITIONS

Although the Colorado River runs along the border of the park, there is no boating within the park proper. You can, however, enjoy a splashy ride nearby on the Fisher Towers stretch of the river north of Moab, and there are plenty of fine outfitters in Moab that can set you up for expeditions.

TOURS AND OUTFITTERS

FAMILY
Fodor's Choice
★

Canyon Voyages Adventure Co. This is an excellent choice for rafting or kayaking adventures on the Colorado or Green rivers. Don and Denise Oblak run a friendly, professional company with a retail store and rental shop that's open year-round. Most of their customers take one-day trips, but they also offer multiday itineraries, guided tours, and rentals. It's also the only company that operates a kayak school for those who want to learn how to run the rapids on their own. Ask about stand-up paddleboarding, biking, and horseback riding, too. ✉ *211 N. Main St., Moab* ☎ *435/259–6007, 800/733–6007* ⊕ *www.canyonvoyages.com* ☜ *From $59.*

Holiday River Expeditions. Since 1966, this outfitter has offered one- to eight-day adventures on the San Juan, Green, and Colorado rivers, including inside Canyonlands National Park. They also offer multisport trips, women's retreats, and bike adventures, including the White Rim Trail. ✉ *2075 E. Main St., Green River* ☎ *435/564–3273, 800/624–6323* ⊕ *www.bikeraft.com* ☜ *From $155.*

DOGS IN THE PARK

Keep in mind that dogs aren't allowed on national park trails and must be on leash in the Devils Garden Campground. However, canines can join you on Bureau of Land Management trails. The heat can be stifling, so remember to bring enough water for you and your four-legged friend and hit the trails in the early morning hours.

FISHING

There is no fishing in Arches National Park, and the Colorado River is too silty to offer good fishing. The nearby La Sal Mountains are dotted with small lakes that are stocked with small trout, but finding good native trout fishing in the area will take some effort.

FOUR-WHEELING

With thousands of acres of nearby Bureau of Land Management lands to enjoy, it's hardly necessary to use the park's limited trails for four-wheel adventures. You can, however, go backcountry in Arches on the Willow Flats Road and the Salt Valley Road—just don't set out for this expedition without first stopping at the visitor center to learn of current conditions. Salt Valley Road is very sandy and requires special driving skills.

TOURS AND OUTFITTERS

Coyote Land Tours. Imposing Mercedes Benz Unimog trucks (which dwarf Hummers) take you to parts of the backcountry where you could never wander on your own. Technical tours challenge drivers with imposing rock formations, washes, and assorted obstacles, and there are tamer sunset excursions and camp-style ride-and-dine trips. They stand by their money-back "great time" guarantee. ✉ *Moab* ☎ *435/260–6056* ⊕ *www.coyotelandtours.com* ☜ *From $59.*

High Point Hummer & ATV. You can rent vehicles, including ATVs, UTVs, Jeeps, and motorcycles, or get a guided tour of the backcountry in open-air Hummer vehicles, ATVs, dirt bikes, or dune buggy–like "side-by-sides" that seat up to six people. The enthusiastic owners love families and small, intimate groups, and offer hiking and canyoneering as well. ✉ *281 N. Main St., Moab* ☎ *435/259–2972, 877/486–6833* ⊕ *www.highpointhummer.com* ☜ *Guided tours from $69.*

HIKING

Getting out on any one of the park trails will surely cause you to fall in love with this Mars-like landscape. But remember, you are hiking in a desert environment and approximately 1 mile above sea level. Many people succumb to heat and dehydration because they do not drink enough water. Park rangers recommend a gallon of water per day per person.

EASY

FAMILY **Balanced Rock Trail.** You'll want to stop at Balanced Rock for photo opportunities, so you may as well walk the easy, partially paved trail around the famous landmark. This is one of the most accessible trails in the park and is suitable for small children and folks who may have difficulty walking. The trail is only about 530 yards round-trip; you should allow 15 minutes for the walk. *Easy.* ✛ *Trailhead: approximately 9¼ miles from park entrance.*

Broken Arch Trail. An easy walk across open grassland, this loop trail passes Broken Arch, which is also visible from the road. The arch gets its name because it appears to be cracked in the middle, but it's not really broken. The trail is 1¼ miles round-trip, and you should allow about an hour for the walk. *Easy.* ✛ *Trailhead: at end of Sand Dune Arch trail, off Devil's Garden Rd., 16½ miles from park entrance.*

Double Arch Trail. If it's not too hot, anyone can walk here from Windows Trail. This relatively flat trail leads you to two massive arches that make for great photo opportunities. The ¾-mile round-trip gives you a good taste of desert flora and fauna. *Easy.* ✛ *Trailhead: 2½ miles from main road, on Windows Section spur road, 9¼ miles from main entrance.*

Landscape Arch. This natural rock opening competes with Kolob Arch at Zion for the title of largest geologic span in the world. Measuring 306 feet from base to base, it appears as a delicate ribbon of rock bending over the horizon. In 1991, a slab of rock about 60 feet long, 11 feet wide, and 4 feet thick fell from the underside, leaving it even thinner. You can reach it by walking a rolling, gravel, 1.6-mile-long trail. *Easy.* ✛ *Trailhead: at Devil's Garden Rd., 18 miles north of park entrance off main road.*

Park Avenue Trail. The first named trail that park visitors encounter, this is an easy, 2-mile round-trip walk (with only one small hill but a somewhat steep descent into the canyon) amid walls and towers that resemble a New York City skyline. You'll walk under the gaze of Queen Nefertiti, a giant rock formation that some observers think has Egyptian-looking features. If you are traveling with companions, make it a one-way, 1-mile downhill trek by having them pick you up at the Courthouse Towers Viewpoint. Allow about 45 minutes for the one-way journey. *Easy.* ✛ *Trailhead: on Arches Scenic Drive, 2 miles from park entrance.*

FAMILY **Sand Dune Arch Trail.** Your kids will return to the car with shoes full of bright red sand from this giant sandbox in the desert and will love exploring in and around the rock. Do not climb or jump off the arch, as doing so has frequently resulted in injuries. Set aside five minutes for this shady, 530-yard walk and as much time as your children's imaginations allow for play. The trail intersects with the Broken Arch Trail, so if you visit both arches it's a 1½-mile round-trip. *Easy.* ✛ *Trailhead: off Arches Scenic Dr., about 16½ miles from park entrance.*

Devils Garden Trail

FAMILY   **Windows Trail.** The first stop for many visitors to the park, Windows Trail gives you an opportunity to get out and enjoy the desert air. Here you'll see three giant openings in the rock and walk on a trail that leads you right through the holes. Allow about an hour on this gently inclined, 1-mile round-trip hike. As 90% of visitors won't follow the "primitive" trail around the backside of the two windows, take advantage if you want some desert solitude. The primitive trail adds an extra half hour to the trip. *Easy.* ✛ *Trailhead: on the Windows Rd., off Arches Scenic Dr., 12 miles from park entrance.*

MODERATE

Fodor's Choice **Delicate Arch Trail.** To see the park's most famous freestanding arch up
★   close takes effort and won't offer you much solitude—but it's worth every step. The 3-mile round-trip trail ascends via steep slickrock, sandy paths, and along one narrow ledge (at the very end) that might give pause to anyone afraid of heights. Plus, there's almost no shade. First-timers should start early to avoid the midday heat in summer. Still, at sunrise, sunset, and every hour in between, it's the park's most popular and busy trail. Heat mixed with lack of shade makes this a strenuous hike in the summer. Bring plenty of water, as heatstroke is a very real possibility. Allow two to three hours for this hike, depending on your fitness level and how long you plan to linger at the arch. If you go at sunset or sunrise, bring a headlamp or flashlight. Don't miss Wolfe Ranch and some ancient rock art near the trailhead. *Moderate.* ✛ *Trailhead: on Delicate Arch Rd., 13 miles from park entrance, 2¼ miles off main road.*

Fodor's Choice **Devils Garden Trail.** Landscape Arch is the highlight of this trail but is just
★   one of several arches within reach depending on your ambitions and the heat. It's an easy ¾-mile one-way trip (mostly gravel, relatively flat) to Landscape Arch, one of the longest stone spans in the world at 306 feet and one of the most fragile-looking. In fact, you can see where a 60-foot-long piece fell off the underside in 1991, leading to the closure of the trail that used to go under the span. This serves as a reminder of the impermanence of the features in the park. Beyond Landscape Arch the scenery changes dramatically and the hike becomes more strenuous, as you must climb and straddle slickrock fins and negotiate some short,

steep inclines. Finally, the stacked spans that compose Double O Arch come into view around a sharp bend. Allow up to three hours for this round-trip hike of just over 4 miles. For a still longer hike, venture on to see a formation called Dark Angel and then return to the trailhead on the primitive loop. The hike to Dark Angel is a difficult route through fins with a short side trip to Private Arch. If you hike all the way to Dark Angel and return on the primitive loop, the trail is about 6 miles round-trip, not including possible (and worthwhile) detours to Navajo Arch, Partition Arch, Tunnel Arch, and Pine Tree Arch. Allow about five hours for this adventure, take plenty of water, and watch your route carefully. Pick up the park's useful guide to Devils Garden, or download it from the website before you go. *Moderate.* ✛ *Trailhead: on Devils Garden Rd., off main road, 18 miles from park entrance.*

Tower Arch Trail. Check with park rangers before attempting the dirt road to Klondike Bluffs parking area. If rains haven't washed out the road, a trip to this seldom-visited area provides a solitude-filled hike climaxed with a giant rock opening. Allow from two to three hours for this 3½-mile round-trip hike, not including the drive. *Moderate.* ✛ *Trailhead: at Klondike Bluffs parking area, 24½ miles from park entrance, 7¾ miles off main road.*

DIFFICULT

Fiery Furnace. This area of the park has taken on a near-mythical lure for park visitors, who are drawn to the forbidden nature of Fiery Furnace. Rangers strongly discourage inexperienced hikers from entering here—in fact, you can't enter without watching a safety video and getting a permit ($6). As a result, up to one month's advance reservations are now required to get a spot on the 2-mile round-trip ranger-led hikes ($16) through this unique formation. A hike here is a challenging but fascinating trip amid rugged rocks and sandy washes into the heart of Arches. The trek may require the use of hands and feet to scramble up and through narrow cracks and along vertigo-inducing ledges above drop-offs, and there are no trail markings. If you're not familiar with the Furnace you can easily get lost and cause resource damage, so watch your step and use great caution. Call or visit the website (*recreation.gov*) for reservations, which are a must. The less intrepid should look into Fiery Furnace from the Overlook off the main road. *Difficult.* ✛ *Trailhead: off main road, about 15 miles from visitor center.*

ROCK CLIMBING AND CANYONEERING

Rock climbers travel from across the country to scale the sheer red rock walls of Arches National Park and surrounding areas. Most climbing routes in the park require advanced techniques. Permits are not required, but climbers are encouraged to register for a free permit, either online or at a kiosk outside the visitor center. Climbers are responsible for knowing park regulations, temporary route closures, and restricted routes. Two popular routes ascend Owl Rock in the Garden of Eden (about 10 miles from the visitor center); the well-worn route has a difficulty of 5.8, while a more challenging option is 5.11 on a scale that goes up to 5.13-plus. Many climbing routes are available in the Park Avenue area, about 2.2 miles from the visitor center. These routes are

also extremely difficult climbs. No commercial outfitters are allowed to lead rock-climbing excursions in the park, but guided canyoneering (which involves ropes, rappelling, and some basic climbing) is permitted. Before climbing, it's imperative that you stop at the visitor center and check with a ranger about climbing regulations.

TOURS AND OUTFITTERS

Desert Highlights. This guide company takes adventurous types on descents and ascents through canyons (with the help of ropes), including those found in the Fiery Furnace at Arches National Park. Full-day and multiday canyoneering treks are available to destinations both inside and outside the national parks. Desert Highlights does not offer guided rock climbing. ⊠ *50 E. Center St., Moab* ☎ *435/259–4433, 800/747–1342* ⊕ *www.deserthighlights.com* ⊠ *From $120.*

Moab Cliffs & Canyons. In a town where everyone seems to offer rafting and 4X4 expeditions, Moab Cliffs & Canyons focuses exclusively on canyoneering, climbing, and rappelling—for novice and veteran adventurers. This is the outfitter that provided technical assistance to the crew on the movie *127 Hours*. ⊠ *253 N. Main St., Moab* ☎ *435/259–3317, 877/641–5271* ⊕ *www.cliffsandcanyons.com* ⊠ *From $84.*

WHAT'S NEARBY

NEARBY TOWNS

Moab is the primary gateway to both Arches and Canyonlands national parks. Don't let its outsize image and status as Grand County seat fool you: only about 5,000 people live here year-round—compared with the 1 million who visit annually. Near the Colorado River in a beautiful valley between red rock cliffs, Moab is an interesting, eclectic place to visit, especially if you would welcome a variety of restaurants, Southwestern-inspired souvenirs, art galleries, and a plethora of lodging options. Also, here you'll find an array of sports outfitters to help you enjoy the parks. For those who want civilization and a sprinkling of culture with their outdoor itineraries, Moab is the place to be.

The next-closest town to Arches, about 47 miles to the northwest, is **Green River.** Unlike hip Moab, this dusty highway outpost is off the tourists' radar screen, except for boaters headed Moab's way on the Green. It's worth a visit for Ray's Tavern. Also, each September the fragrance of fresh cantaloupe, watermelon, and honeydew fills the air, especially during Melon Days, a family-fun event celebrating the harvest on the third weekend of September.

VISITOR INFORMATION

Green River Information Center. ⊠ *John Wesley Powell River History Museum, 1765 E. Main St., Green River* ☎ *435/564–3427* ⊕ *destinationgreenriver.com.* **Moab Information Center.** ⊠ *25 E. Center St., Moab* ☎ *435/259–8825 Moab, 800/635–6622* ⊕ *www.cnha.org or www.discovermoab.com/visitorcenter.htm.*

NEARBY ATTRACTIONS

Canyonlands by Night & Day. For more than 50 years, this outfitter was best known for its two-hour, after-dark boat ride on the Colorado River (March–October). While illuminating the canyon walls with 40,000 watts, the trip includes music and narration highlighting Moab's history, Native American legends, and geologic formations along the river. You can also combine the boat trip with a Dutch-oven dinner. These days, daytime jet boat tours are offered, too, as well as tours by Hummer, airplane, and helicopter (land and air tours are offered year-round). ⊠ *1861 Hwy. 191, Moab* ☎ *435/259–5261* ⊕ *www.canyonlandsbynight.com.*

Courthouse Wash. Although this rock-art panel fell victim to an unusual case of vandalism in 1980, when someone scoured the petroglyphs and pictographs that had been left by four cultures, you can still see ancient images if you take a short walk from the parking area on the left-hand side of the road, heading south. ⊠ *Hwy. 191, about 2 miles south of park entrance.*

FAMILY

Fodor's Choice

★

John Wesley Powell River History Museum. Learn what it was like to travel down the Green and Colorado rivers in the 1800s in wooden boats. A series of displays tracks the Powell Party's arduous, dangerous 1869 journey, and visitors can watch the award-winning film *Journey Into the Unknown* for a cinematic taste of the white-water adventure. The center also houses the River Runner's Hall of Fame, a tribute to those who have followed in Powell's wake. River-themed art occupies a gallery and there's a dinosaur exhibit in the lower level. ⊠ *1765 E. Main St., Green River* ☎ *435/564–3427* ⊕ *www.jwprhm.com* ⊠ *$6* ☉ *Apr.–Oct., daily 8–7; Nov.–Mar., Tues.–Sat. 9–5.*

FAMILY

Museum of Moab. Exhibits on the history, geology, and paleontology of the Moab area include settler-era antiques, and ancient and historic Native Americans are remembered in displays of baskets, pottery, sandals, and other artifacts. Displays also chronicle early Spanish expeditions into the area, regional dinosaur finds, and the history of uranium discovery. ⊠ *118 E. Center St., Moab* ☎ *435/259–7985* ⊕ *www.moabmuseum.org* ⊠ *$5 suggested donation; free Mon.* ☉ *Mar. 15–Oct. 15, Mon.–Sat. 10–6; Oct 16.–Mar. 14, Mon.–Sat. noon–5.*

AREA ACTIVITIES

SPORTS AND THE OUTDOORS

GOLF

Moab Golf Club. A spectacular red rock sandstone backdrop, wide fairways, and lush well-kept greens make for a breathtaking combination. Moab's 4,000-foot elevation and dry air make this municipal course fun to hit. It is open year-round and a relative bargain. ⊠ *2705 S. East Bench Rd., Moab* ☎ *435/259–6488* ⊕ *www.moabcountryclub.com* ⊠ *$48, including cart* ⚐ *18 holes, 6819 yards, par 72.*

NIGHTLIFE AND PERFORMING ARTS

Moab Arts and Recreation Center. Offering a slice of Moab's arts scene, from "Quick Draw Sales" where artists have three hours to create pieces during the annual Plein Air Festival, to dance, crafts, and fitness classes, this has been the spirited hub of arts activities in Moab since 1997. ⊠ *111 E. 100 N, Moab* ☏ *435/259–6272* ⊕ *www.moabrecreation.com.*

SHOPPING

ART GALLERIES

Lema's Kokopelli Gallery. The Lema family has built a reputation for fair prices on a large selection of Native American and Southwest-themed jewelry, art, pottery, rugs, and more. Everything sold here is authentic. ⊠ *70 N. Main St., Moab* ☏ *435/259–5055* ⊕ *www.kokopellioutlet.com* ⊗ *Mar.–Oct., daily 9 am–10 pm; Dec.–Feb., daily 9–5.*

BOOKS

FAMILY **Back of Beyond Books.** A Main Street treasure, this comprehensive bookstore features the American West, environmental studies, Native American cultures, water issues, and Western history, as well as rare antiquarian books on the Southwest. There's also a nice nook for kids. ⊠ *83 N. Main St., Moab* ☏ *435/259–5154, 800/700–2859* ⊕ *www. backofbeyondbooks.com* ⊗ *Daily 9–6 (to 9 pm Mar.–Nov.).*

WESTERN GOODS

Western Image. This is a fun place to browse for Old West antiques, Western art, cowboy hats, boots, belts, coins, badges, and other classy souvenirs. ⊠ *39 N. Main St., Moab* ☏ *435/259–3006* ⊗ *Mar.–Oct., daily 9 am–10 pm; Nov.–Feb., daily 10–6.*

SCENIC DRIVES

Fodor'sChoice **Colorado River Scenic Byway—Highway 128.** One of the most scenic drives
★ in the country, Highway 128 intersects U.S. 191 3 miles south of Arches. The 44-mile highway runs along the Colorado River with 2,000-foot red rock cliffs rising on both sides. This gorgeous river corridor is home to a winery, orchards, and a couple of luxury lodging options. It also offers a spectacular view of world-class climbing destination Fisher Towers before winding north to Interstate 70. The drive from Moab to I–70 takes at least an hour. ⊠ *Hwy. 128, Moab.*

WHERE TO EAT

IN THE PARK

PICNIC AREAS

Balanced Rock. The view is the best part of this picnic spot opposite the Balanced Rock parking area. There are no cooking facilities or water, but there are tables. If you sit just right you might find some shade under a small juniper; otherwise, this is an exposed site. Pit toilets are nearby. ⊠ *Arches Scenic Dr., 9¼ miles from park entrance on main road.*

Devils Garden. There are grills, water, picnic tables, and restrooms here, and depending on the time of day, some shade from junipers and rock walls. It's a good place for lunch before or after a hike. ⊠ *On main road, 18 miles from park entrance.*

OUTSIDE THE PARK

GREEN RIVER

$$ ✕ **La Veracruzana.** The Polito family continues the long tradition of good
MEXICAN food in this older, unassuming building on Green River's main drag. Couples and families should try the *molcajete*, a two-person entrée with meat, chicken, shrimp, and nopal (cactus) served on a volcanic-rock stone mortar. Savory pork and *chile verde* combinations also impress on a menu that offers enchiladas, tacos, and other standard Mexican fare. Ⓢ *Average main: $15* ⊠ *125 W. Main St., Green River* ☎ *435/564–3257.*

$ ✕ **Ray's Tavern.** Ray's is something of a Western legend and a favorite hang-
AMERICAN out for river runners. The bar that runs the length of the restaurant reminds you this is still a tavern and a serious watering hole—but all the photos and rafting memorabilia make it comfortable for families as well. It's worth stopping in for the great tales about working on the river and the coldest beer and the best hamburger in two counties. For dessert, owner Cathy Gardner makes homemade apple pie daily. Ⓢ *Average main: $10* ⊠ *25 S. Broadway, Green River* ☎ *435/564–3511* ⊕ *www.raystavern.com.*

MOAB

$ ✕ **Eklecticafe.** The funky font on the sign makes this place easy to miss
ECLECTIC but worth finding for one of the more creative, healthy menus in Moab.
Fodor's Choice Breakfast and lunch items include a variety of burritos and wraps,
★ scrambled tofu, salmon cakes, Indonesian satay kebabs, and many fresh, organic salads. The *huevos rancheros* have just the right amount of heat and the wakame with either scrambled eggs or tofu is a great way to start the day. Excellent coffee, too. On nice days you can take your meal outside to the large covered patio. In winter you'll want to stay inside by the wood-burning stove. Ⓢ *Average main: $9* ⊠ *352 N. Main St., Moab* ☎ *435/259–6896* ☽ *No dinner.*

$$$$ ✕ **Jeffrey's Steakhouse.** Melt-in-your-mouth tender wagyu beef is this
STEAKHOUSE restaurant's specialty. Jeffrey's offers plenty of salads and side dishes, but remember—this is a steak house, so there's a separate charge for everything, and that can quickly make for a pricey meal. The menu also features lamb and pork chops, chicken and salmon, and a few other entrée options. But it's really the wagyu that brings in the crowds. A good selection of wines is also available and the knowledgeable staff is happy to help you choose a good pairing. With no more than a dozen or so tables in this historic adobe home just off Main Street, it's sometimes hard to get a reservation at this popular eatery, so plan ahead if possible. Ⓢ *Average main: $32* ⊠ *218 N. 100 W, Moab* ☎ *435/259–3588* ⊕ *www.jeffreyssteakhouse.com* ☽ *No lunch* ⌑ *Reservations essential.*

$ ✕ **Moab Brewery.** Southern Utah's award-winning brewery is known for
AMERICAN its Scorpion Pale Ale, Dead Horse Amber Ale, and an assortment of other
FAMILY brews from light to dark. Their on-site restaurant is spacious and comfortable and decorated with kayaks, bikes, and other adventure paraphernalia.

In the bar, you can always find someone to talk to about canyon-country adventure, because river runners, rock climbers, and locals all hang out here. There's a wide selection of menu choices, including fresh salads (try the gazpacho spinach salad), poultry (honey almond), St. Louis–style ribs, vegetarian pasta, and fish (including fish tacos). The house-made gelato is rich but not as good as their beer. $ *Average main: $12* ⊠ *686 S. Main St., Moab* ☎ *435/259–6333* ⊕ *www.themoabbrewery.com.*

$ ✕ **Moab Diner.** For breakfast, lunch, and dinner, this is the place where old-time Moabites go. Try the dishes smothered in green chili (burritos, burgers, omelets, and more), which they claim is Utah's best. The menu offers standard diner fare and the service is always friendly. Breakfast is served all day, and the ice-cream counter is as popular as ever—the diner did start out as an ice-cream parlor after all. $ *Average main: $10* ⊠ *189 S. Main St., Moab* ☎ *435/259–4006* ⊕ *www.moabdiner.com* ⊙ *Closed Sun.*

AMERICAN
FAMILY

$$ ✕ **Pasta Jay's.** Mountain bikers, families, and couples pack this downtown restaurant's patio from noon until well into the evening. This bustling spot's friendly servers rapidly dish up a dozen kinds of pasta in an equal number of preparations, perfect for hungry adventurers. If ravioli and manicotti aren't your thing, there's pizza, sandwiches, and salads, too. Linger over your meal and enjoy the people-watching on Moab's main drag. $ *Average main: 15* ⊠ *4 S. Main St., Moab* ☎ *435/259–2900* ⊕ *www.pastajays.com.*

ITALIAN
FAMILY

$$ ✕ **Peace Tree Juice Café.** Start with your choice of a dozen smoothies, then select from a menu that ranges from wraps to sandwiches to full entrées prepared primarily from local, natural, and organic ingredients for a healthy, filling meal. Try the quinoa-stuffed red pepper, Mediterranean penne, or sweet-and-salty beet salad for interesting new flavor combinations. The dinner menu includes steaks and salmon. Peace Tree's downtown location is as clean and contemporary as its food. For dinner, you may have to wait for a table on the patio. Takeout is also an option. There's another location in Monticello, Utah. $ *Average main: $15* ⊠ *20 S. Main St., Moab* ☎ *435/259–0101* ⊕ *www.peacetreejuicecafe.com.*

CAFÉ

$$$ ✕ **River Grill Restaurant.** The most scenic dining experience in the area is 17 miles upstream from Moab at the Sorrel River Ranch, beside the Colorado River, with views of La Sal Mountains, and the red-rock spires and towers surrounding the ranch. This fine-dining restaurant follows a farm-to-table ethic and its seasonal menu changes regularly; look for local options like buffalo, pheasant, lamb, and trout as well as vegetarian entrées. Even if you don't splurge on a full wine dinner, know that the wine list is high quality and fairly priced. For lunch (which is served until 5 pm) you can sit out on the River Deck, for uninterrupted views. Reservations are recommended. $ *Average main: $28* ⊠ *Sorrel River Ranch, Hwy. 128, mile marker 17.5, Moab* ☎ *435/259–4642* ⊕ *www.sorrelriver.com* ⊙ *Lunch for takeout only, Nov.–Mar.* ⌕ *Reservations essential.*

AMERICAN

$$ ✕ **Sabaku Sushi.** Sushi in the desert? It may seem surprising, but the chefs here know what they're doing. The fish is flown in fresh several times a week, the veggies are crisp and the sauces are spicy—locals particularly love the spicy tuna roll with cucumber and avocado served with sriracha and eel sauce. The tempura is light and crunchy and the stir-fry noodles

ASIAN MODERN
ASIAN
Fodor's Choice
★

5

with vegetables in a spicy miso are a taste treat. For those who aren't so into fish, the menu has chicken and steak options, along with plenty of dishes for vegetarians. The place has a trendy vibe and is often crowded, so call for reservations if you mind waiting for a table. $ *Average main: $15* ⊠ *90 E. Center St, Moab* ☎ *435/259–4455* ⊕ *www.sabakusushi. com* ☾ *Closed Sun.–Tues. No lunch.*

$ ✕ **Sweet Cravings Bakery + Bistro.** Cinda Culton has created a sensation
BAKERY in Moab with some of the largest and most delicious cookies and cin-
FAMILY namon rolls you've ever seen, but the secret here is an amazing roster of breakfast and lunch panini, wraps, and sandwiches, and daily comfort foods like potpies and soups. Baked goods are all from scratch, gluten-free options abound, produce is local, meats are preservative-free, and coffee is 100% Rainforest Alliance and organic. Everything is available to go (in eco-friendly containers), but the Canyon Ham with spinach and tarragon aioli on marbled rye is so good it might not make it to the trail. Breakfast starts at 7 am and lunch is served until 4 pm. $ *Average main: $10* ⊠ *397 N. Main St., Moab* ☎ *435/259–8983* ⊕ *www. cravemoab.com* ☾ *No dinner. Closed weekends Nov.–Feb.*

$$ ✕ **Zax.** Wood-fired pizza ovens are the focal point of this downtown
AMERICAN eatery and sports bar, where baseball bats double as door handles.
FAMILY For $14 you can try the pizza-salad-soup buffet (a popular choice, so the pies are constantly coming out of the oven), but while the pizza is a grand slam, the salad bar is dull as a 1–0 game. The best seats in the house are out on the patio for people-watching. Burgers, sand-wiches, and salads comprise most of the rest of the menu, but there are pasta dishes and steaks, too. The bar has a good selection of local microbrewed beers. $ *Average main: $15* ⊠ *96 S. Main St., Moab* ☎ *435/259–6555* ⊕ *www.zaxmoab.com.*

WHERE TO STAY

OUTSIDE THE PARK

Some of the best nightly lodging values in the area are rental con-dominiums and homes. Accommodations Unlimited is a great place to start, with units ranging from in-town studios to private homes. ☎ *435/259–6575* ⊕ *www.moabcondorentals.com.*

GREEN RIVER

$$ 🏨 **Green River Comfort Inn.** This clean, updated motel is convenient if
HOTEL you're staying only one night, as many do on family rafting outings (Holiday River Expeditions is behind the hotel). **Pros:** clean, and com-fortable; close to town's premier rafting outfitter; kids under 18 stay for free. **Cons:** remote, barren town; no elevator to second floor; Green River's two best restaurants are not in walking distance. $ *Rooms from: $119* ⊠ *1975 E. Main St., Green River* ☎ *435/564–3300* ⊕ *www. comfortinngreenriver.com* ⇆ *54 rooms, 3 suites* ○| *Breakfast.*

MOAB

$$$
B&B/INN

Adobe Abode. A lovely B&B near the nature preserve, this single-story inn surrounds you with solitude. **Pros:** relaxing in the beautifully decorated common area; the entrée-of-the-day (sometimes ham and eggs or waffles) accompanying the Continental breakfast; peace and quiet. **Cons:** you can bicycle to town, but it's too far to walk; no children under 16. $ *Rooms from: $159* ⊠ *778 W. Kane Creek Blvd., Moab* ☎ *435/260–2932 innkeeper's cell, 435/259–7716* ⊕ *www. adobeabodemoab.com* ↩ *4 rooms, 2 suites* ⦿*Breakfast.*

$$$$
HOTEL
FAMILY
Fodor's Choice
★

Best Western Canyonlands Inn. The confluence of Main and Center streets is the epicenter of Moab, and this comfortable, contemporary, impeccably clean hotel anchors the intersection, providing a perfect base camp for families. **Pros:** downtown location; smiling and helpful staff; updated, sparkling rooms; breakfast alfresco on outdoor patio. **Cons:** pricier than some comparable properties due to its location; for those seeking solitude, family-friendliness means the property bustles with happy children. $ *Rooms from: $231* ⊠ *16 S. Main St., Moab* ☎ *435/259–2300, 800/649–5191* ⊕ *www.canyonlandsinn.com* ↩ *34 rooms, 46 suites* ⦿*Breakfast.*

$$
B&B/INN
Fodor's Choice
★

Cali Cochitta Bed & Breakfast. One of the first homes built in Moab, this 19th-century Victorian in the heart of town, two blocks from Main Street shops and restaurants, has been restored to its classic style by owners David and Kim Boger. **Pros:** gracious owners pay attention to the details; easy walk to the hub of town; accomplished chef means scrumptious breakfast in the garden. **Cons:** given its historic construction, some quarters may feel a little tight. $ *Rooms from: $140* ⊠ *110 S. 200 E, Moab* ☎ *435/259–4961* ⊕ *www.moabdreaminn.com* ↩ *3 rooms, 1 suite, 2 cottages* ⦿*Breakfast.*

$$$$
HOTEL

Fairfield Inn and Suites. Views of the Colorado River are sure to wow guests at this new hotel, which opened in November 2014. **Pros:** warm, inviting and very clean; great views of the river and surrounding red rock scenery; buffet, Continental, or hot breakfasts included. **Cons:** about 4 miles from downtown Moab, so not in walking distance to restaurants and shops; pricey (but most Moab hotels are these days). $ *Rooms from: $219* ⊠ *1863 N. Hwy. 191, Moab* ☎ *435/259–5350, 888/236–2427* ⊕ *www.marriott.com* ↩ *65 rooms, 24 suites* ⦿*Breakfast.*

$$$
HOTEL

Gonzo Inn. Unconventional Moab's most original hotel property, this eclectic inn stands out for its design, color, art, and varnished adobe construction. **Pros:** unique, spotless, and hip; steps to Main Street but still one of downtown's quietest properties; friendly staff. **Cons:** interior hallways can be dark; no elevator; not all rooms have a good view. $ *Rooms from: $169* ⊠ *100 W. 200 S, Moab* ☎ *435/259–2515, 800/791–4044* ⊕ *www.gonzoinn.com* ↩ *21 rooms, 22 suites* ⦿*Breakfast.*

$$$$
RENTAL

Moab Springs Ranch. First developed by William Granstaff in the late 19th century, this 18-acre property about 3 miles from Arches and 2 miles from downtown Moab features comfortable hotel rooms and condos set by a meandering spring and decades-old sycamores, mulberries, and cottonwoods. **Pros:** large, green, shaded space filled with a natural spring and ponds; along recently built bike path to town. **Cons:** little within walking distance; some Highway 191 traffic noise. $ *Rooms from: $216*

5

Best Campgrounds In and Around Arches

Campgrounds in and around Moab range from sprawling RV parks with myriad amenities to quaint, shady retreats near a babbling brook. The Devils Garden Campground in the park is a wonderful spot to call home for a few days, though it is often full and does not provide an RV dump station. More than 350 campsites are operated in the vicinity by the Bureau of Land Management—their sites on the Colorado River and near the Slickrock Trail are some of the nicest (and most affordable) in the area. The most centrally located campgrounds in Moab will generally provide services needed by RV travelers.

IN THE PARK
Devils Garden Campground. This campground is one of the most unusual—and gorgeous—in the West, and in the national park system, for that matter. ⊠ *Off main road, 18 miles from park entrance* ☎ *435/719–2299, 435/259–4351 for group reservations, 877/444–6777 for NRRS reservations* ⊕ *www.recreation.gov.*

OUTSIDE THE PARK
Bureau of Land Management Campgrounds. Most of the 350 sites at 25 different BLM campgrounds are in the Moab area, including some stunning sites along the Colorado River (Route 128 and Route 279), Sand Flats Recreation Area (near the Slickrock Trail), and Canyon Flats Recreation Area (outside Needles District of Canyonlands). ☎ *435/259-2100* ⊕ *www.blm.gov/utah/moab.*

Canyonlands Campground. Although this camping park is in downtown Moab, the campground is astride Mill Creek and has many shade trees. ⊠ *555 S. Main St., Moab* ☎ *435/259-6848 or 888/522-6848* ⊕ *www.canyonlandsrv.com.*

Moab Valley RV Resort. Near the Colorado River, this campground with an expansive view feels more like a mall than a campground with its abundant space, activities, and services. ⊠ *1773 N. U.S. 191, Moab* ☎ *435/259-4469* ⊕ *www.moabvalleyrv.com.*

Slickrock Campground. At one of Moab's older campgrounds you find lots of mature shade trees and all the basic amenities—plus three hot tubs where adults have priority. ⊠ *1301½ N. U.S. 191, Moab* ☎ *435/259-7660 or 800/448-8873* ⊕ *www.slickrockcampground.com.*

Up the Creek Campground. Perhaps the quietest of the in-town campgrounds, Up the Creek lies under big cottonwoods on the banks of Mill Creek. ⊠ *210 E. 300 S, Moab* ☎ *435/260-1888* ⊕ *www. moabupthecreek.com.*

⊠ *1266 N. Main St., Moab* ☎ *435/259-7891* ⊕ *www.moabspringsranch. com* ⟿ *19 condos, from studios to larger rentals* ⟦○⟧ *No meals.*

$$ ⟦✕⟧ **Red Stone Inn.** One of the best bargains in town, this timber-frame
HOTEL motel offers small, clean rooms at the south end of the Moab strip near restaurants and shops. **Pros:** walking distance to Moab restaurants and shops; the price is right. **Cons:** pool is at sister property across busy Main Street; no frills. ⟦$⟧ *Rooms from: $114* ⊠ *535 S. Main St., Moab* ☎ *435/259-3500, 800/722-1972* ⊕ *www.moabredstone.com* ⟿ *52 rooms* ⟦○⟧ *No meals.*

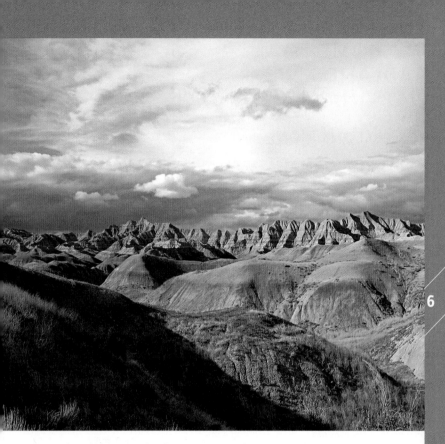

BADLANDS
NATIONAL PARK

WELCOME TO BADLANDS NATIONAL PARK

TOP REASONS TO GO

★ **Fossils:** From the mid-1800s, the fossil-rich Badlands area has welcomed paleontologists, research institutions, and fossil hunters who have discovered the fossil remnants of numerous species from ancient days.

★ **A world of wildlife:** Badlands National Park is home to a wide array of wildlife: bison, pronghorn, deer, black-footed ferrets, prairie dogs, rabbits, coyotes, foxes, badgers.

★ **Missiles:** The Minuteman Missile National Historic Site, north of the entrance to the park, represents the only remaining intact components of a nuclear-missile.

★ **Stars aplenty:** Due to its remote location and vastly open country, Badlands National Park contains some of the clearest and cleanest air in the country, which makes it perfect for viewing the night sky.

★ **Moonscape:** With hundreds of square miles of ragged ridgelines and sawtooth spires, Badlands National Park touts a landscape that is otherworldly.

1 North Unit. This is the most easily accessible of the three units and attracts the most visitors. It includes the Badlands Wilderness Area.

2 Palmer Creek Unit. This is the most isolated section of the park—no recognized roads pass through its borders. You must obtain permission from private landowners to pass through their property (contact the White River Visitor Center on how to do so). If you plan on exploring here, count on spending two days—one day to hike in and one day out.

590

Scenic

589

44

Sheep Mountain Table

Pine Ridge Indian Reservation Boundary

27

40

3
STRONGHOLD UNIT

Stronghold Table

2

Visitor Center

TO WOUNDED KNEE

3 Stronghold Unit. This was used as a gunnery range for the United States Air Force and the South Dakota National Guard from 1942 until the late 1960s. Discarded remnants and unexploded ordnance make this area potentially dangerous, so mind your step here. If you do find fragments of this era, do not handle them. Report the location to a ranger.

SOUTH
DAKOTA

↑ TO WALL AND
RAPID CITY

Roberts Prairie
Dog Town

Sage
Creek

Pinnacles Entrance

← TO MINUTEMAN
MISSILE NHS

Pinnacles Overlook

1 Yellow Mounds Overlook

NORTH UNIT

Conata Conata Basin Overlook

Cactus Flat

Northeast
Entrance

Medicine Root
Loop

Badlands Loop Rd.

Door Trail
Windows Trail
Notch Trail

509

Fossil Exhibit Trail

Cliff Shelf
Nature Trail

Castle Trail
Saddle Pass Trail

Visitor Center

Interior

377

6

**Cedar Pass
Lodge**

0 — 4 mi
0 — 4 km

2

PALMER CREEK UNIT

TO WOUNDED KNEE

KEY	
🚻	Ranger Station
⛺	Campground
⛱	Picnic Area
🍴	Restaurant
🏠	Lodge
🥾	Trailhead
🚻	Restrooms
⚡	Scenic Viewpoint
⋯⋯	Walking/Hiking Trails

GETTING ORIENTED

The park is divided into three units: the North Unit and the southern Stronghold and Palmer units. The two southern units are within Pine Ridge Indian Reservation and are jointly managed by the National Park Service and the Oglala Sioux Tribe. Much of the southern park is accessible only on foot or horseback, or by a high-clearance four-wheel-drive vehicle.

Updated by
T.D. Griffith

So stark and forbidding are the chiseled spires, ragged ridgelines, and deep ravines of South Dakota's badlands that Lieutenant Colonel George Custer once described them as "hell with the fires burned out." Although a bit more accessible than the depths of the underworld, the landscape is easily the strangest in the Great Plains. Ruthlessly ravaged over the ages by wind and rain, the 380 square miles of wild terrain continue to erode and evolve, sometimes visibly changing shape in a few days. Prairie creatures thrive on the untamed territory, and animal fossils are in abundance.

BADLANDS PLANNER

WHEN TO GO

Most visitors see the park between Memorial Day and Labor Day. The park's vast size and isolation prevent it from ever being too packed—though it is usually crowded the first week of August, when hundreds of thousands of motorcycle enthusiasts flock to the Black Hills for the annual Sturgis Motorcycle Rally. In summer, temperatures typically hover around 90°F—though it can get as hot as 116°F—and sudden mid-afternoon thunderstorms are not unusual. Storms put on a spectacular show of thunder and lightning, but it rarely rains for more than 10 or 15 minutes (the average annual rainfall is 16 inches). Autumn weather is generally sunny and warm. Snow usually appears by late October. Winter temperature can be as low as –40°F. Early spring is often wet, cold, and unpredictable. By May the weather usually stabilizes, bringing pleasant 70°F days.

AVG. HIGH/LOW TEMPS.

Jan.	Feb.	Mar.	Apr.	May	June
34/11	40/16	48/24	62/33	72/44	82/56

July	Aug.	Sept.	Oct.	Nov.	Dec.
91/60	92/55	81/46	65/34	48/21	39/17

FESTIVALS AND EVENTS

JANUARY–FEBRUARY **Black Hills Stock Show and Rodeo.** Watch world-champion wild-horse races, bucking horses, timed sheepdog trials, draft-horse contests, and steer wrestling during this two-week-long professional rodeo at the Rushmore Plaza Civic Center in Rapid City. Don't miss the stockman's banquet and ball. ⊠ *Rushmore Plaza Civic Center, 444 Mt. Rushmore Rd., Rapid City* ☎ *605/258–2863* ⊕ *www.blackhillsstockshow.com.*

MARCH **Badlands Quilters Weekend Getaway.** A display of the region's finest hand- and machine-made quilts, plus quilting classes by expert quilters, demonstrations, and sales are held in Wall's community center the second weekend in March. A local church hosts the Saturday night banquet. A group makes patriotic mystery quilts that are then donated to the local VA hospital. ⊠ *Wall Community Center, 5th and Main St., Wall* ☎ *605/279–2889.*

JUNE–AUGUST **Red Cloud Indian Art Show.** American Indian paintings and sculptures are the focus of this 11-week-long exhibition, beginning on the second Sunday in June, at the Red Cloud Indian School in Pine Ridge. ⊠ *Drexel Hall, 100 Mission Dr., Pine Ridge* ☎ *605/867–5491* ⊕ *www.redcloudschool.org.*

PLANNING YOUR TIME

BADLANDS IN ONE DAY

With a packed lunch and plenty of water, arrive at the park via the northeast entrance (off Interstate 90 at exit 131) and follow Route 240 (Badlands Loop Road) southwest toward the **Ben Reifel Visitor Center.** You can pick up park maps and information here, and also pay the park entrance fee (if the booth at the entrance was closed).

Next, stop at the **Big Badlands Overlook,** just south of the northeast entrance, to get a good feel for the landscape. As you head toward the visitor center, hike any one of several trails you'll pass, or if you prefer guided walks, arrive at the visitor center in time to look at the exhibits and talk with rangers before heading down to the Fossil Exhibit Trail. The badlands are one of the richest fossil fields in the world, and along the trail are wayside exhibits describing creatures that once lived here. After your walk, drive a couple of miles to the **Big Foot Pass Overlook,** up on the right. Here you can enjoy a packed lunch amid grassy prairies, with the rocky badland formations all around you.

After lunch, continue driving along Badlands Loop Road, stopping at the various overlooks for views and a hike or two. Near the Conata Picnic Area, you'll find the **Big Pig Dig,** a fossil site that was excavated by paleontologists through the summer of 2008. When you reach the junction with **Sage Creek Rim Road,** turn left and follow it along the northern border of the 100-square-mile **Badlands Wilderness Area,** which is home to hundreds of bison.

Provided the road is dry, take a side trip 5 miles down Sage Creek Rim Road to **Roberts Prairie Dog Town,** inhabited by a huge colony of the chattering critters. Children will love to watch these small rodents, which bark warning calls and dive underground if you get too close to their colony. The animals built burrow networks that once covered the Great Plains, but since European settlers established ranches in the region during the late 19th century, prairie dogs have become a far rarer sight. The park is less developed the farther you travel on Sage Creek Rim Road, allowing you to admire the sheer isolation and untouched beauty of badlands country. Hold out for a glorious sunset over the shadows of the nearby Black Hills, and keep your eyes open for animals stirring about.

GETTING HERE AND AROUND
CAR TRAVEL
The North Unit of Badlands National Park is 75 miles east of Rapid City and about 140 miles northeast of Wind Cave National Park in western South Dakota. It's accessed via exit 110 or 131 off Interstate 90, or Route 44 east to Route 377. Few roads, paved or otherwise, pass within the park. Badlands Loop Road (Route 240) is the most traveled and the only one that intersects Interstate 90. It's well maintained and rarely crowded. Parts of Route 44 and Route 27 run at the fringes of the badlands, connecting the visitor centers and Rapid City. Unpaved roads should be traveled with care when wet. Sheep Mountain Table Road, the only public road into the Stronghold Unit, is impassable when wet, with deep ruts—sometimes only high-clearance vehicles can get through. Off-road driving is prohibited. There's free parking at visitor centers, overlooks, and trailheads.

PARK ESSENTIALS
PARK FEES AND PERMITS
The entrance fee is $7 per person or $15 per vehicle, and is good for seven days. An annual park pass is $30. A backcountry permit isn't required for hiking or camping in Badlands National Park, but it's a good idea to check in at park headquarters before setting out on a backcountry journey. Backpackers may set up camps anywhere except within a half mile of roads or trails. Open fires are prohibited.

PARK HOURS
The park is open 24/7 year-round and is in the Mountain time zone.

CELL-PHONE RECEPTION
Cell-phone service has improved measurably over the last decade in western South Dakota, but you may not get a signal in much of the park. The closest pay phone you'll find will likely be in Wall.

EDUCATIONAL OFFERINGS
RANGER PROGRAMS
Evening Program. Watch a 40-minute outdoor audiovisual presentation on the wildlife, natural history, paleontology, or another aspect of the badlands. The shows typically begin around 9 pm, but check at the visitor center or park website for program times. ⊠ *Cedar Pass*

Campground amphitheater, 20681 Hwy. 240 ⊕ www.nps.gov/badl ⊙ *Mid-June–mid-Aug., daily usually about 9 pm.*

Fossil Talk. What were the badlands like many years ago? This talk about protected fossil exhibits will inspire and answer all your questions. Check at the visitor center or on the park website for exact times. ⊹ *Fossil Exhibit Trail, 5 miles west of the Ben Reifel Visitor Center* ⊕ *www.nps.gov/badl* ⊙ *Mid-June–mid-Aug., daily at 10:30 am, 1:30 pm, and 3:30 pm.*

Geology Walk. Learn the geologic story of the White River badlands in a 45-minute walk. The terrain can be rough in places, so be sure to wear hiking boots or sneakers. A hat is a good idea, too. Check at the visitor center or on the park website for exact times. ⊹ *Door and Window trails parking area, 2 miles east of the Ben Reifel Visitor Center* ⊕ *www. nps.gov/badl* ⊙ *Mid-June–mid-Aug., daily at 8:30 am.*

FAMILY **Junior Ranger Program.** Children ages 5–12 can join in this 45-minute adventure, typically a short hike, game, or other hands-on activity focused on badlands wildlife, geology, or fossils. Parents are welcome. ⊠ *Cedar Pass Campground amphitheater, 20681 Hwy. 240* ☎ *605/433-5361* ⊕ *www.nps.gov/badl* ⊙ *June–Aug. Check at visitor center or on park website for exact times.*

RESTAURANTS

Dining on the prairies of South Dakota has always been a casual and family-oriented experience, and in that sense little has changed in the past century. Even the fare, which consists largely of steak and potatoes, has stayed consistent (in fact, in some towns, "vegetarian" can be a dirty word). But for its lack of comparative sophistication, the grub in the restaurants surrounding Badlands National Park is typically very good. You'll probably never have a better steak—beef or buffalo—outside this area. You should also try cuisine influenced by American Indian cooking. The most popular (and well known) is the Indian taco, made from spiced meat and flat bread. In the park itself there's only one restaurant. The food is quite good, but don't hesitate to explore other options farther afield. You'll find the most choices in Wall.

HOTELS

Badlands National Park is often visited by families on a vacation to see the American West, but few opt to stay overnight here, especially when there's a profusion of accommodations in the Black Hills, situated a mere 50 miles east. As a result, there are few lodging options in and around the park, and if you're determined to bed down within park boundaries, you have only one choice: Cedar Pass Lodge. Though rustic, it's comfortable, inexpensive, and has new cabins.

The rustic-but-comfy formula is repeated by the area's few motels, hotels, and inns. Most are chain hotels in Wall, grouped around the interstate. Whether you stay inside or outside the park, you shouldn't have to worry about making reservations very far in advance, except during the first full week of August, when the entire region is inundated with more than half a million motorcyclists for the annual Sturgis Motorcycle Rally. Rooms for miles around book up more than a year in advance.

Hotel reviews have been shortened. For full information, visit Fodors.com.

WHAT IT COSTS			
$	$$	$$$	$$$$
Restaurants	under $13	$13–$20	$21–$30	over $30
Hotels	under $101	$101–$150	$151–$200	over $200

Restaurant prices are the average cost of a main course at dinner, or if dinner is not served, at lunch. Hotel prices are the lowest cost of a standard double room in high season.

TOURS

Affordable Adventures Badlands Tour. Take a seven-hour narrated tour through the park and surrounding badlands. Tours can easily be customized and are available year-round. ⊠ *5542 Meteor St., Rapid City* ☎ *605/342–7691, 888/888–8249* ⊕ *www.affordableadventuresbh.com* 🖃 *From $120.*

Golden Circle Tours. This company gives a seven- to nine-hour narrated van tour out of Custer to several venues, including Mount Rushmore, Crazy Horse Memorial, and Custer State Park. Other Black Hills tours are available. ⊠ *12023 Hwy. 16, Custer* ☎ *605/673–4349* ⊕ *www. goldencircletours.com* 🖃 *From $99* ⊘ *Mid-Apr.–Oct.*

Gray Line of the Black Hills. This outfit offers bus tours from Rapid City to Mount Rushmore, Black Hills National Forest, Custer State Park, and the Crazy Horse Memorial, as well as other tours tied to special events such as the Mount Rushmore Independence Day festivities and the Custer State Park Buffalo Roundup. ⊠ *1600 E. St. Patrick St., Rapid City* ☎ *800/456–4461* ⊕ *www.blackhillsgrayline.com* 🖃 *From $68* ⊘ *May–Oct.*

FAMILY **Mount Rushmore Tours.** Beginning at Fort Hayes on the *Dances with Wolves* film set and then moving to Mount Rushmore, Custer State Park, and Crazy Horse Memorial, this nine-hour trip around the Black Hills includes a cowboy show plus breakfast and dinner as options. Guests are responsible for their own lunch at the State Game Lodge. ⊠ *2255 Fort Hayes Dr., Rapid City* ☎ *888/343–3113* ⊕ *www. mountrushmoretours.com* 🖃 *From $80* ⊘ *Mid-May–mid-Oct.*

VISITOR INFORMATION

Park Contact Information Badlands National Park. ⊠ Badlands National Park ☎ 605/433-5361 ⊕ www.nps.gov/badl.

VISITOR CENTERS

Ben Reifel Visitor Center. Open year-round, this is the park's main information hub. Stop here to pick up brochures and maps. A 22-minute video about geology and wildlife runs continually. The facility is named for a Sioux activist and the first Lakota to serve in Congress. Born on the nearby Rosebud Indian Reservation, Ben Reifel also served in the Army during World War II. ⊕ *Badlands Loop Rd., near Hwy. 377 junction, 8 miles from northeast entrance* ☎ *605/433–5361* ⊘ *June–mid-Aug., daily 7–7; mid-Aug.–mid-Sept., daily 8–5; mid-Sept–May, daily 8–4.*

White River Visitor Center. Open in summer, this small center serves almost exclusively serious hikers and campers venturing into the Stronghold or

Palmer units. If that's you, stop here for maps and details about road and trail conditions. The center is located on the Pine Ridge Indian Reservation. While you're here you can see fossils and Lakota artifacts, and learn about Sioux culture. ⊹ *25 miles south of Hwy. 44 via Hwy. 27* ☎ *605/455–2878* ⊕ *www.nps.gov/badl* ⊗ *Memorial Day–Labor Day, daily 10–4. Hrs may vary.*

EXPLORING

SCENIC DRIVES

For the average visitor, a casual drive is the essential means by which to see Badlands National Park. To do the scenery justice, drive slowly, and don't hesitate to get out and explore on foot when the occasion calls for it.

Fodor's Choice
★
Badlands Loop Road. The simplest drive is on two-lane Badlands Loop Road. The drive circles from exit 110 off Interstate 90 through the park and back to the interstate at exit 131. Start from either end and make your way around to the various overlooks along the way. Pinnacles and Yellow Mounds overlooks are outstanding places to examine the sandy pink- and brown-toned ridges and spires distinctive to the badlands. At a certain point the landscape flattens out slightly to the north, revealing spectacular views of mixed-grass prairies. The Cedar Pass area of the drive has some of the park's best trails. ⊠ *I–90, Exit 110* ⊕ *www.nps.gov/badl.*

HISTORIC SITES

Big Pig Dig. Until 2008, paleontologists dug for fossils at this site named for a large fossil originally thought to be of a prehistoric pig (it actually turned out to be a small, hornless rhinoceros). There are interpretive signs detailing fossils discovered at the site. ⊹ *Conata Picnic Area, 17 miles northwest of the Ben Reifel Visitor Center.*

Stronghold Unit. With few paved roads and no campgrounds, the park's southwest section is difficult to access without a four-wheel-drive vehicle. If you're willing to trek, its isolation provides a rare opportunity to explore badlands rock formations and prairies completely undisturbed. From 1942 to 1968, the U.S. Air Force and South Dakota National Guard used much of the area as a gunnery range. Hundreds of fossils were destroyed by bomber pilots, who frequently targeted the large fossil remains of an elephant-size titanothere (an extinct relative of the rhinoceros). Beware of unexploded bombs, shells, rockets, and other hazardous materials. Steer clear of it and find another route.

Within the Stronghold Unit, the **Stronghold Table,** a 3-mile-long plateau, can be reached only by crossing a narrow land bridge just wide enough to let a wagon pass. It was here, just before the Massacre at Wounded Knee in 1890, that some 600 Sioux gathered to perform one of the last known Ghost Dances, a ritual in which the Sioux wore white shirts that they believed would protect them from bullets. ⊹ *North and west of White River Visitor Center; entrance off Hwy. 27* ⊕ *www.nps.gov/badl.*

SCENIC STOPS

Fodor's Choice **Badlands Wilderness Area.** Covering about a quarter of the park, this
★ 100-square-mile area is part of the country's largest prairie wilderness.
About two-thirds of the Sage Creek region is mixed-grass prairie, making it the ideal grazing grounds for bison, pronghorn, and many of the
park's other native animals. The Hay Butte Overlook (2 miles northwest
on Sage Creek Rim Road) and the Pinnacles Overlook (1 mile south
of the Pinnacles entrance) are the best places to get an overview of the
wilderness area. Feel free to park at an overlook and hike your own
route into the untamed, unmarked prairie. *⊹ 25 miles northwest of Ben
Reifel Visitor Center ⊕ www.nps.gov/badl.*

Big Badlands Overlook. From this spot just south of the park's northeast
entrance, the vast majority of the park's 1 million annual visitors get
their first views of the White River Badlands. *⊹ 5 miles northeast of
the Ben Reifel Visitor Center.*

FAMILY **Roberts Prairie Dog Town.** Once a homestead, the site today contains one
of the country's largest (if not the largest) colonies of black-tailed prairie dogs. *⊠ Sage Creek Rim Rd. ⊹ 5 miles west of Badlands Loop Rd.*

Yellow Mounds Overlook. Contrasting sharply with the whites, grays, and
browns of the badlands pinnacles, the mounds viewed from here greet
you with soft yet vivid yellows, reds, and purples. *⊹ 16 miles northwest
of the Ben Reifel Visitor Center.*

SPORTS AND THE OUTDOORS

Pure, unspoiled, empty space is the greatest asset of Badlands National
Park, and it can only be experienced to its highest degree if you're on
foot. Spring and autumn are the best times of the year to do wilderness
exploring, because the brutal extremes of summer and winter can—and
do—kill. In fact, the two biggest enemies to hikers and bicyclists in the
badlands are heat and lightning. Before you venture out, make sure you
have at least one gallon of water per person per day, and be prepared
to take shelter from freak thunderstorms, which often strike in the late
afternoon with little warning.

AIR TOURS

Black Hills Balloons. Based in Custer, Black Hills Balloons provides amazing bird's-eye views of some of the Black Hills' most picturesque locations. Reservations are essential. *⊠ 25173 Lower French Creek Rd.,
Custer ☎ 605/673–2520 ⊕ www.blackhillsballoons.com ⊠ From $295.*

BICYCLING

Bicycles are permitted only on designated roads, which may be paved
or unpaved. They are prohibited from closed roads, trails, and the
backcountry. Flat-resistant tires are recommended.

Sheep Mountain Table Road. This 7-mile dirt road in the Stronghold Unit is
ideal for mountain biking, but should be attempted only when dry. The
terrain is level for the first 3 miles, then it climbs and levels out again.

CLOSE UP

Plants and Wildlife in Badlands

The park's sharply defined cliffs, canyons, and mesas are near-deserts with little plant growth. Most of the park, however, is made up of mixed-grass prairies, where more than 460 species of hardy grasses and wildflowers flourish in the warmer months. Prairie coneflower, yellow plains prickly pear, pale-green yucca, buffalo grass, and sideoats grama are just a few of the plants on the badlands plateau. Trees and shrubs are rare and usually confined to dry creek beds. The most common trees are Rocky Mountain junipers and plains cottonwoods.

It's common to see pronghorn antelope and mule deer dart across the flat plateaus, bison grazing on the buttes, prairie dogs and sharp-tailed grouse, and, soaring above, golden eagles, turkey vultures, and hawks. Also present are coyotes, swift foxes, jackrabbits, bats, gophers, porcupines, skunks, bobcats, horned lizards, bighorn sheep, and prairie rattlers. The latter are the only venomous reptiles in the park—watch for them near rocky outcroppings and in prairie-dog towns. Backcountry hikers might consider heavy boots and long pants reinforced with leather or canvas. Although rarely seen, weasels, mountain lions, and the endangered black-footed ferret roam the park.

6

At the top you can take in great views of the area. ⊠ *Badlands National Park* ✛ *About 14 miles north of the White River Visitor Center.*

OUTFITTERS
Two Wheeler Dealer Cycle and Fitness. Family-owned and -operated Two Wheeler Dealer Cycle and Fitness, based in Spearfish, stocks more than 1,000 new bikes for sale or rent. The service is exceptional. Get trail and route information for Badlands National Park and the Black Hills at the counter. ⊠ *305 Main St., Spearfish* ☎ *605/642–7545* ⊕ *www. twowheelerdealer.com.*

BIRD-WATCHING

Especially around sunset, get set to watch the badlands come to life. More than 215 bird species have been recorded in the area, including herons, pelicans, cormorants, egrets, swans, geese, hawks, golden and bald eagles, falcons, vultures, cranes, doves, and cuckoos. Established roads and trails are the best places from which to watch for nesting species. The Cliff Shelf Nature Trail and the Castle Trail, which both traverse areas with surprisingly thick vegetation, are especially good locations. You may even catch sight of a rare burrowing owl at the Roberts Prairie Dog Town. Be sure to bring along a pair of binoculars.

HIKING

The isolation and otherworldliness of the badlands are best appreciated with a walk through them. Take time to examine the dusty rock beneath your feet, and be on the lookout for fossils and animals. Fossil Exhibit Trail and Cliff Shelf Nature Trail are must-dos, but even these popular trails tend to be primitive. You'll find bathrooms at Fossil Exhibit Trail. Both trails feature boardwalks, so you won't be shuffling through dirt and gravel.

Because the weather here can be so variable, rangers suggest that you be prepared for anything. Wear sunglasses, a hat, and long pants, and have rain gear available. It's illegal to interfere with park resources, which includes everything from rocks and fossils to plants and artifacts. Stay at least 100 yards away from wildlife. Due to the dry climate, open fires are never allowed. Tell friends, relatives, and the park rangers if you're going to embark on a multiday expedition. Assume that your cell phone, if you've brought one, won't get a signal in the park. But most important of all, be sure to bring your own water. Sources of water in the park are few and far between, and none of them are drinkable. All water in the park is contaminated by minerals and sediment, and park authorities warn that it's untreatable. If you're backpacking into the wilderness, bring at least a gallon of water per person per day. For day hikes, rangers suggest you drink at least a quart per person per hour.

EASY

FAMILY

Fodor's Choice

★

Fossil Exhibit Trail. The trail, in place since 1964, has fossil replicas of early mammals displayed at wayside exhibits along its ¼-mile length, which is now completely wheelchair accessible. Give yourself at least an hour to fully enjoy this popular hike. *Easy.* ✛ *Trailhead: 5 miles northwest of the Ben Reifel Visitor Center, off Hwy. 240.*

Window Trail. This 200-yard round-trip trail ends at a natural hole, or window, in a rock wall. Looking though, you'll see more of the distinctive badlands pinnacles and spires. *Easy.* ✛ *Trailhead: 2 miles north of the Ben Reifel Visitor Center, off Hwy. 240.*

MODERATE

Cliff Shelf Nature Trail. This ½-mile loop winds through a wooded prairie oasis in the middle of dry, rocky ridges and climbs 200 feet to a peak above White River Valley for an incomparable view. Look for chipmunks, squirrels, and red-winged blackbirds in the wet wood, and eagles, hawks, and vultures at hilltop. Even casual hikers can complete this trail in far less than an hour, but if you want to observe the true diversity of wildlife present here, stay longer. *Moderate.* ✛ *Trailhead: 1 mile east of the Ben Reifel Visitor Center, off Hwy. 240.*

Notch Trail. One of the park's more interesting hikes, this 1½-mile round-trip trail takes you over moderately difficult terrain and up a ladder. Winds at the notch can be fierce, but it's worth lingering for the view of the White River Valley and the Pine Ridge Indian Reservation. If you take a couple of breaks and enjoy the views, you'll probably want to plan on spending a little more than an hour on this hike. *Moderate.* ✛ *Trailhead: 2 miles north of the Ben Reifel Visitor Center, off Hwy. 240.*

DIFFICULT

Saddle Pass Trail. This route, which connects with Castle Trail and Medicine Root Loop, is a steep, ¼-mile climb up and down the side of "The Wall," an impressive rock formation. Plan on spending about an hour on this climb. *Difficult.* ✛ *Trailhead: 2 miles west of the Ben Reifel Visitor Center, off Hwy. 240* ⊕ *www.nps.gov/badl.*

HORSEBACK RIDING

The park has one of the largest and most beautiful territories in the state in which to ride a horse. Riding is allowed in most of the park except for some marked trails, roads, and developed areas. The mixed-grass prairie of the Badlands Wilderness Area is especially popular with riders. However, note that the weather in the Badlands Wilderness Area can be unpredictable. Only experienced riders or people accompanied by experienced riders should venture far from more developed areas.

There are several restrictions and regulations that you must be aware of if you plan to ride your own horse. Potable water for visitors and animals is a rarity. Riders must bring enough water for themselves and their stock. Only certified weed-free hay is approved in the park. Horses are not allowed to run free within the borders of the park.

WHAT'S NEARBY

Badlands National Park is off Interstate 90 with two separate entrances. Badlands can be a one- or two-day stop for visitors who are traveling through the area or a place of frequent visits to locals. Located 50 miles east of the edge of the Black Hills (and Rapid City, the largest community on this side of the state), Badlands allows travelers a unique stop in a highly dense area of national parks, monuments, and memorials. Its close proximity to national treasures such as Mount Rushmore National Memorial, Wind Cave National Park, Jewel Cave National Monument, Devils Tower National Monument, and Custer State Park allows visitors to take in a wealth of sightseeing excursions in a relatively small area. The Black Hills provide a wonderful backdrop for the dry canyon and dusty buttes of the badlands.

NEARBY TOWNS

Built against a steep ridge of badland rock, **Wall** was founded in 1907 as a railroad station, and is among the closest towns to Badlands National Park, 8 miles from the Pinnacles entrance to the North Unit. Wall is home to about 850 residents and the world-famous Wall Drug Store, best known for its fabled jackalopes and free ice water.

Pine Ridge, about 35 miles south of the Stronghold Unit, is on the cusp of Pine Ridge Indian Reservation. The town was established in 1877 as an Indian agency for Chief Red Cloud and his band of followers. With 2,800 square miles, the reservation, home, and headquarters of the Oglala Sioux, is second in size only to Arizona's Navajo Reservation.

Rapid City, in the eastern buttes of the Black Hills, is South Dakota's second-largest city and a good base from which to explore the treasures of the state's southwestern corner, including the neighboring Black Hills National Forest, the badlands 75 miles to the east, and Mount Rushmore and Wind Cave National Park, 25 miles and 140 miles to the southwest respectively.

VISITOR INFORMATION

Oglala Sioux Tribe (Pine Ridge). The Pine Ridge Reservation is home to more than 38,000 Oglala Lakota, members of a major Sioux division known as the Western or Teton Sioux, who live in nine tribal districts on nearly 2 million acres of land. They are led by a Tribal Council President who is advised by an executive committee and a tribal council. ⊠ *Pine Ridge* ☎ *605/867–5821* ⊕ *www.oglalalakotanation.org.*

NEARBY ATTRACTIONS

FAMILY   **Main Street Square.** This attractive plaza in downtown Rapid City is a focal point for a wide array of special events throughout the year, including movies under the stars, food festivals, a farmers' market, musical performances, and ice-skating. At various times of the year, the square features interactive fountains, gardens, a fire pit, and a large oval lawn. ⊠ *Destination Rapid City, 512 Main St., Rapid City* ☎ *605/716–7979* ⊕ *www.mainstreetsquarerc.com.*

Fodor'sChoice   **Mount Rushmore National Memorial.** One of the nation's most iconic
★   attractions, the giant likenesses of Washington, Jefferson, Lincoln, and Theodore Roosevelt, lies just 65 miles west of Badlands. An excellent interpretive center, trail network, and patriotic night lighting ceremony make the trip even more memorable, as does a Youth Exploration Area added in 2015. ⊠ *Rte. 244, Keystone* ☎ *605/574–2523* ⊕ *www.nps. gov/moru* ⊠ *Parking $11* ⊗ *Monument daily 24 hrs; visitor facilities and museums hrs vary.*

Outdoor Campus West. A project of South Dakota Game, Fish, and Parks, this attractive education center opened in 2011. It couples a hands-on museum featuring native habitats and wildlife with a 32-acre outdoor campus offering classes in hunting, fishing, camping, and snowshoeing. Nearby are several miles of hiking trails. ⊠ *4130 Adventure Trail, Rapid City* ☎ *605/394–2310* ⊕ *www.outdoorcampus.org* ⊗ *May–Oct., weekdays 8–5, Sat. 10–4, Sun. 1–4; Nov.–Apr., weekdays 8–5, Sat. 10–4.*

FAMILY   **Wall Drug Store.** This South Dakota original got its start in 1931 by offer-
Fodor'sChoice   ing free ice water to road-weary travelers. Today its four dining rooms
★   seat 520 visitors at a time. A life-size mechanical Cowboy Orchestra and Chuckwagon Quartet greet you inside, and in the back you'll see an animated T. rex and replicas of Mount Rushmore and a native village. The attached Western Mall has 14 shops selling all kinds of keepsakes from cowboy hats, boots, and Black Hills gold jewelry to T-shirts and fudge. Just don't skip the doughnuts. ⊠ *510 Main St., Wall* ☎ *605/279–2175* ⊕ *www.walldrug.com* ⊠ *Free* ⊗ *Late May–early Sept., daily 6 am–10 pm; early Sept.–late May, daily 7–6.*

Wounded Knee Historical Site. A solitary stone obelisk commemorates the site of the 1890 massacre at Wounded Knee, the last major conflict between the U.S. military and American Indians. Only a handful of visitors make pilgrimages to the remote site today, which is simple and largely unchanged from its 1890 appearance. ⊠ *U.S. 18, Pine Ridge* ✛ *12 miles northwest of Pine Ridge* ⊠ *Free* ⊗ *Daily 24 hrs.*

Wounded Knee: The Museum. This modern facility interprets the history of the December 29, 1890, Wounded Knee Massacre through interactive exhibits with historical photos and documents. Although a tour of the museum is an excellent companion to a visit to the actual site of the massacre, many visitors choose to stop at this convenient location off Interstate 90 in lieu of a stop at the isolated battleground 80 miles to the south. ⊠ *600 Main St., Wall* ☎ *605/279–2573* ⊕ *www. woundedkneemuseum.org* ⊠ *$6* ☉ *Mid-May–mid-Oct., daily 9–5:30.*

WHERE TO EAT

IN THE PARK

$
AMERICAN
FAMILY

✕ **Cedar Pass Lodge Restaurant.** Cool off within dark, knotty-pine walls under an exposed-beam ceiling, and enjoy a hearty meal of steak or Indian tacos and fry bread. ⑤ *Average main: $9* ⊠ *20681 Hwy. 240, Interior* ☎ *605/433–5460* ⊕ *www.cedarpasslodge.com* ☉ *Closed Nov.–Mar.*

PICNIC AREAS

Bigfoot Pass Overlook. There is only a handful of tables here and no water, but the incredible view makes it a lovely spot to have lunch. Restrooms are available. ⊠ *Badlands Loop Rd.* ⊕ *7 miles northwest of the Ben Reifel Visitor Center.*

Conata Picnic Area. A half-dozen or so covered picnic tables are scattered over this area, which rests against a badlands wall ½ mile south of Badlands Loop Road. There's no potable water, but there are bathroom facilities and you can enjoy your lunch in peaceful isolation at the threshold of the Badlands Wilderness Area. The Conata Basin area is to the east, and Sage Creek area is to the west. ⊠ *Conata Rd.* ⊕ *15 miles northwest of the Ben Reifel Visitor Center* ⊕ *www.nps.gov/badl.*

OUTSIDE THE PARK

WALL

$
AMERICAN

✕ **Cactus Family Restaurant and Lounge.** Delicious hotcakes and pies await you at this restaurant in downtown Wall. In summer you'll find a buffet large enough to satisfy any appetite. ⑤ *Average main: $10* ⊠ *519 Main St., Wall* ☎ *605/279–2561* ⊕ *www.cactuscafeandlounge.com.*

$
AMERICAN

✕ **Western Art Gallery Restaurant.** More than 200 original oil paintings, all with a Western theme, line the dining room of this eatery in the Wall Drug building. For a tasty meal, try a hot beef sandwich or a buffalo burger. The old-fashioned soda fountain has milk shakes and homemade ice cream. The place serves the area's best donuts. ⑤ *Average main: $11* ⊠ *510 Main St., Wall* ☎ *605/279–2175* ⊕ *www.walldrug.com* ☉ *No dinner.*

WHERE TO STAY

IN THE PARK

$$$
HOTEL

🛏 **Cedar Pass Lodge.** Besides impressive views of the badlands, these cabins include modern touches like flat-screen TVs and Wi-Fi connections. **Pros:** new cabins; the best stargazing in South Dakota. **Cons:**

CLOSE UP

Best Campgrounds in Badlands

Pitching a tent and sleeping under the stars is one of the greatest ways to fully experience the sheer isolation and unadulterated empty spaces of Badlands National Park. You'll find two relatively easy-access campgrounds within park boundaries, but only one has any sort of amenities. The second is little more than a flat patch of ground with some signs. Unless you desperately need a flush toilet to have an enjoyable camping experience, you're just as well off hiking into the wilderness and choosing your own campsite. The additional isolation will be well worth the extra effort. You can set up camp anywhere that's at least a half mile from a road or trail and is not visible from any road or trail.

Cedar Pass Campground. With tent sites and 20 new RV sites as well as coin-operated showers, this is the most developed campground in the park, and it's near the Ben Reifel Visitor Center, Cedar Pass Lodge, and a half-dozen hiking trails. ⊠ *Rte. 377, ¼ mile south of Badlands Loop Rd.* ☎ *605/433–5361* ⊕ *www.cedarpasslodge.com.*

Sage Creek Primitive Campground. The word to remember here is primitive. If you want to get away from it all, this lovely, isolated spot surrounded by nothing but fields and crickets is the right camp for you. ⊠ *Sage Creek Rim Rd., 25 miles west of Badlands Loop Rd.* ☎ *No phone.*

remote location; long drive to other restaurants. $ *Rooms from: $175* ⊠ *20681 Hwy. 240, Interior* ☎ *605/433–5460, 877/386–4383* ⊕ *www. cedarpasslodge.com* ⊗ *Closed Oct.–Apr.* ⊅ *26 cabins* ⊠ *No meals.*

OUTSIDE THE PARK

INTERIOR

$
HOTEL
Badlands Budget Host Motel. Every room in this motel has views of the nearby Buffalo Gap National Grasslands. **Pros:** clean and comfortable; close to the national park. **Cons:** standard rooms with no frills. $ *Rooms from: $72* ⊠ *900 SD Hwy. 377, Interior* ☎ *605/433–5335, 800/388–4643* ⊕ *www.badlandsinteriorcampground.com* ⊗ *Closed Oct.–Mar.* ⊅ *21 rooms, 70 campsites* ⊠ *No meals.*

$$
B&B/INN
FAMILY
Circle View Guest Ranch. Located in the heart of the badlands, this B&B has spectacular views. **Pros:** friendly people; beautiful views; great for groups. **Cons:** small and isolated. $ *Rooms from: $115* ⊠ *20055 Hwy. 44 E, Interior* ☎ *605/433–5582* ⊕ *www.circleviewranch.com* ⊅ *8 rooms, 3 cabins* ⊠ *Breakfast.*

RAPID CITY

$$
B&B/INN
Coyote Blues Village B&B. This European-style lodge on 30 acres displays an unusual mix of antique furnishings and contemporary art. **Pros:** tucked away from the highway; exceptional food. **Cons:** not within walking distance of other restaurants. $ *Rooms from: $125* ⊠ *23165 Horseman's Ranch Rd., Rapid City* ☎ *605/574–4477* ⊕ *www. coyotebluesvillage.com* ⊅ *10 rooms* ⊠ *Breakfast.*

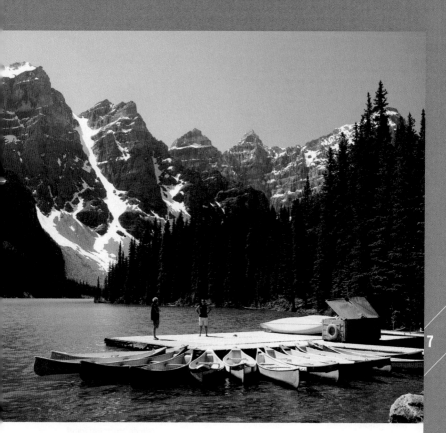

BANFF
NATIONAL PARK

WELCOME TO BANFF NATIONAL PARK

TOP REASONS TO GO

★ **Scenery:** Visitors are often unprepared for the sheer scale of the Canadian Rockies. Scattered between the peaks are glaciers, forests, valleys, meadows, rivers, and the bluest lakes of the planet.

★ **Spectacular ski slopes:** Lake Louise Mountain Resort is Canada's largest single ski area, with skiing on four mountain faces, 4,200 skiable acres, and 113 named trails—and that's only one of Banff's three ski resorts.

★ **Trails galore:** More than 1,600 km (1,000 miles) of defined hiking trails lead to scenic lakes, alpine meadows, glaciers, forests, and deep canyons.

★ **Banff Upper Hot Springs:** Relax in naturally hot mineral springs as you watch snowflakes swirl around you, or gaze at the stars as you "take the waters" on a cool summer's evening.

★ **Icefields Parkway:** One of the most scenic drives on the continent, this 230-km (143-mile) roadway links Banff and Jasper.

1 **Icefields Parkway.** There are many sites to be seen along this spectacular 230-km (143-mile) stretch of road. The Crowfoot Glacier, Bow Pass, Mistaya Canyon, Saskatchewan Crossing, and the Columbia Icefield are the primary highlights in the Banff section.

2 **Lake Louise, Moraine Lake, and the Bow Valley Parkway.** Backed by snowcapped mountains and fantastically ice-blue, Lake Louise is one of the most photographed lakes in the world. Lake Louise, Moraine Lake and the Valley of the Ten Peaks, and stunning Johnston Canyon are highlights of this region.

3 **Banff Townsite.** The hub of the park, Banff Townsite is the place to go to find shops, restaurants, hotels, and other facilities. Highlights of the townsite: the Banff Visitor Centre, Whyte Museum, Banff Centre, Upper Hot Springs Pool, Sulphur Mountain Gondola, and the Hoodoos.

KEY	
🏠	Ranger Station
△	Campground
⛱	Picnic Area
🍴	Restaurant
🏨	Lodge
🚶	Trailhead
🚻	Restrooms
⇀	Scenic Viewpoint
⋯⋯	Walking/Hiking Trails

ALBERTA

GETTING ORIENTED

Areas of majestic beauty fill the 6,641 square km (2,564 square miles) of Banff National Park. Bordered by Jasper National Park to the north, Kootenay and Yoho national parks to the west, the Bighorn Wildland Recreation Area to the east, and Kananaskis Country and Peter Lougheed Provincial Park to the south, Banff is at the center of a huge block of protected wilderness.

7

0   20 mi
0   20 km

Bow Pass &
Peyto Lake Viewpoint
93   Bow Lake
◆ **Crowfoot Glacier**
Hector
Lake
Icefields Pkwy
1

TO
YOHO
NATIONAL
PARK

🌿 **Lake
Louise** 2 ○ Lake Louise
Valley of the
Ten Peaks Moraine
Lake
1A

🌿

**Johnston
Canyon** ◆

Vermilion
Pass
3
TO
KOOTENAY
NATIONAL PARK 93
Cave and Basin NHS ◆ 🍴 📷 Banff
Lake
Minnewanka
**Banff Park
Museum National
Historic Site
of Canada**
Banff Upper Hot Springs ◆
**Fairmont
Banff Springs**
Bow River
Sunshine
Ski Area ●
Canmore

🌿
→
TO
CALGARY

Updated by
Debbie Olsen

Comparing mountains is a subjective and imprecise business. Yet few would deny that the Canadian Rockies are one of the most extravagantly beautiful ranges on Earth. The mountains and vast stretches of wilderness that make up Canada's first national park offer stunning scenery of glaciers, lakes, valleys, and snowcapped mountain peaks. Large mammals such as deer and elk can be observed in all seasons from the roadside.

BANFF PLANNER

WHEN TO GO

Banff National Park is an all-seasons destination. Visit in summer to hike the mountain trails, or go in winter to enjoy some of the world's best skiing. Millions of people visit Banff every year, with the vast majority traveling during July and August, the warmest and driest months. ■TIP➔ **If you can visit in late spring or early fall you will be in shoulder season when prices are lower, the crowds smaller, and the temperatures usually still comfortable.** The downside to an off-season visit is the fact that you miss the summer interpretive programs and the wildflowers that reach their peak from early July to mid-August.

Both of the park's information centers are open all year, with extended hours during the summer months.

AVG. HIGH/LOW TEMPS.

Jan.	Feb.	Mar.	Apr.	May	June
22/5	32/12	39/18	48/30	58/35	66/42
July	Aug.	Sept.	Oct.	Nov.	Dec.
71/45	71/44	61/37	50/30	33/17	22/7

FESTIVALS AND EVENTS

WINTER **Santa Claus Parade of Lights & Festive Fun.** Banff welcomes the holiday season in early December with a day of events that include photo ops with Santa in Central Park, craft shows, children's ice-carving stations, and an evening parade of lights. On Christmas Day, Santa shows off his downhill skills at the three area ski resorts. ☎ *403/762–8421* ⊕ *www.banfflakelouise.com.*

Snow Days. A highlight of this monthlong winter celebration is the Ice Magic winter festival, which features world-class ice-carving and outdoor events. The festivities, which begin in early January, also include a 3-on-3 ball hockey tournament and Mountain Adventure Weekend, during which you can try ice climbing and other exhilarating outdoor activities and watch mountain films. ☎ *403/762–8421* ⊕ *www.banfflakelouise.com.*

SUMMER **Canada Day.** Admission to the national park is free on this July 1 holiday, and big celebrations take place in Canmore and Banff that include parades, fireworks, and live music. ☎ *403/762–1200* ⊕ *www.banff.com.*

Summer Events at the Banff Centre. The center's summer cultural-events lineup, a Banff staple for more than four decades, includes film screenings, visual-arts displays, theater, opera, dance, literary readings, lectures, and musical productions. There's a charge for some events, but many are free or "pay what you can." ☎ *403/762–6300* ⊕ *www. banffcentre.ca.*

FALL **Lake Louise WonderFall.** Part of the magic of the Canadian Rockies is seeing magnificent stands of larch trees glistening golden on a crisp autumn afternoon. WonderFall celebrates this season with special discount packages, larch hikes, photography workshops, and special activities. ☎ *403/762–8421* ⊕ *www.banfflakelouise.com.*

PLANNING YOUR TIME

BANFF NATIONAL PARK IN ONE DAY

Start with a visit to the **Banff Visitor Centre** to pick up maps and information about the major sites. Buy lunch provisions and drive to beautiful **Lake Louise.** Walk the flat shoreline trail and venture upward along the **Lake Agnes Trail** to the teahouse (or turn back once you get a lofty view of Lake Louise). On the drive back to Banff Townsite, stop at Johnston Canyon and allow an hour for the easy round-trip hike to the dramatic waterfall. Have dinner at **Fairmont Banff Springs Hotel.** Afterward, explore the hotel's interior, then end the day with an evening dip in the **Banff Upper Hot Springs.**

GETTING HERE AND AROUND

Banff National Park, in west-central Alberta, is 128 km (80 miles) west of Calgary, 401 km (249 miles) southwest of Edmonton, and 850 km (528 miles) east of Vancouver.

AIR TRAVEL

The closest international airports are in Calgary (YYC) and Edmonton (YEG). Major airlines serve both airports.

BUS TRAVEL

The towns of Banff and Lake Louise have public transit systems and local taxi companies. Public buses run between Canmore, Banff, and Lake Louise, and a ski shuttle in winter picks up passengers at most area hotels and transports them to the park's three ski resorts. Greyhound Canada Transportation provides regular bus service from Calgary, Edmonton, and Vancouver to Banff and Lake Louise. The Canadian Rockies Brewster Shuttle connects Calgary's airport with Kananaskis, Banff, Lake Louise, and Jasper.

Bus Contact Information Brewster Banff Airport Express. ⊠ *100 Gopher St., Banff* ☎ *403/762–6700, 866/606–6700* ⊕ *www.brewster.ca/transportation.* **Greyhound Canada Transportation.** ⊠ *327 Railway Ave., Banff* ☎ *403/762–1092, 800/231–2222 in U.S.*

CAR TRAVEL

The easiest way to get from Calgary to Banff is by car on Trans-Canada Highway 1. Use Icefields Parkway (Highway 93) to get from Jasper to Banff. Car-rental agencies operate at Edmonton and Calgary airports and in Canmore, Banff, Lake Louise, and Jasper.

PARK ESSENTIALS

PARK FEES AND PERMITS

All prices in this chapter are in Canadian dollars, unless stated otherwise. A park entrance pass costs C$9.80 per person or C$19.60 maximum for up to seven people per vehicle per day. An annual pass costs C$67.70 per adult or C$136.40 per family or group. Larger buses and vans pay a group commercial rate. If you're planning to stay a week or more, your best bet is an annual pass.

Permits are required for backcountry camping and some other activities. Backcountry camping permits (C$9.80 per person per night), fire permits (C$8.80 per day), dumping station permits (C$8.80 per day), and fishing permits (C$9.80 per day) are available at the park visitor information center or at some campgrounds. In some cases a fire permit is included in your camping fees. Be sure to check with campground staff.

PARK HOURS

The park, open 24/7 year-round, is in the Mountain time zone.

CELL-PHONE RECEPTION

Cell-phone service is sometimes unpredictable, but is fairly good near the Banff Townsite. Public telephones can be found at the information centers, at most hotels and bars, and at several key spots around the townsite of Banff and the village of Lake Louise.

EDUCATIONAL OFFERINGS

Evening theater programs and guided hikes are among the educational activities the park presents. Check at the visitor centers or online at ⊕ *www.pc.gc.ca/eng/pn-np/ab/banff/edu.aspx.*

FAMILY **Xplorer Program.** Year-round, the park offers the Xplorer Program for kids
Fodor'sChoice age 6 to 11. Pick up an Xplorer Booklet at one of the park's visitor cen-
★ ters. Kids who complete at least six of the booklet's 22 activities receive a souvenir. ⊠ *Banff* ⊕ *www.pc.gc.ca/eng/pn-np/ab/banff/edu.aspx* ▣ *Free.*

RESTAURANTS

More than 100 restaurants operate in Banff National Park, from fast-food outlets to award-winning fine-dining establishments. Trout, venison, elk, moose, and bison appear on the menus of even the most modest eateries. It's a good idea to make reservations at popular places, especially during the peak summer and ski seasons. As at most national parks, prices are slightly inflated. Except for the fanciest spots, casual dress is the norm.

HOTELS

The eclectic accommodations lineup in Banff includes historic mountain resorts, supremely luxurious hotels, quaint inns, roadside motels, and even some backcountry lodges without electricity or running water. Most lodgings do not have meal plans, though some offer breakfast.

With just a few exceptions, room rates are highest from mid-June to late September and between Christmas and New Year's. In many cases, the best rates can be found from October to mid-November and from May to mid-June.

More accommodations can be found just outside the park in Canmore and in Kananaskis Country, a large multiuse provincial recreation area. *Hotel reviews have been shortened. For full information, visit Fodors.com.*

WHAT IT COSTS IN CANADIAN DOLLARS				
	$	$$	$$$	$$$$
Restaurants	under C$13	C$13–C$20	C$21–C$30	over C$30
Hotels	under C$100	C$100–C$150	C$151–C$200	over C$200

Restaurant prices are the average cost of a main course at dinner, or if dinner is not served, at lunch. Hotel prices are the lowest cost of a standard double room in high season.

VISITOR INFORMATION

Park Contact Information Banff National Park. ⌧ *Banff* ☎ *403/762–1550* ⊕ *www.pc.gc.ca/banff.*

VISITOR CENTERS

Banff Visitor Centre. Parks Canada and Banff Lake Louise Tourism (BLLT) run this center jointly. On one side of the building, Parks Canada staffers dispense excellent advice about camping, hiking, interpretive programs, and sightseeing. On the other side, BLLT counselors (*www.banfflakelouise.com*) provide information about restaurants, tour operators, and accommodations. In spring, stop by to find out which hiking trails are open—many remain closed into May due to avalanche risk. ⌧ *224 Banff Ave., Banff* ☎ *403/762–8421* ⊕ *www.pc.gc.ca/banff* ⊙ *Mid-June–early Sept., daily 9–7; early Sept.–mid-June, daily 9–5.*

Lake Louise Visitor Centre. Stop here to get maps and information about area attractions and trails. The Banff Lake Louise Tourism desk can provide information on area accommodations and amenities, and you can purchase educational books and other materials. ⌧ *202 Village Rd., Lake Louise* ☎ *403/522–3833* ⊕ *www.banfflakelouise.com* ⊙ *Mid-June–early Sept., daily 9–7; May–mid-June and early Sept.–mid-Oct., daily 9–5; mid-Oct.–Apr., Thurs.–Sun. 9–4:30.*

EXPLORING

SCENIC DRIVES

Bow Valley Parkway. Formerly known as Highway 1A, this scenic drive between Banff and Lake Louise leads to Hillsdale Meadows, Johnston Canyon, Castle Mountain, and Baker Creek. There are plenty of viewpoints and picnic sites along the way. ⊠ *Banff National Park.*

Fodor'sChoice **Icefields Parkway.** Powerfully rugged
★ mountain scenery, glaciers, waterfalls and icefalls, and wildlife: the Icefields Parkway reveals all of these and more as it snakes its way along the 230 km (143 miles) connecting Banff National Park with Jasper National Park. It is an absolute highlight of the Canadian Rockies.

You could drive this winding road in three to four hours, but your trip will more likely take a full day when you add in stops. The road rises to near the tree line at several points, and the weather can be chilly and unsettled at these high elevations, even in midsummer, so it's a good idea to bring warm clothing along. Only one gas station, open seasonally, operates on the parkway, so check your car's gas gauge before setting out.

Elk, moose, deer, and bighorn sheep are fairly common, and occasionally bears and mountain goats come into view. In summer, alpine wildflowers carpet Bow Pass and Sunwapta Pass. The most dramatic scenery is in the northern end of Banff National Park and the southern end of Jasper National Park, where ice fields and glaciers become common on the high mountains flanking the parkway. (Ice fields are massive reservoirs of ice; glaciers are the slow-moving rivers of ice that flow from the ice fields.) Scenic overlooks and signposted hiking trails abound along the route. ⊠ *Hwy. 93.*

Lake Minnewanka Loop. It's easy to spend the day along this 25-km (15-mile) loop. Traveling clockwise, you can explore Lower Bankhead and Upper Bankhead, an abandoned coal mine and mining community. Just 3 km (2 miles) farther you come to Lake Minnewanka, the park's largest lake. Boat and fishing rentals are available. Still farther along are more lakes and picnic areas. ⊠ *Banff National Park.*

Norquay Drive. The highlight of this 6½-km (4-mile) route is the viewpoint over Banff from near the top. Bighorn sheep and mule deer are often sighted along the twisting road. Trailheads at the top lead to Stoney Squaw Summit and Cascade Amphitheatre. ⊠ *Banff National Park.*

CLOSE UP

Plants and Wildlife in Banff

Awesome forces of nature combined to thrust wildly folded sedimentary and metamorphic rock up into ragged peaks and high cliffs. Add glaciers and snowfields to the lofty peaks, carpet the valleys with forests, mix in a generous helping of small and large mammals, wildflowers, rivers, and crystal-clear lakes, and you've got the recipe for Banff National Park.

COMPLEX LIFE ZONES
This diverse topography has resulted in three complex life zones in Banff: montane, subalpine, and alpine. Each zone has characteristic physical environments along with its own species of plants and animals. The montane zone features valleys and grasslands as well as alders, willows, birches, and cottonwoods. The Douglas firs and lodgepole pines that cover the lower slopes of the mountains are also in the montane

zone. Subalpine forest extends from the montane to about 6,500 feet and is made up of mostly spruce and pine trees. The fragile alpine zone is found at the highest elevations. The rocky terrain and cold, howling winds mean far fewer plants and animals can survive there.

WHERE THE WILD THINGS ARE
Most of the wildlife is found in the montane zone, where bighorn sheep, deer, elk, and caribou abound. Moose and mountain goats can also be seen, as well as the occasional black bear. Other park animals include grizzly bears, wolves, coyotes, and cougars, as well as smaller mammals such as squirrels, marmots, muskrats, porcupines, and beavers. Birds commonly spotted are grouse, larks, finches, ptarmigans, bald eagles, golden eagles, loons, and Canada geese.

7

Tunnel Mountain Drive. On the east side of Banff, Tunnel Mountain Drive makes a scenic 5-km (3-mile) loop. It's closed in winter, but just off the drive, the **hoodoos**—fingerlike, eroded rock formations—are accessible year-round (signs on Banff's main street direct you there). ⊠ *Banff National Park.*

HISTORIC SITES

Banff Park Museum National Historic Site of Canada. A remarkable 1903 log building made chiefly of Douglas fir houses one of western Canada's oldest natural history museums. From bees to bears, the collection, whose origins date to Chicago's fabled World's Columbian Exposition of 1893, encompasses more than 5,000 taxidermied specimens, many of them quite striking. In addition to providing visitors the opportunity to get up close and personal with some of Banff's largest mammals—a grizzly bear, bison, mountain goats, and bighorn sheep among them—this vintage museum offers a window into past generations' priorities regarding the natural world. ⊠ *91 Banff Ave., at Bow River Bridge* ☎ *403/762–1558* ⊕ *www.pc.gc.ca/banff* ⊑ *C$3.90* ⊗ *July–early Sept., daily 10–5; mid-May–June and early Sept.–mid-Oct., Wed.–Sun. 10–5.*

FAMILY   **Banff Upper Hot Springs.** Discovered in 1884, Banff's natural hot mineral springs were the impetus for the development of Canada's first national park. Early travelers to Banff came primarily to experience the "healing waters," and today these can still be experienced at the Banff Upper Hot Springs pools. The popular hot springs are child-friendly during the day—think family swimming pool rather than couples' hot-tub vibe. The water is especially inviting on a dull, cold day or when it's snowing, and the views of the mountains are spectacular. Lockers, bathing suits (circa 1920s or modern), and towels can be rented, and spa services are available. Even though the recommended limit is 20 minutes in the water, you'll likely want to stay an hour or two. The springs can be reached via a short uphill walk from the parking lot. ✉ *1 Mountain Ave., 3 km (2 miles) south of downtown* ☎ *403/762–1515, 800/767–1611* ⊕ *www.hotspring.ca* ✎ *C$7.30* ⊘ *Mid-May–mid-Oct., daily 9 am–11 pm; mid-Oct.–mid-May, Sun.–Thurs. 10–10, Fri. and Sat. 10 am–11 pm.*

FAMILY
Fodor's Choice
★   **Cave and Basin National Historic Site.** This site commemorates the birthplace of Canada's national parks system, which began with the protection of the Banff hot springs in 1885. You'll find restored historic buildings, a plaza, and splendid interpretive displays about Banff and the other national parks in Canada. An interpretive trail explains the area's geology and plant life and has information about the wildlife and history of Banff National Park. While visiting the cave and walking past the warm mineral pools, keep an eye out for the most endangered species in the park, the Banff Springs snail, which makes its home in the warm mineral waters and cannot be found anywhere else in the world. ✉ *311 Cave Ave., 2 km (1 mile) west of downtown* ☎ *403/762–1566* ⊕ *www.pc.gc.ca/banff* ✎ *C$3.90* ⊘ *Mid-July–early Sept., daily 10–5; mid-May–mid-July and early Sept.–mid-Oct., Tues.–Sun. 10–5; mid-Oct.–mid-May, Wed.–Sun. noon–4.*

Fairmont Banff Springs. Banff's architectural showpiece and a National Historic Site, this hotel south of downtown is easily recognized by its castlelike exterior. Heritage Hall, a small museum above the Grand Lobby, has exhibits describing the area's history. On guided tours you can learn additional details about the hotel's grand opening in 1888, the 1920s fire that destroyed the original structure, subsequent construction, and the many illustrious guests who have stayed here. ✉ *405 Spray Ave., 2 km (1 mile) south of downtown* ☎ *403/762–2211, 800/441–1414* ⊕ *www.fairmont.com/banff-springs* ✎ *Hotel and museum free; tours free for hotel guests, C$15 for nonguests* ⊘ *Museum daily 9–9; tours Tues.–Sat. at 3.*

Lake Louise. This is one of the most photographed spots in the park. In summer, you can walk beside the lake and enjoy the nearby hiking trails. Winter offers skating on the ice and sleigh rides. The Fairmont Château Lake Louise hotel sits on the edge of the lake, which is a departure point for several short, moderately strenuous, well-traveled hiking routes, including the popular 3-km (2-mile) trail to Lake Agnes. The tiny lake hangs on a mountain-surrounded shelf that opens to the east with a bird's-eye view of the Beehives and Mount Whitehorn. The teahouse (cash only) by Lake Agnes serves soups, sandwiches, and snacks. ⌧ *Fairmont Château Lake Louise, 111 Lake Louise Dr., Lake Louise* ☎ *403/522–3511.*

Whyte Museum of the Canadian Rockies. Founded by the late Peter and Catharine Whyte, two Banff artists, this museum exhibits artworks, artifacts, and other items relating to the cultural heritage of the Canadian Rockies. Many of the earliest photos of Banff National Park can be found here, either on the walls or in the archives. ⌧ *111 Bear St., Banff* ☎ *403/762–2291* ⊕ *www.whyte.org* ⌧ *C$8* ☉ *Daily 10–5.*

SCENIC STOPS

Many of the most striking scenic stops in Banff National Park are along the Icefields Parkway, also signed as Highway 93, which continues north into Jasper National Park. Other noteworthy diversions include the Banff Gondola ride up Sulphur Mountain, another gondola ride that reveals the beauty of Lake Louise, and a trip to Moraine Lake. You can visit Moraine Lake and many of the stops along the parkway for free, but to get out on a glacier (Athabasca), walk above one on a glass-floored walkway (Glacier Skywalk), or ride the gondolas, you'll need to purchase tickets online or in person from Brewster Attractions, located inside the Columbia Icefield Glacier Discovery Centre and at several other locations. You can purchase tickets to individual attractions or save money by getting a package discount to visit multiple attractions.

Tickets and Reservations Brewster Attractions. ☎ *866/606–6700* ⊕ *www.brewster.ca/activities-in-the-rockies.*

ALONG ICEFIELDS PARKWAY

Icefields Parkway, the 230-km (143-mile) stretch of road between Banff and Jasper national parks, passes by ancient glaciers, cascading waterfalls, turquoise lakes, forested valleys, massive mountain peaks, and abundant and diverse wildlife. You could complete the entire drive in about three hours, but you should plan to take longer. Great viewpoints, hikes, and attractions await you along the way.

The sights are organized from south to north.

WITHIN BANFF NATIONAL PARK

Bow Glacier Falls, Bow Lake, Crowfoot Glacier, and Simpson's Num-Ti-Jah Lodge. You may wish to stop at Bow Lake for the regional Canadian cuisine at Simpson's Num-Ti-Jah Lodge at Bow Lake, but you don't have to dine or stay here to enjoy the trails and views of the lake and Crowfoot Glacier. A trail leads from the bottom of the parking lot to the base of Bow Glacier Falls, where you can feel the spray, hear the roar of the falls, and witness the birth of a river. The Bow River is part of western Canada's largest watershed. The hike is about 4 km (2½ miles) one-way and takes from 1½ to 3 hours to complete depending on how many photos you take. ⌧ *Icefields Pkwy., 40 km (25 miles) north of Lake Louise; 190 km (118 miles) south of Jasper* ☎ *403/522–2167.*

Fodor's Choice ★ **Bow Summit and Peyto Lake Lookouts.** At 2,070 meters (6,791 feet), Bow Summit is the highest drivable pass in the national parks of the Canadian Rockies. The summit's lookout and the one for beautiful, turquoise Peyto Lake—you've likely never seen a shade of blue this exquisite—are

The beautifully blue waters of Moraine Lake reflect the sunlit, snow-drizzled mountains that surround it.

along the same trail. From the parking lot, it's a 15-minute walk on a paved pathway to the Peyto Lake Lookout. To reach the Bow Summit Lookout, follow the self-guided nature trail to the left past the Peyto Lake Lookout, then continue on an old fire road to a spectacular viewpoint that looks to the Bow Valley and Bow Lake to the south and Peyto and Waterfowl Lakes to the north. The hike to see both lookouts is 2.9 km (1.8 miles) one-way with a 230-meter (750-foot) elevation gain and will take about 2½ hours round-trip. The Peyto Lake Lookout is wheelchair accessible from the upper parking lot that tour buses use. ⊠ *Icefields Pkwy., 40 km (25 miles) north of Lake Louise, 190 km (118 miles) south of Jasper.*

Parker Ridge Trail. This short but steep 2½-km (1½-mile) trail delivers you above the tree line. At the top of Parker Ridge, there's an excellent view of the Saskatchewan Glacier, where the Saskatchewan River begins. Snowbanks can persist into early summer, but by late July carpets of wildflowers cover the trail. Stay on the path to keep erosion to a minimum. ⊠ *Icefields Pkwy., 4 km (2½ miles) south of boundary between Banff and Jasper parks, 9 km (5½ miles) south of Columbia Icefield Glacier Adventure Centre.*

BANFF–JASPER BORDER

Sunwapta Pass. Marking the border between Banff and Jasper national parks, Sunwapta is the second-highest drivable pass—6,675 feet—in the national parks. Wildlife is most visible in spring and autumn after a snowfall, when herds of bighorn sheep come to the road to lick up the salt used to melt snow and ice. Be prepared for hairpin turns as you switchback up to the pass summit. ⊠ *Icefields Pkwy., 122 km (76 miles) north of Lake Louise, 108 km (67 miles) south of Jasper.*

OTHER SCENIC STOPS

FAMILY **Banff Gondola.** Views during the steep eight-minute ride to and from the 7,500-foot summit of Sulphur Mountain are spectacular in the enclosed four-person gondolas. From the upper gondola terminal you can hike the short distance to the true summit of Sulphur Mountain on the South East Ridge Trail and perhaps catch sight of grazing bighorn sheep, or visit the gift shop or the reasonably priced restaurant. Be sure to walk the easy 1-km (0.6-mile) boardwalk to the Sulphur Mountain Weather Observatory on Sanson's Peak for excellent views and to break away from the crowds. The gondola is south of the center of Banff; you can catch a Roam public transit bus to get here. Riding the gondola is a very popular activity—go early or late to avoid crowds. ⊠ *1 Mountain Ave., 3 km (2 miles) south of downtown, Banff* ☎ *403/762–2523* ⊕ *www. banffgondola.com* ✉ *C$40 round-trip* ☉ *Late May–late Aug., daily 8 am–9 pm; late Aug.–mid-Oct., daily 8–8; mid-Oct.–early Nov., daily 8:30–4:30; early Nov.–early Dec., daily 10–6.*

FAMILY **Lake Louise Sightseeing Gondola.** Ride this to an alpine plateau for a stunning view that includes more than a dozen glaciers. The deck of the Wildlife Interpretive Centre is a good place to enjoy an ice-cream cone, a cold drink, or a picnic lunch, or you can buy a ticket that includes a buffet breakfast or lunch at the lodge near the gondola's base. Guided interpretive walks (45 minutes) take place at 10:30, 12:30, and 2:30 daily. ⊠ *1 Whitehorn Rd., off Hwy. 1 (Lake Louise exit)* ☎ *403/522–3555* ⊕ *www.lakelouisegondola.com* ✉ *C$32 ride only, C$35 with breakfast, C$40 with lunch* ☉ *Mid-May–late June, daily 9–4; late-June–July, daily 8:30–5:30; Aug.–early Sept., daily 8:30–6; early Sept.–mid.-Oct., daily 10–4.*

Moraine Lake. This beauty, 11 km (7 miles) south of Lake Louise, is a photographic highlight of Banff National Park. Set in the Valley of the Ten Peaks, the lake reflects the snow-clad mountaintops that rise abruptly around it. The lake is a major stop for tour buses as well as a popular departure point for hikers and a place to canoe. Visit early or late in the day to avoid crowds. Moderate hiking trails lead from the lodge at Moraine Lake into some spectacular alpine country. ⊠ *Banff National Park.*

Norquay Sightseeing Chairlift. Great views of the Bow Valley, Banff Townsite, and surrounding mountain peaks can be enjoyed from the top of the Norquay chairlift. The ride up takes 10 minutes. An interpretive path, a viewpoint, and the historic Cliffhouse Bistro, where you can have lunch, dinner, or drinks, are at the top. Free shuttle service operates from Banff's major hotels to the chairlift. ⊠ *2 Mt. Norquay Rd., Banff* ☎ *844/007–7829* ⊕ *summer.banffnorquay.com* ✉ *C$20* ☉ *Daily 9:30–6.*

7

SPORTS AND THE OUTDOORS

MULTISPORT TOURS AND OUTFITTERS

OUTFITTERS

Fodor'sChoice **Bactrax Bike Rentals.** This outfitter has Banff's largest selection of rental skis
★ and snowboards. It rents bikes and camping equipment in the summer.
⊠ *225 Bear St., Banff* ☎ *403/762–8177* ⊕ *www.snowtips-bactrax.com.*

Banff Adventures Unlimited. Rent bikes here, or come by to sign up for
almost any area activity. ⊠ *211 Bear St., Banff* ☎ *403/762–4554,*
800/644–8888 ⊕ *www.banffadventures.com.*

Soul Ski & Bike. This great spot sells, rents, and services bicycles, skis,
and snowboards. Soul Ski is well known for its custom ski boot–fitting
service, and the company rents and sells standard, deluxe, and premium equipment. ⊠ *203A Bear St., Banff* ☎ *403/760–1650* ⊕ *www.
soulskiandbike.com.*

TOURS

Discover Banff Tours. Sign up here for guided sightseeing, wildlife safaris, nature walks, ice walks, and snowshoeing adventures. ⊠ *Sundance
Mall, 215 Banff Ave., Banff* ☎ *403/760–5007, 877/565–9372* ⊕ *www.
banfftours.com* ☎ *From C$56.*

White Mountain Adventures. Daily guided hikes, backpacking, and heli-
hiking can be arranged through this outfitter. In winter, you can try
snowshoeing or a guided ice walk. ⊠ *120A Eagle Crescent, Banff*
☎ *403/760–4403, 800/408–0005* ⊕ *www.whitemountainadventures.
com* ☎ *From C$60.*

Fodor'sChoice **Yamnuska.** Canada's largest mountain-guide company conducts guided
★ mountaineering, rock climbing, backcountry skiing, and ice-climbing
trips and lessons. ⊠ *50 Lincoln Park, Canmore* ☎ *403/678–4164,*
866/678–4164 ⊕ *www.yamnuska.com* ☎ *From C$140.*

AIR TOURS

TOURS AND OUTFITTERS

Alpine Helicopters. Helicopter sightseeing and heli-hiking in the Canadian
Rockies are this company's specialty. ⊠ *91 Bow Valley Tr., Canmore*
☎ *403/678–4802* ⊕ *www.alpinehelicopter.com* ☎ *From C$124.*

CMH. This company offers multiday heli-skiing, heli-hiking, glacier-
climbing, and other adventures with accommodations in remote mountain lodges. ⊠ *217 Bear St., Banff* ☎ *403/762–7100, 800/661–0252*
⊕ *www.canadianmountainholidays.com* ☎ *From C$2,900.*

Rockies Heli Canada. Helicopter tours in Banff, Lake Louise, and Jasper,
including the Columbia Icefield, are conducted by this company that also
arranges heli-camping, hiking, yoga, and horseback-riding trips. ⊠ *Next
to Stoney Nakoda Resort, Nakoda Way, off Trans-Canada Hwy. 1 Exit
118 (Hwy. 40), Kananaskis Village* ☎ *877/591–0222, 403/881–2500,*
403/881–2110 ⊕ *www.rockiesheli.com* ☎ *From C$195.*

BICYCLING

Spectacular road and mountain biking can be found in Banff, and several world-class cycling events take place here. The biking season typically runs from May through October, and there are mountain-bike trails, paved multiuse trails, and excellent road-biking routes. The popular **Legacy Trail,** a 24-km (15-mile) paved route also known as the Rocky Mountain Legacy Trail, allows users to travel safely between Banff and Canmore without having to use the Trans-Canada Highway. Many riders take the Banff to Canmore route, slightly more downhill than in the reverse direction, and return in the Bike 'n Hike Shuttle (☎ 403/762–2282 ⊕ *www.bikeandhikeshuttle.com*).

The park contains more than 189 km (118 miles) of mountain-bike trails, some suitable for beginners, others for advanced bikers. Scenic road-biking rides range from ones of a few hours to several days. Shorter rides include the Bow Lake Trail, Vermilion Lakes Drive, and the loop around Tunnel Mountain. Bikers and hikers often share the trails in the park, with hikers having the right of way. For free riding or down-hilling, head to nearby areas like Calgary's Canada Olympic Park, Fernie, or Golden.

BIRD-WATCHING

Birdlife is abundant in the montane and wetland habitats of the lower Bow Valley, and more than 260 species of birds have been recorded in the park. Come in the spring to observe the annual migration of waterfowl, including common species of ducks and Canada geese as well as occasional tundra swans, cinnamon teal, Northern shovelers, white-winged and surf scoters, and hooded and common mergansers. Bald eagles are also seen regularly. Come in mid-October if you want to observe the annual migration of golden eagles along the "super flyway" of the Canadian Rockies.

BOATING

Lake Minnewanka, near town, is the only place in Banff National Park that allows private motorboats. Aluminum fishing boats with 8-horse-power motors can be rented at the dock (call Lake Minnewanka Boat Tours ☎ 403/762–3473).

Canoe rentals are available at Lake Louise, Moraine Lake, and in Banff, where you launch along the Bow River and explore the waterways of the Bow Valley.

Rafting options range from scenic float trips to family-friendly white-water excursions on the Kananaskis River to the intense white water of the Kicking Horse River, with its Class IV rapids.

TOURS

Canadian Rockies Rafting. Scenic floats and thrilling white-water rafting tours on the Bow, Kananaskis, and Kicking Horse rivers are conducted by these local experts. The rates include pickup in Banff or Canmore.

✉ *701 Bow Valley Tr., Canmore* ☎ *403/678–6535, 877/226–7625* ⊕ *www.rafting.ca* 🖃 *From C$55* ⊘ *Closed Oct.–Apr.*

Chinook Rafting. At Chinook you can book half-day or full-day rafting adventures suitable for families, as well as some for truly adventurous adults. You can choose from three different rivers. Packages combining rafting with other activities represent a discount. ✉ *215 Banff Ave., Banff* ☎ *403/763–2007, 866/330–7238* ⊕ *www.chinookrafting. com* 🖃 *From $86* ⊘ *Closed Oct.–Apr.*

Fairmont Château Lake Louise Voyageur Canoe Experience. Paddle the tranquil waters of Lake Louise in a 26-foot cedar-strip and canvas canoe as part of this 90-minute experience. The accompanying guide shares stories about canoes in Canada from the perspectives of First Nations people, voyagers, explorers, and fur traders. Trips depart from the Fairmont's boathouse, which also rents regular canoes. ✉ *Lake Louise* ☎ *403/522–3511, 800/441–1414* ⊕ *www.fairmont.com/lake-louise/ promotions/canoeing* 🖃 *C$55.*

Hydra River Guides. The guides here lead rides through thrilling Class IV rapids on the Kicking Horse River. ✉ *211 Bear St., Banff* ☎ *403/762– 4554, 800/644–8888* ⊕ *www.raftbanff.com* 🖃 *From C$125.*

Kootenay River Runners. Trips ranging from scenic raft floats on the Toby or Kootenay to Class IV white-water rafting on the Kicking Horse, are available through this company. For Kicking Horse rafting, guests meet at the boat launch about 90 minutes from Banff Townsite. ✉ *4983 Hwy. 93* ☎ *250/347–9210, 800/599–4399* ⊕ *www.raftingtherockies. com* 🖃 *From C$55.*

FAMILY **Minnewanka Lake Cruise.** From mid-May to mid-October, Minnewanka conducts 1½-hour lake tours. ✉ *Minnewanka Lake* ☎ *403/762–3473, 800/760–6934* ⊕ *www.explorerockies.com/minnewanka* 🖃 *From C$54.*

Fodor's Choice ★ **Moraine Lake Lodge.** Moraine Lake is one of the most photographed spots in the Canadian Rockies. From June through September, you can paddle on the beautiful lake in a canoe rented at the lodge's dock. If you want to combine canoeing and walking, trails for several scenic lake hikes begin near the lodge. ✉ *End of Moraine Lake Rd., Lake Louise* ☎ *403/522– 3733, 877/522–2777* ⊕ *www.morainelake.com* 🖃 *From C$55.*

FAMILY **Rocky Mountain Raft Tours.** This Banff-based outfit specializes in one- and two-hour float trips on the Bow River. ✉ *Golf Course Loop Rd., Banff* ☎ *403/762–3632* ⊕ *www.banffrafttours.com* 🖃 *From C$50.*

Wild Water Adventures. Based 40 km (25 miles) north of Lake Louise, this outfitter has trips ranging from gentle floats to intense white-water experiences. Single-day and multiday trips are available. ☎ *403/522– 2211, 888/647–6444* ⊕ *www.wildwater.com* 🖃 *From C$79.*

FISHING

You can experience world-class trout fishing on the Bow River in Banff and enjoy fishing for trophy lake trout on Lake Minnewanka and several other mountain lakes. You will need a national park fishing permit to fish within the park and must follow strict fishing regulations, including no use of live bait. Some waterways are permanently closed to anglers, while others are open only at certain times of the year. Before heading out on your own, read the regulations or speak to the park staff.

TOURS AND OUTFITTERS

Alpine Anglers. This company gives fly-fishing lessons and conducts fly-fishing excursions of a full day or longer. ⊠ *Banff* ☎ *403/760–1133* ⊕ *www.alpineanglers.com* 🖥 *Call for pricing.*

Banff Fishing Unlimited. The experiences this company arranges include fishing for trophy lake trout on Lake Minnewanka and fly-fishing for brown trout on the Bow River. In winter the guides here conduct ice-fishing excursions. ⊠ *Banff* ☎ *403/762–4936, 866/678–2486* ⊕ *www.banff-fishing.com* 🖥 *From C$450 (price per person varies depending on group size).*

Hawgwild Fly Fishing Guides. Learn how to fly-fish from local guide Big Jim Dykstra by signing up with this outfit. ⊠ *Banff* ☎ *403/760–2446* ⊕ *www.banffflyfishingguides.com* 🖥 *From C$395.*

Tightline Adventures. Daylong and multiday fly-fishing trips can be arranged through Tightline. ⊠ *129 Banff Ave., Banff* ☎ *403/763–9669* ⊕ *www.tightlineadventures.com* 🖥 *From C$175.*

GOLF

Fairmont Banff Springs Golf Course. Breathtaking views are the norm at this championship course whose challenging 27 holes wind along the Bow River beneath snowcapped mountain peaks. Stanley Thompson, a major Canadian course architect of his day, designed the original 18-hole course, which opened in 1928. The 9-hole Tunnel Course, designed by Cornish and Robinson (the former a Thompson protégé), opened in the late 1980s. ⊠ *Fairmont Banff Springs, 405 Spray Ave., Banff* ☎ *403/762–6801, 877/591–2525* ⊕ *www.fairmont.com/banff-springs/golf* 🖥 *Stanley Thompson Course, $239; Tunnel Course, $100* ⛳ *Stanley Thompson Course: 18 holes, 6938 yards, par 71; Tunnel course: 9 holes, 3287 yards, par 36* ⊗ *Closed Nov.–Apr.*

HIKING

The trail system in Banff National Park allows you to access the heart of the Canadian Rockies. The scenery is spectacular and you can see wildlife such as birds, squirrels, deer, and sheep along many of the trails. Make noise as you travel the trails so you don't surprise a bear or other large animal. Also, prepare for any and all weather conditions by dressing in layers and bringing at least a half gallon of drinking water along per person on all full-day hikes. Get a trail map at the information center. Some of the more popular trails have bathrooms or outhouses at the trailhead. Dogs should be leashed at all times, and hikers should carry bear spray.

EASY

FAMILY **Discovery Trail and Marsh Trail.** On a hillside above the Cave and Basin Centennial Centre, this 0.8-km (½-mile) boardwalk takes you past the vent of the cave to a spring flowing out of the hillside. Interpretive signage explains the geology and history of the Cave and Basin. Follow the Marsh Trail to observe the birdlife and the lush vegetation fed by the mineral water. Along the boardwalk are telescopes, benches, and interpretive signage as well as a bird blind on the marsh itself. Wheelchairs have limited access to the boardwalk. *Easy.* ⊠ *Banff* ⊹ *Trailhead: at parking lot of Cave and Basin National Historic Site.*

FAMILY **Fenland Trail.** It will take about an hour round-trip to walk the 2-km (1-mile) trail that slowly changes from marsh to dense forest. Watch for beavers, muskrat, and waterfowl. The trail is popular with joggers and cyclists. *Easy.* ⊠ *Banff* ⊹ *Trailhead: at Forty Mile Picnic Area.*

Surprise Corner to Hoodoos. This 4.8-km (3-mile) trail begins with a view of a waterfall on Bow River, leads through meadows and forests and past sheer cliffs, and ends at the hoodoos in the eastern part of Banff Townsite. *Easy.* ⊠ *Banff* ⊹ *Trailhead: at Bow Falls Overlook on Tunnel Mountain Dr.*

MODERATE

Boom Lake Trail. This 5-km (3.2-mile) hike climbs through a forest of pine, fir, and spruce. Surrounded by mountains and glaciers, the waters of the lake are crystal clear. Allow half a day for this hike round-trip. *Moderate.* ⊹ *Trailhead: off Hwy. 93 S, 7 km (4½ miles) west of Castle Junction.*

Castle Lookout Trail. Outstanding views of the mountains above the Bow River Valley are the highlight of this 3.7-km (2.3-mile) one-way trail that is somewhat steep. *Moderate.* ⊹ *Trailhead: off Hwy. 1A at parking lot on north side of Bow Valley Pkwy., 5 km (3.1 miles) west of Castle Junction.*

Fodor's Choice **Johnston Canyon Trail.** Rushing water has carved a path through this lime-
★ stone canyon that is a must-see stop. The first 1.1 km (0.7 mile) is a paved walkway that leads to the 10-meter (33-foot) Lower Falls. From here a slightly more rugged 2.7-km (1¾-mile) trail leads to the nearly 30-meter (100-foot) Upper Falls and a 5-km (3-mile) trail to the Ink Pots. The Ink Pots are six green pools filled with springwater. It will take four to five hours to complete the return trip. *Moderate.* ⊹ *Trailhead: off Hwy. 1A at Johnston Canyon parking lot.*

Lake Agnes Teahouse Trail. Winding north of Lake Louise, this 7-km (4½-mile) trail has stunning views of Lake Agnes and Mirror Lake. The trail passes through an old-growth forest and comes up the right side of a waterfall before ending at a teahouse where you can stop for dessert. It will take four hours or more to make the return trip along this trail. *Moderate.* ⊠ *Lake Louise* ⊹ *Trailhead: accessed from Lake Louise Shoreline Trail, which begins in front of Fairmont Château Lake Louise.*

DIFFICULT

Cory Pass Loop Trail. This 13-km (8-mile) hike is one of the park's most difficult and takes about six hours to do; it is recommended only for experienced hikers who are able to trace a difficult route. Hikers are rewarded with awesome views. The return route loops around Mount Edith and descends the Edith Pass Trail. *Difficult.* ✛ *Trailhead: at Fireside picnic area, eastern end of Bow Valley Pkwy.*

Sulphur Mountain Summit Trail. This well-maintained trail crisscrosses underneath the gondola on Sulphur Mountain and climbs from the parking lot to the summit. You can hike up and take the gondola down, but you should check schedules first. A restaurant and cafeteria are located at the summit along with a viewing platform and interpretive signage. Allow four hours to hike the trail round-trip. *Difficult.* ✛ *Trailhead: at corner of Upper Hot Springs parking lot closest to pool.*

HORSEBACK RIDING

Experiencing the Canadian Rockies on horseback takes you back to the era of Banff's early explorers. Several outfitters conduct guided trips lasting from an hour to a few days. Make your reservations well ahead, though, especially in summer and for multiday journeys. Hourly rides start at $45 per person. Short-term boarding is available in Canmore and a few other communities outside Banff.

TOURS AND OUTFITTERS

Brewster Adventures. This Banff-based outfit conducts daily summer trail rides to the Plain of Six Glaciers, Lake Agnes Tea House, and Paradise Valley. You can also experience the "cowboy way of life" by moving cattle and doing chores on overnight mountain pack tours. In the winter, sleigh rides depart from the lakefront at the Fairmont Château Lake Louise. ⊠ *Lake Louise* ☎ *403/762–5454, 800/691–5085* ⊕ *www.brewsteradventures.com* ☑ *From C$89.*

Great Divide Nature Interpretation. Fun guided interpretive full-day summer hikes and half-day winter snowshoeing trips are this group's specialty. ⊠ *Banff* ☎ *403/522–2735* ⊕ *www.greatdivide.ca* ☑ *From $74 (snowshoeing trips) and $94 (hikes).*

FAMILY **Holiday on Horseback.** Hourly and daily horseback rides are arranged by Holiday on Horseback, which also offers riding lessons and conducts multiday backcountry trips. The company operates carriage rides in summer and sleigh rides in winter. ⊠ *132 Banff Ave., Banff* ☎ *403/762–4551, 800/661–8352* ⊕ *www.horseback.com* ☑ *From C$46.*

Outpost at Warden Rock. Multiday all-inclusive horseback, stagecoach, and bring-your-own horse holidays can be arranged through this operation in the wilderness 80 km (50 miles) north of Banff. ☎ *403/762–2767, 877/762-2767* ⊕ *www.outpostatwardenrock.com* ☑ *From $485* ☉ *Closed mid-Oct.–mid-May.*

Timberline Tours. Trail rides ranging from 10 minutes to 10 days can be arranged with Timberline Tours. ⊠ *St Piran Dr., Lake Louise* ☎ *403/522–3743, 888/858–3388* ⊕ *www.timberlinetours.ca* ☑ *From C$15.*

Johnston Canyon Trail

Rockbound Lake

Silverton Creek

Castle Lookout Trail

Rockbound Lake Trail

Johnston Creek

1A

TO LAKE LOUISE

Silverton Falls Trail

Ink Pots Trail 3.0 mi.

93

Castle Junction

1A Bow Valley Parkway

Johnston Canyon Upper Falls Trail

TO RADIUM

B O W   V A L L E Y

1.6 mi

.6 mi

Johnston Canyon Lower Falls Trail

Trans-Canada Highway

Bow River

TO BANFF

1A

TO BANFF

KEY

------- Trail

2.2 mi Distance in miles

MOUNTAINEERING

Fodor's Choice ★ **Via Ferrata.** Even a novice can climb a mountain safely using Norquay's awesome Via Ferrata. The term "Via Ferrata" is Italian for "iron road," and this protected climbing route uses metal cable fixed to the rock along with iron rungs, pegs, carved footholds, ladders, and bridges. After gearing up, you take a chairlift up the mountain and then follow a certified guide along a route that takes two, four, or six hours to complete. This activity requires good hiking shoes, but shoes are available for loan if you don't have your own. ✉ *2 Mt. Norquay Rd., Banff* ☎ *844/007–7829* ⊕ *summer.banffnorquay.com/plan-your-visit* 💲 *From $139.*

SWIMMING

FAMILY **Banff Centre Sally Borden Fitness Centre.** Amenities here include a 25-meter (82-foot) swimming pool, a wading pool, an outdoor sundeck, a climbing wall, a fitness center, a gymnasium, and a squash center. You can also attend a fitness class. ✉ *107 Tunnel Mountain Rd., Banff* ☎ *403/762–6100* ⊕ *www.banffcentre.ca* 💲 *C$5.50 public swim (free last Sun. of month)* ☉ *Weekdays 6 am–10 pm, weekends 7 am–10 pm.*

WINTER SPORTS

Whether you're driving a dogsled across a frozen lake, ice climbing, snowshoeing, skiing at one of the world's top mountain ski resorts—or simply taking in the northern lights—there's no shortage of winter activities to choose from in Banff.

Skis and snowboards can be rented on the slopes or at many shops in town, concentrated along Bear Street and Banff Avenue.

For ski or boarding instruction, consider booking the program called Club Ski (⊕ *www.skibig3.com*). For C$299, participants receive one day of instruction at each of the three resorts with the same instructor, guided tours of each resort, lift-line priority, and a souvenir photo. Lift tickets are not included.

■ TIP➜ A good bargain is a three-day pass (C$248) that allows you to ski at the Sunshine Village, Mount Norquay, and Lake Louise ski areas. The pass, available at the ski areas and the Banff Ski Hub store or online at www.skibig3.com, includes free shuttle service to the slopes.

CROSS-COUNTRY SKIING

Fodor'sChoice ★ **Canmore Nordic Centre.** This cross-country ski center, built for the 1988 Winter Olympic Games, has rental equipment, a day lodge, and miles of trails to enjoy. You can also take a cross-country lesson, go snowshoeing and fat biking, and play winter disc golf. ⊠ *1988 Olympic Way, Canmore* ☎ *403/678–2400* ⊕ *www.albertaparks.ca/canmore-nordic-centre.aspx* ⬚ *From $15.*

DOWNHILL SKIING

FAMILY **Lake Louise Ski Resort.** Lake Louise is one of the largest ski resorts in North America. With beginner, intermediate, and expert runs from every chair, this is a great hill for families—the downhill terrain on four mountain faces and north-facing back bowls is expansive and varied. Also here are a terrain park, a tube park, a beginner's fun zone, and a snowcross course. The ski school is excellent. **Facilities:** 145 trails; 4,200 acres; 3,250-foot vertical drop; 10 lifts. ⊠ *1 Whitehorn Rd., off Lake Louise Dr., Lake Louise* ☎ *403/522–3555, 877/956–8473* ⊕ *www.skilouise.com* ⬚ *Lift ticket: C$92.*

Ski Banff at Norquay. The oldest ski resort in the Canadian Rockies is only a five-minute drive from Banff. Locals like this five-lift, 28-run mountain, and so do Olympic and World Cup trainees. Night skiing and tubing take place here, too. **Facilities:** 38 trails; 190 acres; 1,650-foot vertical drop; 5 lifts. ☎ *403/762–4421* ⊕ *www.banffnorquay.com* ⬚ *Lift ticket: C$75.*

Sunshine Village. About a 15-minute drive from Banff Townsite, this high-altitude resort with skiable terrain on three mountains has the longest nonglacial ski season in Canada and some of the prettiest views. Sunshine gets as many as 9 meters (30 feet) of dry, powdery snow in a season. Canada's first heated chairlift was installed here for the 2015–2016 season. **Facilities:** 107 trails; 3,358 acres; 3,514-foot vertical drop; 12 lifts. ⊠ *1 Sunshine Access Rd., off Hwy. 1, Banff* ☎ *403/762–6500, 877/542–2633* ⊕ *www.skibanff.com* ⬚ *Lift ticket: $92* ☉ *Closed mid-May–mid-Nov.*

OUTFITTER

Ultimate Ski and Ride. You can rent ski and snowboard equipment and bikes here and take advantage of the shop's free hotel delivery. ✉ *206 Banff Ave., Banff* ☎ *403/762–0547, 866/754–7433* ⊕ *www. ultimatebanff.com* ✆ *From C$29.50.*

NIGHTLIFE AND PERFORMING ARTS

ARTS VENUES

Banff Centre. Most of the cultural activities in the Canadian Rockies take place in and around Banff, and these 16 buildings spread across 43 acres are the hub of that activity. The center presents pop and classical music, theater, and dance throughout the year. The season peaks in summer with concerts, performances, films, and other events, many in an outdoor amphitheater. The Walter Phillips Gallery showcases contemporary artworks by Canadian and international artists. ✉ *107 Tunnel Mountain Dr.* ☎ *403/762–6100, 800/413–8368 in Alberta and British Columbia* ⊕ *www.banffcentre.ca* ✆ *Gallery free* ☉ *Gallery Wed.–Sun. 12:30–5.*

WHAT'S NEARBY

NEARBY TOWNS

Canmore. About 25 km (15 miles) southeast of Banff, Canmore became a modest boomtown with the 1988 Olympic Games. Many of its residents feel that the commute to Calgary for work is a fair trade-off for living in the mountains. For tourists, Canmore makes a good base for exploring Kananaskis Country and Banff National Park. ✉ *Canmore.*

Kananaskis Country. Three provincial parks make up the 4,200-square-km (1,600-square-mile) recreational region known as Kananaskis Country, whose northern entrance is 26 km (16 miles) southeast of Canmore. The area includes grand mountain scenery, and though it's not quite a match for that in the adjacent national parks, Kananaskis allows some activities the parks prohibit, including snowmobiling, motorized boating, and off-road driving. There are also spectacular cross-country and mountain-biking trails.

The main route through Kananaskis Country is Highway 40, also known as the Kananaskis Trail. It runs north–south through the front ranges of the Rockies. Only the northern 40 km (25 miles) of the road remain open from December to mid-June, in part because of the extreme conditions of Highwood Pass (at 7,280 feet, the highest drivable pass in Canada), and in part to protect winter wildlife habitats in Peter Lougheed Provincial Park. Highway 40 continues south to join Highway 541 west of Longview. Access to East Kananaskis Country, a popular area for horseback trips, is on Highway 66, which heads west from the town of Priddis.

Visitor Information Banff Lake Louise Tourism. ⊠ *224 Banff Ave., Banff* ☎ *403/762–8421* ⊕ *www.bannfflakelouise.com.* **Tourism Canmore.** ⊠ *907 7th Ave., Canmore* ☎ *403/678–1295, 855/678–1295* ⊕ *www.tourismcanmore.com.*

AREA ACTIVITIES

SPORTS AND THE OUTDOORS

Many of the outfitters and operators who run tours in Banff National Park are based in Canmore, so if you're staying here, you can often join the tour from Canmore rather than having to drive to the park. Equipment for activities can be rented at most sports shops in Canmore.

GOLF

Silvertip Golf Course. Dramatic elevation changes and views from most holes of the valley and mountains make an outing at this course a memorable event. Designed by Canmore-based Les Furber, responsible for dozens of Canadian courses and many worldwide, Silvertip is the area's only south-oriented one—the resulting extra sun can be a boon when temperatures dip. ⊠ *2000 Silvertip Tr., Canmore* ☎ *403/678–1600, 877/877–5444* ⊕ *www.silvertipresort.com* ⌑ *$175* ⚑ *18 holes, 6534 yards, par 72.*

HIKING

There are many spectacular hikes inside Banff National Park, but there are also wonderful excursions just outside its borders. A good one near Canmore is the two-hour hike to the beautiful spring-fed Grassi Lakes. To get to the lakes, you can take the easy route or a more scenic moderate trail that passes by a waterfall. At the far end of the second lake are some ancient pictographs.

SPELUNKING

FAMILY **Canmore Caverns.** If you have ever wanted to don a headlamp and explore an undeveloped cave, you can have Canmore Caverns arrange a suitable caving experience. The outfitter supplies the equipment, and you bring the enthusiasm. Children must be at least nine years of age to participate. ⊠ *112 Kananaskis Way, Suite 107, Canmore* ☎ *403/678–8819, 877/317–1178* ⊕ *www.canmorecavetours.com* ⌑ *From C$125.*

SUMMER–WINTER SPORTS

FAMILY **Canmore Nordic Centre.** Built for the 1988 Olympic Nordic skiing events, the center has 70 km (43 miles) of groomed cross-country trails in winter that become hiking and mountain-biking trails in summer. Some trails are lighted for night skiing, and a 1½-km (1-mile) paved trail is open in summer for roller skiing and rollerblading. Other winter sports include ice-skating, winter disc golf, and fat biking; in summer you can also play disc golf and participate in a roller biathlon. The state-of-the-art facility is south of Canmore in the northwestern corner of Kananaskis Country. In late January, an international biathlon and dogsled races take place here as part of the **Canmore Winter Carnival.** ⊠ *1988 Olympic Way, Canmore* ☎ *403/678–2400* ⌑ *Trails free Apr.–Oct., C$15 per day Nov.–Mar.* ☉ *Lodge daily 9–5:30; trails open 7 am–11 pm, some trails illuminated until 9 pm.*

WATER SPORTS

FAMILY **Blast Adventures.** Unique guided kayak adventures using inflatable vessels on white water are available through Blast Adventures. Transportation from Banff or Canmore is included. ⊠ *120B Rundle Dr., Canmore* ☎ *403/609–2009, 888/802–5278* ⊕ *www.blastadventures.com* ⊠ *From $94.*

WINTER SPORTS

Nakiska. The site of the 1988 Olympic alpine events, Nakiska is a 45-minute drive southeast of Banff in Kananaskis Country and has wide-trail intermediate skiing and a sophisticated snow-making and grooming system. There's also a tube park. **Facilities:** 71 trails; 1,021 acres; 2,412-foot vertical drop; 6 lifts. ⊠ *3 Mount Allen Dr., off Hwy. 40, Kananaskis Village* ☎ *403/591–7777* ⊕ *www.skinakiska.com* ⊠ *Lift ticket: C$75* ⊗ *Closed mid-Mar.–mid-Nov.*

WHERE TO EAT

IN THE PARK

$$$$ ✕ **1888 Chop House at the Fairmont Banff Springs.** Alberta is world-famous STEAKHOUSE for its beef, and this restaurant is a great place to sample it, along with pork, lamb, and sustainable wild game and seafood. From the butter to the garnishes, everything is made in-house. Try the Brant Lake Wagyu beef tenderloin or share the dry-aged Tomahawk rib eye, which is carved tableside. Seafood choices include Arctic char, East Coast lobster, and scallops with zucchini puree and pork belly. There is one vegetarian option on the menu. $ *Average main: C$50* ⊠ *405 Spray Ave., Banff* ☎ *403/762–2211* ⊕ *www.1888chophouse. com* ⟨ *Reservations essential.*

$$ ✕ **Banff Ave. Brewing Co.** Creating high-quality beer and pairing it with CANADIAN classic Canadian pub fare is the goal of this family-friendly brewpub on Banff's busiest street. Impromptu free tours of the on-site brewery are commonplace. The flagship beer is a heavily hopped pale ale made with Canadian Rockies water. The restaurant is large and open, with plenty of windows and a patio overlooking Banff Avenue—ideal for people-watching. Burgers, steaks, and grilled fish served with fries in paper cones are the menu's mainstays, but there are a few unexpected items like the poached pear and arugula sandwich, lobster maki, and millionaire steak. The pulled pork poutine goes well with any drink. $ *Average main: C$19* ⊠ *Clocktower Village Mall, 110 Banff Ave., Banff* ☎ *403/762–1003* ⊕ *www.banffavebrewingco.ca.*

$$$$ ✕ **The Bison.** "Rocky Mountain comfort food" made with organically CANADIAN grown local ingredients is served here, with bison a specialty. Slow cooking is an emphasis, and everything down to the ketchup and mustard for the bison burgers is made from scratch in-house. The contemporary decor, with hardwood floors and vaulted ceilings, focuses attention on the open kitchen, where the chefs prepare bison onion soup and braised bison short ribs with roasted potatoes. In addition to these signature dishes, wild British Columbia steelhead trout, poached halibut, and Alberta lamb grace the menu. The à la carte

Sunday brunch is very popular. $ *Average main: C$33* ✉ *211 Bear St., Suite 213, Banff* ☎ *403/762–5550* ⊕ *www.thebison.ca* ☉ *No lunch weekdays* ⌨ *Reservations essential.*

$$$$ ✕ **Eden.** Ultraluxe decor and magnificent mountain views provide the
FRENCH   interior and exterior backdrops for a dinner of regionally influenced
Fodor's Choice   French cuisine. The food is prepared à-la-minute from fresh ingredi-
★   ents, and the presentation is awe-inspiring. The prix-fixe menus, one of them vegetarian, cost from C$79 to C$197 for two to 10 courses. The entrées change frequently, but previous ones have included British Columbia sablefish with tomato, watermelon, and onion; rabbit with nuts, wild berries, and foraged mushrooms; and cinnamon-smoked short ribs. The sommeliers offer two astute wine-pairing options, or you can make your own choices from the impressive list. Dining in this Eden is an experience to be savored. Plan to spend at least three hours. $ *Average main: C$79* ✉ *Rimrock Resort Hotel, 100 Mountain Ave., Banff* ☎ *403/762–1865* ⊕ *www.banffeden.com* ☉ *Closed Mon. and Tues. No lunch* ⌨ *Reservations essential.*

$$$ ✕ **Juniper Bistro.** Ask for a window or patio seat at this bistro that
CANADIAN   capitalizes on one of Banff's best views with walls of windows and an engaging outdoor dining area. Cuisine made from fresh local ingredients more than lives up to the expectations the gorgeous setting inspires. The menu changes regularly, but the signature duck breast—smoked in-house and served with du puy lentils, carrots, broccolini, and gooseberry gastrique—is often available. Other strong suits include the beef, lamb, and chicken entrées, all from Canadian sources. Many dishes can be made gluten-free, vegetarian, or both. $ *Average main: C$27* ✉ *1 Juniper Way, Banff* ☎ *403/762–2281, 866/551–2281* ⊕ *thejuniper.com/dining.*

$$$$ ✕ **Le Beaujolais.** Soft music, white tablecloths, and fresh flowers create
FRENCH   an appropriately relaxed atmosphere in this classic French restaurant's upper-floor dining room. This is the place to sample France's greatest hits, including whole Dover sole meunière served tableside, steak au poivre, and roasted duck breast with seared foie gras. Three-course prix-fixe dinner menus start at C$50—the six-course surprise tasting menu (C$99) is a good choice. The wine list is the size of a phone book of yore, but the servers are adept at recommending wine pairings. For a less costly and slightly more casual dining experience, try dining in the on-site Bistro Café de Paris, whose food comes from the same great kitchen as Le Beaujolais. $ *Average main: C$33* ✉ *212 Buffalo St., at Banff Ave., Banff* ☎ *403/762–2712* ⊕ *www.lebeaujolaisbanff.com.*

$$ ✕ **Nourish Bistro.** Vegan-friendly Nourish lives up to its name with
VEGETARIAN   plant-based cuisine so intricate and diverse that even nonvegetarians can find something to love. Twenty different ingredients power the explosion of flavors in each bite of Banff's most intriguing nachos: strawberries, toasted quinoa, smoked blackberry sauce, garlic gherkins, six kinds of beans, Monterey Jack, and nine more items. Other noteworthy dishes on the inventive menu include curry poutine, vegan mac and cheese made with quinoa noodles and a coconut-based sauce, and wild mushroom ravioli covered in garlic, red pepper, and lavender cream sauce. $ *Average main: C$18* ✉ *211 Bear St., Suite 110,*

Often found nibbling, elk like to eat such plants as beargrass, aspen leaves, sagebrush, and chokecherries.

Banff ☎ *403/760–3933* ⊕ *www.nourishbistro.com* 🍴 *Reservations not accepted* ▭ *No credit cards.*

$$$
CANADIAN

✕ **Park Distillery.** With water from six Canadian Rockies glaciers and grain sourced from high-altitude family farms, Park Distillery aims to produce spirits with aromas and flavors like no others. Tours and tastings happen daily at 3:30 at Banff's first distillery restaurant, whose campfire-cuisine theme inspires jolly presentations like bourbon-flambéed oca raclette, cheese and whisky fondue, and Millionaire Hamburger Helper, the last one made with Wagyu chuck and served under a fancy silver cloche. Sprawling over two floors, the restaurant has picnic tables and wall decorations that look right out of a kids' summer camp, though the lively main-floor bar reminds patrons of the grown-up pleasures to be enjoyed. ⑤ *Average main: C$25* ✉ *219 Banff Ave., Banff* ☎ *403/762–5114* ⊕ *www.parkdistillery.com.*

$$$$
CANADIAN
Fodor'sChoice
★

✕ **Post Hotel.** One of the true epicurean experiences in the Canadian Rockies, the Post delivers daring, regionally inspired cuisine accompanied by excellent wines. The low exposed-beam ceiling and a stone fireplace aglow with a wood fire in winter create an in-from-the-cold aura, with white tablecloths and fanned napkins providing a touch of elegance. The menu changes regularly, but past dishes have included warm Alaskan king crab drizzled with lemongrass-ginger butter, sautéed fillet of wild British Columbia halibut with lemongrass thyme sauce, and Alberta beef tenderloin with bordelaise sauce. With more than 24,000 bottles, the restaurant may well have Canada's best wine collection. For a unique dining experience with a group of six or more, inquire about the private cellar dining room. ⑤ *Average main: C$50*

✉ *200 Pipestone Rd., Lake Louise* ☎ *403/522–3989, 800/661–1586* ⊕ *www.posthotel.com* ⌖ *Reservations essential.*

$$$$
ECLECTIC
✕ **Three Ravens.** Its corner location and floor-to-ceiling windows make this restaurant a great spot to catch the often spectacular mountain sunsets while enjoying seasonal creatively prepared cuisine. From the breads and spiced butters to the fruit sorbets, everything is prepared in-house. The menus change twice yearly but often include items such as Alberta bison strip loin with crispy kale and a charred shallot and Merlot glaze, Spanish paprika–crusted British Columbia halibut, and grilled Alberta beef tenderloin with truffle mac and cheese *rissolé* (small croquette). Gluten-free and vegan choices are clearly marked on the menu. The ample wine list showcases the output of top Canadian producers. $ *Average main: C$36* ✉ *Banff Centre, Sally Borden Bldg., 107 Tunnel Mountain Dr., Banff* ☎ *403/762–6300* ⊕ *banffcentre.ca/ three-ravens-restaurant-wine-bar.*

$$$$
SWISS
✕ **Walliser Stube.** For something fun and a little different, sample this Swiss eatery's fondues and raclettes. Choose from bison, beef, tuna, or seafood in broth, or classic cheese fondues. Meat and seafood fondues are served with young vegetables, steamed potatoes, and mushrooms, accompanied by various sauces. If fondue isn't for you, other classic Swiss, German, and Alpine dishes are served à la carte. Whatever your choice, save room for the signature dessert, a Swiss-chocolate fondue served with banana bread, fresh fruit, marshmallows, and whipped cream. The comprehensive wine list roams the globe but favors vintages from Canada and California. $ *Average main: C$45* ✉ *Fairmont Château Lake Louise, Lake Louise Dr., Lake Louise* ☎ *403/522–1818* ⊕ *www.fairmont.com/lakelouise* ⊗ *Closed Sun.* ⌖ *Reservations essential.*

$
BAKERY
✕ **Wild Flour Bakery.** Banff's artisan bakery is a place to enjoy breakfast or lunch without breaking the bank. Breakfast choices include waffles, toast, and house-made granola, which you can enjoy with a regular coffee or espresso, hot chocolate, or tea from the local Banff Tea Company. For lunch are salads, soups, wraps, and sandwiches. Among the innovative standouts are the quinoa salad made with fresh mint, blueberries, almonds, and a raspberry vinaigrette and the chicken wrap with spinach, tomatoes, cucumbers, peach salsa, and honey-soy dressing. Kale salad with fresh apples and toasted nuts is a typical vegan offering. A favorite of locals, Wild Flour is often busy, but the line moves quickly. $ *Average main: C$11* ✉ *211 Bear St., Suite 101, Banff* ☎ *403/760–5074* ⊕ *www.wildflourbakery.ca* ⊗ *No dinner.*

PICNIC AREAS

Bow Lake. Situated on the shores of stunning Bow Lake, this picnic area on the Icefields Parkway has a kitchen shelter, tables, toilets, and fireboxes. ⊹ *Icefields Pkwy., at edge of Bow Lake.*

Cascade. This spot has tables, a kitchen shelter, fireplaces, and flush toilets. ⊹ *Off Lake Minnewanka Rd.*

Fireside. This area has picnic tables and toilets nearby. ⊹ *Off Bow Valley Pkwy.*

FAMILY **Lake Minnewanka picnic area.** A popular spot, this area has picnic shelters, tables, flush toilets, fire rings, and fireplaces. Hike, rent a boat, or try your luck at fishing. ✛ *10 km (6 miles) from Banff on Minnewanka Loop.*

Moraine Lake. One of the most beautiful lakes in the Canadian Rockies is the setting for this picnic area near Lake Louise. There are two kitchen shelters, a few tables, and toilets at this site. ✛ *Off Moraine Lake Rd., 5 km (3 miles) from village of Lake Louise.*

OUTSIDE THE PARK

$$$$ ✕ **The Trough Dining Co.** Fine dining without the attitude is the theme of
ECLECTIC this intimate Canmore restaurant with hardwood floors, a glass water-fall, and terra-cotta walls. The Trough's ever-changing menu incorporates locally grown ingredients prepared with care and creatively displayed. The signature appetizer, bruschetta on house-made dough balls with local organic chèvre, is topped with fresh tomatoes, bacon, truffle oil, fresh basil, caper berries, and a balsamic reduction. The specialty entrée, jerk-spiced Alberta baby back ribs, arguably the best ribs in the Canadian Rockies, takes four days to make and involves 13 spices. Sticky toffee pudding and crème brûlée are among the well-crafted desserts. Dining is indoors or on the outdoor patio. If it gets a touch chilly outside, your server can provide a fleece blanket. ⑤ *Average main: C$35* ✉ *725 9th St., Canmore* ☎ *403/678–2820* ⊕ *www. thetrough.ca* ⊗ *Closed Mon.*

PICNIC AREAS

Barrier Lake. Picnic tables, indoor toilets, a boat launch, a visitor center, free Wi-Fi access, and lovely views are the draws at this day-use area in Kananaskis Country. ✉ *Bow Valley Provincial Park* ✛ *Off Kananaskis Trail (Hwy. 40)* ☎ *403/678–0760 visitor center* ⊕ *www.albertaparks. ca/bow-valley-pp.aspx* ✉ *Free* ⊗ *Closed mid-Oct.–Apr.*

FAMILY **Quarry Lake Park.** One of Canmore's most popular recreational areas, the lake has a small sandy beach and a swimming area fed by an underground mountain spring. There are picnic tables and washrooms, and about 5 km (3 miles) of trails are nearby. The picnic area is adjacent to an off-leash dog park. ✉ *Spray Lakes Rd., Canmore* ✉ *Free* ⊗ *Daily 7 am–11 pm.*

WHERE TO STAY

IN THE PARK

$$$$ 🏨 **Banff Centre.** Perched on the side of Tunnel Mountain, the Banff
HOTEL Centre's lodgings are an especially good choice if you're attending a concert, seminar, or program at the center, but even if you aren't, the varied accommodations, excellent dining, and superb fitness and recreational facilities make it worth considering. **Pros:** free access to superb fitness center; excellent dining; reasonably priced. **Cons:** away from town. ⑤ *Rooms from: C$279* ✉ *107 Tunnel Mountain Dr., Banff*

☎ *403/762–6100, 800/884–7574, 403/762–6444* ⊕ *www.banffcentre.ca/hotels* ⬤ *356 rooms, 32 suites, 23 kitchenette suites, 11 bachelor suites with stove* ⦿ *No meals.*

$$$$ ▦ **Delta Banff Royal Canadian Lodge.** A grotto-style indoor mineral pool
HOTEL intended to mimic natural hot springs is a highlight of this stone-and-wood lodge set among the evergreens. **Pros:** intimate property; 10-minute walk to downtown; mineral pool and steam room. **Cons:** parking fee; small gym. ⑤ *Rooms from: C$309* ⊠ *459 Banff Ave.* ☎ *403/762–3307, 800/661–1379* ⊕ *www.deltahotels.com* ⬤ *99 rooms* ⦿ *No meals.*

$$$$ ▦ **Fairmont Banff Springs.** Affectionately known as "The Castle in the
RESORT Rockies," this massive property originally developed by the Canadian
Fodor's Choice Pacific Railway debuted in 1888, ushering in Banff's tourism boom.
★ **Pros:** ultraluxurious; many amenities; historical property. **Cons:** costly rooms and dining. ⑤ *Rooms from: C$569* ⊠ *405 Spray Ave.* ☎ *403/762–2211, 800/441–1414* ⊕ *www.fairmont.com/banffsprings* ⬤ *768 rooms* ⦿ *No meals.*

$$$$ ▦ **Fairmont Château Lake Louise.** The view out the Fairmont's back
RESORT door is dramatic and then some, with terraces and lawns that reach to the famous aquamarine lake, itself backed by the Victoria Glacier. **Pros:** stunning setting; abundant amenities; luxurious accommodations. **Cons:** costly rooms and dining; a bit away from the townsite. ⑤ *Rooms from: C$419* ⊠ *Lake Louise Dr., Lake Louise* ☎ *403/522–3511, 800/441–1414* ⊕ *www.fairmont.com/lakelouise* ⬤ *433 rooms, 54 suites* ⦿ *No meals.*

$$$$ ▦ **Hidden Ridge Resort.** On a secluded Tunnel Mountain road, this resort
HOTEL with incredible views of the surrounding landscape has large, well-
FAMILY appointed accommodations with wood-burning fireplaces, full kitchens with granite countertops, and flat-screen TVs. **Pros:** large units; great views; nice extras. **Cons:** on a secluded road; long walk to town; parking can be tight during peak times. ⑤ *Rooms from: C$299* ⊠ *901 Hidden Ridge Way, Banff* ☎ *403/762–3544, 800/563–8764* ⊕ *www.banffhiddenridge.com* ⬤ *107 rooms* ⦿ *No meals.*

$$$$ ▦ **Juniper Hotel.** A little oasis only a short drive from downtown, this
HOTEL independently owned hotel sits at the base of Mount Norquay, surrounded by the woodlands of Banff National Park. **Pros:** great restaurant; small and intimate; away from crowds; close to Mount Norquay skiing. **Cons:** away from downtown; no lunch on-site. ⑤ *Rooms from: C$229* ⊠ *1 Juniper Way, Banff* ☎ *403/762–2281, 866/551–2281* ⊕ *thejuniper.com* ⬤ *46 rooms, 4 suites, 2 cabins* ⦿ *No meals.*

$$$$ ▦ **Paradise Lodge & Bungalows.** In a secluded forest setting near beautiful
HOTEL Lake Louise, this property offers comfortable suites and cute cabins that were originally built in the 1930s and have been in the same family for more than 50 years. **Pros:** comfortable, well-appointed cabins; very clean; picturesque setting. **Cons:** frontage road is busy during the day; need to drive to get to lake or townsite; no air-conditioning. ⑤ *Rooms from: C$260* ⊠ *105 Lake Louise Dr., Lake Louise* ☎ *403/522–3595* ⊕ *www.paradiselodge.com* ⦵ *Closed Oct.–Apr.* ⬤ *21 cabins, 24 suites* ⦿ *No meals.*

CLOSE UP

Best Campgrounds in Banff

Parks Canada operates 13 campgrounds in Banff National Park not including backcountry sites for backpackers and climbers. The camping season generally runs from mid-May through October, although the Tunnel Mountain and Lake Louise campgrounds remain open year-round. Hookups are available at most of the campgrounds and at four of the 31 Kananaskis Country campgrounds. Parks Canada also offers Equipped Campsites for $55 per night that include a tent, sleeping pads, and a stove already set up. Another camping option is an oTENTik unit. A cross between a cabin and a tent, each oTENTik can sleep up to six people on foam mattresses and has a heater inside, a fire pit, a bear-proof food locker, a picnic table, and a barbecue. Prices for a one-night stay range from C$16 to C$28 for a tent site. An equipped campsite costs C$55 a night, an oTENTik C$120.

For $50 per day, you can rent camping equipment for up to six people from the BacTrax rental service (⊕ www.campingbanff.com). The company also offers a setup and pack-down service, so you can arrive at your campsite to find everything ready for you, and have it all taken away when your stay is over.

Castle Mountain Campground. This campground is in a beautiful wooded area close to a small store, a gas bar, and a restaurant. ⊠ 34 km (21 miles) from Banff on Bow Valley Pkwy. ⊕ www.pccamping.ca.

Johnston Canyon Campground. The scenery is spectacular and the wildlife abundant in and around this campground across from Johnston Canyon. A small creek flows right by the camping area. ⊠ 25 km (15½ miles) from Banff on Bow Valley Pkwy. ☎ 403/762–1550 or 877/737–3783 ⊕ www.pccamping.ca.

Lake Louise Campground. This forested area next to the Bow River is open year-round, but in early spring and late fall tents and soft-sided trailers are not permitted in order to protect both people and bears. ⊠ 1 km (½ mile) from Lake Louise Village and 4 km (2½ miles) from the lake ☎ 877/737–3783 ⊕ www.pccamping.ca.

Tunnel Mountain Campground. Close to the townsite, this campground has a great view of the valley, hoodoos, and the Banff Springs golf course. ⊠ 2½ km (1½ miles) from Banff Townsite on Tunnel Mountain ☎ 403/762–1550 or 877/737–3783 ⊕ www.pccamping.ca.

Two Jack Lakeside Campground. This secluded campground is on the shores of beautiful Two Jack Lake—one of the park's most scenic areas. There are interpretive programs, and Parks Canada recently built 10 new lakefront oTENTiks that visitors can rent. ⊠ 12 km (7½ miles) from Banff on the Minnewanka Loop ☎ 403/762–1550 or 877/737–3783 ⊕ www.pccamping.ca.

7

$$$$ **Post Hotel.** One of the finest retreats in the Rocky Mountains, this
HOTEL   Swiss chalet–style Relais & Châteaux lodging has an understated elegance, and its outstanding dining and wonderful amenities have garnered
awards and international attention. **Pros:** gourmet dining with famous
wine menu; full-service spa; understated elegance. **Cons:** train nearby;
costly rooms and dining. *⑤ Rooms from: C$405 ⊠ 200 Pipestone Rd.,
Lake Louise ☎ 403/522–3989, 800/661–1586 ⊕ www.posthotel.com
⤵ 69 rooms, 26 suites, 3 cabins �ⓘ◎ⓘ No meals.*

$$$$ **Rimrock Resort Hotel.** This luxurious nine-story hotel on the steep slope
RESORT of Sulphur Mountain has one of Canada's finest restaurants and some
of the best views of any Banff lodging. **Pros:** spectacular views; close to
hot springs and gondola; world-class dining. **Cons:** farther from townsite than other options; parking costs C$16 per day. *⑤ Rooms from:
C$358 ⊠ 300 Mountain Ave. ☎ 403/762–3356, 888/746–7625 ⊕ www.
rimrockresort.com ⤵ 346 rooms, 6 suites �ⓘ◎ⓘ No meals.*

$$$$ **Rundlestone Lodge.** A wood-burning fireplace and rough-hewn front
HOTEL   desk make the lobby of this newly renovated Swiss-style alpine lodge
warm and inviting. **Pros:** comfortable lobby; free underground parking; free Wi-Fi. **Cons:** 15-minute walk to town. *⑤ Rooms from: C$220
⊠ 537 Banff Ave. ☎ 403/762–2201, 800/661–8630 in North America
⊕ www.rundlestone.com ⤵ 75 standard rooms, 19 suites, 2 family
apartments ⓘ◎ⓘ No meals.*

OUTSIDE THE PARK

$$$ **Delta Lodge at Kananaskis.** The location of this lodge in Kananaskis
RESORT Country is second to none, and the numerous amenities, among them
the large indoor pool, indoor-outdoor hot tub, tennis courts, eucalyp-
tus-infused steam room, large fitness area, and spa, make it a destination
in itself. **Pros:** beautiful mountain setting; family-friendly resort; hiking,
biking, golf, and skiing nearby. **Cons:** 30-minute drive to Canmore;
rooms could use an update; no air-conditioning. *⑤ Rooms from: C$199
⊠ Hwy. 40, 28 km (17 miles) south of Hwy. 1, Kananaskis Village
☎ 403/591–7711, 888/244–8666 in North America ⊕ www.deltahotels.
com ⤵ 412 rooms ⓘ◎ⓘ No meals.*

$$$$ **Falcon Crest Lodge.** Just outside the national park in nearby Canmore,
HOTEL   these modern condos are ideal if you enjoy cooking some of your own
meals, as the rooms have fully equipped kitchens with granite coun-
tertops. **Pros:** feels like a home away from home; great views; free
Wi-Fi. **Cons:** 20-minute drive to Banff; no pool; small gym. *⑤ Rooms
from: C$251 ⊠ 190 Kananaskis Way, Canmore ☎ 403/678–6150,
866/609–3222 in North America ⊕ www.falconcrestlodge.ca ⤵ 46
1-bedroom condos, 8 2-bedroom condos, 6 studio suites, 12 deluxe
suites ⓘ◎ⓘ No meals.*

$$$$ **Paintbox Lodge.** Olympic cross-country skiing medalist Sara Renner
B&B/INN and World Cup alpine skiing champion Thomas Grandi own this inti-
mate boutique hotel in the heart of downtown Canmore. **Pros:** down-
town Canmore location; breakfast included; free bikes and Wi-Fi. **Cons:**
small property; not staffed 24 hours. *⑤ Rooms from: C$210 ⊠ 629
10th St., Canmore ☎ 403/609–0482, 888/678–6100 ⊕ paintboxlodge.
com ⤵ 3 rooms, 2 suites ⓘ◎ⓘ Breakfast.*

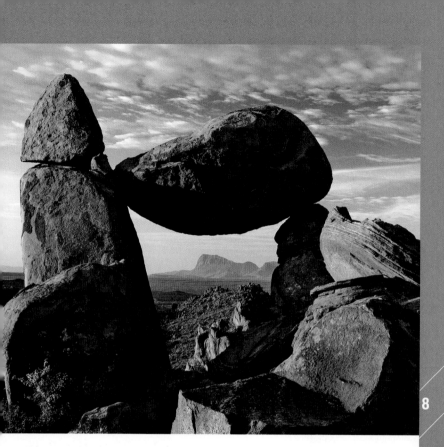

BIG BEND
NATIONAL PARK

WELCOME TO BIG BEND NATIONAL PARK

TOP REASONS TO GO

★ **Varied terrain:** Visit thorny desert, a fabled river, bird-filled woods, and mountain spirals all in the same day.

★ **Wonderful wildlife:** Catch sight of the park's extremely diverse animals, including bands of swarthy javelinas, reclusive mountain lions, and lumbering black bears.

★ **Bird-watching:** Spy a pied-billed grebe or another member of the park's more than 400 bird species, including the Lucifer hummingbird and the unique-to-this-area pato mexicano (Mexican duck).

★ **Hot spots:** Dip into the natural hot springs (105°F) near Rio Grande Village.

★ **Mile-high mountains:** Lace up those hiking boots and climb the Chisos Mountains, reaching almost 8,000 feet skyward in some places and remaining cool even during the most scorching Southwest summer.

1 North Rosillos. Dinosaur fossils have been found in this remote, northern portion of the park. Comprising primarily back roads, this is where nomadic warriors traveled into Mexico via the Comanche Trail.

2 Chisos Basin. This bowl-shaped canyon amid the Chisos Mountains is at the heart of Big Bend. It's a trailhead for numerous hikes and a prime place to watch a sunset through a "fracture" in the bowl known as the Window.

3 Castolon. Just east of Santa Elena Canyon, this cluster of adobe dwellings was once used by ranchers and the U.S. military, earning it a spot on the National Register of Historic Places.

4 Rio Grande Village. Tall, shady cottonwoods highlight the park's eastern fringe along the Mexican border and Rio Grande. It's popular with RVers and bird-watchers.

TEXAS

GETTING ORIENTED

Within its 1,252 square miles, the West Texas park encompasses almost every type of landscape and habitat, from the tall Chisos Mountains, which form its center, to the arid Chihuahuan Desert at its feet—plus a wooded river environment along the Rio Grande. Nature's paint-brush sweeps a surprising abundance of color across the arroyos and canyons, valleys and peaks, while man's efforts have preserved sites to explore, including abandoned ranches, caves with pictographs sketched by extinct civilizations, and mines once used to extract mercury ore.

8

Map labels

385

Persimmon Gap
Visitor Center

2627

1

NORTH   ROSILLOS

• Rosillos Peak
5,445 ft

SIERRA   DEL   CARMEN

• Fossil Bone
Exhibit

Paint Gap

Government
Springs

Panther Junction
Visitor Center

Chisos
Mountain
Lodges

**Chisos
Basin**

2

• Lost Mine Peak
7,550 ft

Visitor Center

Casa Grande
7,325 ft

CHISOS   MOUNTAINS

Chilicotal
Mountain
4,108 ft

JUNIPER CANYON

Emory Peak
7,825 ft

Boquillas Canyon
Overlook

Rio Grande
Overlook

Boquillas del Carmen

Elephant Tusk
5,249 ft

Talley Mountain
3,765 ft

Hot Springs

4 **Rio Grande Village**

Visitor Center

Mariscal
Mine

San Vicente

Rio Grande

TEXAS

CHIHUAHUA
COAHUILA

KEY

🚻	Ranger Station
⛺	Campground
⛱	Picnic Area
🍴	Restaurant
🏠	Lodge
🚶	Trailhead
🚻	Restrooms
⚹	Scenic Viewpoint
⋯⋯	Walking/Hiking Trails

Updated by
Marty Racine

Cradled in the warm, southwestern elbow of Texas, the 801,163 acres of Big Bend National Park hang suspended above the deserts of northern Mexico. From the craggy, forested Chisos Mountains rising up to almost 8,000 feet to the flat, stark plains of the Chihuahuan Desert, Big Bend is one of the nation's most geographically diverse parks, with the kind of dramatic backdrop that inspired Hollywood's first Western sets. Visitors can ride the rapids of the Rio Grande, trek through the classic, Old West landscape, and marvel at the moonscape that skirts Boquillas, Mexico.

BIG BEND PLANNER

WHEN TO GO

There is never a bad time to make a Big Bend foray—except during Thanksgiving, Christmas, and spring break. During these holidays, competition for rooms at the Chisos Mountains Lodge and campsites is fierce—with reservations for campsites and rooms needed up to a year in advance.

Depending on the season, Big Bend sizzles or drizzles, steams up collars or chills fingertips. Many shun the park in the summer, because temperatures skyrocket (up to 120°F), and the Rio Grande lowers.

In winter, temperatures rarely dip below 30°F. During those few times the mercury takes a dive, visitors might be rewarded with a rare snowfall.

The mountains routinely are 5 to 20 degrees cooler than the rest of the park, while the sweltering stretches of the Rio Grande are 5 to 10 degrees warmer.

AVG. HIGH/LOW TEMPS.

Jan.	Feb.	Mar.	Apr.	May	June
61/35	66/38	77/45	81/52	88/59	94/65

July	Aug.	Sept.	Oct.	Nov.	Dec.
93/68	91/66	86/62	79/53	69/42	62/36

FESTIVALS AND EVENTS

FEBRUARY
FAMILY

Texas Cowboy Poetry Gathering. Every February, generally toward the end of the month, ranchers and cowboys congregate for three days at Sul Ross State University to regale audiences with original poetry and washtub-bass tributes to singers like Bob Wills. The idea is to preserve the traditions of the West in words and song. More on-site information is available on the second floor of the University Center. ⊠ *Sul Ross State University, Hwy. 90, Alpine* ⊕ *East end of town* ☎ *432/837–2326, 800/561–3712* ⊕ *www.cowboy-poetry.org.*

JULY

Viva Big Bend. The annual Viva Big Bend music festival in July is a West Texas showcase for Lone Star music. The action—rock, blues, country, Latin, and beyond—takes stage in Alpine, Fort Davis, Marathon, Lajitas, and Marfa, both in large paid-admission venues and free concerts in hotel patios. A shuttle service connecting the four cities is available for those consuming alcohol. ⊠ *Holland Hotel, 209 W. Holland Ave, Alpine* ☎ *432/837–2800 Holland Hotel* ⊕ *www.vivabigbend.com* 🎟 *Cover charge varies.*

SEPTEMBER
FAMILY

Marfa Lights Festival. This Labor Day weekend event celebrates the mysterious multicolored lights that appear at night in the Chinati Mountains east of U.S. 67 and south of U.S. 90 from 10 to 20 times a year. Do they result from pockets of atmospheric gas? The spirits of dead Apaches? Overdriven imaginations? Whatever they are, they draw curious visitors to the center of Marfa for a parade, live music, and food. ⊠ *Presidio County Courthouse lawn, N. Highland Ave., Marfa* ☎ *432/295–0893 Marfa Chamber of Commerce, 432/729–4772 Marfa Visitor Center* ⊕ *www.marfachamber.org.*

NOVEMBER
FAMILY

Alpine Gallery Night Artwalk. For two days each November, the peculiar mix of ranching and artist culture that inhabits Alpine overflows the galleries and seeps into the town's main drag, Holland Avenue. Musicians play at the train depot, barbecue vendors crowd the streets, and local artists display their works in many downtown businesses. ⊠ *Holland Ave., Alpine* ☎ *800/561–3712 Alpine Chamber of Commerce, 432/837–3067 Kiowa Gallery* ⊕ *www.artwalkalpine.com.*

Fodor'sChoice
★

Terlingua International Chili Championship. On the first Saturday of November, top chefs spice up cooling weather with chili cooking, bragging, and partying at two simultaneous chili cookoffs. Rancho CASI stirs the pot for the International Championship on the north side of FM 170, 11 miles west of Study Butte, while the World Championship heats up behind the Terlingua Store in Terlingua Ghost Town. Some of the prize-winning cooks dole out samples. And this is Texas, pardner: no beans allowed. ⊠ *Hwy. 170, Terlingua* ⊕ *West of Terlingua, for both events* ☎ *210/887–8827* ⊕ *www.abowlofred.com.*

8

PLANNING YOUR TIME
BIG BEND IN ONE DAY

Essentially, the park has a west-side and an east-side paved route to its storied attractions, branching apart at the foot of **Chisos Basin Road** in the heart of Big Bend. Attempting both in one day, covering an aggregate 110 miles, could be hectic and ultimately frustrating, and you'll miss the striking details that bring the park and its history to life. To the west, the goal is **Santa Elena Canyon,** carved by the Rio Grande. From Chisos Mountains Lodge, drive 7 miles north on **Chisos Basin Road**, turn west on Route 118 and connect with **Ross Maxwell Scenic Drive**, which curls past silent homesteads, stunning overlooks, the Castolon Historic District (old adobe buildings and a working general store), and a campground near the Rio Grande. Explore as many overlooks and historical sites as time allows on this 30-mile stretch until you reach Santa Elena Canyon at the southwestern rim of the park. From there, walk the **Santa Elena Canyon Trail** (1.7 miles round-trip). You might need to wade Terlingua Creek, then ascend a moderately steep trail cut into the canyon wall, which eventually steps down to a sandy clearing by the river. The majestic canyon is framed by gargantuan rock formations, with the Rio Grande sandwiched between sheer cliffs. Back at the trailhead, return to Route 118 via Ross Maxwell Scenic Drive or unpaved Old Maverick Road (12.8 miles; high-clearance and four-wheel-drive vehicles only) and return east toward Chisos Basin.

A second one-day option is to explore the east side of the park from **Chisos Mountains Lodge:** Head east on Route 118 toward **Rio Grande Village** and explore Panther Junction Visitor Center, Dugout Wells, Mariscal Mine, Hot Springs, Glenn Spring, Daniels Ranch, and Boquillas Canyon. At Rio Grande Village, stroll through cottonwoods by the river, home to many birds. There's also a well-stocked convenience store for a midday snack, with gas pumps. If you have time, and a passport, cross the river at nearby Boquillas Crossing and while away a few hours in the rustic village of Boquillas del Carmen, Mexico. Return to Chisos Basin by the same route, hopefully in time to hike the short Window View Trail, where prime-time hues are captured at sunset.

GETTING HERE AND AROUND
AIR TRAVEL

The nearest major airport is in Midland, 3½ hours north of the park.

BUS TRAVEL

The bus takes you only as far as Marathon.

CAR TRAVEL

Big Bend is 39 miles south of Marathon, off U.S. 385; 81 miles south of Alpine, off Route 118; and 69 miles east of Presidio, off Route 170. Paved park roads have twists and turns, some very extreme in higher elevations; if you have an RV longer than 24 feet or a trailer longer than 20 feet, you should avoid the Chisos Basin Road into higher terrain in Big Bend's central portion. Four-wheel-drive vehicles are needed for many of the backcountry roads. At parking areas take valuables with you.

PARK ESSENTIALS
PARK FEES AND PERMITS
It costs $25 to enter at the gate by car, and your pass is good for seven days. Entry on foot, bicycle, or commercial vehicle is $12; entry by motorcycle is $20. A Big Bend Annual Pass is $40. Camping fees in developed campgrounds are $14 per night, while backcountry camping is $12 for up to 14 days. Mandatory backcountry camping, boating, and fishing permits are available at visitor centers.

PARK HOURS
Big Bend National Park never closes. Visitor centers may be closed Christmas Day. Visitor centers at Rio Grande Village and the Castolon Historic District close in summer. The park is in the Central time zone.

CELL-PHONE RECEPTION
Cell phones do not often work in the park, though service is generally more reliable in flat, open country. Public telephones can be found at the visitor centers.

EDUCATIONAL OFFERINGS
CLASSES AND SEMINARS
Big Bend Seminars. The Big Bend National History Association offers one- and two-day seminars covering subjects such as wildflowers, geology, and desert survival. Classes are generally limited to 15 people and are operated by Far Flung Outdoor Center in Terlingua. ⊠ *1 Adventure Ln., FM 170, Terlingua* ☎ *877/839–5337 Far Flung Outdoor Center, 432/371–2633 office* ⊕ *www.ffoc.net* ✉ *Fees vary.*

RANGER PROGRAMS
FAMILY **Birding Talks.** Rangers lead two-hour birding tours; binoculars are needed. ⊠ *Chisos Basin Visitor Center* ✢ *From Hwy. 118, take Chisos Basin Rd. 7 miles to the lodge parking lot* ☎ *432/477–2264* ⊕ *www. nps.gov/bibe* ☉ *Nov.–Mar., daily 8–3:30; Apr.–Oct., daily 9–4; closed for lunch.*

FAMILY
Fodor's Choice
★ **Interpretive Activities.** Ranger-guided activities are held throughout the park, indoors and outdoors, and include slide shows, talks, and walks on natural and cultural history. Check visitor centers and campground bulletin boards for event postings, which are usually updated on a two-week rotation. ⊠ *Park headquarters at Panther Junction Visitor Center, 1 Panther Dr.* ✢ *Intersection of Hwys. 385 and 118* ☎ *432/477–2251* ⊕ *www.nps.gov/bibe.*

FAMILY **Junior Ranger Program.** This self-guided program for kids of all ages is taught via a $2 booklet of nature-based activities (available at visitor centers). Upon completion of the course, kids are given a Junior Ranger badge or patch, a certificate, and a bookmark. ⊠ *Park headquarters at Panther Junction Visitor Center, 1 Panther Dr.* ✢ *Intersection of Hwys. 385 and 118* ☎ *432/477–2251* ⊕ *www.nps.gov/bibe or www.nps.gov/webrangers.*

8

RESTAURANTS

One word sums up the fare available in the park: casual. You can wear shorts and sneakers to the one park restaurant, which has American-style fare. North of the park, Alpine and Marfa have the biggest selection, while Terlingua, just outside the west park entrance, has a few eateries.

HOTELS

At the Chisos Mountains Lodge, the only hotel in the park, you can select from a freestanding stone cottage or a motel-style room, both within a pace or two of spectacular views—Chisos sunsets are not to be missed. It's convenient to stay here because it's close to trails, and there is a gift shop, general store, visitor center, and the park's only restaurant. Even if you don't stay here, go just to see the stunning view through the wall-sized dining-room windows. The region flanking Big Bend retains its grand historic hotels, such as the glamorous Hotel Paisano in Marfa, the historic Gage Hotel in Marathon, the simple but charming Hotel Limpia in Fort Davis, and the stately Old West Holland Hotel in Alpine, but it also boasts the Lajitas Golf Resort and moderately priced motels in Terlingua.

Hotel reviews have been shortened. For full information, visit Fodors.com.

WHAT IT COSTS			
	$	$$	$$$	$$$$
Restaurants	under $13	$13–$20	$21–$30	over $30
Hotels	under $101	$101–$150	$151–$200	over $200

Restaurant prices are the average cost of a main course at dinner or, if dinner is not served, at lunch. Hotel prices are the lowest cost of a standard double room in high season, excluding taxes and services charges.

VISITOR INFORMATION

PARK CONTACT INFORMATION

FAMILY

Fodor's Choice

★

Big Bend National Park. There are five visitor centers in Big Bend: Panther Junction, considered park headquarters, at the intersection of highways 385 and 118; Persimmon Gap at the park's northern entrance; Rio Grande Village on the eastern border near Mexico; the Castolon Historic District on Ross Maxwell Scenic Drive; and Chisos Basin in the parking area of Chisos Mountains Lodge. Rio Grande Village and Castolon are closed in summer. Cost for vehicles entering the park (from the north and west gates) is $20, good for one week. ⊠ *Big Bend National Park* ☎ *432/477–2251* ⊕ *www.nps.gov/bibe.*

VISITOR CENTERS

FAMILY

Castolon Visitor Center. Here you'll find some of the most hands-on exhibits the park has to offer, with touchable fossils, plants, and implements used by the farmers and miners who settled here in the 1800s and early 1900s. The center closes in summer. Nearby is an old adobe gallery displaying poster boards explaining the U.S.–Mexico "transparent border." ⊹ *In Castolon Historic District, southwest side of park, on Ross Maxwell Scenic Dr.* ☎ *432/477–2666* ⊕ *www.nps.gov/bibe* ☉ *Nov.–Apr., daily 10–5; closed for lunch.*

FAMILY **Chisos Basin Visitor Center.** The center, located at the park's only lodge, is one of the better equipped, as it offers an interactive computer exhibit and a bookstore. An adjacent general store has camping supplies, picnic fare, and some produce. There are plenty of nods to the wild, with natural resource and geology exhibits, a map of bear and mountain lion sightings, and a larger-than-life representation of a mountain lion. The center sponsors educational activities here and at the nearby Chisos Basin Amphitheater. If you are traveling just to see the visitor center, call ahead; opening and closing times are subject to change due to staffing and seasonal transitions. ✢ *From Hwy. 118 take Chisos Basin Rd. 7 miles to Chisos Basin parking area* ☎ *432/477–2264* ⊕ *www.nps.gov/bibe* ☉ *Nov.–Mar., daily 8:30–5; Apr.–Oct., daily 8:30–4; closed for lunch.*

FAMILY **Panther Junction Visitor Center.** The park's main visitor center, near the
Fodor'sChoice base of the Chisos Mountains, includes a bookstore and exhibits on the
★ park's mountain, river, and desert environments. One exhibit poses this question: What is the most dangerous animal in the park? When you open the panel, you're staring into a mirror. A new, elegantly produced 22-minute film detailing the wonders of the park shows on request in the theater, and there's a sprawling board replica of the park's topographical folds. Nearby, a gas station offers limited groceries such as chips, sandwiches, and other picnic items. ✉ *Panther Junction, 1 Panther Junction Dr.* ✢ *Hwy. 118 near the junction of U.S. 385, 70 miles south of Marathon and 30 miles south of park's northern entrance* ☎ *432/477–1158 visitor center, 432/477–2251 park's menu options* ⊕ *www.nps.gov/bibe* ☉ *Daily 9–5.*

FAMILY **Persimmon Gap Visitor Center.** Complete with exhibits and a bookstore, this visitor center is the northern gateway into miles of flatlands that surround the more scenic heart of Big Bend. Dinosaur fossils have been found here; the **Fossil Bone Exhibit** is on the road between Persimmon Gap and Panther Junction. Depending on volunteer help, the center might stay open past posted hours during the busy winter season. ✢ *On Main Park Rd. (U.S. 385), 2 miles south of the park's northern entrance* ☎ *432/477–2393* ⊕ *www.nps.gov/bibe* ☉ *Daily 9:30–4, depending on staffing.*

FAMILY **Rio Grande Village Visitor Center.** Opening days and hours are sporadic and it's closed in summer, but if it's open you can take in the videos of Big Bend's geological and natural features at the minitheater. There are also exhibits dealing with the Rio Grande. ✉ *Rio Grande Village* ✢ *22 miles southeast of Panther Junction* ☎ *432/477–2271* ⊕ *www.nps.gov/ bibe* ☉ *Nov.–Apr., daily 8:30–4; closed for lunch.*

EXPLORING

SCENIC DRIVES

FAMILY **Chisos Basin Road.** Ever-changing, this 7-mile road climbs south from
Fodor'sChoice Chisos Basin Junction, ending at Chisos Mountains Lodge, with a
★ spur leading to a campground. By driving into higher elevations (the heart of Big Bend), you're more likely to spot lions and bears as well as

white-tailed deer amid juniper trees and pinyon pines. You'll also see lovely, red-barked Texas madrone along with some Chisos oaks and Douglas fir trees. Several roadside exhibits along the way explain the various ecosystems. Avoid this drive if you are in an RV longer than 24 feet, because of sharp curves and switchbacks. ✛ *Off Hwy. 118, 3 miles west of Panther Junction* ⊕ *www.nps.gov/bibe.*

FAMILY
Fodor's Choice
★
Ross Maxwell Scenic Drive. Although it extends only 30 miles, you can easily spend a full day on this aptly named route admiring the views, visiting historic sites, taking short hikes, and getting a Big Bend education. There are scenic overlooks, a backside perspective of the Chisos Mountains, plenty of exhibits, and the ruins of old homesteads. If you don't mind a little grate in your gait from the gravel that blankets the road, you can make this drive a loop by reconnecting with Highway 118 from Santa Elena Canyon via unpaved Old Maverick Road for 12.8 miles. If you're in an RV or a low-clearance car, don't even attempt Old Maverick Road. The road isn't paved and is rough going in some spots. ✛ *Off Hwy. 118, about 12 miles west of Panther Junction* ⊕ *www.nps.gov/bibe.*

HISTORIC SITES

FAMILY
Castolon Historic District. Adobe buildings and wooden shacks serve as reminders of the farming and military community of Castolon, near the banks of the Rio Grande. The Magdalena House has historical exhibits. A general store, housed in an old adobe building and fronted by shaded picnic tables, is good for drinks, snacks, and a friendly face. The nearby Castolon Visitor Center closes in summer. ⊠ *Castolon Historic District* ✛ *On Ross Maxwell Scenic Dr., southwest portion of the park* ☎ *432/477–2225 ranger station* ⊕ *www.nps.gov/bibe.*

FAMILY
Hot Springs. Hikers soak themselves in the 105°F waters alongside the Rio Grande, where petroglyphs (rock art) coat the canyon walls nearby. The remains of a post office, motel, and bathhouse point to the old commercial establishment operating here in the early 1900s. The 1.6-mile dirt road leading to the Hot Springs trailhead from Highway 118 is not suggested for RVs or trailers. Nor would it be wise to negotiate it in a rainstorm. Don't leave valuables in your car, as thefts sometimes occur, especially during the slow season. ✛ *18 miles southeast of Panther Junction, near Rio Grande Village* ⊕ *www.nps.gov/bibe.*

FAMILY
Mariscal Mine. Hardy, hard-working men and women once coaxed cinnabar, or mercury ore, from the Mariscal Mine, located at the north end of Mariscal Mountain. They left the mines and surrounding stone buildings behind for visitors to explore. If you stop here, take care not to touch the timeworn stones, as they may contain poisonous mercury residue. ✛ *5 miles west of Rio Grande Village, on River Rd. E* ⊕ *www. nps.gov/bibe/historyculture/mariscalmine.htm.*

SCENIC STOPS

FAMILY
Fodor'sChoice
★

Chisos Basin. Panoramic vistas, a restaurant with an up-close view of jagged mountains, and glimpses of the Colima warbler (which summers in Big Bend) await in the forested Chisos Basin. This central site, considered the spiritual heart of Big Bend at an elevation of 5,400 feet, is ringed by taller peaks and also has hiking trails, a lodge, a campground, a grocery store, a gift shop, an amphitheater, the famous Window rock formation, and one of five park visitor centers. Winter sometimes brings snow, but in summer this is where you find relief from the desert heat below. ✥ *Off Chisos Basin Rd., 7 miles southwest of Chisos Basin Junction and 10 miles southwest of Panther Junction* ⊕ *www.nps.gov/bibe.*

FAMILY
Fodor'sChoice
★

Santa Elena Canyon. The finale of a short but vigorous hike (1.7 miles round-trip) over a steep slope is a spectacular view of the Rio Grande and sheer limestone cliffs that rise 1,500 feet to create a natural box. Summer can feel like a sauna, but you might have this secluded place to yourself. ⊠ *Big Bend National Park* ✥ *30 miles southwest of Panther Junction, 10 miles southwest of Castolon via Ross Maxwell Scenic Dr.; or 14 miles southwest of Hwy. 118 via Old Maverick Rd.* ⊕ *www.nps.gov/bibe.*

SPORTS AND THE OUTDOORS

Spectacular and varied scenery plus more than 300 miles of road spell adventure for hikers, bikers, horseback riders, or those simply in need of a ramble on foot or by ATV or Jeep. A web of dusty, unpaved roads lures adventuresome drivers and experienced hikers deep into the backcountry, while paved roads make shorter trails and scenic overlooks more accessible. Because the park has nearly half of the bird species in North America, birding ranks high. Boating is also popular, because some of the park's most striking features are accessible only via the Rio Grande.

MULTISPORT OUTFITTERS

FAMILY
Big Bend River Tours. Exploring the Rio Grande is this outfitter's specialty. Custom tours can be half a day up to three weeks and include rafting, canoeing, and hiking and horseback trips combined with a river float. Rafting tours include gourmet or music themes. ⊠ *23331 FM 170, Terlingua* ☎ *800/545–4240, 432/371–3033* ⊕ *www.bigbendrivertours.com* ☞ *From $60.*

FAMILY
Desert Sports. From rentals—mountain bikes, boats, and inflatable kayaks—to experienced guides for mountain-bike touring, boating, and hiking, this outfitter has it covered. The company prides itself on its small size and personal touch. ⊠ *FM 170, Terlingua* ✥ *FM 170 near the Terlingua Ghost Town bypass, 5 miles west of the FM 170 and Hwy. 118 intersection* ☎ *432/371–2727, 888/989–6900* ⊕ *www.desertsportstx.com* ☞ *From $75.*

FAMILY
Far Flung Outdoor Center. Call these pros for personalized nature, historical, and geological trips via rafts, ATVs, and 4X4s. Trips include

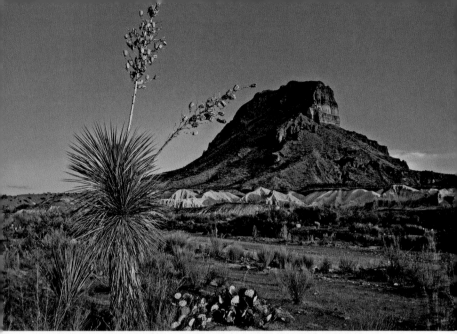

West Texas fauna include prairie dogs, jackrabbits, and roadrunners, while its flora include yuccas.

gourmet rafting tours with cheese and wine served on checkered table-cloths alongside the river, and sometimes spectacular star viewing at night. The property offers overnight "casitas" with kitchenettes and a full range of amenities. ⊠ *FM 170, Terlingua* ✛ *½ mile west of the FM 170–Hwy. 118 intersection* ☎ *800/839–7238, 432/371–2633* ⊕ *www. ffoc.net* 🖃 *ATV tours from $80.*

Red Rock Outfitters. This outfitter sells clothing and gear and arranges river-rafting, canoeing, horseback-riding, zip-line rides, and mountain-biking excursions, as well as Jeep and ATV tours. ⊠ *Lobby of Badlands Hotel, 100 Main St. (FM 170), Lajitas* ☎ *432/424–5170 for resort, 432/424–5000 for front desk* ⊕ *www.lajitasgolfresort.com* 🖃 *From $75.*

BICYCLING

Mountain biking the backcountry roads can be so solitary that you're unlikely to encounter another human being. However, the solitude also means you should be extraordinarily prepared for the unexpected with ample supplies, especially water and sun protection (summer heat is brutal, and you're unlikely to find shade except in forested areas of Chisos Basin). Biking is recommended only during the cooler months (October–April).

On paved roads, a regular road bike should suffice, but you'll have to bring your own—outfitters tend to stock only mountain bikes. Off-road cycling is not allowed in the park. For an easy ride on mostly level ground, try the 13-mile (one-way) unpaved **Old Maverick Road** on the west side of the park off Route 118. For a challenge, take the unpaved

CLOSE UP

Plants and Wildlife in Big Bend

Because Big Bend contains habitats as diverse as spent volcanoes, slick-sided canyons, and the Rio Grande, it follows that species here are extremely diverse, too. Among the park's most notable residents are endangered species like the agave- and cactus-eating Mexican long-nosed bat, shadow-dappled peregrine falcon, swarthy javelina, and fat-bellied horned lizard (Texans call them "horny toads"). More than 450 species of birds wing throughout the park, including the black-capped vireo and the turkey vulture, which boasts a 6-foot wingspan.

In the lower desert, be aware of scorpions and rattlesnakes, especially in the summer at dusk and dawn. The vipers aren't normally aggressive, so try to refrain from sudden movement and give them a wide berth.

In the highlands mountain lions lurk, while black bears loll in the crags and valleys. Your chances of spotting the reclusive creatures are slim, though greater at dusk and dawn. If you do encounter either, don't run away. Instead, stand tall, shout, throw rocks if necessary, and look as scary as possible.

If the winged, furred, and legged denizens of Big Bend are watch-worthy, so, too, are the plants populating the region. Supremely adapted to the arroyos, valleys, and slopes, the plants range from the endangered Chisos Mountains hedgehog cactus (found only in the park) to the towering rasp of the giant dagger yucca. Also here are 60 types of cacti—so be careful where you tread.

8

Old Ore Road for 27 miles from the park's north area to near Rio Grande Village on the east side.

BIRD-WATCHING

Situated on north–south migratory pathways, Big Bend is home to approximately 450 species of birds—more than any other national park. In fact, the birds that flit, waddle, soar, and swim in the park represent more than half the bird species found in North America, including the Colima warbler, found nowhere else in the United States. To glimpse darting hummingbirds, turkey vultures, golden eagles, and the famous Colima, look to the Chisos Mountains. To spy woodpeckers and scaled quail (distinctive for dangling crests), look to the desert scrub. And for cuckoos, cardinals, and screech owls, you must prowl along the river. Rangers lead birding talks.

FAMILY

Fodor's Choice

★

Chisos Basin. Known as a "sky island" towering over the surrounding desert "sea," Chisos Basin shelters the only lodge in the park and is etched by numerous hiking trails of varying difficulty. One takes you to the top of Emory Peak, the highest point in Big Bend. You'll have to hike the high country (above 5,400 feet elevation) to spy the Colima warbler and Lucifer hummingbird, but bear, deer, javelina, and even mountain lions have been known to range closer to the lodge grounds. Your chances of encountering them are rather small, especially during the day. If you do, the animals will likely shy away. At more than a mile high, the basin floor is an especially inviting destination during summer. ✛ *At the end of Chisos Basin Rd., 10 miles southwest of Panther Junction* ☎ *432/477–2291 for Chisos Mountains Lodge, 432/477–2264 for Chisos Basin Visitor Center* ⊕ *www.nps.gov/bibe.*

FAMILY

Fodor's Choice

★

Rio Grande Village. Considered the best birding habitat in Big Bend, this river wetland has summer tanagers and vermilion flycatchers among many other species. The trail's good one for kids, and a portion is wheelchair accessible. ✛ *22 miles southeast of Panther Junction via Hwy. 118* ☎ *432/477–2271 Rio Grande Village Visitor Center (closed in summer)* ⊕ *www.nps.gov/bibe.*

BOATING AND RAFTING

Much is made of the park's hiking trails and the exquisite views they offer. Likewise, the watery pathway that is the Rio Grande should be mentioned for the spectacular views it affords. The 118 miles of the Rio Grande that border the park form its backbone, defining the vegetation, landforms, and animals found at the park's southern rim. By turns shallow and deep, the river flows through stunning canyons and picks up speed over small and large rapids.

Alternately soothing and exciting (Class II and III rapids develop here, particularly after the summer rains), the river can be traversed in several ways, from guided rafting tours to more strenuous kayak and canoe expeditions. In general, rafting trips spell smoother sailing for families, though thrills are inherent when soaring over the river's meringuelike tips and troughs. Always respect this river, however, for fatalities have occurred. ■ TIP➜ Be sure to check the river levels before planning an outing—many times during the year the river's too low to get a decent rafting experience. Conversely, during an especially wet monsoon season, the river rises to levels that even guides won't challenge.

You can bring your own raft to the boat launch at the Rio Grande, but you must obtain a $10 river-use permit (which allows you to camp along the river) from a visitor center. Leave the Jet Skis at home; no motorized vehicles are allowed on the Rio Grande. For less fuss, go with a tour guide or outfitter on trips that range from a few hours to several days. Most outfitters are in the communities of Study Butte, Terlingua, and Lajitas, just west of the park boundary off Route 170. They rent rafts, canoes, kayaks, and inflatable kayaks (nicknamed "duckies") for when the river is low. Their guided trips cost in the tens of dollars to thousands of dollars. Personalized river tours are available all year, and because this is the Lone Star State, they might include gourmet rafting tours that end with beef Wellington and live country music. Though many of the rafting trips are relatively smooth, thus safe for younger boaters, be sure to tell the equipment-rental agent or guide if a party member weighs less than 100 pounds or more than 200, because special life jackets may be necessary.

FISHING

You can cast a line into the Rio Grande all year for free, as long as you obtain a permit from one of the park's visitor centers. You cannot use jug lines, traps, or other nontraditional fishing methods.

HIKING

Each of the park's zones has its own appeal. The east side offers demanding mountain hikes, border canyons, limestone aplenty, and sandy washes with geographic spectacles. Westside trails go down into striking scenery in the Santa Elena Canyon and up into towering volcanic landforms. Descend into gorges, arroyos, and springs or ascend into the must-see scenic windows of Grapevine Hills. The heart of the park has abandoned mines, pine-topped vistas, scrub vegetation around the Chisos, and deserts lying just below soaring Chisos Mountain aeries. ■ TIP➜ Carry enough drinking water—a gallon per person daily (more when extremely hot).

While Big Bend certainly has "expedition level" trails to test the most veteran backpacker, many are very demanding and potentially dangerous (sometimes resulting in fatalities). So no "difficult" trails are noted here. Instead, the ones included here are representative of trails at Big Bend that most physically fit people can accomplish.

EASY

FAMILY **Chihuahuan Desert Nature Trail.** A windmill and spring form a desert oasis, a refreshing backdrop to a ½-mile, hot and flat nature trail; wild doves are abundant, the hike is pleasant, and kids will do just fine. While you're there, keep an eye out for the elf owl, one of the sought-after birds on the Big Bend's "Top 10" list. *Easy, elevation gain minimal.* ⊠ *Hwy. 118* ✛ *Trailhead: at Dugout Wells, 5 miles southeast of Panther Junction* ⊕ *www.nps.gov/bibe.*

FAMILY **Rio Grande Village Nature Trail.** Down by the Rio Grande, this short, ¾-mile trail packs a powerful wildlife punch. The village is considered one of the best spots in the park to see rare birds, and other wildlife isn't in short supply either. Keep a lookout for coyotes, javelinas (they look like wild pigs), and other mammals. This is a good trail for kids, so expect higher traffic. Restrooms are nearby, and the trail can be done in less than an hour, even when lingering. The first ¼ mile is wheelchair accessible. *Easy, elevation gain minimal.* ✛ *Trailhead: 22 miles southeast of Panther Junction via Hwy. 118.*

FAMILY **Window View Nature Trail.** This 0.3-mile paved nature trail is wheelchair accessible and great for little ones. Take in the beautiful, craggy-sided Chisos and look through the V-shaped rock-sided "Window" framing the desert below. This self-guided trail, which is especially captivating at sunset, is easily accomplished in half an hour. Be on the lookout for wild javelina, which occasionally root through here. They're not normally aggressive, but give them a respectful distance. *Easy, elevation gain minimal.* ⊠ *Chisos Basin* ✛ *Trailhead: west of lodge parking lot.*

8

MODERATE

FAMILY **Chisos Basin Loop Trail.** A forested area and higher elevations give you some sweeping views of the lower desert and distant volcanic mountains on this 1.6-mile round-trip. The elevation at the trailhead is 5,400 feet. Set aside about an hour. *Moderate, elevation gain 500 feet.* ⊠ *Chisos Basin* ⊹ *Trailhead: west of lodge parking lot.*

FAMILY **Hot Springs Trail.** An abandoned motel and a bathhouse foundation are among the sights along this 2-mile loop hike. The Rio Grande is heard at every turn, and trees occasionally shelter the walkway. The trailhead is accessed via a 1.6-mile dirt road. It's not suitable for RVs, but most cars can navigate it in dry conditions. Temperatures can soar to 120°F, so hike in the morning or during cooler months. *Easy to moderate, elevation gain 200 feet.* ⊹ *Trailhead: access road off Hwy. 118, about 4 miles west of Rio Grande Village.*

FAMILY **Lost Mine Trail.** Set aside about three hours to leisurely explore the nature of the Chisos Mountains along this elevation-climbing trail. It starts at 5,700 feet, one of the highest elevations in the park, and climbs to an even loftier vantage point. The entire length is 4.8 miles round-trip. If fatigue or time constraints become a factor, the breathtaking view at marker 10, about halfway up, is a worthy destination in itself. *Moderate, elevation gain 1,100 feet.* ⊹ *Trailhead: at mile marker 5 on the Chisos Basin Rd., 2 miles from lodge.*

FAMILY **Santa Elena Canyon Trail.** A 1.7-mile round-trip crosses marshy Terlingua
Fodor'sChoice Creek, scales a rocky staircase, and deposits you on the banks of the
★ Rio Grande for a cathedral-like view of cliff walls boxing in the river. Try to end up here near sunset, when the sun stains the cliffs a rich red-brown chestnut. In clear weather, an overlook on the Ross Maxwell Scenic Drive affords a panoramic view of Santa Elena Canyon from miles away. *Moderate, elevation gain minimal.* ⊹ *Trailhead: 10 miles west of Castolon via Ross Maxwell Scenic Dr. or Old Maverick Rd.*

JEEP TOURS

Wheeled traffic is welcome in the park, up to a point. RVs, trucks, cars, and Jeeps are allowed in designated areas, though personal ATV use is prohibited. Jeep rental isn't available inside the park, but Jeep, SUV, and ATV tours just outside the park are possible through outfitters. Jeep tours can cost as little as $49 for a two-hour tour, while ATV tours ring up at about $135 for the first person, with reduced rates for a second rider.

SWIMMING

Though it might be tempting to doff sweat-drenched T-shirts in favor of bathing suits, be careful where you take your dips. The Rio Grande has ample waters, but swimming isn't recommended due to dangerous currents and high pollution levels.

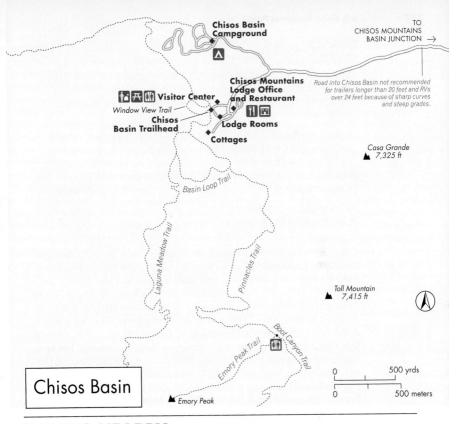

Chisos Basin

WHAT'S NEARBY

Just as many of Big Bend's zones are geographically remote, the park itself is isolated among hundreds upon hundreds of miles of West Texas desert and scrub. The nearest metropolis is El Paso, 329 miles away, while the nearest sizable cities are Odessa and Midland, 222 and 242 miles, respectively, to the northeast.

NEARBY TOWNS

Marathon, just 39 miles to the north, is one of the closest towns to Big Bend. Once a shipping hub, the population-500 town still contains reminders of its Old West railroad days. **Alpine,** a town of about 6,000, hunkers down among the Davis Mountains 81 miles north of the park. The town is known for its extensive college agriculture program at Sul Ross State University. It also attracts celebrities like Will Smith and Jada Pinkett-Smith, who have been spotted at its historic Holland Hotel. About 26 miles west of Alpine is **Marfa,** a population-2,000, middle-of-nowhere West Texas city known for its art scene and spooky, unexplained "Marfa lights," attributed to everything from atmospheric disturbances to imagination.

GOOD READS

■ *Naturalist's Big Bend*, by Roland H. Wauer and Carl M. Fleming, paints a picture of the park's diverse plants and animals.

■ *Big Bend, The Story Behind the Scenery*, by Carol E. Sperling and Mary L. Van Camp, is rife with colorful photos illustrating the park's history and geology.

■ For gleeful and awestruck thoughts on the Big Bend wilderness, check out *God's Country or Devil's Playground*, which collects the writing of nearly 60 authors.

■ The Natural History Association's *Road Guide* ($1.95) gives in-depth information on the web of paved and improved dirt roads running through the park—and the views you can see from them. Find it on sale at park visitor centers.

Once the headquarters of quicksilver mining (now defunct), **Terlingua Ghost Town (populated)** is 7 miles from the park's west entrance on Route 118. Six miles east of Terlingua is **Study Butte**, which also has its roots in the old quicksilver-mining industry. The combined Terlingua–Study Butte population is about 300, many of them iconoclasts and big-city refugees. Follow Route 170 west from Terlingua for 13 miles and you come upon the flat-rock formations of tiny **Lajitas** (pop. 75). Once a U.S. Cavalry outpost, Lajitas, which means "little flat stones," has been converted into a resort area offering plenty of golf and equestrian activities. The border town of **Presidio**, 69 miles from the park's west exit, is regarded as the gateway to northern Mexico. Across the border from Presidio is a spring-break favorite, **Ojinaga, Mexico**, famous for its party-like atmosphere. It's also a springboard to Copper Canyon, a striking series of canyons that run down the west side of the Sierra Tarahumara.

FAMILY **Boquillas del Carmen, Mexico.** Big Bend residents and visitors are thrilled that Boquillas Crossing into Mexico, closed since 9/11, has finally reopened to U.S. citizens. Residents of both countries can now use the crossing, about 2 miles north of Rio Grande Village, from 9 am to 6 pm, Wednesday through Sunday. A passport or birth certificate is required. Once a mining boomtown that fed off rich minerals and silver, Boquillas has shrunk to a small pool of families due in part to the closed border crossing, but there is a restaurant and bar on the other side, plus some shopping. U.S. citizens are allowed to bring back up to $200 in merchandise duty-free. Drive to the crossing past Rio Grande Village, from which you can access a $5 round-trip raft across the Rio Grande. The remaining ¾-mile to the village can be made on foot, by donkey ($5 round-trip), pickup truck ($5), or horseback ($8). △ **If you do not return to the border by 6 pm, Sunday, you'll have an "extended stay" in Mexico until Wednesday.** ⊹ *Near Rio Grande Village; a highway sign will direct you to the crossing* ⊕ *www.nps.gov/bibe.*

VISITOR INFORMATION

Alpine Chamber of Commerce. ⊠ *106 N. 3rd St., Alpine* ☏ *432/837–2326, 800/561–3712* ⊕ *www.alpinetexas.com.* **Big Bend Chamber of Commerce.** ⊠ *Terlingua* ☏ *432/371–2320* ⊕ *www.bigbendchamber.homestead.com.* **Del**

Rio Chamber of Commerce. ⊠ *1915 Veterans Blvd., Del Rio* ☎ *830/775–3551* ⊕ *www.drchamber.com.* **Fort Davis Chamber of Commerce.** ⊠ *No. 4 Memorial Sq., Fort Davis* ☎ *432/426–3015, 800/524–3015* ⊕ *www.fortdavis.com.* **Marfa Chamber of Commerce.** ⊠ *207 N. Highland St., Marfa* ☎ *432/729–4772* ⊕ *www.marfacc.com.* **Presidio Tourism Department.** ⊠ *507 O'Reilly St., Presidio* ☎ *432/229–3517* ⊕ *www.presidiotx.us.*

NEARBY ATTRACTIONS

FAMILY **Barton Warnock Visitor Center.** Affiliated with Big Bend Ranch State Park of Texas, this visitor center offers a self-guided walking tour through a 2½-acre landscaped desert garden. It's a good way to get acquainted with the Trans-Pecos region before adventuring to either the national or state park. Also on the grounds are an interpretive center, a covered picnic area, a bookstore, and a gift shop. ⊹ *FM 170, 1 mile east of Lajitas* ☎ *432/424–3327* ⊕ *www.tpwd. state.tx.us/state-parks* ⊠ *$5 Nov.– Apr.; $3 May–Oct.* ⊗ *Daily 8–4:30.*

FAMILY **Big Bend Ranch State Park.** As a western buffer to Big Bend National Park, this rugged desert wilderness extends along the Rio Grande across more than 300,000 acres from east of Lajitas to Presidio. It's less developed than the national park (if that seems possible), but you can hike, mountain bike, backpack, raft, and ride horseback. A collection of hiking trailheads spoke off from FM 170 across from the Barton Warnock Visitor Center at Lajitas, which serves as the park's eastern information post. The western visitor center is at Fort Leaton State Historical Site near Presidio. ⊠ *Presidio* ☎ *432/358–4444* ⊕ *www.tpwd. state.tx.us/state-parks* ⊠ *Nov.–Apr. $5; May–Oct. $3* ⊗ *Park 24 hrs; visitor centers daily 8–4:30.*

FAMILY
Fodor's Choice ★ **Fort Davis National Historic Site.** The fort for which the city of Fort Davis is named is a serious history lesson on the region from the late 1800s, with exhibits and many original buildings preserved. You can spend hours touring the sprawling grounds, which include barracks, the post hospital, the visitor center, and servants' quarters. Pets are not permitted in public buildings and must be leashed. ⊠ *101 Lt. Henry Flipper Dr., Fort Davis* ⊹ *From north or south via Hwys. 17 and 118; from the west via Hwys. 505, 166, and 17* ☎ *432/426–3224* ⊕ *www.nps.gov/ foda* ⊠ *$7 per person, $15 per carload of more than 2 people.*

FAMILY **Fort Leaton State Historic Site.** The 23-acre site in Presidio County contains a thick-walled adobe fort and trading post that dates back to pioneer days. There are exhibits, a ½-mile nature trail, picnic sites, guided tours, and a store. The park is day-use only—no camping is available. The fort

BEST BETS FOR FAMILIES

■ **Cowboy Poetry.** Cowboys and cowgirls regale with tales at Sul Ross State University's annual event.

■ **McDonald Observatory's Star Parties.** Guides lead observers on a tour of the celestial bodies.

■ **Overnight Rafting Trips.** Far Flung Outdoor Center sometimes offers spring-break trips for families with kids under 12. Trips include short hikes, goggles for stargazing, and canoeing.

8

also doubles as a visitor center for Big Bend Ranch State Park. ⊕ *FM 170, 4 miles southeast of Presidio* ☎ *432/229–3613* ⊕ *www.tpwd.state.tx.us/state-parks* ✉ *Nov.–Apr. $5; May–Oct. $3* ☉ *Daily 8–4:30.*

FAMILY
Fodor'sChoice
★
McDonald Observatory Visitors Center. Check out exhibits, examine sunspots and flares safely via film, or peer into the workings of giant research telescopes. Guided bus tours of the domed observatories depart daily following programs at 11 and 2. After nightfall, the observatory offers star parties. Advance reservations through the website are mandatory for all public programs. On its own, the drive from Fort Davis to the visitor center at 6,235 elevation is worth the trip. ✉ *3640 Dark Sky Dr., Fort Davis* ⊕ *Take Hwy. 118 out of Fort Davis* ☎ *432/426–3640, 877/984–7827 toll-free, recorded information* ⊕ *www.mcdonaldobservatory.org* ✉ *Programs $9, star parties $14* ☉ *Observatory programs, 11 am and 2 pm daily; star parties, after nightfall Tues., Fri., and Sat.*

FAMILY
Museum of the Big Bend. With 5,000 square feet of space, this history-lover's haven has exhibits representing the life and cultures of the region and sponsors an annual show on ranching handiwork (such as saddles, reins, and spurs) held in conjunction with the Cowboy Poetry Gathering each February. The map collection is renowned. ✉ *Sul Ross State University, Hwy. 90, Alpine* ⊕ *Street signs on campus will direct you to the museum* ☎ *432/837–8730 gift shop, 432/837–8143 museum* ⊕ *www.sulross.edu/museum* ✉ *Free, donations accepted* ☉ *Tues.–Sat. 9–5, Sun. 1–5.*

NIGHTLIFE AND PERFORMING ARTS

While recreation and outdoor adventures are alive inside the park, the arts are vibrant outside it. Activities include live poetry readings, an annual four-day music festival, and Cinco de Mayo celebrations that fill up streets and shut down towns.

Ballroom Marfa. Ballroom Marfa is part gallery, part live-music venue. Young, hip, modern, and undeniably cool, the Ballroom welcomes visitors Wednesday through Saturday from 10 to 6 and Sunday 10 to 3. Performers periodically take the stage on Friday and Saturday evenings. Ballroom Marfa closes at times for new installations; see the website for closures and the latest concert information. ✉ *108 E. San Antonio St., Marfa* ☎ *432/729–3600* ⊕ *www.ballroommarfa.org.*

Fodor'sChoice
★
Chinati Foundation. The Chinati Foundation, occupying 15 buildings on a 340-acre campus, is in the vanguard of the "minimalist" movement that defines the Marfa aesthetic. It emphasizes large installations and changes its exhibits regularly, and it has a well-attended annual open house. People fly from all over the country to view the collection, and the foundation conducts guided tours Wednesday through Sunday of its huge contemporary-art holdings. ■TIP➔ Guided tour times are subject to change based on availability. Advance reservations are encouraged via website, email, or phone. ✉ *1 Cavalry Row, Marfa* ☎ *432/729–4362* ⊕ *www.chinati.org* ✉ *From free to $10 for self-guided tours; up to $25 for guided tours* ☉ *Wed.–Sun. 9–5.*

BORDER CROSSING AT BIG BEND

Once upon a time, Big Bend visitors could splash across the Rio Grande and into the confines of Boquillas and Santa Elena, small Mexican towns that buttered their bread by selling Americans handicrafts. Now, if you want to visit one of the border towns, you must do so by entering official checkpoints in Texas; closed since 9/11, the Boquillas Crossing, at the park's southeastern edge, was reopened in 2013.

You'll take a raft across the Rio Grande to reach Boquillas ($5 round-trip), then walk, take a burro ($5), the back of a pickup ($5), or ride a horse ($8) the remaining ¾-mile to town, where you'll find a few bars, restaurants, and shops. To reenter the United States, you'll need a passport, while children 16 and under will also need birth certificates.

Once you get to Mexico, don't fret about language difficulties or money incompatibility. Border towns are very tourist-friendly, and most there speak English. American money is accepted, so it probably won't be necessary to get your greenbacks exchanged. Most Mexican border towns are easy to get to and can be explored in as little as one or two days.

WHERE TO EAT

IN THE PARK

$$$$
SOUTHWESTERN
Fodor's Choice
★

✕ **12 Gage Restaurant.** When the sun sets, this intimate indoor–outdoor restaurant is the best place to eat and socialize in Marathon. The innovative menu, featuring fresh produce from the Gage Hotel Garden across the railroad tracks, changes with the season but maintains a Southwestern flair. Entrées sizzle with prime steaks, smoked cabrito tacos, and roasted game. The chicken-fried steak, a Lone Star staple, is a cut above. Choose from the extensive wine cellar. After dinner you can belly up to the bar at the White Buffalo, where people-watching is always a kick. $ *Average main: $33* ✉ *101 N.W. 1st St., Marathon* ✢ *U.S. 90 in center of town* ☎ *432/386–4205, 800/884–4243 reservations* ⊕ *www.gagehotel.com* ⟁ *Reservations essential.*

$$$
AMERICAN

✕ **Century Bar & Grill.** A simple, select menu defines this cozy restaurant behind the bar in the Holland Hotel. The basics are covered for steaks, seafood, and pasta, plus soups, salads, and appetizers. $ *Average main: $27* ✉ *209 W. Holland Ave., Alpine* ☎ *432/837–2800* ⊕ *www.thehollandhoteltexas.com* ⟁ *Reservations essential.*

$$
AMERICAN
FAMILY

✕ **Chisos Mountains Lodge Restaurant.** The decor of this comfy and casual eatery is unassuming, maybe because the star attraction is the signature view through a wall of windows that brings the craggy Chisos Mountains to your table. Breakfast offers the locally inspired Santa Elena Huevos Rancheros and Emory Peak Omelet. Later, choose from dishes like the Poco Caliente Burger, Rio Grande Chicken-Fried Steak, or Pine Canyon Mango Spinach Salad. There's a soup of the day, and if you're lucky, it'll be the thick and silky Cream of Potato. Each table has an informational booklet about the Big Bend region. ■**TIP**➔ Arrive around sunset to catch the fading rust-color rays through the

8

Window rock formation at the opposite end of the basin. $ *Average main: $16 ✛ 7 miles southwest of Chisos Basin Junction and 10 miles southwest of Panther Junction ☎ 432/477–2292 front desk ⊕ www. chisosmountainslodge.com.*

$ ✕ **Chuy's Restaurant.** This old-school Tex-Mex joint looks a tad shabby
MEXICAN from the outside, but within is some of the tastiest, most authentic, and
FAMILY reasonably priced Mexican food in the territory. Founded in 1959, it was put on the map by football's famed John Madden, a white-knuckle flier who criss-crossed the nation to football games on his decked-out bus. While traveling Texas, he made a point to stop by Chuy's, where a special table is reserved near the TVs just for his entourage. Country music star Dwight Yoakam is also a famous patron. $ *Average main: $8 ✉ 1200 W. Broadway, Van Horn ☎ 432/283–2066 ⊕ www. chuys1959.com.*

$$ ✕ **Starlight Theatre.** This restaurant/saloon/live-music venue is ground
AMERICAN zero for all the ghosts and other characters of Ghost Town Terlingua. The "Feature Presentations" include plenty of local flavor, such as Terlingua chili and the chicken-fried wild boar with Terlingua gold beer gravy. The Starlight is next door to the Terlingua Trading Post, where locals, some of whom look like prospectors from the Old West, sit on the shaded porch, tell stories, drink beer, and play one of the house guitars lying around. Together, these two establishments *are* Ghost Town Terlingua. $ *Average main: $18 ✉ 631 Ivey Rd., Terlingua ✛ Take the Ghost Town turnoff from FM 170 ☎ 432/371–3400 ⊕ www.thestarlighttheatre.com.*

PICNIC AREAS

FAMILY **Dugout Wells Area.** There is a picnic table under the shady cottonwoods off the Dugout Wells Trail loop. There is also a vault toilet here (these kinds of facilities are more pleasant than pit toilets). However, as with all vault toilets in the park, there is no running water to wash your hands. ✛ *6 miles southeast of Panther Junction ☎ 432/477–2251 ⊕ www.nps.gov/bibe.*

Persimmon Gap Area. Quiet and remote, this relatively new picnic area has tables shaded by metal roofs called ramadas. There are no grills, but there is a pit toilet. ✛ *North entrance to Big Bend, on U.S. 385 from Marathon ☎ 432/477–2251 ⊕ www.nps.gov/bibe.*

FAMILY **Rio Grande Village Area.** Half a dozen picnic tables are scattered under cottonwoods south of the convenience store. Half a mile away at Daniels Ranch there are two tables and a grill. Wood fires aren't allowed (charcoal and propane are). ✉ *Hwy. 118 ✛ 22 miles southeast of Panther Junction ☎ 432/477–2251 ⊕ www.nps.gov/bibe.*

FAMILY **Santa Elena Canyon Area.** Two tables sit in the shade next to the parking lot at the trailhead. There is a vault toilet. ✛ *8 miles west of Castolon, accessible via Ross Maxwell Scenic Dr. or Old Maverick Rd. ☎ 432/477–2251 ⊕ www.nps.gov/bibe.*

OUTSIDE THE PARK

$$$
SOUTHWESTERN
Fodor'sChoice
★

✕ **Candelilla Cafe and Thirsty Goat Saloon.** Southwestern dishes, Mexican-inspired fare, and sizzling steaks are the specialties at Candelilla, named for a Mexican succulent from which candle wax is made. It's within walking distance if you're parked at the Lajitas Resort. Order the cream of avocado if it happens to be the soup of the day. The complimentary chips are freshly made, accompanied by a rich, garlicky salsa that's not too hot. Glass walls in this understated yet elegant room give you unobstructed views of sunsets, and a quick stroll next door finds you a nightcap at the Thirsty Goat Saloon, named for a legendary goat who liked Lone Star beer and was even elected "mayor" of Lajitas. ⑤ *Average main: $27 ⊠ Lajitas Golf Resort, Lajitas ✦ FM 170, 17 miles west of Hwy. 118 ☎ 432/424–5000 front desk, 877/525–4827 ⊕ www.lajitasgolfresort.com.*

$$
MODERN ITALIAN
Fodor'sChoice
★

✕ **La Trattoria Ristorante.** A classy if unpretentious bistro and espresso bar, La Trattoria opens at 11 for lunch specials ranging from panini sandwiches to freshly made soups and salads. Candlelight dinners offer antipasti and pasta dishes with an authentic tomato-basil sauce that lend a taste of Italy to the Chihuahuan Desert. If you prefer more traditional West Texas fare, there's Black Angus rib eye. There's a full wine and beer selection, and the restaurant is also vegetarian- and vegan-friendly. ■ TIP➜ It's a good idea to reserve a table on Friday and Saturday and during special events. ⑤ *Average main: $18 ⊠ 901 E. Holland Ave., Alpine ☎ 432/837–2200 ⊕ www.latrattoriacafe.com ✪ Closed Sun. and Mon. ⌚ Reservations essential.*

$$$
SOUTHWESTERN
Fodor'sChoice
★

✕ **Reata.** A favorite of many West Texans spending the day in Alpine, the Reata ("rope" in Spanish) feels both welcoming and upscale, with big, wooden tables and a pleasant rancher/cowboy vibe. It's a "howdy"-type place with a touch of discretion. Service is prompt but down-home. The menu features Tex-Mex accents such as tortilla soup and carne asada, while reflecting its Texas roots with dishes like calf fries and gravy. Of course, here's the beef—from a legendary ranch in the nearby Davis Mountains. The dessert tray is simply a work of art. ⑤ *Average main: $22 ⊠ 203 N. 5th St., Alpine ☎ 432/837–9232 ⊕ www.reata.net ✪ Closed Sun. ⌚ Reservations essential.*

WHERE TO STAY

IN THE PARK

$$
RESORT
FAMILY
Fodor'sChoice
★

▦ **Chisos Mountains Lodge.** With ranger talks just next door at the visitor center, miles of hiking trails to suit all levels of fitness, and plenty of wildlife nearby, these comfortable rooms—some of which have been nicely remodeled—are a great place for families with kids. **Pros:** refrigerators; central location for numerous hiking trails and scenic drives; free Wi-Fi in most rooms. **Cons:** no phones; no TVs. ⑤ *Rooms from: $138 ✦ At the end of Chisos Basin Rd., 10 miles southwest of Panther Junction ☎ 432/477–2291 desk, 877/386–4383 Forever Resorts ⊕ www.chisosmountainslodge.com ⤳ 72 rooms ◎ No meals.*

8

$$
HOTEL
Hotel El Capitan. Famed architect Henry Trost designed this Spanish Revival hotel, which takes its place among such other glamorous Trost landmarks as the Hotel Paisano (Marfa), the Holland Hotel (Alpine) and the Gage Hotel (Marathon). **Pros:** lovely architecture; freeway accessible; pet-friendly. **Cons:** a little farther from the park than some other hotels. ⑤ *Rooms from: $135* ⌧ *100 E. Broadway, Van Horn* ☎ *432/283–1220, 800/283–1220* ⊕ *www.hotelelcapitan.net* ↘ *30 rooms, 6 suites* ⏐⊙⏐ *Breakfast.*

$
RENTAL
FAMILY
Prude Ranch. A historic ranch established in 1897, Prude Ranch is a classic Western getaway for family reunions, church retreats, summer camp, business conferences, and other large gatherings, but also for couples just searching for seclusion. **Pros:** on a scenic loop that includes McDonald Observatory; quiet and peaceful. **Cons:** some of the quarters are rather plain; no phones or TVs in rooms. ⑤ *Rooms from: $95* ⊹ *Hwy. 118 just west of Davis Mountains State Park outside Fort Davis* ☎ *432/426–3202, 800/458–6232 reservations* ⊕ *www. prude-ranch.com* ↘ *41 cabins and lodges, 1 bunkhouse sleeping up to 20, 40 RV sites with full hookups* ⏐⊙⏐ *Some meals.*

OUTSIDE THE PARK

$
RENTAL
El Cosmico. An unusual setup that suits Marfa's quirky personality, El Cosmico is a nomadic draw for adventurers, with tents, teepees, campsites, a yurt, and 1950s-style trailers that provide surprising comfort. **Pros:** a laid-back spread where guests can do their own thing; "well-behaved" dogs are welcome. **Cons:** not suitable for most families. ⑤ *Rooms from: $85* ⌧ *802 S. Highland, Marfa* ☎ *432/729–1950* ⊕ *www.elcosmico.com* ↘ *25 various types of lodging, including 13 safari tents, 3 teepees, 1 yurt, and 8 classic, renovated trailers* ⏐⊙⏐ *No meals.*

$$$$
B&B/INN
Eve's Garden B&B. This whimsical, color-saturated property built with recycled building materials and lots of imagination creates an entirely singular lodging experience. **Pros:** one-of-a-kind property; food is organic and local. **Cons:** not for the average traveler. ⑤ *Rooms from: $210* ⌧ *200 N.W. 3rd St., Marathon* ☎ *432/386–4165* ⊕ *www. evesgarden.org* ↘ *7 rooms* ⏐⊙⏐ *Breakfast.*

$$$
HOTEL
Fodor's Choice
★
Gage Hotel. Cowboy, Indian, and Hispanic cultures are reflected in the furnishings of this picturesque, historic hotel, built in the 1920s facing the life-sustaining railroad tracks. **Pros:** amazing architecture; swimming pool; health center and spa; an intimate bar and restaurant. **Cons:** very popular in spring and fall, so it's often booked well in advance. ⑤ *Rooms from: $185* ⌧ *102 N.W. 1st St., Marathon* ☎ *432/386–4205, 800/884–4243* ⊕ *www.gagehotel.com* ↘ *45 rooms, 2 with shared bath; 3 houses* ⏐⊙⏐ *Breakfast.*

$$
HOTEL
Fodor's Choice
★
Holland Hotel. Once just a stop on the transcontinental railroad, the rancher-themed Holland Hotel is now a historic landmark still hung with its original sign on the main, bustling drag in downtown Alpine— just doors down from shops, cafés, and galleries. **Pros:** complimentary breakfast; elevator (not common to historic properties); pet-friendly; swimming pool available at the co-owned Maverick Inn. **Cons:** noise from nearby trains (earplugs provided in rooms). ⑤ *Rooms from:*

CLOSE UP

Best Campgrounds in Big Bend

The park's copious campsites are separated, roughly, into two categories—frontcountry and backcountry. Each of its four frontcountry sites, except Rio Grande Village RV Campground, has toilet facilities at a minimum. Far more numerous are the primitive backcountry sites, which require $10 permits from the visitor center. Primitive campsites with spectacular views are accessed via River Road, Glenn Springs, Old Ore Road, Paint Gap, Old Maverick Road, Grapevine Hills, Pine Canyon, and Croton Springs.

Chisos Basin Campground. Scenic views and cool shade are the highlights here. ⊠ *7 miles southwest of Chisos Basin Junction* ☏ *432/477–2251* ⊕ *www.reserveusa.com.*

Cottonwood Campground. This Castolon-area campground is a popular bird-watching spot near the Rio Grande. ⊠ *Off Ross Maxwell Scenic Dr., 22 miles southwest of Santa Elena Junction* ☏ *432/477–2251* ⊕ *www.reserveusa.com.*

Maverick Ranch RV Park. Owned by Lajitas Golf Resort, this layout has 101 RV sites and 18 primitive camping sites. RV connections are 30/50 amps, and there is a clubhouse, deli, hot showers, laundry facilities, picnic area, and hiking trails. It's also pet-friendly. ⊠ *FM 170* ☏ *432/424–5180* ⊕ *www.lajitasgolfresort.com*

Rio Grande Village Campground. A shady oasis, this campground is a birding hot spot. It's also a great site for kids and seniors, due to the ease of accessing facilities. There are 100 campsites at $14 a night, coin-operated showers, restrooms, and laundry. ⊠ *22 miles southeast of Panther Junction* ☏ *432/477–2293.*

Rio Grande Village RV Park. Often full during holidays, this is one of the best sites for families because of the minitheater and proximity to the hot spring, which is fun to soak in at night. There are 25 RV sites at $35 a night, full hookups. ⊠ *22 miles southeast of Panther Junction* ☏ *432/477–2293* ⊕ *www.reserveusa.com.*

8

$135 ⊠ *209 W. Holland Ave., Alpine* ☏ *432/837–2800, 800/535–8040* ⊕ *www.hollandhotel.net* ↗ *14 rooms, 11 suites* ⊙| *Breakfast.*

$$$
HOTEL
Fodor'sChoice
★
🏨 **Hotel Paisano.** Once the playground of Liz Taylor, Rock Hudson, and James Dean, who stayed here while filming *Giant,* the Paisano has maintained its glamour with glistening Mediterranean architecture, a fountain in the courtyard dining area, and dress and jewelry shops in downstairs hallways. **Pros:** Hollywood nostalgia; in the center of town. **Cons:** no elevator. Ⓢ *Rooms from: $159* ⊠ *207 N. Highland St., Marfa* ☏ *432/729–3669, 866/729–3669, 432/729–3779* ⊕ *www.hotelpaisano. com* ↗ *32 rooms, 9 suites* ⊙| *Breakfast.*

$$$$
RESORT
Fodor'sChoice
★
🏨 **Lajitas Golf Resort & Spa.** The former cavalry post–turned–ghost town is now a privately owned collection of Western-themed tourist attractions with a golf resort, spa, riding stables, convenience store, RV park, and hiking trails, adding up to the ritziest place to eat, shop, and overnight within 25 miles of the park. **Pros:** resort is a town unto itself, with many luxury activities. **Cons:** quite expensive. Ⓢ *Rooms from: $221*

✉ *Lajitas* ✛ *FM 170, 18 miles west of Hwy. 118* ☎ *432/424–5000, 877/525–4827* ⊕ *www.lajitasgolfresort.com* ⤳ *92 rooms, 10 suites on 5 properties* ⑩ *No meals.*

$$$

B&B/INN

🏚 **La Posada Milagro.** As rustic, yet comfortable, as Terlingua gets, this cozy compound has all the amenities and views that you could hope for in such a faraway outpost. **Pros:** homey feel. **Cons:** far from many services. ⑤ *Rooms from: $200* ✉ *100 Milagro Rd., Terlingua* ☎ *432/371–3044 front desk* ⊕ *www.laposadamilagro.net* ⤳ *3 rooms, 1 suite* ⑩ *No meals.*

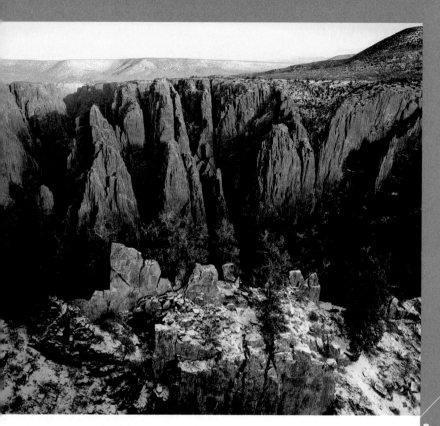

BLACK CANYON
OF THE GUNNISON
NATIONAL PARK

WELCOME TO BLACK CANYON OF THE GUNNISON NATIONAL PARK

TOP REASONS TO GO

★ **Sheer of heights:** Play it safe, but edge as close to the canyon rim as you dare and peer over into an abyss that's more than 2,700 feet deep in some places.

★ **Rapids transit:** Experienced paddlers can tackle Class V rapids and 50°F water with the occasional portage past untamable sections of the Gunnison River.

★ **Fine fishing:** Fish the rare Gold Medal Waters of the Gunnison. Of the 9,000 miles of trout streams in Colorado, only 168 miles have this "gold medal" distinction.

★ **Triple-park action:** Check out Curecanti National Recreation Area and Gunnison Gorge National Conservation Area, which bookend Black Canyon.

★ **Cliff-hangers:** Watch experts climb the Painted Wall—Colorado's tallest vertical wall at 2,250 feet—and other challenging rock faces.

TO GUNNISON GORGE NATIONAL CONSERVATION AREA

BLACK CANYON OF THE GUNNISON

0   1 mi

0   1 km

Warner Point

High Point

1 East Portal. The only way you can get down to the river via automobile in Black Canyon is on the steep East Portal Road. There's a campground and picnic area here, as well as fishing and trail access.

2 North Rim. If you want to access this side of the canyon from the south, expect a drive of up to three hours as you wind around the canyon. The area's remoteness and difficult location mean the North Rim is never crowded; the road is partially unpaved and closes in the winter. There's also a small ranger station here.

3 South Rim. This is the main area of the park. The park's only visitor center is here, along with a campground and a few picnic areas. The South Rim Road closes at Gunnison Point in the winter, when skiers and snowshoers take over.

KEY	
👥🏠	*Ranger Station*
⛰	*Campground*
🌲	*Picnic Area*
🍴	*Restaurant*
🏠	*Lodge*
🏃	*Trailhead*
👥	*Restrooms*
🌟	*Scenic Viewpoint*
┈┈┈	*Walking/Hiking Trails*

COLORADO
●

GETTING ORIENTED

Black Canyon of the Gunnison is a park of extremes—great depths, narrow widths, tall cliffs, and steep descents. It is not a large park, but it offers incredible scenery and unforgettable experiences, whether you're hiking, fishing, or just taking it all in from the car. The adjacent parks and other open spaces offer even more opportunity for adventure.

9

North Rim Road
(closed in winter)

TO CRAWFORD

North Vista Trail

North Rim Ranger Station

North Rim Campground

Chasm View Nature Trail

Chasm View

Painted Wall View

MESA INCLINADO

The Narrows View

Devils Lookout

Balanced Rock View

Dragon Point

Cedar Point

Island Peaks View

Sunset View

VERNAL MESA

Pulpit Rock Overlook

Kneeling Camel View

Gunnison Point

South Rim Road

Visitor Center

Tomichi Point

Deadhorse Trail

3 South Rim Campground

TO HWY 50 AND MONTROSE

347

East Portal Road

Gunnison River

East Portal

CURECANTI NATIONAL RECREATION AREA

Crystal Dam

Updated by
Kellee Katagi

The Black Canyon of the Gunnison River is one of Colorado's—and indeed the West's—most awe-inspiring places. A vivid testament to the powers of erosion, the canyon is roughly 2,000 feet deep. At its narrowest point, it spans 1,000 feet at the rim and only 40 feet at the bottom. The steep angles of the cliffs make it difficult for sunlight to fully break through during much of the day, and ever-present shadows blanket the canyon walls, leaving some places in almost perpetual darkness. No wonder it's called the "Black Canyon."

BLACK CANYON OF THE GUNNISON PLANNER

WHEN TO GO

Summer is the busiest season, with July experiencing the greatest crowds. However, a spring or fall visit gives you two advantages: fewer people and cooler temperatures. In summer, especially in years with little rainfall, daytime temperatures can reach into the 90s. A winter visit to the park brings even more solitude, as all but one section of campsites are shut down and only about 2 miles of South Rim Road, the park main road, are plowed.

November through March is when the snow hits, with an average of about 3 to 8 inches of it monthly. April through May and September and October are the rainiest, with about an inch of precipitation each month. June is generally the driest month. Temperatures at the bottom of the canyon are about 8 degrees warmer than at the rim.

AVG. HIGH/LOW TEMPS.

Jan.	Feb.	Mar.	Apr.	May	June
37/14	42/16	50/18	47/23	67/37	75/44
July	Aug.	Sept.	Oct.	Nov.	Dec.
84/51	81/50	72/42	62/31	48/23	37/12

FESTIVALS AND EVENTS

JULY–AUGUST **Main in Motion.** From 6–8:30 pm every Thursday in the summer, Main Street in Montrose is the place to be. Street performers and other artisans join Historic Downtown Montrose restaurants and shops to make for a pleasant evening stroll. ☏ 970/964–9304 ⊕ *www.montroseinmotion.com.*

JULY **Paonia Cherry Days.** One of Colorado's longest-running annual events, this small-town festival on the 4th of July includes a parade, food, crafts, sidewalk sales, and a variety of entertainment celebrating local cherry crops (and the other fruits that have made Paonia famous). ☏ 970/527–3886 ⊕ *www.paoniacherrydays.com.*

PLANNING YOUR TIME

BLACK CANYON OF THE GUNNISON IN ONE DAY

Pack a lunch and head to the canyon's South Rim, beginning with a stop at the **South Rim Visitor Center.** Before getting back into the car, take in your first view of Black Canyon from **Gunnison Point,** adjacent to the visitor center. Then set out on a driving tour of the 7-mile **South Rim Road,** allowing the rest of the morning to stop at the various viewpoints that overlook the canyon. Don't miss **Chasm View** and **Painted Wall View,** and be sure to stretch your legs along the short (0.4 mile round-trip) **Cedar Point Nature Trail.** If your timing is good, you'll reach **High Point,** the end of the road, around lunchtime.

After lunch, head out on **Warner Point Nature Trail** for an hour-long hike (1.5 miles round-trip). Then retrace your drive along South Rim Road back to the visitor center.

GETTING HERE AND AROUND

AIR TRAVEL

The Black Canyon of the Gunnison lies between the cities of Gunnison and Montrose, both of which have small regional airports.

CAR TRAVEL

The park has three roads. South Rim Road, reached by Route 347, is the primary thoroughfare and winds along the canyon's South Rim. From about late November to early April, the road is not plowed past the visitor center at Gunnison Point. North Rim Road, reached by Route 92, is usually open from May through Thanksgiving; in winter, the road is unplowed. On the park's south side, the serpentine East Portal Road descends abruptly to the Gunnison River below. The road is usually open from the beginning of May through the end of November. Because of the grade, vehicles or vehicle-trailer combinations longer than 22 feet are not permitted. The park has no public transportation.

PARK ESSENTIALS
PARK FEES AND PERMITS

Entrance fees are $15 per week per vehicle. Visitors entering on bicycle, motorcycle, or on foot pay $7 for a weekly pass. To access the inner canyon, you must pick up a wilderness permit (no fee).

PARK HOURS

The park is open 24/7 year-round. It's in the Mountain time zone.

CELL-PHONE RECEPTION

Cell-phone reception in the park is unreliable and sporadic. There are public telephones at South Rim Visitor Center and South Rim Campground.

EDUCATIONAL OFFERINGS
RANGER PROGRAMS

Junior Ranger Program. Kids of all ages can participate in this program with an activities booklet to fill in while exploring the park. Inquire at the South Rim Visitor Center.

WILDLIFE IN BLACK CANYON

You may spot peregrine falcons nesting in May and June, or other birds of prey such as red-tailed hawks, Cooper's hawks, and golden eagles circling overhead at any time of year. In summer, turkey vultures join the flying corps, and in winter, bald eagles. Mule deer, elk, and the very shy bobcat also call the park home. In spring and fall, you may see a porcupine among pinyon pines on the rims. Listen for the high-pitched chirp of the yellow-bellied marmot, which hangs out on sunny, rocky outcrops. Though rarely seen, mountain lions and black bears also live in the park.

RESTAURANTS

The park itself has no eateries, but nearby towns have choices ranging from traditional American to an eclectic café and bakery.

HOTELS

Black Canyon is devoid of hotels. Smaller hotels, some excellent B&Bs, and rustic lodges are nearby, as are a few of the larger chains. *Hotel reviews have been shortened. For full information, visit Fodors.com.*

WHAT IT COSTS				
	$	$$	$$$	$$$$
Restaurants	under $13	$13–$18	$19–$25	over $25
Hotels	under $121	$121–$170	$171–$230	over $230

Restaurant prices are the average cost of a main course at dinner or, if dinner is not served, at lunch. Hotel prices are the lowest cost of a standard double room in high season, excluding taxes and services charges.

VISITOR INFORMATION

Park Contact Information Black Canyon of the Gunnison National Park. ✉ *102 Elk Creek, Gunnison* ☎ *970/641–2337* ⊕ *www.nps.gov/blca.*

VISITOR CENTERS

North Rim Ranger Station. This small facility on the park's North Rim is open only in summer. Rangers can provide information and assistance and can issue permits for wilderness use and rock climbing. If rangers are out in the field, which they often are, guests can find directions for obtaining permits posted in the station. ⊠ *North Rim Rd., 11 miles from Rte. 92 turnoff* ☎ *970/641–2337* ☉ *Late May–Labor Day.*

South Rim Visitor Center. The park's only visitor center offers interactive exhibits and introductory films detailing the park's geology and wildlife. Inquire at the center about free guided tours and informational ranger programs. ✛ *1½ mile from the entrance station on South Rim Rd.* ☎ *970/249–1914* ☉ *Late May–early Sept., daily 8–6; early Sept.–late May, daily 8:30–4.*

EXPLORING

SCENIC DRIVES

The scenic South and North Rim roads offer deep and distant views into the canyon. Both also offer several lookout points and short hiking trails along the rim. The trails that go down into the canyon are steep and strenuous, and essentially unmarked, and so are reserved for experienced (and very fit) hikers.

East Portal Road. The only way to access the Gunnison River from the park by car is via this paved route, which drops approximately 2,000 feet down to the water in only 5 miles, giving it an extremely steep grade. Vehicles longer than 22 feet are not allowed on the road. If you're towing a trailer, you can unhitch it near the entrance to South Rim campground. The bottom of the road is actually in the adjacent Curecanti National Recreation Area. A tour of East Portal Road, with a brief stop at the bottom, takes about 45 minutes.

North Rim Road. Black Canyon's North Rim is much less frequented, but no less spectacular—the walls here are near vertical—than the South Rim. To reach the 15½-mile-long North Rim Road, take the signed turnoff from Route 92 about 3 miles south of Crawford. The road is paved for about the first 4 miles; the rest is gravel. After 11 miles, turn left at the intersection (the North Rim Campground is to the right). There are six overlooks along the road as it snakes along the rim's edge. Kneeling Camel, at the road's east end, provides the broadest view of the canyon. Set aside about two hours for a tour of the North Rim.

South Rim Road. This paved 7-mile stretch from Tomichi Point to High Point is the park's main road. The drive follows the canyon's level South Rim; 12 overlooks are accessible from the road, most via short gravel trails. Several short hikes along the rim also begin roadside. Allow between two and three hours round-trip.

SCENIC STOPS

The vast depths that draw thousands of visitors each year to Black Canyon have also historically prevented any extensive human habitation from taking root, so cultural attractions are largely absent here. But what the park lacks in historic sites it more than makes up for in scenery.

9

Chasm and Painted Wall Views. At the heart-in-your-throat Chasm viewpoint, the canyon walls plummet 1,820 feet to the river, but are only 1,100 feet apart at the top. As you peer down into the depths, keep in mind that this section is where the Gunnison River descends at its steepest rate, dropping 240 feet within the span of a mile. A few hundred yards farther is the best place from which to see Painted Wall, Colorado's tallest cliff. Pinkish swaths of pegmatite (a crystalline, granite-like rock) give the wall its colorful, marbled appearance. ✛ *Approximately 3½ miles from the Visitor Center on South Rim Rd.*

Narrows View. Look upriver from this North Rim viewing spot and you'll be able to see into the canyon's narrowest section, just a slot really, with only 40 feet between the walls at the bottom. The canyon is also taller (1,725 feet) here than it is wide at the rim (1,150 feet). ⊠ *North Rim Rd., first overlook past the ranger station.*

Warner Point. This viewpoint, at the end of the Warner Point Nature Trail, delivers awesome views of the canyon's deepest point (2,722 feet), plus the nearby San Juan and West Elk mountain ranges. ⊠ *End of Warner Point Nature Trail, westernmost end of South Rim Rd..*

> ### GOOD READS
>
> ■ *The Gunnison Country,* by Duane Vandenbusche, contains nearly 500 pages of historical photographs and essays on the park.
>
> ■ *The Essential Guide to Black Canyon of the Gunnison National Park,* by John Jenkins, is one of the definitive guides to the park.
>
> ■ The *South Rim Driving Tour Guide* is enlivened by David Halpern's evocative black-and-white images.
>
> ■ *A Kid's Guide to Exploring Black Canyon of the Gunnison National Park,* by Renee Skelton, is perfect for the 6–12 set.

SPORTS AND THE OUTDOORS

Recreational activities in Black Canyon run the gamut from short and easy nature trails to world-class (and experts-only) rock climbing and kayaking. The cold waters of the Gunnison River are well known to trout anglers.

BIRD-WATCHING

The sheer cliffs of Black Canyon, though not suited for human habitation, provide a great habitat for birds. Peregrine falcons, white-throated swifts, and other cliff-dwelling birds revel in the dizzying heights, while at river level you'll find American dippers foraging for food in the rushing waters. Canyon wrens, which nest in the cliffs, are more often heard than seen, but their hauntingly beautiful songs are unforgettable. Dusky grouse are common in the sagebrush areas above the canyon, and red-tailed and Cooper's hawks and turkey vultures frequent the canyon rims. The best times for birding are spring and early summer.

BOATING AND KAYAKING

FodorsChoice
★
With Class V rapids, the Gunnison River is one of the premier kayak challenges in North America. The spectacular 14-mile stretch of the river that passes through the park is so narrow in some sections that the rim seems to be closing up above your head. Once you're downstream from the rapids (and out of the park), the canyon opens up into what is called the Gunnison Gorge. The rapids ease considerably, and the trip becomes more of a quiet float on Class I to Class IV water.

Kayaking the river through the park requires a wilderness use permit (and lots of expertise), and rafting is not allowed. Access to the Gunnison Gorge is only by foot or horseback. However, several outfitters offer guided raft and kayak trips in the Gunnison Gorge and other sections of the Gunnison River.

For kayaking and rafting outfitters, see Area Activities in the What's Nearby section.

FISHING

The three dams built upriver from the park in Curecanti National Recreation Area have created prime trout fishing in the waters below. Certain restrictions apply: Only artificial flies and lures are permitted, and a Colorado fishing license is required for people aged 16 and older. Rainbow trout are catch-and-release only, and there are size and possession limits on brown trout (check at the visitor center). Most anglers access the river from the bottom of East Portal Road; an undeveloped trail goes along the riverbank for about three-quarters of a mile.

HIKING

All trails can be hot in summer and most don't receive much shade, so bring water, a hat, and plenty of sunscreen. Dogs are permitted, on leash, on Rim Rock, Cedar Point Nature, and Chasm View Nature trails, and at any overlook. Hiking into the inner canyon, while doable, is not for the faint of heart—or slight of step. Six named routes lead down to the river, but they are not maintained or marked. In fact, the park staff won't even call them trails; they refer to them as "controlled slides." These supersteep, rocky routes vary in one-way distance from 1 to 2.75 miles, and the descent can be anywhere from 1,800 to 2,722 feet. Your reward, of course, is a rare look at the bottom of the canyon and the fast-flowing Gunnison. ■TIP➜ Don't attempt an inner-canyon hike without plenty of water (the park's recommendation is one gallon per person, per day). For descriptions of the routes and the necessary permit to hike them, stop at the visitor center at the South Rim or North Rim ranger station. Dogs are not permitted in the inner canyon.

EASY

FAMILY **Cedar Point Trail.** This 0.4-mile round-trip interpretive trail leads out from South Rim Road to two overlooks. It's an easy stroll, and signs along the way detail the surrounding plants. *Easy.* ✚ *Trailhead: off South Rim Rd., 4¼ miles from South Rim Visitor Center.*

Deadhorse Trail. Despite its name, the 5-mile Deadhorse Trail is actually a pleasant hike, starting on an old service road from the Kneeling Camel View on the North Rim Road. The trail's farthest point provides the park's easternmost viewpoint. From this overlook, the canyon is much more open, with pinnacles and spires rising along its sides. *Easy.* ⊠ *Black Canyon of the Gunnison National Park* ✛ *Trailhead: at the southernmost end of North Rim Rd.*

MODERATE

Chasm View Nature Trail. The park's shortest trail (0.3 mile round-trip) starts at North Rim Campground and offers an impressive 50-yard walk right along the canyon rim as well as an eye-popping view of Painted Wall and Serpent Point. This is also an excellent place to spot raptors, swifts, and other birds. *Moderate.* ✛ *Trailhead: at North Rim Campground, 11¼ miles from Rte. 92.*

North Vista Trail. The round-trip hike to Exclamation Point is 3 miles; a more difficult foray to the top of 8,563-foot Green Mountain (a mesa, really) is 7 miles. The trail leads you along the North Rim; keep an eye out for especially gnarled pinyon pines—the North Rim is the site of some of the oldest groves of pinyons in North America, between 400 and 700 years old. *Moderate.* ✛ *Trailhead: at North Rim ranger station, off North Rim Rd., 11 miles from Rte. 92 turnoff.*

Fodor's Choice
★
Warner Point Nature Trail. The 1.5-mile round-trip hike starts from High Point. It provides fabulous vistas of the San Juan and West Elk mountains and Uncompahgre Valley. Warner Point, at trail's end, has the steepest drop-off from rim to river: a dizzying 2,722 feet. *Moderate.* ✛ *Trailhead: at the end of South Rim Rd.*

DIFFICULT

Oak Flat Loop Trail. This 2-mile loop is the most demanding of the South Rim hikes, as it brings you about 400 feet below the canyon rim. In places, the trail is narrow and crosses some steep slopes, but you won't have to navigate any steep drop-offs. Oak Flat is the shadiest of all the South Rim trails; small groves of aspen and thick stands of Douglas fir along the loop offer some respite from the sun. *Difficult.* ✛ *Trailhead: just west of the South Rim Visitor Center.*

HORSEBACK RIDING

Although its name might indicate otherwise, Deadhorse Trail is actually the only trail in the park where horses are allowed. The trail is an easy-to-moderate 5-mile loop that begins east of North Rim Road. Horses are not allowed on the South Rim, and can be on the North Rim only on the Deadhorse Trail, in the North Rim Campground, or on the North Rim Road during transport in a trailer.

Black Canyon of the Gunnison has no facilities geared toward horses. If you bring your own horse, go to the end of North Rim Road and park your trailer at Kneeling Camel Overlook to access Deadhorse Trail. No permit is required.

TOURS

Elk Ridge Ranch and Trail Rides. You can take 90-minute and two-hour rides at this ranch. Elk Ridge also offers a half-day ride to the rim of the Black Canyon. ⊠ *10203 Bostwick Park Rd., Montrose* ☎ *970/240–6007* ☉ *May–Sept., daily.*

ROCK CLIMBING

For expert rock climbers, the sheer cliffs of the Black Canyon represent one of Colorado's premier big-wall challenges. Some routes can take several days to complete, with climbers sleeping on narrow ledges, or "portaledges." Though there's no official guide to climbing in the park, reports from individual climbers are kept on file at the South Rim Visitor Center. Nesting birds of prey may lead to wall closure at certain times of year.

Rock climbing in the park is for experts only, but you can do some bouldering at the Marmot Rocks area, about 100 feet south of South Rim Road between Painted Wall and Cedar Point overlooks (park at Painted Wall). Four boulder groupings offer a variety of routes rated from easy to very difficult; a pamphlet with a diagrammed map of the area is available at the South Rim Visitor Center.

TOURS AND OUTFITTERS

Irwin Guides. Intermediate and expert climbers can take full-day rock-climbing guided tours on routes from 6 to 15 pitches in length. ⊠ *330 Belleview Ave., Crested Butte* ☎ *970/349–5430* ⊕ *www.irwinguides. com* ✆ *From $195 per person, per day.*

Skyward Mountaineering. Intermediate and advanced climbers can take lessons and guided tours on the Black Canyon's fabled climbs with this internationally certified guide and outfitter. ⊠ *2392 Ridgeway Ct., Grand Junction* ☎ *541/639–9913* ⊕ *www.skywardmountaineering.com* ✆ *From $500 per day* ☉ *Closed Dec.–Feb.*

WINTER SPORTS

From late November to early April, South Rim Road is not plowed past the visitor center, offering park guests a unique opportunity to cross-country ski or snowshoe on the road. The Park Service also grooms a cross-country ski trail and marks a snowshoe trail through the woods, both starting at the visitor center. It's possible to ski or snowshoe on the unplowed North Rim Road, too, but it's about 4 miles from where the road closes, through sagebrush flats, to the canyon rim.

WHAT'S NEARBY

While not totally out of the way, Black Canyon of the Gunnison and its two neighboring recreation playgrounds—the Curecanti National Recreation Area and the Gunnison Gorge National Conservation Area—are far enough removed from civilization (i.e., big cities) to maintain a sense of getting-away-from-it-all isolation. They're a good 250 miles from Denver, and 240 miles from Colorado Springs, and touristy towns such as Durango and Telluride are 120 miles and 80 miles away, respectively. Colorado National Monument is about 85 miles distant.

NEARBY TOWNS

The primary gateway to Black Canyon is **Montrose,** 15 miles west of the park. The legendary Ute chief, Ouray, and his wife, Chipeta, lived near here in the late 1800s. Today, Montrose straddles the important agricultural and mining regions along the Uncompahgre River, and is the area's main shopping hub. The closest town to Black Canyon's North Rim is **Crawford,** about 3 miles from the entrance to the North Rim Road, a small hillside enclave amid the sheep and cattle ranches of the North Fork Valley with a small downtown area. Northeast on Route 92 (20 miles) is **Paonia,** a unique and charming blend of the old and new West. Here, career environmentalists and hippie types who have escaped the mainstream mingle with longtime ranchers, miners, and fruit growers. Eleven miles northwest of Crawford on Route 92 is the small ranching and mining community of **Hotchkiss.** The trappings and sensibilities of the Old West are here, from cowboy bars and fields of livestock to the annual summertime rodeo.

VISITOR INFORMATION

Visitor Information **Crawford Area Chamber of Commerce.** ⊠ *Crawford* ☎ *970/921–4000* ⊕ *www.crawfordcountry.org.* **Hotchkiss Community Chamber of Commerce.** ⊠ *Hotchkiss* ☎ *970/872–3226* ⊕ *www.hotchkisschamber.com.* **Paonia Chamber of Commerce.** ⊠ *130 Grand Ave., Paonia* ☎ *970/527–3886* ⊕ *www.paoniachamber.com.*

NEARBY ATTRACTIONS

Fodor's Choice ★ **Colorado National Monument.** Sheer red-rock cliffs open to 23 miles of steep canyons and thin monoliths that sprout as high as 450 feet from the floor of Colorado National Monument. This vast tract of rugged, ragged terrain was declared a national monument in 1911 at the urging of an eccentric visionary named John Otto. Now it's popular for rock climbing, horseback riding, cross-country skiing, biking, and camping. Cold Shivers Point is just one of the many dramatic overlooks along **Rim Rock Drive,** a 23-mile scenic route with breathtaking views. The town of Fruita, at the base of Colorado National Monument, is a haven for mountain bikers and hikers. It makes a great center for exploring the area's canyons—whether from the seat of a bike or the middle of a raft, heading for a leisurely float trip. ⊠ *Fruita* ☎ *970/858–3617* ⊕ *www.nps.gov/colm* ◪ *$10 per wk per vehicle. Visitors entering on bicycle, motorcycle, or foot pay $5 for weekly pass.*

Crawford State Park. The focus of this 337-acre park is Crawford Reservoir, created in 1963 when a dam was built to increase the supply of irrigated water to the surrounding ranches and farms. Boating and waterskiing are permitted on the reservoir, as are swimming and fishing (the lake is stocked with rainbow trout). The park has a 1-mile wheelchair-accessible hiking trail along with the primitive ½-mile

9

Indian Fire Nature Trail, which runs along the reservoir on the park's west side. ⊠ *1 mile south of Crawford, 40468 Hwy. 92, Crawford* ☎ *970/921–5721* ⊕ *parks.state.co.us/Parks/crawford* ✉ *$7.*

Curecanti National Recreation Area. This sprawling recreation area, named in honor of a Ute Indian sub-chief, stretches for 40 miles along U.S. 50, between Gunnison and Montrose. It encompasses three reservoirs along the Gunnison River: Blue Mesa, Colorado's largest lake at almost 20 miles long, and Morrow Point and Crystal, fjord-like reservoirs in the upper Black Canyon of the Gunnison. All three are excellent spots for fishing, boating, and paddling, although only Blue Mesa offers boat ramps. You'll find great fly-fishing east of the Blue Mesa Reservoir, on the Gunnison River. Camping and hiking are also available. The Elk Creek Visitor Center on U.S. 50 is open year-round for trip planning, boat-tour reservations, and pass/permit sales; call for hours. Entrance to the recreation area is free, unless you use the east entrance, which is inside Black Canyon of the Gunnison National Park ($15 entrance fee). ⊠ *102 Elk Creek, Gunnison* ☎ *970/641–2337* ⊕ *www.nps.gov/cure* ✉ *Free.*

AREA ACTIVITIES

SPORTS AND THE OUTDOORS
BOATING
Lake Fork Marina. Located on the western end of Blue Mesa Reservoir off U.S. 92, the Lake Fork Marina rents all types of boats. If you have your own, there's a ramp at the marina and slips for rent. ⊠ *Off U.S. 92, near Lake Fork Campground, Gunnison* ☎ *970/641–3048* ⊕ *www.thebluemesa.com.*

Morrow Point Boat Tours. Starting in neighboring Curecanti National Recreation Area, these guided tours run twice daily (except Tuesday) in the summer, at 10 am and 12:30 pm. Morrow Point Boat Tours take passengers on a 90-minute tour via pontoon boat, and require a 1-mile walk to the boat dock. Reservations are required. ⊠ *Pine Creek Trail and Boat Dock, U.S. 50, milepost 130, 25 miles west of Gunnison, Gunnison* ☎ *970/641–2337* ✉ *$16.*

KAYAKING AND RAFTING
Dvorak Expeditions. This outfitter offers rafting trips on the Dolores River that cover Class II to Class IV rapids and last up to 10 days. Or you can book a "Build-Your-Own-Adventure" trip that pairs rafting with other adventurous options, including ziplining, mountain biking, horseback riding, and rock climbing. ⊠ *17921 U.S. 285, Nathrop* ☎ *719/539–6851, 800/824–3795* ⊕ *www.dvorakexpeditions.com* ✉ *From $122.*

WHERE TO EAT

IN THE PARK

PICNIC AREAS

There are a variety of picnic areas at Black Canyon of the Gunnison, all with pit toilets; all are closed when it snows.

East Portal. This picnic area, located at the bottom of the canyon, accommodates large groups. There are tables, fire grates, bathrooms, and a large shaded shelter. ✉ *East Portal Rd. at the Gunnison River.*

High Point. When the sun is unforgiving, this overlook offers more shade than most of the other picnic areas. There are tables and bathrooms but no fire grates. ✉ *West end of South Rim Rd..*

North and South Rim campgrounds. Feel free to use unoccupied camping sites for picnicking. There are tables, fire grates, and bathrooms. ✉ *North Rim: West end of North Rim Rd.; South Rim: About 1 mile east of South Rim Visitor Center on South Rim Rd..*

OUTSIDE THE PARK

MONTROSE

$$ ✕ **Camp Robber.** This simply decorated restaurant serves some of Montrose's most creative cuisine. Start with the famous green-chili chicken and potato soup, and follow with entrées such as spicy shrimp *chimayo* (New Mexican chili pepper) or the house specialty: pork medallions covered with pistachios. At lunch, salads with housemade dressings, hearty sandwiches, and blue-corn enchiladas fuel hungry hikers. The Sunday brunch will leave you happily stuffed, and locals flock here for the delicious homemade desserts. When the weather permits, you can sit on the shaded patio. ■ **TIP→** The green and red chili is mild, so ask them to spice it up if you prefer your chili sauce with a kick. ⑤ *Average main: $15* ✉ *1515 Ogden Rd., Montrose* ☎ *970/240–1590* ⊕ *www. camprobber.com* ⊗ *No dinner Sun.*

SOUTHWESTERN

PAONIA

$$ ✕ **Flying Fork Cafe & Bakery.** This charming café serves tasty Italian fare in a comfortable dining room and, in the summer, a shady outdoor garden. An assortment of artisan breads and pastries is sold in the small bakery at the front of the building, with a growing selection of gluten-free items. Local ingredients are used whenever possible to create dishes like braised Colorado lamb shank or farfalle in a sauce of smoked chicken, pear, and Gorgonzola. The homemade fettuccine noodles are delicious, and the individual pizzas, made with whole-wheat flour and fresh basil and mozzarella, are good for smaller appetites. ⑤ *Average main: $18* ✉ *101 3rd St., Paonia* ☎ *970/527–3203* ⊕ *www. flyingforkcafe.com* ⊗ *Closed Mon.*

ITALIAN

9

CLOSE UP

Best Campgrounds in Black Canyon of the Gunnison

There are three campgrounds in Black Canyon National Park. The small North Rim Campground is first come, first served, and is closed in the winter. Vehicles longer than 35 feet are discouraged from this campground. South Rim Campground is considerably larger, and has a loop that's open year-round. Reservations are accepted in South Rim Loops A and B. Power hookups only exist in Loop B. The East Portal campground is at the bottom of the steep East Portal Road and is open whenever the road is open. It offers 15 first-come, first-served tent sites in a pretty setting. Water has to be trucked up to the campgrounds, so use it in moderation; it's shut off in mid-to-late September. Generators are not allowed at South Rim and are highly discouraged on the North Rim.

East Portal Campground. Its location next to the Gunnison River makes it perfect for fishing. ⊠ *East Portal Rd., 5 miles from the main entrance.*

North Rim Campground. This small campground, nestled amid pine trees, offers the basics along the quiet North Rim. ⊠ *North Rim Rd., 11¼ miles from Rte. 92.*

South Rim Campground. Stay on the canyon rim at this main campground right inside the park entrance. Loops A and C have tent sites only. The RV hookups are in Loop B, and those sites are priced higher than those in other parts of the campground. It's possible to camp here year-round (Loop A stays open all winter), but the loops are not plowed, so you'll have to hike in with your tent. ⊠ *South Rim Rd., 1 mile from the visitor center.*

WHERE TO STAY

OUTSIDE THE PARK

MONTROSE

$ **Red Arrow Inn & Suites.** This low-key establishment is a great value,
HOTEL with very reasonable prices for one of the nicest lodgings in the area, mainly because of the large, pretty rooms filled with handsome wood furnishings. **Pros:** spacious and comfortable rooms; good breakfast; pleasant pool. **Cons:** motel-style entrances; next to busy street. $ *Rooms from: $89* ⊠ *1702 E. Main St., Montrose* ☎ *970/249–9641* ⊕ *www.redarrowinn.com* ⇶ *57 rooms, 2 suites* ❑ *Breakfast.*

BRYCE CANYON
NATIONAL PARK

WELCOME TO BRYCE CANYON NATIONAL PARK

TOP REASONS TO GO

★ **Hoodoo heaven:** The brashly colored, gravity-defying limestone tentacles reaching skyward—known locally as "hoodoos"— are the main attraction of Bryce Canyon.

★ **Famous fresh air:** With some of the clearest skies anywhere, the park offers views that, on a clear day, extend 200 miles and into three states.

★ **Spectacular sunrises and sunsets:** The deep orange and crimson hues of the park's hoodoos are intensified by the light of the sun at either end of the day.

★ **Dramatically different zones:** From the highest point of the rim to the canyon base, the park spans 2,000 feet, so you can explore three unique climatic zones: spruce-fir forest, ponderosa-pine forest, and pinyon pine–juniper forest.

★ **Snowy fun:** Bryce gets an average of 95 inches of snowfall a year, and is a popular destination for skiers and snowshoe enthusiasts.

1 Bryce Amphitheater. It's the heart of the park. From here you can access the historic Bryce Canyon Lodge as well as Sunrise, Sunset, and Inspiration points. Walk to Bryce Point at sunrise to view the mesmerizing collection of massive hoodoos known as Silent City.

2 Under-the-Rim Trail. This 23-mile trail is the best way to reach Bryce Canyon backcountry. It can be a challenging three-day adventure or a half day of fun via one of the four access points from the main road. A handful of primitive campgrounds lines the route.

3 Rainbow and Yovimpa Points. The end of the scenic road, but not of the scenery, here you can hike a trail to see some ancient bristlecone pines and look south into Grand Staircase–Escalante National Monument.

UTAH

Bryce Canyon Airport

TO HWY 89 & ZION NAT'L PARK

Ruby's Inn

TO ESCALANTE

Tropic Canyon

Pink Cliffs

Rim Trail

Fairyland Point

Fairyland Loop Trail

Visitor Center

Sunrise Point

Bryce Canyon Lodge

Queen's Garden

Sunset Point

Silent City

1 ◆ Bryce Amphitheater

Bryce Canyon

Inspiration Point

Rim Trail

Bryce Point

PAUNSAUGUNT PLATEAU

Swamp Canyon

Paria View

Pink Cliffs

Main Park Rd

Swamp Canyon

Under-the-Rim Trail

2 Under-the-Rim Trail

0   2 mi

0   2 km

Piracy Point

Fairview Point

Natural Bridge

Pink Cliffs

Agua Canyon

Ponderosa Canyon

Under-the-Rim Trail

Black Birch Canyon

Bristlecone Loop Trail

Rainbow Point

3 Yovimpa Point

Pink Cliffs

Riggs Spring Trail

KEY

🏠	Ranger Station
⛺	Campground
🌲	Picnic Area
🍴	Restaurant
🏨	Lodge
🚶	Trailhead
🚻	Restrooms
⚹	Scenic Viewpoint
⋯⋯	Walking/Hiking Trails

GETTING ORIENTED

Bryce Canyon National Park actually isn't a single canyon, but rather a series of natural amphitheaters on the eastern edge of the Paunsaugunt Plateau. The park's scenic drive runs along a formation known as the Pink Cliffs and offers more than a dozen amazing overlooks. Many visitors drive to the end of the 18-mile road and turn around before allowing their jaws to drop in wonder. (It's practical, too, as the scenic overlooks will then be on the right side of the road, making it easy to pull over.) The main park road leads to the most popular hiking trails, which wind their way down into the canyons. A handful of roads veers to the east of the scenic drive to access other points of interest. As relief from the frequent heavy (and slow) traffic during the high season of summer, consider riding in one of the park's shuttle buses.

10

Updated
by Mike
Weatherford

A land that captures the imagination and the heart, Bryce is a favorite among Utah's national parks. Although its splendor had been well known for decades, Bryce Canyon wasn't designated a national park until 1928. The park is named for Ebenezer Bryce, a pioneer cattleman and the first permanent settler in the area. His description of the landscape not being hospitable to cows has oft been repeated. Even more than his famous quote, however, Bryce Canyon is known for its fanciful "hoodoos," best viewed at sunrise or sunset, when the light plays off the red rock.

In geological terms, Bryce is actually an amphitheater, not a canyon. The hoodoos in the amphitheater took on their unusual shapes because the top layer of rock— "cap rock"—is harder than the layers below it. If erosion undercuts the soft rock beneath the cap too much, the hoodoo will tumble. Bryce continues to evolve today, but the hoodoos are a permanent feature; old ones may die, but new ones are constantly forming as the amphitheater rim recedes.

BRYCE CANYON PLANNER

WHEN TO GO

Around Bryce Canyon National Park and the nearby Cedar Breaks National Monument area, elevations approach and surpass 9,000 feet, making for temperamental weather, intermittent and seasonal road closures due to snow, and downright cold nights well into June. The air is cooler on the rim of the canyon than it is at lower altitudes. ■TIP➔ **If you choose to see Bryce Canyon in summer, you'll be visiting with the rest of the world. During these months, traffic on the main road can be crowded with cars following slow-moving RVs, so consider taking one of the park shuttle buses.**

If it's solitude you're looking for, come to Bryce any time between October and March. The park is open all year long, so if you come during the cooler months you might just have a trail all to yourself.

AVG. HIGH/LOW TEMPS.

Jan.	Feb.	Mar.	Apr.	May	June
39/15	39/17	45/23	54/29	64/37	75/45
July	Aug.	Sept.	Oct.	Nov.	Dec.
80/53	80/50	70/42	58/32	45/23	36/15

FESTIVALS AND EVENTS

FEBRUARY
FAMILY

Bryce Canyon Winter Festival. This event at the Best Western Ruby's Inn features cross-country ski races, snow-sculpting contests, ski archery, and ice-skating. Clinics to hone skills such as snowshoeing and photography also take place, and there's entertainment, too. ☎ *435/834–5341* ⊕ *www.rubysinn.com.*

Quilt Walk Festival. During the bitter winter of 1864, Panguitch residents set out over the mountains to fetch provisions from the town of Parowan, 40 miles away. Legend says the men, frustrated and ready to turn back, laid a quilt on the snow and knelt to pray. Soon they realized the quilt had kept them from sinking into the snow. Spreading quilts before them as they walked, leapfrog style, the men traveled to Parowan and back. This three-day event in June commemorates the event with quilting classes, a tour of pioneer homes, tractor pull, dinner-theater, and other events. ☎ *435/676–8585* ⊕ *www.quiltwalk.org.*

Fodor's Choice
★

Utah Shakespeare Festival. For more than 50 years Cedar City has gone Bard-crazy, staging productions of Shakespeare's plays June through October in theaters both indoors and outdoors at Southern Utah University. The Tony award–winning regional theater offers literary seminars, backstage tours, cabarets featuring festival actors, and an outdoor preshow with Elizabethan performers. A new center for the arts, including the open-air Engelstad Shakespeare Theatre, is expected to make its debut during the 2016 season. It helps to reserve in advance as many performances sell out. ☎ *435/586–7878* ⊕ *www.bard.org.*

PLANNING YOUR TIME

BRYCE CANYON IN ONE DAY

Begin your day at the **visitor center** to get an overview of the park and to purchase books and maps. Watch the 20-minute film and peruse exhibits about the natural and cultural history of Bryce Canyon. Then, drive to the historic **Bryce Canyon Lodge.** From here, stroll along the relaxing **Rim Trail.** If you have the time and stamina to walk into the amphitheater, the portion of the Rim Trail near the lodge gets you to the starting point for either of the park's two essential hikes, the **Navajo Loop Trail** from **Sunset Point** or the **Queen's Garden Trail** that connects Sunset to **Sunrise Point.**

Afterward (or if you skip the hike), drive the 18-mile **main park road,** stopping at the overlooks along the way. Allowing for traffic, and if you stop at all 13 overlooks, this drive will take you between two and three hours.

10

If you have the time for more walking, a short, rolling hike along the **Bristlecone Loop Trail** at Rainbow Point rewards you with spectacular views and a cool walk through a forest of bristlecone pines. If you don't have time to drive the 18 miles to the end of the park, skip Bryce Canyon Lodge and drive 2 miles from the visitor center to **Inspiration Point** and then to the next overlook, **Bryce Point.**

End your day with sunset at Inspiration Point or dinner at Bryce Canyon Lodge. As you leave the park, stop at **Ruby's Inn** for American Indian jewelry, souvenirs for the kids, and groceries or snacks for the road.

GETTING HERE AND AROUND

AIR TRAVEL

The nearest commercial airport to Bryce Canyon is 80 miles west in Cedar City, Utah.

BUS TRAVEL

A shuttle bus system operates in Bryce Canyon from late April through September. Buses start at 8 am and run every 10 to 15 minutes, and are free with your admission fee. The route begins at Ruby's Inn and Ruby's Campground outside the park entrance and stops at the visitor center, lodge, campgrounds, and all the main overlooks and trailheads.

CAR TRAVEL

The closest major cities to Bryce Canyon are Salt Lake City and Las Vegas, each about 270 miles away. The park is reached via Route 63, just 3 miles south of the junction with Highway 12. You can see the park's highlights by driving along the well-maintained road running the length of the main scenic area. Bryce has no restrictions on automobiles on the main road, but in the summer you may encounter heavy traffic and full parking lots.

PARK ESSENTIALS

PARK FEES

The entrance fee is $30 per vehicle for a seven-day pass and $15 for pedestrians or bicyclists. The entrance fee includes unlimited use of the park shuttle. An annual Bryce Canyon park pass, good for one year from the date of purchase, costs $35. If you leave your private vehicle outside the park—at the shuttle staging area or Ruby's Inn—the one-time entrance fee, including transportation on the shuttle, is $30 per party.

A $5 backcountry permit, available from the visitor center, is required for camping in the park's interior, allowed only on Under-the-Rim Trail and Rigg's Spring Loop, both south of Bryce Point. Campfires are not permitted.

PARK HOURS

The park is open 24/7, year-round. It's in the Mountain time zone.

CELL-PHONE RECEPTION

Cell-phone reception is hit-and-miss in the park, with the visitor center and lodge your best bet. If you're getting reception, take advantage of it and make your calls; you may not have another chance. Bryce Canyon Lodge, Bryce Canyon Pines General Store, Ruby's Inn, Sunset Campground, and the visitor center all have public telephones.

EDUCATIONAL OFFERINGS
RANGER PROGRAMS

Campfire and Auditorium Programs. Bryce Canyon's natural diversity comes alive in the park's North Campground amphitheater, the Visitor Center Theater, or in the Bryce Canyon Lodge Auditorium. Lectures, multimedia programs, and ranger walks introduce you to geology, astronomy, wildlife, history, and many other topics related to Bryce Canyon and the West. ☎ 435/834–5322.

Full Moon Hike. Rangers lead guided hikes on the nights around each full moon (two per month May–October). You must wear heavy-traction shoes, and reserve a spot on the day of the hike. In peak season the tickets are distributed through a lottery system on the day of the hike. ⊕ www.nps.gov/brca/planyourvisit/fullmoonhikes.htm.

Geology Talk. Rangers regularly host discussions about the long geological history of Bryce Canyon; they are nearly always held at Sunset Point. Talks are free and last 30 minutes.

FAMILY **Junior Ranger Program.** Children ages three and over can sign up to be Junior Rangers at the Bryce Canyon Visitor Center. The park takes that title seriously, so kids have to complete several activities in their free Junior Ranger booklet, as well as collect some litter, and attend a ranger program. Allow three to six hours for all this. Ask a ranger about each day's schedules of events and topics, or look for postings at the visitor center, Bryce Canyon Lodge, and campground bulletin boards.

Fodor's Choice **Night Sky Program.** City folk are lucky to see 2,500 stars in their artifi-
★ cially illuminated skies, but out here among the hoodoos you see three times as many. The Night Sky Program includes low-key astronomy lectures and multimedia presentations, followed by telescope viewing (weather permitting). The program is typically offered on Tuesday, Thursday, and Saturday, May–September. Check at the visitor center for locations, times, and other details. ☎ 435/834–4747 ☑ Free.

Rim Walk. Join a park ranger for a ½-mile, hour-long stroll along the gorgeous rim of Bryce Canyon starting at the Sunset Point overlook. Reservations are not required for the walk, which is usually offered daily from May to September. Start time is usually 5 pm. Check at the visitor center for details. ☑ Free

RESTAURANTS

Dining options in the park proper are limited to Bryce Canyon Lodge; the nearby Ruby's Inn complex is your best eating bet before you pay to enter the park. The restaurants in nearby locales tend to be of the meat-and-potatoes variety. Utah's drinking laws can be confusing, so ask your server what is available: beer is more common than wine and spirits.

HOTELS

Lodging options in and around Bryce Canyon include both rustic and modern amenities, but all fill up fast in summer. Bryce Canyon Lodge is the only hotel inside the park, but there are a number of options in Bryce Canyon City, just north of the park's entrance. Panguitch and Tropic are small towns nearby with good options for budget and

10

CLOSE UP
Plants and Wildlife in Bryce Canyon

Due to elevations approaching 9,000 feet, many of Bryce Canyon's 400 plant species are unlike those you'll see at less lofty places. Look at exposed slopes and you might catch a glimpse of the pygmy pinyon, or the gnarled, 1,000-year-old bristlecone pine. At lower altitudes are the Douglas fir, ponderosa pine, and the quaking aspen, sitting in groves of twinkling leaves. No fewer than three kinds of sagebrush—big, black, and fringed—grow here, as well as the blue columbine.

Mule deer and chipmunks are common companions on the trails and are used to human presence. You might also catch a glimpse of the endangered Utah prairie dog. Give them a wide berth; they may be cute, but they bite. Other animals include elk, black-tailed jackrabbits, and the desert cottontail. More than 170 species of bird live in the park or pass through as a migratory stop. Bird-watchers are often rewarded handsomely for their vigilance: eagles, peregrine falcons, and even the rare California condor have all been spotted in the park.

last-minute travelers. *Hotel reviews have been shortened. For full information, visit Fodors.com.*

WHAT IT COSTS				
	$	$$	$$$	$$$$
Restaurants	under $13	$13–$20	$21–$30	over $30
Hotels	under $101	$101–$150	$151–$200	over $200

Restaurant prices are the average cost of a main course at dinner, or if dinner is not served, at lunch. Hotel prices are the average cost of a standard double room in high season, excluding taxes and service charges.

VISITOR INFORMATION
Park Contact Information Bryce Canyon National Park. ☎ *435/834–5322* ⊕ *www.nps.gov/brca.*

VISITOR CENTER
Bryce Canyon Visitor Center. Even if you're anxious to hit the hoodoos, the visitor center, just to your right after the park-entry pay station, is the best place to start if you want to know what you're looking at and how it got there. Rangers staff a counter where you can ask questions or let them map out an itinerary of "must-sees" based on your time and physical abilities. There are also multimedia exhibits, books, maps, and backcountry camping permits for sale. First aid, emergency, and lost-and-found services are offered here, along with free Wi-Fi. Do all your phone business here; it may be the last place in the park where you get cell reception. ✉ *Hwy. 63* ☎ *435/834–5322* ⊕ *www.nps.gov/brca* ☉ *May–Sept., daily 8–8; Apr. and Oct., daily 8–6; Nov.–Mar., daily 8–4:30.*

EXPLORING

SCENIC DRIVES

Fodor's Choice ★ **Main Park Road.** Following miles of canyon rim, this thoroughfare gives access to more than a dozen scenic overlooks between the park entrance and Rainbow Point. Major overlooks are rarely more than a few minutes' walk from the parking areas, and many let you see more than 100 miles on clear days. Remember that all overlooks lie east of the road. To keep things simple, proceed to the southern end of the park and stop at the overlooks on your northbound return; they will all be on the right side of the road. Allow two to three hours to travel the entire 36-mile round-trip. The road is open year-round, but may close temporarily after heavy snowfalls. Keep your eyes open for wildlife as you drive. Trailers are not allowed at Bryce Point and Paria View, but you can park them at the parking lot across the road from the visitor center. RVs can drive throughout the park, but vehicles longer than 25 feet are not allowed at Paria View. ⊠ *Bryce Canyon National Park.*

HISTORIC SITES

Bryce Canyon Lodge. The lodge's architect, Gilbert Stanley Underwood, was a national park specialist, having designed lodges at Zion and Grand Canyon before turning his T-square to Bryce in 1923. The results are worth a visit as this National Historic Landmark has been faithfully restored, right down to the lobby's huge limestone fireplace, and log and wrought-iron chandelier. Inside the historic building are a restaurant and gift shop, as well as plenty of information on park activities. The lodge operation includes several historic log cabins nearby on the wooded grounds, just a short walk from the rim trail. ⊠ *Hwy. 63* ☎ *435/834–8700.*

SCENIC STOPS

10

Agua Canyon. This overlook in the southern section of the park, 12 miles south of the park entrance, has a nice view of several standout hoodoos. Look for the top-heavy formation called the Hunter, which actually has a few small hardy trees growing on its cap. As the rock erodes, the park evolves; snap a picture because the Hunter may look different the next time you visit. ⊠ *Bryce Canyon National Park.*

Fairyland Point. Best seen as you exit the park, this scenic overlook adjacent to Boat Mesa, ½ mile north of the visitor center and a mile off the main park road, has splendid views of Fairyland Amphitheater and its delicate, fanciful forms. The Sinking Ship and other formations stand before the grand backdrop of the Aquarius Plateau and distant Navajo Mountain. Nearby is the Fairyland Loop trailhead; it's a stunning five-hour hike in summer and a favorite of snowshoers in winter. ⊠ *Off Hwy. 63.*

Inspiration Point. Not far (1½ miles) east along the Rim Trail from Bryce Point is Inspiration Point, site of a wonderful vista on the main

amphitheater and one of the best places in the park to see the sunset. (You will have plenty of company and hear a variety of languages as the sun goes down.) ⊠ *Inspiration Point Rd.*

Natural Bridge. Formed over millions of years by wind, water, and chemical erosion, this 85-foot rusty-orange arch formation—one of several rock arches in the park—is an essential photo op. Beyond the parking lot lies a rare stand of aspen trees, their leaves twinkling in the wind. Watch out for distracted drivers at this stunning viewpoint. ⊠ *Off Hwy. 63, 11 miles south of park entrance.*

Rainbow and Yovimpa Points. Separated by less than half a mile, Rainbow and Yovimpa points offer two fine panoramas facing opposite directions. Rainbow Point's best view is to the north overlooking the southern rim of the amphitheater and giving a glimpse of Grand Staircase–Escalante National Monument. Yovimpa Point's vista spreads out to the south. On a clear day you can see all the way to Arizona, 100 miles away. Yovimpa Point also has a shady and quiet picnic area with tables and restrooms. You can hike between them on the easy Bristlecone Loop Trail or tackle the more strenuous 8¾-mile Riggs Spring Loop Trail, which passes the tallest point in the park. This is the outermost auto stop on the main road, so visitors often drive here first and make it their starting point, then work their way back to the main gate. ⊠ *Off Hwy. 63, 18 miles south of park entrance.*

Fodor's Choice ★ **Sunrise Point.** Named for its stunning views at dawn, this overlook is a short walk from Bryce Canyon Lodge, 2 miles south of the park entrance, and so one of the park's most popular stops. It's also the trailhead for the Queen's Garden Trail and the Fairyland Loop Trail. You have to descend the Queen's Garden Trail to get a regal glimpse of **Queen Victoria,** a hoodoo that appears to sport a crown and glorious full skirt. The trail is popular and marked clearly, but moderately strenuous with 350 feet of elevation change. ⊠ *Off Hwy. 63.*

Sunset Point. Watch the late-day sun paint the hoodoos here. You can see **Thor's Hammer,** a delicate formation similar to a balanced rock, from the rim, but when you hike 550 feet down into the amphitheater on the Navajo Loop Trail, you can walk through the famous and very popular Wall Street—a deep, shady "slot" canyon. The point is 2 miles south of the park entrance near Bryce Canyon Lodge. ⊠ *Bryce Canyon National Park.*

10

SPORTS AND THE OUTDOORS

Most visitors explore Bryce Canyon by car, but the hiking trails are far more rewarding. At these elevations, you'll have to stop to catch your breath more often than you're used to. It gets warm in summer but rarely uncomfortably hot, so hiking farther into the depths of the park is not difficult so long as you don't pick a hike that is beyond your abilities.

AIR TOURS

OUTFITTERS

Bryce Canyon Airlines & Helicopters. For a bird's-eye view of Bryce Canyon National Park, take a dramatic helicopter ride or airplane tour over the fantastic sandstone formations. Longer full-canyon tours and added excursions to sites such as the Grand Canyon, Monument Valley, or Zion are also offered. Flight time can last anywhere from 35 minutes to four hours; family and group rates are available. ☎ *435/619–0017, 435/691–8813* ⊕ *www.rubysinn.com/scenic-flights* ✈ *From $110.*

BIRD-WATCHING

More than 170 bird species have been identified in Bryce. Violet green swallows and white-throated swifts are common, as are Steller's jays, American coots, rufous hummingbirds, and mountain bluebirds. Lucky bird-watchers will see golden eagles floating across the skies above the pink rocks of the amphitheater, and experienced birders might spot an osprey nest high in the canyon wall. The best time in the park for avian variety is from May through July.

HIKING

To get up close and personal with the park's hoodoos, set aside a half day to hike into the amphitheater. There are no elevators, so remember that after you descend below the rim you'll have to get back up. The air gets warmer the lower you go, and the altitude will have you huffing and puffing unless you're a mountain native. The uneven terrain calls for lace-up shoes on even the well-trodden, high-traffic trails and sturdy hiking boots for the more challenging ones. No below-rim trails are paved. For trail maps, information, and ranger recommendations, stop at the visitor center. Bathrooms are at most trailheads but not down in the amphitheater.

EASY

Bristlecone Loop Trail. This 1-mile trail with a modest 200 feet of elevation gain lets you see the park from its highest points of more than 9,000 feet, alternating between spruce and fir forest and wide-open vistas across the Grand Staircase–Escalante National Monument and beyond. You might see yellow-bellied marmots and dusky grouse, critters not found at lower elevations in the park. The most challenging part of the hike is ungluing your eyes from the scenery long enough to read the signage at

Central Bryce Canyon

the many trail forks. Plan on 45 minutes to an hour. *Easy.* ✛ *Trailhead: at Rainbow Point parking area, 18 miles south of park entrance.*

FAMILY
Fodor's Choice
★

Queen's Garden Trail. This hike is the easiest way down into the amphitheater, with 350 feet of elevation change leading to a short tunnel, quirky hoodoos, and lots of like-minded hikers. It's the essential Bryce "sampler." Allow two hours total to hike the 1½-mile trail plus the ½-mile rim-side path and back. *Easy.* ✛ *Trailhead: at Sunrise Point, 2 miles south of park entrance.*

MODERATE

FAMILY
Navajo Loop Trail. One of Bryce's most popular and dramatic attractions is this steep descent via a series of switchbacks leading to Wall Street, a claustrophobic hallway of rock only 20 feet wide in places with walls 100 feet high. After a walk through the Silent City, the northern end of the trail brings Thor's Hammer into view. A well-marked intersection offers a shorter way back or continuing on the Queens Garden Trail to Sunrise Point. For the short version allow at least an hour on this 1½-mile trail with 550 feet of elevation change. *Moderate.* ✛ *Trailhead: at Sunset Point, 2 miles south of park entrance.*

10

Navajo/Queen's Garden Combination Loop. By walking this extended 3-mile loop, you can see some of the best of Bryce; it takes a little more than two hours. The route passes fantastic formations and an open forest of pine and juniper on the amphitheater floor. Descend into the amphitheater from Sunrise Point on the Queens Garden Trail and ascend via the Navajo Loop Trail; return to your starting point via the Rim Trail. *Moderate.* ✛ *Trailheads: at Sunset and Sunrise points, 2 miles south of park entrance.*

DIFFICULT

Fairyland Loop Trail. Hike into whimsical Fairyland Canyon on this trail that gets more strenuous and less crowded as you progress along its 8 miles. It winds around hoodoos, across trickles of water, and finally to a natural window in the rock at Tower Bridge, 1½ miles from Sunrise Point and 4 miles from Fairyland Point. The pink-and-white badlands and hoodoos surround you the whole way. Don't feel like you have to go the whole distance to make it worthwhile. But if you do, allow at least five hours for the round-trip with 1,700 feet of elevation change. You can pick up the loop at Fairyland Point or Sunrise Point. *Difficult.* ✛ *Trailheads: at Fairyland Point, 1 mile off main park road, 1 mile south of park entrance; Sunrise Point, 2 miles south of park entrance.*

Peekaboo Loop. The reward of this steep trail is the Wall of Windows and the Three Wise Men. Horses use this trail in spring, summer, and fall and have the right-of-way. Start at Bryce, Sunrise, or Sunset Point and allow four to five hours to hike the 5-mile trail or 7-mile double-loop. *Difficult.* ✛ *Trailheads: at Bryce Point, 2 miles off main park road, 5½ miles south of park entrance; Sunrise and Sunset points, 2 miles south of park entrance.*

Trail to the Hat Shop. The sedimentary haberdashery sits 2 miles from the trailhead. Hard gray caps balance precariously atop narrow pedestals of softer, rust-color rock. Allow three to four hours to travel this strenuous but rewarding 4-mile round-trip trail, the first part of the longer Under-the-Rim Trail. *Difficult.* ✛ *Trailhead: at Bryce Point, 2 miles off main park road, 5½ miles south of park entrance.*

Under-the-Rim Trail. Starting at Bryce Point, the trail travels 23 miles to Rainbow Point, passing through the Pink Cliffs, traversing Agua Canyon and Ponderosa Canyon, and taking you by several springs. Most of the hike is on the amphitheater floor, characterized by up-and-down terrain among stands of ponderosa pine; the elevation change totals about 1,500 feet. It's the park's longest trail, but four trailheads along the main park road allow you to connect to the Under-the-Rim Trail and cover its length as a series of day hikes. Allow at least two days to hike the route in its entirety, and although it's not a hoodoo-heavy hike there's plenty to see to make it a more leisurely three-day affair. *Difficult.* ✛ *Trailheads: at Bryce Point, Swamp Canyon, Ponderosa Canyon, and Rainbow Point.*

Hikers in Bryce are rewarded with vistas highlighting the park's colorful landscape.

HORSEBACK RIDING

Many of the park's hiking trails were first formed beneath the hooves of cattle wranglers. Today, hikers and riders share the trails. A number of outfitters can set you up with a gentle mount and lead you to the park's best sights. Not only can you cover more ground than you would walking, but equine traffic has the right-of-way at all times. Call ahead to the stables for reservations to find a trip that's right for you, from 90 minutes to all day. The biggest outfitters have more than 100 horses and mules to choose from. People under the age of seven or who weigh more than 220 pounds are prohibited from riding.

TOURS AND OUTFITTERS

Canyon Trail Rides. Descend to the floor of the Bryce Canyon amphitheater via horse or mule—and most visitors have no riding experience, so don't hesitate to join in. A two-hour ride ambles along the amphitheater floor to the Fairy Castle before returning to Sunrise Point. The half-day expedition follows Peekaboo Loop Trail, winds past the Fairy Castle and the Alligator, and passes the Wall of Windows before returning to Sunrise Point. Two rides a day of each type leave in the morning and early afternoon. Trips can now be booked online; there are no rides in winter. ⊠ *Bryce Canyon Lodge, Off Hwy. 63* ☎ *435/679–8665* ⊕ *www. canyonrides.com* ✉ *$60 for 2 hrs; $80 for half-day excursion.*

FAMILY **Ruby's Horseback Adventures.** Ride to the rim of Bryce Canyon, venture through narrow slot canyons in Grand Staircase–Escalante National Monument, or even retrace the trails taken by outlaw Butch Cassidy more than 100 years ago. Rides last from one hour to all day. Kids must be seven or older to ride, in some cases 10. Wagon rides to the rim of Bryce Canyon are available for all ages, as are sleigh rides in winter. ✉ *Bryce Canyon National Park* ☎ *866/782–0002* ⊕ *www.horserides. net* ⌖ *From $55.*

WINTER SPORTS

Unlike Utah's other national parks, Bryce Canyon receives plenty of snow, making it a popular cross-country ski area. Rim Trail, Paria Loop, and other paths above the canyon are popular destinations. The visitor center sells shoe-traction devices, and some of the ranger-guided snowshoe activities include snowshoes and poles.

OUTFITTERS

FAMILY **Ruby's Winter Activities Center.** This facility grooms miles of private, no-cost trails that connect to the ungroomed trails inside the park. Rental snowshoes, ice skates, and cross-country ski equipment are available. ✉ *Hwy. 63, 1 mile north of park entrance, Bryce* ☎ *435/834–5341* ⊕ *www.rubysinn.com/winter.*

WHAT'S NEARBY

Bryce Canyon is a bit off the beaten path, often a side trip for those who visit Zion National Park to the southwest, and far from major roads or large cities (both Las Vegas and Salt Lake City are approximately 270 miles away). The park is just one of a number of beautiful or unique natural areas in southern Utah worth exploring. Towns close to the park pulse with Western personality and are excellent bases for exploring the entire area. To the west, Red Canyon offers an array of activities not available inside the park, such as mountain biking. The expansive and remote Grand Staircase–Escalante National Monument is about an hour to the northeast. Nearby state parks are great side trips: Escalante Petrified Forest and Kodachrome Basin.

NEARBY TOWNS

Panguitch calls itself the "Center of Scenic Utah," and it's an accurate moniker. The small town, 25 miles from Bryce Canyon, boasts restaurants, motels, gas stations, and trinket shops. About 47 miles northeast of Bryce, **Escalante** has modern amenities and is a western gateway to the Grand Staircase–Escalante National Monument. If you're traveling through southwestern Utah on Interstate 15, **Cedar City** will be your exit to Bryce. The largest city you'll encounter in this part of Utah, it's 78 miles from Bryce Canyon. Southern Utah University is here, and the Utah Shakespeare Festival on its campus draws theater buffs from all over the country.

Visitor Information Garfield County Travel Council (Panguitch). ✉ *55 S. Main St., Panguitch* ☎ *800/444–6689* ⊕ *www.brycecanyoncountry.com.* **Cedar City/Brian Head Tourism Bureau.** ✉ *581 N. Main St., Cedar City* ☎ *800/354–4849, 435/586–5124* ⊕ *www.scenicsouthernutah.com.* **Escalante Interagency Visitor Center.** ✉ *755 W. Main St., Escalante* ☎ *435/826–5499* ⊕ *www.blm.gov.*

NEARBY ATTRACTIONS

Cedar Breaks National Monument. From the rim of Cedar Breaks, 23 miles east of Cedar City, a natural amphitheater plunges 2,000 feet into the Markagunt Plateau. Short hiking trails along the rim make this a wonderful summer stop, especially for Cedar City or Shakespeare festival visitors not planning to visit the Zion or Bryce parks. ⊠ *Hwy. 14, Brian Head* ☎ *435/586–0787* ⊕ *www.nps.gov/cebr* 🖾 *$4* ⊙ *Visitor center late May–mid-Oct., daily 9–6.*

Dixie National Forest. The forest's expansive natural area is divided into four noncontiguous swaths covering a total of nearly 2 million acres. Adjacent to three national parks, two national monuments, and several state parks, the forest has 26 campgrounds in a variety of backdrops lakeside, mountainside, and in the depths of pine and spruce forests. Recreational opportunities abound, including hiking, picnicking, horseback riding, and fishing. ⊠ *Dixie National Forest Headquarters, 1789 N. Wedgewood La., Cedar City* ☎ *435/865–3700* ⊕ *www.fs.usda.gov/dixie* 🖾 *Free.*

FAMILY **Escalante Petrified Forest State Park.** This state park was created to protect a huge repository of petrified wood, easily spotted along two moderate-to-strenuous hiking trails. Of equal interest to area locals and visitors is the park's Wide Hollow Reservoir at the base of the hiking trails, which has a swimming beach and is good for boating, fishing, and birding. ⊠ *710 N. Reservoir Rd., Escalante* ☎ *435/826–4466* ⊕ *www.stateparks.utah.gov* 🖾 *$8* ⊙ *Summer, daily 7 am–10 pm; winter, daily 8 am–10 pm.*

FAMILY **Grand Staircase–Escalante National Monument.** In September 1996, President Bill Clinton designated 1.7 million acres in south-central Utah as Grand Staircase–Escalante National Monument. Its three distinct sections—the Grand Staircase, the Kaiparowits Plateau, and the Canyons of the Escalante—offer remote backcountry experiences hard to find elsewhere in the Lower 48. Waterfalls, shoulder-width slot canyons, and improbable colors all characterize this wilderness. Highway 12, which straddles the northern border of the monument, is one of the most scenic stretches in the Southwest. The small towns of Escalante and Boulder offer outfitters, lodging, and dining. ⊠ *Kanab* ☎ *435/644–1200,* ⊕ *www.blm.gov/ut/st/en/fo/grand_staircase-escalante.html* 🖾 *Free.*

FAMILY **Kodachrome Basin State Park.** Yes it is named after the old-fashioned color photo film, and as soon as you see it, you'll understand why the National Geographic Society gave it the name. The stone spires known as "sand pipes" cannot be found anywhere else in the world. Hike any of the trails to spot some of the 67 pipes in and around the park. The short Angels Palace Trail takes you quickly into the park's interior, up, over, and around some of the badlands. ⊠ *Cottonwood Canyon Rd., Cannonville* ☎ *435/679–8562* ⊕ *www.stateparks.utah.gov* 🖾 *$8* ⊙ *Daily 6 am–10 pm.*

10

AREA ACTIVITIES

SPORTS AND THE OUTDOORS

BICYCLING

Hell's Backbone Road. For a scenic and challenging mountain-bike ride, follow the 44-mile Hell's Backbone Road from Panguitch to the Escalante region and beyond. The route, also known as Highway 12, gives riders stunning views and a half-dozen quaint townships as a reward for the steep grades. The road begins 7 miles south of Panguitch.

TOURS AND OUTFITTERS

Excursions of Escalante. Hiking, backpacking, and canyoneering tours in the Escalante region are custom-fit to your needs and abilities by experienced guides whose specialty is taking canyoneers into the slot canyons to move through slot chutes or rappel down walls and other obstacles. All gear and provisions are provided whether it's a day hike or multiday adventure. ✉ *125 E. Main St., Escalante* ☎ *800/839–7567* ⊕ *excursionsofescalante.com* ✎ *$130.*

SCENIC DRIVES

Fodor'sChoice **Highway 12 Scenic Byway.** Keep your camera handy and steering wheel
★ steady along this route between Escalante and Loa, near Capitol Reef National Park. Though the highway starts at the intersection of U.S. 89, west of Bryce Canyon National Park, the stretch that begins in Escalante is one of the most spectacular. The road passes through Grand Staircase–Escalante National Monument and on to Capitol Reef along one of the most scenic stretches of highway in the United States. Be sure to stop at the scenic overlooks; almost every one will give you an eye-popping view, and information panels let you know what you're looking at. Don't get distracted while driving, though; the paved road is twisting and steep, and at times climbs over a hogback with sheer drop-offs on both sides. ⊕ *www.scenicbyway12.com.*

U.S. 89/Utah's Heritage Highway. Winding north from the Arizona border all the way to Spanish Fork Canyon an hour south of Salt Lake City, U.S. 89 is known as the Heritage Highway for its role in shaping Utah history. At its southern end, Kanab is known as "Little Hollywood," having provided the backdrop for many famous Western movies and TV commercials. The town has since grown considerably to accommodate tourists who flock here to see where Ronald Reagan once slept and Clint Eastwood drew his guns. Other towns north along this famous road may not have the same notoriety in these parts, but they do provide a quiet, uncrowded, and inexpensive place to stay near Zion and Bryce Canyon National Parks. East of Kanab, U.S. 89 runs along the southern edge of the Grand Staircase–Escalante National Monument.

WHERE TO EAT

IN THE PARK

$$$ ✗**Bryce Canyon Lodge.** Set among towering pines, this historic lodge, 2
AMERICAN miles south of the park entrance, is the featured place to dine within
the park. Designated as a certified Green Restaurant, the menu includes
organic, regional foods with choices ranging from Utah trout and prime
rib to creative vegetarian-friendly entrées. A beer and wine selection
includes Utah microbrews. No reservations are accepted, so you may
encounter a wait. ⑤ *Average main: $24* ⊠ *Hwy. 63* ☎ *435/834–8700*
⊕ *www.brycecanyonforever.com/lodge-dining* ⊘ *Closed late Nov.–Mar.*
⚑ *Reservations not accepted.*

$ ✗**Valhalla Pizzeria & Coffee Shop.** A former recreation room across the
ITALIAN parking lot from Byrce Canyon Lodge was converted into this 40-seat
FAMILY fast-casual pizzeria and coffee shop which offers breakfast and dinner.
Breakfast choices include homemade pastries and fresh fruit, or kick
back on the tranquil patio in the evening and enjoy fresh pizza, lasagna,
or calzone made from organic ingredients with your choice of beer or
wine. ⑤ *Average main: $12* ⊠ *Off Hwy. 63* ⊹ *2 miles south of park*
entrance ☎ *435/834–8709* ⊕ *www.brycecanyonforever.com/lodge-pizza*
⊘ *Closed mid-Oct.–mid-May. No lunch* ⚑ *Reservations not accepted.*

PICNIC AREAS

FAMILY **North Campground.** Across the road and slightly east of the Bryce Can-
yon visitor center, this campground includes several sites for tents and
RVs, as well as access to scenic trails, a general store, and picnic area.
⊠ *Bryce Canyon National Park* ⚑ *$30 per night.*

Yovimpa Point. At the southern end of the park, 18 miles south of the
park entrance, this shady, quiet spot has tables and restrooms nearby.
A short walk leads to the edge of the Paunsaugunt Plateau and offers
long-distance, panoramic views. ⊠ *Bryce Canyon National Park.*

OUTSIDE THE PARK

10

$$ ✗**Bryce Canyon Restaurant.** Part of the Bryce Canyon Pines motel,
AMERICAN about 15 miles west of Tropic, this cozy eatery is only minutes from
Bryce Canyon National Park and offers large portions of homemade
fare, including soups and a famed selection of pies. ⑤ *Average main:*
$15 ⊠ *Hwy. 12, mile marker 10, Bryce* ☎ *800/892–7923* ⊕ *www.*
brycecanyonmotel.com.

$ ✗**Centro Woodfired Pizzeria.** You can watch your handmade artisanal
ITALIAN pizza being pulled from the fires of the brick oven, then sit back and
Fodor's Choice enjoy a seasonal pie layered with ingredients such as house-made fen-
★ nel sausage and wood-roasted cremini mushrooms. The creamy vanilla
gelato layered with a balsamic reduction and sea salt can actually be
addictive. Wine and beer selections are offered as well. ⑤ *Average main:*
$12 ⊠ *50 W. Center St., Cedar City* ☎ *435/867–8123* ⊘ *Closed Sun.*
⚑ *Reservations not accepted.*

$$ ✗**Cowboy Blues.** This locals' favorite serves up bountiful American food
AMERICAN in a rustic Old West setting and keeps it real by sourcing its Black Angus

beef from Southern Utah ranches and plucking seasonal vegetables from a local garden. You can enjoy a cocktail or beer on the patio, along with a serving of the eatery's one-of-a-kind jalapeño peppers. ⑤ *Average main: $15* ⊠ *530 W. Main St., Escalante* ☎ *435/826–4577* ⊕ *www. cowboyblues.net* ⌖ *Reservations not accepted.*

$$ ✕ **Cowboy's Smokehouse Café.** From the Western-style interior and
AMERICAN creaky floors to the smoker out back, this rustic café has an aura of Texan authenticity with cowboy collectibles and game trophies lining the walls. No surprise that barbecue is the specialty here, with ample portions of favorites such as ribs, mesquite-flavored beef and pulled pork, and the restaurant's own housemade sauce. Lighter fare includes sandwiches and salads. Payment is cash only but there is an ATM on the premises. ⑤ *Average main: $18* ⊠ *95 N. Main St., Panguitch* ☎ *435/676–8030* ⊕ *www.cowboyssmokehousecafe.com* ▭ *No credit cards* ⊘ *Closed Sun.*

$$ ✕ **Esca-Latte Internet Cafe & Pizza Parlor.** When you're spent after a day
CAFÉ of exploration, this is a great place to sit back and relax. Try one of the build-your-own pizzas, known for fresh, local ingredients such as applewood bacon and slow-roasted tomatoes, and pair it with an icy Utah microbrew. There are also sandwiches, salads, homemade desserts, and one of the best cups of coffee in town, fresh ground from fair-trade beans. ⑤ *Average main: $17* ⊠ *310 W. Main St., Escalante* ☎ *435/826–4266* ⊕ *www.escalanteoutfitters.com.*

$$ ✕ **Foster's Family Steakhouse.** This steak house is known for its prime rib
STEAKHOUSE and sautéed mushrooms, but you'll also find seafood on the menu, and some choices include the soup and salad bar. Whatever you choose, be sure to leave room for dessert—try the namesake mixed-berry pie that includes raspberries, rhubarb, and strawberries. Beverages include beer and wine, and you can take out homemade breads and pastries from the bakery. The restaurant is open early for breakfast, too, and you'll find it 2 miles west of the Highway 63 intersection. ⑤ *Average main: $15* ⊠ *1150 Hwy. 12, Bryce* ☎ *435/834–5227* ⊕ *www.fostersmotel. com* ⊘ *Closed Dec. and Jan.*

$$$ ✕ **Milt's Stage Stop.** Locals and an increasing number of tourists have
STEAKHOUSE discovered the lodgelike surroundings, friendly service, and canyon views at this dinner spot a 10-minute drive from Cedar City. It's known for traditional, hearty steak-house cuisine: rib-eye steaks, prime rib, seafood dishes, and sizable salad bar, accompanied by loaded baked potatoes or other sides. Hunting trophies decorate the log cabin–style interior, and in winter deer feed outside while logs blaze away in the big stone fireplace inside. ⑤ *Average main: $25* ⊠ *3560 E. Hwy. 14, Cedar City* ☎ *435/586–9344* ⊕ *www.miltsstagestop.com* ⊘ *No lunch* ⌖ *Reservations essential.*

WHERE TO STAY

IN THE PARK

$$$ 🏨 **Bryce Canyon Lodge.** This historic, rugged stone-and-wood lodge
HOTEL   close to the amphitheater's rim offers motel-style rooms with semipri-
Fodor's Choice   vate balconies or porches and cozy lodgepole-pine cabins, some with
★   cathedral ceilings and gas fireplaces. **Pros:** lodging close to canyon rim,
trails; friendly and attentive staff; cabins have fireplaces. **Cons:** closed
in winter; books up fast; no TV. $ *Rooms from: $193* ⊠ *Off Hwy.*
63 ☎ *435/834–8700, 877/386–4383* ⊕ *www.brycecanyonforever.com/*
lodging ⊘ *Closed Nov.–Mar.* ⇄ *70 rooms, 3 suites, 40 cabins* ⊙ *No*
meals.

OUTSIDE THE PARK

$$ 🏨 **Bard's Inn Bed and Breakfast.** Rooms in this restored turn-of-the-20th-
B&B/INN   century house are named after famous characters from Shakespeare's
plays and handcrafted quilts grace the beds. **Pros:** immaculate rooms;
all rooms have private baths; close to historic downtown. **Cons:** thin
walls and creaky floors; books up fast for festival season. $ *Rooms*
from: $109 ⊠ *150 S. 100 W, Cedar City* ☎ *435/586–6612* ⊕ *www.*
thebardsinn.com ⊘ *Closed Sept.–May* ⇄ *8 rooms* ⊙ *Breakfast.*

$$$ 🏨 **Best Western Bryce Canyon Grand Hotel.** If you're into creature comforts
HOTEL   but can do without charm, this four-story hotel is the place—rooms
are relatively posh, with comfortable mattresses, pillows, and bedding,
spacious bathrooms, and modern appliances. **Pros:** clean, spacious
rooms; lots of indoor amenities. **Cons:** no pets allowed; breakfast can
get crowded. $ *Rooms from: $169* ⊠ *30 N. 100 E, Bryce* ☎ *866/866–*
6634, 435/834–5700 ⊕ *www.brycecanyongrand.com* ⇄ *164 rooms*
⊙ *Breakfast.*

$$ 🏨 **Best Western Plus Ruby's Inn.** This bustling Southwestern-themed hotel
HOTEL   has expanded over the years to include various wings with rooms that
vary widely in terms of size and appeal. **Pros:** one-stop shopping for
tours, amenities. **Cons:** can get very busy, especially when the big tour
buses roll in. $ *Rooms from: $145* ⊠ *26 S. Main St., Bryce* ☎ *435/834–*
5341, 866/866–6616 ⊕ *www.rubysinn.com* ⇄ *370 rooms, 11 suites*
⊙ *No meals.*

$ 🏨 **Bryce View Lodge.** Near the park entrance on Route 63, this motel
HOTEL   is a practical, reasonably priced option, with clean rooms and access
to the pool and other amenities across the way at the Best Western Plus Ruby's Inn, its sister property. **Pros:** good location for park
access; less pricey than surrounding hotels. **Cons:** a bit dated inside
and out. $ *Rooms from: $80* ⊠ *105 E. Center St., Bryce Canyon City*
☎ *435/834–5180, 888/279–2304* ⊕ *www.bryceviewlodge.com* ⇄ *160*
rooms ⊙ *No meals.*

$$ 🏨 **Escalante's Grand Staircase Bed & Breakfast Inn.** Rooms are set apart
B&B/INN   from the main house, giving this property some motel-type privacy
along with bed-and-breakfast amenities. **Pros:** spacious rooms; Wi-Fi.

10

CLOSE UP

Best Campgrounds in Bryce Canyon

The two campgrounds in Bryce Canyon National Park fill up fast, especially in summer, and are family-friendly. All are drive-in, except for the handful of backcountry sites that only backpackers and gung-ho day hikers ever see. Both campgrounds completed a welcome renovation of their restrooms and shared facilities in 2012.

North Campground. A cool, shady retreat in a forest of ponderosa pines, this is a great home base for your exploration of Bryce Canyon. You're near the general store, trailheads, and the visitor center. ⊠ *Main park road, ½ mile south of visitor center* ☎ *435/834–5322.*

Sunset Campground. This serene alpine campground is within walking distance of Bryce Canyon Lodge and many trailheads. All sites are filled on a first-come, first-served basis. ⊠ *Main park road, 2 miles south of visitor center* ☎ *435/834–5322.*

Cons: no pets. $ *Rooms from: $140* ⊠ *280 W. Main St., Escalante* ☎ *435/826–4890* ⊕ *www.escalantebnb.com* ⇨ *8 rooms* ⦿ *Breakfast.*

$

HOTEL **Escalante Outfitters.** A good option if you want a one-stop place to plan and gear up for your outdoor adventure, or if you're on a budget and don't care about amenities. **Pros:** the food is a pleasant surprise; pet-friendly. **Cons:** right on the highway; you may have to wait in line for a shower. $ *Rooms from: $45* ⊠ *310 W. Main St., Escalante* ☎ *435/826–4266* ⊕ *www.escalanteoutfitters.com* ⇨ *7 cabins* ⦿ *No meals.*

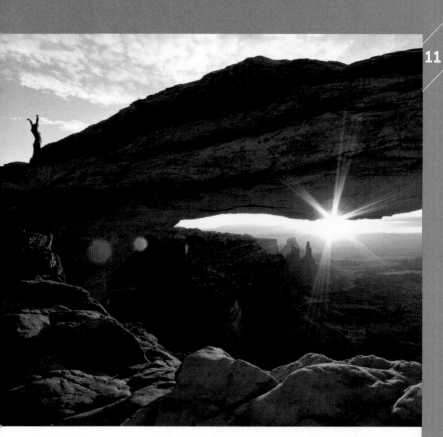

CANYONLANDS NATIONAL PARK

WELCOME TO CANYONLANDS NATIONAL PARK

TOP REASONS TO GO

★ **Endless vistas:** The view from the Island in the Sky stretches for miles as you look out over millennia of sculpting by wind and rain.

★ **Seeking solitude:** Needles, the most interesting part of the park to explore on foot, sees very few visitors, so you'll have it all to yourself.

★ **Radical rides:** The Cataract Canyon rapids and the White Rim Trail are world-class adventures by boat or bike.

★ **American Indian artifacts:** View rock art and Ancestral Puebloan dwellings in the park.

★ **Wonderful wilderness:** Some of the country's most untouched landscapes are within the park's boundaries, and they're worth the extra effort needed to get there.

★ **The night skies:** Far away from city lights, Canyonlands is ideal for stargazing.

1 Island in the Sky. From any of the overlooks here you can see for miles and look down thousands of feet to canyon floors. Chocolate-brown canyons are capped by white rock, and deep-red monuments rise nearby.

2 Needles. Pink, orange, and red rock is layered with white rock and stands in spires and pinnacles around grassy meadows. Extravagantly red mesas and buttes interrupt the horizon, as in a picture postcard of the Old West.

3 The Maze. Only the most intrepid adventurers explore this incredibly remote mosaic of rock formations. There's a reason Butch Cassidy hid out here.

4 Rivers. For many, rafting through the waterways is the best way to see the park. The Green and Colorado are as wild as when John Wesley Powell explored them in the mid-1800s.

5 Horseshoe Canyon. Plan on several hours of dirt-road driving to get here, but the famous rock-art panel "Great Gallery" is a grand reward at the end of a long hike.

GETTING ORIENTED

Canyonlands National Park, in southeastern Utah, is divided into three distinct land districts and the river district, so it can be a little daunting to visit. It's exhausting, but not impossible, to explore the Island in the Sky and Needles in the same day.

KEY	
	Ranger Station
▲	Campground
⊼	Picnic Area
¶¶	Restaurant
⌖	Lodge
⚐	Trailhead
⚥	Restrooms
⇝	Scenic Viewpoint
::::::	Walking/Hiking Trails

UTAH

313

5 Dead Horse Point State Park

TO
MOAB, HWY 191 &
HORSESHOE CANYON UNIT

Dead Horse
Point Overlook

Moses & Zeus

Visitor Center

Shafer Canyon
Overlook

Upheaval Dome

Musselman
Arch

Holeman Spring
Canyon Overlook

**ISLAND IN
THE SKY**

Aztec Butte

Washer Woman Arch

Willow Flat

Mesa Arch

Green River Overlook

Candlestick Tower
Overlook

**GLEN
CANYON
NATIONAL
RECREATION
AREA**

White Rim Rd

Green River

Colorado River

Buck Canyon
Overlook

Orange Cliffs
Overlook

0   4 mi

0   4 km

**Grand View
Point Overlook**

• White Crack

Maze Overlook

3   **The Maze**

Colorado River
Overlook

4   Confluence

Confluence Overlook

Chimney Rock •

Elephant Hill

Big Spring
Canyon Overlook

CATARACT CANYON

Pothole
Point Trail

211

Visitor Center

The Doll House

Cowboy Line Camp

Wooden Shoe Overlook

Squaw Flat

Wooden Shoe
Arch

Colorado River

2   **NEEDLES**

Druid Arch

Gothic Arch

Castle Arch

Fortress Arch

Angel Arch

Caterpillar
Arch

Wedding Ring Arch

Cleft Arch

Updated by
Lisa Church

Canyonlands is truly four parks in one, but the majority of visitors drive through the panoramic vistas of Island in the Sky and barely venture anywhere else. If you've come this far, plan a half day to hike around the Needles district and see the park from the bottom up. To truly experience Canyonlands you should also float down the Green and Colorado rivers on a family-friendly rafting trip. (Rapids-lovers can take on the white water in the legendary Cataract Canyon.) The Maze is so remote that its river beds, slot canyons, and stark rock formations are only for the truly hardy.

CANYONLANDS PLANNER

WHEN TO GO

Gorgeous weather means that spring and fall are most popular for visitors. Canyonlands is seldom crowded, but in the spring backpackers and four-wheelers populate the trails and roads. During Easter week, some of the four-wheel-drive trails in the park are used for Jeep Safari, an annual event drawing thousands of visitors to town.

The crowds thin out by July as the thermostat approaches 100°F and beyond for about four weeks. It's a great time to get out on the Colorado or Green River winding through the park. October can be rainy, but the region receives only 8 inches of rain annually.

The well-kept secret is that winter is the best time in the park. Crowds are gone, roads are good, and snowcapped mountains stand in the background. Winter here is one of nature's most memorable shows, with red rock dusted white and low-floating clouds partially obscuring canyons and towers.

AVG. HIGH/LOW TEMPS.

Jan.	Feb.	Mar.	Apr.	May	June
44/22	52/28	64/35	71/42	82/51	93/60
July	Aug.	Sept.	Oct.	Nov.	Dec.
100/67	97/66	88/55	74/42	56/30	45/23

PLANNING YOUR TIME

CANYONLANDS IN ONE DAY

Your day begins with a choice: Island in the Sky or Needles. If you want expansive vistas looking across southeast Utah's canyons, head for the island, where you stand atop a giant mesa. If you want to walk among Canyonlands' needles and buttes, Needles is your destination. If you have a second or third day in the area, consider contacting an outfitter to take you on a rafting or 4X4 trip. ■TIP→ Before venturing into the park, top off your gas tank, pack a picnic lunch, and stock up on plenty of water.

ISLAND IN THE SKY Make your first stop along the main park road at **Shafer Canyon Overlook.** A short walk takes you out on a finger of land with views of the canyon over both sides. From here you can see Shafer Trail's treacherous descent as it hugs the canyon walls below.

Stop at the visitor center to learn about ranger talks or special programs, then drive to **Mesa Arch.** Grab your camera and water bottle for the short hike out to the arch perched on the cliff's edge. After your excursion, take the spur road to Upheaval Dome, with its picnic spot in the parking lot. A short walk takes you to the first viewpoint of this crater. If you still have energy, 30 more minutes and a little sense of adventure, continue to the second overlook.

Retrace your drive to the main park road and continue to **Grand View Point.** Stroll along the edge of the rim, and see how many landmarks you can spot in the distance. White Rim Overlook is the best of the scenic spots, particularly if you're not afraid of heights and venture all the way out to the end of the rocky cliffs (no guardrail here). On the way back to dinner in Moab, spend an hour in Dead Horse Point State Park.

NEEDLES If you can stay overnight as well, then begin today by setting up camp at Squaw Flat or one of the other wonderful campgrounds in Needles. Then hit the **Joint Trail,** or any of the trails that begin from Squaw Flat, and spend the day hiking in the backcountry of the park. Save an hour for the brief but terrific little hike to **Cave Springs.** Sleep under more stars than you've seen in a long time.

GETTING HERE AND AROUND

AIR TRAVEL

The nearest mid-sized airport to southeastern Utah is Grand Junction Regional Airport in Grand Junction, Colorado, approximately 110 miles from Moab.

CAR TRAVEL

Off U.S. 191, Canyonlands' Island in the Sky visitor center is 21 miles from Arches National Park and 32 miles from Moab on Route 313 west of U.S. 191; the Needles District is reached via Route 211, west of U.S. 191.

Before starting a journey to any of Canyonlands' three districts, make sure your gas tank is topped off, as there are no services inside the large park. Island in the Sky is 32 miles from Moab, Needles District is 80 miles from Moab, and the Maze is more than 100 miles from Moab. The Island in the Sky road from the district entrance to Grand View Point is 12 miles, with one 5-mile spur to Upheaval Dome. The Needles scenic drive is 10 miles with two spurs about 3 miles each. Roads in the Maze, suitable only for rugged, high-clearance, four-wheel-drive vehicles, wind for hundreds of miles through the canyons. Within the parks, safety and courtesy mandate that you always park only in designated pullouts or parking areas.

TRAIN TRAVEL

The nearest train "station" is a solitary Amtrak stop in Green River, about 50 miles northwest of Moab.

PARK ESSENTIALS

PARK FEES AND PERMITS

Admission is $25 per vehicle, $10 per person on foot or bicycle, and $15 per motorcycle, good for seven days. Your Canyonlands pass is good for all the park's districts. There's no entrance fee to the Maze District of Canyonlands. A $50 local park pass grants you admission to both Arches and Canyonlands as well as Natural Bridges and Hovenweep national monuments for one year.

You need a permit for overnight backpacking, four-wheel-drive camping, mountain-bike camping, four-wheel-drive day use in Horse and Lavender canyons, and river trips. Day-use permits are also now required for all motorized vehicles and bicycles on the Elephant Hill and White Rim trails and group sizes are limited. Reservations need to be made at least two weeks (or more) in advance.

PARK HOURS

Canyonlands National Park is open 24 hours a day, seven days a week, year-round. It is in the Mountain time zone.

CELL-PHONE RECEPTION

Cell-phone reception may be available in some parts of the park, but not reliably so. Public telephones are at the park's visitor centers.

EDUCATIONAL OFFERINGS

For more information on current schedules and locations of park programs, contact the visitor centers or check the bulletin boards throughout the park. Note that programs change periodically and may sometimes be canceled because of limited staffing.

FAMILY **Red Rock Explorer Pack.** Just like borrowing a book from a library, kids can check out a backpack filled with tools for learning. The sturdy backpack includes binoculars, a magnifying glass, and a three-ring binder full of activities. It can be cumbersome to carry everything on a hike, but the backpack is great for around the campfire or back in your hotel room. Explorer packs are available in Canyonlands National Park at the Needles and the Island in the Sky visitor centers. ✉ *Canyonlands National Park* ☎ *435/719–4712* ✇ *Free.*

RANGER PROGRAMS

Grand View Point Overlook Talk. Between April and October, rangers lead short presentations at Grand View Point about the geology that created Utah's Canyonlands. ✉ *Grand View Point, 12 miles from park entrance off main park road, Island in the Sky* ✇ *Free* ☉ *Apr.–Oct., daily; check at park visitor centers for times and locations.*

FAMILY **Junior Ranger Program.** Kids ages 5 to 12 can pick up a Junior Ranger booklet at the visitor centers. It's full of puzzles, word games, and fun facts about the park and its wildlife. To earn the Junior Ranger badge, they must complete several activities in the booklet, attend a ranger program, watch the park film, and/or gather a bag of litter. Available at both Needles and Island in the Sky district visitor centers. ✉ *Canyonlands National Park* ☎ *435/259–4712 Island in the Sky, 435/259–4711 Needles* ✇ *Free.*

RESTAURANTS

There are no dining facilities in the park itself. Restaurants in Monticello and Blanding offer simple meals, and most are closed on Sunday and do not serve alcohol. Moab has a multitude of options.

HOTELS

There is no lodging inside Canyonlands. Most visitors use Moab as a base to explore the park. The towns of Monticello and Blanding offer basic motels, both family-owned and national chains. Bluff also has motels and bed-and-breakfasts and offers a quiet place to stay. *Hotel reviews have been shortened. For full information, visit Fodors.com.*

WHAT IT COSTS			
$	**$$**	**$$$**	**$$$$**
Restaurants	under $13	$13–$20	$21–$30	over $30
Hotels	under $101	$101–$150	$151–$200	over $200

Restaurant prices are the average cost of a main course at dinner, or if dinner is not served, at lunch. Hotel prices are the lowest cost of a standard double room in high season.

VISITOR INFORMATION

Park Contact Information Canyonlands National Park. ✉ *2282 S.W. Resource Blvd, Moab* ☎ *435/719-2313* ⊕ *www.nps.gov/cany.*

VISITOR CENTERS

Hans Flat Ranger Station. This remote outpost—46 miles east of Route 24; 21 miles south and east of the Y junction and Horseshoe Canyon kiosk on a dirt road—is a treasure trove of books, maps, and other documents about the unforgiving Maze District of Canyonlands. The slot canyons, pictographs, and myriad rock formations are tempting, but you need to know what you're doing. The rangers will be direct with you—inexperienced off-road drivers and backpackers can get themselves into serious trouble in the Maze. Just to get here you must drive 46 miles on a dirt road that is sometimes impassable even to 4X4 vehicles. There's a pit toilet, but no water, food, or services of any kind. If you're headed for the backcountry, permits cost $30 per group for up to seven days. Rangers offer guided hikes in Horseshoe Canyon on most weekends during the spring and fall. ⊠ *Recreation Rds. 777 and 633, Maze* ☎ *435/259–2652* ⊙ *Daily 8–4:30.*

Island in the Sky Visitor Center. The gateway to the world-famous White Rim Trail, this visitor center, 21 miles from U.S. 191, past the park entrance off the main park road, is often filled with a mix of mountain bikers, hikers, and tourists. Enjoy the orientation film, then browse the bookstore for information about the Canyonlands region. Exhibits help explain animal adaptations as well as some of the history of the park. Rangers give short talks twice a day. ⊠ *Grand View Point Rd., Island in the Sky* ☎ *435/259–4712* ⊙ *Mar.–mid-Dec., daily 9–4, with some extended hrs Mar.–Oct.*

Needles District Visitor Center. This gorgeous building is 34 miles from U.S. 191 and less than 1 mile from the park entrance, off the main park road. Needles is remote, so it's worth stopping to inquire about road, weather, and park conditions. You can also watch the interesting orientation film and get books, trail maps, and other information. ⊠ *Hwy. 211, Needles* ☎ *435/259–4711* ⊙ *Mar.–mid-Dec., daily 9–4, with longer hrs during summer.*

EXPLORING

SCENIC DRIVES

Island in the Sky Park Road. This 12-mile-long main road inside the park is bisected by a 5-mile side road to the Upheaval Dome area. To enjoy dramatic views, including the Green and Colorado rivers, stop at the overlooks and take the short walks. Once you get to the park, allow at least two hours to explore. ⊠ *Island in the Sky.*

Needles District Park Road. You'll feel like you've driven into a Hollywood Western as you roll along the park road in the Needles District. Red mesas and buttes rise against the horizon, blue mountain ranges interrupt the rangelands, and the colorful red-and-white needles stand like soldiers on the far side of grassy meadows. You should get out of the car at a few of the marked roadside stops, including both overlooks at Pothole Point. Allow at least 90 minutes in this less-traveled section of the park. ⊠ *Needles.*

HISTORIC SITES

ISLAND IN THE SKY

Shafer Trail. This road was probably first established by ancient Native Americans, but in the early 1900s ranchers used it to drive cattle into the canyon. Originally narrow and rugged, it was upgraded during the uranium boom, when miners hauled ore by truck from the canyon

CLOSE UP

Plants and Wildlife in Canyonlands

11

Wildlife is not the attraction in Canyonlands, as many of the creatures sleep during the heat of the day. On the bright side, there are fewer people and less traffic to scare the animals away. Cool mornings and evenings are the best time to spot them, especially in summer when the heat keeps them in cool, shady areas. Mule deer are nearly always seen along the roadway as you enter the Needles District, and you'll no doubt see jackrabbits and small rodents darting across the roadway. Approximately 250 bighorn sheep populate the park in the Island in the Sky District, and the Maze shelters about 100 more. If you happen upon one of these regal animals, do not approach it even if it is alone, as bighorn sheep are skittish by nature and easily stressed. Also, report your sighting to a ranger.

---

floor. Check out the road's winding route down canyon walls from Shafer Canyon Overlook before you drive it to see why it's mostly used by daring four-wheelers and energetic mountain bikers. Off the main road, less than 1 mile from the park entrance, it descends 1,400 feet to the White Rim. Check with the visitor center about road conditions before driving the Shafer Trail. It's often impassable after rains or snow. ⊠ *Island in the Sky.*

NEEDLES

FAMILY **Cowboy Line Camp.** This fascinating stop on the **Cave Springs Trail** is an authentic example of cowboy life more than a century ago. You do not need to complete the entire trail (which includes two short ladders and some rocky hiking) to see the 19th-century artifacts at the Cowboy Camp. ⊠ *Off Cave Springs Rd., 2.3 miles from visitor center, Needles.*

SCENIC STOPS

ISLAND IN THE SKY

Fodor'sChoice **Grand View Point.** This 360-degree view is the main event for many
★ visitors to Island in the Sky. Look down on the Colorado and Green rivers and contemplate the power and persistence of water and the vast canyons carved over the millennia. Stretch your legs on the trails along the canyon edge. ⊠ *Off main road, 12 miles from park entrance, Island in the Sky.*

Green River Overlook. From the road it's just 100 yards to this stunning view of the Green River Canyon to the south and west. It's not far from Island in the Sky campground. ⊠ *About 1 mile off Upheaval Dome Rd., 8 miles from park entrance, Island in the Sky.*

Fodor'sChoice **Mesa Arch.** If you don't have time for the 2,000 arches in nearby Arches
★ National Park, you should take the easy, half-mile walk to Mesa Arch. The arch is above a cliff that drops 800 feet to the canyon bottom. Through the arch, views of Washerwoman Arch and surrounding buttes, spires, and canyons make this a favorite photo opportunity. ⊠ *Off main road, 7 miles from park entrance, Island in the Sky.*

Upheaval Dome. This mysterious crater is one of the wonders of Island in the Sky. Some geologists believe it's an eroded salt dome, but others think it was made by a meteorite. It's about a mile, round-trip, to the first overlook; energetic visitors can continue to the second overlook as well for a better perspective. ⊠ *Upheaval Dome Rd., 12 miles from park entrance, Island in the Sky.*

NEEDLES

Pothole Point Trail. Microscopic creatures lie dormant in pools that fill only after rare rainstorms. When the rains do come, some eggs hatch within hours and life becomes visible. If you're lucky, you'll hit Pothole Point after a storm. The dramatic views of the Needles and Six Shooter Peak make this easy, 0.6-mile round-trip worthwhile. Plan for about 45 minutes. There's no shade, so wear a hat and take plenty of water. ⊠ *Off main road, about 10 miles from Needles district park entrance, Needles.*

Wooden Shoe Arch. Kids will enjoy looking for the tiny window in the rock that looks like a wooden shoe with a turned-up toe. If you can't find it on your own, there's a marker to help you. ⊠ *Off main road, about 6 miles from Needles entrance to park, Needles.*

> **MEET ME AT SUNSET**
>
> Sunset is one of the picture-perfect times in Canyonlands, as the slanting sun shines over the vast network of canyons that stretch out below Island in the Sky. A moonlight drive to Grand View Point can also give you lasting memories as the moon drenches the white sandstone in light. Likewise, late-afternoon color in the spires and towers at the Needles District is a humbling, awe-inspiring scene.

SPORTS AND THE OUTDOORS

Canyonlands is one of the world's best destinations for adrenaline junkies. You can rock climb, mountain bike treacherous terrain, tackle world-class white-water rapids, and make your 4X4 crawl over steep cliffs along precipitous drops. Compared with other national parks, Canyonlands allows you to enjoy an amazing amount of solitude while having the adventure of a lifetime.

MULTISPORT OPERATORS

Holiday River Expeditions. Since 1966, this outfitter has offered one- to eight-day adventures on the San Juan, Green, and Colorado rivers, including inside Canyonlands National Park. They also offer multisport trips, women's retreats, and bike adventures, including the White Rim Trail. ⊠ *2075 E. Main St., Green River* ☎ *435/564–3273, 800/624–6323* ⊕ *www.bikeraft.com* ✉ *From $155.*

NAVTEC. Doc Williams was the first physician in Moab in 1896, and some of his descendants have never left, sharing his love for the area through this rafting, canyoneering, and 4X4 company. Whether you want to explore by boat, boots, or wheels, you'll find a multitude of one-day and multiday options here. ⊠ *321 N. Main St., Moab* ☎ *435/259–7983, 800/833–1278* ⊕ *www.navtec.com.*

Sheri Griffith Expeditions. In addition to trips through the white water of Cataract, Westwater, and Desolation canyons, on the Colorado and Green rivers, this company also offers specialty expeditions for women, writers, and families. One of their more luxurious expeditions features dinners cooked by a professional chef and served on linen-covered tables. Cots and other sleeping amenities also make roughing it a little more comfortable. ⌧ *2231 S. U.S. 191, Moab* ☏ *435/259–8229, 800/332–2439* ⊕ *www.griffithexp.com* ✆ *From $82.*

BICYCLING

TOURS AND OUTFITTERS

Magpie Cycling. Seasoned bikers Mike Holme and Maggie Wilson lead groups (or lone riders) on daylong and multiday bike trips exploring the Moab region's most memorable terrain, including the White Rim, Needles, and the Maze. If you need to rent a bike, Magpie will meet you at its preferred shop, Poison Spider Bicycles (*435/259–7882 or 800/635–1792, poisonspiderbicycles.com*). ⌧ *497 N. Main St., Moab* ☏ *435/259–4464, 800/546–4245* ⊕ *www.magpieadventures.com.*

Rim Tours. Reliable, friendly, and professional, Rim Tours has been taking guests on guided one-day or multiday mountain-bike tours, including Klondike Bluffs (which enters Arches) and the White Rim Trail (inside Canyonlands) since 1985. Bike rentals are also available. Bike skills a little rusty? Rim Tours also offers mountain-bike instructional tours and skill clinics. ⌧ *1233 S. U.S. 191, Moab* ☏ *435/259–5223, 800/626–7335* ⊕ *www.rimtours.com* ✆ *Day tours from $140; multiday from $800.*

Western Spirit Cycling Adventures. Head here for fully supported, go-at-your-own-pace, multiday mountain-bike and road-bike tours throughout the western states, including trips to Canyonlands, Trail of the Ancients, and the 140-mile Kokopelli Trail, which runs from Grand Junction, Colorado, to Moab. Guides versed in the geologic wonders of the area cook up meals worthy of the scenery each night. Ask about family rides, too. There's also the option to combine a Green River kayak trip with the three-night White Rim Trail ride. ⌧ *478 Mill Creek Dr., Moab* ☏ *435/259–8732, 800/845–2453* ⊕ *www.westernspirit.com* ✆ *From $925.*

TRAILS

White Rim Road. Mountain bikers from all over the world like to brag that they've conquered this 100-mile ride. The trail's fame is well deserved: it traverses steep roads, broken rock, and dramatic ledges, as well as long stretches that wind through the canyons and look down onto others. If you're biking White Rim without an outfitter, you'll need careful planning, vehicle support, and much sought-after backcountry reservations. Permits are available no more than four months, and no less than two days, prior to permit start date. There is a 15-person, three-vehicle limit for groups. Day-use permits are also now required and can be obtained at the Island in the Sky visitor center or reserved 24 hours in advance through the park's website. Fifty bicycle permits are available each day. ⌧ *Off main park road about*

1 mile from entrance, then about 11 miles on Shafer Trail, Island in the Sky ☎ *435/259–4351* ⊕ *www.nps.gov/cany.*

BIRD-WATCHING

Without getting on the Colorado River, you can see a variety of wrens, including the rock wren, canyon wren, and Bewick's wren. Blue-gray gnatcatchers are fairly common in the summer, along with the solitary vireo and black-throated gray warbler and Virginia's warbler. You'll have the most fun spotting the American kestrel, peregrine falcon, or prairie falcon and watching golden and bald eagles soar overhead. The common raven is everywhere you look, as are the juniper titmouse, mountain chickadee, and a variety of jays. Once on the Colorado River, you'll stand a chance of glimpsing the elusive white-faced ibis, and you'll almost certainly see a great blue heron swooping along the water or standing regally on a sandbar.

BOATING AND RAFTING

Seeing Canyonlands National Park from the river is a great and rare pleasure. Long stretches of calm water on both the Green and Colorado rivers are perfect for lazy canoe or raft trips. Still, be sure to wear life preservers as drownings happen nearly every summer in the area. In Labyrinth Canyon, north of the park boundary, and in Stillwater Canyon, in the Island in the Sky District, the river is quiet and calm and there's plenty of shoreside camping. The Island in the Sky leg of the Colorado River, from Moab to its confluence with the Green River and downstream a few more miles to Spanish Bottom, is ideal for both canoeing and for rides with an outfitter in a large, stable jet boat. If you want to take a self-guided flat-water float trip in the park you must obtain a $30 permit, which you have to request by mail or fax. Make your upstream travel arrangements with a shuttle company before you request a permit. For permits, contact the reservation office at park headquarters (☎ *435/259–4351*).

Below Spanish Bottom, about 64 miles downstream from Moab, 49 miles from the Potash Road ramp, and 4 miles south of the confluence, the Colorado churns into the first rapids of legendary Cataract Canyon. Home of some of the best white water in the United States, this piece of river between the Maze and the Needles districts rivals the Grand Canyon stretch of the Colorado River for adventure. During spring melt-off these rapids can rise to staggering heights and deliver heart-stopping excitement. The canyon cuts through the very heart of Canyonlands, where you can see this amazing wilderness area in its most pristine form. The water calms down a bit in summer but still offers enough thrills for most people. Outfitters will take you for the ride of your life in this wild canyon, where the river drops more steeply than anywhere else on the Colorado River (in ¾ mile, the river drops 39 feet). You can join an expedition lasting anywhere from one to six days, or you can purchase a $30 permit for a self-guided trip from park headquarters.

TOURS

Tag-A-Long Expeditions. This outfitter, more than 50 years in business, has been taking people into the white water of Cataract Canyon and Canyonlands for longer than any other outfitter in Moab. They also run 4X4 expeditions into the backcountry and calm-water excursions on the Colorado and Green rivers. Trips, for three to 11 people, run from a half to six days. ⌧ *452 N. Main St., Moab* ☎ *435/259–8946, 800/453–3292* ⊕ *www.tagalong.com* ✉ *From $170.*

FOUR-WHEELING

Nearly 200 miles of challenging backcountry roads lead to campsites, trailheads, and natural and cultural features in Canyonlands. All of the roads require high-clearance, four-wheel-drive vehicles, and many are inappropriate for inexperienced drivers. The 100-mile White Rim Trail, for example, can be extremely challenging, so make sure that your four-wheel-drive skills are well honed and that you are capable of making basic road and vehicle repairs. Carry at least one full-size spare tire, extra gas, extra water, a shovel, a high-lift jack, and—October through April—chains for all four tires. Double-check to see that your vehicle is in top-notch condition, for you definitely don't want to break down in the interior of the park: towing expenses can exceed $1,000.

Day-use permits, available at the park visitor centers or 24 hours in advance through the park website, are required for motorized and bicycle trips on the Elephant Hill and White Rim trails. For overnight four-wheeling trips you must purchase a $30 permit, which you can reserve no more than four months, and no fewer than two days, in advance by contacting the Backcountry Reservations Office (☎ *435/259–4351*). Cyclists share all roads, so be aware and cautious of their presence. Vehicular traffic traveling uphill has the right-of-way. It's best to check at the visitor center for current road conditions before taking off into the backcountry. You must carry a washable, reusable toilet with you in the Maze District and carry out all waste.

ISLAND IN THE SKY

White Rim Road. Winding around and below the Island in the Sky mesa top, the dramatic, 100-mile White Rim Road offers a once-in-a-lifetime driving experience. As you tackle Murphy's Hogback, Hardscrabble Hill, and more formidable obstacles, you will get some fantastic views of the park. A trip around the loop can be done in one long day, or you can camp overnight with advance reservations. Campsite reservations open in July for the subsequent year, and popular spring and fall weekends fill up immediately. Day-use permits, which are available at the park visitor center or 24 hours in advance through the park website, are required for motorized and bicycle trips on White Rim Road. Bring plenty of water, a spare tire, and a jack, as no services are available on the road. White Rim Road starts at the end of Shafer Trail. ⌧ *Off main park road about 1 mile from entrance, then about 11 miles on Shafer Trail, Island in the Sky* ☎ *435/259–4351* ⊕ *www.nps.gov/cany.*

THE MAZE

Flint Trail. This remote, rugged road is the most popular in the Maze District, but it's not an easy ride. It has 2 miles of switchbacks that drop down the side of a cliff face. You reach Flint Trail from the Hans Flat Ranger Station, 46 miles from the closest paved road. From Hans Flat to the end of the road at the Doll House it's 41 miles, a drive that takes at least six hours one-way. The Maze is not generally a destination for a day trip, so you'll have to purchase an overnight backcountry permit for $30. Despite its remoteness, the Maze District can fill to capacity during spring and fall, so plan ahead. ⊠ *Hans Flat Ranger Station, National Park Rd. 777, 46 miles east of Rte. 24, Maze.*

NEEDLES

Elephant Hill. The first 3 miles of this route are designated as passable by all vehicles, but don't venture out without asking about road conditions. For the rest of the trail, only 4X4 vehicles are allowed. The route is so difficult that many people get out and walk—it's faster than you can drive it in some cases. From Elephant Hill Trailhead to Devil's Kitchen it's 3½ miles; from the trailhead to the Confluence Overlook, it's a 14½-mile round-trip and requires at least eight hours. Don't attempt this without a well-maintained 4X4 vehicle and spare gas, tires, and off-road knowledge. A day-use permit, which is available at the park visitor center or 24 hours in advance through the park website, is required for motorized and bicycle trips on the Elephant Hill Trail. ⊠ *Off main park road, 7 miles from park entrance, Needles.*

HIKING

Canyonlands National Park is a good place to immerse yourself in the intoxicating colors, smells, and textures of the desert. Many of the trails are long, rolling routes over slickrock and sand in landscapes dotted with juniper, pinyon, and sagebrush. Interconnecting trails in the Needles District provide excellent opportunities for weeklong backpacking excursions. The Maze trails are primarily accessed via four-wheel-drive vehicle. In the separate Horseshoe Canyon area, Horseshoe Canyon Trail takes a considerable amount of effort to reach, as it is more than 100 miles from Moab, 32 miles of which are a bumpy, and often sandy, dirt road.

ISLAND IN THE SKY

EASY

Aztec Butte Trail. The highlight of the 2-mile round-trip hike is the chance to see Ancestral Puebloan granaries. The view into Taylor Canyon is also nice. *Easy.* ✛ *Trailhead: on Upheaval Dome Rd., about 6 miles from park entrance.*

Grand View Point Trail. If you're looking for a level walk with some of the best scenery in the West, stop at Grand View Point and wander this 2-mile round-trip trail along the cliff edge. Many people just stop at the paved overlook and drive on, but you'll gain breathtaking perspective by strolling along this flat cliffside trail. On a clear day you can see up to 100 miles to the Maze and Needles districts of the park, the confluence of the Green and Colorado rivers, and each of Utah's major laccolithic mountain ranges: the Henrys, Abajos, and La Sals. *Easy.* ✛ *Trailhead: on main park road, 12 miles from visitor center.*

FAMILY
Fodor's Choice
★
Mesa Arch Trail. After the overlooks, this is the most popular trail in the park, a ½-mile loop that acquaints you with desert plants and terrain and offers vistas of the La Sal Mountains. The highlight of this hike is a natural arch window perched over an 800-foot drop, giving a rare downward glimpse through the arch rather than the usual upward view of the sky. Park rangers say this is one of the best spots to enjoy the sunrise. *Easy.* ✛ *Trailhead: 6 miles from visitor center.*

FAMILY
Whale Rock Trail. If you've been hankering to walk across some of that pavement-smooth stuff they call slickrock, the hike to Whale Rock will make your feet happy. This 1-mile round-trip adventure, complete with handrails to help you make the tough final 100-foot climb, takes you to the very top of the whale's back. Once you get there, you are rewarded with great views of Upheaval Dome and Trail Canyon. *Easy.* ✛ *Trailhead: on Upheaval Dome Rd., 11 miles from park entrance.*

MODERATE

Upheaval Dome Trail. It's fun to imagine that a giant meteorite crashed to earth here, sending shockwaves around the planet. But some people believe that salt, collecting and expanding upward, formed a dome and then exploded, causing the crater. Either way, it's worth the steep hike to see it and decide for yourself. You reach the main overlook after just 0.8 mile, but you can double your pleasure by going on to a second overlook for a better view. The trail is steeper and rougher after the first overlook. Round-trip to the second overlook is 2 miles. *Moderate.* ⊕ *Trailhead: on Upheaval Dome Rd., 12 miles from park entrance.*

DIFFICULT

Syncline Loop Trail. If you're up for a strenuous day of hiking, try this 8-mile trail that circles Upheaval Dome. You get limited views of the dome itself as you actually make a complete loop around the outside of the crater. Stretches of the trail are rocky, rugged, and steep. *Difficult.* ⊕ *Trailhead: on Upheaval Dome Rd., 12 miles from park entrance.*

THE MAZE

DIFFICULT

Horseshoe Canyon Trail. This remote region of Canyonlands National Park is accessible by dirt road, and then only in good weather. Park at the lip of the canyon and hike 6½ miles round-trip to the Great Gallery, considered by some to be the most significant rock-art panel in North America. Ghostly life-size figures in the Barrier Canyon style populate the amazing panel. The hike is moderately strenuous, with a 750-foot descent. Allow at least six hours for the trip and take a gallon of water per person. There's no camping allowed in the canyon, although you can camp on top near the parking lot. *Difficult.* ✛ *Trailhead: 32 miles east of Rte. 24.*

NEEDLES

EASY

Slickrock Trail. Wear a hat if you're on this trail in summer, and carry plenty of water, because you won't find any shade along the 2.4-mile round-trip trek. This is the rare frontcountry site where you might spot one of the few remaining native herds of bighorn sheep in the national park system. Nice panoramic views. *Easy.* ✛ *Trailhead: on main park road, about 10 miles from park entrance.*

MODERATE

FAMILY **Cave Spring Trail.** One of the best, most interesting trails in the park takes you past a historic cowboy camp, prehistoric pictographs, and great views. Two wooden ladders and one short, steep stretch may make this a little daunting for the extremely young or old, but it's also a short hike (0.6 mile), features some shade, and has many features packed into half a mile. Allow about 45 minutes. *Moderate.* ✛ *Trailhead: off main park road on Cave Springs Rd., 2.3 miles from visitor center.*

DIFFICULT

Chesler Park Loop. Chesler Park is a grassy meadow dotted with spires and enclosed by a circular wall of colorful "needles." One of Canyonlands' more popular trails leads through the area to the famous Joint Trail. The trail is 6 miles round-trip to the viewpoint. The entire loop is 11 miles. *Difficult.* ✛ *Trailhead: accessed via Elephant Hill Trailhead, off main park road, about 7 miles from park entrance.*

Joint Trail. Part of the Chesler Park Loop, this well-loved trail follows a series of deep, narrow fractures in the rock. A shady spot in summer, it will give you good views of the Needles formations for which the district is named. The loop travels briefly along a four-wheel-drive road and is 11 miles round-trip; allow at least five hours to complete the hike. *Difficult.* ✛ *Trailhead: accessed by Elephant Hill Trailhead, off main park road, 7 miles from park entrance.*

ROCK CLIMBING

Fodor'sChoice ★ Canyonlands and many of the surrounding areas draw climbers from all over the world. Permits are not required, but because of the sensitive archaeological nature of the park, it's imperative that you stop at the visitor center to pick up regulations pertaining to the park's cultural resources. Popular climbing routes include Moses and Zeus towers in Taylor Canyon, and Monster Tower and Washerwoman Tower on the White Rim Road. Like most routes in Canyonlands, these climbs are for experienced climbers only. Just outside the Needles District, in Indian Creek, is one of the country's best traditional climbing areas.

WHAT'S NEARBY

NEARBY TOWNS

Moab is the major gateway to both Arches and Canyonlands national parks, with the most outfitters, shops, and lodging options of the area. A handful of communities that are much smaller and have fewer amenities is scattered around the Needles and Island in the Sky districts along U.S. 191.

Roughly 55 miles south of Moab is **Monticello.** Convenient to the Needles District, it lies at an elevation of 7,000 feet, making it a cool summer refuge from the desert heat. In winter, it gets downright cold and sees deep snow; the Abajo Mountains, whose highest point is 11,360 feet, rise to the west of town. Monticello motels serve the steady stream of tourists who venture south of Moab, but the town offers few dining or shopping opportunities. **Blanding,** 21 miles south of Monticello, prides itself on old-fashioned conservative values. By popular vote there's a ban on the sale of liquor, beer, and wine, so the town has no state liquor store and its restaurants do not serve alcoholic beverages. Blanding is a good resting point if you're traveling south from Canyonlands to Natural Bridges Natural Monument, Grand Gulch, Lake Powell, or the Navajo Nation. About 25 miles south of Blanding, tiny **Bluff** is doing its best to stay that way. It's a great place to stop if you aren't looking for many amenities but value beautiful scenery, silence, and starry nights. Bluff is the most common starting point for trips on the San Juan River, which serves as the northern boundary for the Navajo Reservation; it's also a wonderful place to overnight if you're planning a visit to Hovenweep National Monument, about 30 miles away.

Visitor Information Blanding Visitor Center. ⊠ *12 N. Grayson Pkwy., Blanding* ☎ *435/678–3662* ⊕ *www.blanding-ut.gov.* **Southwestern Utah Welcome Center.** ⊠ *216 S. Main St., Monticello* ☎ *435/587–3401* ⊕ *www.monticelloutah.org.*

NEARBY ATTRACTIONS

Fodor's Choice ★ **Dead Horse Point State Park.** One of the gems of Utah's state park system, 34 miles southwest from Moab, this park overlooks a sweeping oxbow of the Colorado River, some 2,000 feet below. Dead Horse Point itself is a small peninsula connected to the main mesa by a narrow neck of land. As the story goes, cowboys used to drive wild mustangs onto the point and pen them there with a brush fence. There's a modern visitor center with a coffee shop (March–October) and museum. The park's Intrepid Trail System has become popular with mountain bikers and hikers alike. Be sure to walk the 4-mile rim trail loop and drive to the park's eponymous point if it's a nice day. ⊠ *Hwy. 313* ☎ *435/259–2614, 800/322–3770 camping reservations* ⊕ *www.stateparks.utah.gov* 💲 *$10 per vehicle* ☉ *Park daily 6 am–10 pm; visitor center Mar.–Oct., daily 8–6; Nov.–Feb., daily 9–5.*

Southeast Utah

FAMILY **Edge of the Cedars State Park Museum.** Possibly the most interesting state
Fodor's Choice park in Utah, Edge of the Cedars is one of the nation's foremost muse-
★ ums dedicated to the Ancestral Puebloan culture. Behind the museum,
an interpretive trail leads to an ancient village that they once inhabited.
Portions of the village have been partially excavated and visitors can
climb down a ladder into a 1,000-year-old ceremonial room called a kiva.
The museum displays a variety of pots, baskets, spear points, and rare
artifacts—even a pair of sandals said to date back 1,500 years. ⊠ *660 W.
400 N, Blanding* ☎ *435/678–2238* ⊕ *stateparks.utah.gov/parks/edge-of-
the-cedars* ☎ *$5* ⊗ *Mon.–Sat. 9–5; also Sun. 10–4, Apr.–Sept.*

Natural Bridges National Monument. Stunning natural bridges and ancient
Native American ruins, plus magnificent scenery throughout make Natural Bridges National Monument a must-see for anyone who has time to
make the trip. Sipapu is one of the largest natural bridges in the world,
spanning 225 feet and standing more than 140 feet tall. You can take
in the Sipapu, Owachomo, and Kachina bridges via an 8.6-mile round-
trip hike that meanders around and under them. A 13-site primitive
campground is an optimal spot for stargazing. The national monument
is about 120 miles southwest of the Needles District of Canyonlands
National Park and approximately 45 miles from Blanding. ⊠ *Hwy. 275,
off Hwy. 95, Natural Bridges National Monument* ☎ *435/692–1234*

CLOSE UP

Best Campgrounds in Canyonlands

Canyonlands campgrounds are some of the most beautiful in the national park system. At the Needles District, campers will enjoy fairly private campsites tucked against red rock walls and dotted with pinyon and juniper trees. At Island in the Sky, starry nights and spectacular vistas make the small campground an intimate treasure. Hookups are not available in either of the park's campgrounds; however, the sites are long enough to accommodate units up to 28 feet long.

Squaw Flat Campground. The defining features of the camp sites at Squaw Flat are house-size red rock formations, which provide some shade, offer privacy from adjacent campers, and make this one of the more unique campgrounds in the national park system. ⊠ *Off main road, about 5 miles from park entrance, Needles* ☎ *435/259–7164.*

Willow Flat Campground. From this little campground on a mesa top, you can walk to spectacular views of the Green River. Most sites have a bit of shade from juniper trees. ⊠ *Off main park road, about 9 miles from park entrance, Island in the Sky* ☎ *435/259–4712.*

⊕ *www.nps.gov/nabr* ☎ *$10 per vehicle, $5 for those entering the park on foot, bicycle, or motorcycle* ☉ *May–Sept., daily 8–6; Oct. and Apr., daily 8–5; Nov.–Mar., daily 9–5.*

SHOPPING

Thin Bear Indian Arts. The Hosler family has operated this tiny little trading post in the same location since 1973. Authentic jewelry, rugs, baskets, and pottery are for sale at this friendly spot. ⊠ *1944 S. Main St., Blanding* ☎ *435/678–2940* ☉ *Weekdays 9–5, Sat. 10–2.*

WHERE TO STAY

OUTSIDE THE PARK

$$$
HOTEL 🖭 **Desert Rose Inn and Cabins.** Bluff's largest hotel is an attractive, wood-sided lodge with a huge two-story front porch. **Pros:** clean, comfortable rooms; friendly staff. **Cons:** has no historic charm; town not a culinary hub. ⑤ *Rooms from: $179* ⊠ *701 W. Main St., Bluff* ☎ *435/672–2303, 888/475–7673* ⊕ *www.desertroseinn.com* ⇌ *30 rooms, 16 suites, 7 cabins* ⊚ *No meals.*

$
HOTEL 🖭 **Recapture Lodge.** The knowledgeable owners of this family-owned and -operated inn have detailed tips for exploring the surrounding canyon country. **Pros:** set on shady grounds; owner is a wildlife biologist happy to share his knowledge; horses welcome. **Cons:** older property; small rooms and basic amenities; no phones or Wi-Fi in rooms. ⑤ *Rooms from: $85* ⊠ *220 E. Main St. (U.S. 191), Bluff* ☎ *435/672–2281* ⊕ *www.recapturelodge.com* ⇌ *26 rooms, 2 houses* ⊚ *Breakfast.*

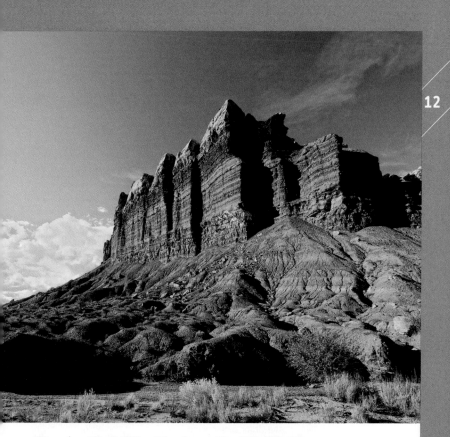

CAPITOL REEF
NATIONAL PARK

WELCOME TO CAPITOL REEF NATIONAL PARK

TOP REASONS TO GO

★ **The Waterpocket Fold:** See an excellent example of a monocline—a fold in the Earth's crust with one very steep side in an area that is otherwise horizontal. This one's almost 100 miles long.

★ **No crowds:** Experience the best of southern Utah weather, rock formations, and wide-open spaces without the crowds of nearby parks such as Zion and Bryce Canyon.

★ **Fresh fruit:** Pick apples, pears, apricots, and peaches in season at the pioneer-planted orchards at historic Fruita. These trees still produce plenty of fruit.

★ **Rock art:** View pictographs and petroglyphs left by ancient Native Americans, who lived in this area from AD 700 to 1300.

★ **Pioneer artifacts:** Buy faithfully reproduced tools and utensils like those used by Mormon pioneers, at the Gifford Farmhouse.

1 Fruita. This historic pioneer village is at the heart of what most people see of Capitol Reef. The one and only park visitor center nearby is the place to get travel and weather information and maps. The scenic drive through Capitol Gorge provides a view of the Golden Throne.

2 Cathedral Valley. The views are stunning and the silence deafening in the park's remote northern section. High-clearance vehicles are required, as is a crossing of the Fremont River. Driving in this valley is next to impossible when the Cathedral Valley Road is wet, so ask at the visitor center about current weather and road conditions.

3 Muley Twist Canyon. At the southern reaches of the park, this canyon is accessed via Notom-Bullfrog Road from the north, and Burr Trail Road from the west and southeast. High-clearance vehicles are required for much of it.

GETTING ORIENTED

At the heart of this 378-square-mile park is the massive natural feature known as the Waterpocket Fold, which runs roughly northwest to southeast along the park's spine. Capitol Reef itself is named for a formation along the fold near the Fremont River. A historic pioneer settlement, the green oasis of Fruita is easily accessed by car, and a 9-mile scenic drive provides a good overview of the canyons and rock formations that populate the park. Colors here range from deep, rich reds to sage greens to crumbling gray sediments. The absence of large towns nearby ensures that night skies are brilliant starscapes.

UTAH

12

Gypsum 2
Sinkhole
Cathedral Valley
Temple of the Sun
Temple of the Moon
The Hartnet
South Desert
WATERPOCKET
Bentonite Hills
Caineville
Twin Rocks
Chimney Rock
The Castle
Fruita Historic District
Fremont Petroglyphs
Capitol Dome
Hickman Bridge
Godsenecks Overlook
Fruita 1
Torrey
Visitor Center
Gifford Farmhouse
Grand Wash
Behunin Cabin
Orientation Pullout
Grover
Golden Throne
Capitol Gorge
Pioneer Register
Larb Hollow Overlook
SOUTH DRAW
Notom-Bullfrog
Steep Creek Overlook
Dry Bench
Homestead Overlook
Cedar Mesa
Bitter Creek Divide
Strike Valley
WATERPOCKET
Boulder
Burr Trail Road
Grand Staircase-Escalante National Monument
Strike Valley Overlook
FOLD
The Post
Burr Trail Switchbacks
Muley Twist Canyon
TO BULLFROG MARINA, LAKE POWELL
TO SAN RAFAEL SWELL
3
0   5 mi
0   5 km
Muley Tanks
Burr Trail Road
Halls Creek Overlook
Glen Canyon National Recreation Area

KEY

Ranger Station
Campground
Picnic Area
Restaurant
Lodge
Trailhead
Restrooms
Scenic Viewpoint
Walking/Hiking Trails

Updated by Mike Weatherford

Capitol Reef National Park is a natural kaleidoscopic feast for the eyes. Here, you are saturated in colors that are more dramatic than anywhere else in the West. The dominant Moenkopi rock formation is a rich, red-chocolate hue. Deep blue-green juniper and pinyon stand out against it. Other sandstone layers are gold, ivory, and lavender. Sunset brings out the colors in an explosion of copper, platinum, and orange, then dusk turns the cliffs purple and blue. The texture of rock deposited in ancient inland seas and worn by subsequent erosion is pure art.

The park preserves the Waterpocket Fold, a giant wrinkle in the earth that extends 100 miles between Thousand Lake Mountain and Lake Powell. When you climb high onto the rocks or into the mountains, you can see this remarkable geologic wonder and the jumble of colorful cliffs, massive domes, soaring spires, and twisting canyons that surround it. It's no wonder American Indians called this part of the country the "land of sleeping rainbow."

But your eyes will not be alone in their joy. The fragrance of pine and sage rises from the earth, and canyon wrens sing to you as you sit by the water. Flowing across the heart of Capitol Reef is the Fremont River, a narrow little creek that can turn into a swollen, raging torrent during desert flash floods. The river sustains cottonwoods, wildlife, and verdant valleys rich with fruit. During the harvest, your sensory experience is complete when you bite into a perfect ripe peach or apple from the park's orchards. Your soul, too, will be gratified here. You can walk the trails in relative solitude and enjoy the beauty without confronting crowds on the roads or paths. All around you are signs of those who came before: ancient American Indians of the Fremont culture, Mormon pioneers who settled the land, and other courageous explorers who traveled the canyons. It is a rare thrill to feel the past overtake the present.

CAPITOL REEF PLANNER

WHEN TO GO

Spring and early summer are most bustling. Folks clear out in the mid-summer heat, and then return for the apple harvest and crisp temperatures of autumn. Still, the park is seldom crowded—though the campground can fill quickly. Annual rainfall is scant, but when it does rain, flash floods can wipe out park roads. Snowfall is usually light. Sudden, short-lived snowstorms—and thunderstorms—are not uncommon in the spring.

AVG. HIGH/LOW TEMPS.

Jan.	Feb.	Mar.	Apr.	May	June
41/20	47/26	558/33	66/40	74/48	87/58
July	Aug.	Sept.	Oct.	Nov.	Dec.
91/65	89/64	80/54	66/44	51/31	41/22

FESTIVALS AND EVENTS

AUGUST
FAMILY
Wayne County Fair. The great American county-fair tradition is at its finest in Loa in mid-August. Horse shows, demolition derby, rodeo, and a parade are part of the fun. There are also crafts such as handmade quilts, agricultural exhibits, children's games, and plenty of good food. ☎ *435/836–2765* ⊕ *waynecountyutah.org.*

Women's Redrock Music Festival. Held at the Robbers Roost Bookstore, this two-day event has been attracting independent female musicians from all corners of the globe, as well as hundreds of fans, since 2007. Run by the nonprofit Entrada Institute, a regional arts and education organization, the festival benefits Utah women through donations and scholarships. ✉ *185 W. Main St., Torrey* ☎ *435/425–3265* ⊕ *womensredrockmusicfest.com.*

OCTOBER
Harvest Time Scarecrow Festival. Events for this monthlong celebration of the end of another busy season are held throughout Wayne County. In addition to a scarecrow contest, there are plenty of family-friendly events, including music, arts and crafts, pumpkin carving and a Halloween party at Torrey's Rim Rock restaurant. ✉ *Torrey* ☎ *435/425–3265* ⊕ *www.entradainstitute.org.*

PLANNING YOUR TIME

CAPITOL REEF IN ONE DAY

Pack a picnic lunch, snacks, and cold drinks to take with you, because there are no restaurants in the park. As you enter the park, look to your left for Chimney Rock; in a landscape of spires, cliffs, and knobs, this deep-red landmark is unmistakable. Start your journey at the **visitor center**, where you can study a three-dimensional map of the area, watch the short film, and browse the many books and maps related to the park. Then head for the park's scenic drive, stopping at the **Fruita Historic District** to see some of the sites associated with the park's Mormon history. Stop at the **Gifford Farmhouse** for a tour and a visit to the gift shop. That lunch you packed can be enjoyed at picnic tables on rolling green lawns lining both sides of the road between the orchard and Gifford Farmhouse.

As you continue on with your tour, check out the **Fremont Indian Petroglyphs,** and if you feel like some exertion, take a hike on the Hickman Bridge Trail. From the trail (or if you skip the hike, from Highway 24 about 2 miles east of the visitor center), you'll see **Capitol Dome.** Along this stretch of Highway 24 stop to see the old one-room **Fruita Schoolhouse,** the **petroglyphs,** and the **Behunin Cabin.** Next you'll have to backtrack a few miles on Highway 24 to find the **Goosenecks Trail.** At the same parking lot you'll find the trailhead for **Sunset Point Trail;** take this short hike in time to watch the setting sun hit the colorful cliffs.

GETTING HERE AND AROUND
AIR TRAVEL
The nearest major airports are in Salt Lake City, about 3½ hours away by car, and Las Vegas, about 5½ hours away.

BUS TRAVEL
Once inside the park, there is no shuttle service as at nearby Zion and Bryce Canyon national parks.

CAR TRAVEL
Though far from big cities, Capitol Reef country can be reached by a variety of approaches. The main high-speed arteries through the region are Interstates 70 and 15, but any route will require travel of some secondary roads such as U.S. 50, U.S. 89, Highway 24, or Route 72. All are well-maintained, safe roads that bisect rich agricultural communities steeped in Mormon history (such as the nearby towns of Bicknell and Loa). Interstate 15 is the fastest way through central Utah, but U.S. 89 and the local roads that feed onto it will give you a more direct path into Utah's past and present-day character. Highway 24 runs across the middle of Capitol Reef National Park, so even those traveling between points west and east of the park with no intention of touring it get a scenic treat on their way.

PARK ESSENTIALS
PARK FEES AND PERMITS
There is no fee to enter the park, but it's $10 per vehicle (or $7 per bicycle) to travel on Scenic Drive beyond Fruita Campground; this fee is good for one week, paid via the "honor system" at a drop box versus a staffed entry gate. Backcountry camping permits are free; pick them up at the visitor center. An annual pass that allows unlimited access to Scenic Drive is $30.

PARK HOURS
The park is open 24/7 year-round. It is in the Mountain time zone.

CELL-PHONE RECEPTION
Cell-phone reception is best near the visitor center and campground areas. Pay phones are at the visitor center and at Fruita Campground.

EDUCATIONAL OFFERINGS
RANGER PROGRAMS

From late May to early September, ranger programs are offered at no charge. You can obtain current information about ranger talks and other park events at the visitor center or campground bulletin boards.

FAMILY **Evening Program.** Learn about Capitol Reef's geology, American Indian cultures, wildlife, and more at the campground amphitheater about a mile from the visitor center. Programs begin typically around sunset. A schedule of topics and times is posted at the visitor center. ⊠ *Amphitheater, Loop C, Fruita Campground, Scenic Dr.* ☎ *435/425–3791.*

FAMILY **Junior Ranger Program.** Each child who participates in this self-guided, year-round program completes a combination of activities in the Junior Ranger booklet, attends a ranger program, watches the park movie, interviews a park ranger, and/or picks up litter. ⊠ *National Park Visitor Center, 16 Scenic Dr.* ☎ *435/425–3791* 🖭 *Free.*

FAMILY **Ranger Talks.** Typically, the park offers a daily morning geology talk at the visitor center and a daily afternoon petroglyph-panel talk. Occasional geology hikes and history tours are also sometimes offered. Times can vary. ⊠ *National Park Visitor Center, 16 Scenic Rd.* ☎ *435/425–3791* 🖭 *Free* ☉ *May–Sept., daily.*

RESTAURANTS

There is no restaurant, just a small store selling baked items and ice cream inside Capitol Reef. But dining options exist close by in Torrey, where you can find everything from one of Utah's best restaurants serving high-end Southwestern cuisine to basic hamburger joints offering up consistently good food.

HOTELS

There are no lodging options within Capitol Reef, but you'll have no problem finding clean and comfortable accommodations no matter what your budget in nearby Torrey and not far beyond in Bicknell and Loa. Drive farther into the region's towns, and you are more likely to find locally owned low- to moderate-priced motels, and a few nice inns and bed-and-breakfasts. Reservations are recommended in summer. *Hotel reviews have been shortened. For full information, visit Fodors.com.*

WHAT IT COSTS			
	$	$$	$$$	$$$$
Restaurants	under $13	$13–$20	$21–$30	over $30
Hotels	under $101	$101–$150	$151–$200	over $200

Restaurant prices are the average cost of a main course at dinner, or if dinner is not served, at lunch. Hotel prices are the lowest cost of a standard double room in high season.

Plants and Wildlife in Capitol Reef

The golden rock and rainbow cliffs are at their finest at sunset, when it seems as if they are lighted from within. That's also when mule deer wander through the orchards near the campground. The deer are quite tame, but do not feed them; their digestive systems are harmed by people food. Many of the park's animals move about only at night to escape the heat of the day, but pinyon jays and black-billed magpies flit around the park all day. The best place to see wildlife is near the Fremont River, where animals are drawn to drink. Ducks and small mammals such as the yellow-bellied marmot live nearby. Desert bighorn sheep also live in Capitol Reef, but they are elusive. Your best chance for spotting the sheep is during a long hike deep within the park. If you should encounter a sheep, do not approach it, as they've been known to charge human beings.

VISITOR INFORMATION

Park Contact Information Capitol Reef National Park. ⊠ *Off Hwy. 24* ☎ *435/425–3791* ⊕ *nps.gov/care.*

VISITOR CENTERS

FAMILY **Capitol Reef Visitor Center.** Watch a park movie, talk with rangers, or peruse the many books, maps, and materials offered for sale in the bookstore. Towering over the center, which is 11 miles east of Torrey, is the Castle, one of the park's most prominent rock formations. ⊠ *Hwy. 24 and Scenic Dr.* ☎ *435/425–3791* ⊙ *Late May–Sept., daily 8–6; Oct.–mid-May, daily 8–4:30.*

EXPLORING

SCENIC DRIVES

FAMILY **Capitol Reef Scenic Drive.** This 8-mile road, called simply Scenic Drive by locals, starts at the visitor center and winds its way through the Fruita Historic District and colorful sandstone cliffs into Capitol Gorge; a side road, Grand Wash Road, provides access into the canyon. At Capitol Gorge, the canyon walls become steep and impressive but the route becomes unpaved for about the last 2 miles, and road conditions may vary due to weather and usage. Check with the visitor center before setting out. ⊠ *Off Hwy. 24, 11 miles east of Torrey.*

SCENIC STOPS

FAMILY **Behunin Cabin.** Elijah Cutlar Behunin used blocks of sandstone to build this cabin in 1882. Floods in the lowlands made life too difficult, and he moved before the turn of that century. The house, 5.9 miles east of the visitor center, is empty, but you can peep through a window. ⊠ *Hwy. 24.*

FAMILY **Capitol Dome.** One of the rock formations that gave the park its name, this giant, sandstone dome is visible in the vicinity of the Hickman Bridge trailhead, 1.9 miles east of the visitor center. ⊠ *Hwy. 24.*

Fodor'sChoice **Capitol Gorge.** At the entrance to
★ this gorge, 9 miles south of the visitor center, Scenic Drive becomes unpaved. The narrow, twisting road on the floor of the gorge was a route for pioneer wagons traversing this part of Utah starting in the 1860s. After every flash flood, pioneers would laboriously clear the route so wagons could continue to go through. The gorge became the main automobile route in the area until 1962, when Highway 24 was built. The short drive to the end of the road has striking views of the surrounding cliffs and leads to one of the park's most popular walks, the hiking trail to the water-holding "tanks" eroded into the sandstone. ⊠ *Scenic Dr.*

> ### GEOLOGY BEHIND THE PARK'S NAME
>
> When water wears away layers of sandstone, basins can appear in the rock. These are called waterpockets. The 100-mile-long Waterpocket Fold—a massive rift in the Earth's crust, where geothermal pressure pushed one side 7,000 feet higher than the other (today it's settled to 2,600 feet)—is full of these waterpockets. Early explorers with seafaring backgrounds called the fold a reef, because it was a barrier to travel. Some of the rocks, due to erosion, also have domelike formations resembling capitol rotundas.

12

Chimney Rock. Even in a landscape of spires, cliffs, and knobs, this deep-red landform, 3.9 miles west of the visitor center, is unmistakable. ⊠ *Hwy. 24.*

FAMILY **Fremont Petroglyphs.** Between AD 600 and 1300 the Capitol Reef area was occupied by Native Americans who were eventually referred to as Fremonts, named after the Fremont River that flows through the park. A nice stroll along a boardwalk bridge, 1.1 miles east of the visitor center, allows close-up views of ancient rock art, which can be identified by the large trapezoidal figures often depicted wearing headdresses and ear baubles. ⊠ *Hwy. 24.*

FAMILY **Fruita Historic District.** In the 1880s Nels Johnson became the first homesteader in the Fremont River Valley, building his home near the confluence of Sulphur Creek and the Fremont River. Other Mormon settlers followed and established small farms and orchards, creating the village of Junction. The orchards thrived, and by 1900 the name was changed to Fruita. The orchards, less than a mile from the visitor center, are preserved and protected as a Rural Historic Landscape. ⊠ *Scenic Dr.*

Pioneer Register. Travelers passing through Capitol Gorge in the 19th and early 20th centuries etched the canyon wall with their names and the date they passed. Directly across the canyon from the Pioneer Register and about 50 feet up are signatures etched into the canyon wall by an early United States Geologic Survey crew. Though it's illegal to write or scratch on the canyon walls today, plenty of damage has been done by vandals over the years. You can reach the register via an easy hike from the sheltered trailhead at the end of Capitol Gorge Road, 10.3

GOOD READS

- *Capitol Reef: Canyon Country Eden,* by Rose Houk, is an award-winning collection of photographs and lyrical essays on the park.

- *Dwellers of the Rainbow, Fremont Culture in Capitol Reef National Park,* by Rose Houk, offers a brief background of the Fremont culture in Capitol Reef.

- *Explore Capitol Reef Trails,* by Marjorie Miller and John Foster, is a comprehensive hiking guide.

- *Geology of Capitol Reef National Park,* by Michael Collier, teaches the basic geology of the park.

- *Red Rock Eden,* by George Davidson, tells the story of historic Fruita, its settlements, and orchards.

miles south of the visitor center; the register is about 10 minutes along the hike to the sandstone "tanks." ⊠ *Off Scenic Dr.*

The Waterpocket Fold. A giant wrinkle in the earth extends almost 100 miles between Thousand Lake Mountain and Lake Powell. You can glimpse the fold by driving south on Scenic Drive, after it branches off Highway 24, past the Fruita Historic District, but for complete immersion enter the park via the 36-mile Burr Trail from Boulder. Travel through the southernmost reaches of the park is largely on unpaved roads. It's accessible to most vehicles during dry weather, but check with the visitor center for current road conditions. ⊠ *Capitol Reef National Park.*

SPORTS AND THE OUTDOORS

The main outdoor activity at Capitol Reef is hiking. There are trails for all levels. Remember: Whenever you venture into the desert—that is, wherever you go in Capitol Reef—take, and drink, plenty of water.

MULTISPORT OUTFITTER

Hondoo Rivers & Trails. This tour company has been providing high-quality backcountry trips into Capitol Reef National Park, Escalante Canyons, and the High Plateaus for 40 years. From April to October, they'll take you on hiking, horseback-riding, and Jeep day tours. Trips are designed to explore the geologic landforms in the area, seek out wildflowers in season, and to encounter free-roaming mustangs, bison, and bighorn sheep when possible. Multiday trips can also be arranged. ⊠ *90 E. Main St., Torrey* 🕾 *435/425–3519* ⊕ *www.hondoo. com* 🖂 *From $120.*

BICYCLING

Bicycles are allowed only on established roads in the park. Highway 24 is a state highway and receives a substantial amount of through traffic, so it's not the best place to pedal. Scenic Drive is better, but the road is narrow, and you have to contend with drivers dazed by the beautiful surroundings. In fact, it's a good idea to traverse it in the morning or evening when traffic is reduced, or in the off-season. Four-wheel-drive roads are certainly less traveled, but they are often sandy, rocky, and steep. You cannot ride your bicycle in washes or on hiking trails.

Cathedral Valley Scenic Backway. In the remote north of the park you can enjoy solitude (but for the occasional off-roader) and a true backcountry ride on this trail. Surfaces include dirt, sand, bentonite clay, and rock, and you will also ford the Fremont River; be prepared to encounter steep hills and switchbacks, wash crossings, and stretches of deep sand. Summer is not a good time to try this ride, as water is very difficult to find and temperatures may exceed 100°F. The entire route is about 58 miles long, and can be accessed at Caineville, off Highway 24, or at River Ford Road, 5 miles west of Caineville; for a multiday trip, there's a primitive campground about midway through the loop. ⊠ *Off Hwy. 24.*

South Draw Road. This is a very strenuous ride that traverses dirt, sand, and rocky surfaces, and crosses several creeks that may be muddy. It's not recommended in winter or spring because of deep snow at higher elevations. The route starts at an elevation of 8,600 feet on Boulder Mountain, 13 miles south of Torrey, and ends 15¾ miles later at 5,500 feet in the Pleasant Creek parking area at the end of Scenic Drive. ⊠ *Bowns Reservoir Rd. and Hwy. 12.*

FOUR-WHEELING

You can explore Capitol Reef in a 4X4 on a number of exciting backcountry routes. Road conditions can vary greatly depending on recent weather patterns. Spring and summer rains can leave the roads muddy, washed out, and impassable even to four-wheel-drive vehicles. Always check at the park visitor center for current conditions before you set out, and take water, supplies, and a cell phone with you.

Cathedral Valley Scenic Backway. The north end of Capitol Reef, along this backcountry road, is filled with towering monoliths, panoramic vistas, two water crossings, and a stark desert landscape. The area is remote and the road through it unpaved, so do not enter without a high-clearance vehicle, some planning, and a cell phone (although reception is virtually nonexistent). The drive through the valley is a 58-mile loop that you can begin at River Ford Road, 11¾ miles east of the visitor center off Highway 24; allow half a day. If your time is limited, you can tour only the Caineville Wash Road, which takes about two hours. Pick up a self-guided auto tour brochure at the visitor center. ⊠ *River Ford Rd., off Hwy. 24.*

HIKING

Many park trails in Capitol Reef include steep climbs, but there are a few easy-to-moderate hikes. A short drive from the visitor center takes you to a dozen trails, and a park ranger can advise you on combining trails or locating additional routes.

EASY

Goosenecks Trail. This nice little walk gives you a good introduction to the land surrounding Capitol Reef. Enjoy the dizzying views from the overlook. It's only a 0.3-mile round-trip. *Easy.* ✛ *Trailhead: at Hwy. 24, about 3 miles west of visitor center.*

Grand Wash Trail. At the end of unpaved Grand Wash Road you can continue on foot through the canyon to its end at Highway 24. You're bound to love the trip. This flat hike takes you through a wide wash between canyon walls. It's an excellent place to study the geology up close. The round-trip hike is 4½ miles; allow two to three hours for your walk. Check at the ranger station for flash-flood warnings before entering the wash. *Easy.* ✛ *Trailhead: at Hwy. 24, east of Hickman Bridge parking lot, or at end of Grand Wash Rd., off Scenic Dr. about 5 miles from visitor center.*

Sunset Point Trail. The trail starts from the same parking lot as the Goosenecks Trail. Benches along this easy, 0.8-mile round-trip invite you to sit and meditate surrounded by the colorful desert. At the trail's end, you will be rewarded with broad vistas into the park; it's even better at sunset. *Easy.* ✛ *Trailhead: at Hwy. 24, about 3 miles west of visitor center.*

MODERATE

Capitol Gorge Trail and the Tanks. Starting at the Pioneer Register, about a mile from the Capitol Gorge parking lot, is a trail that climbs to the Tanks, holes in the sandstone, formed by erosion, that hold water after it rains. After a scramble up about a quarter mile of steep trail with cliff drop-offs, you can look down into the Tanks and can also see a natural bridge below the lower tank. Including the walk to the Pioneer Register, allow an hour or more for this interesting hike, one of the park's most popular. *Moderate.* ✛ *Trailhead: at end of Scenic Dr., 10 miles south of visitor center.*

FAMILY **Cohab Canyon Trail.** Children particularly love this trail for the geological features and native creatures, such as rock wrens and Western pipistrelles (canyon bats), that you see along the way. One end of the trail is directly across from the Fruita Campground on Scenic Drive, and the other is across from the Hickman Bridge parking lot. The first ¼ mile from Fruita is pretty strenuous, but then the walk becomes easy except for turnoffs to the overlooks, which are strenuous but short. Along the way you'll find miniature arches, skinny side canyons, and honeycombed patterns on canyon walls where the wrens make nests. The trail is 3.2 miles round-trip to the Hickman Bridge parking lot. The Overlook Trail adds 1 mile to the journey. Allow one to two hours to overlooks and back; allow two to three hours to Hickman Bridge parking lot and back. *Moderate.* ✛ *Trailheads: Scenic Dr., about 1 mile south of visitor center, or Hwy. 24, about 2 miles east of visitor center.*

Fremont River Trail. What starts as a quiet little stroll beside the river turns into an adventure. The first ½ mile of the trail is wheelchair accessible as you wander past the orchards next to the Fremont River. After you pass through a narrow gate, the trail changes personality and you're in for a steep climb on an exposed ledge with drop-offs. The views at the top of the 480-foot ascent are worth it. It's 2 miles round-trip; allow two hours. *Moderate.* ✛ *Trailhead: near amphitheater off Loop C of Fruita Campground, about 1 mile from visitor center.*

Hickman Bridge Trail. This trail is a perfect introduction to the park. It leads to a natural bridge of Kayenta sandstone, which has a 133-foot opening carved by intermittent flash floods. Early on, the route climbs a set of steps along the Fremont River, and as the trail tops out onto a bench, you'll find a slight depression in the earth. This is what remains of an ancient Fremont pit house, a kind of home that was dug into the ground and covered with brush. The trail splits, leading along the right-hand branch to a strenuous uphill climb to the Rim Overlook and Navajo Knobs. Stay to your left to see the bridge, and you'll encounter a moderate up-and-down trail. As you continue up the wash on your way to the bridge, you'll notice a Fremont granary on the right side of the small canyon. Allow about 2 hours to walk the 2-mile round-trip. The walk is one of the most popular trails in the park, so expect lots of company. *Moderate.* ✛ *Trailhead: Hwy. 24, 2 miles east of visitor center.*

DIFFICULT

Chimney Rock Trail. You're almost sure to see ravens drifting on thermal winds around the deep-red Mummy Cliff that rings the base of this trail. This loop trail begins with a steep climb to a rim above Chimney Rock. The trail is 3.6 miles round-trip, with a 590-foot elevation change. No shade. Use caution during monsoon storms due to lightning hazards. Allow three to four hours. *Difficult.* ✛ *Trailhead: Hwy. 24, about 3 miles west of visitor center.*

Golden Throne Trail. As you hike to the base of the Golden Throne, you may be lucky enough to see one of the park's elusive desert bighorn sheep, but you're more likely to spot their split-hoof tracks. The trail is about 2 miles of gradual rise with some steps and drop-offs. The Golden Throne is hidden until you near the end of the trail, then suddenly you see the huge sandstone monolith. If you hike near sundown the throne burns gold. The round-trip hike is about 3.8 miles and will take two to three hours. *Difficult.* ✛ *Trailhead: at end of Capitol Gorge Rd., 10 miles south of visitor center.*

WHAT'S NEARBY

NEARBY TOWNS

Probably the best home base for exploring the park, the pretty town of **Torrey,** just outside the park, has lots of personality. Giant old cottonwood trees make it a shady, cool place to stay, and the townspeople are friendly and accommodating. A little farther west on Highway 24, tiny **Teasdale** is a charming settlement cradled in a cove of the Aquarius Plateau. The homes, many of which are well-preserved older structures, look out onto brilliantly colored cliffs and green fields. **Bicknell** lies another few miles west of Capitol Reef. Not much happens here, making it a wonderfully quiet place to rest your head. The Wayne County seat of **Loa,** 10 miles west of Torrey, was settled by pioneers in the 1870s. If you head south from Torrey instead of west, you can

Temple of the Sun, a monolith in Capitol Reef's Cathedral Valley, is a favorite with photographers.

take a spectacular 32-mile drive along Highway 12 to **Boulder,** a town so remote that its mail was carried on horseback until 1940. Nearby is Anasazi State Park. In the opposite direction, 51 miles east, **Hanksville** is more a crossroads than anything else.

Visitor Information Wayne County Office of Tourism. ☎ 435/425–3365, 800/858–7951 ⊕ www.capitolreef.org. **Garfield County Office of Tourism.** ⊠ 55 S. Main St., Panguitch ☎ 800/444–6689, 435/676–1160 ⊕ www.brycecanyoncountry.com.

NEARBY ATTRACTIONS

FAMILY **Anasazi State Park.** This former archaeological site includes portions of an Ancestral Puebloan (Anasazi) village occupied sometime between AD 1160 and 1235, a small but informative museum with artifacts discovered on-site, and a reconstructed pueblo dwelling. ⊠ 460 N. Hwy. 12, Boulder ☎ 435/335–7308 ⊕ stateparks.utah.gov ⊠ $5 ☉ Mar.–Oct., daily 8–6; Nov.–Feb., daily 8–4.

FAMILY **Goblin Valley State Park.** Strange-looking "hoodoos" rise up from the desert landscape 12 miles north of Hanksville, making Goblin Valley home to some of the weirdest, goblin-like rock formations in southeast Utah—hundreds of them, with a dramatic orange hue. Short, easy trails wind through the goblins, which delight children. ⊠ Hwy. 24 ☎ 435/275–4584 ⊕ stateparks.utah.gov ⊠ $10 per vehicle ☉ Daily 7 am–10 pm.

Fodor's Choice ★ **San Rafael Swell.** Tremendous geological upheavals pushed through the Earth's surface eons ago, forming a giant oval-shape dome of rock about 80 miles long and 30 miles wide, giving rise to the name "swell." Over the years, the harsh climate beat down the dome, eroding it into a wild array of multicolor sandstone and creating buttes, pinnacles, mesas, and canyons that spread across more than 600,000 acres—an area slightly smaller than the state of Rhode Island.

Managed by the Bureau of Land Management, the Swell offers visitors spectacular sights similar to those in Utah's national parks but without the crowds. In the northern Swell, the Wedge Overlook peers into the Little Grand Canyon and the San Rafael River below, for one of the most scenic vistas in the state. The strata at the edges of the southern Swell are angled near vertical, creating the San Rafael Reef. Both are known for fantastic hiking, canyoneering, and mountain biking.

Interstate 70 bisects the San Rafael Swell, and is the only paved road in the region. Although there are many off-road opportunities, the main gravel road and many of the graded dirt roads through the Swell are accessible to two-wheel-drive vehicles. The Swell is about 25 miles south of Price, and the closest towns—Green River, Castle Dale, and Cleveland—are not that close, so bring whatever supplies you might need, including plenty of water, food, and a spare tire.

Proposals have been made to designate the Swell a national monument. Until then, the San Rafael Swell remains one of the little-known natural wonders of the American West. ⊠ *125 S. 600 W, Price* ☎ *435/636–3600* ⊕ *www.blm.gov/ut.*

AREA ACTIVITIES

SPORTS AND THE OUTDOORS
FISHING
Fishlake National Forest. At an elevation of 8,800 feet is Fish Lake, which lies in the heart of its namesake 1.4-million-acre forest. The area has several campgrounds and wonderful lodges. The lake is stocked annually with lake and rainbow trout, mackinaw, and splake. A large population of brown trout is native to the lake. The Fremont River Ranger District office (*138 S. Main St., Loa*) can provide all the information you need for fishing, camping, and hiking in the forest. ⊠ *Off Hwy. 24* ☎ *435/836–2811* ⊕ *www.fs.usda.gov/fishlake.*

Alpine Adventures. With a stellar reputation for personalized attention during fly-fishing trips into the high backcountry around Capitol Reef and the Fremont River, Alpine Adventures also leads trophy hunting tours. ⊠ *Torrey* ☎ *435/425–3660* ⊕ *alpineadventuresutah.com* 🖃 *From: $225.*

SCENIC DRIVES

Burr Trail Scenic Backway. Branching east off Highway 12 in Boulder, Burr Trail travels through the Circle Cliffs area of Grand Staircase–Escalante National Monument into Capitol Reef. The views are of backcountry canyons and gulches. The road is paved between Boulder and the eastern boundary of Capitol Reef. It leads into a hair-raising set of switchbacks—not suitable for RVs or trailers—that ascend 800 feet in ½ mile. Before attempting to drive this route, check with the Capitol

Reef Visitor Center for road conditions. From Boulder to its intersection with Notom-Bullfrog Road the route is 36 miles long. ⊠ *Off Hwy. 12, Boulder* ⊕ *www.scenicbyway12.com.*

Utah Scenic Byway 24. For 62 miles between Loa and Hanksville, you'll cut right through Capitol Reef National Park. Colorful rock formations in all their hues of red, cream, pink, gold, and deep purple extend from one end of the route to the other. The closer you get to the park the more colorful the landscape becomes. The vibrant rock finally gives way to lush green hills and the mountains west of Loa.

NIGHTLIFE AND PERFORMING ARTS

PERFORMING ARTS

Robbers Roost. This shop, named after Butch Cassidy's hideout, is home base for the Entrada Institute, an alliance of arts and outdoors enthusiasts that holds musical events and talks, usually on Saturday nights, from May through October. The annual women's music festival, held each August, attracts more than 600 attendees to hear performance art, blues, rock, jazz, and folk. ⊠ *185 W. Main St. (Hwy. 24), Torrey* ☎ *435/425–3265* ⊕ *robbersroostbooks.com.*

SHOPPING

Flute Shop Trading Post. Unique and unexpected, the nifty Flute Shop, open year-round, sells American Indian jewelry, rocks, fossils, and flutes, handcrafted by owner Vance Morrill. A quiet and inexpensive four-unit motel has been added to the premises. You'll find it 4 miles south of junction of Highways 12 and 24. ⊠ *1705 S. Scenic Rte. 12, Torrey* ☎ *435/425–3144* ⊕ *www.fluteshopmotel.com* ⊙ *Apr.–Oct., Mon.–Sat. 9–6; hrs vary Nov.–March.*

Gallery 24. This pleasing space sells contemporary fine art from southern Utah–based artists that includes paintings, photography, ceramics, and sculpture. ⊠ *135 E. Main St., Torrey* ☎ *435/425–2124* ⊕ *www. gallery24.biz* ⊙ *Easter–mid-Oct., Thurs.–Mon. 11–5.*

Robbers Roost. The inviting and well-stocked Robbers Roost is part bookstore, part coffee and snack bar, and part performance space, all contained in the late Utah writer Ward Roylance's practically teepee-shape house. It has books by regional authors, guidebooks, maps, T-shirts, and handmade gifts such as authentic Native American jewelry. It's an excellent place to browse, talk about trails, or find out what's going on around town. ⊠ *185 W. Main St. (Hwy. 24), Torrey* ☎ *435/425–3265* ⊕ *robbersroostbooks.com* ⊙ *Mar.–Oct., daily 8–8.*

Torrey Gallery. A new location in a pioneer home off Main Street nearly doubles the space of this lovely gallery which specializes in regional art. Its offerings include paintings, sculpture, and photographs, as well as antique and contemporary Navajo rugs discovered by the owners, longtime collectors. ⊠ *160 W. Main St., Torrey* ☎ *435/425–3909* ⊕ *torreygallery.com* ⊙ *Apr.–Nov., Mon.–Sat. 9:30–6; by appointment Sun. and off-season.*

FAMILY **Torrey Trading Post.** Come here for Native American jewelry and pottery, T-shirts, wood carvings, stone figures, gifts for children, and more. The trading post also has a handful of deluxe and camping cabins for lodging. ⊠ *25 W. Main St., Torrey* ☎ *435/425–3716* ⊕ *torreytradingpost. com* ☾ *Daily 8:30 am–8:30 pm.*

WHERE TO EAT

IN THE PARK

PICNIC AREA

Gifford House Museum and Store. In a grassy meadow with the Fremont River flowing by, this is an idyllic shady spot in the Fruita Historic District for a sack lunch. Picnic tables, drinking water, grills, and a convenient restroom make it perfect. It's 1 mile south of the visitor center. ⊠ *Scenic Dr.*

OUTSIDE THE PARK

$$$ ✕ **Cafe Diablo.** Nestled in the tiny hamlet of Torrey is one of the best
AMERICAN   restaurants in the state, with innovative Southwestern fare that has
Fodor's Choice   included dishes such as pomegranate and chipotle–glazed ribs, and
★   blackened shrimp tacos with baja sauce. The dining room is laced with the work of local artists or you can enjoy the peaceful patio, surrounded by gardens and a view of distant red-rock mountains. Many ingredients are pulled from the restaurant's own organic farm and the international wine list is well chosen. $ *Average main: $26* ⊠ *599 W. Main St. (Hwy. 24), Torrey* ☎ *435/425–3070* ⊕ *cafediablo.net* ☾ *Closed late Oct.–early Apr.*

$$ ✕ **Capitol Reef Café.** For a varied selection of solid and healthy fare,
AMERICAN   visit this unpretentious eatery. Favorites include the vegetable salad and the flaky smoked or grilled fillet of rainbow trout, and the breakfasts are both delicious and hearty. A handful of vegetarian offerings has included mushroom lasagna and there's a surprisingly expansive beer and wine list. Earth tones and tranquil American Indian flute music make for a truly laid-back vibe, and the attached gift shop has an eclectic selection of books about the Southwest. $ *Average main: $14* ⊠ *360 W. Main St. (Hwy. 24), Torrey* ☎ *435/425–3271* ⊕ *capitolreefinn.com* ☾ *Closed late Oct.–mid-Mar.*

$$$ ✕ **Hell's Backbone Grill.** On the grounds of the Boulder Mountain Lodge
ECLECTIC   and voted Best Restaurant in Southern Utah for eight years in a row
Fodor's Choice   by *Salt Lake Magazine,* this remote eatery can be well worth the drive.
★   The menu is inspired by American Indian, Western range, Southwestern, and Mormon pioneer recipes. The owners, who are also the chefs, have a historical connection to the area, and many of the ingredients they use come directly from their own organic farm. Because they insist on fresh ingredients, the menu changes seasonally. The restaurant closes between lunch and dinner, 2:30–5. $ *Average main: $25* ⊠ *20 N. Hwy. 12, Boulder* ☎ *435/335–7464* ⊕ *www.hellsbackbonegrill.com* ☾ *Closed Dec.–early Mar.*

$ ✕**Stan's Burger Shak.** This is the tra-
FAST FOOD ditional pit stop between Lake Powell and Capitol Reef, featuring great
burgers, fries, a generous selection of
flavored shakes, and the best homemade onion rings around. Keep
in mind it generally closes for the
winter. $ *Average main: $8* ✉ *140
S. Hwy. 95, Hanksville* ☎ *435/542-
3330* ⊕ *www.stansburgershak.com*
⊗ *Closed Dec.–early to mid-Feb.*

12

WHERE TO STAY

OUTSIDE THE PARK

$ 🏨**Aquarius Inn.** The large, clean rooms here include amenities such as
HOTEL refrigerators, microwaves, cable TV, and video/DVD players (video
FAMILY rental on-site). **Pros:** not too far from Torrey and Capitol Reef; Laundromat on site; pet-friendly. **Cons:** Bicknell might be too tiny and
quiet for some; can fill quickly on summer weekends. $ *Rooms from:
$77* ✉ *292 W. Main St., Bicknell* ☎ *435/425-3835, 800/833-5379*
⊕ *aquariusinn.com* ⊷ *27 rooms, 1 suite* ⦿ *No meals.*

$ 🏨**Austin's Chuckwagon Motel.** Foremost at this pleasant complex are
HOTEL friendly service and immaculate rooms, including standard-size in the
motel-style lodge or stand-alone cabins that sleep up to six. **Pros:** affordable; great for families; large pool. **Cons:** family atmosphere might
not please solitary travelers. $ *Rooms from: $61* ✉ *12 W. Main St.,
Torrey* ☎ *435/425-3335, 800/863-3288* ⊕ *austinschuckwagonmotel.
com* ⊗ *Closed Nov.–Mar.* ⊷ *25 rooms, 1 suite, 3 cabins* ⦿ *No meals.*

$$$ 🏨**Boulder Mountain Lodge.** If you're traveling scenic Highway 12 between
HOTEL Capitol Reef and Bryce Canyon national parks, don't miss this wonder-
Fodor's Choice ful lodge with a fireplace in the two-story great room and award-winning
★ Hell's Backbone restaurant on the premises. **Pros:** a perfect spot for peace
and solitude; the service and care given to guests is impeccable. **Cons:**
some might find the middle-of-nowhere location too remote. $ *Rooms
from: $168* ✉ *20 N. Hwy. 12, Boulder* ☎ *435/335-7460, 800/556-3446*
⊕ *www.boulder-utah.com* ⊷ *20 rooms, 2 suites* ⦿ *No meals.*

$ 🏨**Fish Lake Resorts.** Here you can find everything from basic cabins
RESORT that sleep two to large ones with six bedrooms, all of which focus on
FAMILY function rather than extra amenities. **Pros:** good place for families and
groups to congregate. **Cons:** some cabins are a little close together.
$ *Rooms from: $65* ✉ *2 N. Hwy. 25, Fish Lake* ☎ *435/638-1000*
⊕ *fishlakeresorts.com* ⊷ *41 cabins* ⦿ *No meals.*

$$$ 🏨**Lodge at Red River Ranch.** The grand log lodge set against a story-
HOTEL book Western landscape where buffalo roam recalls another era. **Pros:**
Fodor's Choice beautiful surroundings; staff can help arrange fly-fishing and horseback
★ riding. **Cons:** dining room only open for breakfast. $ *Rooms from:
$200* ✉ *2900 W. Hwy. 24, Teasdale* ☎ *435/425-3322, 800/205-6343*
⊕ *redriverranch.com* ⊷ *15 rooms* ⦿ *No meals.*

Best Campgrounds in Capitol Reef

Campgrounds in Capitol Reef fill up fast between Memorial Day and Labor Day, though that goes mainly for the superconvenient Fruita Campground and not the more remote backcountry sites. Most of the area's state parks have camping facilities, and the region's two national forests offer many wonderful sites.

Cathedral Valley Campground. You'll find this small, basic, no-fee (no water, pit toilet) campground in the park's remote northern district touts sprawling views, but the bumpy road there is hard to navigate. ✉ *Hartnet Junction, on Caineville Wash Rd.* ☎ *435/425–3791.*

Cedar Mesa Campground. Wonderful views of the Waterpocket Fold and Henry Mountains surround this primitive, no-fee campground in the park's southern district. ✉ *Notom-Bullfrog Rd., 22 miles south of Hwy. 24* ☎ *435/425–3791.*

Fruita Campground. Near the orchards and the Fremont River, the park's developed (flush toilets, running water), shady campground is a great place to call home for a few days. The sites require a $20 nightly fee and those nearest the Fremont River or the orchards are the very best. ✉ *Scenic Dr., about 1 mile south of visitor center* ☎ *435/425–3791.*

$$
B&B/INN
Muley Twist Inn. This gorgeous inn sits on 15 acres of land, with expansive views of the colorful landscape in just about every direction. **Pros:** dramatic setting against a beautiful rock cliff; a place you can slow down and unwind; all rooms have private baths. **Cons:** might be too far away from it all for some. $ *Rooms from: $140* ✉ *249 W. 125 South St., Teasdale* ☎ *435/425–3640, 800/530–1038* ⊕ *www.muleytwistinn. com* ☾ *Closed Nov.–Mar.* ⌐ *5 rooms* ⍟ *Breakfast.*

$
HOTEL
Rim Rock Inn. On a bluff with outstanding views into the desert, this motel was the first one to accommodate visitors to Capitol Reef. **Pros:** immaculate rooms; reasonable price; breakfast included. **Cons:** only five rooms; no shade. $ *Rooms from: $74* ✉ *2523 E. Hwy. 24, Torrey* ☎ *435/425–3398* ⊕ *therimrock.net* ☾ *Closed Nov.–Mar.* ⌐ *19 rooms* ⍟ *Breakfast.*

$$
B&B/INN
SkyRidge Inn Bed and Breakfast. Each of the inn's windows offers an exceptional year-round view of the desert and mountains surrounding Capitol Reef National Park. **Pros:** very comfortable; convenient to gas station and other amenities. **Cons:** no pets. $ *Rooms from: $120* ✉ *1092 E. Hwy 24, Torrey* ☎ *435/425–3222, 877/824–1508* ⊕ *skyridgeinn.com* ⌐ *6 rooms* ⍟ *Breakfast.*

CARLSBAD CAVERNS NATIONAL PARK

WELCOME TO CARLSBAD CAVERNS NATIONAL PARK

TOP REASONS TO GO

★ **400,000 hungry bats:** From mid-May to late October, bats wing to and from the caverns in a swirling, visible tornado.

★ **Take a guided tour through the underworld:** Plummet 75 stories underground and step into enormous caves hung with stalactites and bristling with stalagmites.

★ **Living Desert Zoo and Gardens:** More preserve than zoo, this 1,500-acre park houses scores of rare species, including endangered Mexican wolves, Bolson tortoises, and black bears.

★ **Birding at Rattlesnake Springs:** Nine-tenths of the park's 330 bird species, including roadrunners, golden eagles, and acrobatic cave swallows, visit this green desert oasis.

★ **Pecos River:** A Southwest landmark and recreational oasis, the Pecos River flows through the heart of nearby Carlsbad.

1 Bat Flight. Cowboy Jim White discovered the caverns after noticing that a swirling smokestack of bats appeared there each morning and evening. White is long gone, but the 400,000-member bat colony is still here, snatching up 3 tons of bugs a night. Watch them leave at dusk from the amphitheater near the park visitor center.

2 Carlsbad Caverns Big Room Tour. Travel 75 stories below the surface to visit the Big Room, where you can traipse beneath a 255-foot-tall ceiling and take in immense and eerie cave formations. Situated directly beneath the park visitor center, the room can be accessed via quick-moving elevator or a walking path at the cave mouth.

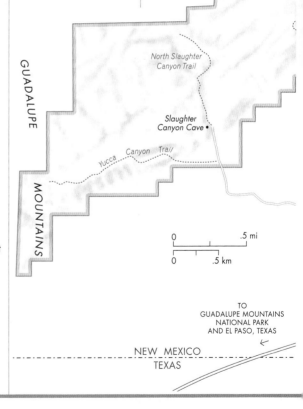

GUADALUPE

MOUNTAINS

North Slaughter Canyon Trail

Slaughter Canyon Cave •

Yucca Canyon Trail

0   .5 mi

0   .5 km

TO
GUADALUPE MOUNTAINS
NATIONAL PARK
AND EL PASO, TEXAS

NEW MEXICO

TEXAS

3 Living Desert Zoo and Gardens State Park.
Endangered river cooters, Bolson tortoises, and Mexican wolves all roam in this sprawling hilltop preserve. You can skip alongside roadrunners and slim wild turkeys in the park's aviary, visit a small group of cougars, and view exhibits of the area's smaller creatures. The Living Desert is on the west side of Carlsbad, New Mexico, 27 miles north of the park.

4 The Pecos River.
Running through the town of Carlsbad, the Pecos River is a landmark of the Southwest that gives life to boating, water-skiing, and fishing. In winter, residents gussy up dozens of riverside homes for the holiday season.

GETTING ORIENTED

13

To reach the essence of Carlsbad Caverns National Park, you have to delve below the surface—literally. Most of the park's key sights are underground in a massive latticework of caves (there are 117 known caves in all, although not all are open to visitors; a variety of tours leave from the visitor center). The park also has a handful of trails and scenic drives aboveground, where you can experience the Chihuahuan Desert and some magnificent geological formations.

KEY	
🏠	Ranger Station
⛺	Campground
⛱	Picnic Area
🍴	Restaurant
🏨	Lodge
🚶	Trailhead
🚻	Restrooms
🔆	Scenic Viewpoint
⋯⋯	Walking/Hiking Trails

5 Rattlesnake Springs.
Despite 30,000-plus acres in which to roam, nine-tenths of the park's 330-plus species of birds show up at Rattlesnake Springs at one time or another—probably because it's one of the few water sources in this area.

Updated by
Marty Racine

On the surface, Carlsbad Caverns National Park is deceptively normal—but all bets are off once visitors set foot in the elevator, which plunges 75 stories underground. The hollow beneath the surface is part silky darkness, part subterranean hallucination. The snaky, illuminated walkway seems less like a trail and more like a foray across the River Styx and into the underworld. Within more than 14 football fields of this netherworld are hundreds of formations that alternately resemble cakes, soda straws, ocean waves, and the large, leering face of a mountain troll.

CARLSBAD CAVERNS PLANNER

WHEN TO GO

While the desert above may alternately bake or freeze, the caverns remain in the mid-50s. If you're coming to see the Brazilian free-tailed bat, arrive between spring and mid-fall.

AVG. HIGH/LOW TEMPS.

Jan.	Feb.	Mar.	Apr.	May	June
57/27	63/32	70/38	79/47	87/56	95/64

July	Aug.	Sept.	Oct.	Nov.	Dec.
95/67	93/66	87/59	79/47	67/35	59/29

FESTIVAL AND EVENTS

FAMILY **Star Parties.** Coinciding with the new or first-quarter moon of every other month, star parties are held outside Living Desert Zoo & Gardens State Park about six times a year. A laser tour and powerful telescope bring the heavens closer. Call for exact scheduling. ⊠ *1504 Miehls Dr., Carlsbad* ☎ *575/887–5516* ⊕ *www.emnrd.state.nm.us.*

MAY
FAMILY

Native American Heritage Days. On the second weekend of May the state park hosts a celebration of Native American history, including vendors, guest speakers, and children's events. ⊠ *1504 Miehls Dr., Carlsbad* ☎ *575/887–5516* ⊕ *www.emnrd.state.nm.us.*

JULY/AUGUST
FAMILY

Bat Flight Breakfast. In midsummer once each year, early risers gather at the cave's entrance to eat breakfast and watch tens of thousands of bats return home from their nocturnal search for food. The breakfast costs $7.50 and is held either in July or August; check with the park for this year's date. ⊠ *727 Carlsbad Caverns Hwy.* ☎ *575/785–2232* ⊕ *www.nps.gov/cave.*

13

DECEMBER
FAMILY
Fodor'sChoice
★

Christmas on the Pecos. Magical Christmas displays decorate Carlsbad mansions along a 3-mile stretch of the Pecos River in a fairyland of seasonal delight. Boat tours ($20 adults Friday and Saturday; $15 adults Sunday–Thursday) run from the day after Thanksgiving through New Year's Eve except Christmas Eve, beginning at 5:30. Vessels depart from the Pecos River Village Conference Center. Purchase tickets there, at the Carlsbad Chamber of Commerce (*302 S. Canal St.*), or online. ⊠ *Pecos River Village Conference Center, 711 Muscatel Ave., Carlsbad* ☎ *575/887–6516 Chamber of Commerce, 575/628–0952 after Oct. 1* ⊕ *www.christmasonthepecos.com.*

PLANNING YOUR TIME

CARLSBAD CAVERNS IN ONE DAY

In a single day, visitors can easily view both the eerie, exotic caverns and the volcano of bats that erupts from the caverns each evening. Unless you're attending the annual Bat Flight Breakfast, when visitors have the morning meal with rangers and then view the early-morning bat return, go ahead and sleep past sunrise and then stroll into the caves.

For the full experience, begin by taking the **Natural Entrance Route Tour,** which allows visitors to trek into the cave from surface level. This tour winds past the Boneyard, with its intricate ossifications and a massive boulder called the Iceberg. After 1¼ miles, or about an hour, the trail links up with the **Big Room Route.** If you're not in good health or are traveling with young children, you might want to skip the Natural Entrance and start with the Big Room Route, which begins at the foot of the elevator. This underground walk extends 1¼ miles on level, paved ground, and takes about 1½ hours to complete. There is a shortcut option that's about two-thirds as long. If you have made reservations in advance or chance upon some openings, you also can take the **King's Palace** guided tour for 1 mile and an additional 1½ hours. It leaves from the Big Room near the elevator. At 83 stories deep, the palace is the lowest part of the cave open to the public. By this time, you will have spent four hours in the cave. Take the elevator back up to the top. If you're not yet tuckered out, consider a short hike along the sunny, self-guided ½-mile **Desert Nature Walk** by the visitor center.

To picnic by the birds, bees, and water of **Rattlesnake Springs,** take U.S. 62/180 south from White's City 5½ miles, and turn back west onto Route 418. You'll find old-growth shade trees, grass, picnic tables, restrooms, and water. Many varieties of birds flit from tree to tree. Return to the Carlsbad Caverns entrance road and take the 9½-mile Walnut

Canyon Desert Drive loop. Leave yourself enough time to return to the **visitor center** for the evening bat flight.

GETTING HERE AND AROUND

AIR TRAVEL

The nearest full-service airport is in El Paso, 145 miles away. Cavern City Air Terminal, located between Carlsbad and the park, is utilized by smaller, regional carriers.

CAR TRAVEL

Carlsbad Caverns is 27 miles southwest of Carlsbad, New Mexico, and 35 miles north of Guadalupe Mountains National Park via U.S. 62/180. The ascending 7-mile Carlsbad Caverns Highway from the turnoff at White's City is paved with pull-outs, which allow motorists to take in the view. Be alert for wildlife crossing roadways, especially in the early morning and at night.

PARK ESSENTIALS

PARK FEES AND PERMITS

No fee is charged for parking or to enter the aboveground portion of the park. It costs $10 to descend into Carlsbad Caverns either by elevator or through the Natural Entrance. Costs for guided tours range from $7 to $20 plus general admission.

Those planning overnight hikes must obtain a free backcountry permit, and all hikers are advised to stop at the visitor center information desk for current information about trails. Trails are poorly defined, but can be followed with a topographic map. Dogs are not allowed in the park, but a kennel is available at the park visitor center for a fee.

PARK HOURS

The park is open year-round, except Christmas Day, New Year's Day, and Thanksgiving. For guided-tour reservations go to ⊕ *www. recreation.gov* or call ☎ *877/444–6777*. From Memorial Day weekend through Labor Day, tours are conducted from 8:30 to 5; the last entry into the cave via the Natural Entrance is at 3:30, and the last entry into the cave via the elevator is at 5. After Labor Day until Memorial Day weekend, tours are conducted from 8:30 to 3:30; the last entry into the cave via the Natural Entrance is at 2, and the last entry into the cave via the elevator is at 3:30. Carlsbad Caverns is in the Mountain time zone.

CELL-PHONE RECEPTION

Cell phones only work about 10% of the time in the park. Public telephones are at the visitor center.

EDUCATIONAL OFFERINGS

RANGER PROGRAMS

FAMILY
Fodor's Choice
★

Evening Bat Flight Program. In the amphitheater at the Natural Cave Entrance (off a short trail from main parking lot) a ranger discusses the park's batty residents before the creatures begin their sundown exodus. The bats aren't on any predictable schedule, so times are a little iffy. Ideally, viewers will first hear the bats preparing to exit, courtesy of an amplified frequency calibrated to human ears, followed by a vortex of black specks swirling out of the cave mouth in search of dinner against the darkening sky. When conditions are favorable, hundreds of thousands of bats will soar off over the span of half an hour or longer. ✉ *727 Carlsbad Caverns Hwy.* ☎ *575/785–3012* ⊕ *www.nps.gov/cave* ⊘ *Mid-May–mid-Oct., nightly at sundown.*

RESTAURANTS

Choice isn't an issue inside Carlsbad Caverns National Park because there are just three dining options—the surface-level café, the underground snack bar near the elevators, and the bring-it-yourself option, for which there are picnic tables at the east end of the parking lot. Luckily, everything is reasonably priced (especially for national park eateries).

13

HOTELS

The only overnight option within the arid, rugged park is to make your own campsite in the backcountry, at least half a mile from any trail.

Outside the park, however, options expand. White's City, 7 miles to the east of the park, has a Rodeway Inn, which is near the boardwalk that connects shopping and entertainment destinations. In Carlsbad there are even more choices, but the oil-field industry booking blocks of rooms has driven rates through the roof. Outside of several new big-box chains, most hotels here are aging and not particularly well maintained, so don't expect a mint on your pillow. Still, most are clean if less than opulent. *Hotel reviews have been shortened. For full information, visit Fodors.com.*

WHAT IT COSTS				
	$	$$	$$$	$$$$
Restaurants	under $13	$13–$20	$21–$30	over $30
Hotels	under $101	$101–$150	$151–$200	over $200

Restaurant prices are the average cost of a main course at dinner, or if dinner is not served, at lunch. Hotel prices are the lowest cost of a standard double room in high season.

VISITOR INFORMATION

Park Contact Information Carlsbad Caverns National Park. ✉ *3225 National Parks Hwy., Carlsbad* ✚ *7 miles from the turnoff at White's City* ☎ *575/785–2232 park menu options, 877/444–6777 cave tour reservations, 575/875–3012 bat flight schedule* ⊕ *www.nps.gov/cave.*

VISITOR CENTERS

FAMILY

Fodor's Choice

★

Carlsbad Caverns National Park Visitor Center. Within this user-friendly facility at the top of an escarpment, a 75-seat theater offers engrossing films and ranger programs about the different types of caves. Exhibits offer a primer on bats, geology, wildlife, and the early tribes and settlers that once lived in and passed through the Carlsbad Caverns area. Friendly rangers staff an information desk, where tickets and maps are sold. A gift shop, café, and bookstore also are on the premises. ✉ *7 miles west of U.S. 62/180, 727 Carlsbad Caverns Hwy.* ☎ *575/785–2232* ⊕ *www.nps.gov/cave* 🖃 *Free admission to the visitor center, $10 for the two self-guided tours (Natural Entrance and Big Room), plus additional fees for guided tours* ⊘ *Late May–early Sept., daily 8–7; early Sept.–late May, daily 8–5.*

EXPLORING

SCENIC DRIVES

Walnut Canyon Desert Drive. This scenic drive begins ½ mile from the visitor center. It travels 9½ miles along the top of a ridge to the edge of Rattlesnake Canyon and sinks back down through upper Walnut Canyon to the main entrance road. The backcountry scenery on this one-way gravel loop is stunning; go late in the afternoon or early in the morning to enjoy the full spectrum of changing light and dancing colors. Along the way, you'll see Big Hill Seep's trickling water, the tall, flowing ridges of the Guadalupe mountain range, and maybe even some robust mule deer. The scenic road is not for RVs or trailers, and it can occasionally be closed for maintenance.

SCENIC STOPS

FAMILY

Fodor's Choice

★

The Big Room. With a floor space equal to about 14 football fields, this subterranean focal point of Carlsbad Caverns clues visitors in to just how large the caverns really are. The White House could fit in one corner of the Big Room, and wouldn't come close to grazing the 255-foot ceiling. Entrance can be accessed by elevator or, for the moderately fit with about an hour to spare, through the Natural Entrance and a 1.25-mile descending trail. Either way, at 750 feet below the surface you will connect with the self-guided 1.25-mile Big Room loop, a relatively level, paved pathway through the almost hallucinatory wonders of various formations and decorations. You also get a layman's lesson on how the cave was carved. An audio guide is available from the visitor center bookstore for a few dollars. This self-guided tour costs $10; kids under 15 are admitted for free but must be accompanied by an adult. Reservations are not necessary. Even in summer, long pants and long-sleeved shirts are advised for cave temperatures in the mid-50s. ⊠ *Visitor Center, 727 Carlsbad Caverns Hwy.* ⊕ *www.nps.gov/cave* ⊠ *$10* ☉ *Late May–early Sept., daily 8:30–5 (last entry into Natural Entrance at 3:30; last entry into elevator at 5); early Sept.–late May, daily 8:30–3:30 (last entry into Natural Entrance at 2; last entry into elevator at 3:30).*

FAMILY

Fodor's Choice

★

Natural Entrance. As natural daylight recedes, a self-guided, paved trail leads downward from the yawning mouth of the main cavern, about 100 yards east of the visitor center. The route is winding and sometimes slick from water seepage above ground. A steep descent of about 750 feet, much of it secured by hand rails, takes you about a mile through the main corridor and past features such as the Bat Cave and the Boneyard. (Despite its eerie name, the formations here don't look much like femurs and fibulas; they're more like spongy bone insides.) Iceberg Rock is a massive boulder that dropped from the cave ceiling millennia ago. After about a mile, you'll link up underground with the 1.25-mile Big Room trail and return to the surface via elevator. Footware with a good grip is recommended. No reservations required. ⊠ *727 Carlsbad Caverns Hwy.* ✛ *7 miles west of U.S. 62/180 at the White's City*

CLOSE UP

Plants and Wildlife in Carlsbad Caverns

Without a doubt, the park's most prominent and popular residents are Brazilian (sometimes called Mexican) free-tailed bats. These bats have bodies that barely span a woman's hand, yet sport wings that would cover a workingman's boot. Female bats give birth to a single pup each year, which usually weighs more than a quarter of what an adult does. Their tiny noses and big ears enable them to search for the many tons of bugs they consume over their lifetime. Numbering nearly a third of a million, these tiny creatures are the park's mascot.

Famous bats aside, there is much more wildlife to recommend in the park. One of New Mexico's best birding areas is at Rattlesnake Springs. Summer and fall migrations give you the best chance of spotting the most varieties of the more than 330 species of birds. Lucky visitors may spot a golden eagle, a rare visitor, or get the thrill of glimpsing a brilliant, gray-and-crimson vermilion flycatcher.

Snakes generally appear in summer, especially at dusk and dawn.

■TIP➔ If you're out walking, be wary of different rattlesnake species, such as banded-rocks and diamondbacks. If you see one, don't panic. Rangers say they are more scared of us than we are of them. Just don't make any sudden moves, and slowly walk away or back around the vipers.

This area is also remarkable because of its location in the Chihuahuan Desert, which sprouts unique plant life. There are thick stands of raspy-leaved yuccas, as well as the agave (mescal) plants that were once a food source for early Native American tribes. The leaves of this leggy plant are still roasted in sand pits by tribal elders during traditional celebrations.

In spring, the stands of yucca plants unfold white flowers on their tall stalks. Blossoming cacti and desert wildflowers are among the natural wonders of Walnut Canyon. You'll see bright red blossoms adorning reach-for-the-sky ocotillo plants, and sunny yellow blooms sprouting from prickly pear cactus.

13

turnoff ⊕ *www.nps.gov/cave* ✉ *$10 for adults; kids 15 and under free* ☉ *Late May–early Sept., daily 8:30–3:30; early Sept.–late May, daily 9–2* ☞ *Children under 16 must be accompanied by an adult.*

FAMILY **Rattlesnake Springs.** Enormous cottonwood trees shade the picnic and recreation area at this cool, secluded oasis near Black River. The rare desert wetland harbors butterflies, mammals, and reptiles, as well as 90% of the park's 330 bird species. Don't let the name scare you; there may be rattlesnakes here, but no more than at any similar site in the Southwest. Restroom facilities are available, but overnight camping and parking are not allowed. ✉ *Hwy. 418* ✛ *Take U.S. 62/180 5½ miles south of White's City and turn west onto Hwy. 418 for 2½ miles* ⊕ *www.nps.gov/cave.*

SPORTS AND THE OUTDOORS

BIRD-WATCHING

From redheaded turkey vultures to svelte golden eagles, about 330 species of birds have been identified in Carlsbad Caverns National Park. Ask for a checklist at the visitor center and then start looking for greater roadrunners, red-winged blackbirds, white-throated swifts, northern flickers, and pygmy nuthatches.

FAMILY
Fodor'sChoice
★

Rattlesnake Springs. Offering one of the best bird habitats in New Mexico, this is a natural wetland with old-growth cottonwoods. Because southern New Mexico is in the northernmost region of the Chihuahuan Desert, you're likely to see birds that can't be found anywhere else in the United States outside extreme southern Texas and Arizona. If you see a flash of crimson, you might have spotted a vermilion flycatcher. Wild turkeys also flap around this oasis, which also has a shaded picnic area. Potable water and permanent toilets are on-site. As elsewhere in the park, you are expected to leave a small footprint. Do not disturb, and if you pack it in, pack it out. ⊠ *Hwy. 418* ✛ *2½ miles west of U.S. 62/180, 5½ miles south of White's City* ⊕ *www.nps.gov/cave.*

HIKING

Deep, dark, and mysterious, the Carlsbad Caverns are such a park focal point that the 40,000-plus acres of wilderness above them have gone largely undeveloped. This is great news for people who pull on their hiking boots when they're looking for solitude. What you find are rudimentary trails that crisscross the dry, textured terrain and lead up to elevations of 6,000 feet or more. These routes often take a half day or more to travel; at least one, Guadalupe Ridge Trail, is long enough that it calls for an overnight stay. Walkers who just want a little dusty taste of desert flowers and wildlife should try the Desert Nature Walk.

Finding the older, less well-maintained trails can be difficult. Pick up a topographical map at the visitor center bookstore, and be sure to pack a lot of water. There's none out in the desert, and you'll need at least a gallon per person per day. The high elevation coupled with a potent sunshine punch can deliver a nasty sunburn, so pack SPF 30 (or higher) sunblock and a hat, even in winter. No pets are allowed on the trails. The day hikes are free, but you do have to obtain a backcountry permit if you're camping. They're free at the visitor center.

EASY

FAMILY
Desert Nature Walk. While waiting for the evening bat-flight program, try taking the ½-mile self-guided hike that begins just east of the visitor center. The tagged and identified flowers and plants make this a good place to get acquainted with much of the local desert flora. Part of the trail is an easy stroll even for the littlest ones, and part is wheelchair accessible. The payoff is great for everyone, too: a big, vivid view of the desert basin. *Easy.* ✛ *Trailhead: east of the visitor center* ⊕ *www.nps.gov/cave.*

Mexican (sometimes referred to as Brazilian) free-tailed bats swarm out of the caves each evening to hunt for food; they return just before dawn.

FAMILY **Rattlesnake Canyon Overlook Trail.** A ¼-mile stroll off Walnut Canyon Scenic Drive offers a nice overlook of the green-carpeted Rattlesnake Canyon. *Easy.* ⊹ *Trailhead: at mile marker 9 on Walnut Canyon Scenic Dr.* ⊕ *www.nps.gov/cave.*

MODERATE

Juniper Ridge Trail. Climb up in elevation as you head north on this nearly 3-mile trail, which leads to the northern edge of the park and then turns toward Crooked Canyon. While not the most notable trail, it's challenging enough to keep things interesting. Allow yourself half a day, and be sure to bring lots of water, especially when the temperature rises. *Moderate.* ⊹ *Trailhead: at mile marker 8.8 of Desert Loop Dr.* ⊕ *www.nps.gov/cave.*

Old Guano Road Trail. Meandering a little more than 3½ miles one-way on mostly flat terrain, the trail dips sharply toward White's City campground, where it ends. Give yourself about half a day to complete the walk. Depending on the temperature, this walk can be taxing, but the high desert sun can be potent any time of the year. Wear a hat and drink lots of water. *Moderate.* ⊹ *Trailhead: at the Bat Flight Amphitheater, near the Natural Cave Entrance* ⊕ *www.nps.gov/cave.*

Rattlesnake Canyon Trail. Rock cairns loom over this trail, which descends from 4,570 to 3,900 feet as it winds into the canyon. Allow half a day to trek down into the canyon and make the somewhat strenuous climb out; the total trip is about 6 miles. *Moderate.* ⊹ *Trailhead: at mile marker 9 on Walnut Canyon Desert Dr.* ⊕ *www.nps.gov/cave.*

Visitor
Center

Entrance

Surface Elevation 4,406 ft

MAIN
CORRIDOR

Bat Cave
200 ft below surface

Devils Den
500 ft below surface

Witches Finger

Elevator Shaft

SCENIC
ROOMS   Green Lake Room

King's Palace
829 ft below surface

Iceberg Rock

Queen's
Chamber

Boneyard

Rest Area and Lunchroom
755 ft below surface

Papoose
Room

Giant Dome   HALL OF
Twin Dome   GIANTS

Painted Grotto

Temple of the Sun

Rock of Ages

Crystal Spring Dome

Totem Pole   BIG ROOM

Top of
the Cross

Mirror Lake

Bottomless Pit

**Subterranean
Trail Network,
Carlsbad Caverns NP**

Fodor's Choice **Yucca Canyon Trail.** Sweeping views of the Guadalupe Mountains and
★ El Capitan give allure to this trail. Drive past Rattlesnake Springs and
stop at the park boundary before reaching the Slaughter Canyon Cave
parking lot. Turn west along the boundary fence line to the trailhead.
The 6-mile round-trip begins at the mouth of Yucca Canyon and climbs
up to the top of the escarpment. Here you find the panoramic view.
Most people turn around at this point; the hearty can continue along
a poorly maintained route that follows the top of the ridge. The first
part of the hike takes half a day. If you continue on, plan on a full day.
Moderate. ✛ *Trailhead: at Slaughter Canyon Cave parking lot, Hwy.
418, 10 miles west of U.S. 62/180.*

DIFFICULT

Guadalupe Ridge Trail. This long, winding ramble follows an old road all
the way to the western edge of the park. Because of its length (about
12 miles), an overnight stay in the backcountry is suggested. The hike
may be long, but for serious hikers the up-close-and-personal views
into Rattlesnake and Slaughter canyons are more than worth it—not
to mention the serenity of being miles and miles away from civilization. *Difficult.* ✛ *Trailhead: 4.8 miles down Desert Loop Dr.* ⊕ *www.
nps.gov/cave.*

North Slaughter Canyon Trail. Beginning at the Slaughter Canyon Cave parking lot, the trail traverses a heavily vegetated canyon bottom into a remote part of the park. As you begin hiking, look off to the east (to your right) to see the dun-colored ridges and wrinkles of the Elephant Back formation, the first of many dramatic limestone formations visible from the trail. The route travels 5½ miles one-way, the last 3 miles steeply climbing onto a limestone ridge escarpment. Allow a full day for the round-trip. *Difficult.* ⊹ *Trailhead: at Slaughter Canyon Cave parking lot, Hwy. 418, 10 miles west of U.S. 62/180.*

13

CAVING

Carlsbad Caverns is famous for the beauty and breadth of its inky depths, as well as for the accessibility of some of its largest caves. All cave tours, except for the self-guided Natural Entrance and Big Room, are ranger-led, so safety is rarely an issue in the caves, no matter how remote. There are no other tour guides in the area, nor is there an equipment retailer other than the Walmart in Carlsbad, 27 miles away. Depending on the difficulty of your cave selection (Spider Cave is the hardest to navigate), you'll need at most knee pads, gloves, flashlight batteries, sturdy pants, hiking boots with ankle support, and some water. The fee for the Natural Entrance and Big Room is $10 for ages 16 and up. Guided tours have an additional fee.

Hall of the White Giant. Plan to squirm through some tight passages for long distances to access a very remote chamber, where you'll see towering, glistening white formations that explain the name. This strenuous, ranger-led tour lasts about four hours. Steep drop-offs might elate you—or make you queasy. Wear sturdy hiking shoes and bring gloves, kneepads, and four AA batteries with you. Visitors must be at least 12 years old. ⊠ *Carlsbad Caverns Visitor Center, 727 Carlsbad Caverns Hwy.* ☎ *877/444–6777 reservations* ⊕ *www.nps.gov/cave* ✉ *$20, plus general admission ticket ($10)* ☉ *Tours: Mon. 8:30 (times subject to change)* ♿ *Reservations essential.*

FAMILY
Fodor's Choice
★

King's Palace. Throughout this regal room, stunningly handsome and indeed fit for a king, you'll see leggy "soda straws" large enough for a giant to sip, plus bizzare formations that defy reality. The tour also winds through the Queen's Chamber, dressed in ladylike, multitiered curtains of stone. The mile-long walk is on a paved trail, but there's one steep hill toward the end. This ranger-guided tour lasts about 1½ hours and gives you a "look" at the natural essence of a cave—a complete blackout, when artificial lights (and sound) are extinguished. While advance reservations are highly recommended, this is the one tour you might be able to sign up for on the spot. Children younger than four aren't allowed on this tour. ⊠ *Carlsbad Caverns Visitor Center, 727 Carlsbad Caverns Hwy.* ⊹ *Departs from the underground rest area near the elevators* ☎ *877/444–6777 reservations* ⊕ *www.nps.gov/cave* ✉ *$8, plus general admission ($10)* ☉ *Tours: summer, daily 9, 10:30, 12, and 3, and Sun., Tues., Thurs., and Sat. 1:30; fall/winter, daily 10:30 and 1:30 (times subject to change).*

Lower Cave. Fifty-foot vertical ladders and a dirt path lead you into undeveloped portions of Carlsbad Caverns. It takes about half a day to negotiate this moderately strenuous side trip led by a knowledgeable ranger. Visitors must supply gloves and four AA batteries. Children younger than 12 are not allowed on this tour. ⊠ *Carlsbad Caverns Visitor Center, 727 Carlsbad Caverns Hwy.* ☎ *877/444–6777 reservations* ⊕ *www.nps.gov/cave* ⊠ *$20, plus general admission ($10)* ⊙ *Tours: summer, Sun., Tues., Thurs., Sat. 8:30; fall/winter, daily 1:30 (times subject to change)* ⌂ *Reservations essential.*

Slaughter Canyon Cave. Discovered in the 1930s by a local goatherd, this cave is one of the most popular secondary sites in the park, about 23 miles southwest of the main Carlsbad Caverns and visitor center. Both the hike to the cave mouth and the tour will take about half a day, but it's worth it to view the deep cavern darkness as it's penetrated only by flashlights and, sometimes, headlamps. From the Slaughter Canyon parking area, give yourself 45 minutes to make the steep ½-mile climb up a trail leading to the mouth of the cave. Arrange to be there a quarter of an hour earlier than the appointed time. You'll find that the cave consists primarily of a single corridor, 1,140 feet long, with numerous side passages.

You can take some worthwhile pictures of this cave. Wear hiking shoes with ankle support, and carry plenty of water. You're also expected to bring your own reliable two-D-cell flashlight. Children younger than six are not permitted. It's a great adventure if you're in shape and love caving. ⊠ *End of Hwy. 418* ✚ *10 miles west of U.S. 62/180* ☎ *877/444–6777 reservations* ⊕ *www.nps.gov/cave* ⊠ *$15, plus general admission ($10)* ⊙ *Tours Fri. 8:30 am* ⌂ *Reservations essential.*

Spider Cave. Visitors may not expect to have an adventure in a cavern system as developed and well stocked as Carlsbad Caverns, but serious cavers and energetic types have the chance to crawl on cave floors, clamber up tight tunnels, stoop under overhangs, and climb steep, rocky pitches. This backcountry cave is listed as "wild," a clue that you might need a similar nature to attempt a visit. Plan to wear your warm, but least-favorite clothes, as they'll probably get streaked with grime. You'll also need soft knee pads, a flashlight (with spare batteries), leather gloves, and water. It will take you half a day to complete this ranger-led tour noted for its adventure and for its continuing role as a living research laboratory. Visitors must be at least 12 years old and absolutely not claustrophobic. The cave is named after the hordes of daddy longlegs that pulsate on the walls of the opening, but they're harmless. ⊠ *Carlsbad Caverns Visitor Center, 727 Carlsbad Caverns Hwy.* ✚ *Meet at the visitor center; a modest overland hike takes you to the cave opening* ☎ *877/444–6777 for reservations* ⊕ *www.nps.gov/cave* ⊠ *$20, plus general admission ($10)* ⊙ *Tours Wed. 8:30 (time subject to change)* ⌂ *Reservations essential.*

TOURS

Cave Resources Office. Those who want to go it alone outside the more established caverns can get permits and information about 10 backcountry caves from the Cave Resources Office in the visitor center.

Heed rangers' advice for these remote, undeveloped, nearly unexplored caves. ⊠ *Carlsbad Caverns Visitor Center, 727 Carlsbad Caverns Hwy.* ☎ *575/785–2232 for the park's main menu* ⊕ *www.nps.gov/cave.*

FAMILY **Ranger-Led Tours.** Cavers who wish to explore both developed and wild caves can go on ranger-led tours, some of which require knee pads, gloves, and flashlights. Reservations for the six different tours (Hall of the White Giant, Lower Cave, Slaughter Canyon Cave, Left-Hand Tunnel, King's Palace, and Spider Cave) are required at least a day in advance. Payment is by credit card over the phone or online, or by mailing a check if you're making reservations 21 days or more in advance; confirm first that space is available. ⊠ *Carlsbad Caverns Visitor Center, 727 Carlsbad Caverns Hwy.* ☎ *877/444–6777 for reservations* ⊕ *www. nps.gov/cave* ⊠ *From $7, plus general admission ($10).*

13

WHAT'S NEARBY

NEARBY TOWNS

On the Pecos River, with 2¾ miles of beaches and picturesque riverside pathways, **Carlsbad, New Mexico,** seems suspended between the past and the present. It's part–university town, part–Old West, with a robust Mexican kick. The town square of mom-and-pop shops, a block from the river, encircles a Pueblo-style county courthouse designed by New Mexican architect John Gaw Meem. Seven miles east of the caverns is **White's City,** grown from a tiny outpost to a small outpost. This privately owned town is the nearest place to Carlsbad Caverns and contains dining and lodging options, plus the essentials.

Visitor Information Carlsbad Chamber of Commerce. ⊠ *302 S. Canal St., Carlsbad* ☎ *575/887–6516* ⊕ *www.carlsbadchamber.com.* **White's City Inc.** ⊠ *17 Carlsbad Caverns Hwy., White's City* ⊹ *At the turnoff from U.S. 62/180 to Carlsbad Caverns* ☎ *800/228–3767* ⊕ *www.hotelscarlsbadcaverns.com.*

NEARBY ATTRACTIONS

FAMILY **Brantley Lake State Park.** In addition to 4,200-acre Brantley Lake and dam, this park 12 miles north of Carlsbad offers primitive camping areas, nature trails, a visitor center, and 51 fully equipped campsites. Half of the campsites are first come, first served, while the other half can be reserved. There's also fishing for largemouth bass, bluegill, crappie, carp, catfish, and walleye pike (though authorities recommend practicing catch-and-release due to the high levels of contaminants). There are boat ramps for those with their own vessel. ⊠ *County Rd. 30 (Capitan Reef Rd.), Carlsbad* ⊹ *5 miles east off U.S. 285, north of Carlsbad* ☎ *575/457–2384, 877/664–7787* ⊕ *www.emnrd.state.nm.us* ⊠ *$5 per vehicle for day use; $14 per vehicle for developed campsites; $8 per vehicle for primitive sites* ☉ *Daily, dawn–dusk.*

Carlsbad Museum and Arts Center. Pueblo pottery, American Indian artifacts, and early cowboy and ranch memorabilia are here, along with exhibitions of contemporary art. The real treasure, though, is the McAdoo Collection, with works by painters of the Taos Society of Artists. ⊠ *418 W. Fox St., Carlsbad* ☎ *575/887–0276* ⊕ *www. cityofcarlsbadnm.com/museum.cfm* ⊙ *Mon.–Sat. 10–5.*

FAMILY

Fodor's Choice

★

Living Desert Zoo and Gardens State Park. More preserve than traditional zoo, the park contains impressive plants and animals native to the Chihuahuan Desert. The Desert Arboretum has hundreds of exotic cacti and succulents, and the Living Desert Zoo is home to mountain lions, javelinas, deer, elk, bobcats, bison, and a black bear. Nocturnal exhibits let you view the area's nighttime wildlife, a walk-through aviary houses birds of prey, and a reptile exhibit. The park also sponsors up to five educational events a month, some of them free. Though there are shaded rest areas, restrooms, and water fountains, in summer it's more comfortable to visit in the morning, before the desert oven heats up. A self-guided tour takes little more than an hour. Don't have time to tour the park? The expansive view from its perchlike setting is the best in town. ⊠ *1504 Miehls Dr., off U.S. 285, Carlsbad* ☎ *575/887–5516* ⊕ *www.emnrd.state.nm.us* ⊠ *$5* ⊙ *Memorial Day weekend–Labor Day, daily 8–5; Labor Day weekend–Memorial Day, daily 9–5; last entry into zoo 3:30 year-round.*

WHERE TO EAT

IN THE PARK

$

AMERICAN

✕ **Carlsbad Caverns Restaurant.** This comfy, cafeteria-style restaurant, the only dining option in the caverns' complex other than an underground snack bar, has the essentials—hamburgers, sandwiches, Mexican fare, and hot roast beef. There are also packaged takeout items. It opens at 8 and closes at 6:30 between Memorial Day and Labor Day, and at 5 the rest of the year. ⑤ *Average main: $8* ⊠ *Carlsbad Caverns Visitor center, 727 Carlsbad Caverns Hwy.* ✛ *7 miles west of U.S. 62/180* ☎ *575/785–2281* ⊕ *www.nps.gov/cave* ⚑ *Reservations not accepted.*

$

FAST FOOD

✕ **Underground Lunchroom.** At 750 feet underground, near the elevators and entrance to the Big Room, you can grab a snack, soft drink, or club sandwich for a quick break. Service is quick, even when there's a crowd. Closes at 5 Memorial Day to Labor Day, at 3:30 the rest of the year. ⑤ *Average main: $8* ⊠ *Carlsbad Caverns visitor center, 727 Carlsbad Caverns Hwy.* ✛ *7 miles west of U.S. 62/180* ☎ *575/785–2232* ⊕ *www. nps.gov/cave* ⊙ *No dinner.*

PICNIC AREAS

Rattlesnake Springs. Of the several places to picnic in the park, this is the best by far. There are about a dozen picnic tables and grills here, many of them tree-shaded, and drinking water and restrooms are available. The seclusion of the site and the oasis-like draw add to the tranquillity. Be alert to the presence of wildlife. ✛ *5½ miles south of White's City on U.S. 62/180, then 2½ miles west on Hwy. 418* ⊕ *www.nps.gov/cave.*

OUTSIDE THE PARK

CARLSBAD

$$ ✗**Lucy's Mexicali Restaurant.** "The
MEXICAN   best margaritas in the world" is the
FAMILY   motto of this long-standing family-
owned Mexican food establishment.
Hyperbole aside, all the staples are
on the menu, plus some not-so-stan-
dard items like chicken fajita burri-
tos and enchiladas served the New
Mexico way—that is, flat with an
egg on top. Try the Tucson-style *chi-*

**CAMPING IN
CARLSBAD CAVERNS**

Backcountry camping is by permit
only. No campfires allowed in the
park, and all camping is hike-to.
Commercial sites can be found in
White's City and Carlsbad.

13

michangas and tasty *carnitas* (beef brisket or chicken sautéed with chili
peppers). Be sure to order Adam's Queso, a cheese dish that's a Lucy's
original. Lucy's also operates a full bar and weekend entertainment cen-
ter across the street at 701 S. Canal Street. ⓢ *Average main: $14* ✉ *710 S.
Canal St., Carlsbad* ☎ *575/887–7714* ⊕ *www.lucysmexicalirestaurant.
com* ⊗ *Closed Sun.* ⌦ *Reservations not accepted.*

$ ✗**Pecos River Cafe.** Stop by this locals' go-to place for savory breakfast
CAFÉ   burritos or an early lunch before traveling to Carlsbad Caverns. Pecos
FAMILY   River Cafe serves Mexican-American favorites, topped with plenty
of New Mexico's famous green chili. There's also a variety of grilled
sandwiches, burgers, and other comfort-food staples. All items are
available for takeout. The service is fast and accommodating, even
during the busy lunch hour. ⓢ *Average main: $10* ✉ *409 S. Canal St.,
Carlsbad* ☎ *575/887–8882* ⊗ *Closed weekends. No dinner* ⌦ *Reserva-
tions not accepted.*

$$ ✗**Red Chimney.** If you hanker for sweet-and-tangy barbecue, this homey,
BARBECUE   log-cabin-style spot is the place for you. Sauce from an old family recipe
FAMILY   is slathered on chicken, pork, beef, turkey, and ham. Fried catfish and
other home-style dishes are also served. If wall-mounted animal heads
make you squeamish, you might want to dine elsewhere. ⓢ *Average
main: $13* ✉ *817 N. Canal St., Carlsbad* ☎ *575/885–8744* ⊗ *Closed
weekends* ⌦ *Reservations not accepted.*

$$ ✗**Trinity Hotel.** In a corner bank building dating from 1892, the Trin-
SOUTHWESTERN   ity Hotel stands elegantly over nearby mundane architecture. With its
Fodor'sChoice   vaulted ceilings, the hotel's cozy dining room is widely regarded as
★   Carlsbad's premier destination for pasta, steaks, and seafood—most
with a distinct New Mexican flavor. Their signature dish is the Chicken
Bolloco, essentially fettuccine Alfredo with fresh green chilis added. For
an appetizer, the Caliente Goat Cheese with blackberries and habañero
sauce is a standout. Unwind at the bar, which features wines from across
the state, including some from the owner's own vineyards in Deming.
Have a sample in the free daily wine tasting from 3 to 7. ⓢ *Aver-
age main: $16* ✉ *201 S. Canal St., Carlsbad* ☎ *575/234–9891* ⊕ *www.
thetrinityhotel.com* ⊗ *Closed Sun.* ⌦ *Reservations essential.*

$$$ ✗**YellowBrix.** This indoor-outdoor restaurant comes as close to "hip"
FUSION   as Carlsbad gets, with a breezy Southwestern ambience graced by fare
with international leanings. The menu spans tapas, panini, and vegetarian dishes, along with grilled entrées customized with *au poivre*

sauce. Housed in a former residence dating to 1928, there are separate dining areas within, flanked by a courtyard patio, where on a warm weekend evening you might find a singer-songwriter playing acoustic guitar for tips. $ *Average main: $25* ⊠ *201 N. Canal St., Carlsbad* ☎ *575/941–2749.*

WHERE TO STAY

OUTSIDE THE PARK

CARLSBAD

$$$
HOTEL
FAMILY

🖵 **Best Western Stevens Inn.** A sprawling local landmark decades old, the Stevens was once Carlsbad's premier motel and entertainment destination for the region, and has kept pace through periodic renovation, such as Wi-Fi in all rooms. **Pros:** established and comfortable; pool; houses the Blue Cactus Lounge with a full bar and a DJ for dancing; fitness center. **Cons:** aging property that needs continual updating. $ *Rooms from: $172* ⊠ *1829 S. Canal St., Carlsbad* ☎ *575/887–2851, 800/730–2851* ⊕ *www. bestwesternnewmexico.com* ⤵ *208 rooms, 12 suites* ⊖ *Breakfast.*

$$$$
HOTEL

🖵 **Hampton Inn and Suites.** On the edge of town leading to the Carlsbad Caverns, the Hampton Inn and Suites is among Carlsbad's newer hotels, within walking distance of a bar and grill, gas station, and Walmart. **Pros:** staff is very friendly and accommodating; clean, new amenities. **Cons:** some rooms need better soundproofing; pricey for the area. $ *Rooms from: $229* ⊠ *120 Esperanza Circle, Carlsbad* ☎ *575/725–5700* ⊕ *www. carlsbadsuites.hamptoninn.com* ⤵ *57 rooms, 28 suites* ⊖ *Breakfast.*

$$$$
HOTEL

🖵 **Holiday Inn Express.** Within walking distance of the only movie theater in Carlsbad, as well as the Carlsbad Mall, the hotel is also close to the Carlsbad hospital and Living Desert Zoo & Gardens State Park. **Pros:** full, hot breakfast; convenient location for the north side of town. **Cons:** a little farther away from the park than other hotels; no pets allowed. $ *Rooms from: $259* ⊠ *2210 W. Pierce St., Carlsbad* ☎ *575/234–1252* ⊕ *www.hiexpress.com* ⤵ *56 rooms, 24 suites* ⊖ *Breakfast.*

$$$
B&B/INN
Fodor's Choice
★

🖵 **Trinity Hotel.** Housed in a gracefully aging building near Carlsbad's historic downtown, the two-story Trinity offers a unique lodging experience in a town known more for its perfunctory motels and big-box chains. **Pros:** one-of-a-kind facility with loads of personality; centrally located; less expensive than some Carlsbad chains; upscale bar and restaurant. **Cons:** no elevator; no interior access to the lobby; no pets allowed. $ *Rooms from: $190* ⊠ *201 S. Canal St., Carlsbad* ☎ *575/234–9891* ⊕ *www.thetrinityhotel.com* ⤵ *7 rooms, 2 suites* ⊖ *Breakfast.*

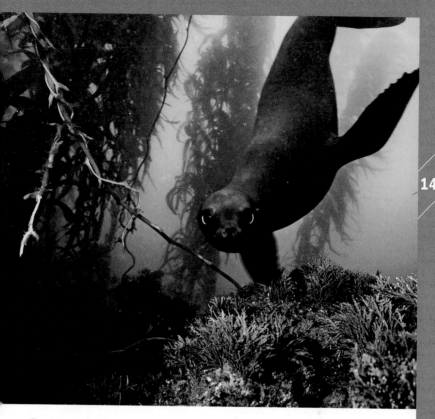

14

CHANNEL ISLANDS
NATIONAL PARK

14

WELCOME TO CHANNEL ISLANDS NATIONAL PARK

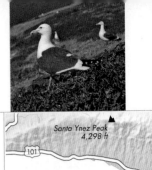

TOP REASONS TO GO

★ **Rare flora and fauna:** The Channel Islands are home to 145 species of terrestrial plants and animals found nowhere else on Earth.

★ **Time travel:** With no cars, phones, or services, these undeveloped islands provide a glimpse of what California was like hundreds of years ago, away from hectic modern life.

★ **Underwater adventures:** The incredibly healthy channel waters rank among the top 10 diving destinations on the planet—but you can also visit the kelp forest virtually via Channel Islands Live, a live underwater program.

★ **Marvelous marine mammals:** More than 30 species of seals, sea lions, whales, and other marine mammals ply the park's waters at various times of year.

★ **Sea-cave kayaking:** Paddle around otherwise inaccessible portions of the park's 175 miles of gorgeous coastline— including one of the world's largest sea caves.

1 Anacapa. Tiny Anacapa is a 5-mile stretch of three islets, with towering cliffs, caves, natural bridges, and rich kelp forests.

2 San Miguel. Isolated, windswept San Miguel, the park's westernmost island (access permit required), has an ancient caliche forest and hundreds of archaeological sites chronicling the Native Americans' 13,000-year history on the islands. More than 100,000 pinnipeds (seals and sea lions) hang out on the island's beaches during certain times of year.

3 Santa Barbara. More than 5 miles of scenic trails crisscross this tiny island, known for its excellent wildlife viewing and native plants. It's a favorite destination for diving, snorkeling, and kayaking.

4 Santa Cruz. The park's largest island offers some of the best hikes and kayaking opportunities, one of the world's largest and deepest sea caves, and more species of flora and fauna than any other park island.

CALIFORNIA

14

GETTING ORIENTED

Channel Islands National Park includes five of the eight Channel Islands and the one nautical mile of ocean that surrounds them. Six nautical miles of surrounding channel waters are designated a National Marine Sanctuary. The park and sanctuary waters are teeming with life, including giant kelp forests, 345 fish species, dolphins, whales, seals, sea lions, and seabirds. The islands range in size from 1-square-mile Santa Barbara to 96-square-mile Santa Cruz. Together they form a magnificent nature preserve with 145 endemic or unique species of plants and animals.

Santa Barbara Island is approximately 52 miles southeast of Santa Cruz Island

Santa Barbara Island Light Beacon

Santa Barbara Island

5 Santa Rosa. Campers love to stay on Santa Rosa, with its myriad hiking opportunities, stunning white-sand beaches, and rare grove of Torrey pines. It's also the only island accessible by plane.

KEY
🏚 Ranger Station
⛺ Campground
🎪 Picnic Area
🍴 Restaurant
🏠 Lodge
🚶 Trailhead
🚻 Restrooms
☀ Scenic Viewpoint
⋯⋯ Walking/Hiking Trails

0 ___ 10 mi

0 ___ 10 km

Updated by Cheryl Crabtree

On crystal-clear days the craggy peaks of Channel Islands are easy to see from the mainland, jutting from the Pacific in such sharp detail it seems you could reach out and touch them. The islands really aren't that far away—a high-speed boat will whisk you to the closest ones in less than an hour—yet very few people ever visit them. Those fearless, adventurous types who do will experience one of the most splendid land-and-sea wilderness areas on the planet.

CHANNEL ISLANDS PLANNER

WHEN TO GO

Channel Islands National Park records about 620,000 visitors each year, but many never venture beyond the visitor center. The busiest times are holidays and summer weekends; if you're going then, make your transportation and accommodation arrangements in advance.

The warm, dry summer and fall months are the best time to go camping. Humpback and blue whales arrive to feed from late June through early fall. The rains usually come December through March—but this is also the best time to spot gray whales and to get discounts at area hotels. In the late spring, thousands of migratory birds descend on the islands to hatch their young, and wildflowers carpet the slopes. The water temperature is nearly always cool, so bring a wet suit if you plan to spend much time in the ocean, even in the summer. Fog, high winds, and rough seas can happen any time of the year.

AVG. HIGH/LOW TEMPS.

Jan.	Feb.	Mar.	Apr.	May	June
66/44	66/45	66/46	68/48	69/51	71/55
July	Aug.	Sept.	Oct.	Nov.	Dec.
74/57	75/59	75/57	74/53	70/48	66/44

PLANNING YOUR TIME
CHANNEL ISLANDS IN ONE DAY

If you have a few hours or a day to visit the Channel Islands, start with viewing the exhibits at the **Channel Islands National Park Visitor Center** in Ventura. Then cruise over to **East Anacapa** for sweeping views of Santa Cruz Island and the mainland—provided it's not too foggy—and hiking, the primary activity here. Wander through western gull rookeries or peer down from steep cliffs and watch the antics of sea lions and seals. Alternatively, zip out to Scorpion Landing or Prisoner's Harbor on **Santa Cruz Island** on a high-speed catamaran run by Island Packers for more extended hiking, snorkeling, or kayaking.

GETTING HERE AND AROUND
AIR TRAVEL

Channel Islands Aviation flies solely to Santa Rosa Island. You can catch a flight to Santa Rosa Island from the Camarillo Airport, south of Ventura, and the Santa Barbara Airport.

BOAT TRAVEL

The visitor center for Channel Islands National Park is on California's mainland, in the town of Ventura, off U.S. 101. From the harbors at Ventura, Santa Barbara, and Oxnard you can board a boat to one of the islands. If you have your own boat, you can land at any of the park islands without a permit, but you should visit the park website for instructions and information on restricted areas. A permit is required to land on the Nature Conservancy property on Santa Cruz Island. Boaters landing at San Miguel must contact the park ranger beforehand.

Island Packers. Sailing on high-speed catamarans from Ventura or a mono-hull vessel from Oxnard, Island Packers goes to Santa Cruz Island daily most of the year, weather permitting. The boats also go to Anacapa several days a week, and to the outer islands from April through November. They also cruise along Anacapa's north shore on three-hour wildlife tours (no disembarking) several times a week. ✉ *3550 Harbor Blvd., Oxnard* ☎ *805/642–1393* ⊕ *islandpackers.com* ✉ *1691 Spinnaker Dr., Ventura* ☎ *805/642–1393* ⊕ *islandpackers.com* 🛥 *From $37.*

TRANSIT TIMES TO THE ISLANDS		
Island	Distance and Time by Boat	Cost (per hiker/camper)
Anacapa Island	14 miles/1 hr from Oxnard	$59/$79
San Miguel Island	58 miles/3 hrs from Ventura	$105/$147
Santa Barbara Island	55 miles/2½–3 hrs from Ventura	$82/$114
Santa Cruz Island	20 miles/1 hr from Ventura	$59/$79
Santa Rosa Island	46 miles/2 hrs from Ventura	$82/$114

CAR TRAVEL

To reach the Ventura harbor, exit U.S. 101 in Ventura at Seaward Boulevard or Victoria Avenue and follow the signs to Ventura Harbor/Spinnaker Drive. To access Channel Islands Harbor in Oxnard, exit U.S. 101

14

at Victoria Avenue and head south approximately 7 miles to Channel Islands Boulevard. To access dive and whale-watching boats in Santa Barbara, exit U.S. 101 at Castillo Street and head south to Cabrillo Boulevard, then turn right for the harbor entrance. Private vehicles are not permitted on the islands. Pets are also not allowed in the park.

TRAIN TRAVEL

Amtrak makes stops in Santa Barbara, Ventura, and Oxnard; from the Amtrak station, just take a taxi or waterfront shuttle bus to the harbor.

PARK ESSENTIALS

PARK FEES AND PERMITS

There is no fee to enter Channel Islands National Park, but unless you have your own boat, you will pay $37 or more per person for a ride with a boat operator. The cost of taking a boat to the park varies depending on which operator you choose. Also, there is a $15-per-day fee for staying in one of the islands' campgrounds.

If you take your own boat, landing permits are not required to visit islands administered by the National Park Service. However, boaters who want to land on the Nature Conservancy preserve on Santa Cruz Island must have a permit. Visit ⊕ *www.nature.org/cruzpermit* for permit information; allow 10 business days to process and return your permit application. If you anchor in a nearby cove at any island, at least one person should remain aboard the boat at all times. San Miguel Island is property of the U.S. Navy. Visitors must obtain an access permit to visit the island. Access permits are available at the boat and air concession offices and at a self-registration station on the island. To hike beyond the ranger station on San Miguel you need a reservation and permit; call ☎ *805/658–5711* to be matched up with a ranger, who must accompany you. Anglers must have a state fishing license; for details, call the California Department of Fish and Wildlife at ☎ *916/653–7664* or visit ⊕ *www.wildlife.ca.gov*. More than a dozen Marine Protected Areas (MPAs) with special resource protection regulations surround the islands, so read the guidelines carefully before you depart.

PARK HOURS

The islands are open every day of the year. Channel Islands National Park Visitor Center in Ventura is closed on Thanksgiving and Christmas. Channel Islands National Park is in the Pacific time zone.

CELL-PHONE RECEPTION

In general, cell-phone reception is spotty and varies by location and service provider. Public telephones are available on the mainland near the Channel Islands National Park Visitor Center but not on the islands.

EDUCATIONAL OFFERINGS

RANGER PROGRAMS

Ranger programs are held at the Channel Islands National Park Visitor Center in Ventura.

FAMILY **Channel Islands Live Program.** Can't make the trip to the islands? Experience them virtually through the Channel Islands Live Program, which takes you on interactive tours of the park. In the Live Dive Program, divers armed with video cameras explore the undersea world of the kelp forest off Anacapa Island; images are transmitted to monitors located on the dock at Landing Cove, in the mainland visitor center, and on the Internet. You see bright red sea stars, spiny sea urchins, and brilliant orange Garibaldis. You can even ask the divers questions via interactive lines. The Live Hike Program takes you on a similar interactive virtual tour of Anacapa Island. Live webcams also connect you 24/7 with panoramic views of Anacapa Island, bald eagle nests, and underwater life in a kelp forest. ⊠ *Landing Cove* ⊕ *www.nps.gov/chis/ planyourvisit/channel-islands-live-nps.htm* ▱ *Free* ⊙ *Summer, Wed.– Sat., visit website for times.*

Tidepool Talk. Explore the area's marine habitat without getting your feet wet. Rangers at the Channel Islands Visitor Center demonstrate how animals and plants adapt to the harsh conditions found in tidal pools of the Channel Islands. ⊠ *Channel Islands National Park Visitor Center, 1901 Spinnaker Rd., Ventura* ☎ *805/658–5730* ▱ *Free* ⊙ *Weekends and holidays at 11:30 (11 in winter) and 3.*

14

RESTAURANTS

Out on the islands, you won't have any trouble deciding where to dine—there are no restaurants, no snack bars, and in some cases, no potable water. Pack a fancy picnic or a simple sandwich—and don't forget it in your car or hotel. For a quick meal before or after your island trip, each of the harbors has a number of decent eateries nearby.

Back on the mainland, though, it's a dining gold mine. Santa Barbara has a long-standing reputation for culinary excellence, and a "foodie" renaissance in recent years has transformed Ventura into a dining destination—with dozens of new restaurants touting nouvelle cuisine made with organic produce and meats. Fresh seafood is a standout, whether it's prepared simply in wharf-side hangouts or incorporated into sophisticated bistro menus. Dining attire is generally casual, though slightly dressy casual wear is the custom at pricier restaurants.

HOTELS

It's easy to choose where to stay in the park—your only option is sleeping in your tent in a no-frills campground. If you hanker for more creature comforts, you can splurge on a bunk and meals on a dive boat.

There's a huge range of lodging options on the mainland, from seaside camping to posh international resorts. The most affordable options are in Oxnard, Ventura, and Carpinteria, a small seaside community between Santa Barbara and Ventura. Despite rates that range from pricey to downright shocking, Santa Barbara's numerous hotels and bed-and-breakfasts attract thousands of patrons year-round. Wherever you stay, be sure to make reservations for the summer and holiday weekends (especially Memorial Day, July 4, Labor Day, and Thanksgiving) well ahead of time; it's not unusual for coastal accommodations to fill completely during these busy times. Also be aware that some hotels double their rates during festivals and other events.

Hotel reviews have been shortened. For full information, visit Fodors.com.

WHAT IT COSTS				
	$	$$	$$$	$$$$
Restaurants	under $16	$16–$22	$23–$30	over $30
Hotels	under $121	$121–$175	$176–$250	over $250

Restaurant prices are the average cost of a main course at dinner, or if dinner is not served, at lunch, excluding sales tax of 8%–8.25% (depending on location). Hotel prices are the lowest cost of a standard double room in high season, excluding service charges and 9%–12% occupancy tax.

VISITOR INFORMATION

VISITOR CENTERS

Channel Islands National Park Visitor Center. The park's Robert J. Lagomarsino Visitor Center has a museum, a bookstore, and a three-story observation tower with telescopes. The museum's exhibits and a 24-minute film, *Treasure in the Sea,* provide an engaging overview of the islands. In the marine life exhibit, sea stars cling to rocks, anemones wave their colorful, spiny tentacles, and a brilliant orange Garibaldi darts around. Also on display are full-size reproductions of a male northern elephant seal and the pygmy mammoth skeleton unearthed on Santa Rosa Island in 1994.

On weekends and holidays at 11 and 3, rangers lead various free public programs describing park resources, and from Wednesday through Saturday in summer the center screens live ranger broadcasts of hikes and dives on Anacapa Island. Webcam images of bald eagles and other land and sea creatures are shown at the center and on the park's website. ⊠ *1901 Spinnaker Dr., Ventura* ☎ *805/658–5730* ⊕ *www.nps.gov/ chis* ☉ *Daily 8:30–5.*

Outdoors Santa Barbara Visitor Center. The small office in the Santa Barbara Harbor provides maps and other information about Channel Islands National Park and Channel Islands National Marine Sanctuary; the Santa Barbara Maritime Museum is housed in the same building. Call ahead to verify hours. ⊠ *113 Harbor Way, Santa Barbara* ☎ *805/456–8752* ⊕ *outdoorsb.sbmm.org* ☉ *Daily 11–5.*

EXPLORING

THE ISLANDS

Anacapa Island. Most people think of Anacapa as an island, but it's actually comprised of three narrow islets. Although the tips of these volcanic formations nearly touch, the islets are inaccessible from one another except by boat. All three have towering cliffs, isolated sea caves, and natural bridges; Arch Rock, on East Anacapa, is one of the best-known symbols of Channel Islands National Park.

Wildlife viewing is the main activity on East Anacapa, particularly in summer when seagull chicks are newly hatched and sea lions and seals

CLOSE UP

Plants and Wildlife on the Channel Islands

Channel Islands National Park is home to species found nowhere else on Earth: mammals such as the island fox and the island deer mouse and birds like the island scrub jay live forever on the endangered species list. Thousands of western gulls hatch each summer on Anacapa, then fly off to the mainland where they spend about four years learning all their bad habits. Then they return to the island to roost and have chicks of their own. It all adds up to a living laboratory not unlike the one naturalist Charles Darwin discovered off the coast of South America 200 years ago, which is why the Channel Islands are often called the North American Galápagos.

lounge on the beaches. Exhibits at East Anacapa's compact **museum** include the original lead-crystal Fresnel lens from the 1932 lighthouse.

Over on West Anacapa, depending on the season and the number of desirable species lurking about there, boats travel to **Frenchy's Cove**. On a voyage here you might see anemones, limpets, barnacles, mussel beds, and colorful marine algae in the pristine tide pools. The rest of West Anacapa is closed to protect nesting brown pelicans. ⊠ *Channel Islands National Park.*

San Miguel Island. The westernmost of the Channel Islands, San Miguel Island is frequently battered by storms sweeping across the North Pacific. The 15-square-mile island's wild windswept landscape is lush with vegetation. Point Bennett, at the western tip, offers one of the world's most spectacular wildlife displays when more than 100,000 pinnipeds hit its beach. Explorer Juan Rodríguez Cabrillo was the first European to visit this island; he claimed it for Spain in 1542. Legend holds that Cabrillo died on one of the Channel Islands—no one knows where he's buried, but there's a memorial to him on a bluff above Cuyler Harbor. ⊠ *Channel Islands National Park.*

Santa Barbara Island. At about 1 square mile, Santa Barbara Island is the smallest of the Channel Islands and nearly 35 miles south of the others. Triangular in shape, Santa Barbara's steep cliffs—which offer a perfect nesting spot for the Scripps's murrelet, a rare seabird—are topped by twin peaks. In spring you can enjoy a brilliant display of yellow coreopsis. Learn about the wildlife on and around the islands at the island's small museum. ⊠ *Channel Islands National Park.*

Fodor's Choice ★ **Santa Cruz Island.** Five miles west of Anacapa, 96-square-mile Santa Cruz Island is the largest of the Channel Islands. The National Park Service manages the easternmost 24% of the island; the rest is owned by the Nature Conservancy, which requires a permit to land. When your boat drops you off on a portion of the 70 miles of craggy coastline, you see two rugged mountain ranges with peaks soaring to 2,500 feet and deep canyons traversed by streams. This landscape is the habitat of a remarkable variety of flora and fauna—more than 600 types of plants, 140 kinds of land birds, 11 mammal species, five varieties of reptiles, and

Santa Rosa, Santa Cruz, and Anacapa Islands

Ventura is approximately 28 miles
Northeast of Prisoners Harbor, Santa Cruz Island

Santa Barbara Channel

Anacapa Passage

Anacapa Island

Arch Rock

Inspiration Point

Light Station and Museum

Summit Peak 936 ft

Scorpion Ranch

San Pedro Point

Smugglers Cove

Sandstone Point

Coche Point

Chinese Harbor

CINP: East Santa Cruz

Prisoners Harbor

Main Ranch

Santa Cruz Island

Painted Cave

CENTRAL VALLEY

West Santa Cruz: The Nature Conservancy

Mount Diablo 2,450 ft

Morse Point

West Point

Santa Cruz Channel

Skunk Point

East Point

Carrington Point

Beckers Bay

Torrey Pines

Santa Rosa Island

Brockway Point

Vail & Vickers Ranch

Black Mtn 1,298 ft

Ford Point

Johnsons Lee

Soledad Peak 1,574 ft

South Point

Cluster Point

Sandy Point

San Miguel Island is approximately 2.5 miles west of Santa Rosa Island

PACIFIC OCEAN

Santa Barbara Island is approximately 52 miles southeast of Santa Cruz Island

0   5 mi

0   5 km

three amphibian species live here. Bird-watchers may want to look for the endemic island scrub jay, which is found nowhere else in the world.

One of the largest and deepest sea caves in the world, **Painted Cave,** lies along the northwest coast of Santa Cruz. Named for the colorful lichen and algae that cover its walls, Painted Cave is nearly ¼ mile long and 100 feet wide. In spring a waterfall cascades over the entrance. Kayakers may encounter seals or sea lions cruising alongside their boats inside the cave. The Channel Islands hold some of the richest archaeological resources in North America; all artifacts are protected within the park. Remnants of a dozen Chumash villages can be seen on the island. The largest of these villages, at the eastern end, occupied the area now called **Scorpion Ranch.** The Chumash mined extensive chert deposits on the island for tools to produce shell-bead money, which they traded with people on the mainland. You can learn about Chumash history and view artifacts, tools, and exhibits on native plant and wildlife at the interpretive visitor center near the landing dock. Visitors can also explore remnants of the early-1900s ranching era in the restored historic adobe and outbuildings. ⊠ *Channel Islands National Park.*

Santa Rosa Island. Between Santa Cruz and San Miguel, Santa Rosa is the second largest of the Channel Islands. The terrain along the coast varies from broad, sandy beaches to sheer cliffs—a central mountain range, rising to 1,589 feet, breaks the island's relatively low profile. Santa Rosa is home to about 500 species of plants, including the rare Torrey pine, and three unusual mammals, the island fox, the spotted skunk, and the deer mouse. They hardly compare, though, to their predecessors: a nearly complete skeleton of a 6-foot-tall pygmy mammoth was unearthed in 1994.

From 1901 to 1998, cattle were raised at the island's **Vail & Vickers Ranch.** The route from Santa Rosa's landing dock to the campground passes by the historic ranch buildings, barns, equipment, and the wooden pier where cattle were brought onto the island. ⊠ *Channel Islands National Park.*

SPORTS AND THE OUTDOORS

DIVING

Some of the best snorkeling and diving in the world can be found in the cool waters surrounding the Channel Islands. In the relatively warm water around Anacapa and eastern Santa Cruz, photographers can get great shots of rarely seen giant black bass swimming among the kelp forests. Here you also find a reef covered with red brittle starfish. If you're an experienced diver, you might swim among five species of seals and sea lions, or try your hand at spearing rockfish or halibut near San Miguel and Santa Rosa. The best time to scuba dive is in summer and fall, when the water is often clear up to a 100-foot depth.

TOURS AND OUTFITTERS

Explorer Diving Adventures. The 65-foot *Explorer* ferries passengers out to all the islands for single- and multiday adventures. Rates include food, snacks, beverages, and air. ⊠ *1583 Spinnaker Dr., Ventura* ☎ *805/890–1142* ⊕ *www.explorerdiveboat.com* ⊠ *From $125 for day trips.*

Peace Dive Boat. Ventura Harbor–based Peace Dive Boat runs single- and multiday diving adventures near all the Channel Islands. Travelers sleep aboard ship. ⊠ *1691 Spinnaker Dr., Dock G, Ventura* ☎ *805/650–3483* ⊕ *www.peaceboat.com* ⊠ *From $110.*

Raptor Dive Boat. Ventura Dive & Sport's 46-foot custom boat, the *Raptor*, takes divers on two- and three-tank trips to Anacapa and Santa Cruz islands and is available for private charters, including offical open-water swims in the channel. ⊠ *Ventura* ☎ *805/650–7700* ⊕ *www.raptordive.com* ⊠ *From $110.*

Spectre Dive Boat. This boat runs single-day diving trips to Anacapa and Santa Cruz. Fees include three dives, air, and food. ⊠ *1575 Spinnaker Dr., Suite 105B-75, Ventura* ☎ *866/225–3483, 805/486–1166* ⊕ *www.calboatdiving.com* ⊠ *From $110.*

Truth Aquatics. Truth runs kayaking, paddleboarding, hiking, snorkeling, and scuba excursions to the National Marine Sanctuary and Channel Islands National Park. ⊠ *Departures from SEA Landing, Santa Barbara Harbor* ☎ *805/962–1127* ⊕ *truthaquatics.com* ⊠ *From $100.*

HIKING

The terrain on most of the islands ranges from flat to moderately hilly. There are no services on the islands (and no public phones; cell-phone reception is dicey). You need to bring all your own food, water (except on Santa Cruz and Santa Rosa, where there are water faucets at campgrounds), and supplies.

TOURS AND OUTFITTERS

Truth Aquatics. This outfitter is authorized to land on some of the park's islands for multiday overnight trips that include naturalist-led hikes (you sleep and eat on board the 65-to-90-foot twin-engine vessels). ⊠ *301 W. Cabrillo Blvd., Santa Barbara* ☎ *805/962–1127* ⊕ *www.truthaquatics.com* ⊠ *From $340.*

EASY

Cuyler Harbor Beach Trail. This easy walk takes you along a 2-mile-long white sand beach on San Miguel. The eastern section is occasionally cut off by high tides. Access permit required. *Easy.* ⊠ *Trailhead: at San Miguel Campground, San Miguel Island.*

FAMILY   **Historic Ranch Trail.** This easy ½-mile walk on Santa Cruz Island takes you to a historic ranch where you can visit an interpretive center in an 1800s adobe and see remnants of a cattle ranch. *Easy.* ⊠ *Trailhead: at Scorpion Beach, Santa Cruz Island.*

FAMILY   **Inspiration Point Trail.** This 1½-mile hike along flat terrain takes in most of East Anacapa; there are great views from Inspiration Point and Cathedral Cove. *Easy.* ⊠ *Trailhead: at Landing Cove, Anacapa Island.*

Water Canyon Trail. Starting at Santa Rosa Campground, this 2-mile walk along a white-sand beach includes some exceptional beachcombing. Frequent strong winds can turn this easy hike into a fairly strenuous excursion, so be prepared. If you extend your walk into Water Canyon, you can follow animal paths to a lush canyon full of native vegetation. *Easy.* ⊠ *Trailhead: at Santa Rosa Campground, Santa Rosa Island.*

MODERATE

FAMILY **Cavern Point Trail.** This moderate 2-mile hike takes you to the bluffs northwest of Scorpion harbor on Santa Cruz, where there are magnificent coastal views and pods of migrating gray whales from December through March. *Moderate.* ⊠ *Trailhead: at Scorpion Ranch Campground, Santa Cruz Island.*

Elephant Seal Cove Trail. This moderate to strenuous walk takes you across Santa Barbara to a point where you can view magnificent elephant seals from steep cliffs. *Moderate.* ⊠ *Trailhead: at Landing Cove, Santa Barbara Island.*

Fodor'sChoice **Prisoners Harbor/Pelican Cove Trail.** Taking in quite a bit of Santa Cruz, ★ this moderate to strenuous 3-mile trail one-way to Pelican Cove is one of the best hikes in the park. You must be accompanied by an Island Packers naturalist or secure a permit (visit *www.nature.org/cruzpermit*; allow 10 to 15 business days to process and return your application), as the hike takes you through Nature Conservancy property. *Moderate.* ⊠ *Trailhead: at Prisoners Harbor, Santa Cruz Island.*

DIFFICULT

Lester Ranch Trail. This short but strenuous 2-mile hike leads up a spectacular canyon filled with waterfalls and lush native plants. At the end of a steep climb to the top of a peak, views of the historic Lester Ranch and the Cabrillo Monument await. If you plan to hike beyond the Lester Ranch, you'll need a hiking permit; call or visit the park website for details. Access permit required. *Difficult.* ⊠ *Trailhead: at San Miguel Campground, San Miguel Island* ☎ 805/658–5730.

Point Bennett Trail. Rangers conduct 15-mile hikes across San Miguel to Point Bennett, where more than 30,000 pinnipeds (three different species) can be seen. Access permit required. *Difficult.* ⊠ *Trailhead: at San Miguel Campground, San Miguel Island.*

KAYAKING

The most remote parts of the Channel Islands are accessible only by a sea kayak. Some of the best kayaking in the park can be found on Anacapa, Santa Barbara, and the eastern tip of Santa Cruz. Anacapa has plenty of sea caves, tidal pools, and even natural bridges you can paddle beneath. Santa Cruz has plenty of secluded beaches to explore, as well as seabird nesting sites and seal and sea lion rookeries. One of the world's largest colonies of Scripps's murrelets resides here, and brown pelicans, cormorants, and storm petrels nest in Santa Barbara's steep cliffs.

It's too far to kayak from the mainland out to the islands, but outfitters have tours that take you to the islands. Tours are offered year-round,

14

but high seas may cause trip cancellations between December and March. ■TIP→ Channel waters can be unpredictable and challenging. Don't venture out alone unless you are an experienced kayaker; guided trips are highly recommended. All kayakers should carry proper safety gear and equipment and be prepared for sudden strong winds and weather changes. Also refrain from disturbing wildlife. Visit the park website for kayaking rules and tips.

The operators listed here hold permits from the National Park Service to conduct kayak tours; if you choose a different company, verify that it holds the proper permits.

TOURS AND OUTFITTERS

Aquasports. This highly regarded company based in Goleta offers guided one-, two-, and three-day trips to Scorpion Cove on Santa Cruz Island for beginner to expert kayakers. They also lead one-day trips to Santa Barbara and Anacapa. Cross-channel passage, instruction, equipment, and guides are included. This is a very popular trip—book early! ☎ *800/773–2309, 805/968–7231* ⊕ *www.islandkayaking.com* ✉ *From $155.*

Channel Islands Outfitters. You can take a one-day trip to Santa Cruz, Anacapa, and Santa Barbara islands, or overnight multiday excursions to all the islands from this outfitter, authorized by the park to guide kayak, snorkel, and hiking adventures. Trips depart from Ventura, Channel Islands, and Santa Barbara harbors; all include equipment and instruction. Boat transportation is an additional charge. ⊠ *117B Harbor Way, Santa Barbara* ☎ *805/899–4925* ⊕ *www.channelislandso.com* ✉ *From $140.*

Santa Barbara Adventure Company. Full-service outfitter Santa Barbara Adventure Company conducts guided kayaking single- and multiday excursions to the Channel Islands. Trips include transportation, equipment, guides, and paddling lessons. ⊠ *32 E. Haley St., Santa Barbara* ☎ *805/884–9283* ⊕ *www.sbadventureco.com* ✉ *From $179.*

WHALE-WATCHING

About a third of the world's cetacean species (27 to be exact) can be seen in the Santa Barbara Channel. In July and August, humpback and blue whales feed off the north shore of Santa Rosa. From late December through March, up to 10,000 gray whales pass through the Santa Barbara Channel on their way from Alaska to Mexico and back again, and on a whale-watching trip during this time frame, you should see one or more of them. Other types of whales, but fewer in number, swim the channel June through August.

TOURS

Island Packers. Depending on the season, you can take a three-hour tour or an all-day tour from either Ventura or Channel Islands harbors with Island Packers. From January through March you're almost guaranteed to see gray whales in the channel. ⊠ *1691 Spinnaker Dr., Ventura* ☎ *805/642–1393* ⊕ *www.islandpackers.com* ✉ *From $37.*

Like much of California's central coast, Santa Cruz looks as rugged and undeveloped as it did centuries ago.

WHAT'S NEARBY

NEARBY TOWNS

With a population of more than 100,000, **Ventura** is the main gateway to Channel Islands National Park. It's a classic California beach town filled with interesting restaurants, a wide range of accommodations, and miles of clean, white beaches. South of Ventura is **Oxnard,** a community of 203,000 boasting a busy harbor and uncrowded beaches. Known for its Spanish ambience, **Santa Barbara** has a beautiful waterfront set against a backdrop of towering mountains—plus glistening palm-lined beaches, whitewashed adobe structures with red-tile roofs, and a hip, youthful vibe in the downtown/waterfront area.

Visitor Information Oxnard Convention & Visitors Bureau. ⊠ *2786 Seaglass Way, Oxnard* ☎ *805/988–0717* ⊕ *www.visitoxnard.com.* **Visit Santa Barbara.** ⊠ *500 E. Montecito St., Santa Barbara* ☎ *805/966–9222, 800/676–1266* ⊕ *www. santabarbaraca.com.* **Ventura Visitors & Convention Bureau.** ⊠ *101 S. Califor- nia St., Ventura* ☎ *805/648–2075* ⊕ *www.visitventuraca.com.*

NEARBY ATTRACTIONS

Mission San Buenaventura. The ninth of the 21 California missions, Mis- sion San Buenaventura was established in 1782 but burned to the ground in the 1790s. It was rebuilt and rededicated in 1809. A self- guided tour takes you through a small museum, a quiet courtyard, and a chapel with 250-year-old paintings. ⊠ *211 E. Main St., at Figueroa*

St., Ventura ☎ *805/643–4318* ⊕ *www.sanbuenaventuramission.org* 🗨 *$4* ⊙ *Sun.–Fri. 10–5, Sat. 9–5.*

Fodor's Choice   **Mission Santa Barbara.** Widely referred to as the "Queen of Missions,"
★   this is one of the most beautiful and frequently photographed buildings in coastal California. Dating to 1786, the architecture evolved from adobe-brick buildings with thatch roofs to more permanent edifices as the mission's population burgeoned. An earthquake in 1812 destroyed the third church built on the site. Its replacement, the present structure, is still a functioning Catholic church. Mission Santa Barbara has a splendid Spanish/Mexican colonial art collection, as well as Chumash sculptures and the only Native American–made altar and tabernacle left in the California missions. Docents lead 60-minute tours ($12 adult) Thursday and Friday at 11 and Saturday at 10:30. ⊠ *2201 Laguna St., at E. Los Olivos St., Santa Barbara* ☎ *805/682–4149 gift shop, 805/682–4713 tours* ⊕ *www.santabarbaramission.org* 🗨 *$8 self-guided tour* ⊙ *Daily 9–4:15.*

Fodor's Choice   **Santa Barbara County Courthouse.** Hand-painted tiles and a spiral staircase
★   infuse the courthouse, a national historic landmark, with the grandeur of a Moorish palace. This magnificent building was completed in 1929. An elevator rises to an arched observation area in the tower that provides a panoramic view of the city. Before or after you take in the view, you can (if it's open) visit an engaging gallery devoted to the workings of the tower's original, still operational Seth Thomas clock. The murals in the ceremonial chambers on the courthouse's second floor were painted by an artist who did backdrops for some of Cecil B. DeMille's films. ⊠ *1100 Anacapa St., at E. Anapamu St., Santa Barbara* ☎ *805/962–6464* ⊕ *www.santabarbaracourthouse.org* ⊙ *Weekdays 8–5, weekends 10–4:30. Free guided tours weekdays at 10:30, daily at 2.*

FAMILY   **Santa Barbara Maritime Museum.** California's seafaring history is the focus here. High-tech, hands-on exhibits, such as a sportfishing activity that lets participants haul in a "big one" and a local surfing history retrospective, make this a fun stop for families. The museum's shining star is a rare, 17-foot-tall Fresnel lens from the historic Point Conception Lighthouse. Ride the elevator to the fourth-floor observation area for great harbor views. ⊠ *113 Harbor Way, off Shoreline Dr., Santa Barbara* ☎ *805/962–8404* ⊕ *sbmm.org* 🗨 *$8* ⊙ *Thurs.–Tues. 10–5.*

FAMILY   **Santa Barbara Museum of Natural History.** The gigantic blue whale skeleton greets you at the entrance to this complex whose major draws include its planetarium, space lab, and gem and mineral display. Startlingly alive-looking stuffed specimens, complete with nests and eggs, roost in the bird hall, and a room of dioramas illustrates Chumash Indian history and culture. Outdoors, nature trails wind through the serene oak-studded grounds. A Nature Pass, available at the museum and the associated Sea Center, is good for discounted admission to both facilities. ⊠ *2559 Puesta del Sol Rd., off Mission Canyon Rd., Santa Barbara* ☎ *805/682–4711* ⊕ *sbnature.org* 🗨 *$12; free 3rd Sun. of month Sept.–Apr.* ⊙ *Daily 10–5.*

FAMILY   **Santa Barbara Museum of Natural History Sea Center.** A branch of the Santa Barbara Museum of Natural History, the Sea Center specializes in Santa Barbara Channel marine life and conservation. It's a fascinating, hands-on marine science laboratory that lets you participate in experiments, projects, and exhibits. The two-story glass walls open to stunning ocean, mountain, and city views. ⊠ *211 Stearns Wharf, Santa Barbara* ☎ *805/962–2526* ⊕ *www.sbnature.org* 🎟 *$8* ⊙ *Daily 10–5.*

Stearns Wharf. Built in 1872, Stearns Wharf is Santa Barbara's most visited landmark. Expansive views of the mountains, cityscape, and harbor unfold from every vantage point on the three-block-long pier. Although it's a nice walk from the Cabrillo Boulevard parking areas, you can also park on the pier and then wander through the shops or stop for a meal at one of the wharf's restaurants. ⊠ *Cabrillo Blvd. and State St., Santa Barbara* ⊕ *stearnswharf.org.*

Fodor's Choice
★
Ventura Oceanfront. Four miles of gorgeous coastline stretch from the county fairgrounds at the northern border of the city of San Buenaventura, through San Buenaventura State Beach, down to Ventura Harbor in the south. The main attraction here is the San Buenaventura City Pier, a landmark built in 1872 and restored in 1993. Surfers rip the waves just north of the pier, and sunbathers relax on white-sand beaches on either side. The mile-long promenade and the Omer Rains Bike Trail north of the pier attract scores of joggers, surrey cyclers, and bikers throughout the year. ⊠ *California St., at ocean's edge, Ventura.*

WHERE TO EAT

IN THE PARK

Picnic Areas. Picnic tables are available on all the islands except San Miguel. You can also picnic on some of the beaches of Santa Cruz, Santa Rosa, and San Miguel; be aware that high winds are always a possibility on Santa Rosa and San Miguel.

OUTSIDE THE PARK

SANTA BARBARA

$$$
SEAFOOD
✕ **Brophy Bros.** The outdoor tables at this casual harborside restaurant have perfect views of the marina and mountains. Staffers serve enormous, exceptionally fresh fish dishes—don't miss the seafood salad and chowder—and provide guests with a pager if there's a long wait for a table. Stroll along the waterfront until the beep lets you know your table's ready. Hugely popular, Brophy Bros. can be crowded and loud, especially on weekend evenings. $ *Average main: $23* ⊠ *119 Harbor Way, off Shoreline Dr., Santa Barbara* ☎ *805/966–4418* ⊕ *brophybros.com.*

$
MEXICAN
✕ **La Super-Rica.** This food stand on the east side of town serves some of the spiciest and most authentic Mexican dishes between Los Angeles and San Francisco. Fans (the late chef Julia Child was one) fill up on the soft tacos served with yummy spicy or mild sauces and legendary beans. Portions are on the small side; order several dishes and share.

$ *Average main: $12* ✉ *622 N. Milpas St., at Alphonse St., Santa Barbara* ☎ *805/963–4940* ▬ *No credit cards* ☉ *Closed Tues. and Wed.*

VENTURA

$
SEAFOOD
✕**Andria's Seafood.** The specialties at this casual, family-oriented restaurant in Ventura Harbor Village are fresh fish-and-chips and homemade clam chowder. After placing your order at the counter, you can sit outside on the patio and enjoy the view of the harbor and marina. $ *Average main: $15* ✉ *1449 Spinnaker Dr., Suite A, Ventura* ☎ *805/654–0546* ⊕ *andriasseafood.com* ⚓ *Reservations not accepted.*

$$$
SEAFOOD
✕**Brophy Bros.** The Ventura outpost of the wildly popular Santa Barbara restaurant provides the same fresh seafood-oriented meals in a spacious second-story setting overlooking the harbor. Feast on everything from fish-and-chips and crab cakes to chowder and delectable fish—often straight from the boats moored below. $ *Average main: $23* ✉ *1559 Spinnaker Dr., in Ventura Harbor Village, Ventura* ☎ *805/639–0865* ⊕ *brophybros.com* ⚓ *Reservations not accepted.*

$
CAFÉ
✕**Harbor Cove Café.** Waterfront views next to Channel Islands National Park visitor center, hearty, cooked-to-order meals, and boxed picnic lunches make this casual dockside eatery a popular spot for island travelers and beachgoers. Fill up on a breakfast burrito before boarding the boat, take a boxed deli-sandwich along, and refuel with a hefty Angus burger, chowder, or fish-and-chips when you return. The café is open for breakfast and lunch daily, plus dinner Friday and Saturday in summer. $ *Average main: $12* ✉ *1867 Spinnaker Dr., Ventura* ☎ *805/658–1639* ☉ *No dinner Sun.–Thurs. in summer, no dinner rest of year.*

$$
SEAFOOD
✕**Lure Fish House.** Fresh, sustainably caught seafood charbroiled over a mesquite grill, a well-stocked oyster bar, specialty cocktails, and a wine list heavy on local vintages lure diners into this slick, nautical-theme space downtown. The menu centers on the mostly local catch and organic vegetables, and includes tacos, sandwiches, and salads. Regulars rave about the shrimp-and-chips, cioppino, and citrus crab-cake salad. $ *Average main: $19* ✉ *60 S. California St., Ventura* ☎ *805/567–4400* ⊕ *www.lurefishhouse.com.*

WHERE TO STAY

OUTSIDE THE PARK

OXNARD

$$$
HOTEL
🛏 **Embassy Suites Mandalay Beach Resort.** Tropical gardens, small waterfalls, and sprawling pool areas surround this Spanish-Mediterranean complex, set on 8 acres of white-sand beach north of Channel Islands Harbor. **Pros:** on the beach, just a mile to island transportation boats; family-friendly. **Cons:** 4 miles from island transportation from Ventura Harbor; fee for Wi-Fi; no full kitchens. $ *Rooms from: $239* ✉ *2101 Mandalay Beach Rd., Oxnard* ☎ *805/984–2500* ⊕ *www.embassysuitesmandalay.com* ⇆ *250 suites* ❑ *Breakfast.*

CLOSE UP

Best Campgrounds on the Channel Islands

Camping is the best way to experience the natural beauty and isolation of Channel Islands National Park. Unrestricted by tour schedules, you have plenty of time to explore mountain trails, snorkel in the kelp forests, or kayak into sea caves. Campsites are primitive, with no water (except on Santa Rosa and Santa Cruz) or electricity. Campfires are not allowed on the islands, though you may use enclosed camp stoves. Use bear boxes for storing your food. You must carry all your gear and pack out all trash. Campers must arrange transportation to the islands before reserving a campsite (and yes, park personnel do check).

National Park Service Reservation System. You can get specifics on each campground and reserve a campsite ($15 per night) by contacting the National Park Service Reservation System up to six months in advance. ☎ *877/444–6777* ⊕ *www.recreation.gov.*

Del Norte Campground. This remote campground on Santa Cruz offers backpackers sweeping ocean views from its 1,500-foot perch. It's accessed via a 3½-mile hike through a series of canyons and ridges. ✉ *Prisoners Harbor landing.*

East Anacapa Campground. You need to walk ½ mile and ascend more than 150 steps to reach this open, treeless camping area above Cathedral Cove. ✉ *East Anacapa landing.*

San Miguel Campground. Accessed by a steep, 1½-mile hike across the beach and through a lush canyon, this campground is on the site of the Lester Ranch; the Cabrillo Monument is nearby. Be aware that strong winds and thick fog are common here. ✉ *Cuyler Harbor landing.*

Santa Barbara Campground. This seldom-visited campground perched on a cliff above Landing Cove is reached via a challenging ½-mile, uphill climb. ✉ *Landing Cove.*

Santa Cruz Scorpion Campground. In a grove of eucalyptus trees, this campground is near the historic buildings of Scorpion Ranch. It's accessed via an easy, ½-mile, flat trail from Scorpion Beach landing. ✉ *Scorpion Beach landing.*

Santa Rosa Campground. Backcountry beach camping is available on this island; it's a 1½-mile, flat walk to the campground. There's a spectacular view of Santa Cruz Island across the water and easy access to fantastic hiking trails. ✉ *Bechers Bay landing.*

14

$$$$
RESORT
Fodor's Choice
★

🍷 **Bacara Resort & Spa.** A luxury resort with four restaurants and a 42,000-square-foot spa and fitness center with 36 treatment rooms, the Bacara provides a gorgeous setting for relaxing retreats. **Pros:** serene natural setting; nature trails; first-rate spa; three zero-edge pools; in-room iPads for quick service orders and lighting and climate control. **Cons:** pricey; not close to downtown; sand on beach not pristine enough for some. Ⓢ *Rooms from: $450* ✉ *8301 Hollister Ave., Goleta* ☎ *844/610–9688* ⊕ *bacararesort.com* ⤳ *313 rooms, 45 suites* ⦿ *No meals.*

$$$$
RESORT
Fodor'sChoice
★

Four Seasons Resort The Biltmore Santa Barbara. Surrounded by lush, perfectly manicured gardens and across from the beach, Santa Barbara's grande dame has long been a favorite for quiet, California-style luxury. **Pros:** first-class resort; historic Santa Barbara character; personal service; steps from the beach. **Cons:** back rooms are close to train tracks; expensive. ⓢ *Rooms from: $795* ✉ *1260 Channel Dr., Santa Barbara* ☎ *805/969–2261, 805/332–3442 reservations* ⊕ *www.fourseasons. com/santabarbara* ⤢ *181 rooms, 26 suites* ⊙*No meals.*

$$
HOTEL

Franciscan Inn. A block from the harbor and West Beach, the family-owned Franciscan has spacious, beach-theme rooms. **Pros:** near waterfront and harbor; friendly staff; good value; family-friendly. **Cons:** busy lobby; pool can be crowded. ⓢ *Rooms from: $175* ✉ *109 Bath St., Santa Barbara* ☎ *805/963–8845* ⊕ *www.franciscaninn.com* ⤢ *33 rooms, 20 suites* ⊙*Breakfast.*

$$$
HOTEL

Hotel Indigo. The closest hotel to the train station, artsy Hotel Indigo is a fine choice for travelers who appreciate contemporary art and want easy access to dining, nightlife, and the beach. **Pros:** multilingual staff; a block from Stearns Wharf; great value for location. **Cons:** showers only (no bathtubs); train whistles early morning; rooms on small side. ⓢ *Rooms from: $189* ✉ *121 State St., Santa Barbara* ☎ *805/966–6586* ⊕ *www.indigosantabarbara.com* ⤢ *41 rooms* ⊙*No meals.*

$$
HOTEL

Motel 6 Santa Barbara Beach. A half block from East Beach amid fancier hotels sits this basic but comfortable motel—the first Motel 6 in existence, and the first in the chain to transform into a contemporary Euro-style abode. **Pros:** very close to zoo and beach; friendly staff; clean. **Cons:** no frills; motel-style rooms; no breakfast. ⓢ *Rooms from: $129* ✉ *443 Corona Del Mar Dr., Santa Barbara* ☎ *805/564–1392, 800/466–8356* ⊕ *motel6.com* ⤢ *51 rooms* ⊙*No meals.*

VENTURA

$$$
RESORT

Four Points by Sheraton Ventura Harbor Resort. An on-site restaurant, spacious rooms, and a slew of amenities make this 17-acre property—which includes sister hotel Holiday Inn Express—a popular and practical choice for Channel Islands visitors. **Pros:** close to island transportation; mostly quiet; short drive to historic downtown. **Cons:** not in the heart of downtown; noisy seagulls sometimes congregate nearby. ⓢ *Rooms from: $179* ✉ *1050 Schooner Dr., Ventura* ☎ *805/658–1212, 800/368–7764* ⊕ *fourpoints.com/ventura* ⤢ *102 rooms, 4 suites* ⊙*No meals.*

$$$
HOTEL

Ventura Beach Marriott. Spacious, contemporary rooms, a peaceful location just steps from San Buenaventura State Beach, and easy access to downtown arts and culture make the Marriott a popular choice. **Pros:** walk to beach and biking/jogging trails; a block from historic pier; great value for location. **Cons:** close to highway; near busy intersection. ⓢ *Rooms from: $189* ✉ *2055 E. Harbor Blvd., Ventura* ☎ *805/643–6000, 888/236–2427* ⊕ *marriottventurabeach.com* ⤢ *270 rooms, 15 suites* ⊙*No meals.*

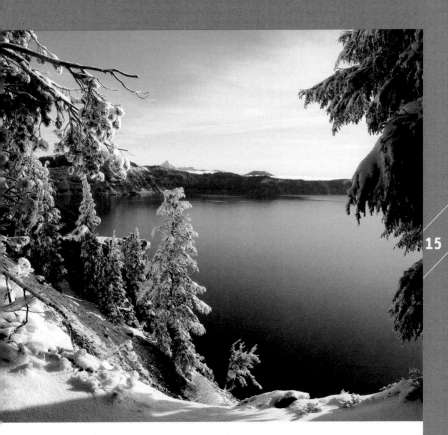

CRATER LAKE
NATIONAL PARK

WELCOME TO CRATER LAKE NATIONAL PARK

TOP REASONS TO GO

★ **The lake:** Cruise inside the caldera basin and gaze into the extraordinary sapphire-blue water of the country's deepest lake, stopping for a ramble around Wizard Island.

★ **Native land:** Enjoy the rare luxury of interacting with totally unspoiled terrain.

★ **The night sky:** Billions of stars glisten in the pitch-black darkness of an unpolluted sky.

★ **Splendid hikes:** Accessible trails spool off the main roads and wind past colorful bursts of wildflowers and cascading waterfalls.

★ **Lake-rim lodging:** Spend the night perched on the lake rim at the rustic yet stately Crater Lake Lodge.

1 Crater Lake. The park's focal point, this nonrecreational, scenic destination is known for its deep blue hue.

2 Wizard Island. Visitors can take boat rides to this protruding landmass rising from the western section of Crater Lake; it's a great place for hiking and picnicking.

3 Mazama Village. About 5 miles south of Rim Drive, the village is your best bet for stocking up on snacks, beverages, and fuel.

4 Cleetwood Cove Trail. The only designated trail to hike down the caldera and reach the lake's edge is on the rim's north side off Rim Drive; all boat tours leave from the dock at trail's end.

GETTING ORIENTED

Crater Lake National Park covers 183,224 acres, and only a relatively small portion of it encompasses the lake for which it's named. In southern Oregon less than 75 miles from the California border, the park is surrounded by several Cascade Range forests, including the Winema and Rogue River national forests. The town of Klamath Falls, 50 miles south of the park, has the most convenient Amtrak stop; Ashland and Medford, to the southwest, are 73 miles and 85 miles, respectively, from the park's southern (Annie Spring) entrance. Roseburg is 85 miles northwest of the park's northern entrance, which is open only seasonally.

KEY	
🏠	*Ranger Station*
⛺	*Campground*
🌲	*Picnic Area*
🍴	*Restaurant*
🏨	*Lodge*
🥾	*Trailhead*
🚻	*Restrooms*
➘	*Scenic Viewpoint*
······	*Walking/Hiking Trails*

OREGON

TO
ROSEBURG
230
138
Pacific Coast
Trail Parking
138
TO
BEND

North Entrance Station

Boundary Springs

Pumice
Desert

North Entrance Rd

Pacific Crest National Scenic Trail

15

4 **Cleetwood
Cove Trail**

Steel
Bay
Cleetwood
Cove

North Junction

Rim Trail

Deepest point
below lake surface:
-1,943 ft

Grotto
Cove

Rim Dr.

Scott Bluffs

The Watchman
8,013 ft

Watchman
Trail

**Wizard
Island**

2

1 *Crater
Lake*

Cloudcap
Bay

Cloudcap Overlook

Pacific Crest Trail

Discovery Point

Rim Village

Danger
Bay

Mount Scott
8,929 ft

Mount Scott
Trail

TO
MEDFORD
AND ASHLAND
62

**Crater Lake
Lodge**

Phantom Ship
Overlook

Sun
Notch

Steel Visitor Center

Rim Dr.

Grayback Dr.
(one way)

Lost
Creek

3

Annie Spring
Entrance Station

Mazama Village

Grayback Ridge

**Crater
Peak**

Pinnacles
Overlook

Pumice
Flat

62

TO
KLAMATH FALLS

0   3 mi

0   3 km

Updated by Andrew Collins

The pure, crystalline blue of Crater Lake astounds visitors at first sight. More than 5 miles wide and ringed by cliffs almost 2,000 feet high, the lake was created approximately 7,700 years ago, following Mount Mazama's fiery explosion. Days after the eruption, the mountain collapsed on an underground chamber emptied of lava. Rain and snowmelt filled the caldera, creating a sapphire-blue lake so clear that sunlight penetrates to a depth of 400 feet (the lake's depth is 1,943 feet). Crater Lake is both the clearest and deepest lake in the United States—and the ninth deepest in the world.

For most visitors, the star attractions of Crater Lake are the lake itself and the breathtakingly situated Crater Lake Lodge. Although it takes some effort to reach it, Wizard Island is another outstanding draw. Other park highlights include the natural, unspoiled beauty of the forest and the geological marvels you can access along the Rim Drive.

CRATER LAKE PLANNER

WHEN TO GO
The park's high season is July and August. September and early October tend to draw smaller crowds. From October well into June, nearly the entire park closes due to heavy snowfall. The road is kept open just from the South Entrance to the rim in winter, except during severe weather.

AVG. HIGH/LOW TEMPS.

Jan.	Feb.	Mar.	Apr.	May	June
34/18	35/18	37/19	42/23	50/28	58/34
July	Aug.	Sept.	Oct.	Nov.	Dec.
68/41	69/41	63/37	52/31	40/23	34/19

FESTIVALS AND EVENTS

Oregon Shakespeare Festival. More than 400,000 Bard lovers descend on charming downtown Ashland (85 miles from Crater Lake) for this nearly yearlong festival that presents works by Shakespeare and other past and contemporary playwrights. ✉ *Ashland* ☎ *541/482–4331* ⊕ *www.osfashland.org.*

PLANNING YOUR TIME

CRATER LAKE IN ONE DAY

Begin at the **Steel Visitor Center,** a short drive from Annie Spring, the only park entrance open year-round. The center's interpretive displays and a short video describe the forces that created the lake and what makes it unique. From here, begin circling the crater's rim by heading northeast on **Rim Drive,** allowing an hour to stop at overlooks—be sure to check out the Phantom Ship rock formation in the lake—before you reach the trailhead of **Cleetwood Cove Trail,** the only safe and legal way to access the lake. If you're game for a good workout, hike down the trail to reach the dock at trail's end and hop aboard a **tour boat** for a two-hour ranger-guided excursion. If you'd prefer to hike on your own, instead take the late-morning shuttle boat to **Wizard Island** for a picnic lunch and a trek to the island's summit.

Back on Rim Drive, continue around the lake, stopping at the **Watchman Trail** for a short but steep hike to this peak above the rim, which affords a splendid view of the lake and a broad vista of the surrounding southern Cascades. Wind up your visit at **Crater Lake Lodge.** Allow time to wander the lobby of this 1915 structure that perches right on the rim. Dinner at the lodge's restaurant, overlooking the lake, caps the day.

GETTING HERE AND AROUND

Rogue Valley International–Medford Airport (MFR) is the nearest commercial airport. About 75 miles southwest of the park, it is served by Alaska, Allegiant, Delta, and United airlines and has rental cars. Amtrak trains stop in downtown Klamath Falls, 50 miles south of the park. Car rentals are available.

Crater Lake National Park's South Entrance, open year-round, is off Highway 62 in southern Oregon. If driving here from California, follow Interstate 5 north to Medford and head east on Highway 62, or take U.S. 97 north past Klamath Falls, exiting northwest on Highway 62. From Portland, Oregon, allow from 5½ to 6 hours to reach the park's South Entrance, via Interstate 5 through the city of Grants Pass. In summer, when the North Entrance is open, the drive from Portland takes just 4½ hours via Interstate 5, Highway 58 (through Oakridge), U.S. 97, and Highway 138. If coming from Portland in summer, staying at an Oakridge or Chemult motel the night before your arrival will have you fairly close to the park the following morning.

Most of the park is accessible only from late June or early July through mid-October. The rest of the year, snow blocks park roadways and entrances except Highway 62 and the access road to Rim Village from Mazama Village. Rim Drive is typically closed because of snow from mid-October to mid-July, and you could encounter icy conditions at any time of year, particularly in the early morning.

15

PARK ESSENTIALS
PARK FEES AND PERMITS

Admission to the park is $15 per vehicle, good for seven days. For all overnight trips, backcountry campers and hikers must obtain a free wilderness permit at Canfield Ranger Station, which is at the park headquarters adjacent to Steel Visitor Center and open daily from 8 to 5.

PARK HOURS

Crater Lake National Park is open 24 hours a day year-round; however, snow closes most park roadways from October to June. Lodging and dining facilities usually are open from late May to mid-October. The park is in the Pacific time zone.

CELL-PHONE RECEPTION

Cell-phone reception in the park is unreliable, although generally it works around Crater Lake Lodge and Mazama Village, which also have public phones.

EDUCATIONAL OFFERINGS
RANGER PROGRAMS

FAMILY **Boat Tours.** The most popular way to tour Crater Lake itself is on a two-hour ranger-led excursion aboard a 37-passenger launch. The first narrated tour leaves the dock at 9:30 am; the last departs at 3:45 pm. Four of the 10 daily boats stop at Wizard Island, where you can get off and reboard three or six hours later. Two of these trips act as shuttles, with no ranger narration. They're perfect if you just want to get to Wizard Island to hike. The shuttles leave at 8:30 and 11:30. To get to the dock you must hike down Cleetwood Cove Trail, a strenuous 1.1-mile walk that descends 700 feet in elevation along the way; only those in excellent physical shape should attempt the hike. Bring adequate water with you. Purchase boat-tour tickets at Crater Lake Lodge, at the top of the trail, or through reservations. Restrooms are available at the top and bottom of the trail. ⊹ *Access Cleetwood Cove Trail off Rim Dr., 11 miles north of Rim Village* ☎ *541/594–2255, 888/774–2728 reservations* ⊕ *www.craterlakelodges.com/activities* ⌑ *$32 shuttle, $40 guided tour, $57 guided tour with island drop-off* ☉ *Daily late June–mid-Sept.*

FAMILY **Junior Ranger Program.** Kids ages 6–12 learn about Crater Lake while earning a Junior Ranger patch in daily sessions during summer months at the Rim Visitor Center, and year-round they can earn a badge by completing the Junior Ranger Activity Booklet, which can be picked up at either visitor center. ☎ *541/594–3100* ⊕ *www.nps.gov/crla/learn/kidsyouth.*

TOURS

Main Street Adventure Tours. This Ashland-based outfitter's guided tours in Southern Oregon include seven-hour ones to Crater Lake. During these tours, available year-round, participants are driven around part of the lake and, seasonally, given the chance to take a boat tour. Along the way to the park there are stops at the Cole M. Rivers Fish Hatchery, the Rogue River Gorge, and Lake of the Woods. ⊠ *Ashland* ☎ *541/482–9852* ⊕ *www.ashland-tours.com* ⌑ *From $179.*

RESTAURANTS

There are just a few casual eateries and convenience stores within the park, all near the main (southern) entrance. For fantastic upscale dining on the caldera's rim, head to the Crater Lake Lodge. Outside the park, Klamath Falls has a smattering of good restaurants, and both Medford and Ashland abound with first-rate eateries serving farm-to-table cuisine and local Rogue Valley wines.

HOTELS

Crater Lake's summer season is relatively brief, and Crater Lake Lodge, the park's main accommodation, is generally booked up a year in advance. If you are unable to get a reservation, check availability as your trip approaches—cancellations are always possible. The other in-park option, the Cabins at Mazama Village, also books up early in summer; as of this writing, for the first time ever, plans were underway to keep the Cabins at Mazama Village open during at least part of the winter—call ahead to confirm exact opening dates. Outside the park there are a couple of options in nearby Prospect, and numerous lodgings in Klamath Falls, Medford, Ashland, and Roseburg. Additionally, if visiting the park via the North Entrance in summer, you might consider staying in one of the handful of motels in Oakridge and Chemult. Even Bend is an option, as it's just a two-hour drive from North Entrance, which is only slightly longer than the drive from Ashland to the main entrance. *Hotel reviews have been shortened. For full information, visit Fodors.com.*

15

WHAT IT COSTS			
	$	**$$**	**$$$**	**$$$$**
Restaurants	under $13	$13–$20	$21–$30	over $30
Hotels	under $100	$100–$150	$151–$200	over $200

Restaurant prices are the average cost of a main course at dinner, or if dinner is not served, at lunch. Hotel prices are the lowest cost of a standard double room in high season.

VISITOR INFORMATION

Park Contact Information Crater Lake National Park. ☎ *541/594–3000* ⊕ *www.nps.gov/crla.* **Park Literature and Information Crater Lake Natural History Association.** ✉ *Crater Lake National Park* ☎ *541/594–3111* ⊕ *www. craterlakeoregon.org.*

VISITOR CENTERS

Rim Visitor Center. In summer you can obtain park information at the center, take a ranger-led tour, or stop into the nearby Sinnott Memorial, which has a small museum and a 900-foot view down to the lake's surface. In winter, snowshoe walks are offered on weekends and holidays. A short walk away, the Rim Village Gift Store and cafeteria are the only services open in winter. ✉ *Rim Dr., 7 miles north of Annie Spring entrance station* ☎ *541/594–3000* ⊕ *www.nps.gov/crla* ☉ *Late May–Sept., daily 9:30–5.*

Steel Visitor Center. Open year-round, the center, part of the park's headquarters, has restrooms, a first-aid station, a small post office, and a shop that sells books, maps, and postcards. There are fewer exhibits than at comparable national park visitor centers, but you can view an engaging 22-minute film, *Crater Lake: Into the Deep,* which describes the lake's formation and geology and examines the area's cultural history. ⊠ *Rim Dr., 4 miles north of Annie Spring entrance station* ☎ *541/594–3000* ⊕ *www.nps.gov/crla* ⊙ *Late Apr.–early Nov., daily 9–5; early Nov.–late Apr., daily 10–4.*

EXPLORING

SCENIC DRIVES

Fodor's Choice ★ **Rim Drive.** Take this 33-mile scenic loop for views of the lake and its cliffs from every conceivable angle. The drive takes two hours not counting frequent stops at overlooks and short hikes that can easily stretch this to a half day. Rim Drive is typically closed due to heavy snowfall from mid-October to mid-June, and icy conditions can be encountered any month of the year, particularly in early morning. ⊹ *Drive begins at Rim Village, 7 miles from (Annie Spring) South Entrance; from North Entrance, follow North Entrance Rd. south for 10 miles* ⊕ *www.nps.gov/crla.*

HISTORIC SITES

Fodor's Choice ★ **Crater Lake Lodge.** Built in 1915, this imposing log-and-stone structure was designed in the classic style of Western national park lodges, and the original lodgepole-pine pillars, beams, and stone fireplaces are still intact. The lobby, fondly referred to as the Great Hall, serves as a warm, welcoming gathering place where you can play games, socialize with a cocktail, or gaze out of the many windows to view spectacular sunrises and sunsets by a crackling fire. Exhibits off the lobby contain historic photographs and memorabilia from throughout the park's history. ⊠ *Rim Village, just east of Rim Visitor Center* ⊕ *www.craterlakelodges.com.*

SCENIC STOPS

Cloudcap Overlook. The highest road-access overlook on the Crater Lake rim, Cloudcap has a westward view across the lake to Wizard Island and an eastward view of Mount Scott, the volcanic cone that is the park's highest point. ⊹ *2 miles off Rim Dr., 13 miles northeast of Steel Visitor Center* ⊕ *www.nps.gov/crla.*

Discovery Point. This overlook marks the spot at which prospectors first spied the lake in 1853. Wizard Island is just northeast, close to shore. ⊠ *West Rim Dr., 1½ miles north of Rim Village* ⊕ *www.nps.gov/crla.*

Mazama Village. In summer, a campground, cabin-style motel, amphitheater, gas station, and small store are open here. No gasoline is available in the park from mid-October to mid-May. Snowfall determines when the village and its facilities open and close for the season. Hours vary; call ahead. ⊠ *Mazama Village Rd., off Hwy. 62, near Annie Spring entrance station* ☎ *541/594–2255, 888/774–2728* ⊕ *www.craterlakelodges.com.*

Phantom Ship Overlook. From this point you can get a close look at Phantom Ship, a rock formation that resembles a schooner with furled masts and looks ghostly in fog. ⊠ *East Rim Dr., 7 miles northeast of Steel Visitor Center* ⊕ *www.nps.gov/crla.*

Pinnacles Overlook. Ascending from the banks of Sand and Wheeler creeks, unearthly spires of eroded ash resemble the peaks of fairy-tale castles. Once upon a time, the road continued east to a former entrance. A path now replaces the old road and follows the rim of Sand Creek (affording more views of pinnacles) to where the entrance arch still stands. ⊠ *Pinnacles Rd., 12 miles east of Steel Visitor Center* ⊕ *www.nps.gov/crla.*

Sun Notch. It's a relatively easy ¼-mile hike through wildflowers and dry meadow to this overlook, which has views of Crater Lake and Phantom Ship. Mind the cliff edges. ⊠ *East Rim Dr., 4.4 miles east of Steel Visitor Center* ⊕ *www.nps.gov/crla.*

Fodor's Choice ★ Wizard Island. The volcanic eruption that led to the creation of Crater Lake resulted in the formation of this magical island a quarter mile off the lake's western shore. The views at its summit—reached on a somewhat strenuous 2-mile hike—are stupendous.

Getting to the island requires a difficult 1.1-mile hike down (and later back up) the steep Cleetwood Cove Trail to the cove's dock. There, board either the shuttle boat to Wizard Island or a Crater Lake narrated tour boat that includes a stop on the island. If you opt for the latter, you can explore Wizard Island a bit and reboard a later boat to resume the lake tour.

The hike to Wizard Summit, 763 feet above the lake's surface, begins at the island's boat dock and steeply ascends over rock-strewn terrain; a path at the top circles the 90-foot-deep crater's rim. More moderate is the 1.8-mile hike on a rocky trail along the shore of Wizard Island, so called because William Steel, an early Crater Lake booster, thought its shape resembled a wizard's hat. ⊹ *Access Cleetwood Cove*

Wildlife in Crater Lake

Wildlife in the Crater Lake area flourishes in the water and throughout the surrounding forest.

SALMON AND TROUT

Two primary types of fish swim beneath the surface of Crater Lake: kokanee salmon and rainbow trout. Kokanees average about 8 inches in length, but they can grow to nearly 18 inches. Rainbow trout are larger than the kokanee but are less abundant in Crater Lake. Trout—including bull, Eastern brook, rainbow, and German

brown—swim in the park's many streams and rivers.

ELK, DEER, AND MORE

Remote canyons shelter the park's elk and deer populations, which can sometimes be seen at dusk and dawn feeding at forest's edge. Black bears and pine martens—cousins of the short-tailed weasel—also call Crater Lake home. Birds such as hairy woodpeckers, California gulls, red-tailed hawks, and great horned owls are more commonly seen in summer in forests below the lake.

Trail off Rim Dr., 11 miles north of Rim Village ☎ *541/594–2255, 888/774–2728* ⊕ *www.craterlakelodges.com/activities* 🛥 *Shuttle boat $32, tour boat $57* ☉ *Daily late June–mid-Sept.; shuttle boats depart 8:30 and 11:30, return 12:45 and 3:35; tour boats depart 9:45 and 12:45, return 3 and 5:50.*

SPORTS AND THE OUTDOORS

FISHING

Fishing is allowed in the lake, but you may find the experience frustrating—in such a massive body of water, the problem is finding the fish. Try your luck near the Cleetwood Cove boat dock, or take poles on the boat tour and fish off Wizard Island. Rainbow trout and kokanee salmon lurk in Crater Lake's aquamarine depths, and some grow to enormous sizes. You don't need a state fishing license, but to protect the lake's pristine waters, the park service prohibits the use of worms, fish eggs, and even some artificial bait (such as powerbait); check with the visitor center for guidance on permissible bait. Private boats are prohibited on the lake.

HIKING

EASY

Castle Crest Wildflower Trail. This short half-mile loop that passes through a spring-fed meadow is one of the park's flatter hikes. Wildflowers burst into full bloom here in July. *Easy.* ⊹ *Trailhead: East Rim Dr., across street from Steel Visitor Center parking lot.*

Godfrey Glen Trail. This 1-mile loop trail is an easy stroll through an old-growth forest with canyon views. Its dirt path is accessible to wheelchairs with assistance. *Easy.* ✛ *Trailhead: Mission Valley Rd., 2.4 miles south of Steel Visitor Center.*

MODERATE

Annie Creek Canyon Trail. This somewhat challenging 1.7-mile hike loops through a deep stream-cut canyon, providing views of the narrow cleft scarred by volcanic activity. This is a good area to look for flowers and deer. *Moderate.* ⊠ *Mazama Campground, Mazama Village Rd.* ✛ *Trailhead: behind amphitheater between D and E campground loops.*

Boundary Springs Trail. If you feel like sleuthing, take this moderate 5-mile round-trip hike to the headwaters of the Rogue River. The trail isn't well marked, so a detailed trail guide is necessary. You'll see streams, forests, and wildflowers along the way before discovering Boundary Springs pouring out of the side of a low ridge. *Moderate.* ✛ *Trailhead: pullout on Hwy. 230, near milepost 19, about 5 miles west of Hwy. 138.*

15

Watchman Peak Trail. This is one of the park's best and most easily accessed hikes. Though it's less than a mile each way, the trail climbs more than 400 feet—not counting the steps up to the actual lookout, which has great views of Wizard Island and the lake. *Moderate.* ✛ *Trailhead: at Watchman Overlook, Rim Dr., 3.8 miles northwest of Rim Village, west side of lake.*

DIFFICULT

Cleetwood Cove Trail. This strenuous 2.2-mile round-trip hike descends 700 feet down nearly vertical cliffs along the lake to the boat dock. Be in very good shape before you tackle this well-maintained trail—it's the hike back up that catches some visitors unprepared. Bring along plenty of water. *Difficult.* ✛ *Trailhead: on Rim Dr., 11 miles north of Rim Village, north side of lake.*

Fodor's Choice ★ **Mt. Scott Trail.** This strenuous 4.4-mile round-trip trail takes you to the park's highest point—the top of Mount Scott, the oldest volcanic cone of Mount Mazama, at 8,929 feet. The average hiker needs 90 minutes to make the steep uphill trek—and nearly 60 minutes to get down. The trail starts at an elevation of about 7,679 feet, so the climb is not extreme, but the trail is steep in spots. The views of the lake and the broad Klamath Basin are spectacular. *Difficult.* ✛ *Trailhead: 14 miles east of Steel Visitor Center on Rim Dr., across from road to Cloudcap Overlook.*

Pacific Crest Trail. You can hike a portion of the Pacific Crest Trail, which extends from Mexico to Canada and winds through the park for 33 miles. For this prime backcountry experience, catch the trail off Highway 138 about a mile east of the North Entrance, where it heads south and then toward the west rim of the lake and circles it for about 6 miles, then descends down Dutton Creek to the Mazama Village area. You'll need a detailed map for this hike; check online or with the PCT association (*www.pcta.org*). *Difficult.* ✛ *Trailhead: at Pacific Crest Trail parking lot, off Hwy. 138, 1 mile east of north entrance.*

SKIING

There are no maintained ski trails in the park, although some backcountry trails are marked with blue diamonds or snow poles. Most cross-country skiers park at Rim Village and follow a portion of West Rim Drive toward Wizard Island Overlook (4 miles). The road is plowed to Rim Village, but it may be closed temporarily due to severe storms. Snow tires and chains are essential. The park's online brochure (available at ⊕ *www.nps.gov/crla*) lists additional trails and their length and difficulty.

SWIMMING

Swimming is allowed in the lake, but it's generally popular only on hot days and among the hardiest of souls. Made up entirely of snowmelt, Crater Lake is very cold—about 45°F to 56°F in summer. The lagoons on Wizard Island and at Cleetwood Cove are your only real choices—but swimming is only advisable when the air temperature rises above 80°F, relatively rare.

WHAT'S NEARBY

NEARBY TOWNS

Klamath Falls and Ashland, both south of the park, and Roseburg, to the west, are the three main gateways to Crater Lake National Park. Other practical bases include Medford, 10 miles from Ashland, and (during the summer, when Crater Lake's north entrance is open), the city of Bend, a 2- to 2½-hour drive north. **Klamath Falls** is about an hour's drive from the park. Klamath Lake, the largest freshwater lake in Oregon, is just north of the city, whose acres of parks and marinas provide endless opportunities to enjoy water sports and bird-watching. **Ashland,** one of Oregon's premier destinations, is set in the foothills of the Siskiyou Mountains. The city's chief appeal is its famed Oregon Shakespeare Festival. Ashland has fine small inns, shops, and restaurants, and the Rogue Valley wine country is nearby. Crater Lake is about a two-hour drive away. **Roseburg's** location at the western edge of the southern Cascades led to its status as a timber-industry center—still the heart of the town's economy—but its site along the Umpqua River has drawn fishermen for years. The drive from Roseburg to Crater Lake takes about two hours.

Visitor Information Ashland Chamber of Commerce. ⊠ *110 E. Main St., Ashland* ☎ *541/482–3486* ⊕ *www.ashlandchamber.com.* **Discover Klamath.** ⊠ *205 Riverside Dr., Klamath Falls* ☎ *541/882–1501, 800/445–6728* ⊕ *www. discoverklamath.com.* **Roseburg Visitors & Convention Bureau.** ⊠ *410 S.E. Spruce St., Roseburg* ☎ *541/672–9731, 800/444–9584* ⊕ *www.visitroseburg.com.*

NEARBY ATTRACTIONS

Fodor's Choice ★ **Klamath Basin National Wildlife Refuge Complex.** As many as 1,000 bald eagles make Klamath Basin their rest stop, amounting to the largest wintering concentration of these birds in the contiguous United States. Located along the Pacific Flyway bird migration route, the nearly 40,000 acres of freshwater wetlands in this complex of six different refuges serve as a stopover for nearly 1 million waterfowl in the fall. Any time of year is bird-watching season; more than 400 species of birds—including about 15 types of raptors—have been spotted in the Klamath Basin. For a leisurely excursion by car, follow the tour routes in the Lower Klamath and Tule Lake refuges—the latter has a superb bookstore and visitor center and is also a short drive from Lava Beds National Monument. ⊠ *Tule Lake Refuge Visitor Center, 4009 Hill Rd., Tulelake* ✛ *27 miles south of Klamath Falls via Hwy. 39* ☎ *530/667–2231* ⊕ *www.fws.gov/refuge/ tule_lake* ⊠ *Free* ☉ *Visitor center, weekdays 8–4:30, weekends 9–4.*

Fodor's Choice ★ **Oregon Caves National Monument.** Marble caves, large calcite formations, and huge underground rooms shape this rare adventure in geology. Guided cave tours take place on the hour in late spring and fall, and every half hour in June, July, and August. The 90-minute half-mile tour is moderately strenuous, with low passageways, twisting turns, and more than 500 stairs; children must be at least 42 inches tall to participate. Cave tours aren't given in winter. Above ground, the surrounding valley holds an old-growth forest with some of the state's largest trees. ⚠ **GPS coordinates for the caves often direct drivers onto a mostly unpaved forest service road meant for four-wheel-drive vehicles. Instead, follow well-signed Highway 46 off U.S. 199 at Cave Junction, which is also narrow and twisting in parts; RVs or trailers more than 32 feet long are not advised.** ⊠ *19000 Caves Hwy. (Hwy. 46), 20 miles east of U.S. 199, 140 miles southwest of Crater Lake, Cave Junction* ☎ *541/592–2100* ⊕ *www.nps.gov/orca* ⊠ *Park free, tours $10* ☉ *Tours late Mar.–Oct.; call for times.*

15

WHERE TO EAT

IN THE PARK

$$ AMERICAN FAMILY ✕ **Annie Creek Restaurant.** This family-friendly dining spot in Mazama Village serves hearty comfort fare. Blue cheese–bacon burgers, Cobb salads, sandwiches, pizzas, lasagna, and a tofu stir-fry are all on the menu. For breakfast expect the American standards, plus a few lighter offerings. Pine trees tower over the outdoor seating area. ⑤ *Average main: $13* ⊠ *Mazama Village Rd. and Ave. C, near Annie Spring entrance station* ☎ *541/594–2255* ⊕ *www.craterlakelodges.com/dining-shopping* ☉ *Closed late Sept.–late May.*

$$$$ PACIFIC NORTHWEST Fodor's Choice ★ ✕ **Dining Room at Crater Lake Lodge.** The only sophisticated dining option inside the park, the lodge emphasizes fresh, regional Northwest cuisine. The dining room is magnificent, with a large stone fireplace and views of Crater Lake's clear-blue waters. Breakfast and lunch are enjoyable here, but the dinner is the main attraction, with tempting dishes such as

smoked salmon crostini with roasted beets and goat cheese, elk chops with a huckleberry-walnut glaze, and bison meatloaf with a mushroom-Merlot sauce. Save room for the blackberry-marionberry-raspberry cobbler. No reservations are accepted for breakfast and lunch, but they're essential for dinner. ⑤ *Average main: $32* ⊠ *Crater Lake Lodge, 1 Lodge Loop Rd., Rim Village* ☎ *541/594–2255* ⊕ *www.craterlakelodges.com* ⊘ *Closed mid-Oct.–mid-May* ⚐ *Reservations essential.*

PICNIC AREAS

Rim Drive. About a half-dozen picnic-area turnouts encircle the lake; all have good views, but they can get very windy. Most have pit toilets, and a few have fire grills, but none have running water. ⊠ *Rim Dr.* ⊕ *www.nps.gov/crla.*

Rim Village. This is the only park picnic area with running water. The tables are set behind the visitor center, and most have a view of the lake below. There are flush toilets inside the visitor center. ⊠ *Rim Dr., south side of lake, by Crater Lake Lodge, Rim Village* ⊕ *www.nps.gov/crla.*

Fodor's Choice
★

Wizard Island. The park's best picnic venue is on Wizard Island; pack a lunch and book yourself on one of the early-morning boat tour departures, reserving space on an afternoon return. There are no formal picnic areas and just pit toilets, but you'll discover plenty of sunny and shaded spots where you can enjoy a quiet meal and appreciate the astounding scene that surrounds you. The island is accessible by boat only, and to get to the boat dock you must hike down 1.1 miles. The hike back up is strenuous. ⚑ *To get to boat dock, access Cleetwood Cove Trail, off Rim Dr., 11 miles north of Rim Village* ⊕ *www.craterlakelodges.com/activities/volcano-boat-cruises.*

OUTSIDE THE PARK

$
AMERICAN

✕ **Beckie's Cafe.** You can get breakfast, lunch, or dinner at this rustic roadhouse diner 15 miles west of Crater Lake's southern entrance, but no one will fault you for skipping your vegetables and plunging into dessert. Since 1926, Beckie's homemade pies have been a must-have treat for travelers on their way to or from the park. Among the year-round selections, very-berry and coconut cream are favorites; savor fresh peach or huckleberry when the fruit is in season—and don't forget to ask for à la mode. ⑤ *Average main: $12* ⊠ *Union Creek Resort, 56484 Hwy. 62, Prospect* ☎ *541/560–3563* ⊕ *www.unioncreekoregon.com/beckies.htm* ⚐ *Reservations not accepted.*

$
CAFÉ

✕ **Gathering Grounds Cafe.** Although this bustling coffeehouse with comfortable seating and exposed-brick walls is a hot spot for espresso drinks made from house-roasted coffee beans, it's also a great option for grabbing healthful, flavorful picnic items. Fresh-fruit parfaits and croissant and English muffin sandwiches are popular for breakfast. Lunch favorites include asparagus-prosciutto panini, sausage-lentil soup, and salads. ⑤ *Average main: $9* ⊠ *116 S. 11th St., Klamath Falls* ☎ *541/887–8403* ⊕ *www.gatheringgroundscafe.com* ⊘ *Closed Sun. No dinner.*

$ | ✕ **Morning Glory.** Breakfast reaches new heights in an eclectically fur-
AMERICAN | nished, blue Craftsman-style bungalow across the street from South-
Fodor'sChoice | ern Oregon University. The extraordinarily good food emphasizes
★ | breakfast fare—omelets filled with crab, artichokes, Parmesan, and smoked-garlic cream; Tandoori tofu scrambles with cherry-cranberry chutney; lemon-poppy waffles with seasonal berries; and cranberry-hazelnut French toast with lemon butter. Expect a wait on weekend mornings, especially for a table on the good-weather patio. $ *Average main: $11* ✉ *1149 Siskiyou Blvd., Ashland* ☎ *541/488–8636* ✪ *No dinner* ⌨ *Reservations not accepted.*

WHERE TO STAY

IN THE PARK

$$$ | 🏠 **The Cabins at Mazama Village.** In a wooded area 7 miles south of the
HOTEL | lake, this complex is made up of several A-frame buildings and has modest rooms with two queen beds and a private bath. **Pros:** clean and well-kept facility. **Cons:** lots of traffic into adjacent campground. $ *Rooms from: $152* ✉ *Mazama Village, near Annie Spring entrance station* ☎ *541/594–2255, 888/774–2728* ⊕ *www.craterlakelodges.com* ✪ *Closed mid-Oct.–late May, but may open some winter months start-ing in 2016* ⇥ *40 rooms* ⦿ *No meals.*

$$$ | 🏠 **Crater Lake Lodge.** The period feel of this 1915 lodge on the caldera's
HOTEL | rim is reflected in its lodgepole-pine columns, gleaming wood floors, and
Fodor'sChoice | stone fireplaces in the common areas. **Pros:** ideal location for watching
★ | sunrise and sunset reflected on the lake; exudes rustic charm; excellent restaurant. **Cons:** books up far in advance; some rooms have tubs only, no shower; relatively simple furnishings and basic amenities. $ *Rooms from: $180* ✉ *1 Lodge Loop Rd., Rim Village, east of Rim Visitor Center, Rim Village* ☎ *541/594–2255, 888/774–2728* ⊕ *www.craterlakelodges. com* ✪ *Closed mid-Oct.–mid-May* ⇥ *71 rooms* ⦿ *No meals.*

OUTSIDE THE PARK

$$ | 🏠 **Prospect Historic Hotel Bed and Breakfast.** Noted individuals such as
B&B/INN | Theodore Roosevelt, Zane Grey, Jack London, and William Jennings Bryan have stayed here in rooms that now bear their names. **Pros:** three waterfalls within walking distance; large property with beautiful grounds and creek; one of the nearest lodgings to the park. **Cons:** small, remote town; breakfast is not included for guests staying in motel units. $ *Rooms from: $150* ✉ *391 Mill Creek Dr., Prospect* ☎ *541/560–3664, 800/944–6490* ⊕ *www.prospecthotel.com* ⇥ *10 main house rooms, 14 motel rooms* ⦿ *Breakfast.*

$$ | 🏠 **Running Y Ranch Resort.** Golfers rave about the Arnold Palmer–
RESORT | designed course at this 3,600-acre Holiday Inn resort in a juniper-and-
FAMILY | ponderosa–shaded canyon overlooking Upper Klamath Lake. **Pros:** kids enjoy indoor pool; walkers and joggers have 8 miles of paved trails. **Cons:** may be too far off the beaten path for some. $ *Rooms from: $140* ✉ *5500 Running Y Rd., 8 miles north of Klamath Falls,*

15

Best Campgrounds in Crater Lake

Tent campers and RV enthusiasts alike will enjoy the heavily wooded and well-equipped setting of Mazama Campground. Lost Creek Campground is much smaller, with minimal amenities and a more "rustic" Crater Lake experience.

Lost Creek Campground. The 16 small, remote tent sites here are usually available on a daily basis; in July and August arrive early to secure a spot. The cost is $10 nightly. ⊠ 3 miles south of Rim Rd. on Pinnacles Spur Rd. at Grayback Dr. ☎ 541/594–3100.

Mazama Campground. This campground is set well below the lake caldera in the pine and fir forest of the Cascades not far from the main access road (Highway 62). Drinking water, showers, and laundry facilities help ensure that you don't have to rough it too much. About half the 200 spaces are pull-throughs, some with electricity and a few with hookups. The best tent spots are on some of the outer loops above Annie Creek Canyon. Tent sites cost $23, RV ones $32. ⊠ *Mazama Village, near Annie Spring entrance station* ☎ *541/594–2255, 888/774–2728* ⊕ *www.craterlakelodges.com.*

Klamath Falls ☎ *541/850–5500, 877/834–3613* ⊕ *www.runningy.com* ⊅ *82 rooms, 43 houses* ⦿ *No meals.*

$$$$
B&B/INN
Fodor's Choice
★

⌂ **Winchester Inn.** You'll find understated elegance and exquisitely comfortable down bedding in this inn's rooms and suites. **Pros:** beautiful tiered gardens; acclaimed restaurant. **Cons:** not a good choice for small children; about a two-hour drive to Crater Lake. $ *Rooms from: $215* ⊠ *35 S. 2nd St., Ashland* ☎ *541/488–1113, 800/972–4991* ⊕ *www.winchesterinn.com* ⊅ *11 rooms, 8 suites* ⦿ *Breakfast.*

DEATH VALLEY
NATIONAL PARK

Visit Fodors.com for advice, updates, and bookings

WELCOME TO DEATH VALLEY NATIONAL PARK

TOP REASONS TO GO

★ **Roving rocks:** Death Valley's Racetrack is home to moving boulders, an unexplained phenomenon that has scientists baffled.

★ **Lowest spot on the continent:** Stand on the lowest spot on the continent at Badwater, 282 feet below sea level.

★ **Wildflower explosion:** During the spring, this desert landscape is ablaze with greenery and colorful flowers, especially between Badwater and Ashford Mill.

★ **Ghost towns:** Death Valley is renowned for its Wild West heritage and is home to dozens of crumbling settlements including Ballarat, Cerro Gordo, Chloride City, Greenwater, Harrisburg, Keeler, Leadfield, Panamint City, Rhyolite, and Skidoo.

★ **Naturally amazing:** From canyons to sand dunes to salt flats and dry lake beds, Death Valley serves up plenty of geological treasures.

1 Central Death Valley. Furnace Creek sits in the heart of Death Valley—if you have only a short time in the park, head here. You can visit gorgeous Golden Canyon, Zabriskie Point, the Salt Creek Interpretive Trail, and Artist's Drive, among other popular points of interest.

2 Northern Death Valley. This region is uphill from Furnace Creek, which means marginally cooler temperatures. Be sure to stop by Rhyolite Ghost Town on Highway 374 before entering the park and exploring Moorish Scotty's Castle, colorful Titus Canyon, and jaw-dropping Ubehebe Crater.

3 Southern Death Valley. This is a desolate area, but there are plenty of sights that help convey Death Valley's rich history. Don't miss the Dublin Gulch Caves.

4 Western Death Valley. Panamint Springs Resort is a nice place to grab a meal and get your bearings before moving on to quaint Darwin Falls, smooth rolling sand dunes, beehive-shaped Wildrose Charcoal Kilns, and historic Stovepipe Wells Village.

CALIFORNIA

GETTING ORIENTED

Death Valley National Park covers 5,310 square miles, ranges from 6 to 60 miles wide, and measures 140 miles north to south. Within the park, the Panamint Range parallels Death Valley to the west, the Amargosa Range to the east. Nearly the entire park lies in southeastern California, with a small eastern portion crossing over into Nevada.

16

Rhyolite (ghost town)
Beatty
374 95
TO LAS VEGAS

Leadfield (ghost town)
Chloride City (ghost town)

Historic Stovepipe Well
Keane Wonder Mine
pipe Wells Village · Sand Dunes
Mesquite Flat
Salt Creek Interpretive Trail

0   10 mi
0   10 km

Devils Cornfield
190

Amargosa Valley

Harmony Borax Works Interpretive Trail
Visitor Center
Furnace Creek
373

Emigrant Canyon Rd. Golden Canyon Interpretive Trail
Zabriskie Point
Twenty Mule Team Canyon

Skidoo (ghost town)
Harrisburg (ghost town)
Artist's Drive Devils Golf Course
Artist's Palette
190
Death Valley Junction

Wildrose Charcoal Kilns
Mahogany Flat
Badwater
Natural Bridge Canyon
Dante's View
TO PAHRUMP

Panamint City (ghost town)
VALLEY
Greenwater (ghost town)
127

Baldwater Basin Lowest elevation in the U.S. 282ft below sea level

Ballard (ghost town)

Tint indicates area below sea level
3
178

Dublin Gulch Caves
Shoshone

Ashford Mill (ruins)

127

Saratoga Spring
TO BAKER & I-15

KEY
🏕 *Ranger Station*
⛺ *Campground*
🌲 *Picnic Area*
🍴 *Restaurant*
🏨 *Lodge*
🥾 *Trailhead*
🚻 *Restrooms*
⟿ *Scenic Viewpoint*
⋯⋯ *Walking/Hiking Trails*
≡≡≡ *4-Wheel Drive Dirt Road*
≡≡≡ *2-Wheel Drive Dirt Road*

Updated by
Deb Hopewell

The desert is no Disneyland. With its scorching summer heat and vast, sparsely populated tracts of land, it's not often at the top of the list when most people plan their California vacations. But the natural riches of Death Valley—the largest national park outside Alaska—are overwhelming: rolling waves of sand dunes, black cinder cones thrusting up hundreds of feet from a blistered desert floor, riotous sheets of wildflowers, bizarrely shaped Joshua trees basking in the orange glow of a sunset, tiny pupfish that enthrall youngsters, and a silence that is both dramatic and startling.

DEATH VALLEY PLANNER

WHEN TO GO

Most of the park's 1 million annual visitors still come between late fall and early spring, taking advantage of moderate temperatures and the lack of rainfall. During these cooler months you will need to book a room in advance, but don't worry: the park never feels crowded. If you visit in summer, believe everything you've ever heard about desert heat—it can be brutal, with temperatures often topping 120°F. The dry air wicks moisture from the body without causing a sweat, so drink plenty of water. Bring sunglasses, a hat, and sufficient clothing to block the sun's rays and the wind. Flash floods are fairly common; sections of roadway can be flooded or washed away. The wettest month is February, when the park receives an average of 0.3 inch of rain.

AVG. HIGH/LOW TEMPS.

Jan.	Feb.	Mar.	Apr.	May	June
65/39	72/46	80/53	90/62	99/71	109/80

July	Aug.	Sept.	Oct.	Nov.	Dec.
115/88	113/85	106/75	92/62	76/48	65/39

FESTIVALS AND EVENTS

MARCH **Annual Art Show & Brunch.** Admission is free for this arts-and-crafts show and sale weekend, held inside and on the lawn of the Furnace Creek Ranch and Inn. ✉ *Furnace Creek Resort, 328 Greenland Blvd., Death Valley* ☎ *760/852-4420* ⊕ *www.deathvalleychamber.org.*

FAMILY **Diaz Lake Trout Derby.** The first Saturday of March, grab your fishing gear and take a shot at the "big one" for a $10 entry fee (free for kids 12 and under). ✉ *Lone Pine* ☎ *760/876–4444* ⊕ *www.lonepinechamber.org.*

MAY **Bishop Mule Days.** Entertainment at this five-day festival over the Memorial Day weekend includes top country-music stars, an arts-and-crafts fair, barbecues, country dances, the longest-running nonmotorized parade in the U.S., and more than 700 mules competing in 181 events. Admission is free. ✉ *1141 N. Main St., Bishop* ☎ *760/872–4263* ⊕ *www.muledays.org.*

OCTOBER **Lone Pine Film Festival.** Every Columbus Day weekend, this town pays tribute to its Hollywood history with three days of tours, films, lectures, and celebrity panels. ✉ *701 S. Main St., Lone Pine* ☎ *760/876–9103* ⊕ *www.lonepinefilmfestival.org.*

NOVEMBER FAMILY **Death Valley 49er Encampment Days.** Originally a centennial celebration held in 1949 to honor the area's first European visitors, this five-day event draws thousands of people from around the world for art shows, a wagon train, live music, artisan booths, dancing, and even a poker tournament. ✉ *Furnace Creek Resort, 328 Greenland Blvd., Death Valley* ⊕ *www.deathvalley49ers.org.*

Shoshone Old West Days. Just outside of Death Valley, this annual three-day festival celebrates Wild West heritage with live performances, arts-and-crafts, and deep-pit barbecue. ✉ *Shoshone* ☎ *760/852–4335* ⊕ *www.shoshonevillage.com.*

PLANNING YOUR TIME

DEATH VALLEY IN ONE DAY

If you begin the day in Furnace Creek, you can see several sights without doing much driving. Bring plenty of water with you, and some food, too. Get up early and drive the 20 miles on Badwater Road to **Badwater,** which looks out on the lowest point in the Western Hemisphere and is a dramatic place to watch the sunrise. Returning north, stop at **Natural Bridge,** a medium-size conglomerate rock formation that has been hollowed at its base to form a span across the canyon, and then at the **Devil's Golf Course,** so named because of the large pinnacles of salt present here. Detour to the right onto **Artist's Drive,** a 9-mile one-way, northbound route that passes **Artist's Palette.** The reds, yellows, oranges, and greens come from minerals in the rocks and the earth. Four miles

16

north of Artist's Drive you will come to the **Golden Canyon Interpretive Trail,** a 2-mile round-trip that winds through a canyon with colorful rock walls. Just before Furnace Creek, take Highway 190 3 miles east to **Zabriskie Point,** overlooking dramatic, furrowed red-brown hills and the **Twenty Mule Team Canyon.** Return to Furnace Creek, where you can grab a meal and visit the museum at the Furnace Creek Visitor Center. Heading north from Furnace Creek, pull off the highway and take a look at the **Harmony Borax Works.**

GETTING HERE AND AROUND

AIR TRAVEL

The closest airport to the park with commercial service, Las Vegas McCarren International Airport, is 130 miles away, so you'll still need to drive a couple of hours to reach the park. Roughly 160 miles to the west, Burbank's Bob Hope Airport is the second-closest airport.

CAR TRAVEL

It can take more than three hours to cross from one side of the park to another, so it's important to choose an entrance point that makes sense for what you want to see. If you're driving from Los Angeles, enter through the western portion along Highway 395; if you're coming from Las Vegas, enter from the north at Beatty, Nevada, or via the central entrance at Death Valley Junction. Travelers from Orange County, San Diego, and the Inland Empire should access the park via Interstate 15 North at Baker.

Distances can be deceiving within the park: what seems close can be very far away. Much of the park can be viewed on regularly scheduled bus tours, but these often don't allow time for hikes to sites not seen from the road, such as Salt Creek, Golden Canyon, and Natural Bridge. The best option is to drive to a number of the sites, get out of the car, and walk.

When driving in Death Valley, reliable maps are important, as signage is often limited or, in a few places, nonexistent. Other important accessories include a compass, a mobile phone (though these don't always work in remote areas), and extra food and water (3 gallons per person per day is recommended, plus additional radiator water). If you're able to take a four-wheel-drive vehicle, bring it: many of Death Valley's most spectacular canyons are otherwise inaccessible. Be aware of possible winter closures or driving restrictions due to snow or other weather by checking the park's website.

Driving Information California Highway Patrol. ☏ *800/427–7623 recorded info from CalTrans, 760/872–5900 live dispatcher* ⊕ *www.chp.ca.gov.* **California State Department of Transportation Hotline.** ☏ *800/427–7623* ⊕ *www.dot.ca.gov.*

PARK ESSENTIALS

PARK FEES AND PERMITS

The entrance fee is $20 per vehicle and $10 for those entering on foot, bus, bike, or motorcycle. The payment, valid for seven consecutive days, is collected at the park's entrance stations and at the visitor center at Furnace Creek. (If you enter the park on Highway 190, you won't find an entrance station; remember to stop by the visitor center to pay the fee.) Annual park passes, valid only at Death Valley, are $40.

A permit is not required for groups of 14 or fewer, but if you're planning an overnight visit to the backcountry, complete a registration form at the Furnace Creek Visitor Center. Backcountry camping is allowed in areas that are at least 2 miles from maintained campgrounds and the main paved or unpaved roads and ¼ mile from water sources. Most abandoned mining areas are restricted to day use.

PARK HOURS

The park is open year-round, and can be visited day or night. Most facilities within the park remain open year-round, daily 8–6.

CELL-PHONE RECEPTION

Results vary, but in general you should be able to get fairly good cell-phone reception on the valley floor. In the surrounding mountains, however, don't count on it.

EDUCATIONAL OFFERINGS

RANGER PROGRAMS

FAMILY **Junior Ranger Program.** Children can join this program at any of the three visitor centers, where they can pick up a workbook and complete up to 15 projects (based on their age) to earn a souvenir badge. ✉ *Death Valley National Park.*

16

RESTAURANTS

Inside the park, if you're looking for a special evening out in Death Valley, head to the Inn at Furnace Creek Dining Room, where you'll be spoiled with fine wines and juicy steaks. It's also a great spot to start the day with a hearty gourmet breakfast. Most other eateries within the park are mom-and-pop-type places with basic American fare. Outside the park, dining choices are much the same, with little cafés and homey diners serving up coffee shop–style burgers, chicken, and steaks. If you're vegetarian or vegan, BYOB (bring your own beans).

HOTELS

It's difficult to find lodging anywhere in Death Valley that doesn't have breathtaking views of the park and surrounding mountains. Most accommodations, aside from the Inn at Furnace Creek, are homey and rustic. Rooms fill up quickly during the fall and spring seasons, and reservations are required about three months in advance for the prime weekends.

Outside the park, head to Beatty or Amargosa Valley in Nevada for a bit of nightlife and casino action. The western side of Death Valley, along the eastern Sierra Nevada, is a gorgeous setting, though it's quite a distance from Furnace Creek. Here, you can stay in the historic Dow Villa Motel, where John Wayne spent many a night, or head farther south to the ghost towns of Randsburg or Cerro Gordo for a true Wild West experience. *Hotel reviews have been shortened. For full information, visit Fodors.com.*

WHAT IT COSTS				
	$	$$	$$$	$$$$
Restaurants	under $13	$13–$20	$21–$30	over $30
Hotels	under $101	$101–$150	$151–$200	over $200

Restaurant prices are the average cost of a main course at dinner, or if dinner is not served, at lunch. Hotel prices are the lowest cost of a standard double room in high season.

TOURS

Death Valley Adventure Tour (*Adventure Motorcycle [AdMo] Tours*). Motorcycle enthusiasts can sign up for a guided Death Valley Adventure Tour that starts and ends in Las Vegas. The five-day tour through Death Valley covers 100–180 miles a day. The tours, which run October through May, include hotel accommodations, gasoline, breakfasts, two dinners, snacks, a support vehicle, and a professional guide. To join, you'll need a motorcycle driver's license and experience with off-road and all-terrain riding. ⊠ *Death Valley* ☎ 760/249–1105 ⊕ *www. admotours.com* ⚑ *From $2,325 with your own bike; rentals from $778.*

Furnace Creek Visitor Center tours. This center has many tour options, including a weekly 2-mile Harmony Borax Walk and guided hikes to Mosaic Canyon and Golden Canyon. Less strenuous options include wildflower, birding, and geology walks, and a Furnace Creek Inn historical tour. Visit the website for a complete list. The visitor center also shows a movie about the park every half hour daily from 8 to 5 in winter, 9 to 6 in summer. ⊠ *Furnace Creek Visitor Center, Rte. 190, 30 miles northwest of Death Valley Junction, Death Valley* ☎ 760/786–2331 ⊕ *www.nps.gov/deva/planyourvisit/tours.htm.*

Pink Jeep Tours Las Vegas. Hop aboard a 10-passenger luxury vehicle with oversized viewing windows with Pink Jeep Tours Las Vegas to visit landmarks such as Dante's Peak, Furnace Creek, Devil's Golf Course, and Zabriskie Point. The all-day tours take place September through May, are professionally narrated, and include lunch and bottled water. ⊠ *3629 W. Hacienda Ave., Las Vegas* ☎ 888/900–4480 ⊕ *pinkjeeptourslasvegas.com* ⚑ *From $235.*

VISITOR INFORMATION

Park Contact Information Death Valley National Park. ⊠ *Death Valley National Park* ☎ *760/786–3200* ⊕ *www.nps.gov/deva.*

VISITOR CENTERS

Furnace Creek Visitor Center and Museum. The exhibits and artifacts here provide a broad overview of how Death Valley formed; you can pick up maps at the bookstore run by the Death Valley Natural History Association. This is also the place to learn about or sign up for ranger-led walks (available November through April) or check out a live presentation about the valley's cultural and natural history. The helpful center offers a 20-minute movie about the park every 30 minutes. Your children are likely to receive plenty of individual attention from the enthusiastic rangers. ✉ *Hwy. 190, Death Valley* ✛ *30 miles northwest of Death Valley Junction* ☎ *760/786–3200* ⊕ *www.nps.gov/deva* ⊘ *Daily 8–5.*

Scotty's Castle Visitor Center and Museum. During your visit to Death Valley, make sure you make the hour's drive north from Furnace Creek to Scotty's Castle. In addition to living-history tours, you'll find a nice display of exhibits, books, self-guided tour pamphlets, and displays about the castle's creators, Death Valley Scotty and Albert M. Johnson. Fuel up with sandwiches or souvenirs (there's no gasoline sold here anymore) before heading back out to the park. ✉ *Rte. 267, Death Valley* ✛ *53 miles northwest of Furnace Creek and 45 miles northwest of Stovepipe Wells Village* ☎ *760/786–2392* ⊕ *www.nps.gov/deva* ⊘ *Daily 9–4:15 (hrs vary seasonally).*

EXPLORING

SCENIC DRIVE

Artist's Drive. This 9-mile, one-way route skirts the foothills of the Black Mountains and provides intimate views of the changing landscape. Once inside the palette, the huge expanses of the valley are replaced by the small-scale natural beauty of pigments created by volcanic deposits or sedimentary layers. It's a quiet, lonely drive, and shouldn't be rushed. Reach Artist's Palette by heading south on Badwater Road from its intersection with Route 190. ✉ *Death Valley National Park.*

HISTORIC SITES

Charcoal Kilns. Ten well-preserved stone kilns, each 25 feet high and 30 feet wide, stand as if on parade. The kilns, built by Chinese laborers for a mining company in 1877, were used to burn wood from pinyon pines to turn it into charcoal. The charcoal was then transported over the mountains into Death Valley, where it was used to extract lead and silver from the ore mined there. If you hike nearby Wildrose Peak, you will be rewarded with terrific views of the kilns. ✉ *Wildrose Canyon Rd., Death Valley* ✛ *37 miles south of Stovepipe Wells.*

Harmony Borax Works. Death Valley's mule teams hauled borax from here to the railroad town of Mojave, 165 miles away. The teams plied the route until 1889, when the railroad finally arrived in Zabriskie. Constructed in 1883, one of the oldest buildings in Death Valley houses the Borax Museum, 2 miles south of the borax works at the Inn at Furnace Creek (between the restaurants and the post office). Originally a miners' bunkhouse, the building once stood in Twenty Mule Team Canyon. Now it displays mining machinery and historical exhibits. The adjacent structure is the original mule-team barn. ✉ *Harmony Borax Works Rd., west of Hwy. 190, 2 miles north of Furnace Creek* ⊕ *www.nps.gov/deva/ historyculture/harmony.htm* ⊘ *Daily 10–6.*

Keane Wonder Mine. The tram towers and cables from the old mill used to process gold from Keane Wonder Mine are still here, leading up to the mine. Due to safety concerns about the site, the National Park

Plants and Wildlife in Death Valley

There's a general misconception that Death Valley National Park consists of mile upon endless mile of flat desert sands, scattered cacti, and an occasional cow skull. Many people don't realize that across the valley floor from Badwater—the lowest point in the Western Hemisphere—Telescope Peak towers at 11,049 feet above sea level. The extreme topography of Death Valley is a lesson in geology. Two hundred million years ago seas covered the area, depositing layers of sediment and fossils. Between 3.5 million and 5 million years ago faults in the Earth's crust and volcanic activity pushed and folded the ground, causing mountain ranges to rise and the valley floor to drop. The valley was then filled periodically by lakes, which eroded the surrounding rocks into fantastic formations and deposited the salts that now cover the floor of the basin.

Most animal life in Death Valley (51 mammal, 36 reptile, 307 bird, and 3 amphibian species) is found near the limited sources of water. The bighorn sheep spend most of their time in the secluded upper reaches of the park's rugged canyons and ridges. Coyotes often can be seen lazing in the shade next to the golf course and have been known to run onto the fairways to steal a golf ball. The only native fish in the park is the pupfish, which grows to slightly longer than 1 inch. In winter, when the water is cold, the fish lie dormant in the bottom mud, becoming active again in spring. Because they are wary of large moving shapes, you must stand quietly over a pool at Salt Creek to see them.

Botanists say there are more than 1,000 species of plants here (21 exist nowhere else in the world), though many annual plants lie dormant as seeds for all but a few months in spring, when rains trigger a bloom. The rest congregate around the few water sources. Most of the low-elevation vegetation grows around the oases at Furnace Creek and Scotty's Castle, where oleanders, palms, and salt cedar grow. At higher elevations you will find pinyon, juniper, and bristlecone pine.

Service has temporarily closed access to the mine and surrounding area. ⊠ *Access road off Beatty Cutoff Rd., Death Valley* ✛ *17½ miles north of Furnace Creek.*

FAMILY

Fodor's Choice

★

Scotty's Castle. This Moorish-style mansion, begun in 1924 and never completed, takes its name from Walter Scott, better known as Death Valley Scotty. An ex-cowboy, prospector, and performer in Buffalo Bill's Wild West Show, Scotty always told people the castle was his, financed by gold from a secret mine. In reality, there was no mine, and the house belonged to a Chicago millionaire named Albert Johnson, whom Scott had finagled into investing in the fictitious mine. Despite the con, Johnson and Scott became great friends. The house functioned for a while as a hotel and still contains works of art, imported carpets, handmade European furniture, and a tremendous pipe organ. To see both floors of the house, you must book a tour—purchase tickets in advance to reserve a space during holidays and some weekends. Park rangers dressed in period attire re-create life at the castle circa the 1930s. Check out the

Underground Tour (separate admission ticket required), which takes you through a ¼-mile tunnel in the castle basement. ⊠ *Scotty's Castle Rd. (Hwy. 267), Death Valley* ✛ *53 miles north of Salt Creek Interpretive Trail* ☎ *760/786–2392* ⊕ *www.nps.gov/deva* ⊠ *$15* ⊙ *Daily 8:30–4:15; tours daily 10–3:30 (hrs vary seasonally).*

SCENIC STOPS

Artist's Palette. So called for the contrasting colors of its volcanic deposits and sedimentary layers, this is one of the signature sights of Death Valley. Artist's Drive, the approach to the area, is one-way heading north off Badwater Road, so if you're visiting Badwater from Furnace Creek, come here on the way back. The drive winds through foothills of sedimentary and volcanic rocks. About 4 miles into the drive, a short side road veers right to a parking lot that's a few hundred feet before the "palette," whose natural colors include shades of green, gold, and pink. ⊠ *Off Badwater Rd., Death Valley* ✛ *11 miles south of Furnace Creek.*

Badwater. At 282 feet below sea level, Badwater is the lowest spot on land in North America—and also one of the hottest. Stairs and wheelchair ramps descend from the parking lot to a wooden platform that overlooks a sodium chloride pool, a small but remarkably persistent reminder that the valley floor used to contain a lake. You can continue past the platform on a broad, white path that peters out after a half mile or so. Badwater is one of the most popular and easily accessible sites within the park. From this lowest point, be sure to look across to Telescope Peak, which towers more than 2 miles above the valley floor. ⊠ *Badwater Rd., Death Valley* ✛ *19 miles south of Furnace Creek.*

Fodor'sChoice ★ **Dante's View.** This lookout is 5,450 feet above sea level in the Black Mountains. In the dry desert air you can see across most of 160-mile-long Death Valley. The view is astounding. Take a 10-minute, mildly strenuous walk from the parking lot toward a series of rocky overlooks, where with binoculars you can spot some of Death Valley's signature sites. A few interpretive signs point out the highlights below in the valley and across, in the Sierra. Getting here from Furnace Creek takes about an hour—time well invested. ⊠ *Dante's View Rd., Death Valley* ✛ *Off Hwy. 190, 35 miles from Badwater, 20 miles south of Twenty Mule Team Canyon.*

Devil's Golf Course. Thousands of miniature salt pinnacles carved into surreal shapes by the desert wind dot this wildly varied landscape. The salt was pushed up to the earth's surface by pressure created as underground salt- and water-bearing gravel crystallized. Get out of your vehicle and take a closer look; you'll see perfectly round holes descending into the ground. ⊠ *Badwater Rd., Death Valley* ✛ *13 miles south of Furnace Creek. Turn right onto dirt road and drive 1 mile.*

Golden Canyon. Just South of Furnace Creek, these glimmering mountains are perhaps best known for their role in the original *Star Wars*. The canyon is also a fine hiking spot, with gorgeous views of the Panamint Mountains, ancient dry lake beds, and alluvial fans. ⊠ *Hwy. 178, Death Valley* ✛ *From the Furnace Creek Visitor Center, drive 2 miles south on*

16

Hwy. 190, then 2 miles south on Hwy. 178 to the parking area. The lot has a kiosk with trail guides.

Racetrack. Getting here involves a 28-mile journey over a rough dirt road, but the reward is well worth the trip. Where else in the world do rocks move on their own? This phenomenon has baffled scientists for years and is perhaps one of the last great natural mysteries. No one has actually seen the rocks in motion, but theory has it that when it rains, the hard-packed lake bed becomes slippery enough that gusty winds push the rocks along—sometimes for several hundred yards. When the mud dries, a telltale trail remains. The trek to the Racetrack can be made in a sedan, but beware—sharp rocks can slash tires; a truck or SUV with thick tires, high clearance, and a spare tire are suggested. ⊠ *Death Valley* ✛ *27 miles west of Ubehebe Crater via dirt road.*

Sand Dunes at Mesquite Flat. These dunes, made up of minute pieces of quartz and other rock, are ever-changing products of the wind-rippled hills, with curving crests and a sun-bleached hue. The dunes are the most photographed destination in the park, and you can see them at their best at sunrise and sunset. Keep your eyes open for animal tracks—you may even spot a coyote or fox. Bring plenty of water, and note where you parked your car: it's easy to become disoriented in this ocean of sand. If you lose your bearings, climb to the top of a dune and scan the horizon for the parking lot. ⊠ *Death Valley* ✛ *19 miles north of Hwy. 190, northeast of Stovepipe Wells Village.*

Stovepipe Wells Village. This tiny 1926 town, the first resort in Death Valley, takes its name from the stovepipe that an early prospector left to indicate where he found water. The area contains a motel, restaurant, convenience store, RV hookups, swimming pool, and landing strip, though first-time park visitors are better off staying in Furnace Creek, which is more central. Off Highway 190, on a 3-mile gravel road immediately southwest, are the multicolor walls of Mosaic Canyon. ⊠ *Hwy. 190, Death Valley* ✛ *2 miles from Sand Dunes, 77 miles east of Lone Pine* ☎ *760/786–2387* ⊕ *www.escapetodeathvalley.com.*

Titus Canyon. This popular one-way, 27-mile drive starts at Nevada Highway 374 (Daylight Pass Road), 2 miles from the park's boundary. Along the way you'll see Leadville Ghost Town and spectacular limestone and dolomite narrows at the end of the canyon. Toward the end, a two-way section of gravel road leads you into the mouth of the canyon from Scotty's Castle Road. High-clearance vehicles are strongly recommended. ⊠ *Death Valley National Park* ✛ *Access road off Nevada Hwy. 374, 6 miles west of Beatty, NV.*

Twenty Mule Team Canyon. This canyon was named in honor of the 20-mule teams that, between 1883 and 1889, carried 10-ton loads of borax through the burning desert (though they didn't actually pass through this canyon). Along the 2.7-mile, one-way loop road off Highway 190, you'll find the soft rock walls reach high on both sides, making it seem like you're on an amusement-park ride. Remains of prospectors' tunnels are visible here, along with some brilliant rock formations. ⊠ *20 Mule Team Rd.* ✛ *Off Hwy. 190, 4 miles south of Furnace Creek, 20 miles west of Death Valley Junction.*

Ubehebe Crater. At 500 feet deep and ½ mile across, this crater resulted from underground steam and gas explosions about 3,000 years ago. Volcanic ash spreads out over most of the area, and the cinders lie as deep as 150 feet, near the crater's rim. Trek down to the crater's floor or walk around it on a fairly level path. Either way, you need about an hour and will be treated to fantastic views. ⊠ *N. Death Valley Hwy., Death Valley* ⊹ *8 miles northwest of Scotty's Castle.*

Zabriskie Point. Although only about 710 feet in elevation, this is one of Death Valley National Park's most scenic spots, overlooking a striking panorama of wrinkled, multicolor hills. It's a great place to watch the sunrise, but it can be bustling any time of day. Pair it with a drive out to magnificent Dante's View. ⊠ *Hwy. 190, Death Valley* ⊹ *5 miles south of Furnace Creek.*

SPORTS AND THE OUTDOORS

BICYCLING

Mountain biking is permitted on any of the back roads and roadways open to the public (bikes aren't permitted on hiking trails). Visit ⊕ *www.nps.gov/deva/planyourvisit/bikingandmtbiking.htm* for a list of suggested routes for all levels of ability. Bicycle Path, a 4-mile round-trip trek from the visitor center to Mustard Canyon, is a good place to start. Bike rentals are available at the Furnace Creek Resort, by the hour or by the day (☎ *760/786–3371*).

16

TOURS AND OUTFITTERS

Spirit of the Mojave Mountain Biking Tour (*Escape Adventures*). Mountain bike into the heart of Death Valley during a six-day adventure through the national park. The 110-mile journey (on single-track trails) includes accommodations (both camping and inns). Bikes, tents, sleeping bags, helmets, and other gear may be rented for an additional price. Tours are available February–April and October only. ⊠ *Death Valley National Park* ☎ *800/596–2953, 702/838–6966* ⊕ *www.escapeadventures.com* 🖃 *From $1,190.*

BIRD-WATCHING

Approximately 350 bird species have been identified in Death Valley. The best place to see the park's birds is along the Salt Creek Interpretive Trail, where you can spot ravens, common snipes, killdeer, spotted sandpipers, and great blue herons. Along the fairways at Furnace Creek Golf Club, you can see kingfishers, peregrine falcons, hawks, Canada geese, yellow warblers, and the occasional golden eagle. Scotty's Castle draws wintering birds from around the globe that are attracted to its running water, shady trees, and shrubs. Other good spots to find birds are at Saratoga Springs, Mesquite Springs, Travertine Springs, and Grimshaw Lake near Tecopa.

You can download a complete park bird checklist, divided by season, at ⊕ *www.nps.gov/deva/learn/nature/upload/death-valley-bird-checklist.*

"I loved how soft the dunes in Death Valley National Park looked from a distance in the early morning light. I ventured out far from the road to capture the serene isolation, and found these unexpected print trails." —photo by Evan Spiler, Fodors.com member

pdf. Rangers at Furnace Creek Visitor Center often lead birding walks through various locations between November and March.

FOUR-WHEELING

Maps and SUV guidebooks for four-wheel-drive and other backcountry roads (including the popular Cottonwood/Marble canyons, Racetrack, Eureka Dunes, Saratoga Springs, and Warm Springs Canyon) are offered at the Furnace Creek Visitor Center. Remember: Never travel alone and be sure to pack plenty of water and snacks. The park recommends checking ⊕ *www.nps.gov/deva/planyourvisit/backcountryroads. htm* for back-road conditions before setting out. Driving off established roads is strictly prohibited in the park.

ROADS

Butte Valley. This 21-mile road in the southwest part of the park climbs from 200 feet below sea level to an elevation of 4,000 feet. The geological formations along the drive reveal the development of Death Valley. ⊠ *Trailhead on Warm Spring Canyon Rd., Death Valley ✛ 50 miles south of Furnace Creek Visitor Center.*

Warm Springs Canyon. If you have a four-wheel-drive vehicle and nerves of steel, this route takes you past Warm Springs talc mine and through Butte Valley, over Mengel Pass and toward **Geologists Cabin,** a charming and cheery little cabin where you can spend the night, if nobody else beats you to it. The park suggests checking their website or asking a ranger to check current conditions on all backcountry roads. The cabin, which sits under a cottonwood tree, has a fireplace, table and chairs, and a sink. Farther up the road, the cabins at Mengel's Home and Russell Camp are also open for public use. Keep the historic cabins clean and restock any items that you use. ⊠ *Warm Springs Canyon Rd., off Hwy. 190/Badwater Rd., Death Valley.*

GOLF

Furnace Creek Golf Club. Play 9 or 18 holes at the lowest golf course in the world (214 feet below sea level). Its improbably green fairways are lined with date palms and tamarisk trees, and its level of difficulty is rated surprisingly high. You can rent clubs and carts, and there are golf packages available for Furnace Creek Ranch or Furnace Creek Inn guests. In winter, reservations are essential. ⊠ *Hwy. 190, Furnace Creek* ☎ *760/786–2301* ⊕ *www.furnacecreekresort.com* ✉ *From $30* ⅄ *18 holes, 6215 yards, par 70.*

HIKING

Plan to hike before or after midday in the spring, summer, or fall, unless you're in the mood for a masochistic baking. Carry plenty of water, wear protective clothing, and keep an eye out for black widows, scorpions, snakes, and other potentially dangerous creatures. Some of the best trails are unmarked; if the opportunity arises, ask for directions.

16

EASY

FAMILY **Darwin Falls.** This lovely 2-mile round-trip hike rewards you with a
Fodor's Choice refreshing waterfall surrounded by thick vegetation and a rocky gorge.
★ No swimming or bathing is allowed, but it's a beautiful place for a picnic. Adventurous hikers can scramble higher toward more rewarding views of the falls. *Easy.* ⊹ *Trailhead: access the 2-mile graded dirt road and parking area off Hwy. 190, 1 mile west of Panamint Springs Resort.*

Natural Bridge Canyon. A rough 2-mile access road leads to a parking lot. From there, set off to see interesting geological features in addition to the bridge, which is ¼ mile away. The one-way trail continues for a few hundred meters, but scenic returns diminish quickly and eventually you're confronted with climbing boulders. *Easy.* ⊹ *Trailhead: access road off Badwater Rd., 15 miles south of Furnace Creek.*

FAMILY **Salt Creek Interpretive Trail.** This trail, a ½-mile boardwalk circuit, loops through a spring-fed wash. The nearby hills are brown and gray, but the floor of the wash is alive with aquatic plants such as pickleweed and salt grass. The stream and ponds here are among the few places in the park to see the rare pupfish, the only native fish species in Death Valley. Animals such as bobcats, fox, coyotes, and snakes visit the spring, and you may also see ravens, common snipes, killdeer, and great blue herons. *Easy.* ⊹ *Trailhead: off Hwy. 190, 14 miles north of Furnace Creek.*

MODERATE

Fall Canyon. This is a 3-mile, one-way hike from the Titus canyon parking area. First, walk ½ mile north along the base of the mountains to a large wash, then go 2½ miles up the canyon to a 35-foot dry fall. You can continue by climbing around to the falls on the south side.

Moderate. ✛ *Trailhead: access road off Scotty's Castle Rd., 33 miles northwest of Furnace Creek.*

FAMILY **Mosaic Canyon.** A gradual uphill trail (4 miles round-trip) winds through the smoothly polished, marbleized limestone walls of this narrow canyon. There are dry falls to climb at the upper end. *Moderate.* ✛ *Trailhead: access road off Hwy. 190, ½ mile west of Stovepipe Wells Village.*

DIFFICULT

Fodor's Choice **Telescope Peak Trail.** The 14-mile round-trip begins at Mahogany Flat
★ Campground, which is accessible by a rough dirt road. The steep and at some points treacherous trail winds through pinyon, juniper, and bristlecone pines, with excellent views of Death Valley and Panamint Valley. Ice axes and crampons may be necessary in winter—check at the Furnace Creek Visitor Center. It takes a minimum of six grueling hours to hike to the top of the 11,049-foot peak and then return. Getting to the peak is a strenuous endeavor; take plenty of water and only attempt it in fall unless you're an experienced hiker. *Difficult.* ✛ *Trailhead: off Wildrose Rd., south of Charcoal Kilns.*

HORSEBACK AND CARRIAGE RIDES

TOURS AND OUTFITTERS

FAMILY **Furnace Creek Stables.** Set off on a one- or two-hour guided horseback, carriage, or haywagon ride from Furnace Creek Stables. The rides traverse trails with views of the surrounding mountains, where multicolor volcanic rock and alluvial fans form a background for date palms and other vegetation. Evening carriage rides take passengers around the golf course and Furnace Creek Ranch. The stables are open October–May only. ✉ *Hwy. 190, Furnace Creek* ☎ *760/614–1018* ⊕ *www. furnacecreekstables.net* 🖼 *From $55.*

SHOPPING

Experienced desert travelers carry an ice chest stocked with food and beverages. You're best off replenishing your food stash in Ridgecrest, Barstow, or Pahrump, larger towns that have a better selection and nontourist prices.

Furnace Ranch General Store. This convenience store carries groceries, souvenirs, camping supplies, and other basics. ✉ *Hwy. 190, Furnace Creek* ☎ *760/786–2345* ⊕ *www.furnacecreekresort.com/activities/ shopping* ☉ *Daily 7 am–10 pm.*

WHAT'S NEARBY

NEARBY TOWNS

Founded at the turn of the 20th century, **Beatty** sits 16 miles east of the California-Nevada border on Death Valley's northern side. Named for a single pine tree found at the bottom of the canyon of the same name, **Lone Pine,** on the park's west side, is where you'll find Mount Whitney, the highest peak in the continental United States, at 14,496 feet. The nearby Alabama Hills have been used in many movies and TV scenes, including segments in *The Lone Ranger*. Down south, unincorporated **Shoshone,** a very small town at the edge of Death Valley, started out as a mining town. The area, dotted with tamarisk trees and date palms, is home to a natural warm-springs pool fed by an underwater river.

Visitor Information Beatty Chamber of Commerce. ⊠ *119 E. Main St.* ☎ *775/553–2424* ⊕ *www.beattynevada.org.* **Death Valley Chamber of Commerce.** ⊠ *860 Tecopa Hot Springs Rd., Tecopa* ☎ *888/600–1844* ⊕ *www. deathvalleychamber.org.* **Lone Pine Chamber of Commerce.** ⊠ *120 S. Main St., Lone Pine* ☎ *760/876–4444* ⊕ *www.lonepinechamber.org.*

NEARBY ATTRACTIONS

Air Flight Test Museum at Edwards Air Force Base. This museum, at what many consider to be the birthplace of supersonic flight, chronicles the rich history of flight testing. Numerous airplanes are on exhibit, from the first F-16B to the only remaining YF-22. The 3½-hour walking and driving tour is open to the public once a month, and requires a reservation. To take the tour, you have to provide basic information for a background check at least a week in advance (a month for non-U.S. residents), but be aware that tours fill up months in advance. On the base's website, click Tours for details. ⊠ *405 S. Rosamond Blvd., off Yeager Blvd., Edwards* ☎ *661/277–3517* ⊕ *www.edwards.af.mil* ⤢ *Free* ⊗ *1 day a month, 9:30–1.*

FAMILY **Ancient Bristlecone Pine Forest.** About an hour's drive from Independence or Bishop you can view some of the oldest living trees on Earth, some of which date back more than 40 centuries. The world's largest bristlecone pine can be found in Patriarch Grove, while the world's oldest known living tree is along Methusula Trail in Schulman Grove. Getting to Patriarch Grove is slow going along the narrow dirt road, especially for sedans with low clearance. ⊠ *Schulman Grove visitor center, White Mountain Rd., Bishop* ⊹ *From U.S. 395, turn east onto Hwy. 168 and follow signs for 23 miles* ⊕ *www.fs.usda.gov/main/inyo/home* ⤢ *$3* ⊗ *Mid-May–Nov., weather permitting.*

Ballarat Ghost Town. This crusty, dusty town saw its heyday between 1897 and 1917. There's a store-museum where you can grab a cold soda before venturing out to explore the crumbling landscape. For years Ballarat's more infamous draw was **Barker Ranch,** where convicted murderer Charles Manson and his "family" were captured after the 1969 Sharon Tate murder spree; the house burned down in 2009. ⊠ *Death Valley* ⊹ *From Hwy. 395, exit SR-178 and travel 45 miles to the historic marker; Ballarat is 3½ miles from the pavement.*

Fodor's Choice **Manzanar National Historic Site.** A reminder of an ugly episode in U.S. history, the former Manzanar War Relocation Center is where more than
★ 11,000 Japanese-Americans were confined behind barbed-wire fences between 1942 and 1945. A visit here is both deeply moving and inspiring—the former because it's hard to comprehend that the United States was capable of confining its citizens in such a way, the latter because

"I'd always wanted to photograph this remote location, and on my drive into Death Valley I was rewarded at Zabriskie Point with this amazing view." —photo by Rodney Ee, Fodors.com member

those imprisoned here showed great pluck and perseverance in making the best of a bad situation. Most of the buildings from the 1940s are gone, but two sentry posts, the auditorium, and numerous Japanese rock gardens remain. One of eight guard towers and two barracks have been reconstructed, and a mess hall has been restored. Interactive exhibits inside the barracks include audio and video clips from people who were incarcerated in Manzanar during WWII. You can drive the one-way dirt road on a self-guided tour past various ruins to a small cemetery, where a monument stands. Signs mark where the barracks, a hospital, a school, and the fire station once stood. An outstanding 8,000-square-foot interpretive center has exhibits and documentary photographs and screens a short film. ⊠ *Independence* ✛ *West side of U.S. 395 between Independence and Lone Pine* ☎ *760/878–2194* ⊕ *www.nps.gov/manz* ✉ *Free* ☉ *Park daily dawn–dusk; center Nov.– Mar., daily 9–4:30; Apr.–Oct., daily 9–5:30.*

FAMILY **Mt. Whitney Fish Hatchery.** A delightful place for a family picnic, the hatchery was one of California's first trout farms. The Tudor Revival–style structure, completed in 1917, is an architectural stunner, its walls nearly 3 feet thick with locally quarried granite. Fish production ceased in 2007 after a fire and subsequent mudslide, but dedicated volunteers staff the facility and raise trout for display purposes in a large pond out front. Bring change for the fish-food machines. ⊠ *Fish Hatchery Rd., 2 miles north of town, Independence* ☎ *760/876–4128* ⊕ *mtwhitneyfishhatchery.org* ✉ *Free (donations welcomed)* ☉ *Mid-Apr.–mid-Dec., Thurs.–Mon. 10–3:30* ☉ *Closed mid-Dec.–mid-Apr.*

Fodor'sChoice **Petroglyph Canyons.** Two canyons in the Coso Mountain range, com-
★ monly called Big Petroglyph and Little Petroglyph, hold a superlative
concentration of ancient rock art, the largest of its kind in the Northern Hemisphere. Thousands of well-preserved images of animals and
humans are scratched or pecked into dark basaltic rocks. The canyons
lie within the million-acre U.S. Naval Weapons Center at China Lake.
Only the drawings of Little Petroglyph can be visited, and only on a
guided tour arranged in advance through the Maturango Museum.
Tour participants must be U.S. citizens over 10 years of age, and must
supply birthdate, birthplace, and Social Security information before
visiting. Because vehicles caravan during the tour, a valid ID, vehicle
registration, and proof of insurance must be presented upon arrival.
⊠ *Ridgecrest* ☎ *760/375–6900* ⊕ *www.maturango.org* ⬚ *$40* ⊗ *Mar.–
June and Sept.–Dec., call or check website for times.*

FAMILY **Randsburg.** The Rand Mining District first boomed when gold was dis-
Fodor'sChoice covered in the Rand Mountains in 1895. Along with neighboring settle-
★ ments, it grew further due to the success of the Yellow Aster Mine,
which yielded $3 million worth of gold before 1900. Rich tungsten ore,
used in World War I to make steel alloy, was discovered in 1907, and
silver was found in 1919. Randsburg is one of the few gold-rush communities not to have become a ghost town; the tiny city jail is among
the original buildings still standing in this town with a population under
100. In nearby Johannesburg, 1 mile south of Randsburg, spirits are
said to dwell in the stunning Old West cemetery in the hills above town.
⊠ *Hwy. 395, near the junction with Rte. 14, Death Valley.*

FAMILY **Rhyolite.** Though it's not within the boundary of Death Valley National
Park, this Nevada ghost town, named for the silica volcanic rock
nearby, is still a big draw. Around 1904, Rhyolite's Montgomery Shoshone Mine caused a financial boom, and fancy buildings sprung up all
over town. Today you can still explore many of the crumbling edifices.
The Bottle House, built by miner Tom Kelly out of almost 50,000 Adol-
phus Busch beer bottles, is a must-see. ⊠ *Hwy. 374* ✛ *35 miles north of
Furnace Creek Visitor Center and 5 miles west of Beatty* ⊕ *www.nps.
gov/deva/learn/historyculture/rhyolite-ghost-town.htm.*

Shoshone Museum. This museum chronicles the local history of Death
Valley and houses a unique collection of period items, and minerals and
rocks from the area. ⊠ *Rte. 127, Shoshone* ☎ *760/852–4524* ⊕ *www.
shoshonevillage.com/shoshone-museum.html* ⬚ *Free* ⊗ *Wed.–Mon. 9–3.*

Trona Pinnacles National Natural Landmark. Fantastic-looking formations
of calcium carbonate, known as tufa, were formed underwater along
fault lines in the bed of what is now Searles Dry Lake. Some of the
more than 500 spires stand as tall as 140 feet, creating a landscape so
surreal that it doubled for outer-space terrain in the film *Star Trek V.*

An easy-to-walk ½-mile trail allows you to see the tufa up close, but
wear sturdy shoes—tufa cuts like coral. The best road to the area can be
impassable after a rainstorm. ⊠ *Pinnacle Rd.* ✛ *5 miles south of Hwy.
178, 18 miles east of Ridgecrest* ☎ *760/384–5400 Ridgecrest BLM
office* ⊕ *www.blm.gov/ca/st/en/fo/ridgecrest/trona.3.html.*

16

WHERE TO EAT

IN THE PARK

$
AMERICAN
✕ **19th Hole.** Next to the clubhouse of the world's lowest golf course, this open-air spot serves hamburgers, hot dogs, chicken, and sandwiches. The full-service bar has a drive-through service for golfers in carts. $ *Average main: $8* ⊠ *Furnace Creek Golf Club, Hwy. 190, Furnace Creek* ☎ *760/786–2345* ⊕ *www.furnacecreekresort.com/activities/dining* ⊘ *Closed mid-May–mid-Oct. No dinner.*

$$$
CAFÉ
FAMILY
✕ **Forty-Niner Cafe.** This casual coffee shop serves basic American fare for breakfast, lunch, and dinner. It's done up in a rustic mining style with whitewashed pine walls, vintage map–covered tables, and prospector-branded chairs. Menu items include custom-made omelets, homemade soups, burgers, and sandwiches. $ *Average main: $22* ⊠ *Ranch at Furnace Creek, Hwy. 190, Furnace Creek* ☎ *760/786–2345* ⊕ *www.furnacecreekresort.com.*

$$$$
AMERICAN
Fodor's Choice
★
✕ **Inn at Furnace Creek Dining Room.** Fireplaces, beamed ceilings, and spectacular views provide a visual feast to match this restaurant's ambitious menu. Dishes include fare such as salmon, free-range chicken, and filet mignon, and there's a seasonal menu of vegetarian dishes. Unique touches include the signature prickly-pear margarita, or you can always have afternoon tea in the lobby, an inn tradition since 1927. Lunch, breakfast, and Sunday brunch are also served. Reservations are essential for dinner only. $ *Average main: $38* ⊠ *Inn at Furnace Creek, Hwy. 190, Furnace Creek* ☎ *760/786–2345* ⊕ *www.furnacecreekresort.com* ⊘ *Closed mid-May–mid-Oct.* ⚐ *Reservations essential.*

$$
AMERICAN
✕ **Panamint Springs Resort Restaurant.** This is a great place for steak and a beer—choose from more than 150 different beers and ales—or pasta and a salad. In summer, evening meals are served outdoors on the porch, which has spectacular views of Panamint Valley. Breakfast and lunch are also served. Reservations are suggested for dinner. $ *Average main: $20* ⊠ *Hwy. 190, Death Valley* ✛ *31 miles west of Stovepipe Wells* ☎ *775/482–7680* ⊕ *www.panamintsprings.com/services/dining-bar.*

$$$$
STEAKHOUSE
FAMILY
✕ **Wrangler Buffet and Steakhouse.** This casual, family-style restaurant has a buffet for breakfast and lunch, and steak-house favorites (chicken, fish, barbecue platter) for dinner. It's slightly more formal than the other restaurant at the Ranch at Furnace Creek, the Forty-Niner Cafe. Still, there's no dress code and reservations aren't required. $ *Average main: $31* ⊠ *Furnace Creek Ranch, Hwy. 190, Furnace Creek* ☎ *760/786–2345* ⊕ *www.furnacecreekresort.com.*

OUTSIDE THE PARK

$$
AMERICAN
✕ **Crowbar Café and Saloon.** In an old wooden building where antique photos adorn the walls and mining equipment stands in the corners, the Crowbar serves enormous helpings of regional dishes such as steak and taco salads. Home-baked fruit pies make fine desserts, and frosty beers are surefire thirst quenchers. $ *Average main: $15* ⊠ *Rte. 127,*

CLOSE UP

Best Campgrounds in Death Valley

You'll need a high-clearance or 4X4 vehicle to reach these locations. To find out where you can camp in the backcountry, pick up a copy of the backcountry map at the visitor center, or check the website ⊕ www.nps.gov/deva/planyourvisit/camping.htm.

You can only build fires in the metal fire grates that are available at most campgrounds, though fires may be restricted in summer (check with rangers about current conditions). Wood gathering is prohibited at all campgrounds. A limited supply of firewood is available at general stores in Furnace Creek and Stovepipe Wells, but because prices are high and supplies limited, you're better off bringing your own if you intend to have a campfire. Camping is prohibited in the historic Inyo, Los Burro, and Ubehebe Crater areas, as well as all day-use spots, including Aguerberry Point Road, Cottonwood Canyon Road, Racetrack Road, Skidoo Road, Titus Canyon Road, Wildrose Road, and West Side Road.

Furnace Creek. This campground, 196 feet below sea level, has some shaded tent sites and is open all year. ⊠ Hwy. 190, Furnace Creek ☏ 800/365–2267.

Mahogany Flat. If you have a four-wheel-drive vehicle and want to scale Telescope Peak, the park's highest mountain, you might want to sleep at one of the few shaded spots in Death Valley, at a cool 8,133 feet. ⊠ Off Wildrose Rd., south of Charcoal Kilns ☏ No phone.

Panamint Springs Resort. Part of a complex that includes a motel and cabin, this campground is surrounded by cottonwoods. The daily fee includes use of the showers and restrooms. ⊠ Hwy. 190, 28 miles west of Stovepipe Wells ☏ 775/482–7680.

Sunset Campground. This first-come, first-served campground is a gravel-and-asphalt RV city. ⊠ Sunset Campground Rd., 1 mile north of Furnace Creek ☏ 800/365–2267.

Texas Spring. This campsite south of the Furnace Creek Visitor Center has good views and facilities and is a few dollars cheaper than Furnace Creek. ⊠ Off Badwater Rd., south of Furnace Creek Visitor Center ☏ 800/365–2267.

16

Shoshone ☏ 760/852–4123 ⊕ www.shoshonevillage.com/shoshone-crowbar-cafe-saloon.html.

$ ✕ **Mt. Whitney Restaurant.** A boisterous family-friendly restaurant with four flat-screen televisions, this place serves the best burgers in town. In addition to the usual beef variety, you can choose from ostrich, elk, venison, and buffalo burgers. ⑤ Average main: $10 ⊠ 227 S. Main St., Lone Pine ☏ 760/876–5751.

AMERICAN

$ ✕ **Randsburg General Store.** Built as Randsburg's Drug Store in 1896, this popular biker and family spot is one of the area's few surviving ghost-town buildings with original furnishings intact, such as a tin ceiling, light fixtures, and a 1904 marble-and-stained-glass soda fountain. You can still enjoy a phosphate soda from that same fountain, or lunch on slow-roasted barbecue sandwiches and blueberry milk shakes along with chili, hamburgers, and breakfast. ⑤ Average main: $10 ⊠ 35 Butte Ave., Randsburg ☏ 760/374–2143 ⊙ Closed Tues. and Wed.

AMERICAN

FAMILY

WHERE TO STAY

IN THE PARK

During the busy season (November–March) you should make reservations for lodgings within the park several months in advance.

$$$$
HOTEL
Fodor'sChoice
★

🏨 **The Inn at Furnace Creek.** Built in 1927, this adobe-brick-and-stone lodge nestled in one of the park's greenest oases is Death Valley's most luxurious accommodation, going so far as to have valet parking. **Pros:** refined; comfortable; great views. **Cons:** a far cry from roughing it; expensive. $ *Rooms from: $390* ⊠ *Furnace Creek Village, near intersection of Hwy. 190 and Badwater Rd., Death Valley* ☎ *760/786–2345* ⊕ *www.furnacecreekresort.com* ⊘ *Closed mid-May–mid-July and Sept.–mid-Oct.* ⤳ *66 rooms* ⑩ *No meals.*

$
B&B/INN

🏨 **Panamint Springs Resort.** Ten miles inside the west entrance of the park, this low-key resort overlooks the sand dunes and peculiar geological formations of the Panamint Valley. **Pros:** slow-paced; friendly; peaceful and quiet after sundown. **Cons:** far from the park's main attractions. $ *Rooms from: $84* ⊠ *Hwy. 190, Death Valley* ⤓ *28 miles west of Stovepipe Wells* ☎ *775/482–7680* ⊕ *www.deathvalley.com/psr* ⤳ *14 rooms, 1 cabin* ⑩ *No meals.*

$$$
RESORT

🏨 **The Ranch at Furnace Creek.** Originally the crew headquarters for the Pacific Coast Borax Company, the four buildings here have motel-style rooms that are good for families. **Pros:** good family atmosphere; central location. **Cons:** rooms can get hot despite air-conditioning; parking near your room can be problematic. $ *Rooms from: $175* ⊠ *Hwy. 190, Furnace Creek* ☎ *760/786–2345, 800/236-7916* ⊕ *www.furnacecreekresort.com* ⤳ *224 rooms* ⑩ *No meals.*

$$
HOTEL

🏨 **Stovepipe Wells Village.** If you prefer quiet nights and an unfettered view of the night sky and nearby sand dunes and Mosaic Canyon, this property is for you. **Pros:** intimate, relaxed; no big-time partying; authentic desert-community ambience. **Cons:** isolated; a bit dated. $ *Rooms from: $150* ⊠ *Hwy. 190, Stovepipe Wells* ☎ *760/786–2387* ⊕ *www.escapetodeathvalley.com* ⤳ *83 rooms* ⑩ *No meals.*

OUTSIDE THE PARK

$$
HOTEL

🏨 **Dow Villa Motel and Dow Hotel.** Built in 1923 to cater to the film industry, the Dow Villa Motel and the historic Dow Hotel sit in the center of Lone Pine. **Pros:** clean rooms; great mountain views; in-room whirlpool tubs in motel. **Cons:** some rooms share bathrooms. $ *Rooms from: $115* ⊠ *310 S. Main St., Lone Pine* ☎ *760/876–5521, 800/824–9317* ⊕ *www.dowvillamotel.com* ⤳ *92 rooms* ⑩ *No meals.*

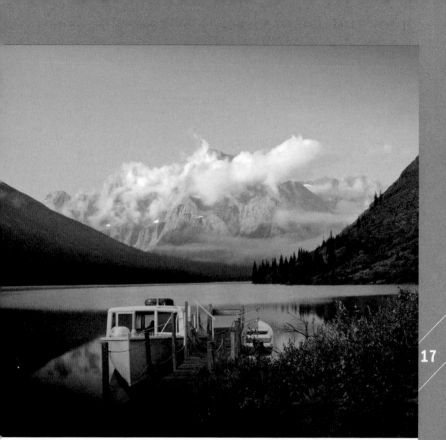

GLACIER AND WATERTON LAKES NATIONAL PARKS

WELCOME TO GLACIER AND WATERTON LAKES NATIONAL PARKS

TOP REASONS TO GO

★ **Witness the Divide:** The rugged mountains that weave their way through Glacier and Waterton along the Continental Divide seem to have glaciers in every hollow melting into tiny streams, raging rivers, and icy-cold mountain lakes.

★ **Just hike it:** Hundreds of miles of trails of all levels of difficulty lace the park, from flat and easy half-hour strolls to steep, strenuous all-day hikes.

★ **Go to the sun:** Crossing the Continental Divide at the 6,646-foot-high Logan Pass, Glacier's Going-to-the-Sun Road is a spectacular drive.

★ **View the wildlife:** This is one of the few places in North America where all native carnivores, including grizzlies, black bears, coyotes, and wolves, still survive.

★ **See glaciers while you still can:** Approximately 150 glaciers were present in Glacier National Park in 1850; by 2015, there were only 25 left.

1 **West Glacier.** Known to the Kootenai people as "sacred dancing lake," Lake McDonald is the largest glacial water basin lake in Glacier National Park.

2 **Logan Pass.** At 6,646 feet, the pass is the highest point on the Going-to-the-Sun Road. From mid-June to mid-October, a 1½-mile boardwalk leads to an overlook that crosses an area filled with lush meadows and wildflowers.

3 **East Glacier.** St. Mary Lake and Many Glacier are the major highlights of the eastern side of Glacier. Services and amenities are located at both sites.

4 **Backcountry.** This is some of the most incredible terrain in North America and provides the right combination of beautiful scenery and isolation. Although Waterton is a much smaller park, its backcountry trails connect with hiking trails in both Glacier and British Columbia's Akamina-Kishinena Provincial Park.

5 **Waterton Lakes.** The Canadian national park is the meeting of two worlds: the flatlands of the prairie and the abrupt upthrust of the mountains.

GETTING ORIENTED

In the rocky northwestern corner of Montana, Glacier National Park encompasses 1.2 million acres (1,563 square miles) of untrammeled wilds. Within the park, there are 25 named glaciers, 200 lakes, and 1,000 miles of streams. Neighboring Waterton Lakes National Park, across the border in Alberta, Canada, covers another 124,788 acres (505 square kilometers). In 1932, the parks were unified to form the Waterton-Glacier International Peace Park—the first international peace park in the world—in recognition of the two nations' friendship and dedication to peace.

KEY
🏢 *Ranger Station*
🔺 *Campground*
🌳 *Picnic Area*
🍴 *Restaurant*
🏠 *Lodge*
🚶 *Trailhead*
🚻 *Restrooms*
⤳ *Scenic Viewpoint*
⋯⋯ *Walking/Hiking Trails*

ALBERTA

MONTANA

BRITISH
COLUMBIA

Waterton Lakes
National Park 5

4

Mount Custer
8,883 ft

CANADA
UNITED STATES

Goat
Haunt

Upper
Waterton
Lake

Kintla Peak
10,101 ft

Thunderbird
Mountain
8,790 ft

Cleveland Mtn.

Chief
Mountain
9,080 ft

17

Continental Divide

Apikuni Mountain
9,068 ft

Many Glacier Rd.

Two Medicine Valley

Granite Park
Chalet

Longfellow Peak
8,904 ft

Many Glacier

The Garden Wall

Visitor Center

Salamander Glacier
Grinnell Glacier

Logan
Pass **2**

Visitor Center

St Mary

17

Trail of the Cedars

Going-to-
the-Sun Mtn.

Rising
Sun

0   10 miles

0   10 km

**Hidden
Lake**

St. Mary Lake

Lake
McDonald

Sprague
Creek

Gunsight Mtn.
9,258 ft

Jackson Gl.

Jackson Glacier
Overlook

Lake
McDonald

Going-to-
the-Sun Road

Jackson Mtn.

Pumpelly Gl.

Mount Logan
9,239 ft

**Two Medicine
Entrance**

Visitor Center

Apgar
West Entrance

Triple Divide Peak
8,020 ft

Two Medicine Valley

**Two
Medicine**

1 West
Glacier

2

Rising Wolf Mtn.
9,513 ft

89

Running Eagle Falls

89

Flathead

Upper Two
Medicine

Mount
St. Nicholas
9,376 ft

49

Pinnacle

East Glacier

3

River

Essex Walton

2

Goat Lick
Overlook

Updated by
Debbie Olsen

The massive peaks of the Continental Divide in northwestern Montana form the backbone of Glacier National Park and its sister park in Canada, Waterton Lakes, which together make up the International Peace Park. From their slopes, melting snow and alpine glaciers yield the headwaters of rivers that flow west to the Pacific Ocean, north to the Arctic Ocean, and southeast to the Atlantic Ocean via the Gulf of Mexico. Coniferous forests, thickly vegetated stream bottoms, and green-carpeted meadows provide homes and sustenance for all kinds of wildlife.

GLACIER AND WATERTON PLANNER

WHEN TO GO

Of the 2 million annual visitors to Glacier and 400,000 to Waterton, most come between July and mid-September, when the streams are flowing, wildlife is roaming, and naturalist programs are fully underway. Snow removal on the alpine portion of Going-to-the-Sun Road is usually completed by mid-June; the opening of Logan Pass at the road's summit marks the summer opening of Glacier. Canada's Victoria Day in late May marks the beginning of the season in Waterton. Spring and fall are quieter.

AVG. HIGH/LOW TEMPS.
Glacier

Jan.	Feb.	Mar.	Apr.	May	June
28/15	35/19	42/23	53/30	64/37	71/44
July	Aug.	Sept.	Oct.	Nov.	Dec.
79/47	78/46	67/39	53/32	37/25	30/18

Waterton Lakes

Jan.	Feb.	Mar.	Apr.	May	June
32/12	34/14	42/22	50/29	59/37	66/43
July	Aug.	Sept.	Oct.	Nov.	Dec.
73/46	72/44	63/38	53/33	38/22	33/15

FESTIVALS AND EVENTS

WINTER **Ski Fest.** This annual celebration of cross-country skiing is a great way to introduce newcomers to kick-and-glide skiing. Equipment demonstrations, free ski lessons, and family activities are scheduled at the Izaak Walton Inn in Essex, Montana, and free trail passes are dispensed. ☎ *406/888–5700* ⊕ *www.izaakwaltoninn.com.*

Whitefish Winter Carnival. For more than 40 years this February fest has been the scene of lively activities, including a grand parade with more than 100 entries, a torchlight parade on skis, fireworks, a penguin dip, and other family-friendly activities. ✉ *Whitefish* ☎ *406/862–3501* ⊕ *www.whitefishwintercarnival.com.*

SUMMER **Canada Day.** On July 1, all guests get into the national parks free of charge in honor of Canada's birthday. Waterton also has special activities for families such as treasure hunts and evening theater programs. ✉ *Waterton Townsite* ☎ *403/859–5133.*

Montana Dragon Boat Festival. Held on Flathead Lake, this captivating event features 95 teams of 20 paddlers each racing 46-foot-long Hong Kong–style boats. ☎ *888/888–2308, 406/758–2820* ⊕ *www.montanadragonboat.com.*

Summer Concert Series. Running each Thursday from mid-June to early August, the series is held in the Don Lawrence Amphitheater at Marantette Park in Columbia Falls. Types of music vary, but the Don Lawrence Big Band performs every year. ☎ *406/892–2072.*

Waterton Wildflower Festival. Wildflower walks, horseback rides, hikes, watercolor workshops, photography classes, and family events help visitors and locals celebrate the annual blooming of Waterton's bountiful wildflowers. ✉ *Waterton Lakes National Park* ☎ *800/215–2395* ⊕ *www.watertonwildflowers.com.*

FALL **NW Montana Antique Threshing Bee.** Steam threshing machines, steam plows, antique tractors, and engines flex muscles in the Parade of Power, organized by the Northwest Montana Antique Power Association in Kalispell. Participants challenge friends and neighbors to tractor barrel races and shingle-making events, while children of all ages enjoy miniature steam-train rides, music, food, and entertainment. ☎ *406/756–5577, 406/862–0890* ⊕ *nwantiquepower.com.*

Waterton Wildlife Weekend. Wildlife viewing is at its best in Waterton during the fall. The weekend's events include viewing on foot, on horseback, and by boat. There are also photography, drawing, and sketching courses. ✉ *Waterton Lakes National Park* ☎ *800/215–2395* ⊕ *www.watertonwildlife.com.*

17

PLANNING YOUR TIME

GLACIER IN ONE DAY

It's hard to beat the **Going-to-the-Sun Road** for a one-day trip in Glacier National Park. This itinerary takes you from west to east—if you're starting from St. Mary, take the tour backward. First, however, call the Glacier Park Boat Company (☎ *406/257–2426*) to make a reservation for the **St. Mary Lake** or **Lake McDonald boat tour**, depending on where you end up. Then drive up Going-to-the-Sun Road to **Avalanche Creek Campground**, and take a 30-minute stroll along the fragrant **Trail of the Cedars**. Afterward, continue driving up—you can see views of waterfalls and wildlife to the left and an awe-inspiring, precipitous drop to the right. At the summit, **Logan Pass**, your arduous climb is rewarded with a gorgeous view of immense peaks, sometimes complemented by the sight of a mountain goat. Stop in at the **Logan Pass Visitor Center**, then take the 1½-mile **Hidden Lake Nature Trail** up to prime wildlife-viewing spots. Have a picnic at the overlook above Hidden Lake. In the afternoon, continue driving east over the mountains. Stop at the **Jackson Glacier Overlook** to view one of the park's largest glaciers. Continue down; eventually the forest thins, the vistas grow broader, and a gradual transition to the high plains begins. When you reach **Rising Sun Campground**, take the one-hour St. Mary Lake boat tour to St. Mary Falls. The Going-to-the-Sun Road is generally closed from mid-September to mid-June.

WATERTON IN ONE DAY

Begin your day with a stop at the **Waterton Information Centre** to pick up free maps and information about interpretive programs and schedules.

Behind the reception center is the **Bear's Hump Trailhead**, where you can enjoy a relatively easy 1.4-km (0.9-mile) hike to a beautiful scenic overlook. After the hike, drive up the hill to the historic **Prince of Wales Hotel** to enjoy the view.

Next, visit **Waterton Townsite** for an early lunch. Afterward, walk the easy 3-km (2-mile) **Townsite Loop Trail**, stopping to view **Cameron Falls** and explore the trail behind the falls.

End the day with a scenic two-hour **Waterton Inter-Nation Shoreline Cruise** across the border to **Goat Haunt Ranger Station** and back.

GETTING HERE AND AROUND

AIR TRAVEL

The nearest airports to Glacier are in Kalispell (25 miles) and Great Falls (157 miles), both in Montana. The nearest airport to Waterton Lakes is in Calgary (271 km [168 miles]).

BUS TRAVEL

Glacier National Park operates a free shuttle along the Going-to-the-Sun Road from July through early September. The shuttle runs from Apgar to St. Mary Visitor Center; park visitor centers have information about departure times.

CAR TRAVEL

On the east, U.S. 89 accesses Many Glacier and St. Mary, while Highway 49 reaches Two Medicine. On the west, U.S. 2 goes to West Glacier. At the northwestern edge of Glacier, North Fork Road connects to Polebridge. Take the Chief Mountain Highway (Highway 17) to access

Waterton Lakes during the summer or U.S. 89 to Alberta Highway 2 through Cardston and then west to the park via Highway 5 any time of the year.

The roads in both parks are either paved or gravel and become deteriorated from freezing and thawing. Drive slowly and anticipate that rocks and wildlife may be around the corner. Road reconstruction is part of the park experience as there are only a few warm months during which road crews can complete projects. Gasoline is available along most paved roads. Scenic pull-outs are frequent; watch for other vehicles pulling in or out, and watch for children in parking areas. Most development and services center on St. Mary Lake in the east and Lake McDonald in the west.

BORDER CROSSINGS A passport is required of everyone crossing the Canadian/U.S. border. When you arrive at the border crossing, customs officers will ask you where you are going, where you are from, and similar questions. You and your vehicle are subject to random search. Firearms are prohibited, except hunting rifles, which require permission you must obtain in advance. Soil, seeds, meat, and many fruits are also prohibited. Kids traveling with only one parent need a notarized letter from the other parent giving permission to enter Canada or the United States. If you are traveling with pets, you need proof of up-to-date immunizations to cross the border in either direction. Citizens from most countries (Canada, Mexico, and Bermuda are exceptions) entering the United States from Canada must pay $6 (cash only) at the border for a required I–94 or I–94W Arrival-Departure Record form, to be returned to border officials when leaving the United States. Contact United States Customs (☎ 406/335–2611 ⊕ *www.cbp. gov*) or the Canada Border Services Agency (☎ 403/344–3767 ⊕ *www. cbsa-asfc.gc.ca*) for more information.

PARK ESSENTIALS

PARK FEES AND PERMITS

Entrance fees for Glacier are $25 per vehicle or $12 for one person on foot or bike from May to October. Entrance fees drop to $15 per vehicle or $10 per person from November to April. Entrance fees are good for seven days, or you can purchase an annual pass for $35. A day pass to Waterton Lakes costs C$7.80 for an individual or C$19.60 per seven people per vehicle, and an annual pass costs C$39.20 for an individual or C$98.10 for a family. *Passes to Glacier and Waterton must be paid separately.*

At Glacier the required backcountry permit is $5 per person per day or $60 per year from the Apgar Backcountry Permit Center after mid-April for the upcoming summer. Reservations cost $30. On the park's official website (⊕ *www.nps.gov/glac/planyourvisit/backcountry.htm*), you can find the latest backcountry information and a form that can be faxed to the backcountry office.

Waterton requires backcountry camping permits for use of its 13 backcountry camping spots, with reservations available up to 90 days ahead. Buy the permit for C$9.80 per adult per night—reserve for an additional C$11.70—at the visitor reception center (☎ 403/859–5133).

17

PARK HOURS

The parks are open year-round, but most roads and facilities close from October through May. The parks are in the Mountain time zone.

CELL-PHONE RECEPTION

Cell-phone coverage is improving, but in mountainous terrain it is common to have poor reception. Depending on your cell-phone carrier, cell service is best available in West Glacier or St. Mary in Glacier National Park and in the Waterton Townsite in Waterton Lakes National Park. Find pay phones at Avalanche Campground, Glacier Highland Motel and Store, Apgar, St. Mary Visitor Center, Two Medicine Camp Store, and all lodges except Granite Park Chalet and Sperry Chalet. Several pay phones are also available in the townsite of Waterton Lakes National Park.

EDUCATIONAL OFFERINGS

Evening interpretive programs at Waterton Lakes National Parks are offered from late June until Labor Day at the Falls Theatre, near Cameron Falls, and the townsite campground. These one-hour sessions begin at 8. A guided International Peace Park hike is held every Wednesday and Saturday in July and August. The 14-km (9-mile) hike begins at the Bertha trailhead, and is led by Canadian and American park interpreters. You take lunch at the International Border before continuing on to Goat Haunt in Glacier National Park, Montana, and returning to Waterton via boat. A fee is charged for the return boat trip. You must preregister for this hike at the Waterton Information Centre.

CLASSES AND SEMINARS

FAMILY **Glacier Institute.** Based near West Glacier at the Field Camp and on the remote western boundary at the Big Creek Outdoor Education Center, this learning institute offers more than 75 field courses for kids and adults. Year-round, experts in wildlife biology, native plants, and river ecology lead treks into Glacier's backcountry on daylong and multiday programs. The Youth Adventure Series for children ages 6 to 11 features one-day naturalist courses; preteens and teens can take weeklong trips. Three-day family camps for ages 7 and up are also on offer. ⊠ *137 Main St., Kalispell* ☎ *406/755–1211, 406/755–7154* ⊕ *www.glacierinstitute.org* ✉ *$50–$725.*

FAMILY **Ranger-led Activities.** Free ranger-led programs, most of them daily from
Fodor's Choice July to early September, include guided hikes, group walks, evening talks,
★ historical tours, gaze-at-the-stars parties, and naturalist discussions. For the Native America Speaks program, tribal members share their history and culture through stories, poetry, music, and dance. In winter, guided two-hour snowshoe treks take place in the Apgar area. Among the activities for children is the **Junior Ranger Program,** for which children between ages 6 and 12 complete fun educational tasks to become Junior Rangers. To learn more about ranger-led activities, check online or at the visitor centers or refer to the park newspaper. ☎ *406/888–7800* ⊕ *www.nps.gov/glac/planyourvisit/ranger-led-activities.htm* ✉ *Free.*

RESTAURANTS

Steak houses serving certified Angus beef are typical of the region; in recent years, resort communities have diversified their menus to include bison meat, fresh fish, and vegetarian options. Small cafés offer hearty, inexpensive meals and perhaps the chance to chat with locals. Trout, venison, elk, moose, and bison appear on the menus inside the park. Attire everywhere is casual.

HOTELS

The parks' lodgings in the parks tend to be rustic and simple, though there are a few grand lodges. Some modern accommodations have swimming pools, hot tubs, boat rentals, guided excursions, and fine dining. The supply of rooms within both parks is limited, but the prices are relatively reasonable. It's best to reserve well ahead, especially for July and August. *Hotel reviews have been shortened. For full information, visit Fodors.com.*

WHAT IT COSTS			
$	$$	$$$	$$$$
Restaurants	under $13	$13–$20	$21–$30	over $30
Hotels	under $100	$100–$150	$151–$200	over $200

Restaurant prices are the average cost of a main course at dinner, or if dinner is not served, at lunch. Hotel prices are the lowest cost of a standard double room in high season.

17

TOURS

Red Jammer Bus Tours. Glacier National Park Lodges operates driver-narrated bus tours that cover most of the park accessible by road. The tour of Going-to-the-Sun Road, a favorite, is conducted in "jammers," vintage 1936 red buses with roll-back tops—photo opportunities are plentiful. In addition to tours, which last from a few hours to a full day, hiker shuttles and transfers from the West Glacier train station to Lake McDonald Lodge or the Village Inn are available. Reservations are essential. ☎ *855/733–4522, 303/265–7010, 303/297–3175* ⊕ *www. glaciernationalparklodges.com/red-bus-tours* 🖃 *From $40 for tours; shuttles $5–$10* ⊗ *June–Sept.*

Sun Tours. Tour the park in an air-conditioned coach and learn the Blackfeet perspective from native guides who concentrate on how Glacier's features are relevant to the Blackfeet Nation, past and present. These tours depart from East Glacier and the St. Mary Visitor Center. ⊠ *29 Glacier Ave., East Glacier* ☎ *406/226–9220, 800/786–9220* ⊕ *www. glaciersuntours.com* 🖃 *From $45* ⊗ *June–Sept., daily from East Glacier at 8 am, St. Mary Visitor Center at 9:15 am.*

VISITOR INFORMATION

Park Contact Information Glacier National Park. ☎ *406/888-7800* ⊕ *www.nps.gov/glac.* **Waterton Lakes National Park.** ☎ *403/859-5133, 403/859-2224 year-round* ⊕ *www.pc.gc.ca/waterton.*

GLACIER VISITOR CENTERS

FAMILY **Apgar Visitor Center.** This is a great first stop if you're entering the park from the west. Here you can get all kinds of information, including maps, permits, books, and the *Junior Ranger* newspaper, and you can check out displays that will help you plan your tour of the park. In winter, the rangers offer free snowshoe walks. Snowshoes can be rented for $2 at the visitor center. ✉ *2 miles north of West Glacier in Apgar Village, Glacier National Park* ☎ *406/888–7800* ☺ *Mid-May–mid-June, daily 9–4:30; mid-June–Aug., daily 8–5:30; Sept.–mid-Oct., daily 8:30– 5; mid-Oct.–mid-May, weekends 9–4:30.*

Logan Pass Visitor Center. Built of stone, this center stands sturdy against the severe weather that forces it to close in winter. When it's open, rangers give 10-minute talks on the alpine environment, and you can get advice from them and buy books and maps. ✉ *Going-to-the-Sun Rd., 34 miles east of West Glacier, 18 miles west of St. Mary, Glacier National Park* ☎ *406/888–7800* ☺ *Mid-June–Aug., daily 9–7; Sept., daily 9:30–4.*

St. Mary Visitor Center. The park's largest visitor complex has a huge relief map of the park's peaks and valleys and screens a 15-minute orientation video. Exhibits are designed to help visitors understand the park from the perspective of its original inhabitants—the Blackfeet, Salish, Kootenai, and Pend d'Orielle tribes. Rangers host evening presentations during the summer. The center has books and maps for sale, backcountry camping permits, and large viewing windows facing the 10-mile-long St. Mary Lake. ✉ *Going-to-the-Sun Rd., off U.S. 89, Glacier National Park* ☎ *406/732–7750* ☺ *Mid-May–mid-Sept., daily 8–5, with extended hrs during summer.*

WATERTON VISITOR CENTER

Waterton Information Centre. Stop here on Waterton Townsite's eastern edge to pick up brochures, maps, and books. You can also pick up the booklet for the free Xplorer Program for kids between ages six and 11. Park interpreters are on hand to answer questions and give directions. ✉ *Waterton Rd., before townsite, Waterton Lakes National Park* ☎ *403/859–5133* ☺ *Mid-May–mid-June, daily 8–6; mid-June–early Sept., daily 8–8; early Sept.–early Oct., daily 9–6.*

GLACIER NATIONAL PARK

EXPLORING

SCENIC DRIVES

Fodor's Choice **Going-to-the-Sun Road.** This magnificent, 50-mile highway—the only
★ American roadway designated both a National Historic Landmark and a National Civil Engineering Landmark—crosses the crest of the Continental Divide at Logan Pass and traverses the towering Garden Wall. Open from mid-June to mid-September only (due to heavy snowfalls), this is one of the most stunning drives in Glacier National Park. A multiyear Sun Road rehabilitation project will result in some driving delays due to reconstruction. The drive is susceptible to frequent delays

Plants and Wildlife in Glacier and Waterton

In summer, a profusion of new flowers, grasses, and budding trees covers the landscape high and low. Spring attracts countless birds, from golden eagles riding thermals north to Canada and Alaska to rare harlequin ducks dipping in creeks. Snow-white mountain goats, with their wispy white beards and curious stares, are seen in alpine areas, and sure-footed bighorn sheep graze the high meadows in the short summers. The largest population of grizzly bears in the lower 48 states lives in the wild in and around the park. Feeding the animals is illegal.

Visiting Glacier in winter makes for easy tracking of many large animals like moose, elk, deer, mountain lions, wolf, lynx, and their smaller neighbors—the snowshoe hare, pine marten, beaver, and muskrat.

In park lakes, sportfishing species include burbot (ling), northern pike, whitefish, grayling, cutthroat, rainbow, lake (Mackinaw), kokanee salmon, and brook trout.

in summer. To avoid traffic jams and parking problems, take the road early in the morning or late in the evening (when the lighting is ideal for photography and wildlife is most likely to appear). Vehicle size is restricted to under 21 feet long, 10 feet high, and 8 feet wide, including mirrors, between Avalanche Creek Campground and Sun Point. Cyclists enjoy traveling the open part of the road in early June before it is open to vehicular traffic. ⊠ *Glacier National Park.*

Many Glacier Road. This 12-mile drive enters Glacier on the northeast side of the park, west of Babb, and travels along Sherburne Lake for almost 5 miles, penetrating a glacially carved valley surrounded by mountains. It passes through meadows and a scrubby forest of lodgepole pines, aspen, and cottonwood. The farther you travel up the valley, the more clearly you'll be able to see Grinnell and Salamander glaciers. The road, which passes Many Glacier Hotel and ends at the Swiftcurrent Campground, is usually closed from October to May. ⊠ *Glacier National Park.*

HISTORIC SITES

FAMILY **Apgar.** On the southwest end of Lake McDonald, this tiny hamlet has a few stores, an ice-cream shop, motels, ranger buildings, a campground, and a historic schoolhouse. A store called the Montana House is open year-round in the village, but except for the weekend-only visitor center, no other services remain open from November to mid-May. Across the street from the Apgar visitor center, **Apgar Discovery Cabin** is filled with animal posters, kids' activities, and maps. ⊠ *2 miles north of west entrance, Glacier National Park* ☎ *406/888–7939* ⊙ *Cabin: mid-June–Labor Day, daily 1:30–3.*

SCENIC STOPS

ALONG THE GOING-TO-THE-SUN ROAD

The Going-to-the-Sun Road, arguably the most beautiful drive in the country, connects Lake McDonald on the western side of Glacier with St. Mary Lake on the east. Turnoffs provide views of the high country

17

and glacier-carved valleys. If you don't want to drive the Going-to-the-Sun Road, consider making the ride in a "jammer," an antique red bus operated by Glacier National Park Lodges. The drivers double as guides, and they can roll back the tops of the vehicles to give you improved views.

The Garden Wall. An abrupt and jagged wall of rock juts above the road and is visible for about 10 miles as it follows Logan Creek from just past Avalanche Creek Campground to Logan Pass. ⊠ *Going-to-the-Sun Rd., 24–34 miles northeast of West Glacier, Glacier National Park.*

Hidden Lake Overlook. Take a walk from Logan Pass up to see the crystalline Hidden Lake, which often still has ice clinging to it in early July. It's a 1½-mile hike on an uphill grade, partially on a boardwalk that protects the abundant wildflowers. ⊠ *Trailhead: behind Logan Pass Visitor Center, Glacier National Park.*

Jackson Glacier Overlook. On the eastern side of the Continental Divide, you come into view of Jackson Glacier looming in a rocky pass across the upper St. Mary River valley. If it isn't covered with snow, you'll see sharp peaks of ice. The glacier is shrinking and may disappear in another 100 years. ⊠ *5 miles east of Logan Pass, Glacier National Park.*

Logan Pass. At 6,646 feet, this is the highest point in the park accessible by motor vehicle. Crowded with tourists in July and August, it offers unparalleled views of both sides of the Continental Divide. Mountain goats, bighorn sheep, and grizzly bears frequent the area. The Logan Pass Visitor Center is just east of the pass. ⊠ *34 miles east of West Glacier, 18 miles west of St. Mary, Glacier National Park.*

St. Mary Lake. When the breezes calm, the second-largest lake in Glacier National Park mirrors the snowcapped granite peaks that line the St. Mary Valley. To get a good look at the beautiful scenery, follow the Sun Point Nature Trail (closed for renovation in 2016) along the lake's shore. The hike is 1 mile each way. ⊠ *1 mile west of St. Mary, Glacier National Park.*

OTHER SCENIC STOPS

Goat Lick Overlook. Mountain goats frequent this natural salt lick on a cliff above the Middle Fork of the Flathead River. You can watch the wildlife from an observation stand. ⊠ *U.S. 2, 2½ miles east of Walton Ranger Station, Glacier National Park.*

Grinnell and Salamander Glaciers. These glaciers formed as one ice mass, but in 1926 they broke apart and have been shrinking ever since. The best viewpoint is reached by the 5½-mile Grinnell Glacier Trail from Many Glacier. The trailhead is at the far northwestern end of Lake Josephine. You can get there by boat or via the trail behind the Many Glacier Hotel. In summer, rangers lead six-hour hikes to Grinnell Valley that depart each morning from the Many Glacier Picnic Area. ⊠ *Glacier National Park.*

Lake McDonald. This beautiful 10-mile-long lake, the parks' largest lake, is accessible year-round from Going-to-the-Sun Road. Take a boat ride to the middle for a view of the surrounding glacier-clad mountains. You can go fishing and horseback riding at either end, and in winter, snowshoe and cross-country ski. ⊠ *2 miles north of west entrance, Glacier National Park.*

The scenic, 50-mile Going-to-the-Sun Road takes about two hours to drive, depending on how often you stop.

Running Eagle Falls (Trick Falls). Cascading near Two Medicine, these are actually two different waterfalls from two different sources. In spring, when the water level is high, the upper falls join the lower falls for a 40-foot drop into Two Medicine River; in summer, the upper falls dry up, revealing the lower 20-foot falls that start midway down the precipice. ⊠ *2 miles east of Two Medicine entrance, Glacier National Park.*

Two Medicine Valley. Rugged, often windy, and always beautiful, the valley is a remote 9-mile drive from Highway 49 and is surrounded by some of the park's most stark, rocky peaks. On and around the valley's lake you can rent a canoe, take a narrated boat tour, camp, and hike. Bears frequent the area. The road is closed from late October through late May. ⊠ *Two Medicine entrance, 9 miles east of Hwy. 49, Glacier National Park* ☎ *406/888–7800, 406/257–2426 boat tours.*

SPORTS AND THE OUTDOORS

MULTISPORT OUTFITTERS

Glacier Guides and Montana Raft Company. Take a raft trip through the Wild-and-Scenic–designated white water of the Middle Fork of the Flathead and combine it with a hike, horseback ride, or a barbecue. Guided hikes, fly-fishing trips, and multiday adventures can also be arranged. ⊠ *11970 U.S. 2 E, 1 mile west of West Glacier, Glacier National Park* ☎ *406/387–5555, 800/521–7238* ⊕ *www.glacierguides.com* ✍ *From $55* ⊙ *May–Oct.*

Glacier Raft Company and Outdoor Center. In addition to running fishing trips, family float rides, saddle and paddle adventures, and

high-adrenaline white-water adventure rafting (including multiday excursions), this outfitter will set you up with camping, backpacking, and fishing gear. There's also a full-service fly-fishing shop and outdoor store. You can stay in one of 13 log cabins or a glacier-view home. ⊠ *12400 U.S 2 E, West Glacier* ☎ *406/888–5454, 800/235–6781* ⊕ *www.glacierraftco.com* ✉ *From $54* ⊙ *Year-round; rafting mid-May–Sept.*

Great Northern Whitewater. Sign up for daily white-water, kayaking, and fishing trips. Multiday trips can also be arranged. This outfitter also rents Swiss-style chalets with views of Glacier's peaks. ⊠ *12127 U.S. 2 E, 1 mile south of West Glacier, Glacier National Park* ☎ *406/387–5340, 800/735–7897* ⊕ *www.greatnorthernresort.com* ✉ *From $54* ⊙ *May–Oct.*

Wild River Adventures. Brave the white water in an inflatable kayak or a traditional raft or enjoy a scenic float with these guys, who will paddle you over the Middle Fork of the Flathead, and peddle you tall tales all the while. They also conduct trail rides and scenic fishing trips on rivers around Glacier National Park. ⊠ *11900 U.S. 2 E, 1 mile west of West Glacier, Glacier National Park* ☎ *406/387–9453, 800/700–7056* ⊕ *www.riverwild.com* ✉ *From $52* ⊙ *Mid-May–Sept.*

BICYCLING

Cyclists in Glacier must stay on roads or bike routes and are not permitted on hiking trails or in the backcountry. The one-lane, unpaved Inside North Fork Road from Apgar to Polebridge is well suited to mountain bikers. Two Medicine Road is an intermediate paved route, with a mild grade at the beginning, becoming steeper as you approach Two Medicine Campground. Much of the western half of Going-to-the-Sun Road is closed to bikes from 11 am to 4 pm. Other restrictions apply during peak traffic periods and road construction. Many cyclists enjoy the Going-to-the-Sun Road prior to its opening to vehicular traffic in mid-June. You cannot cycle all the way over the pass in early June, but you can cycle as far as the road is plowed and ride back down without encountering much traffic besides a few snowplows and construction vehicles. You can find thrilling off-road trails just outside the park near Whitefish. There are no bike-rental shops inside the park, but there are two in the town of Whitefish.

OUTFITTERS

Glacier Cyclery. Daily and weekly bike rentals of touring, road, and mountain bikes for all ages and skill levels are available here. The shop also sells bikes, equipment, and attire and does repairs. Information about local trails is available on its website and in the store. ⊠ *326 E. 2nd St., Whitefish* ☎ *406/862–6446* ⊕ *www.glaciercyclery.com* ✉ *From $30.*

Great Northern Cycle & Ski. You can rent road bikes and mountain bikes from this outfitter that also services and repairs bikes and sells cycling and skiing attire and gear. The shop's website has trail and ride information. ⊠ *328 Central Ave., Whitefish* ☎ *406/862–5321* ⊕ *www. greatnortherncycles.com* ✉ *From $39.*

BOATING AND RAFTING

Glacier has many stunning lakes and rivers, and boating is a popular park activity. Many rafting companies provide adventures along the border of the park on the Middle and North Forks of the Flathead River. The Middle Fork has some excellent white water, while the North Fork has both slow-moving and fast-moving sections. If you bring your own raft or kayak—watercraft such as Sea-Doos or Jet Skis are not allowed in the park—stop at the Hungry Horse Ranger Station in the Flathead National Forest near West Glacier to obtain a permit. Consider starting at Ousel Creek and floating to West Glacier on the Middle Fork of the Flathead River.

> ### SHRINKING GLACIERS
>
> The effects of climate change are on full display at Glacier National Park. In 1850 there were approximately 150 glaciers here; as of 2015, only 25 remained. Some climate scientists predict that by 2050 even these will be gone.

TOURS AND OUTFITTERS

Glacier Park Boat Company. This company conducts tours of five lakes. A **Lake McDonald cruise** takes you from the dock at Lake McDonald Lodge to the middle of the lake for an unparalleled view of the Continental Divide's Garden Wall. **Many Glacier tours** on Swiftcurrent Lake and Lake Josephine depart from Many Glacier Hotel and provide views of the Continental Divide. Two **Medicine Lake cruises** leave from the dock near the ranger station and lead to several trails. **St. Mary Lake cruises** leave from the launch near Rising Sun Campground and head to Red Eagle Mountain and other spots. The tours last from 45 to 90 minutes. You can rent small watercraft at Apgar, Lake McDonald, Two Medicine, and Many Glacier. ☎ 406/257–2426 ⊕ *www.glacierparkboats.com* ✉ *Tours from $12.50, rentals from $10* ☼ *May–Sept.*

FISHING

Within Glacier there's an almost unlimited range of fishing possibilities, with catch-and-release encouraged. You can fish in most waters of the park, but the best fishing is generally in the least accessible spots. A fishing license is not required inside the park, but you must stop by a park office to pick up a copy of the regulations. The fishing season runs from the third Saturday in May through November. Several companies offer guided fishing trips in the area. ■TIP→ **Fishing on both the North Fork and the Middle Fork of the Flathead River requires a Montana conservation license ($10) and a Montana fishing license ($15 for two consecutive days or $60 for a season). They are available at most convenience stores, sports shops, and from the Montana Department of Fish, Wildlife, and Parks** (☎ 406/752–5501 ⊕ *www.fwp.mt.gov*).

HIKING

With more than 730 miles of marked trails, Glacier is a hiker's paradise. Trail maps are available at all visitor centers and entrance stations. Before hiking, ask about trail closures due to bear or mountain lion activity. Never hike alone. For backcountry hiking, pick up a permit from park headquarters or the Apgar Backcountry Permit Center (☎ 406/888–7939) near Glacier's west entrance.

TOURS

Glacier Guides. The exclusive backpacking guide service in Glacier National Park can arrange guided day hikes or multiday hikes. Guided hiking tours are customized to match the skill level of the hikers, and include stops to identify plants, animals, and habitats. ⊠ *11970 U.S. 2 E, West Glacier* ☎ *406/387–5555, 800/521–7238* ⊕ *www.glacierguides. com* ✉ *From $85.*

EASY

Avalanche Lake Trail. From Avalanche Creek Campground, take this 3-mile trail leading to mountain-ringed Avalanche Lake. The walk is relatively easy (it ascends 500 feet), making this one of the park's most accessible backcountry lakes. Crowds fill the parking area and trail during July and August and on sunny weekends in May and June. *Easy.* ✛ *Trailhead: across from Avalanche Creek Campground, 15 miles north of Apgar on Going-to-the-Sun Rd.*

Hidden Lake Nature Trail. This uphill, 1½-mile trail runs from Logan Pass southwest to Hidden Lake Overlook, from which you get a beautiful view of the lake and McDonald Valley. In spring, ribbons of water pour off the rocks surrounding the lake. *Easy.* ✛ *Trailhead: behind Logan Pass Visitor Center.*

Sun Point Nature Trail. This 1.3-mile well-groomed trail, closed in 2016 for renovation but reopening in 2017, allows you to walk along the cliffs and shores of picturesque St. Mary Lake. A stunning waterfall awaits at the end of the hike. You can hike one-way and take a boat transfer back. *Easy.* ✛ *Trailhead: 11 miles east of Logan Pass on Going-to-the-Sun Rd., at Sun Point parking area.*

FAMILY **Trail of the Cedars.** This wheelchair-accessible, ½-mile boardwalk loop through an ancient cedar and hemlock forest is a favorite of families with small children and people with disabilities. Interpretive signs describe the habitat and natural history of the rain forest. *Easy.* ✛ *Trailhead: across from Avalanche Creek Campground, 15 miles north of Apgar on Going-to-the-Sun Rd.*

MODERATE

Fodor's Choice **Highline Trail.** From the Logan Pass parking lot, hike north along the
★ Garden Wall and just below the craggy Continental Divide. Wildflowers dominate the 7.6 miles to Granite Park Chalet, a National Historic Landmark, where hikers with reservations can overnight. Return to Logan Pass along the same trail or hike down 4½ miles (a 2,500-foot descent) on the Loop Trail. *Moderate.* ✛ *Trailhead: at Logan Pass Visitor Center.*

Iceberg Lake Trail. This moderately strenuous 9-mile round-trip hike passes the gushing Ptarmigan Falls, then climbs to its namesake, where icebergs bob in the chilly mountain loch. Mountain goats hang out on sheer cliffs above, bighorn sheep graze in the high mountain meadows, and grizzly bears dig for glacier lily bulbs, grubs, and other delicacies. Rangers lead hikes here almost daily in summer, leaving at 8:30 am. *Moderate.* ✛ *Trailhead: at Swiftcurrent Inn parking lot, off Many Glacier Rd.*

17

Many Glacier

Lake
Sherburne

Swiftcurrent Pass Trail

Redrock
Lake

Grinnell Glacier
Trail

Bullhead
Lake

Swiftcurrent
Lake

Upper
Grinnell
Lake

Lake
Josephine

Craker Lake Trail

Grinnell
Lake

Grinnell
Glacier

Craker
Lake

**Weeping
Wall**

GARDEN WALL

Piegan Pass Trail

Triple Arches

Otokomi
Lake

Rose

Creek

Siyeh Bend
Cut-off Trail

Hidden Lake
Nature Trail

Siyeh Pass Trail

Baring Creek

Goat
Lake

**Rising
Sun**

**Logan Pass
Visitor Center**

Saint Mary
Lake

Hidden
Lake

CONTINENTAL DIVIDE

Going-to-the-Sun Road

Florence
Falls

St. Mary
Falls

Virginia
Falls

0   2 mi

0   2 km

DIFFICULT

Grinnell Glacier Trail. The strenuous 5½-mile hike to Grinnell Glacier, the park's largest and most accessible glacier, is marked by several spectacular viewpoints. You start at Swiftcurrent Lake's picnic area, climb a moraine to Lake Josephine, then climb to the Grinnell Glacier overlook. Halfway up, turn around to see the prairie land to the northeast. You can shortcut the trail by 2 miles each way by taking scenic boat rides across Swiftcurrent Lake and Lake Josephine. From July to mid-September, a ranger-led hike departs from the Many Glacier Hotel boat dock on most mornings at 8:30. *Difficult.* ✤ *Trailhead: at Lake Josephine boat dock.*

Two Medicine Valley Trails. One of the least-developed areas of Glacier, the southeastern corner of the park is a good place for a quiet day hike, although you should look out for signs of bears. The trailhead to Upper Two Medicine Lake and Cobalt Lake begins west of the boat dock and camp supply store, where you can make arrangements for a boat pickup or drop-off across the lake. *Difficult.* ✤ *Trailhead: west of Two Medicine Campground boat dock, 9 miles west of Hwy. 49.*

CLOSE UP

The History of Glacier National Park

The history of Glacier National Park started long before Congress named the spectacular wilderness a national park.

SPIRITUALLY CHARGED TERRAIN

Native Americans, including the Blackfeet, Kootenai, and Salish, regularly traversed the area's valleys for centuries before white immigrants arrived. For the most part, these migratory people foraged the Rocky Mountains for sustenance in the form of roots, grasses, berries, and game. Many tribes felt that the mountain terrain, with its unusual glacier-carved horns, cirques, and arêtes, was spiritually charged. Later, white people would be similarly inspired by region's beauty and would nickname the area atop the Continental Divide the "Crown of the Continent."

TRAPPERS ARRIVE

White trappers arrived as early as the 1780s. In 1805, Lewis and Clark passed south of what is now Glacier National Park. Attracted by the expedition's reports of abundant beaver, many more trappers, primarily British, French, and Spanish, migrated to the region. For the next few decades, though, human activity was limited to lone trappers and migrating Indians.

ELUSIVE PASS

Lewis and Clark sought but did not find the elusive pass over the Rockies, now known as Marias Pass, on the park's southern edge at elevation 5,200 feet. Their scouts may have been unaware of the relatively low elevation, or perhaps they feared the Blackfeet, who controlled the region. The pass went undiscovered until 1889, when surveyors for the Great Northern Railway found it. By 1891 the company's tracks had crossed Marias Pass, and by 1895 the railroad had completed its westward expansion.

NATIVE POPULATION DECLINES

As homesteaders, miners, and trappers poured into the Glacier area in the late 1800s, the Native American population seriously declined. The Blackfeet were devastated by smallpox epidemics from the mid-1800s until the early 1900s. The disease and a reduced food supply due to the overhunting of buffalo stripped the Blackfeet of their power and, eventually, their land. In 1895, the tribe sold the area now within the park to the U.S. government, which opened it to miners. Returns on the mines were never substantial, and most were abandoned by 1905.

PROTECTING THE BEAUTY

Between the late 1880s and 1900, the Great Northern Railway company built seven backcountry chalets to house guests, and promised tourists from the East a back-to-nature experience with daylong hikes and horseback rides between the chalets. Visitors arrived by train at West Glacier, took a stagecoach to Lake McDonald, a boat to the lakeside Snyder Hotel, and began their nature adventures from there. Congress found reason enough to establish Glacier National Park and in 1910, President William Howard Taft signed the bill that did so.

17

HORSEBACK RIDING

Horses are permitted on many trails within the parks; check for seasonal exceptions. Horseback riding is prohibited on paved roads. You can pick up a brochure with suggested routes and lists of outfitters from any visitor center or entrance station. The **Sperry Chalet Trail** to the view of Sperry Glacier above Lake McDonald is a tough 7-mile climb.

TOURS AND OUTFITTERS

Glacier Gateway Outfitters. On this East Glacier company's trips, a Blackfoot cowboy guides riders on Blackfeet Nation land adjacent to the Two Medicine area of Glacier National Park. Rides, from an hour to all day, climb through aspen groves to high-country views of Dancing Lady and Bison mountains. Riders must be seven or older. Reservations are essential. ✉ *East Glacier* ☏ *406/226–4408 in season, 406/338–5560 off season* 🖘 *From $35* ⊙ *June–Sept.*

Swan Mountain Outfitters. The only outfitter that offers horseback riding inside the park, Swan begins its rides at Apgar, Lake McDonald, Many Glacier, and West Glacier. Trips for beginning to advanced riders cover both flat and mountainous terrain. Fishing can also be included. Riders must be seven or older and weigh less than 250 pounds. Reservations are essential. ✉ *Coram* ☏ *877/888–5557 central reservations, 406/381–4405 Apgar Corral* ⊕ *www.swanmountainoutfitters.com/glacier* 🖘 *From $45* ⊙ *Late May–mid-Sept.*

SKIING AND SNOWSHOEING

Cross-country skiing and snowshoeing are increasingly popular in the park. Glacier distributes a free pamphlet entitled *Ski Trails of Glacier National Park,* with 16 noted trails. You can start at Lake McDonald Lodge and ski cross-country up Going-to-the-Sun Road. The 2½-mile Apgar Natural Trail is popular with snowshoers. No restaurants are open in winter in Glacier, but you can pop into Montana House (⊕ *montanahouse.info*) for hot cider, coffee, cookies, and a little shopping. The park website (⊕ *home.nps.gov/applications/glac/ski/xcski. htm*) has ski trail maps.

TOURS AND OUTFITTERS

Glacier Adventure Guides. This organization leads one-day and multiday guided snowshoe trips on scenic winter trails. On overnight trips, you stay in igloos and snow caves. During the summer, the company conducts guided hiking and rock-climbing adventures outside the park. ✉ *Glacier National Park* ☏ *877/735–9514, 406/892–2173* ⊕ *www. glacieradventureguides.com* 🖘 *From $35* ⊙ *Mid-Nov.–May.*

Izaak Walton Inn. Just outside the southern edge of the park, the inn has more than 20 miles of groomed cross-country ski trails on its property. It offers equipment rentals and lessons as well as guided ski and snowshoe tours inside the park. Inn guests can ski for free, but others must purchase a ski pass. The inn is one of the few places in the area that is both open in winter and accessible by Amtrak train, which saves you the worry of driving on icy mountain roads. ✉ *290 Izaak Walton Inn Rd., off U.S. 2, Essex* ☏ *406/888–5700* ⊕ *www.izaakwaltoninn.com/ activities/winter-activities* 🖘 *From $10* ⊙ *Mid-Nov.–May.*

WATERTON LAKES NATIONAL PARK

A World Heritage Site, Waterton Lakes National Park represents the meeting of two worlds—the flatlands of the prairie and the abrupt upthrust of the mountains—squeezing an unusual mix of wildlife, flora, and climate zones into its 505 square km (200 square miles).

EXPLORING

SCENIC DRIVES

Akamina Parkway. Take this winding 16-km (10-mile) road up to Cameron Lake, but drive slowly and watch for wildlife: it's common to see bears along the way. At the lake you will find a relatively flat, paved, 1.6-km (1-mile) trail that hugs the western shore and makes a nice walk. Bring your binoculars. Grizzly bears are often spotted on the lower slopes of the mountains at the far end of the lake. ⊠ *Waterton Lakes National Park.*

Red Rock Parkway. The 15-km (9-mile) route takes you from the prairie up the Blakiston Valley to Red Rock Canyon, where water has cut through the earth, exposing red sedimentary rock. It's common to see bears just off the road, especially in autumn, when the berries are ripe. ⊠ *Waterton Lakes National Park.*

HISTORIC SITES

First Oil Well in Western Canada. Alberta is known worldwide for its oil and gas production, and the first oil well in western Canada was established in 1902 in what is now the park. Stop at this National Historic Site to explore the wellheads, drilling equipment, and remains of the Oil City boomtown. ✛ *Watch for sign 7.7 km (4.8 miles) up the Akamina Pkwy.* ⌫ *Free.*

Prince of Wales Hotel. Named for the prince who later became King Edward VIII, this hotel was constructed between 1926 and 1927 and was designated a National Historic Site in 1995. Stand on the ridge outside the hotel and take in the magnificent view or pop inside and enjoy it from the comfort of the expansive lobby. Tea is served in the lobby in the afternoon. ⊠ *Off Hwy. 5, Waterton Lakes National Park* ☎ *406/892–2525, 403/236–3400 mid-May–late Sept.* ⊕ *www.glacierparkinc.com/prince_of_wales.php* ⌫ *Free* ☉ *Mid-May–late Sept.*

SCENIC STOPS

Cameron Lake. The jewel of Waterton, Cameron Lake sits in a land of glacially carved cirques (steep-walled basins). In summer, hundreds of varieties of alpine wildflowers fill the area, including 22 kinds of wild orchids. Canoes, rowboats, kayaks, and fishing gear can be rented here. ⊠ *Akamina Pkwy., 13 km (8 miles) southwest of Waterton Townsite, Waterton Lakes National Park.*

Goat Haunt Ranger Station. Reached only by foot trail or tour boat from Waterton townsite, this spot on the U.S. end of Waterton Lake is the stomping ground for mountain goats, moose, grizzlies, and black bears. The ranger posted at this remote station gives thrice-daily 10-minute overviews of Waterton Valley history. Bring your passport if you want

17

to explore the U.S. side of Waterton Lake beyond the ranger station. ⊠ *Southern end of Waterton Lake, Waterton Lakes National Park* ☎ *403/859–2362* ⊕ *www.watertoncruise.com* ✇ *Tour boat C$45* ⊙ *May–mid-Oct.*

Waterton Townsite. A low-key community in roughly the park's geographical center, the townsite swells with tourists in summer, and restaurants and shops open to serve them. In winter only a few motels are open, and services are limited. ⊠ *Waterton Townsite.*

SPORTS AND THE OUTDOORS

The park contains numerous short hikes for day-trippers and some longer treks for backpackers. Upper and Middle Waterton and Cameron lakes provide peaceful havens for boaters. A tour boat cruises across Upper Waterton Lake, crossing the U.S.–Canada border, and the winds that rake across that lake create an exciting ride for windsurfers—bring a wet suit, though; the water remains numbingly cold throughout summer.

BICYCLING

Bikes are allowed on some trails, such as the 3-km (2-mile) **Townsite Loop Trail.** A great family bike trail is the 4.3-mile (one-way) paved **Kootenai Brown Trail,** which leads from the townsite to the park gates along the edges of the lakes. A ride on mildly sloping **Red Rock Canyon Road** isn't too difficult (once you get past the first hill). The **Crandell Loop** trail provides a slightly more challenging ride for mountain bikers.

OUTFITTERS

FAMILY   **Pat's Waterton.** Choose from surrey bikes, mountain bikes, or motorized scooters at Pat's, which also rents tennis rackets, strollers, and binoculars. ⊠ *224 Mt. View Rd., Waterton Townsite* ☎ *403/859–2266* ⊕ *www.patswaterton.com* ✇ *From $10.*

BOATING

Nonmotorized boats can be rented at Cameron Lake in summer; private craft can be used on Upper and Middle Waterton lakes.

TOURS AND OUTFITTERS

Waterton Inter-Nation Shoreline Cruise Co. This company's two-hour round-trip boat tour along Upper Waterton Lake from Waterton Townsite to Goat Haunt Ranger Station is one of the most popular activities in Waterton. The narrated tour passes scenic bays, sheer cliffs, and snow-clad peaks. Because Goat Haunt is in the United States, you must clear customs to stay there and hike into Glacier. ⊠ *Waterton Townsite Marina, northwest corner of Waterton Lake near Bayshore Inn, Waterton Lakes National Park* ☎ *403/859–2362, 403/938–5019, 403/859–2362* ⊕ *www.watertoncruise.com* ✇ *C$45* ⊙ *May–mid-Oct., cruises several times daily.*

HIKING

There are 225 km (191 miles) of trails in Waterton Lakes that range in difficulty from short strolls to strenuous treks. Some trails connect with the trail systems of Glacier and British Columbia's Akamina-Kishenina Provincial Park. The wildflowers in June are particularly stunning along most trails. *Hiking Glacier and Waterton National Parks,* by Erik Molvar, has detailed information including pictures and GPS-compatible maps for 60 of the best hiking trails in both parks.

TOURS

Waterton Outdoor Adventures. This is the headquarters for hiker shuttle services that run throughout Waterton to most major trailheads; you can reserve shuttles up to two months ahead. Waterton Outdoor Adventures can also arrange certified hiking guides for groups. ⊠ *Tamarack Outdoor Outfitters, 214 Mt. View Rd., Waterton Townsite* ☎ *403/859–2378* ⊕ *www.hikewaterton.com* ✉ *From C$13.50* ☽ *May–Sept.*

EASY

FAMILY **Bear's Hump Trail.** This steep 2.8-km (1.4-mile) trail climbs up the mountainside to an overlook with a great view of Upper Waterton Lake and the townsite. *Easy.* ✛ *Trailhead: behind Waterton Information Centre.*

FAMILY **Cameron Lake Shore Trail.** This relatively flat paved trail, 1.6 km (1 mile) one-way, is a peaceful place for a walk. Look for wildflowers along the shoreline and grizzlies on the lower slopes of the mountains at the far end of the lake. *Easy.* ✛ *Trailhead: at lakeshore in front of parking lot, 13 km (8 miles) southwest of Waterton Townsite.*

Crandell Lake Trail. This 2½-km (1½-mile) trail winds through fragrant pine forest, ending at a popular mountain lake. *Easy.* ✛ *Trailhead: about halfway up Akamina Pkwy.*

MODERATE

Bertha Lake Trail. This 11.4-km (7.1-mile) round-trip trail leads from the Waterton Townsite through a Douglas fir forest to a beautiful overlook of Upper Waterton Lake, then continues on to Lower Bertha Falls. From there, a steeper climb takes you past Upper Bertha Falls to Bertha Lake. In June, the wildflowers along the trail are stunning. *Moderate.* ✛ *Trailhead: at parking lot off Evergreen Ave., west of Townsite Campground.*

DIFFICULT

Fodor's Choice **Crypt Lake Trail.** Awe-inspiring and strenuous, this 17.2-km (11-mile)
★ round-trip trail is one of the most stunning hikes in the Canadian Rockies. Conquering the trail involves taking a boat taxi across Waterton Lake, climbing 700 meters (2,300 feet), crawling through a tunnel nearly 30 meters (100 feet) long, and scrambling across a sheer rock face. The reward, and well worth it: views of a 183-meter (600-foot) cascading waterfall and the turquoise waters of Crypt Lake. *Difficult.* ✛ *Trailhead: at Crypt Landing, accessed by ferry from Waterton Townsite.*

HORSEBACK RIDING

Rolling hills, grasslands, and rugged mountains make riding in Waterton Lakes a real pleasure. Scenery, wildlife, and wildflowers are easily viewed from the saddle, and horses are permitted on many park trails.

TOURS AND OUTFITTERS

Alpine Stables. At these stables you can arrange hourlong trail rides and full-day guided excursions within the park as well as multiday pack trips through the Rockies foothills. ⊠ *Waterton Lakes National Park* ☎ *403/859–2462 May–Sept., 403/653–2449 Oct.–Apr.* ✉ *From C$40* ☽ *May–Sept.*

17

FAMILY FUN

Opportunities for family fun at Glacier and Waterton include canoeing, climbing, hiking, biking, and touring.

Canoe Lake McDonald. Rent a canoe and paddle around the lake. If you work up a sweat, jump in. *Glacier.*

Climb Bear's Hump. This 2.8-km (1.7-mile) trail winds up a mountainside to an overlook with a great view of Upper Waterton Lake and the townsite. *Waterton.*

Hike Hidden Lake Nature Trail. A 2.4-km (1½-mile) trail runs uphill from Logan Pass to the Hidden Lake Overlook, yielding beautiful views

of the lake and McDonald Valley. In spring, ribbons of water pour off the rocks surrounding the lake. A boardwalk protects the abundant wildflowers and spongy tundra on the way. *Glacier.*

Surrey Around Town. Rent a surrey bike at Pat's Waterton store and pedal around the townsite. A surrey bike has a flat seat and a canopy and can hold up to three people. *Waterton.*

Tour Going-to-the Sun in a Jammer Bus. With amazing vistas and many stops for photo ops, the Going-to-the-Sun Road tour in a vintage Jammer Bus is a beloved park tradition. *Glacier.*

SWIMMING

FAMILY **Waterton Health Club.** The club has an 18-meter (56-foot) saltwater pool, a hot tub, a sauna, and a gym. Towels are provided. ⊠ *Waterton Lakes Lodge Resort, 101 Clematis Ave., Waterton Townsite* ☎ *403/859–2150, 888/985–6343* ⊕ *watertonlakeslodge.com* 💷 *C$18.90/week* ☉ *Daily 7 am–10 pm.*

FAMILY **Waterton Lakes.** The lakes are chilly year-round, but they're a great place to cool off after a long hot day of hiking. Most visitors can only handle dipping in a toe or two, some wade, and a few brave souls join the "polar bear club" and plunge in completely. ⊠ *Waterton Townsite* 💷 *Free.*

WHAT'S NEARBY

You could easily spend a week exploring Waterton and Glacier, but you may wish to take in some nearby sights as well. Outside Glacier National Park are the gateway towns of **East Glacier,** 30 miles south of St. Mary Visitor Center; **West Glacier,** 2½ miles south of Apgar Visitor Center; and **Columbia Falls,** 17 miles southwest of West Glacier, where you can find tour operators, accommodations, restaurants, and stores. Not far from Glacier Park are **Essex, Kalispell, Whitefish, Browning,** and **Bigfork,** home to excellent golf courses, world-class cross-country and downhill skiing, summer and winter festivals, diverse recreational opportunities, accommodations, and restaurants. The main attractions in the Canadian town of **Cardston,** east of Waterton Townsite, are an intriguing museum of horse-drawn vehicles and the nearly nightly theater performances in summer.

NEARBY TOWNS

Bigfork. About 45 minutes from Glacier's west entrance on Flathead Lake's pristine northeast shore, Bigfork twinkles with decorative lights that adorn its boutique shops and fine restaurants. Bigfork is a wonderful art community with excellent galleries and one of the finest repertory theaters in the Northwest. ⊠ *Bigfork* ⊕ *www.bigfork.org.*

Browning. About 35 miles east of Glacier, Browning is the center of the Blackfeet Nation, whose name is thought to derive from the color of its members' painted or dyed black moccasins. These days there are about 13,000 enrolled tribal members. The city's main attractions are the Museum of the Plains Indian and the Blackfeet Heritage Center and Art Gallery. ⊠ *Browning* ⊕ *www.browningmontana.com.*

Cardston. Just 45 km (28 miles) east of Waterton, Cardston is home to the Alberta Temple, built by the Mormon pioneers who established the town. The Remington Carriage Museum contains North America's largest collection of horse-drawn vehicles. The Carriage House Theatre (*www.carriagehousetheatre.com*) presents entertaining live theatrical performances on most summer evenings. ⊕ *cardston.ca.*

Columbia Falls. This small town 19 miles southwest of the Apgar Visitor Center has restaurants, services, and accommodations. Near the town are two excellent golf courses, a water park, and more than 80 miles of groomed snowmobile trails in winter. ⊠ *Columbia Falls* ⊕ *www.columbiafallschamber.org.*

East Glacier. Early tourists to Glacier National Park first stopped in East Glacier, where the Great Northern Railway had established a station. Although most people coming from the east now enter by car through St. Mary, East Glacier, about 30 miles south, U.S. 89 to Highway 49, attracts visitors with its quiet, secluded surroundings and lovely Glacier Park Lodge. ⊠ *East Glacier* ⊕ *www.eastglacierpark.info.*

Essex. The village of Essex, along U.S. 2, 30 miles southeast of West Glacier, borders the southern tip of the park and is the site of the main rail and bus terminals for park visitors. ⊠ *Essex.*

Fort Macleod. Named for its Northwest Mounted Police fort, the town of Fort Macleod is 105 km (65 miles) northwest of Waterton Townsite. You can still explore the old fort, and nearby is Head-Smashed-In Buffalo Jump, a UNESCO World Heritage Site and museum where you can learn about the history of the Plains Indians. ⊠ *Fort Macleod* ⊕ *www.fortmacleod.com/visiting.*

West Glacier. The green waters of the Flathead River's Middle Fork and several top-notch outfitters make West Glacier, 2½ miles south of the Apgar Visitor Center, an ideal base for river sports such as rafting and fishing. There are several good accommodations and restaurants here. ⊠ *West Glacier.*

Whitefish. The best base for the park is Whitefish, 28 miles west of the Apgar Visitor Center. With a population of 6,000, the town has a well-developed nightlife scene and good restaurants, galleries, and shops. ⊠ *Whitefish* ⊕ *www.explorewhitefish.com.*

17

Visitor Information Bigfork Area Chamber of Commerce. ✉ *8155 Hwy. 35, Bigfork* ☎ *406/837–5888* ⊕ *www.bigfork.org.* **East Glacier Chamber of Commerce.** ✉ *909 Hwy. 49 N, East Glacier* ☎ *406/226–4403.* **Glacier Country Montana.** ✉ *140 N. Higgens Ave., Suite 204, Missoula* ☎ *800/338–5072* ⊕ *www.glaciermt.com.* **Town of Cardston.** ✉ *67 3rd Ave. W* ☎ *403/653–3366, 888/434–3366* ⊕ *www.cardston.ca.* **Waterton Lakes Chamber of Commerce.** ✉ *Waterton Lakes National Park* ⊕ *www.mywaterton.ca.* **Whitefish Chamber of Commerce.** ✉ *307 Spokane Ave., Suite 103, Whitefish* ☎ *403/862–3501, 877/862–3548* ⊕ *www.whitefishchamber.org.*

NEARBY ATTRACTIONS

FAMILY **Big Sky Waterpark.** During summer, the water park is a popular place. Besides the 10 waterslides and a golf course, there are arcade games, bumper cars, a carousel, barbecue grills, a picnic area, and food service. ✉ *7211 U.S. 2 E, at Hwy. 206, Columbia Falls* ☎ *406/892–5025, 406/892–5026* ⊕ *www.bigskywp.com* 🎟 *$25* ⊙ *Late May–early Sept., daily 11–7.*

Museum of the Plains Indian. The impressive collection of artifacts from the Blackfeet at this museum includes clothing, saddlebags, and artwork. ✉ *19 Museum Loop, Browning* ☎ *406/338–2230* ⊕ *www. browningmontana.com* 🎟 *$5, June–Sept., free Oct.–May* ⊙ *June–Sept., daily 9–4:45; Oct.–May, weekdays 10–4:30.*

AREA ACTIVITIES

SPORTS AND THE OUTDOORS
DOGSLEDDING
Dog Sled Adventures. The dogs are raring to run from late November to mid-April at Dog Sled Adventures. Your friendly musher will gear the ride to the passengers, from kids to senior citizens; bundled up in a sled, you'll be whisked from Stillwater State Forest on a 1½-hour ride over a 12-mile trail. Reservations are necessary. ✉ *U.S. 93, 20 miles north of Whitefish, 2 miles north of Olney, Glacier National Park* ☎ *406/881–2275* ⊕ *www.dogsledadventuresmt.com* 🎟 *From $110 per person.*

SKIING AND SNOWBOARDING
Whitefish Mountain Resort. Eight miles from Whitefish, this has been one of Montana's top ski areas since the 1930s, yet it remains comfortably small. The resort is popular among train travelers from the Pacific Northwest and the upper Midwest. Whitefish mountain has good powder skiing, nice glades, and groomed trails for all ski levels. In summer there are bike trails, an alpine slide, an aerial adventure park, and a zip line. The terrain is 25% beginner, 50% intermediate, and 25% advanced; there are two high-speed quad chairs, one quad chair, four triple chairs, one double chair, and three surface lifts. **Facilities:** 105 trails; 3,000 acres; 2,500-foot vertical drop; 11 lifts. ✉ *1015 Glades Dr.* ☎ *406/862–2900, 800/858–3930, 406/862–7669 snow report* ⊕ *www. skiwhitefish.com* 🎟 *Lift ticket: $73* ⊙ *Late-Nov.–early Apr. and mid-June–mid-Sept., daily 9–4:30.*

WHERE TO EAT

IN THE PARKS

GLACIER

$$$ **✕ Lake McDonald Lodge Restaurants.** In Russell's Fireside Dining Room,
AMERICAN take in a great view while choosing between standards such as pasta,
steak, wild game, and salmon. There are also some delicious salads and
other local favorites on the menu such as Montana Rainbow trout.
Check out the pastry chef's daily dessert special, which has included
such items as strawberry shortcake and apple bread pudding with car-
amel-cinnamon sauce. The restaurant has an excellent breakfast buffet,
and box lunches are prepared on request. Across the parking lot, **Jam-
mer Joe's Grill & Pizzeria** serves burgers and pasta for lunch and dinner.
The all-day bar menu at **Lucke's Lounge** includes burgers, sandwiches,
salads and appetizers. There's a great view of Lake McDonald from
the lounge. ⑤ *Average main: $22* ✉ *Glacier National Park* ⊹ *Going-to-
the-Sun Rd., 10 miles north of Apgar* ☎ *406/888–5431, 406/892–2525*
⊕ *www.glaciernationalparklodges.com* ⊘ *Closed early Oct.–early June.*

$$$ **✕ Ptarmigan Dining Room.** The picturesque Ptarmigan's massive windows
AMERICAN afford stunning views of Grinnell Point over Swiftcurrent Lake. Known
for using regional, sustainably sourced ingredients, the restaurant specializes in dishes such as smoked Montana trout, bison tenderloin, and
seared duck breast with cherry chutney. Gluten-free and vegan dishes
are also served. Save room for the huckleberry cobbler for dessert.
Before or after dinner, pop into the adjacent Swiss Lounge to enjoy a
Montana microbrew or a huckleberry daiquiri. ⑤ *Average main: $21*
✉ *Many Glacier Rd., Glacier National Park* ☎ *303/265–7010* ⊕ *www.
glaciernationalparklodges.com* ⊘ *Closed late Sept.–early June.*

PICNIC AREAS

There are picnic spots at or near most campgrounds in Glacier National
Park. Each has tables, grills, and drinking water in summer. You can get
a map at the visitor center that identifies all the picnic sites in the park.

Apgar. In a tree-shaded area at the southern end of Lake McDonald, the
Apgar Campground has tables, drinking water, and restrooms. ⊹ *Off
Going-to-the-Sun Rd., north of campground, 4 km (2½ miles) north
of west entrance.*

Fish Creek. In a forested area adjacent to Lake McDonald, this picnic
area has tables, drinking water, and restrooms. There's a swimming
area nearby, and the trailheads for several good hikes. ⊹ *Off Camas
Rd. before Fish Creek Campground, 4 miles northwest of west entrance.*

Rising Sun. In a cottonwood grove adjacent to St. Mary Lake, this area
has tables, restrooms, and drinking water in summer. ⊹ *Off Going-
to-the-Sun Rd., 10 km (6 miles) southwest of St. Mary Visitor Center.*

Sprague Creek. This picnic site on Lake McDonald's eastern shore has
tables, restrooms, and drinking water in summer. ⊹ *Off Going-to-the-
Sun Rd., adjacent to Sprague Creek Campground, 15 km (9 miles)
northeast of west entrance.*

17

WATERTON LAKES

$$$ ✕ **Lakeside Chophouse.** Grab a window seat or a spot on the patio to
STEAKHOUSE enjoy the spectacular view from Waterton's only lakefront restaurant.
This is the place in the park for a steak dinner—locally produced
Alberta beef plays a starring role on the globally inspired menu. The
petite filet mignon with garlic butter, the ribeye with chimichurri sauce,
and the Cajun-blackened New York steak are all good bets, but you can
also order Mumbai butter chicken, teriyaki-glazed salmon, and Asian-
style stir-fried vegetables. $ *Average main: C$28* ⊠ *111 Waterton Ave.,
Waterton Townsite* ☎ *888/527–9555, 403/859–2211, 403/859–2291*
⊕ *www.bayshoreinn.com* ⊗ *Closed mid-Oct.–Apr.*

$ ✕ **Wieners of Waterton.** If there is such a thing as a gourmet hot dog, then
HOT DOG this is the place to find it. The buns here are baked fresh daily, and the
FAMILY all-beef wieners and smokies are sourced locally with one exception:
the genuine Nathan's dogs, which are shipped from New York City.
There's even an anti-dog for the vegetarian set. Made with falafel, it's
topped with hummus, tzatziki sauce, and fresh vegetables. For all the
dogs, there are plenty of homemade sauces and tons of interesting top-
pings to choose from. Sides include sweet potato fries, fried pickles,
kettle chips, and classic Canadian poutine (fries served with gravy and
cheese curds). $ *Average main: C$8* ⊠ *301 Wildflower Ave., Waterton
Townsite* ☎ *403/859–0007* ⊕ *www.wienersofwaterton.com* ⊗ *Closed
Oct.–Apr.* ⌣ *Reservations not accepted.*

OUTSIDE THE PARKS

$$$ ✕ **Belton Chalet Grill Dining Room.** The hotel's handsome restaurant still
AMERICAN has its original wainscoting and leaded-glass windows, but in fine
Fodor's Choice weather ask to dine on the deck outside to watch the sun set behind the
★ mountains. The signature dishes include buffalo meatloaf, wild salmon
in lime-ginger coconut broth, and bacon-wrapped beef fillet cured in
bourbon and brown sugar. Try the wonderful berry crisp with huckleberry ice cream for dessert. The menu in the lounge is more casual, with
items like Southern chicken salad and Korean steak tacos. During summer, if you place an order at the front desk by 6 pm, a box lunch will be
ready for pickup the next morning. $ *Average main: $27* ⊠ *12575 U.S.
2 E, next to railroad station, West Glacier* ☎ *406/888–5000, 888/235–
8665, 406/888–5005* ⊕ *www.beltonchalet.com/dining_near_glacier.php*
⊗ *Closed early Oct.–early Dec. and late Mar.–late May. Closed Mon.–
Thurs. early Dec.–late Mar. (brunch only on Sun. Dec.–Mar.). No lunch.*

$$ ✕ **Serrano's.** Mexican food in Montana! After a day on the dusty trail,
MEXICAN Serrano's is a treat whether dining inside or on the back patio. Try a
taco salad, a beef burrito, or a chicken enchilada with one of the res-
taurant's famous margaritas; dinners are served with complimentary
chips and homemade salsa. The Mexican flan is delicious, but you
may want to try the less traditional huckleberry carrot cake for dessert.
Don't be surprised if there's a line in July, August, and early September.
The restaurant is a favorite with locals and visitors, and it doesn't take
reservations. $ *Average main: $15* ⊠ *29 Dawson Ave., East Glacier*
☎ *406/226–9392* ⊕ *www.serranosmexican.com* ⊗ *Closed Oct.–Apr.*
⌣ *Reservations not accepted.*

$$$
STEAKHOUSE

✕ **Summit Mountain Steakhouse.** The drive to this slightly off-the-beaten-track steak house southwest of East Glacier is well worth the detour. The small dining room seats 30 and has large windows with mountain views shared by an outdoor patio with additional seating. Two good starters are the roasted tomato bruschetta and the flatbread. They'll set you up nicely for the excellent handmade burgers and steaks or the signature slow-roasted pork tenderloin in smoked Burgundy-huckleberry sauce. Cocktails, reasonably priced steak-friendly wines, and several craft beers complement the cuisine. The mountain huckleberry is Montana's prized wild fruit. Here it goes into the marvelous huckleberry cheesecake for dessert. Ⓢ *Average main: $22* ✉ *16900 U.S. 2 W, East Glacier* ☎ *406/226–9319* ⊕ *www.summitmtnlodge.com* ⊙ *Closed Mid-Sept.–mid-June. No lunch* ⊟ *No credit cards.*

$$
AMERICAN

✕ **Three Forks Grille and Deli.** Italian-influenced classic mountain cuisine is prepared with care at the two-level Grille, which emphasizes local, sustainably produced ingredients. The regional focus extends to the artworks that adorn the walls; many are by area artists. The menu changes regularly depending on what is in season, but it always includes hand-cut steaks, wild game, and fresh seafood, and there are vegetarian, gluten-free, and dairy-free choices. Grilled Montana rainbow trout marinated in lime, herbs, and olive oil is another staple, as is the bison burger, served here with pickled red onions and white cheddar. All the desserts are made in-house from scratch. The Grille is open daily for dinner; the Deli serves soups, salads, sandwiches, panini, and a few entrées like lasagna for lunch. Ⓢ *Average main: $19* ✉ *729 Nucleus Ave., Columbia Falls* ☎ *406/892–2900* ⊕ *threeforksgrille.com* ⊙ *No lunch Sun.*

17

PICNIC AREAS

Waterton has 14 picnic sites in some of the most scenic areas of the park. All sites are equipped with picnic tables and washroom facilities, and most have a water source nearby. Some picnic sites are equipped with barbecues or outdoor fire pits. Firewood is not supplied, but it can be purchased in the village.

Cameron Bay. There are several picnic shelters along Upper Waterton Lake in the Cameron Bay area. These lakefront sites are equipped with tables, water taps, and wood-burning stoves. ✉ *Waterton Townsite* ⊕ *Along Upper Waterton Lake.*

Pass Creek. Open year-round, this picnic site is adjacent to a burbling creek. It has a large enclosed picnic shelter with an indoor wood-burning stove and there's an outdoor fire ring. ✉ *Waterton Lakes National Park* ⊕ *Across bridge from Red Rock Pkwy. turnoff.*

WHERE TO STAY

IN THE PARKS

GLACIER

$$ **Lake McDonald Lodge.** On the shores of Lake McDonald not far from
HOTEL Apgar and West Glacier, this lodge is an ideal base for exploring the
Fodor's Choice western side of the park and is one of the great historic lodges of the
★ West. **Pros:** lakeside setting; historic property; close to Apgar, West
Glacier, and Going-to-the-Sun Road. **Cons:** rustic; no TV (except for in
the suites); small bathrooms. ⑤ *Rooms from: $140* ⊠ *Going-to-the-Sun
Rd., Glacier National Park* ☎ *855/733–4522, 406/888–5431* ⊕ *www.
glaciernationalparklodges.com* ⤳ *32 standard lodge rooms, 36 cabins,
8 hostel dorms, 4 suites* ⫟⊙⫟ *No meals.*

$$$ **Many Glacier Hotel.** On Swiftcurrent Lake in the park's northeastern
HOTEL section, this is the most isolated of the grand hotels, and—especially
if you are able to book a lake-view balcony room—among the most
scenic. **Pros:** stunning views from lodge; secluded; good hiking trails
nearby. **Cons:** rustic rooms; no TV; no Internet. ⑤ *Rooms from: $165*
⊠ *Many Glacier Rd., 12 miles west of Babb, Glacier National Park*
☎ *855/733–4522, 406/732–4411* ⊕ *www.glaciernationalparklodges.
com* ☉ *Closed mid-Sept.–mid-June* ⤳ *206 rooms, 6 family rooms, 2
suites* ⫟⊙⫟ *No meals.*

$$ **Village Inn.** On the shores of beautiful Lake McDonald, this motel on
HOTEL the National Register of Historic Places was fully renovated in 2015: all
rooms have Wi-Fi, new beds, and furnishings that fit with the historic
style. **Pros:** great views; convenient Apgar village location; all rooms
have Wi-Fi; kitchenettes in some rooms. **Cons:** rustic motel; no air-con-
ditioning; no restaurant. ⑤ *Rooms from: $150* ⊠ *Apgar Village, Glacier
National Park* ☎ *855/733–4522* ⊕ *www.glaciernationalparklodges.com*
⤳ *36 rooms* ⫟⊙⫟ *No meals.*

WATERTON

$$$ **Bayshore Inn.** On the shores of Waterton Lake, this inn right in town
HOTEL has a lot going for it: lovely views, the only on-site spa in Waterton,
multiple eating establishments on property, and easy access to many
services. **Pros:** lakefront views; spa; townsite location; multiple restaurants. **Cons:** older-style rooms; motor inn. ⑤ *Rooms from: C$199*
⊠ *111 Waterton Ave., Waterton Townsite* ☎ *888/527–9555, 403/859–
2211, 403/859–2291* ⊕ *www.bayshoreinn.com* ☉ *Closed mid-Oct.–
Apr.* ⤳ *66 rooms, 4 suites* ⫟⊙⫟ *No meals.*

$$$$ **Waterton Glacier Suites.** In the heart of the townsite, this all-suite
HOTEL property is within walking distance of restaurants, shopping, and the
dock on beautiful Waterton Lake. **Pros:** modern suites with mini-refrig-
erators; open year-round; convenient location. **Cons:** no views; pull-
out sofas uncomfortable. ⑤ *Rooms from: C$244* ⊠ *107 Wildflower
Ave., Waterton Lakes National Park* ☎ *403/859–2004, 866/621–3330*
⊕ *www.watertonsuites.com* ⤳ *26 rooms* ⫟⊙⫟ *No meals.*

CLOSE UP

Best Campgrounds in Glacier and Waterton

There are 10 major campgrounds in Glacier National Park, and excellent backcountry sites for backpackers. Reservations for St. Mary campground are available through the National Park Reservation Service (☎ 877/444–6777 or 518/885–3639 ⊕ www.recreation.gov). Reservations may be made up to five months in advance. Parks Canada operates four campgrounds in Waterton Lakes that range from fully serviced to unserviced sites. There are also some backcountry campsites. Visitors can prebook campsites for a fee of C$11 online or C$13.50 by phone. The reservation service is available at ⊕ www.reservation.parkscanada.gc.ca or by phone at ☎ 877/737–3783.

BEST OPTIONS IN GLACIER

Apgar Campground. This popular and large campground on the southern shore of Lake McDonald has many activities and services. ⊠ Apgar Rd. ☎ 406/888–7800.

Avalanche Creek Campground. This peaceful campground on Going-to-the-Sun Road is shaded by huge red cedars and bordered by Avalanche Creek. ⊠ 25 km (15.7 miles) from west entrance on Going-to-the-Sun Rd. ☎ 406/888–7800.

Kintla Lake Campground. Beautiful and remote, this is a trout fisherman's dream. ⊠ 23.5 km (14 miles) north of Polebridge Ranger Station on Inside North Fork Rd.

Many Glacier Campground. One of the most beautiful spots in the park is also a favorite for bears. ⊠ Next to Swiftcurrent Motor Inn on Many Glacier Rd.

Sprague Creek Campground. This sometimes noisy roadside campground for tents, RVs, and truck campers (no towed units) offers spectacular views of the lake and sunsets, and there's fishing from shore. ⊠ Going-to-the-Sun Rd., 1.6 km (1 mile) south of Lake McDonald Lodge ☎ 406/888–7800.

St. Mary Campground. This large, grassy spot alongside the lake and stream has mountain views and cool breezes. ⊠ 1.4 km (0.9 mile) from St. Mary entrance to Going-to-the-Sun Rd. ☎ 406/888–7800.

BEST OPTIONS IN WATERTON

Crandell Campground. Along the Red Rock Parkway a short hike from Crandell Lake, this campground is surrounded by montane forest. ⊠ On Red Rock Pkwy., 2 km (1.2 miles) before Crandell Lake ☎ 403/859–5133.

Waterton Townsite Campground. Though the campground is busy and windy, sites here are grassy and flat with access to kitchen shelters and have views down the lake into the U.S. part of the Peace Park. ⊠ Waterton and Vimy Aves. ☎ 877/737–3783.

17

OUTSIDE THE PARKS

$$$
HOTEL
🍴 **Belton Chalet.** This carefully restored 1910 railroad hotel, the original winter headquarters for the park, has a great location just outside the West Glacier entrance and cozy, bright rooms with period furnishings and original woodwork around the windows. **Pros:** excellent restaurant; wraparound decks with lovely views; historic property. **Cons:**

train noise; rustic; no air-conditioning or TVs. $ *Rooms from: $160* ✉ *12575 U.S. 2 E, West Glacier* ☎ *406/888–5000, 888/235–8665* ⊕ *www.beltonchalet.com* ⇝ *25 rooms, 2 cottages* ⦿ *Breakfast.*

$$$
B&B/INN

🖼 **Garden Wall Inn B&B.** This antiques-filled 1923 home has individually decorated guest rooms with down duvets. **Pros:** historic home; nice personal touches; spacious rooms. **Cons:** small property; no view. $ *Rooms from: $155* ✉ *504 Spokane Ave., Whitefish* ☎ *406/862–3440, 888/530–1700* ⊕ *www.gardenwallinn.com* ⇝ *4 rooms, 1 suite* ⦿ *Breakfast.*

$$$$
RENTAL
FAMILY

🖼 **Glacier Outdoor Center Cabins.** Five minutes from the entrance to West Glacier, these cozy cabins with living rooms, barbecues, private decks, and fully equipped kitchens are ideal for families. **Pros:** great for families; can accommodate large groups; kitchens in cabins. **Cons:** outside the townsite; no restaurant. $ *Rooms from: $329* ✉ *12400 U.S. 2 E, West Glacier* ☎ *800/235–6781, 406/888–5454* ⊕ *www.glacierraftco. com* ☉ *Closed Nov.–Apr.* ⇝ *12 cabins* ⦿ *No meals.*

$$$$
HOTEL

🖼 **Glacier Park Lodge.** Just east of the park, across from the Amtrak station, this beautiful full-service hotel built in 1913 is supported by 500- to 800-year-old fir and 3-foot-thick cedar logs. **Pros:** golf course; scenic location; lots of activities. **Cons:** small bathrooms; no elevator; no air-conditioning. $ *Rooms from: $202* ✉ *Off U.S. 2, East Glacier* ☎ *406/892–2525, 406/226–9311* ⊕ *www.glacierparkinc.com* ☉ *Closed late Sept.–May* ⇝ *161 rooms* ⦿ *No meals.*

$$$$
B&B/INN

🖼 **Great Bear Inn.** This cozy inn has a wraparound deck that provides wonderful mountain views; inside is a comfortable lounge area where guests can relax and mingle. **Pros:** intimate lodge; room rate includes breakfast; close to West Glacier; complimentary laundry facilities. **Cons:** isolated location; cannot accommodate walk-in guests; can be tricky to find. $ *Rooms from: $230* ✉ *5672 Blankenship Rd., West Glacier* ☎ *406/250–4577* ⊕ *www.thegreatbearinn.com* ⇝ *9 rooms, 2 cabins* ⦿ *Breakfast.*

$$$
HOTEL

🖼 **Izaak Walton Inn.** This historic railway lodge just south of Glacier National Park is popular with railway buffs: originally built to house railway workers, it is decorated with railroad memorabilia. **Pros:** good location between East and West Glacier; open year-round; fun railway theme. **Cons:** train noise can be a problem; no phones or TVs in rooms; no cell-phone access; Wi-Fi signal not always strong. $ *Rooms from: $159* ✉ *290 Izaak Walton Inn Rd., off U.S. 2, Essex* ☎ *406/888–5700, 406/888–5200* ⊕ *www.izaakwaltoninn.com* ⇝ *33 rooms, 9 cottages, 6 cabins* ⦿ *No meals.*

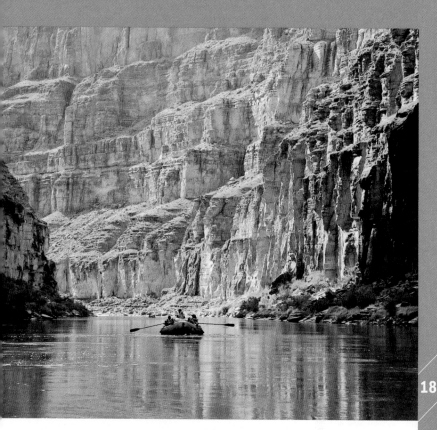

GRAND CANYON
NATIONAL PARK

WELCOME TO GRAND CANYON NATIONAL PARK

TOP REASONS TO GO

★ **Its iconic status:** This is one of those places where you really want to say, "Been there, done that!"

★ **Awesome vistas:** Painted Desert, sandstone canyon walls, pine and fir forests, mesas, plateaus, volcanic features, the Colorado River, streams, and waterfalls make for some jaw-dropping moments.

★ **Year-round adventure:** Outdoor junkies can bike, boat, camp, fish, hike, ride mules, white-water raft, watch birds and wildlife, cross-country ski, and snowshoe.

★ **Continuing education:** Adults and kids can have fun learning, thanks to free park-sponsored nature walks and interpretive programs.

★ **Sky-high and river-low experiences:** Experience the canyon via plane, train, and automobile, as well as by helicopter, row- or motorboat, bike, mule, or foot.

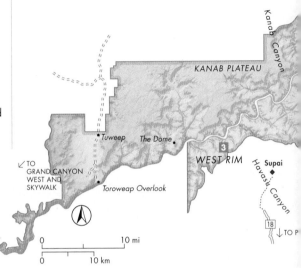

1 South Rim. The South Rim is where the action is: Grand Canyon Village's lodging, camping, eateries, stores, and museums, plus plenty of trailheads into the canyon. Visitor services and facilities are open and available daily, including holidays. Four free shuttle routes cover more than 35 stops, and visitors who'd rather relax than rough it can treat themselves to comfy hotel rooms and elegant restaurant meals (lodging and camping reservations are essential).

2 North Rim. Of the nearly 5 million people who visit the park annually, 90% enter at the South Rim, but many consider the North Rim even more gorgeous—and worth the extra effort. Open only from mid-May to the end of October (or the first good snowfall), the North Rim has legitimate bragging rights: at more than 8,000 feet above sea level (1,000 feet higher than the South Rim), it has precious solitude and seven developed viewpoints. Rather than staring into the canyon's depths, you get a true sense of its expanse.

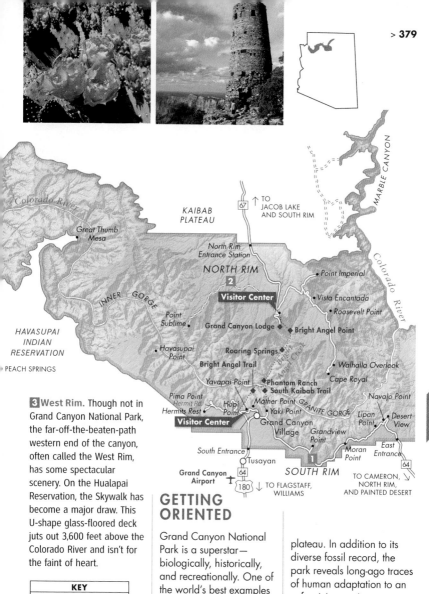

KAIBAB PLATEAU

↑ TO JACOB LAKE AND SOUTH RIM

North Rim Entrance Station

NORTH RIM

Visitor Center

Point Sublime

Grand Canyon Lodge

Havasupai Point

Roaring Springs

Bright Angel Trail

Yavapai Point

Point Imperial

Vista Encantada

Roosevelt Point

Bright Angel Point

Walhalla Overlook

Cape Royal

Phantom Ranch

South Kaibab Trail

HAVASUPAI INDIAN RESERVATION

▸ PEACH SPRINGS

Great Thumb Mesa

Colorado River

INNER GORGE

MARBLE CANYON

Colorado River

Pima Point
Hermit Rd.
Hermits Rest

Hopi Point

Mather Point

Yaki Point

GRANITE GORGE

Navajo Point

Lipan Point

Desert View

Visitor Center

Grand Canyon Village

Grandview Point

Moran Point

East Entrance

South Entrance

Tusayan

Grand Canyon Airport

SOUTH RIM

↓ TO FLAGSTAFF, WILLIAMS

TO CAMERON, NORTH RIM, AND PAINTED DESERT

18

3 West Rim. Though not in Grand Canyon National Park, the far-off-the-beaten-path western end of the canyon, often called the West Rim, has some spectacular scenery. On the Hualapai Reservation, the Skywalk has become a major draw. This U-shape glass-floored deck juts out 3,600 feet above the Colorado River and isn't for the faint of heart.

KEY

👥	Ranger Station
⛺	Campground
🧺	Picnic Area
🍴	Restaurant
🏨	Lodge
🚶	Trailhead
🚻	Restrooms
⚜	Scenic Viewpoint
⋯⋯	Walking/Hiking Trails

GETTING ORIENTED

Grand Canyon National Park is a superstar—biologically, historically, and recreationally. One of the world's best examples of arid-land erosion, the canyon provides a record of three of the four eras of geological time. Almost 2 billion years' worth of Earth's history is written in the colored layers of rock stacked from the river bottom to the top of the plateau. In addition to its diverse fossil record, the park reveals long-ago traces of human adaptation to an unforgiving environment. It's also home to several major ecosystems, five of the world's seven life zones, three of North America's four desert types, and all kinds of rare, endemic, and protected plant and animal species.

Updated by
Mara Levin
and Elise Riley

When it comes to the Grand Canyon, there are statistics and there are sensations. While the former are impressive—the canyon measures in at an average width of 10 miles, length of 277 river miles, and depth of 1 mile—they don't truly prepare you for that first impression. Seeing the canyon for the first time is an astounding experience—one that's hard to wrap your head around. In fact, it's more than an experience, it's an emotion, one that's only just beginning to be captured with the superlative "Grand." Hike or ride a trusty mule down into the canyon, bike or ramble along its rim, fly over, or raft through on the Colorado River—there are manifold ways to soak up the canyon's magnificence.

Roughly 5 million visitors come to the park each year. You can access the canyon via two main points—the South Rim and the North Rim—but the South Rim is much easier to get to and therefore much more visited. The width from the North Rim to the South Rim varies from 600 feet to 18 miles, but traveling between rims by road requires a 215-mile drive. Hiking arduous trails from rim to rim is a steep and strenuous trek of at least 21 miles, but it's well worth the effort. You'll travel through five of North America's seven life zones. (To do this any other way, you'd have to journey from the Mexican desert to the Canadian woods.) West of Grand Canyon National Park, the tribal lands of the Hualapai and the Havasupai lie along the so-called West Rim of the canyon.

GRAND CANYON PLANNER

WHEN TO GO

There's no bad time to visit the canyon, though the busiest times of year are summer and spring break. Visiting during these peak seasons, as well as holidays, requires patience and a tolerance for crowds. Note that weather changes on a whim in this exposed high-desert region. The North Rim shuts down mid-October through mid-May due to weather conditions and related road closures.

AVG. HIGH/LOW TEMPS.
South Rim

Jan.	Feb.	Mar.	Apr.	May	June
41/18	45/21	51/25	60/32	70/39	81/47
July	Aug.	Sept.	Oct.	Nov.	Dec.
84/54	82/53	76/47	65/36	52/27	43/20

North Rim

Jan.	Feb.	Mar.	Apr.	May	June
37/16	39/18	44/21	53/29	62/34	73/40
July	Aug.	Sept.	Oct.	Nov.	Dec.
77/46	75/45	69/39	59/31	46/24	40/20

Inner Canyon

Jan.	Feb.	Mar.	Apr.	May	June
56/36	62/42	71/48	82/56	92/63	101/72
July	Aug.	Sept.	Oct.	Nov.	Dec.
106/78	103/75	97/69	84/58	68/46	57/37

FESTIVALS AND EVENTS

AUGUST **Grand Canyon Music Festival.** For three weekends in late August–early September, this festival brings mostly chamber music to the Shrine of Ages amphitheater at Grand Canyon Village. In the early 1980s, music aficionados Robert Bonfiglio and Clare Hoffman hiked through the Grand Canyon and decided the stunning spectacle should be accompanied by the strains of a symphony. One of the park rangers agreed, and the wandering musicians performed an impromptu concert. Encouraged by the experience, Bonfiglio and Hoffman started the festival. ☎ *928/638–9215, 800/997–8285* ⊕ *www.grandcanyonmusicfest.org.*

DECEMBER **Mountain Village Holiday.** The city of Williams hails the winter holidays with a parade of lights, holiday decorations downtown, and live entertainment from early December to early January. ☎ *928/635–1418* ⊕ *www.experiencewilliams.com.*

18

PLANNING YOUR TIME

Plan ahead: Mule rides require at least a six-month advance reservation, and longer for the busy season (most can be reserved up to 13 months in advance). Multiday rafting trips should be reserved at least a year in advance.

The park is most crowded on the South Rim, especially near the south entrance and in Grand Canyon Village, as well as on the scenic drives, particularly the 23-mile Desert View Drive.

THE SOUTH RIM IN ONE DAY

Start early, pack a picnic lunch, and drive to the South Rim's **Grand Canyon Visitor Center,** just north of the south entrance, to pick up info and see your first incredible view at **Mather Point.** Continue east along **Desert View Drive** for about 2 miles to **Yaki Point.** Next, continue driving 7 miles east to **Grandview Point** for a good view of the buttes Krishna Shrine and Vishnu Temple. Go 4 miles east and catch the view at **Moran Point,** then 3 miles to the **Tusayan Ruin and Museum,** where a small display is devoted to the history of the Ancestral Puebloans. Continue another mile east to **Lipan Point** to view the Colorado River. In less than a mile, you'll arrive at **Navajo Point,** the highest elevation on the South Rim. **Desert View and Watchtower** is the final attraction along Desert View Drive.

On your return drive, stop off at any of the picnic areas for lunch. Once back at Grand Canyon Village, walk the paved **Rim Trail** to **Maricopa Point.** Along the way, pick up souvenirs in the village and stop at historic **El Tovar Hotel** for dinner (be sure to make reservations well in advance). If you have time, take the shuttle on **Hermit Road** to **Hermits Rest,** 7 miles away. Along that route, Hopi Point and Powell Point are excellent spots to watch the sunset.

GRAND CANYON IN 3 DAYS

On Day 1, follow the one-day itinerary for the morning, but spend more time exploring Desert View Drive and enjoy a leisurely picnic lunch. Later, drive 30 miles beyond Desert View to **Cameron Trading Post,** which has a good restaurant and is an interesting side trip. Travel Hermit Road on your second morning, and drive to Grand Canyon Airport for a late-morning small-plane or helicopter tour. Have lunch in **Tusayan** and cool off at the IMAX film *Grand Canyon: The Hidden Secrets.* Back in the village, take a ranger-led program. On your third day, hike partway down the canyon on **Bright Angel Trail.** It takes twice as long to hike back up, so plan accordingly. Get trail maps at **Grand Canyon Visitor Center,** and bring plenty of water.

Alternatively, spend Days 2 and 3 exploring the remote **West Rim,** 150 miles toward Nevada or California and far away from major highways. Fill the first day with a horseback ride along the rim, a helicopter ride into the canyon, or a pontoon boat ride on the Colorado River. The next day, raft the Class V–VII rapids. Another option is to get a tribal permit and spend Days 2 and 3 in **Havasu Canyon,** a truly spiritual backcountry experience. You can opt to hike, ride horseback, or take a helicopter 8 miles down to the small village of Supai and the Havasupai Lodge.

Tips for Avoiding Grand Canyon Crowds

It's hard to commune with nature while you're searching for a parking place, dodging video cameras, and stepping away from strollers. However, this scenario is likely only during the peak summer months. One option is to bypass Grand Canyon National Park altogether and head to the West Rim of the canyon, tribal land of the Hualapai and Havasupai. If only the park itself will do, the following tips will help you to keep your distance and your cool.

TAKE ANOTHER ROUTE

Avoid road rage by choosing a different route to the South Rim, forgoing traditional Highway 64 and U.S. 180 from Flagstaff. Take U.S. 89 north from Flagstaff instead, passing near Sunset Crater and Wupatki national monuments. When you reach the junction with Highway 64, take a break at Cameron Trading Post (1 mile north of the junction)—or stay overnight. This is a good place to shop for Native American artifacts, souvenirs, and the usual postcards, dream-catchers, recordings, and T-shirts. There are also high-quality Navajo rugs, jewelry, and other authentic handicrafts, and you can sample Navajo tacos. U.S. 64 to the west takes you directly to the park's east entrance; the scenery along the Little Colorado River gorge en route is eye-popping. It's 23 miles from the east entrance to the visitor center at Grand Canyon Visitor Center.

EXPLORE THE NORTH RIM

Although the North Rim is just 10 miles across from the South Rim, the trip to get there by car is a five-hour drive of 215 miles. At first it might not sound like the trip would be worth it, but the payoff is huge. Along the way, you'll travel through some of the prettiest parts of the state and be granted even more stunning views than those on the more easily accessible South Rim. Those who make the North Rim trip often insist it has the canyon's most beautiful views and best hiking. To get to the North Rim from Flagstaff, take U.S. 89 north past Cameron, turning left onto U.S. 89A at Bitter Springs. En route you'll pass the area known as Vermilion Cliffs. At Jacob Lake, take Highway 67 directly to the Grand Canyon North Rim. North Rim services are closed from November through mid-May because of heavy snow, but in summer months and early fall, it's a wonderful way to beat the crowds at the South Rim.

18

GETTING HERE AND AROUND
SOUTH RIM

AIR TRAVEL Several carriers fly from North Las Vegas Airport to the **Grand Canyon National Park Airport** in Tusayan (GCN ☎ 928/638–2446) including Grand Canyon Express (☎ 800/940–2550 ⊕ www.scenic.com), and Vision Holidays (☎ 702/261–3850 ⊕ www.visionholidays.com).

CAR TRAVEL The best route into the park from the east or south is from Flagstaff. Take U.S. 180 northwest to the park's southern entrance and Grand Canyon Village. From the west on Interstate 40, the most direct route to the South Rim is taking Highway 64 from Williams to U.S. 180.

PARK SHUTTLE TRAVEL   The South Rim is open to car traffic year-round, though access to Hermits Rest is limited to shuttle buses part of the year. There are four free shuttle routes: The **Hermits Rest Route** operates March through November, between Grand Canyon Village and Hermits Rest. The **Village Route** operates year-round in the village area, stopping at lodgings, the general store, and the Grand Canyon Visitor Center. The **Kaibab Rim Route** goes from the visitor center to five viewpoints, including the Yavapai Geology Museum and Yaki Point (where cars are not permitted). The **Hiker's Express** shuttles hikers from the village to the South Kaibab Trailhead each morning. ■ TIP→ **In summer, South Rim roads are congested, and it's easier, and sometimes required, to park your car and take the free shuttle.** Running from one hour before sunrise until one hour after sunset, shuttles arrive every 15 to 30 minutes at 30 clearly marked stops.

TAXI AND SHUTTLE TRAVEL   Although there's no public transportation into the Grand Canyon, you can hire a taxi to take you to or from the Grand Canyon Airport or any of the Tusayan hotels.

TRAIN TRAVEL   **Grand Canyon Railway.** There's no need to deal with all of the other drivers racing to the South Rim. Sit back and relax in the comfy train cars of the Grand Canyon Railway. Live music and storytelling enliven the trip as you journey past the landscape through prairie, ranch, and national park land to the log-cabin train station in Grand Canyon Village. You won't see the Grand Canyon from the train, but you can walk (¼ mile) or catch the shuttle at the restored, historic Grand Canyon Railway Station. The vintage train departs from the Williams Depot every morning and makes the 65-mile journey in 2¼ hours. You can do the round-trip in a single day; however, it's a more relaxing and enjoyable strategy to stay for a night or two at the South Rim before returning to Williams. ☎ 800/843–8724 ⊕ www.thetrain. com ✉ $70–$178 round-trip ☞ Rates include $8 park entry fee but not tax. Add-ons, like snacks, increase your fare.

NORTH RIM

AIR TRAVEL   The nearest airport to the North Rim is **St. George Municipal Airport** (☎ 435/627–4080 ⊕ www.flysgu.com) in Utah, 164 miles north, with regular service provided by both Delta and United Airlines.

CAR TRAVEL   To reach the North Rim by car, take U.S. 89 north from Flagstaff past Cameron, turning left onto U.S. 89A at Bitter Springs. At Jacob Lake, take Highway 67 directly to the Grand Canyon North Rim. You can drive yourself to the scenic viewpoints and trailheads; the only transportation offered in the Park is a shuttle twice each morning that brings eager hikers from Grand Canyon Lodge to the North Kaibab Trailhead (a 2-mile trip). Note that services on the North Rim shut down in mid-October, and the road closes after the first major snowfall (usually the end of October); Highway 67 south of Jacob Lake is closed.

SHUTTLE TRAVEL   From mid-May to mid-October, the **Trans Canyon Shuttle** (☎ 928/638–2820 ⊕ www.trans-canyonshuttle.com) travels daily between the South and North rims—the ride takes 4½ hours each way. One-way fare is $85, round-trip $160. Reservations are required.

PARK ESSENTIALS
PARK FEES AND PERMITS

A fee of $30 per vehicle or $15 per person for pedestrians and cyclists is good for one week's access at both rims.

The $50 Grand Canyon Pass gives unlimited access to the park for 12 months.

No permits are needed for day hikers; but **backcountry permits** (☎ *928/638–7875* ⊕ *www.nps.gov/grca $10, plus $8 per person per night*) are necessary for overnight hikers camping below the rim. Permits are limited, so make your reservation as far in advance as possible—they're taken by fax (☎ *928/638–2125*), by mail (1824 S. Thompson St., Suite 201, Flagstaff, AZ 86001), or in person at the Backcountry Information centers (in the village on the South Rim and near the visitor center on the North Rim) up to four months ahead of arrival. **Camping** in the park is restricted to designated campgrounds (☎ *877/444–6777* ⊕ *www.recreation.gov*).

PARK HOURS

The South Rim is open continuously every day of the year (weather permitting), while the North Rim is open mid-May through October. The park is in the Mountain Standard time zone year-round. Daylight saving time isn't observed.

CELL-PHONE RECEPTION

Cell-phone coverage can be spotty at both the South Rim and North Rim—though Verizon customers report better reception at the South Rim. Don't expect a strong signal anywhere in the park.

EDUCATIONAL OFFERINGS
RANGER PROGRAMS

SOUTH RIM **Interpretive Ranger Programs.** The National Park Service sponsors all sorts of orientation activities, such as daily guided hikes and talks, which change with the seasons. The focus may be on any aspect of the canyon—from geology and flora and fauna to history and early inhabitants. For schedules on the South Rim, go to any of the Grand Canyon visitor centers, pick up a free copy of the *Guide,* or check online. ☎ *928/638–7888* ⊕ *www.nps.gov/grca* ✉ *Free.*

FAMILY **Junior Ranger Program for Families.** The Junior Ranger Program provides a free, fun way to look at the cultural and natural history of this sublime destination. These hands-on educational activities for children ages four and up, available at the visitor centers, include guided adventure hikes, ranger-led "discovery" talks, and book readings. ☎ *928/638–7888* ⊕ *www.nps.gov/grca/forkids/beajuniorranger.htm* ✉ *Free.*

NORTH RIM **Discovery Pack Junior Ranger Program.** In summer, children ages four and
FAMILY up can take part in hands-on educational programs and earn a Junior Ranger certificate and badge. Sign up at the North Rim Visitor Center for these independent and ranger-led activities. ☎ *928/638–7967* ⊕ *www.nps.gov/grca* ✉ *Free.*

Interpretive Ranger Programs. Daily guided hikes and talks may focus on any aspect of the canyon—from geology and flora and fauna to history and the canyon's early inhabitants. For schedules, go to the

18

Grand Canyon Lodge or pick up a free copy of *The Guide to the North Rim* from the park visitor center. ☎ 928/638–7967 ⊕ *www.nps.gov/ grca* ☜ *Free.*

RESTAURANTS

Within the park on the South Rim, you can find everything from cafeteria food to casual café fare to creatively prepared, Western- and Southwestern-inspired American cuisine—there's even a coffeehouse with organic joe. Reservations are accepted (and recommended) only for dinner at El Tovar Dining Room; they can be made up to six months in advance with El Tovar room reservations, 30 days in advance without. You should also make dinner reservations at the Grand Canyon Lodge Dining Room on the North Rim—as the only "upscale" dining option, the restaurant fills up quickly at dinner throughout the season (the two other choices on the North Rim are a cafeteria and a chuck-wagon-style Grand Cookout experience). The dress code is casual across the board, but El Tovar is your best option if you're looking to dress up a bit and thumb through an extensive wine list. Drinking water and restrooms aren't available at most picnic spots.

Eateries outside the park generally range from mediocre to terrible—you didn't come all the way to the Grand Canyon for the food, did you? Our selections highlight your best options. Of towns near the park, Williams definitely has the leg up on culinary variety and quality, with Tusayan (near the South Rim) and Jacob Lake (the closest town to the North Rim) offering mostly either fast food or merely adequate sit-down restaurants. Near the park, even the priciest places welcome casual dress. On the Hualapai and Havasupai reservations in Havasu Canyon and on the West Rim, dining is limited and basic.

HOTELS

The park's accommodations include three "historic-rustic" facilities and four motel-style lodges, all of which have undergone significant upgrades over the past decade. Of the 922 rooms, cabins, and suites, only 203 are at the North Rim, all at the Grand Canyon Lodge. Outside El Tovar Hotel, the canyon's architectural highlight, accommodations are relatively basic but comfortable, and the most sought-after rooms have canyon views. Rates vary widely, but most rooms fall in the $100 to $180 range, though the most basic units at the South Rim go for just $89.

Reservations are a must, especially during the busy summer season. ■TIP→ **If you want to get your first choice (especially Bright Angel Lodge or El Tovar), make reservations as far in advance as possible; they're taken up to 13 months ahead. You might find a last-minute cancellation, but you shouldn't count on it.** Although lodging at the South Rim will keep you close to the action, the frenetic activity and crowded facilities are off-putting to some. With short notice, the best time to find a room on the South Rim is in winter. And though the North Rim is less crowded than the South Rim, the only lodging available is at Grand Canyon Lodge.

Just south of the South Rim park boundary, Tusayan's hotels are in a convenient location but without bargains, while Williams (about an hour's drive) can provide price breaks on food and lodging, as well as a respite from the crowds. Extra amenities (e.g., swimming pools and gyms) are also more abundant. Reservations are always a good idea. At Grand Canyon West, lodging options are extremely limited; you can purchase a "package," which includes lodging and a visitation permit, through Hualapai Tourism.

Hotel reviews have been shortened. For full information, visit Fodors.com.

Lodging Contacts Xanterra Parks & Resorts. ☎ *888/297-2757*
⊕ *www.grandcanyonlodges.com.*

WHAT IT COSTS			
$	**$$**	**$$$**	**$$$$**
Restaurants	under $12	$12–$20	$21–$30	over $30
Hotels	under $101	$101–$175	$176–$250	over $250

Restaurant prices are the average cost of a main course at dinner or, if dinner is not served, at lunch. Hotel prices are the lowest cost of a standard double room in high season, excluding taxes and service charges.

TOURS

Grand Canyon Field Institute. Instructors lead guided educational tours, hikes around the canyon, and weekend programs at the South Rim. With more than 200 classes a year, tour topics include everything from archaeology and backcountry medicine to photography and natural history. Contact GCFI for a schedule and price list. Private hikes can be arranged. Discounted classes are available for members; annual dues are $35. ⊠ *GCA Warehouse, 2-B Albright Ave., Grand Canyon Village* ☎ *928/638–2841, 866/471–4435* ⊕ *www.grandcanyon.org/fieldinstitute* ⊠ *From $235.*

Xanterra Motorcoach Tours. Narrated by knowledgeable guides, tours include the Hermits Rest Tour, which travels along the old wagon road built by the Santa Fe Railway; the Desert View Tour, which glimpses the Colorado River's rapids and stops at Lipan Point; Sunrise and Sunset Tours; and combination tours. Children 16 and younger are free when accompanied by a paying adult. ☎ *303/297-2757, 888/297-2757* ⊕ *www.grandcanyonlodges.com* ⊠ *From $22.*

VISITOR INFORMATION
PARK CONTACT INFORMATION
Grand Canyon National Park. Before you go into the park, get the complimentary *Trip Planner,* updated regularly, from the Grand Canyon National Park. At the main visitor center, pick up a copy of the *Guide,* a weekly listing of ranger talks and other park activities. ☎ *928/638-7888* ⊕ *www.nps.gov/grca.*

SOUTH RIM VISITOR CENTERS
Desert View Information Center. Near the watchtower, at Desert View Point, this nonprofit Grand Canyon Association store and information center has a nice selection of books, park pamphlets, gifts, and educational materials. It's also a handy place to pick up maps and info if you enter the park at the Eastern entrance. All sales from the Association

18

stores go to support the park programs. ⊠ *Eastern entrance, Grand Canyon National Park* ☏ *800/858–2808, 928/638–7888* ☉ *Daily 9–5; hrs vary in winter.*

Grand Canyon Verkamp's Visitor Center. This small visitor center is named for the Verkamp family, who operated a curios shop on the South Rim for more than a hundred years. The building serves as an official visitor center, ranger station (get your Junior Ranger badges here), bookstore, and museum, with compelling exhibits on the Verkamps and other pioneers in this region. ⊠ *Desert View Dr. across from El Tovar Hotel, Grand Canyon Village* ☏ *928/638–7146* ☉ *Daily 8–7; ranger station 8–5.*

Grand Canyon Visitor Center. The park's main orientation center provides pamphlets and resources to help plan your visit. It also holds engaging interpretive exhibits on the park. Rangers are on hand to answer questions and aid in planning canyon excursions. A daily schedule of ranger-led hikes and evening lectures is posted on a bulletin board inside, and a 20-minute film about the history, geology, and wildlife of the canyon plays every 30 minutes in the theater. The bicycle rental office, a small café, and a huge gift store are also in this complex. There's ample parking by the information center; from here, it's a short walk out to Mather Point, or a short ride on the shuttle bus, which can take you into Grand Canyon Village. The visitor center is also accessible via a leisurely 1-mile walk on the Greenway Trail, a paved pathway that meanders through the forest. ⊠ *East side of Grand Canyon Village, 450 Hwy. 64* ☏ *928/638–7888* ⊕ *www.explorethecanyon.com* ☉ *Daily 9–5, outdoor exhibits may be viewed anytime.*

Yavapai Geology Museum. Learn about the geology of the canyon at this Grand Canyon Association museum and bookstore. You can also catch the park shuttle bus or pick up information for the Rim Trail here. The views of the canyon and Phantom Ranch from inside this historic building are stupendous. ⊠ *1 mile east of Market Plaza, Grand Canyon Village* ☏ *928/638–7888* ☉ *Daily 8–6.*

NORTH RIM VISITOR CENTER
North Rim Visitor Center. View exhibits, peruse the bookstore, and pick up useful maps and brochures at this visitor center. Interpretive programs are often scheduled in summer. If you're craving coffee, it's a short walk from here to the Roughrider Saloon at the Grand Canyon Lodge. ⊠ *Near parking lot on Bright Angel Peninsula, Grand Canyon National Park* ☏ *928/638–7864* ⊕ *www.nps.gov/grca* ☉ *Mid-May–mid-Oct., daily 8–6.*

GRAND CANYON SOUTH RIM

EXPLORING

Visitors to the canyon converge mostly on the South Rim, and mostly in summer. Grand Canyon Village is here, with a majority of the park's lodging and camping, trailheads, restaurants, stores, and museums, along with a nearby airport and railroad depot. Believe it or not, the average stay in the park is a mere half day or so; this is not advised! You need to spend several days to truly appreciate this marvelous place, but at the very least, give it a full day. Hike down into the canyon, or along the rim, to get away from the crowds and experience nature at its finest.

SCENIC DRIVES

Desert View Drive. This heavily traveled 23-mile stretch of road follows the rim from the east entrance to Grand Canyon Village. Starting from the less-congested entry near Desert View, road warriors can get their first glimpse of the canyon from the 70-foot-tall watchtower, the top of which provides the highest viewpoint on the South Rim. Eight overlooks, the remains of an Ancestral Puebloan dwelling at the Tusayan Ruin and Museum, and the secluded and lovely Buggeln picnic area make for great stops along the South Rim. The Kaibab Trail Route shuttle bus travels a short section of Desert View Drive and takes 50 minutes to ride round-trip without getting off at any of the stops: Grand Canyon Visitor Center, South Kaibab Trailhead, Yaki Point, Pipe Creek Vista, Mather Point, and Yavapai Geology Museum. ⊠ *Grand Canyon National Park.*

Hermit Road. The Santa Fe Company built Hermit Road, formerly known as West Rim Drive, in 1912 as a scenic tour route. Nine overlooks dot this 7-mile stretch, each worth a visit. The road is filled with hairpin turns, so make sure you adhere to posted speed limits. A 1.5-mile Greenway trail offers easy access to cyclists looking to enjoy the original 1912 Hermit Rim Road. From March through November, Hermit Road is closed to private auto traffic because of congestion; during this period, a free shuttle bus carries visitors to all the overlooks. Riding the bus round-trip without getting off at any of the viewpoints takes 75 minutes; the return trip stops only at Pima, Mohave, and Powell points. ⊠ *Grand Canyon National Park.*

HISTORIC SITES

Tusayan Ruin and Museum. Completed in 1932, this museum offers a quick orientation to the lifestyles of the prehistoric and modern Indian populations associated with the Grand Canyon and the Colorado Plateau. Adjacent, an excavation of an 800-year-old dwelling gives a glimpse of the lives of some of the area's earliest residents. Of special interest are split-twig figurines dating back 2,000 to 4,000 years ago, a replica of a 10,000-year-old spear point, and other artifacts left behind by ancient cultures. A ranger leads twice-daily interpretive tours of the Ancestral Puebloan village along a 0.1-mile paved loop trail. ⊕ *About 20 miles east of Grand Canyon Village on E. Rim Dr.* ☎ *928/638–7888* ⊠ *Free* ☉ *Daily 9–5.*

SCENIC STOPS

The Abyss. At an elevation of 6,720 feet, the Abyss is one of the most awesome stops on Hermit Road, revealing a sheer drop of 3,000 feet to the Tonto Platform, a wide terrace of Tapeats sandstone about two-thirds of the way down the canyon. From the Abyss you'll also see several isolated sandstone columns, the largest of which is called the Monument. ⊕ *About 5 miles west of Hermit Rd. Junction on Hermit Rd.*

18

Desert View and Watchtower. From the top of the 70-foot stone-and-mortar watchtower, even the muted hues of the distant Painted Desert to the east and the Vermilion Cliffs rising from a high plateau near the Utah border are visible. In the chasm below, angling to the north toward Marble Canyon, an imposing stretch of the Colorado River reveals itself. Up several flights of stairs, the watchtower houses a glass-enclosed observatory with powerful telescopes. ⊕ *About 23 miles east of Grand Canyon Village on Desert View Dr.* ☎ *928/638–2736* ☽ *Daily 8–8; hrs vary in winter.*

Grandview Point. At an elevation of 7,399 feet, the view from here is one of the finest in the canyon. To the northeast is a group of dominant buttes, including Krishna Shrine, Vishnu Temple, Rama Shrine, and Sheba Temple. A short stretch of the Colorado River is also visible. Directly below the point, and accessible by the steep and rugged Grandview Trail, is Horseshoe Mesa, where you can see remnants of Last Chance Copper Mine. ⊕ *About 12 miles east of Grand Canyon Village on Desert View Dr.*

Hermits Rest. This westernmost viewpoint and Hermit Trail, which descends from it, were named for "hermit" Louis Boucher, a 19th-century French-Canadian prospector who had a number of mining claims and a roughly built home down in the canyon. The trail served as the original mule ride down to Hermit Camp beginning in 1914. Views from here include Hermit Rapids and the towering cliffs of the Supai and Redwall formations. You can buy curios and snacks in the stone building at Hermits Rest. ⊕ *About 8 miles west of Hermit Rd. Junction on Hermit Rd.*

Fodor's Choice ★
Hopi Point. From this elevation of 6,800 feet, you can see a large section of the Colorado River; although it appears as a thin line, the river is nearly 350 feet wide. The overlook extends farther into the canyon than any other point on Hermit Road. The unobstructed views make this a popular place to watch the sunset.

Across the canyon to the north is Shiva Temple, which remained an unexplored section of the Kaibab Plateau until 1937. That year, Harold Anthony of the American Museum of Natural History led an expedition to the rock formation in the belief that it supported life that had been cut off from the rest of the canyon. Imagine the expedition members' surprise when they found an empty Kodak film box on top of the temple—it had been left behind by Emery Kolb, who felt slighted for not having been invited to join Anthony's tour.

Directly below Hopi Point lies Dana Butte, named for a prominent 19th-century geologist. In 1919, an entrepreneur proposed connecting Hopi Point, Dana Butte, and the Tower of Set across the river with an aerial tramway, a technically feasible plan that fortunately has not been realized. ⊕ *About 4 miles west of Hermit Rd. Junction on Hermit Rd.*

Lipan Point. Here, at the canyon's widest point, you can get an astonishing visual profile of the gorge's geologic history, with a view of every eroded layer of the canyon and one of the longest visible stretches of Colorado River. The spacious panorama stretches to the Vermilion Cliffs on the northeastern horizon and features a multitude of imaginatively

Plants and Wildlife in the Grand Canyon

Eighty-nine mammal species inhabit Grand Canyon National Park, as well as 355 species of birds, 56 kinds of reptiles and amphibians, and 17 kinds of fish. The rare Kaibab squirrel is found only on the North Rim—you can recognize them by their all-white tails and black undersides. The pink Grand Canyon rattlesnake lives at lower elevations within the canyon. Hawks and ravens are visible year-round. The endangered California condor has been reintroduced to the canyon region. Park rangers give daily talks on the magnificent birds, whose wingspan measures 9 feet. In spring, summer, and fall, mule deer, recognizable by their large ears, are abundant at the South Rim. Don't be fooled by gentle appearances; these guys can be aggressive. It's illegal to feed them, as it'll disrupt their natural habitats, and increase your risk of getting bitten or kicked.

The best times to see wildlife are early in the morning and late in the afternoon. Look for out-of-place shapes and motions, keeping in mind that animals occupy all layers in a natural habitat and not just at your eye level. Use binoculars for close-up views. While out and about try to fade into the woodwork by keeping your movements limited and noise at a minimum.

More than 1,700 species of plants color the park. The South Rim's Coconino Plateau is fairly flat, at an elevation of about 7,000 feet, and covered with stands of pinyon and ponderosa pines, junipers, and Gambel's oak trees. On the Kaibab Plateau on the North Rim, Douglas fir, spruce, quaking aspen, and more ponderosas prevail. In spring you're likely to see asters, sunflowers, and lupine in bloom at both rims.

18

---

named spires, buttes, and temples—intriguing rock formations named after their resemblance to ancient pyramids. You can also see Unkar Delta, where a creek joins the Colorado to form powerful rapids and a broad beach. Ancestral Puebloan farmers worked the Unkar Delta for hundreds of years, growing corn, beans, and melons. ✣ *About 25 miles east of Grand Canyon Village on Desert View Dr.*

FodorsChoice **Mather Point.** You'll likely get your first glimpse of the canyon from
★ this viewpoint, one of the most impressive and accessible (next to the main visitor center plaza) on the South Rim. Named for the National Park Service's first director, Stephen Mather, this spot yields extraordinary views of the Grand Canyon, including deep into the inner gorge and numerous buttes: Wotans Throne, Brahma Temple, and Zoroaster Temple, among others. The Grand Canyon Lodge, on the North Rim, is almost directly north from Mather Point and only 10 miles away—yet you have to drive 215 miles to get from one spot to the other. ✉ *Near Grand Canyon Visitor Center, Grand Canyon National Park* ☎ *928/638-7888* ⊕ *www.nps.gov/grca.*

Moran Point. This point was named for American landscape artist Thomas Moran, who was especially fond of the play of light and shadows from this location. He first visited the canyon with John Wesley Powell in 1873. "Thomas Moran's name, more than any other, with the

BEST GRAND CANYON VIEWS

The best time of day to see the canyon is before 10 and after 4, when the angle of the sun brings out the colors of the rock, and clouds and shadows add dimension. Colors deepen dramatically among the contrasting layers of the canyon walls just before and during sunrise and sunset.

Hopi Point is the top spot on the South Rim to watch the sun set; **Yaki** and **Pima** points also offer vivid views. For a grand sunrise, try **Mather** or **Yaki** points.

■TIP→ Arrive at least 30 minutes early for sunrise views and as much as 90 minutes for sunset views at these points. For another point of view, take a leisurely stroll along the Rim Trail and watch the color change along with the views. Timetables are listed in the *Guide* and are posted at park visitor centers.

possible exception of Major Powell's, is to be associated with the Grand Canyon," wrote noted canyon photographer Ellsworth Kolb. It's fitting that Moran Point is a favorite spot of photographers and painters. ✛ *About 17 miles east of Grand Canyon Village on Desert View Dr.*

Trailview Overlook. Look down on a dramatic view of the Bright Angel and Plateau Point trails as they zigzag down the canyon. In the deep gorge to the north flows Bright Angel Creek, one of the region's few permanent tributary streams of the Colorado River. Toward the south is an unobstructed view of the distant San Francisco Peaks, as well as Bill Williams Mountain (on the horizon) and Red Butte (about 15 miles south of the canyon rim). ✛ *About 2 miles west of Hermit Rd. Junction on Hermit Rd.*

Yaki Point. Stop here for an exceptional view of Wotans Throne, a flat-top butte named by François Matthes, a U.S. Geological Survey scientist who developed the first topographical map of the Grand Canyon. The overlook juts out over the canyon, providing unobstructed views of inner-canyon rock formations, South Rim cliffs, and Clear Creek canyon. About a mile south of Yaki Point is the trailhead for the South Kaibab Trail. The point is one of the best places on the South Rim to watch the sunset. ✛ *2 miles east of Grand Canyon Village on Desert View Dr.*

Fodor's Choice ★ **Yavapai Point.** This is one of the best locations on the South Rim to watch the sunset. Dominated by the Yavapai Geology Museum and Observation Station, this point displays panoramic views of the mighty gorge through a wall of windows. Exhibits at the museum include videos of the canyon floor and the Colorado River, a scaled diorama of the canyon with national park boundaries, fossils and rock fragments used to re-create the complex layers of the canyon walls, and a display on the natural forces used to carve the chasm. Dig even deeper into Grand Canyon geology with free daily ranger programs. Check ahead for special events, guided walks, and program schedules. There's also a bookstore. ⊠ *Grand Canyon Village* ✛ *1 mile east of Market Plaza* 🖾 *Free* ⊙ *Museum daily 8–6.*

SPORTS AND THE OUTDOORS

AIR TOURS

Flights by plane and helicopter over the canyon are offered by a number of companies, departing from the Grand Canyon Airport at the south end of Tusayan. Though the noise and disruption of so many aircraft buzzing the canyon is controversial, flightseeing remains a popular, if expensive, option. You'll have more visibility from a helicopter but they're louder and more expensive than the fixed-wing planes. Prices and lengths of tours vary, but you can expect to pay about $169 per adult for short plane trips and approximately $179–$250 for brief helicopter tours (and about $500 for tours leaving from Vegas). These companies often have significant discounts in winter—check the company websites to find the best deals.

TOURS

Grand Canyon Airlines. This company offers a variety of plane tours, from a 50-minute fixed-wing tour of the eastern edge of the Grand Canyon, the North Rim, and the Kaibab Plateau to an all-day tour that combines flightseeing with four-wheel-drive tours and float trips on the Colorado River. They also schedule combination tours that leave from Las Vegas (plane flight from Las Vegas to Grand Canyon Airport, then helicopter flight into the canyon). ⊠ *Grand Canyon Airport, Tusayan* ☎ *928/638– 2359, 866/235–9422* ⊕ *www.grandcanyonairlines.com* ✈ *From $169.*

Maverick Helicopters. Maverick Helicopters has 25- and 45-minute tours of the South Rim, North Rim, and Dragon Corridor of the Grand Canyon. Airplane tours out of Las Vegas are also provided. A landing tour option for those flying from Las Vegas to the West Rim sets you down in the canyon for a short snack below the rim. ⊠ *Grand Canyon Airport* ☎ *928/638–2622, 800/962–3869* ⊕ *www.flymaverick.com* ✈ *From $165.*

Papillon Grand Canyon Helicopters. Leaving from Grand Canyon Airport, Papillon Grand Canyon Helicopters operates in tandem with Grand Canyon Airlines to offer combination fixed-wing and helicopter tours of the canyon. Add-on options include off-road jeep tours and smooth-water rafting trips. ⊠ *Grand Canyon Airport, Tusayan* ☎ *928/638– 2764, 888/635–7272* ⊕ *www.papillon.com* ✈ *From $124.*

HIKING

Although permits are not required for day hikes, you must have a back-country permit for longer trips (⇨ *see Park Fees and Permits at the start of this chapter*). Some of the more popular trails are listed here; more detailed information and maps can be obtained from the Back-country Information centers. Also, rangers can help design a trip to suit your abilities.

Remember that the canyon has significant elevation changes and, in summer, extreme temperature ranges, which can pose problems for people who aren't in good shape or who have heart or respiratory problems. ■TIP➔ **Carry plenty of water and energy foods.** The majority of each year's 400 search-and-rescue incidents result from hikers

18

Grand Canyon South Rim

PALISADES OF THE DESERT

Desert View and Watchtower

East Entrance

Tusayan Ruin and Museum

Cardenas Butte

Navajo Point

Lipan Point

Colorado River

TO CAMERON AND NORTH RIM

4 mi

4 km

Jupiter Temple

Venus Temple

Apollo Temple

Walhalla Overlook

Cape Royal

Cape Royal Rd.

Siegfried Pyre

WALHALLA PLATEAU

Vishnu Temple

Solomon Temple

Zuni Point

Moran Point

Hance Rapids

Horseshoe Mesa

GRANITE GORGE

Wotans Throne

Grandview Point

Hermit Trail

Desert View Dr.

North Kaibab Trailhead

North Rim Visitor Center

North Rim Lodge

Bright Angel Point

Obi Point

Brahma Temple

Zoroaster Temple

Phantom Ranch

North Kaibab Trail

Bright Angel Trail

Grapevine Rapids

Shoshone Point

South Kaibab Trail

Yaki Point

SOUTH RIM

NORTH RIM

see Grand Canyon North Rim map

Wildforss Trail

Bright Angel Trail

Isis Temple

Horn Creek Rapids

Powell Point

Maricopa Point

Yavapai Point

Mather Point

Grand Canyon Village

see Grand Canyon Village map

Bright Angel Trailhead

64

180

South Entrance

Tusayan

64

Grand Canyon Airport

TO FLAGSTAFF, WILLIAMS

Shiva Temple

Tower of Ra

Osiris Temple

Granite Rapids

Hopi Point

Mohave Point

The Abyss

Trailview Overlook

Pima Point

Hermit Road

Hermits Rest

Dripping Springs

Diana Temple

Point Sublime

Boucher Rapids

UPPER GRANITE GORGE

KEY

Ranger Station

Campground

Picnic Area

Restaurant

Lodge

underestimating the size of the canyon, hiking beyond their abilities, or not packing sufficient food and water.

■ TIP➜ **Under no circumstances should you attempt a day hike from the rim to the river and back.** Remember that when it's 80°F on the South Rim, it's 110°F on the canyon floor. Allow two to four days if you want to hike rim to rim (it's easier to descend from the North Rim, as it's more than 1,000 feet higher than the South Rim). Hiking steep trails from rim to rim is a strenuous trek of at least 21 miles and should only be attempted by experienced canyon hikers.

EASY

Fodor's Choice
★

Rim Trail. The South Rim's most popular walking path is the 12-mile (one-way) Rim Trail, which runs along the edge of the canyon from Pipe Creek Vista (the first overlook on Desert View Drive) to Hermits Rest. This walk, which is paved to Maricopa Point and for the last 1.5 miles to Hermits Rest, visits several of the South Rim's historic landmarks. Allow anywhere from 15 minutes to a full day, depending on how much of the trail you want to cover; the Rim Trail is an ideal day hike, as it varies only a few hundred feet in elevation from Mather Point (7,120 feet) to the trailhead at Hermits Rest (6,650 feet). The trail also can be accessed from several spots in Grand Canyon Village and from the major viewpoints along Hermit Road, which are serviced by shuttle buses during the busy summer months. On the Rim Trail, water is only available in the Grand Canyon Village area and at Hermits Rest. *Easy.*

MODERATE

Bright Angel Trail. This well-maintained trail is one of the most scenic hiking paths from the South Rim to the bottom of the canyon (9.6 miles each way). Rest houses are equipped with water at the 1.5- and 3-mile points from May through September, and at Indian Garden (4 miles) year-round. Water is also available at Bright Angel Campground, 9¼ miles below the trailhead. Plateau Point, on a spur trail about 1.5 miles below Indian Garden, is as far as you should attempt to go on a day hike; the round-trip will take six to nine hours.

Bright Angel Trail is the easiest of all the footpaths into the canyon, but because the climb out from the bottom is an ascent of 5,510 feet, the trip should be attempted only by those in good physical condition and should be avoided in midsummer due to extreme heat. The top of the trail can be icy in winter. Originally a bighorn sheep path and later used by the Havasupai, the trail was widened late in the 19th century for prospectors and is now used for both mule and foot traffic. Also note that mule trains have the right-of-way—and sometimes leave unpleasant surprises in your path. *Moderate.* ✣ *Trailhead: Kolb Studio, Hermit Rd.*

DIFFICULT

South Kaibab Trail. This trail starts near Yaki Point, 4 miles east of Grand Canyon Village, and is accessible via the free shuttle bus. Because the route is so steep (and sometimes icy in winter)—descending from the trailhead at 7,260 feet down to 2,480 feet at the Colorado River—and has no water, many hikers take this trail down, then ascend via the less-demanding Bright Angel Trail. Allow four to six hours to reach the Colorado River on this 6.4-mile trek. At the river, the trail crosses

18

Grand Canyon Village and The Rim Trail

KEY

🛈	Ranger Station
🔼	Campground
🅿	Picnic Area
🍴	Restaurant
🏠	Lodge

a suspension bridge and runs on to Phantom Ranch. Along the trail there is no water and little shade. There are no campgrounds, though there are portable toilets at Cedar Ridge (6,320 feet), 1.5 miles from the trailhead. An emergency phone is available at the Tipoff, 4.6 miles down the trail (3 miles past Cedar Ridge). The trail corkscrews down through some spectacular geology. Look for (but don't remove) fossils in the limestone when taking water breaks. Even though an immense network of trails winds through the Grand Canyon, the popular corridor trails (Bright Angel and South Kaibab) are recommended for hikers new to the region. *Difficult.* ⊹ *Trailhead: Yaki Point Rd., off Desert View Dr.*

MULE RIDES

Fodor's Choice ★ Mule rides provide an intimate glimpse into the canyon for those who have the time, but not the stamina, to see the canyon on foot. ■**TIP**➔ Reservations are essential and are accepted up to 13 months in advance.

These trips have been conducted since the early 1900s. A comforting fact as you ride the narrow trail: no one's ever been killed while riding a mule that fell off a cliff. (Nevertheless, the treks are not for the faint of heart or people in questionable health.)

TOURS AND OUTFITTERS

Fodor's Choice ★ **Xanterra Parks & Resorts Mule Rides.** These trips delve into the canyon from the South Rim to Phantom Ranch, or east along the canyon's edge (the Plateau Point rides were discontinued in 2009). Riders must be at least 55 inches tall, weigh less than 200 pounds (for the Phantom Ranch ride), and understand English. Children under 15 must be accompanied by an adult. Riders must be in fairly good physical condition, and pregnant women are advised not to take these trips.

The three-hour ride along the rim costs $118. An overnight with a stay at Phantom Ranch at the bottom of the canyon is $515 ($901 for two riders). Two nights at Phantom Ranch, an option available from November through March, will set you back $732 ($1,206 for two). Meals are included. Reservations (by phone), especially during the busy summer months, are a must, but you can check at the Bright Angel Transportation Desk to see if there's last-minute availability. ☎ *888/297–2757* ⊕ *www.grandcanyonlodges.com* ☻ *Phantom Ranch rides daily; Rim rides mid-Mar.–Oct., twice daily; Nov.–mid-Mar., once daily* ⚠ *Reservations essential.*

GRAND CANYON NORTH RIM

The North Rim stands 1,000 feet higher than the South Rim and has a more alpine climate, with twice as much annual precipitation. Here, in the deep forests of the Kaibab Plateau, the crowds are thinner, the facilities fewer, and the views even more spectacular. Due to snow, the North Rim is off-limits in winter. The buildings and concessions are closed November through mid-May. The road and entrance gate close when the snow makes them impassable—usually by the end of November.

18

Lodgings are limited in this more remote park, with only one historic lodge (with cabins and hotel-type rooms as well as a restaurant) and a single campground. Dining options have opened up a little with the addition of the Grand Cookout, offered nightly with live entertainment under the stars. Your best bet may be to pack your camping gear and hiking boots and take several days to explore the lush Kaibab Forest. The canyon's highest, most dramatic rim views also can be enjoyed on two wheels (via primitive dirt access roads) and on four legs (courtesy of a trusty mule).

EXPLORING

SCENIC DRIVE

Fodor's Choice ★ **Highway 67.** Open mid-May to roughly mid-November (or the first big snowfall), this two-lane paved road climbs 1,400 feet in elevation as it passes through the Kaibab National Forest. Also called the "North Rim Parkway," this scenic route crosses the limestone-capped Kaibab Plateau—passing broad meadows, sun-dappled forests, and small lakes and springs—before abruptly falling away at the abyss of the Grand Canyon. Wildlife abounds in the thick ponderosa pine forests and lush mountain meadows. It's common to see deer, turkeys, and coyotes as you drive through such a remote region. Point Imperial and Cape Royal branch off this scenic drive, which runs from Jacob Lake to Bright Angel Point. ⊠ *Hwy. 67, Grand Canyon National Park.*

HISTORIC SITE

Grand Canyon Lodge. Built in 1937 by the Union Pacific Railroad (replacing the original 1928 building, which burned in a fire), this massive stone structure is listed on the National Register of Historic Places. Its huge sunroom has hardwood floors, high-beam ceilings, and a marvelous view of the canyon through plate-glass windows. On warm days, visitors sit in the sun and drink in the surrounding beauty on an outdoor viewing deck, where National Park Service employees deliver free lectures on geology and history. The dining room serves breakfast, lunch, and dinner; the Roughrider Saloon is a bar by night and a coffeeshop in the morning. ⊠ *10 Albright St., off Hwy. 67 near Bright Angel Point, Grand Canyon National Park* ☎ *928/638–2631* ⊕ *www. grandcanyonforever.com.*

SCENIC STOPS

Fodor's Choice
★

Bright Angel Point. This trail, which leads to one of the most awe-inspiring overlooks on either rim, starts on the grounds of the Grand Canyon Lodge and runs along the crest of a point of rocks that juts into the canyon for several hundred yards. The walk is only 0.5 mile round-trip, but it's an exciting trek accented by sheer drops on each side of the trail. In a few spots where the route is extremely narrow, metal railings ensure visitors' safety. The temptation to clamber out on precarious perches to have your picture taken should be resisted at all costs. ⊠ *North Rim Dr., Grand Canyon National Park.*

Cape Royal. A popular sunset destination, Cape Royal showcases the canyon's jagged landscape; you'll also get a glimpse of the Colorado River, framed by a natural stone arch called Angels Window. In autumn, the aspens turn a beautiful gold, adding even more color to an already magnificent scene of the forested surroundings. The easy and rewarding 1-mile round-trip hike along **Cliff Springs Trail** starts here; it takes you through a forested ravine and terminates at Cliff Springs, where the forest opens to another impressive view of the canyon walls. ⊠ *Cape Royal Scenic Dr., 23 miles southeast of Grand Canyon Lodge, Grand Canyon National Park.*

Point Imperial. At 8,803 feet, Point Imperial has the highest vista point at either rim; it offers magnificent views of both the canyon and the distant country: the Vermilion Cliffs to the north, the 10,000-foot Navajo Mountain to the northeast in Utah, the Painted Desert to the east, and the Little Colorado River canyon to the southeast. Other prominent points of interest include views of Mount Hayden, Saddle Mountain, and Marble Canyon. ⊠ *Point Imperial Rd., 3 miles off Cape Royal Rd., 11 miles northeast of Grand Canyon Lodge, Grand Canyon National Park.*

Fodor's Choice
★

Point Sublime. You can camp within feet of the canyon's edge at this awe-inspiring site. Sunrises and sunsets are spectacular. The winding road, through gorgeous high country, is only 17 miles, but it will take you at least two hours one-way. The road is intended only for vehicles with high road clearance (pickups and four-wheel-drive vehicles). It is also necessary to be properly equipped for wilderness road travel. Check with a park ranger or at the information desk at Grand Canyon Lodge before taking this journey. You may camp here only with a permit from the Backcountry Information Center. ⊠ *North Rim Dr., about 20 miles west of North Rim Visitor Center, Grand Canyon National Park*.

Roosevelt Point. Named after the president who gave the Grand Canyon its national monument status in 1908 (it was upgraded to national park status in 1919), Roosevelt Point is the best place to see the confluence of the Little Colorado River and the Grand Canyon. The cliffs above the Colorado River south of the junction are known as the Palisades of the Desert. A short woodland loop trail leads to this eastern viewpoint. ⊠ *Cape Royal Rd., 18 miles east of Grand Canyon Lodge, Grand Canyon National Park*.

SPORTS AND THE OUTDOORS

HIKING

EASY

Cape Final Trail. This 4-mile (round-trip) gravel path follows an old jeep trail through a ponderosa pine forest to the canyon overlook at Cape Final with panoramic views of the northern canyon, the Palisades of the Desert, and the impressive spectacle of Juno Temple. *Easy.* ⊹ *Trailhead: dirt parking lot 5 miles south of Roosevelt Point on Cape Royal Rd.*

FAMILY **Roosevelt Point Trail.** This easy 0.2-mile round-trip trail loops through the forest to the scenic viewpoint. Allow 20 minutes for this relaxed, secluded hike. *Easy.* ⊹ *Trailhead: Cape Royal Rd.* ⊕ *www.nps.gov/grca.*

FAMILY **Transept Trail.** This 3-mile (round-trip), 1½-hour trail begins near the Grand Canyon Lodge at 8,255 feet. Well maintained and well marked, it has little elevation change, sticking near the rim before reaching a dramatic view of a large stream through Bright Angel Canyon. The route leads to a side canyon called Transept Canyon, which geologist Clarence Dutton named in 1882, declaring it "far grander than Yosemite." Check the posted schedule to find a ranger talk along this trail; it's also a great place to view fall foliage. Flash floods can occur any time of the year, especially June through September when thunderstorms develop rapidly. *Easy.* ⊹ *Trailhead: near the Grand Canyon Lodge's east patio.*

MODERATE

Uncle Jim Trail. This 5-mile, three-hour loop starts at 8,300 feet and winds south through the forest, past Roaring Springs and Bright Angel canyons. The highlight of this rim hike is Uncle Jim Point, which, at 8,244 feet, overlooks the upper sections of the North Kaibab Trail. *Moderate.* ⊹ *Trailhead: North Kaibab Trail parking lot.*

Fodor'sChoice **Widforss Trail.** Round-trip, Widforss Trail is 9.8 miles, with an elevation ★ change of only 200 feet. Allow five to six hours for the hike, which starts at 8,080 feet and passes through shady forests of pine, spruce, fir, and aspen on its way to Widforss Point, at 7,900 feet. Here you'll have good views of five temples: Zoroaster, Brahma, and Deva to the southeast, and Buddha and Manu to the southwest. You are likely to see wildflowers in summer, and this is a good trail for viewing fall foliage.

18

It's named in honor of artist Gunnar M. Widforss, renowned for his paintings of national park landscapes. *Moderate.* ⊹ *Trailhead: Point Sublime Rd., near intersection of Hwy. 67.*

DIFFICULT

North Kaibab Trail. At 8,241 feet, this trail leads into the canyon and down to Phantom Ranch. It is recommended for experienced hikers only, who should allow four days for the round-trip hike. The long, steep path drops 5,840 feet over a distance of 14.5 miles to Phantom Ranch and the Colorado River, so the National Park Service suggests that day hikers not go farther than Roaring Springs (5,020 feet) before turning to hike back up out of the canyon. After about 7 miles, Cottonwood Campground (4,080 feet) has drinking water in summer, restrooms, shade trees, and a ranger. *Difficult.* ■ TIP➔ A free shuttle takes hikers to the North Kaibab trailhead twice daily from Grand Canyon Lodge; reserve a spot the day before. ⊹ *Trailhead: 2 miles north of Grand Canyon Lodge.*

MULE RIDES

TOURS AND OUTFITTERS

FAMILY **Canyon Trail Rides.** This company leads mule rides on the easier trails of the North Rim. A one-hour ride (minimum age seven) runs $40. Half-day trips on the rim or into the canyon (minimum age 10) cost $80. Weight limits are 200 pounds for canyon rides and 220 pounds for the rim rides. Available daily from May 15 to October 15, these excursions are popular, so make reservations in advance. ☎ 435/679–8665 ⊕ *www.canyonrides.com.*

18

GRAND CANYON WEST RIM

The West Rim is a 5-hour drive from the South Rim of Grand Canyon National Park or a 2½-hour drive from Las Vegas. From Kingman, drive north 30 miles on U.S. 93, and then turn right onto Pierce Ferry Road and follow it for 28 miles. (A more scenic alternative is to drive 42 miles north on Stockton Hill Road, turning right onto Pierce Ferry Road for 7 miles, but this takes a bit longer because Stockton Hill Road has a lower speed limit than the wide, divided U.S. 93 highway.) Turn right (east) onto Diamond Bar Road and follow for 21 miles to Grand Canyon West entrance.

Visitors aren't allowed to travel in their own vehicles to the viewpoints once they reach the West Rim, and must purchase a tour package—which can range from day use to horseback or helicopter rides to lodging and meals—from Hualapai Tourism.

EXPLORING

Hualapai Tourism. At the Welcome Center, Hualapai Tourism, run by the Hualapai tribe, offers the basic Hualapai Legacy tour package ($44 per person, including taxes and fees), which includes a Hualapai visitation permit and hop-on, hop-off shuttle transportation to three sites. The shuttle will take you to Eagle Point, where the Indian Village walking tour visits authentic dwellings. Educational displays there uncover

Grand Canyon North Rim

0 _____ 5 mi
0 _____ 5 km

KEY

🏠	Ranger Station
⛺	Campground
🪑	Picnic Area
🍴	Restaurant
🏛	Lodge
·······	Walking/Hiking Trails
===	Dirt Road

SOUTH CANYON

MARBLE CANYON

445

Tatahatso Point

Point Hansbrough

PAINTED DESERT

TO JACOB LAKE, MARBLE CANYON AND SOUTH RIM

KAIBAB PLATEAU

NAVAJO INDIAN RESERVATION

67

North Rim Entrance Station

Highway 67

Nankoweap Rapids

Point Sublime

Point Imperial

Bourke Point

Nankoweap Mesa

Kwagunt Butte

NORTH RIM

Point Imperial Road

Ken Patrick Trail

Vista Encantada

Tritle Peak

Roosevelt Point

Atoko Point

Siegfried Pyre

Chuar Butte

Wildforss Trail

North Rim Visitor Center

TRANSEPT CANYON

Transept Trail

Grand Canyon Lodge

Bright Angel Point

WALHALLA PLATEAU

Temple Butte

Cottonwood Campground

BRIGHT ANGEL CANYON

Obi Point

Cape Royal Road

Cape Final Trail

Jupiter Temple

Shiva Temple

Brahma Temple

Walhalla Ruins

Venus Temple

Apollo Temple

Osiris Temple

Isis Temple

Zoroaster Temple

Cliff Springs Trail

Walhalla Overlook

Cape Royal

North Kaibab Trail

Bright Angel Trail

Granite Rapids

Horn Creek Rapids

Phantom Ranch

Cape Royal Trail

Wotan's Throne

Vishnu Temple

Cardenas Butte

Bright Angel Trail

Hopi Point

The Abyss

Mather Point

SOUTH RIM

South Kaibab Trail

GRANITE GORGE

Solomon Temple

PALISADES OF THE DESERT

Hermit Road

Yaki Point

Grapevine Rapids

Hance Rapids

Desert View

Navajo Point

TO FLAGSTAFF, WILLIAMS

64

Grand Canyon Village

Lipan Point

Colorado River

the culture of five different Native American tribes (Havasupai, Plains, Hopi, Hualapai, and Navajo), and intertribal, powwow-style dance performances entertain visitors at the nearby amphitheater. The shuttle also goes to Hualapai Ranch, site of Western performances, cookouts, horseback and wagon rides, and the only lodging on the West Rim; and Guano Point, where the "High Point Hike" offers panoramic views of the Colorado River. At all three areas, local Hualapai guides and roaming "ambassadors" add a Native American perspective that you won't find on North and South Rim tours.

For extra fees, you can add meals (there are cafés at each of the three stops), overnight lodging at Hualapai Ranch, a helicopter trip into the canyon, a pontoon boat trip on the Colorado, a horseback ride along the canyon rim, or a walk on the Grand Canyon Skywalk. ⊠ *Grand Canyon West* ☎ *928/769–2636, 888/868–9378* ⊕ *www.hualapaitourism. com* 🖃 *$44* ⊙ *Daily.*

Grand Canyon Skywalk. This cantilevered glass terrace is suspended nearly 4,000 feet above the Colorado River and extends 70 feet from the edge of the Grand Canyon. Approximately 10 feet wide, the bridge's deck, made of tempered glass several inches thick, has 5-foot glass railings on each side creating an unobstructed open-air platform. Admission to the skywalk is a separate add-on to the basic Grand Canyon West admission. Visitors must store personal items, including cameras, cell phones, and video cameras, in lockers before entering. A professional photographer takes photographs of visitors, which can be purchased from the gift shop. ⊕ *www.hualapaitourism.com* 🖃 *$32.*

SPORTS AND THE OUTDOORS

Hualapai River Runners. One-day combination river trips are offered by the Hualapai Tribe through the Hualapai River Runners from mid-March through October. The trips leave from Peach Springs (a 2-hour drive from the West Rim) and include rafting, a hike, a helicopter ride up to the West Rim, and transport. Lunch, snacks, and beverages are provided. Children must be eight or older to take the trip, which runs several rapids with the most difficult rated as Class VII, depending on the river flow. ⊠ *5001 Buck N Doe Rd., Peach Springs* ☎ *928/769–2636, 888/868–9378* ⊕ *www.hualapaitourism.com* 🖃 *From $387.*

WHAT'S NEARBY

The northwest section of Arizona is geographically fascinating. In addition to the Grand Canyon, it's home to national forests, national monuments, and national recreation areas. Towns, however, are small and scattered. Many of them cater to visiting adventurers, and Native American reservations dot the map.

NEARBY TOWNS

Towns near the canyon's South Rim include the tiny town of Tusayan, 1 mile south of the entrance station, and Williams, the "Gateway to the Grand Canyon," 58 miles south.

Tusayan has basic amenities and an airport that serves as a starting point for airplane and helicopter tours of the canyon. The cozy mountain town of **Williams**, founded in 1882 when the railroad passed through, was once a rough-and-tumble joint, replete with saloons and bordellos. Today, it reflects a much milder side of the Wild West, with 3,300 residents and more than 25 motels and hotels. Wander along the main street—part of historic Route 66, but locally named, like the town, after trapper Bill Williams—and indulge in Route 66 nostalgia inside antiques shops or souvenir and T-shirt stores.

The communities closest to the North Rim—all of them tiny and with limited services—include Fredonia, 76 miles north; Marble Canyon, 80 miles northeast; Lees Ferry, 85 miles east; and Jacob Lake, 45 miles north.

Fredonia, a small community of about 1,050, approximately an hour's drive north of the Grand Canyon, is often referred to as the gateway to the North Rim; it's also relatively close to Zion and Bryce Canyon national parks in Utah. **Marble Canyon** marks the geographical beginning of the Grand Canyon at its northeastern tip. It's a good stopping point if you're driving U.S. 89 to the North Rim. En route from the South Rim to the North Rim is **Lees Ferry,** where most of the area's river rafts start their journey. The tiny town of **Jacob Lake,** nestled high in pine country at an elevation of 7,925 feet, was named after Mormon explorer Jacob Hamblin, also known as the "Buckskin Missionary." It has a hotel, café, campground, and lush mountain countryside.

VISITOR INFORMATION

Kaibab National Forest, North Kaibab Ranger District. ⊠ *430 S. Main St., Fredonia* ☎ *928/643-7395* ⊕ *www.fs.usda.gov/kaibab.* **Kaibab National Forest, Tusayan Ranger District.** ⊠ *176 Lincoln Log Loop, Grand Canyon National Park* ☎ *928/638-2443* ⊕ *www.fs.usda.gov/kaibab.* **Kaibab Plateau Visitor Center.** ⊠ *U.S. 89A at Hwy. 67, Jacob Lake* ☎ *928/643-7298* ⊕ *www.fs.usda.gov/kaibab.* **Williams Visitor Center.** ⊠ *200 W. Railroad Ave., at Grand Canyon Blvd., Williams* ☎ *928/635-4061* ⊕ *www.experiencewilliams.com.*

NEARBY ATTRACTIONS

National Geographic Visitor Center Grand Canyon. Here you can schedule and purchase tickets for air and jeep tours, and buy a national park pass, which enables you to access the park by special entry lanes. However, the biggest draw is the six-story IMAX screen that features the short movie, *Grand Canyon: The Hidden Secrets.* You can learn about the geologic and natural history of the canyon, soar above stunning rock formations, and ride the rapids through the rocky gorge. The film is shown every hour on the half hour; the adjoining gift store is huge and well stocked. ⊠ *450 Hwy. 64/U.S. 180, 2 miles south of the Grand Canyon's south entrance, Tusayan* ☎ *928/638-2468* ⊕ *www.explorethecanyon.com* 🎟 *$12.50 for IMAX movies* ☉ *Mar.–Oct., daily 8 am–10 pm; Nov.–Feb., daily 9:30–6:30.*

Vermilion Cliffs National Monument. West of the town of Marble Canyon are these spectacular cliffs, more than 3,000 feet high in many places. Keep an eye out for condors; the giant endangered birds were reintroduced into the area in 1996. Reports suggest that the birds, once in captivity, are surviving well in the wilderness. ☎ *435/688–3200* ⊕ *www.blm.gov/az.*

AREA ACTIVITIES

SPORTS AND THE OUTDOORS

FISHING

The stretch of ice-cold, crystal-clear water at Lees Ferry off the North Rim provides arguably the best trout fishing in the Southwest. Many rafters and anglers stay the night in a campground near the river or in nearby Marble Canyon before hitting the river at dawn.

Arizona Game and Fish Department. Fish for trout, crappie, catfish, and smallmouth bass at a number of lakes surrounding Williams. To fish on public land, anglers age 14 and older are required to obtain a fishing license from the Arizona Game and Fish Department, either at their office or online. ✉ *Flagstaff* ☎ *928/774–5045* ⊕ *www.azgfd.gov.*

RAFTING

Fodor's Choice ★ The National Park Service authorizes 16 concessionaires to run rafting trips through the canyon—you can view a full list at the park's website (⊕ *www.nps.gov/grca/planyourvisit/river-concessioners.htm*). Trips run from three to 16 days, depending on whether you opt for the upper canyon, lower canyon, or full canyon. You can also experience a one-day rafting trip, running a few rapids in Grand Canyon West with the Hualapai tribe.

Arizona Raft Adventures. Arizona Raft Adventures organizes six- to 16-day paddle and/or motor trips through the upper, lower, or "full" canyon, for all skill levels. Trips depart April through October. ✉ *4050 East Huntington Dr., Flagstaff* ☎ *928/526–8200, 800/786–7238* ⊕ *www.azraft.com* ▭ *From $2,025.*

Canyoneers. With a reputation for high quality and a roster of three- to 14-day trips, Canyoneers is popular with those who want to do some hiking as well. The five-day "Best of the Grand" trip includes a hike down to Phantom Ranch. The motorized and oar trips are available April through September. ✉ *7195 N. U.S. 89, Flagstaff* ☎ *928/526–0924, 800/525–0924* ⊕ *www.canyoneers.com* ▭ *From $1,080.*

Grand Canyon Expeditions. You can count on Grand Canyon Expeditions to take you down the Colorado River safely and in style: evening meals might include filet mignon, pork chops, or shrimp. The eight-day motorized and 14-day Dory trips range from $2,590 to $3,804, and some trips focus on special interests like archaeology and photography. ☎ *435/644–2691, 800/544–2691* ⊕ *www.gcex.com.*

Wilderness River Adventures. One of the canyon's larger rafting outfitters, Wilderness River Adventures runs a wide variety of trips from three to 16 days, oar or motorized, from April to October. Their most popular trip is the seven-day motor trip. ✉ *2040 E. Frontage Rd., Page* ☎ *928/645–3296, 800/992–8022* ⊕ *www.riveradventures.com.*

18

Continued on page 414

EXPLORING THE
COLORADO RIVER

High in Colorado's Rocky Mountains, the Colorado River begins as a catch-all for the snowmelt off the mountains west of the Continental Divide. By the time it reaches the Grand Canyon, the Colorado has been joined by multiple tributaries to become a raging river, red with silt as it sculpts spectacular landscapes. A network of dams can only partially tame this mighty river.

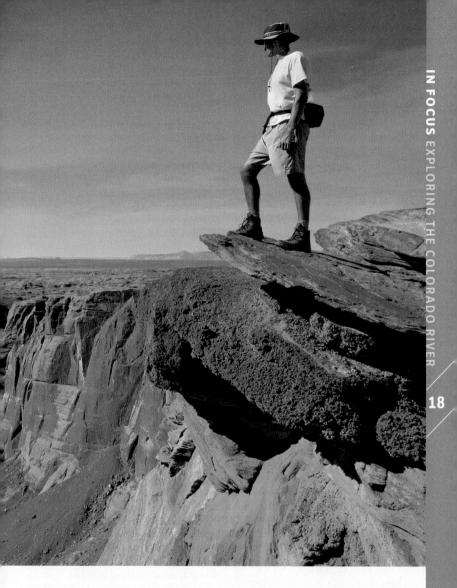

Snaking its way through five states, the Colorado River is an essential water source to the arid Southwest. Its natural course runs 1,450 miles from its origin in Colorado's La Poudre Pass Lake in Rocky Mountain National Park to its final destination in the Gulf of California, also called the Sea of Cortez. In northern Arizona, the Colorado River has been a powerful force in shaping the Grand Canyon, where it flows 4,000 to 6,000 feet below the rim. Beyond the canyon, the red river takes a lazy turn at the Arizona–Nevada border, where Hoover Dam creates the reservoir at Lake Mead. The Colorado continues at a relaxed pace along the Arizona–California border, providing energy and irrigation in Arizona, California, and Nevada before draining into northwestern Mexico.

A RIVER RUNS THROUGH IT

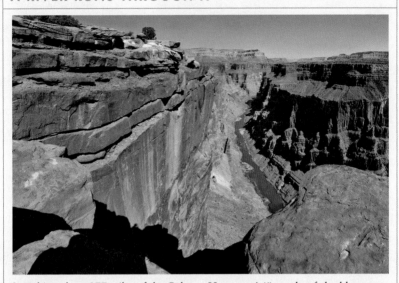

Stretching along 277 miles of the Colorado River is one of the seven natural wonders of the world: the Grand Canyon ranges in width from 4 to 18 miles, while the walls around it soar up to a mile high. Nearly 2 billion years of geologic history and majesty are revealed in exposed tiers of rock cut deep in the Colorado Plateau. What caused this incredible marvel of nature? Erosion by water coupled with driving wind are most likely the major culprits: under the sculpting power of wind and water, the shale layers eroded into slopes and the harder sandstone and limestone layers created terraced cliffs. Other forces that may have helped shape the canyon include ice, volcanic activity, continental drift, and earthquakes.

WHO LIVES HERE
Native tribes have lived in the canyon for thousands of years and continue to do so, looking to the river for subsistence. The plateau-dwelling Hualapai ("people of the tall pines") live on a million acres along 108 miles of the Colorado River in the West Rim. The Havasupai ("people of the blue green water") live deep within the walls of the 12-mile-long Havasu Canyon—a major side canyon connected to the Grand Canyon.

ENVIRONMENTAL CONCERNS
When the Grand Canyon achieved national park status in 1919, only 44,173 people made the grueling overland trip to see it—quite a contrast from today's nearly 5 million annual visitors. The tremendous increase in visitation has greatly impacted the fragile ecosystems, as has Lake Powell's Glen Canyon Dam, which was constructed in the 1950s and '60s. The dam has changed the composition of the Colorado River, replacing warm water rich in sediments (nature's way of nourishing the riverbed and banks) with mostly cool, much clearer water. This has introduced nonnative plants and animals that threaten the extinction of several native species. Air pollution has also affected visibility and the constant buzz of aerial tours has disturbed the natural solitude.

Above and right, views of Colorado River in the Grand Canyon from Toroweap.

DID YOU KNOW?

The North Rim's isolated Toroweap overlook (also called Tuweep) is perched 3,000 feet above the canyon floor: a height equal to stacking the Sears Tower and Empire State Building on top of each other.

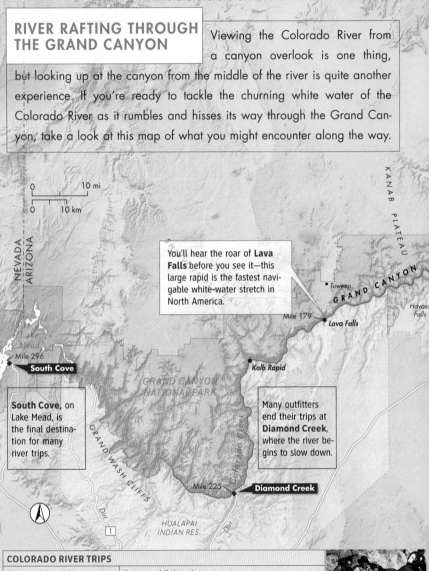

RIVER RAFTING THROUGH THE GRAND CANYON

Viewing the Colorado River from a canyon overlook is one thing, but looking up at the canyon from the middle of the river is quite another experience. If you're ready to tackle the churning white water of the Colorado River as it rumbles and hisses its way through the Grand Canyon, take a look at this map of what you might encounter along the way.

0 ___ 10 mi
0 ___ 10 km

You'll hear the roar of **Lava Falls** before you see it—this large rapid is the fastest navigable white-water stretch in North America.

• Tuweep

GRAND CANYON

KANAB PLATEAU

Havasu Falls

Mile 179 • Lava Falls

Lake Mead

Mile 296
South Cove

Kolb Rapid

GRAND CANYON NATIONAL PARK

South Cove, on Lake Mead, is the final destination for many river trips.

GRAND WASH CLIFFS

Colorado River

Many outfitters end their trips at **Diamond Creek**, where the river begins to slow down.

Mile 225 **Diamond Creek**

Dirt

1

HUALAPAI INDIAN RES.

Dirt

COLORADO RIVER TRIPS

Time and Length	Entry and Exit points
1 day Float trip	Glen Canyon Dam to Lees Ferry (no rapids)
1 day Combo trip	Diamond Creek, then helicopter to West Rim
3–4 days	Lees Ferry to Phantom Ranch
6 days, 89 miles	Phantom Ranch to Diamond Creek
9–10 days, 136 miles	Lees Ferry to Diamond Creek
14–16 days, 225 miles	Lees Ferry to South Cove

*Trips either begin or end at Phantom Ranch/Bright Angel Beach at the bottom of the Grand Canyon, at river mile 87

Kanab
89

UTAH
ARIZONA

Lake
Powell

Glen Canyon Dam

PARIA CANYON

Direction
of Flow

Page

89

Lees Ferry

Mile 0

Marble Canyon

VERMILLION CLIFFS

AIT 89

Bitter
Springs

House Rock
Rapids

ECHO CLIFFS

89

KAIBITO PLATEAU

One-day float trips (no white-water) go through beautiful **Glen Canyon**.

Longer trips begin at **Lees Ferry**, a few miles below the Glen Canyon Dam near Page.

Deer Creek Falls

Great Thumb
Mesa

Bedrock Rapid

NORTH RIM

Point
Imperial

Fossil Rapid

Point
Sublime

67

Forester
Rapid

Sapphire
Rapid

Bright
Angel
Point

Mile 61

Serpentine
Rapid

Mile 98

Unkar Rapid

Crystal Rapid

Phantom Ranch

Granite Rapid

Mile 87

Grapevine Rapid

HAVASUPAI
INDIAN RES.

Mather Pt.

Bright
Angel
Trail

Hance
Rapid

Desert View

Grand Canyon
Village

Grandview
Point

64

Tusayan

Colorado River

MARBLE CANYON

Little Colorado River

⚠ You need to be very fit to hike the arduous 9.6-mile **Bright Angel Trail**, especially if you choose to hike up when departing from Phantom Ranch.

Phantom Ranch allows you to begin or end your trip in between the scenic North and South Rims.

If you begin at Phantom Ranch, you will soon plunge through the colossal waves of **Granite** and **Crystal Rapids**.

Cameron

TO
FLAGSTAFF, ↓
49 Miles

COCONINO PLATEAU

180

64

NOT JUST RAPIDS

Don't think that your experience will be nonstop white-water adrenaline. Most of the Colorado River features long, relaxing stretches of water, where you drift amid grandiose rock formations. You might even spot a mountain goat or two. Multiday trips include camping on the shore.

PLANNING YOUR RIVER RAFTING TRIP

OAR, MOTOR, OR HYBRID?

Base the type of trip you choose on the amount of effort you want to put in. Motor rafts, which are the roomiest of the choices, cover the most miles in less time and are the most comfortable. Guides do the rowing on oar boats and these smaller rafts offer a wilder ride. All-paddle trips are the most active and require the most involvement from guests. Hybrid trips are popular because they offer both the opportunity to paddle and to relax.

THE GEAR

Life jackets, beverages, tents, sheets, tarps, sleeping bags, dry bags, first aid, and food are provided—but you'll still need to plan ahead by packing clothing, hats, sunscreen, toiletries, and other sundries. Commercial outfitters allow each river runner two waterproof bags to store items during the day—just keep in mind that one of these will be filled up with the provided sleeping bag and tarp. ■ TIP➜ Bring a rain suit: summer thunderstorms are frequent and chilly.

WHEN TO GO

Lots of people book trips for summer's peak period: June through August. If you're flexible, take advantage of the Arizona weather and go from May to early June or in September. ■ TIP➜ Seats fill up quickly; make reservations for multi-day trips a year or two in advance.

TRIP LENGTH

Rafting options on the Colorado River range from one-day trips at either the east or west end of the Grand Canyon to leisurely, two-week paddle trips through the full length of Grand Canyon National Park. If you're short on time, take a one-day trip near Grand Canyon West, where you'll run several rapids and fly back to the West Rim by helicopter. Another action-packed choice is to raft the river for 3 or 4 days, disembark at Phantom Ranch, then hike up to the Grand Canyon South Rim. "Full Canyon" rafting trips can take 9 to 16 days.

DID YOU KNOW?

As you're hanging on for dear life, consider this: Civil War veteran John Wesley Powell chartered these treacherous rapids in 1869—not only were conditions more dangerous then, but he had only one arm.

WHERE TO EAT

IN THE PARK

SOUTH RIM

$$$
STEAKHOUSE
✕ **Arizona Room.** The canyon views from this casual Southwestern-style steak house are the best of any restaurant at the South Rim. The menu includes such delicacies as chili-crusted pan-seared wild salmon, chipotle barbecue baby back ribs, and half-pound buffalo burgers with Gorgonzola aioli. For dessert, try the cheesecake with prickly-pear syrup paired with one of the house's specialty coffee drinks. Seating is first-come, first-served, so arrive early to avoid the crowds. $ *Average main: $22* ⊠ *Bright Angel Lodge, Desert View Dr., Grand Canyon Village* ☎ *928/638–2631* ⊕ *www.grandcanyonlodges.com* ♡ *Closed Jan. and Feb. No lunch Nov. and Dec.* ⚐ *Reservations not accepted.*

$$
SOUTHWESTERN
✕ **Bright Angel Restaurant.** No surprises, affordable dishes here will fill your belly at breakfast, lunch, or dinner. Entrées include such basics as salads, steaks, lasagna, burgers, fajitas, and fish tacos (sandwiches are options at lunch). Or you can step it up a notch and order some of the same selections straight from the Arizona Room menu, including prime rib, baby back ribs, and wild salmon. For dessert try the warm apple grunt cake topped with vanilla ice cream. Be prepared to wait for a table: the dining room bustles all day long. The plain decor is broken up with large-pane windows and original artwork. $ *Average main: $12* ⊠ *Bright Angel Lodge, Desert View Dr., Grand Canyon Village* ☎ *928/638–2631* ⊕ *www.grandcanyonlodges.com* ⚐ *Reservations not accepted.*

$
AMERICAN
✕ **Canyon Café at Yavapai Lodge.** Open for breakfast, lunch, and dinner, this cafeteria in the Yavapai Lodge, across from Market Plaza, serves down-home staples like chicken potpie, fried catfish, and fried chicken. Fast-food favorites include pastries, burgers, and pizza. There isn't a fancy bar, but you can order beer and wine with your meal. Resembling an old-fashioned diner, the large cafeteria has easy-to-read signs that point the way to your favorite foods. $ *Average main: $7* ⊠ *Yavapai Lodge, Desert View Dr., Grand Canyon Village* ☎ *928/638–2631* ⊕ *www.visitgrandcanyon.com/dining-and-shopping* ♡ *Closed Nov.–Feb. (except during Thanksgiving weekend and Christmas week)* ⚐ *Reservations not accepted.*

$$$
SOUTHWESTERN
Fodor's Choice
★
✕ **El Tovar Dining Room.** No doubt about it—this is the best restaurant for miles. Modeled after a European hunting lodge, this rustic 19th-century dining room built of hand-hewn logs is worth a visit. The cuisine is modern Southwestern with an exotic flair. Start with the smoked salmon–and–goat cheese crostini or the acclaimed black bean soup. The dinner menu includes such hearty yet creative dishes as prickly-pear-and-orange–glazed duck with roasted poblano black bean rice, grilled New York strip steak with au gratin potatoes, and a vegetarian ratatouille over polenta. The dining room also has an extensive wine list. ■ **TIP→ Dinner reservations can be made up to six months in advance with room reservations, and 30 days in advance for all other visitors.** If you can't get a dinner table, consider lunch or

breakfast—the best in the region with dishes like polenta corncakes with prickly pear–pistachio butter and prime rib hash. $ *Average main: $27* ✉ *El Tovar Hotel, Desert View Dr., Grand Canyon Village* ☎ *303/297–2757, 888/297–2757 for reservations only* ⊕ *www.grandcanyonlodges.com* ⊜ *Reservations essential.*

$ ✕ **Maswik Cafeteria.** You can get a burger, hot sandwich, pasta, or Mexican fare at this food court, as well as pizza by the slice and wine and beer in the adjacent Maswik Pizza Pub. This casual eatery is ¼ mile from the rim, and the Pizza Pub stays open until 11 pm (you can also order pizza to take out). Lines can be long during high-season lunch and dinner, but everything moves fairly quickly. $ *Average main: $7* ✉ *Maswik Lodge, Desert View Dr., Grand Canyon Village* ⊕ *www.grandcanyonlodges.com* ⊜ *Reservations not accepted.*

AMERICAN

NORTH RIM

$ ✕ **Deli in the Pines.** Dining choices are limited on the North Rim, but this is your best bet for a meal on a budget. Selections include pizza, salads, deli sandwiches, hot dogs, homemade breakfast pastries and burritos, and soft-serve ice cream. Best of all, there is an outdoor seating area for dining alfresco. It's open for lunch and dinner. $ *Average main: $6* ✉ *Grand Canyon Lodge, Bright Angel Point, North Rim* ☎ *928/638–2611* ⊕ *www.grandcanyonforever.com* ⊙ *Closed mid-Oct.–mid-May* ⊜ *Reservations not accepted.*

AMERICAN

$$ ✕ **Grand Canyon Lodge Dining Room.** This historic lodge has a huge, high-ceilinged dining room with spectacular views and decent food, though the draw here is definitely the setting. You might find smoked, chipotle-glazed pork chop, bison flank steak, and grilled ruby trout for dinner. The filling, simply prepared food takes a flavorful turn with Southwestern spices and organic selections. It's also open for breakfast and lunch. A full-service bar and an impressive wine list add to the relaxed atmosphere of the only full-service, sit-down restaurant on the North Rim. Dinner reservations are essential in summer and on spring and fall weekends. $ *Average main: $20* ✉ *Grand Canyon Lodge, Bright Angel Point, North Rim* ☎ *928/638–2611* ⊕ *www.grandcanyonforever.com* ⊙ *Closed mid-Oct.–mid-May.*

AMERICAN
Fodor's Choice
★

18

$$$ ✕ **Grand Cookout.** Dine under the stars and enjoy live entertainment at this chuck wagon–style dining experience—a popular family-friendly choice among the North Rim's limited dining options. Fill up on Western favorites at the all-you-can-eat buffet, including barbecue beef brisket, roasted chicken, baked beans, and cowboy biscuits. The food is basic and tasty, but the real draw is the nightly performance of Western music and tall tales. Transportation from the Grand Canyon Lodge to the cookout (1 mile away) is included in the price. Be sure to call before 4 pm for dinner reservations. Advance reservations are taken by phone (during winter months) or at the Grand Canyon Lodge registration desk. $ *Average main: $30* ✉ *Grand Canyon Lodge, North Rim* ☎ *928/638–2611, 928/645–6865 in winter* ⊕ *www.grandcanyonforever.com* ⊙ *Closed Oct.–May. No lunch* ⊜ *Reservations essential.*

AMERICAN
FAMILY

OUTSIDE THE PARK

TUSAYAN

$$$
AMERICAN
FAMILY

✕ **Canyon Star Steakhouse and Saloon.** Relax in the rustic timber-and-stone dining room at the Grand Hotel for reliable if uninspired American food, with an emphasis on steaks and barbecue at dinner. Popular options include barbecue chicken and ribs, and Mexican fare. Most nights there's live guitar or banjo music. There's a kids' menu, and breakfast and lunch are served daily. In summer, be sure to reserve a table at dinner. ⑤ *Average main: $21* ✉ *Hwy. 64/U.S. 180, Tusayan* ☎ *928/638–3333* ⊕ *www.grandcanyongrandhotel.com.*

$$$
AMERICAN

✕ **The Coronado Room.** Inside the Best Western Grand Canyon Squire Inn is the most sophisticated cuisine in Tusayan. The menu includes well-prepared, hearty American food, with an emphasis on game (elk, venison, buffalo), plus grilled seafood, escargot, and oversize desserts. There's a good-size wine list, too. Although classier than most eateries in these parts, dress is still casual and the vibe relaxed. Service is attentive. Reservations are a good idea, particularly in the busy season. ⑤ *Average main: $22* ✉ *100 Hwy. 64/U.S. 180, Tusayan* ☎ *928/638–2681* ⊕ *www.grandcanyonsquire.com* ⊗ *No lunch.*

WILLIAMS

$$
AMERICAN
FAMILY

✕ **Cruisers Café 66.** Patterned after a '50s-style high-school hangout (but with cocktail service), this diner pleases kids and adults with a large menu of family-priced American classics—good burgers and fries, barbecue pork sandwiches, salads, and thick malts, plus a choice steak that'll set you back about $20. The Grand Canyon Brewery, accessed by a side entrance, adds to the casual fun—just saddle up to a hand-carved log bar stool and order one of five microbrews on tap. A large mural of the town's heyday along the "Mother Road" and historic cars out front make this a Route 66 favorite. Kids enjoy the relaxed atmosphere and jukebox tunes. ⑤ *Average main: $15* ✉ *233 W. Rte. 66, Williams* ☎ *928/635–2445* ⊕ *www.cruisers66.com.*

$$$
ECLECTIC
Fodor'sChoice
★

✕ **Red Raven Restaurant.** This dapper storefront bistro in the heart of downtown Williams features warm lighting and romantic booth seating. Creatively presented fare blends American, Italian, and Asian ingredients. Specialties include a starter of crisp tempura shrimp salad with a ginger-sesame dressing, and mains like charbroiled salmon with basil butter over cranberry–pine nut couscous, and pork tenderloin with cilantro pesto, served with mashed potatoes and sautéed local vegetables. The well-selected wine and beer list is one of the most extensive in the region. ⑤ *Average main: $21* ✉ *135 W. Rte. 66, Williams* ☎ *928/635–4980* ⊕ *www.redravenrestaurant.com.*

WHERE TO STAY

IN THE PARK

SOUTH RIM

$ ⛺ **Bright Angel Lodge.** Famed architect Mary Jane Colter designed this

HOTEL 1935 log-and-stone structure, which sits within a few yards of the can-

FAMILY yon rim and blends superbly with the canyon walls. **Pros:** some rooms have canyon vistas; all are steps away from the rim; Internet kiosks and transportation desk for the mule ride check-in are in the lobby; good value for the amazing location. **Cons:** the popular lobby is always packed; parking is a bit of a hike. $ *Rooms from: $92* ✉ *Desert View Dr., Grand Canyon Village* ☎ *888/297–2757 for reservations only, 928/638–2631* ⊕ *www.grandcanyonlodges.com* 🛏 *37 rooms (18 with bath), 50 cabins* ⦿ *No meals.*

$$$ ⛺ **El Tovar Hotel.** The hotel's proximity to all of the canyon's facilities,

HOTEL European hunting-lodge atmosphere, attractively updated rooms and

Fodor's Choice tile baths, and renowned dining room make it the best place to stay on

★ the South Rim. A registered National Historic Landmark, the "architectural crown jewel of the Grand Canyon" was built in 1905 of Oregon pine logs and native stone. **Pros:** historic lodging just steps from the South Rim; fabulous lounge with outdoor seating and canyon views; best in-park dining on-site. **Cons:** books up quickly. $ *Rooms from: $197* ✉ *Desert View Dr., Grand Canyon Village* ☎ *888/297–2757 for reservations only, 928/638–2631* ⊕ *www.grandcanyonlodges.com* 🛏 *66 rooms, 12 suites* ⦿ *No meals.*

$$$ ⛺ **Kachina Lodge.** The well-appointed rooms at this motel-style lodge on

HOTEL the South Rim are a good bet for families and are within easy walking distance of dining facilities at nearby lodges. **Pros:** partial canyon views in half the rooms; family-friendly; steps from the best restaurants in the park. **Cons:** check-in takes place at nearby El Tovar Hotel; limited parking. $ *Rooms from: $205* ✉ *Desert View Dr., Grand Canyon Village* ☎ *888/297–2757 for reservations only, 928/638–2631* ⊕ *www.grandcanyonlodges.com* 🛏 *49 rooms* ⦿ *No meals.*

$$ ⛺ **Maswik Lodge.** Far from the noisy crowds, Maswik accommodations are

HOTEL in two-story motel-style buildings nestled in a shady ponderosa pine forest.

FAMILY **Pros:** north units are well equipped; good for families; affordable dining options. **Cons:** rooms lack historic charm; tucked away from the rim in the forest; south units don't have a/c. $ *Rooms from: $102* ✉ *Grand Canyon Village* ☎ *888/297–2757 for reservations only, 928/638–2631* ⊕ *www.grandcanyonlodges.com* 🛏 *278 rooms* ⦿ *No meals.*

$ ⛺ **Phantom Ranch.** In a grove of cottonwood trees on the canyon floor,

B&B/INN Phantom Ranch is accessible only to hikers and mule trekkers; there are 40 dormitory beds and 14 beds in cabins, all with shared baths. **Pros:** only inner-canyon lodging option; fabulous canyon views; remote access limits crowds. **Cons:** accessible only by foot or mule; few amenities or means of outside communication. $ *Rooms from: $45* ✉ *On canyon floor, at intersection of Bright Angel and Kaibab trails, Grand Canyon National Park* ☎ *303/297–2757, 888/297–2757* ⊕ *www.*

18

grandcanyonlodges.com ⟿ *4 dormitories, 9 cabins (some cabins with outside showers reserved for mule riders)* ⦿ *Some meals.*

$$$ ⊞ **Thunderbird Lodge.** This motel with comfortable, simple rooms and
HOTEL partial canyon views has all the modern amenities you'd expect at a typical mid-price chain hotel—even pod coffeemakers. **Pros:** canyon views in some rooms ($16 extra); family-friendly. **Cons:** check-in takes place at nearby Bright Angel Lodge; limited parking nearby. $ *Rooms from: $205* ⊠ *Desert View Dr., Grand Canyon Village* ☎ *888/297–2757 reservations only, 928/638–2631* ⊕ *www.grandcanyonlodges.com* ⟿ *55 rooms* ⦿ *No meals.*

$$ ⊞ **Yavapai Lodge.** The largest motel-style lodge in the park is tucked
HOTEL in a pinyon and juniper forest at the eastern end of Grand Canyon Village, across from Market Plaza. **Pros:** transportation-activities desk on-site in the lobby; walk to Market Plaza in Grand Canyon Village; forested grounds. **Cons:** farthest in-park lodging from the rim (½ mile); no a/c in west rooms. $ *Rooms from: $147* ⊠ *10 Yavapai Lodge Rd., Grand Canyon Village* ☎ *877/404–4611 reservations only* ⊕ *www.visitgrandcanyon.com* ⟿ *358 rooms* ⦿ *No meals.*

NORTH RIM

$$ ⊞ **Grand Canyon Lodge.** This historic property, constructed mainly in the
HOTEL 1920s and '30s, is the premier lodging facility in the North Rim area.
Fodor's Choice **Pros:** steps away from gorgeous North Rim views; close to several easy
★ hiking trails. **Cons:** as the only in-park North Rim lodging option, it fills up fast; few amenities and limited Internet access. $ *Rooms from: $124* ⊠ *Hwy. 67, North Rim* ☎ *877/386–4383, 928/638–2611 May–Oct., 928/645–6865 Nov.–Apr.* ⊕ *www.grandcanyonforever.com* ⊘ *Closed mid-Oct.–mid-May* ⟿ *40 rooms, 178 cabins* ⦿ *No meals.*

OUTSIDE THE PARK

TUSAYAN

$$ ⊞ **Best Western Grand Canyon Squire Inn.** About 2 miles from the park's
HOTEL south entrance, this motel lacks the historic charm of the older lodges
FAMILY at the canyon rim, but has more amenities, including a small cowboy museum, an upscale gift shop, and one of the better restaurants in the region. **Pros:** a cool pool in summer and a hot tub for cold winter nights; children's activities at the Family Fun Center; close to South Rim. **Cons:** hall noise can be an issue with all of the in-hotel activities. $ *Rooms from: $170* ⊠ *100 Hwy. 64/U.S. 180* ☎ *928/638–2681, 800/622–6966* ⊕ *www.grandcanyonsquire.com* ⟿ *250 rooms, 4 suites* ⦿ *No meals.*

$$$ ⊞ **The Grand Hotel.** At the south end of Tusayan, this popular hotel has
HOTEL bright, clean rooms decorated in Southwestern colors, a cozy stone-
FAMILY and-timber lobby, and free Wi-Fi. **Pros:** Western entertainment; gift shop stocked with Native American art, outdoor gear, and regional books. **Cons:** somewhat generic property. $ *Rooms from: $179* ⊠ *149 Hwy. 64/U.S. 180* ☎ *928/638–3333, 888/634–7263* ⊕ *www.grandcanyongrandhotel.com* ⟿ *121 rooms* ⦿ *No meals.*

CLOSE UP

Best Campgrounds in the Grand Canyon

Within the national park, camping is permitted only in designated campsites. Some campgrounds charge nightly camping fees in addition to entrance fees, and some accept reservations up to five months in advance through ⊕ www. recreation.gov. Others are first-come, first-served.

In-park camping in a spot other than a developed rim campground requires a permit from the Backcountry Information Center, which also serves as your reservation. Permits can be requested by mail or fax only; applying well in advance is recommended. Call ☏ 928/638-7875 between 1 pm and 5 pm Monday through Friday for information.

Outside the park boundaries, there are campgrounds near the South and North rims, and in Havasu Canyon and the Kaibab National Forest. There's no camping on the West Rim, but you can pitch a tent on the beach near the Colorado River.

SOUTH RIM
Bright Angel Campground. This backcountry campground is near Phantom Ranch, at the bottom of the canyon. There are toilet facilities and running water, but no showers. ⊠ Intersection of South and North Kaibab trails ☏ 928/638-7875.

Desert View Campground. Popular for spectacular views of the canyon from the nearby watchtower, this campground doesn't take reservations; show up before noon, as it fills up fast in summer. ⊠ Desert View Dr., 23 miles east of Grand Canyon Village off Hwy. 64.

Indian Garden. Halfway down the canyon is this backcountry campground, en route to Phantom Ranch on the Bright Angel Trail. Running water and toilet facilities are available, but not showers. ⊠ Bright Angel Trail ☏ 928/638-7875.

NORTH RIM
North Rim Campground. The only designated campground at the North Rim of Grand Canyon National Park sits 3 miles north of the rim, near the general store, and has 84 RV and tent sites (no hookups). ⊠ Hwy. 67 ☏ 928/638-7888 ⊕ www.recreation.gov.

OUTSIDE THE PARK
Diamond Creek. You can camp on the banks of the Colorado River, but your peace might be interrupted by the fact that this smooth beach is a launch point for river runners. The Hualapai permit camping on their tribal lands here, with an overnight camping permit of $32.55 per person per night, which can be purchased at the Hualapai Lodge. ☏ 928/769-2210 or 888/255-9550 ⊕ www. hualapaitourism.com.

Havasu Canyon. You can stay in the primitive campgrounds in Havasu Canyon for $17 per person per night (in addition to the $40-per-person entry fee). ☏ 928/448-2174 ⊕ www.havasupaitribe.com.

Kaibab National Forest. Both developed and undeveloped campsites are available on a first-come, first-served basis May through September at this forest that surrounds Williams and extends to the Grand Canyon. ☏ 928/699-1239 or 928/638-2443 ⊕ www.fs.usda.gov/kaibab.

18

WILLIAMS

$ 🚂 **Canyon Motel and RV Park.** Railcars, cabooses, and cottages make up this
HOTEL 13-acre property on the outskirts of Williams. **Pros:** family-friendly prop-
FAMILY erty with hiking, horseshoes, playground, and indoor swimming pool;
general store and Wi-Fi; friendly and helpful owners. **Cons:** short drive
to restaurants and shops; RV-park traffic. ⑤ *Rooms from: $76* ⊠ *1900 E.
Rodeo Rd., Rte. 66, Williams* ☎ *928/635–9371, 800/482–3955* ⊕ *www.
thecanyonmotel.com* ⇒ *18 rooms, 5 railcar suites* ⦿ *No meals.*

$$ 🚂 **Grand Canyon Railway Hotel.** Designed to resemble the train depot's
HOTEL original Fray Marcos lodge, this hotel features attractive Southwest-
ern-style accommodations with large bathrooms and comfy beds with
upscale linens. **Pros:** railway package options; game room and outdoor
playground; short walk from historic downtown restaurants and bars.
Cons: large-scale property. ⑤ *Rooms from: $169* ⊠ *233 North Grand
Canyon Blvd., Williams* ☎ *928/635–4010, 800/843–8724* ⊕ *www.
thetrain.com* ⇒ *287 rooms, 11 suites* ⦿ *No meals.*

NORTH RIM

$$ 🚂 **Jacob Lake Inn.** The bustling lodge at Jacob Lake Inn is a popular stop
HOTEL for those heading to the North Rim, 45 miles south. **Pros:** grocery store,
bakery, and restaurant; quiet rooms. **Cons:** only the newer rooms have
TVs; old-fashioned key locks. ⑤ *Rooms from: $108* ⊠ *U.S. 89A and
Hwy. 67, Jacob Lake* ☎ *928/643–7232* ⊕ *www.jacoblake.com* ⇒ *32
rooms, 26 cabins* ⦿ *No meals.*

$ 🚂 **Marble Canyon Lodge.** Popular with anglers and rafters, this Arizona
HOTEL Strip lodge offers two types of accommodations: standard rooms in the
original lodge building and two-bedroom apartments in a newer building. **Pros:** convenience store, restaurant, and trading post; great fishing
on the Colorado River. **Cons:** no-frills rustic lodging. ⑤ *Rooms from:
$70* ⊠ *¼ mile west of Navajo Bridge on U.S. 89A, Marble Canyon*
☎ *928/355–2225, 800/726–1789* ⊕ *www.marblecanyoncompany.com*
⇒ *46 rooms, 8 apartments* ⦿ *No meals.*

WEST RIM

$$ 🚂 **Hualapai Ranch.** Accommodations at the comfortable Hualapai
B&B/INN Ranch, the only lodging on the West Rim, are available through Huala-
FAMILY pai Tourism, and hotel rates include Continental breakfast. **Pros:** front
porches have nice desert views; rustlers tell tall tales while you roast
s'mores at campfire programs; dining room serves meals all day long.
Cons: no phones, Internet, or TVs. ⑤ *Rooms from: $142* ⊠ *Quarter-
master Point Rd., Grand Canyon West* ☎ *928/769–2636, 888/868–
9378* ⊕ *www.hualapaitourism.com* ⇒ *26 cabins* ⦿ *Breakfast.*

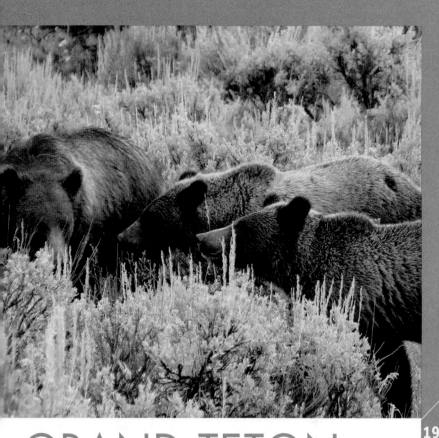

GRAND TETON NATIONAL PARK

WELCOME TO GRAND TETON NATIONAL PARK

TOP REASONS TO GO

★ **Heavenward hikes:** Trek where grizzled frontiersmen roamed. Jackson Hole got its name from mountain man Davey Jackson; now there are hundreds of trails for you to explore.

★ **Wildlife big and small:** Keep an eye out for little fellows like short-tailed weasels and beaver, as well as bison, elk, wolves, and both black and grizzly bears.

★ **Waves to make:** Float the Snake River or take a canoe onto Jackson Lake or Jenny Lake.

★ **Homesteader history:** Visit the 1890s barns and ranch buildings of Mormon Row or Menor's Ferry.

★ **Cycling paradise:** Take to two wheels for safe, speedy transport to and through Grand Teton on miles of pathways and rural roads, then get off the beaten path for spectacular singletrack.

★ **Trout trophies:** Grab your rod and slither over to the Snake River, where cutthroat trout are an angler's delight.

1 Antelope Flats. Buffalo and antelope frequently roam across this sagebrush-covered area northeast of Moose; it's also where the homesteader barns along Mormon Row dot the landscape. This is a popular place for wildflower viewing and bicycle rides.

2 Jenny Lake. In this developed area, you can go to the visitor center, purchase supplies, and talk to a ranger—plus ride a boat across the lake, hike around it, have a picnic, or camp nearby.

3 Moose. Just north of Craig Thomas Discovery and Visitor Center, this historical area is home to the tranquil Chapel of the Transfiguration and Menor's Ferry, the only way across the Snake until a bridge was built in 1927.

4 Oxbow Bend. At this famously scenic spot, the Snake River, its inhabitants, and the Tetons all converge, especially in early morning or near dusk. You're likely to see moose feeding in willows, elk grazing in aspen stands, and birds such as bald eagles, osprey, sandhill cranes, ducks, and American white pelicans.

GETTING ORIENTED

Grand Teton's rugged peaks jut more than a mile above the valley floor in Jackson Hole. Without any foothills as prelude, the sight of these glacier-scoured crags is striking indeed. Several piedmont lakes reflect the mountains, and the winding Snake River cuts south through the expansive sagebrush flats in the heart of the park. The northern portion of the park is outstanding wildlife-watching territory—you can see everything from rare birds to lumbering moose to the big predators (wolves and black and grizzly bears). Two main roads run through the 310,000-acre park; highway U.S. 26/89/191 curves along the eastern or outer side, and Teton Park Road (closed during winter) runs close to the foot of the mountain range.

> 191
> 287
> 89
TO
YELLOWSTONE
NATIONAL PARK

Survey Peak
9,277 ft

WYOMING

Lizard Creek

MOOSE BASIN

0   5 miles
0   7 km

Moose
Mountain
10,054 ft

Ranger Peak
11,355 ft

Jackson
Lake

Two
Ocean
Lake

Visitor Center

Eagles Rest Peak
11,258 ft

Colter Bay

Emma
Matilda Lake

Rolling Thunder Mountain
10,908 ft

Jackson
Lake Lodge

Traverse Peak
11,051 ft

Half Moon
Bay

TO
DUBOIS

Willow Flats

Chapel of the Sacred Heart

Oxbow Bend

Moran
Bay

Signal Mountain Lodge

Moran
Junction

4

26
287

Mount Moran
12,605 ft

Leigh
Lake

Signal Mountain Drive

Signal
Mountain

R A N G E

Spalding
Bay

Mount Woodring
11,590 ft

String
Lake
Trailhead

Teton Park Rd.

191

Cathedral Group
Turnout

THE
POTHOLES

Cunningham Cabin
Historic Site

String
Lake

Mount St John
11,430 ft

Hidden Falls

2

Jenny Lake Lodge

Snake River
Overlook

CASCADE CANYON

Jenny
Lake

River

CASCADE CANYON

Triangle X Ranch

Mount Owen
12,928 ft

Teewinot Mtn
12,325 ft

Visitor Center

Grand Teton
13,770 ft

Middle Teton

South Teton
12,514 ft

Nez
Perce

Taggart Lake
Trailhead

1

ANTELOPE FLATS

T E T O N

Buck
Mountain

Taggart
Lake

Glacier View
Turnout

Teton
Science School
Kelly Campus

19

DEATH CANYON

Chapel of the
Transfiguration

Menor's Ferry
Historic Area

Lower
Slide Lake

Death Canyon Trailhead

Phelps Lake

Visitor Center

Mount Hunt
10,783 ft

Moose Junction

3

Mormon Row
Historic Area

River

GRANITE CANYON

Blacktail Butte
7,688 ft

Rendezvous Peak
10,927 ft

Granite Canyon
Trailhead

J A C K S O N

Visitor Center

Kelly

Teton
Village

Jackson Hole
Airport

Gros Ventre

Gros
Ventre
Junction

H O L E

Multiuse
Pathway

TO
DRIGGS, ID

River

Gros

Ventre

191

Wilson

Multiuse
Pathway

22

Jackson

WEST GROS VENTRE

EAST GROS VENTRE

KEY	
🧍	Ranger Station
⛺	Campground
⛱	Picnic Area
🍴	Restaurant
🏠	Lodge
🥾	Trailhead
🚻	Restrooms
⚜	Scenic Viewpoint
⋮⋮⋮⋮	Walking/Hiking Trails

Updated by
Lea Brayton

Your jaw might drop the first time you see the Teton Range rising above the Jackson Hole valley floor. With no foothills to get in the way, you'll have a close-up, unimpeded view of magnificent, jagged, snowcapped peaks. This massif is long on natural beauty, dominated by the 13,770-foot Grand Teton. Before your eyes, mountain glaciers creep down 12,605-foot Mount Moran. Large and small lakes gleam along the range's base. Many of the West's iconic animals— elk, bears, bald eagles among them—call this park home.

GRAND TETON PLANNER

WHEN TO GO

In July and August all the roads, trails, and visitor centers are open, and the Snake River's float season is in full swing. Lower rates and smaller crowds can be found in spring and fall, but some services and roads are limited. Grand Teton Lodge Company, the park's major concessionaire, winds down its activities in late September, and most of Teton Park Road closes from November through April (highway U.S. 26/191/89 stays open all winter). In spring and fall, Teton Park Road is open to pedestrians, cyclists, and in-line skaters; in winter, it's transformed into a cross-country ski trail. ■ TIP➔ To have access to most services without the crowds, plan a trip in late May, June, or September.

Towns outside the park rev up in winter. Teton Village and Jackson both buzz with the energy of Snow King Resort and Jackson Hole Mountain Resort, the former conveniently in town, the latter an international skiing hot spot 13 miles from Jackson. Prices rise for the peak winter season.

AVG. HIGH/LOW TEMPS.

Jan.	Feb.	Mar.	Apr.	May	June
28/5	33/8	43/17	53/24	63/31	74/37
July	Aug.	Sept.	Oct.	Nov.	Dec.
82/41	81/39	71/31	59/23	40/16	28/6

FESTIVALS AND EVENTS

YEAR-ROUND **Grand Teton Music Festival.** Since 1962, these summer symphony concerts have been wowing audiences in the world-renowned Walk Festival Hall in Teton Village. Under the direction of Maestro Donald Runnicles, the festival presents full orchestra concerts on Friday and Saturday in July and the first half of August, and smaller ensembles from Tuesday to Thursday. In winter, concerts take place at least monthly. Tickets cost between $25 and $55, but many performances are free. ⊠ *Walk Festival Hall, 3330 Cody La., Teton Village* ☎ *307/733–1128* ⊕ *www.gtmf.org.*

MARCH **Pole-Pedal-Paddle.** Individuals and teams competing seriously or just out for fun participate in this four-part race that has alpine and cross-country skiing segments as well as bicycling and boating legs. Usually held on the last Saturday of March, the race, a fund-raiser, starts at the Jackson Hole Mountain Resort and ends in the Snake River Canyon. ⊠ *Jackson Hole* ☎ *307/733–6433* ⊕ *jhskiclub.org/polepedalpaddle.*

MAY **ElkFest.** The centerpiece of this free two-day festival on the third weekend of May is the Jackson Hole Boy Scout Elk Antler Auction, at which thousands of pounds of naturally shed antlers are sold to the highest bidder. Pick up some horns for your decor, get a taste of the High Noon Chili Cookoff, or just enjoy the spectacle of khaki-clad lads hauling around massive racks. ⊠ *Jackson* ☎ *307/733–3316* ⊕ *www.elkfest.org.*

Old West Days. This festival's Memorial Day weekend activities include a rodeo, a parade, a brew fest, cowboy music, and the Mountain Man Rendezvous—atlatl (dart-hurling) competition, anyone?—plus the start of the Jackson Hole Shootout's summer performances. ⊠ *Town Square, Jackson* ☎ *307/733–3316* ⊕ *www.jacksonholechamber.com/ old_west_days.*

MAY– **JH Shootout.** Following a tradition more than half a century old, gun-
SEPTEMBER slingers stage a shootout on summer evenings at 6 pm (except Sunday), at the Town Square's northeastern corner. Don't worry, the bullets aren't real. ⊠ *Jackson Hole* ☎ *307/733–3316* ⊕ *www.jacksonholechamber. com/events/jh-shootout.php.*

SEPTEMBER **Fall Arts Festival.** More than 50 events celebrate art, music, food, and wine throughout Jackson Hole during the 11-day annual festival, which runs from the first to the second weekend of September. Catch live painting and sculpting demonstrations in the popular quickdraw event, then bid for the spontaneous art. ⊠ *Town Square, Jackson* ☎ *307/733– 3316* ⊕ *www.jacksonholechamber.com/fall_arts_festival.*

19

PLANNING YOUR TIME
GRAND TETON IN ONE DAY

Begin the day by packing a picnic lunch or picking one up at a Jackson eatery. Arrive at **Craig Thomas Discovery and Visitor Center** in time for a 9 am, two-hour, guided Snake River scenic float trip (make required reservations with one of the half-dozen outfitters that offer the trip). When you're back on dry ground, drive north on Teton Park Road, stopping at scenic turnouts—don't miss Teton Glacier—until you reach South Jenny Lake Junction.

Park at the Jenny Lake ranger station and take the 20-minute boat ride to the **west shore boat dock** for a short but breathtaking hike to **Hidden Falls** or **Inspiration Point.** Return to your car by mid-afternoon, drive back to Teton Park Road, and head north to Signal Mountain Road to catch an elevated view of the Tetons. In late afternoon descend the mountain and continue north on Teton Park Road.

At Jackson Lake Junction, you can go east to **Oxbow Bend** or north to **Willow Flats,** both excellent spots for wildlife viewing before you head to **Jackson Lake Lodge** for dinner and an evening watching the sun set over the Tetons. Or if you'd like to get back on the water, drive to **Colter Bay Village Marina,** where you can board a 1½-hour sunset cruise across Jackson Lake to Elk Island. You can reverse this route if you're heading south from Yellowstone: start the day with a 7:30 breakfast cruise from Colter Bay and end it with a sunset float down the Snake River.

GETTING HERE AND AROUND
AIR TRAVEL

Jackson Hole Airport (JAC), the only commercial airport inside a national park, was established before the park opened. Five airlines service the modern airport.

BUS TRAVEL

Grand Teton Lodge Company has shuttle service that makes six trips a day between Colter Bay and Jackson, with several stops in between. It's free for guests of the lodge and $12 for everyone else.

CAR TRAVEL

The best way to see Grand Teton National Park is by car. Unlike Yellowstone's Grand Loop, Grand Teton's road system doesn't allow for easy tour-bus access to the major sights. Only a car will get you close to Jenny Lake, into the remote Gros Ventre Range on the east side of the valley, and to the top of Signal Mountain. You can stop at many points along the roads within the park for a hike or to take in the view. Be extremely cautious in winter when whiteouts and ice are not uncommon. There are adequate road signs throughout the park, but a map is handy to have in the vehicle.

Jackson Hole's main highway (U.S. 89/191) runs the entire length of the park, from Jackson to Yellowstone National Park's south entrance. This highway is also called U.S. 26 south of Moran Junction and U.S. 287 north of Moran Junction. This road is open all year from Jackson to Moran Junction and north to Flagg Ranch, 2 miles south of Yellowstone. In light traffic, the southern (Moose) entrance to Grand Teton is a drive of about 15 minutes from downtown Jackson via the highway. Coming from the opposite direction on the same road, the northern boundary of the park is about 15 minutes south of Yellowstone National Park. Also open year-round, U.S. 26/287 runs east from Dubois over Togwotee Pass to the Moran entrance station, a drive of about one hour.

Two back-road entrances to Grand Teton require high-clearance vehicles. Both roads are closed by snow from November through mid-May and can be heavily rutted through June. Moose-Wilson Road (Wyoming Highway 390) starts at Highway 22 in Wilson (5 miles west of Jackson) and travels 7 miles north past Teton Village to the Granite Canyon entrance station. Of the 9 miles from here to Moose, 1½ are gravel. This route is closed to large trucks, trailers, and RVs. Even rougher is 60-mile Grassy Lake Road, which heads east from Highway 32 in Ashton, Idaho, through Targhee National Forest. It connects with U.S. 89/287 in the John D. Rockefeller Jr. Memorial Parkway, sandwiched between Grand Teton and Yellowstone.

PARK ESSENTIALS

PARK FEES AND PERMITS

Park entrance costs $30 per car, truck, or RV; $20 per motorcycle; and $12 per person on foot or bicycle, good for seven days in Grand Teton. The cost is $50 for the same car, truck, or RV pass to both Grand Teton and Yellowstone parks. Annual park passes cost $60. The winter day-use fee is $5.

Backcountry permits, which must be retrieved in person at the Craig Thomas Discovery and Visitor Center, Colter Bay Visitor Center, or Jenny Lake Ranger Station, cost $25, with an additional $10 fee for reservations. Permits are required for all overnight stays outside designated campgrounds.

For those bringing boats into the park, seven-day permits are available year-round at Craig Thomas Discovery and Visitor Center and in summer at the Jenny Lake and Colter Bay visitor centers. Annual permits cost $40 for motorized craft and $10 for nonmotorized craft, including stand-up paddleboards. State law also requires a special Aquatic Invasive Species decal. Wyoming residents pay $10 for motorized watercraft and $5 for nonmotorized craft; out-of-state visitors pay $30 and $15, respectively.

19

PARK HOURS

The park is open 24/7 year-round. It's in the Mountain time zone.

CELL-PHONE RECEPTION

Cell phones work in most developed areas and occasionally on trails. Public phones are at Dornan's, south Jenny Lake, Signal Mountain Lodge, Moran Entrance Station, Jackson Lake Lodge, Colter Bay Village, Leeks Marina, and Flagg Ranch.

RANGER PROGRAMS

FOR CHILDREN

FAMILY **Junior Ranger Program.** Children and even adults can earn a Junior Ranger badge or patch by attending a program and picking up a Junior Ranger booklet at any visitor center in the park. Learn about the natural world of the park on an easy 1-mile round-trip hike with a ranger. Kids should wear old clothes and bring water, rain gear, and insect repellent. ⊠ *Grand Teton National Park* ✛ *Meet outside Jenny Lake Visitor Center* ☎ *307/739–3399, 307/739–3594.*

FAMILY **Nature Explorer's Backpack Program.** Rangers lend a nature journal and a backpack full of activities to children ages six through 12 before sending them out along the trails at the Rockefeller Preserve. ⊠ *Laurance S. Rockefeller Preserve Interpretive Center, east side of Moose-Wilson Rd.* ✛ *4 miles south of Moose, 3 miles north of Granite Canyon Entrance Station* ☎ *307/739–3654* ☉ *Late May–early Sept., daily 9–5.*

GENERAL

Campfire Programs. In summer, park rangers give free slide-show presentations at Colter Bay and sometimes elsewhere. For locations and schedules of topics, check at the visitor centers or in the *Grand Teton Guide* park newspaper. ⊠ *Grand Teton National Park* ☎ *307/739–3399, 307/739–3594* ☉ *June and July, nightly.*

RESTAURANTS

Though the park itself has some excellent restaurants, don't miss dining in Jackson, where chefs apply European and other cooking techniques to game, fowl, and fish dishes and generally include vegetarian entrées. Steaks are usually cut from grass-fed Wyoming or Montana beef, but you'll also find buffalo and elk on the menu; poultry and pasta are offered by most restaurants, as are fresh salads and fish (trout, tilapia, and salmon are most common). Just about everywhere, you can order a burger or a bowl of soup. Casual is the word for most dining within and outside the park. An exception is Jenny Lake Lodge, where jackets and ties for men are recommended for dinner. Breakfast is big: steak and eggs, pancakes, biscuits and gravy; lunches are lighter, often taken in a sack to enjoy on the trail.

HOTELS

The choice of lodging properties within the park is as diverse as the landscape itself. You'll find simple campgrounds, cabins, and standard motel rooms, but you can also settle into a homey bed-and-breakfast or a luxurious suite in a full-service resort. Between June and August, rates go up and rooms are harder to get unless you make a reservation well ahead of your visit.

For information on lodging and dining in the park, contact the park's largest concessionaire, Grand Teton Lodge Company. ☎ *307/543–2811* ⊕ *www.gtlc.com. Hotel reviews have been shortened. For full information, visit Fodors.com.*

WHAT IT COSTS				
	$	**$$**	**$$$**	**$$$$**
Restaurants	under $13	$13–$20	$21–$30	over $30
Hotels	under $100	$100–$150	$151–$200	over $200

Restaurant prices are the average cost of a main course at dinner, or if dinner is not served, at lunch. Hotel prices are the lowest cost of a standard double room in high season.

TOURS

Alltrans Tours. Full-day bus tours from Jackson provide an overview of Grand Teton National Park. You'll learn about the park's geology, history, birds, plants, and wildlife. ⊠ *940 W. Broadway, Jackson* ☏ *307/733–3135, 800/443–6133* ⊕ *www.jacksonholealltrans.com* ⊠ *From $129* ⊗ *Daily June–Sept.*

Grand Teton Lodge Company Bus Tours. Half-day tours depart from Jackson Lake Lodge and include visits to scenic viewpoints, visitor centers, and other park sites. Guides provide information about park geology, history, wildlife, and ecosystems. Buy tickets in advance at Colter Bay or Jackson Lake Lodge activities desks. Full-day tours continue into Yellowstone. ⊠ *Jackson Lake Lodge* ☏ *307/543–2811, 800/628–9988* ⊕ *www.gtlc.com/activities* ⊠ *From $67* ⊗ *Mid-May–early Oct., Mon.–Sat.*

Jackson Lake Cruises. Grand Teton Lodge Company runs 1½-hour Jackson Lake cruises from Colter Bay Village Marina throughout the day, as well as three-hour breakfast cruises and sunset cruises. Guides explain how forest fires and glaciers have shaped the Grand Teton landscape. ⊹ *2 miles off U.S. 89/191/287, 5 miles north of Jackson Lake Junction* ☏ *307/543–3100, 800/628–9988* ⊕ *www.gtlc.com/activities* ⊠ *From $30* ⊗ *Late May–mid-Sept.*

FAMILY **Teton Science School.** The school conducts wildlife expeditions in Grand Teton, Yellowstone, and surrounding forests—participants see and learn about wolves, bears, bighorn sheep, and other animals. Full-day and half-day excursions are offered, as well as custom trips. The bear and wolf expedition is a thrilling three-day, two-night field adventure during spring and fall. ⊠ *700 Coyote Canyon Rd., Jackson* ☏ *307/733–1313* ⊕ *www.tetonscience.org* ⊠ *Half-day tours $130; full-day tour $210, multiday programs $1,200–$3,300.*

VISITOR INFORMATION

Park Contact Information Grand Teton National Park. ⊠ *Jackson Hole* ☏ *307/739–3300* ⊕ *www.nps.gov/grte.*

VISITOR CENTERS

Colter Bay Visitor Center. A small display shows off items from the park's collection of American Indian artifacts. (Hundreds more are being cleaned and restored for future displays.) In summer, rangers lead various hikes from here. On the back deck they present short evening programs about bear safety and the park's history. ⊠ *Colter Bay*

19

Marina Rd., off Colter Bay Village Rd., ½ mile west of U.S. 89/191/287, Oxbow Bend ☎ *307/739–3594* ☉ *June–early Sept., daily 8–7.*

Craig Thomas Discovery and Visitor Center. This sleek center has interactive and interpretive exhibits dedicated to themes of preservation, mountaineering, and local wildlife. There's also a 3-D map of the park and streaming video along a footpath showing the area's intricate natural features. Dozens of Native American artifacts from the David T. Vernon Collection are housed here. A plush, 155-seat theater occasionally screens nature documentaries. ⊠ *Moose* ⊹ *½ mile west of Moose Junction* ☎ *307/739–3399* ☉ *Early June–late Sept., daily 8–7; call for fall and spring hrs.*

Jenny Lake Visitor Center. This historic log cabin was used as a studio by the first official park photographer, Harrison Crandall. Geology exhibits explain how faults moved the mountains. ⊠ *Jenny Lake* ⊹ *S. Jenny Lake Junction, 8 miles north of Moose Junction, off Teton Park Rd.* ☎ *307/739–3392* ☉ *May–late Sept., daily 8–7; call for spring and fall hrs.*

Laurance S. Rockefeller Preserve Interpretive Center. This contemporary structure feels more like an art gallery than an interpretive facility. The elegant, eco-friendly building is more than just eye candy—you can experience the sounds of the park in a cylindrical audio chamber, and laminated maps in the reading room are great for trip planning., Rangers here promote "contemplative hiking" and are well informed about the many birds around the center's trailheads. It's best to get here in the early morning or late evening because the small parking area fills quickly. ⊹ *East side of Moose-Wilson Rd., about 4 miles south of Moose and 3 miles north of Granite Canyon Entrance Station* ☎ *307/739–3654* ☉ *Early June–mid Sept., daily 9–5; call for off-season hrs* ☞ *Limited group size (no more than 10 to a party); vehicle-size restrictions on Moose-Wilson Rd.*

EXPLORING

SCENIC DRIVES

FAMILY **Antelope Flats Road.** Off U.S. 191/26/89, about 2 miles north of Moose Junction, this narrow road wanders eastward over sagebrush flats. The road intersects the gravel Mormon Row, where you can turn off to see abandoned homesteaders' barns and houses from the turn of the 20th century. Less than 2 miles past Mormon Row is a three-way intersection where you can turn right to loop around past the town of Kelly and Gros Ventre campground and rejoin U.S. 191/26/89 at Gros Ventre Junction. Keep an eye out for abundant pronghorn, bison, moose, raptors, and cyclists. ⊠ *Grand Teton National Park.*

Fodor's Choice ★ **Jenny Lake Scenic Drive.** This 4-mile, one-way loop provides the park's best roadside close-ups of the Tetons as it winds south through groves of lodgepole pine and open meadows. Roughly 1½ miles off Teton Park Road, the Cathedral Group Turnout faces 13,770-foot Grand Teton (the range's highest peak), flanked by 12,928-foot Mount Owen and 12,325-foot Mount Teewinot. ⊠ *Jenny Lake.*

Plants and Wildlife in Grand Teton

CLOSE UP

Grand Teton's short growing season and arid climate create a complex ecosystem and hardy plant species. The dominant elements are big sagebrush—which gives the valley its gray-green cast—lodgepole pine trees, quaking aspen, and ground-covering wildflowers such as bluish-purple lupine.

SHORT GROWING SEASON
In spring and early summer you will see the vibrant yellow arrowleaf balsamroot and low larkspur. Jackson Hole's short growing season gives rise to spectacular if short-lived displays of wildflowers, best seen between mid-June and early July. The changing of the aspen and cottonwood leaves in early fall can be equally dazzling.

OFT AND RARELY SEEN WILDLIFE
On almost any trip to Grand Teton, you will see bison, pronghorn antelope, and moose. More rarely you will see a black or grizzly bear, a fox, or a wolf. Watch for elk along the forest edge, and, in the summer, on Teton Park Road. Oxbow Bend and Willow Flats are good places to look for moose, beaver, and otter in twilight hours any time of year. Pronghorn and bison appear in summer along the highway and Antelope Flats Road.

SMALLER ANIMALS
The park's smaller animals—yellow-bellied marmots, pikas, and Uinta ground squirrels, as well as a variety of birds and waterfowl—are commonly seen along park trails and waterways. Seek out water sources—the Snake River, the glacial lakes, and marshy areas—to see birds such as bald eagles, ospreys, ducks, and trumpeter swans. Your best chance to see wildlife is at dawn or dusk.

FAMILY **Signal Mountain Summit.** This exciting drive climbs 700 feet along a 4-mile stretch of winding road. As you travel through forest you can catch glimpses of Jackson Lake and Mount Moran. At the top of the road, park and follow the well-marked path to one of the park's best panoramas. From 7,593 feet above sea level your gaze can sweep over all of Jackson Hole and the 40-mile Teton Range. The views are particularly dramatic at sunset. The road is not appropriate for long trailers and is closed in winter. ✛ *Off Teton Park Rd., south of Jackson Lake Junction.*

19

HISTORIC SITES

Cunningham Cabin Historic Site. At the end of a gravel spur road, an easy ¾-mile trail runs through sagebrush around Pierce Cunningham's 1890 log-cabin homestead. Although you can peer inside, the building has no furnishings or displays. Watch for badgers, coyotes, and Uinta ground squirrels in the area. ⊠ *Antelope Flats* ✛ *½ mile off Jackson Hole Hwy., 5 miles south of Moran Junction.*

Menor's Ferry Historic Area. Down a path from the Chapel of the Transfiguration, the ferry on display here is not the original, but it's an accurate re-creation of the double-pontoon craft built by Bill Menor in 1894. It demonstrates how people crossed the Snake River before bridges were built. In the cluster of turn-of-the-20th-century buildings there are historical displays. Pick up a pamphlet for a self-guided tour, and check out the nearby general store, where candy and soda are sold in the summer. The ferry typically runs after spring runoff, between June and August, and only when a park ranger is available to operate it. ✛ *½ mile off Teton Park Rd., 1 mile north of Moose Junction* ☉ *Daily sunrise–sunset.*

Mormon Row Historic Area. Settled by homesteaders between 1896 and 1907, this area received its name because many of them were members of the Church of Jesus Christ of Latter-day Saints, also known as Mormons. The remaining barns, homes, and outbuildings are representative of early homesteading in the West. You can wander around, hike the row, and take photographs. The century-old T.A. Moulton Barn is said to be the most-photographed barn in the state. ✛ *Off Antelope Flats Rd., 2 miles north of Moose Junction* ☉ *Daily.*

SCENIC STOPS

Chapel of the Sacred Heart. This small log Catholic chapel sits in the pine forest with a view of Jackson Lake. It's open only for services, but you can enjoy the view anytime. ✛ *½ mile north of Signal Mountain Lodge, off Teton Park Rd.* ☎ *307/733–2516* ☉ *Services mid-June–late Sept., weekends at 5.*

Chapel of the Transfiguration. This tiny chapel built in 1925 on land donated by Maud Noble is still a functioning Episcopal church. Couples come here to exchange vows with the Tetons as a backdrop, and tourists snap photos of the small church with its awe-inspiring view. ✉ *Chapel of the Transfiguration Rd., ½ mile off Teton Park Rd., Moose* ☎ *307/733–2603* ⊕ *www.stjohnsjackson.org* ☉ *Services late May–late Sept., Sun. at 8 and 10.*

Jackson Lake. The biggest of Grand Teton's glacier-carved lakes, this body of water in the park's northern reaches was enlarged by construction of the Jackson Lake Dam in 1906. You can fish, sail, and windsurf here. Three marinas (Colter Bay, Leeks, and Signal Mountain) provide access for boaters, and several picnic areas, campgrounds, and lodges overlook the lake. ✛ *U.S. 89/191/287 from Lizard Creek to Jackson Lake Junction, and Teton Park Rd. from Jackson Lake Junction to Signal Mountain Lodge.*

Jenny Lake. Named for the Shoshone wife of Beaver Dick Leigh, a mountain man, this glacier-carved lake south of Jackson Lake draws paddlesports enthusiasts to its pristine waters and hikers to its tree-shaded trails. ✛ *Off Teton Park Rd. midway between Moose and Jackson Lake.*

Oxbow Bend. This peaceful spot overlooks a quiet backwater left by the Snake River when it cut a new southern channel. White pelicans stop here on their spring migration (many stay on through summer), sandhill cranes and trumpeter swans visit frequently, and great blue herons nest amid the cottonwoods along the river. Use binoculars to search for bald eagles, osprey, moose, beaver, and otter. The Oxbow is known for the reflection of Mount. Moran that marks its calm waters in early morning. ✛ *U.S. 89/191/287, 2½ miles east of Jackson Lake Junction.*

Willow Flats. You will almost always see moose grazing in this marshy area, in part because of its flourishing willow bushes, where moose both eat and hide. This is also a good place to see birds and waterfowl. ⊹ *U.S. 89/191/287, 1 mile north of Jackson Lake Junction.*

SPORTS AND THE OUTDOORS

BICYCLING

Since the first paved pathways were completed in Jackson Hole in 1996, the valley has become a cyclist's paradise. Almost 60 miles of paved pathways thread through Jackson Hole, with more in the works. Those on two wheels can access Grand Teton on a path that begins at the north end of town and travels 21 miles to South Jenny Lake Junction. A bike lane permits two-way bike traffic along the one-way Jenny Lake Loop Road, a one-hour ride. The River Road, 4 miles north of Moose, is an easy four-hour mountain-bike ride along a ridge above the Snake River on a gravel road. Bicycles are not allowed on trails or in the backcountry.

In the Bridger-Teton National Forest that surrounds Jackson, the Snow King Mountain trail system offers miles of singletrack, from easy to challenging. The Cache Creek to Game Creek loop is a 25-mile ride on dirt roads, trails, and a paved pathway. Roadies can enjoy the rural Fish Creek or Fall Creek roads, and downhillers revel in the Bike Park at Jackson Hole Mountain Resort. Maps can be obtained at the Jackson Hole and Greater Yellowstone Visitor Center at the north end of town on Cache Street.

OUTFITTERS

Hoback Sports. Get your own bike tuned up or rent one: road, mountain, hybrid, kids', and trailers. The shop also sells bikes, clothing, and mountain sporting accessories, and offers daily mountain-bike tours. ✉ *520 W. Broadway, Suite 3, Jackson* ☎ *307/733–5335* ⊕ *www.hobacksports. com* ⊗ *Daily 9–7.*

19

BIRD-WATCHING

With more than 300 species of birds, the Tetons make excellent bird-watching country. Here you might spot both the calliope hummingbird (the smallest North American hummingbird) and the trumpeter swan (the world's largest waterfowl). Birds of prey circle around Antelope Flats Road—the surrounding fields are good hunting turf for red-tailed hawks and prairie falcons. At Taggart Lake you might see woodpeckers, bluebirds, and hummingbirds. Look for songbirds, such as pine and evening grosbeaks and Cassin's finches, in surrounding open pine and aspen forests.

Oxbow Bend. Impressive birds congregate at this quiet spot. In spring, white pelicans stop by during their northerly migration; in summer, bald eagles, great blue herons, and osprey nest nearby. Year-round, you'll have a good chance of seeing trumpeter swans. Nearby **Willow Flats**

has similar bird life, plus sandhill cranes. ⊠ *U.S. 89/191/287, 2 miles east of Jackson Lake Junction.*

Phelps Lake. The moderate, 1.8-mile round-trip Phelps Lake Overlook Trail takes you from the Death Canyon trailhead up conifer- and aspen-lined glacial moraine to a view that's accessible only on foot. Expect abundant bird life: Western tanagers, northern flickers, and ruby-crowned kinglets thrive in the bordering woods, and hummingbirds feed on scarlet gilia beneath the overlook. Don't neglect the Phelps Lake Trail, which circles the lake and is accessible from either Death Canyon or the Rockefeller Preserve. ⊠ *Moose-Wilson Rd., about 3 miles off Teton Park Rd..*

BOATING AND WATER SPORTS

Water sports in Grand Teton are diverse. You can float the Snake River, which runs high and fast early in the season (May and June) and more slowly during the latter part of the summer. Canoes, kayaks, and stand-up paddleboards dominate the smaller lakes and share the water with motorboats on large Jackson Lake. Motorboats also are allowed on Jenny Lake, but there's an engine limit of 10 horsepower. You can launch your boat at Colter Bay, Leek's Marina, Signal Mountain, and Spalding Bay on Jackson Lake.

If you're floating the Snake River on your own, you are required to purchase a permit ($20 per boat for the entire season, or $10 per raft for seven days). Permits are available year-round at Craig Thomas Discovery and Visitor Center and in summer at Colter Bay. Before you set out, check with park rangers about current conditions.

You may prefer to take one of the many guided float trips through calm-water sections of the Snake; outfitters pick you up at the float-trip parking area near Craig Thomas Discovery and Visitor Center for a 15-minute drive to upriver launch sites. Ponchos and life preservers are provided. Early morning and evening floats are your best bets for wildlife viewing. Be sure to carry a jacket or sweater. Float season runs from mid-April to mid-December.

Colter Bay Village Marina. All types of services are available to boaters, including free parking for boat trailers and vehicles, free mooring, guided fishing trips, boat rentals, and fuel. ⊠ *On Jackson Lake* ☎ *307/543–3100, 800/628–9988.*

Leek's Marina. Parking for boat trailers and other vehicles is available for up to three nights. There are no boat rentals, but there is free short-term docking. The pizza restaurant here is superb. Park concessionaire Signal Mountain Lodge operates the marina. ⊠ *U.S. 89/191/287, 6 miles north of Jackson Lake Junction* ☎ *307/543–2831* ☉ *Mid-May–late Sept.*

Signal Mountain Lodge Marina. The marina rents pontoon boats, deck cruisers, motorboats, kayaks, and canoes by the hour or all day; rates run from $19 an hour for a kayak to $129 an hour for a deck cruiser. ⊠ *Teton Park Rd., 3 miles south of Jackson Lake Junction* ☎ *307/543–2831* ⊕ *signalmountainlodge.com/boat-rentals* ☉ *Mid-May–late Sept.*

Spalding Bay. You can launch your boat here and park your trailer and vehicle for the day. No docking or mooring is available. ⊹ *2 miles off Teton Park Rd., 7 miles south of Jackson Lake Junction.*

TOURS AND OUTFITTERS

Barker-Ewing Scenic Float Trips. Travel the peaceful parts of the Snake River within the park and look for wildlife as knowledgeable guides talk about area history, geology, plants, and animals. ⊠ *Moose* ☎ *307/733–1800, 800/365–1800* ⊕ *barkerewing.com* ✉ *From $70* ⊗ *May–Sept.*

Colter Bay Village Marina. You can rent motorboats, kayaks, and canoes at Colter Bay from park concessionaire Grand Teton Lodge Company, which also conducts scenic raft trips on the Snake River. ⊹ *2 miles off U.S. 89/191/287, 5 miles north of Jackson Lake Junction* ☎ *307/543–3100, 800/628–9988* ⊕ *www.gtlc.com/activities* ✉ *Kayaks and canoes $18.50 per hr, motorboats $42 per hr, scenic trips from $67* ⊗ *Late May–Sept.*

Mad River Boat Trips. Mad River leads a variety of white-water and scenic float trips, some combined with breakfast, lunch, or dinner. ⊠ *Jackson* ☎ *307/733–6203, 800/458–7238* ⊕ *www.mad-river.com* ✉ *From $52* ⊗ *Mid-May–Sept.*

Rendezvous River Sports. Join the stand-up paddleboard craze with help from the river rats at Rendezvous. Kayaking instruction and guided trips on area rivers and lakes, as well backcountry trips in the national parks, are other options. The shop rents kayaks, canoes, rafts, and paddleboards. ⊠ *Jackson* ☎ *307/733–2471* ⊕ *www.jacksonholekayak.com* ✉ *From $95 for half-day clinic; from $145 for full-day* ⊗ *Mar.–Nov.*

Triangle X National Park Float Trips. The knowledgeable and charismatic Triangle X guides will row you down 10 miles of the Snake River through pristine riparian habitat in Grand Teton National Park. For the best wildlife viewing, book a dawn or sunset supper float. ⊠ *Moose* ☎ *307/733–5500, 888/860–0005* ⊕ *nationalparkfloattrips. com* ✉ *From $70* ⊗ *Mid-May–Sept.*

19

CLIMBING

The Teton Range has some of the nation's most diverse mountaineering. Excellent rock, snow, and ice routes abound. Unless you're already a pro, it's recommended that you take a course from one of the park's concessionaire climbing schools before tackling the tough terrain. Practice your moves at Teton Boulder Park, a free outdoor artificial climbing wall in Phil Baux Park at the base of Snow King Mountain.

TOURS

Exum Mountain Guides. The climbing experiences offered by the oldest guide service in North America include one-day mountain climbs, weeklong clinics culminating in a two-day ascent of the Grand Teton, and backcountry adventures on skis and snowboards. ⊠ *Grand Teton National Park* ☎ *307/733–2297* ⊕ *www.exumguides.com* ✉ *From $255.*

Jackson Hole Mountain Guides. Beginning to advanced climbers can get instruction or explore classic granite routes in the Tetons and beyond. ✉ *1325 U.S. 89, Suite 104, Jackson* ☎ *307/733–4979, 800/239–7642* ⊕ *www.jhmg.com* 🖃 *From $185.*

FISHING

Rainbow, brook, lake, and native cutthroat trout inhabit the park's waters. The Snake's 75 miles of river and tributary are world-renowned for their fishing. To fish in Grand Teton National Park, you need a Wyoming fishing license, which you can purchase from the state game and fish department or at Colter Bay Village Marina, Dornan's, Signal Mountain Lodge, and area sporting-goods stores. A day permit for nonresidents costs $14, and an annual permit costs $92 plus $12.50 for a conservation stamp; for state residents a license costs $24 per season plus $12.50 for a conservation stamp. Children under age 14 can fish free with an adult who has a license.

Wyoming Game and Fish Department. You can purchase a fishing license from the department. ✉ *420 N. Cache St., Jackson* ☎ *307/733–2321, 307/733–2321* ⊕ *wgfd.wyo.gov.*

TOURS

Grand Teton Lodge Company. The park's major concessionaire operates guided fishing trips on Jackson Lake and guided fly-fishing trips on the Snake River. Make reservations at the activities desks at Colter Bay Village or Jackson Lake Lodge, where trips originate. ✉ *Grand Teton National Park* ☎ *307/543–3100, 800/628–9988* ⊕ *www.gtlc. com/activities* 🖃 *From $184* ⊘ *June–Sept.*

Signal Mountain Lodge. Hourly and half-day Jackson Lake guided fishing trips depart from the marina at Signal Mountain Lodge, weather permitting. The rates include equipment and tackle. ✉ *Teton Park Rd., 3 miles south of Jackson Lake Junction* ☎ *307/543–2831* ⊕ *www. signalmountainlodge.com/signal-mountain-fishing* 🖃 *From $290* ⊘ *Mid-May–mid-Sept.* ☞ *Minimum age 6.*

HIKING

Most of Grand Teton's trails are unpaved, with just a few short paved sections in the vicinity of developed areas. You can get trail maps and information about hiking conditions from rangers at the park visitor centers at Moose, Jenny Lake, and Colter Bay, where you will also find bathrooms or outhouses; there are no facilities along trails themselves. Of the more than 250 miles of maintained trails, the most popular are those around Jenny Lake, the Leigh and String lakes area, and Taggart Lake Trail, with views of Avalanche Canyon.

Frontcountry or backcountry you may see moose and bears—keep your distance. Pets are not permitted on trails or in the backcountry, but you can take them along roadsides as long as they are on a leash no more than 6 feet long. Always let someone know where you are going and when you expect to return, and carry plenty of water, snacks, rain gear, warm clothes, bear spray, and a cell phone.

EASY

Cascade Canyon Trail. Take Jenny Lake Boating's 20-minute boat ride from the dock near the Jenny Lake Visitor Center to the start of a gentle, ½-mile climb to 200-foot Hidden Falls, the park's most popular and crowded trail destination. With the boat ride ($15 round-trip), plan on a couple of hours to experience this trail. Listen here for the distinctive bleating of the rabbitlike pikas among the glacial boulders and pines. The trail continues ½ mile to Inspiration Point over a rocky path that is moderately steep. There are two points on the climb that afford good views of Jenny Lake and the surrounding area, but keep climbing; after passing a rock wall you'll finally reach the true Inspiration Point, with the best views. *Easy.* ⊹ *Trailhead: at Jenny Lake Visitor Center, ¼ mile off Teton Park Rd., 8 miles north of Moose Junction* ⊕ *www. jennylakeboating.com.*

Colter Bay Nature Trail Loop. This very easy 1¾-mile round-trip excursion treats you to views of Jackson Lake and the Tetons. As you follow the level trail along the forest's edge, you may see moose and bald eagles. Allow two hours to complete the walk. *Easy.* ⊹ *Trailhead: at Colter Bay Visitor Center, 1 mile off U.S. 89/191/287, 5 miles north of Jackson Lake Junction.*

Lunchtree Hill Trail. One of the park's easiest trails begins at Jackson Lake Lodge and leads ½ mile to the top of a hill above Willow Flats. The area's willow thickets, beaver ponds, and wet, grassy meadows make it a birder's paradise. Look for sandhill cranes, hummingbirds, and the many types of songbirds described in the free bird guide available at visitor centers. You might also see moose. Round-trip the walk takes no more than half an hour. *Easy.* ⊹ *Trailhead: at Jackson Lake Lodge, U.S. 89/191/287, ½ mile north of Jackson Lake Junction.*

MODERATE

FAMILY **Jenny Lake Loop Trail.** You can walk to Hidden Falls from Jenny Lake ranger station by following the mostly level trail around the south shore of the lake to Cascade Canyon Trail. Jenny Lake Trail continues around the lake for 6½ miles. It's an easy trail—classed here as moderate because of its length—that will take you from two to three hours. You'll walk through a lodgepole-pine forest, have expansive views of the lake and the land to the east, and hug the shoulder of the massive Teton range itself. Along the way you are likely to see elk, pikas, golden-mantled ground squirrels, a variety of ducks and water birds. You may also hear elk bugling, birdsong, and the chatter of squirrels. *Moderate.* ⊹ *Trailhead: at Jenny Lake Visitor Center, S. Jenny Lake Junction, ½ mile off Teton Park Rd., 8 miles north of Moose Junction.*

Leigh Lake Trail. This flat trail follows String Lake's northeastern shore to Leigh Lake's southern shore, covering 2 miles in a round-trip of about an hour. You can extend your hike into a moderate 7½-mile, four-hour round-trip by following the forested east shore of Leigh Lake to Bearpaw Lake. Along the way you'll have views of Mount Moran across the lake, and you may be lucky enough to spot a moose or a bear. *Moderate.* ⊹ *Trailhead: at northwest corner of String Lake Picnic*

19

Jenny Lake Loop Trail

TO STRING LAKE

TO STRING LAKE

one way

TO CASCADE CANYON

Inspiration Point

Western Shore Boat Dock

Jenny Lake Overlook

Hidden Falls

Jenny Lake

Hidden Falls Trail

Jenny Lake Shuttle Boat

Teton Park Road

Eastern Shore Boat Dock

Visitor Center

Jenny Lake Campground

Bike Trail

TO MOOSE JUNCTION

Area, ½ mile west of Jenny Lake Rd., 2 miles off Teton Park Rd., 12 miles north of Moose Junction.

String Lake Trail. The 3½-mile loop around String Lake lies in the shadows of 11,144-foot Rockchuck Peak and 11,430-foot Mount Saint John. This is also a good place to see moose and elk, hear songbirds, and view wildflowers. The trail, which takes about three hours to hike, is a bit more difficult than other mid-length trails in the park, which means it's also less crowded. *Moderate.* ✛ *Trailhead: ¼ mile west of Jenny Lake Rd., 2 miles off Teton Park Rd., 12 miles north of Moose Junction.*

Taggart Lake Trail. Hike 1½ miles from the trailhead to the lake and then continue on a 4-mile route around the lake where the terrain becomes steeper near Beaver Creek. There are views of Avalanche Canyon and areas where you might see moose. Plan on two to three hours to enjoy this trail. *Moderate.* ✛ *Trailhead: 4 miles south of S. Jenny Lake Junction on Teton Park Rd.*

DIFFICULT

Amphitheater Lake. A little more than 10 miles round-trip, this hike starts at Lupine Meadows and switches back through steep pines and flowered meadows to Surprise Lake and the regal Amphitheater Lake, tucked away in an expansive rock basin. The strenuous trail weaves out for views of Jenny Lake and the sprawling valley, while Disappointment

Peak looms above. Get to the trail early and allow at least five hours to tackle the 3,000-foot gain. *Difficult.* ⊠ *Jenny Lake* ⊹ *Trailhead: at Lupine Meadows parking area, south of Jenny Lake.*

TOURS

Hole Hiking Experience. Guides lead hikes for all ages and ability levels in the Greater Yellowstone Ecosystem. They provide information about the history, geology, and ecology of the area. Many trips incorporate yoga or have a holistic bent. In winter, snowshoe tours are offered. ⊠ *Jackson* ☎ *307/690–4453, 866/733–4453* ⊕ *www.holehike.com.*

HORSEBACK RIDING

You can arrange a guided horseback tour at Colter Bay Village and Jackson Lake Lodge corrals or with private outfitters. Most offer rides from an hour or two up to all-day excursions. If you want to spend even more time riding in Grand Teton and the surrounding mountains, consider a stay at a dude ranch. Most shorter rides are appropriate for novice riders. More experienced riders will enjoy the longer journeys where the terrain gets steeper and you may wind through deep forests. For any ride be sure to wear long pants and boots (cowboy boots or hiking boots). Because you may ride through trees, a long-sleeve shirt is also a good idea and a hat is always appropriate, but it should have a stampede string to make sure it stays on your head if the wind comes up.

TOURS

Colter Bay Village Corral. One- and two-hour rides leave the corral for various destinations. Short jaunts head around several secluded ponds on Hermitage Point. ⊹ *2 miles off U.S. 89/191/287, 5 miles north of Jackson Lake Junction* ☎ *307/543–3100, 800/628–9988* ⊕ *www.gtlc. com/activities* ▤ *From $42* ⊙ *June–Sept.*

Jackson Lake Lodge Corral. One- and two-hour trail rides follow secluded paths to peaceful Emma Matilda Lake and Oxbow Bend. ⊠ *U.S. 89/191/287, ½ mile north of Jackson Lake Junction* ☎ *307/543–3100, 800/628–9988* ⊕ *www.gtlc.com* ▤ *From $45* ⊙ *Mid-May–Sept.* ☞ *Call to book in advance.*

19

WINTER SPORTS

Grand Teton has some of North America's finest and most varied cross-country skiing. Ski the gentle 3-mile Swan Lake–Heron Pond Loop near Colter Bay, the mostly level 10-mile Jenny Lake Trail, or the moderate 4-mile Taggart Lake–Beaver Creek Loop and 5-mile Phelps Lake Overlook Trail. Teton Park Road is groomed for classic and skate-skiing from early January to mid-March. In winter, overnight backcountry travelers must register or make a reservation at the Craig Thomas Discovery and Visitor Center.

Snowmobiling is permitted on Jackson Lake only for ice fishing. Since snowmobiles must be towed into the park, sledders pay only the regular park entrance fees. Snowmobilers wishing to proceed north from Flagg Ranch into Yellowstone National Park must be with a commercial tour guide.

The Flagg Ranch Information Station is closed in winter but ski and snowshoe trails are open and marked with flagging tape. Pick up a map at the Flagg Ranch convenience store. For information about a free, ranger-guided snowshoe walk, call the Craig Thomas Discovery and Visitor Center.

TOURS AND OUTFITTERS

Pepi Stiegler Sports. Buy or rent skis or snowboards at Pepi's, conveniently located at the base of Jackson Hole Mountain Resort. The selection of clothing and accessories is the valley's largest. ⊠ *3395 W. Village Dr., Teton Village* ☎ *307/733–4505, 307/733–4505* ⊕ *www. pepistieglers.com* 🎿 *Ski or snowboard rental $28–$52.*

Skinny Skis. The valley's hub for Nordic skiing sells and rents equipment for snowshoeing, skate-skiing, and classic cross-country skiing. This is the place to find the latest and greatest down jackets, and wool base layers. Staffers here can give you advice about what trails to explore. ⊠ *65 W. Deloney Ave., Jackson* ☎ *307/733–6094* ⊕ *www.skinnyskis.com* ☽ *June–Aug., Mon.–Sat. 9–8, Sun. 9–7; Sept.–May, Mon.–Sat. 9–6, Sun. 10–5.*

Togwotee Mountain Lodge. Here you can rent a snowmobile and explore 600-plus miles of groomed trails and endless powder-filled meadows along the Continental Divide. ⊠ *27655 U.S. 26/287, Moran* ☎ *307/543–2847, 800/543–2847, 866/278–4245* ⊕ *www.togwoteelodge.com* 🎿 *Snowmobile rental $164–$209* ☽ *Nov.–Apr.*

WHAT'S NEARBY

NEARBY TOWNS

The major gateway to Grand Teton National Park is **Jackson**—but don't confuse this with Jackson Hole. Jackson Hole is the mountain-ringed valley that includes Jackson and much of Grand Teton National Park. The town of Jackson, south of the park, is a small community (roughly 9,700 residents) that gets flooded with 3 to 4 million visitors annually. Expensive homes and fashionable shops have sprung up all over, but with its wooden boardwalks and old-fashioned storefronts, the town center still looks like a Western movie set. There's a lot to do here, both downtown and in the surrounding countryside.

If it's skiing you're after, **Snow King Resort** is the oldest resort in the valley, and its 7,808-foot mountain overlooks the town of Jackson and the National Elk Refuge. It's at the end of Snow King Avenue. **Teton Village,** on the southwestern side of the park, is a cluster of businesses centered around the facilities of the Jackson Hole Mountain Resort. This ski and snowboard area has the longest continuous vertical rise in the U.S. at 4,139 feet, accessed by an aerial tram to the top of Rendezvous Mountain (10,450 feet). A gondola and various other lifts take skiers to other sections of the mountain. There are plenty of places to eat, stay, and shop here.

On the "back side of the Tetons," as eastern Idaho is known, is **Driggs,** the western gateway to Yellowstone and Grand Teton. Easygoing and rural, Driggs resembles the Jackson of a few decades ago. To reach the park from here you have to cross a major mountain pass that is sometimes closed in winter by avalanches. **Dubois,** about 85 miles east of Jackson, is the least known of the gateway communities to Grand Teton and Yellowstone, but this town of 1,000 has all the services of the bigger towns. You can still get a room for the night here during the peak summer travel period without making a reservation weeks or months in advance (though it's a good idea to call a week or so before you intend to arrive).

About an hour to the south is **Pinedale,** another small Wyoming town with lodging, restaurants, and attractions. Energy development has made the area a hopping place these days, so be sure to plan ahead if you want to stay in town.

VISITOR CENTER

Jackson Hole and Greater Yellowstone Visitor Center. Stop at the center for information about area attractions and to see wildlife displays that include bronze elk sculptures outside and a herd of stuffed elk in the lobby. Several organizations and governmental agencies—among them the U.S. Forest Service, U.S. Fish and Wildlife Service, U.S. Department of the Interior, and Wyoming Game and Fish Department—operate the center jointly, so you can get information about the entire region. From early December to late March, buses depart every 15 minutes to take visitors 2½ miles north for sleigh rides that glide close to grazing elk on the refuge. ⊠ *532 N. Cache St., Jackson* ☎ *307/733–3316* ⊕ *www.fws. gov/nwrs/threecolumn.aspx?id=2147509813* ☉ *Late May–Sept., daily 8–7; Oct.–late May, daily 9–5.*

Visitor Information Colter Bay Visitor Center. ⊠ *U.S. 89/191/287, 6 miles north of Jackson Lake Junction, Moran* ☎ *307/739–3594* ⊕ *www.nps. gov/grte/planyourvisit/cbvc.htm.* **Dubois Chamber of Commerce.** ⊠ *616 W. Ramshorn St., Dubois* ☎ *888/455–2556* ⊕ *www.duboiswyomingchamber. org.* **Eastern Idaho Visitor Information Center.** ⊠ *425 N. Capitol Ave., Idaho Falls* ☎ *208/523–1010, 866/365–6943* ⊕ *www.visitidaho.org/regions/eastern.* **Jackson Hole Chamber of Commerce.** ⊠ *Jackson* ☎ *307/733–3316* ⊕ *www. jacksonholechamber.com.* **Sublette County Chamber of Commerce.** ⊠ *19 E. Pine St., Pinedale* ☎ *307/367–2241* ⊕ *www.sublettechamber.com.* **Teton Valley Chamber of Commerce.** ⊠ *57 S. Main St., Driggs* ☎ *208/354–2500* ⊕ *www. tetonvalleychamber.com.*

19

NEARBY ATTRACTIONS

DUBOIS

FAMILY **National Bighorn Sheep Interpretive Center.** The local variety is known as the Rocky Mountain bighorn, but you can learn about all kinds of bighorn sheep here. Among the exhibits of mounted specimens here are the Super Slam diorama, with one of each type of wild sheep in the world, and two bighorn rams fighting during the rut. Hands-on exhibits illustrate a bighorn's body language, characteristics, and habitat. Reserve ahead for winter wildlife-viewing tours ($75) to Whiskey Mountain. ⊠ *907 W. Ramshorn St., Dubois* ☎ *307/455–3429, 888/209–2795,*

CLOSE UP

Granite Hot Springs

Soothing thermal baths in pristine outback country await in the heart of the Bridger-Teton National Forest, just a short drive south of Jackson. At Hoback Junction, about 11 miles south of Jackson, head east (toward Pinedale) on U.S. Highway 189/191 and follow the Hoback River through its beautiful canyon. A tributary canyon 10 miles east of the junction is followed by a well-maintained and -marked gravel road to Granite Hot Springs (☎ 307/734-7400), in the Bridger-Teton National Forest. Drive 9 miles off U.S. 189/191 (northeast) on Granite Creek Road to reach the hot springs. The thermal bath at the end of the road, from 93°F to 112°F, is pure bliss, but it's closed from November through December 10 and from April to May 20. The cost is $6 per person, cash or check only. Call for hours, which vary by season.

307/455-3429 ⊕ www.bighorn.org ≝ $4 ⊙ Late May–early Sept., daily 9–6; early Sept.–late May, Mon.–Sat. 10–4.

JACKSON

Bridger-Teton National Forest. This 3.4-million-acre forest has something for everyone: history, hiking, camping, and wildlife. It encompasses the Teton Wilderness east of Grand Teton National Park and south of Yellowstone National Park, the Gros Ventre Wilderness southeast of Jackson, and the Bridger Wilderness farther south and east. No motor vehicles are allowed in the wilderness areas, but between them are many scenic drives, natural springs where you can swim or soak throughout the year, and cultural sights like abandoned lumber camps in the forest. The peaks reach higher than 13,000 feet, and the area is liberally sprinkled with more than a thousand high-mountain lakes, where fishing is generally excellent. ⊠ *Forest headquarters, 340 N. Cache St., Jackson* ☎ *307/739-5500* ⊕ *www.fs.fed.us/r4/btnf* ≝ *Free.*

FAMILY **Jackson Hole Museum.** At this museum open year-round you can learn about historic homesteaders, dude ranches, and hunters, as well as Jackson's all-female town government of yore—a lady sheriff of that era claimed to have killed three men before hanging up her spurs. Native American, ranching, and cowboy artifacts are on display. A free app with a self-guided tour of Jackson is available on the museum's website. ⊠ *225 N. Cache St., Jackson* ☎ *307/733-2414, 307/733-2414* ⊕ *www.jacksonholehistory.org* ≝ *$5* ⊙ *Mon.–Sat. 10–6; Tues.–Sat. 10–5 in winter.*

FAMILY **National Elk Refuge.** Wildlife abounds on this 25,000-acre refuge. From late November to March, more than 7,000 elk, many with enormous antler racks, winter here. Elk can be observed from various pull-outs along U.S. 191 or by slowly driving your car on the refuge's winding, unpaved roads. You can take a horse-drawn sleigh ride for the chance to see the elk up close. Among the other animals that make their home here are buffalo, bighorn sheep, and coyotes, as well as trumpeter swans and other waterfowl. In summer, the refuge is light on big game, but you can tour a historic homestead from June to September. From mid-December to early April, sleigh rides operated by Bar T 5 (*www.bart5.com*) depart every 15 minutes or so from the Jackson Hole and Greater Yellowstone Visitor Center. Wear warm clothing, including hats, gloves, boots, long johns, and coats. ⊠ *Refuge Rd., northeast of Jackson* ☎ *307/733–9212 for refuge, 307/734–9378 for visitor center, 307/733–0277 for sleigh rides* ⊕ *www.fws.gov/refuge/national_elk_refuge* ⊠ *Sleigh rides $20* ⊗ *Daily sunrise–sunset.*

Fodor's Choice **National Museum of Wildlife Art.** See an impressive collection of wildlife ★ art—most of it devoted to North American species—in 14 galleries displaying the work of artists that include Karl Bodmer, Charles Russell, John Clymer, Robert Bateman, and Carl Rungius. A deck here affords views across the National Elk Refuge, where you can see wildlife in a natural habitat. An elaborate ¾-mile outdoor sculpture trail includes a monumental herd of bronze bison by Richard Loffler trudging across the butte. ⊠ *2820 Rungius Rd., Jackson* ☎ *307/733–5771* ⊕ *www. wildlifeart.org* ⊠ *$14* ⊗ *Mid-May–mid-Oct., daily 9–5; mid-Oct.–mid-May, Mon.–Sat. 9–5, Sun. 11–5.*

PINEDALE

FAMILY **Museum of the Mountain Man.** Preserving the area's trapper heritage, this museum displays 19th-century guns, traps, clothing, and beaver pelts. An interpretive exhibit details the area's pioneer and ranch history, and there's an overview of the Western fur trade. In the early summer the museum hosts living-history demonstrations, children's events, and lectures. In July, a reenactment of the early-19th-century Green River Rendezvous, when mountain men, Native Americans, and others got together to barter and socialize, takes place. ⊠ *700 E. Hennick Rd., Pinedale* ☎ *307/367–4101, 877/686–6266* ⊕ *www. museumofthemountainman.com* ⊠ *$7* ⊗ *May–Sept., daily 9–5; Oct., weekdays 9–4.*

AREA ACTIVITIES

19

BOATING

The companies that operate in Grand Teton also generally have trips on other area waters. The Snake River outside the park has spectacular white-water stretches. The rafting season runs from late May through August, with the wildest water during June.

GOLF

Jackson Hole Golf and Tennis Club. This 18-hole course redesigned by Robert Trent Jones has views of the Teton Range and an eco-friendly and elegant clubhouse. It has been ranked among Wyoming's top courses. ⊠ *5000 Spring Gulch Rd., 9 miles north of Jackson on U.S. 89, then 2 miles west at Gros Ventre Junction* ☎ *307/733–3111* ⊕ *www.jhgtc.com* ⊠ *$65–$185* ⅃ *18 holes, 7409 yards, par 72* ⊗ *Late Apr.–mid-Oct.*

Teton Pines Resort and Country Tennis Club. Arnold Palmer and Ed Seay designed this relatively flat 18-hole course near Teton Village. It has views of the Tetons, abundant wildlife, and is certified as an Audubon course. In winter it becomes a well-groomed cross-country ski track with a full-service shop. The restaurant is excellent. ⊠ *3450 N. Clubhouse*

Dr., Wilson ☎ *307/733–1005, 800/238–2223* ⊕ *www.tetonpines.com* ✉ *$120–$160 mid-June–mid-Sept.; from $65 in spring and fall* ⛳ *18 holes, 7412 yards, par 72* ⊙ *May–mid-Oct.*

WINTER SPORTS

Jackson Hole Mountain Resort. Skiers and snowboarders love Jackson Hole, one of the great skiing experiences in America. There are thousands of routes up and down the mountain, and despite Jackson's reputation not all of them are hellishly steep. Early, regular, and peak season prices vary, and some online discounts are available. In the summer, a mountain-bike park takes advantage of the legendary terrain. **Facilities:** 116 trails; 2,500 acres; 4,139-foot vertical drop; 13 lifts. ✉ *Jackson Hole* ☎ *307/733–2292, 800/333–7766* ⊕ *www.jacksonhole.com* ✉ *Lift ticket regular season: full-day $115, half-day $88.*

NIGHTLIFE AND PERFORMING ARTS

MUSIC

$$$

BARBECUE

FAMILY

Fodor'sChoice

★

✕ **Bar J Chuckwagon.** This may be the best value in Jackson Hole: you get a complete ranch-style meal plus a rollicking Western show. Served on a tin plate, the food is barbecue beef, chicken, pork ribs, or rib-eye steak with potatoes, beans, biscuits, applesauce, and spice cake, along with lemonade or ranch coffee. The talented Bar J Wranglers croon, play instruments, share cowboy stories, and even yodel. The dinner and show take place inside, so don't let the weather keep you away. The doors open at 5:30. You can explore the Bar J's Western village—including a saloon and several shops—before the dinner bell rings at 7. Reservations are a good idea. $ *Average main: $27* ✉ *Off Moose-Wilson Rd., 1 mile north of Hwy. 22, Wilson* ☎ *307/733–3370* ⊕ *www. barjchuckwagon.com* ⊙ *Closed Oct.–late May.*

SHOPPING

ART GALLERIES

Tayloe Piggott Gallery. A hot spot for contemporary work, this gallery downplays wildlife and landscape art in favor of hip and bright painting, sculpture, and jewelry. It's a bit of SoHo nestled in the Rockies. ✉ *62 S. Glenwood St., Jackson* ☎ *307/733–0555* ⊕ *www.tayloepiggottgallery.com.*

Trailside Galleries. This gallery's grand selection of traditional Western art includes paintings by the biggest names—Charles M. Russell, John Clymer, and Howard Terpning among them—along with works by talented contemporary artists such as Z.S. Liang, Nancy Glazier, and Bill Anton. ✉ *130 E. Broadway, Jackson* ☎ *307/733–3186* ⊕ *www. trailsidegalleries.com.*

Under the Willow Photo Gallery. Abi Garaman has been capturing images of Jackson Hole and Grand Teton National Park on film for more than 50 years. The gallery displays many of his photographs of wildlife, mountains, barns, and other subjects. ✉ *50 S. Cache St., Jackson* ☎ *307/733–6633* ⊕ *www.underthewillow.com.*

Fodor's Choice **Wild by Nature Gallery.** At this bright gallery you'll find wildlife and
★ landscape photography by Henry H. Holdsworth, plus books, note
cards, and gifts. Several coffee-table books contain striking Tetons
imagery. Wild by Nature offers photography workshops year-round,
and multiday photo tours in the Greater Yellowstone area alongside
the artist himself. ⊠ *95 W. Deloney Ave., Jackson* ☎ *307/733–8877*
⊕ *www.wildbynaturegallery.com.*

CLOTHING

Cowboy Shop. From silk scarves to big shiny buckles, if cowboys wear it,
here's the place to get it. Western-style clothing includes hats, boots, and
leather goods. ⊠ *129 W. Pine St., Pinedale* ☎ *307/367–4300* ⊕ *www.
cowboyshop.com* ⊗ *Closed Sun.*

Hide Out Leathers. Men's and women's clothing and accessories, including
locally designed coats and vests, are the specialty here. You'll also find
home decor such as pillows and throws. ⊠ *40 N. Center St., Jackson*
☎ *307/733–2422* ⊕ *www.hideoutleathers.com.*

JD High Country Outfitters. Well stocked with the best in outdoor equipment for winter and summer, the shop carries everything from backpacks to skis and hunting rifles, as well as clothing and other supplies.
Fishing gear can be rented. ⊠ *50 E. Broadway, Jackson* ☎ *307/733–
3270, 307/733–3270* ⊕ *www.jdhcoutfitters.com.*

SPAS

Bear and Doe Massage Works. The only Russian-style banya in Wyoming is a locals' favorite for massage. With a cedar sauna, an infrared
sauna, a steam room, and a cold plunge, it's the perfect place to soothe
overworked muscles, relax with friends, and even get thwacked with
birch branches to improve circulation. ⊠ *35 E. Simpson Ave., Jackson*
☎ *307/732–0863* ⊕ *www.bearanddoebanya.com* ⊗ *Mon.–Sat. 10–8.*

19

WHERE TO EAT

IN THE PARK

$$ ✕ **Dornan's Chuck Wagon.** Hearty portions of beef, beans, potatoes, short
AMERICAN ribs, stew, and lemonade or hot coffee are the dinner standbys at Dor-
FAMILY nan's. Locals come here for the barbecue cooked over wood fires. At
breakfast, count on old-fashioned staples such as sourdough pancakes
or biscuits and gravy. You can eat your chuck-wagon meal inside the
restaurant's teepee if it happens to be raining or windy; otherwise, sit
at outdoor picnic tables with views of the Snake River and the Tetons.
The quick service and inexpensive prices make this a good choice for
families. $ *Average main: $20* ⊠ *10 Moose Rd., off Teton Park Rd.*
☎ *307/733–2415* ⊕ *www.dornans.com* ⊗ *Closed mid-Oct.–mid-June.*

$$ ✕ **Dornan's Pizza & Pasta Company.** Tasty Italian fare is the draw here, but
PIZZA you'll also find generous margaritas, a diverse wine list, and occasional
live music. Place your order at the front counter, then head to a table
inside, on the side deck, or upstairs on the roof, which has stunning

mountain views. This extremely popular eatery also serves sandwiches and salads. The long inside bar has stellar views and friendly barkeeps. Check Dornan's schedule for live music, and be sure to explore the wine shop next door: it's one of the most varied and well stocked in the state, and there's no corkage fee when you buy wine for your meal. $ *Average main: $14 ✉ 10 Moose Rd., off Teton Park Rd.* ☎ *307/733–2415* ⊕ *www.dornans.com.*

$$$ ✕ **Jackson Lake Lodge Mural Room.** One of the park's best restaurants
AMERICAN   gets its name from a 700-square-foot mural painted by the Western artist Carl Roters. The mural details an 1837 Wyoming mountain man rendezvous and covers two walls of the dining room. Select from a menu that includes elk, beef, salmon, duck, and chicken. The plantain-crusted trout is a great choice, as is the bison prime rib. The tables face tall windows with panoramic views of Willow Flats and Jackson Lake to the northern Tetons. There's no official dress code, but wearing jeans or open-toed shoes is not advised. $ *Average main: $28 ✉ U.S. 89/191/287, ½ mile north of Jackson Lake Junction* ☎ *307/543–3463, 800/628–9988* ⊕ *www.gtlc.com/dining* ⊙ *Closed mid-Oct.–late May.*

$$ ✕ **Jackson Lake Lodge Pioneer Grill.** With an old-fashioned soda fountain,
AMERICAN   friendly service, and seats along a winding counter, this eatery recalls a 1950s-era luncheonette. Tuck into burgers, sundaes, and other classic American fare. $ *Average main: $15 ✉ U.S. 89/191/287, ½ mile north of Jackson Lake Junction* ☎ *307/543–2811* ⊕ *www.gtlc.com/dining* ⊙ *Closed early Oct.–late May.*

$$$$ ✕ **Jenny Lake Lodge Dining Room.** Elegant yet rustic, Grand Teton's finest
AMERICAN   dining space is extremely ambitious for a national park restaurant. The five-course menu might include dishes like lavender-poached nectarine and house-corned buffalo hash. The thoughtfully assembled wine list is sufficiently versatile to keep pace. The menus for breakfast and dinner are prix-fixe; lunch, for which the inventive soups and salads are popular with regulars and tourists, is à la carte. Jackets are strongly encouraged for men at dinner. $ *Average main: $88 ✉ Jenny Lake Rd., 2 miles off Teton Park Rd., 12 miles north of Moose Junction* ☎ *307/733–4647, 800/628–9988* ⊕ *www.gtlc.com/dining* ⊙ *Closed early Oct.–late May* ⚐ *Reservations essential.*

$ ✕ **John Colter Cafe Court.** Quick and cheap is the name of the game
AMERICAN   at this no-frills cafeteria. Simple sandwiches and salads, plus a few bottled beers, are on the menu. $ *Average main: $8 ✉ 5 miles north of Jackson Lake Lodge* ☎ *307/543–2811* ⊕ *www.gtlc.com* ⊙ *Closed early Sept.–early June.*

$$ ✕ **John Colter's Ranch House and Restaurant-Bar.** The casual Ranch House
AMERICAN   offers friendly service and inexpensive prices, making it a good choice for travelers on a budget or families who can't take another cafeteria meal. Western-style meals—thick steaks, barbecue ribs, rotisserie chicken—dominate the menu. The kitchen will prep your day's catch if you deliver it at least three hours in advance of dinner. $ *Average main: $20 ✉ 2 miles off U.S. 89/191/287, 5 miles north of Jackson Lake Junction, Colter Bay* ☎ *307/543–2811* ⊕ *www.gtlc.com/dining* ⊙ *Closed early Sept.–late May.*

$$ **✕ The Peaks.** At Signal Mountain Lodge, this casual Western-style bistro
AMERICAN has exposed ceiling beams and expansive windows overlooking Jackson Lake and the Tetons. Fish is the specialty. Wild-caught salmon is served in a sauce of lemon, capers, and parsley, and the trout cakes are a superb appetizer. The Trapper Grill next door also serves lunch, and in the adjacent Deadman's Bar, the mountain of nachos and huckleberry margaritas are crowd favorites. $ *Average main: $19* ✉ *Teton Park Rd., 4 miles south of Jackson Lake Junction* ☎ *307/543–2831* ⊕ *www. signalmountainlodge.com* ◷ *Closed mid-Oct.–mid-May.*

PICNIC AREAS

The park has 11 designated picnic areas, each with tables and grills, and most with pit toilets and water pumps or faucets. In addition to those listed here you can find picnic areas at Colter Bay Village Campground, Cottonwood Creek, the east shore of Jackson Lake, and South Jenny Lake and String Lake trailhead.

Chapel of the Sacred Heart. From this intimate lakeside picnic area you can look across southern Jackson Lake to Mount Moran. ⊹ *¼ mile east of Signal Mountain Lodge, off Teton Park Rd.*

Colter Bay. This big picnic area, spectacularly located right on the beach at Jackson Lake, gets crowded in July and August. It's close to flush toilets and stores. ⊹ *2 miles off U.S. 89/191/287, 5 miles north of Jackson Lake Junction.*

Jenny Lake. Shaded and pine-scented, this picnic site adjacent to the Jenny Lake shuttle boat dock is a good place to have lunch before heading across the lake for the ½-mile hike to Hidden Falls. ⊹ *Near Jenny Lake Visitor Center.*

OUTSIDE THE PARK

$ **✕ The Bunnery.** Lunch is served year-round and dinner is served in sum-
AMERICAN mer, but it's the breakfasts of savory omelets and home-baked pastries that are irresistible. Try a giant almond stick, a sticky bun, or a slice of raspberry, strawberry, or blueberry pie. There's also a decent vegetarian selection. All the breads are house-made, most from flour that includes oats, sunflower, and millet; the OSM waffle is dense and delectable. The Bunnery is elbow to elbow inside, so you may have to wait to be seated on busy mornings, but any inconvenience is well worth it. In summer there's outdoor seating. $ *Average main: $11* ✉ *Hole-in-the-Wall Mall, 130 N. Cache St., Jackson* ☎ *307/734–0075* ⊕ *www.bunnery.com* ◷ *No dinner Sept.–May.*

$$$$ **✕ Couloir.** The gondola at Teton Village whisks you to this stylish dining
AMERICAN room at 9,095 feet. Gaze down on Jackson Hole while lingering over
Fodor'sChoice signature cocktails and a smart, contemporary prix-fixe dinner menu.
★ Entrées might include house-smoked bison cuts or fork-ready Kurobuta pork, along with clever sides like chickpea pancakes and fried-green "Wyomatoes," locally grown tomatoes. Faux cowhide upholstery and a towering bar give the room a fun, modern feel. Days and hours can change with the seasons, so call for reservations. For the same view in summer but with a smaller price tag, step outside on the Deck from 4:30

19

to sunset and enjoy live music, distinctive drinks like the infused jalapeño-ginger margaritas, and tempura-fried vegetables and other huge portions of upscale bar food. $ *Average main: $85* ✉ *Jackson Hole Mountain Resort, Teton Village* ☎ *307/739–2675* ⊕ *www.jacksonhole. com/couloir-restaurant.html* ☾ *Closed late Sept.–late Nov. and Apr.–mid-June. No lunch mid-June–late-Sept.* ⚐ *Reservations essential.*

$$$
MODERN ITALIAN

✕ **Il Villaggio Osteria.** Underneath rustic barnwood timbers and columns or on an open-air patio, diners enjoy the flavors of Italy fused with fresh, inventive touches. Try the bone-marrow bruschetta, house-pulled mozzarella figs stuffed with blue cheese, or a generous slice of gooey lasagna. Part of the eco-chic Hotel Terra, the popular restaurant has a wine list with bottles from several continents. $ *Average main: $27* ✉ *3335 W. Village Dr., Teton Village* ☎ *307/739–4100* ⊕ *www.jhosteria.com* ☾ *No lunch.*

$$
AMERICAN

✕ **Lift Jackson Hole.** Off the beaten path with one of Jackson's best views, this mountain-chic restaurant serves heaping portions of updated pub-style food. From the upper deck you can take in Snow King Mountain vistas while enjoying rock shrimp and goat cheese wonton cigars and sipping a locally produced craft beer. Live music from the adjacent park frequently provides the soundtrack. In winter the après-ski crowd assembles around the stone fireplace to rewarm and refuel, the latter done perfectly with a half-pound fried crab cake burger livened up with a lemon-caper aioli and accompanied by piping-hot waffle fries. The warm brownie smothered in a Wyoming huckleberry compote completes the uplifting picture. $ *Average main: $16* ✉ *645 S. Cache St., at the base of Snow King Resort, Jackson* ☎ *307/733–5438* ⊕ *liftjacksonhole. com* ☾ *Closed 1st 3 wks in Apr. and 1 wk in late Nov. (Thanksgiving).*

$$$
ITALIAN

✕ **Nani's Ristorante and Bar.** The menu at this spacious local favorite focuses on a different Italian region each month. Depending on the locale, the dishes might include braised veal shanks with saffron risotto, lasagna, or other Italian specialties; vegan and gluten-free plates are prepared as well. The grandly presented Teton Tiramisu is a must for dessert. Tucked behind a motel, this place attracts gourmets who appreciate the fine cuisine and the selection of Italian and non-Italian wines, including many sparklers. $ *Average main: $28* ✉ *242 N. Glenwood St., Jackson* ☎ *307/733–3888* ⊕ *www.nanis.com* ☾ *No lunch.*

$
MEXICAN
FAMILY

✕ **Pica's Taqueria.** A locals' favorite a mile from the bustle of Town Square, Pica's serves authentic Mexican dishes at an affordable price. From fish tacos and huge wet burritos to delectable chopped salads, the food is consistently fresh, and the margaritas are strong. Bright, colorful folk art surrounds the basic counters and tables. In summer, the sunny patio tables are dog-friendly. $ *Average main: $10* ✉ *1160 Alpine La., Jackson* ☎ *307/734–4457* ⊕ *www.picastaqueria.com.*

$$$
AMERICAN
Fodor'sChoice
★

✕ **Snake River Grill.** One of Jackson's best restaurants, this sophisticated dining room serves creatively prepared dishes like free-range veal chops, grilled venison, buffalo strip steak, elk chops, and grilled Idaho trout. The menu changes seasonally and reflects what is available in the market. The extensive wine list seems to pick up another award every year or so. $ *Average main: $28* ✉ *84 E. Broadway Ave., Jackson* ☎ *307/733–0557* ⊕ *www.snakerivergrill.com* ☾ *Closed Apr. and Nov. No lunch.*

$$ ✕ **Teton Thai.** By the Ranch Lot at the base of Jackson Hole Mountain
THAI   Resort, the restaurant is owned by people of Thai heritage, and the
Fodor'sChoice   cuisine reflects it. Try the *gang khio wan* (green curry), *tom yum hai*
★   (hot and sour soup with chicken), or Crying Tiger (wine-soaked beef
with a tangy dipping sauce). The pad thai is the state's finest. There's a
full bar. ⑤ *Average main: $14* ⊠ *7342 Granite Loop Rd., Teton Village*
☎ *307/733–0022* ⊕ *www.tetonthai.com.*

WHERE TO STAY

IN THE PARK

$$$ ⌂ **Colter Bay Village.** Near Jackson Lake, this cluster of Western-style
HOTEL   cabins—some with one room, others with two—is within walking dis-
tance of the lake. **Pros:** prices are good for what you get; many nearby
facilities. **Cons:** little sense of privacy; not all cabins have bathrooms.
⑤ *Rooms from: $160* ⊠ *Colter Bay* ✛ *2 miles off U.S. 89/191/287, 10
miles north of Jackson Lake Junction* ☎ *307/543–3100, 800/628–9988*
⊕ *www.gtlc.com/lodging* ☼ *Closed Oct.–late May* ⏎ *166 cabins (9 with
shared baths), 66 tent cabins* ⑂ *No meals.*

$$$ ⌂ **Dornan's Spur Ranch Cabins.** Part of Dornan's shopping, dining, and
RESORT   recreation development at Moose, this clutch of one- and two-bedroom
cabins has great views of the Tetons and the Snake River. **Pros:** cabins
are simple but clean; full kitchens can save you money. **Cons:** not much
privacy; little atmosphere; no fireplaces. ⑤ *Rooms from: $195* ⊠ *10
Moose Rd., off Teton Park Rd. at Moose Junction, Moose* ☎ *307/733–
2522* ⊕ *www.dornans.com* ⏎ *8 1-bedroom cabins, 4 2-bedroom cabins*
⑂ *No meals.*

$$$$ ⌂ **Jackson Lake Lodge.** This sprawling resort stands on a bluff with spec-
HOTEL   tacular views across Jackson Lake to the Tetons. **Pros:** central location
for visiting Grand Teton and Yellowstone; heated outdoor pool. **Cons:**
rooms without views are pricey for what you get; the hotel hosts many
large meetings. ⑤ *Rooms from: $280* ⊠ *U.S. 89/191/287, ½ mile north
of Jackson Lake Junction* ☎ *307/543–3100, 800/628–9988* ⊕ *www.gtlc.
com/lodging* ☼ *Closed early Oct.–mid-May* ⏎ *385 rooms* ⑂ *No meals.*

$$$$ ⌂ **Jenny Lake Lodge.** This lodge, the most expensive and arguably the
RESORT   most elegant in any national park, has been serving travelers since the
Fodor'sChoice   1920s. **Pros:** maximum comfort in a pristine setting; perhaps the best
★   hotel in the national park system. **Cons:** very expensive; not suitable
for kids under 17; pretty formal for a national-park property. ⑤ *Rooms
from: $689* ⊠ *Jenny Lake Rd., 2 miles off Teton Park Rd., 12 miles
north of Moose Junction* ☎ *307/733–4647, 800/628–9988* ⊕ *www.gtlc.
com/lodging* ☼ *Closed early Oct.–late May* ⏎ *37 cabins* ⑂ *Some meals.*

$$ ⌂ **Moulton Ranch Cabins.** Along Mormon Row, these cabins stand a few
B&B/INN   dozen yards south of the famous Moulton Barn seen on park bro-
chures. **Pros:** quiet and secluded; picturesque setting. **Cons:** fairly basic
accommodations; little nightlife nearby; no Sunday check-in. ⑤ *Rooms
from: $110* ⊠ *202 Mormon Row Rd., off Antelope Flats Rd., east and
then south from U.S. 26/89/191* ☎ *307/733–3749 summer* ⊕ *www.
moultonranchcabins.com* ☼ *Closed Oct.–May* ⏎ *5 cabins* ⑂ *No meals.*

19

$$$ **Signal Mountain Lodge.** The main building of this lodge on Jackson
HOTEL Lake's southern shoreline has a cozy lounge and a grand pine deck
overlooking the lake; some of the pine-shaded cabins are equipped with
sleek kitchens. **Pros:** popular restaurants and bar; on-site gas station;
pets allowed; some rooms updated. **Cons:** motel-basic rooms. $ *Rooms
from: $185* ✉ *Teton Park Rd., 3 miles south of Jackson Lake Junction*
☎ *307/543–2831* ⊕ *www.signalmountainlodge.com* ⊘ *Closed mid-
Oct.–mid-May* ⇌ *51 rooms, 28 cabins* ⦿ *No meals.*

OUTSIDE THE PARK

$$$$ **Alpenhof Lodge.** With more atmosphere than anywhere else in Teton
HOTEL Village, this Austrian-style hotel sits next to the tram in the heart of
Jackson Hole Mountain Resort. **Pros:** quaint feel; cozy surroundings;
spa treatments available; pet-friendly. **Cons:** some rooms are small,
especially for the price. $ *Rooms from: $219* ✉ *3255 West Village Dr.,
Teton Village* ☎ *307/733–3242, 800/732–3244* ⊕ *www.alpenhoflodge.
com* ⊘ *Closed early Apr.–mid-May, restaurants closed in Nov.* ⇌ *42
rooms* ⦿ *Breakfast.*

$$$$ **Amangani.** This exclusive resort built of sandstone and redwood
RESORT blends into the landscape of Gros Ventre Butte, affording beautiful
views of Spring Creek Gulch from its cliff-top location. **Pros:** extremely
luxurious; impeccable service; excellent Tetons views; extensive ame-
nities. **Cons:** very expensive; too detached from the mundane world
below. $ *Rooms from: $1,075* ✉ *1535 N.E. Butte Rd., Jackson*
☎ *307/734–7333, 877/734–7333* ⊕ *www.amangani.com* ⇌ *40 suites*
⦿ *Some meals* ⌖ *Rates dependent on season.*

$$$ **Antler Inn.** No motel in Jackson has a better location than the Antler,
HOTEL a block south of Town Square. **Pros:** restaurants nearby; family-run
operation; good prices in the off-season; dogs allowed. **Cons:** frequently
booked-up in summer. $ *Rooms from: $160* ✉ *43 W. Pearl St., Jackson*
☎ *307/733–2535, 800/522–2406* ⊕ *www.townsquareinns.com/antler-
inn* ⇌ *105 rooms* ⦿ *No meals.*

$$$$ **Hotel Terra.** The opulent Hotel Terra takes green hospitality to the
HOTEL next level, but it's also luxe to the core, with a hip, urban feel and all
the amenities the price tag suggests. **Pros:** extremely green; expert staff;
organic spa. **Cons:** not for budget-conscious; in a crowded corner of
Teton Village. $ *Rooms from: $399* ✉ *Teton Village, just west of Mangy
Moose* ☎ *307/379–4000, 800/631–6281, 307/379–4000, 800/631–
6281* ⊕ *www.hotelterrajacksonhole.com* ⇌ *132 rooms* ⦿ *Some meals.*

$$$$ **The Lexington at Jackson Hole.** Within walking distance of Town Square,
HOTEL this lodging has some of the town's best-appointed rooms for people
with disabilities. **Pros:** walking distance to town; small pool and Jacuzzi;
appealing base; friendly and helpful staff. **Cons:** limited views; must
drive to mountains. $ *Rooms from: $299* ✉ *285 N. Cache St., Jackson*
☎ *307/733–2648, 888/771–2648* ⊕ *www.lexingtonhoteljacksonhole.
com* ⇌ *91 rooms, 53 suites* ⦿ *Breakfast.*

$$$$ **R Lazy S Ranch.** Jackson Hole, with the spectacle of the Tetons in the
RESORT background, is true dude-ranch country, and the R Lazy S is one of
FAMILY the finest in the area. **Pros:** authentic all-inclusive dude ranch experi-
ence; very popular with older kids; beautiful setting. **Cons:** few modern

CLOSE UP

Best Campgrounds in Grand Teton

You'll find a variety of campgrounds, from small areas where only tents are allowed to full RV parks with all services. If you don't have a tent but want to bring your sleeping bags, you can take advantage of the tent cabins at Colter Bay, where you have a hard floor, cots, and canvas walls for shelter. Standard campsites include a place to pitch your tent or park your trailer/camper, a fire pit for cooking, and a picnic table. All developed campgrounds have toilets and water; plan to bring your own firewood. Check in at National Park Service campsites as early as possible—sites are assigned on a first-come, first-served basis.

DEVELOPED SITES
Colter Bay Campground. Busy, noisy, and filled by noon, this centrally located campground has tent and trailer or RV sites. ⊠ *2 miles off U.S. 89/191/287, 5 miles north of Jackson Lake Junction, Colter Bay* ☎ *307/543–3100, 800/628–9988.*

Flagg Ranch. In a shady pine grove overlooking the headwaters of the Snake River, these sites provide a great base for exploring Grand Teton or Yellowstone. The showers and laundry facilities are a bonus, and camper cabins are available. ⊠ *U.S. 89/191/287, 20 miles north of Jackson Lake Junction* ☎ *307/543–2861, 800/443–2311.*

Gros Ventre. The park's biggest campground is set in an open, grassy area on the bank of the Gros Ventre River, away from the mountains but not far from the town of Kelly. ⊠ *4½ miles off U.S. 26/89/191, 2½ miles west of Kelly on Gros Ventre Rd., 6 miles south of Moose Junction* ☎ *307/543–3100, 800/628–9988.*

Jenny Lake. Wooded sites and Teton views make this tent-only spot the most desirable campground in the park, and it fills early. ⊠ *Jenny Lake, ½ mile off Teton Park Rd., 8 miles north of Moose Junction* ☎ *307/543–3100, 800/628–9988.*

Lizard Creek. Views of Jackson Lake, wooded sites, and the relative isolation of this campground make it a relaxing choice. ⊠ *U.S. 89/191/287, 13 miles north of Jackson Lake Junction* ☎ *307/543–2831, 800/672–6012.*

Signal Mountain. This campground in a hilly setting on Jackson Lake has boat access to the lake. ⊠ *Teton Park Rd., 3 miles south of Jackson Lake Junction* ☎ *307/543–2831, 800/672–6012.*

BACKCOUNTRY PERMITS
You can reserve a backcountry campsite between January 5 and mid-May for a $25 nonrefundable fee using the online reservation system. Two-thirds of all sites are set aside for in-person, day-before permits, so you can also take a chance that the site you want will be open when you arrive. In that case you pay no fee at all, but a trip to Craig Thomas Visitor and Discovery Center or Jenny Lake Ranger Station is still required for a permit and mandatory bear-proof food storage canister. The Jackson Hole Mountain Resort tram provides quick access to the park's backcountry, which can also be reached on foot from various trailheads. ☎ *307/739–3443* ⊕ *www.nps.gov/grte/planyourvisit/bcres.htm.*

19

trappings; not for the high-maintenance traveler. $ *Rooms from: $238* ⊠ *Teton Village* ✛ *1 mile north of Teton Village, off Moose Wilson Rd.* ☎ *307/733–2655* ⊕ *www.rlazys.com* ▭ *No credit cards* ☾ *Closed Oct.–mid-June* ⇗ *12 cabins* ⦿ *All meals* ⌇ *1-week minimum stay.*

$$$$
HOTEL

⛑ **Snake River Lodge & Spa.** Anchored by an expansive four-level spa, Snake River combines the best elements of a genteel resort and a faux-folksy lodge. **Pros:** cool public spaces; vast spa menu. **Cons:** labyrinthine hallways; most rooms have no real view. $ *Rooms from: $339* ⊠ *7710 Granite Loop Rd., Teton Village* ☎ *307/732–6000, 855/342–4712* ⊕ *www.snakeriverlodge.com* ⇗ *148 rooms* ⦿ *Breakfast.*

$$$$
HOTEL
FAMILY

⛑ **Snow King Hotel.** At the base of Snow King Mountain and eight blocks from Town Square, this hotel with a modern Western feel has a popular restaurant, a cycling and ski shop, and outdoor fire pits near the beautiful pool. **Pros:** central location; ski-in, ski-out; cycling and ski shop. **Cons:** large groups often dominate the property; somewhat expensive. $ *Rooms from: $295* ⊠ *Snow King Resort, 400 E. Snow King Ave., Jackson* ☎ *307/733–5200* ⊕ *www.snowking.com* ⇗ *201 rooms, 2 suites* ⦿ *No meals.*

$$$$
B&B/INN

⛑ **Teton Tree House.** On a steep hillside and surrounded by trees, this lodgepole-pine bed-and-breakfast is a real retreat. **Pros:** scenic locale; good breakfast; knowledgeable hosts. **Cons:** small climb to the inn; must drive to town; no kids under five. $ *Rooms from: $280* ⊠ *6175 Heck of a Hill Rd., Wilson* ☎ *307/733–3233* ⊕ *www.atetontreehouse-jacksonhole.com* ⇗ *6 rooms* ⦿ *Breakfast.*

$$$$
B&B/INN
Fodor's Choice
★

⛑ **The Wildflower Inn.** You'll enjoy gourmet breakfasts and an afternoon beverage and snack at this country inn that's surrounded by 3 acres of aspen and pine trees frequented by moose, deer, and other wildlife. **Pros:** excellent views; frequent wildlife sightings; loaner gear available; clean and comfortable. **Cons:** books out far in advance; 12 miles from Jackson. $ *Rooms from: $360* ⊠ *3725 Shooting Star La., off Moose-Wilson Rd., Jackson* ☎ *307/733–4710, 307/733–4710, 800/893–7910* ⊕ *www.jacksonholewildflower.com* ⇗ *5 rooms* ⦿ *Breakfast.*

$$$$
HOTEL
Fodor's Choice
★

⛑ **The Wort Hotel.** Built in 1941, this brick Victorian hotel a block from Town Square seems to have been around as long as the Tetons, but it feels up-to-date inside. **Pros:** charming old building with lots of history; convenient downtown location; some good package deals. **Cons:** limited views; must drive to parks and mountains. $ *Rooms from: $399* ⊠ *50 N. Glenwood St., Jackson* ☎ *307/733–2190, 800/322–2727* ⊕ *www.worthotel.com* ⇗ *55 rooms, 5 suites* ⦿ *Breakfast.*

GREAT BASIN
NATIONAL PARK

WELCOME TO GREAT BASIN NATIONAL PARK

TOP REASONS TO GO

★ **Ancient tree spottings:** The twisting, windswept bristlecone pines in Great Basin are thousands of years old.

★ **Desert skyscraper:** Wheeler Peak rises out of the vast desert basin with summit temperatures often 20–30 degrees below that of the visitor center.

★ **Rare shields:** Look for hundreds of these unique disk-shape formations inside Lehman Caves.

★ **Gather your pine nuts while you may:** Come in the fall and go a little nutty, as you can gather up to three gunnysacks of pinyon pine nuts, found in abundance throughout the park. They're great on salads.

★ **Celestial show:** Pitch-dark nights make for dazzling stars. Gaze on your own or attend a seasonal nighttime talk, led by a park ranger.

1 Lehman Caves. Highlighted by the limestone caverns, this is the primary destination of most Great Basin visitors. It includes a popular visitor center and two campgrounds (both accessible for RVers). Nearby is the start of the Wheeler Peak Scenic Drive.

2 Wheeler Peak. Rarely is a crown jewel truly so—but just look at this 13,063-footer when it's capped with snow. Hikers can climb the mountain via day-use-only trails, which also lead to three small alpine lakes, a glacier, and some ancient bristlecone pines.

3 Granite Basin. This is the less crowded part of an already sparsely visited park. Trails follow a handful of creeks around Pyramid Peak, and six primitive campgrounds line Snake Creek. A bristlecone pine grove is nearby, though far off any beaten path.

4 Arch Canyon. A high-clearance, four-wheel-drive vehicle is recommended, and stout boots are critical if you want to get to Lexington Arch, which is unusual in that it is formed of limestone, not sandstone as most arches are. This is a day-use-only area.

GETTING ORIENTED

One of the smallest (77,180 acres) and one of the least visited national parks in the lower 48 states, Great Basin National Park, on the Nevada–Utah border, occupies only a minute fraction of the almost 200,000 square miles of the Great Basin desert—yet it exemplifies the landscape and ecology of the region. The surrounding high desert (4,500–6,200 feet in elevation) is the largest desert in the United States, bordered by the Sierra Nevada range, the Rocky Mountains, the Columbia Plateau, and the Mojave and Sonoran deserts. It covers 75% of the state of Nevada and extends into California, Oregon, Utah, and Idaho.

NEVADA

> 6
> 50

487

TO ELY

488

Baker

487

BLUE RIDGE

Wheeler Peak Scenic Drive

Buck Mountain 10,972 ft

Bald Mountain 11,562 ft

Mather Overlook

Upper Lehman Campground

Lower Lehman Campground

Wheeler Park Campground

Bristlecone Pine Trail

1 Lehman Caves ♦
Visitor Center

Baker Creek Rd.

Grey Cliffs Group Camping

2 Wheeler Peak 13,063 ft

Jeff Davis Peak 12,771 ft

Glacier

Baker Creek ♦

Baker Peak 12,298 ft

S N A K E   R A N G E

KIOUS BASIN

Pyramid Peak 11,926 ft

3

GRANITE BASIN

Bristlecone Pine Grove

HORSE HEAVEN

Shoshone Campground

Snake

Creek

Mount Washington 11,658 ft

Bristlecone Pine Grove

Bristlecone Pine Grove

0   2 mi

0   2 km

20

Lexington Arch ♦

4 ARCH CANYON

KEY

🏕 Ranger Station
△ Campground
🌲 Picnic Area
🍴 Restaurant
🏨 Lodge
🥾 Trailhead
🚻 Restrooms
✳ Scenic Viewpoint
⋯⋯ Walking/Hiking Trails

Updated by Stina Sieg

As you drive the staight, desolate road into Great Basin National Park, it's hard not to feel moved—or at least tiny. Massive Wheeler Peak rises up 13,063 feet in front of you, as the terrain transitions from dry desert to alpine forest. There's plenty to see here, from the ancient, otherworldly bristlecone pines to the surreal formations in Lehman Caves. But the real beauty of Great Basin isn't its best-known attractions. It's the extraordinary solitude.

Roughly 100,000 people visit every year (compared with 5 million at the Grand Canyon), which means that even in the high season, your experience will be overwhelmingly personal. That's especially true on the park's many trails, which take you into lush meadows and up steep mountains, and past alpine lakes, historic ruins, and Nevada's only glacier. The farther into the backcountry you go, the more you'll feel like you have Great Basin's 77,000 acres all to yourself—just the way fans of this off-the-beaten-path park like it.

GREAT BASIN PLANNER

WHEN TO GO

As one of the least-visited national parks in the country, Great Basin National Park is never crowded. The small number of visitors ensures that most any time is a fine time to visit this park, though of course much of that number will pass through the entry gates during the warmer months. In summer the high-desert weather here is typically mild, so you'll be comfortable in shorts and T-shirts during the day— though temperatures drop at night, and get colder the higher up you climb, so bring light jackets and pants

A winter visit can be sublime in its solitude, but the hardy visitor must be prepared for the elements, especially if the backcountry is a destination. With temperatures hovering in the low teens, heavy coats, boots, and other appropriate winter gear is necessary. Some roads might be impassable in inclement weather; check ahead with a park ranger.

AVG. HIGH/LOW TEMPS.

Jan.	Feb.	Mar.	Apr.	May	June
41/18	44/21	48/24	56/31	66/40	76/48

July	Aug.	Sept.	Oct.	Nov.	Dec.
86/57	83/56	75/47	62/47	49/26	42/20

FESTIVALS AND EVENTS

SUMMER **Silver State Classic Challenge.** Twice a year, car enthusiasts of all stripes close Route 318 for the country's largest (and most venerable) open-road race for amateur fast-car drivers. The event occurs south of Ely on Route 318, from Lund to Hiko, and is open to just about any four-wheeled vehicle. ☎ 702/631–6166 ⊕ *www.silverstateclassic.com.*

FAMILY **White Pine County Fair.** Livestock, flower, and vegetable competitions, plus horse races, food booths, dancing, and a barbecue dinner make this fair, held at the White Pine County Fairgrounds in Ely, the real thing. The dates fluctuate every August. ☎ 775/289–4691 ⊕ *www.wpcfair.com.*

PLANNING YOUR TIME
GREAT BASIN IN ONE DAY

Start your visit with the 90-minute tour of the fascinating limestone caverns of **Lehman Caves,** the park's most famous attraction. If you have time before or after the tour, hike the short and family-friendly **Mountain View Nature Trail,** near the Lehman Caves Visitor Center, to get your first taste of the area's pinyon-juniper forests. Stop for lunch at the Lehman Caves Cafe (open mid-April–mid-October) or at least plan on a hand-scooped ice-cream treat—or have a picnic near the visitor center.

In the afternoon, take a leisurely drive up to **Wheeler Peak,** the park's tallest mountain (and the second highest in Nevada) at just over 13,000 feet. You can stop about halfway along your drive to hike the short **Osceola Ditch Trail,** a remnant of the park's gold-mining days, or, alternatively, just enjoy the fantastic views from the two overlooks. If you're feeling energetic when you reach Wheeler Peak, hike some of the trails there.

20

GETTING HERE AND AROUND
AIR TRAVEL

The nearest airport is in Cedar City (142 miles) but will likely be pricey. Salt Lake City (234 miles) and Las Vegas (286 miles) are better bets, though you'll probably get the cheapest fares (and might have the most fun) flying into Vegas.

CAR TRAVEL

The entrance to Great Basin is on Route 488, 5 miles west of its junction with Route 487. From Ely, take U.S. 6/50 to Route 487. From Salt Lake City or Cedar City, Utah, take Interstate 15 South to U.S. 6/50 West; from Las Vegas, drive north on Interstate 15 and then north on Route 93 to access U.S. 6/50.

In the park, Baker Creek Road and portions of Wheeler Peak Scenic Drive, above Upper Lehman Creek, are closed from November to June. The road to the visitor center and the roads to the developed campgrounds are paved, but two-wheel-drive cars don't do well in winter storms. RVs and trailers over 24 feet aren't allowed above Lower Lehman Creek. With an 8% grade, the road to Wheeler Peak is steep and curvy, but not dangerous if you take it slow. Motorcyclists should watch for gravel on the road's surface.

PARK ESSENTIALS

PARK FEES AND PERMITS

Admission to the park is free, but if you want to tour Lehman Caves there's a fee ($4–$10, depending on age and tour length). To fish in Great Basin National Park, those 12 and older need a state fishing license from the Nevada Department of Wildlife (⊕ *www.ndow.org*). The one-day nonresident license is $18, plus $7 for each additional day at time of purchase. Backcountry hikers do not need permits, but for your own safety you should fill out a form at the visitor center before setting out.

PARK HOURS

The park is open 24/7 year-round. It's in the Pacific time zone.

CELL-PHONE RECEPTION

Now that a cell tower has been placed in Baker, there's decent coverage close to Lehman Caves; the more remote you get, the spottier it becomes. The only public phone in the park is at the visitor center.

EDUCATIONAL OFFERINGS

RANGER PROGRAMS

FAMILY **Junior Ranger Program.** Youngsters answer questions and complete activities related to the park and then are sworn in as Junior Rangers and receive a Great Basin Bristlecone badge. ⊠ *Great Basin National Park* ☎ *775/234–7331* ⊕ *www.nps.gov/grba.*

FAMILY **Weekly Astronomy Programs.** You'll find some of the country's darkest skies—and brightest stars—at Great Basin. Expect to be dazzled, especially on moonless nights, as you get a chance to see the wild blue yonder through a telescope at these ranger-led events. ⊠ *Lehman Caves Visitor Center, Baker* ☉ *Memorial Day–Labor Day, Tues., Thurs., and Sat.; Sept., Oct., Apr., and May, Sat.*

RESTAURANTS

Dining in the park itself is limited to the basic breakfast and lunch fare at the Lehman Caves Cafe and Gift Shop. Nearby Baker, a town of less than 100 people, has an option or two.

HOTELS

There is no lodging in the park, so unless you're willing and able to snag one of the park's first-come, first-served campsites, or expect to camp in the backcountry, plan on lodging in nearby Baker or in Ely. *Hotel reviews have been shortened. For full information, visit Fodors.com.*

WHAT IT COSTS				
	$	$$	$$$	$$$$
Restaurants	under $13	$13–$20	$21–$30	over $30
Hotels	under $101	$101–$150	$151–$200	over $200

Restaurant prices are the average cost of a main course at dinner, or if dinner is not served, at lunch. Hotel prices are the lowest cost of a standard double room in high season.

TOURS

Alaska Mountain Guides. Outdoor enthusiasts looking for adventure may want to consider a guided trip with virtually the only outfitter working in the park. These strenuous excursions last 5–12 days and can have various focuses, including rock climbing, mountaineering, hiking, and technical skill-building. Salt Lake City is typically the jumping-off point, and many of the trips take place November–June. ⊠ *57 Mud Bay Rd., Haines* ☎ *800/766–3396, 801/206–0115* ⊕ *www. alaskamountainguides.com.*

VISITOR INFORMATION

Park Contact Information Great Basin National Park. ⊠ *Rte. 488, Baker* ☎ *775/234-7331* ⊕ *www.nps.gov/grba.*

VISITOR CENTERS

Great Basin Visitor Center. Here you can see exhibits on the flora, fauna, and geology of the park, or ask a ranger to suggest a favorite hike. Books, videos, and souvenirs are for sale; water is available, but for snacks continue up the road to the Lehman Caves Visitor Center. ⊠ *Rte. 487, just north of Baker* ☎ *775/234–7520* ☉ *Oct.–mid-May, daily 8–4:30; mid-May–Sept., daily 8–5:30.*

Lehman Caves Visitor Center. Regularly scheduled cave tours lasting 60 or 90 minutes depart from here. Mountain View Nature Trail encircles the visitor center and includes Rhodes Cabin and the historic cave entrance. Exhibits highlight the gnarled and ancient bristlecone pine and other park flora, plus cave formations. Buy gifts for friends and family back home at the bookstore, and take advantage of the free Wi-Fi. ⊠ *Rte. 488, ½ mile inside park boundary* ☎ *775/234–7331* ☉ *Daily 8–5.*

20

EXPLORING

SCENIC DRIVES

Baker Creek Road. Though less popular than the Wheeler Peak Scenic Drive, this gravel road affords gorgeous views of Wheeler Peak, the Baker Creek Drainage, and Snake Valley. Beautiful wildflowers are an extra treat in spring and early summer. The road is closed in the winter, and there are no pull-outs or scenic overlooks. ⊠ *½ mile inside the park boundary off Rte. 488.*

Fodor's Choice   **Wheeler Peak Scenic Drive.** A must for any Great Basin trip. Less than
★   a mile from the visitor center off Route 488, turn onto this paved
road that winds its way up to elevations of 10,000 feet. You'll go past
pinyon-juniper forest in lower elevations; as you climb, the air cools as
much as 20–30 degrees. Along the way, overlooks offer awe-inspiring
views of the Snake Range mountains, and a short hiking trail leads to
views of the Osceola mining site. Turn off at Mather Overlook, elevation 9,000 feet, for the best photo ops. Wheeler Overlook is the best
place to see Wheeler Peak, as well as fall colors. Allow 1½ hours for the
24-mile round-trip, not including hikes. ⊠ *Just inside park boundary,
off Rte. 488 about 5 miles west of Baker, Baker.*

SCENIC STOPS

FAMILY   **Lehman Caves.** In 1885, rancher and miner Absalom Lehman discovered
this underground wonder—a single limestone and marble cavern 2½
miles long. Inside, stalactites, stalagmites, helictites, flowstone, popcorn, and other bizarre mineral formations cover almost every surface.
Lehman Caves is one of the best places to see rare shield formations,
created when calcite-rich water is forced from tiny cracks in a cave
wall, ceiling, or floor. Year-round the cave maintains a constant, damp
temperature of 50°F, so wear a light jacket and nonskid shoes when
you take the tour, which takes you ¼ mile into the cave. Go for the full
90-minute tour if you have time; during summer, it's offered four or five
times per day, as is the 60-minute tour. Expect daily tours during the
winter. Children under age five are not allowed on the 90-minute tours,
except during the winter; those under 16 must be accompanied by an
adult. Take the 0.3-mile Mountain View Nature Trail beforehand to see
the original cave entrance and **Rhodes Cabin,** where black-and-white
photographs of the park's earlier days line the walls. If you're planning
a visit during a holiday, get your cave tickets in advance as the tours
can book up quickly. ⊠ *Lehman Caves Visitor Center* ☎ *775/234–7331*
💲 *$4–$10* ⊙ *Daily 8–4:30.*

SPORTS AND THE OUTDOORS

Great Basin National Park is a great place for experienced outdoor
enthusiasts. Only one outfitter does guided trips here, and the closest
outdoor store is miles away in Ely, so bring everything you might need
and be prepared to go it alone. Permits are not required to go off the
beaten path, but such adventurers are encouraged to register with a
ranger just in case. The effort is worth it, for the backcountry is wide
open and not at all crowded no matter the time of year (just keep an
eye on the weather). As is the case in all national parks, bicycling is
restricted to existing roads, but as the park sees fewer visitors than
other national parks, road cyclists will find few cars to trouble them.
Still, be extra careful on Wheeler Drive, which can become busy any
time of the year.

Lehman Caves: It's amazing what a little water and air can do to a room.

BIRD-WATCHING

Great Basin National Park might not be crowded with people, but it sports an impressive list of bird species sighted—238, according to the National Park Service checklist. Some species, such as the common raven and American robin, can be seen at most locations. Others, such as the red-naped sapsucker, are more commonly seen near Lehman Creek. In the higher elevations, listen for the loud shriek of Clark's nutcracker, storing nuts.

CROSS-COUNTRY SKIING

Lehman Creek Trail. In summer, descend 2,050 feet by hiking Lehman Creek Trail one-way (downhill) from Wheeler Peak campground to Upper Lehman Creek campground. In winter, it is the most popular cross-country skiing trail in the park. You may need snowshoes to reach the skiable upper section, with free rentals available at the Lehman Cave Visitor Center.

HIKING

You'll witness beautiful views by driving along the Wheeler Peak Scenic Drive and other park roads, but hiking allows an in-depth experience that just can't be matched. Trails at Great Basin run the gamut from relaxing ¼-mile jaunts to multiday backpacking excursions, so everyone can find a path that matches personal ability, fitness level, and desired destination, be it mountain peak, flowered meadow, or evergreen forest.

CLOSE UP

Plants and Wildlife in Great Basin

Despite the cold, dry conditions in Great Basin, 925 plant species thrive; 13 are considered sensitive species. The region gets less than 10 inches of rain a year, so plants have developed some ingenious methods of dealing with the desert's harshness. For instance, many flowering plants will only grow and produce seeds in a year when there is enough water. Spruces, pines, and junipers have set down roots here, and the bristlecone pine has been doing so for thousands of years.

The park's plants provide a variety of habitats for animals and for more than 230 bird species. In the sagebrush are jackrabbits, ground squirrels, chipmunks, and pronghorn. Mule deer and striped skunks abound in the pygmy forest of pinyon pine and juniper trees. Shrews, ringtail cats, and weasels make their homes around the springs and streams. Mountain lions, bobcats, and sheep live on the rugged slopes and in valleys. The park is also home to coyotes, kit fox, and badgers. Treat the Great Basin rattlesnake with respect. Bites are uncommon and rarely fatal, but if you're bitten, remain calm and call 911.

When you pick up a trail map at the visitor center, ask about trail conditions (many are unpaved, and some are maintained less than others) and bring appropriate clothing when you set out from any trailhead. No matter the trail length, always carry water, and remember that the trails are at high elevations, so pace yourself accordingly. Never enter abandoned mineshafts or tunnels, because they are unstable and dangerous. Those headed into the backcountry don't need to obtain a permit, but are encouraged to register at either of the two visitor centers. Though Great Basin is a high desert, winters can be harsh, so always inquire about the weather ahead of time at the visitor center.

EASY

FAMILY **Mountain View Nature Trail.** Just past the Rhodes Cabin on the right side of the visitor center, this short and easy trail (0.3 mile) through pinyon pine and juniper trees is marked with signs describing the plants. The path passes the original entrance to Lehman Caves and loops back to the visitor center. It's a great way to spend a half hour or so while you wait for your cave tour to start. *Easy.* ⊹ *Trailhead: at Lehman Caves Visitor Center.*

Osceola Ditch Trail. In 1890, at a cost of $108,223, the Osceola Gravel Mining Company constructed an 18-mile-long trench. The ditch was part of an attempt to glean gold from the South Snake Range, but water shortages and the company's failure to find much gold forced the mining operation to shut down in 1905. You can reach portions of the eastern section of the ditch on foot via the Osceola Ditch Trail, which passes through pine and fir trees. Allow 30 minutes for this easy 0.3-mile round-trip hike. *Easy.* ⊹ *Trailhead: Wheeler Peak Scenic Dr.*

MODERATE

Alpine Lakes Trail. This moderate, 2.7-mile trek loops past the beautiful Stella and Teresa lakes from the trailhead at the top of the Wheeler Park Scenic Drive. You'll rise and fall about 600 feet in elevation as you pass through subalpine and alpine forest. The views of Wheeler Peak, amid wildflowers (in summer), white fir, twisted aspens, and towering ponderosa pines, make this a memorable hike. The trailhead is at nearly 10,000 feet, so make sure you're adjusted to the altitude and prepared for changing weather. Allow three hours. *Moderate.* ✛ *Trailhead: at Bristlecone parking area, near end of Wheeler Peak Scenic Dr.*

> **GOOD READS**
>
> ■ *Hiking Great Basin National Park,* by Bruce Grubbs, will get your Great Basin trip off on the right foot.
>
> ■ *Trails to Explore in Great Basin National Park,* by Rose Houk, is all about hiking in the park.
>
> ■ *Geology of the Great Basin,* by Bill Fiero, and *Basin and Range,* by John McPhee, present geological tours of the Great Basin.

FAMILY
Fodor's Choice
★

Bristlecone Pine Trail. Though the park has several bristlecone pine groves, the only way to see the gnarled, ancient trees up close is to hike this trail. From the parking area to the grove, it's a moderate 1.4-mile hike that takes about an hour each way. Rangers offer informative talks in season; inquire at the visitor center. The Bristlecone Pine Trail also leads to the **Glacier Trail**, which skirts the southernmost permanent ice field on the continent and ends with a view of a small alpine glacier, the only one in Nevada. From there it's less than 3 miles back to the parking lot. Allow three hours for the moderate hike and remember the trailhead is at 9,800 feet above sea level. *Moderate.* ✛ *Trailhead: Summit Trail parking area, Wheeler Peak Scenic Dr., 12 miles from Lehman Caves Visitor Center.*

DIFFICULT

Baker Lake Trail. This full-day, 12-mile hike can easily be made into a two-day backpacking trip. You'll gain a total of 2,620 feet in elevation on the way to Baker Lake, a jewel-like alpine lake with a backdrop of mountainous cliffs. *Difficult.* ✛ *Trailhead: Baker Creek Rd., going south from just east of the Lehman Caves Visitor Center.*

Fodor's Choice
★

Wheeler Peak Summit Trail. Begin this full-day, 8.6-mile hike early in the day so as to minimize exposure to afternoon storms. Depart and return to Summit Trailhead near the end of Wheeler Peak Scenic Drive. Most of the route follows a ridge up the mountain to the summit. Elevation gain is 2,900 feet to 13,063 feet above sea level, so hikers should have good stamina and watch for altitude sickness and/or hypothermia due to drastic temperature and weather changes. *Difficult.* ✛ *Trailhead: Wheeler Peak Scenic Dr., Summit Trail parking area.*

20

WHAT'S NEARBY

NEARBY TOWNS

An hour's drive west of the park, at the intersection of three U.S. highways, **Ely** (population 4,262) has the biggest population in the area and has been called "where Eastern Nevada goes to town." It grew up in the second wave of the early Nevada mining boom, right at the optimistic turn of the 20th century. For 70 years copper kept the town in business, but when it ran out in the early 1980s Ely declined fast. Then, in 1986, the National Park Service designated Great Basin National Park 68 miles to the east and the town got a boost. Ely has since been rebuilt and revitalized, though it's kept a quirky, faded feel. Downtown is dotted with vintage neon signs and a few abandoned buildings. It's home to a railroad museum, the county seat, and a great old hotel-casino (Hotel Nevada), as well as plenty of hotels and tourist amenities. If you want to get closer to the park, you can stay in tiny **Baker** (population roughly 75), which sits at the main park entrance. Little more than a cluster of small businesses a few miles south of U.S. 6/50 on Route 487, the desert oasis is 5 miles from the visitor center.

> **BEST BETS FOR FAMILIES**
>
> ■ **Bristlecone Pine Hike.** Enjoy this hike (2 miles long and almost 2 miles high) to see the park's signature trees in the Wheeler Peak cirque. Bristlecone pines are ancient, often thousands of years old, and gnarled—in other words, pretty cool for kids.
>
> ■ **Lehman Caves.** The consistently cool cave air will give you goose bumps, as will the array of stalactites, stalagmites, and fantasylike chambers.
>
> ■ **Nevada Northern Railway Museum.** Ride the rails year-round at this attraction in Ely.

Visitor Information White Pine County Tourism and Recreation Board. ⊠ *Bristlecone Convention Center, 150 6th St., Ely* ☎ *800/496–9350, 775/289–3720* ⊕ *www.elynevada.net.* **Great Basin Business and Tourism Council.** ⊠ *10 Main St., Baker* ⊕ *www.greatbasinpark.com.*

NEARBY ATTRACTIONS

Cave Lake State Park. At 7,350 feet above sea level in the pine and juniper forest of the big Schell Creek Range that borders Ely on the east, this is an idyllic spot. You can spend a day fishing for rainbow and brown trout in the reservoir and a night sleeping under the stars. Arrive early; it gets crowded. Access may be restricted in winter. ⊠ *15 miles southeast of Ely via U.S. 50/6/93* ☎ *775/296–1505* ⊕ *www.parks.nv.gov/parks/cave-lake-state-park* 🔖 *$5 for Nevada residents, $7 for nonresidents* ☉ *Daily, 24 hrs.*

FAMILY **Nevada Northern Railway Museum.** During the mining boom the Nevada Northern Railroad connected East Ely, Ruth, and McGill to the transcontinental rail line in the northeast corner of Nevada. The whole operation is now a museum, and the biggest attraction in Ely, visited by happy train aficionados from near and far. You can tour the depot, offices, warehouses, yard, engine houses, and repair shops, and catch a ride on one of the trains daily in July and August. If you're lucky, you'll get a lively history lesson from Sean Pitts, the resident historian, who knows how to spin a yarn. ⊠ *1100 Ave. A, Ely* ☎ *866/407–8326* ⊕ *www.nnry.com* 🖃 *$6* ⊗ *July and Aug., daily 8–5; Sept.–June, Wed.–Mon. 8–5.*

U.S. 93 Scenic Byway. The 68 miles between the park and Ely make a beautiful drive with diverse views of Nevada's paradoxical geography: dry deserts and lush mountains. You'll catch an occasional glimpse of a snake, perhaps a rattler, slithering on the road's shoulder, or a lizard sunning on a rock. Watch for deer. A straight drive to Ely takes a little more than an hour; if you have the time to take a dirt-road adventure, don't miss the Ward Charcoal Ovens or a peek at Cave Lake.

Ward Charcoal Ovens State Historic Park. In the desert south of Ely is this row of six beehive-shaped, 30-foot-tall ovens that could process 35 cords of wood at once. From 1876 to 1879, the ovens turned pinyon, juniper, and mountain mahogany into charcoal, which was used for refining local silver and copper ore. It's a well-preserved piece of unique mining history. ⊠ *7 miles south of Ely on U.S. 50/93, and 11 miles southwest on Cave Valley Rd.* ☎ *775/289–1693* ⊕ *www.parks.nv.gov/ parks/ward-charcoal-ovens-state-historic-park* 🖃 *$7* ⊗ *Daily, 24 hrs.*

WHERE TO EAT

IN THE PARK

$ ✕ **Lehman Caves Cafe and Gift Shop.** This casual spot is a great place to
AMERICAN cool your heels and soak in the vast desert view between park aventures.
FAMILY The basic menu includes light breakfasts, soup-and-sandwich lunches, freshly baked desserts, and giant ice-cream sandwiches, made by hand. ⑤ *Average main: $5* ⊠ *Next to visitor center* ☎ *775/234–7221* ⊕ *www. greatbasinpark.com/lehmangifts.htm* ⊗ *Closed Nov.–Mar. No dinner.*

PICNIC AREAS

Lehman Caves Visitor Center Picnic Area. This full-service picnic site, with tables, fire grills, water, and restrooms (the latter two available during the summer), is a short walk from the visitor center. Summer hours are often extended beyond the standard 8 am–4:30 pm. ⊠ *Just north of Lehman Caves Visitor Center.*

Pole Canyon Trailhead Picnic Area. Inaccessible when Baker Creek Road is closed in the winter, this picnic area at the mouth of a canyon has a handful of tables and fire grills but no water. It does have a restroom. Access is via a narrow, one-lane road. ⊠ *East of entrance to Grey Cliffs Group Camping site, at the mouth of Pole Canyon.*

Upper Lehman Creek Campground. There are a handful of places here where you can sit down for a bite and a breather. A group picnic site requires advance reservations, but areas near the host site and

20

amphitheater are first come, first served. Water is available. ✉ *4 miles from the Lehman Caves Visitor Center on Wheeler Peak Scenic Dr..*

OUTSIDE THE PARK

$ ✕**The Border Inn.** Restaurants come and go in nearby Baker, but this little
AMERICAN spot on the Utah–Nevada line can be counted on for a hearty breakfast, lunch, or dinner. It's a meat-and-potatoes kind of place, with classic American fare like hamburgers, chicken-fried steak, sandwiches, and steaks. There is also a full bar and a few slot machines in an adjacent room. ⑤ *Average main: $10* ✉ *U.S. 6/50, 13 miles east of Great Basin National Park, Baker* ☎ *775/234–7300* ⊕ *www.borderinncasino.com.*

$$$ ✕**Cellblock Steakhouse.** The only fine-dining in Ely, this low-lighted spot
STEAKHOUSE comes with a big helping of local color. Each table is its own "cell," complete with metal bars and old-timey photos on the wall. The portions are big and satisfying, and you can choose your libation from a full bar. Try The Rustler (filet mignon wrapped in bacon) or the prime rib (deputy's, sheriff's, or judge's cut), and end with a calorie-worthy dessert (dubbed Parole Options), like the smooth crème brûlée. ⑤ *Average main: $23* ✉ *211 5th St., Ely* ☎ *775/289–3033* ⊕ *www.jailhousecasino. com/dining.php* ◷ *No lunch.*

$$ ✕**Lectrolux Cafe.** Expect Mediterranean offerings at this Baker social
MEDITERRANEAN spot, but with different chefs coming most seasons, menu items tend
FAMILY to flunctuate. The brightly painted dining room, heavy with art, is something to be seen: equal parts deli, gift shop, and hotel lobby. It also boasts the best-stocked bar in the Great Basin, with several single-malt scotches, a variety of grappas, and dozens of wines and beers to choose from. ⑤ *Average main: $15* ✉ *Silver Jack Inn, Rte. 487, 5 miles south of U.S. 50 near park entrance, Baker* ☎ *775/299–5428* ⊕ *www. silverjackinn.com* ◷ *Closed Nov.–Feb.*

WHERE TO STAY

OUTSIDE THE PARK

$ 🏨**All Aboard Cafe & Inn.** After a dusty journey to far-flung Ely, there may
B&B/INN be no better spot to bed down than this charming, early-20th-century house just a block from the historic train station. **Pros:** inviting front porch; bright, cheery rooms; café serves breakfast, lunch, and dinner. **Cons:** no elevator to second floor; far away from Ely's gambling scene (if that's your thing). ⑤ *Rooms from: $90* ✉ *220 E. 11th St., Ely* ☎ *775/289– 3959* ⊕ *www.allaboardcafeandinn.com* ⤴ *5 rooms* ⦿*Breakfast.*

$ 🏨**The Border Inn.** Located on the Nevada side of the border with Utah on
HOTEL Route 50, the Border Inn has all the basics: clean, simple rooms with air-conditioning including 11 with kitchenettes, the area's only gas station, a full-service restaurant, and a casino to boot. **Pros:** restaurant, gas, and groceries all here; most reliable food and lodging in the area. **Cons:** gravel parking lot is dusty; Wi-Fi and cell service can be iffy. ⑤ *Rooms from: $69* ✉ *U.S. 6/50, Baker* ✛ *13 miles east of Great Basin National Park* ☎ *775/234–7300* ⊕ *www.borderinncasino.com* ⤴ *29 rooms* ⦿*No meals.*

CLOSE UP

Best Campgrounds in Great Basin

Great Basin has four developed campgrounds, all easily accessible by car, but only the Lower Lehman Creek Campground is open year-round. All are first come, first served, and can be paid for on-site with cash, check, or credit card.

Primitive campsites around Snake and Strawberry creeks are open year-round and are free; however, snow and rain can make access to the sites difficult. None have RV hookups (but RVers can stay at Whispering Elms in nearby Baker).

Baker Creek Campground. The turnoff is just past the park entrance, on the left as you approach the Lehman Caves Visitor Center. ⊠ 2½ miles south of Rte. 488, 3 miles from visitor center. ☎ No phone.

Lower Lehman Creek Campground. Other than Great Basin's primitive sites, this is the only campground in the park that is open year-round.

It's the first turnoff past the Lehman Caves Visitor Center. ⊠ 2½ miles from visitor center on Wheeler Peak Scenic Dr. ☎ No phone.

Upper Lehman Creek Campground. About a mile past the Lower Lehman Creek turnoff, this camp fills up quickly in the summer. ⊠ 4 miles from visitor center on Wheeler Peak Scenic Dr. ☎ No phone.

Wheeler Park Campground. This cool high-elevation campground at the end of Wheeler Peak Scenic Drive has stunning views and is near trailheads. ⊠ 12 miles from Lehman Caves Visitor Center on Wheeler Peak Scenic Dr. ☎ No phone.

Whispering Elms Campground. The largest camping facility close to but not inside the park is also the nearest to offer hookups for RVs. It is open year-round. ⊠ Rte. 487, behind Great Basin Lodge, Baker ☎ 775/234–9900.

$$$
B&B/INN
Fodor'sChoice
★

▦ Hidden Canyon Bed & Breakfast at the Lodge and Roseberry Court. The most luxurious lodging for hours in any direction, this elegant spot is surrounded by mountains and hundreds of acres of rugged, high-desert beauty. **Pros:** beautiful, lush, and serene setting make this feel like a retreat; airy, elegant rooms; hiking, fishing, and snowshoeing opportunities abound. **Cons:** no TV or cell service; the road in can be rough; far from services and more than a 30-minute drive to Great Basin National Park. ⑤ *Rooms from: $186 ⊠ 2000 Hidden Canyon Pkwy., Baker* ☎ *775/234–7172* ⊕ *www.greatbasinpark.com/hiddencanyon. htm* ➪ *4 lodge rooms (1 without a bathroom), 11 Roseberry Court rooms* ⊙ *Breakfast* ▭ *No credit cards.*

$
HOTEL

▦ Jailhouse Motel and Casino. This motel at Ely's main intersection was built near the town's old-time jail, so no wonder the rooms are assigned cell numbers and there are prison bars around the booths at its fancy steak house (although they don't pass the food through a slot). **Pros:** Main Street location; on-site casino, two restaurants, and a bar. **Cons:** smoky casino adjacent to registration and restaurant entrance. ⑤ *Rooms from: $59 ⊠ 211 5th St., Ely* ☎ *775/289–3033, 800/841–5430* ⊕ *www. jailhousecasino.com* ➪ *60 rooms.*

20

$$ ⚐ **La Quinta Inn & Suites.** The newest and largest hotel in Ely, the La
HOTEL Quinta Inn & Suites is a clean, fresh, comfortable stay in a small town
filled with aging options. **Pros:** complimentary hot breakfast; pool;
full grocery store next door. **Cons:** on an unattractive strip of motels;
too far to walk to Main Street; often seems understaffed, with over-
whelmed desk clerks. ⑤ *Rooms from: $120* ✉ *1591 Great Basin Blvd.,
Ely* ☎ *775/289–8833* ⊕ *www.lq.com* ⤳ *100 rooms* ❍| *Breakfast.*

$ ⚐ **Prospector Hotel & Gambling Hall.** This big, comfortable hotel walks
HOTEL the line between classy and kitschy, with Western-themed rooms, on-
site gambling, and a tasty Mexican restaurant. **Pros:** a good value,
with quality that far surpasses many other local options; clean, inviting
rooms; pets and RVs welcome. **Cons:** have to walk through casino to
get to restaurant; not walking distance to downtown and most services.
⑤ *Rooms from: $89* ✉ *1501 E. Aultman St., Ely* ☎ *775/289–8900,
800/750–0557* ⊕ *www.prospectorhotel.us* ⤳ *61 rooms* ❍| *No meals.*

$ ⚐ **Silver Jack Inn.** For being about as far off the beaten track as you
HOTEL can get in the Nevada desert, this tiny motel is a cozy oasis of rooms
surrounding a tree-filled lawn and a relaxing patio. **Pros:** funky, artis-
tic decor; great location; on-site restaurant serving breakfast, lunch,
and dinner. **Cons:** rooms have not been updated in years, and may
not be up to everyone's standards; "overflow" rooms across the street
are bare-bones; staff changes often. ⑤ *Rooms from: $69* ✉ *Rte. 487,
Baker* ✛ *1 block south of the turnoff for Great Basin National Park*
☎ *775/299–5428* ⊕ *www.silverjackinn.com* ⤳ *10 rooms* ❍| *No meals.*

$ ⚐ **Whispering Elms Motel & RV Park.** The strip of rooms in the back of
HOTEL this friendly RV park may look plain from the outside but are some of
the cleanest and best-equipped in town, with microwaves, fridges, and
a/c. **Pros:** great location, just at the turnoff for Great Basin; bar is a
local hangout; clean rooms with reliable Wi-Fi. **Cons:** no pool or other
big-city amenities; gravel parking lot. ⑤ *Rooms from: $62* ✉ *Rte. 487,
Baker* ✛ *Just south of the Great Basin Visitor Center and north of the
turnoff for the park* ☎ *775/234–9900* ⊕ *www.camptheelms.wix.com/
the-elms* ⤳ *6 rooms* ❍| *No meals.*

GREAT SAND DUNES NATIONAL PARK

WELCOME TO GREAT SAND DUNES NATIONAL PARK

TOP REASONS TO GO

★ **Dune climbing:** Trek through the 30 square miles of main dunes in this landlocked dune field.

★ **Unrivaled diversity:** You can see eight completely different life zones in this park, ranging from salty wetlands and lush forests to parched sand sheet and frozen alpine peaks, all in a single day.

★ **Bounty of bison:** Take a ride around the west end of the park, where more than 2,000 bison roam in the grasslands and wetlands.

★ **Aspens in autumn:** Take a hike—or, if you've got a high-clearance four-wheel-drive vehicle and good driving skills, take the rough road—up to Medano Pass during fall foliage season when the aspens turn gold.

★ **Vigorous hikes:** Pack a picnic lunch and climb up to High Dune, followed by the more strenuous stretch over to Star Dune. Or tackle the dramatic Music Pass Trail, which takes you to the tree line and covers 3.5 miles (and 2,000 feet in elevation change) each way.

1 Sand dunes. The 30-square-mile field of sand has no designated trails. The highest dune in the park—and, in fact, in North America—is 750-foot-high Star Dune.

2 Sangre de Cristo Mountains. Named the "Blood of Christ" Mountains by Spanish explorers because of their ruddy color—especially at sunrise and sunset—the range contains 10 of Colorado's 54 Fourteeners (mountains taller than 14,000 feet). Six that are more than 13,000 feet tall are within the preserve itself.

3 Forest. Ponderosa pines populate the forested areas around the Sangre de Cristo Mountains in the preserve and park's eastern boundaries.

4 Grasslands. Wildlife, such as elk and bison, feed on the park's grassy areas, primarily found in the park's southern area and the Great Sand Dunes National Preserve.

5 Wetlands. Popular with a variety of birds and amphibians, these seasonal wetlands form in the area around Medano Creek, where cottonwood and willow trees also thrive.

SAN LUIS VALLEY

SAND SHEET

SABKHA

← TO MOSCA

COLORADO
●

21

Music Pass

0 ———— 2 mi
0 ———— 2 km

S A N G R E   D E   C R I S T O   M O U N T A I N S

Medano Pass

Mt Herard
13,297 ft

STAR DUNE
COMPLEX

4x4 only

3

2

Mt Zwischen
12,006 ft

D U N E F I E L D   Point of No Return
4-wheel drive vehicles
only beyond this point

1

Castle Creek 🏕
Sand Pit 🏕   Dunes
Overlook
Trail

ESCAPE
DUNES   **Pinyon Flats**

Mosca Creek

◆**Star Dune**
750 ft
(tallest dune in park)▲

◆**High Dune**
650 ft

Visitor Center
Montville
Nature Trail

Mosca Pass Trail

Medano
Creek

5

4

150

TO
HWY160

KEY

👫	Ranger Station
🔺	Campground
🏕	Picnic Area
🍴	Restaurant
📷	Lodge
🚶	Trailhead
🚻	Restrooms
🔆	Scenic Viewpoint
⋯⋯	Walking/Hiking Trails

GETTING ORIENTED

The Great Sand Dunes National Park and Preserve encompasses 150,000 acres (about 234 square miles) of land and mountains surrounding the dunes. Looking at the dunes from the west, your eye sweeps over the grassland and sand sheet, a vast expanse of smaller dunes and flatter sections of sand and knee-high brush. The Sangre de Cristo Mountains rear up in the east behind the dunes, forming a dramatic backdrop and creating a stunning juxtaposition of color and form. Depending on the time of year, you'll hear a quiet gurgle or a real rush from Medano Creek, which flows along the eastern edge of the dunes (*medano* is Spanish for "sand dune," pronounced *meh*-dah-noh). Hiking trails thread these mountains—the "preserve" area—where you can walk quietly through aspens and evergreens.

Updated by
Whitney Bryen

Created by winds that sweep the San Luis Valley floor, the enormous sand dunes that form the heart of Great Sand Dunes National Park and Preserve are an improbable, unforgettable sight. The dunes, as curvaceous as Rubens's nudes, stretch for more than 30 square miles. Because they're made of sand, the dunes' very existence seem tenuous, as if they might blow away before your eyes, yet they're solid enough to have withstood 440,000 years of Mother Nature—and the modern stress of hikers and saucer-riding thrill seekers.

GREAT SAND DUNES PLANNER

WHEN TO GO

About 300,000 visitors come to the park each year, most on summer weekends; they tend to congregate around the main parking area and Medano Creek. To avoid the crowds, hike away from the main area up to the High Dune. Or come in the winter, when the park is a place for contemplation and repose—as well as skiing and sledding.

Fall and spring are the prettiest times to visit, with the surrounding mountains still capped with snow in May, and leaves on the aspen trees turning gold in September and early October. In summer, the surface temperature of the sand can climb to 140°F in the afternoon, so climbing the dunes is best in the morning or late afternoon. Since you're at a high altitude—about 8,200 feet at the visitor center—the air temperatures in the park itself remain in the 70s most of the summer.

AVG. HIGH/LOW TEMPS.

Jan.	Feb.	Mar.	Apr.	May	June
35/10	39/14	47/21	56/28	66/37	77/45
July	Aug.	Sept.	Oct.	Nov.	Dec.
81/51	78/49	71/42	60/32	46/20	36/11

FESTIVALS AND EVENTS

FAMILY **Alamosa Round-Up Rodeo.** The last week in June marks the annual rodeo competition in Alamosa, a genuine Wild West event including barrel racers, bulls, broncos, and bareback riding. ⊕ *www.alamosaroundup. com* 🎫 *$12.*

PLANNING YOUR TIME

GREAT SAND DUNES IN ONE DAY

Arrive early in the day during the summer so you can hike up to **High Dune** and get a view of the entire dune field. Round-trip, the walk itself should take about 1½ to 2 hours (plus time to jump off or slide down the dunes). In the afternoon, hop into the car and head to Zapata Falls, hike on the short-and-shady Montville Nature Trail, or head for the longer Mosca Pass Trail, which follows a small creek through cool aspens and evergreens to one of the lower mountain passes.

In the spring and early summer or fall, when the temperatures are cooler, first walk up to the High Dune to enjoy the view. If you're game to hike farther, head to **Star Dune** for a picnic lunch. Hike down the eastern ridge to Medano Creek, then head to the western end of the park to explore the sand sheet, grasslands, and wetlands. If you're here on a morning when there's a hayride (or four-wheel-drive) tour to see the bison, take it and then head off on your hikes.

GETTING HERE AND AROUND

CAR TRAVEL

Great Sand Dunes National Park and Preserve is about 240 miles from both Denver and Albuquerque, and roughly 180 miles from Colorado Springs and Santa Fe. The fastest route from Denver is Interstate 25 south to U.S. 160, heading west to just past Blanca, to Highway 150 north, which goes right to the park's main entrance. For a more scenic route, take U.S. 285 over Kenosha, Red Hill, and Poncha Passes, turn onto Highway 17 just south of Villa Grove, then take County Lane 6 to the park (watch for signs just south of Hooper). From Albuquerque, go north on Interstate 25 to Santa Fe, then north on U.S. 285 to Alamosa, then U.S. 160 east to Highway 150. From the west, Highway 17 and County Lane 6 take you to the park. The park entrance station is about 3 miles from the park boundary, and it's about a mile from there to the visitor center; the main parking lot is about a mile farther.

PARK ESSENTIALS

PARK FEES AND PERMITS

Entrance fees are $3 per adult above age 15 and are valid for one week from date of purchase. Children are admitted free at all times. Pick up camping permits ($20 per night per site at Pinyon Flats Campground) and backpacking permits (free) at the visitor center.

PARK HOURS

The park is open 24/7. It is in the Mountain time zone.

CELL-PHONE RECEPTION

Cell-phone reception in the park is sporadic. Public telephones are at the visitor center, dunes parking lot, and at the Pinyon Flats campground—you need a calling card (these aren't coin-operated phones).

EDUCATIONAL OFFERINGS

RANGER PROGRAMS

FAMILY **Interpretive Programs.** Family-friendly nature walks designed to help visitors learn more about the Great Sand Dunes National Park are scheduled most days from late May through September, and sporadically in April and October. Call or drop in to ask about sunset walks, afternoon weekend tours, and evening stargazing programs. ⊠ *Programs begin at the visitor center* ☎ *719/378–6399* ⊠ *Free.*

FAMILY **Junior Ranger Programs.** In summer, children ages 3 through 12 can join age-appropriate activities to learn about plants, animals, and the park's ecology, and they can become Junior Rangers by working successfully through an activity booklet available at the visitor center. If they complete the self-led program, they'll receive a patch or a badge. ⊠ *Visitor Center, 11999 Hwy. 150* ☎ *719/378–6399.*

RESTAURANTS

There are no dining establishments in the park. In the visitor center and at the campground there are vending machines with drinks that are stocked mid-spring through mid-fall. There is one picnic area in the park.

HOTELS

There are no hotels, motels, or lodges in the park. The nearest lodge is right outside the park entrance, and there are many hotels in Alamosa and a handful of them in other surrounding towns including Salida, Walsenburg, and Monte Vista. *Hotel reviews have been shortened. For full information, visit Fodors.com.*

WHAT IT COSTS				
	$	**$$**	**$$$**	**$$$$**
Restaurants	under $13	$13–$18	$19–$25	over $25
Hotels	under $121	$121–$170	$171–$230	over $230

Restaurant prices are the average cost of a main course at dinner or, if dinner is not served, at lunch. Hotel prices are the lowest cost of a standard double room in high season, excluding taxes and service charges.

CLOSE UP

Plants and Wildlife in Great Sand Dunes

The salty wetlands are dotted with sedges, rushes, and other plants that are tolerant of changes in water salinity and levels, while the sand sheet and grasslands have prickly pear, rabbit brush, and yucca. The dune field looks barren from afar, but up close you see various grasses have rooted in swales among the dunes. Juniper, pinyon, and ponderosa pine trees grow on the lower portions of the mountain, hardy spruce and fir trees survive in the subalpine forest zone, and lichens and tiny flowers cling to the rock at the top.

Birds inhabit the wetlands; short-horned lizards, elk, and pronghorns live in the sand sheet and grassland; and Great Sand Dunes tiger beetles and Ord's kangaroo rats breed in the dune field. In the forests and on the mountainsides, raptors fly overhead, while mule deer and Rocky Mountain bighorn sheep graze.

TOURS

FAMILY **Bison Tour.** The Nature Conservancy, an international nonprofit conservation organization, owns a 103,000-acre ranch that includes a herd of roughly 2,000 bison in the 50,000-acre Medano Ranch section, in the southwest corner of the park. The conservancy offers a two-hour tour focused on the section of the park, where bison—along with coyotes, elk, deer, pronghorns, porcupines, and birds such as great horned owls and red-tailed hawks—roam in the grasslands and wetlands. Depending on the season, the tour will be led by wagon or a four-wheel-drive vehicle. Tours begin at the Nature Conservancy's Zapata Ranch Headquarters and reservations are required at least 24 hours in advance. ⊠ *Zapata Ranch Headquarters, 5305 Hwy. 150, Mosca* ☎ *888/592–7282, 719/378–2356* ⊕ *www.zranch.org* 🖃 *Tours $50* ☉ *daily 8–5; tours Wed., Fri., and Sat. 9 am and noon.*

VISITOR INFORMATION

Park Contact Information Great Sand Dunes National Park and Preserve. ⊠ *11999 Hwy. 150, Mosca* ☎ *719/378–6399* ⊕ *www.nps.gov/grsa.*

VISITOR CENTERS

Great Sand Dunes Visitor Center. View exhibits and artwork, browse in the bookstore, and watch a 20-minute film with an overview of the dunes. Rangers are on hand to answer questions. Facilities include restrooms and a vending machine stocked with soft drinks and snacks, but no other food. (The Great Sand Dunes Oasis, just outside the park boundary, has a café that is open generally late April through early October.) ⊠ *Near the park entrance* ☎ *719/378–6399* ⊕ *www.nps.gov/grsa/planyourvisit/visitor-center.htm* ☉ *Late May–early Sept., daily 8:30–6; early Sept.–late May, daily 9–4:30 (sometimes until 5 in late spring and early fall—call ahead).*

EXPLORING

SCENIC DRIVES

Medano Pass Primitive Road. This 22-mile road connects Great Sand Dunes with the Wet Mountain Valley and Highway 69 on the east side of the Sangre de Cristo Mountains via a climb to Medano Pass (about 10,000 feet above sea level) and affords stunning views, especially in late September when the aspen trees change color. It also provides access to campsites in the national preserve. It is a four-wheel-drive-only road that is best driven by someone who already has good driving skills on rough, unpaved roads. (Your four-wheel-drive vehicle must have high clearance and be engineered to go over rough roads, and you may need to drop your tires' air pressure.) The road has sections of deep, loose sand, and it crosses Medano Creek nine times. Before you go, stop at the visitor center for a map and ask about current road conditions. Drive time pavement to pavement is 2½ to 3 hours. ⊠ *Great Sand Dunes National Park.*

SCENIC STOPS

Dune Field. The more than 30 square miles of big dunes in the heart of the park are the main attraction, although the surrounding sand sheet does have some smaller dunes. You can start putting your feet in the sand 3 miles past the main park entrance. ⊠ *Great Sand Dunes National Park.*

High Dune. This isn't the park's highest dune, but it's high enough in the dune field to provide a view of all the dunes from its summit. It's on the first ridge of dunes you see from the main parking area. ⊠ *Great Sand Dunes National Park.*

SPORTS AND THE OUTDOORS

BIRD-WATCHING

The San Luis Valley is famous for its migratory birds, many of which stop in the park. Great Sand Dunes also has many permanent feathered residents. In the wetlands, you might see American white pelicans and the American avocet. On the forested sections of the mountains there are goshawks, northern harriers, gray jays, and Steller's jays. And in the alpine tundra there are golden eagles, hawks, horned larks, and white-tailed ptarmigan.

HIKING

Visitors can walk just about anywhere on the sand dunes in the heart of the park. The best view of all the dunes is from the top of High Dune. There are no formal trails because the sand keeps shifting, but you don't really need them: It's extremely difficult to get lost out here.

■ TIP→ Before taking any of the trails in the preserve, rangers recommend stopping at the visitor center and picking up the handout that lists the trails, including their degree of difficulty. The dunes can get very hot in the summer, reaching up to 140°F in the afternoon. If you're hiking, carry plenty of water; if you're going into the backcountry to camp overnight, carry even more water and a water filtration system. A free permit is required to backpack in the park. Also, watch for weather changes. If there's a thunderstorm and lightning, get off the dunes or trail immediately, and seek shelter. Before hiking, leave word with someone indicating where you're going to hike and when you expect to be back. Tell that contact to call 911 if you don't show up when expected.

EASY

FAMILY **Hike to High Dune.** Get a panoramic view of all the surrounding dunes from the top of High Dune. Since there's no formal path, the smartest approach is to zigzag up the dune ridgelines. High Dune is 650 feet high, and to get there and back takes about 1½ to 2 hours. It's just over a mile each way, but it can feel like a lot longer if there's been no rain for some time and the sand is soft. If you add on the walk to the 750-foot Star Dune, which is another 1 mile there and back, plan on another two hours and a strenuous workout up and down the dunes. *Easy.* ✛ *Start from main dune field.*

MODERATE

Fodor's Choice **Mosca Pass Trail.** This moderately challenging route follows the Montville Trail laid out centuries ago by Native Americans, which became ★ the Mosca Pass toll road used in the late 1800s and early 1900s. This is a good afternoon hike, because the trail rises through the trees and subalpine meadows, often following Mosca Creek. It is 3½ miles one-way, with a 1,500-foot gain in elevation. Hiking time is two to three hours each way. *Moderate.* ✛ *Trailhead: lower end of trail begins at Montville Trailhead, just north of visitor center.*

DIFFICULT

Music Pass Trail. This steep trail offers superb views of the glacially carved Upper Sand Creek Basin, ringed by several 13,000-foot peaks and the Wet Mountain Valley to the east. The top of the pass can be covered in snow through midsummer and reaches about 11,000 feet above sea level, surrounded by even higher mountain peaks. It's 3½ miles and a 2,000-foot elevation gain one-way from the lower parking lot on the east side of the preserve, off Forest Service Road 119, and 1 mile from the upper parking lot (reachable only by four-wheel drive). Depending on how fit you are and how often you stop, it can take six hours round-trip from the lower lot. *Difficult.* ✛ *Trailhead: on eastern side of park, reached via Hwy. 69, 4½ miles south of Westcliffe. Turn off Hwy. 69 to the west at the sign for Music Pass and South Colony Lakes Trails. At the "T" junction, turn left onto South Colony Rd. At the end of the ranch fence on the right you'll see another sign for Music Pass.*

WHAT'S NEARBY

The vast expanse one sees from the dunes is the San Luis Valley. Covering 8,000 square miles (and with an average altitude of 7,500 feet), the San Luis Valley is the world's largest alpine valley, sprawling on a broad, flat, dry plain between the San Juan Mountains to the west and the Sangre de Cristo range to the east, and extending south into northern New Mexico. The area is one of the state's major agricultural producers.

NEARBY TOWNS

Alamosa, the San Luis Valley's major city, is 35 miles southwest of Great Sand Dunes via U.S. 160 and Highway 150. It's a casual, central base for exploring the park and the surrounding region. The rest of the area is dotted with tiny towns, including **Mosca, Blanca, Antonito,** and **Fort Garland,** to the south of the park, and **Monte Vista, Del Norte,** and **Hooper** to the west. They are all within an hour's drive from the park.

Visitor Information Alamosa Convention & Visitors Bureau. ⊠ *610 State Ave., Alamosa* ☎ *800/258–7597, 719/589–3681* ⊕ *www.alamosa.org.* **Del Norte Chamber of Commerce.** ⊠ *505 Grand Ave., Del Norte* ⊕ *www.delnortechamber. org.* **Monte Vista Chamber of Commerce.** ⊠ *947 1st Ave., Monte Vista* ☎ *719/852–2731* ⊕ *www.monte-vista.org.*

NEARBY ATTRACTIONS

Alamosa National Wildlife Refuge. Less than an hour's drive southwest of Great Sand Dunes is a sanctuary for songbirds, waterbirds, and raptors (it's also home to many other types of birds, along with mule deer, beavers, and coyotes). The Rio Grande runs through the park comprising more than 12,000 acres of natural and man-made wetlands. You can take a 4-mile hike round-trip along the river or a 3½-mile wildlife drive on the park's western side or a drive along Bluff Road to an overlook on the park's eastern side. The refuge office is staffed by volunteers sporadically from March through November and closed in winter—it's wise to call first. ⊠ *9383 El Rancho La., off U.S. 160, Alamosa* ☎ *719/589–4021* ⊕ *www.fws.gov/alamosa* 🎫 *Free* ☉ *Daily sunrise–sunset.*

FAMILY **Cumbres & Toltec Scenic Railroad.** Take a day trip on the Cumbres & Toltec Scenic Railroad, an 1880s steam locomotive that chugs through portions of Colorado's and northern New Mexico's rugged mountains that you can't reach via roads. It's the country's longest and highest narrow-gauge railroad. The company offers two round-trip train routes—either Antonito to Osier, or Chama, New Mexico, to Osier—plus several bus-and-train combinations and one-way trips. Cumbres & Toltec offers themed rides, including a special Christmastime train ride called "The Cinder Bear." ⊠ *5234 U.S. 285, Antonito* ☎ *888/286–2737* ⊕ *www. cumbrestoltec.com* 🎫 *$95–$179* ☉ *Late May–mid-Oct.*

Fort Garland Museum. Colorado's first military post was established here in 1858 to protect settlers in the San Luis Valley, which was then part of the Territory of New Mexico. The legendary Kit Carson once served here, and the six original adobe structures are still standing. The fort

Near water in the park's grasslands area is where you might see elk, mule deer, and lizards.

features a re-creation of the commandant's quarters from Carson's era, as well as period military displays, and a rotating local folk-art exhibit. ✉ 29477 Hwy. 159, Fort Garland ☎ 719/379–3512 ⊕ museumtrail. org/fortgarlandmuseum.asp ✉ $5 ⊙ Apr.–Oct., daily 9–5; Nov.–Mar., Thurs.–Mon. 10–4.

Monte Vista National Wildlife Refuge. Just west of the Alamosa wildlife refuge is its sister sanctuary, the Monte Vista National Wildlife Refuge, a 15,000-acre park that's a stopping point for up to 20,000 migrating cranes in the spring and fall. It hosts an annual Crane Festival, held one weekend in mid-March in the nearby town of Monte Vista and a children's Crane Festival in mid-October at the park with kid-friendly activities. You can see the sanctuary via a 2½-mile driving tour. ✉ 6120 Hwy. 15, south off U.S. 160/285, Monte Vista ☎ 719/589–4021 ⊕ www.fws.gov/refuge/monte_vista/ ✉ Free ⊙ Daily sunrise–sunset.

FAMILY **Rio Grande Scenic Railroad.** This railroad carries passengers on excursions between Alamosa and La Veta some weekdays. You can also take a weekend ride from Alamosa to the Fir Summit Amphitheater where a wind- and solar-powered performance stage at 9,400 feet attracts regional and national Western and folk artists. The Rio Grande also offers a round-trip "Train to Christmas Town" from Alamosa to La Veta several times in late November and December. ✉ 610 State Ave., Alamosa ☎ 877/726–7245, 719/587–0509 ⊕ www.coloradotrain.com ✉ $19–$169 ⊙ Late May–mid-Oct.

FAMILY **Zapata Falls Recreation Area.** If it's a hot day, take a drive to the falls section of the Zapata Falls Recreation Area, about 7 miles south of Great Sand Dunes National Park (and about 10 miles north of Alamosa).

From the trailhead, it's a ½-mile hike to the 40-foot waterfall and a mildly steep trail, which can include wading in a stream and walking through a narrow gorge to view the falls (depending on water levels). Air temperatures in the gorge are always cool and inviting, and the falls are beautiful, but be careful of the current (and slippery rocks) here. A picnic area and restrooms are at the entrance. The trailhead is 3½ miles off Highway 150, between mile markers 10 and 11. ⊠ *Rio Grande National Forest Supervisor's Office, 1803 W. U.S. 160, Monte Vista* ☎ *719/852–5941* ⊕ *www.fs.usda.gov/riogrande* ⌨ *Free* ☉ *Daily.*

AREA ACTIVITIES

SPORTS AND THE OUTDOORS
FISHING
Colorado fishing license. There are plenty of fisheries in the area where you can catch trout, pike, and perch, including the Rio Grande, the Conejos River, and Sanchez, Smith, and Platoro reservoirs. A Colorado fishing license is required ($9 for one day, $21 for five days). ⊠ *Colorado Division of Wildlife, SE Region Service Center, 4255 Sinton Rd., Colorado Springs* ☎ *800/244–5613* ⊕ *wildlife.state.co.us/fishing.*

EDUCATIONAL OFFERINGS
Colorado Field Institute. This nonprofit teams up with the experts at the park and other area organizations, such as the Rio Grande National Forest, San Luis Valley National Wildlife Refuges Complex, and the Nature Conservancy's Medano/Zapata Ranch to conduct in-depth outdoor educational programs on the natural and cultural resources of the area. Check its website for the lecture and field-trip schedule. ⊕ *www.coloradofieldinstitute.org* ☉ *Times and locations vary; call ahead.*

ARTS AND ENTERTAINMENT
ART GALLERIES
Luther Bean Museum and Art Gallery. This Adams State College museum displays American Indian pottery and textiles, European porcelain, photography, and furniture collections in a handsome, wood-paneled 19th-century drawing room, as well as changing exhibits of regional arts and crafts. ⊠ *Richardson Hall, Room 256, 208 Edgemont Blvd., Alamosa* ☎ *719/587–7827* ⊕ *www.adams.edu/lutherbean* ⌨ *Free* ☉ *Weekdays 10–2.*

SCENIC DRIVES

Manassa, San Luis, and Fort Garland Loop. To get a real feel for this area, take an easy driving loop from Alamosa through much of the San Luis Valley (the whole trip is about 95 miles). Head east on U.S 160 to Fort Garland, south on Highway 159 to San Luis, west on Highways 159 and 142 to Manassa, then north on U.S. 285 back to Alamosa. More than half of the route is part of the Los Caminos Antiguos Drive, one of Colorado's Scenic Byways.

WHERE TO EAT

IN THE PARK

PICNIC AREAS

Mosca Creek. Great Sand Dunes National Park's only picnic area is shaded by cottonwood trees. It has a dozen places where visitors can park a car or small RV near a picnic table and a grill. ⊠ *South of the dunes parking lot.*

OUTSIDE THE PARK

$ ✕ **East West Grill.** Noodles, salads, and teriyaki top the menu at this
ASIAN casual, almost fast-food-style place with dine-in or carry-out options.
⑤ *Average main: $8* ⊠ *408 4th St., Alamosa* ☎ *719/589–4600* ⊕ *www. east-westgrill.com.*

$ ✕ **Milagros Coffeehouse.** The coffee is full-bodied at this combination
CAFÉ coffeehouse, café, and used-book store, where all profits go to local charities. The breakfast bagels are especially tasty and organic; local food dominates the menu, which includes plenty of vegetarian and gluten-free options. ⑤ *Average main: $7* ⊠ *529 Main St., Alamosa* ☎ *719/589–9299.*

$ ✕ **The Oasis Cafe.** The no-frills restaurant in the Great Sand Dunes Oasis
AMERICAN (which includes a grocery store and gas station as well as motel rooms and campsites), just outside the park entrance, is open for breakfast, lunch, and dinner. The Navajo taco (served on fry bread) and beef or chicken burritos are among the most popular items, although the menu ranges from grilled-cheese sandwiches to steaks. ⑤ *Average main: $11* ⊠ *5400 Hwy. 150, Mosca* ☎ *719/378–2222* ⊕ *www.greatdunes.com* ⊘ *Closed mid-Sept.–late-Apr.*

WHERE TO STAY

OUTSIDE THE PARK

$ ⊡ **Best Western Alamosa Inn.** This sprawling, well-maintained complex
HOTEL is your best bet for reasonably priced lodgings. **Pros:** reliable basic accommodations; easy to find. **Cons:** noisy street; nothing but fast food nearby. ⑤ *Rooms from: $108* ⊠ *2005 Main St., Alamosa* ☎ *719/589– 2567, 800/459–5123* ⊕ *www.bestwestern.com/alamosainn* ⇌ *52 rooms, 1 suite* ⦿ *Breakfast.*

$ ⊡ **Conejos Canyon River Ranch.** Located within the Rio Grande National
HOTEL Forest on the Conejos River, 42 miles southwest of Alamosa, this
FAMILY peaceful, family-friendly retreat is an excellent base for fishing. **Pros:** gorgeous riverfront setting; access to national forest; plenty of activities for adults and kids; on-site gift shop. **Cons:** no amenities nearby; more than an hour from the Great Sand Dunes. ⑤ *Rooms from: $98* ⊠ *25390 Hwy. 17, Antonito* ☎ *719/376–2464* ⊕ *www.conejosranch. com* ⊘ *Limited rooms and cabins available Dec.–Apr.* ⇌ *8 rooms, 8 cabins* ⦿ *Breakfast.*

CLOSE UP

Best Campgrounds in Great Sand Dunes

Great Sand Dunes has one campground, open year-round. During weekends in the summer, it can fill up with RVs and tents by midafternoon. Black bears live in the preserve, so when camping there, keep your food, trash, and toiletries in the trunk of your car (or use bear-proof containers). There is one campground and RV park near the entrance to Great Sand Dunes, and several others in the area.

Pinyon Flats Campground. Set in a pine forest about a mile past the visitor center, this campground has a trail leading to the dunes. Sites are available on a first-come, first-served basis; RVs are allowed, but there are no hookups. ⊠ *On the main park road, near the visitor center* ☎ *719/378–6399.*

$ 🍴 **Great Sand Dunes Lodge.** Located right at the entrance of the park,
HOTEL   behind the Oasis, this simple lodge offers clean, comfortable rooms with private balconies (and great views of the dunes and mountains). **Pros:** closest hotel rooms to the dunes; great views. **Cons:** with the exception of the nearby Oasis Cafe, the nearest restaurants are more than 20 miles away. ⑤ *Rooms from: $95* ⊠ *7900 Hwy. 150 N, Mosca* ☎ *719/378–2900* ⊕ *www.gsdlodge.com* ✆ *Closed mid-Oct.–mid-Mar* 🛏 *12 rooms.*

$$$$ 🍴 **Zapata Ranch.** Part of a 103,000-acre working cattle and bison ranch
B&B/INN   owned by the Nature Conservancy, the Zapata Ranch is focused mainly on all-inclusive, weeklong stays, during which guests learn about bison, land conservation, and renewable ranching practices, and participate in ranch activities (including branding cattle and mending fences). **Pros:** beautiful setting among mature cottonwoods; historic lodge buildings; terrific restaurant with indoor and outdoor seating. **Cons:** much pricier than other area accommodations; limited capacity (the ranch rents only those rooms that aren't reserved for guest ranch visitors). ⑤ *Rooms from: $285* ⊠ *5305 State Hwy. 150* ☎ *888/592–7282, 719/378–2356* ⊕ *www.zranch.org* 🛏 *15 rooms* 🍽 *All-inclusive.*

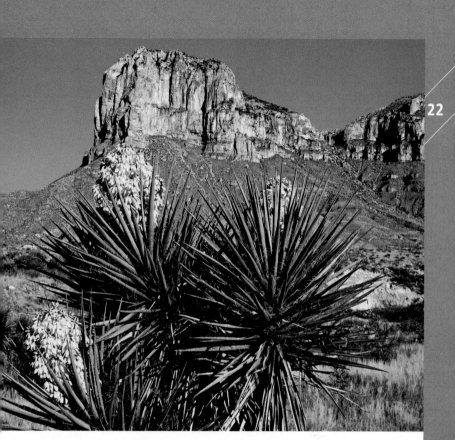

GUADALUPE MOUNTAINS NATIONAL PARK

WELCOME TO GUADALUPE MOUNTAINS NATIONAL PARK

TOP REASONS TO GO

★ **Tower over Texas:** The park is home to 8,749-foot Guadalupe Peak, the highest point in the state.

★ **Fall for fiery foliage:** Though surrounded by arid desert and rocky soil, the park has miles of beautiful foliage in McKittrick Canyon. In late October you can watch it burst into flaming colors.

★ **Hike unhindered:** The main activity at the park is hiking its rugged, remote, and often challenging trails: 80 miles' worth will keep you captivated and spry—and far away from civilization.

★ **Marvel at wildlife:** Despite the surrounding arid region, a variety of wildlife—including shaggy brown elk, furtive mountain lions, and shy black bears—traipse the mountains, woods, and desert here.

★ **The Old West whispers:** Rock ruins and former homesteads dot a hardscrabble landscape challenged by pioneers.

1 **Guadalupe Peak.** This crude, rocky pinnacle tops 8,700 feet and towers over the rest of the park's peaks. Those who brave the seven-hour-plus round-trip to the summit are rewarded with breathtaking views of New Mexico and southwestern Texas.

2 **McKittrick Canyon.** In late October and early November, the lush green foliage along McKittrick Canyon's trout-filled desert stream bursts into russet, amber, and gold hues. An easy, wheelchair-accessible ramble takes visitors through this geological wonder.

3 **El Capitan.** Not to be confused with equally impressive El Capitan in Yosemite National Park, this 3,000-foot cliff dominates the southern skyline of the Guadalupe Range. It has visitors talking and hikers walking: a 6- to 11-mile-plus trail winds around the base of this massive limestone formation.

NEW MEXICO
TEXAS

Cutoff Mountain
6,933 ft

Butterfield Route

4 **Manzanita Spring.** The area around this idyllic stream and picnic spot has a little bit of everything: a spring feeds lush grasses and trees, giving life to hundreds of wildflowers. Birds hang out here to enjoy the tasty seeds and insects that the water, shade, and vegetation provide. Plus, it's only a 0.2-mile stroll from here to the Frijole Ranch History Museum.

5 **Frijole Ranch History Museum.** This easily accessible former ranch home is

TEXAS

22

GETTING ORIENTED

The park is off U.S. 62/180, 110 miles east of El Paso, Texas; 35 miles southwest of Carlsbad Caverns National Park; and 55 miles southwest of Carlsbad, New Mexico. White's City, New Mexico, gateway to Carlsbad Caverns, is 35 miles northeast of the park on U.S. 62/180.

the oldest intact structure in the park, set amid several rock-walled outbuildings and a landscaped yard. The museum injects a bit of man-made history into the natural surroundings, which include two nearby springs.

KEY

🏠	Ranger Station
🔺	Campground
⛱	Picnic Area
🍴	Restaurant
▦	Lodge
🚶	Trailhead
🚻	Restrooms
➤	Scenic Viewpoint
⋯	Walking/Hiking Trails

Updated by Marty Racine

Guadalupe Mountains National Park is a study in extremes: it has mountaintop forests but also rocky canyons, arid deserts, and a stream that winds through verdant woods. The park is home to the Texas madrone tree, found commonly only here and in Big Bend National Park. Guadalupe Mountains National Park also has the distinction of hosting the loftiest spot in Texas: 8,749-foot Guadalupe Peak. The mountain dominates the view from every approach, but it's just one member of a rugged range carved by wind, water, and time.

GUADALUPE MOUNTAINS PLANNER

WHEN TO GO

Trails here are rarely crowded, except in fall, when foliage changes colors in McKittrick Canyon, and during spring break in March. Still, this is a very remote area, and you probably won't find too much congestion at any time. Hikers are more apt to explore backcountry trails in spring and fall, when it's cooler but not too cold. Snow, not uncommon in the winter months, can linger in the higher elevations. The windy season is March through May, and the rainy months are July and August.

AVG. HIGH/LOW TEMPS.

Jan.	Feb.	Mar.	Apr.	May	June
53/30	58/35	63/38	71/46	78/55	88/63
July	Aug.	Sept.	Oct.	Nov.	Dec.
87/63	84/62	78/57	71/49	61/38	57/33

PLANNING YOUR TIME
GUADALUPE IN ONE DAY

Start your tour at **Headquarters Visitor Center,** also known as the Pine Springs Ranger Station, where an exhibit and slide show introduce the park's plants, wildlife, and geology. Nearby is the 0.75-mile, round-trip, wheelchair-accessible **Pinery Trail,** which rambles to the Pinery Butterfield Stage Station ruins. As you take in the sights, do not touch the ruins' fragile walls; the site is quite vulnerable. Next, head to the **Frijole Ranch History Museum,** housed in a vacated yet well-preserved ranch home built in 1876.

Once you're done exploring the shaded grounds and admiring the labor that built the compound, turn onto the trailhead behind the ranch house for the 0.2-mile stroll to the calming waters of **Manzanita Spring,** one of two watering holes that gurgle within a couple of miles of the museum. Park staff call such areas riparian zones. These oases supply the fragile wildlife here, and can sometimes look like Pre-Raphaelite paintings, with mirrored-surface ponds and delicate flowers and greenery.

Afterward, pay a visit to the famed **McKittrick Canyon.** Regardless of the season, the dense foliage and basin stream are worth the hike—though it's best to visit it in late October and early November when the trees burst into color. There isn't a direct route, but you can get here quickly by driving northeast from the visitor center on U.S. 62/180. Follow it to the gate at the McKittrick turnoff, which is locked at sunset. Head northwest through the gate (ignoring the service road) in your car, and you'll arrive at the canyon.

Take your time walking the **McKittrick Canyon Trail,** which leads to Pratt Lodge, or the strenuous but rewarding 8.4-mile **Permian Reef Trail,** which takes you up thousands of feet, past monumental geological formations. Or traverse the easy, short (less than 1 mile) **McKittrick Canyon Nature Loop.**

GETTING HERE AND AROUND
AIR TRAVEL

To get within striking distance of Guadalupe Mountains National Park by air, Carlsbad's Cavern City Air Terminal, 55 miles northeast, hosts regional carriers. El Paso International Airport is 110 miles to the west.

CAR TRAVEL

About half of the Guadalupe Mountains is a designated wilderness, so few roadways penetrate the park. Most sites are accessible off U.S. 62/180. Dog Canyon Campground, on the north end of the park, can be reached via Route 137 from New Mexico.

PARK ESSENTIALS
PARK FEES AND PERMITS

An admission fee of $5 for everyone 16 and older planning to hike is collected at the visitor center, and is good for one week. Camping is $8 a night per site; pay at the visitor center or at self-registration boards in campgrounds. For overnight backpacking trips, you must get a free permit from either Headquarters Visitor Center or Dog Canyon Ranger Station.

PARK HOURS

The park is open 24/7, year-round. It's in the Mountain time zone.

CELL-PHONE RECEPTION

Cell phones with far-reaching service can pick up signals at key points along trails. Alternatively, public phones are located at Dog Canyon Ranger Station, Headquarters Visitor Center, McKittrick Contact Station, and Pine Springs Campground.

EDUCATIONAL OFFERINGS

RANGER PROGRAMS

FAMILY **Junior Ranger Program.** The park offers a self-guided Junior Ranger Program: kids choose activities from a workbook—including taking nature hikes and answering questions based on park exhibits—and earn a badge once they've completed four. If they complete six, they earn an additional patch. Workbooks are available at Headquarters Visitor Center, or they can be downloaded from the park's website. ⊠ *Headquarters Visitor Center, about ¾ mile north of U.S. 62/180* ☎ *915/828–3251* ⊕ *www.nps.gov/gumo* ☽ *Daily 8–4:30.*

RESTAURANTS

Dining in the park is a do-it-yourself affair. Ranger stations don't serve meals or sell picnic items, though nearby White's City has a café and offers some convenience-store basics—sodas, snacks, and the like.

HOTELS

There are no hotels within the park. Your best options are in White's City, NM (35 miles), Carlsbad, NM (55 miles), or Van Horn, Texas (65 miles). *Hotel reviews have been shortened. For full information, visit Fodors.com.*

WHAT IT COSTS				
	$	$$	$$$	$$$$
Restaurants	under $13	$13–$20	$21–$30	over $30
Hotels	under $101	$101–$150	$151–$200	over $200

Restaurant prices are the average cost of a main course at dinner, or if dinner is not served, at lunch. Hotel prices are the lowest cost of a standard double room in high season, excluding taxes and service charges.

VISITOR INFORMATION

VISITOR CENTERS

Fodor's Choice ★ **Headquarters Visitor Center.** You can pick up maps, brochures, hiking permits, and other information at the Headquarters Visitor Center, aka Pine Springs Ranger Station, with easy access off the highway. A slide show and a 12-minute movie provide a quick introduction to the park, half of which is protected as a designated wilderness area. Intricately crafted exhibits depict typical wildlife and plant scenes ranging from lowland desert to forested mountaintop, while outside the entrance native flora are marked for identification. ⊠ *400 Pine Canyon Dr.* ✛ *Accessible from U.S. 62/180, 55 miles southwest of Carlsbad, 110 miles east of El Paso* ☎ *915/828–3251, 915/828–3269* ⊕ *www.nps.gov/gumo* ☛ *Free admission to the center; $5*

for a one-week hiking permit; $8 a site for overnight camping ⊙ *Daily
8–4:30* ☞ *Flora and fauna displays, film room, bookstore.*

Fodor's Choice **McKittrick Contact Station.** Poster-size illustrations in a shaded, out-
★ door patio area tell the geological story of the Guadalupe Mountains,
believed to have been carved from an ancient sea. You can also hear the
recorded memoirs of oilman Wallace Pratt, who donated his ranch and
surrounding area to the federal government for preservation. Nearby
trailheads access a 0.9-mile nature loop and lengthier hikes. ⊠ *4 miles
off U.S. 62/180, 7 miles northeast of Headquarters Visitor Center*
☎ *915/828–3251, 915/828–3269* ⊕ *www.nps.gov/gumo* ✉ *Exhibits are
free; $5 for hiking permit, available at nearby trailheads* ⊙ *June–Aug.,
daily 8–6; Sept.–May, daily 8–4:30.*

22

EXPLORING

SCENIC DRIVES

Williams Ranch Road. Take in panoramic views and see limestone cliffs
up close on this 7¼-mile, one-way drive over what was once the Butterfield Overland Mail Stage Line. The closest highway, U.S. 62/180,
parallels a segment of the old trail. The route is rough—you need a
high-clearance, four-wheel-drive vehicle—but enjoyable. It takes about
an hour. The road leads to an old ranch house at the base of a 3,000-
foot cliff, where James "Dolph" Williams worked with his partner, an
Indian named Geronimo (no relation to the historical figure). This is
a day-trip only; overnight parking prohibited. The drive is locked, so
pick up a gate key at Headquarters Visitor Center. ✛ *Drive west on
U.S. 62/180 from Headquarters Visitor Center for 8¼ miles until you
see brown metal gate on north side with National Park Service sign.
Continue through 2 locked gates (lock them behind you)* ⊕ *www.nps.
gov/gumo* ⊙ *Daily dawn–dusk.*

HISTORIC SITES

FAMILY **Frijole Ranch History Museum.** Displays and photographs depict ranch
Fodor's Choice life and early park history inside this ranch-house museum, occupy-
★ ing what is believed to be the region's oldest intact structure. Hiking
trails, which are easy to travel and great for kids, spoke off from the
shady, tree-lined grounds; one leads to wildlife oases Manzanita Spring
and Smith Spring. Due to staffing shortages, the museum might be
closed, especially in summer "low" season, so call ahead. Still, this is a
worthwhile (and accessible) destination, as you can explore the ranch
grounds replete with outbuildings, an orchard, and still-functioning irrigation system. It is also a peaceful setting reflecting echoes of the past.
⊠ *Frijole Ranch Rd. north of U.S. 62/180* ✛ *Access road 1 mile northeast of Headquarters Visitors Center* ☎ *915/828–3251, 915/828–3269*
⊕ *www.nps.gov/gumo* ⊙ *Ranch grounds daily; museum has irregular
hrs depending on staffing.*

FAMILY **Pinery Butterfield Stage Station Ruins.** In the mid-1800s passengers en route from St. Louis to California on the Butterfield Overland Mail stagecoach route would stop here for rest and refreshment. At more than a mile elevation, the station was the highest on the journey, but it operated for only about a year. The ruins provide a reasonable peek into the past: several buildings with rock walls (but no roofs) layered on the desert floor. Please do not touch. You can drive here from Highway 62/180 or take a paved ¾-mile round-trip trail from Headquarters Visitor Center. ✛ *½ mile east of Headquarters Visitor Center* ⊕ *www.nps.gov/gumo.*

SCENIC STOPS

Fodor'sChoice **McKittrick Canyon.** A desert creek flows through this canyon, considered
★ one of the wondrous sights in Texas, lined with walnut, maple, and other trees that explode into brilliant hues each autumn. Call the visitor center to chart the progress of the colorful fall foliage; the spectacular changing of the leaves often extends into November, depending on the weather. You're likely to spot mule deer heading for the water here. The canyon is ground zero for several hiking trails, including Pratt Cabin (two to three hours) and the Grotto (four hours). ⊠ *Guadalupe Mountains National Park* ✛ *4 miles north of U.S. 62/180, about 7 miles northeast of Headquarters Visitor Center* ⊕ *www.nps. gov/gumo* ✉ *$5 hiking permit good for 1 week at the trailhead or Headquarters Visitor Center.*

SPORTS AND THE OUTDOORS

BIRD-WATCHING

More than 300 species of birds have been spotted in the park, including the ladder-backed woodpecker, Scott's oriole, Say's phoebe, and white-throated swift. Many migratory birds—such as fleeting hummingbirds and larger but less graceful turkey vultures—stop at Guadalupe during spring and fall migrations. **Manzanita Springs**, near the Frijole Ranch History Museum, is an excellent birding spot. As with hiking, there aren't any local guides, but rangers at the Dog Canyon and Pine Springs ranger stations can help you spot some native species.

Books on birding are available at the Pine Springs Ranger Station in the Headquarters Visitor Center; bird lovers might find the Natural History Association's birding checklist for Guadalupe Mountains National Park especially helpful. It will be easy to spot the larger birds of prey circling overhead, such as keen-beaked golden eagles and swift, red-tailed hawks. Be on the lookout for owls in the **Bowl** area, and watch for swift-footed roadrunners in the desert areas (they're quick, but not as speedy as their cartoon counterpart).

CLOSE UP

Plants and Wildlife in Guadalupe Mountains

22

Despite the constant wind and the arid conditions, more than a thousand species of plants populate the mountains, chasms, and salt dunes that comprise the park's different geologic zones. Some grow many feet in a single night; others bloom so infrequently they're called "century plants." In fall, McKittrick Canyon's oaks, bigtooth maples, and velvet ashes go Technicolor above the little stream that traverses it. Barren-looking cacti burst into yellow, red, and purple bloom in spring, and wildflowers can carpet the park for thousands of acres after unusually heavy rains.

More than 86,000 acres of mountains, chasms, canyons, woods, and deserts house an incredible diversity of wildlife, including hallmark Southwestern species like roadrunners and long-limbed jackrabbits, which run so fast they appear to float on their enormous, black-tipped ears. Other furry residents include coyotes,

black bears, mountain lions, fox, deer, elk, and badgers. You may also spot numerous winged creatures: 300 different bird species, 90 types of butterflies, and 16 species of bats.

Plenty of reptiles and insects make their homes here, too: coachwhip snakes, diamondback rattlers, whiptail lizards, scorpions, and lovelorn taran-tulas (the only time you might spy them is in the fall, when they search for mates), to name a few. Texas's famous (and threatened) horned lizards—affectionately called "horny toads"—can also be seen waddling across the soil in search of ants and other insects. Rangers caution parents not to let little ones run too far ahead on the trails. ■ TIP→ Rattle-snakes are common here but they hibernate in winter. In summer, overnight campers should be cautious at dusk and dawn. The snakes are not aggressive, so try to remain calm and give a wide berth to any you spot.

HIKING

No matter which trail you select, be sure to pack wisely—the park doesn't sell anything. This includes the recommended gallon of water per day per person, as well as sunscreen, sturdy footwear, and hats. (Bring $5, too— that's the additional cost to use the trails, payable at the visitor centers.) The area has a triple-whammy regarding sun ailments: it's very open, very sunny, and has a high altitude (which makes sunburns more likely). Slather up. And be sure to leave Fido at home—few of the park's trails allow pets.

HIKING RESOURCES

FAMILY **Dog Canyon Ranger Station.** The staff at the Dog Canyon Ranger Station can help plan your day hike, horseback ride, or overnight backpacking trip. Dog Canyon is an excellent gateway to the high country of the park's northern boundary mere miles from the New Mexico state line. The ranger station can be accessed from New Mexico by NM 137 off U.S. 285 (12 miles north of Carlsbad, NM) or by County Road 408 off U.S. 62/180 (9 miles south of Carlsbad), which links to 137. ✉ *Hwy. 137* ☎ *575/981–2418* ⊕ *www.nps.gov/gumo* ✉ *$5 for day hikes, more for other activities.*

EASY

FAMILY **Indian Meadows Nature Trail.** A mostly level trail in Dog Canyon, this 0.5-mile hike crosses an arroyo into meadowlands. It's a good way to spend about 45 minutes savoring the countryside. *Easy.* ⊕ *Trailhead: directly across from Dog Canyon Ranger Station* ⌨ *$5 hiking permit is good for one week from the nearby ranger station (irregular hours) or the trailhead.*

FAMILY **McKittrick Nature Loop.** Signs along this mile-long loop explain the geological and botanical history of the area, and the views, while not spectacular, are engaging enough to hold your interest. The trail is not wheelchair- or stroller-accessible due to the narrow pathway and rocky terrain. You can take the loop in either of two directions when you come to a fork in the trail. *Easy to moderate.* ⊕ *Trailhead: accessed via McKittrick Canyon Trailhead at northeast corner of park* ⌨ *$5 hiking permit at the trailhead or Headquarters Visitor Center.*

MODERATE

El Capitan/Salt Basin Overlook Trails. Several trails combine to form a popular loop through the low desert. El Capitan skirts the base of El Capitan peak for about 3.5 miles, leading to a junction with Salt Basin Overlook. The 4.5-mile Salt Basin Overlook trail begins at the Pine Springs Trailhead and has views of the stark, white salt flat below and loops back onto the El Capitan Trail. The 11.3-mile round-trip is not recommended during the intense heat of summer, since there is absolutely no shade. *Moderate to difficult.* ⊕ *Trailhead: access for El Capitan begins at the Pine Springs trailhead behind Headquarters Visitor Center* ⌨ *A 7-day, $5 hiking permit is available at nearby Headquarters Visitor Center.*

FAMILY **Frijole/Foothills Trail.** Branching off the Frijole Ranch Trail, this hike leads to Pine Springs Campground behind Headquarters Visitor Center. The 5.5-mile round-trip through desert vistas takes about four hours. *Moderate.* ⊕ *Trailhead: at Frijole Ranch History Museum* ⌨ *A 7-day, $5 hiking permit is available at the trailhead or nearby Headquarters Visitor Center.*

FAMILY **Marcus Overlook.** A 4.5-mile round-trip rewards you with a panoramic view of West Dog Canyon. Set aside about half a day for it. *Moderate, elevation gain 800 feet.* ⊕ *Trailhead: accessed at Rte. 137, 60 miles southwest of U.S. 285* ⌨ *A 7-day, $5 hiking permit is available at the trailhead or the nearby Dog Canyon Ranger Station (irregular hours).*

FAMILY **Pratt Lodge Trail.** View stream and canyon woodlands along a 4½-mile round-trip excursion that leads to the vacant Pratt Lodge, a stone cabin built during the Great Depression in the "most beautiful spot in Texas," according to its original owner, Wallace Pratt. Perhaps he was enthralled by an oasis of running water carving through the canyon floor or a colorful riot of autumn foliage. Plan on at least two hours if you walk at a brisk pace, but give yourself another hour or two if you want to take your time. *Moderate.* ⊕ *Trailhead: accessed 4 miles north of U.S. 62/180 at McKittrick Canyon Ranger Station, about 7 miles northeast of Headquarters Visitors Center* ⌨ *A 7-day, $5 hiking permit is available at the trailhead.*

Fodor'sChoice
★

The sun sets over the desert landscape of west Texas at Guadalupe Mountains National Park.

FAMILY
Fodor'sChoice
★

Smith Spring Trail. Departing from the Frijole Ranch, the trail heads for a shady oasis where you're likely to spot mule deer and elk drawn to the miracle of water in the desert. As a bonus, the route passes Manzanita Spring, another wildlife refuge only 0.2 mile past Frijole Ranch. Allow 1½ hours to complete the 2.2-mile round-trip walk. This is a good hike for older kids whose legs won't tire as easily, but it is not wheelchair accessible past Manzanita Spring. *Easy to moderate.* ⊹ *Trailhead: off access road 1 mile northeast of Headquarters Visitor Center* 🚩 *A 7-day, $5 hiking permit is available at the trailhead or nearby Headquarters Visitor Center.*

FAMILY

Trail to Grotto Picnic Area. The 6.75-mile round-trip trek to this picnic area affords views of a flowing stream and surface rock that resembles formations in an underground cave with jagged overhangs. Plan on about five hours at a leisurely pace. *Moderate, elevation gain minimal.* ⊹ *Trailhead: McKittrick Contact Station, 4 miles north of 62/180, 7 miles northeast of Headquarters Visitor Center* 🚩 *A 7-day, $5 hiking pass is available at the trailhead or Headquarters Visitor Center.*

DIFFICULT

Fodor'sChoice
★

The Bowl. Cutting through forests of pine and Douglas fir, this trail to an aptly named mountaintop valley is considered one of the most gorgeous in the park. The strenuous 9-mile round-trip—which can take up to 10 hours, depending on your pace—is where rangers go when they want to enjoy themselves. Don't forget to bring (and drink) lots of water. *Difficult.* ⊹ *Trailhead: accessed from Pine Springs Trailhead. From Pine Springs Campground, follow Frijole/Foothills Trail and Bear Canyon*

Trail to top; then turn left onto Bowl Trail 🖃 *A 7-day, $5 hiking permit is available at the trailhead or nearby Headquarters Visitor Center.*

Fodor's Choice ★ **Guadalupe Peak Trail.** An 8.5-mile workout over a steep grade to the top of Texas pays off with a passage through various ecosystems and some great views. The round-trip hike can take up to eight hours to complete, but the trail is clearly defined and does not require undue athleticism. The steepest climbs are in the beginning, when you are likely to be freshest. In summer, start this hike in early morning to allow a descent before afternoon thunderstorms flare up. Lightning targets high peaks. Be alert to changing weather and head for lower ground if conditions worsen. Also, Guadalupe Peak is considered one of the windiest points in the U.S. *Difficult, elevation gain 3,000 feet.* ✛ *Trailhead: accessed via Pine Springs Trail, in RV section of Pine Springs Campground* ⊕ *www.nps. gov/gumo* 🖃 *A 7-day, $5 hiking permit is available at the trailhead or nearby Headquarters Visitor Center.*

Lost Peak. The somewhat strenuous trek from Dog Canyon into a coniferous forest is 6.5 miles round-trip and will take about six hours to complete at a fairly slow pace. There is no defined trail the last ¼ mile to the peak, but adventurers are rewarded with terrific views. *Difficult, elevation gain 1,500 feet.* ✛ *Trailhead: access via Dog Canyon Trailhead. From there, follow Tejas Trail into canyon and to junction with McKittrick Ridge Trail* ⊕ *www.nps.gov/gumo* 🖃 *A 7-day, $5 hiking permit is available at the trailhead or nearby Dog Canyon Ranger Station (irregular hours).*

WHERE TO EAT

IN THE PARK

The park has no snack bars or restaurants, but several picnic areas are available. Wood and charcoal fires are not allowed anywhere in the park. If you want to cook a hot meal, bring a camp stove.

PICNIC AREAS

FAMILY **Fodor's Choice** ★ **Dog Canyon Campground.** Thirteen campsites have picnic tables, which you can use during the day for free. This is a lovely shaded area at 6,300 elevation where you're likely to see mule deer. Drinking water and restrooms are available on the grounds, about a two-hour drive from the Headquarters Visitor Center. ✛ *Off Rte. 137, 65 miles southwest of Carlsbad.*

FAMILY **Frijole Ranch Campground.** It's not very secluded, but Frijole sports newly constructed picnic shelters that can accommodate large groups near the parking area. Two picnic tables are also set up under tall trees. Restrooms are available nearby and at the Frijole Ranch History Museum, but hours of operation there can be inconsistent. ✛ *Access road 1 mile northeast of Headquarters Visitor Center.*

Best Campgrounds in Guadalupe Mountains

CLOSE UP

22

The park has two developed campgrounds that charge fees, and 10 designated primitive, backcountry sites where you can camp for free. First, obtain a permit at Headquarters Visitor Center or Dog Canyon Ranger Station. Visitors haul their supplies for miles to stretch out on the unspoiled land of these backcountry sites. In the backcountry, no restrooms are provided; visitors may dig their own privies, but toilet paper and other waste should be packed out. Wood and charcoal fires are prohibited throughout the park, but you can use your camp stove at both the developed and backcountry sites.

Dog Canyon Campground. This campground is remote and a little tricky to find, but well worth the effort. The very well-maintained camping area is in a coniferous forest, with 9 tent sites and 4 RV sites (no hookups). ⊠ Rte. 137, just within park northern entrance ☎ 575/981–2418.

Pine Springs Campground. You'll be snuggled amid pinyon and juniper trees near the base of a tall mountain peak at this resting place behind the Headquarters Visitor Center. It has 20 tent sites, 18 RV sites (no hookups), one wheelchair-accessible site, and two group sites. ⊠ At park east entrance, off U.S. 62/180 ☎ 915/828–3251.

FAMILY **Pine Springs Campground.** Drinking water, restrooms, and a picnic area are available at this central campground near the Headquarters Visitor Center. Shade, however, can be a bit sparse in the intense summer heat. A network of hiking trails will help you walk off that hearty lunch. ⊹ *Behind Headquarters Visitor Center* ☞ *Free for day picnic use.*

OUTSIDE THE PARK

Tiny **White's City, New Mexico,** 35 miles to the northeast off U.S. 62/180, is more a collection of services and tourist attractions than a town, but it does have the Cactus Café. The town of **Carlsbad, New Mexico,** 55–60 miles northeast of the park, has more amenities. *For dining options near the park, see Where to Eat in Carlsbad Caverns National Park (Chapter 13).*

WHERE TO STAY

OUTSIDE THE PARK

For lodging options near the park, see Where to Stay in Carlsbad Caverns National Park (Chapter 13).

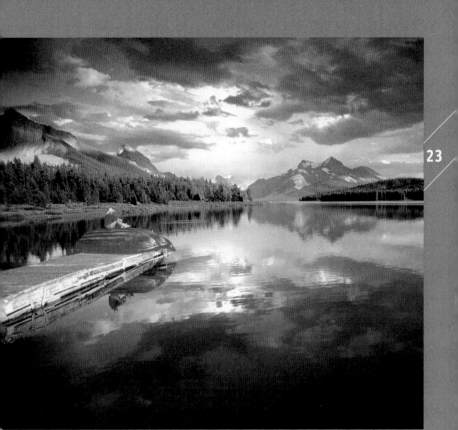

JASPER NATIONAL PARK

WELCOME TO JASPER NATIONAL PARK

TOP REASONS TO GO

★ **Larger than life:** Almost the size of the state of Connecticut, Jasper is the largest of the Canadian Rocky Mountain national parks, and it's one of the world's largest protected mountain ecosystems.

★ **Spectacular scenery:** Jasper's scenery is rugged and mountainous. Within its boundaries are crystal-clear mountain lakes, thundering waterfalls, jagged mountain peaks, and ancient glaciers.

★ **Wonderful wildlife:** The Canadian Rockies provide a diverse habitat for 277 bird species and 69 species of mammals, including deer, elk, moose, sheep, goats, and bears.

★ **Columbia Icefield:** The largest ice field south of Alaska, the Columbia Icefield is also the hydrographic apex of North America, with water flowing to three different oceans from one point.

★ **Authentic mountain community:** The town of Jasper makes a great home base for forays into the park. With hotels, restaurants, and shopping, it has all the amenities you need.

1 Yellowhead Corridor. Trans-Canada Highway 16 (Yellowhead Highway) travels through the foothills and main ranges of the Canadian Rockies. Highlights are views of the Jasper Lake sand dunes (Km 27), Disaster Point Animal Lick (Km 39½), Pocahontas Coal Mine Interpretive Trail (Km 39½), and Miette Hot Springs (Km 58).

2 Jasper Townsite. Shops, restaurants, nightclubs, and the main park information center are here. Just outside town are Lac Beauvert, Lake Annette, and Lake Edith, plus Old Fort Point, and Jasper Skytram.

3 Maligne Valley. Highlights of this region include the Athabasca Valley Lookout (Km 5.8), Maligne Canyon (Km 7), Medicine Lake (Km 20.7), and Maligne Lake (Km 45), where the paved road ends.

4 Cavell Road. The road is just past the Astoria River bridge (Km 11.7) on Highway 93A, south of Jasper Townsite. Weather permitting, it's generally open from mid-June to mid-October. Highlights include Astoria Valley Viewpoint, Mount Edith Cavell, and Cavell Meadows.

5 Icefields Parkway. Highway 93 spans 230 km (143 miles) between Jasper Townsite and Lake Louise and is one of the world's most spectacular drives. Highlights include Athabasca Falls (Km 31), Sunwapta Falls (Km 55), Columbia Icefield (Km 103), Sunwapta Pass (Km 108), and the Weeping Wall (Km 125).

Chown Glacier

Twintree Lake

Calumet Icefield

BRITISH COLUMBIA

ALBERTA

GETTING ORIENTED

23

Wild and untamed, the 11,228 square km (4,335 square miles) of Jasper National Park encompass rugged mountain terrain, natural hot springs, crystal-clear lakes, rivers, raging waterfalls, glaciers, and an abundance of wildlife.

ALBERTA

Miette River

Celestine Lake

Jasper Lake

Talbot Lake

Visitor Center

Miette Hot Springs◆

Whistlers Mtn.◆

Jasper

Tonquin Valley

Mt. Edith Cavell◆

Athabasca Falls◆

MALIGNE CANYON

Beaver Lake

Medicine Lake

Maligne Lake

Sunwapta Falls◆

Hooker Icefield

Icefields Parkway

Brazeau Icefield

Columbia Icefield◆

Columbia Icefield

Athabasca Glacier

TO BANFF, LAKE LOUISE AND BANFF NATIONAL PARK

KEY	
👫	Ranger Station
▲	Campground
🛆	Picnic Area
🍴	Restaurant
🏠	Lodge
🚶	Trailhead
🚻	Restrooms
⚡	Scenic Viewpoint
⋯⋯	Walking/Hiking Trails

0   10 mi
0   10 km

Updated by
Debbie Olsen

Jagged mountain peaks, shimmering glaciers, and crystal-clear lakes are just part of the incredible scenery that makes up the largest and wildest of Canada's Rocky Mountain parks. Situated along the eastern slopes of the Rockies in west-central Alberta, Jasper National Park is home to an astonishing variety of wildlife. Part of a collective UNESCO World Heritage Site, Jasper National Park is the planet's second-largest dark sky preserve. Light pollution is so minimal here that conditions are ideal for viewing the night sky, which both professional and amateur astronomers come here to do.

JASPER PLANNER

WHEN TO GO

An old saying in the Canadian Rockies states, "If you don't like the weather, just wait a minute." The weather in Jasper National Park is unpredictable and ever changing, so you need to prepare for all weather conditions, especially when hiking. In summer it can be hot enough for swimming in Lake Edith one day and icy cold the next. Temperatures in winter are usually well below freezing, but occasionally warm air blows in and causes snow and ice to melt.

July and August are the peak travel months for visitors—and the best time for hiking and viewing wildflowers. If you are traveling then, book accommodations well in advance and expect to pay a bit more than at other times of the year.

Temporary road closures may occur due to adverse weather conditions.

AVG. HIGH/LOW TEMPS.

Jan.	Feb.	Mar.	Apr.	May	June
24/5	38/12	42/23	55/24	66/34	66/43

July	Aug.	Sept.	Oct.	Nov.	Dec.
70/44	70/40	58/35	52/29	38/21	29/10

FESTIVALS AND EVENTS

SUMMER **Canada Day.** July 1, Canada's birthday, is celebrated with a parade, a
FAMILY full day of activities, and fireworks at dusk. On Canada Day, admission
is free to all the country's national parks. ✉ *Jasper* ☎ *780/852–6176*
⊕ *www.jaspercanadaday.com.*

FAMILY **Jasper Heritage Rodeo.** This rodeo that debuted in 1926 is the only one
that takes place inside a Canadian national park. On the second weekend in August, cowboys compete in bull riding, bareback riding, barrel racing, and steer wrestling events. An evening dance and a pancake
breakfast are also part of the festivities. ✉ *Jasper* ☎ *780/852–6236*
⊕ *www.jasperheritagerodeo.com.*

FAMILY **Parks Day.** Celebrating the country's natural wonders, this event takes
place on the third Saturday in July. There are activities for the whole
family, a fair on the lawn in the middle of town, and free guided hikes
to some of Jasper National Park's most interesting spots. ✉ *Jasper*
☎ *780/852–6176* ⊕ *www.friendsofjasper.com.*

FALL **Jasper Dark Sky Festival.** Held since 2011, when Jasper was declared an
FAMILY official Dark Sky Preserve (the world's second largest), this October
event welcomes stargazing adventurers for nine days of outdoor activities, lectures, scientific presentations, photography workshops, food,
and family-friendly fun. Science celebrities like astronaut Chris Hadfield
often attend. ✉ *Jasper* ☎ *780/852–6236* ⊕ *jasperdarksky.travel.*

WINTER **Jasper in January.** Jasper's biggest winter celebration takes place during
FAMILY the last half of January. A street festival, fireworks, wine tasting, great
Fodor's Choice live music, and a chili cook-off, are among the highlights. ✉ *Jasper*
★ ☎ *780/852–6236* ⊕ *jasperinjanuary.com.*

SPRING **Jasper Pride.** This four-day festival in March is the only gay pride festival
in the Canadian Rockies. Activities include movie nights, canyon walks,
ski events, music, and food. ✉ *Jasper* ☎ *780/852–6236* ⊕ *jasperpride.ca.*

PLANNING YOUR TIME

JASPER IN ONE DAY

Make a stop at the **Jasper Information Centre** to get maps of the park and
information about any special activities before driving up to **Mount Edith
Cavell.** The 1 km (½-mile) trail from the parking lot leads to the base
of an imposing cliff where you can see the stunning Angel Glacier. If
you are feeling energetic, take the steep 3-km (2-mile) trail that climbs
up the valley to **Cavell Meadows,** which are carpeted with wildflowers
from mid-July to mid-August. Return to Jasper Townsite for lunch. In
the afternoon, take the 45-minute drive southeast of the townsite to
beautiful **Maligne Lake,** the second-largest glacier-fed lake in the world.
Explore the lake and make a stop at **Spirit Island** on a 1½-hour guided

boat tour with **Maligne Lake Scenic Cruises.** Return to the townsite for supper and end your day by participating in a free evening interpretive program at **Jasper Heritage Fire Hall,** in the center of the Jasper Townsite.

GETTING HERE AND AROUND

Jasper National Park is in central Alberta in the Canadian Rockies. It borders Banff National Park to the south. Jasper Townsite is 287 km (178 miles) northwest of Banff Townsite.

AIR TRAVEL

The closest international airports are in Edmonton, 362 km (225 miles) to the east, and Calgary, 480 km (298 miles) to the southeast.

BUS TRAVEL

Greyhound Canada (☎ *800/661–8747, 800/231–2222 in U.S.* ⊕ *www. greyhound.ca*) provides regular service to Jasper from Calgary, Edmonton, and Vancouver; and **Brewster Sightseeing Excursions** (☎ *800/760– 6934* ⊕ *www.explorerockies.com*) provides transportation between the Calgary and Edmonton airports and Jasper. **SunDog Tours** (☎ *888/786– 3641* ⊕ *www.sundogtours.com*) operates shuttles between Jasper and Edmonton, Hinton, Edson, Lake Louise, Banff, and Calgary.

CAR TRAVEL

Driving is the easiest way to get from Edmonton or Calgary airport to Jasper. Car-rental agencies do business at both airports and in Jasper.

TRAIN TRAVEL

VIA Rail Canada (☎ *888/842–7245* ⊕ *www.viarail.ca*) provides train service three times a week from Edmonton, twice from Vancouver, and five times from Prince Rupert. **Rocky Mountaineer** (☎ *877/460–3200* ⊕ *www.rockymountaineer.com*) offers luxury train journeys between Jasper and Vancouver twice per week. There is no train service from Calgary to Jasper.

PARK ESSENTIALS

PARK FEES AND PERMITS

A park entrance pass is C$9.80 per person or C$19.60 maximum per vehicle per day. Larger buses and vans pay a group rate. An annual pass costs C$67.70 per adult or C$136.40 per family or group.

Permits, obtained from the park's information center (☎ *780/852–6176*) are required for backcountry camping (C$9.80 per day), campfires (C$8.80 per day), using dumping stations (C$8.80 per day), and fishing (C$9.80 per day).

PARK HOURS

The park is open 24/7 year-round. It is in the Mountain time zone.

CELL-PHONE RECEPTION

Cell phones generally work only in and around the town of Jasper.

EDUCATIONAL OFFERINGS

INTERPRETIVE PROGRAMS

FAMILY **Friends of Jasper National Park.** This group's excellent summer offerings include a junior naturalist program, birding tours, hiking tours, and historical walks. At the information center shop, you can borrow a Friends hiking kit with binoculars, maps, and first-aid and other materials.

✉ *Jasper Information Centre, 500 Connaught Dr.* ☎ *780/852–4767*
⊕ *www.friendsofjasper.com* ✉ *Free.*

Jasper Planetarium. The planetarium has the largest telescope in the Canadian Rockies. In the planetarium dome, an astronomy expert conducts an interactive tour of the night sky. ✉ *86 Connaught Dr., Jasper* ☎ *888/786–3641, 780/852–4056* ⊕ *www.jasperplanetarium.ca* ✉ *C$20.*

FAMILY **Parks Canada Interpretive Programs.** Park interpretive activities include campground sing-alongs, wildlife presentations, aboriginal programs, and guided hikes. Many events take place on Patricia Street at the Jasper Heritage Fire Hall. ✉ *414 Patricia St., Jasper* ☎ *780/852–6176* ⊕ *www.pc.gc.ca/eng/pn-np/ab/jasper/activ.aspx* ✉ *Free.*

RESTAURANTS

Canadian Rocky Mountain cuisine focuses on sustainably grown, regionally sourced ingredients. Look for beef, lamb, pheasant, venison, elk, bison, and trout from Alberta, and salmon from British Columbia. In addition to places serving local cuisine, Jasper also has Greek, Italian, Japanese, French, Indian, and Mexican restaurants.

HOTELS

Accommodations in this area include luxury resorts, fine hotels, reasonably priced motels, rustic cabins, bed-and-breakfast inns, and backcountry lodges. Reserve your accommodations well ahead if traveling here in summer. *Hotel reviews have been shortened. For full information, visit Fodors.com.*

WHAT IT COSTS IN CANADIAN DOLLARS			
$	**$$**	**$$$**	**$$$$**
Restaurants	under $13	$13–$20	$21–$30	over $30
Hotels	under $100	$100–$150	$151–$200	over $200

Restaurant prices are the average cost of a main course at dinner or, if dinner is not served, at lunch. Hotel prices are the lowest cost of a standard double room in high season, excluding taxes and service charges.

TOURS

FAMILY **Jasper Adventure Centre.** Guided tours, birding trips, ice walks, and snowshoeing tours are all available here. Most tours last three hours. The center also books canoeing, rafting, and other types of excursions. ✉ *611 Patricia St.* ☎ *780/852–5595* ⊕ *www.jasperadventurecentre.com* ✉ *From C$65.*

Maligne Adventures. Day treks, overnight backpacking trips, whitewater rafting, and heli-hiking excursions are among the offerings here. The Maligne Canyon Icewalk is popular in winter. ✉ *616 Patricia St.* ☎ *780/852–3370, 866/625–4463* ⊕ *www.maligneadventures.com* ✉ *From C$65.*

Maligne Tours. This outfit's tours include a 90-minute interpretive cruise to Spirit Island, one of the most beautiful spots in the Canadian Rockies. Photography and other cruises are also conducted, and you can rent a canoe to explore Maligne Lake on your own. ✉ *Jasper National*

Park ☎ *780/852–3370, 866/625–4463, 403/852–3405* ⊕ *www. malignelake.com* ✉ *From C$67* ☞ *Arrange tours/rentals at Maligne Lake tour building.*

SunDog Tour Co. Sightseeing and group coach excursions are this Jasper-based tour company's specialty. Some Jasper and Banff tours are offered in partnership with the Jasper Adventure Centre. ⊠ *414 Connaught Dr., Jasper* ☎ *780/852–5595, 888/786–3641* ⊕ *www.sundogtours.com* ✉ *From C$65.*

Walks and Talks Jasper. Most of this company's nature walks and hiking, snowshoe, ice-field, and other tours last about three hours. ⊠ *626 Connaught Dr.* ☎ *780/852–4994, 888/242–3343* ⊕ *www.walksntalks. com* ✉ *From C$70.*

VISITOR INFORMATION
Park Contact Information Jasper National Park. ☎ *780/852–6176* ⊕ *www.pc.gc.ca/jasper.*

VISITOR CENTERS
Jasper Information Centre. The 1914 cobblestone-and-timber structure that houses the Jasper Townsite visitor center is a superb example of rustic Canadian architecture. Parks Canada staffers here have information about trails, backcountry hiking, wildlife viewing, and interpretive programs, and representatives of Tourism Jasper provide advice about tours, restaurants, and accommodations. You can pick up maps, brochures, and other helpful materials as well. Parks Canada also operates an information desk at the Columbia Icefield Glacier Discovery Centre, 103 km (64 miles) south of Jasper Townsite. ⊠ *500 Connaught Dr.* ☎ *780/852–6176* ⊕ *www.pc.gc.ca/eng/pn-np/ab/jasper/visit.aspx* ✉ *Free* ☉ *Apr.–June 14 and Oct., daily 9–5; June 15–Sept. 4, daily 8:30–7; Sept. 5–30, daily 9–6; Nov.–Mar., daily 9–4.*

EXPLORING

SCENIC DRIVES

Scenic drives skirt the base of glaciers, stunning lakes, and exceptional wildlife-viewing areas. The 230-km (143-mile) **Icefields Parkway** that connects Jasper with Banff provides access to the largest ice field in the Rocky Mountains of North America and takes you to the very edge of the treeless alpine tundra. ⇨ *For more details on the parkway, see Banff National Park, Chapter 7.*

Within Jasper, **Maligne Lake Road** and **Pyramid Lake Road** are good scenic drives, south and north of the townsite, respectively.

SCENIC STOPS

Athabasca Falls. At 23 meters (75 feet), these falls are not the highest in the Canadian Rockies, but they are the most powerful. The Athabasca River carries more water than any other Rocky Mountains river, and all that water is funneled over the falls and into a narrow gorge, creating a powerful surge. The falls are especially dramatic in late spring and early summer when the river is at its highest. Trails and overlooks provide good viewpoints. Don't give into temptation and climb past the guard rails. The rocks and vegetation can be deceivingly slippery and people have died trying to get a photo of themselves standing on a rock near the falls. ⊠ *199 km (113 miles) north of Lake Louise, 31 km (19 miles) south of Jasper, Jasper National Park.*

Fodor'sChoice **Athabasca Glacier.** The glacier is a 7-km (4½-mile) tongue of ice flowing
★ from the immense Columbia Icefield almost to the Icefields Parkway. A century ago the ice flowed over the current location of the highway; signposts depict the gradual retreat of the ice since that time. Several other glaciers are visible from here; they all originate from the Columbia Icefield, a giant alpine lake of ice covering 325 square km (125 square miles). Its edge is visible from the highway. You can hike up to the toe of the glacier, but venturing farther without a trained guide is extremely dangerous because of hidden crevasses.

Athabasca Glacier Ice Walks (*800/565–7547, www.icewalks.com*) conducts three-, five-, and six-hour guided walks costing from C$75 to C$105. Reserve a space at the Columbia Icefield Glacier Discovery Centre or through **Jasper Adventure Centre** (*780/852–5595 or 800/565–7547, www.jasperadventurecentre.com*), in Jasper. **Brewster Tours' Ice Explorers** (*columbiaicefield.com*) trips in vehicles modified to drive on ice are another way to tour the glacier. You can purchase tickets (C$55) for these trips online or at the Discovery Centre. ⊠ *Icefields Pkwy., 127 km (79 miles) north of Lake Louise, 103 km (64 miles) south of Jasper.*

Columbia Icefield Glacier Discovery Centre. Opposite the Athabasca Glacier, this facility houses interpretive exhibits, a gift shop, and cafeteria- and buffet-style dining facilities. The summer midday rush between 11 and 3 can be intense. The 32 rooms at the Glacier View Inn, on the center's second floor, are available from early May to mid-October. ⊠ *Icefields Pkwy., 127 km (79 miles) north of Lake Louise, 103 km (64 miles) south of Jasper* 🕾 *877/423–7433* ⊕ *www.explorerockies. com* 🎟 *Free* 🕙 *Mid-June–Aug., daily 10–7; late May–mid-June and Sept.–early Oct., daily 10–5.*

Glacier Skywalk. This fully accessible cliff-edge walkway leads to a glass-floor observation platform 280 meters (918 feet) above the Sunwapta Valley. From this vantage point, you'll get a bird's-eye view of the surrounding ice-capped mountain peaks and deep glacier-carved valleys of the Canadian Rockies. A five-minute shuttle from the Columbia Icefield Glacier Discovery Centre delivers you to the walkway. ⊠ *Discovery Centre, Icefields Pkwy., 127 km (79 miles) north of Lake Louise, 103 km (64 miles) south of Jasper* 🕾 *866/606–6700, 403/762–6700* ⊕ *www. glacierskywalk.com* 🎟 *C$30* 🕙 *June–early Aug., daily 9–6; early Aug.–early Sept., daily 9–7; May and early Sept.–end of Sept., daily 10–5; early Oct.–mid-Oct., daily 10–4.*

FAMILY **Jasper SkyTram.** The tram whisks you 3,191 vertical feet up the steep flank of Whistlers Mountain to an impressive overlook of the townsite and the surrounding mountains. The seven-minute ride takes you to

23

the upper station, above the tree line (be sure to bring warm clothes). A 30- to 45-minute hike from here leads to the summit, which is 8,085 feet above sea level. Several unmarked trails lead through the alpine meadows beyond. ⊠ *Whistlers Mountain Rd., 3 km (2 miles) south of Jasper off Hwy. 93* ☎ *780/852–3093* ⊕ *www.jaspertramway.com* 🖃 *C$37 round-trip* ⊗ *June–early Sept., daily 9–8; Apr., May, and early Sept.–Oct., daily 10–5.*

Maligne Canyon. The Maligne River cut 50 meters (165 feet) deep through limestone bedrock to create Maligne Canyon. An interpretive trail winds along the river, switching from side to side over six bridges as the canyon progressively deepens. The 4-km (2½-mile) trail along the canyon can be crowded, especially near the trailhead. Just off the path, you'll find the Maligne Canyon Restaurant and a good Native American crafts store. On a wintertime ice walk, the views from the bottom of the frozen canyon are spectacular. ⊠ *Maligne Lake Rd., 11 km (7 miles) south of Jasper.*

Maligne Lake. The remarkably blue, 22-km-long (14-mile-long) Maligne Lake is one of the world's largest glacier-fed lakes. The first outsider known to visit the lake was Henry MacLeod, a surveyor looking for a possible route for the Canadian Pacific Railway, in 1875. A couple of day hikes (approximately four hours round-trip), with some steep sections, lead to alpine meadows that have panoramic views of the lake and the surrounding mountain ranges. You can also take canoeing and fishing trips, and there's an excellent cafeteria. ⊠ *Maligne Lake Rd., 44 km (27 miles) southeast of Jasper* ⊕ *www.malignelake.com.*

Miette Hot Springs. The naturally heated mineral waters here originate in three springs and are cooled to 40°C (104°F) to allow bathing in the two pools. At 15°C (59°F), the adjacent pool refreshingly negates all that heat. A short walk leads to the remnants of the original hot-springs facility, where several springs still pour hot sulfurous water into the nearby creek. Day passes and bathing suit, locker, and towel rentals are available. ⊠ *Miette Hot Springs Rd., off Hwy. 16, 58 km (36 miles) northeast of Jasper* ☎ *780/866–3939* ⊕ *www.parkscanada. gc.ca/hotsprings* 🖃 *C$6.05* ⊗ *Mid-May–late June and early Sept.–early Oct., daily 10:30–9; late June–early Sept., daily 8:30 am–10:30 pm.*

Fodor's Choice
★
Mount Edith Cavell. The Jasper area's highest mountain stands 3,363 meters (11,033 feet) tall. Showing its permanently snow-clad north face to the town, the peak was named for a World War I British nurse who stayed in Belgium to treat wounded Allied soldiers after Brussels fell to the Germans and was subsequently executed for helping prisoners of war escape. The mountain is arguably the most spectacular site in the park reachable by car. From Highway 93A, a narrow, winding 14½-km (9-mile) road (often closed until the beginning of June) leads to a parking lot at the mountain's base. Trailers aren't permitted on this road, but they can be left at a separate parking lot near the junction with 93A. Several scenic lookouts along the route offer access to trails leading up the **Tonquin Valley,** one of the premier hiking areas. ⊠ *Off Hwy. 93A, 27 km (17 miles) south of Jasper.*

Plants and Wildlife in Jasper

In Jasper it is possible to stand in a field of wildflowers, hike through a thick subalpine forest, stand on a glacier, and revel in the solitude of the fragile alpine zone all in one day. An array of plants occupies the three life zones of montane, alpine, and subalpine. About 1,300 species of plants and 20,000 types of insects and spiders are part of the complex web of life in the Canadian Rockies.

VAST WILDERNESS

Jasper's vast wilderness is one of the few remaining places with a full range of carnivores, such as grizzly bears, black bears, wolves, coyotes, cougars, and wolverines. There are also large populations of elk, deer, woodland caribou, bighorn sheep, and mountain goats among the more than four dozen species of mammals, many of which are often seen right from the roadsides. Each year hundreds of animals are killed along Jasper's highways, so it is vital to observe all speed limits and especially to slow down in special animal-sighting speed-zone areas. When hiking, keep your distance from wild animals and make a lot of noise as a means of avoiding contact with large mammals, especially bears.

23

Stutfield Glacier. This stunning glacier stretches down 914 meters (3,000 feet) of cliff face, forming a set of double icefalls visible from a roadside viewpoint. ⊠ *135 km (86 miles) north of Lake Louise, 95 km (57 miles) south of Jasper Townsite, Jasper National Park.*

Sunwapta Falls. "Sunwapta" is the Stoney Indian word for "turbulent river." There are two sets of falls at this site, but most people just see the Upper Falls, which are a short walk from the parking area. They have a drop of about 18.5 meters (60 feet) and are prettiest in the late spring when the spring melt is at its peak. They are smaller than the Athabasca Falls to the north. ⊠ *Jasper National Park ✢ Off Icefields Pwky. 1 km (½ mile) west of Sunwapta Falls Rocky Mountain Lodge; 173 km (110 miles) north of Lake Louise, 57 km (33 miles) south of Jasper.*

SPORTS AND THE OUTDOORS

In the northern half of the park, backpacking and horse-packing trips offer wilderness seclusion. The park's southern half rewards trekkers with dramatic glacial scenery. Day hikes are popular around Mount Edith Cavell, Miette Hot Springs, and Maligne Lake; Pyramid Lake and the Fairmont Jasper Park Lodge are destinations for horseback riding.

MULTISPORT OUTFITTERS

Alpine Club of Canada. Reservations for backcountry huts can be made through the club. ☎ *403/678–3200* ⊕ *www.alpineclubofcanada.ca.*

FAMILY **Alternative Adventures.** This outfitter operates out of a camping resort 10 km (6.2 miles) west of Hinton on Highway 16, about a 35-minute drive from Jasper. Zip-lining, eco-adventures, and hang-gliding, paragliding, and power-kiting instruction are on offer. ⊠ *Hwy. 16, 10 km (6.2 miles) east of east Jasper National Park Gate* ☎ 780/817–9696 ⊕ *www.alternativeadventures.ca* ✉ *From C$62.50.*

Boat House. You can rent a kayak, paddle boat, canoe, or other equipment here. ⊠ *Fairmont Jasper Park Lodge, Hwy. 16* ☎ 780/852–3301 ⊕ *www.fairmont.com/jasper* ✉ *From C$25.*

Canadian Skyline Adventures. Hire an experienced guide to take you to the most scenic places in Jasper National Park, including the world-famous Skyline Trail. Guides can also take you on an epic backcountry hiking trip. ⊠ *Jasper* ☎ 780/820–0772 ⊕ *www.canadianskylineadventures. com* ✉ *From C$55.*

Gravity Gear. Gear for ice climbing, backcountry skiing, and mountaineering can be rented or purchased at this company whose staffers can also refer certified guides for these activities. ⊠ *618 Patricia St.* ☎ 780/852–3155, 888/852–3155 ⊕ *www.gravitygearjasper.com* ✉ *From C$125.*

Jasper Adventure Centre. Guided hikes, ice walks on the Athabasca Glacier, tours of the Icefields Parkway, and train excursions are among the adventures this outfitter organizes. ⊠ *611 Patricia St.* ☎ 780/852–5595, 800/565–7547 ⊕ *www.jasperadventurecentre.com* ✉ *From C$65.*

Jasper Dive Adventures. During World War II, a top-secret British mission known as Project Habbakuk took place in Jasper National Park. The goal was to produce an unsinkable aircraft carrier from pykrete, a mixture of wood pulp and ice. When the project was canceled, the unfinished ship was sunk in Patricia Lake. This company offers guided diving tours of the remains. It also rents equipment and conducts scuba certification courses. ⊠ *Jasper* ☎ 780/852–3560 ⊕ *www. jasperdiveadventures.com* ✉ *From C$75.*

Jasper Motorcycle Tours. Experience the Canadian Rockies in comfort on a thrilling chauffeured motorcycle tour. A professional driver can carry up to two guests per sidecar-style motorcycle. Rentals of Harley Davidson Heritage Classic and Harley Fatboy motorcycles are also available to licensed drivers. ⊠ *610 Patricia St., Jasper* ☎ 780/931–6100 ⊕ *www. jaspermotorcycletours.com* ✉ *From C$99.*

Jasper Source for Sports. Here you can rent bikes, fishing and camping supplies, and ski and snowboard equipment. ⊠ *406 Patricia St.* ☎ 780/852–3654 ⊕ *www.jaspersports.com.*

Pyramid Lake Boat House. Canoes, rowboats, kayaks, paddleboats, and electric boats are available from this company that also sells fishing licenses and has rod and reel rentals. ⊠ *Pyramid Lake Resort, Pyramid Lake Rd., 5 km (3 miles) north of Jasper Townsite* ☎ 780/852–4900, 888/717–1277 ⊕ *www.mpljasper.com* ✉ *From C$25.*

Totem Ski Shop. Come here for summer and winter sports equipment and clothing. ⊠ *408 Connaught Dr.* ☎ 780/852–3078 ⊕ *www. totemskishop.com.*

AIR TOURS

OUTFITTERS

Icefield Helicopter Tours. This outfitter offers a bird's-eye view of the Columbia Icefields. They also have heli-yoga, heli-horseback riding, heli-hiking, heli-fishing, romance tours, and other helicopter tours outside the park. Flights take off from their Icefield heli-base. ☏ 888/844–3514, 403/721–2100 ⊕ www.icefieldheli.com ✉ From C$185.

Rockies Heli Canada. You can arrange heli-hiking, yoga, camping, and snowshoeing adventures with this company whose flights depart from its Icefield Adventure Base, 43 km (27 miles) east of the Icefields Parkway on Highway 11 East. ☏ 888/844–3514, 403/721–2100 ⊕ www.rockiesheli.com ✉ From C$195.

23

BIRD-WATCHING

An astonishing 277 species of birds make their home in the Canadian Rockies. The golden eagle migration, which occurs in spring and fall, is the park's biggest birding event. During migration period, you might see more than 200 eagles in one day at the east end of the park (Pocahontas area). At other times of year, the best place to observe birds is at **Cottonwood Slough,** along Pyramid Lake Road. This is a good place to spot Barrow's goldeneye, warblers, snipes, soras and hummingbirds, and red-necked grebe.

BOATING AND RAFTING

Boating in rowboats and canoes is allowed on most ponds and lakes. Boats with electric motors without on-board generators are allowed on most road-accessible lakes, but the use of gas-powered motors is restricted. It's wise to ask park staff about restrictions before launching your boat.

The rafting season runs from May through September. Children as young as six years of age can participate on some of the float trips. The Athabasca River has Class II white-water rapids; the Sunwapta and Fraser rivers have Class III rapids.

TOURS AND OUTFITTERS

Jasper Raft Tours. Take a half-day float trip on the Athabasca with Jasper Raft Tours. ☏ 780/852–2665, 888/553–5628 ⊕ www.jasperrafttours.com ✉ From C$67.

Jasper's Whitewater Rafting Ltd. This well-regarded outfit conducts half-day and shorter trips on the Athabasca and Sunwapta rivers. ✉ 618 Connaught Dr., Jasper ☏ 780/852–7238, 800/557–7238 ⊕ www.whitewaterraftingjasper.com ✉ From C$64.

Maligne Rafting Adventures. This operator conducts rafting tours on the Athabasca, Sunwapta, and Fraser rivers. Day trips are available on Class II, III, and IV rapids. ✉ 616 Patricia St., Jasper ☏ 780/852–3370 ⊕ www.raftjasper.com ✉ From C$59.

Mount Robson Whitewater Rafting. Rafting excursions on the Fraser River leave from the Mount Robson Lodge, 95 km (59 miles) west of Jasper in

British Columbia. Choices include a two-hour scenic float trip, a three-hour white-water excursion, or a full-day rafting adventure on Class I and Class III rapids. Free overnight group camping is available with the purchase of any rafting trip. ⊠ *Mount Robson Lodge, Hwy. 16, 5 km (3 miles) west of Mt. Robson Provincial Park* ☎ *250/566–4879, 888/566–7238* ⊕ *www.mountrobsonwhitewater.com* ✉ *From C$59.*

Rocky Mountain River Guides. The guides conduct trips for rafters of all experience levels. ⊠ *626 Connaught Dr., Jasper* ☎ *780/852–3777* ⊕ *www.rmriverguides.com* ✉ *From C$68.*

GOLF

Fairmont Jasper Park Lodge. Stanley Thompson designed the championship course at this upscale resort. Packages that include accommodations and golfing can be found on the website. ⊠ *1 Lodge Rd.* ☎ *780/852–6090* ⊕ *www.fairmont.com/jasper* ✉ *C$199* ⅄ *18 holes, 6663 yards, par 71.*

HIKING

Long before Jasper was established as a national park, a vast network of trails provided an essential passageway for wildlife, First Nations people, explorers, and fur traders. Nearly 1,000 km (621 miles) of hiking trails in Jasper provide an opportunity to truly experience wilderness, and hardcore backpackers will find multiday loops of more than 160 km (100 miles). The trails at Mount Edith Cavell and Maligne Canyon should not be missed.

A few of these trails are restricted to pedestrians, but hikers, mountain bikers, and equestrian users may share most of them. Several paved trails are suitable for wheelchairs and strollers, while others are rugged backcountry trails designed for backpacking trips. Bathrooms can be found along the most used day-use trails. You might see elk, bighorn sheep, moose, bears, and mountain goats along the way. It is never a good idea to surprise a large animal such as an elk or bear, so make plenty of noise as you go along, avoid hiking alone, stick to designated trails, and carry bear spray and know how to use it.

EASY

FAMILY **Lake Annette Loop.** This kid-friendly 2.4-km (1½-mile) loop trail with interpretive signage is paved and mostly level. It takes most people less than two hours to complete. Toilets are at two locations, and there is a shelter halfway around. *Easy.* ⚘ *Trailhead: on right side of Lake Annette picnic area's western parking lot. From townsite take Hwy. 16 north to Maligne Lake Rd. east to Old Lodge Rd. and Lake Annette Rd.*

FAMILY **Maligne Canyon.** This 2.1-km (1.3-mile), one-way trail east of Jasper Townsite leads to views of the area's famous limestone gorge. Starting at the fifth of six bridges spanning the canyon, the winding trail gains about 100 meters (330 feet) in elevation. There's a waterfall at the head of the canyon. *Easy.* ⚘ *From townsite take Hwy. 16 north to Maligne Lake Rd. east. Trailhead: at Fifth Bridge, 8 km (5 miles) east of Jasper.*

Old Fort Point Loop. Shaped by glaciers, Old Fort Point is a bedrock knob that provides an excellent view of Jasper. It will take an hour or two to complete the 3½-km (2.2-mile) loop trail. A wide, easy path that begins behind the information kiosk leads to a very steep section of trail. It's common to see Rocky Mountain bighorn sheep, the provincial mammal of Alberta, from this trail. Along the way you'll pass Jasper National Park's oldest rock, but the real highlight is the view from the top. *Easy.* ⊹ *Trailhead: 1.6 km (1 mile) east of Jasper Townsite. Follow Hwy. 93A to Old Fort Point/Lac Beauvert access road. Turn left, cross the Athabasca River, and park in lot on right.*

FAMILY **Path of the Glacier Trail.** This must-do 1.6-km (1-mile) trail only takes
Fodor's Choice about an hour. The kid-friendly path, paved at the start, runs across
★ a rocky landscape once covered in glacial ice. Eventually you come to a viewpoint overlooking Cavell Pond, which is fed by Cavell Glacier. Small icebergs often float in the water. The view across the valley takes in Angel Glacier, resting her wings between Mount Edith Cavell and Sorrow Peak. *Easy.* ⊹ *Trailhead: at parking lot at west end of Cavell Rd. From Icefields Pkwy., take Hwy. 93A south 5½ km (3.4 miles) and Cavell Rd. west 15 km (9.3 miles).*

FAMILY **Valley of the Five Lakes.** It takes two to three hours to complete this family-friendly 4.2-km (2.3-mile) hike. Five small lakes are the highlight of the trip, which takes you through a lodgepole-pine forest, across the Wabasso Creek wetlands, and through a flowery meadow. Watch for birds, beavers, and other wildlife along the way. Turn this into a moderately difficult hike by continuing another 10 km (6.2 miles) to Old Fort Point. *Easy.* ⊹ *Trailhead: 9 km (5.6 miles) south of Jasper Townsite on Hwy. 93.*

MODERATE

Fodor's Choice **Cavell Meadows Loop.** This moderately steep 8-km (5-mile) trail will take
★ four to six hours. Into early summer the upper section is still covered in snow and not recommended, but from mid-July to mid-August you can enjoy the carpet of wildflowers. There's also an excellent view of the Angel Glacier. *Moderate.* ⊹ *Trailhead: parking lot at west end of Cavell Rd. From Icefields Pkwy., take Hwy. 93A south 5½ km (3.4 miles) and Cavell Rd. west 15 km (9.3 miles).*

DIFFICULT

Wilcox Pass. Excellent views of the Athabasca Glacier are the highlight of this strenuous, 8-km (5-mile) hike near the Columbia Icefield Glacier Discovery Centre. This pass was originally used by explorers and First Nations people and is fairly steep. Keep an eye out for wildflowers and bighorn sheep. Be sure to dress in warm layers, because this pass can be snowy until late July. *Difficult.* ⊹ *Trailhead: off Wilcox Creek Campground entrance road, 3.1 km (2 miles) south of Icefield centre. From townsite take Icefields Pkwy. (Hwy. 93) south 106 km (66 miles) to campground.*

WILDERNESS HIKING

Jasper's backcountry is some of the wildest and most pristine of any mountain park in the world. Check at the visitor center for information about the hundreds of hiking and mountain-biking trails and the overnight camping quotas on the Skyline and Tonquin Valley trails.

Skyline Trail. The trail meanders at or above the tree line for 44 km (27 miles) past some of the park's best scenery. Reservations are recommended. *Difficult.* ☎ *780/852–6177.*

Tonquin Valley. Near Mount Edith Cavell, Tonquin Valley is a classic Canadian backpacking area. Its high mountain lakes bounded by steep rocky peaks known as the Ramparts, attract many hikers in summer and fall. *Difficult.*

HORSEBACK RIDING

Several outfitters offer one-hour, half-day, full-day, and multiday guided trips within the park. Participants must be at least age six to participate in a riding trip, but pony rides are available for younger children. It's wise to make your reservations well ahead during July and August and for multiday journeys. Contact the Cottonwood Corral Association (☎ *780/852–3121*) about horse boarding.

TOURS AND OUTFITTERS

Jasper Riding Stables and Outfitters. These stables offer rides and full-day excursions into the hills overlooking Jasper; there are also carriage rides and winter sleigh rides. ✉ *Pyramid Resort, Pyramid Lake Rd.* ☎ *780/852–7433* ⊕ *www.jasperstables.com* ☞ *From C$47.*

Skyline Trail Rides. This company offers backcountry horseback trips and horse-assisted hiking, and it operates Shovel Pass Lodge, midway on the famous Skyline Trail. Riders and hikers can book a stay at the lodge and enjoy comfortable accommodations and delicious meals. ✉ *Fairmont Jasper Park Lodge, Hwy. 16* ☎ *780/852–4215* ⊕ *www.skylinetrail.com* ☞ *From C$195.*

Tonquin Valley Adventures. Guided multiday horseback and hiking trips into the Tonquin Valley are the specialty of this company that also operates the valley's Amethyst Lake Lodge. In the summer there's a cook on-site; all meals are included in the guided trips. There is also a cabin that can be rented by hikers and skiers who wish to cook their own meals. Bring your fishing gear—there are boats at the cabin and a lake with wild rainbow trout. ✉ *Jasper* ☎ *780/852–1188* ⊕ *www. tonquinadventures.com* ☞ *From C$795 for 3-day, 2-night horse trip.*

Tonquin Valley Backcountry Lodge. The lodge offers guided multiday horseback trips in the Tonquin Valley that include accommodations and all meals. It also provides accommodations and meals for hikers and skiers on self-guided trips. ✉ *Jasper* ☎ *780/852–3909* ⊕ *www.tonquinvalley. com* ☞ *From C$410.*

SWIMMING

FAMILY **Lake Annette and Lake Edith.** These two lakes with women's names have sandy beaches and water that reaches the low 70s°F during warm spells. ⊠ *On Hwy. 16 near Fairmont Jasper Park Lodge* 🎫 *Free.*

FAMILY **Jasper Aquatic Center.** This recreation facility has a three-story-high indoor waterslide, a 25-meter (82-foot) swimming pool, and a kiddie pool. A steam room and a hot tub are also on-site, and towel and suit rentals are available. The center closes for two weeks in the fall. ⊠ *305 Bonhomme St., Jasper* 🕾 *780/852–3663* ⊕ *www.jasper-alberta.com/2249/fitness-aquatic-centre* 🎫 *C$7* 🕙 *Daily 2–9.*

23

WINTER SPORTS

Jasper has more than 50 km (31 miles) of groomed cross-country ski trails and it is a very popular snowshoe and fat-bike destination. There is a wide choice of groomed and natural trails, and equipment and local guides can be arranged through local ski shops. Current cross-country ski information is available at the park visitor center. Ice climbing, ice walks, skating, and wildlife watching are also popular winter activities. Downhill skiers will enjoy Marmot Basin, a 20-minute drive from town.

Marmot Basin. At 1,698 meters (5,570 feet), Marmot Basin has the highest base elevation of any Canadian ski area. The resort includes a mix of downhill skiing terrain, and the slopes are a little less crowded than those around Banff, especially on weekdays. There are three day lodges, two of which are at mid-mountain. Shuttles between Marmot Basin and the Jasper Townsite run every day of the season. Discounted lift tickets are available during the Jasper in January winter festival. **Facilities:** 86 trails; 1,675 acres; 2,612-meter drop; 7 lifts. ⊠ *1 Marmot Rd., off Hwy. 93A* 🕾 *780/852–3816, 866/952–3816* ⊕ *www.skimarmot.com* 🎫 *Lift ticket: C$88.*

FAMILY **Mildred Lake.** The Fairmont Jasper Park Lodge maintains a skating rink and an oval skating trail on nearby Mildred Lake. Groomed cross-country ski and snowshoe trails are also in the area. ⊠ *1 Old Lodge Rd., off Maligne Lake Rd., Jasper.*

Pyramid Lake. At this pretty lake you can ski groomed cross-country trails, go snowshoeing or ice-skating, or take a sleigh ride. ⊠ *Pyramid Lake Rd., 6½ km (4 miles) north of Jasper, off Hwy. 16A* 🎫 *Free.*

WHAT'S NEARBY

The Jasper Townsite is 287 km (178 miles) north of the **Banff Townsite**, 400 km (249 miles) northwest of **Calgary**, 360 km (224 miles) west of **Edmonton**, and 82 km (51 miles) west of **Hinton**. Most visitors arrive from Calgary or Edmonton—both near the major highway—where the two international airports are located.

Visitor Information Tourism Jasper. 🕾 *780/852–6236* ⊕ *www.jasper.travel.*

516 <   **Jasper National Park**

WHERE TO EAT

IN THE PARK

PICNIC AREAS

Athabasca Day Use Site. This large area has a shelter and is ideal for family reunions because it can be reserved ahead for a fee of C$50. It has beautiful views of the river and mountains. ⊠ *Off Hwy. 16E, 15 km (9 miles) from Jasper* ☎ *780/852–6176* ⊕ *www.pc.gc.ca/jasper.*

FAMILY **Lake Annette picnic area.** Beside Lake Annette, this picnic area has shelters and tables. It's a favorite with families who come to the lake to swim. ⊠ *Near junction of Maligne Lake Rd. and Hwy. 16.*

Pyramid Lake Beach. At Pyramid Lake's small but nice beach area there are picnic tables with fire boxes. ⊠ *Off Pyramid Lake Rd., 6½ km (4 miles) north of townsite.*

Sixth Bridge picnic area. This picnic area sits beside the Maligne River near where it flows into the Athabasca River. There are no shelters, but it's a favorite with locals because of the scenic location. ⊠ *Off Maligne Lake Rd., 2.2 km (1.3 miles) from Hwy. 16 junction.*

OUTSIDE THE PARK

$ ✕ **Bear's Paw Bakery.** This cozy little downtown bakery is a great stop
BAKERY for breakfast or lunch. Tasty muffins, scones, and fresh cinnamon buns are served for breakfast, sandwiches and wraps for lunch. Freshly baked cookies, cakes, and artisan breads are also available, along with a wide variety of coffees and teas. Popular with locals and visitors, this place with just a few tables for dining inside can be packed during peak times. The owners also run the Other Paw, two blocks away. Ⓢ *Average main: C$9* ⊠ *4 Cedar Ave., near Connaught Dr., Jasper* ☎ *780/852–3233* ⊕ *www.bearspawbakery.com* ⊙ *No dinner* ⟂ *Reservations not accepted.*

$$$ ✕ **Evil Dave's.** A funky atmosphere and an "evil"-inspired menu make
CANADIAN this downtown restaurant a fun place to dine. Local favorites among the globally inspired, locally sourced entrées include the Malicious Salmon (blackened salmon with sweet curry aioli), Malevolent Meatloaf (Alberta bison wrapped in wild boar bacon), and Diabolical Tenderloin (Alberta beef tenderloin with pico de gallo and red wine demi-glace). Save room for Wicked Cheesecake for dessert. Some dishes can be served family style for larger groups. Ⓢ *Average main: C$26* ⊠ *622 Patricia St., Jasper* ☎ *780/852–3323* ⊕ *www.evildavesgrill.com* ⊙ *No lunch* ⟂ *Reservations essential.*

$$ ✕ **Famoso.** Authentic fire-roasted Neapolitan-style pizzas made in a real
PIZZA bell oven are the specialty at this small pizzeria in the upper level of a downtown building. The atmosphere is casual, and though you seat yourself and order over a counter, servers bring the food and drinks to your table. The pizzas range from a classic margherita to interesting combinations like cavoletti (brussels sprouts, prosciutto crisps, Gorgonzola cheese, dates, and walnuts) and prosciutto with arugula. Enjoy

a gelato for dessert. $ *Average main: C$16* ⊠ *607 Patricia St., Jasper* ☎ *780/852–5577* ⊕ *www.famoso.ca.*

$$$ ✕ **Fiddle River.** This pine-finished, second-floor dining room has great
CANADIAN views of the railway station, downtown Jasper, and the mountains, and the Canadian seafood, wild game, and Alberta beef dishes are classic and delicious. Daily specials are noted on a chalkboard menu. This is a good place to sample halibut or lobster from Atlantic Canada or enjoy Alberta game meats like elk or bison. The wine list includes some noteworthy Canadian wines. $ *Average main: C$30* ⊠ *620 Connaught Dr., Jasper* ☎ *780/852–3032* ⊕ *www.fiddleriverrestaurant.com* ⊗ *No lunch.*

23

$$$ ✕ **Jasper Brewing Company.** The park's only brewery is a fine stop for a
AMERICAN beer and a burger after a big hike or a day of skiing. Premium hops and natural mountain water go into the six signature beers brewed on-site. You can watch sports action on the big screens near the bar or dine in the restaurant. Wings, poutine, fish-and-chips, sandwiches, burgers, and other classic pub fare predominate on the menu, but there are also well-made salads, steaks, and seafood dishes. $ *Average main: C$23* ⊠ *624 Connaught Dr., Jasper* ☎ *780/852–4111* ⊕ *www.jasperbrewingco.ca* ▭ *No credit cards.*

$$$ ✕ **Oka Sushi.** This is slow food at its best, with just one chef and one
JAPANESE server and patrons sitting either at tables along the perimeter or at the small bar, watching the sushi as it's prepared *à la minute*. Tatsuhiko Okaki, the owner and chef, is famous for fashioning tantalizing combinations from the freshest ingredients. Try the Jasper Roll, made with crab meat and shrimp and served with a spicy sauce. Sapporo beer and sake complement chef Okaki's creations perfectly. Only about a dozen people can fit in this sushi bar at once. Reservations—only possible for the earliest seatings, at 6 and 6:30—should be made well in advance. $ *Average main: C$27* ⊠ *Fairmont Jasper Park Lodge, 1 Old Lodge Rd., Jasper* ☎ *780/852–1114* ⊕ *www.fairmont.com/jasper/ dining/okasushi* ⊗ *Closed Sun. year-round, Mon. in winter. No lunch* ⟡ *Reservations essential.*

$$$$ ✕ **ORSO Trattoria.** Get a taste of northern Italy at this must-visit restau-
ITALIAN rant for osso buco aficionados. The braised Alberta veal osso buco is slow cooked for 10 hours with gremolata braising juices and served over a delicate saffron risotto. Close your eyes and you might believe you're in Milan, but don't keep them closed too long or you'll miss some of the best views in the Canadian Rockies. On warm evenings you can dine on the heated outdoor patio and enjoy vistas of Lac Beauvert, Mount Edith Cavell, and Whistlers Mountain. All the pastas on the menu are handmade, and the produce is locally sourced from the well-respected Twin Meadows Farms. Be sure to save room for tiramisu for dessert. Children age five and under eat for free, and those 12 and under can order from a special menu or, for half price, the regular menu. $ *Average main: C$38* ⊠ *1 Old Lodge Rd., Jasper* ☎ *780/852–6090* ⊕ *www. fairmont.com/jasper/dining/orso-trattoria* ⟡ *Reservations essential* ▭ *No credit cards.*

$$$$ ✕ **Tekarra.** In a log cabin near the confluence of the Athabasca and Miette
CANADIAN rivers, this restaurant has an engagingly rustic feel, but don't let the
Fodor'sChoice simple architecture fool you: the cuisine is among the finest in the Cana-
★ dian Rockies. Chef David Husereau sources local ingredients and does
his own baking, smoking, and curing. A recent menu addition are small
plates that work well for sharing. These include sides such as brussels
sprouts with maple and bacon or spaghetti squash with honey and fresh
nutmeg. A good entrée might be the macadamia-crusted rack of Alberta
lamb, iron-seared Arctic char with sweet crab butter, or Alberta beef tenderloin with caramelized onions. The signature dessert is a hot chocolate
soufflé with homemade vanilla ice cream. Excellent gluten-free dishes
are available. The wine list has been thoughtfully assembled, and there's
an extensive martini menu. ⑤ *Average main: C$35* ⊠ *Tekarra Lodge
Resort, Hwy. 93A, Jasper* ☎ 780/852–4624 ⊕ *www.tekarrarestaurant.
com* ⊘ *Closed early Oct.–mid-May* ⚖ *Reservations essential.*

WHERE TO STAY

IN THE PARK

$$$ ⊞ **Alpine Village.** Facing the Athabasca River, this cabin resort feels like
HOTEL it's miles away from civilization even though the drive to Jasper takes
FAMILY only three minutes. **Pros:** well-kept property; kitchen suites; location
across from the Athabasca River. **Cons:** outside town; closed in win-
ter; no in-room phones; limited Wi-Fi access. ⑤ *Rooms from: C$195*
⊠ *On Hwy. 93A N, 2½ km (1½ miles) southeast of Jasper Townsite*
☎ 780/852–3285, 780/852–1955 ⊕ *www.alpinevillagejasper.com* ⏎ *49
rooms* ⦶ *No meals.*

$$$$ ⊞ **The Crimson Jasper.** Jasper received a mild jolt of style when this mod-
HOTEL ern-looking hotel opened 2014. **Pros:** newly renovated, air-conditioned
rooms; one block from downtown; mini-refrigerators and microwaves
in all rooms. **Cons:** across from train tracks; small elevator; rooms
are spread out. ⑤ *Rooms from: C$308* ⊠ *200 Connaught Dr., Jasper*
☎ 780/852–3394, 888/852–7737, 780/852–3833 ⊕ *www.mpljasper.
com/hotels/the_crimson* ⏎ *33 standard rooms, 65 kitchenette rooms,
1 suite* ⦶ *No meals* ⊟ *No credit cards.*

$$$$ ⊞ **Fairmont Jasper Park Lodge.** On the shores of magnificent Lac Beau-
RESORT vert about 7 km (4½ miles) northeast of Jasper Townsite, the lodge,
FAMILY a thoughtful blend of civilized luxury and rustic Canadian charm, is
Fodor'sChoice a destination itself. **Pros:** many amenities; beautiful setting; top-notch
★ dining. **Cons:** 10-minute drive to townsite; on-site dining can be
pricey. ⑤ *Rooms from: C$457* ⊠ *1 Old Lodge Rd.* ☎ 780/852–3301,
866/441–1414 ⊕ *www.fairmont.com/jasper* ⏎ *446 rooms, 100 suites*
⦶ *No meals.*

$$$ ⊞ **Patricia Lake Bungalows.** Lakefront solitude is the highlight of these
HOTEL comfortable lodgings on the shores of tranquil Patricia Lake. **Pros:** good
FAMILY value; quiet location; well-tended grounds. **Cons:** five-minute drive from
town; limited Wi-Fi access. ⑤ *Rooms from: C$195* ⊠ *Pyramid Lake Rd.*
☎ 780/852–3560, 888/499–6848 ⊕ *www.patricialakebungalows.com*
⊘ *Closed mid-Oct.–Apr.* ⏎ *10 rooms, 18 suites, 22 cabins* ⦶ *No meals.*

Best Campgrounds in Jasper

Parks Canada operates campgrounds in Jasper National Park that have a total of 1,772 available frontcountry sites during the peak season. There is winter camping at Wapiti campground. Hookup sites are available at Whistlers and Wapiti campgrounds only, so reserve a site in advance if you are traveling during the peak summer season. In addition to standard camping sites, Parks Canada operates oTENTiks at Whistlers Campground. These accommodations are a cross between a cabin and a tent and sleep up to six people on foam mattresses. Call ☎ 780/852–6176 or 877/737–3783 or go online at ⊕ www.pccamping.ca for reservations.

Columbia Icefield Campground. This rustic tent campground is near a creek and has great views of the Columbia Icefield. ⊠ Hwy. 93, 106 km (66 miles) south of Jasper Townsite.

Honeymoon Lake Campground. This rustic campground is just down the road from Sunwapta Falls. With 35 sites on the shores of Honeymoon Lake, this is a good spot to bring a canoe and enjoy a peaceful paddle. ⊠ Hwy. 93, 35 km (22 miles) south of Jasper Townsite.

Jonas Creek Campground. This small, primitive campground is in a quiet spot along a creek off the Icefields Parkway. Sites are first come, first served. ⊠ Just off Icefields Pkwy., 75 km (47 miles) south of Jasper Townsite.

Wabasso Campground. Families flock to this campground because of its playground and many amenities. ⊠ Hwy. 93A, 16 km (10 miles) south of Jasper Townsite.

Wapiti Campground. Close to Jasper, this campground is near a number of good hiking trails. A portion of Wapiti remains open during the winter. ⊠ Hwy. 93, 5 km (3 miles) south of Jasper Townsite.

Whistlers Campground. This campground is the largest and has the most amenities and the greatest variety of camping options. It's the number-one choice for families because of the on-site interpretive programs at Whistlers Outdoor Theatre. ⊠ Hwy. 93, 3 km (2 miles) south of Jasper Townsite.

$$$$ ⬚ **Sawridge Inn and Conference Centre.** A three-story hotel on the edge of
HOTEL Jasper, the Sawridge is built around a spacious and impressive atrium
FAMILY filled with lush plants. **Pros:** many amenities; free Wi-Fi; in-room
refrigerators; free shuttle to downtown. **Cons:** atrium-restaurant noise
audible in some rooms; popular with tour groups; 15-minute walk
to downtown. ⑤ *Rooms from: C$298* ⊠ *82 Connaught Dr., Jasper*
☎ *780/852–5111, 888/729–7343* ⊕ *www.sawridgejasper.com* ⇆ *153
rooms, 4 suites* ❍❘ *No meals.*

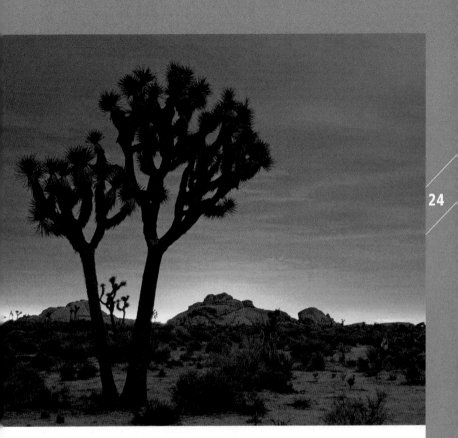

JOSHUA TREE
NATIONAL PARK

WELCOME TO JOSHUA TREE NATIONAL PARK

TOP REASONS TO GO

★ **Rock climbing:** Joshua Tree is a world-class site with challenges for climbers of just about every skill level.

★ **Peace and quiet:** Savor the solitude of one of the last great wildernesses in America.

★ **Stargazing:** You'll be mesmerized by the Milky Way flowing across the summer sky. For spectacular natural fireworks, visit in mid-August during the Perseid meteor shower and watch shooting stars streak overhead.

★ **Wildflowers:** In spring, the hillsides explode in a patchwork of yellow, blue, pink, and white.

★ **Sunsets:** Twilight is a magical time here, especially during the winter, when the setting sun casts a golden glow on the mountains.

247 • Yucca Valley • Visitor Center • Twentynine Palms • Adobe Rd. • Visitor Center • 62 • Twentynine Palms Hwy. • Joshua Tree • Yucca Trail • West Entrance Station • Fortynine Palms Oasis • Oasis of Mara • Utah Trail Rd. • North Entrance Station • Park Boulevard • Black Rock Canyon • Keys Ranch • Barker Dam • Hidden Valley • LOST HORSE VALLEY • QUEEN VALLEY • California Riding Trail • Ryan Mtn. • L I T T L E   S A N   B E R N A R D I N O   M T S. • Desert Hot Springs • Keys View • Lost Horse Mine • Geology Tour Road • PLEASANT VALLEY • TO LOS ANGELES • Dillon Road • Palm Springs • Cathedral City • 10 • Rancho Mirage • Palm Desert • 111 • Indio • Coachella • 86 • 111

1 Keys View. This is the most dramatic overlook in the park—on clear days you can see Signal Mountain in Mexico.

2 Hidden Valley. Crawl between the big rocks and you'll understand why this boulder-strewn area was once a cattle rustlers' hideout.

3 Cholla Cactus Garden. Come here in the late afternoon, when the spiky stalks of the bigelow (jumping) cholla cactus are backlit against an intense blue sky.

4 Oasis of Mara. Walk the nature trail around this desert oasis, which the first settlers, the Serrano, dubbed "the place of little springs and much grass."

CALIFORNIA

Utah Trail Rd.

62

24

62

0   5 mi

0   5 km

PINTO   MOUNTAINS

COXCOMB   MOUNTAINS

3

PINTO   BASIN

**Cholla
Cactus
Garden**

• Ocatillo
Patch

Pinto Basin Rd.

HEXIE
MOUNTAINS

Kaiser Road

EAGLE   MOUNTAINS

177

Visitor Center

♦ **Cottonwood Spring**

COTTONWOOD MTS

**Lost Palms
Oasis** ♦

Desert Center

• Bajada Nature Trail

10

Chiriaco
Summit

TO
⬏ MECCA

KEY

🚹🚺	*Ranger Station*
🔺	*Campground*
🪑	*Picnic Area*
🍴	*Restaurant*
🏨	*Lodge*
🥾	*Trailhead*
🚻	*Restrooms*
⤳	*Scenic Viewpoint*
┄┄┄	*Walking/Hiking Trails*

GETTING ORIENTED

Daggerlike tufts grace the branches of the namesake of Joshua Tree National Park in south-eastern California, where the arid Mojave Desert meets the sparsely veg-etated Colorado Desert (part of the Sonoran Desert, which lies across California, Arizona, and Northern Mexico). Passenger cars are fine for paved areas, but you'll need four-wheel drive for many of the rugged backcountry roadways. At the park's most popular sites, parking is limited. Joshua Tree does not have public transportation.

Updated
by Sarah
Amandolare

One of the last great wildernesses in the continental United States, Joshua Tree National Park teems with fascinating landscapes and life forms. It attracts around 1.5 million visitors each year, yet is mysteriously quiet at dawn and dusk. The park features ruggedly beautiful desert scenery, enormous boulders and jagged rocks, natural cactus gardens, and lush oases shaded by elegant fan palms. The landscape shifts abruptly from the arid stubble of the low Sonoran Desert to vast stands of the park's namesake Joshua trees in the higher, wetter Mojave Desert. Members of the yucca family of shrubs, the plants' unruly limbs are said to have reminded Mormon pioneers of the prophet Joshua's outstretched arms reaching toward heaven.

JOSHUA TREE PLANNER

WHEN TO GO

October through May, when the desert is cooler, is when most visitors arrive. Daytime temperatures range from the mid-70s in December and January to mid-90s in October and May. Lows can dip to near freezing in midwinter, and you may even encounter snow at the higher elevations. Summers can be torrid, with daytime temperatures reaching 110°F.

AVG. HIGH/LOW TEMPS.

Jan.	Feb.	Mar.	Apr.	May	June
62/32	65/37	72/40	80/50	90/55	100/65
July	Aug.	Sept.	Oct.	Nov.	Dec.
105/70	101/78	96/62	85/55	72/40	62/31

FESTIVALS AND EVENTS

FEBRUARY **Riverside County Fair & National Date Festival.** Head to Indio for camel and
FAMILY ostrich races. ⊠ *Riverside County Fairgrounds, 82-503 Hwy. 111, Indio*
☎ *800/811–3247* ⊕ *www.datefest.org.*

OCTOBER **Pioneer Days.** Outhouse races, live music, and arm wrestling mark this
FAMILY annual mid-October celebration in Twentynine Palms. The event also
features a parade, carnival, chili dinner, and an old timers' gathering.
⊠ *Twentynine Palms* ☎ *760/367–3445* ⊕ *www.visit29.org.*

PLANNING YOUR TIME

JOSHUA TREE IN ONE DAY

After stocking up on water, snacks, and lunch in Yucca Valley or Joshua
Tree (you won't find any supplies inside the park), begin your visit at
the **Joshua Tree Visitor Center,** where you can pick up maps and peruse
exhibits to get acquainted with what awaits you. Enter the park itself at
the nearby **West Entrance Station** and continue driving along the highly
scenic and well-maintained **Park Boulevard.** Stop first at **Hidden Valley,** where you can relax at the picnic area or hike the easy 1-mile loop
trail. After a few more miles turn left onto the spur road that takes you
to the trailhead for the **Barker Dam Nature Trail.** Walk the easy 1.3-
mile loop to view a water tank ranchers built to quench their cattle's
thirst; along the way you'll spot birds and a handful of cactus varieties.
Return to Park Boulevard and head south; you'll soon leave the main
road again for the drive to **Keys View.** The easy loop trail here is only
0.25 mile, but the views extend for miles in every direction—look for
the San Andreas Fault, the Salton Sea, and nearby mountains. Return
to Park Boulevard, where you'll find **Cap Rock,** another short loop trail
winding amid rock formations and Joshua trees.

Continuing along Park Boulevard, the start of the 18-mile self-guided
Geology Tour Road will soon appear on your right. A brochure outlin-
ing its 16 stops is available here; note that the round-trip will take about
two hours, and high-clearance vehicles are recommended after stop 9.
■**TIP→** Do not attempt if it has recently rained. Back on Park Boulevard, you'll soon arrive at the aptly named **Skull Rock.** This downright
spooky formation is next to the parking lot; a nearby trailhead marks
the beginning of a 1.7-mile nature trail. End your day with a stop at the
Oasis Visitor Center in Twentynine Palms, where you can stroll through
the historic **Oasis of Mara,** popular with area settlers.

GETTING HERE AND AROUND

AIR TRAVEL

Palm Springs International Airport is the closest major airport to Joshua
Tree National Park. It's about 45 miles from the park. The drive from
Los Angeles International Airport to Joshua Tree takes about two hours.

CAR TRAVEL

An isolated island of pristine wilderness—a rarity these days—Joshua
Tree National Park is within a short drive of 11 million Southern California residents. Most visitors, in fact, make the two-hour drive from
the Los Angeles area to enjoy a weekend of solitude in 792,726 acres
of untouched desert. The urban sprawl of Palm Springs (home to the
nearest airport) is 45 miles away, but gateway towns Joshua Tree, Yucca

Valley, and Twentynine Palms are just north of the park. If you're staying in the Palm Springs area, you can enjoy the highlights of the park in one day, including a stop for a picnic at a scenic spot.

■ TIP➜ If you'd prefer not to drive, most Palm Springs area hotels can arrange a half- or full-day tour that hits the highlights of Joshua Tree National Park. But you'll need to spend two or three days camping here to truly experience the quiet beauty of the desert.

PARK ESSENTIALS

PARK FEES AND PERMITS

Park admission is $20 per car, $10 per person on foot, bicycle, motorcycle, or horse. The Joshua Tree Pass, good for one year, is $30.

PARK HOURS

The park is open every day, around the clock. The park is in the Pacific time zone.

CELL-PHONE RECEPTION

Cell phones don't work in most areas of the park. There are no telephones in the interior of the park.

EDUCATIONAL OFFERINGS

LECTURES

The Desert Institute at Joshua Tree National Park. This organization offers a full schedule of educational lectures on topics such as the birds of Joshua Tree National Park, hiking, gourmet campfire cuisine, and photography. Classes meet at various locations; many include field trips within the park. ⊠ *74485 National Park Dr., Twentynine Palms* ☎ *760/367–5535* ⊕ *www.joshuatree.org.*

Stargazing. At Joshua Tree National Park you can tour the Milky Way on summer evenings using binoculars. Rangers also offer programs on some evenings when the moon isn't visible. Pick up a schedule at a visitor center. ⊠ *Cottonwood Campground Amphitheater and Oasis Visitor Center.*

RANGER PROGRAMS

Evening Programs. Rangers present hour-long lectures, usually on Friday or Saturday evening, at Black Rock Canyon Nature Center, Cottonwood Amphitheater, Indian Cove Amphitheater, and Jumbo Rocks Campground. Topics range from natural history to local lore. The schedule is posted at the visitor centers. ⊠ *Joshua Tree National Park* ⊡ *Free* ☉ *Fri. and/or Sat. at 7 or 8:30 pm, depending on staffing.*

Fodor's Choice **Keys Ranch Tour.** A guide takes you through the former home of a family
★ that homesteaded here for 60 years. In addition to the ranch, a workshop, store, and schoolhouse are still standing, and the grounds are strewn with vehicles and mining equipment. The 90-minute tour, which begins at the Keys Ranch gate, tells the history of the family that built the ranch. Tickets are $10, and reservations are required. ⊠ *Hidden Valley Picnic Area* ☎ *760/367–5522* ⊕ *www.nps.gov/jotr.*

RESTAURANTS

Dining options in the gateway towns around Joshua Tree National Park are extremely limited—you'll mostly find fast-food outlets and a few casual cafés in Yucca Valley and Twentynine Palms. The exception is the restaurant at 29 Palms Inn, which has an interesting California-cuisine menu that features lots of veggies. Still, you'll have to travel to the Palm Springs desert resort area for a fine-dining experience.

HOTELS

Lodging choices in the Joshua Tree National Park area are limited to a few motels, chain hotels, and a luxury bed-and-breakfast establishment in the gateway towns. In general, most offer few amenities and are modestly priced. Book ahead for the spring wildflower season—reservations may be difficult to obtain then.

For a more extensive range of lodging options, you'll need to head to Palm Springs and the surrounding desert resort communities. *Hotel reviews have been shortened. For full information, visit Fodors.com.*

24

WHAT IT COSTS				
	$	$$	$$$	$$$$
Restaurants	under $13	$13–$20	$21–$30	over $30
Hotels	under $101	$101–$150	$151–$200	over $200

Restaurant prices are the average cost of a main course at dinner, or if dinner is not served, at lunch. Hotel prices are the lowest cost of a standard double room in high season, excluding taxes and service charges.

TOURS

Big Wheel Tours. Based in Palm Desert, Big Wheel Tours offers van excursions, Jeep tours, and hiking trips through the park. Pickups are available at Palm Springs area hotels. ⊠ *74850 42nd Ave., Palm Desert* ☎ *760/779–1837* ⊕ *www.bwbtours.com* 🗐 *From $119.*

Trail Discovery. You can get a full day of exploring Joshua Tree with Trail Discovery, along with information on the park's plants, animals, geography, and history. Park admission, bottled water, hip-packs, snacks, and fruit are included. Transportation is not provided. ☎ *760/413–1575* ⊕ *www.palmspringshiking.com* 🗐 *From $95.*

VISITOR INFORMATION

Park Contact Information Joshua Tree National Park. ⊠ *74485 National Park Dr., Twentynine Palms* ☎ *760/367–5500* ⊕ *www.nps.gov/jotr.*

VISITOR CENTERS

Cottonwood Visitor Center. Exhibits in this small center, staffed by rangers and volunteers, illustrate the region's natural history. The center also has restrooms. ⊠ *Cottonwood Spring, Pinto Basin Rd.* ⊕ *www.nps. gov/jotr* ⊗ *Daily 8:30–4.*

Joshua Tree Visitor Center. This visitor center has interesting exhibits illustrating park geology, cultural and historic sites, and hiking and rock-climbing activities. There's also a small bookstore. Restrooms with flush toilets are on the premises. ⊠ *6554 Park Blvd., Joshua Tree* ☎ *760/366–1855* ⊕ *www.nps.gov/jotr* ⊗ *Daily 8–5.*

Oasis Visitor Center. Exhibits here illustrate how Joshua Tree was formed, reveal the differences between the park's two types of desert, and demonstrate how plants and animals eke out an existence in this arid climate. Take the ½-mile nature walk through the nearby Oasis of Mara, which is alive with cottonwood trees, palm trees, and mesquite shrubs. Facililities include picnic tables, restrooms, and a bookstore. ⊠ *74485 National Park Dr., Twentynine Palms* ☎ *760/367–5500* ⊕ *www.nps.gov/jotr* ⊗ *Daily 8:30–5.*

EXPLORING

You can experience Joshua Tree National Park on several levels. Even on a short excursion along Park Boulevard between the Joshua Tree entrance station and Oasis of Mara, you'll see some of the best desert scenery in North America—including a staggering abundance of flora visible along a dozen self-guided nature trails. You'll also see remnants of homesteads from a century ago, now mostly abandoned and wind-worn. If rock climbing is your passion, this is the place for you; boulder-strewn mountaintops and slopes beckon. But in the end, Joshua Tree National Park is a pristine wilderness where you can enjoy a solitary stroll along an animal trail and commune with nature. Be sure to take some time to explore on your own and enjoy the peace and quiet.

SCENIC DRIVES

Geology Motor Tour. Some of the park's most fascinating landscapes can be observed from this 18-mile dirt road. Parts of the journey are rough, so make sure you have a 4X4. Sights to see include a 100-year-old stone dam called Squaw Tank, defunct mines, and a large plain with an abundance of Joshua trees. There are 16 stops along the way, so give yourself about two hours to make the round-trip. ⊠ *South of Park Blvd., west of Jumbo Rocks.*

Park Boulevard. If you have time only for a short visit, driving Park Boulevard is your best choice. Traversing the most scenic portions of Joshua Tree, this well-paved road connects the north and west entrances in the park's high desert section. Along with some sweeping desert views, you'll see jumbles of splendid boulder formations, stands of Joshua trees, and Hidden Valley and Barker Dam, remnants of the area's wild and woolly past. From the Oasis Visitor Center, drive south. After about 5 miles, the road forks; turn right and head west toward Jumbo Rocks (clearly marked with a road sign). ⊠ *Joshua Tree National Park.*

Pinto Basin Road. This paved road takes you from high Mojave desert to low Colorado desert. A long, slow drive, the route runs from the main part of the park to Interstate 10; it can add as much as an hour to and from Palm Springs (round-trip), but the views and roadside exhibits make it worth the extra time. From the Oasis Visitor Center, drive south. After about 5 miles, the road forks; take a left and continue another 9 miles to the Cholla Cactus Garden, where the sun fills the cactus needles with light. Past that is the Ocotillo Patch, filled with spindly plants bearing razor-sharp thorns and, after a rain, bright green leaves and brilliant red flowers. Side trips from this route require a 4X4. ⊠ *Joshua Tree National Park.*

HISTORIC SITES

FAMILY **Hidden Valley.** This legendary cattle-rustlers' hideout is set among big boulders, which kids love to scramble over and around. There are shaded picnic tables here. ⊠ *Park Blvd., 14 miles south of west entrance.*

Fodor'sChoice **Keys Ranch.** This 150-acre ranch,
★ which once belonged to William and Frances Keys and is now on the National Historic Register, illustrates one of the area's most successful attempts at homesteading. The couple raised five children under extreme desert conditions. Most of the original buildings, including the house, school, store, and workshop, have been restored to the way they were when William died in 1969. The only way to see the ranch is on one of the 90-minute walking tours usually offered Friday–Sunday, October–May, and weekends in summer; advance reservations required. ✛ *2 miles north of Barker Dam Rd.* ☎ *760/367–5522* ⊕ *www.nps.gov* ✉ *$10, available at Joshua Tree and Oasis visitor centers* ☉ *Oct.–May, Fri. and Sat. at 2 pm, Sun. at 10 am; June–Sept., Sat. at 6 pm, Sun. at 9 am.*

> **PLANTS AND WILDLIFE IN JOSHUA TREE**
>
> Joshua Tree will shatter your notions of the desert as a wasteland. Life flourishes here, as flora and fauna have adapted to heat and drought. In most areas you'll be walking among native Joshua trees, ocotillos, and yuccas. One of the best spring desert wildflower displays in Southern California blooms here. You'll see plenty of animals—reptiles such as nocturnal sidewinders, birds like golden eagles or burrowing owls, and occasionally mammals like coyotes and bobcats.

24

Lost Horse Mine. This historic mine, which produced 10,000 ounces of gold and 16,000 ounces of silver between 1894 and 1931, was among Southern California's most productive mines. The 10-stamp mill is considered one of the best preserved of its type in the park system. The site is accessed via a fairly strenuous 2-mile hike. ⊠ *Keys View Rd., about 15 miles south of west entrance.*

SCENIC STOPS

Barker Dam. Built around 1900 by ranchers and miners to hold water for cattle and mining operations, the dam now collects rainwater and is a good place to spot wildlife such as the elusive bighorn sheep. ⊠ *Barker Dam Rd.* ✛ *Off Park Blvd., 10 miles south of west entrance.*

Cholla Cactus Garden. This stand of bigelow cholla (sometimes called jumping cholla, since its hooked spines seem to jump at you) is best seen and photographed in late afternoon, when the backlit spiky stalks stand out against a colorful sky. ⊠ *Pinto Basin Rd.* ✛ *20 miles north of Cottonwood Visitor Center.*

Cottonwood Spring. Home to the native Cahuilla people for centuries, this spring provided water for travelers and early prospectors. The area, which supports a large stand of fan palms, is one of the best stops for bird-watching, as migrating birds (and bighorn sheep) rely on the water as well. A number of gold mines were located here, and the area still has some remains, including an *arrastra* (a gold ore–grinding tool) and concrete pillars. Flash floods in 2011 and 2013, however, have necessitated that some areas no longer be open to the public. ⊠ *Cottonwood Visitor Center.*

Fortynine Palms Oasis. A short drive off Highway 62, this site is a bit of a preview of what the park's interior has to offer: stands of fan palms, interesting petroglyphs, and evidence of fires built by early American Indians. Since animals frequent this area, you may spot a coyote, bobcat, or roadrunner. ⊠ *End of Canyon Rd.* ✛ *4 miles west of Twentynine Palms.*

Fodor's Choice
★

Keys View. At 5,185 feet, this point affords a sweeping view of the Santa Rosa Mountains and Coachella Valley, the San Andreas Fault, the peak of 11,500-foot Mount San Gorgonio, the shimmering surface of Salton Sea, and—on a rare clear day—Signal Mountain in Mexico. Sunrise and sunset are magical times, when the light throws rocks and trees into high relief before bathing the hills in brilliant shades of red, orange, and gold. ⊠ *Keys View Rd.* ✛ *16 miles south of park's west entrance.*

Lost Palms Oasis. More than 100 fan palms comprise the largest group of the exotic plants in the park. A spring bubbles from between the rocks, but disappears into the sandy, boulder-strewn canyon. The 7-mile round-trip hike is not for everyone. Don't forget to bring water. . ⊠ *Cottonwood Visitor Center.*

Ocotillo Patch. Stop here for a roadside exhibit on the dramatic display made by the red-tipped succulent after even the shortest rain shower. ⊠ *Pinto Basin Rd.* ✛ *About 3 miles east of Cholla Cactus Gardens.*

SPORTS AND THE OUTDOORS

BICYCLING

Mountain biking is a great way to see Joshua Tree. Bikers are restricted to roads that are used by motorized vehicles, including the main park roads and a few four-wheel-drive trails. Most scenic stops and picnic areas, and the Wallstreet trailhead, have bike racks.

Black Eagle Mine Road. This 9-mile dead-end road is peppered with defunct mines, which should be approached with caution. It runs along the edge of a former lake bed, then crosses a number of dry washes before navigating several of Eagle Mountain's canyons. ✛ *Trailhead: off Pinto Basin Rd., 6½ miles north of Cottonwood Visitor Center.*

Covington Flats. This 4-mile route takes you past impressive Joshua trees as well as pinyon pines, junipers, and areas of lush desert vegetation. It's tough going toward the end, but once you reach 5,518-foot Eureka Peak you'll have great views of Palm Springs, the Morongo Basin, and the surrounding mountains. ✛ *Trailhead: at Covington Flats picnic area, La Contenta Rd., 10 miles south of Rte. 62.*

Pinkham Canyon and Thermal Canyon Roads. This challenging 20-mile route begins at the Cottonwood Visitor Center and loops through the Cottonwood Mountains. The unpaved trail follows Smoke Tree Wash through Pinkham Canyon, rounds Thermal Canyon, and loops back to the beginning. Rough in places, the road travels through soft sand and rocky floodplains. ✢ *Trailhead: at Cottonwood Visitor Center.*

Queen Valley. This 13.4-mile network of mostly level roads winds through one of the park's most impressive groves of Joshua trees. You can also leave your bike at one of the racks placed in the area and explore on foot. ✢ *Trailhead: at Hidden Valley Campground, and accessible opposite Geology Tour Road at Big Horn Pass.*

BIRD-WATCHING

Joshua Tree, located on the inland portion of the Pacific Flyway, hosts about 240 species of birds, and the park is a popular seasonal location for bird-watching. During the fall migration, which runs mid-September through mid-October, there are several reliable sighting areas. At Barker Dam you might spot white-throated swifts, several types of swallows, or red-tailed hawks. Lucy's warbler, flycatchers, and Anna's hummingbirds cruise around Cottonwood Spring, a serene palm-shaded setting where you'll likely see the largest and most random concentrations of birds in the park; occasional ducks, herons, and egrets, as well as migrating rufous and calliope, wintering prairie falcons, and a resident barn owl could show up. Black Rock Canyon sees pinyon jays, while Covington Flats reliably gets mountain quail, and you may see La Conte's thrashers, ruby-crowned kinglets, and warbling vireos at either locale. Rufus hummingbirds, Pacific slope flycatchers, and various warblers are frequent visitors to Indian Cove. Lists of birds found in the park, as well as information on recent sightings, are available at visitor centers.

HIKING

There are more than 190 miles of hiking trails in Joshua Tree, ranging from quarter-mile nature trails to 35-mile treks. Some connect with each other, so you can design your own desert maze. Remember that drinking water is hard to come by—you won't find water in the park except at the entrances. Bring along at least a gallon per person for all but the shortest hikes, more if the weather is hot.

EASY

Bajada All Access. Learn all about what plants do to survive in the desert on this wheelchair-accessible ¼-mile loop. *Easy.* ✢ *Trailhead: south of Cottonwood Visitor Center, ½ mile from park entrance.*

Cap Rock. This ½-mile wheelchair-accessible loop—named after a boulder that sits atop a huge rock formation like a cap—winds through fascinating rock formations and has signs that explain the geology of the Mojave Desert. *Easy.* ✢ *Trailhead: at junction of Park Blvd. and Keys View Rd.*

FAMILY **Hidden Valley.** Crawl through the rocks surrounding Hidden Valley to see where cattle rustlers supposedly hung out on this 1-mile loop. *Easy.* ✢ *Trailhead: at Hidden Valley Picnic Area.*

Indian Cove Trail. Look for lizards and roadrunners along this ½-mile loop that follows a desert wash. A walk along this well-signed trail reveals signs of Indian habitation, animals, and flora such as desert willow and yucca. *Easy.* ⊹ *Trailhead: at west end of Indian Cove Campground.*

Oasis of Mara. A stroll along this short, wheelchair-accessible trail, located just outside the visitor center, reveals how early settlers took advantage of this oasis, which was first settled by the Serrano Indians. *Mara* means "place of little springs and much grass" in their language. The Serrano, who farmed the oasis until the mid-1850s, planted one palm tree for each male baby born during the first year of the settlement. *Easy.* ⊹ *Trailhead: at Oasis Visitor Center.*

Skull Rock Trail. The 1.7-mile loop guides hikers through boulder piles, desert washes, and a rocky alley. It's named for what is perhaps the park's most famous rock formation, which resembles a human head. Access the trail from within Jumbo Rocks Campground or from a small parking area on the highway just east of the campground. *Easy.* ⊹ *Trailhead: at Jumbo Rocks Campground.*

MODERATE

California Riding and Hiking Trail. This well-traveled route stretches for 35 miles between the Black Rock Canyon entrance and the north entrance. You can access the trail for a short or long hike at several points. The visitor centers have trail maps. *Moderate.* ⊹ *Trailheads: at Upper Covington Flats, Ryan Campground, Twin Tanks, south of north park entrance, and Black Rock Campground.*

Hi-View Nature Trail. This 1.3-mile loop climbs nearly to the top of 4,500-foot Summit Peak. The views of nearby Mount San Gorgonio (snow-capped in winter) make the moderately steep journey worth the effort. You can pick up a pamphlet describing the vegetation you'll see along the way at any visitor center. *Moderate.* ⊹ *Trailhead: ½ mile west of Black Rock Canyon Campground.*

Fodor'sChoice   **Ryan Mountain Trail.** The payoff for hiking to the top of 5,461-foot Ryan
★   Mountain is one of the best panoramic views of Joshua Tree. From here you can see Mount San Jacinto, Mount San Gorgonio, Lost Horse Valley, and the Pinto Basin. You'll need two to three hours to complete the 3-mile round-trip with 1,000-plus feet of elevation gain. *Moderate.* ⊹ *Trailhead: at Ryan Mountain parking area, 16 miles southeast of park's west entrance, or Sheep Pass, 16 miles southwest of Oasis Visitor Center.*

DIFFICULT

Boy Scout Trail. The moderately strenuous 8-mile trail, suitable for backpackers, extends from Indian Cove to Park Boulevard. It runs through the westernmost edge of the Wonderland of Rocks (where you're likely to see climbers on the outcroppings), passing through a forest of Joshua trees, past granite towers, and around willow-lined pools. Completing the round-trip journey requires camping along the way, so you may want to hike only part of the trail or have a car waiting at the other end. *Difficult.* ⊹ *Trailhead: between Quail Springs Picnic Area and Indian Cove Campground.*

Lost Palms Oasis Trail. Allow four to six hours for the moderately strenuous, 7¼-mile round-trip, which leads to the most impressive oasis in

the park. You'll find more than 100 fan palms and an abundance of wildflowers here. *Difficult.* ✛ *Trailhead: at Cottonwood Spring Oasis.*

Mastodon Peak Trail. Some boulder scrambling is required on this 3-mile hike that loops up to the 3,371-foot Mastodon Peak, but the journey rewards you with stunning views of the Salton Sea. The trail passes through a region where gold was mined from 1919 to 1932, so be on the lookout for open mines. The peak draws its name from a large rock formation that early miners believed looked like the head of a prehistoric behemoth. *Difficult.* ✛ *Trailhead: at Cottonwood Spring Oasis.*

ROCK CLIMBING

Fodor's Choice
★

With an abundance of weathered igneous boulder outcroppings, Joshua Tree is one of the nation's top winter-climbing destinations. There are more than 4,500 established routes offering a full menu of climbing experiences—from bouldering for beginners in the Wonderland of Rocks to multiple-pitch climbs at Echo Rock and Saddle Rock. The best-known climb in the park is Hidden Valley's Sports Challenge Rock. A map inside the *Joshua Tree Guide* shows locations of selected wilderness and nonwilderness climbs.

TOURS AND OUTFITTERS

Joshua Tree Rock Climbing School. The school offers several programs, from one-day introductory classes to multiday programs for experienced climbers, and provides all needed equipment. Beginning classes, offered year-round on most weekends, are limited to six people age eight or older. ✉ *Joshua Tree National Park* ☎ *760/366–4745, 800/890–4745* ⊕ *www.joshuatreerockclimbing.com* ✉ *From $175.*

Vertical Adventures Rock Climbing School. About 1,000 climbers each year learn the sport in Joshua Tree National Park through this school. Classes, offered September–May, meet at a designated location in the park, and all equipment is provided. ✉ *Joshua Tree National Park* ☎ *800/514–8785* ⊕ *www.verticaladventures.com* ✉ *From $145.*

WHAT'S NEARBY

NEARBY TOWNS

Palm Springs, about a 45-minute drive from the North Entrance Station at Joshua Tree, serves as the home base for most park visitors. This city of 46,000 has 95 golf courses, 600 tennis courts, and 50,000 swimming pools. A hideout for Hollywood stars since the 1920s, Palm Springs offers a glittering array of shops, restaurants, and hotels. Stroll down Palm Canyon Drive and you're sure to run into a celebrity or two.

About 9 miles north of Palm Springs and closer to the park is **Desert Hot Springs,** which has more than 1,000 natural hot mineral pools and 40 health spas ranging from low-key to luxurious. **Yucca Valley** is the largest and fastest growing of the communities straddling the park's

Joshua Tree NP
Western Area

northern border. The town boasts a handful of motels, supermarkets, and a Walmart. Tiny **Joshua Tree**, the closest community to the park's west entrance, is where the serious rock climbers make their headquarters. **Twentynine Palms**, known as "two-nine" by locals, is sandwiched between the Marine Corps Air Ground Task Force Center to the north and Joshua Tree National Park to the south. Here you'll find a smattering of coffeehouses, antiques shops, and cafés.

Visitor Information California Welcome Center Yucca Valley. ⊠ 56711 *Twentynine Palms Hwy., Yucca Valley* ☎ 760/365-5464 ⊕ *www.visitcwc. com.* **Joshua Tree Chamber of Commerce.** ⊠ *6448 Hallee Rd., Joshua Tree* ☎ 760/366-3723 ⊕ *www.joshuatreechamber.org.* **Palm Springs Bureau of Tourism.** ⊠ *2109 N. Palm Canyon Dr., Palm Springs* ☎ 760/778-8415, 800/348-7746 ⊕ *www.visitpalmsprings.com.* **Twentynine Palms Chamber of Commerce.** ⊠ *73484 Twentynine Palms Hwy., Twentynine Palms* ☎ 760/367-3445 ⊕ *www.29chamber.org.* **Yucca Valley Chamber of Commerce.** ⊠ *56711 Twentynine Palms Hwy., Yucca Valley* ☎ 760/365-6323 ⊕ *www.yuccavalley.org.*

NEARBY ATTRACTIONS

FAMILY   **Hi-Desert Nature Museum.** Creatures that make their homes in Joshua Tree National Park are the focus here. A small live-animal display includes scorpions, snakes, lizards, and small mammals. You'll also find rocks, minerals, and fossils from the Paleozoic era, taxidermy, and Native American artifacts. There's also a children's area and art exhibits. ⊠ *Yucca Valley Community Center, 57116 Twentynine Palms Hwy., Yucca Valley* ☎ *760/369–7212* ⊕ *hidesertnaturemuseum.org* ▭ *Free* ⊗ *Thurs.–Sat. 10–5.*

Oasis of Murals. Twenty-three murals painted on the sides of buildings depict the history and current lifestyle of Twentynine Palms. If you drive around town, you can't miss the murals, but you can also pick up a free map from the Twentynine Palms Chamber of Commerce. ⊠ *Twentynine Palms.*

Pioneertown. In 1946 Roy Rogers, Gene Autry, the Sons of the Pioneers (the music group for whom the town is named), and Russ Hayden built Pioneertown, an 1880s-style Wild West movie set complete with hitching posts, saloon, and an OK Corral. You can stroll past wooden and adobe storefronts and feel like you're back in the Old West. Or not: Pappy and Harriet's Pioneertown Palace, now the town's top draw, has evolved into a hip venue for indie and mainstream performers such as Dengue Fever, Neko Case, and Robert Plant. ⊠ *53688 Pioneertown Rd., 4 miles north of Yucca Valley, Pioneertown* ⊕ *pappyandharriets.com.*

WHERE TO EAT

IN THE PARK

PICNIC AREAS
Black Rock Canyon. Set among Joshua trees, pinyon pines, and junipers, this popular picnic area has barbecue grills and drinking water. It's one of the few with flush toilets. ⊹ *End of Joshua La. at the Black Rock Canyon Campground.*

Covington Flats. This is a great place to get away from crowds. There's just one table, and it's surrounded by flat, open desert dotted here and there by Joshua trees. ⊠ *La Contenta Rd., 10 miles from Rte. 62.*

Hidden Valley. Set among huge rock formations, with picnic tables shaded by dense trees, this is one of the most pleasant places in the park to stop for lunch. ⊠ *Park Blvd., 14 miles south of the west entrance.*

OUTSIDE THE PARK

$ ✕ **C&S Coffee Shop.** If you're yearning for pork chops and gravy for
AMERICAN   breakfast or eggs over easy for dinner, head to this tidy diner, which has been a local hangout since 1946. The typical diner menu also features soups, salads, and sandwiches, all cooked to order and presented in heaping portions. Don't miss the perfectly cooked fries. Expect a cheery

Learn about the park's flora and fauna by attending the ranger programs.

welcome and prompt service. $ *Average main: $8* ✉ *55795 Twentynine Palms Hwy., Yucca Valley* ☎ *760/365–9946.*

$
MEXICAN
✕ **Edchada's.** Rock climbers who spend their days in Joshua Tree swear by the margaritas at this Mexican eatery. Specialties include prodigious portions of fajitas, carnitas, seafood enchiladas, and fish tacos. $ *Average main: $12* ✉ *73502 Twentynine Palms Hwy., Twentynine Palms* ☎ *760/367–2131.*

$$$
AMERICAN
FAMILY
Fodor's Choice
★
✕ **Pappy & Harriet's Pioneertown Palace.** Smack in the middle of a Western-movie-set town is this Western-movie-set saloon where you can have dinner, relax over a drink at the bar, or check out some great indie and other bands—Leon Russell, Sonic Youth, the Get Up Kids, and Robert Plant have all played here, as have many Cali groups. The food ranges from Tex-Mex to Santa Maria–style barbecue to steak and burgers. No surprises, but plenty of fun. Pappy & Harriet's may be in the middle of nowhere, but you'll need reservations for dinner on weekends, especially on Sunday night. $ *Average main: $22* ✉ *53688 Pioneertown Rd., Pioneertown* ☎ *760/365–5956* ⊕ *www.pappyandharriets.com* ⊗ *Closed Tues. and Wed.* ⌔ *Reservations essential.*

$
CAFÉ
✕ **Park Rock Café.** If you're on your way to the national park on Highway 62, stop in the town of Joshua Tree to grab a hearty breakfast bagel sandwich and order a box lunch to take with you. The café creates some tasty sandwiches, including a healthy option with avocado and pesto mayo. The lentil barley soup is a favorite. Outside dining is pleasant here. $ *Average main: $9* ✉ *6554 Park Blvd., Joshua Tree* ☎ *760/366–8200* ⊕ *jtparkrockcafe.com* ⊗ *No dinner.*

WHERE TO STAY

OUTSIDE THE PARK

$$$
B&B/INN
FAMILY
Fodor's Choice
★

29 Palms Inn. The closest lodging to the entrance to Joshua Tree National Park, the funky 29 Palms Inn scatters a collection of adobe and wood-frame cottages, some dating back to the 1920s and 1930s, over 70 acres of grounds that include the ancient Oasis of Mara, a popular destination for birds and bird-watchers year-round. **Pros:** gracious hospitality; exceptional bird-watching; popular with artists. **Cons:** rustic accommodations; limited amenities. $ *Rooms from: $165* ⊠ *73950 Inn Ave., Twentynine Palms* ☎ *760/367–3505* ⊕ *www.29palmsinn.com* ↩ *20 rooms, 3 guesthouses* ❑ *Breakfast* ⊹.

$
B&B/INN

Casa Cody. The service is personal and gracious at this historic bed-and-breakfast near the Palm Springs Art Museum; spacious studios and one- and two-bedroom suites hold Santa Fe–style rustic furnishings. **Pros:** family-size digs; friendly ambience; good value. **Cons:** old buildings; limited amenities. $ *Rooms from: $99* ⊠ *175 S. Cahuilla Rd., Palm Springs* ☎ *760/320–9346, 800/231–2639* ⊕ *www.casacody.com* ↩ *18 rooms, 9 suites, 2 cottages* ❑ *Breakfast.*

$$$
B&B/INN
Fodor's Choice
★

Orbit In Hotel. The architectural style of this hip inn on a quiet back-street dates back to the late 1940s and '50s—nearly flat roofs, wide overhangs, glass everywhere—and the period feel continues inside. **Pros:** saltwater pool; in-room spa services; Orbitini cocktail hour. **Cons:** best for couples; style not to everyone's taste; staff not available 24 hours. $ *Rooms from: $169* ⊠ *562 W. Arenas Rd., Palm Springs* ☎ *760/323–3585, 877/996–7248* ⊕ *www.orbitin.com* ↩ *9 rooms* ❑ *Breakfast.*

$$
B&B/INN

Roughley Manor. To the wealthy pioneer who erected the stone mansion now occupied by this bed-and-breakfast, expense was no object, which is evident in the 50-foot-long planked maple floor in the great room, the intricate carpentry on the walls, and the huge stone fireplaces that warm the house on the rare cold night. **Pros:** elegant rooms and public spaces; good stargazing in the gazebo; great horned owls on property. **Cons:** somewhat isolated location; three-story main building doesn't have an elevator. $ *Rooms from: $135* ⊠ *74744 Joe Davis Dr., Twentynine Palms* ☎ *760/367–3238* ⊕ *www.roughleymanor.com* ↩ *2 suites, 7 cottages* ❑ *Breakfast.*

24

Best Campgrounds in Joshua Tree

Camping is the best way to experience the stark, exquisite beauty of Joshua Tree. You'll also have a rare opportunity to sleep outside in a semi-wilderness setting. The campgrounds, set at elevations from 3,000 to 4,500 feet, have only primitive facilities; few have drinking water. Black Rock and Indian Cove campgrounds, on the northern edge of the park, accept reservations up to six months in advance, and only for October through Memorial Day. Campsites elsewhere are on a first-come, first-served basis. Belle and White Tank campgrounds, and parts of Black Rock Canyon, Cottonwood, and Indian Cove campgrounds, are closed from the day after Memorial Day to September.

Belle Campground. This small campground is popular with families, as there are a number of boulders kids can scramble over and around. ✉ *9 miles south of Oasis of Mara* ☎ *760/367–5500* ⊕ *www.nps.gov/jotr.*

Black Rock Canyon Campground. Set among juniper bushes, cholla cacti, and other desert shrubs, Black Rock Canyon is one of the prettiest campgrounds in ✉ *Joshua Tree. Joshua La., south of Hwy. 62 and Hwy. 247* ☎ *760/367–5500* ⊕ *www.recreation.gov.*

Cottonwood Campground. In spring this campground, the southernmost one in the park (and therefore often the last to fill up), is surrounded by some of the desert's finest wildflowers and is a great spot to watch the night sky. ✉ *Pinto Basin Rd., 32 miles south of North Entrance Station* ☎ *760/367–5500* ⊕ *www.nps.gov/jotr.*

Hidden Valley Campground. This campground is a favorite with rock climbers, who make their way up valley formations that have names like the Blob, Old Woman, and Chimney Rock. ✉ *Off Park Blvd., 20 miles southwest of Oasis of Mara* ☎ *760/367–5500* ⊕ *www.nps.gov/jotr.*

Indian Cove Campground. This is a sought-after spot for rock climbers, primarily because it lies among the 50 square miles of rugged terrain at the Wonderland of Rocks. ✉ *Indian Cove Rd., south of Hwy. 62* ☎ *760/367–5500* ⊕ *www.nps.gov/jotr.*

Jumbo Rocks. Each campsite at this well-regarded campground tucked among giant boulders has a bit of privacy. It's a good home base for visiting many of Joshua Tree's attractions. ✉ *Park Blvd., 11 miles from Oasis of Mara* ☎ *760/367–5500* ⊕ *www.nps.gov/jotr.*

White Tank. This small, quiet campground is popular with families because a nearby trail leads to a natural arch. ✉ *Pinto Basin Rd., 11 miles south of Oasis of Mara* ☎ *760/367–5500* ⊕ *www.nps.gov/jotr.*

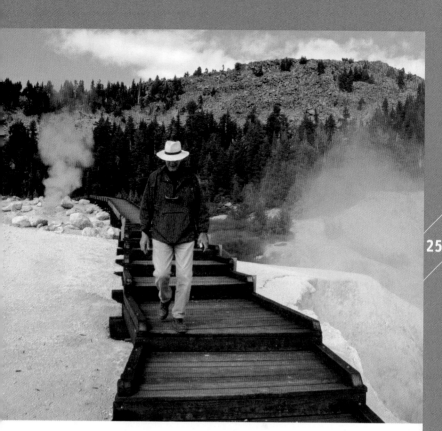

LASSEN VOLCANIC NATIONAL PARK

WELCOME TO LASSEN VOLCANIC NATIONAL PARK

TOP REASONS TO GO

★ **Hike a volcano:** The 2½-mile trek up Lassen Peak rewards you with a spectacular view of far northern California.

★ **Spot a rare bloom:** The Lassen Smelowskia, a small white-to-pinkish flower, grows only in Lassen Volcanic National Park, mainly on Lassen Peak.

★ **View volcano varieties:** All four types of volcanoes found in the world—shield, plug dome, cinder cone, and composite—are represented here.

★ **Listen to the Earth:** The park's thumping mud pots and venting fumaroles roil, gurgle, and belch a raucous symphony from beneath the Earth's crust.

★ **Escape the crowds:** Lassen, in sparsely populated far northern California, is one of the lesser-known national parks.

1 Southwest. Hydrothermal activity is greatest in the southwestern area; you'll see evidence on hikes to Bumpass Hell and Devils Kitchen. Walkways beside the former Sulphur Works on Lassen Park Highway, just past the Kohm Yah-mah-nee Visitor Center, provide easy access to smelly, belching fumaroles.

2 Middle. Marsh meadows and stunning falls highlight the Kings Creek area in the park's southern midsection. Farther north, Summit Lake—amid a red fir forest at an elevation of about 6,700 feet—has two campgrounds and a trail leading to several smaller lakes.

Prospect Peak
8,338 ft
Butte Lake

Cinder Cone

PAINTED DUNES

Fairfield
Peak

FANTASTIC LAVA BEDS

Ash Butte

Snag
Lake

Crater Butte

GRASSY SWALE

Horseshoe
Lake

Juniper
Lake

Warner Valley

Pacific Crest Trail

TO
CHESTER ↓

CALIFORNIA

GETTING ORIENTED

From gurgling mud pots and hissing steam vents, to tranquil lakes and lily-covered ponds, to jagged mountain peaks bordered by flowering meadows, Lassen Volcanic National Park's varied landscapes are certain to soothe, awe, and intrigue. Whether you want to climb to the top of a dormant volcano or simply loll at the water's edge as birdsong drifts down from tall pines, you'll find unexpected pleasures in this park formed by molten lava.

25

3 Northwest. Lassen Park Highway winds past the barren rubble of Devastated Area, providing stunning views of Lassen Peak and passing Chaos Jumbles before reaching lush, wooded Manzanita Lake.

4 Eastern. Among the delights found in the least accessible and least visited part of the park are Cinder Cone and Ash Butte, lava beds, and meadows, plus beautiful Snag and Juniper lakes and the many creeks that flow out of them.

KEY	
🏕	Ranger Station
▲	Campground
⊞	Picnic Area
🍴	Restaurant
🏨	Lodge
🚶	Trailhead
🚻	Restrooms
⤳	Scenic Viewpoint
⋯⋯	Walking/Hiking Trails

Updated by Andrew Collins

A dormant plug dome, Lassen Peak is the main focus of Lassen Volcanic National Park, but this 165-square-mile tract of dense forests and alpine meadows also abounds with memorable opportunities for hiking, camping, and wildlife photography. The famed peak began erupting in May 1914, sending pumice, rock, and snow thundering down the mountain, and gas and hot ash billowing into the atmosphere. Lassen's most spectacular outburst was in 1915, when it blew a cloud of ash almost 6 miles high. The resulting mudflow destroyed vegetation for miles; the evidence is still visible today, especially in Devastated Area. The volcano finally came to rest in 1921.

LASSEN VOLCANIC PLANNER

WHEN TO GO

The park is open year-round, though most roads are closed from late October to mid-June due to snow.

AVG. HIGH/LOW TEMPS.

Jan.	Feb.	Mar.	Apr.	May	June
50/13	51/13	53/16	61/23	70/29	79/34
July	Aug.	Sept.	Oct.	Nov.	Dec.
84/40	85/40	78/36	69/30	56/21	50/14

PLANNING YOUR TIME

LASSEN VOLCANIC IN ONE DAY

Start your day early at the park's northwest entrance, accessible via Highway 44 from Redding. Make a stop at the **Loomis Museum**, where you can view exhibits before taking the easy, 1-mile round-trip **Lily Pond Nature Trail**. Back at the museum, drive down to **Manzanita Lake**. Take a mid-morning break and pick up supplies at the **Camper Store** for a picnic lunch before taking the main road toward **Lassen Peak**. As you circle the peak on its northern flank, you come on **Devastated Area,** testimony to the damage done by the 1915 eruptions. Continue to **Summit Lake,** where you can picnic and swim, or to **Kings Creek,** an area of lush meadows where you can hike to **Kings Creek Falls.** Allow at least two hours to make the 3-mile round-trip hike, which ends in a 700-foot descent to the falls. If time permits, continue to the **Sulphur Works** to stroll sidewalks that skirt sulfur-emitting steam vents.

GETTING HERE AND AROUND

AIR TRAVEL

Redding Municipal Airport (RDD), the nearest commercial airport to the park, is about an hour's drive west of either entrance. United Express flies twice daily from San Francisco. Most major airlines serve the airports in Reno, a 2½-hour drive, and Sacramento, a three-hour drive.

CAR TRAVEL

From the north, take the Highway 44 exit off Interstate 5 in Redding and drive east about 48 miles to the park entrance, at the junction with Highway 89. Turn right and drive 1 mile to the northwest entrance station. From the south, take the Highway 36 exit off Interstate 5 in Red Bluff and head east 45 miles, turning left onto Highway 89. From here it's about 4 miles to the southwest entrance ranger station. The 30-mile main park road, officially called Lassen Volcanic National Park Highway but often called simply Lassen Park Highway, starts at the southwest entrance. The highway skirts around the southern, eastern, and northern sides of Lassen Peak and exits the park on the northwestern side.

PARK ESSENTIALS

PARK FEES AND PERMITS

From mid-April through November the fee to enter the park is $20 per car ($15 for motorcycles); the rest of the year the fee is $10 for cars and motorcycles. The fee covers seven consecutive days. Those entering by bus, bicycle, horse, or on foot pay $10. An annual park pass costs $40. For backcountry camping, pick up a free wilderness permit at the Loomis Museum or the north and south entrance ranger stations, or download one at ⊕ *www.nps.gov/lavo.*

PARK HOURS

The park is open 24/7 year-round. It is in the Pacific time zone.

CELL-PHONE RECEPTION

Cell phones don't work in many parts of the park. There are pay telephones outside the Manzanita Camper Store and the Loomis Museum.

25

EDUCATIONAL OFFERINGS

If you're wondering why fumaroles fume, how lava tubes are formed, or which critter left those tracks beside the creek, check out the array of ranger-led programs. Most groups meet outside Loomis Museum or near Manzanita Lake. To learn what's available and at what time, see park bulletin boards.

RANGER PROGRAMS

Bear Necessities. Learn about black bears at this ranger-led talk that takes less than an hour. ⊠ *Outside Loomis Museum, north entrance* ☎ *530/595–4480* ⊕ *www.nps.gov/lavo* ☺ *Mid-June–mid-Aug.*

Early Birds. Take a morning stroll and learn about the birds of Manzanita Lake. ⊠ *Lassen Volcanic National Park* ✚ *Meet outside the Manzanita Lake Camp Store* ☎ *530/595–4480* ⊕ *www.nps.gov/lavo.*

FAMILY **Kids Program.** Junior Rangers, ages seven to 12, meet for 45 minutes three times a week with rangers. Junior Firefighters gather on Thursday morning to learn about the role wildfires have in shaping our national parks. Youngsters unable to attend the sessions can earn patches by completing certain requirements. Those under seven can join the Chipmunk Club and get a sticker after filling out a nature sheet. ⊠ *Lassen Volcanic National Park* ☎ *530/595–4480* ⊕ *www.nps.gov/lavo* ☞ *Call or check at visitor centers for meeting places.*

Starry Nights. Beneath the night sky, rangers discuss myths and contemporary theories about galaxies, stars, and planets in a 45-minute program. ⊠ *Devastated Area parking lot, Lassen Park Hwy., 2½ miles north of Summit Lake* ☎ *530/595–4480* ⊕ *www.nps.gov/lavo.*

Volcanoes! Explore the park's geology and volcanic history. ⊠ *Lassen Volcanic National Park* ✚ *Meet outside Loomis Museum* ☎ *530/595–4480* ⊕ *www.nps.gov/lavo* ☺ *Call for times.*

RESTAURANTS

Dining options within the park are limited to simple fare at Lassen Café & Gift in Kohm Yah-mah-nee Visitor Center and at the Manzanita Lake Camper Store, and the delicious meals at Drakesbad Guest Ranch. Nonguests can call ahead to make reservations for breakfast, lunch, and dinner at the ranch (☎ 866/999–0914). The nearest community with a good mix of mostly casual dining options is Chester, about a half-hour drive from the southwest entrance station. About an hour away, the small cities of Red Bluff and Redding have more extensive restaurant selections.

HOTELS

Other than the camping cabins at Manzanita Lake, Drakesbad Guest Ranch is the only lodging available inside Lassen. It's rustic (no electricity, just old-fashioned kerosene lamps), expensive, and popular: the ranch is often fully booked a year or more in advance for summer stays. The towns surrounding the park have bed-and-breakfasts, chain hotels, motels, and other lodgings. *Hotel reviews have been shortened. For full information, visit Fodors.com.*

WHAT IT COSTS				
	$	$$	$$$	$$$$
Restaurants	under $13	$13–$20	$21–$30	over $30
Hotels	under $100	$100–$150	$151–$200	over $200

Restaurant prices are the average cost of a main course at dinner, or if dinner is not served, at lunch. Hotel prices are the lowest cost of a standard double room in high season, excluding taxes and service charges.

VISITOR INFORMATION

Park Contact Information Lassen Volcanic National Park Headquarters.
⊠ *38050 Hwy. 36 E, Mineral* ☎ *530/595–6100* ⊕ *www.nps.gov/lavo.*

VISITOR CENTER

Kohm Yah-mah-nee Visitor Center. A handsome contemporary structure at the southwest entrance, the center is a handy stop. You can pick up maps and trail and road guides, inquire about children's activities and ranger-led programs, view an engaging film about the park, and check out the well-conceived interactive exhibits. There are restrooms and first-aid facilities here, and an excellent bookstore. The casual Lassen Café & Gift is a good light-lunch option—the best spot to dine is outdoors at one of the mountain-view picnic tables. ⊠ *Lassen Volcanic National Park Hwy., north of Mineral* ☎ *530/595–4480* ⊕ *www.nps.gov/lavo/ planyourvisit/visitorcenters.htm* ☉ *Visitor center Apr.–Nov., daily 9–5; Dec.–Mar., Wed.–Sun. 9–5. Café closed weekdays mid-Oct.–late May.*

EXPLORING

SCENIC DRIVES

Fodor's Choice ★ **Volcanic Legacy Scenic Byway.** This 185-mile scenic drive begins in Chester and loops through the forests, volcanic peaks, hydrothermal springs, and lava fields of Lassen National Forest and Lassen Volcanic National Park, providing an all-day excursion into dramatic wilderness. From Chester, take Highway 36 west to Highway 89 north, which within the park is called Lassen Volcanic National Park Highway, or Lassen Park Highway. Upon exiting the park at the north, follow Highway 44 east and then south to Highway 36, on which you can head back west to Chester. Parts of this route are inaccessible in winter. ⊠ *Lassen Volcanic National Park* ☎ *800/427–7623 CA Highway info service, 530/595–4480 Lassen Park visitor center.*

HISTORIC SITES

Loomis Museum. Here you can view artifacts from the park's 1914 and 1915 eruptions, including dramatic original photographs taken by Benjamin Loomis, who was instrumental in the park's establishment. The museum also has a bookstore, and there are excellent exhibits about the area's American Indian heritage. ⊠ *Lassen Park Hwy. at Manzanita Lake* ☎ *530/595–6140* ☜ *Free* ☉ *Memorial Day–late Oct., daily 9–5.*

Plants and Wildlife in Lassen Volcanic

Because of its varying elevations, Lassen has several different ecological habitats.

BELOW 6,500 FEET

Below 6,500 feet you can find ponderosa pine, Jeffrey pine, sugar pine, white fir, and several species of manzanita, gooseberry, and Ceanothus. Wildflowers—wild iris, spotted coralroot, pyrola, violets, and lupine—surround the hiking trails in spring and early summer.

MANZANITA LAKE AREA

The Manzanita Lake area has the best bird-watching opportunities, with yellow warblers, pied-billed grebes, white-headed and hairy woodpeckers, golden-crowned kinglets, and Steller's jays. The area is also home to rubber boas, garter snakes, brush rabbits, Sierra Nevada red foxes, black-tailed deer, coyotes, and the occasional mountain lion.

FROM 6,500 TO 8,000 FEET

At elevations of 6,500 to 8,000 feet are red fir forests populated by many of the same wildlife as the lower regions, with the addition of black-backed three-toed woodpeckers, blue grouse, snowshoe hare, pine martens, and the hermit thrush.

ABOVE 8,000 FEET

Above 8,000 feet the environment is harsher, with bare patches of land between subalpine forests. You'll find whitebark pine, groves of mountain hemlock, small pikas, yellow-bellied marmots, and the occasional black bear. Bird-watchers should look for gray-crowned rosy finches, rock wrens, golden eagles, falcons, and hawks. California tortoiseshell butterflies are found on the highest peaks. If you can visit in winter, you'll see one of the park's most magnificent seasonal sights: massive snowdrifts up to 30 and 40 feet high.

SCENIC STOPS

Boiling Springs Lake. A worthwhile, if occasionally muddy, 3-mile hike leads from the Drakesbad Guest Ranch to Boiling Springs Lake, which is surrounded by steep cliffs topped with trees. Constant bubbles release sulfuric steam into the air. ✛ *Trailhead parking near end of Warner Valley Rd., close to Drakesbad Guest Ranch.*

Fodor's Choice ★ **Bumpass Hell.** This site's quirky name came about when a man with the last name of Bumpass was severely burned after falling into the boiling springs. A scenic but strenuous 3-mile round-trip hike brings you close to hot springs, hissing steam vents, and roiling mud pots. ✛ *Trailhead at paved parking area off Lassen Park Hwy., 6 miles from southwest entrance ranger station.*

Chaos Jumbles. More than 350 years ago, an avalanche from the Chaos Crags lava domes scattered hundreds of thousands of rocks—many of them from 2 to 3 feet in diameter—over a couple of square miles. ✉ *Lassen Park Hwy., 2 miles northeast of the northwest entrance ranger station.*

Devils Kitchen. One of the park's three main geothermal areas, this is a great place to view mud pots, steam vents, and boiling pools. It's much

less frequented than Bumpass Hell, so you can expect more wildlife during your moderately difficult 4.2-mile round-trip hike. You need to drive on a partially paved road to reach the trailhead. ⊹ *Trailhead parking near end of Warner Valley Rd., close to Drakesbad Guest Ranch.*

Fodor's Choice
★
Lassen Peak. When this now-dormant plug dome volcano erupted in 1915, it spewed a huge mushroom cloud of debris almost 6 miles into the air. A fabulous panoramic view makes the strenuous 2½-mile hike to the 10,457-foot summit worth the effort. ⊠ *Lassen Park Hwy., 7 miles from southwest entrance ranger station* ☎ *530/595–4480.*

Manzanita Lake. Lassen Peak is reflected in the waters of the lake, which has good catch-and-release trout fishing and a pleasant trail for exploring the area's abundant wildlife. ⊠ *Lassen Park Hwy., at northwest entrance ranger station.*

FAMILY
Sulphur Works Thermal Area. Proof of Lassen Peak's volatility becomes evident shortly after you enter the park at the southwest entrance. Sidewalks skirt boiling springs and sulfur-emitting steam vents. This area is usually the last site to close because of snow. ⊠ *Lassen Park Hwy., 1 mile from the southwest entrance ranger station.*

Summit Lake. The midpoint between the northern and southern entrances, Summit Lake is a good place to take an afternoon swim. A trail leads around the lakeshore, and several other trails diverge toward a cluster of smaller lakes in the more remote eastern section of the park. ⊠ *Lassen Park Hwy., 17½ miles from southwest entrance ranger station.*

SPORTS AND THE OUTDOORS

Lassen is a rugged adventurer's paradise, but be prepared for sudden changes in the weather: fierce thunderstorms sometimes drench the mountains, and blizzard conditions can develop quickly in winter. In summer, hot temperatures can make high-altitude hikers woozy.

BICYCLING

Biking is allowed on park roads but not trails. Cyclists under 18 must wear a helmet. Skateboarding and rollerblading are prohibited.

OUTFITTERS
Bodfish Bicycles & Quiet Mountain Sports. Rent mountain bikes here for $10 an hour or $33 a day. ⊠ *149 Main St., Chester* ☎ *530/258–2338* ⊕ *www.bodfishbicycles.com.*

Redding Sports Ltd. Bike rentals here run $40 for the first 24 hours, $25 for each additional day. ⊠ *950 Hilltop Dr., Redding* ☎ *530/221–7333* ⊕ *www.reddingsportsltd.com.*

FISHING

The best place to fish is in Manzanita Lake, though it's catch and release only. Butte, Snag, and Horseshoe lakes, along with several creeks and streams, are also popular fishing destinations within the park. Anglers will need a California freshwater fishing license; you can pick up an application at most sporting-goods stores or download it from the California Department of Fish and Wildlife's website (⊕ *www.dfg.ca.gov*). Ask about fishing conditions at bait-and-tackle shops.

OUTFITTERS

Ayoobs Hardware. Stop by Ayoobs for tackle, bait, and local lore. ⊠ *201 Main St., Chester* ☎ *530/258–2611.*

The Fishen Hole. A couple of miles from the lake, this bait-and-tackle shop sells fishing licenses and provides information about conditions. ⊠ *3844 Shasta Dam Blvd., at Red Bluff Ave., Shasta Lake* ☎ *530/275–4123.*

The Sports Nut. Buy fishing and camping gear at the Sports Nut. ⊠ *208 Main St., Chester* ☎ *530/258–3327.*

HIKING

Of the 150 miles of hiking trails within the park, 18 miles are part of the Pacific Crest Trail through California, Oregon, and Washington. Trails vary greatly, some winding through coniferous forest and others across rocky alpine slopes or along meandering waterways.

EASY

FAMILY **Lily Pond Nature Trail.** This 1-mile jaunt loops past a small lake and through a wooded area, ending at a pond that is filled with yellow water lilies in summer. Marked with interpretive signs, this easy trail is a good choice for families with kids. *Easy.* ✛ *Trailhead: across road from Loomis Museum, Lassen Park Hwy., near northwest entrance ranger station.*

MODERATE

Fodor's Choice **Bumpass Hell Trail.** Boiling springs, steam vents, and mud pots are the ★ highlights of this 3-mile round-trip hike. Expect the loop to take about two hours. During the first mile there's a gradual climb of 500 feet before a steep 300-foot descent to the basin. You'll encounter rocky patches, so wear hiking boots. Stay on trails and boardwalks near the thermal areas, as what appears to be firm ground may be only a thin crust over scalding mud. *Moderate.* ✛ *Trailhead: at end of paved parking area off Lassen Park Hwy., 6 miles from southwest entrance ranger station.*

Kings Creek Falls Hike. Nature photographers love this 3-mile round-trip hike through forests dotted with wildflowers. A steep 700-foot descent leads to the spectacular falls. It can be slippery in spots, so watch your step. Be in good shape for this hike. *Moderate.* ✛ *Trailhead: on southeast side of Lassen Park Hwy., 12 miles from southwest entrance ranger station.*

Mill Creek Falls. This 2½-hour 3.8-mile round-trip hike through forests and wildflowers takes you to where East Sulphur and Bumpass creeks merge to create the park's highest waterfall. *Moderate.* ✛ *Trailhead: on east side of Southwest Walk-In Campground parking lot.*

DIFFICULT

Fodor's Choice
★
Lassen Peak Hike. This trail winds 2½ miles to the mountaintop. It's a tough climb—2,000 feet uphill on a steady, steep grade—but the reward is a spectacular view. At the peak you can see into the rim and view the entire park (and much of California's far north). Bring sunscreen, water, snacks, a first-aid kit, and, because it can be windy and cold at the summit, a jacket. ⚓ *Trailhead: at parking area off Lassen Park Hwy., 7 miles north of the southwest entrance ranger station* ☎ *530/595–4480.*

HORSEBACK RIDING

Drakesbad Guest Ranch. This property operated by the park's concessionaire offers guided rides to nonguests who make reservations. Among the options is a two-hour lope to Devils Kitchen. There's also a five-lake loop for advanced riders. ✉ *End of Warner Valley Rd., Chester* ☎ *866/999–0914* ⊕ *www.drakesbad.com* ▧ *From $55* ◷ *Early June–mid-Oct.*

SNOWSHOEING

You can try snowshoeing anywhere in the park. The gentlest places are in the northern district, while more challenging terrain is in the south.

■**TIP→** Beware of hidden cavities in the snow. Park officials warn that heated sulfur emissions, especially in the Sulphur Works Area, can melt out dangerous snow caverns, which may be camouflaged by thin layers of fresh snow that skiers and snowshoers can easily fall through.

TOURS AND OUTFITTERS

Lassen Mineral Lodge. The lodge rents snowshoes for $12 a day, skis and poles for $16. ✉ *38348 Hwy. 36, Mineral* ☎ *530/595–4422* ⊕ *www. minerallodge.com.*

Redding Sports Ltd. The shop rents snowshoes for $15 a day; skis, boots, and poles go for $20 per day. ✉ *950 Hilltop Dr., Redding* ☎ *530/221–7333* ⊕ *www.reddingsportsltd.com.*

Snowshoe Walks. On weekends from late December through early April, park rangers lead two-hour snowshoe walks that explore the park's geology and winter ecology. The hikes require moderate exertion at an elevation of 7,000 feet; children under age eight are not allowed. If you don't have snowshoes you can borrow a pair; $1 donation suggested. Walks are first come, first served; meet outside the Kohm Yah-mah-nee Visitor Center. ✉ *Lassen Park Hwy., near southwest entrance ranger station* ☎ *530/595–4480* ⊕ *www.nps.gov/lavo* ▧ *Free* ◷ *Late Dec.– early Apr., weekends at 1:30.*

WHAT'S NEARBY

NEARBY TOWNS

The tiny logging town of **Chester**, 30 miles from the southwest park entrance on Highway 36, serves as the commercial center for the Lake Almanor area. With a population of about 2,100, it contains a handful of accommodations and services and is a good base for exploring the park. **Susanville**, population 18,000, a high-desert town 35 miles east of Chester, has some basic motels and restaurants. **Red Bluff**, population 14,000, blends Old West toughness and late-1800s gentility: restored Victorians line the streets west of Main Street, while the downtown looks like a stage set for a Western. Red Bluff is a good place to stock up before heading into the park; it's 52 miles from Lassen's southwest entrance via Highway 36.

With a population of 92,000, **Redding** is the largest city in far Northern California and the area's main commercial center. Redding is 32 miles north of Red Bluff via Interstate 5, and 50 miles west of the park's northwest entrance via Highway 44.

Red Bluff and Redding have the most accommodations and services in the area; each is an hour's drive from the park.

Visitor Information Lake Almanor Area Chamber of Commerce. ⊠ *328 Main St., Suite 6, Chester* ☎ *530/258–2426* ⊕ *www.lakealmanorarea.com.* **Lassen County Chamber of Commerce.** ⊠ *75 N. Weatherlow St., Susanville* ☎ *530/257–4323* ⊕ *www.lassencountychamber.org.* **Red Bluff–Tehama County Chamber of Commerce.** ⊠ *100 Main St., Red Bluff* ☎ *530/527–6220, 800/655–6225* ⊕ *www.redbluffchamber.com.* **Redding Convention and Visitors Bureau.** ⊠ *844 Sundial Bridge Dr., Redding* ☎ *800/874–7562, 530/225–4100* ⊕ *www. visitredding.com.* **Shasta Cascade Wonderland Association.** ⊠ *1699 Hwy. 273, Anderson* ☎ *530/365–1258, 800/474–2784* ⊕ *www.shastacascade.com.*

NEARBY ATTRACTIONS

Fodor's Choice ★ **Lake Shasta Caverns National Natural Landmark.** Stalagmites, stalactites, flowstone deposits, and crystals entice visitors to the Lake Shasta Caverns. To see this impressive spectacle, you must take the two-hour tour, which includes a catamaran ride across the McCloud arm of Lake Shasta and a bus ride up North Grey Rocks Mountain to the cavern entrance. The temperature in the caverns is 58°F year-round, making them a cool retreat on a hot summer day. The most awe-inspiring of the limestone rock formations is the glistening Cathedral Room, which appears to be gilded. ⊠ *20359 Shasta Caverns Rd., Exit 695 off I–5, 17 miles north of Redding, Lakehead* ☎ *530/238–2341, 800/795–2283* ⊕ *www.lakeshastacaverns.com* ⊠ *$24* ⊙ *June–Aug., tours on the half hr, daily 9–4; Apr., May, and Sept., tours on the hr, daily 9–3; Oct.– Mar., tours at 10, noon, and 2.*

FAMILY
Fodor's Choice ★ **Turtle Bay Exploration Park.** This park has walking trails, an arboretum and botanical gardens, and many interactive exhibits for kids, including a gold-panning area. The main draw is the stunning **Sundial Bridge,**

which links the Sacramento River Trail and the park's arboretum and gardens. Access to the bridge and arboretum is free, but there's a fee for the museum. ⊠ *844 Sundial Bridge Dr., Redding* ☎ *530/243–8850, 800/887–8532* ⊕ *www.turtlebay.org* ⊡ *Museum $16* ☉ *Mid-Mar.–early Sept., Mon.–Sat. 9–5, Sun. 10–5; early Sept.–mid-Mar., Wed.–Sat. 9–4, Sun. 10–4.*

AREA ACTIVITIES

Whether you want to camp in national forests, wade in creeks, watch dragonflies dip over meadows thick with wildflowers, or stargaze while listening to a chorus of crickets, the great outdoors is the draw here. When you're ready to merge with civilization, the towns near Lassen Volcanic offer shopping, movies, dining, and a bit of people-watching.

SPORTS AND THE OUTDOORS

BOATING AND FISHING

Twenty-one types of fish, including rainbow trout and salmon, inhabit Lake Shasta, which is about a 75-minute drive northwest of Lassen Volcanic National Park. The lake area also has one of the state's largest nesting populations of bald eagles. Rent boats, Jet Skis, and windsurfing boards at marinas and resorts along the 370-mile shoreline. The Sacramento River and its numerous creeks and tributaries also attract fishing enthusiasts from across the country.

WHERE TO EAT

IN THE PARK

$ ✕ **Lassen Café & Gift.** Coffee and hot cocoa, wine and beer (including
CAFÉ local brews from Lassen Ale Works), and sandwiches, burgers, soups, salads, bagels, and pizzas are on the menu here. Indoors, there's a fireplace, but if the weather is fine the patio, with its mountain views, is the place to be. ⑤ *Average main: $9* ⊠ *Kohm Yah-mah-nee Visitor Center, Lassen Park Hwy.* ☎ *530/595–3555* ⊕ *www.lassenrecreation. com* ☉ *Closed weekdays mid-Oct.–late May.*

$ ✕ **Manzanita Lake Camper Store.** Pick up simple prepared foods, grocer-
CAFÉ ies, and beverages—local wines and beers among them—at the store, which has an ATM and a pay phone. ⑤ *Average main: $9* ⊠ *Manzanita Lake Campground, Lassen Park Hwy.* ☎ *530/335–7557* ⊕ *www. lassenrecreation.com* ☉ *Closed mid-Oct.–late May.*

PICNIC AREAS

Kings Creek. Trees shade these creekside picnic tables. Vault toilets are the only amenities. ⊹ *Off Lassen Park Hwy., 11½ miles north of southwest entrance ranger station* ⊕ *www.nps.gov/lavo.*

Lake Helen. This site with picnic tables and vault toilets has views of several peaks, including Lassen Peak. ⊠ *Lassen Park Hwy.* ⊹ *6 miles north of southwest entrance ranger station, near Bumpass Hell trailhead* ⊕ *www.nps.gov/lavo.*

OUTSIDE THE PARK

$$$ ✕ **Artisan's View Restaurant.** Dining at this contemporary roadhouse is in
AMERICAN a stained-wood, high-ceiling room indoors, or out on the deck, which
has views of a broad serene meadow and the hillside beyond. Opened
in 2015 as part of the luxurious Highlands Ranch Resort and among
the few sophisticated eating options within Lassen's orbit, Artisan's
View deservedly became an instant hit. Favorites on the regional Ameri-
can menu include blackened medium-rare ahi with carrot-cucumber
slaw, and balsamic-marinated Muscovy duck with blackberries and
wild mushrooms. Lighter bar fare like beef sliders with whiskey bar-
becue sauce is served, too. ⑤ *Average main: $27* ✉ *Highlands Ranch
Resort, 41515 Hwy. 36 E* ☎ *530/595–3388* ⊕ *highlandsranchresort.
com/artisans-view-restaurant.*

$ ✕ **Lassen Ale Works.** Installed within the atmospheric confines of Susan-
AMERICAN ville's 1860s Pioneer Saloon, this brewery earns kudos for its expertly
crafted ales, many of them named for local sites. The Lassen-inspired
Volcanic Double IPA is a standout. The kitchen turns out deftly pre-
pared comfort food such as Basque-style fall-off-the-bone lamb stew
and beer-braised-sausage sandwiches. ⑤ *Average main: $11* ✉ *724
Main St., Susanville* ☎ *530/257–7666* ⊕ *www.lassenaleworks.com.*

WHERE TO STAY

IN THE PARK

$$$$ 🏨 **Drakesbad Guest Ranch.** With propane furnaces and kerosene lamps,
B&B/INN everything about this century-old property in the park's remote but
Fodor's Choice beautiful southeastern corner harks back to a simpler time. **Pros:** back-
★ to-nature experience; great for family adventures; only full-service lodg-
ing inside the park. **Cons:** accessible only via a partially paved road
leading out of Chester; rustic, with few in-room frills. ⑤ *Rooms from:
$354* ✉ *End of Warner Valley Rd., Chester* ☎ *866/999–0914* ⊕ *www.
drakesbad.com* ☉ *Closed mid-Oct.–early June* ⇆ *19 rooms* ⏧ *All meals.*

OUTSIDE THE PARK

$$ 🏨 **Bidwell House.** Some guest rooms at this 1901 ranch house have
B&B/INN wood-burning stoves, claw-foot tubs, and antique furnishings; a sepa-
Fodor's Choice rate cottage with a kitchen sleeps six. **Pros:** unique decor in each room;
★ beautiful wooded setting; near Lake Almanor. **Cons:** not ideal for kids.
⑤ *Rooms from: $125* ✉ *1 Main St., Chester* ☎ *530/258–3338* ⊕ *www.
bidwellhouse.com* ⇆ *14 rooms, 2 with shared bath* ⏧ *Breakfast.*

$ 🏨 **High Country Inn.** Rooms are spacious in this colonial-style motel east
HOTEL of Lassen National Park in Susanville, about a 75-minute drive away
from either of the main park entrances. **Pros:** great mountain views;
seasonal heated pool. **Cons:** lots of traffic in the area; more than an
hour's drive from the park. ⑤ *Rooms from: $93* ✉ *3015 Riverside Dr.,
Susanville* ☎ *530/257–3450, 866/454–4566* ⊕ *www.high-country-inn.
com* ⇆ *66 rooms* ⏧ *Breakfast.*

25

Best Campgrounds in Lassen Volcanic

Lassen's eight campgrounds draw a broad range of campers, from large groups singing around a mesmerizing fire to solitary hikers seeking a quiet place under the stars. You can drive a vehicle to all campgrounds except the Southwest Walk-In. This is the only campground open year-round; the others usually open in June and close in early fall. Campfires are restricted to fire rings. Lassen has black bears, so be sure to secure your food and garbage properly by using the bear boxes provided at the park's campsites. For more camping information, go to ⊕ www.nps.gov/lavo/planyourvisit/camping_in_campgrounds.htm. For reservations, visit ⊕ www.recreation.gov.

Juniper Lake. On the east shore of the park's largest lake, these campsites are close to the water in a wooded area. To reach them, you have to take a rough gravel road that leads 13 miles north of Chester and enters at the park's southeast corner; trailers are not advised. There is no potable water here. ⊠ Chester Juniper Lake Rd., about 13 miles north of Hwy. 36. No reservations.

Manzanita Lake. The largest of Lassen campgrounds accommodates RVs up to 35 feet and has 20 rustic cabins. Many ranger programs begin here, and a trail nearby leads to the crater that holds Crags Lake. ⊠ Off Lassen Park Hwy., 2 miles east of junction of Hwys. 44 and 89 ☎ 530/595–6121 or 877/444–6777.

Southwest Walk-In. Relatively small and Lassen's only campground open year-round, Southwest lies within a red fir forest and has views of Brokeoff Peak. Snow camping is allowed, but from October to June no drinking water is available. ⊠ Near southwest entrance, beside Kohm Yah-mah-nee Visitor Center. No reservations.

Summit Lake North. This completely forested campground has easy access to backcountry trails. You'll likely observe deer grazing. ⊠ Lassen Park Hwy., 12 miles south of Manzanita Lake and 17½ miles north of southwest entrance. ☎ 530/595–6121 or 877/444–6777.

Summit Lake South. Less crowded than its neighbor to the north, this campground has wet meadows where wildflowers grow in the spring. No potable water is available after mid-September. ⊠ Lassen Park Hwy., 12 miles south of Manzanita Lake and 17½ miles north of southwest entrance ☎ 530/595–6121 or 877/444–6777.

$$$$
B&B/INN
Fodor's Choice
★

Highlands Ranch Resort. Opened in 2015 on a gorgeous 175-acre alpine meadow 10 miles from Lassen National Park's southwest entrance, this cluster of smartly designed upscale bungalows is peaceful and luxurious. **Pros:** stunning views; most luxurious accommodations near the park; friendly and helpful staff. **Cons:** pricey for the area, but you get a lot for what you pay. ⑤ Rooms from: $239 ⊠ 41515 Hwy. 36 E ☎ 530/595–3388 ⊕ www.highlandsranchresort.com ➪ 7 cottages ❧ Breakfast.

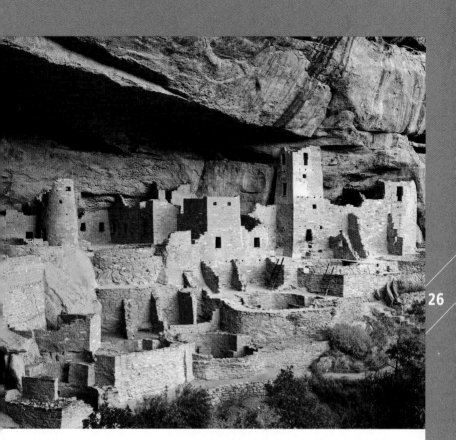

MESA VERDE
NATIONAL PARK

WELCOME TO MESA VERDE NATIONAL PARK

TOP REASONS TO GO

★ **Ancient artifacts:** Mesa Verde is a time capsule for the Ancestral Puebloan culture; more than 4,000 archaeological sites and 3 million objects have been unearthed here.

★ **Bright nights:** Mesa Verde's lack of light and air pollution, along with its high elevation make for spectacular views of the heavens.

★ **Active adventures:** Get your heart pumping outdoors with hiking, biking, and exploring on trails of varying difficulties.

★ **Cliff dwellings:** Built atop the pinyon-covered mesa tops and hidden in the park's valleys are 600 ancient dwellings, some carved directly into the sandstone cliff faces.

★ **Geological marvels:** View the unique geology that drew the Ancient Puebloan people to the area: protected desert canyons, massive alcoves in the cliff walls, thick bands of sandstone, continuous seep springs, and soils that could be used for both agriculture and architecture.

1 Morefield Campground. Near the park entrance, this large campground (the only one in Mesa Verde) includes a village area with a gas station and store. The best-known sites are farther in, but this one is close to some of the best hiking trails in the park.

2 Visitor and Research Center. Turn left at the entrance for the park's visitor center. Buy tickets for the popular ranger-led tours here and learn everything you need to know to plan a great trip.

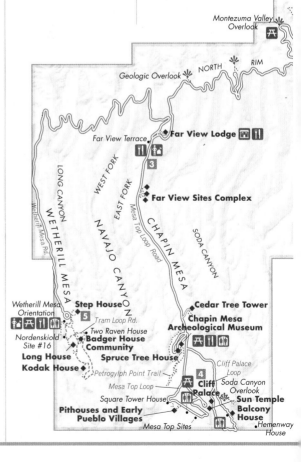

← TO CORTEZ

Montezuma Valley Overlook

Geologic Overlook

NORTH RIM

Far View Terrace

Far View Lodge

3

Far View Sites Complex

LONG CANYON

WEST FORK

EAST FORK

Wetherill Mesa Rd.

WETHERILL MESA

NAVAJO CANYON

Mesa Top Loop Road

CHAPIN MESA

SODA CANYON

Wetherill Mesa Orientation

5

Step House

Tram Loop Rd.

Two Raven House

Nordenskiold Site #16

Badger House Community

Long House

Kodak House

Spruce Tree House

Petroglyph Point Trail

Mesa Top Loop

Square Tower House

Pithouses and Early Pueblo Villages

Mesa Top Sites

Cedar Tree Tower

Chapin Mesa Archeological Museum

Cliff Palace Loop

4

Cliff Palace

Soda Canyon Overlook

Sun Temple

Balcony House

Hemenway House

COLORADO

3 **Far View.** Almost an hour's drive (but just 18 miles) from Mesa Verde's entrance, Far View is the park's epicenter, with several restaurants and the park's only overnight lodge. The fork in the road here takes you west toward the sites at Wetherill Mesa or south toward Chapin Mesa.

4 **Chapin Mesa.** Home to the park's most famous cliff dwellings and archaeological sites, the Chapin Mesa area includes the famous 150-room Cliff House dwelling and other man-made and natural wonders. It's also home to the Chapin Mesa Archeological Museum, where you can take a free tour of nearby Spruce Tree House.

GETTING ORIENTED

Perhaps no other area offers as much evidence about the Ancestral Puebloan culture as Mesa Verde National Park. Several thousand archaeological sites have been found, and research is ongoing to discover more. The carved-out homes and assorted artifacts, many of which are displayed at the park's Chapin Mesa Archeological Museum, belonged to ancestors of today's Hopi, Zuni, and Pueblo tribes, among others. Due to the sensitive nature of these sites, hiking in the park is restricted to designated trails, and certain cliff dwellings may be accessed only on ranger-led tours during the peak summer season.

26

5 **Wetherill Mesa.** It's less visited than Chapin Mesa, but just as rewarding for visitors. See Long House, Two Raven House, Kodak House, and the Badger House Community.

KEY	
👫	*Ranger Station*
🔺	*Campground*
🅰	*Picnic Area*
🍴	*Restaurant*
🏨	*Lodge*
🥾	*Trailhead*
🚻	*Restrooms*
⟫	*Scenic Viewpoint*
⋯⋯	*Walking/Hiking Trails*

Updated by
Aimee Heckel

Unlike the other national parks, Mesa Verde earned its status from its ancient cultural history rather than its geological treasures. President Theodore Roosevelt established it in 1906 as the first national park to "preserve the works of man," in this case that of the Ancestral Puebloans, also known as the Anasazi. They lived in the region from roughly 550 to 1300; they left behind more than 4,000 archaeological sites spread out over 80 square miles. Their ancient dwellings, set high into the sandstone cliffs, are the heart of the park.

Mesa Verde (which in Spanish means, literally, "Green Table," but translates more accurately to something like "green flat-topped plateau") is much more than an archaeologist's dreamland, however. It's one of those windswept places where man's footprints and nature's paintbrush—some would say chisel—meet. Rising dramatically from the San Juan Basin, the jutting cliffs are cut by a series of complex canyons and covered in several shades of green, from pines in the higher elevations down to sage and other mountain brush on the desert floor. From the tops of the smaller mesas, you can look across to the cliff dwellings in the opposite rock faces. Dwarfed by the towering cliffs, the sand-color dwellings look almost like a natural occurrence in the midst of the desert's harsh beauty.

MESA VERDE PLANNER

WHEN TO GO

The best times to visit the park are late May, early June, and most of September, when the weather is fine but the summer crowds have thinned. Mid-June through August is Mesa Verde's most crowded time.

In July and August, lines at the museum and visitor center may last half an hour. Afternoon thunderstorms are common in July and August.

The park gets as much as 100 inches of snow in winter. Snow may fall as late as May and as early as October, but there's rarely enough to hamper travel. In winter, the Wetherill Mesa Road is closed, but you can still get a glimpse of some of the Wetherill Mesa sandstone dwellings, sheltered from the snow in their cliff coves, from the Chapin Mesa area.

AVG. HIGH/LOW TEMPS.

Jan.	Feb.	Mar.	Apr.	May	June
40/18	44/19	50/26	52/34	71/44	83/52
July	Aug.	Sept.	Oct.	Nov.	Dec.
88/58	85/56	76/48	66/39	51/28	42/21

FESTIVALS AND EVENTS

MAY OR JUNE **Mountain Ute Bear Dance.** This traditional dance, the local version of a Sadie Hawkins (in which the women choose their dance partners—and the selected men can't refuse), is held in May or June on the Towaoc Ute reservation south of Cortez. The event celebrates spring and the legacy of a mythical bear who taught the Ute people her secrets. It's part of a multiday festival that includes music, races, and softball games, and culminates with an hour-long dance that's over when only one couple remains. ⊠ *124 Mike Wash Rd., Towaoc* ☎ *970/565–3751* ⊕ *www.utemountainutetribe.com.*

JULY **Durango Fiesta Days.** A parade, rodeo, barbecue, street dance, cook-offs, live music, and more come to the Durango Fairgrounds in July. ⊠ *La Plata County Fairgrounds, 2500 Main Ave., Durango* ☎ *970/749–4960* ⊕ *www.durangofiestadays.com.*

OCTOBER **Durango Cowboy Poetry Gathering.** A parade and dance accompany FAMILY art exhibitions, poetry readings, music, and storytelling in this four-day event run by the Durango Cowboy Poetry Gathering, a non-profit set up to preserve the traditions of the American West. It's held the first weekend in October. ⊠ *Durango* ☎ *970/749–2995* ⊕ *www.durangocowboypoetrygathering.org.*

PLANNING YOUR TIME

MESA VERDE IN ONE DAY

For a full experience, take at least one ranger-led tour of a major cliff dwelling site, as well as a few self-guided walks. Arrive early and stop first at the Visitor and Research Center, where you can purchase tickets for Cliff Palace and Balcony House tours on Chapin Mesa. If it's going to be a hot day, you might want to take an early-morning or late-afternoon bus tour. Drive to the **Chapin Mesa Museum** to watch a 25-minute film introducing you to the area and its history. Just behind the museum is the trailhead for the 0.5-mile-long **Spruce Tree House Trail**, which leads to the best-preserved cliff dwelling in the park. Then drive to **Balcony House** for an hour-long, ranger-led tour.

Have lunch at the Spruce Tree House cafeteria or the Cliff Palace picnic area. Afterward take the ranger-led tour of **Cliff Palace** (one hour). Use the rest of the day to explore the overlooks and trails off the 6-mile loop of **Mesa Top Loop Road.** Or head back to the museum and take **Petroglyph Point Trail** to see a great example of Ancestral Puebloan rock carvings. A leisurely walk along the Mesa Top's **Soda Canyon Overlook Trail** (off Cliff Palace Loop Road) gives you a beautiful bird's-eye view of the canyon below. On the drive back toward the park entrance, be sure to check out the view from **Park Point.**

GETTING HERE AND AROUND

AIR TRAVEL

The cities of Durango (36 miles east of the park entrance) and Cortez (11 miles to the west) have airports.

CAR TRAVEL

The park has just one entrance, off U.S. 160, between Cortez and Durango in what's known as the Four Corners area (which spans the intersection of Colorado, New Mexico, Arizona, and Utah). Most of the roads at Mesa Verde involve steep grades and hairpin turns, particularly on Wetherill Mesa. Vehicles over 8,000 pounds or 25 feet are prohibited on this road. Trailers and towed vehicles are prohibited past Morefield Campground. Check the condition of your vehicle's brakes before driving the road to Wetherill Mesa. For the latest road information, tune to 1610 AM, or call ☎ *970/529–4461.* Off-road vehicles are prohibited in the park. At less-visited Wetherill Mesa, you must leave your car behind and hike to the Long House, Kodak House, and Badger House Community.

PARK ESSENTIALS

PARK FEES AND PERMITS

Admission is $15 per vehicle for a seven-day permit. An annual pass is $30. Ranger-led tours of Cliff Palace, Long House, and Balcony House are $3 per person. You can also take ranger-guided bus tours from the Far View Lodge, which last between 3½ and 4 hours and cost $41–$48 ($26–$35 for kids; under 5 free). Backcountry hiking and fishing are not permitted at Mesa Verde.

PARK HOURS

Mesa Verde's facilities each operate on their own schedule, but most are open daily, from Memorial Day through Labor Day, between about 8 am and sunset. The rest of the year, they open at 9. In winter, the Spruce Tree House is open only to offer a few scheduled tours each day. Wetherill Mesa (and all the sites it services) is open only from Memorial Day through Labor Day. Far View Visitor Center, Far View Terrace, and Far View Lodge are open between April and October. Morefield Campground and the sites nearby are open from mid-May through mid-October. Specific hours are subject to change, so check with the visitor center upon arrival.

CELL-PHONE RECEPTION AND INTERNET

You can get patchy cell service in the park. Best service is typically at the Morefield Campground area, which is the closest to the neighboring towns of Cortez and Mancos. Public telephones can be found at all the major visitor areas (Morefield, Far View, and Spruce Tree). You can get free Wi-Fi throughout the Far View Lodge and at the Morefield Campground store.

EDUCATIONAL OFFERINGS

RANGER PROGRAMS

FAMILY **Evening Ranger Campfire Program.** Every night in summer at the Morefield Campground Amphitheater, park rangers present a different 45- to 60-minute program on topics such as stargazing, history, wildlife, and archaeology. Several evenings a week, you can also find free, hour-long ranger talks in the Far View Lodge library. ⊠ *Morefield Campground Amphitheater, 4 miles south of park entrance* ☎ *970/529–4465* ⌖ *Free* ☉ *Memorial Day–Labor Day, daily at 9 pm. Lodge program time and days vary.*

Far View Sites Walk. This one-hour, self-guided walk winds through the mesa-top sites in the Far View area. ⊠ *Far View House, 1 mile south of Far View Visitor Center* ☎ *970/529–4465* ⊕ *www.nps.gov/meve* ⌖ *Free* ☉ *Daily 8 am–sunset during open seasons.*

FAMILY **Junior Ranger Program.** Children ages 4 through 12 can earn a certificate and badge for successfully completing at least three activities in the park's Junior Ranger booklet (available at the park or online). ⊠ *Mesa Verde Visitor and Research Center or Chapin Mesa Archeological Museum* ☎ *970/529–4465* ⊕ *www.nps.gov/meve/forkids/beajuniorranger.htm.*

Ranger-Led Tours. The cliff dwellings known as Balcony House, Cliff Palace, and Long House can be explored only on ranger-led tours; the first two last about an hour, the third is 90 minutes. Buy tickets at the Visitor and Research Center. These are active tours and may not be suitable for some children; each requires climbing ladders without handrails and squeezing through tight spaces. Be sure to bring water and sunscreen. ⊠ *Mesa Verde National Park* ☎ *970/529–4465* ⊕ *www.nps.gov/meve/planyourvisit/visitcliffdwelling.htm* ⌖ *$4 per site.*

RESTAURANTS

Dining options in Mesa Verde are limited inside the park, but comparatively plentiful and varied if you're staying in Cortez or Durango. In surrounding communities, Southwestern restaurants and steak houses are common options.

HOTELS

All 150 rooms of the park's Far View Lodge, open April through October, fill up quickly—so reservations are recommended, especially if you plan to visit on a weekend in summer. Options in the surrounding area include chain hotels, cabins, and bed-and-breakfast inns. Durango in particular has a number of hotels in fine old buildings reminiscent of the Old West. *Hotel reviews have been shortened. For full information, visit Fodors.com.*

26

WHAT IT COSTS				
	$	**$$**	**$$$**	**$$$$**
Restaurants	under $13	$13–$18	$19–$25	over $25
Hotels	under $121	$121–$170	$171–$230	over $230

Restaurant prices are the average cost of a main course at dinner or, if dinner is not served, at lunch. Hotel reviews are the lowest cost of a standard double room in high season, excluding taxes and service charges.

TOURS
BUS TOURS
FAMILY **ARAMARK Tours.** If you want a well-rounded visit to Mesa Verde's most popular sites, consider a group tour. The park concessionaire provides all-day and half-day guided tours of the Chapin Mesa and Far View sites, departing in buses from either Morefield Campground or Far View Lodge. Tours are led by Aramark guides or park rangers, who share information about the park's history, geology, and excavation processes. Cold water is provided, but you'll need to bring your own snacks. Buy tickets at Far View Lodge, Far View Terrace, the Morefield Campground, or online. Tours sell out, so reserve in advance. ⊠ *1 Navajo Hill, Box 277* ☎ *970/529–4422, 800/449–2288* ⊕ *www.visitmesaverde.com* ⊠ *From $41* ☉ *Mid-Apr.–mid-Oct., daily, departs at 8 am and 1:30 pm.*

VISITOR INFORMATION
Park Contact Information Mesa Verde National Park. ⊠ *Mesa Verde National Park* ☎ *970/529–4465* ⊕ *www.nps.gov/meve.*

VISITOR CENTERS
Chapin Mesa Archeological Museum. This is an excellent first stop for an introduction to Ancestral Puebloan culture, as well as the area's development into a national park. Exhibits showcase original textiles and other artifacts, and a theater plays an informative film every 30 minutes. Rangers are available to answer your questions, and there's also a sign-in sheet for hiking trails. The museum sits at the south end of the park entrance road and overlooks Spruce Tree House. Nearby, you'll find park headquarters, a gift shop, a post office, snack bar, and bathrooms. ⊠ *Park entrance road, 5 miles south of Far View Visitor Center, 20 miles from park entrance* ☎ *970/529–4465* ⊕ *www.nps.gov/meve/planyourvisit/museum.htm* ⊠ *Free* ☉ *Daily. Hrs vary by season.*

Mesa Verde Visitor and Research Center. Mesa Verde's visitor center is the place to go to sign up for tours and get the information you need to plan a successful trip. This is the only place in the park to buy tickets for the Cliff Palace, Balcony House, and Long House ranger-led tours. The sleek, energy-efficient research center is filled with more than 3 million artifacts and archives. The center features indoor and outdoor exhibits, a gift shop, picnic tables, and a museum. A selection of books, maps, and videos on the history of the park is available, and rangers are on hand to answer questions and explain the history of the Ancestral Puebloans. ⊠ *Park entrance on the left* ☎ *970/529–4465* ⊕ *www.nps.gov/meve/planyourvisit/meve_vc.htm* ☉ *Daily. Hrs vary by season.*

The Cliff Palace at Mesa Verde National Park is lit up for Christmas.

EXPLORING

SCENIC DRIVES

Mesa Top Loop Road. This 6-mile drive skirts the scenic rim of Chapin Mesa and takes you to several overlooks and short, paved trails. You'll get great views of Sun Temple and Square Tower, as well as Cliff Palace, Sunset House, and several other cliff dwellings visible from the Sun Point Overlook. ⊠ *Mesa Verde National Park*.

Park Entrance Road. The main park road, also known as SH 10, leads you from the entrance off U.S. 160 to the Far View complex, 15 miles from the park entrance. As a break from the switchbacks, you can stop at a couple of pretty overlooks along the way, but hold out for Park Point, which, at the mesa's highest elevation (8,572 feet), gives you unobstructed, 360-degree views. Note that trailers and towed vehicles are not permitted beyond Morefield Campground. ⊠ *Mesa Verde National Park*.

Wetherill Mesa Road. This 12-mile mountain road, stretching from the Far View Visitor Center to the Wetherill Mesa, has sharp curves and steep grades (and is restricted to vehicles less than 25 feet long and 8,000 pounds). Roadside pull-outs offer unobstructed views of the Four Corners region. At the end of the road, you can access Step House, Long House, and Badger House. ⊠ *Mesa Verde National Park* ⊗ *Memorial Day–Labor Day, weather permitting*.

CLOSE UP

Plants and Wildlife in Mesa Verde

Mesa Verde is home to 640 species of plants, including a number of native plants found nowhere else. Its lower elevations feature many varieties of shrubs, including rabbitbrush and sagebrush. Higher up, you'll find mountain mahogany, yucca, pinyon, juniper, and Douglas fir. During warmer months, brightly colored blossoms, like the yellow perky Sue, blue lupines, and bright-red Indian paintbrushes, are scattered throughout the park.

The park is also home to a variety of migratory and resident animals, including 74 species of mammals. Drive slowly along the park's roads; mule deer are everywhere. You may spot wild turkeys, and black bear encounters are not unheard of on the hiking trails. Bobcats, coyotes, and mountain lions are also around, but they are seen less frequently. About 200 species of birds, including threatened Mexican spotted owls, red-tailed hawks, golden eagles, and noisy ravens, also live here. On the ground, you should keep your eyes and ears open for lizards and snakes, including the poisonous—but shy— prairie rattlesnake. As a general rule, animals are most active in the early morning and at dusk.

Many areas of the park have had extensive fire damage over the years. In fact, wildfires here have been so destructive they are given names, just like hurricanes. For example, the Bircher Fire in 2000 consumed nearly 20,000 acres of brush and forest, much of it covering the eastern half of the park. It will take several centuries for the woodland there to look as verdant as the area atop Chapin Mesa, which escaped the fire. But in the meantime, you'll have a chance to glimpse nature's powerful rejuvenating processes in action; the landscape in the fire-ravaged sections of the park is already filling in with vegetation.

HISTORIC SITES

Badger House Community. A self-guided walk along paved and gravel trails takes you through a group of four mesa-top dwellings. The community, which covers nearly 7 acres, dates back to the year 650, the Basketmaker Period, and includes a primitive, semisubterranean pit house and what's left of a multistoried stone pueblo. Allow about 45 minutes to see the sites. The trail is 2.4 miles round-trip. The park plans to offer bike rentals, too. ⊠ *Wetherill Mesa Rd., 12 miles from Far View Visitor Center* ⊕ *www.nps.gov/meve/historyculture/mt_badger_house.htm* ⊠ *Free.*

Balcony House. The stonework of this 40-room cliff dwelling, which housed about 40 or 50 people, is impressive, but you're likely to be even more awed by the skill it must have taken to reach this place. Perched in a sandstone cove 600 feet above the floor of Soda Canyon, Balcony House seems almost suspended in space. Even with the aid of modern passageways and a partially paved trail, today's visitors must climb a 32-foot ladder and crawl through a 12-foot-long tunnel to enter. Surrounding the house is a courtyard with a parapet wall and the intact balcony for which the house is named. A favorite with kids, the dwelling is accessible only on a ranger-led tour. Purchase tickets at the

Visitor and Research Center, Morefield Ranger Station, or the Colorado Welcome Center in Cortez. ⊠ *Cliff Palace/Balcony House Rd., 10 miles south of Far View Visitor Center, Cliff Palace Loop* ⌧ *$4.*

Fodor's Choice
★ **Cliff Palace.** This was the first major Mesa Verde dwelling seen by cowboys Charlie Mason and Richard Wetherill in 1888. It is also the largest, containing about 150 rooms and 23 kivas on three levels. Getting there involves a steep downhill hike and three ladders. Purchase tickets at the Visitor and Research Center, Morefield Ranger Station, and at the Colorado Welcome Center in Cortez. From Memorial Day through Labor Day, rangers in historical costumes lead a 90-minute

26

Twilight Tour of the site. These tours run daily just before twilight; tickets are available only at the Visitor and Research Center. Also check out 90-minute, small-group photography tours at sunset. ⊠ *Cliff Palace Overlook, about 2½ miles south of Chapin Mesa Archeological Museum* ⌧ *Basic tour $4; twilight tour $12; photography tour $20.*

FAMILY **Far View Sites Complex.** This was probably one of the most densely populated areas in Mesa Verde, comprising as many as 50 villages in a ½-square-mile area at the top of Chapin Mesa. Most of the sites here were built between 900 and 1300. Begin the self-guided tour at the interpretive panels in the parking lot, then proceed down a ½-mile, level trail. ⊠ *Park entrance road, near the Chapin Mesa area* ⊕ *www. nps.gov/meve* ⌧ *Free.*

Long House. This Wetherill Mesa cliff dwelling is the second largest in Mesa Verde. It is believed that about 150 people lived in Long House, so named because of the size of its cliff alcove. The spring at the back of the cave is still active today. The in-depth, ranger-led tour begins a short distance from the parking lot and takes about 90 minutes. Even though you will hike less than a mile, be prepared to climb two 15-foot ladders. Buy your ticket at the Visitor and Research Center, Morefield Ranger Station, or at the Colorado Welcome Center in Cortez. ⊠ *On Wetherill Mesa, 29 miles past the visitor center, near mile marker 15* ⊕ *www.nps.gov/meve* ⌧ *Tours $4.*

FAMILY **Spruce Tree House.** This 138-room complex is the best-preserved site in the park, and the rooms and ceremonial chambers are more accessible to visitors than those in other sites. Here you can actually enter a kiva, via a short ladder that goes underground, just as the original inhabitants did. It's a great place for kids to explore, but because of its location in the heart of the Chapin Mesa area, Spruce Tree House can resemble a crowded playground during busy periods. Tours are self-guided from spring to fall (allow 45 minutes to an hour), but a park ranger is on-site to answer questions. Sign up for ranger-guided tours in the winter. The trail leading to Spruce Tree House starts behind the museum and leads you 100 feet down into the canyon. You may find yourself breathing hard by the time you make it back up to the parking lot. ⊠ *At the Chapin Mesa Archeological Museum, 5 miles south of Far View Visitor Center* ⊑ *Free.*

Step House. So named because of a crumbling prehistoric stairway leading up from the dwelling, Step House is reached via a paved (but steep) trail that's ¾ mile long. The house is unique in that it shows clear evidence of two separate occupations: the first around 626, the second a full 600 years later. The self-guided tour takes about 45 minutes. ⊠ *Wetherill Mesa Rd., 12 miles from Far View Visitor Center* ⊕ *www. nps.gov/meve/historyculture/cd_step_house.htm* ⊑ *Free.*

Sun Temple. Although researchers assume it was probably a ceremonial structure, they're unsure of the exact purpose of this complex, which has no doors or windows in most of its chambers. Because the building was not quite half-finished when it was left in 1276, some researchers surmise it might have been constructed to stave off whatever disaster caused its builders—and the other inhabitants of Mesa Verde—to leave. ⊠ *Mesa Top Loop Rd., about 2 miles south of Chapin Mesa Archeological Museum* ⊕ *www.nps.gov/meve/historyculture/mt_sun_ temple.htm* ⊑ *Free.*

Pit Houses and Early Pueblo Villages. Three dwellings, built on top of each other from 700 to 950, at first look like a mass of jumbled walls, but an informational panel helps identify the dwellings—and the stories behind them are fascinating. The 325-foot trail from the walking area is paved, wheelchair accessible, and near a restroom. ⊠ *Mesa Top Loop Rd., about 2½ miles south of Chapin Mesa Archeological Museum* ⊑ *Free.*

SCENIC STOPS

Cedar Tree Tower. A self-guided tour takes you to, but not through, a tower and kiva built between 1100 and 1300 and connected by a tunnel. The tower-and-kiva combinations in the park are thought to have been either religious structures or signal towers. ⊠ *Near the four-way intersection on Chapin Mesa; park entrance road, 1½ miles north of Chapin Mesa Archeological Museum* ⊑ *Free.*

Kodak House Overlook. Get an impressive view into the 60-room Kodak House and its several small kivas from here. The house, closed to the public, was named for a Swedish researcher who absentmindedly left his Kodak camera behind here in 1891. ⊠ *Wetherill Mesa Rd.* ⊕ *www. nps.gov/meve.*

Soda Canyon Overlook. Get your best view of Balcony House here. You can also read interpretive panels about the site and the surrounding canyon geology. ⊠ *Cliff Palace Loop Rd., about 1 mile north of Balcony House parking area.*

SPORTS AND THE OUTDOORS

At Mesa Verde, outdoor activities are restricted, due to the fragile nature of the archaeological treasures here. Hiking (allowed on marked trails only) is the best option, especially as a way to view some of the Ancestral Puebloan dwellings.

BIRD-WATCHING

Turkey vultures soar between April and October, and large flocks of ravens hang around all summer. Among the park's other large birds are red-tailed hawks, great horned owls, and a few golden eagles. The Steller's jay (the male looks like a blue jay with a dark hat on) frequently pierces the pinyon-juniper forest with its cries, and hummingbirds dart from flower to flower in the summer and fall. Any visit to cliff dwellings late in the day will include frolicking white-throated swifts, which make their home in rock crevices overhead.

Pick up a copy of the park's "Checklist of the Birds" brochure or visit the National Park Service's website (⊕ *www.nps.gov/meve/ planyourvisit/birdwatching.htm*) for a detailed listing of the feathered inhabitants here.

HIKING

A handful of trails lead beyond Mesa Verde's most visited sites and offer more solitude than the often-crowded cliff dwellings. The best canyon vistas can be reached if you're willing to huff and puff your way through elevation changes and switchbacks. Carry more water than you think you'll need, wear sunscreen, and bring rain gear—cloudbursts can come seemingly out of nowhere. Certain trails are open seasonally, so check with a ranger before heading out. No backcountry hiking is permitted in Mesa Verde, and pets are prohibited.

EASY

FAMILY **Farming Terrace Trail.** This 30-minute, ½-mile loop begins and ends on the spur road to Cedar Tree Tower, about 1 mile north of the Chapin Mesa area. It meanders through a series of check dams, which the Ancestral Puebloans built to create farming terraces. *Easy.* ✛ *Trailhead: park entrance road, 4 miles south of Far View Visitor Center.*

Knife Edge Trail. Perfect for a sunset stroll, this easy 2-mile (round-trip) walk around the north rim of the park leads to an overlook of the Montezuma Valley. If you stop at all the flora identification points that the trail guide pamphlet suggests, the hike should take about 1½ to 2 hours. The patches of asphalt you're likely to spot along the way are leftovers from old Knife Edge Road, built in 1914 as the main entryway into the park. *Easy.* ✛ *Trailhead: Morefield Campground, 4 miles from park entrance.*

FAMILY **Soda Canyon Overlook Trail.** One of the easiest and most rewarding hikes in the park, this little trail travels 1½ miles round-trip through the forest on almost completely level ground. The overlook is an excellent point from which to photograph the Chapin Mesa–area cliff dwellings. *Easy.* ✛ *Trailhead: Cliff Palace Loop Rd., about 1 mile north of Balcony House parking area.*

MODERATE

Petroglyph Point Trail. Scramble along a narrow canyon wall to reach the largest and best-known petroglyphs in Mesa Verde. Older literature occasionally refers to the destination of this 2.4-mile loop hike as "Pictograph Point," but that's a misnomer. Pictographs are painted onto the rock, and petroglyphs are carved into it. If you pose for a photo just right, you can just manage to block out the gigantic "don't touch" sign next to the rock art. A map—available at any ranger station—points out three dozen points of interest along the trail. The trail is open only when Spruce Tree House is open; check with a ranger to verify times. *Moderate.* ⟴ *Trailhead: at Spruce Tree House, next to Chapin Mesa Archeological Museum.*

Spruce Canyon Trail. While Petroglyph Point Trail takes you along the side of the canyon, this trail ventures down into its depths. It's only 2.4 miles long, but you descend about 600 feet in elevation. Remember to save your strength; what goes down must come up again. Access to the trail is limited to times when Spruce Tree House is open; check with a ranger beforehand. *Moderate.* ⟴ *Trailhead: at Spruce Tree House, next to Chapin Mesa Archeological Museum* ☞ *Registration required.*

DIFFICULT

Prater Ridge Trail. This 7.8-mile round-trip loop, which starts and finishes at Morefield Campground, is the longest hike you can take inside the park. It provides fine views of Morefield Canyon to the south and the San Juan Mountains to the north. About halfway through the hike, you'll see a cut-off trail that you can take, which shortens the trip to 5 miles. *Difficult.* ⟴ *Trailhead: west end of Morefield Campground, 4 miles from park entrance.*

26

STARGAZING

There are no large cities in the Four Corners area, so there is little artificial light to detract from the stars in the night sky. Far View Lodge and Morefield Campground are great for sky watching.

SHOPPING

Chapin Mesa Archeological Museum Shop. Books and videos are the primary offering here, with more than 400 titles on Ancestral Puebloan and Southwestern topics. You can also find a selection of touristy T-shirts and hats. ✉ *Spruce Tree Terrace, near Chapin Mesa Archeological Museum, 5 miles from Far View Visitor Center* ☎ *970/529–4445.*

Far View Terrace Shop. In the same building as the Far View Terrace Cafe, this is the largest gift shop in the park, with gifts, souvenirs, Native American art, toys, and T-shirts galore. ✉ *Mesa Top Loop Rd., 15 miles south of park entrance* ☎ *970/529–4421, 800/449–2288* ☼ *Daily 7 am–8 pm.*

WHAT'S NEARBY

NEARBY TOWNS

A onetime market center for cattle and crops, **Cortez**, 11 miles west of the park, is now the largest gateway town to Mesa Verde and a base for tourists visiting the Four Corners region. You can still see a rodeo here at least once a year. **Dolores**, steeped in a rich railroad history, is on the Dolores River, 19 miles north of Mesa Verde. Near both the San Juan National Forest and McPhee Reservoir, Dolores is a favorite of outdoor enthusiasts. East of Mesa Verde by 36 miles, **Durango**, the region's main hub, comes complete with a variety of restaurants and hotels, shopping, and outdoor-equipment shops. Durango became a town in 1881 when the Denver and Rio Grande Railroad pushed its tracks across the neighboring San Juan Mountains.

NEARBY ATTRACTIONS

FAMILY **Anasazi Heritage Center.** Operated by the Federal Bureau of Land Management, this museum houses artifacts culled from more than 1,500 excavations in the region. The center has permanent exhibits showcasing the archaeology, history, and culture of the Ancestral Puebloans and other indigenous peoples. There are also two 12th-century pueblos, named after the Spanish friars Dominguez and Escalante, within walking distance. A full-scale replica of an ancient pit-house dwelling illustrates how the people lived around AD 850. It also houses the visitor center and jumping-off point for the **Canyons of the Ancients National Monument.** ✉ 27501 State Hwy. 184, Dolores ✛ 3 miles west of Dolores ☎ 970/882–5600 ⊕ www.blm.gov/co/st/en/fo/ahc.html 🎫 $3 ⏰ Mar.–Oct., daily 9–5; Nov.–Feb., daily 10–4.

Crow Canyon Archaeological Center. Professionals, students, and any would-be Indiana Joneses come here to learn about ancient relics. Among the more popular offerings of the center's educational programs are weeklong "Archaeology Adventures," which allow visitors to work alongside professional archaeologists as they search for pottery, stone tools, and other artifacts at excavation sites throughout the area, then clean and catalog their finds in the lab. The program includes a special guided tour of Mesa Verde National Park. ✉ 23390 County Rd. K, Cortez ☎ 970/565–8975, 800/422–8975 ⊕ www.crowcanyon.org.

FAMILY **Durango & Silverton Narrow Gauge Railroad.** The most entertaining way
Fodor'sChoice to relive the halcyon days of the Old West is to take a ride on the
★ Durango & Silverton Narrow Gauge Railroad, a nine-hour round-trip journey along the 45-mile railway to Silverton. You'll travel in comfort in lovingly restored coaches or in the open-air cars called gondolas as you listen to the train's shrill whistle as it chugs along. On the way, you get a good look at the Animas Valley, which in some parts is broad and green and in others narrow and rimmed with rock. A shorter excursion—to Cascade Canyon, 26 miles away—in heated coaches is available in winter. The train departs from the Durango Depot, constructed in 1882 and beautifully restored. Next door is the

Durango & Silverton Narrow Gauge Railroad Museum. ✉ *479 Main Ave., Durango* ☎ *970/247–2733, 877/872–4607* ⊕ *www.durangotrain. com* ⊠ *$91–$199* ⊙ *Train: early May–late Oct., daily; Cascade Canyon Train: late Nov.– early May.*

Four Corners Monument. The Navajo Nation manages this interesting landmark about 65 miles southeast of Bluff and 6 miles north of Teec Nos Pos, Arizona. Primarily a photo op, you'll also find Navajo and Ute artisans selling authentic jewelry and crafts, as well as traditional foods. It's the only place in the United States where four states meet at one single point. Bring plenty of water. You'll need cash for the entry fee. No cards or checks are accepted, and the nearest ATM is in Teec Nos Pos. ✉ *Four Corners Monument Rd., off U.S. 160, Teec Nos Pos* ⊕ *www.navajonationparks.org* ⊠ *$5* ⊙ *May–mid-Sept., daily 8–8; mid-Sept.–Apr., 8–6.*

Ute Mountain Tribal Park. The only way to see this spectacular 125,000-acre park, located inside the Ute reservation, is by taking a guided tour. Expert tribal guides lead strenuous daylong hikes into this dazzling repository of Ancestral Puebloan ruins, including beautifully preserved cliff dwellings, pictographs, and petroglyphs. There are also less-demanding half-day tours, as well as private and custom tour options. Tours start at the park's visitor center, off Highway 160. ✉ *Hwy. 160/491, Cortez* ☎ *970/565–3751, 800/847–5485* ⊕ *www. utemountaintribalpark.info* ⊠ *From $29.*

AREA ACTIVITIES

SPORTS AND THE OUTDOORS

FISHING

McPhee Reservoir. In 1985, crews completed construction of an irrigation dam across the Dolores River, forming the McPhee Reservoir, the second largest in the state. It draws anglers looking to bag a variety of warm- and cold-water fish along its 50 miles of shoreline, which is surrounded by spectacular specimens of juniper and sage as well as large stands of pinyon pine. There are two boat ramps; the McPhee Boat Ramp also has a new marina and convenience store. The area also has camping, hiking, and a relatively easy mountain-bike trail, and the mesa offers panoramic views of the surrounding San Juan National Forest. ✉ *Forest Service Rd. 271, off State Hwy. 184, Dolores* ⊕ *About 9 miles northwest of Dolores* ⊠ *Free.*

HIKING

Animas View Overlook Trail. If you're looking for a great view without the effort, try the ¾-mile Animas View Overlook Trail. It takes you past signs explaining local geology, flora, and fauna before bringing you to a precipice with an unparalleled view of the valley and the surrounding Needle Mountains. It's the only wheelchair-accessible trail in the area. From town, it's a 45-minute drive up Junction Creek Road. ⊕ *Trailhead: at Forest Rd. 171, milepost 8.*

Fodor's Choice ★ **Colorado Trail.** This epic trail starts a few miles northwest of Durango and covers about 500 miles on its way to Denver. You're not obliged to go that far, of course. Just a few miles in and out will give you a taste

Marketing the Four Corners Monument

There's no view to speak of at Four Corners Monument, but it's a popular photo op nonetheless. Set on Navajo land, about one usually dusty mile off U.S. 60, the monument is the only place in the nation where the borders of four states meet. The first permanent marker, a simple "look-what's-here," was erected at the intersection of Colorado, Utah, New Mexico, and Arizona in 1912. As long as there have been cameras, people have gone out of their way just to stand in such a way as to be in four states at once.

The monument was refurbished in 1992, and a larger marker, consisting of a bronze disk embedded in granite, was put in place. Though bigger and more ornate than the first marker, it still seems far too unassuming to have attracted the bazaar that surrounds it. In response to a ready market of tourists and trinket hounds, the main drive is rimmed with plywood booths

hawking Ute, Navajo, Apache, and other American Indian artwork, crafts, artifacts, and rugs. You can also buy fry bread and corn on the cob. It's all genuine, but the opportunistic nature of the site—it costs $5 per person just to enter (cash only; kids 6 and under are free)—detracts from what began as the simple fascination of standing at the very point where four southwestern states meet.

No major cities are nearby. Cortez, Colorado, is 40 miles away on U.S. 60; tiny Teec Nos Pos, Arizona, is 6 miles away; Shiprock, New Mexico, is about 27 miles to the east; and Bluff, Utah, is 53 miles distant.

The Navajo Nation Parks and Recreation Department administers the Four Corners Monument, along with numerous natural sites and thousands of square miles of pristine wilderness. For more information, email nslim@navajonationparks.org.

of the grandeur of this trail, which winds through mountain ranges and high passes and some of the most amazing mountain scenery around. ⊠ *Trailhead off County Rd. 204, Durango* ✛ *From town, take 25th St. west; it turns into Junction St. and continues on to the lower parking lot* ⊕ *www.coloradotrail.org.*

RAFTING

Beginning in the San Juan Mountains of southwestern Colorado, the Dolores River runs north for more than 150 miles before joining the Colorado River near Moab, Utah. This is one of those rivers that tends to flow madly in spring and diminish considerably by midsummer, and for that reason rafting trips are usually run in April and May, and occasionally early June.

Durango Rivertrippers. This outfitter runs two- and four-hour trips down the Animas River. You can up your adrenaline output by swapping the raft for an inflatable kayak on any of the Animas River trips. Or ask about zip-line and rafting packages, or Jeep tours or rentals. ⊠ *724 Main Ave., Durango* ☎ *970/259–0289* ⊕ *www.durangorivertrippers.com.*

NIGHTLIFE AND PERFORMING ARTS

Cortez Cultural Center. The cultural center has exhibits on regional artists and Ancestral Puebloan culture, as well as events and fairs. Summer evening programs include Native American dances and storytelling. ⊠ *25 N. Market St., Cortez* ☎ *970/565–1151* ⊕ *www.cortezculturalcenter. org* ☐ *Free* ☉ *Memorial Day–Labor Day, daily 10–10; Sept. and May, daily 10–6; Oct.–Apr., daily 10–5.*

ART GALLERIES

Toh-Atin Gallery. Recognized as one of the region's best Native American galleries, Toh-Atin specializes in Navajo rugs and weavings. There's also a wide range of paintings and prints, pottery, baskets, and jewelry made by the artisans of many Southwestern tribes. ⊠ *145 W. 9th St., Durango* ☎ *970/247–8277, 800/525–0384* ⊕ *www.toh-atin.com.*

NIGHTLIFE

Diamond Belle Saloon. Awash in flocked wallpaper and lace, the Diamond Belle Saloon is dominated by a gilt-and-mahogany bar. With its prime location—on the ground floor of the historic Strater Hotel—and a staff of ragtime piano players and waitresses dressed as saloon girls, the Diamond Belle can really pack them in. Be sure to try the Brazilian mint martini; if you're hungry, try the much-hailed Diamond burger. ⊠ *699 Main Ave., Durango* ☎ *970/247–4431* ⊕ *www.diamondbelle.com.*

26

SHOPPING

Notah Dineh Trading Company and Museum. This store specializing in Navajo rugs has the largest collection in the area. There are also handmade baskets, beadwork, pottery, and jewelry. If you stop in the free museum you can see relics of the Old West. ⊠ *345 W. Main St., Cortez* ☎ *800/444–2024* ⊕ *www.notahdineh.com.*

WHERE TO EAT

IN THE PARK

$ ✕ **Far View Terrace Cafe.** This full-service cafeteria offers great views,
AMERICAN but it's nothing fancy. Grab a simple coffee here or head across the dining room to Mesa Mocha for a latte. Order an omelet cooked to order, or if you're in a hurry to hit the park trails, you can grab a to-go lunch. Dinner options include a Navajo taco piled high with all the fixings. ⑤ *Average main: $8* ⊠ *Across from Far View Visitor Center* ☎ *970/529–4444* ⊕ *www.visitmesaverde.com/dining/far-view-terrace-cafe.aspx* ☉ *Closed late Oct.–early May.*

$ ✕ **Knife Edge Cafe.** Located in the Morefield Campground, this simple
CAFÉ restaurant in a covered outdoor terrace with picnic tables serves a hearty
FAMILY all-you-can-eat pancake breakfast with sausage every morning. Coffee and beverages are also available. It also offers lunch and dinner. ⑤ *Average main: $6* ⊠ *4 miles south of park entrance* ☎ *970/565–2133* ⊕ *www.nps.gov/meve/planyourvisit/restaurants.htm* ☉ *Closed mid-Sept.–early May.*

$$$
AMERICAN
Fodor'sChoice
★

✕**Metate Room.** The park's rugged terrain contrasts with this relaxing space just off the lobby of the Far View Lodge. The well-regarded dining room is upscale, but the atmosphere remains casual. A wall of windows affords wonderful Mesa Verde vistas. The menu is based on regional heritage foods, including corn, beans, and squash (all staples for the Ancestral Puebloans). Many entrées are unique, such as cinnamon-chili pork tenderloin or regional quail with prickly pear–red pepper jam. Every table gets mesa bread and black bean hummus for starters. There's an array of local wines (try Cortez's own Guy Drew) and cocktails with kitschy names, like the "Long House Lemonade." Gluten-free and vegan options are available. ⑤ *Average main: $25* ✉ *Far View Lodge, 1 Navajo Road, across from Far View Visitor Center, 15 miles southwest of park entrance* ☎ *970/529–4421* ⊕ *www.visitmesaverde. com/dining/metate-room.aspx* ⊗ *Closed late Oct.–mid Apr. No lunch.*

$
AMERICAN

✕**Spruce Tree Terrace Cafe.** This small cafeteria has a limited selection of hot food, coffee, salads, and sandwiches. The patio is pleasant, and it's conveniently located across the street from the museum. The Spruce Tree Terrace is also the only food concession in the park that's open year-round. Try the popular Navajo tacos. ⑤ *Average main: $8* ✉ *Near Chapin Mesa Archeological Museum, 5 miles south of the Far View Visitor Center* ☎ *970/529–4521* ⊕ *www.visitmesaverde.com/dining/ spruce-tree-terrace-cafe.aspx* ⊗ *No dinner.*

PICNIC AREAS

FAMILY **Chapin Mesa Picnic Area.** This is the nicest and largest picnic area in the park. It has about 40 tables under shade trees and a great view into Spruce Canyon, as well as flushing toilets. ✉ *Near Chapin Mesa Archeological Museum, 5 miles south of Far View Visitor Center.*

FAMILY **Wetherill Mesa Picnic Area.** Ten tables placed under lush shade trees, along with nearby drinking water and restrooms, make this a pleasant spot for lunch. ✉ *12 miles southwest of Far View Visitor Center.*

OUTSIDE THE PARK

$$
MODERN
AMERICAN

✕**Ken & Sue's.** Plates are big and the selection is creative at Ken & Sue's, one of Durango's favorite restaurants. Locals are wild for the contemporary American cuisine with an Asian flair, served in an intimate space. Try the pistachio-crusted grouper with vanilla-rum butter, or Aunt Lydia's meatloaf with red-wine gravy and mashed potatoes. If the weather allows, ask for a table on the large, pretty patio in the back. ⑤ *Average main: $18* ✉ *636 Main Ave., Durango* ☎ *970/385–1810* ⊕ *www.kenandsues.com* ⊗ *No lunch weekends.*

$
AMERICAN

✕**Olde Tymers Cafe.** If you're looking for the locals, look no further than Olde Tymers Cafe—known in these parts as OTC—a bustling café and bar in a beautiful old building on Main Avenue with an inviting patio in the back. The hamburger is a huge specimen on a fat, fresh bun, and the salads and sandwiches are piled high. There's a different special every night—including $6 burgers on Monday—and a respectable roster of beers on tap, including local Durango brews. ⑤ *Average main: $10* ✉ *1000 Main Ave., Durango* ☎ *970/259–2990* ⊕ *www.otcdgo.com.*

CLOSE UP

Best Campgrounds in Mesa Verde

Morefield Campground is the only option within the park, and it's an excellent one. Reservations are accepted; it's open late May through early September. In nearby Mancos, just across the highway from the park entrance, there's a campground with full amenities (but no electrical hookups), while the San Juan National Forest offers backcountry camping.

Morefield Campground. With 267 campsites, including 15 full-hookup RV sites, access to trailheads, and plenty of amenities, the only campground in the park is an appealing mini-city for campers. It's a 40-minute drive to reach the park's most popular sites. Reservations are accepted. ⊠ *4 miles south of park entrance* ☎ *970/564–4300, 800/449–2288* ⊕ *www. visitmesaverde.com.*

$$$$ ✕**Ore House.** Durango is a meat-and-potatoes kind of town, and
STEAKHOUSE the rustic Ore House is Durango's idea of a steak house. The aroma of beef smacks you in the face as you walk past, but there are also chicken, pork, and wild-caught seafood dishes available. This local favorite serves enormous slabs of aged Angus that are hand cut daily. For a special occasion try the chateaubriand for two ($73). **$** *Average main: $37* ⊠ *147 E. College Dr., Durango* ☎ *970/247–5707* ⊕ *www. orehouserestaurant.com.*

WHERE TO STAY

IN THE PARK

$$ ⊞ **Far View Lodge.** Talk about a view—all rooms have a private balcony,
HOTEL from which you can admire views of the neighboring states of Arizona,
Fodor's Choice Utah, and New Mexico up to 100 miles in the distance. **Pros:** close to
★ the key sites; views are spectacular. **Cons:** simple rooms and amenities, with no TV; walls are thin and less than soundproof; limited cell-phone service. **$** *Rooms from: $135* ⊠ *Across from Far View Visitor Center, 1 Navajo Road, 15 miles southwest of park entrance* ☎ *602/331–5210, 800/449–2288* ⊕ *www.visitmesaverde.com* ⊗ *Closed Nov.–Mar.* ⌐ *150 rooms* ⎮⊙⎮*No meals.*

OUTSIDE THE PARK

$ ⊞ **American Holiday Mesa Verde Inn.** This is arguably the nicest motel
HOTEL on the strip, mostly because its air-conditioned rooms are spacious and pleasantly decorated. **Pros:** reasonably priced; near the national park; outdoor pool. **Cons:** can get noisy; nothing fancy. **$** *Rooms from: $65* ⊠ *640 S. Broadway, Cortez* ☎ *970/565–3773* ⊕ *www. mesaverdeinncolorado.com* ⌐ *84 rooms* ⎮⊙⎮*No meals.*

$$$ ⊞ **Rochester Hotel.** The renovated Rochester Hotel is funky yet chic,
B&B/INN with marquee-lighted movie posters from Hollywood Westerns filmed nearby lining the airy hallways. **Pros:** free guest parking; large rooms;

free use of cruiser bikes in town. **Cons:** can be noisy; no counter space in bathrooms. ⑤ *Rooms from: $179* ✉ *726 E. 2nd Ave., Durango* ☎ *970/385–1920, 800/664–1920* ⊕ *www.rochesterhotel.com* ⤳ *19 rooms, 8 suites* ❍| *Breakfast.*

$$$
HOTEL
Fodor's Choice
★

Strater Hotel. Still the hottest spot in town, this Western grande dame opened for business in 1887 and has been visited by Butch Cassidy, Louis L'Amour (he wrote many of the *Sacketts* novels here), Francis Ford Coppola, John Kennedy, and Marilyn Monroe (the latter two stayed here at separate times). **Pros:** right in the thick of things; genuine Old West feel. **Cons:** breakfast not included in all rates; when the bar gets going, rooms above it get no peace. ⑤ *Rooms from: $190* ✉ *699 Main Ave., Durango* ☎ *970/247–4431, 800/247–4431* ⊕ *www.strater. com* ⤳ *93 rooms* ❍| *No meals.*

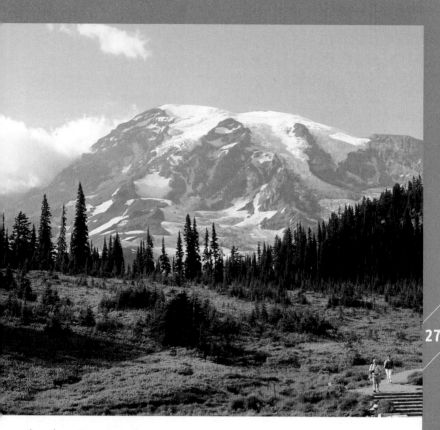

MOUNT RAINIER
NATIONAL PARK

WELCOME TO MOUNT RAINIER NATIONAL PARK

TOP REASONS TO GO

★ **The mountain:** Some say Mount Rainier is the most magical mountain in America. At 14,411 feet, it is a popular peak for climbing, with more than 10,000 attempts per year—half of which are successful.

★ **The glaciers:** About 35 square miles of glaciers and snowfields encircle Mount Rainier, including Carbon Glacier and Emmons Glacier, the largest glaciers by volume and area, respectively, in the continental United States.

★ **The wildflowers:** More than 100 species of wildflowers bloom in the park's high meadows; the display dazzles from midsummer until the snow flies.

★ **Fabulous hiking:** More than 240 miles of maintained trails provide access to old-growth forest, river valleys, lakes, and rugged ridges.

★ **Unencumbered wilderness:** Under the provisions of the 1964 Wilderness Act and the National Wilderness Preservation System, 97% of the park is preserved as wilderness.

1 **Longmire.** Inside the Nisqually Gate explore Longmire historic district's museum and visitor center, ruins of the park's first hotel, or the nature loop. Nearby, delicate footbridges span the thundering Christine and Narada falls.

2 **Paradise.** The park's most popular destination is famous for wildflowers in summer and skiing in winter. Skyline Trail is one of many hiking routes that crisscross the base of the mountain; the larger of the two park lodges is also here.

3 **Ohanapecosh.** Closest to the southeast entrance and the town of Packwood, the giant old-growth trees of the Grove of the Patriarchs are a must-see. Another short trail around nearby Tipsoo Lake has great views.

4 **Sunrise and White River.** This side of the park is easy to visit in summer if you enter from the east side, but it's a long drive from the southwest entrance. Sunrise is the highest stretch of road in the park and a great place to take in the alpenglow—reddish light on the peak of the mountain near sunrise and sunset. Mount Rainier's premier mountain-biking area, White River, is also the gateway to more than a dozen hiking trails.

5 **Carbon River and Mowich Lake.** Near the Carbon River Entrance Station is a swath of temperate forest, but to really get away from it all, follow the windy gravel roads to remote Mowich Lake.

GETTING ORIENTED

The jagged white crown of Mount Rainier is the showpiece of the Cascades and the focal point of this 337-square-mile national park. The most popular destination in the park, Paradise, is in the southern region; Ohanapecosh, the Grove of the Patriarchs, and Tipsoo Lake are in the southeastern corner. Mount Rainier National Park's eastern and northern areas are dominated by wilderness. The snowy folds of the Cascade mountain range stretch out from this Washington park; Seattle is roughly 50 miles north and the volcanic ruins of Mount St. Helens 100 miles south.

27

KEY	
🏠	Ranger Station
�△	Campground
⛩	Picnic Area
🍴	Restaurant
🏨	Lodge
🚶	Trailhead
🚻	Restrooms
✦	Scenic Viewpoint
⋯⋯	Walking/Hiking Trails

Updated by Shelley Arenas

Like a mysterious, white-clad chanteuse, veiled in clouds even when the surrounding forests and fields are bathed in sunlight, Mount Rainier is the centerpiece of its namesake park. The impressive volcanic peak stands at an elevation of 14,411 feet, making it the fifth-highest peak in the lower 48 states. Nearly 2 million visitors a year enjoy spectacular views of the mountain and return home with a lifelong memory of its image.

The mountain holds the largest glacial system in the contiguous United States, with more than two dozen major glaciers. On the lower slopes you find silent forests made up of cathedral-like groves of Douglas fir, western hemlock, and western red cedar, some more than 1,000 years old. Water and lush greenery are everywhere in the park, and dozens of thundering waterfalls, accessible from the road or by a short hike, fill the air with mist.

MOUNT RAINIER PLANNER

WHEN TO GO

Rainier is the Puget Sound's weather vane: if you can see it, skies will be clear. Visitors are most likely to see the summit July through September. Crowds are heaviest in summer, too, meaning the parking lots at Paradise and Sunrise often fill before noon, campsites are reserved months in advance, and other lodgings are reserved as much as a year ahead.

True to its name, Paradise is often sunny during periods when the lowlands are under a cloud layer. The rest of the year, Rainier's summit gathers flying-saucer-like lenticular clouds whenever a Pacific storm approaches; once the peak vanishes from view, it's time to haul out rain gear. The rare periods of clear winter weather bring residents up to Paradise for cross-country skiing.

AVG. HIGH/LOW TEMPS.

Jan.	Feb.	Mar.	Apr.	May	June
36/24	40/26	44/28	53/32	62/37	66/43

July	Aug.	Sept.	Oct.	Nov.	Dec.
75/47	74/47	68/43	57/38	45/31	39/28

PLANNING YOUR TIME
MOUNT RAINIER IN ONE DAY
The best way to get a complete overview of Mount Rainier in a day is to enter via Nisqually and begin your tour by browsing in **Longmire Museum.** When you're done, get to know the environment in and around Longmire Meadow and the overgrown ruins of Longmire Springs Hotel on the 0.5-mile **Trail of the Shadows** nature loop.

From Longmire, Highway 706 East climbs northeast into the mountains toward Paradise. Take a moment to explore two-tiered **Christine Falls,** just north of the road 1½ miles past Cougar Rock Campground, and the cascading **Narada Falls,** 3 miles farther on; both are spanned by graceful stone footbridges. Fantastic mountain views, alpine meadows crosshatched with nature trails, a welcoming lodge and restaurant, and the excellent **Jackson Memorial Visitor Center** combine to make lofty Paradise the primary goal of most park visitors. One outstanding (but challenging) way to explore the high country is to hike the 5-mile round-trip **Skyline Trail** to Panorama Point, which rewards you with stunning 360-degree views.

Continue eastward on Highway 706 East for 21 miles and leave your car to explore the incomparable, 1,000-year-old **Grove of the Patriarchs.** Afterward, turn your car north toward White River and **Sunrise Visitor Center,** where you can watch the alpenglow fade from Mount Rainier's domed summit.

GETTING HERE AND AROUND
AIR TRAVEL
Seattle–Tacoma International Airport, 15 miles south of downtown Seattle, is the nearest airport to the national park.

CAR TRAVEL
The Nisqually entrance is on Highway 706, 14 miles east of Route 7; the Ohanapecosh entrance is on Route 123, 5 miles north of U.S. 12; and the White River entrance is on Route 410, 3 miles north of the Chinook and Cayuse passes. These highways become mountain roads as they reach Rainier, winding up and down many steep slopes, so cautious driving is essential: use a lower gear, especially on downhill sections, and take care not to overheat brakes by constant use. These roads are subject to storms any time of year and are repaired in the summer from winter damage and washouts.

Side roads into the park's western slope are narrower, unpaved, and subject to flooding and washouts. All are closed by snow in winter except Highway 706 to Paradise and Carbon River Road, though the

27

latter tends to flood near the park boundary. (Route 410 is open to the Crystal Mountain access road entrance.)

Park roads have a maximum speed of 35 mph in most places, and you have to watch for pedestrians, cyclists, and wildlife. Parking can be difficult during peak summer season, especially at Paradise, Sunrise, Grove of the Patriarchs, and at the trailheads between Longmire and Paradise; arrive early if you plan to visit these sites. All off-road-vehicle use—4X4 vehicles, ATVs, motorcycles, snowmobiles—is prohibited in Mount Rainier National Park.

PARK ESSENTIALS

PARK FEES AND PERMITS

The entrance fee of $25 per vehicle and $10 for those on foot, motorcycle, or bicycle is good for seven days. Annual passes are $50. Climbing permits are $44 per person per climb or glacier trek. Wilderness camping permits must be obtained for all backcountry trips, and advance reservations are highly recommended.

PARK HOURS

Mount Rainier National Park is open 24/7 year-round, but with limited access in winter. Gates at Nisqually (Longmire) are staffed year-round during the day; facilities at Paradise are open daily from late May to mid-October; and Sunrise is open daily July to early September. During off-hours you can buy passes at the gates from machines that accept credit and debit cards. Winter access to the park is limited to the Nisqually entrance, and the Jackson Memorial Visitor Center at Paradise is open on weekends and holidays in winter. The road from Longmire to Paradise is closed Tuesday and Wednesday during the winter; the Paradise snowplay area is open Thursday to Monday when there is sufficient snow.

CELL-PHONE RECEPTION

Cell-phone reception is unreliable throughout much of the park, although access is clear at Paradise, Sunrise, and Crystal Mountain. Public telephones are at all park visitor centers, at the National Park Inn at Longmire, and at Paradise Inn at Paradise.

EDUCATIONAL OFFERINGS

RANGER PROGRAMS

FAMILY **Junior Ranger Program.** Youngsters ages 6 to 11 can pick up an activity booklet at a visitor center and fill it out as they explore the park. When they complete it, they can show it to a ranger and receive a Mount Rainier Junior Ranger badge. ✉ *Visitor centers, Mt. Rainier National Park* ☎ *360/569–2211* ⊕ *www.nps.gov/mora/forkids/index.htm* ✆ *Free.*

Ranger Programs. Park ranger-led activities include **guided snowshoe walks** in the winter (most suitable for those older than eight) as well as **evening programs** during the summer at Longmire/Cougar Rock, Ohanapecosh, and White River campgrounds, and at the Paradise Inn. Evening talks may cover subjects such as park history, its flora and fauna, or interesting facts on climbing Mount Rainier. There are also daily guided programs that start at the Jackson Visitor Center, including meadow and vista walks, tours of the Paradise Inn, a morning ranger chat, and evening astronomy program. ✉ *Visitor centers, Mt. Rainier National Park* ☎ *360/569–2211* ⊕ *www.nps.gov/mora/planyourvisit/ rangerprograms.htm* ✆ *Free.*

RESTAURANTS

A limited number of restaurants are inside the park, and a few worth checking out lie beyond its borders. Mount Rainier's picnic areas are justly famous, especially in summer, when wildflowers fill the meadows. Resist the urge to feed the yellow pine chipmunks darting about.

HOTELS

The Mount Rainier area is remarkably bereft of quality lodging. Rainier's two national park lodges, at Longmire and Paradise, are attractive and well maintained. They exude considerable history and charm, especially Paradise Inn, but unless you've made summer reservations a year in advance, getting a room can be a challenge. Dozens of motels, cabin complexes, and private vacation-home rentals are near the park entrances; while they can be pricey, the latter are convenient for longer stays. *Hotel reviews have been shortened. For full information, visit Fodors.com.*

WHAT IT COSTS			
$	**$$**	**$$$**	**$$$$**
Restaurants	under $13	$13–$20	$21–$30	over $30
Hotels	under $101	$101–$150	$151–$200	over $200

Restaurant prices are the average cost of a main course at dinner, or if dinner is not served, at lunch. Hotel prices are the lowest cost of a standard double room in high season, excluding taxes and service charges.

27

VISITOR INFORMATION

Park Contact Information Mount Rainier National Park. ⊠ *55210 238th Ave. East, Ashford* ☎ *360/569-2211, 360/569-6575* ⊕ *www.nps.gov/mora.*

VISITOR CENTERS

Jackson Memorial Visitor Center. High on the mountain's southern flank, this center houses exhibits on geology, mountaineering, glaciology, and alpine ecology. Multimedia programs are staged in the theater; there's also a snack bar and gift shop. This is the park's most popular visitor destination, and it can be quite crowded in summer. ⊠ *Hwy. 706 E, 19 miles east of Nisqually park entrance, Mt. Rainier National Park* ☎ *360/569-6571* ⊕ *www.nps.gov/mora/planyourvisit/paradise. htm* ☉ *Mid-June–Labor Day, daily 10–7; early Sept., daily 10–6; mid-Sept.–mid-Oct., daily 10–5; late Oct.–early June, weekends 10–5; food service closes 15 mins earlier year-round.*

Longmire Museum and Visitor Center. Glass cases inside this museum preserve the park's plants and animals, including a stuffed cougar. Historical photographs and geographical displays provide a worthwhile overview of the park's history. The adjacent visitor center has some perfunctory exhibits on the surrounding forest and its inhabitants, as well as pamphlets and information about park activities. ⊠ *Hwy. 706, 10 miles east of Ashford, Longmire* ☎ *360/569-6575* ⊕ *www.nps.gov/ mora/planyourvisit/longmire.htm* 🎟 *Free* ☉ *July–mid-Oct., daily 9–5; mid-Oct.–June, daily 9–4:30.*

Sunrise Visitor Center. Exhibits at this center explain the region's sparser alpine and subalpine ecology. A network of nearby loop trails leads you through alpine meadows and forest to overlooks that have broad views of the Cascades and Rainier. The visitor center has a snack bar and gift shop. ⊠ *Sunrise Rd., 15 miles from the White River park entrance, Mt. Rainier National Park* ☎ 360/663–2425 ⊕ *www.nps.gov/mora/planyourvisit/ sunrise.htm* ☉ *Early July–early Sept., daily 10–6.*

EXPLORING

SCENIC DRIVES

Chinook Pass Road. Route 410, the highway to Yakima, follows the eastern edge of the park to Chinook Pass, where it climbs the steep, 5,432-foot pass via a series of switchbacks. At its top, take in broad views of Rainier and the east slope of the Cascades. The pass usually closes for the winter in November. ⊠ *Mt. Rainier National Park* ⊕ *www.wsdot. wa.gov/traffic/passes/chinook.*

Mowich Lake Road. In the northwest corner of the park, this 24-mile mountain road begins in Wilkeson and heads up the Rainier foothills to Mowich Lake, traversing beautiful mountain meadows along the way. Mowich Lake is a pleasant spot for a picnic. The road is open mid-July to mid-October. ⊕ *www.nps.gov/mora/planyourvisit/carbon- and-mowich.htm.*

Paradise Road. This 9-mile stretch of Highway 706 winds its way up the mountain's southwest flank from Longmire to Paradise, taking you from lowland forest to the ever-expanding vistas of the mountain above. Visit early on a weekday if possible, especially in peak summer months, when the road is packed with cars. The route is open year-round though there may be some weekday closures in winter. From November through April, all vehicles must carry chains. ⊠ *Mt. Rainier National Park* ⊕ *www.nps.gov/mora/planyourvisit/paradise.htm.*

Sunrise Road. This popular (and often crowded) scenic road to the highest drivable point at Mount Rainier carves its way 11 miles up Sunrise Ridge from the White River Valley on the northeast side of the park. As you top the ridge there are sweeping views of the surrounding lowlands. The road is open late June to October. ⊠ *Mt. Rainier National Park* ⊕ *www.nps.gov/mora/planyourvisit/sunrise.htm.*

HISTORIC SITES

National Park Inn. Even if you don't plan to stay overnight, you can stop by year-round to view the architecture of this inn, built in 1917 and on the National Register of Historic Places. While you're here, relax in front of the fireplace in the lounge, stop at the gift shop, or dine at the restaurant. ⊠ *Longmire Visitor Complex, Hwy. 706, 10 miles east of Nisqually entrance, Longmire* ☎ 360/569–2411 ⊕ *www. mtrainierguestservices.com/accommodations/national-park-inn.*

SCENIC STOPS

Christine Falls. These two-tiered falls were named in honor of Christine Louise Van Trump, who climbed to the 10,000-foot level on Mount Rainier in 1889 at the age of nine, despite having a crippling nervous-system disorder. ☒ *Next to Hwy. 706, about 2½ miles east of Cougar Rock Campground, Mt. Rainier National Park.*

Fodor's Choice ★ **Grove of the Patriarchs.** Protected from the periodic fires that swept through the surrounding areas, this small island of 1,000-year-old trees is one of Mount Rainier National Park's most memorable features. A 1½-mile loop trail heads through the old-growth forest of Douglas fir, cedar, and hemlock. ☒ *Rte. 123, west of the Stevens Canyon entrance, Mt. Rainier National Park* ⊕ *www.nps.gov/mora/planyourvisit/ ohanapecosh.htm.*

> ### PLANTS AND WILDLIFE IN MOUNT RAINIER
>
> Wildflower season in the meadows at and above timberline is mid-July through August. Large mammals like deer, elk, black bears, and cougars tend to occupy the less accessible wilderness areas of the park and thus elude the average visitor; smaller animals like squirrels and marmots are easier to spot. The best times to see wildlife are at dawn and dusk at the forest's edge. Fawns are born in May, and the bugling of bull elk on the high ridges can be heard in late September and October, especially on the park's eastern side.

27

Narada Falls. A steep but short trail leads to the viewing area for these spectacular 168-foot falls, which expand to a width of 75 feet during peak flow times. In winter the frozen falls are popular with ice climbers. ☒ *Along Hwy. 706, 1 mile west of the turnoff for Paradise, 6 miles east of Cougar Rock Campground, Mt. Rainier National Park* ⊕ *www.nps. gov/mora/planyourvisit/longmire.htm.*

FAMILY **Tipsoo Lake.** The short, pleasant trail that circles the lake—ideal for families—provides breathtaking views. Enjoy the subalpine wildflower meadows during the summer months; in early fall there is an abundant supply of huckleberries. ☒ *Off Cayuse Pass east on Hwy. 410, Mt. Rainier National Park* ⊕ *www.nps.gov/mora/planyourvisit/sunrise.htm.*

SPORTS AND THE OUTDOORS

MULTISPORT OUTFITTERS

RMI Expeditions. Reserve a private hiking guide through this highly regarded outfitter, or take part in its one-day mountaineering classes (mid-May through late September), where participants are evaluated on their fitness for the climb and must be able to withstand a 16-mile round-trip hike with a 9,000-foot gain in elevation. The company also arranges private cross-country skiing and snowshoeing guides. ☒ *30027 Hwy. 706 E, Ashford* ☎ *888/892–5462, 360/569–2227* ⊕ *www.rmiguides.com* ☛ *From $1,026 for 4-day package.*

Whittaker Mountaineering. You can rent hiking and climbing gear, skis, snowshoes, snowboards, and other outdoor equipment at this all-purpose Rainier Base Camp outfitter, which also arranges for private cross-country skiing and hiking guides. ✉ *30027 SR 706E, Ashford* ☎ *800/238–5756, 360/569–2982* ⊕ *www.whittakermountaineering.com.*

BIRD-WATCHING

Be alert for kestrels, red-tailed hawks, and, occasionally, golden eagles on snags in the lowland forests. Also present at Rainier, but rarely seen, are great horned owls, spotted owls, and screech owls. Iridescent rufous hummingbirds flit from blossom to blossom in the drowsy summer lowlands, and sprightly water ouzels flutter in the many forest creeks. Raucous Steller's jays and gray jays scold passersby from trees, often darting boldly down to steal morsels from unguarded picnic tables. At higher elevations, look for the pure white plumage of the white-tailed ptarmigan as it hunts for seeds and insects in winter. Waxwings, vireos, nuthatches, sapsuckers, warblers, flycatchers, larks, thrushes, siskins, tanagers, and finches are common throughout the park.

HIKING

Although the mountain can seem remarkably benign on calm summer days, hiking Rainier is not a city-park stroll. Dozens of hikers and trekkers annually lose their way and must be rescued—and lives are lost on the mountain each year. Weather that approaches cyclonic levels can appear quite suddenly, any month of the year. All visitors venturing far from vehicle access points, with the possible exception of the short loop hikes listed here, should carry day packs with warm clothing, food, and other emergency supplies.

EASY

Nisqually Vista Trail. Equally popular in summer and winter, this trail is a 1¼-mile round-trip through subalpine meadows to an overlook point for Nisqually Glacier. The gradually sloping path is a favorite venue for cross-country skiers in winter; in summer, listen for the shrill alarm calls of the area's marmots. *Easy.* ⊕ *Trailhead: at Jackson Memorial Visitor Center, Rte. 123, 1 mile north of Ohanapecosh, at the high point of Hwy. 706* ⊕ *www.nps.gov/mora/planyourvisit/day-hiking-at-mount-rainier.htm.*

Sunrise Nature Trail. The 1.5-mile-long loop of this self-guided trail takes you through the delicate subalpine meadows near the Sunrise Visitor Center. A gradual climb to the ridgetop yields magnificent views of Mount Rainier and the more distant volcanic cones of Mount Baker, Mount Adams, and Glacier Peak. *Easy.* ⊕ *Trailhead: at Sunrise Visitor Center, Sunrise Rd., 15 miles from the White River park entrance* ⊕ *www.nps.gov/mora/planyourvisit/sunrise.htm.*

Trail of the Shadows. This 0.7-mile loop is notable for its glimpses of meadowland ecology, its colorful soda springs (don't drink the water), James Longmire's old homestead cabin, and the foundation of the old Longmire Springs Hotel, which was destroyed by fire around 1900.

Easy. ⊕ *Trailhead: at Hwy. 706, 10 miles east of Nisqually entrance*
⊕ *www.nps.gov/mora/planyourvisit/day-hiking-at-mount-rainier.htm.*

MODERATE

Fodor's Choice
★

Skyline Trail. This 5-mile loop, one of the highest trails in the park, beckons day-trippers with a vista of alpine ridges and, in summer, meadows filled with brilliant flowers and birds. At 6,800 feet, Panorama Point, the spine of the Cascade Range, spreads away to the east, and Nisqually Glacier tumbles downslope. *Moderate.* ⊕ *Trailhead: Jackson Memorial Visitor Center, Rte. 123, 1 mile north of Ohanapecosh at the high point of Hwy. 706* ⊕ *www.nps.gov/mora/planyourvisit/skyline-trail.htm.*

Van Trump Park Trail. You gain an exhilarating 2,200 feet on this route while hiking through a vast expanse of meadow with views of the southern Puget Sound. The 5.8-mile track provides good footing, and the average hiker can make it up and back in five hours. *Moderate.* ⊕ *Trailhead: Hwy. 706 at Christine Falls, 4.4 miles east of Longmire* ⊕ *www.nps.gov/mora/planyourvisit/van-trump-trail.htm.*

DIFFICULT

Fodor's Choice
★

Wonderland Trail. All other Mount Rainier hikes pale in comparison to this stunning 93-mile trek, which completely encircles the mountain. The trail passes through all the major life zones of the park, from the old-growth forests of the lowlands to the alpine meadows and goat-haunted glaciers of the highlands—pick up a mountain-goat sighting card from a ranger station or visitor center if you want to help in the park's effort to learn more about these elusive animals. Wonderland is a rugged trail; elevation gains and losses totaling 3,500 feet are common in a day's hike, which averages 8 miles. Most hikers start out from Longmire or Sunrise and take 10–14 days to cover the 93-mile route. Snow lingers on the high passes well into June (sometimes July); count on rain any time of the year. Campsites are wilderness areas with pit toilets and water that must be purified before drinking. Only hardy, well-equipped, and experienced wilderness trekkers should attempt this trip, but those who do will be amply rewarded. Wilderness permits are required, and reservations are strongly recommended. *Difficult.* ⊕ *Trailheads: Longmire Visitor Center, Hwy. 706, 17 miles east of Ashford; Sunrise Visitor Center, Sunrise Rd., 15 miles west of the White River park entrance* ⊕ *www.nps.gov/mora/planyourvisit/the-wonderland-trail.htm.*

27

MOUNTAIN CLIMBING

Climbing Mount Rainier is not for amateurs; each year, adventurers die on the mountain, and many become lost and must be rescued. Near-catastrophic weather can appear quite suddenly, any month of the year. If you're experienced in technical, high-elevation snow, rock, and ice-field adventuring, Mount Rainier can be a memorable adventure. Climbers can fill out a climbing card at the Paradise, White River, or Carbon River ranger stations and lead their own groups of two or more. Climbers must register with a ranger before leaving and check out on return. A $45 annual climbing fee applies to anyone heading above 10,000 feet or onto one of Rainier's glaciers. During peak season it is recommended that climbers make their camping reservations ($20 per site) in advance;

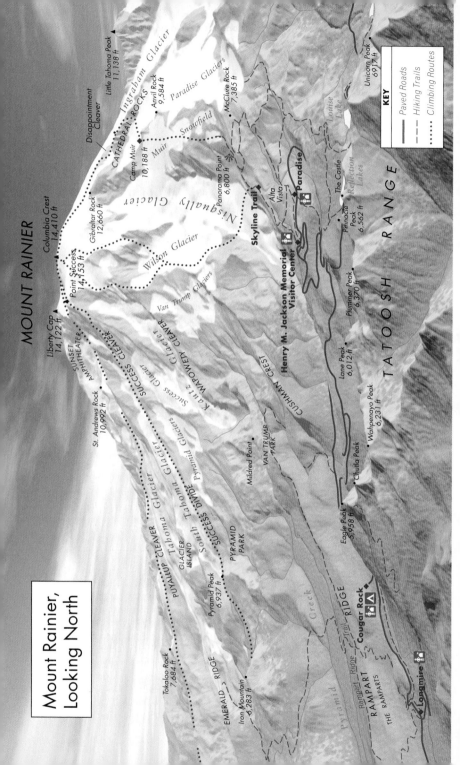

Mount Rainier, Looking North

MOUNT RAINIER

Little Tahoma Peak
11,138 ft

Disappointment Cleaver

Ingraham Glacier

CATHEDRAL ROCKS

Anvil Rock
9,584 ft

Paradise Glaciers

McClure Rock
7,385 ft

Snowfield

Camp Muir
10,188 ft

Muir

Panorama Point
6,800 ft

Columbia Crest
14,410 ft

Gibraltar Rock
12,660 ft

Nisqually Glacier

Skyline Trail

Alta Vista

Paradise

Louise Lake

The Castle

Reflection Lakes

Unicorn Peak
6,917 ft

Point Success
14,153 ft

Wilson Glacier

Henry M. Jackson Memorial
Visitor Center

Pinnacle Peak
6,562 ft

Liberty Cap
14,122 ft

SUNSET AMPHITHEATER

Van Trump Glaciers

Plummer Peak
6,370 ft

SUCCESS CLEAVER

St. Andrews Rock
10,992 ft

KAUTZ CLEAVER

Kautz Glacier

CUSHMAN CREST

Lane Peak
6,012 ft

TATOOSH RANGE

Success Glacier

VAN TRUMP PARK

PUYALLUP CLEAVER

Tahoma Glacier

Pyramid Glaciers

Mildred Point

Wahpenayo Peak
6,231 ft

Chutla Peak

GLACIER ISLAND

South Tahoma Glacier

SUCCESS DIVIDE

PYRAMID PARK

Eagle Peak
5,958 ft

Tokaloo Rock
7,684 ft

Pyramid Peak
6,937 ft

Cougar Rock

EMERALD RIDGE

Iron Mountain
6,283 ft

Creek

Pyramid

Trail Ridge Trail

RAMPART RIDGE

THE RAMPARTS

Longmire

KEY

—— Paved Roads
– – – Hiking Trails
······· Climbing Routes

reservations are taken by fax and mail beginning in mid-March on a first-come, first-served basis (find the reservation form at ⊕ *www.nps. gov/mora/planyourvisit/climbing.htm*).

SKIING AND SNOWSHOEING

Mount Rainier is a major Nordic ski center for cross-country and telemark skiing. Although trails are not groomed, those around Paradise are extremely popular. If you want to ski with fewer people, try the trails in and around the Ohanapecosh–Stevens Canyon area, which are just as beautiful and, because of their more easterly exposure, slightly less subject to the rains that can douse the Longmire side, even in the dead of winter. Never ski on plowed main roads, especially around Paradise—the snowplow operator can't see you. Rentals aren't available on the eastern side of the park.

Deep snows make Mount Rainier a snowshoeing pleasure. The Paradise area, with its network of trails, is the best choice. The park's east-side roads, Routes 123 and 410, are unplowed and provide other good snowshoeing venues, although you must share the main routes with snowmobilers.

Paradise Snowplay Area and Nordic Ski Route. Sledding on flexible sleds (no toboggans or runners), inner tubes, and plastic saucers is allowed only in the Paradise snow-play area adjacent to the Jackson Visitor Center. The area is open when there is sufficient snow, usually Thursday through Monday from late December through mid-March. The easy, 3½-mile Paradise Valley Road Nordic ski route begins at the Paradise parking lot and follows Paradise Valley/Stevens Canyon Road to Reflection Lakes. Equipment rentals are available at Whittaker Mountaineering in Ashford or at the National Park Inn's General Store in Longmire. ⊠ *Adjacent to the Jackson Visitor Center at Paradise, Mt. Rainier National Park* ☎ *360/569–2211* ⊕ *www.nps.gov/mora/planyourvisit/ winter-recreation.htm.*

TOURS AND OUTFITTERS

General Store at the National Park Inn. The store at the National Park Inn in Longmire rents cross-country ski equipment and snowshoes. It's open daily in winter, depending on snow conditions. ⊠ *National Park Inn, Longmire* ☎ *360/569–2411* ⊕ *www.mtrainierguestservices.com/ activities-and-events/winter-activities/cross-country-skiing.*

WHAT'S NEARBY

NEARBY TOWNS

Ashford sits astride an ancient trail across the Cascades used by the Yakama Indians to trade with the coastal tribes of western Washington. The town began as a logging railway terminal; today it's the main gateway to Mount Rainier—and the only year-round access point to the park—with lodges, restaurants, grocery stores, and gift shops. Surrounded by Cascade peaks, **Packwood** is a pretty mountain village on

DID YOU KNOW?

Named after British admiral Peter Rainier in the late 18th century, Mount Rainier had an earlier name. Tahoma (also Takhoma), its American Indian name, means "the mountain that was God." Various unsuccessful attempts have been made to restore the aboriginal name to the peak. Of course, to most Puget Sound residents, Rainier is simply "the mountain."

U.S. 12, below White Pass. Between Mount Rainier and Mount St. Helens, it's a perfect jumping-off point for exploring local wilderness areas.

Visitor Information Destination Packwood Association. ⊠ *13011B U.S. Hwy. 12, Packwood* ☎ *360/494–2223* ⊕ *www.destinationpackwood.com.*

NEARBY ATTRACTIONS

Goat Rocks Wilderness. The crags in Gifford Pinchot National Forest, south of Mount Rainier, are aptly named. You often see mountain goats here, especially when you hike into the backcountry. Goat Lake is a particularly good spot for viewing these elusive creatures. See the goats without backpacking by taking Forest Road 21 to Forest Road 2140, south from U.S. 12. The goats will be on Stonewall Ridge looming up ahead of you. ⊠ *NF-21 and NF-2140, Randle* ☎ *360/891–5000* ⊕ *www.fs.usda.gov/giffordpinchot.*

Johnston Ridge Observatory. With the most spectacular views of the crater and lava dome of Mount St. Helens, this observatory also has exhibits that interpret the geology of the mountain and explain how scientists monitor an active volcano. ⊠ *Rte. 504, 53 miles east of I–5, 24000 Spirit Lake Hwy., Castle Rock* ☎ *360/274–2140* ⊕ *www.fs.usda.gov/recarea/mountsthelens/recarea/?recid=31562* 🎫 *$8* ⊙ *Mid-May–Oct., daily 10–6.*

FAMILY **Mt. Rainier Scenic Railroad and Museum.** This trip takes you through lush forests and across scenic bridges, covering 14 miles of incomparable beauty. Trains depart from Elbe, 11 miles west of Ashford, then bring passengers to a lovely picnic area near Mineral Lake before returning. Seasonal theme trips, such as the Great Pumpkin Express and the Snowball Express, are also available. Back at the station in Mineral Lake, guests can tour the museum containing old train memorabilia and artifacts, as well as exhibits on the area's old railroad camps, which served as the hub of logging operations by rail. ⊠ *349 Mineral Creek Rd., Mineral* ☎ *360/569–7959, 888/783–2611* ⊕ *www.mrsr.com* 🎫 *Rides $32, museum $15 (free with train ride)* ⊙ *Mid-May–Oct., weekends (also Fri. in summer); some seasonal trips in Dec. and Easter weekend.*

Mount St. Helens Science and Learning Center. Exhibits at this multimillion-dollar facility document the great 1980 blast of Mount St. Helens and its effects on the surrounding 150,000 acres, which were devastated but are in the process of a remarkable recovery. A ¼-mile trail leads from the visitor center to Coldwater Lake, which has a recreation area. ⊠ *Rte. 504, 43 miles east of I–5, 19000 Spirit Lake Hwy., Toutle* ☎ *360/274–2114* ⊕ *www.mshslc.org* 🎫 *Free* ⊙ *Weekends 10–6.*

Mount St. Helens Visitor Center. This facility, one of three visitor centers along Route 504 on the west side of the mountain, has exhibits documenting the eruption, plus a walk-through volcano. ⊠ *Rte. 504, 5 miles east of I–5, 3029 Spirit Lake Hwy., Silver Lake* ☎ *360/274–2131* ⊕ *www.mountsthelens.com/visitorcenters.html* 🎫 *$5* ⊙ *Mid-May–mid-Sept., daily 9–5; mid-Sept.–Oct. and Mar.–mid-May, daily 9–4; Nov.–Feb., Thurs.–Mon. 9–4.*

FAMILY **Northwest Trek Wildlife Park.** This spectacular, 435-acre wildlife park 35 miles south of Puyallup is devoted to native creatures of the Pacific Northwest. Walking paths wind through natural surroundings—so natural that in 1998 a cougar entered the park and started snacking on the deer (it was finally trapped and relocated to the North Cascades). See beavers, otters, and wolverines; get close to wolves, foxes, coyotes; and observe several species of big cats and bears in wild environments. Admission includes a 50-minute tram ride through fields of wandering moose, bighorn sheep, elk, bison, and mountain goats. The most adventurous way to see the park is via one of five zip lines, which traverse the park canopy—rides are available early May through late September. ⊠ *11610 Trek Dr. E, Eatonville* ☎ *360/832–6117* ⊕ *www.nwtrek.org* 🖼 *$19.75* ☉ *Late June–Labor Day, daily 9:30–6; early Sept.–early Oct. and mid-Mar.–late June, weekdays 9:30–4, weekends 9:30–5; Oct.– early Mar., Fri.–Sun. 9:30–3.*

AREA ACTIVITIES

SPORTS AND THE OUTDOORS
SKIING
Crystal Mountain Ski Area. Washington State's biggest and best-known ski area has 10 lifts (plus a children's lift and a gondola), and 57 runs. In summer, it's open for hiking, rides on the Mt. Rainier Gondola, and meals at the Summit House, all providing sensational views of Rainier and the Cascades. **Facilities:** 57 trails; 2,600 acres; 3,100-foot vertical drop; 12 lifts. ⊠ *Crystal Mountain Blvd., off Rte. 410, Crystal Mountain* ☎ *360/663–2265* ⊕ *www.crystalmountainresort.com* 🎫 *Lift ticket: $76 including gondola, $68 without; $25 gondola only* ☉ *Mid.-Nov.– mid.-Apr., daily 9–4; gondola open in summer: June–Aug., weekends 10–7:30, weekdays 10–5:30; Sept. daily 10–5:30.*

WHERE TO EAT

IN THE PARK

$$$ ✕ **National Park Inn Dining Room.** Photos of Mount Rainier taken by top
ECLECTIC photographers adorn the walls of this inn's large dining room, a bonus on the many days the mountain refuses to show itself. Meals are simple but tasty: pot roast with fingerling potatoes, seared halibut, cedar-plank trout, and blackberry cobbler à la mode. For a hearty start to the day, try the country breakfast or oatmeal brûlée. $ *Average main: $24* ⊠ *Hwy. 706, Longmire* ☎ *360/569–2411* ⊕ *www.mtrainierguestservices.com* 🍴 *Reservations not accepted.*

$ ✕ **Paradise Camp Deli.** Grilled meats, sandwiches, salads, and soft drinks
AMERICAN are served daily from May through early October and on weekends
FAMILY and holidays during the rest of the year. $ *Average main: $9* ⊠ *Jackson Visitor Center, Paradise Rd. E, Paradise* ☎ *360/569–2400* ⊕ *www. mtrainierguestservices.com* ☉ *Closed weekdays early Oct.–Apr.* 🍴 *Reservations not accepted.*

27

$$$ ✕**Paradise Inn.** Where else can you enjoy Sunday brunch in a historic,
AMERICAN heavy-timbered lodge halfway up a mountain? Tall windows provide
terrific views of Rainier, and the warm glow of native wood perme-
ates the large dining room. The lunch menu is simple and healthy—
three kinds of burgers (black bean, bison, and beef), salads, and the
like. For dinner, there's nothing like a hearty plate of the inn's signa-
ture bourbon buffalo meat loaf. ⑤ *Average main: $24* ✉ *E. Paradise
Rd., near Jackson Visitor Center, Paradise* ☎ *360/569-2275* ⊕ *www.
mtrainierguestservices.com* ⊘ *Closed Oct.–late May* ⚅ *Reservations
not accepted.*

$ ✕**Sunrise Day Lodge Food Service.** A cafeteria and grill serve inexpen-
AMERICAN sive hamburgers, chili, and hot dogs from early July through August.
FAMILY ⑤ *Average main: $9* ✉ *Sunrise Rd., 15 miles from the White River
park entrance, Mt. Rainier National Park* ☎ *360/663-2425* ⊕ *www.
mtrainierguestservices.com* ⊘ *Closed early Sept.–late June* ⚅ *Reserva-
tions not accepted.*

PICNIC AREAS
Park picnic areas are usually open only from late May through
September.

Sunrise Picnic Area. Set in an alpine meadow that's filled with wildflow-
ers in July and August, this picnic area provides expansive views of
the mountain and surrounding ranges in good weather. ✉ *Sunrise Rd.,
11 miles west of the White River entrance, Mt. Rainier National Park*
⊕ *www.nps.gov/mora/planyourvisit/sunrise.htm.*

OUTSIDE THE PARK

$$ ✕**Alexander's Country Inn & Restaurant.** This woodsy country inn serves
AMERICAN some of the best food in the area. Ceiling fans and wooden booths lining
the walls add a touch of whimsy to the 1912 building. Try the steak or
trout—freshly caught from the pond on the grounds. The homemade
bread is fantastic, and the blackberry pie is a must for dessert. Dine inside
or outside on a patio overlooking a waterfall. Box lunches for adventurers are available. ⑤ *Average main: $20* ✉ *37515 Hwy. 706 E, Ashford*
☎ *360/569-2323, 800/654-7615* ⊕ *www.alexanderscountryinn.com*
⊘ *No lunch. Closed Mon.–Thurs. fall–spring.*

$ ✕**Scaleburgers.** Once a 1939 logging-truck weigh station, the build-
AMERICAN ing is now a popular restaurant serving homemade hamburgers, fries,
FAMILY and shakes. Eat outside on tables overlooking the hills and scenic railroad. ⑤ *Average main: $8* ✉ *54109 Mountain Hwy. E, 11 miles west
of Ashford, Elbe* ☎ *360/569-2247* ▭ *No credit cards* ⊘ *Limited hrs in
winter; call ahead.*

$$$ ✕**Summit House.** On top of Crystal Mountain at 6,872 feet is Washing-
PACIFIC ton's highest-elevation restaurant. The menu features Northwest cui-
NORTHWEST sine, including halibut fish-and-chips, coho salmon, and huckleberry ice
cream. On Fridays there's a prime rib special. With stunning views of
Mount Rainier, the Summit House is a popular stop for skiers, hikers,
and summer tourists, too. Sit inside to stay warm by the fireplace, or sit
outside on the patio and watch chipmunks run along the nearby rocks.
The restaurant is reached by riding the scenic Mt. Rainier Gondola from

the base of Crystal Mountain; note that gondola tickets ($25/adults) must be purchased separately. As the only restaurant at the summit, reservations are strongly advised, though walk-ins are accepted when space is available. $ *Average main: $23* ✉ *33914 Crystal Mountain Blvd., Crystal Mountain* ☎ *360/663–3085* ⊕ *crystalmountainresort. com* ☉ *Open seasonally during summer and ski season; check website or call for current hrs.*

WHERE TO STAY

IN THE PARK

$$$
B&B/INN

🏠 **National Park Inn.** A large stone fireplace warms the common room of this country inn, the only one of the park's two inns that's open year-round. **Pros:** classic ambience; open all year. **Cons:** jam-packed in summer; must book far in advance; some rooms have shared bath. $ *Rooms from: $169* ✉ *Longmire Visitor Complex, Hwy. 706, 6 miles east of Nisqually entrance, Longmire* ☎ *360/569–2275, 855/755–2275* ⊕ *www. mtrainierguestservices.com* ⤳ *25 rooms, 18 with bath* ⵔ *No meals.*

$$$
HOTEL
Fodor's Choice
★

🏠 **Paradise Inn.** With its hand-carved Alaskan cedar logs, burnished parquet floors, stone fireplaces, Indian rugs, and glorious mountain views, this 1917 inn is a classic example of a national park lodge. **Pros:** central to trails; pristine vistas; nature-inspired details. **Cons:** rooms are small and basic; many rooms have shared bathrooms; no elevators, a/c, cell service, or Wi-Fi. $ *Rooms from: $174* ✉ *E. Paradise Rd., near Jackson Visitor Center, Paradise* ☎ *360/569–2275, 855/755–2275* ⊕ *www. mtrainierguestservices.com* ☉ *Closed Oct.–mid-May* ⤳ *121 rooms* ⵔ *No meals.*

27

OUTSIDE THE PARK

$$
B&B/INN

🏠 **Alexander's Country Inn.** At this top-notch lodging just a mile from Mount Rainier's Nisqually Entrance, antique furnishings and fine linens lend romance to rooms in the main building; there are also two adjacent guesthouses. **Pros:** luxurious amenities, especially considering moderate rates; on-site day spa; serving guests since 1912 and also home to one of the region's most popular restaurants. **Cons:** lots of breakables means it's not great for children. $ *Rooms from: $130* ✉ *37515 Hwy. 706 E, 4 miles east of Ashford, Ashford* ☎ *360/569–2300, 800/654–7615* ⊕ *www.alexanderscountryinn.com* ⤳ *12 rooms, 2 3-bedroom houses* ⵔ *Breakfast.*

$$$$
B&B/INN
FAMILY

🏠 **Alta Crystal Resort.** In the national forest, this small resort with family-friendly amenities feels remote yet is close to Mount Rainier's Sunrise entrance and Crystal Mountain Ski Resort. **Pros:** very family-friendly; easy access to trails; owners are knowledgeable about the area. **Cons:** not close to restaurants or grocery store; limited cell-phone reception. $ *Rooms from: $280* ✉ *68317 SR 410 E, Greenwater* ☎ *360/663–2556, 800/277–6475, 360/663–2500* ⊕ *www.altacrystalresort.com* ⤳ *23 suites, 1 cabin* ⵔ *No meals.*

Best Campgrounds in Mount Rainier

Three drive-in campgrounds are in the park—Cougar Rock, Ohanapecosh, and White River—with almost 500 sites for tents and RVs. None has hot water or RV hookups. The more primitive Mowich Lake Campground has 10 walk-in sites for tents only. For backcountry camping, get a free wilderness permit at a visitor center on a first-come, first-served basis (permits for specific dates can be reserved for a fee of $20 per group for up to 14 days of camping). Primitive sites are spaced at 7- to 8-mile intervals along the Wonderland Trail.

Cougar Rock Campground.
A secluded, heavily wooded campground with an amphitheater, Cougar Rock is one of the first to fill up. Reservations are accepted for summer only. ⊠ *2½ miles north of Longmire* ☎ *877/444–6777.*

Mowich Lake Campground. This is Rainier's only lakeside campground and has just 10 primitive campsites. At 4,959 feet, it's also peaceful and secluded. ⊠ *Mowich Lake Rd., 6 miles east of park boundary* ☎ *360/569–2211.*

Ohanapecosh Campground. This lush, green campground in the park's southeast corner has an amphitheater and self-guided trail. It's one of the first campgrounds to open for the season. ⊠ *Rte. 123, 1½ miles north of park boundary* ☎ *877/444–6777.*

White River Campground. At an elevation of 4,400 feet, White River is one of the park's highest and least wooded campgrounds. Here you can enjoy campfire programs, self-guided trails, and partial views of Mount Rainier's summit. ⊠ *5 miles west of White River entrance* ☎ *360/569–2211.*

$$$$
B&B/INN
⌂ **Stormking Spa and Cabins.** In a forest setting a mile from the Nisqually entrance of Mount Rainier National Park, Stormking features five luxury cabins for adults: four are shaped like yurts, and all have cozy gas fireplaces, hot tubs, private outdoor seating areas, and natural finishes of wood and stone. **Pros:** very romantic and secluded; reasonably priced for special occasion getaways; deer and other wildlife frequent the property. **Cons:** no full kitchens; Wi-Fi available at spa but not in cabins. ⑤ *Rooms from: $205* ⊠ *37311 SR 706 E, Ashford* ☎ *360/569–2964* ⊕ *www.stormkingspa.com* ⇥ *5 cabins* ⓘ⊙⌐ *Breakfast.*

$$$
B&B/INN
⌂ **Wellspring.** Deep in the woods outside Ashford, the accommodations here include tastefully designed log cabins, tent cabins, a tree house, and a room in a greenhouse. **Pros:** unique lodging with a wide range of prices, depending on the room; some options good for groups; relaxing spa and hot soaking tubs. **Cons:** limited amenities; no cell service; no on-site assistance for guests. ⑤ *Rooms from: $155* ⊠ *54922 Kernehan Rd., Ashford* ☎ *360/569–2514* ⊕ *www.wellspringspa.com* ⇥ *5 rooms, 6 cabins, 3 tent cabins, 1 cottage, 1 tree house, 1 lodge* ⓘ⊙⌐ *Breakfast.*

NORTH CASCADES NATIONAL PARK

WELCOME TO NORTH CASCADES NATIONAL PARK

TOP REASONS TO GO

★ **Pure wilderness:** Nearly 400 miles of mountain and meadow trails immerse hikers in pristine natural panoramas, with sure sightings of bald eagles, deer, elk, and other wildlife.

★ **Majestic glaciers:** The North Cascades are home to several hundred moving ice masses, more than half of the glaciers in the United States.

★ **Splendid flora:** A bright palette of flowers blankets the hillsides in midsummer, while October's colors paint the landscape in vibrant autumn hues.

★ **Thrilling boat rides:** Lake Chelan, Ross Lake, and the Stehekin River are the starting points for kayaking, white-water rafting, and ferry trips.

★ **19th-century history:** Delve into the state's farming, lumber, and logging pasts in clapboard towns and homesteads around the park.

1 **North Unit.** The park's creek-cut northern wilderness, centered on snowy Mount Challenger, stretches north from Highway 20 over the Picket Range toward the Canadian border. It's an endless landscape of pine-topped peaks and ridges.

2 **South Unit.** Hike lake-filled mountain foothills in summer to take in vistas of blue skies and flower-filled meadows. Waterfalls and wildlife are abundant here.

3 **Ross Lake National Recreation Area.** Drawing a thick line from British Columbia all the way down to the North Cascades Scenic Highway, placid Ross Lake is edged with pretty bays that draw swimmers and boaters.

4 **Lake Chelan National Recreation Area.** Ferries cruise between small waterfront villages along this pristine waterway, while kayakers and hikers follow quiet trails along its edges. This is one of the Northwest's most popular summer escapes, with nature-bound activities and rustic accommodations.

KEY	
🏠	Ranger Station
⛺	Campground
🪧	Picnic Area
🍴	Restaurant
🏨	Lodge
🚶	Trailhead
🚻	Restrooms
➤	Scenic Viewpoint
⋯⋯	Walking/Hiking Trails

WASHINGTON

CANADA
BRITISH COLUMBIA
WASHINGTON
UNITED STATES   Hozomeen

EASY RIDGE
Mt. Challenger

ROSS
LAKE

ROSS LAKE
NATIONAL
RECREATION
AREA
3

CRESCENT SPIRES

Gorge   Diablo
Powerhouse
Newhalem
Creek   Colonial Creek
Visitor Center
20
Goodell Creek
Ladder
Creek Falls
and Rock Gardens

McAllister
Creek
Panther Creek
Fisher Creek
Thunder Creek

NORTH CASCADE
NATIONAL PARK
SOUTH UNIT
2

Ross Lake

North Cascades Highway

20

Rainy Pass

Cottonwood

Bridge Creek
Campground

LAKE CHELAN
NATIONAL RECREATION
AREA
4

Buckner
Homestead

Visitor Center
Stehekin

Lake
Chelan

0   5 mi
0   5 km

GETTING ORIENTED

The park rises upward from the massive Cascade ranges seen northeast of Seattle, widening in a swath of snow-covered peaks all the way to the Canadian border. The broad Skagit River and many large creeks cut through the valleys; most end in the long arm of Lake Chelan in the south or in the snakelike expanse of Ross Lake at the park's northern edge. Even in summer, valleys can start the day shrouded in fog; it's best to drive the highway west to east in the afternoon. A morning start is a good choice coming the other way. However, you'll find the most sensational scenery by hiking to one of the high park passes or mountain lookouts.

28

Updated by
Shelley Arenas

Countless snow-clad mountain spires dwarf narrow glacial valleys in this 505,000-acre expanse of the North Cascades, which encompasses three diverse natural areas. North Cascades National Park is the core of the region, flanked by Lake Chelan National Recreation Area to the south and Ross Lake National Recreation Area to the north; all are part of the Stephen T. Mather Wilderness Area. It's a spectacular gathering of snowy peaks, glacial meadows, plunging canyons, and cold deep-blue lakes. Traditionally the lands of several American Indian tribes, it's fitting that it's still completely wild—and wildlife-filled.

NORTH CASCADES PLANNER

WHEN TO GO

The spectacular, craggy peaks of the North Cascades—often likened to the Alps—are breathtaking anytime. Summer is peak season, especially along the alpine stretches of Highway 20; weekends and holidays can be crowded. Summer is short and glorious in the high country, extending from snowmelt (late May to July, depending on the elevation and the amount of snow) to early September.

The North Cascades Highway is a popular autumn drive in September and October, when the changing leaves put on a colorful show. The lowland forest areas, such as the complex around Newhalem, can be visited almost any time of year. These are wonderfully quiet in early spring or late autumn on mild rainy days. Snow closes the North Cascades Highway from mid-November through mid-April.

AVG. HIGH/LOW TEMPS.

Jan.	Feb.	Mar.	Apr.	May	June
39/30	43/32	49/34	56/38	64/43	70/49

July	Aug.	Sept.	Oct.	Nov.	Dec.
76/52	76/53	69/49	57/42	45/36	39/31

PLANNING YOUR TIME
NORTH CASCADES IN ONE DAY

The **North Cascades Highway,** with its breathtaking mountain and meadow scenery, is one of the most memorable drives in the United States. Although many travelers first head northeast from Seattle into the park and make this their grand finale, if you start from Winthrop, at the south end of the route, traffic is lighter and there's less morning fog. Either way, the main highlight is **Washington Pass,** the road's highest point, where an overlook affords a sensational panorama of snow-covered peaks.

Rainy Pass, where the road heading north drops into the west slope valleys, is another good vantage point. Old-growth forest begins to appear, and after about an hour you reach **Gorge Creek Falls overlook** with its 242-foot cascade. Continue west to Newhalem and stop for lunch, then take a half-hour stroll along the **Trail of the Cedars.** Later, stop at the **North Cascades Visitor Center** and take another short hike. It's an hour drive down the Skagit Valley to Sedro-Woolley, where bald eagles are often seen along the river in winter.

GETTING HERE AND AROUND
AIR TRAVEL

The nearest commercial airports are in Bellingham to the northwest and in Wenatchee south of Chelan. Chelan Seaplanes has daily 30-minute flights to Stehekin from Chelan.

CAR TRAVEL

Highway 20, the North Cascades Highway, splits the park's north and south sections. The gravel Cascade River Road, which runs southeast from Marblemount, peels off Highway 20; Sibley Creek/Hidden Lake Road (USFS 1540) turns off Cascade River Road to the Cascade Pass trailhead. Thornton Creek Road is another rough four-wheel-drive track. For the Ross Lake area in the north, the unpaved Hozomeen Road (Silver–Skagit Road) provides access between Hope, British Columbia, and Silver Lake and Skagit Valley provincial parks. From Stehekin, the Stehekin Valley Road continues to High Bridge and Car Wash Falls—although seasonal floods may cause washouts. Note that roads are narrow and some are closed seasonally, many sights are off the beaten path, and the scenery is so spectacular that, once you're in it, you'll want to make more than a day trip.

28

PARK ESSENTIALS

PARK FEES AND PERMITS

There are no entrance fees to the national park and no parking fees at trailheads on park land. A Northwest Forest Pass, required for parking at Forest Service trailheads, is $5 per vehicle for a calendar day or $30 for a year. A free wilderness permit is required for all overnight stays in the backcountry; these are available in person only. Dock permits for boat-in campgrounds are also $5 per day. Car camping is $16 per night at Colonial Creek, Goodell Creek, and Newhalem Creek campgrounds during the summer (when water and other services are available) and free off-season; free at the primitive Gorge Lake and Hozomeen campgrounds. Passes and permits are sold at visitor centers and ranger stations around the park area.

PARK HOURS

The park never closes, but access is limited by snow in winter. Highway 20 (North Cascades Highway), the major access to the park, is partially closed from mid-November to mid-April.

CELL-PHONE RECEPTION

Cell-phone reception in the park is unreliable. Public telephones are found at the North Cascades Visitor Center and Skagit Information Center in Newhalem, and the Golden West Visitor Center and North Cascades Stehekin Lodge in Stehekin.

EDUCATIONAL OFFERINGS

Seattle City Light Information and Tour Center. Based at a history museum that has exhibits about the onset of electric power through the Cascade ranges, Seattle's public electric company offers tours and programs during summer. Several trails start at the building, and the group offers sightseeing excursions on Diablo Lake in partnership with the North Cascades Institute, Friday through Monday in summer by advance reservation. The tour includes a visit to the Diablo Dam. Free 45-minute walking tours through the historic town of Newhalem are offered daily from July through Labor Day. ⊠ *Milepost 120, North Cascades Hwy., Newhalem* ☎ *360/854–2589* ⊕ *www.skagittours.com* ☞ *Walking tour free, other tours $40–$45 (includes lunch)* ⊗ *May–Sept.*

RANGER PROGRAMS

In summer, rangers conduct programs at the visitor centers, where you also can find exhibits and other park information. At the North Cascades Visitor Center (in Newhalem) you can learn about rain-forest ecology, while at the Golden West Visitor Center (in Stehekin) there's an arts and crafts gallery as well as audiovisual and children's programs. Check center bulletin boards for schedules.

RESTAURANTS

There are no formal restaurants in North Cascades National Park, just a lakeside café at the North Cascades Environmental Learning Center. The only other place to eat out is in Stehekin, at the Stehekin Valley Ranch dining room, North Cascades Lodge, or the Stehekin Pastry Company; all serve simple, hearty, country-style meals and sweets. Towns within a few hours of the park on either side have a few small eateries, and a few lodgings have small dining rooms with skilled chefs who craft high-end meals of locally grown products, matched with extensive wine lists. Otherwise, don't expect fancy decor or gourmet frills—just friendly service and generally delicious homemade stews, roasts, grilled fare, soups, salads, and baked goods.

HOTELS

Accommodations in North Cascades National Park are rustic, cozy, and comfortable. Options range from plush Stehekin lodges and homey cabin rentals to spartan Learning Center bunks and campgrounds. Expect to pay roughly $50 to $200 per night, depending on the rental size and the season. Book at least three months in advance, or even a year for popular accommodations in summer. Outside the park are numerous resorts, motels, bed-and-breakfasts, and even overnight boat rentals in Chelan, Concrete, Glacier, Marblemount, Sedro-Woolley, Twisp, and Winthrop. *Hotel reviews have been shortened. For full information, visit Fodors.com.*

WHAT IT COSTS				
	$	$$	$$$	$$$$
Restaurants	under $13	$13–$20	$21–$30	over $30
Hotels	under $101	$101–$150	$151–$200	over $200

Restaurant prices are the average cost of a main course at dinner or, if dinner is not served, at lunch. Hotel prices are the lowest cost of a standard double room in high season, excluding taxes and service charges.

TOURS

Chelan Seaplanes. Daily flights run between Chelan and Stehekin and take 25–30 minutes. One-way fare is $89. Tours of the national park's glaciers are also offered and run $195–$295 per person. ⊠ *1328 W. Woodin Ave., Chelan* ☎ *509/682–5555* ⊕ *www.chelanseaplanes.com* ⌨ *From $89 one-way.*

FAMILY
Fodor's Choice
★
North Cascades Environmental Learning Center. Come here for information on park hiking, wildlife watching, horseback riding, climbing, boat rentals, and fishing, as well as classroom education and hands-on nature experiences. Guided tours staged from the center include lake and dam tours, mountain climbs, pack-train excursions, and guided canoe trips on Diablo Lake. Other choices range from forest ecology and backpacking trips to writing and art retreats. Family getaway weekends in summer are a fun way to unplug from technology and introduce kids to nature. There's also a research library, a dock on Diablo Lake, an amphitheater, and overnight lodging. The center is operated by the North Cascades Institute, in partnership with the National Parks Service and Seattle City Light. ⊠ *1940 Diablo Dam Rd., Diablo* ☎ *360/854–2599 Headquarters, 206/526–2599 Environmental Learning Center* ⊕ *www.ncascades.org* ⌨ *Tours and day programs from $40; overnight lodging (including meals) from $200 per couple.*

VISITOR INFORMATION

Park Contact Information North Cascades National Park. ⊠ *810 Rte. 20, Sedro-Woolley* ☎ *360/854–7200* ⊕ *www.nps.gov/noca.*

28

VISITOR CENTERS

Chelan Ranger Station. The base for the Chelan National Recreation Area and Wenatchee National Forest has an information desk and a shop selling regional maps and books. ⊠ *428 W. Woodin Ave., Chelan* ☎ *509/682–4900* ⊕ *www.nps.gov/noca/planyourvisit/visitorcenters. htm* ⊗ *Weekdays 7:45–4:30.*

Glacier Public Service Center. This office doubles as a headquarters for the Mount Baker–Snoqualmie National Forest; it has maps, a book and souvenir shop, and a permits desk. The center is also right on the way to some of the park's main trailheads. ⊠ *10091 Mt. Baker Hwy., Glacier* ☎ *360/599–2714* ⊕ *www.nps.gov/noca/planyourvisit/ visitorcenters.htm* ⊗ *Late May, Fri.–Mon. 8–4:30; June–mid-Oct., daily 8–4:30; mid-Oct.–mid-May, weekends 9–3.*

Golden West Visitor Center. Rangers here offer guidance on hiking, camping, and other activities, as well as audiovisual and children's programs and bike tours. There's also an arts and crafts gallery. Maps and concise displays explain the layered ecology of the valley, which encompasses in its length virtually every ecosystem in the Northwest. Campers can pick up free backcountry permits. Note that access is by floatplane, ferry, or trail only. ⊠ *Stehekin Valley Rd., ¼ mile north of Stehekin Landing, Stehekin Valley Rd., Stehekin* ☎ *360/854–7365* ⊕ *www.nps. gov/noca/planyourvisit/visitorcenters.htm* ⊗ *Mid-Oct.–Nov. and mid-Feb.–Apr., Mon., Wed., and Fri. 12:30–1:30; May, weekdays 12:30–2, weekends 10–2; Memorial Day–Sept., daily 8:30–5; early Oct.–mid-Oct., daily 10–2.*

North Cascades Park & Forest Information Center. This is the park's major administrative center and the place to pick up passes, permits, and information about current conditions. ⊠ *810 Rte. 20, Sedro-Woolley* ☎ *360/854–7200* ⊕ *www.nps.gov/noca/planyourvisit/visitorcenters. htm* ⊗ *Mid-Oct.–mid-May, weekdays 8–4:30; mid-May–mid-Oct., daily 8–4:30.*

North Cascades Visitor Center. The main visitor facility for the park complex has extensive displays on the surrounding landscape. Learn about the history and value of old-growth trees, the many creatures that depend on the rain-forest ecology, and the effects of human activity on the ecosystem. Park rangers frequently conduct programs; check bulletin boards for schedules. ⊠ *Milepost 120, North Cascades Hwy., Newhalem* ☎ *206/386–4495* ⊕ *www.nps.gov/noca/planyourvisit/ visitorcenters.htm* ⊗ *Early May, weekends 9–5; mid-May–Sept., daily 9–6; Oct.–mid-Nov., weekends 9–5.*

Wilderness Information Center. The main stop to secure backcountry and climbing permits for North Cascades National Park and the Lake Chelan and Ross Lake recreational areas, this office has maps, a bookshop, and nature exhibits. If you arrive after hours, there's a self-register permit stop outside. ⊠ *Off milepost 105.9, N. Cascades Hwy., 7280 Ranger Station Rd., Marblemount* ☎ *360/854–7245* ⊕ *www.nps.gov/ noca/planyourvisit/visitorcenters.htm* ⊗ *May, June, and Sept.–mid-Oct., Sun.–Thurs. 8–4:30, Fri. and Sat. 7–6; July and Aug., Sun.–Thurs. 7–6, Fri. and Sat. 7–8.*

EXPLORING

SCENIC DRIVES

North Cascades Highway. Also known as Highway 20, this classic scenic route first winds through the green pastures and woods of the upper Skagit Valley, the mountains looming in the distance. Beyond Concrete, a former cement-manufacturing town, the highway climbs into the mountains, passes the Ross and Diablo dams, and traverses Ross Lake National Recreation Area. Here several pull-outs offer great views of the lake and the surrounding snowcapped peaks. From June to September, the meadows are covered with wildflowers, and from late September through October, the mountain slopes flame with fall foliage. The pinnacle point of this stretch is 5,477-foot-high Washington Pass: look east, to where the road descends quickly into a series of hairpin curves between Early Winters Creek and the Methow Valley. Remember, this section of the highway is closed from roughly November to April, depending on snowfall, and sometimes closes temporarily during the busy summer season due to mudslides from storms. From the Methow Valley, Highway 153 takes the scenic route along the Methow River's apple, nectarine, and peach orchards to Pateros, on the Columbia River; from here, you can continue east to Grand Coulee or south to Lake Chelan. ⊕ *www.cascadeloop.com.*

> ### PLANTS AND WILDLIFE IN NORTH CASCADES
>
> Bald eagles are present year-round along the Skagit River and the lakes—in December, hundreds flock to the Skagit to feed on a rare winter salmon run, and remain through January. Spring and early summer bring black bears to the roadsides in the high country. Deer and elk can often be seen in early morning and late evening, grazing and browsing at the forest's edge. Other mountain residents include beaver, marmots, pika, otters, skunks, opossums, and smaller mammals, as well as forest and field birds.

28

HISTORIC SITES

Buckner Homestead. Dating from 1889, this restored pioneer farm includes an apple orchard, farmhouse, barn, and many ranch buildings. You can pick up a self-guided tour booklet from the drop box. Feel free to enjoy apples from the trees in season. A harvest festival is held in October. ⊠ *Stehekin Valley Rd., 3½ miles north of Stehekin Landing, Stehekin* ⊕ *www.bucknerhomestead.org.*

SCENIC STOPS

Gorge Powerhouse/Ladder Creek Falls and Rock Gardens. A powerhouse is just that, but the rock gardens overlooking Ladder Creek Falls, 7 miles west of Diablo, are beautiful and inspiring. ⊠ *North Cascades Hwy., 2 miles east of North Cascades Visitor Center, Newhalem* ☎ *360/854–2589* ⊕ *www.seattle.gov/light/tours/skagit* ⊠ *Free* ☉ *May–Sept., daily dawn–dusk.*

Stehekin. One of the most beautiful and secluded valleys in the Pacific Northwest, Stehekin was homesteaded by hardy souls in the late 19th century. It's actually not a town, but rather a small community set at the scenic northwest end of Lake Chelan, and it's accessible only by boat, floatplane, or trail. Year-round residents—there's about 100 of them—enjoy a wilderness lifestyle. They have intermittent outside communications, boat-delivered supplies, and just two-dozen cars among them—vehicles must be barged in, after all. Even on a peak summer season day, only around 200 visitors make the trek here. ☒ *Stehekin* ⊕ *www.stehekin.com.*

SPORTS AND THE OUTDOORS

BICYCLING

Mountain bikes are permitted on highways, unpaved back roads, and a few designated tracks around the park; however, there is no biking on footpaths. Ranger stations have details on the best places to ride in each season, as well as notes on spots that are closed due to weather, mud, or other environmental factors. It's $27 round-trip to bring a bike on the Lake Chelan ferry to Stehekin.

OUTFITTERS

Discovery Bikes. You can rent mountain bikes at a self-serve rack in front of the Stehekin Log office in Stehekin. Helmets are included. ☒ *Stehekin Valley Rd., 5-minute walk from boat landing, Stehekin* ☎ *509/682–3014* ⊕ *www.stehekindiscoverybikes.com* ☞ *From $5 per hr.*

BOATING

The boundaries of North Cascades National Park touch two long and sinewy expanses: Lake Chelan in the far south, and Ross Lake, which runs toward the Canadian border. Boat ramps, some with speed- and sailboat, paddleboat, kayak, and canoe rentals, can be found all around Lake Chelan, and passenger ferries cross between towns and campgrounds. Hozomeen, accessible via a 39-mile dirt road from Canada, is the boating base for Ross Lake; the site has a large boat ramp, and a boat taxi makes drops at campgrounds all around the shoreline. Diablo Lake, in the center of the park, also has a ramp at Colonial Creek. Gorge Lake has a public ramp near the town of Diablo.

HIKING

⚠ Black bears are often sighted along trails in the summer; do not approach them. Back away carefully, and report sightings to the Golden West Visitor Center. Cougars, which are shy of humans and well aware of their presence, are rarely sighted in this region. Still, keep kids close and don't let them run too far ahead or lag behind on a trail. If you do spot a cougar, pick up children, have the whole group stand close together, and make yourself look as large as possible.

EASY

FAMILY **Happy Creek Forest Walk.** Old-growth forests are the focus of this kid-friendly boardwalk route, which loops just 0.3 mile through the trees right off the North Cascades Highway. Interpretive signs provide details about flora along the way. *Easy.* ✛ *Trailhead: at milepost 135, North Cascades Hwy.* ⊕ *www.nps.gov/noca.*

Rainy Pass. An easy and accessible 1-mile paved trail leads to Rainy Lake, a waterfall, and glacier-view platform. *Easy.* ✛ *Trailhead: off Hwy. 20, 38 miles east of visitor center at Newhalem* ⊕ *www.nps.gov/noca.*

River Loop Trail. Take this flat and easy, 1.8-mile, wheelchair-accessible trail down through stands of huge old-growth firs and cedars toward the Skagit River. *Easy.* ✛ *Trailhead: near North Cascades Visitor Center* ⊕ *www.nps.gov/noca/planyourvisit/newhalem-area-trails.htm.*

Sterling Munro Trail. Starting from the North Cascades Visitor Center, this popular introductory stroll follows a short 300-foot path over a boardwalk to a lookout above the forested Picket Range peaks. *Easy.* ✛ *Trailhead: milepost 120, near Newhalem Creek Campground* ⊕ *www.nps.gov/noca/planyourvisit/newhalem-area-trails.htm.*

Trail of the Cedars. Only 0.3 mile long, this trail winds its way through one of the finest surviving stands of old-growth western red cedar in Washington. Some of the trees on the path are more than 1,000 years old. *Easy.* ✉ *Newhalem* ✛ *Trailhead: near North Cascades Visitor Center, milepost 120, Hwy. 20* ⊕ *www.nps.gov/noca/planyourvisit/newhalem-area-trails.htm.*

MODERATE

Fodor's Choice **Cascade Pass.** This extremely popular 3.7-mile, four-hour trail is known
★ for stunning panoramas from the great mountain divide. Dozens of peaks line the horizon as you make your way up the fairly flat, hairpin-turn track, the scene fronted by a blanket of alpine wildflowers from July to mid-August. Arrive before noon if you want a parking spot at the trailhead. *Moderate.* ✛ *Trailhead: at end of Cascade River Rd., 14 miles from Marblemount* ⊕ *www.nps.gov/noca/planyourvisit/cascade-pass-trail.htm.*

Diablo Lake Trail. Explore nearly 4 miles of waterside terrain on this route, which is accessed from the Sourdough Creek parking lot. An excellent alternative for parties with small hikers is to take the Seattle City Light Ferry one-way. *Moderate.* ✛ *Trailhead: at milepost 135, Hwy. 20* ⊕ *www.nps.gov/noca.*

DIFFICULT

Thornton Lakes Trail. A 5-mile climb into an alpine basin with three pretty lakes, this steep and strenuous hike takes about five to six hours round-trip. *Difficult.* ✛ *Trailhead: off Hwy. 20, 3 miles west of Newhalem, Thornton Lake Rd. and Hwy. 20* ⊕ *www.nps.gov/noca/planyourvisit/thornton-lake-trail.htm.*

HORSEBACK RIDING

Many hiking trails and backwoods paths are also popular horseback-riding routes, particularly around the park's southern fringes.

TOURS AND OUTFITTERS

Cascade Corrals. This subsidiary of Stehekin Outfitters organizes 2½-hour horseback trips to Coon Lake and full-day rides (lunch included) to Moore Point and Bridge Creek. English- and western-style riding lessons are also available. Reservations are taken at the Courtney Log Office at Stehekin Landing. Some rides depart from the Landing, others from Stehekin Valley Ranch. ⊠ *North Cascades National Park* ⊕ *stehekinoutfitters.com* ✉ *From $60* ☉ *June–mid-Sept., half-day rides daily at 8:15 and 2:15.*

KAYAKING

The park's tangles of waterways offer access to remote areas inaccessible by road or trail; here are some of the most pristine and secluded mountain scenes on the continent. Bring your own kayak and you can launch from any boat ramp or beach; otherwise, companies in several nearby towns and Seattle suburbs offer kayak and canoe rentals, portage, and tours. The upper basin of Lake Chelan (at the park's southern end) and Ross Lake (at the top edge of the park) are two well-known kayaking expanses, but there are dozens of smaller lakes and creeks between. The Stehekin River also provides many kayaking possibilities.

TOURS AND OUTFITTERS

Ross Lake Resort. The resort rents kayaks, motor boats, canoes, and fishing equipment, and offers portage service for exploring Ross Lake. A water-taxi service is also available; the resort is not accessible by road. ⊠ *503 Diablo St., Rockport* ☎ *206/386–4437, 206/708–3980 off-season (Jan.–May)* ⊕ *www.rosslakeresort.com.*

Stehekin Valley Ranch. Kayak tours of the upper estuary of Lake Chelan are offered daily at 10 am. ⊠ *Stehekin Valley Rd., Stehekin* ✛ *3½ miles from Stehekin Landing* ☎ *509/682–4677, 800/536–0745* ⊕ *www. stehekinvalleyranch.com* ✉ *From $40* ☉ *June–Sept.*

RAFTING

June through August is the park's white-water season, and rafting trips run through the lower section of the Stehekin River. Along the way take in views of cottonwood and pine forests, glimpses of Yawning Glacier on Magic Mountain, and placid vistas of Lake Chelan.

TOURS AND OUTFITTERS

North Cascades River Expeditions. June through October, North Cascades River Expeditions focuses on regional rivers; trips are offered on the Upper Skagit year-round. ☎ *800/634–8433* ⊕ *www.riverexpeditions. com* ✉ *From $60.*

FAMILY **Orion River Expeditions.** Introductory family-oriented floats are offered in August on the Skagit River for ages six and up. More lively white-water tours run on other area rivers April through September. ☎ *509/548–1401, 800/553–7466* ⊕ *www.orionexp.com* ✉ *From $60.*

FAMILY **Wildwater River Guides.** Half-day rafting excursions on the Skagit River depart from Goodell Creek Campground near Newhalem, March through September. The mild waters are great for beginners and families. ⊠ *Goodell Creek Campground, Newhalem* ☎ *509/470–8558, 800/522–9453* ⊕ *www.wildwater-river.com* ✉ *From $69.*

WINTER SPORTS

Mount Baker, just off the park's far northwest corner, is one of the Northwest's premier skiing, snowboarding, and snowshoeing regions—the area set a world record for most snow in a single season during the winter of 1998–99 (1,140 inches). The Mount Baker Highway (Route 542) cuts through the slopes toward state sno-parks; Salmon Ridge Sno-Park, 46 miles east of Bellingham at exit 255, has groomed trails and parking. Mt. Baker Ski Area, 17 miles east of the town of Glacier, has eight chairlifts and access to backcountry skiing; its season runs roughly from November to April.

Stehekin is another base for winter sports. The Stehekin Valley alone has 20 miles of trails; some of the most popular are around Buckner Orchard, Coon Lake, and the Courtney Ranch (Cascade Corrals).

Mt. Baker. Off the park's northwest corner, this is the closest winter-sports area, with facilities for downhill and Nordic skiing, snowboarding, and other recreational ventures. The main base is the town of Glacier, 17 miles west of the slopes, where lodging is available. Equipment rental and food service are on-site. **Facilities:** 38 trails; 1,000 acres; 1,500-foot vertical drop; 10 lifts (8 quad-chairs, 2 rope-tows). ⊠ *Hwy. 542, Glacier* ✛ *52 miles east of Bellingham* ☎ *360/734–6771, 360/671–0211 for snow reports* ⊕ *www.mtbaker.us* ✉ *Lift ticket: weekdays $52, weekends and holidays $57* ☉ *Nov.–Apr.*

WHAT'S NEARBY

NEARBY TOWNS

Heading into North Cascades National Park from Seattle on Interstate 5 to Highway 2, **Sedro-Woolley** (pronounced "*see*-droh *wool*-lee") is the first main town you encounter. A former logging and steel-mill base settled by North Carolina pioneers, the settlement still has a 19th-century ambience throughout its rustic downtown area. Surrounded by farmlands, it's a pretty spot to stop and has basic visitor services like hotels, gas stations, and groceries. It's also home to the North Cascades National Park Headquarters. From here, it's about 40 miles to the park's western edges. Along the way, you still have a chance to stop for supplies in **Concrete,** about 20 miles from the park along Highway 2.

Marblemount is 10 miles farther east, about 12 miles west of the North Cascades Visitor Center. It's another atmospheric former timber settlement nestled in the mountain foothills, and its growing collection of motels, cafés, and tour outfitters draw outdoor enthusiasts each summer. The park's base town, though, is **Newhalem,** tucked right along the highway between the north and south regions. This is the place to explore the visitor center and its surrounding trails, view exhibits, and pick up maps, permits, and tour information.

Still traveling east on Highway 20, it's about 5 miles from Newhalem to **Diablo,** where the local lake, dam, and overlook are all good reasons to stop. Keep going until the road turns south along the park's eastern side: this is the famed North Cascades Scenic Highway. From top to bottom, including Rainy Pass and the curve through the chilly Washington Pass overlook, this section is about 20 miles.

Winthrop, a relaxed, riverside rodeo town complete with clapboard cafés and five-and-dime charm, is about a 30-mile drive east of Washington Pass. This is also an outdoor-recreation base, offering activities that range from cross-country skiing to hiking, mountain biking, and whitewater rafting. Less than 10 miles southeast of Winthrop, the tiny town of **Twisp** is settled in the farmlands and orchards, its streets lined with a few small lodgings and eateries.

The resort town of **Chelan,** nestled around its serene namesake lake, lies about 60 miles due south of Winthrop along Highway 153. It's a serene summer getaway for boating and swimming, as well as an access point for small villages and campgrounds along the shoreline. **Stehekin,** at the lake's northern end, is a favorite tourist stop for its peaceful isolation; without road connections, your options for getting here are by boat, floatplane, or trail. A ferry runs between Chelan and Stehekin.

VISITOR INFORMATION

Lake Chelan Chamber of Commerce. ⊠ *216 E. Woodin Ave., Chelan* ☎ *509/682–3503* ⊕ *www.lakechelan.com.* **Sedro-Woolley Chamber of Commerce.** ⊠ *810 Metcalf St., Sedro-Woolley* ☎ *360/855–1841, 888/225–8365* ⊕ *www.sedro-woolley.com.* **Twisp Visitor Information Center and Chamber of Commerce.** ⊠ *201 S. Methow Valley Hwy., Twisp* ☎ *509/997–2020* ⊕ *www. twispinfo.com.* **Winthrop Chamber of Commerce.** ⊠ *202 Hwy. 20, Winthrop* ☎ *509/996–2125* ⊕ *www.winthropwashington.com.*

NEARBY ATTRACTIONS

FodorsChoice
★

Lake Chelan. This sinewy, 50½-mile-long fjord—Washington's deepest lake—works its way from the town of Chelan, at its south end, to Stehekin, at the far northwest edge. The scenery is striking, the flat blue water encircled by plunging gorges, with a vista of snow-slathered mountains beyond. No roads access the lake except for the shoreline around Chelan, so a floatplane or boat is needed to see the whole thing. Resorts dot the warmer eastern shores. ⊠ *U.S. 97A, Chelan* ☎ *509/682–3503* ⊕ *www.lakechelan.com.*

Lake Chelan Boat Co. The *Lady of the Lake II* makes journeys from May to October, departing Chelan at 8:30 and returning at 6 ($40.50 round-trip). The *Lady Express,* a speedy catamaran, runs between Stehekin, Holden Village, the national park, and Lake Chelan year-round; schedules vary with the seasons. Tickets are $61 round-trip May to October and $40.50 round-trip the rest of the year. The vessels also can drop off and pick up at lakeshore trailheads. ⊠ *1418 Woodin Ave., Chelan* ☎ *509/682–4584, 888/682–4584* ⊕ *www.ladyofthelake.com.*

FAMILY **Lake Whatcom Railway.** The steam-powered train makes short jaunts through the woods 11 miles north of Sedro-Woolley. Excursions run in July and August and during special events, such as the Christmas train rides with Santa in December. During peak weekends, tours depart at noon and children pay half price. Note that the schedule changes seasonally. ⊠ *Hwy. 9, Wickersham* ☎ *360/441–0719* ⊕ *www. lakewhatcomrailway.com* 💲*$25* ⊗ *Call for hrs.*

WHERE TO EAT

IN THE PARK

$$ ✗ **Restaurant at Stehekin Valley Ranch.** Meals in the rustic log ranch house,
AMERICAN served at polished wood tables, include buffet dinners of steak, ribs, hamburgers, fish, salad, beans, and dessert. Note that breakfast is served 7 to 9, lunch is noon to 1, and dinner is 5:30 to 7. Show up later than that and you'll find the kitchen is closed. If you want to enjoy a drink with your meal, bring your own alcohol—it's not otherwise served. For guests not staying at the ranch, dinner reservations are required and transportation from the Stehekin Landing costs $7. ⑤ *Average main: $18* ⊠ *Stehekin Valley Rd., 9 miles north of Stehekin Landing, Stehekin* ☎ *509/682–4677, 800/536–0745* ⊕ *www.stehekinvalleyranch. com* ⊗ *Closed Oct.–mid-June* ⚄ *Reservations essential.*

$ ✗ **Stehekin Pastry Company.** As you enter this lawn-framed timber cha-
CAFÉ let, you're immersed in the tantalizing aromas of a European bakery. Glassed-in display cases are filled with trays of homemade baked goods, and the pungent espresso is eye-opening. Sit down at a window-side table and dig into an over-filled sandwich or rich bowl of soup—and don't forget dessert: the pie is sublime, made with fruit fresh-picked from local orchards. Although it's outside of town, the shop is conveniently en route to Rainbow Falls. ⑤ *Average main: $7* ⊠ *Stehekin Valley Rd., about 2 miles north of Stehekin Landing, Stehekin* ☎ *509/682–7742* ⊕ *www.stehekinpastry.com* ⊗ *Closed mid-Oct.–mid-May.*

PICNIC AREAS

Developed picnic areas at both Rainy Pass (Highway 20, 38 miles east of the park visitor center) and Washington Pass (Highway 20, 42 miles east of the visitor center) have a half-dozen picnic tables, drinking water, and pit toilets. The vistas of surrounding peaks are sensational at these two overlooks. More picnic facilities are located near the visitor center in Newhalem and at Colonial Creek Campground, 10 miles east of the visitor center on Highway 20.

OUTSIDE THE PARK

$$$$ ✗ **Dining Room at Sun Mountain Lodge.** In a sylvan hilltop setting overlook-
PACIFIC ing the Methow Valley, intimate tables and a woodsy interior design set
NORTHWEST the scene for an extraordinary dining experience. The upscale Pacific Northwest cuisine is based on often-organic, locally grown, raised, caught, and crafted ingredients, providing for exquisite flavors to match

28

the artful presentation and elegant yet unpretentious atmosphere. Highlights include chicken curry soup, melt-in-your-mouth pork chops, quinoa garlic cakes, and filet of beef with potato soufflé. The dessert menu has many tempting choices, including apple pie with house-made vanilla ice cream and Chocolate Fantasy—a quintet of chocolate delights. The 5,000-bottle wine cellar is one of the best and most extensive in the region. $ *Average main: $38* ⊠ *604 Patterson Lake Rd., Winthrop* ☎ *509/996–4707, 800/572–0493* ⊕ *www.sunmountainlodge.com/ dining* ⊘ *Closed Sun.–Thurs. in winter and spring; closed 2 weeks in Nov. and Mar.–early Apr. No lunch.*

$$
AMERICAN

✕**Twisp River Pub.** This popular, family-friendly riverfront brewpub produces a range of house beers, incuding the top-selling IPA, ESB, and Oatmeal Stout as well as seasonal ales and hard apple and pear ciders. Within the spacious, folksy yet semi-industrial interior, dine on hearty pub grub like beef or buffalo burgers, fish-and-chips, housemade soups, and meaty sandwiches and wraps. Dinners include steak, salmon, coconut curry, and Thai peanut noodles—one of the most frequently requested dishes. Or nosh on buffalo wings, nachos, hummus, calamari, or sweet potato fries. Brunch—omelets, scrambles, Benedicts—is served on Sunday. There's live music every weekend and jazz in the riverside beer garden on summer Wednesday evenings. Keep an eye out for bald eagles and deer down by the river. $ *Average main: $13* ⊠ *201 Hwy. 20, 9 miles south of Winthrop, Twisp* ☎ *509/997–6822, 888/220–3360* ⊕ *www.methowbrewing.com* ⊘ *Closed Mon.–Wed. mid-Oct.–mid-May (except Christmas–New Year period). No brunch Mon.–Sat.*

WHERE TO STAY

IN THE PARK

$$
HOTEL

North Cascades Lodge at Stehekin. Crackling fires and Lake Chelan views are provided both in standard rooms in the Alpine House, with its shared lounge and lakeside deck, and in larger rooms in the Swiss Mont building, with private decks overlooking the water. **Pros:** on the water; recreation center with pool table; tent-to-tent hiking excursions; kayaking. **Cons:** no air-conditioning; TV is only available in the recreation building; limited Internet service and no cell-phone service. $ *Rooms from: $128* ⊠ *955 Stehekin Valley Rd., Stehekin* ☎ *509/682–4494* ⊕ *www.lodgeatstehekin.com* ⇩ *28 rooms, 1 house* ⍾ *No meals.*

$$$$
B&B/INN

Silver Bay Inn Resort. Perched on a slip of land at the head of Lake Chelan, Silver Bay's accommodations feature water and mountain views; all have their own kitchens. **Pros:** hot-tub vistas; free use of boats and bikes. **Cons:** summertime mosquitoes; five-night minimum in summer; not for families with kids under 12. $ *Rooms from: $225* ⊠ *Silver Bay Rd., Stehekin* ☎ *509/670–0693* ⊕ *www.silverbayinn.com* ⊘ *Closed Nov.–May* ⇩ *1 room, 1 cabin, 1 house* ⍾ *No meals.*

$$$$
B&B/INN
FAMILY

Stehekin Valley Ranch. Alongside pretty meadows at the edge of pine forest, this rustic ranch is a center for hikers and horseback riders, who stay in barnlike cabins with cedar paneling, tile floors, and a private bath,

Best Campgrounds in North Cascades

Tent campers can choose between forest sites, riverside spots, lake grounds, or meadow spreads encircled by mountains. Here camping is as easy or challenging as you want to make it; some campgrounds are a short walk from ranger stations, while others are miles from the highway. Note that many campsites, particularly those around Stehekin, are completely remote and without road access anywhere, so you have to walk, boat, ride a horse, or take a floatplane to reach them. Most don't accept reservations, and spots fill up quickly May through September. If there's no ranger on-site, you can often sign yourself in—and always check in at a ranger station before you set out overnight. Note that some areas are occasionally closed due to flooding, forest fires, or other factors.

Lake Chelan National Recreation Area. Many backcountry camping areas are accessible via park shuttles or boat. All require a free backcountry permit. Purple Point, the most popular campground due to its quick access to Stehekin Landing, has six tent sites, bear boxes, and nearby road access. ✉ *Stehekin Landing, Stehekin* ☎ *509/699–2080.*

or canvas-roof tent cabins with bunk beds, kerosene lamps, and shared bathrooms. **Pros:** easy access to recreation; playground and outdoor game fields; hearty meals included. **Cons:** no bathrooms in tent cabins; many repeat guests so book early. ⑤ *Rooms from: $250* ✉ *Stehekin Valley Rd., 9 miles north of Stehekin Landing, Stehekin* ☎ *509/682–4677, 800/536–0745* ⊕ *www.stehekinvalleyranch.com* ☾ *Closed Oct.–mid-June* ↪ *7 tent cabins (shared bathroom), 8 cabins* ⑩ *All meals.*

OUTSIDE THE PARK

$$$$ 🏨 **Campbell's Resort.** More than a century old, this sprawling resort sits
RESORT on landscaped grounds alongside Lake Chelan; every room has a bal-
FAMILY cony with mountain and beach views, and some have a kitchen or fireplace. **Pros:** plenty of summer programs to keep kids busy; on-site day
spa; great base for winter sports. **Cons:** tour buses, weddings, and con-
ferences bring noisy crowds. ⑤ *Rooms from: $265* ✉ *104 W. Woodin
Ave., Chelan* ☎ *509/682–2561, 800/553–8225* ⊕ *www.campbellsresort.
com* ↪ *163 rooms, 5 suites, 2 cabins* ⑩ *No meals.*

$ 🏨 **Chewuch Inn.** Set on 5 acres just south of Winthrop, lodgings at the
B&B/INN inn have modern amenities and luxurious touches. **Pros:** free cookies in
afternoon; excellent service; short walk to town. **Cons:** basement rooms
have no windows; a bit hard to find off the main highway. ⑤ *Rooms
from: $100* ✉ *223 White Ave., Winthrop* ☎ *509/996–3107, 800/747–
3107* ⊕ *www.chewuchinn.com* ↪ *11 rooms, 7 cabins* ⑩ *Breakfast.*

$ 🏨 **Duck Brand Hotel and Cantina.** Named for the town's original 19th-
HOTEL century saloon and retaining its frontier feel, this eclectic, casual and
comfortable timber hotel has five small, simple rooms with big wood
beams, flowered fabrics, and country accents facing a second-floor
porch along the town's main street. **Pros:** small-town charm; fun and

28

friendly; restaurant on-site. **Cons:** might be a bit rustic for the sophisticated city traveler. ⓢ *Rooms from: $85* ✉ *248 Riverside Ave., Winthrop* ☎ *509/996–2408* ⊕ *www.duckbrandhotel.com* ☉ *Closed Mar.* ⬿ *5 rooms* ⎮⚪⎮ *No meals.*

$$$$
RESORT
FAMILY
Fodor'sChoice
★

Freestone Inn. At the heart of the 120-acre, historic Wilson Ranch, amid more than 2 million acres of forest, this upscale mountain retreat embraces the pioneer spirit in spacious rooms, suites, and wood-paneled cabins snuggled up to Early Winters Creek. **Pros:** gorgeous scenery; myriad activities; close to North Cascades National Park (17 miles west). **Cons:** limited cell-phone and TV service; some resort amenities may be limited in shoulder season. ⓢ *Rooms from: $229* ✉ *31 Early Winters Dr., about 14 miles northwest of Winthop, Mazama* ☎ *509/996–3906, 800/639–3809* ⊕ *www.freestoneinn.com* ⬿ *10 rooms, 7 suites, 15 cabins, 3 lodges* ⎮⚪⎮ *Breakfast.*

$$$
HOTEL
FAMILY

Lakeside Lodge & Suites. Adjacent to Lakeside Park, a couple miles from downtown Chelan, this four-story property has all lake-facing rooms to enjoy sunset over the lake, and plenty of family-friendly amenities, including two pools and two hot tubs. **Pros:** lake views; adjacent to park with beach, playground, and sports courts; hot breakfast included. **Cons:** some room views are blocked by a giant tree; rooms open to outside (no halls); no on-site restaurant. ⓢ *Rooms from: $179* ✉ *2312 W. Woodin Ave., Chelan* ☎ *800/468–2781, 509/682–4396* ⊕ *www.lakesidelodgeandsuites.com* ⬿ *93 rooms* ⎮⚪⎮ *Breakfast.*

$$
B&B/INN

Mazama Country Inn. Ideal as a base for outdoor-recreation enthusiasts, the inn offers clean, no-frills accommodations and nearby access to the Pasayten Wilderness and North Cascades National Park. **Pros:** inclusive meal option available in winter; off-season specials; rooms very clean. **Cons:** no TV; no kids under 10 during winter months. ⓢ *Rooms from: $105* ✉ *15 Country Rd., Mazama* ☎ *800/843–7951, 509/996–2681* ⊕ *www.mazamacountryinn.com* ⬿ *18 rooms* ⎮⚪⎮ *No meals.*

$$
B&B/INN
FAMILY

River Run Inn. The rooms and cabins aren't fancy here, but the inn's riverfront location and amenities—including picnic tables, hammocks, playground, lawn games, and indoor pool—make it a popular place to stay. **Pros:** free use of bikes; serene riverfront setting; free DVD library. **Cons:** hot tub is only big enough for a few people; bathrooms are small. ⓢ *Rooms from: $120* ✉ *27 Rader Rd., Winthrop* ☎ *800/757–2709, 509/996–2173* ⊕ *www.riverrun-inn.com* ⬿ *10 rooms, 5 cabins* ⎮⚪⎮ *No meals.*

$$$$
RESORT
Fodor'sChoice
★

Sun Mountain Lodge. The stunning North Cascades and all its attractions are the stars of this outdoor-oriented resort set 3,000 feet up in the foothills, with luxurious accommodations, spectacular mountain views, and a range of activities that make it a year-round destination, whether the peaks are covered in snow or wildflowers. **Pros:** stunning setting; a wide array of outdoor activities year-round; panoramic views; award-winning dining; warm hospitality. **Cons:** limited cell service; roundabout route from Seattle in winter. ⓢ *Rooms from: $315* ✉ *604 Patterson Lake Rd., Winthrop* ☎ *509/996–2211, 800/572–0493* ⊕ *www.sunmountainlodge.com* ☉ *Closed 2 wks in early Nov. and Mar.–early Apr.* ⬿ *86 rooms, 10 suites, 16 cabins* ⎮⚪⎮ *Breakfast.*

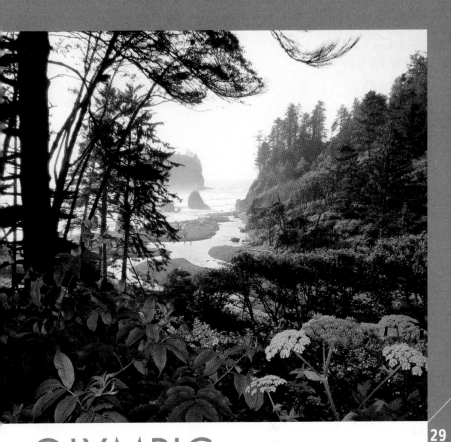

OLYMPIC
NATIONAL PARK

WELCOME TO OLYMPIC NATIONAL PARK

TOP REASONS TO GO

★ **Exotic rain forest:** A rain forest in the Pacific Northwest? Indeed, Olympic National Park is one of the few places in the world with this unique temperate landscape.

★ **Beachcombing:** Miles of rugged, spectacular coastline hemmed with sea stacks and tidal pools edge the driftwood-strewn shores of the Olympic Peninsula.

★ **Nature's hot tubs:** A dip in Sol Duc's natural geothermal mineral pools offers a secluded spa experience in the wooded heart of the park.

★ **Lofty vistas:** The hardy can hike up meadowed foothill trails or climb the frosty peaks throughout the Olympics—or just drive up to Hurricane Ridge for endless views.

★ **A sense of history:** American Indian history is key to this region, where eight tribes have traditional ties to the park lands— there's 12,000 years of human history to explore.

1 Coastal Olympic.
Here the Pacific smashes endlessly into the rugged coastline, carving out some of the park's most memorable scenes in the massive, rocky sea stacks and islets just offshore. Back from the water are beaches and tide pools full of sea stars, crabs, and anemones.

WASHINGTON

2 The Rain Forest.
Centered on the Hoh, Queets, and Quinault river valleys, this is the region's most unique landscape. Fog-shrouded Douglas firs and Sitka spruces, some more than 300 feet tall, huddle in this moist, pine-carpeted area, shading fern- and moss-draped cedars, maples, and alders.

3 The Mountains.
Craggy gray peaks and snow-covered summits dominate the skyline. Low-level foliage and wildflower meadows make for excellent hiking in the plateaus. Even on the sunniest days, temperatures are brisk. Some roads are closed in winter months.

4 Alpine Meadows. In midsummer, the swath of colors is like a Monet canvas spread over the landscape, and wildlife teems among the honeyed flowers. Trails are never prettier, and views are crisp and vast.

GETTING ORIENTED

The Olympic Peninsula's elegant snowcapped and forested landscape is edged on all sides by water: to the north the Strait of Juan de Fuca separates the United States from Canada, a network of Puget Sound bays laces the east, the Chehalis River meanders along the southern end, and the massive gray Pacific Ocean guards the west side.

29

KEY	
🛉	Ranger Station
⛺	Campground
🎪	Picnic Area
🍴	Restaurant
🏨	Lodge
🚶	Trailhead
🚻	Restrooms
⇗	Scenic Viewpoint
⋯⋯	Walking/Hiking Trails

Updated by
Shelley Arenas

A spellbinding setting is tucked into the country's far northwestern corner, within the heart-shape Olympic Peninsula. Edged on all sides by water, the forested landscape is remote and pristine, and works its way around the sharpened ridges of the snowcapped Olympic Mountains. Big lakes cut pockets of blue in the rugged blanket of pine forests, and hot springs gurgle up from the foothills. Along the coast the sights are even more enchanting: wave-sculpted boulders, tidal pools teeming with sea life, and tree-topped sea stacks.

OLYMPIC PLANNER

WHEN TO GO

Summer, with its long stretches of sun-filled days, is prime touring time for Olympic National Park. June through September are the peak months; Hurricane Ridge, the Hoh Rain Forest, Lake Crescent, and Ruby Beach are bustling by 10 am.

Late spring and early autumn are also good bets for clear weather; anytime between April and October, you'll have a good chance of fair skies. Between Thanksgiving and Easter, it's a toss-up as to which days will turn out fair; prepare for heavy clouds, rain showers, and chilly temperatures, then hope for the best.

Winter is a great time to visit if you enjoy isolation. Locals are usually the only hardy souls during this time, except for weekend skiers heading to the snowfields around Hurricane Ridge. Many visitor facilities have limited hours or are closed from October to April.

AVG. HIGH/LOW TEMPS.

Jan.	Feb.	Mar.	Apr.	May	June
45/33	48/35	51/36	55/39	60/44	65/48
July	Aug.	Sept.	Oct.	Nov.	Dec.
68/50	69/51	66/48	58/42	50/37	45/34

FESTIVALS AND EVENTS

FEBRUARY
FAMILY
Chocolate on the Beach Festival. Venues in the North Beach towns of Seabrook, Moclips, and Pacific Beach host this annual celebration of chocolate the last weekend of February. Activities include classes, contests, demonstrations, and dining and sampling events. ⊠ *Pacific Beach* ⊕ *www.chocolateonthebeachfestival.com.*

MAY
Irrigation Festival. For more than a century, the people of Sequim have been celebrating the irrigation ditches that brought life-giving water here. Highlights of the 10-day festival include a beauty pageant, logging demonstrations, arts and crafts, a classic car show, a strongman competition, parades, and a picnic. ⊠ *Sequim* ⊕ *www.irrigationfestival.com.*

JUNE–AUGUST
Centrum Summer Arts Festival. This summer-long lineup of concerts and workshops is held at Fort Worden State Park, a 19th-century army base near Port Townsend. ⊠ *Port Townsend* ☎ *360/385–3102* ⊕ *www. centrum.org.*

JUNE–
SEPTEMBER
Olympic Music Festival. A variety of classical concerts are performed in a renovated barn on weekends from late June through early September; picnic on the farm while you listen. ☎ *360/732–4800* ⊕ *www. olympicmusicfestival.org.*

JULY
Forks Old-Fashioned Fourth of July. A salmon bake, parade, demolition derby, arts and crafts exhibits, kids' activities, and plenty of fireworks mark Forks's weekend-long celebration. ⊠ *Forks* ☎ *360/374–2531, 800/443–6757* ⊕ *www.forkswa.com.*

FAMILY
Fourth of July Porch Illumination and Festival. The pretty Cape Cod–style cottages of Seabrook get lit up and decked out in full Americana splendor for the Independence Day weekend. The event kicks off with the evening porch illumination walk. Other weekend events include a flag presentation, bike parade, seafood boil, market with vendors and food trucks, magic show, live music, and fireworks. ⊠ *Seabrook, 204 Front St., Pacific Beach* ☎ *206/276–0099* ⊕ *www.seabrookwa.com.*

Sequim Lavender Festival. Mid-July, a street fair and free self-guided farm tours celebrate Sequim's many fragrant lavender fields. ⊠ *Sequim* ☎ *360/681–3035* ⊕ *www.lavenderfestival.com.*

SEPTEMBER
Wooden Boat Festival. Hundreds of antique boats sail into Port Townsend for the weekend; there's also live music, education programs, and demonstrations. ⊠ *Port Townsend* ☎ *360/385–3628* ⊕ *www.woodenboat.org.*

29

PLANNING YOUR TIME
OLYMPIC IN ONE DAY

Start at the **Lake Quinault Lodge,** in the park's southwest corner. From here, drive a half hour into the Quinault Valley via **South Shore Road.** Tackle the forested **Graves Creek Trail,** then head up **North Shore Road** to the Quinault Rain Forest Interpretive Trail. Next, head back to U.S. 101 and drive to **Ruby Beach,** where a shoreline walk presents a breathtaking scene of sea stacks and sparkling, pink-hued sands.

Forks, and its **Timber Museum,** are your next stop; have lunch here, then drive 20 minutes to the beach at **La Push.** Next, head to **Lake Crescent,** around the corner to the northeast, where you can rent a boat, take a swim, or enjoy a picnic next to the sparkling teal waters. Drive through **Port Angeles** to **Hurricane Ridge;** count on an hour's drive from bottom to top if there aren't too many visitors. At the ridge, explore the visitor center or hike the 3-mile loop to **Hurricane Hill,** where you can see over the entire park north to Vancouver Island and south past Mount Olympus.

GETTING HERE AND AROUND
You can enter the park at a number of points, but since the park is 95% wilderness, access roads do not penetrate far. The best way to get around and to see many of the park's top sites is on foot.

AIR TRAVEL
Seattle–Tacoma International Airport is the nearest airport to Olympic National Park. It's roughly a two-hour drive from the park.

BOAT TRAVEL
Ferries provide another unique (though indirect) link to the Olympic area from Seattle; contact **Washington State Ferries** (☎ 800/843–3779, 206/464–6400 ⊕ www.wsdot.wa.gov/ferries) for information.

BUS TRAVEL
Grays Harbor Transit runs buses on weekdays only from Aberdeen and Hoquiam to Amanda Park, on the west end of Lake Quinault. Jefferson Transit operates a Forks–Amanda Park route Monday through Saturday.

Bus Contacts Grays Harbor Transit. ☎ 360/532–2770, 800/562–9730 ⊕ www.ghtransit.com. **Jefferson Transit.** ☎ 800/371–0497, 360/385–4777 ⊕ www.jeffersontransit.com.

CAR TRAVEL
U.S. 101 essentially encircles the main section of Olympic National Park, and a number of roads lead from the highway into the park's mountains and toward its beaches. You can reach U.S. 101 via Interstate 5 at Olympia, via Route 12 at Aberdeen, or via Route 104 from the Washington state ferry terminals at Bainbridge or Kingston.

PARK ESSENTIALS
ADMISSION FEES AND PERMITS
Seven-day vehicle admission is $20; an annual pass is $40. Individuals arriving on foot, bike, or motorcycle pay $7. An overnight wilderness permit, available at visitor centers and ranger stations, is $5 per person per night. A frequent-hiker pass, which covers all wilderness-use fees, is $35 per year. Fishing in freshwater streams and lakes within Olympic National Park does not require a Washington state fishing license; however, anglers must acquire a salmon-steelhead catch record card when fishing for those species. Ocean fishing and harvesting shellfish require licenses, which are available at sporting-goods and outdoor-supply stores.

GOOD READS

■ Robert L. Wood's *Olympic Mountains Trail Guide* is a great resource for both day hikers and those planning longer excursions.

■ Craig Romano's *Day Hiking Olympic Peninsula: National Park/Coastal Beaches/Southwest Washington* is a detailed guide to day hikes in and around the national park.

■ Stephen Whitney's *A Field Guide to the Cascades and Olympics* is an excellent trailside reference, covering more than 500 plant and animal species found in the park.

■ The park's newspaper, the *Olympic Bugler*, is a seasonal guide for activities and opportunities in the park. You can pick it up at the visitor centers.

■ A handy online catalog of books, maps, and passes for northwest parks is available from Discover Your Northwest (⊕ www.discovernw.org).

ADMISSION HOURS

Six park entrances are open 24/7; gate kiosk hours (for buying passes) vary according to season and location, but most are staffed during daylight hours. Olympic National Park is in the Pacific time zone.

CELL-PHONE RECEPTION

Note that cell reception is sketchy in wilderness areas. There are public telephones at the Olympic National Park Visitor Center, Hoh River Rain Forest Visitor Center, and lodging properties within the park—Lake Crescent, Kalaloch, and Sol Duc Hot Springs. Fairholme General Store also has a phone.

EDUCATIONAL OFFERINGS

CLASSES AND SEMINARS

FAMILY **NatureBridge.** This rustic educational facility offers talks and excursions focusing on park ecology and history. Trips range from canoe trips to camping excursions, with a strong emphasis on family programs. ⊠ *111 Barnes Point Rd., Port Angeles* ☎ *360/928–3720* ⊕ *www. naturebridge.org/olympic.*

RANGER PROGRAMS

FAMILY **Junior Ranger Program.** Anyone can pick up the booklet at visitor centers and ranger stations and follow this fun program, which includes assignments to discover park flora and fauna, ocean life, and Native American lore. Kids get a badge when they turn in the finished work. ⊠ *Olympic National Park* ☎ *360/565–3130* ⊕ *www.nps.gov/olym/ forkids/beajuniorranger.htm.*

RESTAURANTS

The major resorts are your best bets for eating out in the park. Each has a main restaurant, café, and/or kiosk, as well as casually upscale dinner service, with regional seafood, meat, and produce complemented by a range of microbrews and good Washington and international wines. Reservations are either recommended or required.

29

Outside the park, small, easygoing cafés and bistros line the main thoroughfares in Sequim, Port Angeles, and Port Townsend, offering cuisine that ranges from hearty American-style fare to more eclectic local flavor.

HOTELS

Major park resorts run from good to terrific, with generally comfortable rooms, excellent facilities, and easy access to trails, beaches, and activity centers. Midsize accommodations, like Sol Duc Hot Springs Resort, are often shockingly rustic—but remember, you're here for the park, not for the rooms.

The towns around the park have motels, hotels, and resorts for every budget. For a full beach-town vacation experience, base yourself in a home or cottage in the coastal community of Seabrook (near Pacific Beach). Sequim and Port Angeles have many attractive, friendly B&Bs, plus lots of inexpensive chain hotels and motels. Forks is basically a motel town, with a few guesthouses around its fringes.

Hotel reviews have been shortened. For full information, visit Fodors.com.

WHAT IT COSTS				
	$	**$$**	**$$$**	**$$$$**
Restaurants	under $13	$13–$20	$21–$30	over $30
Hotels	under $101	$101–$150	$151–$200	over $200

Restaurant prices are the average cost of a main course at dinner, or if dinner is not served, at lunch. Hotel prices are the lowest cost of a standard double room in high season, excluding taxes and service charges.

VISITOR INFORMATION

Park Contact Information Olympic National Park. ⊠ *Olympic National Park Visitor Center, 3002 Mount Angeles Rd., Port Angeles* ☎ *360/565–3130* ⊕ *www. nps.gov/olym.*

VISITOR CENTERS

Hoh Rain Forest Visitor Center. Pick up park maps and pamphlets, permits, and activities lists in this busy, woodsy chalet; there's also a shop and exhibits on natural history. Several short interpretive trails and longer wilderness treks start from here. ⊠ *Hoh Valley Rd., Forks ✛ 31 miles south of Forks* ☎ *360/374–6925* ⊕ *www.nps.gov/olym/planyourvisit/ visitorcenters.htm* ⊘ *May–Labor Day, daily 9–5; early Sept.–Apr., Fri.– Sun. 10–4.*

Hurricane Ridge Visitor Center. The upper level of this visitor center has exhibits and nice views; the lower level has a gift shop and snack bar. Guided walks and programs start in late June. In winter, find details on the surrounding ski and sledding slopes and take guided snowshoe walks. ⊠ *Hurricane Ridge Rd.* ☎ *360/565–3131 for road conditions* ⊕ *www.nps.gov/olym/planyourvisit/visitorcenters.htm* ⊘ *Apr.–mid-Dec., daily 9–6; late-Dec.–Mar., weekends 9–4 (if road is open).*

Olympic National Park Visitor Center. This modern, well-organized facility, staffed by park rangers, provides everything: maps, trail brochures, campground advice, weather forecasts, listings of wildlife sightings, educational programs and exhibits, information on road and trail closures, and a gift shop. ⊠ *3002 Mount Angeles Rd., Port Angeles* ☎ *360/565–3130* ⊕ *www.nps.gov/olym/planyourvisit/visitorcenters. htm* ⊙ *May–Sept., daily 8:30–5; Oct.–Apr., daily 9–4.*

South Shore Quinault Ranger Station. The National Forest Service's ranger station near the Lake Quinault Lodge has maps, campground information, and program listings. ⊠ *353 S. Shore Rd., Quinault* ☎ *360/288– 2525* ⊕ *www.fs.usda.gov/main/olympic/home* ⊙ *Sept.–May, weekdays 8–4:30; Memorial Day–Labor Day, Mon.–Thurs. 8–4, Fri.–Sat. 8–6, Sun. 9–4.*

Wilderness Information Center (WIC). Located behind Olympic National Park Visitor Center, this facility provides all the information you'll need for a trip in the park, including trail conditions, safety tips, and weather bulletins. The office also issues camping permits, takes campground reservations, and rents bear-proof food canisters. ⊠ *3002 Mount Angeles Rd., Port Angeles* ☎ *360/565–3100* ⊕ *www.nps.gov/ olym/planyourvisit/wic.htm* ⊙ *May and June, daily 8–5; July–Labor Day, daily 8–6; Sept.–Apr., daily 8–4.*

EXPLORING

Most of the park's attractions are found either off U.S. 101 or down trails that require hikes of 15 minutes or longer. The west coast beaches are linked to the highway by downhill tracks; the number of cars parked alongside the road at the start of the paths indicates how crowded the beach will be.

SCENIC DRIVES

Fodor'sChoice
★ **Port Angeles Visitor Center to Hurricane Ridge.** The premier scenic drive in Olympic National Park is a steep ribbon of curves, which climbs from thickly forested foothills and subalpine meadows into the upper stretches of pine-swathed peaks. At the top, the visitor center at Hurricane Ridge has some spectacular views over the heart of the peninsula and across the Strait of Juan de Fuca. A mile past the visitor center, there are picnic tables in open meadows with photo-worthy views of the mountains to the east. Hurricane Ridge also has an uncommonly fine display of wildflowers in spring and summer. In winter, vehicles must carry chains and the road is usually open Friday–Sunday only (call first to check conditions). ⊠ *Olympic National Park* ⊕ *www.nps.gov/olym.*

29

HISTORIC SITES

La Push. At the mouth of Quileute River, La Push is the tribal center of the Quileute Indians. In fact, the town's name is a variation on the French *la bouche,* which means "the mouth." Offshore rock spires known as sea stacks dot the coast here, and you may catch a glimpse of bald eagles nesting in the nearby cliffs. ⊠ *Rte. 110, 14 miles west of Forks, La Push* ⊕ *www.nps.gov/olym/planyourvisit/upload/mora.pdf.*

Lake Ozette. The third-largest glacial impoundment in Washington anchors the coastal strip of Olympic National Park at its north end. The small town of Ozette, home to a coastal tribe, is the trailhead for two of the park's better one-day hikes. Both 3-mile trails lead over boardwalks through swampy wetland and coastal old-growth forest to the ocean shore and uncrowded beaches. ⊠ *Ozette* ✛ *At the end of Hoko-Ozette Rd., 26 miles southwest of Hwy. 112 near Sekiu* ☎ *360/565–3130 Ozette Ranger Station* ⊕ *www.nps.gov/olym/planyourvisit/visiting-ozette.htm.*

SCENIC STOPS

Fodor's Choice ★ **Hoh River Rain Forest.** South of Forks, an 18-mile spur road links Highway 101 with this unique temperate rain forest, where spruce and hemlock trees soar to heights of more than 200 feet. Alders and big-leaf maples are so densely covered with mosses they look more like shaggy prehistoric animals than trees, and elk browse in shaded glens. Be prepared for precipitation: the region receives 140 inches or more each year. ⊠ *Olympic National Park* ✛ *From Hwy. 101, at about 20 miles north of Kalaloch, turn onto Upper Hoh Rd. 18 miles east to Hoh Rain Forest Visitor Center* ☎ *360/374–6925* ⊕ *www.nps.gov/olym/planyourvisit/visiting-the-hoh.htm* ☉ *Visitor Center: May–Labor Day, daily 9–5; Labor Day–Apr., Fri.–Sun. 10–4.*

Fodor's Choice ★ **Hurricane Ridge.** The panoramic view from this 5,200-foot-high ridge encompasses the Olympic range, the Strait of Juan de Fuca, and Vancouver Island. Guided tours are given in summer along the many paved and unpaved trails, where wildflowers and wildlife such as deer and marmots flourish. ⊠ *Hurricane Ridge Rd., 17 miles south of Port Angeles* ☎ *360/565–3130 visitor center* ⊕ *www.nps.gov/olym/planyourvisit/visiting-hurricane-ridge.htm* ☉ *Visitor center open daily in summer; rest of year on days road is open.*

Kalaloch. With a lodge, a huge campground, miles of coastline, and easy access from the highway, this is a popular spot. Keen-eyed beachcombers may spot sea otters just offshore; they were reintroduced here in 1970. ⊠ *Hwy. 101, 32 miles northwest of Lake Quinault, Kalaloch* ☎ *360/565–3130 visitor center* ⊕ *www.nps.gov/olym/planyourvisit/visiting-kalaloch-and-ruby-beach.htm.*

Lake Crescent. Visitors see Lake Crescent as Highway 101 winds along its southern shore, giving way to gorgeous views of teal waters rippling in a basin formed by Tuscan-like hills. In the evening, low bands of clouds caught between the surrounding mountains often linger over its reflective surface. ⊠ *Hwy. 101, 16 miles west of Port Angeles and 28 miles northeast of Forks* ☎ *360/565–3130 visitor center* ⊕ *www.nps.gov/olym/planyourvisit/visiting-lake-crescent.htm.*

Lake Quinault. This glimmering lake, 4½ miles long and 300 feet deep, is the first landmark you'll reach when driving the west-side loop of U.S. 101. The rain forest is thickest here, with moss-draped maples and alders, and towering spruce, fir, and hemlock. Enchanted Valley, high up near the Quinault River's source, is a deeply glaciated valley that's closer to the Hood Canal than to the Pacific Ocean. A scenic loop drive circles the lake and travels around a section of the Quinault River. ⊠ *Hwy. 101, 38*

29

CLOSE UP

Plants and Wildlife in Olympic

Along the high mountain slopes hardy cedar, fir, and hemlock trees stand tough on the rugged land; the lower montane forests are filled with thickets of silver firs; and valleys stream with Douglas firs and western hemlock. The park's famous temperate rain forests are on the peninsula's western side, marked by broad western red cedars, towering red spruces, and ferns festooned with strands of mosses and patchwork lichens. This lower landscape is also home to some of the Northwest's largest trees: massive cedar and Sitka spruce near Lake Quinault can measure more than 700 inches around, and Douglas firs near the Queets and Hoh rivers are nearly as wide.

These landscapes are home to a variety of wildlife, including many large mammals and 15 creatures found nowhere else in the world. Hikers often come across Roosevelt's elk, black-tailed deer, mountain goats, beavers, raccoons, skunks, opossums, and foxes; Douglas squirrels and flying squirrels populate the heights of the forest. Less common are black bears (most prevalent from May through August); wolves, bobcats,

and cougar are rarely seen. Birdlife includes bald eagles, red-tailed hawks, osprey, and great horned owls. Rivers and lakes are filled with freshwater fish, while beaches hold crabs, sea stars, anemones, and other shelled creatures. Get out in a boat on the Pacific to spot seals, sea lions, and sea otters—and perhaps a pod of porpoises, orcas, or gray whales.

Beware of jellyfish around the shores—beached jellyfish can still sting. In the woods, check for ticks after every hike and after each shower. Biting nasties include black flies, horseflies, sand fleas, and the ever-present mosquitoes. Yellow-jacket nests populate tree hollows along many trails; signs throughout the Hoh Rain Forest warn hikers to move quickly through these sections. If one or two chase you, remain calm and keep walking; these are just "guards" making sure you're keeping away from the hive. Poison oak is common, so familiarize yourself with its appearance. Bug repellent, sunscreen, and long pants and sleeves will go a long way toward making your experience more comfortable.

---

miles north of Hoquiam ☎ *360/288–2525 Quinault Rain Forest ranger station* ⊕ *www.nps.gov/olym/planyourvisit/visiting-quinault.htm.*

Second and Third Beaches. During low tide these flat, driftwood-strewn expanses are perfect for long afternoon strolls. Second Beach, accessed via an easy forest trail through Quileute lands, opens to a vista of Pacific Ocean and sea stacks. Third Beach offers a 1.3-mile forest hike for a warm-up before reaching the sands. ⊠ *Hwy. 101, 32 miles north of Lake Quinault* ☎ *360/565–3130 visitor center* ⊕ *www.nps.gov/olym.*

Sol Duc. Sol Duc Valley is one of those magical places where all the Northwest's virtues seem at hand: lush lowland forests, sparkling river scenes, salmon runs, and serene hiking trails. Here, the popular Sol Duc Hot Springs area includes three attractive sulfuric pools ranging in temperature from 98°F to 104°F. ⊠ *Sol Duc Rd.* ⊹ *South of U.S. 101, 12*

Olympic's
Coastal Region

miles past the west end of Lake Crescent ☎ *360/565–3130 visitor center* ⊕ *www.nps.gov/olym/planyourvisit/visiting-the-sol-duc-valley.htm.*

Staircase. Unlike the forests of the park's south and west sides, Douglas fir is the dominant tree on the east slope of the Olympic Mountains. Fire has played an important role in creating the majestic forest here, as the Staircase Ranger Station explains in interpretive exhibits. ⊠ *Olympic National Park* ✢ *At end of Rte. 119, 15 miles from U.S. 101 at Hoodsport* ☎ *360/565–3130 visitor center* ☉ *Hrs vary but generally open daily in summer.*

SPORTS AND THE OUTDOORS

BEACHCOMBING

The wild, shell-strewn Pacific coast teems with tide pools and crustaceans. Crabs, sand dollars, anemones, sea stars, and all sorts of shellfish are exposed at low tide, when flat beaches can stretch out for hundreds of yards. The most easily accessible sand-strolling spots are Rialto, Ruby, First, and Second beaches, near Mora and La Push, and Kalaloch Beach and Fourth Beach in the Kalaloch stretch.

The Wilderness Act and the park's code of ethics instruct visitors to leave all nonliving materials where they are for others to enjoy.

BICYCLING

The rough gravel car tracks to some of the park's remote sites were meant for four-wheel-drive vehicles, but can double as mountain-bike routes. The Quinault Valley, Queets River, Hoh River, and Sol Duc River roads have bike paths through old-growth forest. Graves Creek Road, in the southwest, is a mountain-bike path; Lake Crescent's north side is also edged by the bike-friendly Spruce Railroad Trail. More bike tracks run through the adjacent Olympic National Forest. Note that U.S. 101 has heavy traffic and isn't recommended for cycling, although the western side has broad roads with beautiful scenery and can be biked off-season. Bikes are not permitted on foot trails.

TOURS AND OUTFITTERS

All Around Bikes. This bike, gear, and repair shop is a great resource for advice on routes around the Olympic Peninsula. Bike rentals cost $30 per half day, $50 all day, and $60 for 24 hours. ⊠ *150 W. Sequim Bay Rd., Sequim* ☎ *360/681–3868* ⊕ *www.allaroundbikes.com.*

Sound Bike & Kayak. This sports outfitter rents and sells bikes, kayaks, and related equipment. Kayak rentals run $15 per hour and $50 per day. Bikes rent for $10 per hour, $45 per day, or $55 for 24 hours. ⊠ *120 E. Front St., Port Angeles* ☎ *360/457–1240* ⊕ *www.soundbikeskayaks.com.*

CLIMBING

At 7,980 feet, Mount Olympus is the highest peak in the park and the most popular climb in the region. To attempt the summit, climbers must register at the Glacier Meadows Ranger Station. Mount Constance, the third-highest Olympic peak at 7,743 feet, has a well-traversed climbing route that requires technical experience; reservations are recommended for the Lake Constance stop, which is limited to 20 campers. Mount Deception is another possibility, though tricky snows have caused fatalities and injuries in the last decade.

Climbing season runs from late June through September. Note that crevasse skills and self-rescue experience are highly recommended. Climbers must register with park officials and purchase wilderness permits before setting out. The best resource for climbing advice is the Wilderness Information Center in Port Angeles.

TOURS AND OUTFITTERS

Mountain Madness. Adventure through the rain forest to the glaciated summit of Mount Olympus on a five-day trip, offered several times per year by Mountain Madness. ☎ *800/328–5925, 206/937–8389* ⊕ *www. mountainmadness.com* ✉ *From $1,200 for 5-day climb.*

FISHING

There are numerous fishing possibilities throughout the park. Lake Crescent is home to cutthroat and rainbow trout, as well as petite kokanee salmon; Lake Cushman, Lake Quinault, and Ozette Lake have trout, salmon, and steelhead. As for rivers, the Bogachiel and Queets have steelhead salmon in season. The glacier-fed Hoh River is home to chinook salmon April to November, and coho salmon from August through November; the Sol Duc River offers all five species of salmon. Rainbow trout are found in the Dosewallips, Elwha, and Skykomish rivers. Other places to go after salmon and trout include the Duckabush, Quillayute, Quinault, and Salmon rivers. A Washington state punch card is required during salmon-spawning months; fishing regulations vary throughout the park. Licenses are available from sporting-goods and outdoor-supply stores.

TOURS AND OUTFITTERS

Bob's Piscatorial Pursuits. This company, based in Forks, offers salmon and steelhead fishing trips around the Olympic Peninsula from mid-September through May. ✉ *Forks* ☎ *866/347–4232* ⊕ *www.piscatorialpursuits. com* ✉ *From $225 per person for 2 people; $340 for 1 person.*

HIKING

Know your tides, or you might be trapped by high water. Tide tables are available at all visitor centers and ranger stations. Remember that a wilderness permit is required for all overnight backcountry visits.

29

EASY

FAMILY

Fodor's Choice

★

Hoh River Trail. From the Hoh Visitor Center, this rain-forest jaunt takes you into the Hoh Valley, wending its way for 17.4 miles alongside the river, through moss-draped maple and alder trees and past open meadows where elk roam in winter. *Easy.* ⊹ *Trailhead: Hoh Visitor Center, 18 miles east of U.S. 101* ⊕ *www.nps.gov/olym/planyourvisit/ hoh-river-trail.htm.*

Hurricane Ridge Meadow Trail. A ¼-mile alpine loop, most of it wheelchair accessible, leads through wildflower meadows overlooking numerous vistas of the interior Olympic peaks to the south and a panorama of the Strait of Juan de Fuca to the north. *Easy.* ⊹ *Trailhead: Hurricane Ridge Rd., 17 miles south of Port Angeles* ⊕ *www.nps.gov/olym/planyourvisit/ visiting-hurricane-ridge.htm.*

MODERATE

FAMILY

Cape Alava Trail. Beginning at Ozette, this 3-mile boardwalk trail leads from the forest to wave-tossed headlands. *Moderate.* ⊠ *Ozette* ⊹ *Trailhead: end of the Hoko-Ozette Rd., 26 miles south of Hwy. 112, west of Sekiu* ⊕ *www.nps.gov/olym/planyourvisit/visiting-ozette.htm.*

Graves Creek Trail. This 6-mile-long moderately strenuous trail climbs from lowland rain forest to alpine territory at Sundown Pass. Due to spring floods, a fjord halfway up is often impassable in May and June. *Moderate.* ⊹ *Trailhead: end of S. Shore Rd., 23 miles east of U.S. 101* ⊕ *www.nps.gov/olym.*

FAMILY

Fodor's Choice

★

Sol Duc River Trail. The 1.5-mile gravel path off Sol Duc Road winds through thick Douglas fir forests toward the thundering, three-chute Sol Duc Falls. Just 0.1 mile from the road, below a wooden platform over the Sol Duc River, you'll come across the 70-foot Salmon Cascades. In late summer and autumn, thousands of salmon negotiate 50 miles or more of treacherous waters to reach the cascades and the tamer pools near Sol Duc Hot Springs. The popular 6-mile **Lovers Lane Loop Trail** links the Sol Duc falls with the hot springs. You can continue up from the falls 5 miles to the **Appleton Pass Trail,** at 3,100 feet. From there you can hike on to the 8.5-mile mark, where views at the High Divide are from 5,050 feet. *Moderate.* ⊹ *Trailhead: Sol Duc Rd., 12 miles south of U.S. 101* ⊕ *www.nps.gov/olym/planyourvisit/sol-duc-river-trail.htm.*

DIFFICULT

High Divide Trail. A 9-mile hike in the park's high country defines this trail, which includes some strenuous climbing on its last 4 miles before topping out at a small alpine lake. A return loop along High Divide wends its way an extra mile through alpine territory, with sensational views of Olympic peaks. This trail is only for dedicated, properly equipped hikers who are in good shape. *Difficult.* ⊹ *Trailhead: end of Sol Duc River Rd., 13 miles south of U.S. 101* ⊕ *www.nps.gov/olym/ planyourvisit/high-divide-loop.htm.*

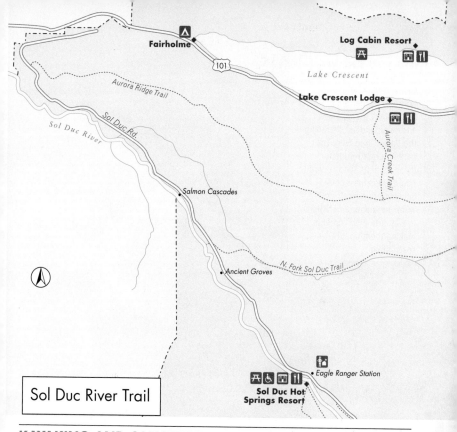

Sol Duc River Trail

KAYAKING AND CANOEING

Lake Crescent, a serene expanse of teal-color waters surrounded by deep-green pine forests, is one of the park's best boating areas. Note that the west end is for swimming only; no speedboats are allowed here.

Lake Quinault has boating access from a gravel ramp on the north shore. From U.S. 101, take a right on North Shore Road, another right on Hemlock Way, and a left on Lakeview Drive. There are plank ramps at Falls Creek and Willoughby campgrounds on South Shore Drive, 0.1 mile and 0.2 mile past the Quinault Ranger Station, respectively.

Lake Ozette, with just one access road, is a good place for overnight trips. Only experienced canoe and kayak handlers should travel far from the put-in, since fierce storms occasionally strike—even in summer.

TOURS AND OUTFITTERS

Fairholm General Store. Kayaks and canoes on Lake Crescent are available to rent from $20 per hour to $55 for eight hours. The store is at the lake's west end, 27 miles west of Port Angeles. ⊠ 221121 U.S. 101, Port Angeles ☎ 360/928–3020 ☉ Closed after Labor Day–Apr. and Mon.–Thurs. in May.

Lake Crescent Lodge. You can rent canoes and kayaks here for $20 per hour and $45 per half day. Hour-long guided kayak tours are offered

daily for $35 in a single kayak and $45 in a double kayak. ⊠ 416 *Lake Crescent Rd.* ☎ 360/928–3211 ⊕ *www.olympicnationalparks. com* ⊗ *Closed Jan.–Apr.*

Log Cabin Resort. This resort, 17 miles west of Port Angeles, has paddleboat, kayak, canoe, and paddleboard rentals for $20 per hour and $55 per day. The dock provides easy access to Lake Crescent's northeast section. ⊠ *3183 E. Beach Rd., Port Angeles* ☎ 360/928–3325 ⊕ *www. olympicnationalparks.com* ⊗ *Closed Oct.–mid-May.*

Rainforest Paddlers. This company takes kayakers down the Lizard Rock and Oxbow sections of the Hoh River. They also offer river rafting and kayak rentals. ⊠ *4883 Upper Hoh Rd., Forks* ☎ 360/374–5254, *866/457–8398* ⊕ *www.rainforestpaddlers.com* ✑ *Tours from $45; kayak rentals from $11/hr.*

RAFTING

Olympic has excellent rafting rivers, with Class II to Class V rapids. The Elwha River is a popular place to paddle, with some exciting turns. The Hoh is better for those who like a smooth, easy float.

TOURS AND OUTFITTERS

Olympic Raft and Kayak. Based in Port Angeles, this is the only rafting outfit that offers trips on the restored Elwha River in Olympic National Park. It also offers half-day kayaking trips on the Salish Sea, launching from a county park in Port Angeles. ⊠ *123 Lake Aldwell Rd., Port Angeles* ☎ 888/452–1443 ⊕ *www.raftandkayak.com* ✑ *From $60.*

WINTER SPORTS

Hurricane Ridge is the central spot for winter sports. Miles of downhill and Nordic ski tracks are open late December through March, and a ski lift, towropes, and ski school are open 10 to 4 weekends and holidays. A snow-play area for children ages eight and younger is near the Hurricane Ridge Visitors Center. Hurricane Ridge Road is open Friday through Sunday in the winter season; all vehicles are required to carry chains.

TOURS AND OUTFITTERS

Hurricane Ridge Visitor Center. Rent snowshoes and ski equipment here December through March. ⊠ *Hurricane Ridge Rd., Port Angeles* ☎ *360/565–3131 road condition information* ⊕ *www.nps.gov/olym/ planyourvisit/hurricane-ridge-in-winter.htm* ⊗ *Closed Mon.–Thurs.*

WHAT'S NEARBY

NEARBY TOWNS

Although most Olympic Peninsula towns have evolved from their exclusive reliance on timber, **Forks,** outside the national park's northwest tip, remains one of the region's logging capitals. Washington state's wettest town (100 inches or more of rain a year), it's a small, friendly place with just 3,500 residents and a modicum of visitor facilities. **Port Angeles,** a city of 19,000, focuses on its status as the main gateway to Olympic National Park and Victoria, British Columbia. Set below the Strait of Juan de Fuca and looking north to Vancouver Island, it's an enviably scenic settlement filled with attractive, Craftsman-style homes.

The Pacific Northwest has its very own "Banana Belt" in the waterfront community of **Sequim,** 15 miles east of Port Angeles along U.S. 101. The town of 6,000 is in the rain shadow of the Olympics and receives only 16 inches of rain per year (compared with the 40 inches that drench the Hoh Rain Forest just 40 miles away). The beach community of **Seabrook,** near Pacific Beach, is 25 miles from the southeast corner of the national park via the Moclips Highway. Many of its several hundred high-end vacation homes are available for short-term rentals; the community has parks, swimming pools, bike trails, special events, and a growing retail district.

Visitor Information Forks Chamber of Commerce Visitor Center. ⊠ *1411 S. Forks Ave. (U.S. 101), Forks* ☎ *800/443–6757, 360/374–2531* ⊕ *www.forkswa. com.* **Port Angeles Chamber of Commerce Visitor Center.** ⊠ *121 E. Railroad Ave., Port Angeles* ☎ *360/452–2363* ⊕ *www.portangeles.org.* **Sequim-Dungeness Valley Chamber of Commerce.** ⊠ *1192 E. Washington St., Sequim* ☎ *360/693–6197, 800/737–8462* ⊕ *www.sequimchamber.com.*

NEARBY ATTRACTIONS

FAMILY   **Dungeness Spit.** Curving 5½ miles into the Strait of Juan de Fuca, the
Fodor'sChoice   longest natural sand spit in the United States is a wild, beautiful sec-
★   tion of shoreline. More than 30,000 migratory waterfowl stop here each spring and fall, but you'll see plenty of birdlife any time of year. The entire spit is part of the **Dungeness National Wildlife Refuge.** Access it through the **Dungeness Recreation Area,** which serves as a portal to the shoreline. ⊠ *554 Voice of America Rd., Sequim* ✛ *Entrance 3 miles north from U.S. 101, 4 miles west of Sequim* ☎ *360/457–8451 wildlife refuge* ⊕ *www.clallam.net/parks/dungeness.html* 🎫 *$3 per family* 🕙 *Daily dawn–dusk.*

New Dungeness Lighthouse. At the end of the Dungeness Spit is the towering white 1857 New Dungeness Lighthouse; tours are available, though access is limited to those who can hike or kayak out 5 miles to the end of the spit. Guests also have the opportunity to serve as lighthouse keepers for a week at a time. An adjacent, 66-site camping area, on the bluff above the Strait of Juan de Fuca, is open year-round. ⊠ *Sequim* ✛ *Entrance 3 miles north of Hwy. 101 via Kitchen Dick Rd.* ☎ *360/683–6638* ⊕ *www.newdungenesslighthouse.com.*

Port Angeles Fine Arts Center. This small, sophisticated museum is inside the former home of late artist and publisher Esther Barrows Webster, one of Port Angeles's most energetic and cultured citizens; displays are modern, funky, and intriguing. Outside, Webster's Woods Art Park is dotted with oversize sculptures set before a vista of the city and harbor. Exhibitions emphasize the works of emerging and well-established Pacific Northwest artists. ⊠ *1203 E. Lauridsen Blvd., Port Angeles*

☎ *360/457–3532* ⊕ *www.pafac.org* ✉ *Free* ⊙ *Mar.–Oct., Thurs.–Sun. 11–5; Nov.–Feb., Thurs.–Sun. 10–4 and by appointment; Art Park daily sunrise–sunset.*

Timber Museum. The museum highlights Forks's logging history since the 1870s; a garden and fire tower are also on the grounds. ✉ *1421 S. Forks Ave., Forks* ☎ *360/374–9663* ⊕ *www.forkstimbermuseum.org* ⊙ *Mon.–Sat. 10–5, Sun. 11–4.*

WHERE TO EAT

IN THE PARK

$$$
AMERICAN

✕ **Creekside Restaurant.** A tranquil country setting and ocean views at Kalaloch Lodge's restaurant create the perfect backdrop for savoring local dinner specialties like grilled salmon, fresh shellfish, and Moroccan-spiced organic chicken breast. Tempting desserts include local berry tart and warm chocolate cake. Reservations are recommended for dinner. Hearty breakfasts feature sourdough pancakes and make-your-own omelets with cage-free eggs. Lunch favorites include a salmon BLT, fish-and-chips, and clam chowder, as well as burgers, soups, and salads made with local produce. ⑤ *Average main: $24* ✉ *157151 Hwy. 101, Forks* ☎ *866/662–9928, 360/962–2271* ⊕ *www.thekalalochlodge.com/dine.aspx.*

$$$$
AMERICAN

✕ **Lake Crescent Lodge.** Part of the original 1916 lodge, the fir-paneled dining room overlooks the lake; you won't find a better spot for sunset views. Hearty breakfast selections include biscuits and gravy, omelets and scrambles made with cage-free eggs, and raspberry-filled French toast. Lunch features a variety of burgers and sandwiches, including grilled cheese with crab. Dinner entrées include grilled salmon, seared weathervane scallops, filet mignon, pork shank, and roasted chicken breast. A good Northwest wine list complements the menu. Note that meals are offered only during set hours, but a more casual menu of appetizers, sandwiches, burgers, and desserts is available from the lounge all day for dining in the lobby or out on the Sun Porch. ⑤ *Average main: $32* ✉ *416 Lake Crescent Rd., Port Angeles* ☎ *360/928–3211, 888/723–7127* ⊕ *www.olympicnationalparks.com/stay/dining/lake-crescent-lodge.aspx* ⊙ *Closed Jan.–Apr.*

$$$
AMERICAN

✕ **The Springs Restaurant.** The main Sol Duc Hot Springs Resort restaurant is a rustic, fir-and-cedar–paneled dining room surrounded by trees. In summer big breakfasts are turned out daily 7:30 to 10:30; dinner is served between 5 and 9:30 (lunch and snacks are available 11 to 4 at the Poolside Deli). Evening choices include Northwest seafood, rotisserie chicken, burgers, and steaks. ⑤ *Average main: $21* ✉ *12076 Sol Duc Rd., at U.S. 101, Port Angeles* ☎ *360/327–3583* ⊕ *www. olympicnationalparks.com/stay/dining/sol-duc-hot-springs-resort-.aspx* ⊙ *Closed mid-Oct.–late Mar.*

PICNIC AREAS

All Olympic National Park campgrounds have adjacent picnic areas with tables, some shelters, and restrooms, but no cooking facilities. The same is true for major visitor centers, such as Hoh Rain Forest.

29

Drinking water is available at ranger stations, interpretive centers, and inside campgrounds.

East Beach Picnic Area. Set on a grassy meadow overlooking Lake Crescent, this popular swimming spot has six picnic tables and vault toilets. ⊠ *East Beach Rd., Port Angeles* ✛ *At far east end of Lake Crescent, off Hwy. 101, 17 miles west of Port Angeles.*

La Poel Picnic Area. Tall firs lean over a tiny gravel beach at this small picnic area, which has several picnic tables and a splendid view of Pyramid Mountain across Lake Crescent. ⊠ *Olympic National Park* ✛ *Off Hwy. 101, 22 miles west of Port Angeles* ☉ *Closed mid-Oct.–mid-May.*

Rialto Beach Picnic Area. Relatively secluded at the end of the road from Forks, this is one of the premier day-use areas in the park's Pacific coast segment. This site has 12 picnic tables, fire grills, and vault toilets. ⊠ *Rte. 110, 14 miles west of Forks, Forks.*

OUTSIDE THE PARK

$$
ECLECTIC

✕ **Alder Wood Bistro.** An inventive menu of local and organic dishes makes this one of the most popular restaurants in Sequim. Pizzas from the wood-fired oven include unique creations, like one featuring oyster, shiitake and cremini mushrooms, bacon, morel crème fraîche, caramelized onions, mozzarella, and finished with mixed greens. The menu's sustainably harvested seafood selections highlight whatever is in season and also get the wood-fire treatment. Even the bacon-wrapped meat loaf features local grass-fed beef, along with buttermilk mashed potatoes and greens. For dessert, try the wood-fired organic apple pie. On warmer days, enjoy alfresco dining in the pretty garden courtyard. ⑤ *Average main: $20* ⊠ *139 W. Alder St., Sequim* ☎ *360/683–4321* ⊕ *www.alderwoodbistro.com* ☉ *Closed Sun.–Wed.*

$$$
PACIFIC
NORTHWEST
Fodor's Choice
★

✕ **Blondie's Plate.** This Sequim bistro in a former church is a popular spot for both locals and tourists. Many of the menu choices are "small-plate" or tapas style, which makes it easy to mix and match different tastes and share with dining companions. Categories include starters, garden, surf, pasture, and starch; servers can recommend good matches. The grilled pear salad with blue cheese goes well with the crispy-skin salmon, served with ginger miso and sautéed vegetables. Traditional full plates like roast chicken with roasted baby potatoes and asparagus are also available. Cocktails are noteworthy, too, and a changing dessert menu may include flourless chocolate cake or croissant bread pudding. Unlike many of the downtown restaurants in quiet Sequim, Blondie's stays open every night of the week. The restaurant is small, so reserve ahead. ⑤ *Average main: $25* ⊠ *134 S. 2nd Ave., Sequim* ☎ *360/683–2233* ⊕ *www.blondiesplate.com* ☉ *No lunch.*

$$$$
FRENCH

✕ **C'est Si Bon.** The interior design as well as the food is far more Euro-savvy than is typical on the Olympic Peninsula. A fanciful dining room is done up in bold red hues, with crisp white linens, huge oil paintings, and glittering chandeliers; the spacious solarium takes an equally formal approach. A changing menu highlights house-made French onion soup, escargots, magret de canard with berry sauce, Dungeness crab soufflé, filet mignon, and rack of lamb. The wine list is superb, with French,

Australian, and Northwest choices to pair with everything. $ *Average main: $32* ✉ *23 Cedar Park Rd., Port Angeles* ☎ *360/452–8888* ⊕ *www.cestsibon-frenchcuisine.com* ⊗ *Closed Mon. No lunch* ⚑ *Reservations essential.*

$$ ✕ **Dockside Grill.** With tremendous views of John Wayne Marina and
PACIFIC Sequim Bay, this is a fun place to watch boats placidly sail by. The casual
NORTHWEST yet elegant menu includes Dungeness crab fritters, steamed clams, cedar-plank salmon, bouillabaisse, cioppino, and pasta. The kitchen also serves up excellent steak. The lunch menu includes burgers, fish-and-chips, and several sandwich choices, including an oyster po' boy and Dungeness crab melt. $ *Average main: $20* ✉ *2577 W. Sequim Bay Rd., Sequim* ☎ *360/683–7510* ⊕ *www.docksidegrill-sequim.com* ⊗ *Closed Mon. and Tues.*

$$ ✕ **Fountain Café.** Artwork lines the walls of the small, funky café tucked
ECLECTIC inside a historic clapboard building a block off the main drag, where seafood and pasta dishes carry Mediterranean, Moroccan, Italian, and Pacific Northwest influences. Start with pan-fried oysters or mussels and clams in a pesto-chardonnay broth. Chicken marsala and paella are mainstays. Full-bodied Pacific Northwest and Italian wines as well as simple sweets like tiramisu and gingerbread round out the menu. $ *Average main: $18* ✉ *920 Washington St., Port Townsend* ☎ *360/385–1364* ⊕ *www.fountaincafept.com* ⚑ *Reservations not accepted.*

$$ ✕ **Oak Table Café.** Carefully crafted breakfasts and lunches, made with
AMERICAN high-grade, fresh ingredients, are the focus of this well-run, family-friendly eatery, a Sequim institution since 1981. Breakfast is served throughout the day, and on Sunday, when the large, well-lighted dining room is especially bustling, it's the only meal. The selection is extensive. Thickly sliced bacon and eggs are a top seller, but the restaurant is best known for its creamy blintzes, golden-brown waffles, crepes, and variety of pancakes, particularly the cinnamony sweet soufflé-style apple pancake. Egg dishes include eggs Nicole—a medley of sautéed mushrooms, onions, spinach, and scrambled eggs served over an open-face croissant and covered with hollandaise sauce. Lunches include burgers, salads, and sandwiches. $ *Average main: $13* ✉ *292 W. Bell St., Sequim* ☎ *360/683–2179* ⊕ *www.oaktablecafe.com* ⊗ *No dinner.*

29

WHERE TO STAY

IN THE PARK

$$$ 🏨 **Kalaloch Lodge.** Overlooking the Pacific, Kalaloch has cozy lodge
HOTEL rooms with sea views and separate cabins along the bluff. **Pros:** ranger
FAMILY tours; clam digging; supreme storm-watching in winter. **Cons:** no
Fodor'sChoice Internet and most units don't have TVs; some rooms are two blocks
★ from main lodge; limited cell-phone service. $ *Rooms from: $199* ✉ *157151 U.S. 101, Forks* ☎ *360/962–2271, 866/662–9928* ⊕ *www.thekalalochlodge.com* ⤳ *10 lodge rooms, 6 motel rooms, 4 motel suites, 40 cabins, 6 duplex cabins* ⦿❘ *No meals.*

$$$ 🏨 **Lake Crescent Lodge.** Deep in the forest at the foot of Mount Storm
HOTEL King, this 1916 lodge has a variety of comfortable accommodations,

Best Campgrounds in Olympic

Note that only a few places take reservations; if you can't book in advance, you'll have to arrive early to get a place. Each site usually has a picnic table and grill or fire pit, and most campgrounds have water, toilets, and garbage containers; for hookups, showers, and laundry facilities, you'll have to head into the towns. Firewood is available from camp concessions, but if there's no store you can collect dead wood within 1 mile of your campsite. Dogs are allowed in campgrounds, but not on most trails or in the backcountry. Trailers should be 21 feet long or less (15 feet or less at Queets Campground) though a few campgrounds can accommodate up to 35 feet. There's a camping limit of two weeks. Nightly rates run $15–$22 per site.

If you have a backcountry pass, you can camp virtually anywhere through-out the park's forests and shores. Overnight wilderness permits are $5 per person per night and are available at visitor centers and ranger stations. Note that when you camp in the backcountry, you must choose a site at least ½ mile inside the park boundary.

Elwha Campground. The larger of the Elwha Valley's two campgrounds, this is one of Olympic's year-round facilities. ⌧ *Elwha River Rd., 7 miles south of U.S. 101* ☎ *No phone.*

Kalaloch Campground. Kalaloch is the biggest and most popular Olympic campground, and it's open all year. Its vantage of the Pacific is unmatched on the park's coastal stretch. ⌧ *U.S. 101, ½ mile north of Kalaloch Information Station, Olympic National Park* ☎ *877/444–6777 for reservations.*

Lake Quinault Rain Forest Resort Village Campground. Stretching along the south shore of Lake Quinault, this RV campground has many recreation facilities, including beaches, canoes, ball fields, and horseshoe pits. The 31 RV sites, which rent for $35 per night, are open year-round but bathrooms are closed in winter. ⌧ *3½ miles east of U.S. 101, South Shore Rd., Lake Quinault* ☎ *360/288–2535, 800/255–6936* ⊕ *www.rainforestresort.com.*

Mora Campground. Along the Quillayute estuary, this campground doubles as a popular staging point for hikes northward along the coast's wilderness stretch. ⌧ *Rte. 110, 13 miles west of Forks* ☎ *No phone.*

Ozette Campground. Hikers heading to Cape Alava, a scenic promontory that is the westernmost point in the lower 48 states, use this lakeshore campground as a jumping-off point. ⌧ *Hoko-Ozette Rd., 26 miles south of Hwy. 112* ☎ *No phone.*

Sol Duc Campground. Sol Duc resembles virtually all Olympic campgrounds save one distinguishing feature—the famed hot springs are a short walk away. ⌧ *Sol Duc Rd., 11 miles south of U.S. 101* ☎ *No phone.*

Staircase Campground. In deep woods away from the river, this campground is a popular jumping-off point for hikes into the Skokomish River Valley and the Olympic high country. ⌧ *Rte. 119, 16 miles north-west of U.S. 101* ☎ *No phone.*

from basic rooms with shared baths to spacious two-bedroom fireplace cottages. **Pros:** gorgeous setting; free wireless access in the wilderness. **Cons:** no laundry; Roosevelt Cottages must be booked a year in advance for summer stays. $ *Rooms from: $188* ✉ *416 Lake Crescent Rd., Port Angeles* ☎ *360/928–3211, 888/723–7127* ⊕ *www.olympicnationalparks.com* ☽ *Closed Jan.–Apr., except Roosevelt fireplace cabins open weekends* ⚓ *30 motel rooms, 17 cabins, 5 lodge rooms with shared bath* ᵀᴼᴵ *No meals.*

$$$$ ⏴ **Lake Quinault Lodge.** On a lovely glacial lake in Olympic National Forest, this beautiful early-20th-century lodge complex is within walking distance of the lakeshore and hiking trails in the spectacular old-growth forest. **Pros:** hosts summer campfires with s'mores; family-friendly ambience; year-round pool and sauna. **Cons:** no TV in some rooms; lake is sometimes closed to fishing and boating; some units are noisy and not very private. $ *Rooms from: $219* ✉ *345 South Shore Rd., Quinault* ☎ *360/288–2900, 800/562–6672* ⊕ *www.olympicnationalparks.com* ⚓ *91 rooms, 1 suite* ᵀᴼᴵ *No meals.*

HOTEL

$$ ⏴ **Log Cabin Resort.** This rustic resort has an idyllic setting at the northeast end of Lake Crescent with lodging choices that include A-frame chalet units, standard cabins, small camper cabins, motel units, and RV sites with full hookups. **Pros:** boat rentals available on-site; convenient general store; pets allowed in some cabins. **Cons:** cabins are extremely rustic; no plumbing in the camper cabins; no TVs. $ *Rooms from: $122* ✉ *3183 E. Beach Rd., Port Angeles* ☎ *888/896–3818, 360/928–3325* ⊕ *www.olympicnationalparks.com* ☽ *Closed Oct.–late May* ⚓ *4 rooms, 24 cabins, 22 RV sites, 4 tent sites* ᵀᴼᴵ *No meals.*

HOTEL
FAMILY

$$$ ⏴ **Sol Duc Hot Springs Resort.** Deep in the brooding forest along the Sol Duc River and surrounded by 5,000-foot-tall mountains, the main draw of this remote 1910 resort is the pool area, with soothing mineral baths and a freshwater swimming pool. **Pros:** nearby trails; peaceful setting; some units are pet-friendly. **Cons:** units are dated; no air-conditioning; pools get crowded. $ *Rooms from: $172* ✉ *12076 Sol Duc Hot Springs Rd.* ☎ *866/476–5382* ⊕ *www.olympicnationalparks.com* ☽ *Closed mid-Oct.–late Mar.* ⚓ *32 cabins, 1 suite* ᵀᴼᴵ *No meals.*

HOTEL

29

OUTSIDE THE PARK

$$$ ⏴ **Colette's Bed & Breakfast.** A contemporary oceanfront mansion set on a 10-acre sanctuary of gorgeous gardens offers more space, service, and luxury than any other property in the area, with water-view suites that have fireplaces, patios, and two-person spa tubs. **Pros:** water views extend to Victoria, BC; discreet personal service. **Cons:** does not cater to families. $ *Rooms from: $195* ✉ *339 Finn Hall Rd., 10 miles east of town, Port Angeles* ☎ *360/457–9197, 888/457–9777* ⊕ *www.colettes.com* ⚓ *5 suites* ᵀᴼᴵ *Breakfast.*

B&B/INN
Fodor's Choice
★

$$$ ⏴ **Domaine Madeleine.** Perched on a bluff above the Strait of Juan de Fuca, the luxurious accommodations here have either impressionist or Asian accents, fireplaces, and water and mountain views. **Pros:** colorful waterfront lodgings; abundant wildlife; well-appointed rooms. **Cons:** no children under 12; the gourmet breakfast costs extra. $ *Rooms from: $180* ✉ *146 Wildflower La., 8 miles east of town, Port Angeles*

B&B/INN

☎ *360/457–4174* ⊕ *www.domainemadeleine.com* ⬉ *4 rooms, 1 cottage* ⦿ *No meals.*

$$$$ ⛶ **Fort Worden State Park Conference Center.** The 330-acre Fort Worden,
RENTAL built as a late-19th-century gun emplacement to guard the mouth of the
Puget Sound, gained a new purpose when enterprising souls turned the
spacious Victorian homes on officer's row into some of the more memorable lodgings on the Olympic Peninsula. **Pros:** myriad activities; acres
of waterfront for play; historic ambience. **Cons:** summer crowds; no
TV, Internet, or air-conditioning in the houses; few amenities. ⑤ *Rooms
from: $249* ⊠ *200 Battery Way, Port Townsend* ☎ *360/344–4434*
⊕ *www.fortworden.org/stay-here/#lodging* ⬉ *35 houses, 3 dorms, 80
camp sites with full hookups* ⦿ *Breakfast.*

$ ⛶ **Ocean Crest Resort.** Set on a forested bluff above the Pacific Ocean, 30
RESORT minutes from Olympic National Park and Lake Quinault, Ocean Crest
has small budget studios, large studios with ocean views, and one- and
two-bedroom units. **Pros:** windows open to hear the ocean's roar; some
rooms are pet-friendly; off-season specials. **Cons:** remote; rooms are
dated. ⑤ *Rooms from: $69* ⊠ *4651 Rte. 109, Moclips* ☎ *360/276–4465*
⊕ *www.oceancrestresort.com* ⬉ *45 rooms* ⦿ *No meals.*

$$ ⛶ **Quality Inn Uptown.** South of Port Angeles, at the green edge of the
HOTEL Olympic Mountain foothills, this no-frills choice has a great thing going
for it: a stunning panorama of mountain and harbor views. **Pros:** central location; great views. **Cons:** basic interior design and amenities;
somewhat dated; no elevators. ⑤ *Rooms from: $143* ⊠ *101 E. 2nd
St., Port Angeles* ☎ *360/457–9434* ⊕ *www.qualityinnportangeles.com*
⬉ *51 rooms* ⦿ *Breakfast.*

$$$$ ⛶ **Sea Cliff Gardens Bed & Breakfast.** A gingerbread-style porch fronts
B&B/INN this antiques-furnished waterfront Victorian home on 2 acres of land-
Fodor's Choice scaped grounds; all of the exquisitely appointed guest rooms have fire-
★ places and panoramic water views through large picture windows. **Pros:**
sumptuous accommodations with stunning views; gorgeous flower gardens; romantic setting. **Cons:** a bit off the beaten path. ⑤ *Rooms from:
$215* ⊠ *397 Monterra Dr., Port Angeles* ☎ *360/452–2322* ⊕ *www.
seacliffgardens.com* ⬉ *5 suites* ⦿ *Breakfast.*

$$$$ ⛶ **Seabrook Cottage Rentals.** Crushed seashells line pathways throughout
RENTAL this charming collection of some 300 Cape Cod–style homes, more
FAMILY than half of which are available to rent. **Pros:** recreational activities
Fodor's Choice and beach within walking distance; homes are new with many ameni-
★ ties; some are pet-friendly. **Cons:** ongoing construction; added cleaning
fees; limited services outside of village. ⑤ *Rooms from: $279* ⊠ *4275
State Rte. 109, Pacific Beach* ☎ *360/276–0265, 877/779–9990* ⊕ *www.
seabrookcottagerentals.com* ⬉ *150 cottages* ⦿ *No meals.*

PETRIFIED FOREST
NATIONAL PARK

WELCOME TO PETRIFIED FOREST NATIONAL PARK

TOP REASONS TO GO

★ **Terrific timber:** Be mesmerized by the clusters of petrified (fossilized) wood. The trees look like they're made of colorful stone.

★ **Walls with words:** Don't scratch the surface, but see how others did. Ancestors of the Hopi, Zuni, and Navajo left their mark in petroglyphs cut, scratched, or carved into stone.

★ **Route 66 kicks:** A section of the fabled road is preserved in the park, the only section of the highway protected in a national park.

★ **Triassic treasures:** Find an oasis of water in the desert, or at least evidence that it once existed. Clam fossils in the park indicate that waterways once prevailed where sand, stone, and trees now define the land.

★ **Corps creations:** The Painted Desert Inn, a National Historic Landmark, was modernized by the Civilian Conservation Corps (CCC) during the throes of the Great Depression. It is now a museum and bookstore.

1 Painted Desert. The main area of the park, in the northern section, is where park headquarters, the Painted Desert Inn, and Route 66 are located. It's also the best place for hiking. A permit is required for overnight camping in the wilderness area, but day users need not obtain one. The 28-mile park road begins here, off Interstate 40.

2 Blue Mesa. In the heart of the Painted Desert, this 1-mile loop trail begins off a loop road accessed from the park road. Petrified trees lie among hills of bluish bentonite clay.

3 Rainbow Forest Museum. Get a trail guide here for the short Giant Logs Trail located behind the museum, and keep an eye out for Old Faithful, a log almost 10 feet wide. The southern terminus for the park road is here.

ARIZONA

GETTING ORIENTED

There are few places where the span of geologic and human history is as wide or apparent as it is at Petrified Forest National Park. Fossilized trees and countless other fossils date back to the Triassic Period, while a stretch of the famed Route 66 of more modern lore is protected within park boundaries. Ancestors of the Hopi, Zuni, and Navajo left petroglyphs, pottery, and even structures built of petrified wood. Nine park sites are on the National Register of Historic Places; one, the Painted Desert Inn, is one of only 3% of such sites that are also listed as National Historic Landmarks.

30

KEY
🏠 *Ranger Station*
▲ *Campground*
⛱ *Picnic Area*
🍴 *Restaurant*
🏨 *Lodge*
🚶 *Trailhead*
🚻 *Restrooms*
⚘ *Scenic Viewpoint*
⋯⋯ *Walking/Hiking Trails*

Updated by
Elise Riley

Petrified logs scattered about a vast pink-hued lunarlike landscape resemble a fairy-tale forest turned to stone at Petrified Forest National Park. The park's 218,533 acres, which include portions of the Painted Desert, are covered with petrified tree trunks whose wood cells were fossilized over centuries by brightly hued mineral deposits—silica, iron oxide, carbon, manganese, aluminum, copper, and lithium. The park holds plenty of other fossils; remnants of humans and their artifacts have been recovered at more than 500 sites in the park.

PETRIFIED FOREST PLANNER

WHEN TO GO

The park is rarely crowded. Weather-wise, the best time to visit is autumn, when nights are chilly but daytime temperatures hover near 70°F. Half of all yearly rain falls between June and August, so it's a good time to spot blooming wildflowers. The park is least crowded in winter, because of cold winds and occasional snow, though daytime temperatures are in the 50s and 60s.

AVG. HIGH/LOW TEMPS.

Jan.	Feb.	Mar.	Apr.	May	June
48/21	54/25	60/29	70/35	79/43	89/52
July	Aug.	Sept.	Oct.	Nov.	Dec.
92/60	89/59	84/52	72/40	59/28	48/22

FESTIVALS AND EVENTS

MAY **National Wildflower Week.** Activities include wildflower walks and an interactive wildflower display.

DECEMBER **Petrified Forest Park Anniversary.** A national monument since 1906 and a national park since 1962, Petrified Forest throws a party for its birthday, with homemade cider, cookies, and cultural demonstrations.

PLANNING YOUR TIME

PETRIFIED FOREST IN ONE DAY

A nonstop drive through the park (28 miles) takes only 45 minutes, but you can spend a half day or more exploring if you stop along the way. From almost any vantage point you can see the multicolored rocks and hills that were home to prehistoric humans and ancient dinosaurs.

Entering from the north, stop at **Painted Desert Visitor Center** for a 20-minute introductory film. Two miles in, the **Painted Desert Inn National Historic Landmark** provides guided ranger tours. Drive south 8 miles to reach **Puerco Pueblo,** a 100-room pueblo built before 1400. Continuing south, you'll find Puebloan petroglyphs at **Newspaper Rock** and, just beyond, the **Tepees,** cone-shape rock formations.

Blue Mesa is roughly the midpoint of the drive, and the start of a 1-mile, moderately steep loop hike that leads you around badland hills made of bentonite clay. Drive on for 5 miles until you come to **Jasper Forest,** just past **Agate Bridge,** with views of the landscape strewn with petrified logs. **Crystal Forest,** about 20 miles south of the north entrance, is named for the smoky quartz, amethyst, and citrine along the 0.8-mile loop trail. **Rainbow Forest Museum,** at the park's south entrance, has restrooms, a bookstore, and exhibits. Just behind Rainbow Forest Museum is **Giant Logs,** a 0.4-mile loop that takes you to "Old Faithful," the largest log in the park, estimated to weigh 44 tons.

GETTING HERE AND AROUND

AIR TRAVEL

The nearest major airports are in Phoenix, Arizona (259 miles away via U.S. 17 and U.S. 40), and Albuquerque, New Mexico (204 miles via U.S. 40).

CAR TRAVEL

Holbrook, the nearest large town with services such as gas or food, is on U.S. 40, roughly 30 miles from either of the park's two entrances.

30

Parking is free, and there's ample space at all trailheads, as well as at the visitor center and the museum. The main park road extends 28 miles from the Painted Desert Visitor Center (north entrance) to the Rainbow Forest Museum (south entrance). For park road conditions, call ☎ *928/524–6228.*

PARK ESSENTIALS

PARK FEES AND PERMITS

Entrance fees are $20 per car for seven consecutive days or $10 per person on foot, bicycle, motorcycle, or bus. Backcountry hiking and camping permits are free (limit of 15 days) at the Painted Desert Visitor Center or the Rainbow Forest Museum before 4 pm.

PARK HOURS

It's a good idea to call ahead or check the website, since the park's hours vary so much; as a rule of thumb, the park is open daily from sunrise to sunset, and keep in mind that the area does not observe daylight saving time. Hours are approximately: daily 8–5 from November to February, daily 7–6:30 in March and April, daily 7 am–7:30 pm from May to August, and daily 7–6 in September and October.

EDUCATIONAL OFFERINGS

Ask at either park visitor center for the availability of special ranger-led tours, such as the after-hours lantern tour of the Painted Desert Inn Museum.

RANGER PROGRAMS

Ranger Walks and Talks. Park rangers lead regular programs along the Great Logs Trail, inside the Painted Desert Inn Museum, and to the Puerco Pueblo. You can view which ranger programs are currently being offered at the visitor centers or online at *www.nps.gov/pefo*. ⊠ *Petrified Forest National Park*.

FAMILY   **Junior Ranger.** Children 12 and younger can learn more about the park's extensive human, animal, and geologic history as they train to become a Junior Ranger. ⊠ *Petrified Forest National Park*.

RESTAURANTS

Dining in the park is limited to a cafeteria in the Painted Desert Visitor Center and snacks in the Rainbow Forest Museum. In and around the Navajo and Hopi reservations, be sure to sample Indian tacos, an authentic treat made with scrumptious fry bread, beans, and chilies. If you're searching for burger-and-fries fare, Holbrook is your best bet.

HOTELS

There is no lodging within Petrified Forest. Outside the park, lodging choices include modern resorts, rustic cabins, and small bed-and-breakfasts. Note that air-conditioning is not a standard amenity in the mountains, where the nights are cool enough for a blanket even in summer. Closer to the Navajo and Hopi reservations many establishments are run by American Indians, tribal enterprises intent on offering first-class service and hospitality. Nearby Holbrook offers most national chain hotels and comfortable accommodations. *Hotel reviews have been shortened. For full information, visit Fodors.com.*

WHAT IT COSTS				
	$	**$$**	**$$$**	**$$$$**
Restaurants	under $13	$13–$20	$21–$30	over $30
Hotels	under $101	$101–$150	$151–$200	over $200

Restaurant prices are the average cost of a main course at dinner, or if dinner is not served, at lunch. Hotel prices are the lowest cost of a standard double room in high season.

VISITOR INFORMATION

Park Contact Information Petrified Forest National Park. ⊠ *1 Park Rd., Petrified Forest* ☎ *928/524-6228* ⊕ *www.nps.gov/pefo.*

VISITOR CENTERS

Painted Desert Inn National Historic Landmark. This visitor center isn't as large as the other two, but here you can get information as well as view cultural history exhibits. ⊠ *Main park rd., 2 miles north of Painted Desert Visitor Center* ☎ *928/524–6228.*

Painted Desert Visitor Center. This is the place to go for general park information and an informative 20-minute film. Proceeds from books purchased here will fund continued research and interpretive activities for the park. ⊠ *North entrance* ✛ *Off I–40, 27 miles east of Holbrook* ☎ *928/524–6228.*

Rainbow Forest Museum and Visitor Center. View displays of prehistoric animals, watch an orientation video, and—perhaps most important—use the restroom facilities at this visitor center at the southern end of the park. ⊠ *South entrance* ✛ *Off U.S. 180, 18 miles southeast of Holbrook* ☎ *928/524–6228.*

EXPLORING

SCENIC DRIVES

Painted Desert Scenic Drive. A 28-mile scenic drive takes you through the park from one entrance to the other. If you begin at the north end, the first 5 miles of the drive take you along the edge of a high mesa, with spectacular views of the Painted Desert. Beyond lies the desolate Painted Desert Wilderness Area. After the 5-mile point, the road crosses Interstate 40, then swings south toward the Puerco River across a landscape covered with sagebrush, saltbrush, sunflowers, and Apache plume. Past the river, the road climbs onto a narrow mesa leading to Newspaper Rock, a panel of Pueblo Indian rock art. Then the road bends southeast, enters a barren stretch, and passes teepee-shaped buttes in the distance. Next you come to Blue Mesa, roughly the park's midpoint and a good place to stop for views of petrified logs. The next stop on the drive is Agate Bridge, really a 100-foot log over a wide wash. The remaining overlooks are Jasper and Crystal forests, where you can get further glimpses of the accumulated petrified wood. On your way out of the park, stop at the Rainbow Forest Museum for a rest and to shop for a memento. ⊠ *Begins at Painted Desert Visitor Center.*

30

HISTORIC SITES

Agate House. This eight-room pueblo is thought to have been built entirely of petrified wood 700 years ago. Researchers believe it might have been used as a temporary dwelling by seasonal farmers or traders from one of the area tribes. ⊠ *Rainbow Forest Museum parking area.*

Newspaper Rock. See huge boulders covered with petroglyphs believed to have been carved by the Pueblo Indians more than 500 years ago. ■TIP➔ **Look through the binoculars that are provided here—you'll be surprised at what the naked eye misses.** ⊠ *Main park rd.* ✛ *6 miles south of Painted Desert Visitor Center.*

Different minerals in different concentrations cause the rich colors in petrified wood and in the Painted Desert.

Painted Desert Inn National Historic Landmark. A nice place to stop and rest in the shade, this site offers vast views of the Painted Desert from several lookouts. Inside, cultural history exhibits, murals, and Native American crafts are on display. ⊠ *Main park rd.* ✛ *2 miles north of Painted Desert Visitor Center.*

Puerco Pueblo. This is a 100-room pueblo, built before 1400 and said to have housed ancestral Puebloan people. Many visitors come to see petroglyphs, as well as a solar calendar. ⊠ *Main park rd.* ✛ *10 miles south of Painted Desert Visitor Center.*

SCENIC STOPS

Agate Bridge. Here you'll see a 100-foot log spanning a 40-foot-wide wash. ⊠ *Main park rd.* ✛ *19 miles south of Painted Desert Visitor Center.*

Crystal Forest. The fragments of petrified wood strewn here once held clear quartz and amethyst crystals. ⊠ *Main park rd.* ✛ *20 miles south of Painted Desert Visitor Center.*

Giant Logs Interpretive Loop Trail. A short walk leads you past the park's largest log, known as Old Faithful. It's considered the largest because of its diameter (9 feet 9 inches), as well as how tall it once was. ⊠ *Main park rd.* ✛ *28 miles south of Painted Desert Visitor Center.*

Jasper Forest. More of an overlook than a forest, this spot has a large concentration of petrified trees in jasper or red. ⊠ *Main park rd.* ✛ *17 miles south of Painted Desert Visitor Center.*

Plants and Wildlife in Petrified Forest

Engelmann's asters and sunflowers are among the blooms in the park each summer. Juniper trees, cottonwoods, and willows grow along Puerco River wash, providing shelter for all manner of wildlife. You might spot mule deer, coyotes, prairie dogs, and foxes, while other inhabitants, like porcupines and bobcats, tend to hide. Bird-watchers should keep an eye out for mockingbirds, red-tailed and Swainson's hawks, roadrunners, swallows, and hummingbirds. Look for all three kinds of lizards—collared, side-blotched, and southern prairie—in rocks.

Beware of rattlesnakes. They're common but can generally be easily avoided: Watch where you step, and don't step anywhere you can't see. If you do come across a rattler, give it plenty of space, and let it go its way before you continue on yours. Other reptiles are just as common but not as dangerous. The gopher snake looks similar to a rattlesnake, but is nonpoisonous. The collared lizard, with its yellow head, can be seen scurrying out of your way in bursts measured at up to 15 mph. They aren't poisonous, but will bite in the rare instance of being caught.

The Tepees. Witness the effects of time on these cone-shaped rock formations colored by iron, manganese, and other minerals. ⊠ *Main park rd.* ✣ *8 miles south of Painted Desert Visitor Center.*

SPORTS AND THE OUTDOORS

Because the park goes to great pains to maintain the integrity of the fossil- and artifact-strewn landscape, sports and outdoor options in the park are limited to on-trail hiking.

HIKING

All trails begin off the main road, with restrooms at or near the trailheads. Most maintained trails are relatively short, paved, clearly marked, and, with a few exceptions, easy to moderate in difficulty. Hikers with greater stamina can make their own trails in the wilderness area, located just north of the Painted Desert Visitor Center. Watch your step for rattlesnakes, which are common in the park—if left alone and given a wide berth, they're passed easily enough.

EASY

Crystal Forest Trail. This easy ¾-mile loop leads you past petrified wood that once held quartz crystals and amethyst chips. *Easy.* ✣ *Trailhead: 20 miles south of the Painted Desert Visitor Center.*

Giant Logs Trail. At 0.4 mile, Giant Logs is the park's shortest trail. The loop leads you to Old Faithful, the park's largest petrified log—9 feet, 9 inches at its base, weighing an estimated 44 tons. *Easy.* ✣ *Trailhead: directly behind Rainbow Forest Museum, 28 miles south of Painted Desert Visitor Center.*

30

Petroglyphs: The Writing on the Wall

Like some other historic sites in eastern Arizona, Petrified Forest National Park is a great place to view petroglyphs and pictographs—designs pecked or scratched into the stone are called petroglyphs; those that are painted on the surface are pictographs. Few pictographs remain because of the deleterious effects of weathering, but the more durable petroglyphs number in the thousands.

The rock art of early Native Americans is carved or painted on basalt boulders, on canyon walls, and on the underside of overhangs throughout the area. No one knows the exact meaning of these signs, and interpretations vary; they've been seen as elements in shamanistic or hunting rituals, as clan signs, maps, or even indications of visits by extraterrestrials.

WHERE TO FIND IT

Susceptible to (and often already damaged by) vandalism, many rock-art sites aren't open to the public. Two good petroglyphs to check out at **Petrified Forest National Park** are Newspaper Rock, an overlook near mile marker 12, and Puerco Pueblo, near mile marker 11. Other sites in Arizona include **Hieroglyphic Point** in Salt River Canyon, and **Five-Mile Canyon** in Snowflake.

DETERMINING ITS AGE

It's just as difficult to date a "glyph" as it is to understand it. Archaeologists try to determine a general time frame by judging the style, the date of the ruins and pottery in the vicinity, the amount of patination (formation of minerals) on the design, or the superimposition of newer images on top of older ones. Most of eastern Arizona's rock art is estimated to be at least 1,000 years old, and many of the glyphs were created even earlier.

VARIED IMAGES

Some glyphs depict animals like bighorn sheep, deer, bear, and mountain lions; others are geometric patterns. The most unusual are the anthropomorphs, strange humanlike figures with elaborate headdresses. Concentric circles are a common design. A few of these circles served as solstice signs, indicating the summer and winter solstice and other important dates. At the solstice, when the angle of the sun is just right, a shaft of light shines through a crack in a nearby rock, illuminating the center of the circle. Archaeologists believe that these solar calendars helped determine the time for ceremonies and planting.

Many solstice signs are in remote regions, but you can visit Petrified Forest National Park around June 20 to see a concentric circle illuminated during the summer solstice. The glyph, reached by a paved trail just a few hundred yards from the parking area, is visible year-round, but light shines directly in the center during the week of the solstice. The phenomenon occurs at 9 am, a reasonable hour for looking at the calendar.

■ TIP➔ Do not touch petroglyphs or pictographs—the oil from your hands can damage the images.

The stones tell a story with ancient etchings on Newspaper Rock.

Long Logs Trail. Although barren, this easy 1.6-mile loop passes the largest concentration of wood in the park. *Easy.* ⊹ *Trailhead: 26 miles south of Painted Desert Visitor Center.*

FAMILY **Puerco Pueblo Trail.** A relatively flat and interesting 0.3-mile trail takes you past remains of a home of the Ancestral Puebloan people, built before 1400. The trail is paved and wheelchair accessible. *Easy.* ⊹ *Trailhead: 10 miles south of Painted Desert Visitor Center.*

MODERATE

Agate House. A fairly flat 1-mile trip takes you to an eight-room pueblo sitting high on a knoll. *Moderate.* ⊹ *Trailhead: 26 miles south of Painted Desert Visitor Center.*

Fodor's Choice **Blue Mesa.** Although it's only 1 mile long and significantly steeper than ★ the rest, this trail at the park's midway point is one of the most popular and worth the effort. *Moderate.* ⊹ *Trailhead: 14 miles south of Painted Desert Visitor Center.*

Painted Desert Rim. The 1-mile trail is at its best in early morning or late afternoon, when the sun accentuates the brilliant red, blue, purple, and other hues of the desert and petrified forest landscape. *Moderate.* ⊹ *Trail runs between Tawa Point and Kachina Point, 1 mile north of Painted Desert Visitor Center; drive to either point from visitor center.*

DIFFICULT

Kachina Point. This is the trailhead for wilderness hiking at Petrified Forest National Park. A 1-mile trail leads to the Wilderness Area, but from there you're on your own. There are no developed trails, so hiking here is cross-country style. Expect to see strange formations, beautifully colored landscapes, and maybe, just maybe, a pronghorn antelope. *Difficult.* ✛ *Trailhead: on the northwest side of the Painted Desert Inn National Historic Landmark.*

WHAT'S NEARBY

Located in eastern Arizona just off Interstate 40, Petrified Forest National Park is set in an area of grasslands, overlooked by mountains in the distance. At nearly an hour from **American Indian Nations**, nearly two hours from **Flagstaff**, and three hours from the **Grand Canyon**, the park is relatively remote and separated from many comforts of travel. Just a half hour away, **Holbrook**, the nearest town, is the best place to grab a quick bite to eat or take a brief rest.

> **LOOK AND TOUCH— BUT DON'T TAKE**
>
> One of the most commonly asked questions about the Petrified Forest is, "Can I touch the wood?" Yes! Feel comfortable to touch anything, pick it up, inspect it... just make sure you put it back where you found it. It's illegal to remove even a small sliver of fossilized wood from the park.

NEARBY ATTRACTIONS

Fodor's Choice ★ **Canyon de Chelly.** Home to Ancestral Puebloans from AD 350 to 1300, the nearly 84,000-acre Canyon de Chelly (pronounced d'*shay*) is one of the most spectacular natural wonders in the Southwest. On a smaller scale, it rivals the Grand Canyon for beauty. Its main gorges—the 26-mile-long Canyon de Chelly ("canyon in the rock") and the adjoining 35-mile-long Canyon del Muerto ("canyon of the dead")—comprise sheer, heavily eroded sandstone walls that rise to 1,100 feet over dramatic valleys. Ancient pictographs and petroglyphs decorate some of the cliffs, and within the canyon complex there are more than 7,000 archaeological sites. Stone walls rise hundreds of feet above streams, hogans, tilled fields, and sheep-grazing lands.

You can view prehistoric sites near the base of cliffs and perched on high, sheltering ledges, some of which you can access from the park's two main drives along the canyon rims. The dwellings and cultivated fields of the present-day Navajo lie in the flatlands between the cliffs, and those who inhabit the canyon today farm much the way their ancestors did. Most residents leave the canyon in winter but return in early spring to farm.

Canyon de Chelly's South Rim Drive (36 miles round-trip with seven overlooks) starts at the visitor center and ends at **Spider Rock Overlook**, where cliffs plunge nearly 1,000 feet to the canyon floor. The view here is of two pinnacles, Speaking Rock and Spider Rock. Other highlights on the South Rim Drive are Junction Overlook, where Canyon del Muerto joins Canyon de Chelly; White House Overlook, from which a 2½-mile round-trip trail leads to the **White House Ruin**, with remains of nearly 60 rooms and several kivas; and Sliding House Overlook, where you can see dwellings on a narrow, sloped ledge across the canyon. The carved and sometimes narrow trail down the canyon side to White House Ruin is the only access into Canyon de Chelly without a guide—if you have a fear of heights, this may not be the hike for you.

The only slightly less breathtaking **North Rim Drive** (34 miles round-trip with four overlooks) of Canyon del Muerto also begins at the visitor center and continues northeast on Indian Highway 64 toward the town of Tsaile. Major stops include **Antelope House Overlook,** a large site named for the animals painted on an adjacent cliff; **Mummy Cave Overlook,** where two mummies were found inside a remarkably unspoiled pueblo dwelling; and **Massacre Case Overlook,** which marks the spot where an estimated 115 Navajo were killed by the Spanish in 1805. (The rock walls of the cave are still pockmarked by the Spaniards' ricocheting bullets.) ⊠ *Indian Hwy. 7, 3 miles east of U.S. 191, Chinle* ☎ *928/674–5500 for visitor center* ⊕ *www.nps.gov/ cach* ⊒ *Free* ⊙ *Daily 8–5.*

Homolovi Ruins State Park. *Homolovi* is a Hopi word meaning "place of the little hills." The pueblo sites here at Homolovi Ruins State Park are thought to have been occupied between AD 1200 and 1425, and include 40 ceremonial kivas and two pueblos containing more than 1,000 rooms each. The Hopi believe their immediate ancestors inhabited this place, and they consider the site sacred. Many rooms have been excavated and recovered for protection; rangers conduct guided tours. The Homolovi Visitor Center has a small museum with Hopi pottery and Ancestral Puebloan artifacts; it also hosts workshops on native art, ethnobotany, and traditional foods. Campsites, with or without hookups, are $25 and can be reserved in advance. ⊠ *AZ 87, 3½ miles northeast of Winslow, Winslow* ☎ *928/289–4106* ⊕ *www.azstateparks. com* ⊒ *$7* ⊙ *Visitor center daily 8–5.*

Rock Art Ranch. The Ancestral Puebloan petroglyphs of this working cattle ranch in Chevelon Canyon are startlingly vivid after more than 1,000 years. Ranch owner Brantly Baird will guide you along the ¼-mile trail, explaining Western and archaeological history. It's mostly easy walking, except for the climb in and out of Chevelon Canyon, where there are handrails. Baird houses his Native American artifacts and pioneer farming implements in his own private museum. It's out of the way and on a dirt road, but you'll see some of the best rock art in northern Arizona. Reservations are required. ⊠ *Off AZ 87, 13 miles southeast of Winslow, Winslow* ☎ *928/288–3260* ⊒ *$35 per person, price varies by size of group* ⊙ *By appointment only.*

30

WHERE TO EAT

INSIDE THE PARK

$ ✕ **Painted Desert Visitor Center Cafeteria.** Serving standard (but pretty
AMERICAN decent) cafeteria fare, this is the only place in the park where you can get a full meal. ⑤ *Average main: $7* ⊠ *North entrance* ☎ *928/524–6228.*

PICNIC AREAS

Chinde Point Picnic Area. Near the north entrance, this small spot has tables and restrooms. ✛ *2 miles north of Painted Desert Visitor Center.*

Rainbow Forest Museum Picnic Area. There are restrooms and tables at this small picnic area near the south entrance. ✛ *Off I–40, 27 miles east of Holbrook.*

WHERE TO STAY

OUTSIDE THE PARK

HOLBROOK

$ **Wigwam Motel.** On the National
HOTEL Register of Historic Places, the Wigwam consists of 15 bright-white concrete teepees. **Pros:** impeccably kitschy; one of the signature spots along Route 66. **Cons:** very sparse accommodations that can fit no more than two. ⑤ *Rooms from: $62* ✉ *811 West Hopi Dr., Holbrook* ☎ *928/524–3048* ⊕ *www.sleepinawigwam.com* ⌫ *15 rooms* ⊺⊙⊦ *No meals.*

WINSLOW

$$ **La Posada Hotel.** One of the great
HOTEL railroad hotels, La Posada ("rest-
Fodor'sChoice ing place") exudes the charm of an
★ 18th-century Spanish hacienda and its restoration has been a labor of love. **Pros:** historic charm; unique architecture; impressive restaurant. **Cons:** mazes of staircases aren't wheelchair-friendly. ⑤ *Rooms from: $139* ✉ *303 E. 2nd St., Winslow* ☎ *928/289–4366* ⊕ *www.laposada.org* ⌫ *53 rooms* ⊺⊙⊦ *No meals.*

> ### BEST CAMPGROUNDS IN PETRIFIED FOREST
>
> There are no campgrounds in the park. Backpacking or minimal-impact camping is allowed in a designated zone north of Lithodendron Wash in the Wilderness Area; a free permit must be obtained (pick up at the visitor center or museum), and group size is limited to eight. RVs are not allowed. There are no fire pits or designated sites, nor is any shade available. Note that if it rains, that pretty Painted Desert formation turns to sticky clay.

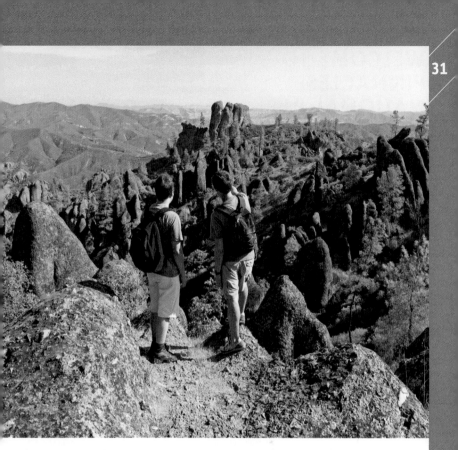

PINNACLES
NATIONAL PARK

WELCOME TO PINNACLES NATIONAL PARK

TOP REASONS TO GO

★ **Condor encounters:** There are only 240 California condors alive in the wild today, and Pinnacles is home to more than 30 of the critically endangered bird.

★ **Cave exploring:** The park contains two talus caves—a unique type of cave formed when boulders fall into narrow canyons, creating ceilings, passageways, and small rooms.

★ **Hiking the pinnacles:** There aren't many roads, so the best way to see the otherworldly rock formations of the ancient volcano found in the middle of the park is to hike the more than 30 miles of trails.

★ **Climbing sans crowds:** Despite achieving National Park status a few years back, Pinnacles has a remote location, so it gets far fewer visitors than parks like Yosemite, leaving the hundreds of rock-climbing routes crowd-free.

★ **Star appeal:** Far from cities, the park is a popular stargazing destination, especially during the annual Perseid meteor shower.

1 East Entrance. There are only two entrances to Pinnacles, and this is the family-friendly choice. It has the park's only campground—including a visitor center, a small swimming pool that's especially inviting on hot days, and a modest store for food, drinks, and other camping essentials and incidentals. This entrance is also the best access point for Bear Gulch Cave, the most popular hike in the park.

2 West Entrance. The park's western side tends to be quieter than the eastern one, and it has fewer amenities, but coming here is the best way to sneak a peek at the high-peak formations without having to hike. Just drive to the Chaparral Trailhead parking lot, and you can view them from there. The Balconies Cave Trail is also popular on this side of the park. The towering rocks keep the canyon trail shady and relatively cool.

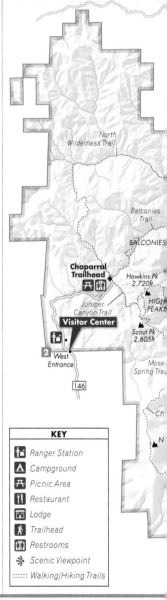

KEY

🏠	Ranger Station
⛺	Campground
🌲	Picnic Area
🍴	Restaurant
🏨	Lodge
🚶	Trailhead
🚻	Restrooms
�	Scenic Viewpoint
┈┈	Walking/Hiking Trails

CALIFORNIA

25

BEAR VALLEY

McCABE CANYON

East Entrance

146

1

25

Balconies Trail

BALCONIES

Visitor Center

Condor Gulch Trail

•Bacon and Butterfield
Homesteads\ private
Pinnacles property
Campground

*Hawkins Pk
2,720ft*

*East Entrance
Station*

**Bear
Gulch**

**Peaks
View**

HIGH
PEAKS

*Scout Pk
2,605ft*

LITTLE PINNACLES

FROG CANYON

BEAR VALLEY

GRASSY CANYON

*Moses
Spring Trail*

▲ *Mt. Defiance
2,657ft*

*Chalone Peak
Trail*

▲ *N Chalone Pk
3,304ft*

▲ *S Chalone Pk
3,269ft*

0   1 Mi

0   1 km

GETTING ORIENTED

Bounded on the west by Steinbeck's Salinas Valley and busy U.S. 101 and on the east by pastoral Highway 25, Pinnacles can almost seem like two parks, with the ancient volcanic peaks at its center barring cars from getting from one side to the other—only hikers can make this trek. From San Francisco the drive south to either of the park's entrances, both along Highway 146, is about 130 miles (2½ hours); the drive south from San Jose is about 80 miles (1¾ hours), and from the Monterey/Carmel area it's about 50 miles (1 hour) to the west entrance. To drive from one entrance to the other, allow at least an hour and a half. If you're entering the park from the west, Highway 146 becomes winding and hilly after Soledad, and it's only one lane wide in many places.

Updated by
Deb Hopewell

Pinnacles may be the nation's newest national park, but President Theodore Roosevelt recognized the uniqueness of this ancient volcano—its jagged spires and monoliths thrusting upward from chaparral-covered mountains—when he made it a national monument in 1908. Legends abound of robbers and banditos who used the park's talus caves as hideouts, though the most famous denizens of Pinnacles these days are the magnificent California condors that thrive in its wilderness. The bustling Bay Area is only about two hours away, but the outside world seems to recede even before you reach the entrance gates.

PINNACLES PLANNER

WHEN TO GO

Summers tend to be very warm, and triple-digit temperatures are not uncommon; luckily this means fewer crowds, especially on weekdays. Spring, particularly March and April, is the most popular season, as this is the prime time for viewing spectacular displays of lupine, poppies, and other wildflowers. Though late September can still be quite warm, fall is a great time to visit if you want to enjoy cooler temperatures and fewer crowds. Winters are cold by California standards, but this is an opportune time to hike, especially the High Peaks, where most of the trails are in the sun. On the other hand, the temperatures in the deeply shaded areas such as the Balconies Trail can reach below freezing.

One thing to keep in mind: Bear Gulch Cave, on the east side, is one of the most popular hikes and attractions, but it's also home to a large colony of Townsend's big-eared bats. This protected species raises its young in the late spring and summer, so the cave is closed from about mid-May to mid-July. If your plans include visiting the cave, check the park's website (⊕ *www.nps.gov/pinn/planyourvisit/cavestatus.htm*), which provides updates on closures.

AVG. HIGH/LOW TEMPS.

Jan.	Feb.	Mar.	Apr.	May	June
62/27	63/30	67/32	72/33	80/37	88/41
July	Aug.	Sept.	Oct.	Nov.	Dec.
95/45	95/45	90/42	81/36	69/31	61/27

FESTIVALS AND EVENTS

MAY **Steinbeck Festival.** This biannual three-day festival celebrates the life and works of author and Salinas native John Steinbeck, whose Pulitzer and Nobel prize–winning novels were often set in the areas of Monterey County he knew and loved so well. Films, tours, talks, and visual- and performing-arts activities take place in both Monterey and Salinas. ⊠ *1 Main St., Salinas* ☎ *831/775–4721* ⊕ *www.steinbeck.org.*

JULY **California Salinas Rodeo.** More than a century old, this rodeo is the largest in California and one of the best professional rodeos in the country. Hundreds of top-ranked wranglers compete for prizes in events that include bareback riding, saddle bronc riding, steer wrestling, and bull riding. ⊠ *1034 N. Main St., Salinas* ☎ *831/775–3100* ⊕ *www.carodeo. com.*

PLANNING YOUR TIME

PINNACLES IN ONE DAY

Begin your day early by arriving at the west entrance, stopping briefly at the **West Pinnacles Visitor Contact Station** to pick up maps. Continue on Highway 146 about 2 miles to the **Chaparral Trailhead** parking lot, where you can view the park's impressive peaks. The best way to experience them is by hiking, so grab your flashlight and some water and follow the **Balconies Trail** from the parking lot. This mostly level 1-mile hike takes you along the shaded canyon floor to the **Balconies Cave,** where you must duck under boulders and sometimes squeeze through talus passages. From the cave you can hike an extra ½-mile on the **Balconies Cliff Trail,** climbing to fantastic views east to Machete Ridge. Follow the trail down to the back side of the caves, and return through the caves to the original trail. Upon returning to your car, head west to Soledad.

From Soledad follow U.S. 101 south about 19 miles to King City, and exit at 1st Street. Follow the East Pinnacles signs to Highway 25 and continue north until you reach Highway 146 and the park's east entrance.

If the store adjacent to the **Pinnacles Visitor Center** is open, pick up a drink or a snack before continuing on Highway 146 a little more than 2 miles to the turnoff for the Bear Gulch Day Use Area. The **Bear Gulch Nature Center** is open seasonally as staffing permits. If the center is open, check out its displays, which include a seismograph (the park lies near the San Andreas Fault). Just past the nature center, there's a small parking lot with shaded tables, a perfect place for a picnic. Make sure you have your water and flashlight with you as you take the **Bear Gulch Trail** from the picnic area to the **Moses Spring Trail** (0.2 mile). Once you get to the caves (about 0.3 mile), you'll scramble through until you come to a long staircase cut into the stone; very shortly the trail will bring you to the **Bear Gulch Reservoir.** Follow the Rim Trail as it leaves the reservoir for views of the peaks to the east and west. After a switchback descent, it connects again with the Moses Spring Trail (0.7 mile), which leads back to the parking lot.

GETTING HERE AND AROUND
AIR TRAVEL
The nearest major airport is Mineta San Jose International Airport (SJC), about 80 miles north of the park. San Francisco International Airport (SFO) is about 100 miles north.

CAR TRAVEL
One of the first things you need to decide when visiting Pinnacles is which entrance—east or west—you'll use. There is no through road. Entering from Highway 25 on the east side of the park is straightforward. The gate is only a mile or so from the turnoff. From the west, once you head east out of Soledad on Highway 146, the road quickly becomes narrow and hilly, with many blind curves. Park rangers discourage visitors from driving RVs, large vehicles, or vehicles towing trailers on this road. Drive slowly and cautiously along the 11 miles or so before you reach the west entrance.

PARK ESSENTIALS
PARK FEES AND PERMITS
Park admission is $15 per car or motorcycle, $10 per person on foot or bicycle. The Pinnacles National Park Annual Pass ($25) is valid for one year from the month of purchase.

PARK HOURS
The east entrance is open 24 hours a day, 7 days a week. The west entrance opens daily at 7:30 am and closes at 8 pm. An automatic gate opens for cars leaving the park after closing time.

CELL-PHONE RECEPTION
The closer you get to Pinnacles, the less reliable cell-phone service will be; it's nearly nonexistent within the park. There's a pay phone at the visitor center at the east entrance and at the Bear Gulch Nature Center. There are no public phones at the west entrance or in the interior of the park.

EDUCATIONAL OFFERINGS
INTERPRETIVE PROGRAMS
Illustrated Ranger Talks. On some weekend evenings, rangers give free presentations at the east entrance's campground amphitheater. The topics depend on the ranger's particular interests but always relate to the park's main stories and its geology, plants, or wildlife. Times vary, so check the Pinnacles website or the Activity Boards at the east or west entrances or the Bear Gulch Nature Center. ✉ *5000 Hwy. 146* ☎ *831/389–4486* ⊕ *www.nps.gov/pinn/planyourvisit/programs.htm.*

RANGER PROGRAMS

Junior Ranger Program. Kids can pick up a free Junior Ranger booklet at the Bear Gulch Nature Center, Pinnacles Visitor Center, or the West Pinnacles Visitor Contact Station. Once they explore the park and complete the activities in the booklet, they'll earn a Junior Ranger Badge. ⊠ *5000 Hwy. 146* ☎ *831/389–4486* ⊕ *www.nps.gov/pinn/planyourvisit/events. htm.*

Night Hikes. Rangers occasionally lead night hikes, including ones under the full moon or to view stars or explore caves. Check the park's website to see if any hikes, which are from easy to moderate in difficulty and take between one and two hours, will coincide with your visit. Groups are limited to 20 people. To reserve a spot, drop by the Pinnacles Visitor Center or call no more than one week ahead of the hike. ⊠ *5000 Hwy. 146, Paicines* ☎ *831/389–4486 east side, 831/537–7220 west side* ⊕ *www.nps.gov/pinn/planyourvisit/programs.htm.*

Ranger-Guided Hikes and Activities. From President's Day weekend through the end of May, park rangers conduct free guided hikes, usually on the weekends. On the east side of the park, the hikes are typically to Bear Gulch Cave; on the west side, they're to the Balconies Cliffs and Caves. When you get to the park, ask a ranger about the day's opportunities or consult one of the Ranger Activity Boards outside the Pinnacles Visitor Center, the Bear Gulch Nature Center, or the West Pinnacles Visitor Contact Station. ⊠ *5000 Hwy. 146* ☎ *831/389–4486* ⊕ *www.nps.gov/ pinn/planyourvisit/programs.htm.*

RESTAURANTS

The park has no restaurants, so it's a good idea to pack a cooler before you arrive, especially if you plan on staying for more than a day. If coming from the north, you'll find supermarkets and grocery stores in Hollister; at the southern end, King City is the best option. Soledad, the gateway to the park's western entrance, also has a supermarket. The small camp store adjacent to the eastern entrance's visitor center carries mostly canned goods and snacks, as well as bags of ice. Food or drink aren't available at the western entrance. Because you can't drive through to the other entrance, you'll need to come prepared.

HOTELS

There aren't any hotels or lodges within the park, so if you want to stay overnight, camping at the Pinnacles Campground, near the east entrance, is your only option. Outside the park, King City, Hollister, and Soledad have mostly budget-class motels. *Hotel reviews have been shortened. For full information, visit Fodors.com.*

WHAT IT COSTS			
$	**$$**	**$$$**	**$$$$**
Restaurants	under $13	$13–$20	$21–$30	over $30
Hotels	under $100	$100–$150	$151–$200	over $200

Restaurant prices are the average cost of a main course at dinner, or if dinner is not served, at lunch. Hotel prices are the lowest cost of a standard double room in high season.

VISITOR INFORMATION

Park Contact Information Pinnacles National Park. ✉ *5000 Hwy. 146, Paicines* ☎ *831/389–4486* ⊕ *www.nps.gov/pinn.*

VISITOR CENTERS

Pinnacles Visitor Center. At the park's main visitor center, located at the eastern entrance, you can purchase admission passes, get maps, browse books, and buy gifts. The adjacent campground store sells snacks and drinks. ✉ *Hwy. 146, 2 miles west of Hwy. 25, Paicines* ☎ *831/389–4485* ⊕ *www.nps.gov/pinn.*

West Pinnacles Visitor Contact Station. This station is just past the park's western entrance, about 10 miles east of Soledad. Here you can get maps and information, watch a 13-minute film about Pinnacles, and view some displays. Food and drink aren't available here. ✉ *Hwy. 146, off U.S. 101, Soledad* ☎ *831/389–4427* ⊕ *www.nps.gov/pinn* ☉ *Daily 9–4:30, call or check website to confirm hrs.*

EXPLORING

HISTORIC SITES

Bacon and Butterfield Homesteads. On the park's eastern side, these two preserved homesteads in the heart of the 331-acre Ben Bacon Ranch Historic District illustrate what subsistence farming in the area looked like from 1865 to 1941, before large-scale agriculture and ranching became the norm. ✉ *Pinnacles National Park* ⊕ *www.nps.gov/cultural_landscapes/snp/725493.html.*

SCENIC STOPS

Chaparral Trailhead. This is the end of the road on the west side of the park, but it's also the best view of the Peaks you can get without having to hit the trails. Look for knifelike Machete Ridge looming in the distance. ✛ *About 2 miles northeast of West Pinnacles Visitor Contact Station on Hwy. 146.*

Peaks View. Short of hiking up to the rugged High Peaks, this east-side viewing area is the best place to catch a glimpse of them (off to the west). You might spot hawks and other birds as well. The area has restrooms and a few picnic tables, and drinking water is available. ✛ *About 1½ miles west of Pinnacles Visitor Center on Hwy. 146, east side.*

SPORTS AND THE OUTDOORS

BIRD-WATCHING

You don't have to be an avid bird-watcher to appreciate the diversity of birds at Pinnacles, so don't forget to bring your binoculars, especially for that charged moment when you realize you've spotted a highly rare California condor suspended on a thermal draft. You're most likely to

Plants and Wildlife in Pinnacles National Park

Pinnacles doesn't have the wildlife superstars found at other national parks—bison, bear, elk, bighorn sheep. Here, California condors rule the roost.

MAGNIFICENT BIRDS

These magnificent birds, which when fully grown have wingspans approaching 10 feet, were nearly extinct in the 1980s. Only 22 remained in the world just three decades ago, but thanks to an intensive captive breeding program, there are now more than 400, with 240 of them in the wild. Pinnacles is one of the five release locations for California condors, and about 30 make their home in the park. It is also the preferred habitat for prairie falcons, which breed here in one of the highest densities in the world.

FROM BOBCATS TO BEETLES

Bobcats and cougars also roam Pinnacles, and California quail are abundant. In addition, there are 14 species of bats, including a colony of Townsend's big-eared bats in Bear Gulch Cave, hibernating in winter and raising their young throughout the summer. The park has the most bee species—400 per unit area—of

any place ever studied. It's also an essential refuge for native species, among them the big-eared kangaroo rat, the Gabilan slender salamander, the Pinnacles shield-back katydid, and the Pinnacles riffle beetle, that have been challenged by nearby human encroachment.

WILDFLOWERS AND CHAPARRAL

Springtime sets the stage for a wildflower extravaganza, especially from March through early May, when more than 80% of the park's plants are in bloom. The most prodigious early bloomers include manzanita, shooting stars, and Indian warriors; by March the park is awash in California poppies, bush poppies, buck brush, fiesta flower, and monkey flower. Late bloomers include suncups, bush lupine, and Johnny-jump-ups. Most of the park is covered in chaparral, which has adapted to the high-heat, low-moisture conditions. This particular plant community is mostly shrubs that grow to around 6 feet tall; the dominant species is chamise, which grows alongside buck brush, manzanita, black sage, and holly-leaved cherry.

see a condor in the early morning or in the early evening in the relatively remote High Peaks area, or on the Balconies Cliff Trail above the caves as you look toward Machete Ridge. Condors are often seen just southeast of the campground, riding the morning thermals along the ridge, and in the evening coming in to roost on their favorite trees. There are two spotting scopes in the campground (on the Bench Trail near Pinnacles Visitor Center) that may help you get a closer look. If you happen to find yourself especially close to a condor, do not under any circumstances approach it. Condors are a federally protected species, and you can be fined for doing so.

The High Peaks are a good place to spot other raptors, such as prairie and peregrine falcons, golden eagles, red-tailed hawks, and American kestrels. But you don't have to undertake a strenuous uphill hike to catch some of the best bird-watching in the park. The campground and visitor center on the east side lies at the convergence of habitats—riparian, oak/

pine trees, chaparral, and human-made. Many species take advantage of water sources provided by the swimming pool and water fountain, and on the paved road past the parking lot, a riparian corridor is the prime habitat for coveys of California quail and wild turkeys.

HIKING

Hiking is the most popular activity at Pinnacles, which has more than 30 miles of trails for every interest and level of fitness. Because there isn't a through road, hiking is the only way to experience the park's interior, including the High Peaks, the talus caves, and the reservoir.

Moses Spring Trail, Bear Gulch Trail, and Balconies Trail are self-guided "interpretive" trails. At the visitor centers you can purchase a trail guide (75¢) that points out different geological, botanical, and habitat facts.

Several trails start near the Bear Gulch Day Use Area. On weekends and holidays year-round, you can catch a shuttle that operates between the east side visitor center and the Bear Gulch parking lot, which sometimes fills up.

Flashlights are required in the Bear Gulch and Balconies cave systems— you won't be able to get through the caves without one. Penlights won't do the job; the best choice is a hands-free, head-mounted light. Also, although the hikes to the caves themselves are easy and short, getting through the caves requires much scrambling, ducking, climbing, and squeezing. Make sure you have suitable, closed-toe shoes.

EASY

Balconies Cliffs-Cave Loop. Grab your flashlight before heading out from the Chaparral Trailhead parking lot for this 2.4-mile loop that takes you through the Balconies Caves. This trail is especially beautiful in spring, when wildflowers carpet the canyon floor. About 0.6 mile from the start of the trail, turn left to begin ascending the Balconies Cliffs Trail, where you'll be rewarded with close-up views of Machete Ridge and other steep, vertical formations; you may run across rock climbers testing their skills. *Easy.* ⊠ *West side of park* ⊹ *Trailhead: from West Pinnacles Visitor Contact Station, drive about 2 miles to Chaparral Trailhead parking lot. Trail picks up on west side of lot.*

FAMILY **Moses Spring-Rim Trail Loop.** Perhaps the most popular hike at Pinnacles, this relatively short (2.2 miles) trail is fun for kids and adults. It leads to the Bear Gulch cave system, and if your timing is right, you'll pass by several seasonal waterfalls inside the caves. If it has been raining, check with a ranger, as the caves could be flooded. The upper side of the cave is usually closed in spring and early summer to protect the Townsend's big-ear bats and their pups. *Easy.* ⊠ *East side of park* ⊹ *Trailhead: just past Bear Gulch Nature Center, on south side of overflow parking lot.*

MODERATE

Condor Gulch Trail. The trailhead starts at the Bear Gulch Day Use area, and it's an easy 1-mile hike up to the Condor Gulch Overlook, where you can get a good view of the High Peaks above and look back down to the trail behind you. Take the moderately easy 2-mile loop back down, or continue another 0.7 mile up to where the Condor Gulch meets the

High Peaks Trail and extend your hike by following the trail in either direction. *Moderate.* ⊠ *East side of park* ✛ *Trailhead: opposite Nature Center at Bear Gulch Day Use Area.*

Pinnacles Visitor Center to Bear Gulch Day Use Area. This 4.6-mile round-trip hike (about three hours) follows the Chalone and Bear creeks first along the Bench Trail for about 1½ miles, where it meets up with the Bear Gulch Trail. Purchase an interpretive map at the visitor center and keep your eyes open for signs pointing out where you might be able to spot the rare red-legged frog or the native three-spined stickleback fish. *Moderate.* ⊠ *East side of park* ✛ *Trailhead: Pinnacles Visitor Center; follow signs to Bench Trail.*

South Wilderness Trail. This 6½-mile hike with no elevation gain is an easy stroll alongside the Chalone River that eventually reaches the park's eastern boundary. Listen to birds sing along the creek as you meander among this unmaintained trail's magnificent groves of valley oaks. *Moderate.* ⊠ *East side of park* ✛ *Trailhead: follow Bench Trail out of Pinnacles Campground for 0.6 mile, then turn left onto fire road to access South Wilderness Trail.*

DIFFICULT

Chalone Peak Trail. If you choose this strenuous 9-mile round-trip hike (2,040 feet of elevation gain), you'll be rewarded with views of the surrounding valleys from the highest point in the park at 3,304 feet (where there are restrooms). If you want to extend the hike, proceed south along the unmaintained portion of the trail for 1.6 miles to South Chalone Peak (3,269 feet). *Difficult.* ⊠ *East side of park* ✛ *Trailhead: at Bear Gulch Reservoir where Moses Spring, Rim, and Chalone Peak trails meet near caves.*

Juniper Canyon Loop. This steep 4.3-mile loop climbs into the heart of the dramatic High Peaks with a 1,215-foot elevation gain. In summer the temperature can get very high. From the trailhead follow the switchbacks up for 1.2 miles, where the trail veers right; be sure to stop at Scout Peak, where you'll find restrooms and fantastic views in all directions—keep an eye out for the occasional California condor in flight. From Scout Peak, follow the High Peaks Trail through a steep and narrow section, where you hug the side of rock faces until reaching a short, nearly vertical staircase that has a railing to help you up. *Difficult.* ⊠ *West side of park* ✛ *Trailhead: Chaparral Trailhead parking lot.*

ROCK CLIMBING

Pinnacles has been a favorite of Bay Area and Central Coast climbers for years, but luckily it remains a relatively quiet spot without the hassle and crowds of better-known parks like Yosemite and Joshua Tree. One important thing to consider is that unlike Yosemite and other granite playgrounds, Pinnacles is largely made of volcanic rock that can be soft and crumbly. The park service suggests that if you have never climbed at Pinnacles before, your first attempts should be well below your usual level to allow you to familiarize yourself with the strength and character of the rocks. In general, the east side of the park has stronger rock, but the west side has much higher peaks.

A good resource for first-time climbers is the Friends of Pinnacles (⊕ *www.pinnacles.org*), a nonprofit that works directly with the park to offer useful tips, guidelines, and updates regarding climbing closures due to nesting raptors. Some formations might also be closed from January through June or July if falcons or eagles are nesting. If you want to know if a specific route is open, check with a ranger or look for the climbing information boards at both the east and west trailheads. Complying with closures is voluntary, but climbers or hikers caught disturbing nesting birds will be fined.

STARGAZING

Though the populous Bay Area is only a couple of hours away, Pinnacles remains nearly untouched by light pollution, making it an outstanding place to watch meteor showers, stars, or the full moon. It's popular with astronomy clubs, whose members occasionally set up their telescopes for public use. Park rangers sometimes lead nighttime activities, usually on the weekends, that include dark-sky and full-moon hikes and "star parties" to watch meteor showers and other celestial phenomena. Campsites often fill up well in advance when meteor showers are expected. These activities are usually limited to 25 or fewer visitors per program, and reservations are required (no more than one week in advance) by calling ☎ *831/389–4485* or visiting the Pinnacles Visitor Center.

WHAT'S NEARBY

NEARBY TOWNS

Soledad, at the park's western entrance, is most famous for being the setting of John Steinbeck's *Of Mice and Men,* but it's also a part of the Monterey County wine region. There are many good wineries with tasting rooms within about 30 miles. Hahn, Scheid, Pessagno, and Ventana, all on the **River Road Wine Trail** (⊕ *www.riverroadwinetrail.com*), are open daily.

To the north in San Benito County is **Hollister,** a farming town that is fast becoming a bedroom community of San Jose. This area is not as well known for wine as is Monterey County, but you can spend a low-key afternoon visiting tasting rooms along the San Benito County Wine Trail. Most are on or near Cienega Road, just south of Hollister off Highway 25. Calera and Léal are among the wineries with tasting rooms open daily.

Popular Monterey and Carmel are a little more than an hour's drive from Pinnacles. Visiting them can enhance a park vacation.

Visitor Information San Benito County Chamber of Commerce. ✉ *243 6th St., Suite 100, Hollister* ☎ *831/637–5315* ⊕ *sanbenitocountychamber.com/ visit.* **Soledad-Mission Chamber of Commerce.** ✉ *641 Front St., Soledad* ☎ *831/678–3941* ⊕ *www.soledadchamber.com.*

WHERE TO EAT

IN THE PARK

PICNIC AREAS

Chaparral Trailhead Picnic Area. This is the only designated picnic area on the west side of the park, but there are great views of the nearby High Peaks. There are few trees for shade, however, and it can be quite warm in summer. Restrooms are close by, and drinking water is available. ⊠ *West side of park* ✛ *About 2 miles northeast of West Pinnacles Visitor Contact Station on Hwy. 146.*

Moses Spring Picnic Area. The park's most pleasant picnic area, shaded by live oaks, sits alongside a seasonal creek. It's a convenient spot to picnic before or after a hike to the reservoir via the Moses Spring or Rim trail. The nearby Bear Gulch Day Use Area has bathrooms (across from the Bear Gulch Nature Center) and drinking water. ⊠ *East side of park* ✛ *About 0.3 mile past Bear Gulch Nature Center on Bear Gulch Trail.*

Peaks View Picnic Area. A nice spot for a picnic, Peaks View is one of the few places on the east side of the park where you can catch a glimpse of the High Peaks without getting on a trail. Restrooms and drinking water are available. ⊠ *East side of park* ✛ *About 1.5 miles west of Pinnacles Visitor Center on Hwy. 146.*

WHERE TO STAY

OUTSIDE THE PARK

$$$$
B&B/INN
Fodor'sChoice
★

Inn at the Pinnacles. Set amid 160 acres of hilltop vineyards overlooking the Salinas Valley and the coastal Santa Lucia Mountains, this Mediterranean-style bed-and-breakfast is an oasis of comfort just off the winding road leading to the park's western entrance. **Pros:** gorgeous vineyard setting and sunset views; tasty breakfast; close to the park. **Cons:** 20 minutes to closest Soledad restaurants; better for couples than families. ⑤ *Rooms from: $235* ⊠ *3025 Stonewall Canyon Rd., Soledad* ⊕ *www.innatthepinnacles.com* ↝ *6 rooms* ⑩ *Breakfast* ⌖ *2-night minimum.*

$$
RENTAL

Paicines Ranch. Comfortable, somewhat rustic rooms and cottages are tucked into a corner of this 7,000-acre working cattle ranch that's within an easy 30-minute drive of the park's east entrance. **Pros:** easy access to park's east entrance; good for large groups or families; peaceful; cooking facilities available. **Cons:** no amenities outside of rooms; closest restaurants 15 minutes away. ⑤ *Rooms from: $100* ⊠ *13388 Old Airline Hwy., Paicines* ⊕ *www.paicinesranch.com* ↝ *8 rooms* ⑩ *No meals.*

$$
HOTEL
FAMILY

Peacock Inn at Casa de Fruta. You can decide for yourself if the surprisingly pleasant accommodations at one end of a popular fruit stand–cum–amusement park are charming or cheesy, but they're clean and fairly spacious, and the updated fixtures lend the place a fresh,

Best Campgrounds in Pinnacles

Pinnacles has only one camping option, on the park's eastern side, next to the Pinnacles Visitor Center.

Pinnacles Campground. Set under a canopy of live oaks that provides welcome shade over most of its 134 sites (83 nonelectric tent-only sites, 14 nonelectric group sites, and 37 electric RV sites), this campground is open year-round. The bathrooms, which have flush toilets, are clean if somewhat dated; showers are available for a small fee. Each site has a picnic table and a fire ring, but because of high fire danger, especially in the dry summer and early fall, campfires often aren't allowed. The swimming pool behind the visitor center is open from April through September. Leashed pets are allowed in the campground, but not on trails. The campground store, which shares space next to the visitor center, carries basic food supplies, snacks, soft drinks, beer, and ice. ⊠ *5000 Hwy. 146* ☎ *877/444–6777 for reservations, 831/389–4538 for campground store.*

contemporary feel. **Pros:** great for families with young kids; reasonably priced; convenient for travel to or from Interstate 5. **Cons:** location near highway means noise; next door to large RV park. $ *Rooms from: $139* ⊠ *10021 Pacheco Pass Hwy., Hollister* ⊕ *www.casadefruta.com* ⇥ *14 rooms* ⫶⊚⫶ *No meals.*

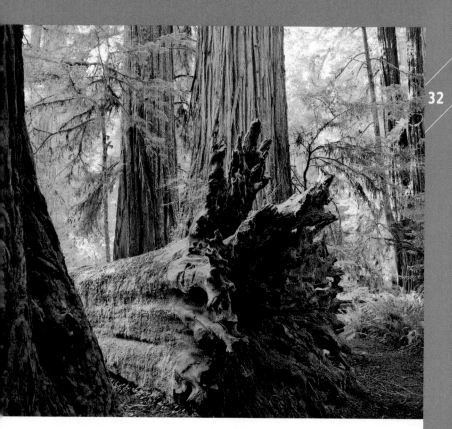

REDWOOD
NATIONAL PARK

WELCOME TO REDWOOD NATIONAL PARK

TOP REASONS TO GO

★ **Giant trees:** These mature coastal redwoods are the tallest trees in the world.

★ **Hiking to the sea:** The park's trails wind through majestic redwood groves, and many connect to the Coastal Trail, which runs along the western edge of the park.

★ **Rare wildlife:** Mighty Roosevelt elk favor the park's flat prairie and open lands; seldom-seen black bears roam the backcountry; trout and salmon leap through streams; and Pacific gray whales swim along the coast during their spring and fall migrations.

★ **Stepping back in time:** Hike mossy and mysterious Fern Canyon Trail and explore a prehistoric scene of lush vegetation and giant ferns—a memorable scene in *Jurassic Park 2* was shot here.

★ **Cheeps, not beeps:** Amid the majestic redwoods you're out of cell-phone range but well within range of warbling songbirds and burbling creeks.

1 Del Norte Coast Redwoods State Park. The rugged terrain of this far northwestern corner of California combines stretches of treacherous surf, steep cliffs, and forested ridges. On a clear day it's postcard-perfect; with fog, it's mysteriously mesmerizing.

2 Jedediah Smith Redwoods State Park. Gargantuan old-growth redwoods dominate the scenery here. The Smith River cuts through canyons and splits across boulders, carrying salmon to the inland creeks where they spawn.

3 Prairie Creek Redwoods State Park. The forests here give way to spacious, grassy plains where abundant wildlife thrives. Roosevelt elk are a common sight in the meadows and down to Gold Bluffs Beach, where a short trail leads to Fern Canyon.

4 Orick Area. The highlight of the southern portion of Redwood National and State Parks is the Tall Trees Grove. It's difficult to reach and requires a special pass, but it's worth the hassle—this section has some of the tallest coast redwood trees. The current world-record holder, a 379-footer named Hyperion, was discovered outside the grove in 2006.

GETTING ORIENTED

U.S. 101 weaves through the southern portion of Redwood National Park, skirts around the center, and then slips back through redwoods in the north and on to Crescent City. The entire park spans about 50 miles north to south. The Kuchel Visitor Center, Prairie Creek Redwoods State Park, Tall Trees Grove, Fern Canyon, and Lady Bird Johnson Grove are in the southern section. In the central section, where the Klamath River Overlook is the dominant feature, the narrow, mostly graveled Coastal Drive loop yields ocean vistas. To the north are Mill Creek Trail, Enderts Beach, and Crescent Beach Overlook in Del Norte Coast Redwoods State Park, as well as Jedediah Smith Redwoods State Park, Stout Grove, Little Bald Hills, and Simpson-Reed Grove.

KEY	
🏠	*Ranger Station*
⛺	*Campground*
🏕	*Picnic Area*
🍴	*Restaurant*
🏨	*Lodge*
🥾	*Trailhead*
🚻	*Restrooms*
✳	*Scenic Viewpoint*
::::::	*Walking/Hiking Trails*

Updated
by Andrew
Collins

Soaring more than 350 feet high, the coastal redwoods that give this park its name are miracles of efficiency—some have survived hundreds of years, a few more than two millennia. These massive trees glean nutrients from the rich alluvial flats at their feet and from the moisture and nitrogen trapped in their uneven canopy. Their huge, thick-bark trunks can hold thousands of gallons of water, reservoirs that have helped them withstand centuries of firestorms.

REDWOOD PLANNER

WHEN TO GO

Campers and hikers flock to the park from mid-June to early September. The crowds disappear in winter, but you'll have to contend with frequent rains and nasty potholes on side roads. Temperatures fluctuate widely: the foggy coastal lowland is much cooler than the higher-altitude interior.

The average annual rainfall is between 90 and 100 inches, most of it falling between November and April. During the dry summer, thick fog rolling in from the Pacific veils the forests, providing the redwoods a large portion of their moisture intake.

AVG. HIGH/LOW TEMPS.

Jan.	Feb.	Mar.	Apr.	May	June
54/39	56/40	57/41	59/42	62/45	65/48
July	Aug.	Sept.	Oct.	Nov.	Dec.
67/50	67/51	68/49	64/46	58/43	55/40

PLANNING YOUR TIME
REDWOOD IN ONE DAY

From Crescent City head south on U.S. 101. A mile south of Klamath, detour onto the 8-mile-long, narrow, and mostly unpaved **Coastal Drive** loop. Along the way, you'll pass the old **Douglas Memorial Bridge,** destroyed in the 1964 flood. Coastal Drive turns south above Flint Ridge. In less than a mile you'll reach the **World War II Radar Station,** which looks like a farmhouse, its disguise in the 1940s. Continue south to the intersection with Alder Camp Road, stopping at the **High Bluff Overlook.**

From the Coastal Drive turn left to reconnect with U.S. 101. Head south to reach **Newton B. Drury Scenic Parkway,** a 10-mile drive through an old-growth redwood forest with access to numerous trailheads. This road is open to all noncommercial vehicles. Along the way, stop at **Prairie Creek Visitor Center,** housed in a small redwood lodge. Enjoy a picnic lunch and an engaging tactile walk in a grove behind the lodge on the Revelation Trail, which was designed for vision-impaired visitors. Back on the parkway head north less than a mile and drive out unpaved **Cal-Barrel Road,** which leads east through redwood forests. Return to the parkway, continue south about 2 miles to reconnect with U.S. 101, and turn west on mostly unpaved **Davison Road** (motorhomes/RVs and trailers are prohibited). In about 30 minutes you'll curve right to **Gold Bluffs Beach.** Continue north to the **Fern Canyon** trailhead. Return to U.S. 101, and drive south to the turnoff for the **Thomas H. Kuchel Visitor Center.** Pick up free permits—only 50 a day are granted—to visit the **Tall Trees Grove** and head north on U.S. 101 to the turnoff for **Bald Hills Road,** a steep route (motorhomes/RVs and trailers are not advised). If you visit the grove, allow at least four hours round-trip from the information center. You could also bypass the turnoff to the grove and continue south on Bald Hills Road to 3,097-foot **Schoolhouse Peak.** For a simpler jaunt, turn onto Bald Hills Road and follow it for 2 miles to the **Lady Bird Johnson Grove Nature Loop Trail.** Take the footbridge to the easy 1-mile loop, which follows an old logging road through a mature redwood forest. ■ TIP➔ Motorhomes/RVs and trailers are not allowed on Coastal Drive, Cal-Barrel Road, and Davison Road, and are not advised on Bald Hills Road.

GETTING HERE AND AROUND
AIR TRAVEL

United Airlines flies a few times daily between San Francisco and the most practical gateway, Arcata/Eureka Airport, 9 miles north of Arcata and 16 miles north of Eureka. In September 2015, the regional carrier PenAir began offering daily service from Portland, Oregon, to Del Norte County Regional Airport in Crescent City. Another option is Oregon's Rogue Valley International Medford Airport, which is served by Alaska, Allegiant, Delta, and United. The drive from Medford's airport to the park takes about 2½ hours.

CAR TRAVEL

U.S. 101 runs north–south the entire length of the park. You can access all the main park roads via U.S. 101 and U.S. 199, which runs east–west through the park's northern portion. Many roads within the park aren't paved, and winter rains can turn them into obstacle courses; sometimes they're closed completely. Motorhomes/RVs and trailers aren't permitted on some routes. The drive from San Francisco to the park's southern end takes about five hours via U.S. 101. From Portland it takes roughly the same amount of time to reach the park's northern section by way of Interstate 5 to U.S. 199. ■TIP➔ Don't rely solely on GPS, which is not always accurate; closely consult park maps, available at the visitor information centers.

PARK ESSENTIALS

PARK FEES AND PERMITS

Admission to Redwood National Park and the related state parks is free. To visit Tall Trees Grove, you must get a free permit at the Kuchel Visitor Center in Orick. The fee to camp at the state parks is $35. Free permits, available at the Kuchel, Crescent City, and (summer only) Hiouchi visitor centers, are needed to stay at all designated backcountry camps.

PARK HOURS

The park is open year-round, 24 hours a day.

CELL-PHONE RECEPTION

It's difficult to pick up a signal in much of the park, especially in the camping and hiking areas. If you need a public telephone, go to the Prairie Creek or Jedediah Smith visitor center.

EDUCATIONAL OFFERINGS

RANGER PROGRAMS

All summer long, ranger-led programs explore the mysteries of both the redwoods and the sea. Topics include how the trees grow from fleck-size seeds to towering giants, what causes those weird fungi on old stumps, why the ocean fog is so important to redwoods, and exactly what those green-tentacled creatures are that float in tide pools. Campfire programs can include slide shows, storytelling, music, and games. Check with visitor centers for offerings and times.

Field Seminars. State park rangers and other experts conduct seminars with an emphasis on natural history. Subjects may include photography, wildflowers, tide pools, Roosevelt elk, and stargazing. The programs, sponsored by the Redwood Parks Association, are usually free; a few, like the December Candlelight Walk, are fund-raisers. ☎ *707/464–9150* ⊕ *www.redwoodparksassociation.org.*

FAMILY **Junior Ranger Program.** From June to early September, rangers lead one-hour programs for children between ages seven and 12. Activities include nature walks and lessons in bird identification and outdoor survival. ☎ *707/465–7335* ⊕ *www.nps.gov/redw/learn/kidsyouth* ☒ *Free.*

Ranger Talks. From late May through mid-September, state park rangers regularly lead discussions on the redwoods, tide pools, geology, and American Indian culture. Pick up a schedule at the visitor centers. ☎ *707/465–7335* ⊕ *www.nps.gov/redw/planyourvisit* ☒ *Free.*

FAMILY **Redwood EdVentures.** Fun and engaging nature Redwood EdVentures scavenger hunts for kids, called Quests, include ones in the park. Visit the website for "treasure map" PDFs detailing the Quests, which typically take no more than an hour. Participants receive a patch upon completion. ⊕ *www.redwood-edventures.org* ✉ *Free.*

RESTAURANTS

The park has no restaurants, but Eureka and Arcata have diverse dining establishments—everything from hip oyster bars to various ethnic restaurants. The selection is decent in Crescent City, and there are a few, generally good, choices in Klamath, Orick, and Trinidad. Most small-town restaurants close early, around 7:30 or 8 pm.

HOTELS

The only lodgings within park boundaries are the Elk Meadow Cabins, near the Prairie Creek Redwoods Visitor Center. Orick, to the south of Elk Meadow, and Klamath, to the north, have basic motels, and in Klamath there's the Requa Inn bed-and-breakfast. Elegant Victorian inns, seaside motels, and fully equipped vacation rentals are among the options in towns north and south of the park. In summer, try to book at least a week ahead at lodgings near the park entrance. *Hotel reviews have been shortened. For full information, visit Fodors.com.*

WHAT IT COSTS				
	$	**$$**	**$$$**	**$$$$**
Restaurants	under $13	$13–$20	$21–$30	over $30
Hotels	under $100	$100–$150	$151–$200	over $200

Restaurant prices are the average cost of a main course at dinner, or if dinner is not served, at lunch. Hotel prices are the lowest cost of a standard double room in high season, excluding taxes and service charges.

VISITOR INFORMATION

Park Contact Information Redwood National and State Parks. ✉ *1111 2nd St., Crescent City* ☎ *707/465–7335* ⊕ *www.nps.gov/redw.*

VISITOR CENTERS

Crescent City Information Center. At the park's headquarters, this downtown visitor center with a gift shop and picnic area is the main information stop if you're approaching the Redwoods from the north. ✉ *1111 2nd St., Crescent City* ☎ *707/465–7335* ⊕ *www.nps.gov/redw* ⊗ *Mid-May–mid-Oct., daily 9–5; mid-Oct.–mid-May, daily 9–4.*

Hiouchi Information Center. This small seasonal center at Jedediah Smith Redwoods State Park has exhibits about the area flora and fauna and screens a park film. A starting point for ranger programs, the center has restrooms and a picnic area. ✉ *U.S. 199, 2 miles west of Hiouchi and 9 miles east of Crescent City* ✛ *Southeast of entrance to Jedediah Smith Campground* ☎ *707/458–3294* ⊕ *www.nps.gov/redw* ⊗ *Late May–early Sept., daily 9–5.*

Jedediah Smith Visitor Center. Adjacent to the Jedediah Smith Redwoods State Park main campground, this seasonal center has information about ranger-led walks and evening campfire programs. Also here are nature and history exhibits, a gift shop, and a picnic area. ✉ *Off U.S. 199, Hiouchi* ☎ *707/458–3496* ⊕ *www.parks.ca.gov* ⊗ *Late May–early Sept., daily noon–8.*

Fodor's Choice **Prairie Creek Visitor Center.** In a small redwood lodge, this center has a
★ massive stone fireplace. The wildlife displays include a section of a tree
a young elk died beside. Because of the peculiar way the redwood grew
around the elk's skull, the tree appears to have antlers. The center has
information about summer programs in Prairie Creek Redwoods State
Park, and you'll find a gift shop, a picnic area, restrooms, and exhibits
on flora and fauna. Roosevelt elk often roam the vast field adjacent to
the center, and several trailheads begin nearby. Stretch your legs with
an easy stroll along **Revelation Trail,** a short loop that starts behind the
lodge. ⊠ *Prairie Creek Rd., off U.S. 101 near southern end of Newton
B. Drury Scenic Pkwy., Orick* ☎ *707/488–2039* ⊕ *www.parks.ca.gov/
prairiecreek* ⊙ *Mid-May–mid-Oct., daily 9–5; mid-Oct.–mid-May,
Wed.–Sun. 9–4.*

Fodor's Choice **Thomas H. Kuchel Visitor Center.** The park's southern section contains the
★ largest and best of the Redwoods visitor centers. Rangers here dispense
brochures, advice, and free permits to drive up the access road to Tall
Trees Grove. Whale-watchers find the center's deck an excellent observation point, and bird-watchers enjoy the nearby Freshwater Lagoon, a
popular layover for migrating waterfowl. Many of the center's exhibits
are hands-on and kid-friendly. ⊠ *Off U.S. 101 beside Redwood Creek
Beach County Park, Orick* ☎ *707/465–7765* ⊕ *www.nps.gov/redw*
⊙ *Mid-May–mid-Oct., daily 9–5; mid-Oct.–mid-May, daily 9–4.*

EXPLORING

SCENIC DRIVES

Coastal Drive. The 8-mile, narrow, and mostly unpaved Coastal Drive
takes about one hour to traverse. Weaving through stands of redwoods,
the road yields close-up views of the Klamath River and expansive panoramas of the Pacific. Recurring landslides have closed sections of the
original road; this loop, closed to trailers and RVs, is all that remains.
Hikers access the Flint Ridge section of the Coastal Trail off the drive.
⊠ *Klamath* ✛ *1 mile south of Klamath off U.S. 101; take Klamath
Beach Rd. exit and follow signs.*

Howland Hill Road/Stout Grove. Take your time as you drive this 10-mile
route along Mill Creek, which winds through old-growth redwoods
and past the Smith River. Trailers and RVs are prohibited on this route.
✛ *Access from Elk Valley Rd., off U.S. 101.*

Fodor's Choice **Newton B. Drury Scenic Parkway/Big Tree Wayside.** This paved 10-mile
★ route accessed a little south of Klamath or a bit north of Orick threads
through Prairie Creek Redwoods State Park and old-growth redwoods.
It's open to all noncommercial vehicles. North of the Prairie Creek Visitor Center you can make the 0.8-mile walk to Big Tree Wayside and
observe Roosevelt elk in the prairie. ⊠ *Orick* ✛ *Entrances off U.S. 101
about 5 miles south of Klamath and 5 miles north of Orick.*

SCENIC STOPS

Crescent Beach Overlook. The scenery here includes ocean views and, in the distance, Crescent City and its working harbor. In balmy weather this is a great place for a picnic. From the overlook you can spot migrating gray whales going south from November through January and returning north between February and April. ⊠ *Off Enderts Beach Rd., 2 miles south of Crescent City.*

Del Norte Coast Redwoods State Park. This park southeast of Crescent City contains 15 memorial redwood groves. The growth extends down steep slopes almost to the shore. ⊠ *Off U.S. 101, about 9 miles southeast of Crescent City, Crescent City* ☎ *707/465–7335* ⊕ *www.parks.ca.gov* ⊙ *Mid-May–mid-Oct., daily 9–6; mid-Oct.–mid-May, daily 9–4.*

Fodor's Choice ★ **Fern Canyon.** Enter another world and be surrounded by 50-foot canyon walls covered with sword, deer, and five-finger ferns. Allow an hour to explore the ¼-mile-long vertical garden along a 0.7-mile loop. From the northern end of Gold Bluffs Beach it's an easy walk, although you'll have to wade across or scamper along planks that traverse a small stream several times (in addition to driving across a couple of streams on the way to the parking area). But the lush, otherworldly surroundings, which appeared in *Jurassic Park 2*, are a must-see when creeks aren't running too high. Motorhomes/RVs and all trailers are prohibited on the road to Fern Canyon. You can also hike to the canyon from Prairie Creek Visitor Center along the moderately challenging West Ridge–Friendship Ridge–James Irvine Loop, 12½ miles round-trip. ⊠ *North of Gold Bluffs Beach, Orick* ✛ *2¾ miles north of Orick, take Davison Rd. northwest off U.S. 101 and follow signs to Gold Bluffs Beach* ⊕ *www.nps.gov/redw.*

Jedediah Smith Redwoods State Park. Home to the Stout Memorial Grove, this park with 20 miles of hiking and nature trails is named after a trapper who in 1826 became the first white man to explore northern California's interior. If you're coming from interior Oregon, the park provides the first opportunity to drive and hike among stands of soaring redwoods. ⊠ *Jedediah Smith Visitor Center, U.S. 199, Hiouchi* ✛ *2 miles west of Hiouchi, 9 miles east of Crescent City* ☎ *707/458–4396* ⊕ *www.parks.ca.gov.*

Lady Bird Johnson Grove. One of the park's more easily accessible spots to view big trees, the grove was dedicated by, and named for, the former first lady. A 1-mile nature loop follows an old logging road through a mature redwood forest. Allow 45 minutes to complete the trail. ⊠ *Bald Hills Rd., Orick* ✛ *1 mile north of Orick off U.S. 101, then 2½ miles to trailhead* ⊕ *www.nps.gov/redw.*

Fodor's Choice ★ **Prairie Creek Redwoods State Park.** Spectacular redwoods and lush ferns make up this park traversed by the stunning Newton B. Drury Scenic Parkway. Extra space has been paved alongside the parklands, providing fine places to observe herds of Roosevelt elk, which at one time neared extinction, in adjoining meadows. Another section of the park, reached via unpaved Davison Road or by hiking on trails from the park's interior, fringes gorgeous Gold Bluffs Beach. If your time in Redwood National Park is limited, Prairie Creek is one of the best in the system to spend a full day hiking and exploring. ⊠ *Prairie Creek Information Center, Prairie Creek Rd., near southern end of Newton B. Drury Scenic Pkwy., Orick* ✛ *5 miles north of Orick off U.S. 101* ☎ *707/488–2039* ⊕ *www.parks.ca.gov.*

Tall Trees Grove. At the Kuchel and other visitor centers you can obtain a free permit to make the steep 14-mile drive to this redwood grove that once contained the world-record holder for tallest tree. Rangers dispense only 50 permits maximum a day, first come, first served. The last 6½ or so miles to the trailhead are on an unpaved access road. The hike from the trailhead parking lot is 4 miles round-trip. ⊠ *Tall Trees Access Rd., off Bald Hills Rd., Orick* ✛ *1 mile north of Orick, head east and south from U.S. 101 on Bald Hills Rd. for about 7 miles, then southwest on unpaved access road about 6½ miles to trailhead* ☞ *Trailers and RVs not allowed in trailhead parking lot.*

SPORTS AND THE OUTDOORS

BICYCLING

Besides the roadways, you can bike on several trails. Best bets include the 11-mile Lost Man Creek Trail, which begins 3 miles north of Orick; the 12-mile round-trip Coastal Trail (Last Chance Section), which starts at the southern end of Enderts Beach Road and becomes steep and narrow as it travels through dense slopes of foggy redwood forests; and the 19-mile, single-track Ossagon Trail Loop, on which you're likely to see elk as you cruise through redwoods before coasting oceanside toward the end.

BIRD-WATCHING

Many rare and striking winged specimens inhabit the area, including chestnut-backed chickadees, brown pelicans, great blue herons, pileated woodpeckers, northern spotted owls, and marbled murrelets.

FISHING

Deep-sea and freshwater fishing are popular here. Anglers often stake out sections of the Klamath and Smith rivers in their search for salmon and trout. A single fishing license covers both ocean and river fishing. You can go crabbing and clamming on the coast, but check the tides carefully: rip currents and sneaker waves can be deadly.

OUTFITTERS
Coast True Value. This store that sells fishing gear, bait, and tackle is a good place to purchase a state fishing license, valid for both river and ocean fishing. An annual license costs just under $50 for California residents and about $128 for nonresidents. Anyone can purchase a two-day license for about $24. ⊠ *900 Northcrest Dr., Crescent City* ☎ *707/464–3535* ⊕ *www.truevalue.com/ctv.*

KEY

🏚 Ranger Station
🔺 Campground
🎔 Picnic Area
🍴 Restaurant
↘ Scenic Viewpoint
    State Parklands
    National Parklands

Lake Earl State Wildlife Area Headquarters

Lake Earl

Tolowa Dunes State Park

Simpson-Reed Grove

Hiouchi Information Center

197

199

199

Information

POINT ST. GEORGE

Old Mill Rd.

Lake Earl Dr.

Elk Valley Rd.

101

Jedediah Smith Redwoods State Park

Stout Grove

Hiouchi

Crescent City

Northcrest Dr.

Howland Hill Rd.

Little Bald Hills

Castle Rock

Park Headquarters Information

Battery Point Lighthouse

Humboldt Rd.

Crescent Beach

Enderts Beach Rd.

Crescent Beach Overlook

Nickel Creek

Enderts Beach

Mill Creek

101

P A C I F I C

Del Norte Coast Redwoods State Park

SISTER ROCKS

C O A S T

DeMartin

Overlook

FOOTSTEPS ROCKS

Wilson Creek

False Klamath Cove

Lagoon Creek

R A N G E

101

O C E A N

Klamath River Overlook

Requa

Requa Rd.

Coastal Drive

Flint Ridge

Klamath

169

0   3 mi
0   3 km

High Bluff Overlook

Alder Camp Rd.

Klamath Glen

Coastal Trail

Klamath River

Redwood NP
Northern Areas

32

Plants and Wildlife in Redwood

CLOSE UP

Coast redwoods, the world's tallest trees, grow in the moist, temperate climate of California's North Coast. The current record holder, topping out at 379 feet, was found in the Redwood Creek watershed in 2006. These ancient giants thrive in an environment that exists in only a few hundred coastal miles along the Pacific Ocean. They commonly live 600 years—though some have been around for 2,000 years.

DIVERSE, COMPLEX
A healthy redwood forest is diverse and includes Douglas firs, western hemlocks, tan oaks, and madrone trees. The complex soils of the forest floor support a profusion of ferns, mosses, and fungi, along with numerous shrubs and berry bushes. In spring, California rhododendron bloom all over, providing a dazzling purple and pink contrast to the dense greenery.

OLD-GROWTH FORESTS
Redwood National and State Parks hold 45% of California's old-growth redwood forests. Of the original 3,125 square miles (2 million acres) in the Redwoods Historic Range, only 4% survived logging that began in 1850. A quarter of these trees are privately owned and managed land. The rest are on public tracts.

WILDLIFE SPECIES
In the park's backcountry, you might spot mountain lions, black bears, black-tailed deer, river otters, beavers, and minks. Roosevelt elk roam the flatlands, and the rivers and streams teem with salmon and trout. Gray whales, seals, and sea lions cavort near the coastline. More than 400 species of birds have been recorded in the parks, which are located along the Pacific Flyway.

HIKING

MODERATE

Coastal Trail. This easy-to-difficult trail runs most of the park's length; smaller sections that vary in difficulty are accessible at frequent, well-marked trailheads. The moderate-to-difficult **DeMartin section** leads past 6 miles of old-growth redwoods and through prairie. If you're up for a real workout, hike the brutally difficult but stunning **Flint Ridge section,** 4½ miles of steep grades and numerous switchbacks past redwoods and Marshall Pond. The moderate 5½-mile-long **Klamath section,** which connects the Wilson Creek Picnic Area and the Klamath River Overlook, with a short detour to Hidden Beach and its tide pools, provides coastal views and whale-watching opportunities. *Moderate.* ⊠ *Klamath* ✛ *Trailheads: DeMartin, U.S. 101 mile markers 12.8 (south) and 15.6 (north); Flint Ridge, Douglas Bridge parking area, north end of Coastal Dr. (east), and off Klamath Beach Rd. (west); Klamath, Requa Rd. at Klamath River Overlook (south), Wilson Creek Picnic Area, off U.S. 101 (north)* ⊕ *www.nps.gov/redw.*

DIFFICULT

West Ridge–Friendship Ridge–James Irvine Loop. For a moderately strenuous trek, try this 12½-mile loop. The difficult West Ridge segment passes redwoods looming above a carpet of ferns. The difficult Friendship Ridge portion slopes down toward the coast through forests of spruce and hemlock and accesses iconic Fern Canyon. The moderate James Irvine Trail portion winds along a small creek and amid dense stands of redwoods. *Difficult.* ⊠ *Orick* ⊹ *Trailhead: at Prairie Creek Visitor Center, Prairie Creek Rd., off Newton B. Drury Scenic Pkwy.* ⊕ *www. nps.gov/redw.*

KAYAKING

With many miles of often shallow rivers, streams, and estuarial lagoons, kayaking is a popular pastime in the park.

OUTFITTERS

Humboats Kayak Adventures. You can rent kayaks and take lessons here and book group kayaking tours that from December to June include whale-watching trips. Half-day river kayaking trips pass beneath massive redwoods; the whale-watching outings get you close enough for good photos of migrating gray whales and resident humpback whales. ⊠ *Woodley Island Marina, 601 Startare Dr., Dock A, Eureka* ☏ *707/443–5157* ⊕ *www.humboats.com* ⊠ *From $55.*

Fodor's Choice ★ **Kayak Zak's.** This outfit rents kayaks and stand-up paddleboards, good for touring the beautiful estuarial and freshwater lagoons of Humboldt Lagoons State Park. You can also book a guided nature paddle. Rentals at the Stone Lagoon Visitor Center take place year-round, and on most summer weekends Kayak Zak's sets up a trailer at nearby Big Lagoon. The lagoons are stunning. Herds of Roosevelt elk sometimes traipse along the shoreline of Big Lagoon; raptors, herons, and waterfowl abound in both lagoons; and you can paddle across Stone Lagoon to a spectacular secluded Pacific-view beach. ⊠ *Stone Lagoon Visitor Center, 115336 U.S. 101, about 5½ miles south of Orick, Trinidad* ☏ *707/498–1130* ⊕ *www.kayakzak.com* ⊠ *From $25.*

WHALE-WATCHING

Good vantage points for whale-watching include Crescent Beach Overlook, the Kuchel Visitor Center in Orick, points along the Coastal Trail, and the Klamath River Overlook. From late November through January is the best time to see their southward migrations; from February through April the whales return, usually passing closer to shore.

WHAT'S NEARBY

NEARBY TOWNS

Crescent City, north of the park, is Del Norte County's largest town (population 7,185) and home to the Redwood National and State Parks headquarters. Though it curves around a beautiful stretch of ocean,

32

rain and bone-chilling fog often prevail. Very small **Klamath** is outside park boundaries though near to the middle section. The town has a few lodgings but not much dining. Roughly 50 miles south of Crescent City (20 miles north of Eureka), **Trinidad** has a cove harbor that attracts fishermen and photographers. The picturesque town has a few notable dining and lodging options and is a good base for exploring Prairie Creek Redwoods State Park and other southerly attractions. Farther south, **Arcata** began life in 1850 as a base camp for miners and lumberjacks and had fewer than 1,000 residents until the early 1900s. Today this artsy, progressive town's 17,700 citizens include the 8,100 students of Humboldt State University. Activity centers around the grassy Arcata Plaza, which is surrounded by restored buildings containing funky bars, cafés, and indie shops. Nearby **Eureka,** population 27,000 and the Humboldt County seat, was named after a gold miner's hearty exclamation. Its Old Town has an alluring waterfront boardwalk, several excellent restaurants and shops, and the region's largest selection of lodgings. The visitor center here is the area's best overall resource for tourism information. Strip malls dominate much of Eureka, but the city center has much to recommend it.

> **GOOD READS**
>
> ■ The *Redwood Official National and State Parks Handbook,* published by the Redwood Parks Association, covers the area's ecology, botany, natural and cultural history, and common wildlife.
>
> ■ *The Tallest Tree,* by Robert Lieber, is a beautifully illustrated board book for children.
>
> ■ Richard Preston's spellbinding *The Wild Trees: A Story of Passion and Daring* chronicles the redwood-climbing exploits of several botanists fiercely passionate about California's endangered tall trees and the ecosystem that supports them.

Visitor Information Arcata Chamber of Commerce. ⊠ *1635 Heindon Rd., Arcata* ☎ *707/822–3619* ⊕ *www.arcatachamber.com.* **Crescent City/Del Norte County Chamber of Commerce.** ⊠ *1001 Front St., Crescent City* ☎ *707/464–3174, 800/343–8300* ⊕ *www.delnorte.org.* **Humboldt County Convention and Visitors Bureau.** ⊠ *322 1st St., Eureka* ☎ *707/443–5097, 800/346–3482* ⊕ *www.redwoods.info.*

NEARBY ATTRACTIONS

Battery Point Lighthouse. At low tide, you can walk from the pier across the ocean floor to this working lighthouse, which was built in 1856. It houses a museum with nautical artifacts and photographs of shipwrecks. There's even a resident ghost. Call ahead for guided group tours. ⊠ *A St., Crescent City* ☎ *707/464–3089* ⊕ *www.delnortehistory. org* ☜ *$3* ⊙ *Apr.–Sept., daily 10–4; Oct.–Mar., weekends 10–4.*

Northcoast Marine Mammal Center. The nonprofit center rescues and rehabilitates stranded, sick, and injured seals, sea lions, dolphins, and porpoises. Its facility isn't a museum or an aquarium, but placards and kiosks provide information about marine mammals and coastal ecosystems, and even when the place is closed you can observe the rescued animals through a fence enclosing individual pools. The gallery and gift shop is open on most weekends and some weekdays, especially in summer, and volunteers are often on hand to answer questions. It's worth calling the day of your visit to find out when feedings will take place. ⊠ *424 Howe Dr., Crescent City* ☎ *707/465–6265* ⊕ *www. northcoastmmc.org* ⊠ *Free* ☉ *Call for hrs.*

FAMILY **Trees of Mystery.** Since opening in 1946, this unabashedly goofy but endearing roadside attraction has been doling out family fun. From the moment you pull your car up to the 49-foot-tall talking statue of Paul Bunyan (alongside Babe the Blue Ox), the kitschy thrills begin. You can then explore a genuinely informative museum of Native American artifacts, admire intricately carved redwood figures, and browse tacky souvenirs. For a fee you can ride a six-passenger gondola over the redwood treetops for a majestic view of the forest canopy, and stroll along several mostly easy trails through the adjacent forest of redwoods, Sitka spruce, and Douglas firs. ⊠ *15500 U.S. 101 N, between Klamath and Del Norte Coast Redwoods State Park, Klamath* ☎ *707/482–2251* ⊕ *www.treesofmystery.net* ⊠ *Museum free, trails $15* ☉ *Museum June– Sept., daily 8:30–6:30; Oct.–May, daily 9:30–4:30. Trails June–Sept., daily 8–7; Oct.–May, daily 9–3:30.*

WHERE TO EAT

IN THE PARK

PICNIC AREAS

Crescent Beach. This beach has a grassy picnic area with tables, fire pits, and restrooms. There's an overlook south of the beach. ⊠ *Enderts Beach Rd., 4 miles south of Crescent City, Crescent City.*

Elk Prairie. In addition to many elk, this spot has a campground, a nature trail, and a ranger station. ⊠ *Prairie Creek Redwoods State Park, 127011 Newton B. Drury Scenic Pkwy., Orick.*

High Bluff Overlook. This picnic area's sunsets and whale-watching are unequaled. A ½-mile trail leads from here to the beach. ⊠ *Coastal Dr. loop, off U.S. 101, via Alder Camp Rd., Klamath.*

OUTSIDE THE PARK

ARCATA

$$ ✕ **Cafe Brio.** With an inviting indoor dining room and outside seat-
CAFÉ ing overlooking bustling Arcata Plaza, this artisan bakery and restau-
Fodor's Choice rant is known for its savory and sweet breads. Notable noshes include
★ ham-and-cheese breakfast croissants, focaccia sandwiches with avocado and Humboldt Fog goat cheese from Arcata's Cypress Grove creamery, and farm-to-table dinner fare. Lemon cream tarts are among the pastries available all day. The wine selection is small but terrific, and Blue Bottle coffees are served. $ *Average main: $17* ⊠ *791 G St., Arcata* ☎ *707/822–5922* ⊕ *www.cafebrioarcata.com* ☉ *No dinner Sun.–Tues.*

$ ✕ **Wildberries Marketplace.** This market with juice and salad bars and a
DELI small café carries a great selection of deli items and picnic provisions,
many of them produced locally or in-state. ⑤ *Average main: $8* ✉ *747
13th St., Arcata* ☎ *707/822–0095* ⊕ *www.wildberries.com* ▭ *No credit
cards.*

CRESCENT CITY

$$ ✕ **Good Harvest Cafe.** The café, which serves great breakfasts and superb
AMERICAN espresso drinks, lives up to its name with ample use of locally grown
and organic ingredients. For lunch and dinner there are salads, burgers,
sandwiches, vegetarian specialties, and several fish entrées. ⑤ *Average
main: $16* ✉ *575 U.S. 101 S, Crescent City* ☎ *707/465–6028.*

$ ✕ **Vita Cucina.** Set in a nondescript downtown shopping center, this
AMERICAN casual café, bakery, and takeout market serves fresh, creative food
that's anything but ordinary. Come by in the morning for pastries or
quiche. The fare later on includes Vietnamese *banh mi* and sushi-grade
ahi sandwiches, whole smoked chicken with garlic-mashed potatoes,
and barbecue-pork pizzas. Open only until 6 or 7 on most weekday
evenings, this is more of a daytime venue and a great stop for picnic
supplies before venturing into the park. The big drawback is that it's
closed on weekends. ⑤ *Average main: $12* ✉ *1270 Front St., Crescent
City* ☎ *707/464–1076* ⊕ *www.vitacucina.com* ⊘ *Closed weekends. No
dinner.*

EUREKA

$$ ✕ **Café Waterfront Oyster Bar and Grill.** Amid Old Town's vibrant din-
SEAFOOD ing district, the café serves consistently fresh locally caught seafood.
Steamed clams, grilled snapper, oyster burgers, and chowders are all on
the menu—one of the West Coast's top oyster beds, in the bay across
the street, supplies the oysters on the half shell. Steaks and burgers
are served, too. The historic building served as a saloon and brothel
until the 1950s. The two Victorian-style bed-and-breakfast rooms
upstairs are named for former ladies of the house. After dinner, stroll
a short way to Living the Dream Ice Cream for a gelato by the harbor.
⑤ *Average main: $19* ✉ *102 F St., Eureka* ☎ *707/443–9190* ⊕ *www.
cafewaterfronteureka.com.*

TRINIDAD

$ ✕ **Beachcomber Cafe.** Before a day of hiking and exploring, fuel up in
BAKERY downtown Trinidad on organic espresso or coffee drinks, freshly baked
breads and pastries, housemade granola, and bagels with lox, chèvre,
local jams, poached eggs, and other toppings. The lineup for lunch
includes soups, salads, and panini. Cozy and art-filled, the Beachcomber
is a great place for people-watching and mingling with locals. ⑤ *Average
main: $7* ✉ *363 Trinity St., Trinidad* ☎ *707/677–0106* ⊘ *No dinner.*

$$$ ✕ **Trinidad Bay Eatery and Gallery.** A short stroll from Trinidad's lovely
AMERICAN bayfront and near the park's southern end, this unpretentious combina-
tion gallery and seafood-oriented restaurant cooks up tasty meals. But-
termilk pancakes and Dungeness crab Benedict are among the favorites
for breakfast; at lunchtime burgers, specialty sandwiches, and chow-
ders and solids dominate the menu. For dinner, consider the starter of
ahi poke with crème fraîche, followed by lemon-caper calamari steak,

Redwood trees, and the moss that often coats them, grow best in damp, shady environments.

red-coconut-curry scallops, or cioppino in chipotle broth. You'll easily find an appropriate wine on the well-chosen list to accompany your meal. Save room for the locally beloved blackberry cobbler. $ *Average main: $24* ✉ *607 Parker St., Trinidad* ☎ *707/677–3777* ⊕ *www.trinidadeatery.com.*

WHERE TO STAY

IN THE PARK

$$$$
B&B/INN
FAMILY
Fodor's Choice
★
🏠 **Elk Meadow Cabins.** From the porches of these beautifully restored 1,200-square-foot former millworkers' cottages, guests often see Roosevelt elk meandering in the meadows. **Pros:** in a stunning part of Prairie Creek State Park yet conveniently located on U.S. 101; spacious enough for four to six guests; kitchens. **Cons:** a bit of a drive from most area restaurants; expensive for just two occupants, though reasonable for families or groups. $ *Rooms from: $289* ✉ *7 Valley Green Camp Rd., off U.S. 101 north of Davison Rd., Orick* ☎ *707/488–2222, 866/733–9637* ⊕ *www.redwoodparklodge.com/cabins* ⤴ *7 cabins* ⦿ *No meals.*

OUTSIDE THE PARK

CRESCENT CITY

$
HOTEL
🏠 **Curly Redwood Lodge.** A single redwood tree produced the 57,000 board feet of lumber used to build this budget 1957 motor lodge. **Pros:** large rooms; several restaurants within walking distance; cool retro

32

CLOSE UP

Best Campgrounds in Redwood

Within a 30-minute drive of Redwood National and State Parks are roughly 60 public and private camping facilities. None of the four primitive areas in Redwood—DeMartin, Flint Ridge, Little Bald Hills, and Nickel Creek—is a drive-in site. You will need to get a free permit from any visitor center except Prairie Creek before camping in these campgrounds, and along Redwood Creek in the backcountry. Bring your own water because drinking water isn't available at any of these sites. These campgrounds, plus Gold Bluffs Beach, are first come, first served.

If you'd rather drive than hike in, Redwood has four developed campgrounds—Elk Prairie, Gold Bluffs Beach, Jedediah Smith, and Mill Creek—that are within the state-park boundaries. None has RV hookups, and some length restrictions apply. Fees are $35 in state park campgrounds. For details and reservations, call ☎ 800/444–7275 or check ⊕ www.reserveamerica.com.

Elk Prairie Campground. Roosevelt elk frequent this popular campground adjacent to a prairie and old-growth

redwoods. ⊠ On Newton B. Drury Scenic Pkwy., 5 miles north of Orick in Prairie Creek Redwoods State Park ☎ 800/444–7275.

Gold Bluffs Beach Campground. You can camp in tents right on the beach at this Prairie Creek Redwoods State Park campground near Fern Canyon. ⊠ At end of Davison Rd., 5 miles south of Prairie Creek Visitor Center off U.S. 101 ☎ 800/444–7275.

Jedediah Smith Campground. This is one of the few places to camp—in tents or RVs—within groves of old-growth redwood forest. ⊠ 8 miles east of Crescent City on U.S. 199 ☎ 800/444–7275.

Mill Creek Campground. Redwoods tower over large Mill Creek, in Del Norte Coast Redwoods State Park. ⊠ East of U.S. 101, 7 miles southeast of Crescent City ☎ 800/444–7275.

Nickel Creek Campground. An easy hike gets you to these five primitive sites in Redwood National Park; near tide pools, they have great ocean views. ⊠ On Coastal Trail ½ mile from end of Enderts Beach Rd. ☎ 707/465–7335.

furnishings. **Cons:** road noise can be bothersome; very basic amenities. ⑤ Rooms from: $75 ⊠ 701 U.S. 101 S, Crescent City ☎ 707/464–2137 ⊕ www.curlyredwoodlodge.com ⇌ 33 rooms, 3 suites ⑩ No meals.

EUREKA

$$$
HOTEL
Fodor'sChoice
★

🛉 **Carter House Inns.** Owner Mark Carter says he trains his staff always to say yes; whether it's breakfast in bed or an in-room massage, someone here will get you what you want. **Pros:** elegant; every detail in place; aim-to-please service. **Cons:** though kids are allowed, this is best for grown-ups; breakfast is a little ordinary considering how upscale everything else is. ⑤ Rooms from: $189 ⊠ 301 L St., Eureka ☎ 707/444–8062, 800/404–1390 ⊕ www.carterhouse.com ⇌ 22 rooms, 8 suites, 2 cottages ⑩ Breakfast.

$$ Eagle House Victorian Inn. By the bustling waterfront and steps from
B&B/INN   Old Town's inviting shops and restaurants, this towering 1880s Vic-
torian inn exudes character and abounds with opulent architectural
details and florid period-style bedding, wallpapers, and furnishings.
Pros: easy walk to Old Town Eureka dining and shopping; fascinating
old building; reasonable rates. **Cons:** when inn is full up, the hot water
isn't always reliable; older TVs and other amenities. $ *Rooms from:*
$115 ⊠ 139 2nd St., Eureka ☎ 707/444–3344 ⊕ www.eaglehouseinn.
com ↝ 24 rooms ⊙ *Breakfast.*

KLAMATH

$$ Historic Requa Inn. This serene 1914 inn overlooks the Klamath River
B&B/INN   a mile east of where it meets the ocean. **Pros:** serene; relaxing yet central
Fodor'sChoice   location with river views; excellent restaurant. **Cons:** walls are thin; not
★   a good choice for children. $ *Rooms from: $139 ⊠ 451 Requa Rd.,*
Klamath ☎ 707/482–1425, 866/800–8777 ⊕ www.requainn.com ↝ 12
rooms ⊙ *Breakfast.*

$ Ravenwood Motel. Attentive on-site owners converted a dowdy road-
HOTEL   side motel into this class act consisting of 10 rooms and five suites—
four with full kitchens—beautifully decorated with different themes.
Pros: handy to park's central section; exceptionally clean rooms. **Cons:**
nonsuite rooms a bit small; along a prosaic strip of businesses with no
view to speak of. $ *Rooms from: $75 ⊠ 151 Klamath Blvd., Klamath*
☎ *707/482–5911, 866/520–9875 ⊕ www.ravenwoodmotel.com ↝ 10*
rooms, 5 suites ⊙ *Breakfast.*

NEAR PARK'S SOUTHERN SECTION

$$ Redwood Coast Vacation Rentals. Given the relatively limited num-
RENTAL   ber of hotels and inns close to the park, renting a vacation home in
the area can be a good strategy, especially if you are traveling as a
family or with a few friends and appreciate having kitchen facilities.
Pros: properties for all budgets; all rentals have kitchens; many rentals
have multiple bedrooms and baths. **Cons:** 10 am checkout; one-time
cleaning fee adds a lot to the cost for travelers only staying a night or
two. $ *Rooms from: $140 ⊠ McKinleyville ☎ 707/834–6555 ⊕ www.*
redwoodcoastvacationrentals.com ↝ 75 units of varying size ⊙ *No*
meals.

TRINIDAD

$$ Trinidad Inn. These quiet cottage rooms nestled in the evergreens are
HOTEL   2 miles north of Trinidad Bay's harbor, restaurants, and shops. **Pros:**
FAMILY   idyllic setting; walking path through adjacent redwood grove; good for
kids. **Cons:** older facility. $ *Rooms from: $115 ⊠ 1170 Patrick's Point*
Dr., Trinidad ☎ 707/677–3349 ⊕ www.trinidadinn.com ↝ 7 rooms, 3
suites ⊙ *Breakfast.*

ROCKY MOUNTAIN NATIONAL PARK

WELCOME TO ROCKY MOUNTAIN NATIONAL PARK

TOP REASONS TO GO

★ **Awesome ascents:**
Seasoned climbers can trek to the summit of 14,259-foot Longs Peak or attack the rounded granite domes of Lumpy Ridge. Novices can summit Twin Sisters Peaks or Mount Ida, both reaching more than 11,000 feet.

★ **Continental Divide:**
Straddle this great divide, which cuts through the western part of the park, separating water's flow to either the Pacific or Atlantic Ocean.

★ **Gorgeous scenery:**
Peer out over more than 100 lakes, gaze up at majestic mountain peaks, and soak in the splendor of lush wetlands, pine-scented woods, forests of spruce and fir, and alpine tundra in the park's four distinct ecosystems.

★ **More than 355 miles of trails:** Hike on dozens of marked trails, from easy lakeside strolls to strenuous mountain climbs.

★ **Wildlife viewing:**
Spot elk and bighorn sheep, along with moose, otters, and more than 280 species of birds.

Long Draw Reservoir

Skeleton Gulch

Cache la Poudre River

Lulu City

Flatiron Mountain 12,335 ft

Mummy Range

Ypsilon Mountain 13,514 ft

Visitor Center

Mount Chiquita 13,069 ft

Old Fall River Road

Trail Ridge Road

Continental Divide

Big Thompson River

Trail

3

Alluvial Fan

34

Roaring Forest Canyon

Forest Canyon

4 Timber Creek

Colorado River

Holzwarth Lodge Historic Site

Mt. Ida

Mount Julian 12,928 ft

Trail Ridge

Kawuneeche Valley

Long Meadows

Spruce Canyon

Bighorn Flats

34

Snowdrift Peak 12,274 ft

1 Bear Lake

Lc

Glacier Gorge

Visitor Center

Grand Lake

Shadow Mountain Lake

Grand Lake

Ptarmigan Mountain 12,324 ft

Isolation Peak 13,118 ft

Paradise Park

Mount Adams 12,121 ft

0   3 mi

0   3 km

1 Bear Lake. One of the most photographed (and crowded) places in the park, Bear Lake is the hub for many trailheads and a major stop on the park's shuttle service.

2 Longs Peak. The highest peak in the park and the toughest to climb, this Fourteener pops up in many park vistas. A round-trip trek to the top takes 10 to 15 hours, so most visitors forego summit fever and opt for a (still spectacular) partial journey.

3 Trail Ridge Road. The alpine tundra of the park is the highlight here, as the road—the highest continuous highway in the United States—climbs to more than 12,000 feet (almost 700 feet above timberline).

COLORADO

GETTING ORIENTED

33

Rocky Mountain National Park's 416-square-mile wilderness of meadows, mountains, and mirrorlike lakes lies about 70 miles from Denver. The park is roughly an eighth of the size of Yellowstone, yet it receives almost as many visitors—3 million a year.

Bighorn Mountain
11,463 ft
Black Canyon
Lumpy Ridge
Visitor Center
34
Estes Park
34
Beaver Meadows
36
Moraine Park
36
Visitor Center and Park Headquarters
66
7
Sprague Lake *Glacier Basin*
Bear Lake Rd.
Twin Sisters Peaks
Boulder Brook
Longs Peak
2
Longs Peak 14,255 ft
Meeker Park
North St. Vrain Creek
7
Wild Basin Area
5
Allenspark

4 Timber Creek Campground. The park's far western area is much less crowded than most other sections, though it has its share of amenities and attractions, including evening programs, 98 camping sites, and a visitor center.

5 Wild Basin Area. Far from the crowds, the park's southeast quadrant consists of lovely expanses of subalpine forest punctuated by streams and lakes.

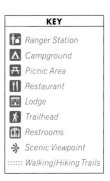

KEY
🏚 Ranger Station
⛺ Campground
⛩ Picnic Area
🍴 Restaurant
🏨 Lodge
🥾 Trailhead
🚻 Restrooms
⤳ Scenic Viewpoint
┈┈ Walking/Hiking Trails

Updated by Lindsey Galloway

Anyone who delights in alpine lakes, dense forests, and abundant wildlife—not to mention dizzying heights—should consider Rocky Mountain National Park. Here, a single hour's drive leads from a 7,800-foot elevation at park headquarters to the 12,183-foot apex of the twisting and turning Trail Ridge Road. More than 355 miles of hiking trails take you to the park's many treasures: meadows flush with wildflowers, cool dense forests of lodgepole pine and Engelmann spruce, and the noticeable presence of wildlife, including elk and bighorn sheep.

ROCKY MOUNTAIN PLANNER

WHEN TO GO

More than 80% of the park's annual 3 million visitors come in summer and fall. For thinner high-season crowds, come in early June or September. But there is a good reason to put up with summer crowds: only from Memorial Day to mid-October will you get the chance to make the unforgettable drive over Trail Ridge Road (note that the road may still be closed during those months if the weather turns bad).

Spring is capricious—75°F one day and a blizzard the next (March sees the most snow). June can range from hot and sunny to cool and rainy. July typically ushers in high summer, which can last through September. Up on Trail Ridge Road, it can be 15°F–20°F cooler than at the park's lower elevations. Wildlife viewing and fishing is best in any season but winter. In early fall, the trees blaze with brilliant foliage. Winter, when backcountry snow can be 4 feet deep, is the time for cross-country skiing, snowshoeing, and ice fishing.

AVG. HIGH/LOW TEMPS.

Jan.	Feb.	Mar.	Apr.	May	June
39/16	41/17	45/21	53/27	62/34	73/41

July	Aug.	Sept.	Oct.	Nov.	Dec.
78/46	76/45	70/38	60/30	46/23	40/18

FESTIVALS AND EVENTS

JUNE
FAMILY
Fiber Affair & Wool Market. Watch shearing, spinning, and sheepdog herding contests, plus angora goats, sheep, llamas, and alpacas being judged for their wool. Shop for knitting and weaving supplies as well as finished woolen items, such as hats, coats, and mittens. ⊠ *Estes Park Events Complex, 1125 Rooftop Way, Estes Park* ☎ *970/586–6104* ⊕ *www. visitestespark.com/events-calendar/special-events/wool-market.*

FAMILY
Jazz Fest & Art Walk. Pack a picnic and bring the kids for a weekend afternoon of free jazz performances and an art walk at the outdoor theater in downtown Estes Park. ⊠ *Performance Park Amphitheater, 417 W. Elkhorn Ave., Estes Park* ☎ *970/586–6104* ⊕ *www.visitestespark.com/ events-calendar/special-events/jazz-fest-and-art-walk.*

JULY
Estes Park Music Festival. In July and August, the Colorado Music Festival Chamber Orchestra teams with the Estes Park Music Festival for a series of concerts at the historic Stanley Hotel Concert Hall ($31 for adults; children are free). Come winter, concerts featuring a variety of performances are held at 2 pm on Sunday afternoon from November through April ($7). ⊠ *Stanley Hotel, 333 E. Wonderview Ave., Estes Park* ☎ *970/586–9519, 800/443–7837* ⊕ *www.estesparkmusicfestival. org.*

FAMILY
Rooftop Rodeo. Consistently ranked one of the top small rodeos in the country (and a tradition since 1908), this six-day event features a parade and nightly rodeo events, such as barrel racing and saddle bronc riding. ⊠ *Estes Park Fairgrounds, 1209 Manford Ave, Estes Park* ☎ *970/586–6104* ⊕ *www.rooftoprodeo.com.*

SEPTEMBER–
NOVEMBER
FAMILY
Fodor'sChoice
★
Elk Fest. In early October, the calls of bull elk fill the forest as the animals make their way down the mountains for mating season. Estes Park celebrates with elk bugle contests, Native American music and performances, and elk educational seminars. For $5, tour buses take visitors to the best elk-viewing spots. ⊠ *Bond Park, E. Elkhorn Ave. and MacGregor Ave., Estes Park* ⊕ *www.visitestespark.com/events-calendar/ special-events/elk-fest.*

Fall Back Beer Fest. In late October or early November, you can get a taste of the booming Colorado craft-beer craze and sample one of the 100 different beers created by 30 Colorado breweries at the Fall Back Beer Fest. DIYers can attend the Learn to Homebrew day, which includes equipment demonstrations and hops samples. ⊠ *Estes Parks Event Complex, 1125 Rooftop Way, Estes Park* ⊕ *www.fallbackbeerfest. com* 💵 *From $30.*

Longs Peak Scottish-Irish Highland Festival. A traditional tattoo (drum-and bugle-filled parade) kicks off this four-day fair of ancient Scottish

33

athletic competitions, including full-armor jousting and throwing contests involving hammers and 20-foot-long, 140-pound wooden poles (called cabers). The festival also features Celtic music, Irish dancing, and events for dogs of the British Isles (such as terrier racing and sheepdog demonstrations). ⊠ *Estes Park Fairgrounds, 1209 Manford Ave., Estes Park* ☎ *970/586–6308, 800/903–7837* ⊕ *www.scotfest.com.*

JANUARY **Estes Park Winter Festival.** You'll find plenty of cures for cabin fever during
FAMILY this festival, including chili cook-offs, toboggan races, and ice-skating. Be sure to check out the annual Winter Trails Day, which gives families the chance to try out snowshoeing equipment and learn proper techniques from instructors. ⊠ *Estes Park Events Complex, 1125 Rooftop Way, Estes Park* ⊕ *www.visitestespark.com/events-calendar/special-events/winter-festival.*

PLANNING YOUR TIME
ROCKY MOUNTAIN IN ONE DAY

Starting out in Estes Park, begin your day at the **Bighorn Restaurant**, a classic breakfast spot and a local favorite. While you're enjoying your short stack with apple-cinnamon-raisin topping, you can put in an order for a packed lunch (it's a good idea to bring your food with you, as dining options in the park consist of a single, seasonal snack bar at the top of Trail Ridge Road).

Drive west on U.S. 34 into the park, and stop at the **Beaver Meadows Visitor Center** to watch the orientation film and pick up a park map. Also inquire about road conditions on Trail Ridge Road, which you should plan to drive either in the morning or afternoon, depending on the weather. If possible, save the drive for the afternoon, and use the morning to get out on the trails, before the chance of an afternoon lightning storm.

For a beautiful and invigorating hike, head to Bear Lake and follow the route that takes you to **Nymph Lake** (an easy 0.5-mile hike), then onto **Dream Lake** (an additional 0.6 miles with a steeper ascent), and finally to **Emerald Lake** (an additional 0.7 miles of moderate terrain). You can stop at several places along the way. The trek down is much easier, and quicker, than the climb up. ■TIP➔ **If you prefer a shorter, simpler (yet still scenic) walk, consider the Bear Lake Nature Trail, a 0.6-mile loop that is wheelchair and stroller accessible.**

You'll need the better part of your afternoon to drive the scenic **Trail Ridge Road.** Start by heading west toward Grand Lake, stop at the lookout at the Alluvial Fan, and consider taking Old Fall River Road the rest of the way across the park. This single-lane dirt road delivers unbeatable views of waterfalls and mountain vistas. You'll take it westbound from Horseshoe Park (the cutoff is near the Endovalley Campground), then rejoin Trail Ridge Road at its summit, near the Alpine Visitor Center. If you're traveling on to Grand Lake or other points west, stay on Trail Ridge Road. If you're heading back to Estes Park, turn around and take Trail Ridge Road back (for a different set of awesome scenery). End your day with a ranger-led talk or evening campfire program.

GETTING HERE AND AROUND
AIR TRAVEL
The closest commercial airport is **Denver International Airport** (DEN). Its **Ground Transportation Information Center** (☎ 800/247–2336 or 303/342–4059 ⊕ www.flydenver.com) assists visitors with car rentals, door-to-door shuttles, and limousine services. From the airport, the eastern entrance of the park is 80 miles (about two hours). **Estes Park Shuttle** (☎ 970/586–5151 ⊕ www.estesparkshuttle.com; reservations essential) serves Estes Park and Rocky Mountain from both Denver International Airport and Longmont/Boulder.

CAR TRAVEL
Estes Park and Grand Lake are the Rocky Mountain's gateway communities; from these you can enter the park via U.S. 34 or 36 (Estes Park) or U.S. 34 (Grand Lake). U.S. 36 runs from Denver through Boulder, Lyons, and Estes Park to the park; the portion between Boulder and Estes Park is heavily traveled—especially on summer weekends. Though less direct, Colorado Routes 119, 72, and 7 have much less traffic (and better scenery). If you're driving directly to Rocky Mountain from the airport, take the E–470 tollway from Peña Boulevard to Interstate 25.

The **Colorado Department of Transportation** (for road conditions ☎ 303/639–1111 ⊕ www.cotrip.org) plows roads efficiently, but winter snowstorms can slow traffic and create wet or icy conditions. In summer, the roads into both Grand Lake and Estes Park can see heavy traffic, especially on weekends.

CAR TRAVEL WITHIN THE PARK The main thoroughfare in the park is Trail Ridge Road (U.S. 34); in winter, it's closed from the first storm in the fall (typically in October) through the spring (depending on snowpack, this could be at any time between April and June). During that time, it's plowed only up to Many Parks Curve on the east side and the Colorado River trailhead on the west side. (For current road information: ☎ 970/586–1222 ⊕ www.coloradodot.info.)

The spectacular Old Fall River Road runs one-way between the Endovalley Picnic Area on the eastern edge of the park and the Alpine Visitor Center at the summit of Trail Ridge Road, on the western side. It is typically open from July to September, depending on snowfall. It's a steep, narrow road (no wider than 14 feet), and trailers and vehicles longer than 25 feet are prohibited, but a trip on this 90-year-old thoroughfare is well worth the effort. For information on road closures, contact the park: ☎ 970/586–1206 ⊕ www.nps.gov/romo.

SHUTTLES Rocky Mountain has limited parking, but offers three free shuttle buses, which operate daily from 7 to 7, late May to early October. All three shuttles can be accessed from a large Park & Ride located within the park, 7 miles from the Beaver Meadows entrance. Visitors who don't want to drive into the park at all can hop on the Hiker Shuttle at the Estes Park Visitor Center. The hourly shuttle makes stops at the Beaver Meadows Visitor Center and the Park & Ride, where visitors can switch to one of the other two shuttles, which head to various trailheads. The Moraine Park Route shuttle runs every 30 minutes and stops at the Moraine Park Visitor Center and then continues on to the Fern Lake

Trailhead. The Bear Lake Route shuttle runs every 15 minutes from the Park & Ride to the Bear Lake Trailhead.

TRAIN TRAVEL

Amtrak trains stop in downtown Denver, Winter Park/Fraser (80 miles away), and Granby (66 miles). ☎ *800/872–7245* ⊕ *www.amtrak.com.*

PARK ESSENTIALS

PARK FEES AND PERMITS

Entrance fees are $20 per automobile for a weekly pass, or $10 if you enter on bicycle, motorcycle, or foot. An annual pass costs $40.

Backcountry camping requires a permit that's $26 per party from May through October, and free the rest of the year. Visit ⊕ *www.nps.gov/ romo/planyourvisit/backcntry_guide.htm* before you go for a planning guide to backcountry camping. You can get your permit online, by phone (☎ *970/586–1242*), or in person. In person, you can get a day-of-trip permit year-round at one of the park's two backcountry offices, located next to the Beaver Meadows Visitor Center and in the Kawuneeche Visitor Center.

PARK HOURS

The park is open 24/7 year-round; some roads close in winter. It is in the Mountain time zone.

CELL-PHONE RECEPTION

Cell phones work in some sections of the park, and free Wi-Fi can be accessed in and around the Beaver Meadows Visitor Center and the Kawuneeche Visitor Center.

EDUCATIONAL OFFERINGS

ART PROGRAM

Artist-in-Residence. Professional writers, sculptors, composers, and visual and performing artists can stay in a rustic cabin for two weeks in summer while working on their art. During their stay, they must make two presentations and donate a piece of original work to the park that relates to their stay. Applications must be received by November for requests for the following summer. ⊠ *Rocky Mountain National Park* ☎ *970/586–1206.*

CLASSES AND SEMINARS

FAMILY **Rocky Mountain Conservancy.** Each year, the Rocky Mountain Conservancy sponsors more than 200 hands-on field institute adventures for adults and children on such topics as natural history, fishing, geology, bird-watching, wildflower identification, wildlife biology, photography, and sketching. Classes range from lectures of a few hours to overnight and multiday camping trips. Most are fairly rigorous, incorporating hiking and other outdoor activities. All are taught by expert instructors. ⊠ *1895 Fall River Rd., Estes Park* ☎ *970/586–3262* ⊕ *rmconservancy. org* 🔊 *$10–$360 per class* ☉ *Jan.–Oct.*

RANGER PROGRAMS

FAMILY **Junior Ranger Program.** Stop by the Junior Ranger Headquarters off Trail Ridge Road for ranger-led talks during the summer months. You can also pick up a Junior Ranger activity book (in English or Spanish) here or at any visitor center in the park. Program content has been developed for children ages 6 to 12; the material focuses on environmental education, identifying birds and wildlife, and outdoor safety skills. Once a child has completed all of the activities in the book, a ranger will look over his or her work and award a Junior Ranger badge. ⊠ *Rocky Mountain National Park* ☎ *970/586–1206* ⊕ *www.nps.gov/romo/forkids* ⊠ *Free.*

FAMILY **Ranger Programs.** Join in on free hikes, talks, and activities conducted by those who know the park best. Topics may include wildlife, geology, vegetation, or park history. Don't miss special programs like "Skins and Things," a popular hands-on learning experience, and "Exploring with a Camera," which offers photography tips. In the evening, rangers lead twilight hikes, stargazing sessions, and storytelling around the campfire. Look for the extensive program schedule in the park's newspaper available at the main entrances. ⊠ *Rocky Mountain National Park* ☎ *970/586–1206* ⊠ *Free.*

RESTAURANTS

Restaurants in north central Colorado run the gamut from simple diners with tasty, homey basics to elegant establishments with extensive wine lists. Some restaurants take reservations, but many—particularly midrange spots—seat on a first-come, first-served basis. In the park itself, there are no real dining establishments, though you can get snacks and light fare at the Trail Ridge Store, adjacent to the Alpine Visitor Center at the top of the Trail Ridge Road. The park also has a handful of scenic picnic areas, all with tables and pit or flush toilets.

HOTELS

Bed-and-breakfasts and small inns in north central Colorado vary from old-fashioned fluffy cottages to sleek, modern buildings with understated lodge themes. If you want some pampering, there are guest ranches and spas.

In Estes Park, Grand Lake, and other nearby towns, the elevation keeps the climate cool, and you'll scarcely need (and you'll have a tough time finding) air-conditioned lodging. For a historic spot, try the Stanley Hotel in Estes Park, which dates to 1909 and features 160 guestrooms. The park has no hotels or lodges. *Hotel reviews have been shortened. For full information, visit Fodors.com.*

WHAT IT COSTS			
$	$$	$$$	$$$$
Restaurants	under $13	$13–$18	$19–$25	over $25
Hotels	under $121	$121–$170	$171–$230	over $230

Restaurant prices are the average cost of a main course at dinner or, if dinner is not served, at lunch. Hotel prices are the lowest cost of a standard double room in high season, excluding taxes and service charges.

TOURS

FAMILY **Green Jeep Tours.** From the back of an open-air, neon-green Jeep on these tours, you can enjoy the majestic scenery while your experienced guide points out wildlife along the way. Green Jeep Tours also offers a two-hour tour in September and October that focuses on finding elk. Admission includes the cost of the seven-day pass into the park. ⊠ *157 Moraine Ave., Estes Park* ☎ *970/577–0034* 🖃 *From $40.*

Rocky Mountain Rush. This company's most popular tour, the "Top of the World," takes visitors in an open-top vehicle all the way to Old Fall River Road and back down Trail Ridge. A waterfall tour and sunset valley tour offer great wildlife spottings at lower elevations. ⊠ *212 E. Elkhorn Ave., Estes Park* ☎ *970/586–8687* ⊕ *www.rockymountainrush. com* 🖃 *From $65.*

FodorśChoice ★ **Yellow Wood Guiding.** Guided photo safaris, offered year-round, ensure visitors leave the Rocky Mountain National Park with more than just memories. Customized for either beginners or experts, the tours offer the use of professional digital cameras for visitors who don't have their own and plenty of tips on how to take animal and landscape photos. Yellow Wood Guiding also offers hiking, snowshoe, and wildlife tours seasonally. ⊠ *212 E. Elkhorn Ave., Estes Park* ☎ *970/586–8687* ⊕ *www.ywguiding.com* 🖃 *From $95.*

VISITOR INFORMATION

Park Contact Information Rocky Mountain National Park. ⊠ *1000 U.S. 36, Estes Park* ☎ *970/586–1206* ⊕ *www.nps.gov/romo.*

VISITOR CENTERS

Alpine Visitor Center. At the top of Trail Ridge Road, this visitor center is open only when that road is navigable. The center also houses the park's only gift shop and snack bar. ⊠ *Fall River Pass, at junction of Trail Ridge and Old Fall River Rds., 22 miles from Beaver Meadows entrance* ☎ *970/586–1206* ⊘ *Late May–mid-June and Labor Day–Columbus Day, daily 10:30–4:30; mid-June–Labor Day, daily 9–5.*

Beaver Meadows Visitor Center. Housing the park headquarters, this visitor center was designed by students of the Frank Lloyd Wright School of Architecture at Taliesin West using the park's popular rustic style, which integrates buildings into their natural surroundings. Completed in 1966, it was named a National Historic Landmark in 2001. The surrounding utility buildings are noteworthy examples of the rustic-style buildings that the Civilian Conservation Corps constructed during the Depression. The center has a terrific 20-minute orientation film and a large relief map of the park. ⊠ *U.S. 36, 3 miles west of Estes Park and 1 mile east of Beaver Meadows Entrance Station* ☎ *970/586–1206* ⊘ *Daily 8–4:30.*

FAMILY **Fall River Visitor Center.** The Discovery Room, which houses everything from old ranger outfits to elk antlers, coyote pelts, and bighorn sheep skulls for hands-on exploration, is a favorite with kids at this visitor center. ⊠ *U.S. 34, at the Fall River Entrance Station* ☎ *970/586–1206* ⊘ *Daily 9–5.*

FAMILY **Kawuneeche Visitor Center.** The only visitor center on the park's far west side, Kawuneeche has exhibits on the plant and animal life of the area, as well as a large three-dimensional map of the park and an orientation film. ⊠ *U.S. 34, 1 mile north of Grand Lake and ½ mile south of Grand Lake Entrance Station* ☎ *970/586–1206* ⊘ *Daily 8–4:30.*

Plants and Wildlife in Rocky Mountain

Volcanic uplifts and the savage clawing of receding glaciers created Rocky Mountain's majestic landscape. You'll find four distinct ecosystems here—a riparian (wetland) environment with 150 lakes and 450 miles of streams; verdant montane valleys teeming with proud ponderosa pines and lush grasses; higher and colder subalpine mountains with wind-whipped trees (krummholz) that grow at right angles; and harsh, unforgiving alpine tundra with dollhouse-size versions of familiar plants and wildflowers. Alpine tundra is seldom found outside the Arctic, yet it makes up one-third of the park's terrain. Few plants can survive at this elevation of 11,000–11,500 feet, but many beautiful wildflowers—including alpine forget-me-nots—bloom here briefly in late June or early July.

The park has so much wildlife that you can often enjoy prime viewing from the seat of your car. Fall, when many animals begin moving down from higher elevations, is an excellent time to spot some of the park's animal residents. This is also when you'll hear the male elk bugle mating calls (popular spots to see and hear bugling elk are Kawuneeche Valley, Horseshoe Park, Moraine Park, and Upper Beaver Meadows).

May through mid-October is the best time to see the bighorn sheep that congregate in the Horseshoe Park/Sheep Lakes area, just past the Fall River entrance. If you want to glimpse a moose, try Kawuneeche Valley. Other animals in the park include mule deer, squirrels, chipmunks, pikas, beavers, and marmots. Common birds include broad-tailed and rufous hummingbirds, peregrine falcons, woodpeckers, mountain bluebirds, and Clark's nutcracker, as well as the white-tailed ptarmigan, which live year-round on the alpine tundra.

Mountain lions, black bears, and bobcats also inhabit the park but are rarely seen by visitors. Altogether, the park is home to roughly 60 species of mammals and 280 bird species.

EXPLORING

SCENIC DRIVES

Bear Lake Road. This 23-mile round-trip drive offers superlative views of Longs Peak (14,259-foot summit) and the glaciers surrounding Bear Lake, winding past shimmering waterfalls shrouded with rainbows. You can either drive the road yourself (open year-round) or hop on one of the park's free shuttle buses. ⊠ *Runs from the Beaver Meadow Entrance Station to Bear Lake.*

Old Fall River Road. Nearly 100 years old and never more than 14 feet wide, this road stretches for 11 miles, from the park's east side to the Fall River Pass (11,796 feet above sea level) on the west. The drive provides spectacular views and a few white-knuckle moments, as the road is steep, serpentine, and lacking in guardrails. Start at West Horseshoe Park, which has the park's largest concentrations of sheep and elk, and head up the gravel road, passing Chasm Falls (there are a few places to park for a quick hike). ⊠ *Runs north of and roughly parallel to Trail Ridge Road, starting near Endovalley Campground (on east) and ending at Fall River Pass/Alpine Visitor Center (on west)* ☉ *July–Oct.*

Fodor's Choice **Trail Ridge Road.** This is the park's star attraction and the world's high-
★ est continuous paved highway, topping out at 12,183 feet. The 48-mile road connects the park's gateways of Estes Park and Grand Lake. The views around each bend—of moraines and glaciers, and craggy hills framing emerald meadows carpeted with columbine and Indian paint-brush—are truly awesome. As it passes through three ecosystems—montane, subalpine, and arctic tundra—the road climbs 4,300 feet in elevation. As you drive the road, take your time at the numerous turn-outs to gaze over the verdant valleys, brushed with yellowing aspen in fall, that slope between the glacier-etched granite peaks. **Rainbow Curve** affords views of nine separate mountain peaks, each more than 10,000 feet high, and of the **Alluvial Fan,** a 42-acre swath of rocks and boulders (some the size of cars) left behind after an earthen dam broke in 1982. You can complete a one-way trip across the park on Trail Ridge Road in two hours, but it's best to give yourself three or four hours to allow for leisurely breaks at the overlooks. Note that the middle part of the road closes with the first big snow (typically by mid-October) and most often reopens around Memorial Day, though you can still drive up about 10 miles from the west and 8 miles from the east. ⊠ *Trail Ridge Rd. (U.S. 34), runs between Estes Park and Grand Lake* ☉ *June–mid-Oct.*

HISTORIC SITES

Rocky Mountain has more than 1,000 archaeological sites and 150 buildings of historic significance; 47 of the buildings are listed in the National Register of Historic Places, which is reserved for structures that tie in strongly to the park's history in terms of architecture, archae-ology, engineering, or culture. Most buildings at Rocky Mountain are done in the rustic style, a design preferred by the National Park Service's first director, Stephen Mather, that works to incorporate nature into these man-made structures.

FAMILY **Holzwarth Historic Site.** A scenic ½-mile interpretive trail leads you over the Colorado River to the original dude ranch that the Holzwarth fam-ily, some of the park's original homesteaders, ran between the 1920s and 1950s. Allow about an hour to view the buildings—including a dozen small guest cabins—and chat with a ranger. Though the site is open year-round, the inside of the buildings can be seen only in sum-mer. It's a great place for families to learn about homesteading. ⊠ *Off U.S. 34, about 8 miles north of Kawuneeche Visitor Center, Estes Park.*

Lulu City. The remains of a few cabins are all that's left of this one-time silver-mining town, established around 1880. Reach it by hiking the 3.6-mile Colorado River Trail. Look for wagon ruts from the old Stewart Toll Road and mine tailings in nearby Shipler Park (this is also a good place to spot moose). The Colorado River is a mere stream at this point, flowing south from its headwaters at nearby La Poudre Pass. ⊠ *Off Trail Ridge Rd., 9½ miles north of Grand Lake Entrance Station.*

SCENIC STOPS

Bear Lake. Thanks to its picturesque location, easy accessibility, and the good hiking trails nearby, this small alpine lake below Flattop Mountain and Hallett Peak is one of the most popular destinations in the park. Free park shuttle buses can take you there May through October. ⊠ *Bear Lake Rd., 7 miles southwest of Moraine Park Visitor Center, off U.S. 36.*

Forest Canyon Overlook. Park at a dedicated lot to disembark on a wildflower-rich, 0.2-mile trail. Easy to access for all skill levels, this glacial valley overlook offers views of ice-blue pools (the Gorge Lakes) framed by ragged peaks. ⊠ *Trail Ridge Rd., 6 miles east of Alpine Visitor Center.*

> ### ELK BUGLING
>
> In September and October, there are traffic jams in the park as people drive up to listen to the elk bugling. Rangers and park volunteers keep track of where the elk are and direct visitors to the mating spots. The bugling is high-pitched, and if it's light enough, you can see the elk put his head in the air.

33

SPORTS AND THE OUTDOORS

BIRD-WATCHING

Spring and summer, early in the morning, are the best times for bird-watching in the park. **Lumpy Ridge** is a nesting ground for several kinds of birds of prey. Migratory songbirds from South America have summer breeding grounds near the **Endovalley Picnic Area.** The **alpine tundra** is habitat for white-tailed ptarmigan. The **Alluvial Fan** is the place for viewing broad-tailed hummingbirds, hairy woodpeckers, ouzels, and the occasional raptor.

FISHING

Rocky Mountain is a wonderful place to fish, especially for trout—German brown, brook, rainbow, cutthroat, and greenback cutthroat—but check at a visitor center about regulations and information on specific closures, catch-and-release areas, and limits on size and possession. No fishing is allowed at Bear Lake. To avoid the crowds, rangers recommend angling in the more-remote backcountry. To fish in the park, anyone 16 and older must have a valid Colorado fishing license, which you can obtain at local sporting-goods stores. See ⊕ *www.wildlife.state.co.us/fishing* for details.

TOURS AND OUTFITTERS

Estes Angler. This popular fishing guide arranges four-, six-, and eight-hour fly-fishing trips—as well as full-day horseback excursions—into the park's quieter regions, year-round, with a maximum of three people per guide. The best times for fishing are generally from April to mid-November. Equipment is also available for rent. ⊠ *338 W. Riverside*

Dr., Estes Park ☎ *970/586–2110, 800/586–2110* ⊕ *www.estesangler. com* ✉ *From $125* ⊙ *Daily 8–6.*

Kirks Fly Shop. This Estes Park outfitter offers various guided fly-fishing trips, as well as backpacking, horseback, and llama pack trips. The store also carries fishing and backpacking gear. ⊠ *230 E. Elkhorn Ave., Estes Park* ☎ *970/577–0790, 877/669–1859* ⊕ *www.kirksflyshop.com* ✉ *From $50* ⊙ *Daily 7–7.*

Scot's Sporting Goods. This shop rents and sells fishing gear, and provides four-, six-, and eight-hour instruction trips daily from May through mid-October. Clinics, geared toward first-timers, focus on casting, reading the water, identifying insects for flies, and properly presenting natural and artificial flies to the fish. Half-day excursions into the park are available for three or more people. A range of camping and hiking equipment is also for sale. ⊠ *870 Moraine Ave., Estes Park* ☎ *970/586–2877 May–Sept., 970/443–4932 Oct.–Apr.* ⊕ *www.scotssportinggoods. com* ✉ *From $210* ⊙ *June–Aug., daily 8–8; May and Sept.–mid-Oct., daily 9–5.*

HIKING

Fodor'sChoice
★

Rocky Mountain National Park contains more than 355 miles of hiking trails, so you could theoretically wander the park for weeks. Most visitors explore just a small portion of these trails—those that are closest to the roads and visitor centers—which means that some of the park's most accessible and scenic paths can resemble a backcountry highway on busy summer days. The high-alpine terrain around Bear Lake is the park's most popular hiking area, and although it's well worth exploring, you'll get a more frontierlike experience by hiking one of the trails in the less-explored sections of the park, such as the far northern end or in the Wild Basin area to the south.

Keep in mind that trails at higher elevations may have some snow on them, even in late summer. And because of afternoon thunderstorms on most summer days, an early morning start is highly recommended: the last place you want to be when a storm approaches is on a peak or anywhere above the tree line. All trail mileages are round-trip unless stated otherwise.

EASY

Bear Lake Trail. The virtually flat nature trail around Bear Lake is an easy, 0.6-mile loop that's wheelchair and stroller accessible. Sharing the route with you will likely be plenty of other hikers as well as songbirds and chipmunks. *Easy.* ⊕ *Trailhead: at Bear Lake, Bear Lake Rd.*

FAMILY **Copeland Falls.** The 0.3-mile hike to these Wild Basin Area falls is a good option for families, as the terrain is relatively flat (there's only a 15-foot elevation gain). *Easy.* ⊕ *Trailhead: at Wild Basin Ranger Station.*

East Inlet Trail. An easy hike of 0.3 miles from East Inlet trailhead, just outside the park in Grand Lake, will get you to **Adams Falls** in about 15 minutes. The area around the falls is often packed with visitors, so if you have time, continue east to enjoy more solitude, see wildlife, and catch views of **Mount Craig** from near the East Meadow campground.

Note, however, that the trail beyond the falls has an elevation gain of between 1,500 and 1,900 feet, making it a more challenging hike. *Easy.* ⊠ *Grand Lake* ⊹ *Trailhead: at East Inlet, end of W. Portal Rd. (CO 278) in Grand Lake.*

Fodor's Choice
★

Glacier Gorge Trail. The 2.8-mile hike to **Mills Lake** can be crowded, but the reward is one of the park's prettiest lakes, set against the breathtaking backdrop of Longs Peak, Pagoda Mountain, and the Keyboard of the Winds. There's a modest elevation gain of 750 feet. On the way, about 1 mile in, you pass **Alberta Falls**, a popular destination in and of itself. The hike travels along Glacier Creek, under the shade of a subalpine forest. Give yourself at least four hours for hiking and lingering. *Easy.* ⊹ *Trailhead: off Bear Lake Rd., about 1 mile southeast of Bear Lake.*

Sprague Lake. With virtually no elevation gain, this 0.5-mile, pine-lined looped path near a popular backcountry campground is wheelchair accessible and provides views of Hallet Peak and Flattop Mountain. *Easy.* ⊹ *Trailhead: at Sprague Lake, Bear Lake Rd., 4½ miles southwest of Moraine Park Visitor Center.*

MODERATE

Fodor's Choice
★

Bear Lake to Emerald Lake. This scenic, calorie-burning hike begins with a moderately level, 0.5-mile journey to **Nymph Lake.** From here, the trail gets steeper, with a 425-foot elevation gain, as it winds around for 0.6 miles to **Dream Lake.** The last stretch is the most arduous part of the hike, an almost all-uphill 0.7-mile trek to lovely **Emerald Lake,** where you can perch on a boulder and enjoy the view. All told, the hike is 3.6 miles, with an elevation gain of 605 feet. Allow two hours or more, depending on stops. *Moderate.* ⊹ *Trailhead: at Bear Lake, off Bear Lake Rd., 8 miles southwest of the Moraine Park Visitor Center.*

Cub Lake. This 4.6-mile, three-hour (round-trip) hike takes you through meadows and stands of aspen trees and up 540 feet in elevation to a lake with water lilies. *Moderate.* ⊹ *Trailhead: at Cub Lake, about 1¾ miles from Moraine Park Campground.*

Colorado River Trail. This walk to the ghost town of Lulu City on the west side of the park is excellent for looking for the bighorn sheep, elk, and moose that reside in the area. Part of the former stagecoach route that went from Granby to Walden, the 3.7-mile trail parallels the infant Colorado River to the meadow where Lulu City once stood. The elevation gain is 350 feet. *Moderate.* ⊹ *Trailhead: at Colorado River, off Trail Ridge Rd., 1¾ miles north of the Timber Creek Campground.*

Fern Lake Trail. Heading to Odessa Lake from the north involves a steep hike, but on most days you'll encounter fewer other hikers than if you had begun the trip at Bear Lake. Along the way, you'll come to the Arch Rocks; the Pool, an eroded formation in the Big Thompson River; two waterfalls; and Fern Lake (3.8 miles from your starting point). Less than a mile farther, Odessa Lake itself lies at the foot of Tourmaline Gorge, below the craggy summits of Gabletop Mountain, Little Matterhorn, Knobtop Mountain, and Notchtop Mountain. For a full day of spectacular scenery, continue past Odessa to Bear Lake (9 miles total), where you can pick up the shuttle back to the Fern Lake Trailhead. *Moderate.* ✛ *Trailhead: off Fern Lake Rd., about 2½ miles south of Moraine Park Visitor Center.*

DIFFICULT

Chasm Lake Trail. Nestled in the shadow of Longs Peak and Mount Meeker, Chasm Lake offers one of Colorado's most impressive back-drops, which also means you can expect to encounter plenty of other hikers on the way. The 4.2-mile Chasm Lake Trail, reached via the Longs Peak Trail, has a 2,360-foot elevation gain. Just before the lake, you'll need to climb a small rock ledge, which can be a bit of a challenge for the less sure-footed; follow the cairns for the most straightforward route. Once atop the ledge, you'll catch your first memorable view of the lake. *Difficult.* ✛ *Trailhead: at Longs Peak Ranger Station, off Rte. 7, 10 miles from the Beaver Meadows Visitor Center.*

Deer Mountain Trail. This 6-mile round-trip trek to the top of 10,083-foot Deer Mountain is a great way for hikers who don't mind a bit of a climb to enjoy the views from the summit of a more manageable peak. You'll gain more than 1,000 feet in elevation as you follow the switchbacking trail through ponderosa pine, aspen, and fir trees. The reward at the top is a panoramic view of the park's eastern mountains. *Difficult.* ✛ *Trailhead: at Deer Ridge Junction, about 4 miles west of Moraine Park Visitor Center, U.S. 34 at U.S. 36.*

Longs Peak Trail. Climbing this 14,259-foot mountain (one of 53 "Four-teeners" in Colorado) is an ambitious goal for almost anyone—but only those who are very fit and acclimated to the altitude should attempt it. The 16-mile round-trip climb requires a predawn start (3 am is ideal), so that you're off the summit before the typical summer afternoon thunderstorm hits. Also, the last 2 miles or so of the trail are very exposed—you have to traverse narrow ledges with vertigo-inducing drop-offs. That said, summiting Longs can be one of the most reward-ing experiences you'll ever have. The Keyhole route is the most popular means of ascent, and the number of people going up it on a summer day can be astounding, given the rigors of the climb. Though just as scenic, the Loft route, between Longs and Mount Meeker from Chasm Lake, is less crowded but not as clearly marked and therefore more difficult to navigate. *Difficult.* ✛ *Trailhead: at Longs Peak Ranger Station, off Rte. 7, 10 miles from Beaver Meadows Visitor Center.*

HORSEBACK RIDING

Horses and riders can access 260 miles of trails in Rocky Mountain National Park.

TOURS AND OUTFITTERS

FAMILY **Glacier Creek Stable.** Located within the park near Sprague Lake, Gla-cier Creek Stable offers two- to 10-hour rides to Glacier Basin, Odessa Lake, and Storm Pass. ⊠ *Glacier Creek Campground, off Bear Lake Rd. near Sprague Lake* ☎ *970/586–3244 stables, 970/586–4577 off-season reservations* ⊕ *sombrero.com* ☏ *From $55.*

Bear Lake Region

0 — 1 mi
0 — 1 km

Cub Lake

Bierstadt Lake

Bierstadt

0.7mi

Bear Lake

0.5mi

Bear Lake

Nymph Lake

Glacier Gorge

Emerald Lake

0.7mi

0.6mi

Dream Lake

0.5mi

1.7mi

Lake Haiyaha

0.9mi

2.3mi

0.2mi

1.9mi

0.5mi

3.0mi

0.9mi

0.6mi

Mills Lake

The Loc

0.6mi

Jewel Lake

KEY
------- Trail
------- Horse/Hiking Trail
2.2 mi Distance in miles

FAMILY **Moraine Park Stable.** Located inside the park just before the Cub Lake Trailhead, Moraine Park Stable offers two- to eight-hour trips to Beaver Meadows, Fern Lake, and Tourmaline Gorge. ☒ *549 Fern Lake Rd* ☎ *970/586–2327 stables, 970/586–4577 off-season reservations* ⊕ *www.sombrero.com* ☒ *From \$55.*

ROCK CLIMBING

Expert rock climbers as well as novices can try hundreds of classic and big-wall climbs here (there's also ample opportunity for bouldering and mountaineering). The burgeoning sport of ice climbing also thrives in the park. The Diamond, Lumpy Ridge, and Petit Grepon are the places for serious rock climbing, while well-known ice-climbing spots include Hidden Falls, Loch Vale, and Emerald and Black lakes.

TOURS AND OUTFITTERS

FAMILY
Fodor's Choice
★

Colorado Mountain School. Guiding climbers since 1877, Colorado Mountain School is an invaluable resource for climbers in the Rocky Mountain area (they're also the park's only official provider of technical climbing services). They can teach you rock climbing, mountaineering, ice climbing, avalanche survival, and many other skills. Take introductory half-day and one- to five-day courses on climbing and rappelling technique, or sign up for guided introductory trips, full-day climbs, and longer expeditions. Make reservations a month in advance for summer climbs. ✉ *341 Moraine Ave., Estes Park* ☎ *800/836–4008, 303/447–2804* ⊕ *coloradomountainschool.com* 🖃 *From $90.*

WINTER SPORTS

Each winter, the popularity of snowshoeing in the park increases. It's a wonderful way to experience Rocky Mountain's majestic winter side, when the jagged peaks are softened with a blanket of snow and the summer hordes are nonexistent. You can snowshoe any of the summer hiking trails that are accessible by road; many of them also become well-traveled cross-country ski trails. Two trails to try are Tonahutu Creek Trail (near Kawuneeche Visitor Center) and the Colorado River Trail to Lulu City (start at the Timber Creek Campground).

Backcountry skiing within the park ranges from gentle cross-country outings to full-on, experts-only

> ### LONGS PEAK
>
> At 14,259 feet above sea level, **Longs Peak** has long fascinated explorers to the region. Longs Peak is the northernmost of the Fourteeners—the 54 mountains in Colorado that reach above the 14,000-foot mark—and one of more than 114 named mountains in the park that are higher than 10,000 feet. The peak, in the park's southeast quadrant, has a distinctive flat-topped, rectangular summit that is visible from many spots on the park's east side and on Trail Ridge Road.

33

adventures down steep chutes and open bowls. Ask a ranger about conditions, and gear up as if you were spending the night. If you plan on venturing off trail, take a shovel, probe pole, and avalanche transceiver. Only on the west side of the park are you permitted to snowmobile, and you must register at Kawuneeche Visitor Center before traveling the unplowed section of Trail Ridge Road up to Milner Pass. Check the park newspaper for ranger-guided tours.

TOURS AND OUTFITTERS

Estes Park Mountain Shop. You can rent or buy snowshoes and skis here, as well as fishing, hiking, and climbing equipment. The store is open year-round and gives four-, six-, and eight-hour guided snowshoeing, fly-fishing, and climbing trips to areas in and around Rocky Mountain National Park. ✉ *2050 Big Thompson Ave., Estes Park* ☎ *970/586–6548, 866/303–6548* ⊕ *www.estesparkmountainshop.com* 🖃 *From $54.*

Never Summer Mountain Products. This well-stocked shop sells and rents all sorts of outdoor equipment, including cross-country skis, hiking gear, kayaks, and camping supplies. ✉ *919 Grand Ave., Grand Lake* ☎ *970/627–3642* ⊕ *www.neversummermtn.com.*

WHAT'S NEARBY

NEARBY TOWNS

Estes Park, 5 miles east of Rocky Mountain, is the park's most popular gateway. The town sits at an altitude of more than 7,500 feet, with 14,259-foot Longs Peak and a legion of surrounding mountains as its stunning backdrop. Many of the small hotels lining the roads are mom-and-pop outfits that have been passed down through several generations.

Estes Park's quieter cousin, **Grand Lake,** 1½ miles outside the park's west entrance, gets busy in summer, but has a low-key, quintessentially Western graciousness. In winter, it's *the* snowmobiling and ice-fishing destination for Front Range Coloradans. At the park's southwestern entrance are the Arapaho and Roosevelt National Forests, Arapaho National Recreational Area, and the small town of **Granby,** the place to go for big-game hunting and mountain biking. There are also skiing and other mountain activities (both summer and winter varieties) at nearby SolVista Basin and the Winter Park/Mary Jane ski areas.

SCENIC DRIVES

Peak to Peak Scenic and Historic Byway. The Peak to Peak Scenic and Historic Byway (Highways 119, 72, and 7), a 55-mile stretch that winds from Central City through Nederland to Estes Park, is not the quickest route to the eastern gateway to Rocky Mountain National Park, but it's certainly the most scenic. You'll pass through the old mining towns of Ward and Allenspark and enjoy spectacular mountain vistas. Mount Meeker and Longs Peak rise magnificently behind every bend in the road. The descent into Estes Park provides grand vistas of snow-covered mountains and green valleys.

An afternoon drive along this route is especially memorable in fall, when the sky is deeper blue and stands of aspens contrast with the evergreen pine forests. ⊠ *Nederland ✚ From Central City, drive north on Hwy. 119. From Nederland, drive north on Hwy. 72. Turn left at intersection with Hwy. 7 and continue to Estes Park ⊕ www.codot.gov/travel/scenic-byways.*

AREA ACTIVITIES

SPORTS AND THE OUTDOORS

BIRD-WATCHING

Windy Gap Watchable Wildlife Area. On the path alongside the reservoir at Windy Gap Watchable Wildlife Area, you're likely to spot geese, pelicans, swans, eagles, killdeer, osprey, and more. The park has information kiosks, spotting scopes, viewing areas, covered picnic tables, and a nature trail that's wheelchair accessible. ⊠ *Granby ✚ 5 miles west of Granby on U.S. 40 where it meets Rte. 125* ☎ *970/725–6200* ⊕ *www.northernwater.org/waterprojects/howwindygapworks.aspx* ⊗ *May–Sept., daily dawn–dusk.*

33

FISHING

Anglers in the Grand Lake and Granby area enjoy plentiful trout, mackinaw, and kokanee salmon. Ice fishers will not want to miss the big contest held the first weekend in January on Lake Granby, where winners collect $20,000 in cash and prizes. Anyone older than 16 needs a Colorado fishing license, which you can obtain at local sporting-goods stores. See ⊕ *www.wildlife.state.co.us/fishing* for more information.

The Big Thompson River, which runs east of Estes Park along U.S. 34, is popular for its good stock of rainbow and brown trout.

Trail Ridge Marina. The Trail Ridge Marina is on the western shore of Shadow Mountain Lake, which is connected to Grand Lake by a channel. The marina rents pontoon, pleasure, and fishing boats, as well as kayaks and stand-up paddleboards. ✉ *12634 U.S. 34, Grand Lake* ✛ *2 miles south of Grand Lake on U.S. 34* 📞 *970/627–3586* ⊕ *www. trailridgemarina.com* 🕙 *Closed Oct.–Apr.*

GOLF

Grand Elk Golf Club. Designed by PGA great Craig Stadler, this challenging mountain course is reminiscent of traditional heathland greens in Britain yet brings its own blend of Colorado style, with expansive views of sagebrush-covered hills, aspen groves, and the Continental Divide. The semi-private club is an excellent value compared to other Colorado mountain courses. Green fees include a cart, although it is a very walkable course. ✉ *1300 Tenmile Dr., Granby* 📞 *970/887–9122* ⊕ *www. grandelk.com* 💲 *$85 weekdays, $95 weekends* ⛳ *18 holes, 7144 yards, par 71* 🕙 *Closed mid-Oct.–mid-May* ⚐ *Reservations essential.*

WINTER SPORTS

Many consider Grand Lake to be Colorado's snowmobiling capital, with more than 300 miles of trails (150 miles groomed), many winding through virgin forest. There are several rental and guide companies in the area. If you're visiting during the winter holidays, it's wise to make reservations about three weeks ahead.

Grand Adventures. Take a two- or four-hour guided snowmobile tour, or rent a machine and head out on your own. ✉ *304 W. Portal Rd., Grand Lake* 📞 *970/726–9247* ⊕ *www.grandadventures.com* 💲 *From $55* 🕙 *Closed late spring–late fall.*

Never Summer Mountain Products. Rent skis and snowshoes in the winter, or buy backpacks, tents, and other camping equipment for summer sports. Rocky Mountain National Park requires backpackers to use bear canisters (for overnight food storage), which Never Summer rents for $5 for 24 hours. ✉ *919 Grand Ave., Grand Lake* 📞 *970/627–3642* ⊕ *www.neversummermtn.com.*

On The Trail Rentals. This handy outfit a few miles northwest of town rents snowmobiles and also offers guided tours into Arapaho National Forest. During the summer, you can rent mountain bikes, ATVs, and side-by-sides here. ✉ *1447 County Rd. 491, Grand Lake* 📞 *970/627–0171, 888/627–2429* ⊕ *www.onthetrailrentals.com* 💲 *From $110* 🕙 *Snowmobile rental late Nov.–Mar.; ATV rental late May–Nov.*

NIGHTLIFE AND PERFORMING ARTS

PERFORMING ARTS

Rocky Ridge Music Center. Relax with some chamber music while taking in views of the mountains at the much-respected Rocky Ridge Music Center. Faculty members hold their own classical chamber music concerts June to September. ⊠ *465 Longs Peak Rd., Estes Park* ⊹ *South of Estes Park off Hwy. 7 at turnoff to Longs Peak Campground (mile marker 9)* ☎ *970/586–4031* ⊕ *www.rockyridge.org* ⊑ *$22.*

NIGHTLIFE

Lariat Saloon. A local hot spot, this rustic bar has pinball, pool, and video games, plus live music on summer weekends. It's also the only spot in town for late-night eats. Look for the buffalo and dreadlock-adorned fox amid the eclectic Western decor. ⊠ *1121 Grand Ave., Grand Lake* ☎ *970/627–9965.*

Lonigans Saloon, Nightclub & Grill. If you're in the mood for a fun Irish pub with "altitude," head over to Lonigans for drinks, bar food, and pool. Wednesday is open-mike night, and Friday and Saturday have karaoke. ⊠ *110 W. Elkhorn Ave., Estes Park* ☎ *970/586–4346* ⊕ *www.lonigans.com.*

SHOPPING

Rocky Mountain Chocolate Factory. Indulge in fudge, truffles, and fantastic caramel apples at this paradise of sweets. ⊠ *517 Big Thompson Ave., Estes Park* ☎ *970/586–6601* ⊕ *www.rmcf.com.*

WHERE TO EAT

IN THE PARK

$ ⨯ **Cafe at Trail Ridge.** The park's only source for food, this small café
AMERICAN offers snacks, sandwiches, hot dogs, and soups. A coffee bar also serves fair-trade coffee, espresso drinks, and tea, plus water, juice, and salads. The café is in the same building as the Trail Ridge Store, adjacent to the Alpine Visitor Center, and is open seasonally, whenever Trail Ridge Road is open. ⑤ *Average main: $7* ⊠ *Trail Ridge Rd., at Alpine Visitor Center* ☎ *970/586–3097* ⊕ *www.trailridgegiftstore.com* ⊗ *Closed mid-Oct.–mid-May. No dinner.*

PICNIC AREAS

Endovalley. With 32 tables and 30 fire grates, this is the largest picnic area in the park. Here, you'll find aspen groves, nice views of Fall River Pass—and lovely Fan Lake a short hike away. ⊠ *Off U.S. 34, at beginning of Old Fall River Rd., about 4½ miles from Fall River Visitor Center.*

Hollowell Park. In a meadow near Mill Creek, this lovely spot for a picnic has 10 tables and is open year-round. It's also close to the Hollowell Park and Mill Creek Basin Trailheads. ⊠ *Off Bear Lake Rd., about 2½ miles from Moraine Park Visitor Center.*

FAMILY **Sprague Lake.** With 27 tables and 16 pedestal grills, there's plenty of room for the whole gang at this alfresco dining spot. It's open year-round, with flush toilets in the summer and vault toilets the rest of the year. ⌧ *About ½ mile from intersection of Bear Lake Rd. and U.S. 36, 4 miles from Bear Lake.*

OUTSIDE THE PARK

ESTES PARK

33

$ ✕**Bighorn Restaurant.** An Estes Park staple since 1972, this family-run
AMERICAN outfit is where the locals go for breakfast. Try a double-cheese omelet,
FAMILY *huevos rancheros*, or grits before heading into the park in the morning. The owners are happy to pack a lunch for you—just place your order along with breakfast, and it will be ready when you leave. This homey spot also serves lunch and dinner, with specialties such as house-smoked pulled pork, housemade meatballs, and rib eye cut on-site. Expect a wait in the summer. ⑤ *Average main: $12* ⌧ *401 W. Elkhorn Ave., Estes Park* ☎ *970/586–2792* ⊕ *www.estesparkbighorn.com.*

$$ ✕**Ed's Cantina & Grill.** The fajitas and well-stocked bar make this lively
MEXICAN Mexican restaurant popular with locals and visitors alike. The decor
FAMILY is bright, with light woods and large windows. When the sun is shining, ask for patio seating by the river. If you're hungry, try one of the enchilada platters (choose from bison, chicken mole, or vegetarian) or *carne asada*. The fish and bison tacos are other popular options. ⑤ *Average main: $13* ⌧ *390 E. Elkhorn Ave., Estes Park* ☎ *970/586–2919.*

$ ✕**Estes Park Brewery.** If you want to sample some local brews, check out
AMERICAN the Estes Park Brewery, which has been crafting beer since 1993. Not sure what you will like? Head downstairs to the tasting area to sample a variety of brews on tap. The Stinger Wild Honey Wheat is the most popular, while the Bear Lake Blueberry Wheat has a hint of blueberries and is served with fruit in the glass. The food is no-frills (beer chili is the specialty), and the menu includes things like pizza, burgers, sandwiches, and house-made bratwurst. After eating, you can amuse yourself at the pool table or video games. ⑤ *Average main: $11* ⌧ *470 Prospect Village Dr., Estes Park* ☎ *970/586–5421* ⊕ *www.epbrewery.com.*

$ ✕**Poppy's Pizza & Grill.** This casual riverside eatery serves creative signa-
PIZZA ture pizzas. Try the spinach, artichoke, and feta pie made with sundried
FAMILY tomato pesto. You can also create your own pie from five sauces and nearly 40 toppings. Other options include sandwiches, wraps, salads, and burgers. Poppy's has patio seating at the river and an extensive selection of beer. ⑤ *Average main: $10* ⌧ *342 E. Elkhorn Ave., Estes Park* ☎ *970/586–8282* ⊕ *www.poppyspizzaandgrill.com* ⊗ *Closed Jan.* ⚲ *Reservations not accepted.*

GRAND LAKE

$ ✕**Fat Cat Cafe.** Located on the boardwalk, this cozy family-run café
CAFÉ specializes in delicious breakfast and lunch at reasonable prices. The
Fodor's Choice friendly owners serve up hearty helpings, as well as advice on local
★ sightseeing. The $14.50 ($7.95 for kids) weekend breakfast buffet is downright amazing, with nearly 50 items—including biscuits and gravy, *huevos rancheros* casserole with house-made green chili sauce, and a

wide selection of scones, pastries, and pies that are baked in-house. If you have to wait for a table (which you might on a summer Sunday), Fat Cat offers coffee and cinnamon rolls to tide you over. $ *Average main: $10* ⊠ *916 Grand Ave., Grand Lake* ☎ *970/627–0900* ⊗ *Closed Tues. No dinner.*

$
SOUTHERN
Fodor'sChoice
★

✕ **Sagebrush BBQ & Grill.** Falling-off-the-bone, melt-in-your-mouth barbecue pork, chicken, and beef draw local and out-of-town attention to this homey café. You can munch on peanuts (and toss the shells on the floor) while dining at tables with cowhide-patterned tablecloths set against a backdrop of license plates from across the country. Comforting sides such as baked beans, corn bread, coleslaw, and potatoes top off the large plates. The breakfast menu includes omelets, pancakes, eggs Benedict, and biscuits, as well as chicken-fried steak and *huevos rancheros* platters for heartier appetites. Dinner reservations are recommended on summer weekends. $ *Average main: $12* ⊠ *1101 Grand Ave., Grand Lake* ☎ *970/627–1404* ⊕ *www.sagebrushbbq.com.*

WHERE TO STAY

OUTSIDE THE PARK

ESTES PARK

$$$$
HOTEL

Boulder Brook. Watch elk stroll past your spacious luxury suite at this smart, secluded spot on the river amid towering pines, just 2 miles from Rocky Mountain National Park. **Pros:** scenic location; quiet area; attractive grounds. **Cons:** not within walking distance of attractions; no nearby dining. $ *Rooms from: $250* ⊠ *1900 Fall River Rd., Estes Park* ☎ *970/586–0910, 800/238–0910* ⊕ *www.boulderbrook.com* ⌁ *20 suites* ⍾ *No meals.*

$$$$
RESORT
FAMILY

C Lazy U Guest Ranch. Secluded in a broad, verdant valley, this deluxe dude ranch offers a smorgasbord of activites as well as plush, Western-style accommodations with wood-paneled walls, beautiful furnishings, and bathrooms with copper sinks and custom vanities. **Pros:** kid- and family-friendly; helpful staff; deluxe in every respect. **Cons:** distant from other area attractions; no pets; very expensive. $ *Rooms from: $3000* ⊠ *3640 Hwy. 125, Granby* ✛ *3½ miles north on Hwy. 125 from U.S. 40 junction* ☎ *970/887–3344* ⊕ *www.clazyu.com* ⌁ *43 rooms, 1 private house* ⍾ *All-inclusive.*

$$
RESORT
FAMILY

Glacier Lodge. Families are the specialty at this secluded, 22-acre guest resort on the banks of the Big Thompson River. **Pros:** great place for families; attractive grounds on the river; on free bus route. **Cons:** not within walking distance of attractions; along rather busy road. $ *Rooms from: $160* ⊠ *2166 Hwy. 66, Estes Park* ☎ *800/523–3920* ⊕ *www.glacierlodge.com* ⊗ *Closed Nov.–Apr.* ⌁ *22 single-family cabins, 4 cabins for 12–30, 2 sleeping rooms* ⍾ *No meals.*

$$
HOTEL

The Historic Mary's Lake Lodge. The sound of a baby grand piano greets you in the lobby of this 1913 chalet-style lodge, which sits at the base of Rams Horn Mountain and overlooks peaceful Mary's Lake, a few miles south of town. **Pros:** historic charm; beautiful views. **Cons:** not within walking distance of attractions or other dining; large, older

Best Campgrounds in Rocky Mountain

CLOSE UP

33

The park's five campgrounds accommodate campers looking to stay in a tent, trailer, or RV (only three campgrounds accept reservations—up to six months in advance at ⊕ *www.recreation.gov* or ⊕ *www.reserveamerica.com*; the others fill up on a first-come, first-served basis).

Aspenglen Campground. This quiet, eastside spot near the north entrance is set in open pine woodland along Fall River. There are a few excellent walk-in sites for those who want to pitch a tent away from the crowds but still be close to the car. Reservations are recommended in summer. ⊠ *Drive past Fall River Visitor Center on U.S. 34 and turn left at the campground road.*

Glacier Basin Campground. This spot offers expansive views of the Continental Divide, easy access to the free summer shuttles to Bear Lake and Estes Park, and ranger-led evening programs in the summer. Reservations are essential. ⊠ *Drive 5 miles south on Bear Lake Rd. from U.S. 36* ☎ *877/444–6777.*

Longs Peak Campground. Open May to November, this campgound is only a short walk from the Longs Peak trailhead, making it a favorite among hikers looking to get an early start there. The tent-only sites, which are first come, first served, are limited to eight people; firewood, lighting fluid,

and charcoal are sold in summer. ⊠ *9 miles south of Estes Park on Rte. 7.*

Moraine Park Campground. The only campground in Rocky Mountain open year-round, this spot connects to many hiking trails and has easy access to the free summer shuttles. Rangers lead evening programs in the summer. You'll hear elk bugling if you camp here in September or October. Reservations are essential from mid-May to late September. ⊠ *Drive south on Bear Lake Rd. from U.S. 36, 1 mile to campground entrance.*

Timber Creek Campground. Anglers love this spot on the Colorado River, 10 miles from Grand Lake village and the only east-side campground. In the evening you can sit in on ranger-led campfire programs. The 98 campsites are first come, first served. ⊠ *1 Trail Ridge Rd., 2 miles west of Alpine Visitor Center.*

Backcountry Camping, Rocky Mountain National Park. Experienced hikers can camp at one of the park's many designated backcountry sites with advance reservations or a day-of-trip permit (which comes with a $26 fee in May through October). Contact the Backcountry Permits office before starting out to get a sense of current conditions. ⊠ *Beaver Meadows Visitor Center, Kawuneeche Visitor Center* ☎ *970/586–1242.*

---

hotel. $ *Rooms from: $149* ⊠ *2625 Mary's Lake Rd., Estes Park* ☎ *970/586–5958, 877/442–6279* ⊕ *www.maryslakelodge.com* ⤶ *13 rooms, 3 suites* ❏| *No meals.*

$$
HOTEL
🏨 **Riverview Pines.** Cast a line for stocked brown and rainbow trout, watch widlife visit the river's edge, or just sit and read on the expansive lawn at this peaceful property, the best value along beautiful Fall River Road between Estes and Rocky Mountain National Park. **Pros:** friendly and helpful owner-managers; quiet and scenic location on river;

low rates for the area. **Cons:** very basic rooms without much decoration; on a busy road. $ *Rooms from: $135* ⊠ *1150 W. Elkhorn Ave., Estes Park* ☎ *970/586–3627* ⊕ *www.riverviewpines.com* ⤳ *12 rooms, 8 cabins* ⊘ *No meals.*

$$$$
HOTEL
Fodor'sChoice
★

☷ **Stanley Hotel.** Perched regally on a hill, with a commanding view of town, the Stanley is one of Colorado's great old hotels, featuring Georgian colonial–style architecture and a storied, haunted history that includes being the inspiration for Stephen King's novel *The Shining.* **Pros:** historic hotel; many rooms have been updated; good restaurant. **Cons:** some rooms are small and tight; building is old; no air-conditioning. $ *Rooms from: $279* ⊠ *333 Wonderview Ave., Estes Park* ☎ *970/577–4000, 800/976–1377* ⊕ *www.stanleyhotel.com* ⤳ *150 rooms, 10 suites, 18 condos* ⊘ *No meals.*

$$
RESORT
FAMILY

☷ **YMCA of the Rockies – Estes Park Center.** Established in 1907—eight years before Rocky Mountain National Park—this 860-acre family-friendly property abuts the park and has an abundance of attractive, clean lodging options among its nine lodges and 217 cabins. **Pros:** good value for large groups and longer stays; lots of family-oriented activities and amenities; stunning scenery. **Cons:** very large, busy, and crowded property; fills fast; location requires vehicle to visit town or the national park. $ *Rooms from: $129* ⊠ *2515 Tunnel Rd., Estes Park* ☎ *970/586–3341, 888/613–9622 family reservations, 800/777–9622 group reservations* ⊕ *www.ymcarockies.org* ⤳ *553 rooms, 217 cabins* ⊘ *Some meals.*

GRAND LAKE

$
HOTEL
Fodor'sChoice
★

☷ **Historic Rapids Lodge & Restaurant.** This handsome lodgepole-pine structure, which dates to 1915, is tucked on the banks of the Tonahutu River, and gives guests a dose of history amid a natural setting. **Pros:** in-house restaurant; condos are great for longer stays; quiet area of town. **Cons:** unpaved parking area; lodge rooms are above restaurant; all lodge rooms are on second floor and there's no elevator. $ *Rooms from: $95* ⊠ *210 Rapids La., Grand Lake* ☎ *970/627–3707* ⊕ *www.rapidslodge.com* ⊘ *Closed Apr. and Nov.* ⤳ *6 rooms, 9 suites, 4 cabins, 12 condos* ⊘ *No meals.*

$
HOTEL
FAMILY

☷ **Mountain Lakes Lodge.** Families and dog-lovers enjoy these comfortable, charming, whimsically decorated log cabins, which have such unique touches as cow-spotted walls, canoe-paddle headboards, and wooden ducks swimming on the ceiling. **Pros:** dog-friendly; close to fishing; good value. **Cons:** outside of town (and services); two-night minimum; no daily housekeeping. $ *Rooms from: $99* ⊠ *10480 U.S. 34, Grand Lake* ☎ *970/627–8448* ⊕ *www.grandlakelodging.net* ⊘ *Closed for 10 days in Apr.* ⤳ *10 units, 2 houses* ⊘ *No meals.*

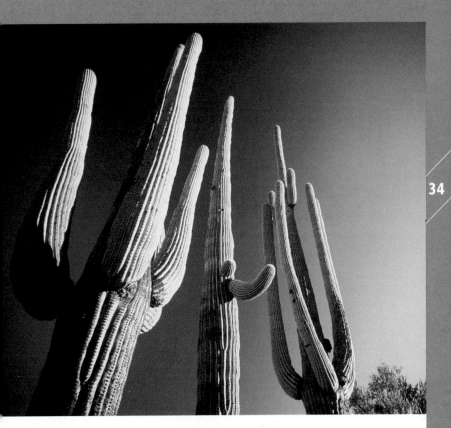

SAGUARO
NATIONAL PARK

WELCOME TO SAGUARO NATIONAL PARK

TOP REASONS TO GO

★ **Saguaro sightseeing:** Hike, bike, or drive through dense saguaro stands for an up-close look at this king of all cacti.

★ **Wildlife watching:** Diverse wildlife roams through the park, including such ground dwellers as javelinas, coyotes, and rattlesnakes, and winged residents ranging from the migratory lesser long-nosed bat to the diminutive elf owl.

★ **Ancient artwork:** Get a glimpse into the past at the numerous petroglyph rock-art sites where ancient peoples etched into the stones as far back as 5000 BC.

★ **Desert hiking:** Take a trek through the undisturbed and magical Sonoran Desert, and discover that it's more than cacti.

★ **Two districts, one park:** Split into two districts, the park offers a duo of separate experiences on opposite sides of Tucson.

1 Saguaro West: Tucson Mountain District. This popular district makes up less than one-third of the park. Here you'll find an American Indian video orientation to saguaros at the visitor center, hiking trails, an ancient Hohokam petroglyph site at Signal Hill, and a scenic drive through the park's densest desert growth.

ARIZONA

34

KEY

🏢	Ranger Station
⛺	Campground
🏕	Picnic Area
🍴	Restaurant
🏨	Lodge
🥾	Trailhead
🚻	Restrooms
⚞	Scenic Viewpoint
⋯⋯	Walking/Hiking Trails

2 Saguaro East: Rincon Mountain District. In the Rincon Mountains, Saguaro East encompasses nearly 60,000 acres of designated wilderness area, an easily accessible scenic loop drive, several easy and intermediate trails through the cactus forest, and opportunities for adventure and backcountry camping at six rustic campgrounds.

3 Rincon Valley Area. This roughly 4,000-acre expansion along the southern border of Saguaro's Rincon Mountain District offers access to the riparian area along Rincon Creek.

4 Saguaro Wilderness Area. In the Rincon Mountain District, this backcountry area travels from desert scrublands at 3,000 feet to mixed conifer forests at 9,000 feet.

GETTING ORIENTED

Saguaro National Park preserves some of the densest stands of these massive cacti, which can live up to 200 years and weigh up to 2 tons. Today more than 90,000 acres include habitats stretching from the arid Sonoran Desert up to high mountain forests. The park is split into two sections, with Tucson, Arizona, sandwiched in the middle. The urban base proves useful, but the park is no less rugged. More than half of it is designated wilderness area.

Updated by
Mara Levin
And Elise Riley

Standing sentinel in the desert, the towering saguaro is perhaps the most familiar emblem of the Southwest. Known for their height (often 50 feet) and arms reaching out in weird configurations, these slow-growing giants can take 15 years to grow a foot high and up to 75 years to grow their first arm. A typical saguaro lives 150 years, but many survive more than 200 years. They are found only in the Sonoran Desert, and the largest concentration is in Saguaro National Park. In late spring (usually May), the succulent's top is covered with tiny white blooms—the Arizona state flower. The cacti are protected by state and federal laws, so don't disturb them.

SAGUARO PLANNER

WHEN TO GO

Saguaro never gets crowded; however, most people visit in milder weather, October through April. December through February can be cool, and are likely to see gentle rain showers. The spring days from March through May are bright and sunny with wildflowers in bloom. Because of high temperatures, from June through September it's best to visit the park in the early morning or late afternoon. The intense summer heat puts off most hikers, at least at lower elevations, but lodging prices are much cheaper—rates at top resorts in Tucson drop by as much as 70%. Cooler temperatures return in October and November, providing perfect weather for hiking and camping throughout the park.

AVG. HIGH/LOW TEMPS.

Jan.	Feb.	Mar.	Apr.	May	June
63/38	66/40	72/44	80/50	89/57	98/67

July	Aug.	Sept.	Oct.	Nov.	Dec.
98/73	96/72	93/67	84/57	72/45	65/39

PLANNING YOUR TIME

SAGUARO IN ONE DAY

Before setting off, choose which section of the park to visit and pack a lunch (there's no food service in either park district). Also bring plenty of water—you're likely to get dehydrated in the dry climate—or purchase a reusable bottle at the visitor center (there are water stations in both districts of the park).

In the western section, start out by watching the 15-minute video at the **Red Hills Visitor Center,** then stroll along the 0.5-mile-long **Desert Discovery Trail.**

Drive north along Kinney Road, then turn right onto the graded dirt **Bajada Loop Drive.** Before long you'll see a turnoff for the **Hugh Norris Trail** on your right. If you're game for a steep 45-minute hike uphill, this trail leads to a perfect spot for a picnic. Hike back down and drive along the Bajada Loop Drive until you reach the turnoff for **Signal Hill.** From here it's a short walk to the **Hohokam petroglyphs.**

Alternatively, in the eastern section, pick up a free map of the hiking trails at the **Rincon Mountain Visitor Center.** Drive south along the paved **Cactus Forest Drive** to the Javelina picnic area, where you'll see signs for the **Freeman Homestead Trail,** an easy 1-mile loop that winds through a stand of mesquite as interpretive signs describe early inhabitants in the Tucson basin. If you're up for more difficult hiking, you might want to tackle part of the **Tanque Verde Ridge Trail,** which affords excellent views of saguaro-studded hillsides.

Along the northern loop of Cactus Forest Drive is **Cactus Forest Trail,** which branches off into several fairly level paths. You can easily spend the rest of the afternoon strolling among the saguaros.

GETTING HERE AND AROUND

Both districts of Saguaro National Park are approximately a 30-minute drive from the Tucson International Airport.

Both districts are about a half-hour drive from central Tucson. To reach Rincon Mountain District (east section) from Interstate 10, take Exit 275, then go north on Houghton Road for 10 miles. Turn right on Escalante and left onto Old Spanish Trail, and the park will be on the right side. If you're coming from town, go east on Speedway Boulevard to Houghton Road. Turn right on Houghton and left onto Old Spanish Trail.

To reach the Tucson Mountain District (west section) from Interstate 10, take Exit 242 or Exit 257, then go west on Speedway Boulevard (the name will change to Gates Pass Road), follow it to Kinney Road, and turn right.

34

As there's no public transportation to or within Saguaro, a car is a necessity. In the western section, Bajada Loop Drive takes you through the park and to various trailheads; Cactus Forest Drive does the same for the eastern section.

PARK ESSENTIALS

PARK FEES AND PERMITS

Admission to Saguaro is $10 per vehicle and $5 for individuals on foot or bicycle; it's good for seven days from purchase at both park districts. Annual passes cost $25. For camping at one of the primitive campsites in the east district (the closest campsite is 6 miles from the trailhead), obtain a required backcountry permit for $6 nightly from the Rincon Mountain Visitor Center up to two months in advance.

PARK HOURS

The park opens at sunrise and closes at sunset every day but Christmas day. It's in the Mountain time zone. The visitor center is open daily from 9 am to 5 pm.

CELL-PHONE RECEPTION

Cell-phone reception is generally good in the eastern district but is unreliable in the western district. The visitor centers have pay phones.

EDUCATIONAL OFFERINGS

Orientation Programs. Daily programs at both park districts introduce visitors to the desert. You might find presentations on bats, birds, or desert blooms, and naturalist-led hikes (including moonlight hikes). Check online or call for the current week's activities. ⊠ *Rincon Mountain and Red Hills visitor centers* ☎ *520/733–5100* ⊕ *nps.gov/sagu* ⬚ *Free.*

RANGER PROGRAMS

FAMILY **Junior Ranger Program.** In the Junior Ranger Discovery program, young visitors can pick up an activity pack any time of the year at either visitor center and complete it within an hour or two. There also are daylong camps for kids ages 5 through 12 in the east district. ⊠ *Rincon Mountain and Red Hills visitor centers* ☎ *520/733–5100* ⊕ *nps.gov/sagu.*

Ranger Talks. The assortment of talks by national park rangers are a great way to hear about wildlife, geology, and archaeology. ⊠ *Rincon Mountain and Red Hills visitor centers* ☎ *520/733–5100* ⬚ *Free* ☽ *Nov.–Apr.*

RESTAURANTS

At Saguaro, you won't find more than a sampling of Southwest jams, hot sauces, and candy bars at the two visitor centers' gift shops. Vending machines outside sell bottled water and soda, but pack some lunch for a picnic if you don't want to drive all the way back into town. Five picnic areas in the west district, and two in the east, offer scenery and shade. However, the city of Tucson, sandwiched neatly between the two park districts, offers some of the best Mexican cuisine in the country. A genuine college town, Tucson also has excellent upscale Southwestern cuisine, as well as good sushi, Thai, Italian, and Ethiopian food.

HOTELS

Although there are no hotels within the park, its immediate proximity to Tucson makes finding a place to stay easy. A couple of B&Bs are a short drive from the park. Some ranches and smaller accommodations close during the hottest months of summer, but many inexpensive B&Bs and hotels are open year-round, and offer significantly lower rates from late May through August. *Hotel reviews have been shortened. For full information, visit Fodors.com.*

WHAT IT COSTS			
$	**$$**	**$$$**	**$$$$**
Restaurants	under $13	$13–$20	$21–$30	over $30
Hotels	under $101	$101–$150	$151–$200	over $200

Restaurant prices are the average cost of a main course at dinner, or if dinner is not served, at lunch. Hotel prices are the lowest cost of a standard double room in high season.

34

VISITOR INFORMATION

Park Contact Information Saguaro National Park. ⊠ *3693 S. Old Spanish Trail, Tucson* ☎ *520/733–5158 for Saguaro West, 520/733–5153 for Saguaro East* ⊕ *www.nps.gov/sagu.*

VISITOR CENTERS

The visitor centers in both districts have orientation slide shows and rangers who can answer your questions, as well as loads of books and maps. Both sell bottled water and soda.

Red Hills Visitor Center. Take in gorgeous views of nearby mountains and the surrounding desert from the center's large windows and shaded outdoor terrace. A spacious gallery is filled with educational exhibits, and a lifelike display simulates the flora and fauna of the region. A 15-minute slide show, "Voices of the Desert," provides a poetic, Native American perspective on the Saguaro. Park rangers and volunteers hand out maps and suggest hikes to suit your interests. The gift shop sells books, trinkets, a few local items like honey and prickly-pear jellies, and reusable water bottles that you can fill at water stations outside. ⊠ *2700 N. Kinney Rd., Saguaro West* ☎ *520/733–5158* ⊕ *www.nps. gov/sagu* ☉ *Daily 9–5.*

Rincon Mountain Visitor Center. Stop here to pick up free maps and printed materials on various aspects of the park, including maps of hiking trails and backcountry camping permits (Red Hills Visitor Center, in Saguaro West, does not offer permits). Exhibits at the center are comprehensive, and a relief map of the park lays out the complexities of this protected landscape. Two 20-minute slide shows explain the botanical and cultural history of the region, and there is a short self-guided nature walk along the paved Cactus Garden Trail. A small, select variety of books and other gift items, along with energy bars, beef jerky, and refillable water bottles, are sold here. ⊠ *3693 S. Old Spanish Trail, Saguaro East* ☎ *520/733–5153* ⊕ *www.nps.gov/sagu* ☉ *Daily 9–5.*

EXPLORING

SCENIC DRIVES

Unless you're ready for a long desert hike, the best way to see Saguaro is from the comfort of your car.

Bajada Loop Drive. This 6-mile drive winds through thick stands of saguaros and past two picnic areas and trailheads to a few short hikes, including one to a petroglyph site. Although the road is unpaved and somewhat bumpy, it's a worthwhile trade-off for access to some of the park's densest desert growth. It's one-way between Hugh Norris Trail and Golden Gate Road, so if you want to make the complete circuit, travel counterclockwise. The road is susceptible to flash floods during the monsoon season (July and August), so check road conditions at the visitor center before proceeding. This loop route is also popular among bicyclists, and dogs on leash are permitted along the road. ⊠ *Saguaro West.*

Cactus Forest Drive. This paved 8-mile drive provides a great overview of all Saguaro East has to offer. The one-way road, which circles clockwise, has several turnouts with roadside displays that make it easy to pull over and admire the scenery; you can also stop at two picnic areas and three easy nature trails. This is a good bicycling route as well, but watch out for snakes and javelinas crossing in front of you. This road is open from 7 am to sunset daily. ⊠ *Cactus Forest Dr., Saguaro East.*

HISTORIC SITES

Manning Camp. The summer home of Levi Manning, onetime Tucson mayor, was a popular gathering spot for the city's elite in the early 1900s. The cabin can be reached only on foot or horseback via one of several challenging high-country trails: Douglas Spring Trail to Cow Head Saddle Trail (12 miles), Turkey Creek Trail (7.5 miles), or Tanque Verde Ridge Trail (15.4 miles). The cabin itself is not open for viewing. ⊠ *Saguaro East* ✛ *Douglas Spring Trail (6 miles) to Cow Head Saddle Trail (6 miles).*

SCENIC STOPS

FAMILY **Signal Hill.** The most impressive petroglyphs, and the only ones with explanatory signs, are on the Bajada Loop Drive in Saguaro West. An easy five-minute stroll from the signposted parking area takes you to one of the largest concentrations of rock carvings in the Southwest. You'll have a close-up view of the designs left by the Hohokam people between AD 900 and 1200, including large spirals some believe are astronomical markers. ⊠ *Bajada Loop Dr., Saguaro West* ✛ *4½ miles north of visitor center.*

Plants and Wildlife in Saguaro

The saguaro may be the centerpiece of Saguaro National Park, but more than 1,200 plant species, including 50 types of cactus, thrive in the park. Among the most common cacti here are the prickly pear, barrel cactus, and teddy bear cholla—so named because it appears cuddly, but rangers advise packing a comb to pull its barbed hooks from unwary fingers.

For many of the desert fauna, the saguaro functions as a high-rise hotel. Each spring the Gila woodpecker and gilded flicker create holes in the cactus and then nest there. When they give up their temporary digs, elf owls, cactus wrens, sparrow hawks,

and other birds move in, as do dangerous Africanized honeybees.

You may not encounter any of the park's six species of rattlesnake or the Gila monster, a venomous lizard, but avoid sticking your hands or feet under rocks or into crevices. Look where you're walking; if you do get bitten, get to a clinic or hospital as soon as possible. Not all snakes pass on venom; 50% of the time the bite is "dry" (nonpoisonous).

Wildlife, from bobcats to jackrabbits, is most active in early morning and at dusk. In spring and summer, lizards and snakes are out and about but tend to keep a low profile during the midday heat.

34

SPORTS AND THE OUTDOORS

BICYCLING

TOURS AND OUTFITTERS

Fair Wheel Bikes. Mountain bikes and road bikes can be rented by the day or week here. The company also organizes group rides of varying difficulty. ✉ *1110 E. 6th St., University* ☎ *520/884–9018* ⊕ *fairwheelbikes.com.*

BIRD-WATCHING

To check out the more than 200 species of birds living in or migrating through the park, begin by focusing your binoculars on the limbs of the saguaros, where many birds make their home. In general, early morning and early evening are the best times for sightings. In winter and spring, volunteer-led birding hikes begin at the visitor centers.

The finest areas to flock to in Saguaro East (the Rincon Mountain District) are the Desert Ecology Trail, where you may find rufous-winged sparrows, verdins, and Cooper's hawks along the washes, and the Javelina picnic area, where you'll most likely spot canyon wrens and black-chinned sparrows. At Saguaro West (the Tucson Mountain District), sit down on one of the visitor center benches and look for ash-throated flycatchers, Say's phoebes, curve-billed thrashers, and Gila woodpeckers. During the cooler months, keep a lookout for wintering neotropical migrants such as hummingbirds, swallows, orioles, and warblers.

A saguaro grows under the protection of another tree, such as a paloverde or mesquite, before superseding it.

TOURS

Borderland Tours. Bird-watching tours throughout the state and internationally are led by this company, whose owner, Richard Taylor, has written several photo field guides, including *Birds of Southeastern Arizona.* Seven-day tours of Southeastern Arizona include all meals, accommodations, and transportation from Tucson. ✉ *2550 W. Calle Padilla, Northwest* ☎ *520/882–7650* ⊕ *www.borderland-tours.com* ✉ *From $2,195 for a 7-day tour of Southeastern Arizona.*

Wild Bird Store. This shop is an excellent resource for birding information, feeders, books, and trail guides. Free bird walks are offered most Sundays. ✉ *3160 E. Fort Lowell Rd., Central* ☎ *520/322–9466* ⊕ *www.wildbirdsonline.com.*

Wings. This elite Tucson-based company leads ornithological expeditions worldwide and locally. Its Southern Arizona tours—sighting owls, hawks, warblers, hummingbirds, and more—have a maximum group size of seven and range from eight to 10 days. ✉ *Tucson* ☎ *520/320–9868, 866/547–9868* ⊕ *www.wingsbirds.com* ✉ *From $2,400.*

HIKING

The park has more than 100 miles of trails. The shorter hikes, such as the Desert Discovery and Desert Ecology trails, are perfect for those looking to learn about the desert ecosystem without expending too much energy.

■ TIP→ Rattlesnakes are commonly seen on trails; so are coyotes, javelinas, roadrunners, Gambel's quail, and desert spiny lizards. Hikers should keep their distance from all wildlife.

SAGUARO WEST

EASY

FAMILY **Desert Discovery Trail.** Learn about plants and animals native to the region on this paved path in Saguaro West. The 0.5-mile loop is wheelchair accessible, and has resting benches and ramadas (wooden shelters that supply shade). Dogs on leash are permitted here. *Easy.* ✛ *Trailhead: 1 mile north of Red Hills Visitor Center.*

Signal Hill Trail. This ¼-mile trail in Saguaro West is a simple, rewarding ascent to ancient petroglyphs carved a millennium ago by the Hohokam people. *Easy.* ✛ *Trailhead: 4½ miles north of Red Hills Visitor Center on Bajada Loop Dr.*

MODERATE

Sendero Esperanza Trail. Follow a sandy mine road for the first section of this 6-mile trail in Saguaro West, then ascend via a series of switchbacks to the top of a ridge and cross the Hugh Norris Trail. Descending on the other side, you'll meet up with the King Canyon Trail. The Esperanza ("Hope") Trail is often rocky and sometimes steep, but rewards include ruins of the Gould Mine, dating back to 1907. *Moderate.* ✛ *Trailhead: 1½ miles east of the intersection of Bajada Loop Dr. and Golden Gate Rd.*

Sweetwater Trail. Though technically within Saguaro West, this trail is on the eastern edge of the district, and affords access to Wasson Peak from the eastern side of the Tucson Mountains. After gradually climbing 3.4 miles, it ends at King Canyon Trail (which would then take you on a fairly steep 1.2-mile climb to Wasson Peak). Long and meandering, this little-used trail allows more privacy to enjoy the natural surroundings than some of the more frequently used trails. *Moderate.* ✛ *Trailhead: western end of El Camino del Cerro Rd.*

Valley View Overlook Trail. On clear days you can spot the distinctive slope of Picacho Peak from this 1.5-mile trail in Saguaro West. Even on an overcast day there are splendid vistas of Avra Valley. *Moderate.* ✛ *Trailhead: 3 miles north of Red Hills Visitor Center on Bajada Loop Dr.*

DIFFICULT

Fodor's Choice **Hugh Norris Trail.** This 10-mile trail through the Tucson Mountains is
★ one of the most impressive in the Southwest. It's full of switchbacks, and some sections are moderately steep, but the top of 4,687-foot Wasson Peak treats you to views of the saguaro forest spread across the *bajada* (the gently rolling hills at the base of taller mountains). *Difficult.* ✛ *Trailhead: 2½ miles north of Red Hills Visitor Center on Bajada Loop Dr.*

King Canyon Trail. This 3.5-mile trail is the shortest, but steepest, route to the top of Wasson Peak in Saguaro West. It meets the Hugh Norris Trail less than half a mile from the summit. The trail, which begins across from the Arizona–Sonora Desert Museum, is named after the Copper King Mine. It leads past many scars from the search for mineral

34

wealth. Look for petroglyphs in this area. *Difficult.* ✛ *Trailhead: 2 miles south of Red Hills Visitor Center.*

SAGUARO EAST

EASY

Cactus Forest Trail. This 2.5-mile one-way loop in Saguaro East is open to pedestrians, bicyclists, and equestrians. It is a moderately easy walk along a dirt path that passes historic lime kilns and a wide variety of Sonoran Desert vegetation. While walking this trail, keep in mind that it is one of the only off-road trails for bicyclists. *Moderate.* ✉ *Saguaro East* ✛ *Trailhead: 2 miles south of Rincon Mountain Visitor Center, off Cactus Forest Dr.*

Cactus Garden Trail. This 100-yard paved trail in front of the Rincon Mountain Visitor Center is wheelchair accessible and has resting benches and interpretive signs about common desert plants. *Easy.* ✛ *Trailhead: next to Rincon Mountain Visitor Center.*

FAMILY **Desert Ecology Trail.** Exhibits on this ¼-mile loop near the Mica View picnic area explain how local plants and animals subsist on limited water. *Easy.* ✛ *Trailhead: 2 miles north of Rincon Mountain Visitor Center.*

Freeman Homestead Trail. Learn a bit about the history of homesteading in the region on this 1-mile loop. Look for owls living in the cliffs above as you make your way through the lowland vegetation. *Easy.* ✛ *Trailhead: next to Javelina picnic area, 2 miles south of Rincon Mountain Visitor Center.*

MODERATE

Douglas Spring Trail. This challenging 6-mile trail, steep in some parts, leads almost due east into the Rincon Mountains. After a half mile through a dense concentration of saguaros, you reach the open desert. About 3 miles in is Bridal Wreath Falls, worth a slight detour in spring when melting snow creates a larger cascade. Blackened tree trunks at the Douglas Spring Campground are one of the few traces of a huge fire that swept through the area in 1989. *Moderate.* ✛ *Trailhead: eastern end of Speedway Blvd.*

Fodor's Choice **Hope Camp Trail.** Well worth the 5-mile round-trip trek, this Rincon
★ Valley Area route rewards hikers with gorgeous views of the Tanque Verde Ridge and Rincon Peak. The trail is also open to mountain bicyclists. *Moderate.* ✛ *Trailhead: from Camino Loma Alta trailhead to Hope Camp.*

DIFFICULT

Tanque Verde Ridge Trail. Be rewarded with spectacular scenery on this 18-mile round-trip trail that takes you through desert scrub, oak, alligator juniper, and pinyon pine at the 6,000-foot peak, where views of

GOOD READS

■ The *Tucson Hiking Guide*, by Betty Leavengood, is a useful and entertaining book with day hikes in the park.

■ Books that give a general introduction to the park include *Saguaro National Park*, by Doris Evans, and *Sonoran Desert: The Story Behind the Scenery*, by Christopher L. Helms.

■ *All About Saguaros*, by Carle Hodge and published by Arizona Highways Books, includes fabulous color photos of the cactus.

the surrounding mountain ranges from both sides of the ridge delight. *Difficult.* ✛ *Trailhead: Javelina picnic area, 2 miles south of Red Hills Visitor Center.*

WHAT'S NEARBY

NEARBY TOWNS

Saguaro stands as a protected desert oasis, with metropolitan **Tucson,** Arizona's second-largest city, lying between the two park sections. Spread over 227 miles, and with a population of nearly a half million, Tucson averages 340 days of sunshine a year.

34

NEARBY ATTRACTIONS

FAMILY **Arizona–Sonora Desert Museum.** The name "museum" is a bit misleading, Fodor'sChoice since this delightful site is actually a zoo, aquarium, and botanical gar-★ den featuring the animals, plants, and even fish of the Sonoran Desert. Hummingbirds, coatis, rattlesnakes, scorpions, bighorn sheep, bobcats, and Mexican wolves all busy themselves in ingeniously designed habitats.

An Earth Sciences Center has an artificial limestone cave to climb through and an excellent mineral display. The coyote and javelina (a wild, piglike mammal with an oddly oversize head) exhibits have "invisible" fencing that separates humans from animals, and at the Raptor Free Flight show (October through April, daily at 10 and 2), you can see the powerful birds soar and dive, untethered, inches above your head.

The restaurants are above average, and the gift shop, which carries books, jewelry, and crafts, is outstanding. ■TIP➔ **June through August, the museum stays open until 10 pm every Saturday, which provides a great opportunity to see nocturnal critters.** ✉ *2021 N. Kinney Rd., Westside* ☎ *520/883–2702* ⊕ *www.desertmuseum.org* 🖃 *$19.50* ☽ *Mar.–Sept., daily 7:30–5; Oct.–Feb., daily 8:30–5.*

FAMILY **Bear Canyon Trail.** Also known as Seven Falls Trail, this route in Sabino Fodor'sChoice Canyon is a three- to four-hour, 7.8-mile round-trip that is moderately ★ easy and fun, crossing the stream several times on the way up the canyon. Be sure to bring plenty of water. Kids enjoy the boulder-hopping, and all hikers are rewarded with pools and waterfalls as well as views at the top. The trailhead can be reached from the parking area by either taking a five-minute Bear Canyon Tram ride ($3) or walking the 1.8-mile tram route. *Moderate.* ✉ *Sabino Canyon Rd., at Sunrise Dr., Foothills* ☎ *520/749–2861* ⊕ *www.fs.usda.gov/coronado or www. sabinocanyon.com.*

FAMILY **Colossal Cave Mountain Park.** This limestone grotto 20 miles east of Tucson is the largest dry cavern in the world. Guides discuss the fascinating crystal formations and relate the many romantic tales surrounding the cave, including the legend that an enormous sum of money stolen in a stagecoach robbery is hidden here.

Forty-five-minute cave tours begin every 30 minutes and require a ½-mile walk and a climb of 363 steps. The park includes a ranch area with trail rides (from $30), a gemstone-sluicing area, a small museum, a desert tortoise habitat, nature trails, a butterfly garden, and a gift shop. Parking is $5 per vehicle. Take Broadway Boulevard or 22nd Street east to Old Spanish Trail. ⊠ *16721 E. Old Spanish Trail, Eastside* ☎ *520/647–7275* ⊕ *www.colossalcave.com* ⊠ *Cave tour $13* ☉ *Oct.– mid-Mar., daily 9–5; mid-Mar.–Sept., daily 8–5.*

FAMILY **Old Tucson.** This film studio–theme park, originally built for the 1940 motion picture *Arizona,* has been used to shoot countless movies, such as *Rio Bravo* (1959) and *The Quick and the Dead* (1994), and the TV shows *Gunsmoke, Bonanza,* and *Highway to Heaven.* Actors in Western garb perform and roam the streets talking to visitors.

Youngsters enjoy the simulated gunfights, rides, stunt shows, and petting farm, while adults might appreciate the screenings of old Westerns, studio tour, and the little-bit-bawdy Grand Palace Hotel's Dance Hall Revue. There are plenty of places to eat and to buy souvenirs. Horseback riding and stagecoach rides are available for an additional charge. ⊠ *Tucson Mountain Park, 201 S. Kinney Rd., Westside* ☎ *520/883– 0100* ⊕ *www.oldtucson.com* ⊠ *$17.95* ☉ *Hrs vary by season, typically daily 10–5; closed mid-Aug.–early Oct.*

St. Augustine Cathedral. Although the imposing white-and-beige, late-19th-century, Spanish-style building was modeled after the Cathedral of Queretaro in Mexico, a number of its details reflect the desert setting. For instance, above the entryway, next to a bronze statue of St. Augustine, are carvings of local desert scenes with saguaro cacti, yucca, and prickly pears—look closely and you'll find the horned toad. Compared with the magnificent facade, the modernized interior is a bit disappointing. Call for the schedule of English and Spanish masses. ■TIP➔ **For a distinctly Southwestern experience, attend the mariachi mass celebrated Sunday at 8 am.** ⊠ *192 S. Stone Ave., Downtown* ☎ *520/623–6351* ⊕ *cathedral-staugustine.org* ⊠ *Free* ☉ *Daily 9–5.*

AREA ACTIVITIES

SPORTS AND THE OUTDOORS
BALLOONING
Fleur de Tucson Balloon Tours. Operating out of Northwest Tucson from October through April, this company flies over the Tucson Mountains and Saguaro National Park West. Flights include photos as well as a Continental champagne brunch after you arrive back on the ground. Meet your balloon guide at a parking lot near Ina Road and Interstate 10. ⊠ *Northwest* ☎ *520/403–8547* ⊕ *www.fleurdetucson.net* ⊠ *From $275.*

WHERE TO EAT

IN THE PARK

PICNIC AREAS

Mam-A-Gah. This is the most isolated picnic area in Saguaro West. It's on King Canyon Trail, a good area for birding and wildflower viewing. It's about a mile walk to reach the site, and the undeveloped trail isn't wheelchair accessible. ⊠ *King Canyon Trail, Saguaro West.*

Mica View. Talk about truth in advertising: This picnic area gives you an eyeful of Mica Mountain, the park's highest peak. None of the tables are in the shade. ⊠ *Cactus Forest Dr., Saguaro East.*

Signal Hill. Because of the nearby petroglyphs, this is the park's most popular picnic site. Its many picnic tables, sprinkled around palo verde and mesquite trees, can accommodate large groups. ⊠ *Bajada Loop Dr., Saguaro West.*

OUTSIDE THE PARK

$ CAFÉ Fodor'sChoice ★

✕ **Beyond Bread.** Twenty-seven varieties of bread are made at this bustling bakery with Central, Eastside, and Northwest locations, and highlights from the menu of generous sandwiches include Annie's Addiction (hummus, tomato, sprouts, red onion, and cucumber) and Brad's Beef (roast beef, provolone, onion, green chilies, and Russian dressing); soups, salads, and breakfast items are equally scrumptious. Eat inside or on the patio, or order takeout, but either way, splurge on one of the incredible desserts. The other locations—larger and just as busy—are at 6260 East Speedway Boulevard and 421 West Ina Road. ⑤ *Average main: $8* ⊠ *3026 N. Campbell Ave., Central* ☎ *520/322–9965* ⊕ *www. beyondbread.com* ☉ *No dinner Sun.*

$$ MEXICAN Fodor'sChoice ★

✕ **Café Poca Cosa.** At what is arguably Tucson's most creative Mexican restaurant, the chef prepares recipes inspired by different regions of her native country. The menu, which changes daily, might include chicken mole or pork *pibil* (made with a tangy Yucatecan barbecue seasoning). Servings are plentiful, and each table gets a stack of warm corn tortillas and a bowl of beans to share. Order the daily Plato Poca Cosa, and the chef will select one beef, one chicken, and one vegetarian entrée for you to sample. The bold-color walls of the contemporary interior are hung with Latin American art. ⑤ *Average main: $18* ⊠ *110 E. Pennington St., Downtown* ☎ *520/622–6400* ⊕ *www.cafepocacosatucson.com* ☉ *Closed Sun. and Mon.* ⌲ *Reservations essential.*

$$$$ SOUTHWESTERN

✕ **The Grill at Hacienda del Sol.** Tucked into the foothills and surrounded by spectacular flowers and cactus gardens, this special-occasion restaurant, a favorite among locals hosting out-of-town visitors, provides an alternative to the chili-laden dishes of most Southwestern nouvelle cuisine. Wild-mushroom bisque, grilled buffalo in dark-chocolate mole, and pan-seared sea bass are among the menu choices at this luxurious guest ranch resort. Lower-priced tapas such as tequila-steamed mussels and carne asada tacos can be enjoyed on the more casual outdoor bar patio, accompanied by live flamenco guitar music on weekends.

34

The lavish Sunday brunch buffet is worth a splurge. $ *Average main: $32 ⊠ Hacienda del Sol Guest Ranch Resort, 5501 N. Hacienda Del Sol Rd., Foothills ☎ 520/529–3500 ⊕ www.haciendadelsol.com/dining/the-grill.htm.*

$ ✕ **Mi Nidito.** A perennial favorite among locals (the wait is worth it), Mi
MEXICAN   Nidito ("my little nest") has also hosted its share of visiting celebrities. Following President Clinton's lunch here, the rather hefty Presidential Plate (bean tostada, taco with barbecued meat, chiles rellenos, chicken enchilada, and beef tamale with rice and beans) was added to the menu. Top that off with the mango chimichangas for dessert, and you're talkin' executive privilege. $ *Average main: $10 ⊠ 1813 S. 4th Ave., South ☎ 520/622–5081 ⊕ www.minidito.net ۞ Closed Mon. and Tues.*

$$$$ ✕ **Vivace.** A nouvelle Italian bistro in a lovely Foothills setting, Vivace
ITALIAN   has long been a favorite with Tucsonans. Wild mushrooms and goat cheese in puff pastry is hard to resist as a starter. The fettuccine with grilled salmon is a nice, lighter alternative to such entrées as a rich osso buco. For dessert, the molten chocolate cake with spumoni is worth the 20 minutes it takes to create. Patio seating, with either city or mountain views, is especially inviting on warm evenings. $ *Average main: $32 ⊠ 6440 N. Campbell Ave., Foothills ☎ 520/795–7221 ⊕ www.vivacetucson.com ۞ Closed Sun.*

$ ✕ **Zinburger.** Have a glass of wine or a cocktail with your gourmet burger
AMERICAN and fries at this high-energy, somewhat noisy, and unquestionably hip burger joint. Zinburger delivers tempting burgers—try the Kobe beef with cheddar and wild mushrooms—and decadent milk shakes made of exotic combinations like dates and honey or melted chocolate with praline flakes. A few creative salads, including one with ahi tuna, round out the menu. The restaurant also has a second location on the northeast side of town. $ *Average main: $10 ⊠ 1865 E. River Rd., Foothills ☎ 520/299–7799 ⊕ www.foxrc.com.*

WHERE TO STAY

OUTSIDE THE PARK

$$$$ ☐ **Arizona Inn.** Although near the university and many sights, the beauti-
HOTEL   fully landscaped lawns and gardens of this 1930 inn seem far from the
Fodor'sChoice hustle and bustle. **Pros:** unique historical property; emphasis on service.
★   **Cons:** rooms may not be modern enough for some; close to University Medical Center but long walk (1½ miles) from the main campus. $ *Rooms from: $299 ⊠ 2200 E. Elm St., University ☎ 520/325–1541, 800/933–1093 ⊕ www.arizonainn.com ⇨ 72 rooms, 20 suites, 2 casitas |◯| No meals ✛ C4.*

$$$ ☐ **Casa Tierra.** For a real desert experience, head to this B&B on 5
B&B/INN   acres near the Desert Museum and Saguaro National Park West. **Pros:**
Fodor'sChoice peaceful; great Southwest character. **Cons:** far from town (30-minute
★   drive); two-night minimum stay; closed in summer. $ *Rooms from: $165 ⊠ 11155 W. Calle Pima, Westside ☎ 520/578–3058, 866/254–0006 ⊕ www.casatierratucson.com ۞ Closed mid-June–mid-Aug. ⇨ 3 rooms, 1 suite |◯| Breakfast ✛ A4.*

CLOSE UP

Best Campgrounds in Saguaro

There's no drive-up camping in the park. All six primitive campgrounds are in the eastern district and require a hike to reach—the shortest hikes are to Douglas Spring Campground (6 miles) and to Happy Valley (5 miles). All are open year-round. Pick up your backcountry camping permit ($6 per night) at the Rincon Mountain Visitor Center. Before choosing a camping destination, look over the relief map of hiking trails and the book of wilderness campground photos taken by park rangers. You can camp in the backcountry for a maximum of 14 days. Each site can accommodate up to six people. Reservations can be made via mail or in person up to two months in advance. Hikers are encouraged to set out before noon. If you haven't the time or the inclination

to hike in, several more camping opportunities exist within a few miles of the park.

Douglas Spring. Getting to this 4,800-foot-elevation campground takes a not-too-rough 6-mile hike up the Douglas Spring Trail. ⊠ *6 miles on Douglas Spring Trail, off Speedway Blvd.* ☏ *No phone.*

Grass Shack. This pretty campground is among juniper and small oak trees in a transitional area midway up Mica Mountain. ⊠ *10.3 miles via Douglas Spring Trail to Manning Camp Trail* ☏ *No phone.*

Juniper Basin. Vegetation here is oak forest, and the expansive views are worth the challenging 7-mile ascent. ⊠ *7 miles on Tanque Verde Ridge Trail.* ☏ *No phone.*

34

$$$$
RESORT
Fodor's Choice
★
🏨 **Hacienda del Sol Guest Ranch Resort.** This 32-acre hideaway in the Santa Catalina Foothills is a charming and more intimate alternative to the larger resorts, and is partly a guest ranch, with riding stables down the road. **Pros:** outstanding restaurant and bar; buildings and landscaping are stunningly beautiful. **Cons:** not enough resort amenities for some (no golf or spa, just a few massage rooms). ⑤ *Rooms from: $209* ⊠ *5501 N. Hacienda Del Sol Rd., Foothills* ☏ *520/299–1501, 800/728–6514* ⊕ *www.haciendadelsol.com* ⇥ *54 rooms, 8 suites* ⦿ *No meals* ✛ *D2.*

$$
HOTEL
Fodor's Choice
★
🏨 **Hotel Congress.** This hotel, built in 1919, has been artfully restored to its original Western version of art deco; it's now the center of Tucson's hippest scene and a great place for younger and adventurous travelers to stay. **Pros:** prime location; good restaurant; funky and fun. **Cons:** no elevator to guest rooms; no TVs in rooms (only in common areas); noise from nightclub. ⑤ *Rooms from: $149* ⊠ *311 E. Congress St., Downtown* ☏ *520/622–8848, 800/722–8848* ⊕ *www.hotelcongress.com* ⇥ *40 rooms* ⦿ *No meals* ✛ *B4.*

$$$
RESORT
FAMILY
🏨 **Tanque Verde Ranch.** The most upscale of Tucson's guest ranches and one of the oldest in the country, the Tanque Verde sits on 640 beautiful acres in the Rincon Mountains next to Saguaro National Park East. **Pros:** authentic Western experience; loads of all-inclusive activities; great riding. **Cons:** at the eastern edge of town; all-inclusive package excludes alcohol. ⑤ *Rooms from: $169* ⊠ *14301 E. Speedway Blvd.,*

Eastside ☎ *520/296–6275, 800/234–3833* ⊕ *www.tanqueverderanch. com* ⌂ *49 rooms, 25 suites* ⦿*All-inclusive* ✛ *H4.*

$$$$
RESORT
FAMILY
Fodor'sChoice
★

⊞ **White Stallion Ranch.** A 3,000-acre working cattle ranch run by the hospitable True family since 1965, this place is the real deal, satisfying for families as well as singles or couples. **Pros:** solid dude-ranch experience; charming hosts; airport shuttle. **Cons:** no TV in rooms; alcohol not included in the rate—pay extra or bring your own. ⑤ *Rooms from: $480* ⊠ *9251 W. Twin Peaks Rd., Northwest* ☎ *520/297–0252, 888/977–2624* ⊕ *www.wsranch.com* ⌂ *24 rooms, 17 suites* ⦿*All-inclusive* ✛ *A1.*

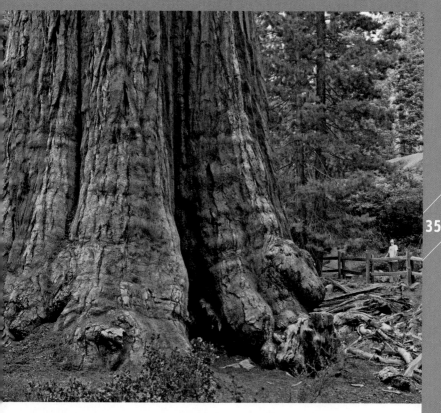

SEQUOIA AND KINGS CANYON NATIONAL PARKS

WELCOME TO SEQUOIA AND KINGS CANYON NATIONAL PARKS

TOP REASONS TO GO

★ **Gentle giants:** You'll feel small—in a good way—walking among some of the world's largest living things in Sequoia's Giant Forest and Kings Canyon's Grant Grove.

★ **Because it's there:** You can't even glimpse it from the main part of Sequoia, but the sight of majestic Mount Whitney is worth the trip to the eastern face of the High Sierra.

★ **Underground exploration:** Far older even than the giant sequoias, the gleaming limestone formations in Crystal Cave will draw you along dark, marble passages.

★ **A grander-than-Grand Canyon:** Drive the twisting Kings Canyon Scenic Byway down into the jagged, granite Kings River Canyon, deeper in parts than the Grand Canyon.

★ **Regal solitude:** To spend a day or two hiking in a subalpine world of your own, pick one of the many trailheads at Mineral King.

1 Giant Forest–Lodgepole Village. One of the most heavily visited areas of Sequoia contains major sights such as Giant Forest, General Sherman Tree, Crystal Cave, and Moro Rock.

2 Grant Grove Village–Redwood Canyon. The "thumb" of Kings Canyon National Park is its busiest section, where Grant Grove, General Grant Tree, Panoramic Point, and Big Stump are the main attractions.

3 Cedar Grove. The drive through the high-country portion of Kings Canyon National Park to Cedar Grove Village, on the canyon floor, reveals magnificent granite formations of varied hues. Rock meets river in breathtaking fashion at Zumwalt Meadow.

4 Mineral King. In the southeast section of Sequoia, the highest road-accessible part of the park is a good place to hike, camp, and soak up the unspoiled grandeur of the Sierra Nevada.

5 Mount Whitney. The highest peak in the Lower 48 stands on the eastern edge of Sequoia; to get there from Giant Forest you must either backpack eight days through the mountains or drive nearly 400 miles around the park to its other side.

KEY

🏛	Ranger Station
⛺	Campground
🌲	Picnic Area
🍴	Restaurant
🏠	Lodge
🚶	Trailhead
🚻	Restrooms
⋇	Scenic Viewpoint
⋮⋮⋮⋮	Walking/Hiking Trails

CALIFORNIA

35

GETTING ORIENTED

The two parks comprise 865,964 acres (1,353 square miles), mostly on the western flank of the Sierra. A map of the adjacent parks looks vaguely like a mitten, with the palm of Sequoia National Park south of the north-pointing, skinny thumb and long fingers of Kings Canyon National Park. Between the western thumb and eastern fingers, north of Sequoia, lies part of Sequoia National Forest, which includes Giant Sequoia National Monument.

LE CONTE DIVIDE

McClure Meadow

Le Conte Canyon

John Muir Trail

Bench Lake

MONARCH DIVIDE

Woods Creek Trail

Kings Canyon Scenic Byway

KINGS / CANYON **3**

Cedar Grove

Roads End Permit Station

Rae Lakes

Charlotte Lake

Visitor Center

Roaring River

KINGS-KERN DIVIDE

0   5 mi
0   5 km

Hwy

Stony Creek Village

Table Mountain 13,630 ft

Tyndall Creek

Whitney Portal

Wuksachi Village

Lodgepole Village

Visitor Center

Crystal Cave

Giant Forest

Mount Whitney 14,491 ft

1

Giant Forest Museum

General Sherman Tree

Bearpaw Meadow

John Muir Trail

Crabtree

5

Moro Rock

Buckeye Flat

Mount Kaweah 13,802 ft

Rock Creek

Potwisha

Mount Guyot 12,300 ft

Visitor Center

Ash Mountain Entrance

Little Five Lakes

Mineral King Rd.

Mineral King

4

Lookout Point Entrance

Cold Springs

KERN CANYON

Hockett Meadows

South Fork

Sheep Mountain 10,050 ft

Kern Canyon

Updated
by Cheryl
Crabtree

Although *Sequoiadendron giganteum* is the formal name for the redwoods that grow here, everyone outside the classroom calls them sequoias, big trees, or Sierra redwoods. Their monstrously thick trunks and branches, remarkably shallow root systems, and neck-craning heights are almost impossible to believe, as is the fact they can live for more than 2,500 years. Many of these towering marvels are in the Giant Forest stretch of Generals Highway, which connects Sequoia and Kings Canyon national parks.

Next to or a few miles off the 46-mile Generals Highway are most of Sequoia National Park's main attractions and Grant Grove Village, the orientation hub for Kings Canyon National Park. The two parks share a boundary that runs from the Central Valley in the west, where the Sierra Nevada foothills begin, to the range's dramatic eastern ridges. Kings Canyon has two portions: the smaller is shaped like a bent finger and encompasses Grant Grove Village and Redwood Mountain Grove (two of the parks' largest concentration of sequoias), and the larger is home to stunning Kings River Canyon, whose vast, unspoiled peaks and valleys are a backpacker's dream. Sequoia is in one piece and includes Mount Whitney, the highest point in the lower 48 states (although it is impossible to see from the western part of the park and is a chore to ascend from either side).

SEQUOIA AND KINGS CANYON PLANNER

WHEN TO GO

The best times to visit are late spring and early fall, when temperatures are moderate and crowds thin. Summertime can draw hordes of tourists to see the giant sequoias, and the few, narrow roads mean congestion at peak holiday times. If you must visit in summer, go during the week. By contrast, in wintertime you may feel as though you have the parks all to yourself. But because of heavy snows, sections of the main park roads can be closed without warning, and low-hanging clouds can move in and obscure mountains and valleys for days. From early October to late April, check road and weather conditions before venturing out. ■TIP➔ **Even in summer, you can escape hordes of people just walking ¼ to ½ mile off the beaten path on a less-used trail.**

Temperatures in the chart below are for the mid-level elevations, generally between 4,000 and 7,000 feet.

AVG. HIGH/LOW TEMPS.

Jan.	Feb.	Mar.	Apr.	May	June
42/24	44/25	46/26	51/30	58/36	68/44
July	Aug.	Sept.	Oct.	Nov.	Dec.
76/51	76/50	71/45	61/38	50/31	44/27

FESTIVALS AND EVENTS

MARCH **Blossom Days Festival.** On the first Saturday of March, communities along Fresno County's Blossom Trail celebrate the flowering of the area's orchards, citrus groves, and vineyards. ☎ 559/600–4271 ⊕ *www. gofresnocounty.com/blossomtrail/blossomindex.asp.*

APRIL **Jazzaffair.** On the second weekend of April, a festival of mostly traditional jazz takes place at several venues just south of the parks. ☎ *559/561–4549.*

MAY **Woodlake Rodeo.** The local Lions Club sponsors this rousing rodeo that draws large crowds to Woodlake on Mother's Day weekend. ☎ *559/564–8555* ⊕ *www.woodlakelionsrodeo.com.*

OCTOBER **Big Fresno Fair.** Over 12 days in October, agricultural, home-arts, and other competitions, plus horse racing and a carnival make for a lively county fair. ✉ *Fresno* ☎ *559/650–3247* ⊕ *www.fresnofair.com.*

DECEMBER **Annual Trek to the Tree.** On the second Sunday of December, thousands of carolers gather at the base of General Grant Tree, the nation's official Christmas tree. ☎ *559/565–3341.*

PLANNING YOUR TIME

SEQUOIA NATIONAL PARK IN ONE DAY

After spending the night in Visalia or Three Rivers—and provided your vehicle's length does not exceed 22 feet—shove off early on Route 198 to Sequoia National Park's **Ash Mountain entrance.** Pull over at the **Hospital Rock** picnic area to gaze up at the imposing granite formation of Moro Rock, which you later will climb. Heed signs that advise "10 mph" around tight turns as you climb 3,500 feet on **Generals Highway** to the **Giant Forest Museum.** Spend a half hour there, then examine some firsthand by circling the lovely **Round Meadow** on the **Big Trees Trail,** to which you must walk from the museum or from its parking lot across the road.

Get back in your car and continue a few miles north on Generals Highway to see the jaw-dropping **General Sherman Tree.** Then set off on the **Congress Trail** so that you can be further awed by the Senate and House big-tree clusters. Buy lunch at the **Lodgepole** complex, 2 miles to the north, and eat at the nearby **Pinewood** picnic area. Now you're ready for the day's big exercise, the mounting of **Moro Rock.**

You can drive there or, if it is summer, park at the museum lot and take the free shuttle. Count on spending at least an hour for the 350-step ascent and descent, with a pause on top to appreciate the 360-degree view. Get back in the car, or on the shuttle, and proceed past the **Tunnel Log** to **Crescent Meadow.** Spend a relaxing hour or two strolling on the trails that pass by, among other things, **Tharp's Log.** By now you've probably renewed your appetite; head to **Wolverton Barbeque** (summer evenings only) or the restaurant at **Wuksachi Lodge.**

KINGS CANYON NATIONAL PARK IN ONE DAY

Enter the park via the **Kings Canyon Scenic Byway** (Route 180), having spent the night in Fresno or Visalia. Better yet, wake up already in **Grant Grove Village,** perhaps in the **John Muir Lodge.** Stock up for a picnic with takeout food from the **Grant Grove Restaurant,** or purchase prepackaged food from the nearby market. Drive east a mile to see the **General Grant Tree** and compact **Grant Grove's** other sequoias. If it's no later than midmorning, walk up the short trail at **Panoramic Point,** for a great view of Hume Lake and the High Sierra. Either way, return to Route 180 and continue east. Stop at Junction View to take in several noteworthy peaks that tower over Kings Canyon. From here, visit **Boyden Cavern** or continue to **Cedar Grove Village,** pausing along the way for a gander at **Grizzly Falls.** Eat at a table by the **South Fork of the Kings River,** or on the deck off the Cedar Grove Snack Bar. Now you are ready for the day's highlight, strolling **Zumwalt Meadow,** which lies a few miles past the village.

After you have enjoyed that short trail and the views it offers of **Grand Sentinel** and **North Dome,** you might as well go the extra mile to **Roads End,** where backpackers embark for the High Sierra wilderness. Make the return trip—with a quick stop at **Roaring River Falls**—past Grant Grove and briefly onto southbound **Generals Highway.** Pull over at the **Redwood Mountain Overlook** and use binoculars to look down upon the world's largest sequoia grove, then drive another couple of miles to the **Kings Canyon Overlook,** where you can survey some of what you have done today. If you've made reservations and have time, have a late dinner at **Wuksachi Lodge.**

GETTING HERE AND AROUND

AIR TRAVEL

The closest airport to Sequoia and Kings Canyon national parks is Fresno Yosemite International Airport (FAT).

CAR TRAVEL

Sequoia is 36 miles east of Visalia on Route 198; Grant Grove Village in Kings Canyon is 56 miles east of Fresno on Route 180. There is no automobile entrance on the eastern side of the Sierra. Routes 180 and 198 are connected by Generals Highway, a paved two-lane road that sometimes sees delays at peak times due to ongoing improvements. The road is extremely narrow and steep from Route 198 to Giant Forest, so keep an eye on your engine temperature gauge, as the incline and congestion can cause vehicles to overheat; to avoid overheated brakes, use low gears on downgrades.

If you are traveling in an RV or with a trailer, study the restrictions on these vehicles. Do not travel beyond Potwisha Campground on Route 198 with an RV longer than 22 feet; take straighter, easier Route 180 instead. Maximum vehicle length on Generals Highway is 40 feet, or 50 feet combined length for vehicles with trailers.

Generals Highway between Lodgepole and Grant Grove is sometimes closed by snow. The Mineral King Road from Route 198 into southern Sequoia National Park is closed 2 miles below Atwell Mill either on November 1 or after the first heavy snow. The Buckeye Flat–Middle Fork Trailhead road is closed from mid-October to mid-April when the Buckeye Flat Campground closes. The lower Crystal Cave Road is closed when the cave closes (typically in November). Its upper 2 miles, as well as the Panoramic Point and Moro Rock–Crescent Meadow roads, close with the first heavy snow. Because of the danger of rockfall, the portion of Kings Canyon Scenic Byway east of Grant Grove closes in winter. For current road and weather conditions, call ☎ 559/565–3341.

35

■TIP→ Snowstorms are common from late October through April. Unless you have a four-wheel-drive vehicle with snow tires, you should carry chains and know how to install them.

PARK ESSENTIALS

PARK FEES AND PERMITS

The admission fee is $20 per vehicle and $10 for those who enter by bus, on foot, bicycle, motorcycle, or horse; it is valid for seven days in both parks. U.S. residents over the age of 62 pay $10 for a lifetime pass, and permanently disabled U.S. residents are admitted free.

If you plan to camp in the backcountry, you need a permit, which costs $15 for hikers or $30 for stock users (e.g., horseback riders). One permit covers the group. Availability of permits depends upon trailhead quotas. Reservations are accepted by mail or fax for a $15 processing fee, beginning March 1, and must be made at least 14 days in advance (☎ 559/565–3766). Without a reservation, you may still get a permit on a first-come, first-served basis starting at 1 pm the day before you plan to hike. For more information on backcountry camping or travel with pack animals (horses, mules, burros, or llamas), contact the Wilderness Permit Office (☎ 530/565–3761).

PARK HOURS

The parks are open 24/7 year-round. They are in the Pacific time zone.

CELL-PHONE RECEPTION

Cell-phone reception is poor to nonexistent in the higher elevations and spotty even on portions of Generals Highway, where you can (on rare clear days) see the Central Valley. Public telephones may be found at the park entrance stations, visitor centers, ranger stations, some trailheads, and at all restaurants and lodging facilities in the park.

EDUCATIONAL OFFERINGS

Educational programs at the parks include museum-style exhibits, ranger- and naturalist-led talks and walks, film and other programs, and sightseeing tours, most of them conducted by either the park service or the nonprofit Sequoia Natural History Association. Exhibits at the visitor centers and the Giant Forest Museum focus on different aspects of the park: its history, wildlife, geology, climate, and vegetation—most notably the giant sequoias. Weekly notices about programs are posted at the visitor centers and elsewhere.

Grant Grove Visitor Center at Kings Canyon National Park has maps of self-guided park tours. Ranger-led walks and programs take place throughout the year in Grant Grove. Cedar Grove and Forest Service campgrounds have activities from Memorial Day to Labor Day. Check bulletin boards or visitor centers for schedules.

EXHIBITS

Giant Forest Museum. Well-imagined and interactive displays at this worthwhile stop provide the basics about sequoias, of which there are 2,161 with diameters exceeding 10 feet in the approximately 2,000-acre Giant Forest. ⊠ *Sequoia National Park ⊹ Generals Hwy., 4 miles south of Lodgepole Visitor Center* ☎ *559/565–4480* ⊠ *Free* ☉ *Hrs vary, but usually late May–early Sept., daily 9–5 (sometimes until 6), and weekends and holidays the rest of the year* ☞ *Shuttle: Giant Forest or Moro Rock–Crescent Meadow.*

PROGRAMS AND SEMINARS

Evening Programs. The Sequoia Parks Conservancy presents films, hikes, and evening lectures during the summer and winter. From May through October the popular Wonders of the Night Sky programs celebrate the often stunning views of the heavens experienced at both parks. ⊠ *Sequoia National Park* ☎ *559/565–4251* ⊕ *www. exploresequoiakingscanyon.com.*

Free Nature Programs. Almost any summer day, half-hour to 1½-hour ranger talks and walks explore subjects such as the life of the sequoia, the geology of the park, and the habits of bears. Giant Forest, Lodgepole Visitor Center, and Wuksachi Village are frequent starting points. Look for less frequent tours in the winter from Grant Grove. Check bulletin boards throughout the park for the week's offerings. ⊕ *www. exploresequoiakingscanyon.com.*

Seminars. Expert naturalists lead seminars on a range of topics, including birds, wildflowers, geology, botany, photography, park history, backpacking, and pathfinding. Reservations are required. Information about times and prices is available at the visitor centers or through the Sequoia Parks Conservancy. ⊠ *Sequoia National Park* ☎ *559/565–4251* ⊕ *www. exploresequoiakingscanyon.com.*

TOURS

Fodor's Choice ★ **Sequoia Field Institute.** The Sequoia Parks Conservancy's highly regarded educational division conducts single-day and multiday "EdVenture" tours that include backpacking hikes, natural-history walks, cross-country skiing, kayaking excursions, and motorcoach tours. ⊠ *47050 Generals Hwy., Unit 10, Three Rivers* ☎ *559/565–4251* ⊕ *www.*

exploresequoiakingscanyon.com ✉ *From $275 for a half-day guided tour.*

Sequoia Sightseeing Tours. This locally owned operator's friendly, knowledgeable guides conduct daily interpretive sightseeing tours in Sequoia and Kings Canyon. Reservations are essential. The company also offers private tours. ✉ *Three Rivers* ☎ *559/561-4189* ⊕ *www.sequoiatours. com* ✉ *From $69 tour of Sequoia; from $129 tour of Kings Canyon.*

RESTAURANTS

In Sequoia and Kings Canyon national parks, you can treat yourself (and the family) to a high-quality meal in a wonderful setting in the Peaks restaurant at Wuksachi Lodge, but otherwise you should keep your expectations modest. A good strategy is to embrace outdoor eating. You can grab bread, spreads, drinks, and fresh produce at one of several small grocery stores, or get take-out food from the Grant Grove Restaurant, the Cedar Grove snack bar, or one of the two small Lodgepole eateries. The summertime Wolverton Barbecue is a hybrid experience between dining in and picnicking out; the all-you-can-eat feast is staged on a patio that overlooks a sublime meadow. Between the parks and just off Generals Highway, the Montecito Sequoia Lodge has a year-round buffet.

HOTELS

Hotel accommodations in Sequoia and Kings Canyon are limited, and—although they are clean and comfortable—tend to lack much in-room character. Keep in mind, however, that the extra money you spend on lodging here is offset by the time you'll save by being inside the parks. You won't be faced with a 60- to 90-minute commute from the less-expensive motels in Three Rivers (by far the most charming option), Visalia, and Fresno. Reserve as far in advance as you can, especially for summertime stays. *Hotel reviews have been shortened. For full information, visit Fodors.com.*

WHAT IT COSTS			
$	**$$**	**$$$**	**$$$$**
Restaurants	under $13	$13–$20	$21–$30	over $30
Hotels	under $101	$101–$150	$151–$200	over $200

Restaurant prices in the reviews are the average cost of a main course at dinner, or if dinner is not served, at lunch. Hotel prices are the lowest cost of a standard double room in high season, excluding taxes and service charges.

VISITOR INFORMATION

National Park Service Sequoia and Kings Canyon National Parks. ✉ *47050 Generals Hwy. (Rte. 198), Three Rivers* ☎ *559/565–3341* ⊕ *www.nps.gov/seki.*

SEQUOIA VISITOR CENTERS

Foothills Visitor Center. Exhibits here focus on the foothills and resource issues facing the parks. You can pick up books, maps, and a list of ranger-led walks, and get wilderness permits. ✉ *47050 Generals Hwy., Rte. 198, 1 mile north of Ash Mountain entrance, Sequoia National*

Park ☎ *559/565–3341* ⊘ *Hrs vary, but typically open daily 8–4:30 in summer.*

Lodgepole Visitor Center. Along with exhibits on the area's history, geology, and wildlife, the center screens an outstanding 22-minute film about bears. You can buy books, maps, and tickets to cave tours and the Wolverton barbecue here. ⊹ *Generals Hwy. (Rte. 198), 21 miles north of Ash Mountain entrance* ☎ *559/565–3341* ⊘ *Days and hrs vary, but typically daily 7–7 in summer* ☞ *Shuttle: Giant Forest or Wuksachi-Lodgepole-Dorst.*

KINGS CANYON VISITOR CENTERS

Cedar Grove Visitor Center. Off the main road and behind the Sentinel Campground, this small ranger station has books and maps, plus information about hikes and other activities. ⊹ *Kings Canyon Scenic Byway, 30 miles east of Rte. 180/198 junction* ☎ *559/565–3341* ⊘ *Days and hrs vary, but typically open late May–early Sept., Tues.–Sun. 9–5.*

Kings Canyon Park Visitor Center. The center's 15-minute film and various exhibits provide an overview of the park's canyon, sequoias, and human history. Books, maps, and weather advice are dispensed here, as are (if available) free wilderness permits. ⊠ *Kings Canyon National Park* ⊹ *Grant Grove Village, Generals Hwy. (Rte. 198), 3 miles northeast of Rte. 180, Big Stump entrance* ☎ *559/565–3341* ⊘ *Days and hrs vary, but typically open daily 9–4:30.*

SEQUOIA NATIONAL PARK

EXPLORING

SCENIC DRIVES

Generals Highway. One of California's most scenic drives, this 46-mile road is the main asphalt artery between Sequoia and Kings Canyon national parks. Some portions are also signed as Route 180, others as Route 198. Named after the landmark Grant and Sherman trees that leave so many visitors awestruck, Generals Highway runs from Sequoia's Foothills Visitor Center north to Kings Canyon's Grant Grove Village. Along the way, it passes the turnoff to Crystal Cave, the Giant Forest Museum, Lodgepole Village, and other popular attractions. The lower portion, from Hospital Rock to the Giant Forest, is especially steep and winding. If your vehicle is 22 feet or longer, avoid that stretch by entering the parks via Route 180 (from Fresno) rather than Route 198 (from Visalia or Three Rivers). Take your time on this road—there's a lot to see, and wildlife can scamper across at any time. ⊠ *Sequoia National Park.*

Mineral King Road. Vehicles longer than 22 feet are prohibited on this side road into southern Sequoia National Park, and for good reason: it contains 589 twists and turns, according to one reputable source. Anticipating an average speed of 20 mph is optimistic. The scenery is splendid as you climb nearly 6,000 feet from Three Rivers to the Mineral King Area. In addition to maneuvering the blind curves and

narrow stretches, you might find yourself sharing the pavement with bears, rattlesnakes, and even softball-size spiders. Allow 90 minutes each way. The road is usually open from late May through October. ⊠ *Sequoia National Forest* ✛ *East off Sierra Dr. (Rte. 198), 3.5 miles northeast of Three Rivers.*

SCENIC STOPS

Sequoia National Park is all about the trees, and to understand the scale of these giants you must walk among them. If you do nothing else, get out of the car for a short stroll through one of the groves. But there is much more to the park than the trees. Try to access one of the vista points that provide a panoramic view over the forested mountains. Generals Highway (on Routes 198 and 180) will be your route to most of the park's sights. A few short spur roads lead from the highway to some sights, and Mineral King Road branches off Route 198 to enter the park at Lookout Point, winding east from there to the park's southernmost section.

Auto Log. Before its wood showed signs of severe rot, cars drove right on top of this giant fallen sequoia. Now it's a great place to pose for pictures or shoot a video. ✛ *Moro Rock–Crescent Meadow Rd., 1 mile south of Giant Forest.*

Crescent Meadow. A sea of ferns signals your arrival at what John Muir called the "gem of the Sierra." Walk around for an hour or two and you might decide that the Scotland-born naturalist was exaggerating a wee bit, but the verdant meadow is quite pleasant and you just might see a bear. Wildflowers bloom here throughout the summer. ✛ *End of Moro Rock–Crescent Meadow Rd., 2.6 miles east off Generals Hwy.* ☞ *Shuttle: Moro Rock–Crescent Meadow.*

Fodor'sChoice ★ **Crystal Cave.** One of more than 200 caves in Sequoia and Kings Canyon, Crystal Cave is composed largely of marble, the result of limestone being hardened under heat and pressure. It contains several eye-popping formations. There used to be more, but some were damaged or obliterated by early-20th-century dynamite blasting. You can only see the cave on a tour. The Daily Tour ($16), a great overview, takes about 50 minutes. To immerse yourself in the cave experience—at times you'll be crawling on your belly—book the exhilarating Adventure Tour ($135). Purchase Daily Tour tickets at either the Foothills or Lodgepole visitor center; they're not sold at the cave itself. ⊠ *Crystal Cave Rd., off Generals Hwy.* ☎ *559/565–4251* ⊕ *www.explorecrystalcave.com* ⊡ *$16* ⊙ *Mid-May–Nov., daily 10–4.*

Fodor'sChoice ★ **General Sherman Tree.** The 274.9-foot-tall General Sherman is one of the world's tallest and oldest sequoias, and it ranks No. 1 in volume, adding the equivalent of a 60-foot-tall tree every year to its approximately 52,500 cubic feet of mass. The tree doesn't grow taller, though—it's dead at the top. A short, wheelchair-accessible trail leads to the tree from Generals Highway, but the main trail (½ mile) winds down from a parking lot off Wolverton Road. The walk back up the main trail is steep, but benches along the way provide rest for the short of breath. ✛ *Main trail Wolverton Rd. off Generals Hwy. (Rte. 198)* ☞ *Shuttle: Giant Forest or Wolverton–Sherman Tree.*

Mineral King Area. A subalpine valley of fir, pine, and sequoia trees, Mineral King sits at 7,500 feet at the end of a steep, winding road. This is the highest point to which you can drive in the park. It is open only from Memorial Day through late October. ✧ *Mineral King Rd., 25 miles east of Generals Hwy. (Rte. 198)* ⊗ *June–late Oct., daily.*

Fodor's Choice **Moro Rock.** Sequoia National Park's best non-tree attraction offers panoramic views to those fit and determined enough to mount its 350 or so steps. In a case where the journey rivals the destination, Moro's stone stairway is so impressive in its twisty inventiveness that it's on the National Register of Historic Places. The rock's 6,725-foot summit overlooks the Middle Fork Canyon, sculpted by the Kaweah River and approaching the depth of Arizona's Grand Canyon, although smoggy, hazy air often compromises the view. ✧ *Moro Rock–Crescent Meadow Rd., 2 miles east off Generals Hwy. (Rte. 198) to parking area* ☞ *Shuttle: Moro Rock–Crescent Meadow.*

Tunnel Log. This 275-foot tree fell in 1937, and soon a 17-foot-wide, 8-foot-high hole was cut through it for vehicular passage (not to mention the irresistible photograph) that continues today. Large vehicles take the nearby bypass. ✧ *Moro Rock–Crescent Meadow Rd., 2 miles east of Generals Hwy. (Rte. 198)* ☞ *Shuttle: Moro Rock–Crescent Meadow.*

35

SPORTS AND THE OUTDOORS

The best way to see Sequoia is to take a hike. Unless you do so, you'll miss out on the up-close grandeur of mist wafting between deeply scored, red-orange tree trunks bigger than you've ever seen. If it's winter, put on some snowshoes or cross-country skis and plunge into the snow-swaddled woodland. There are not too many other outdoor options: no off-road driving is allowed in the parks, and no special provisions have been made for bicycles. Boating, rafting, and snowmobiling are also prohibited.

BICYCLING
Steep, winding roads and shoulders that are either narrow or nonexistent make bicycling here more of a danger than a pleasure. Outside of campgrounds, you are not allowed to pedal on unpaved roads.

BIRD-WATCHING
More than 200 species of birds inhabit Sequoia and Kings Canyon national parks. Not seen in most parts of the United States, the white-headed woodpecker and the pileated woodpecker are common in most mid-elevation areas here. There are also many hawks and owls, including the renowned spotted owl. Species are diverse in both parks due to the changes in elevation, and range from warblers, kingbirds, thrushes, and sparrows in the foothills to goshawk, blue grouse, red-breasted nuthatch, and brown creeper at the highest elevations. The Sequoia Parks Conservancy (☎ 559/565–4251 ⊕ *www.sequoiaparksconservancy.org*) has information about bird-watching in the southern Sierra.

CROSS-COUNTRY SKIING

For a one-of-a-kind experience, cut through the groves of mammoth sequoias in Giant Forest. Some of the Crescent Meadow trails are suitable for skiing as well; none of the trails is groomed. You can park at Giant Forest. Note that roads can be precarious in bad weather. Some advanced trails begin at Wolverton.

Wuksachi Lodge Rentals. Rent cross-country skis and snowshoes here. Depending on snowfall amounts, instruction may also be available. Reservations are recommended. Marked trails cut through Giant Forest, about 5 miles south of the lodge. ✣ *Off Generals Hwy. (Rte. 198), 2 miles north of Lodgepole* ☎ *559/565–4070* ☉ *Nov.–May (unless no snow), daily 9–4* ☞ *Shuttle: Wuksachi-Lodgepole-Dorst.*

FISHING

There's limited trout fishing in the creeks and rivers from late April to mid-November. The Kaweah River is a popular spot; check at visitor centers for open and closed waters. Some of the park's secluded backcountry lakes have good fishing. A California fishing license, required for persons 16 and older, costs about $15 for one day, $24 for two days, and $47 for 10 days (discounts are available for state residents and others). For park regulations, closures, and restrictions, call the parks at ☎ *559/565–3341* or stop at a visitor center. Licenses and fishing tackle are usually available at Hume Lake.

California Department of Fish and Game. The department supplies fishing licenses and provides a full listing of regulations. ☎ *916/928–5805* ⊕ *www.wildlife.ca.gov.*

HIKING

The best way to see the park is to hike it. The grandeur and majesty of the Sierra is best seen up close. Carry a hiking map and plenty of water. Visitor center gift shops sell maps and trail books and pamphlets. Check with rangers for current trail conditions, and be aware of rapidly changing weather. As a rule of thumb, plan on covering about a mile per hour.

EASY

Fodor'sChoice ★ **Big Trees Trail.** This hike is a must, as it does not take long and the setting is spectacular: beautiful Round Meadow surrounded by many mature sequoias, with well-thought-out interpretive signs along the path that explain the ecology on display. The 0.7-mile Big Trees Trail is wheelchair accessible. Parking at the trailhead lot off Generals Highway is for cars with handicap placards only. The round-trip loop from the Giant Forest Museum is about a mile long. *Easy.* ✣ *Trailhead: off Generals Hwy. (Rte. 198), near the Giant Forest Museum* ☞ *Shuttle: Giant Forest.*

Fodor'sChoice ★ **Congress Trail.** This 2-mile trail, arguably the best hike in the parks in terms of natural beauty, is a paved loop that begins near General Sherman Tree. You'll get close-up views of more big trees here than on any other Sequoia hike. Watch for the clusters known as the House and Senate. The President Tree, also on the trail, supplanted the General Grant Tree in 2012 as the world's second largest in volume (behind the General Sherman). An offshoot of the Congress Trail leads to Crescent Meadow, where in summer you can catch a free shuttle back to the

Sherman parking lot. *Easy.* ✛ *Trailhead: off Generals Hwy. (Rte. 198),
2 miles north of Giant Forest* ☞ *Shuttle: Giant Forest.*

Crescent Meadow Trails. A 1-mile trail loops around lush Crescent
Meadow to Tharp's Log, a cabin built from a fire-hollowed sequoia.
From there you can embark on a 60-mile trek to Mount Whitney, if
you're prepared and have the time. Brilliant wildflowers bloom here
in midsummer. *Easy.* ✛ *Trailhead: the end of Moro Rock–Crescent
Meadow Rd., 2.6 miles east off Generals Hwy. (Rte. 198)* ☞ *Shuttle:
Moro Rock–Crescent Meadow.*

Muir Grove Trail. You will attain solitude and possibly see a bear or
two on this unheralded gem of a hike, a 4-mile round-trip from the
Dorst Creek Campground. The remote grove is small but lovely, its
soundtrack provided solely by nature. The trailhead is subtly marked.
In summer, park in the amphitheater lot and walk down toward the
group campsite area. *Easy.* ✛ *Trailhead: Dorst Creek Campground,
Generals Hwy. (Rte. 198), 8 miles north of Lodgepole Visitor Center*
☞ *Shuttle: Lodgepole-Wuksachi-Dorst.*

MODERATE

Little Baldy Trail. Climbing 700 vertical feet in 1.75 miles of switchbacking, this trail ends at a granite dome with a great view of the peaks of
the Mineral King area and the Great Western Divide. The walk to the
summit and back takes about four hours. *Moderate.* ✛ *Trailhead: Little
Baldy Saddle, Generals Hwy. (Rte. 198), 9 miles north of General Sherman Tree* ☞ *Shuttle: Lodgepole-Wuksachi-Dorst.*

Tokopah Falls Trail. This trail with a 500-foot elevation gain follows the
Marble Fork of the Kaweah River for 1.75 miles one-way and dead-ends
below the impressive granite cliffs and cascading waterfall of Tokopah
Canyon. The trail passes through a mixed-conifer forest. It takes 2½
to 4 hours to make the round-trip journey. *Moderate.* ✛ *Trailhead: off
Generals Hwy. (Rte. 198), ¼ mile north of Lodgepole Campground*
☞ *Shuttle: Lodgepole-Wuksachi-Dorst.*

DIFFICULT

Marble Falls Trail. The 3.7-mile trail to Marble Falls crosses through the
rugged foothills before reaching the cascading water. Plan on three to
four hours one-way. *Moderate.* ✛ *Trailhead: off the dirt road across
from the concrete ditch near site 17 at Potwisha Campground, off
Generals Hwy. (Rte. 198).*

Mineral King Trails. Many trails to the high country begin at Mineral
King. Two popular day hikes are Eagle Lake (6.8 miles round-trip) and
Timber Gap (4.4 miles round-trip). At the Mineral King Ranger Station
(*559/565–3768*) you can pick up maps and check about conditions from
late May to late September. *Difficult.* ✛ *Trailheads: at end of Mineral
King Rd., 25 miles east of Generals Hwy. (Rte. 198).*

HORSEBACK RIDING

Trips take you through forests and flowering meadows and up mountain slopes.

TOURS AND OUTFITTERS

Grant Grove Stables. Grant Grove Stables isn't too far from parts of Sequoia National Park, and is perfect for short rides from June to September. Reservations are recommended. ☎ *559/335–9292 summer, 559/799–7247 off-season* ⊕ *www.visitsequoia.com/grant-grove-stables. aspx* ✉ *From $40.*

SLEDDING AND SNOWSHOEING

The Wolverton area, on Route 198 near Giant Forest, is a popular sledding spot, where sleds, inner tubes, and platters are allowed. You can buy sleds and saucers, with prices starting at $10, at the Wuksachi Lodge (☎ *559/565–4070*), 2 miles north of Lodgepole.

You can rent snowshoes for $20–$27 at the Wuksachi Lodge, 2 miles north of Lodgepole. Naturalists lead snowshoe walks around Giant Forest and Wuksachi Lodge, conditions permitting, on Saturdays and holidays. Make reservations and check schedules at Giant Forest Museum (☎ *559/565–3341*) or Wuksachi Lodge.

SWIMMING

Drowning is the number-one cause of death in both Sequoia and Kings Canyon parks. Though it is sometimes safe to swim in the parks' rivers in the late summer and early fall, it is extremely dangerous to do so in the spring and early summer, when the snowmelt from the high country causes swift currents and icy temperatures. Stand clear of the water when the rivers are running, and stay off wet rocks to avoid falling in. Check with rangers for safety information.

35

KINGS CANYON NATIONAL PARK

EXPLORING

SCENIC DRIVES

Fodor'sChoice
★
Kings Canyon Scenic Byway. The 30-mile stretch of Route 180 between Grant Grove Village and Zumwalt Meadow delivers eye-popping scenery—granite cliffs, a roaring river, waterfalls, and Kings River Canyon itself—much of which you can experience at vista points or on easy walks. The canyon comes into view about 10 miles east of the village at **Junction View.** Five miles beyond, at **Yucca Point,** the canyon is thousands of feet deeper than the more famous Grand Canyon. **Canyon View,** a special spot 1 mile east of the Cedar Grove Village turnoff, showcases evidence of the area's glacial history. Here, perhaps more than anywhere else, you'll understand why John Muir compared Kings Canyon vistas with those in Yosemite. Driving the byway takes about an hour each way without stops. ✛ *Rte. 180 north and east of Grant Grove village.*

HISTORIC SITES

Fallen Monarch. This toppled sequoia's hollow base was used in the second half of the 19th century as a home for settlers, a saloon, and even to stable U.S. Cavalry horses. As you walk through it (assuming entry is permitted, which is not always possible), notice how little the wood has decayed, and imagine yourself tucked safely inside, sheltered from a storm or protected from the searing heat. ✛ *Grant Grove Trail, 1 mile north of Kings Canyon Park Visitor Center.*

SCENIC STOPS

Kings Canyon National Park consists of two sections that adjoin the northern boundary of Sequoia National Park. The western portion, covered with sequoia and pine forest, contains the park's most visited sights, such as Grant Grove. The vast eastern portion is remote high country, slashed across half its southern breadth by the deep, rugged Kings River Canyon. Separating the two is Sequoia National Forest, which encompasses Giant Sequoia National Monument. The Kings Canyon Scenic Byway (Route 180) links the major sights within and between the park's two sections. *As of this writing, a fire that started in mid-2015 has burned more than 140,000 acres in the Kings Canyon National Forest and portions of the national park. Check the park website before you travel for updated information on road conditions and possible sight closures as repairs are ongoing.*

General Grant Tree. President Coolidge proclaimed this to be the "nation's Christmas tree," and 30 years later President Eisenhower designated it as a living shrine to all Americans who have died in wars. Bigger at its base than the General Sherman Tree, it tapers more quickly. It's estimated to be the world's third-largest sequoia by volume. A spur trail winds behind the tree, where scars from a long-ago fire remain visible. ✛ *Trailhead: 1 mile north of Grant Grove Visitor Center.*

Redwood Mountain Sequoia Grove. One of the world's largest sequoia groves, Redwood contains within its 2,078 acres nearly 2,200 sequoias whose diameters exceed 10 feet. You can view the grove from afar at an overlook or hike 6 to 10 miles down into the richest regions, which include two of the world's 25 heaviest trees. ✛ *Drive 6 miles south of Grant Grove on Generals Hwy. (Rte. 198), then turn right at Quail Flat; follow it 2 miles to the Redwood Canyon trailhead.*

SPORTS AND THE OUTDOORS

The siren song of beauty, challenge, and relative solitude (by national parks standards) draws hard-core outdoors enthusiasts to the Kings River Canyon and the backcountry of the park's eastern section. Backpacking, rock-climbing, and extreme-kayaking opportunities abound, but the park also has day hikes for all ability levels. Winter brings sledding, skiing, and snowshoeing fun. No off-road driving or bicycling is allowed in the park, and snowmobiling is also prohibited.

BICYCLING

Bicycles are allowed only on the paved roads in Kings Canyon. Cyclists should be extremely cautious along the steep highways and narrow shoulders.

CROSS-COUNTRY SKIING

Roads to Grant Grove are accessible even during heavy snowfall, making the trails here a good choice over Sequoia's Giant Forest when harsh weather hits.

Kings Canyon's Cedar Grove Area

0   1 mi

0   1 km

FISHING

There is limited trout fishing in the park from late April to mid-November, and catches are minor. Still, Kings River is a popular spot. Some of the park's secluded backcountry lakes have good fishing. Licenses are available, along with fishing tackle, in Grant Grove and Cedar Grove. *See Sports and the Outdoors, in Sequoia National Park, above, for more information about licenses.*

HIKING

You can enjoy many of Kings Canyon's sights from your car, but the giant gorge of the Kings River Canyon and the sweeping vistas of some of the highest mountains in the United States are best seen on foot. Carry a hiking map—available at any visitor center—and plenty of water. Check with rangers for current trail conditions, and be aware of rapidly changing weather. Except for one trail to Mount Whitney, permits are not required for day hikes.

Roads End Permit Station. You can obtain wilderness permits, maps, and information about the backcountry at this station, where bear canisters, a must for campers, can be rented or purchased. When the station is closed, complete a self-service permit form. ⊠ *Kings Canyon National Park* ✛ *Eastern end of Kings Canyon Scenic Byway, 6 miles east of Cedar Grove Visitor Center* ☉ *Hrs vary, but typically Mid-May–Sept., daily 7–4.*

CLOSE UP

Plants and Wildlife in Sequoia and Kings Canyon

The parks can be divided into three distinct zones. In the west (1,500–4,500 feet) are the rolling, lower-elevation foothills, covered with shrubby chaparral vegetation or golden grasslands dotted with oaks. Chamise, red-barked manzanita, and the occasional yucca plant grow here. Fields of white popcorn flower cover the hillsides in spring, and the yellow fiddleneck flourishes. In summer, intense heat and absence of rain cause the hills to turn golden brown. Wildlife includes the California ground squirrel, noisy blue-and-gray scrub jay, black bears, coyotes, skunks, and gray fox.

At middle elevation (5,000–9,000 feet), where the giant sequoia belt resides, rock formations mix with meadows and huge stands of evergreens—red and white fir, incense cedar, and

ponderosa pines, to name a few. Wildflowers like yellow blazing star and red Indian paintbrush bloom in spring and summer. Mule deer, golden-mantled ground squirrels, Steller's jays, and black bears (most active in fall) inhabit the area, as does the chickaree.

The high alpine section of the parks is extremely rugged, with a string of rocky peaks reaching above 13,000 feet to Mount Whitney's 14,494 feet. Fierce weather and scarcity of soil make vegetation and wildlife sparse. Foxtail and whitebark pines have gnarled and twisted trunks, the result of high wind, heavy snowfall, and freezing temperatures. In summer you can see yellow-bellied marmots, pikas, weasels, mountain chickadees, and Clark's nutcrackers.

EASY

Big Stump Trail. From 1883 until 1890, logging was done here, complete with a mill. The 1-mile loop trail, whose unmarked beginning is a few yards west of the Big Stump entrance, passes by many enormous stumps. *Easy.* ⊠ *Kings Canyon National Park* ✛ *Trailhead: near Big Stump Entrance, Generals Hwy. (Rte. 180).*

Fodor'sChoice ★ **Grant Grove Trail.** Grant Grove is only 128 acres, but it's a big deal. More than 120 sequoias here have a base diameter that exceeds 10 feet, and the **General Grant Tree** is the world's third-largest sequoia by volume. Nearby, the Confederacy is represented by the **Robert E. Lee Tree,** recognized as the world's 11th-largest sequoia. Also along the easy-to-walk trail are the **Fallen Monarch** and the **Gamlin Cabin,** built by 19th-century pioneers. *Easy.* ⊠ *Kings Canyon National Park* ✛ *Trailhead: off Generals Hwy. (Rte. 180), 1 mile north of Kings Canyon Park Visitor Center.*

Roaring River Falls Walk. Take a shady five-minute walk to this forceful waterfall that rushes through a narrow granite chute. The trail is paved and mostly accessible. *Easy.* ⊠ *Kings Canyon National Park* ✛ *Trailhead: 3 miles east of Cedar Grove Village turnoff from Kings Canyon Scenic Byway.*

Fodor'sChoice ★ **Zumwalt Meadow Trail.** Rangers say this is the best (and most popular) day hike in the Cedar Grove area. Just 1.5 miles long, it offers three visual treats: the South Fork of the Kings River, the lush meadow, and the high granite walls above, including those of Grand Sentinel and North Dome. *Easy.* ⊠ *Kings Canyon National Park* ✛ *Trailhead: 4½ miles east of Cedar Grove Village turnoff from Kings Canyon Scenic Byway.*

MODERATE

Big Baldy. This hike climbs 600 feet and 2 miles up to the 8,209-foot summit of Big Baldy. Your reward is the view of Redwood Canyon. Round-trip the hike is 4 miles. *Moderate.* ⊠ *Kings Canyon National Park* ✛ *Trailhead: 8 miles south of Grant Grove on Generals Hwy. (Rte. 198).*

Mist Falls Trail. This sandy trail follows the glaciated South Fork Canyon through forest and chaparral, past several rapids and cascades, to one of the largest waterfalls in the two parks. Nine miles round-trip, the hike is relatively flat, but climbs 600 feet in the last 2 miles. It takes from four to five hours to complete. *Moderate.* ⊠ *Kings Canyon National Park* ✛ *Trailhead: at end of Kings Canyon Scenic Byway, 5½ miles east of Cedar Grove Village.*

Panoramic Point Trail. You'll get a nice view of whale-shape Hume Lake from the top of this Grant Grove path, which is paved and only 300 feet long. It's fairly steep—strollers might work here, but not wheelchairs. Trailers and RVs are not permitted on the steep and narrow road that leads to the trailhead parking lot. *Moderate.* ⊠ *Kings Canyon National Park* ✛ *Trailhead: at end of Panoramic Point Rd., 2.3 miles from Grant Grove Village.*

Redwood Canyon Trails. Two main trails lead into Redwood Canyon Grove, the world's largest sequoia grove. The 6.5-mile **Hart Tree and Fallen Goliath Loop** passes by a 19th-century logging site, pristine Hart Meadow, and the hollowed-out Tunnel Tree before accessing a side trail to the grove's largest sequoia, the 277.9-foot-tall Hart Tree. The 6.4-mile **Sugar Bowl Loop** provides views of Redwood Mountain and Big Baldy before winding down into its namesake, a thick grove of mature and young sequoias. *Moderate.* ⊠ *Kings Canyon National Park* ✛ *Trailhead: off Quail Flat. Drive 5 miles south of Grant Grove on Generals Hwy. (Rte. 198), turn right at Quail Flat and proceed 1½ miles to trailhead.*

DIFFICULT

Buena Vista Peak. For a 360-degree view of Redwood Canyon and the High Sierra, make the 2-mile ascent to Buena Vista. *Difficult.* ⊠ *Kings Canyon National Park* ✛ *Trailhead: off Generals Hwy. (Rte. 198), south of Kings Canyon Overlook, 7 miles southeast of Grant Grove.*

Don Cecil Trail. This trail climbs 4,000 feet up the cool north-facing slope of the Kings River Canyon, passing Sheep Creek Cascade and providing several fine glimpses of the canyon and the 11,000-foot Monarch Divide. The trail leads to Lookout Peak, which affords a panorama of the park's backcountry. This strenuous, all-day hike covers 13 miles round-trip. *Difficult.* ⊠ *Kings Canyon National Park* ✛ *Trailhead: at Sentinel Campground, Cedar Grove Village.*

35

Mount Whitney

At 14,494 feet, Mount Whitney is the highest point in the contiguous United States and the crown jewel of Sequoia National Park's wild eastern side. The peak looms high above the tiny, high-mountain desert community of Lone Pine, where numerous Hollywood Westerns have been filmed. The high mountain ranges, arid landscape, and scrubby brush of the eastern Sierra are beautiful in their vastness and austerity.

Despite the mountain's scale, you can't see it from the more traveled west side of the park because it is hidden behind the Great Western Divide. The only way to access Mount Whitney from the main part of the park is to circumnavigate the Sierra Nevada via a 10-hour, nearly 400-mile drive outside the park. No road ascends the peak; the best vantage point from which to catch a glimpse of the mountain is at the end of Whitney Portal Road. The 13 miles of winding road leads from U.S. 395 at Lone Pine to the trailhead for the hiking route to the top of the mountain. Whitney Portal Road is closed in winter.

Mt. Whitney Trail. The most popular route to the summit, the Mt. Whitney Trail can be conquered by very fit and experienced hikers. If there's snow on the mountain, this is a challenge for expert mountaineers only. All overnighters must have a permit, as must day hikers on the trail beyond Lone Pine Lake, about 2½ miles from the trailhead. From May through October, permits are distributed via a lottery run each February by Recreation.gov. The Eastern Sierra Interagency Visitor Center (*760/876–6222*), on Route 136 at U.S. 395 about a mile south of Lone Pine, is a good resource for information about permits and hiking. ⊠ *Kings Canyon National Park* ☎ *760/873–2483 trail reservations* ⊕ *www.fs.usda.gov/inyo.*

Hotel Creek Trail. For gorgeous canyon views, take this trail from Cedar Grove up a series of switchbacks until it splits. Follow the route left through chaparral to the forested ridge and rocky outcrop known as Cedar Grove Overlook, where you can see the Kings River Canyon stretching below. This strenuous 5-mile round-trip hike gains 1,200 feet and takes three to four hours to complete. *Difficult.* ⊠ *Kings Canyon National Park* ⊹ *Trailhead: at Cedar Grove Pack Station, 1 mile east of Cedar Grove Village.*

HORSEBACK RIDING

One-day destinations by horseback out of Cedar Grove include Mist Falls and Upper Bubb's Creek. In the backcountry, many equestrians head for Volcanic Lakes or Granite Basin, ascending trails that reach elevations of 10,000 feet. Costs per person range from $35 for a one-hour guided ride to around $250 per day for fully guided trips for which the packers do all the cooking and camp chores.

Hiking in the Sierra Mountains is a thrilling experience, putting you amid some of the world's highest trees.

TOURS AND OUTFITTERS

Cedar Grove Pack Station. Take a day ride or plan a multiday adventure along the Kings River Canyon with Cedar Grove Pack Station. Popular routes include the Rae Lakes Loop and Monarch Divide. ✉ *Kings Canyon National Park ✛ Kings Canyon Scenic Byway, 1 mile east of Cedar Grove Village* ☎ *559/565–3464* ⊕ *www.nps.gov/seki/planyourvisit/horseride.htm* ✉ *From $40 per hr or $100 per day* ☉ *Late May–early Sept.*

Grant Grove Stables. A one- or two-hour trip through Grant Grove leaving from the stables provides a taste of horseback riding in Kings Canyon. ✉ *Kings Canyon National Park ✛ Rte. 180, ½ mile north of Grant Grove Visitor Center* ☎ *559/335–9292 mid-June–Sept.* ⊕ *www.nps.gov/seki/planyourvisit/horseride.htm* ✉ *From $45* ☉ *June–Labor Day, daily 8–6.*

SLEDDING AND SNOWSHOEING

In winter, Kings Canyon has a few great places to play in the snow. Sleds, inner tubes, and platters are allowed at both the Azalea Campground area on Grant Tree Road, ¼ mile north of Grant Grove Visitor Center, and at the Big Stump picnic area, 2 miles north of the lower Route 180 entrance to the park.

Snowshoeing is good around Grant Grove, where you can take occasional naturalist-guided snowshoe walks from mid-December through mid-March as conditions permit. Grant Grove Market rents sleds and snowshoes.

WHAT'S NEARBY

The already remote Sierra National Forest encircles much of Sequoia and Kings Canyon national parks, making them a wilderness within a wilderness.

NEARBY TOWNS

Numerous towns and cities tout themselves as "gateways" to the parks, with some more deserving of the title than others. One that certainly merits the name is frisky **Three Rivers**, a Sierra foothills hamlet (population 2,200) along the Kaweah River. Close to Sequoia's Ash Mountain and Lookout Point entrances, Three Rivers is a good spot to find a room when park lodgings are full. Either because Three Rivers residents appreciate their idyllic setting or because they know that tourists are their bread and butter, you'll find them almost uniformly pleasant and eager to share tips about the best spots for "Sierra surfing" the Kaweah's smooth, moss-covered rocks or where to find the best cell-phone reception (it's off to the cemetery for Verizon customers).

Visalia, a Central Valley city of about 128,000 people, lies 58 miles southwest of Sequoia's Wuksachi Village and 56 miles southwest of the Kings Canyon Park Visitor Center. Its vibrant downtown contains several good restaurants. Closest to Kings Canyon's Big Stump entrance, **Fresno**, the main gateway to the southern Sierra region, is about 55 miles west of Kings Canyon and about 85 miles northwest of Wuksachi Village. This Central Valley city of nearly a half-million people is sprawling and unglamorous, but it has all the cultural and other amenities you'd expect of a major crossroads.

Visitor Information Fresno/Clovis Convention & Visitors Bureau. ⊠ *1550 E. Shaw Ave., Ste. 101, Fresno* ☎ *559/981–5500, 800/788–0836* ⊕ *www.playfresno. org.* **Sequoia Foothills Chamber of Commerce.** ⊠ *42268 Sierra Dr., Three Rivers* ☎ *559/561–3300* ⊕ *www.threerivers.com.* **Visalia Convention & Visitors Bureau.** ⊠ *Kiosk, 303 E. Acequia Ave., at S. Bridge St., Visalia* ☎ *559/334–0141, 800/524–0303* ⊕ *www.visitvisalia.org.*

NEARBY ATTRACTIONS

Boyden Cavern. The Kings River has carved out hundreds of caverns, including Boyden, which brims with stalagmite, stalactite, drapery, flowstone, and other formations. In summer, the Bat Grotto shelters a slew of bats. If you can't make it to Crystal Cave in Sequoia, Boyden is a reasonable substitute. Reservations aren't taken for regular tours, which take about 45 minutes and start with a steep walk uphill. As of this writing, tours of Boyden Cavern are closed because of the fire in the region, but they should reopen by spring 2016. ⊠ *74101 E. Kings Canyon Rd. (Rte. 180), between Grant Grove and Cedar Grove* ☎ *888/965–8243* ⊕ *caverntours.com/boyden-cavern* ⊠ *$15* ⊙ *June–Aug., daily 10–5; May and Sept.–Nov., daily 11–5; tours on the hr.*

Exeter Murals. More than two dozen murals in the Central Valley city of Exeter's cute-as-a-button downtown make it worth a quick detour if you're traveling on Route 198. Several of the murals, which depict the area's agricultural and social history, are quite good. All adorn buildings within a few blocks of the intersection of Pine and E streets. If you're hungry, the **Wildflower Cafe**, at 121 South E Street, serves inventive salads and sandwiches. Shortly after entering Exeter head west on Pine Street (it's just before the water tower) to reach downtown. ⊠ *Exeter* ✛ *Rte. 65, 2 miles south of Rte. 198, about 11 miles east of Visalia* ⊕ *cityofexeter.com/about-8187/gallery/murals.*

FAMILY
Fodor's Choice
★

Forestiere Underground Gardens. Sicilian immigrant Baldassare Forestiere spent four decades (1906–46) carving out an odd, subterranean realm of rooms, tunnels, grottoes, alcoves, and arched passageways that once extended for more than 10 acres between Highway 99 and busy, mall-pocked Shaw Avenue. Though not an engineer, Forestiere called on his memories of the ancient Roman structures he saw as a youth and on techniques he learned digging subways in New York and Boston. Only a fraction of his prodigious output is on view, but you can tour his underground living quarters, including bedrooms (one with a fireplace), the kitchen, living room, and bath, as well as a fishpond and auto tunnel. Skylights allow exotic full-grown fruit trees to flourish more than 20 feet belowground. ⊠ *5021 W. Shaw Ave., 2 blocks east of Hwy. 99, Fresno* ☎ *559/271–0734* ⊕ *www.undergroundgardens.com* ☒ *$15* ⏱ *Tours June–Aug., Wed.–Sun. on the hr 10–4 (weather permitting). Sept.–Nov. and Mar.–May, hrs vary rest of year.*

Project Survival's Cat Haven. Take the rare opportunity to glimpse a Siberian lynx, a clouded leopard, a Bengal tiger, and other endangered wild cats at this conservation facility that shelters more than 30 big cats. A guided hour-long tour along a quarter mile of walkway leads to fenced habitat areas shaded by trees and overlooking the Central Valley. ⊠ *38257 E. Kings Canyon Rd. (Rte. 180), 15 miles west of Kings Canyon National Park, Dunlap* ☎ *559/338–3216* ⊕ *www.cathaven. com* ☒ *$12* ⏱ *May–Sept., Wed.–Mon. 10–5; Oct.–Apr., Thurs.–Mon. 10–4. Last tour leaves 1 hr before closing.*

Sequoia National Forest and Giant Sequoia National Monument. Delicate spring wildflowers, cool summer campgrounds, and varied winter-sports opportunities—not to mention more than half of the world's giant sequoia groves—draw outdoorsy types year-round to this sprawling district surrounding the national parks. Together, the forest and monument cover nearly 1,700 square miles, south from the Kings River and east from the foothills along the San Joaquin Valley. The monument's groves are both north and south of Sequoia National Park. One of the most popular is the **Converse Basin Grove,** home of the Boole Tree, the forest's largest sequoia. The grove is accessible by car on an unpaved road.

The Hume Lake Forest Service District Office, at 35860 Kings Canyon Scenic Byway (Route 180), has information about the groves, along with details about recreational activities. In springtime, diversions include hiking among the wildflowers that brighten the foothills.

The floral display rises with the heat as the mountain elevations warm up in summer, when hikers, campers, and picnickers become more plentiful. The abundant trout supply attracts anglers to area waters, including 87-acre **Hume Lake,** which is also ideal for swimming and nonmotorized boating. By fall the turning leaves provide the visual delights, particularly in the Western Divide, Indian Basin, and the Kern Plateau. Winter activities include downhill and cross-country skiing, snowshoeing, and snowmobiling. ⊠ *Sequoia National Park* ✛ *Northern Entrances: Generals Hwy. (Rte. 198), 7 miles southeast of Grant Grove; Hume Lake Rd. between Generals Hwy. (Rte. 198) and Kings Canyon Scenic Byway (Rte. 180); Kings Canyon Scenic Byway (Rte. 180) between Grant Grove and Cedar Grove. Southern Entrances: Rte. 190 east of Springville; Rte. 178 east of Bakersfield* ☎ *559/784–1500 forest and monument, 559/338–2251 Hume Lake* ⊕ *www.fs.usda.gov/ sequoia.*

AREA ACTIVITIES

SPORTS AND THE OUTDOORS
BOATING AND RAFTING
Kings River Expeditions. This outfit arranges one- and two-day whitewater rafting trips on the Kings River. ⊠ *1840 W. Shaw Ave., Clovis* ☎ *559/233–4881, 800/846–3674* ⊕ *www.kingsriver.com* ☑ *From $110.*

WHERE TO EAT

IN THE PARKS

SEQUOIA
$ ✕ **Lodgepole Market, Deli, and Snack Bar.** The choices here run the gamut
CAFÉ from simple to very simple, with the three counters only a few strides apart in a central eating complex. For hot food, including burgers, hot dogs, and pizzas, venture into the snack bar. The deli sells prepackaged salads, sandwiches, and wraps along with ice cream scooped from tubs. You'll find other prepackaged foods in the market. ⑤ *Average main: $8* ⊠ *Next to Lodgepole Visitor Center, Sequoia National Park* ☎ *559/565–3301* ⊘ *Closed Dec.–mid-Apr.*

$$$ ✕ **The Peaks.** Huge windows run the length of the Wuksachi Lodge's
MODERN high-ceilinged dining room, and a large fireplace on the far wall warms
AMERICAN both body and soul. The diverse dinner menu—by far the best at both parks—reflects a commitment to locally sourced and sustainable products. The menu might include venison, pan-seared mountain trout, and vegetarian options like pho and chili. The wine selection is serviceable but lacks imagination. Breakfast and lunch are also served, and pizzas are available for takeout. ⑤ *Average main: $28* ⊠ *Wuksachi Lodge, 64740 Wuksachi Way, Wuksachi Village* ☎ *559/565–4070* ⊕ *www. visitsequoia.com/the-peaks-restaurant.aspx* ⌂ *Reservations essential.*

$$$ ✕ **Wolverton Barbeque.** Weather permitting, diners congregate nightly
BARBECUE on a wooden porch that looks directly out onto a small but strikingly verdant meadow. In addition to the predictable meats such as ribs and

chicken, the all-you-can-eat buffet has sides that include baked beans, corn on the cob, and potato salad. Following the meal, listen to a naturalist talk, join in an interactive living history presentation, and clear your throat for a campfire sing-along. Purchase tickets at Lodgepole Market, Wuksachi Lodge, or Wolverton Recreation Area's office. $ *Average main: $25 ⊠ Sequoia National Park ✛ Wolverton Rd., 1½ mile northeast off Generals Hwy. (Rte. 198) ☎ 559/565–4070 ☺ No lunch. Closed early Sept.–mid-June.*

PICNIC AREAS

Take care to dispose of your food scraps properly (the bears might not appreciate this short-term, but the practice helps ensure their long-term survival).

Crescent Meadow. A mile or so past Moro Rock, this comparatively remote picnic area has meadow views and, quite handily, is by a lovely trail on which you can burn off those potato chips and cookies. Tables are under the giant sequoias, off the parking area. There are restrooms and drinking water. Fires are not allowed. ✛ *End of Moro Rock–Crescent Rd., 2.6 miles east off Generals Hwy. (Rte. 198).*

Foothills Picnic Area. Near the parking lot at the southern entrance of the park, this area has tables, drinking water, and restrooms. ✛ *Across Generals Hwy. from Foothills Visitor Center.*

Hospital Rock. American Indians once ground acorns into meal at this site; outdoor exhibits tell the story. The picnic area's name, however, stems from a Caucasian hunter/trapper who was treated for a leg wound here in 1873. Look up, and you'll see Moro Rock. Grills, drinking water, and restrooms are available. ✛ *Generals Hwy. (Rte. 198), 6 miles north of Ash Mountain entrance.*

Pinewood Picnic Area. Picnic in Giant Forest, in the vicinity of sequoias if not actually under them. Drinking water, restrooms, grills, and wheelchair-accessible spots are provided in this expansive setting near Sequoia National Park's most popular attractions. ✛ *Generals Hwy. (Rte. 198), 2 miles north of Giant Forest Museum, halfway between Giant Forest Museum and General Sherman Tree.*

Wolverton Meadow. At a major trailhead to the backcountry, this is a great place to stop for lunch before a hike. The area sits in a mixed-conifer forest adjacent to parking. Drinking water, grills, and restrooms are available. ✛ *Wolverton Rd., 1½ miles northeast off Generals Hwy. (Rte. 198).*

KINGS CANYON

$$ ✕ **Cedar Grove Snack Bar.** The menu here is surprisingly extensive, with
AMERICAN dinner entrées such as pasta, pork chops, trout, and steak. For breakfast, try the biscuits and gravy, French toast, pancakes, or cold cereal. Burgers (including vegetarian patties) and hot dogs dominate the lunch choices. Outside, a patio dining area overlooks the Kings River. $ *Average main: $15 ⊠ Cedar Grove Village, Kings Canyon National Park ☎ 559/565–0100 ☺ Closed Oct.–May.*

$$ ✕ **Grant Grove Restaurant.** In a no-frills, open room, this restaurant
AMERICAN offers standard American fare such as pancakes for breakfast or hot sandwiches and chicken for later meals. Takeout service is available

year-round, and during the summer there's also a pizza parlor. $ *Average main: $16* ⊠ *Grant Grove Village, Kings Canyon National Park* ☎ *559/335–5500.*

PICNIC AREAS

Big Stump. Some trees still stand at this site at the edge of a logged sequoia grove. Near the park's entrance, the area is paved and next to the road. It's the only picnic area in either park that is plowed in the wintertime. Restrooms, grills, and drinking water are available, and the area is entirely accessible. ⊹ *Generals Hwy. (Rte. 180), just inside Big Stump entrance.*

Grizzly Falls. This little gem is worth a pull-over, if not a picnic at the roadside tables. A less-than-a-minute trek from the parking lot delivers you to the base of the delightful, 100-foot-plus falls. On a hot day, nothing feels better than dipping your feet in the cool water. An outhouse is on-site, but grills are not, and water is unavailable. ⊹ *Off Rte. 180, 2½ miles west of Cedar Grove entrance.*

OUTSIDE THE PARKS

$ ╳ **Antoinette's Coffee and Goodies.** For smoothies, well-crafted espresso
CAFÉ drinks, breakfast bowls, and pumpkin chocolate-chip muffins and other homemade baked goods, stop for a spell at this convivial coffee shop. Antoinette's is known as the town's hub for vegan and gluten-free items. There's Wi-Fi here, too. $ *Average main: $6* ⊠ *41727 Sierra Dr., Three Rivers* ☎ *559/561–2253* ⊕ *www.antoinettescoffeeandgoodies. com* ⊗ *Closed Tues. No dinner* ⚐ *Reservations not accepted.*

$$ ╳ **Café 225.** High ceilings and contemporary decor contribute to the
MODERN relaxed and sophisticated atmosphere at this popular downtown res-
AMERICAN taurant. Chef-owner Karl Merten can often be spotted at area markets seeking out locally grown ingredients for his seasonally changing dishes. Meats and fish grilled on a wood-fired rotisserie figure prominently on the menu, which also includes pastas and unusual treats such as artichoke fritters and slow-roasted pork loin adobo. The green-chili burger, grilled over oak coals and served with sharp cheddar and chipotle aioli, is a town favorite. $ *Average main: $19* ⊠ *225 W. Main St., Visalia* ☎ *559/733–2967* ⊕ *www.cafe225.com* ⊗ *Closed Sun.*

$$$ ╳ **Elbow Room.** A classic San Francisco–style steak house and bar, the
AMERICAN Elbow Room has been a Fresno social hub since opening in 1955. The steak sandwich, served open face on jalapeño cheese bread, has been a menu staple since the beginning; other classics include deviled eggs and an iceberg wedge with blue cheese. Among the more contemporary dishes are grilled Alaskan salmon and a salad with quinoa, mixed greens, asparagus, and artichoke hearts. The restaurant has indoor seating areas and a covered patio with year-round temperature controls, a boon in summer. $ *Average main: $22* ⊠ *Fig Garden Village Shopping Center, 731 W. San Jose Ave., near W. Shaw Ave., Fresno* ☎ *559/227– 1234* ⊕ *elbowroomfresno.com.*

$$$ ╳ **Gateway Restaurant and Lodge.** The view's the draw at this roadhouse
AMERICAN that overlooks the Kaweah River as it plunges out of the high country.

The Gateway serves everything from osso buco and steaks to shrimp in Thai chili sauce. Some menu items are pricey, but you can also order a pizza or a beef or salmon burger. For the best results, stick to the simpler preparations. Dinner reservations are essential on summer weekends. $ *Average main: $29* ✉ *45978 Sierra Dr., Three Rivers* ☎ *559/561–4133* ⊕ *www.gateway-sequoia.com.*

$ ✕ **The Lunch Box.** A casual downtown café and bakery, the Lunch Box

AMERICAN serves healthful meals at reasonable prices. Choose from nearly 50 types of hot and cold sandwiches and wraps, more than 20 different salads, and soups such as chicken noodle and Tuscan tomato. Tandoori-seasoned salmon fillet and chicken verde enchiladas are typical daily specials. ■TIP➔ **This is good place for a quick bite or to pick up picnic items before or after a visit to Sequoia National Park.** $ *Average main: $10* ✉ *112 N. Court St., at Main St., Visalia* ☎ *559/635–8624* ⊕ *lunchboxcateringcompany.com* ⊗ *Closed Sun.*

$ ✕ **ol' Buckaroo.** Set on a bluff overlooking the Kaweah River, the boho-

AMERICAN chic ol' Buckaroo serves fresh, housemade dishes made with organic ingredients. A local couple started the restaurant in 2014, first operating out of a food truck and later expanding into a building that housed the original Buckaroo restaurant for decades. The menu changes seasonally, but don't miss regulars like lemon ricotta pancakes for brunch (weekends only), or the buttermilk-dipped and fried organic chicken for dinner. Ask about the daily specials. $ *Average main: $12* ✉ *41695 Sierra Dr., Three Rivers* ☎ *559/799–3665* ⊕ *olbuckaroo.com* ⊗ *No lunch weekdays.*

$$$ ✕ **School House Restaurant & Tavern.** A Wine Country–style establishment

MODERN that sources ingredients from the on-site gardens and surrounding farms
AMERICAN and orchards, this popular restaurant occupies a red-brick 1921 schoolhouse in the town of Sanger. Chef Ryan Jackson, who grew up on local fruit farms, returned home after stints cooking at prestigious Napa Valley restaurants to create seasonal menus from the bounty of familiar backyards. The fare might include salmon ratatouille with summer vegetables, braised duck Stroganoff in a mushroom-Cabernet sauce, or lobster salad tossed with local peaches, arugula, goat cheese, almonds, and roasted peach vinaigrette. With salads, pizza, pasta, and sandwiches, lunch is more basic. You can eat in the main dining room (the former school auditorium), the more casual tavern, or by the outdoor patio's fire pits. $ *Average main: $25* ✉ *1018 S. Frankwood Ave., at Hwy. 180 (King's Canyon Rd.), 20 miles east of Fresno, Sanger* ☎ *559/787–3271* ⊕ *schoolhousesanger.com* ⊗ *Closed Mon. and Tues.*

$ ✕ **Sierra Subs and Salads.** This well-run sandwichery satisfies carni-

AMERICAN vores and vegetarians alike with crispy-fresh ingredients prepared with panache. Depending on your preference, the centerpiece of the Bull's Eye sandwich, for instance, will be roast beef or a portobello mushroom, but whichever you choose, the accompanying flavors—of ciabatta bread, horseradish-and-garlic mayonnaise, roasted red peppers, Havarti cheese, and spinach—will delight your palate. $ *Average main: $8* ✉ *41717 Sierra Dr., Three Rivers* ☎ *559/561–4810* ⊕ *www.sierrasubsandsalads.com* ⊗ *Closed Mon. No dinner.*

35

$$$$ ✕**The Vintage Press.** Built in 1966, this is the best restaurant in the
EUROPEAN   Central Valley. Cut-glass doors and bar fixtures decorate the artfully
Fodor'sChoice   designed rooms. The California–Continental cuisine includes dishes
★   such as crispy veal sweetbreads with a port-wine sauce and filet mignon
with a cognac-mustard sauce. The chocolate Grand Marnier cake is a
standout among the homemade desserts and ice creams. The wine list
has more than 900 selections. ⑤ *Average main: $32* ⊠ *216 N. Willis St.,
Visalia* ☎ *559/733–3033* ⊕ *www.thevintagepress.com.*

WHERE TO STAY

IN THE PARKS

SEQUOIA

$$ 🏨 **Silver City Mountain Resort.** High on Mineral King Road, this privately
RESORT   owned resort has rustic cabins and Swiss-style chalets, all with at least
a stove, refrigerator, and sink. **Pros:** rustic setting; friendly staff; "off
the grid" ambience. **Cons:** electricity (by generator) available only
between noon and 10 pm. ⑤ *Rooms from: $120* ⊠ *Sequoia National
Park* ✛ *Mineral King Rd., 21 miles southeast of Rte. 198* ☎ *559/561–
3223* ⊕ *www.silvercityresort.com* ☉ *Closed Nov.–late May* ⇗ *11 units,
6 with shared bath* ⦿ *No meals.*

$$$$ 🏨 **Wuksachi Lodge.** The striking cedar-and-stone main building is a fine
HOTEL   example of how a structure can blend effectively with lovely moun-
Fodor'sChoice   tain scenery. **Pros:** best place to stay in the parks; lots of wildlife.
★   **Cons:** rooms can be small; main lodge is a few-minutes' walk from
guest rooms; slow Wi-Fi. ⑤ *Rooms from: $229* ⊠ *64740 Wuksachi
Way, Wuksachi Village* ☎ *559/565–4070, 888/252–5757* ⊕ *www.
visitsequoia.com/lodging.aspx* ⇗ *102 rooms* ⦿ *No meals.*

KINGS CANYON

$$ 🏨 **Cedar Grove Lodge.** Backpackers like to stay here on the eve of long
HOTEL   treks into the High Sierra wilderness, so bedtimes tend to be early. **Pros:**
a definite step up from camping in terms of comfort. **Cons:** impersonal;
not everybody agrees it's clean enough. ⑤ *Rooms from: $138* ⊠ *Kings
Canyon Scenic Byway, Kings Canyon National Park* ☎ *877/522–6966*
⊕ *www.visitsequoia.com/kings-canyon.aspx* ☉ *Closed mid-Oct.–mid-
May* ⇗ *21 rooms* ⦿ *No meals.*

$ 🏨 **Grant Grove Cabins.** Some of the wood-panel cabins here have heaters,
HOTEL   electric lights, and private baths, but most have woodstoves, battery
lamps, and shared baths. **Pros:** warm, woodsy feel; clean. **Cons:** can be
difficult to walk up to if you're not in decent physical shape; costly for
what you get. ⑤ *Rooms from: $94* ⊠ *Kings Canyon Scenic Byway in
Grant Grove Village, Kings Canyon National Park* ☎ *877/522–6966*
⊕ *www.visitsequoia.com/kings-canyon.aspx* ⇗ *33 cabins, 9 with bath;
17 tent cabins* ⦿ *No meals.*

$ 🏨 **John Muir Lodge.** In a wooded area in the hills above Grant Grove
HOTEL   Village, this modern, timber-sided lodge has rooms and suites with
queen- or king-size beds and private baths. **Pros:** open year-round; common room stays warm; quiet. **Cons:** check-in is down in the village.

Best Campgrounds in Sequoia and Kings Canyon

Campgrounds in Sequoia and Kings Canyon occupy wonderful settings, with lots of shade and nearby hiking trails. Some campgrounds are open year-round, others only seasonally. Except for Bearpaw (around $350 a night including meals), fees at the campgrounds listed *below* range from $12 to $35, depending on location and size. There are no RV hookups at any of the campgrounds; expect a table and a fire ring with a grill at standard sites. Only Bearpaw, Lodgepole, Dorst Creek, Potwisha, and Buckeye Flat accept reservations, and for all of these you'll need to book well ahead. The rest are first come, first served. Campgrounds around Lodgepole and Grant Grove get busy in summer with vacationing families. Keep in mind that this is black-bear country. Carefully follow posted instructions about storing food—you'll be fined if you don't. Bear-proof metal containers are provided at many campgrounds.

IN SEQUOIA

Atwell Mill Campground. At 6,650 feet, this peaceful, tent-only campground is just south of the Western Divide. ⊠ *Mineral King Rd., 20 miles east of Rte. 198* ☎ *559/565–3341.*

Bearpaw High Sierra Camp. Classy camping is the order of the day at this tent hotel and restaurant. Make reservations starting on January 2nd. ⊠ *High Sierra Trail, 11.5 miles from Lodgepole Village* ☎ *888/252–5757* ⊕ *www.visitsequoia.com.*

Dorst Creek Campground. Wildlife sightings are common at this large campground at elevation 6,700 feet. ⊠ *Generals Hwy., 8 miles north of*

Lodgepole Visitor Center ☎ *559/565–3341 or 877/444–6777.*

Lodgepole Campground. The largest Lodgepole-area campground is also the noisiest, though things quiet down at night. ⊠ *Off Generals Hwy. beyond Lodgepole Village* ☎ *559/565–3341 or 877/444–6777.*

Potwisha Campground. On the Marble Fork of the Kaweah River, this midsize campground, open year-round, at elevation 2,100 feet gets no snow in winter and can be hot in summer. ⊠ *Generals Hwy., 4 miles north of Foothills Visitor Center* ☎ *559/565–3341 or 877/444–6777.*

IN KINGS CANYON

Azalea Campground. Of the three campgrounds in the Grant Grove area, Azalea is the only one open year-round. It sits at 6,500 feet amid giant sequoias. ⊠ *Kings Canyon Scenic Byway, ¼ mile north of Grant Grove Village* ☎ *559/565–3341.*

Sentinel Campground. At 4,600 feet and within walking distance of Cedar Grove Village, Sentinel fills up fast in summer. ⊠ *Kings Canyon Scenic Byway, ¼ mile west of Cedar Grove Village* ☎ *559/565–3341.*

Sheep Creek Campground. Of the overflow campgrounds, this is one of the prettiest. ⊠ *Off Kings Canyon Scenic Byway, 1 mile west of Cedar Grove Village* ☎ *No phone.*

Sunset Campground. Many of the easiest trails through Grant Grove are adjacent to this large camp, near the giant sequoias at 6,500 feet. ⊠ *Off Generals Hwy., near Grant Grove Visitor Center* ☎ *No phone.*

35

⑤ *Rooms from: $94* ⊠ *Kings Canyon Scenic Byway, ¼ mile north of Grant Grove Village, 86728 Highway 180, Kings Canyon National Park* ☎ *559/335–5500* ⊕ *www.visitsequoia.com/john-muir-lodge.aspx* ⤲ *36 rooms* ⦿⦿ *No meals.*

OUTSIDE THE PARKS

The only lodging immediately outside the parks is in Three Rivers. Options include inns, chain and mom-and-pop motels, and riverside cabins. Numerous chain properties operate in Visalia or Fresno (your favorite is likely represented in one or both cities), about an hour from the south and north entrances, respectively.

$$$
HOTEL
FAMILY

▦ **Montecito-Sequoia Lodge.** Outdoor activities are what this year-round family resort is all about, including many that are geared toward teenagers and small children. **Pros:** friendly staff; great for kids; lots of fresh air and planned activities. **Cons:** can be noisy with all the activity; some complaints about cleanliness; not within national park. ⑤ *Rooms from: $179* ⊠ *63410 Generals Hwy., 11 miles south of Grant Grove, Sequoia National Forest* ☎ *559/565–3388, 800/227–9900* ⊕ *www.montecitosequoia.com* ⊙ *Closed 1st 2 wks of Dec.* ⤲ *37 rooms, 13 cabins* ⦿⦿ *All meals.*

$$$
B&B/INN
Fodor'sChoice
★

▦ **Rio Sierra Riverhouse.** Guests at Rio Sierra come for the river views, the sandy beach, and the proximity to Sequoia National Park (6 miles away), but invariably end up raving equally about the warm, laid-back hospitality of proprietress Mars Roberts. **Pros:** seductive beach; winning hostess; river views from all rooms; contemporary ambience. **Cons:** books up quickly in summer; some road noise audible in rooms. ⑤ *Rooms from: $170* ⊠ *41997 Sierra Dr., Hwy. 198, Three Rivers* ☎ *559/561–4720* ⊕ *www.rio-sierra.com* ⊙ *Closed Jan.* ⤲ *5 rooms* ⦿⦿ *No meals* ⌨ *2-night minimum stay on summer weekends.*

$
B&B/INN

▦ **The Spalding House.** This restored Colonial Revival inn is decked out with antiques, oriental rugs, handcrafted woodwork, and glass doors. **Pros:** warm feel; old-time atmosphere; great place for a twilight stroll. **Cons:** no TVs in rooms. ⑤ *Rooms from: $95* ⊠ *631 N. Encina St., Visalia* ☎ *559/739–7877* ⊕ *www.thespaldinghouse.com* ⤲ *3 suites* ⦿⦿ *Breakfast.*

THEODORE ROOSEVELT NATIONAL PARK

Visit Fodors.com for advice, updates, and bookings

WELCOME TO THEODORE ROOSEVELT NATIONAL PARK

TOP REASONS TO GO

★ **The "Granddaddy Trail":** Hike the Maah Daah Hey Trail, which means "grandfather" or "been here long." It's one of the most popular and well-maintained trails in western North Dakota.

★ **Views from above:** Get an encompassing 360-degree view of the badlands from Buck Hill.

★ **History lessons from the frontier:** View Maltese Cross Ranch Cabin, which once belonged to Theodore Roosevelt.

★ **Badlands Broadway:** Come experience a theatrical tribute to the history and personalities that make up the Old West at the Medora Musical, located in the town, not the park.

★ **Great clubbing—golf, that is:** Perfect your swing at Bully Pulpit Golf Course in Medora, one of America's premier courses near the national park.

★ **Away from it all:** As this is not a heavily visited park, you'll likely encounter more wild horses than people here.

1 North Unit. Visitors looking to enjoy the great outdoors should be sure to travel along the 14-mile scenic drive and stop at one of the many hiking trailheads along the way. These trailheads give easy access to the backcountry of the North Unit.

2 South Unit. Often considered the main unit of Theodore Roosevelt National Park and adjacent to the famous town of Medora, the South Unit is home to some of the former president's personal artifacts and even his cabin.

3 Elkhorn Ranch. This area of the park is the actual location of one of T.R.'s ranches in the badlands. None of the ranch buildings are still standing, but signs show their former location.

GETTING ORIENTED

The Little Missouri River winds throughout this western North Dakota park, and plenty of bison, deer, pronghorn, coyote, prairie dogs, and eagles inhabit the land. Climb the peaks and you will get exceptional views of the canyons, caprocks, petrified forest, and other bizarre geological formations that make up the badlands.

KEY
🚹 *Ranger Station*
⛰ *Campground*
🎋 *Picnic Area*
🍴 *Restaurant*
🏨 *Lodge*
🚶 *Trailhead*
🚻 *Restrooms*
⇲ *Scenic Viewpoint*
⋯⋯ *Walking/Hiking Trails*

NORTH DAKOTA

Man and Grass Overlook

Bentonitic Clay Overlook

North Unit Scenic Drive

Buckhorn Trail

Caprock Coulee Trailhead

North

Oxbow Overlook

Long X Trailhead

Visitor Center

85

Achenbach Trail

Little Missouri River

Juniper Campground

Slump Block Pullout

Sperati Point

Achenbach

1

NORTH UNIT

Little Mo Trailhead

CCC Campground

36

Achenbach Trail

Achenbach Hills

0   2 mi

0   2 km

Maah Daah Hey Trail

Little Missouri River

Mike Auney Bottom

Horse Camp

Petrified Forest Plateau

3

ELKHORN RANCH

South Unit Scenic Loop Drive

0   2 mi

0   2 km

Big Plateau

Beef Corral Pullout

Peaceful Valley Ranch

Halliday Well Site

Cottonwood

2

SOUTH UNIT

Boicourt Overlook

River Woodland Overlook

North Dakota Badlands Overlook

Maltese Cross Ranch Cabin

Painted Canyon Overlook

Medora

Visitor Center

Ridgeline Trail

Chateau DeMores State Historic Site

Buck Hill

10   94

Sully Creek State Park

Sully Creek State Park

Visitor Center

Updated by
T.D. Griffith

Across much of North Dakota, for a century and a quarter, the terrain remained virtually unchanged from the day Theodore Roosevelt stepped off the train here in 1883, eager to shoot his first bison. Within two weeks, the future 26th president purchased an open-range cattle ranch, and the following year he returned to establish a second, which is part of the 110-square-mile national park that today bears his name. Despite its remote location, Theodore Roosevelt National Park is ideal for those intrepid travelers who revel in bird and wildlife viewing, hiking and backpacking, photography, picnicking, stargazing, and scenic drives.

Today, some 600,000 annual visitors are attracted to North Dakota's lone national park as much by its namesake as by its vast landscape of craggy ravines, tablelands, and gorges, an otherworldly moonscape that ranks among the least inhabited places in the U.S. For those who seek the road less traveled, a day trekking its backcountry trails or remote gravel roads can be a solitary pursuit, uninterrupted by any other humans.

THEODORE ROOSEVELT PLANNER

WHEN TO GO
The park is open year-round, but North Dakota winters can be brutal—very cold and windy. Portions of some roads close during winter months, depending on snowfall. Rangers discontinue their outdoor programs when autumn comes, and they recommend that only experienced hikers do any winter explorations. Check the park's website for current conditions.

■ TIP→ **Although July and August tend to be the busiest months, the park is rarely crowded.** About 600,000 people visit each year, with the South Unit receiving the greatest number of visitors. The best times to see wildlife and hike comfortably are May through October. The park is all but desolate December through February, but it's a beautiful time to see the wildlife—also, winter sunsets can be very vivid as the colors reflect off the snow and ice. The park gets an average of 30 inches of snow per year.

AVG. HIGH/LOW TEMPS.

Jan.	Feb.	Mar.	Apr.	May	June
27/1	34/8	43/18	58/30	71/40	79/50

July	Aug.	Sept.	Oct.	Nov.	Dec.
87/55	87/52	75/41	62/30	43/17	32/7

FESTIVALS AND EVENTS

JULY **Killdeer Mountain Roundup Rodeo.** Begun in 1923, this is North Dakota's oldest rodeo sanctioned by the PRCA. The community goes all out, hosting a parade, street dance, community barbecue, and fireworks display on July 3 and 4. ⊠ *Killdeer* ☎ *701/764–5777* ⊕ *www.killdeer.com.*

AUGUST **Founder's Day.** Each August 25, this holiday commemorates the establishment of the National Park Service in 1916. The visitor centers host special programs and serve cookies and lemonade. ☎ *701/623–4466* ⊕ *www.nps.gov/thro.*

SEPTEMBER **Dakota Nights Astronomy Festival.** Without light pollution from nearby towns, Theodore Roosevelt National Park is ideal for astronomical observation any cloudless night of the year. To enjoy the stars with others, come during the annual Dakota Nights Astronomy Festival in September (dates vary). Check the park website for a current schedule. ⊠ *Theodore Roosevelt National Park* ⊕ *www.nps.gov/thro* ☎ *Free.*

DECEMBER **Old-Fashioned Cowboy Christmas.** Held the first full weekend in December
FAMILY in downtown Medora, the Old-Fashioned Cowboy Christmas begins with a wreath-hanging ceremony at the community center, followed by a children's carnival, sleigh rides, magic acts, and a dance. ⊠ *Medora* ☎ *701/623–4910.*

PLANNING YOUR TIME

THEODORE ROOSEVELT IN ONE DAY

With just one day, focus on the South Unit. Arrive early at the **Painted Canyon Scenic Overlook,** near the visitor center, for a sweeping and colorful vista of the canyon's rock formations. Stay awhile to watch the effect of the sun's progress across the sky, or come back in the evening to witness the deepening colors and silhouettes in the fading sunlight.

Continue to the **South Unit Visitor Center** in Medora, spending about an hour here touring the Theodore Roosevelt exhibit and the Maltese Cross Ranch Cabin. Circle the 36-mile **Scenic Loop Drive** twice: once to stop and walk a few trails and visit the overlooks, and once at sundown to watch the wildlife. Your first time around, go counterclockwise. Stop at **Scoria Point Overlook** and hike 0.6 mile on **Ridgeline Nature Trail.** Back

36

Plants and Wildlife in Theodore Roosevelt

The park's landscape is one of prairies marked by cliffs and rock chasms made of alternating layers of sandstone, siltstone, mudstone, and bentonite clay. In spring the prairies are awash with tall grasses, wildflowers, and shrubs including the ubiquitous poison ivy. The pesky plant also inhabits the forests, where you find box elders, ash, and junipers among the trees. To avoid the rash-inducing plant—and scrapes and bruises that may come from rocks and thick undergrowth—it's always advisable to hike with long pants and sturdy boots.

More than 400 American bison live in the park. These normally docile beasts look tame, but with a set of horns, up to a ton of weight, and legs that will carry them at speeds in excess of 35 mph, they could be the most dangerous animals within park boundaries. Rangers tell visitors repeatedly not to approach them. Some mountain lions also live in the park but are rarely seen. The same goes for prairie rattlers.

On the less threatening side of the park's fauna, a herd of more than 200 to 300 elk live in the South Unit. As many as 150 feral horses are also in the South Unit. The North Unit has some longhorn steers, which are often found in the bison corral area, about 2½ miles west of the visitor center.

on the drive, stop next at the North Dakota Badlands and Boicourt overlooks to gaze at the strange, ever-changing terrain. When you pass through Peaceful Valley, look for prairie dogs. Have a packed lunch at the **Cottonwood picnic area,** then use a couple of hours to hike Jones Creek Trail or Coal Vein Nature Trail—or sign up for a horseback ride at **Peaceful Valley Ranch.**

Return to your car at least an hour before sunset, and drive slowly around Scenic Loop Drive, clockwise this time, to view the wildlife. Plan to be at **Buck Hill** for one of the most spectacular sunsets you'll ever see. Bring a jacket, because it's a bit windy and it gets chilly as the sun sets. After dark, drive carefully out of the park—elk and other animals may still be on the road.

GETTING HERE AND AROUND
AIR TRAVEL
Planes fly into the North Dakota towns of Bismarck, Dickinson, and Williston.

CAR TRAVEL
Getting to and from the park is relatively easy due to its close proximity to Medora, as well as exceptional signage. The South Unit entrance and visitor center is just off Interstate 94 in Medora at exits 24 and 27. The Painted Canyon Visitor Center is 7 miles east of Medora on Interstate 94 at exit 32. The North Unit entrance is south of Watford City on U.S. 85. Bus transportation is available along Interstate 94, with a stop in Medora that is only three blocks from the park entrance.

There's ample parking space at all trailheads, and parking is free. Some roads are closed in winter. You may encounter bison and other wildlife on the roadway.

TRAIN TRAVEL
Amtrak serves Williston.

PARK ESSENTIALS

PARK FEES AND PERMITS
The entrance pass is $20 per vehicle, $15 per motorcycle, and $10 for an individual, good for seven days. A variety of annual passes are available. A backcountry permit, free from the visitor centers, is required for overnight camping away from campgrounds.

PARK HOURS
The park is open year-round. The North Unit is in the Central time zone. The South Unit and the Painted Canyon Visitor Center are in the Mountain time zone. The South Unit Visitor Center is open year-round; the North Unit and Painted Canyon Visitor Centers are open May–October. Check the park website for current operating hours.

CELL-PHONE RECEPTION
Cell-phone reception occurs in some areas of the park, but many places receive no signal. Public telephones can be found at the South Unit's Cottonwood Campground, at the Painted Canyon Visitor Center, and at the North Unit Visitor Center.

EDUCATIONAL OFFERINGS

RANGER PROGRAMS
FAMILY **Evening Campfires.** Rangers host hour-long presentations and discussions on such subjects as park history, astronomy, fires, and wildlife. Look for times and subjects posted at park campgrounds. ⊠ *Cottonwood Campground, South Unit; Juniper Campground, North Unit ⊕ www. nps.gov/thro ☾ June–mid-Sept., daily.*

FAMILY **Ranger-Led Talks and Walks.** Rangers take visitors on the trails of both units and through the backcountry and Elkhorn Ranch, discussing such subjects as geology, paleontology, wildlife, and natural history. Check at campground entrances or at the visitor centers for times, topics, departure points, and destinations. ⊠ *Theodore Roosevelt National Park* ☏ *701/623–4466 ⊕ www.nps.gov/thro ✉ Free ☾ June–mid-Sept., daily.*

FILM
T.R. Country. All three visitor centers show a 13-minute film focusing on the unique beauty and breathtaking landscape of North Dakota's badlands, its wildlife, and its history, narrated with Roosevelt's own words. ⊠ *South Unit, North Unit, and Painted Canyon visitor centers* ☏ *701/623–4466 ⊕ www.nps.gov/thro ✉ Free ☾ Daily, every half hr.*

RESTAURANTS
One does not visit Theodore Roosevelt National Park for the fine dining. In fact, the only venues within the park are the picnic areas, and provided you're prepared, this can be a perfectly simple and satisfying way to experience the open spaces and natural wonder of the badlands. In the towns near the park you'll find casual, down-to-earth family establishments that largely cater to the locals. Expect steak and

potatoes, and lots of them. Fortunately, the beef here is among the best in the country.

HOTELS

If you're set on sleeping within the park, be sure to pack your tent. Outside the park are mostly small chain hotels catering to interstate travelers—largely retired couples in RVs and young families in minivans. However, there is a handful of historic properties and working ranches that offer guests a truly Western experience. Due to the current oil boom in the region, it's essential to book ahead during summer months. *Hotel reviews have been shortened. For full information, visit Fodors.com.*

WHAT IT COSTS				
	$	**$$**	**$$$**	**$$$$**
Restaurants	under $13	$13–$20	$21–$30	over $30
Hotels	under $101	$101–$150	$151–$200	over $200

Restaurant prices are the average cost of a main course at dinner or, if dinner is not served, at lunch. Hotel prices are the lowest cost of a standard double room in high season.

VISITOR INFORMATION

Park Contact Information Theodore Roosevelt National Park. ⊠ *Theodore Roosevelt National Park* ☎ *701/623-4466 South Unit,* ⊕ *www.nps.gov/thro.*

VISITOR CENTERS

North Unit Visitor Center. Here you'll find a bookstore and small auditorium where you can watch park films to acquaint you with the park. ⊠ *North Unit entrance, off U.S. 85, North Unit* ☎ *701/842-2333* ⊕ *www.nps.gov/thro* ⬛ *Free* ⊗ *Memorial Day–Labor Day, daily 9–5:30; check park website for off-season hrs.*

Painted Canyon Visitor Center. Easily reached off Interstate 94, this South Unit Visitor Center has a bookstore and exhibits. ⊠ *Exit 32 off I–94, South Unit* ☎ *701/575-4020* ⊕ *www.nps.gov/thro* ⬛ *Free* ⊗ *Mid-June–Labor Day, daily 8–6; May–mid-June and early Sept. and Oct., daily 8:30–4:30.*

South Unit Visitor Center. This building houses a large auditorium screening films about the park, plus an excellent exhibit on Theodore Roosevelt's life. On display are artifacts such as the clothing Roosevelt wore while ranching in the Dakota Territory, his firearms, and several writings in his own hand reflecting his thoughts on the nation's environmental resources. A bookstore and public restrooms are available. ⊠ *South Unit entrance, exits 24 and 27 off I–94* ☎ *701/623-4466* ⊕ *www.nps. gov/thro* ⬛ *Free* ⊗ *June–Sept., daily 8–6; Oct.–May, daily 8–4:30.*

EXPLORING

SCENIC DRIVES

North Unit Scenic Drive. The 14-mile, two-way drive follows rugged terrain above spectacular views of the canyons, and is flanked by more than a dozen turnouts with interpretive signs. Notice the slump blocks, massive segments of rock that have slipped down the cliff walls over time. Farther along pass through badlands coulees, deep-water clefts that are now dry. There's a good chance of meeting bison, mule deer, and bighorn sheep along the way, also keep an eye out for longhorn steers, just like the ones you would see in Texas. ⊠ *From the unit entrance to the Oxbow Overlook, North Unit.*

South Unit Scenic Loop Drive. A 36-mile, two-way scenic loop takes you past prairie-dog towns, coal veins, trailheads, and panoramic views of the badlands. Information on the park's natural history is posted at the various overlooks—stop at all of the interpretive signs to learn about the park's natural and historical phenomena. Some of the best views can be seen from Scoria Point Overlook, Boicourt Overlook, North Dakota Badlands Overlook, Skyline Vista, and Buck Hill. If you hit the road at dusk, be prepared to get caught in a buffalo traffic jam, as the huge creatures sometimes block the road and aren't in any hurry to move. Don't get out of your car or honk at them—they don't like it. ⊠ *Loop begins near Peaceful Valley Ranch, South Unit.*

HISTORIC SITES

Elkhorn Ranch. This unit of the park is composed of the 218 acres of ranchland where Theodore Roosevelt ran cattle on the open range. Today there are no buildings, but foundation blocks outline the original structures. Check with visitor center staff about road conditions. ⊕ *35 miles north of South Unit Visitor Center* ☎ *701/623–4466 South Unit* ⊒ *Free.*

Maltese Cross Ranch Cabin. About 7 miles from its original site in the river bottom sits the cabin Theodore Roosevelt commissioned to be built on his Dakota Territory property. Inside are Roosevelt's original writing table and rocking chair. Interpretive tours are scheduled every day June–September. ⊠ *South Unit entrance, exits 24 and 27 off I–94* ☎ *701/623–4466 South Unit* ⊒ *Free.*

SCENIC STOPS

Fodor'sChoice ★ **Buck Hill.** At 2,855 feet, this is one of the highest points in the park and provides a spectacular 360-degree view of the badlands. Come here for the sunset. ⊕ *17 miles east of the South Unit Visitor Center.*

Oxbow Overlook. The view from this spot at the end of the North Unit drive looks over the unit's westerly badlands and the Little Missouri River, where it takes a sharp turn south. This is the place to come for stargazing. ⊕ *14 miles west of the North Unit Visitor Center.*

36

Don't let these bulky beasts fool you: even though a bison may weigh 2,000 pounds, it can run 35 mph.

Painted Canyon Scenic Overlook. Catch your first glimpse of badlands majesty here—the South Unit canyon's colors change dramatically with the movement of the sun across the sky. ⊠ *Exit 32 off I–94, South Unit.*

Petrified Forest. Although bits of petrified wood have been found all over the park, the densest collection is in the South Unit's west end, accessible on foot or horseback via the Petrified Forest Loop Trail from Peaceful Valley Ranch (10 miles round-trip) or from the park's west boundary (3 miles round-trip). ⊠ *Trailheads: Peaceful Valley Ranch, 7 miles north of the South Unit Visitor Center; west boundary, 10 miles north of exit 23 off I–94/U.S. 10.*

Sperati Point. For a great view of the Missouri River's 90-degree angle, hike a 1½-mile round-trip trail to this spot 430 feet above the riverbed. ⊹ *14 miles west of the North Unit Visitor Center.*

SPORTS AND THE OUTDOORS

During the summer months, the park is best seen by hiking its many trails. If visitors want to take in the park the way the West's original settlers did, there are ample opportunities to saddle up and view the park on horseback.

BICYCLING

Bikes are allowed on interior roads but not off-road. Cyclists on the multiuse Maah Daah Hey Trail aren't allowed on the portions of the trails within the park.

FISHING

Catfish, little suckers, northern pikes, and goldeyes are among the underwater inhabitants of the Little Missouri River. If you wish to fish in the park or elsewhere in the state and are over age 16, you must obtain a North Dakota fishing license. For out-of-state residents, a three-day permit is $15, a 10-day permit is $25, and a one-year permit is $45. For in-state residents, a one-year permit is $10.

Buffalo Gap Guest Ranch. Eight miles west of Medora, the Buffalo Gap Guest Ranch sells hunting and fishing licenses. ⊠ *3100 Buffalo Gap Rd., Medora* ☎ *701/623–4200* ⊕ *www.buffalogapguestranch.com.*

> ## BEST BETS FOR FAMILIES
>
> ■ **Horseback Riding.** Saddling up and riding astride a horse for a while lets kids relive the days of the Old West.
>
> ■ **Medora Musical.** This show is a fun summer event with surprisingly diverse acts. For the complete package, hit the Pitchfork Fondue before the show.
>
> ■ **Stargazing Party.** Look upon the seemingly endless stars in the vast North Dakota sky.

36

HIKING

Particularly in the South Unit, there are numerous opportunities to jump on a trail right from the park road. The North and South units are connected by the 96-mile Maah Daah Hey Trail. Backcountry hiking is allowed, but you need a permit (free from any visitor center) to camp in the wild. Park maps are available at all three visitor centers. If you plan to camp overnight, let several people know about where you plan to pitch your tent, and inquire about river conditions, maps, regulations, trail updates, and additional water sources before setting out.

NORTH UNIT

EASY

FAMILY **Buckhorn Trail.** A thriving prairie-dog town is just 1 mile from the trailhead of this 11-mile North Unit trail. It travels over level grasslands, then it loops back along the banks of Squaw Creek. If you're an experienced hiker, you'll complete the entire trail in about half a day. Novices or families might want to plan on a whole day, however. *Easy.* ✛ *Trailhead: Caprock Coulee Nature Trail, 1½ miles west of the Juniper Campground.*

FAMILY **Little Mo Nature Trail.** Flat and only 1.1 miles long, this trail in the North Unit passes through badlands and woodlands to the river's edge. The first 0.7 mile is wheelchair accessible. It's a great way to see the park's diverse terrain and wildlife, and because it shouldn't take you longer than an hour, it's a great trail for families with children. *Easy.* ✛ *Trailhead: Juniper Campground in the North Unit.*

DIFFICULT

Upper Caprock Coulee Trail. This 4.3-mile round-trip trail follows a loop around the pockmarked lower-badlands coulees. There's a slow incline that takes you up 300 feet. Portions of the trail are slippery. Beginners should plan a half day for this hike. *Difficult.* ⬦ *Trailhead: 8 miles west of North Unit Visitor Center.*

SOUTH UNIT
MODERATE

FAMILY **Maah Daah Hey Trail.** Hike, bike, or ride horseback on the 96-mile and
Fodor's Choice growing Maah Daah Hey Trail, the most popular and well-maintained
★ trail in western North Dakota. An expansion project, completed in the summer of 2010, opened up new vistas that were previously inaccessible. The trail traverses both park units and the Little Missouri National Grasslands. Maps are available at the park visitor centers. Walking the entire trail is a true wilderness adventure and will probably take you at least five days. If you want to do something shorter, such as a two- or three-hour hike, leave from the South Unit and walk an hour or hour and a half in one direction, and then return. *Moderate.* ⬦ *Trailhead: Sully Creek State Park, 3 miles south of South Unit Visitor Center.*

HORSEBACK RIDING

The best way to see many of the park's sights is on horseback. You are allowed to bring your own horse to the park, or you can sign up for a guided trip. Horses are allowed only on backcountry trails or cross-country. Like campers, riders must obtain free backcountry-use permits. Riders taking multiday trips through the park must also have a permit. Horses are not allowed on park roadways, in developed campgrounds, picnic areas, or on developed nature trails. Overnight parties in the backcountry are limited to a maximum of eight horses and eight riders per group. Horses must be tied down securely when not being ridden. Be sure to bring enough water for the animals and certified weed-free hay.

WHAT'S NEARBY

NEARBY TOWNS

Medora, gateway to the park's South Unit, may have a population of only 96, but it is a walkable town with several museums, tiny shops, and plenty of restaurants and places to stay. Its Wild West history is reenacted in a madcap musical production each night in summer. To the east is **Dickinson** (pop. 28,000), the largest town near the national park. North of Dickinson and about 35 miles east of the park's North Unit, **Killdeer** (pop. about 825) is known for its Roundup Rodeo—North Dakota's oldest—and its gorgeous scenery. Killdeer is the place to fill your tank, because there isn't another gas station around for 40 miles. **Williston** (pop. about 30,000) is 60 miles north of the North Unit, just over the Missouri River. The Amtrak stop nearest to the national park is here.

VISITOR INFORMATION
Dickinson Convention and Visitors Bureau. ✉ *72 W. Museum Dr., Dickinson* ☎ *701/483-4988, 800/279-7391* ⊕ *www.visitdickinson.com.* **Killdeer City Hall.** ✉ *165 Railroad St., Killdeer* ☎ *701/764-5295* ⊕ *www.killdeer.com.* **Medora**

Chamber of Commerce. ⊠ *475 4th St., Medora* ☎ *701/623–4830* ⊕ *www. medorand.com.* **Williston Convention and Visitors Bureau.** ⊠ *212 Airport Rd., Williston* ☎ *701/774–9041, 800/615–9041* ⊕ *www.visitwilliston.com.*

NEARBY ATTRACTIONS

Little Missouri National Grasslands. This is the largest and most diverse of 19 national grasslands in the western United States, spanning a million acres in western North Dakota. It takes three hours to complete a self-guided 58-mile driving tour known as the Custer Auto Trail, beginning and ending in Medora. The best time to see wildlife is in early morning or late afternoon. Don't forget a camera and binoculars. There are no designated hiking trails, but off-road hiking is permitted. For a copy of the driving tour, contact the U.S. Forest Service office in Dickinson or the South Unit Visitor Center. ⊠ *U.S. Forest Service, 99 23rd Ave. W, Dickinson* ☎ *701/227–7800* ⊕ *www.fs.usda.gov/dpg* ⊠ *Free.*

Little Missouri State Park. Called *Mako Shika* or "Land Bad" by the Sioux, the Little Missouri State Park has unusual land formations that create the state's most awe-inspiring scenery. The beehive-shaped rock formations resulted from the erosion of sedimentary rock deposited millions of years ago by streams flowing from the Rocky Mountains. Undeveloped and rugged, this wilderness area has primitive and modern camping and 50 miles of horse trails. ⊠ *Killdeer* ✛ *Off Rte. 22, 18 miles north and 2 miles east of Killdeer* ☎ *701/764–5256 summer, 701/794–3731 winter* ⊕ *www.parkrec.nd.gov/parks/lmosp/lmosp.html* ⊠ *$5 per vehicle* ⊙ *Daily.*

North Dakota Cowboy Hall of Fame. This $4 million museum features six galleries and rotating exhibits, hosts special events, and is dedicated to the horse culture of the plains. ⊠ *250 Main St., Medora* ☎ *701/623–2000* ⊕ *www.northdakotacowboy.com* ⊠ *$8* ⊙ *May–Sept., daily 9–6.*

Roadside Art. Known as the "Enchanted Highway," this self-guided 30-mile driving tour on Route 21 south of Dickinson features seven giant metal sculptures designed by a local artist, including a 51-foot Teddy Roosevelt. Massive sculptures include a deer crossing, grasshopper family, pheasants on the prairie, a 150-foot-long gaggle of geese, and a tin family with a 45-foot father, 44-foot mother, and 23-foot son. ⊠ *Exit 72 off I–94, Rte. 21 between Lefor and Regent, Dickinson* ☎ *701/483–4988, 800/279–7391* ⊠ *Free.*

AREA ACTIVITIES

SPORTS AND THE OUTDOORS
GOLF

Fodor'sChoice
★
Bully Pulpit Golf Course. This impressive golf course weaves its way through the badlands buttes, giving players a truly breathtaking backdrop for a round of golf, and some exceptional vertical teeboxes and greens. It's one of the best and most challenging public courses in the United States. ⊠ *3731 Bible Camp Rd., Medora* ☎ *701/623–4653* ⊠ *$89, includes cart* ⌿ *18 holes, 7166 yards, par 72* ⊙ *Mid-Apr.–Oct., daily dawn–dusk.*

NIGHTLIFE AND PERFORMING ARTS

FAMILY **Medora Musical.** Well worth your while in summer is this theatrical tribute to the Old West, its history, and its personalities. It's been in operation for five decades. ⊠ *3422 Chateau Rd., Medora* ☎ *701/623–4444, 800/633–6721* ⊕ *www.medora.com* ✉ *$37* ⊙ *Early June–Labor Day, daily 7:30 pm.*

WHERE TO EAT

IN THE PARK

PICNIC AREAS

Cottonwood. This is in a lovely valley near the river. There are fire pits, drinking water, restrooms, eight open tables, and eight covered tables. ⊕ *5½ miles north of South Unit Visitor Center.*

Juniper. This area has restrooms, grills, drinking water, and 28 tables (eight with shelter). ⊕ *5 miles west of North Unit Visitor Center.*

Painted Canyon Scenic Overlook. This area has eight covered tables, drinking water, restrooms, and a spectacular view. ⊠ *Exit 32 off I–94.*

OUTSIDE THE PARK

$$ ✗ **Boots Bar and Grill.** This watering hole is the type of place your
STEAKHOUSE grandpa probably talked about. It has Medora's largest tavern, an
FAMILY upstairs dining room, and breezy patios, as well as live music, dancing, and microbrews. Diners feast primarily on pizzas, burgers, and steak and it's kid-friendly until 10 pm, even friendlier afterward. ⑤ *Average main: $20* ⊠ *300 Pacific Ave., Medora* ☎ *701/623–2668* ⊕ *www. bootsbarmedora.com.*

$$ ✗ **Buckskin Bar and Grill.** This steak house, with a saloon and dance hall,
STEAKHOUSE was built in 1915. The building has rough-hewn walls, original wood floors, and tin ceilings. It's still the local hangout for the ranching community, who saunter in for the prime rib and latest local news. Photos of local cowboy celebrities who dined here line the walls. Steak and seafood are the kitchen's main focus, with prime rib a specialty. For dessert, the homemade peach and cherry cobbler is a must. ⑤ *Average main: $17* ⊠ *64 Central Ave. S, Killdeer* ☎ *701/764–5321* ⊕ *www. buckskinbargrill.com.*

$ ✗ **Cowboy Cafe.** This locally owned-and-operated café specializes in
AMERICAN homemade soups, caramel rolls, and delicious roast beef dishes. Be prepared for a (short) wait, since the cozy dining room is popular with both locals and visitors, particularly at breakfast. ⑤ *Average main: $8* ⊠ *215 4th St., Medora* ☎ *701/623–4343* ⊟ *No credit cards.*

$$$ ✗ **Theodore's.** Theodore's offers the best fine dining in Medora and, per-
AMERICAN haps, in western North Dakota. The lunch menu features salads, prime-
Fodor's Choice rib sandwiches, and buffalo burgers, while dinner fare includes shrimp
★ with pineapple dipping sauce, a crusted South American rib eye, and tenderloin with Gorgonzola cream sauce. The stained glass and wood paneling make this restaurant inside the Rough Riders Hotel feel like

Best Campgrounds in Theodore Roosevelt

CLOSE UP

For the adventurous traveler, camping in Theodore Roosevelt is well worth the effort. The unadulterated isolation, epic views, and relationship with nature afforded by the Spartan campgrounds within the park create an experience you'll be hard-pressed to find elsewhere in the United States. Just remember that the park's campgrounds are relatively undeveloped—you'll have to pack in everything you need. If you pick a campsite in the surrounding wilderness, you must obtain a backcountry camping permit (available free) from a visitor center first.

Cottonwood Campground. Nestled under juniper and cottonwood trees on the bank of the Little Missouri River, this is a wonderful place to watch buffalo, elk, and other wildlife drink from the river at sunrise and just before sunset. ✉ *½ mile north of South Unit Visitor Center* ☎ *701/623–4466.*

Juniper Campground. The sites here are surrounded by junipers, hence the name. Don't be surprised if you see a bison herd wander through on its way to the Little Missouri River. ✉ *5 miles west of North Unit Visitor Center* ☎ *701/842–2333.*

36

a little hideaway for a quiet lunch or dinner. The fireplace was built from bricks taken from the North Dakota Capitol that burned in 1930. T.R.'s Tavern has a full-service bar. $ *Average main: $25* ✉ *Rough Riders Hotel, 301 3rd Ave., Medora* ☎ *701/623–4433* ⚲ *Reservations not accepted.*

WHERE TO STAY

OUTSIDE THE PARK

$$$
HOTEL
AmericInn Motel and Suites. A Western theme, complete with mounted animals, dominates the public areas of this contemporary hotel. **Pros:** near shops and restaurants; indoor pool; ideal after long hikes in the park. **Cons:** right on the railroad tracks; no elevator; chain-hotel feel. $ *Rooms from: $189* ✉ *75 E. River Rd. S, Medora* ☎ *701/623–4800, 800/634–3444* ⊕ *www.americinn.com* ⬎ *77 rooms, 8 suites* ⦿ *Breakfast.*

$$
RESORT
Buffalo Gap Guest Ranch. Perched on a bluff 8 miles west of Medora, this rustic property commands a view of the Dakota badlands and has access to the Maah Daah Hey Trail. **Pros:** great prices on lodging and food; exceptional view; large outdoor patio. **Cons:** bar can be smoky; 10 minutes from town. $ *Rooms from: $125* ✉ *3100 Buffalo Gap Rd., Medora* ☎ *701/623–4200* ⊕ *www.buffalogapguestranch.com* ⬎ *22 cabins, 10 RV sites* ⦿ *No meals.*

$
HOTEL
Ramada Grand Dakota Hotel. Across from the Prairie Hills Mall, this three-story motel lets you relax on couches before the fireplace in the huge lobby. **Pros:** full-service restaurant; great customer service. **Cons:** can be busy; pool can be quite popular, particularly in the summer.

⑤ *Rooms from: $99* ✉ *532 15th St. W, Dickinson* ☎ *701/483–5600, 800/422–0949* ⊕ *www.ramada.com* ↩ *192 rooms, 47 suites* ⏀ *No meals.*

$$$ ⛭ **Rough Riders Hotel.** Renovations over the years have made this place
HOTEL   decidedly posh, but it retains the red velvet chairs, antique armoires, and
Fodor's Choice   iron-rod and oak bed frames that have made this property a favorite
★   for decades. **Pros:** historic, downtown location; dining on the premises. **Cons:** relatively expensive; occasional railroad noise. ⑤ *Rooms from: $189* ✉ *301 3rd Ave., Medora* ☎ *701/623–4444, 800/633–6721* ⊕ *www.medora.com/stay/hotel/rough-riders-hotel* ↩ *76 rooms* ⏀ *No meals.*

WIND CAVE
NATIONAL PARK

WELCOME TO
WIND CAVE NATIONAL PARK

TOP REASONS
TO GO

★ **Underground exploring:** Wind Cave offers visitors the chance to get their hands and feet dirty on guided tours through long and complex caves.

★ **The call of the wild:** Wind Cave National Park boasts a wide variety of animals: bison, coyote, deer, antelope, elk, and prairie dogs.

★ **Education by candlelight:** Wind Cave offers numerous educational and interpretive programs, including the Candlelight Cave Tour, which allows guests to explore the cave by candlelight only.

★ **Historic cave:** On January 3, 1903, President Theodore Roosevelt signed a bill that made Wind Cave the first cave in the nation protected by the federal government.

★ **Noteworthy neighbors:** With its proximity to national parks, state parks, and other monuments, Wind Cave is situated perfectly to explore some of America's greatest national treasures.

1 The Surface. Wind Cave lies at the confluence of western mountains and central plains, which blesses the park with a unique landscape. A series of established trails weave in and out of forested hillsides and grassy meadows, providing treks of varying difficulty.

2 The Cave. With an explored maze of caverns totaling 145 miles, Wind Cave is considered one of the longest caves in the world. Notably, scientists estimate that only 5% of the cave has been explored to date. It is also estimated that 95% of the world's boxwork formations are found in Wind Cave, which means that visitors here are treated to some of the rarest geological features on the planet.

SOUTH DAKOTA

GETTING ORIENTED

Bounded by Black Hills National Forest to the west and windswept prairie to the east, Wind Cave National Park, in southwestern South Dakota, encompasses the transition between two distinct ecosystems: mountain forest and mixed-grass prairie. Abundant wildlife, including bison and elk, roam the 33,851 acres of the park's diverse terrain. Underground, a year-round 53°F temperature gives summer visitors a cool oasis—and winter visitors a warm escape.

37

Highland Creek Trail

Boland Ridge

Boland Ridge Trail

Red Valley

5

6

1

5

101

0   2 mi
0   2 km

KEY

- 👫 *Ranger Station*
- ⛺ *Campground*
- 🌲 *Picnic Area*
- 🍴 *Restaurant*
- 🏨 *Lodge*
- 🚶 *Trailhead*
- 🚻 *Restrooms*
- ⚜ *Scenic Viewpoint*
- ⋯ *Walking/Hiking Trails*

Updated by
T.D. Griffith

If you don't get out of your car at Wind Cave, you haven't scratched the surface—literally. The park has more than 145 miles of underground passageways. Curious cave formations include 95% of the world's mineral boxwork, and gypsum beard so sensitive it reacts to the heat of a lamp. This underground wilderness is part of a giant limestone labyrinth beneath the Black Hills. Wind Cave ranks as the sixth-longest cave in the world, but experts believe 95% of it has yet to be mapped.

WIND CAVE PLANNER

WHEN TO GO

The biggest crowds come to Wind Cave from June to September, but the park and surrounding Black Hills are large enough to diffuse the masses. Neither the cave nor grounds above are ever too packed, although on busy summer days tours sometimes sell out over an hour ahead of time, so come early in the day and reserve your spot. Park officials contend it's actually less busy during the first full week in August, when the Sturgis Motorcycle Rally brings roughly a half-million bikers to the region, clogging highways for miles around. Most hotels within a 100-mile radius are booked up to a year in advance.

The colder months are the least crowded, though you can still explore underground, thanks to the cave's constant 53°F temperature. The shoulder seasons are also unpopular, though autumn is a perfect time to visit. The days are warm, the nights are cool, and in late September/ early October the park's canyons and coulees display incredible colors.

AVG. HIGH/LOW TEMPS.

Jan.	Feb.	Mar.	Apr.	May	June
37/8	41/14	49/21	58/30	67/40	77/49
July	Aug.	Sept.	Oct.	Nov.	Dec.
84/55	84/53	76/44	63/32	46/20	39/12

FESTIVALS AND EVENTS

JUNE
FAMILY
Fodor's Choice
★

Crazy Horse Volksmarch. This 6.2-mile hike up the mountain where the massive Crazy Horse Memorial is being carved is the largest event of its kind and gives hikers the opportunity to stand on the Lakota leader's outstretched arm. It's held the first full weekend in June. ⊠ *12151 Ave. of the Chiefs, Crazy Horse Memorial ✥ 5 miles north of Custer* ☎ *605/673–4681* ⊕ *www.crazyhorse.org.*

JULY
FAMILY

Days of '76. This award-winning PRCA outdoor rodeo includes the usual riding, roping, and bull riding, two parades with vintage carriages and coaches, and Western arts and crafts. This five-day affair is one of the most popular events in South Dakota, featuring the top cowboys and cowgirls in the sport. ⊠ *Days of '76 Rodeo Grounds, 18 Seventy Six Dr., Deadwood ✥ North side of Deadwood across from First Gold Hotel* ☎ *800/999–1876* ⊕ *www.daysof76.com.*

FAMILY

Gold Discovery Days. A parade, carnival, car show, stick-horse rodeo, hot-air balloon rally, hunt for gold nuggets, and bed races are all part of the fun at this three-day event in late July in Custer. ⊠ *Main St., Custer* ☎ *800/992–9818* ⊕ *www.golddiscoverydays.com.*

SEPTEMBER
FAMILY
Fodor's Choice
★

Custer State Park Buffalo Roundup. The nation's largest buffalo roundup is one of South Dakota's most exciting events. Early on a Friday or Monday morning in late September or early October, cowboys and rangers saddle up and corral the park's 1,400 head of bison so they can be vaccinated. You'll hear the thunder of nearly 6,000 hooves before you even see the bison. ⊠ *Custer State Park, 13329 U.S. Hwy. 16A, Custer ✥ Travel south on the Wildlife Loop until you see the corrals and the crowd* ☎ *605/255–4515.*

Deadwood Jam. A quarter century strong and still filling the streets of Deadwood with live music, the Black Hills' premier music festival showcases an eclectic collection of country, rock, and blues for two days in mid-September. ⊠ *Deadwood History & Information Center, 3 Siever St., Deadwood* ☎ *800/999–1876* ⊕ *www.deadwood.com/events/ deadwoodjam.*

PLANNING YOUR TIME

WIND CAVE IN ONE DAY

Pack a picnic lunch, then head to the visitor center to purchase tickets for a morning tour of Wind Cave. Visit the exhibit rooms in the center afterward. Then drive or walk the quarter mile to the picnic area north of the visitor center. The refreshing air and deep emerald color of the pine woodlands will flavor your meal.

In the afternoon, take a leisurely drive through the parklands south of the visitor center, passing through **Gobbler Pass** and **Bison Flats**, for an archetypal view of the park and to look for wildlife. On the way back north, follow U.S. 385 east toward **Wind Cave Canyon**. If you enjoy bird-watching, park at the turnout and hike the 1.8-mile trail into the canyon, where you can spot swallows and great horned owls in the cliffs and woodpeckers in the trees.

Get back on the highway going north, take a right on Highway 87, and continue a half mile to the turnout for **Centennial Trail**. Hike the trail about 2 miles to the junction with **Lookout Point Trail**, turn right and return to Highway 87. The whole loop is about 4.75 miles. As you continue driving north to the top of Rankin Ridge, a pull-out to the right serves as the starting point for 1.25-mile **Rankin Ridge Trail**. It loops around the ridge, past **Lookout Tower**—the park's highest point—and ends up back at the pull-out. This trail is an excellent opportunity to enjoy the fresh air, open spaces, and diversity of wildlife in the park.

GETTING HERE AND AROUND

AIR TRAVEL
The nearest commercial airport is in Rapid City.

BUS TRAVEL
Bus lines serve Rapid City and Wall.

Gray Line of the Black Hills. This outfit offers bus tours from Rapid City to Mount Rushmore, Black Hills National Forest, Custer State Park, and the Crazy Horse Memorial, as well as other tours tied to special events. ✉ *1600 E. St. Patrick St., Rapid City* ☎ *605/342–4461, 800/456–4461* ⊕ *www.blackhillsgrayline.com.*

CAR TRAVEL
Wind Cave is 56 miles from Rapid City, via U.S. 16 and Highway 87, which runs through the park, and 73 miles southwest of Badlands National Park.

U.S. 385 and Highway 87 travel the length of the park on the west side. Additionally, two unpaved roads, NPS Roads 5 and 6, traverse the northeastern part of Wind Cave. NPS Road 5 joins Highway 87 at the park's north border.

PARK ESSENTIALS

PARK FEES AND PERMITS
There's no fee to enter the park; cave tours cost $7–$23. The requisite backcountry camping and horseback-riding permits are both free from the visitor center.

PARK HOURS
The park is open year-round. It is in the Mountain time zone.

CELL-PHONE RECEPTION
Cell-phone reception is hit and miss in the park, and western South Dakota is serviced only by Verizon Wireless and AT&T, so those with other carriers may be charged roaming fees. You will find a public phone outside the visitor center.

EDUCATIONAL OFFERINGS
RANGER PROGRAMS

FAMILY **Junior Ranger Program.** Kids 12 and younger can earn a Junior Ranger badge by completing activities that teach them about the park's ecosystems, the cave, the animals, and protecting the environment. Pick up the Junior Ranger guidebook for free at the Wind Cave Visitor Center. ✉ *Wind Cave National Park, 26611 Hwy. 385* ☎ *605/745–4600.*

Prairie Hike. This two-hour exploration of parkland habitats begins with a short talk at the visitor center, then moves to a trailhead. ✉ *26611 Hwy. 385* ☎ *605/745–4600* ⊕ *www.nps.gov/wica* ☉ *Late June–early-Aug., Mon. and Sat. 9 am.*

RESTAURANTS

If you're determined to dine in Wind Cave National Park, be sure to pack your own meal because, other than vending machines, the only dining venues inside park boundaries are the two picnic areas near the visitor center and Elk Mountain Campground. The towns beyond the park offer additional options. Deadwood claims some of the best-ranked restaurants in South Dakota. Buffalo, pheasant, and elk are relatively common ingredients in the Black Hills. No matter where you go, beef is king.

HOTELS

While Wind Cave claims a singular campground, you'll have to look outside park boundaries if you want to bed down in something more substantial than a tent. New chain hotels with modern amenities are plentiful in the Black Hills, but when booking accommodations consider a stay at one of the area's historic properties. From grand brick downtown hotels to intimate Queen Anne homes converted to bed-and-breakfasts, historic lodgings are easy to locate. Other distinctive lodging choices include the region's mountain lodges and forest retreats.

It may be difficult to obtain quality accommodations during summer—and downright impossible during the Sturgis Motorcycle Rally, held the first full week of August every year—so plan ahead and make reservations (three or four months out is a good rule of thumb) if you're going to travel during peak season. To find the best value, choose a hotel far from Interstate 90. *Hotel reviews have been shortened. For full information, visit Fodors.com.*

WHAT IT COSTS				
	$	$$	$$$	$$$$
Restaurants	under $13	$13–$20	$21–$30	over $30
Hotels	under $101	$101–$150	$151–$200	over $200

Restaurant prices are the average cost of a main course at dinner or, if dinner is not served, at lunch. Hotel prices are the lowest cost of a standard double room in high season.

VISITOR INFORMATION

Park Contact Information Wind Cave National Park. ✉ *26611 U.S. 385, Hot Springs* ☎ *605/745–4600* ⊕ *www.nps.gov/wica.*

CLOSE UP

Plants and Wildlife in Wind Cave

About three-quarters of the park is grassland. The rest is forested, mostly by the ponderosa pine. Poison ivy is common in wetter, shadier areas, so wear long pants and boots when hiking. The convergence of forest and prairies makes an attractive home for bison, elk, coyotes, pronghorn antelope, prairie dogs, and mule deer. Wild turkey and squirrels are less obvious in this landscape, but commonly seen by observant hikers.

Mountain lions also live in the park; although usually shy, they will attack if surprised or threatened. Make noise while hiking to prevent chance encounters. Bison appear docile, but can be dangerous. The largest land mammal in North America, they weigh up to a ton and run at speeds in excess of 35 mph.

VISITOR CENTERS

Wind Cave Visitor Center. The park's sole visitor center is the primary place to get general information. Located on top of the cave, it has three exhibit rooms, with displays on cave exploration, the Civilian Conservation Corps, park wildlife, and resource management. Other than vending machines, there's no coffee or snacks here or elsewhere in the park. ⊠ *26611 U.S. 385, Hot Springs* ✛ *Off U.S. 385, 3 miles north of park's southern border* ☎ *605/745–4600* ⊕ *www.nps.gov/wica* ✉ *Free* ⊙ *Mid-Apr.–mid-Oct., daily 8–5; mid-Oct.–early Apr., daily 8–4:30.*

EXPLORING

SCENIC DRIVES

Bison Flats Drive (South Entrance). Entering the park from the south on U.S. 385 takes you past Gobbler Ridge and into the hills commonly found in the southern Black Hills region. After a couple of miles, the landscape gently levels onto the Bison Flats, one of the mixed-grass prairies on which the park prides itself. You might see a herd of grazing buffalo between here and the visitor center. You can also catch panoramic views of the parklands, surrounding hills, and limestone bluffs. ⊠ *Hwy. 385.*

Fodor's Choice ★ **Rankin Ridge Drive (North Entrance).** Entering the park across the north border via Highway 87 is perhaps the most beautiful drive into the park. As you leave behind the grasslands and granite spires of Custer State Park and enter Wind Cave, you see the prairie, forest, and wetland habitats of the backcountry and some of the oldest rock in the Black Hills. The silvery twinkle of mica, quartz, and feldspar crystals dots Rankin Ridge east of Highway 87, and gradually gives way to limestone and sandstone formations. ⊠ *Hwy. 87.*

SCENIC STOPS

Rankin Ridge Lookout Tower. Some of the best panoramic views of the park and surrounding hills can be seen from this 5,013-foot tower, which is typically not staffed or open to the public. Hike the 1-mile Rankin Ridge loop to get there. ⊠ *Wind Cave National Park ⊹ 6 miles north of the visitor center on Hwy. 87.*

Fodor'sChoice
★

Wind Cave. Known to American Indians for centuries, Wind Cave was named for the strong currents of air that alternately blow in and out of its entrance. The cave's winds are related to the difference in atmospheric pressure between the cave and the surface. When the atmospheric pressure is higher outside than inside the cave, the air blows in, and vice versa. With more than 145 miles of known passageway divided into three different levels, Wind Cave ranks the sixth longest in the world. It's host to an incredibly diverse collection of geologic formations, including more boxwork than any other known cave, plus a series of underground lakes. The cave tours sponsored by the National Park Service allow you to see unusual and beautiful formations with names such as popcorn, frostwork, and boxwork. ⊠ *Wind Cave National Park ⊹ U.S. 385 to Wind Cave Visitor Center ⊕ www.nps.gov/wica/ planyourvisit/guidedtours.htm.*

DID YOU KNOW?

Theodore Roosevelt made Wind Cave one of the country's earliest national parks, and the first dedicated to preserving a cave resource, on January 3, 1903. It is now known to be one of the longest caves in the world, with 145 miles of explored passageways.

37

SPORTS AND THE OUTDOORS

Many visitors come to Wind Cave solely to descend into the park's underground passages. While there are great ranger-led tours for casual visitors—and more daring explorations for experienced cavers—the prairie and forest above the cave shouldn't be neglected.

MULTISPORT OUTFITTERS

Edge Sports—Rapid City. Rock climbers will find a good selection of equipment at Edge Sports, cavers will find a solid inventory of clothing and gear, while winter-sports lovers can explore an ample inventory of snowboards. Its store in Lead, open only in winter, is right on the way to the slopes and offers ski rentals. ⊠ *619 Main St., Rapid City* ☎ *605/716–9912.*

Granite Sports. Several miles north of Wind Cave Park in Hill City, Granite Sports sells hiking boots, Gore-Tex jackets, packs, and water bottles; they also know the best local guides. ⊠ *201 Main St., Hill City* ☎ *605/574–2121* ⊕ *www.granitesports.biz.*

Scheels All Sport. In the 118,000-square-foot Rushmore Crossing Mall, off Interstate 90 at East-North Street or Lacrosse Street exits, Scheels All Sport carries a wide selection of all-weather hiking clothes and binoculars suitable for bird-watchers and has shooting simulators. ✉ *1225 Eglin St., Rapid City* ☎ *605/342–9033* ⊕ *www.scheels.com.*

BIRD-WATCHING

Rankin Ridge. See large birds of prey here, including turkey vultures, hawks, and golden eagles. ⊹ *6 miles north of the visitor center on Hwy. 87.*

Fodor's Choice ★

Wind Cave Canyon. Here's one of the best birding areas in the park. The limestone walls of the canyon are ideal nesting grounds for cliff swallows and great horned owls, while the standing dead trees on the canyon floor attract red-headed and Lewis woodpeckers. As you hike down the trail, the steep-sided canyon widens to a panoramic view east across the prairies. ⊹ *About ½ mile east of visitor center* ⊕ *www.nps.gov/wica.*

HIKING

There are more than 30 miles of hiking trails within the boundaries of Wind Cave National Park, covering ponderosa forest and mixed-grass prairie. The landscape has changed little over the past century, so a hike through the park is as much a historical snapshot of pioneer life in the 1890s as it is exercise. Be sure to hit the Wind Cave Canyon Trail, where limestone cliffs attract birds like cliff swallows and great horned owls, and the Cold Brook Canyon Trail, a short but fun trip past a prairie-dog town to the park's edge. Besides birds and small animals such as squirrels, you're apt to see deer and pronghorn while hiking, and probably some bison.

Hiking into the wild, untouched backcountry is perfectly safe, provided you have a map (available from the visitor center) and a good sense of direction. Don't expect any developments, however; bathrooms and a water-bottle filling station are available only at the visitor center, and the trails are dirt or gravel. There are no easily accessible sources along the trails, and water from backcountry sources must be treated, so pack your own.

EASY

Wind Cave Canyon Trail. This easy 1.8-mile trail follows Wind Cave Canyon to the park boundary fence. The canyon, with its steep limestone walls and dead trees, provides the best opportunity in the park for bird-watching. Be especially vigilant for cliff swallows, great horned owls, and red-headed and Lewis woodpeckers. Deer, least chipmunks, and other small animals also are attracted to the sheltered environment of the canyon. Even though you could probably do a round-trip tour of this trail in less than an hour and a half, be sure to spend more time here to observe the wildlife. *Easy.* ⊹ *Trailhead: east side of Hwy. 385, 1 mile north of southern access road to visitor center.*

MODERATE

Centennial Trail. Constructed to celebrate South Dakota's centennial in 1989, this trail bisects the Black Hills, covering 111 miles from north to south. Designed for bikers, hikers, and horses, the trail is rugged but accommodating (note, however, that bicycling on the trail is not allowed within park boundaries). It will take you at least a half day to cover the 6 miles of this trail that traverse the park. *Moderate.* ⚜ *Trailhead: off Hwy. 87, 2 miles north of visitor center.*

FAMILY **Cold Brook Canyon Trail.** Starting on the west side of U.S. 385, 2 miles south of the visitor center, this 1.5-mile, mildly strenuous hike runs past a former prairie-dog town, the edge of an area burned by a controlled fire in 1986, and through Cold Brook Canyon to the park boundary fence. Experienced hikers can conquer this trail and return to the trailhead in an hour or less, but more leisurely visitors will probably need more time. *Moderate.* ⚜ *Trailhead: west side of U.S. 385, 2 miles south of visitor center.*

DIFFICULT

Boland Ridge Trail. Get away from the crowds for a half day via this strenuous, 2.5-mile round-trip hike. The panorama from the top is well worth it, especially at night. *Difficult.* ⚜ *Trailhead: off Park Service Rd. 6, 1 mile north of junction with Park Service Rd. 5.*

Highland Creek Trail. This difficult, roughly 8.5-mile trail is the longest and most diverse trail within the park, traversing mixed-grass prairies, ponderosa pine forests, and the riparian habitats of Highland Creek, Beaver Creek, and Wind Cave Canyon. Even those in good shape will need a full day to cover this trail round-trip. *Difficult.* ⚜ *Southern trailhead stems from Wind Cave Canyon trail 1 mile east of U.S. 385. Northern trailhead on Forest Service Rd. 5.*

SPELUNKING

Fodor's Choice ★ You may not explore the depths of Wind Cave on your own, but you can choose from five ranger-led cave tours, available from June through August; the rest of the year, only one or two tours are available. On each tour you pass incredibly beautiful cave formations, including extremely well-developed boxwork. The least crowded times to visit in summer are mornings and weekends.

The cave is 53°F year-round, so bring a sweater. Note that the uneven passages are often wet and slippery. Rangers discourage those with heart conditions and physical limitations from taking the organized tours. However, with some advance warning (and for a nominal fee) park rangers can arrange private, limited tours for those with physical disabilities. For wild caving tours, the park provides hard hats, knee pads, and gloves, and all cavers are required to have long pants, a long-sleeved shirt, and hiking boots or shoes with nonslip soles. If you prefer lighted passages and stairways to dark crawl spaces, a tour other than the Wild Caving Tour might appeal to you.

Tours depart from the visitor center. A schedule can be found online at ⊕ *www.nps.gov/wica*. To make a reservation, call ☎ *605/745–1134.*

EASY

Garden of Eden Cave Tour. You don't need to go far to see boxwork, pop-corn, and flowstone formations. Just take the relatively easy, one-hour tour, which covers about 0.25 mile and 150 stairs. It's available four times daily, June through Labor Day, and three times daily, October to early June. (It is unavailable most of September.) *Easy.* ✉ *26611 U.S. 385 ✚ 3 miles north of park's southern border* ⊕ *www.nps.gov/wica/ planyourvisit/tour-garden-of-eden.htm* ✆ *$10.*

Natural Entrance Cave Tour. This 1¼-hour tour takes you 0.5 mile into the cave, onto more than 300 stairs (most heading down), and out an elevator exit. Along the way are some significant boxwork deposits on the middle level. The tour leaves 15 times daily from June through Labor Day, and seven times daily for the rest of September. *Easy.* ✉ *26611 U.S. 385 ✚ Off U.S. 385, 3 miles north of park's southern border* ⊕ *www. nps.gov/wica/planyourvisit/tour-natural-entrance.htm* ✆ *$12.*

MODERATE

Candlelight Cave Tour. Available twice daily, early June through Labor Day, this tour goes into a section of the cave with no paved walks or lighting. Everyone on the tour carries a lantern similar to those used in expeditions in the 1890s. The tour lasts two hours and covers 1 mile; reservations are essential. Children younger than eight are not admitted. *Moderate.* ✉ *26611 U.S. 385 ✚ Off U.S. 385, 3 miles north of park's southern boundary* ⊕ *www.nps.gov/wica/planyourvisit/tour- candlelight.htm* ✆ *$12.*

Fairgrounds Cave Tour. View examples of nearly every type of calcite formation found in the cave on this 1½-hour tour, available eight times daily, June through Labor Day. There are some 450 steps, leading up and down. *Moderate.* ✉ *26611 U.S. 385 ✚ Off U.S. 385, 3 miles north of the park's southern boundary* ⊕ *www.nps.gov/wica/planyourvisit/ tour-fairgrounds.htm* ✆ *$12.*

DIFFICULT

Fodor's Choice   **Wild Cave Tour.** For a serious caving experience, sign up for this chal-
★   lenging four-hour tour. After some basic training in spelunking, you crawl and climb through fissures and corridors, most lined with gypsum needles, frostwork, and boxwork. Expect to get dirty. Wear shoes with good traction, long pants, and a long-sleeve shirt. The park provides knee pads, gloves, and hard hats with headlamps. Parents or guardians must sign a consent form for 16- and 17-year-olds. Tours are available at 1 pm daily, early June through mid-August, and at 1 pm weekends mid-August through Labor Day. Reservations are essential. *Difficult.* ✉ *26611 U.S. 385 ✚ Off U.S. 385, 3 miles north of park's southern boundary* ⊕ *www.nps.gov/wica/planyourvisit/tour-caving.htm* ✆ *$30.*

WHAT'S NEARBY

Wind Cave is part of South Dakota's Black Hills, a diverse region of alpine meadows, ponderosa pine forests, and creek-carved, granite-walled canyons covering 2 million acres in the state's southwest quadrant. This mountain range contrasts sharply with the sheer cliffs and dramatic buttes of the badlands to the north and east, and the wide, windswept plains of most of the state. Though anchored by Rapid City—the largest city for 350 miles in any direction—the Black Hills' crown jewel is Mount Rushmore National Memorial, visited by nearly 3 million people each year. U.S. 385 is the backbone of the Black Hills.

Subterranean Trail Network

KEY

Cave passage

Mound Builder's Rest

Bachelor's Quarters

Three-way Stair

Monte Cristo's Palace

Elks Room 3911 ft

Crossroads 3885 ft

Elevator Building

Garden of Eden

Wild Cave Tour

Garden of Eden Tour

Rome

Muddle Room

Omnibus Hall

Assembly Room

Model Room

Blue Grotto 3835 ft

Temple Room

Tour

Fairgrounds

Fairgrounds 3967 ft

Chert Room

Methodist Church

Trail

Candlelight Tour

The Attic

Brown's Canyon

Overland

Trail

Standing Rock Chamber

Pearly Gates

Devils Lookout 3931 ft

Visitor Center

Parking

The Amphitheater

Roe's Misery

Back Room

Post Office 3960 ft

Parking

Rainbow Falls

Snowdrift Avenue

Natural Entrance Tour

Upper Specimen Route

Trail

Fairy Palace

North Room 3983 ft

Cave Entrance

Guide's Discovery

COMMON CAVE TERMS

Sound like a serious spelunker with this cavemen cheat sheet for various *speleothems* (cave formations).

Boxwork: Composed of interconnecting thin blades that were left in relief on cave walls when the bedrock was dissolved away.

Cave balloons: Thin-walled formations resembling partially deflated balloons, usually composed of hydromagnesite.

Flowstone: Consists of thin layers of a mineral deposited on a sloping surface by flowing or seeping water.

Frostwork: Sprays of needles that radiate from a central point that are usually made of aragonite.

Gypsum beard: Composed of bundles of gypsum fibers that resemble a human beard.

Logomites: Consist of popcorn and superficially resemble hollowed-out stalagmites.

Pool Fingers: Deposited underneath water around organic filaments.

Stalactites: Carrot-shape formations formed from dripping water that hang down from a cave ceiling.

Stalagmites: Mineral deposits from dripping water built up on a cave floor.

NEARBY TOWNS

Custer. About 30 miles north of Hot Springs is the town of Custer, the Mother City of the Black Hills. Near here, George Armstrong Custer and his expedition first discovered gold in 1874, leading to the gold rush of 1875 and '76. ⊠ *Custer* ⊕ *www.visitcuster.com.*

Fodor'sChoice ★ **Deadwood.** In one of America's longest ongoing historic preservation projects, you'll discover brick streets fronted by Victorian architecture, with Main Street shops, restaurants, and gaming halls. Deadwood owes its historical character to gold and gaming halls, just as it did in its late-19th-century heyday. You can walk in the footsteps of Wild Bill Hickok and Calamity Jane, who swore she could outdrink, outspit, and outswear any man—and usually did. Both of the Western legends are buried in Deadwood's Boot Hill–Mt. Moriah Cemetery. ⊠ *Deadwood* ⊕ *www.deadwood.com.*

Hill City. The small, quiet mountain town of Hill City is the gateway to Mount Rushmore. Despite having just 780 residents, the community claims no fewer than seven art galleries, a natural history museum, a winery, a vintage steam railroad, and a classy visitor center on its eastern flank. ⊠ *Hill City* ⊕ *www.hillcitysd.com.*

Hot Springs. Noted for its striking sandstone structures, the small and historic community of Hot Springs is the gateway to Wind Cave National Park. It is also the entry point to scores of other natural and historical sites, including Evans Plunge, a naturally heated indoor-outdoor pool; the Mammoth Site, where more than 50 woolly and Columbian mammoths have been unearthed, the Black Hills Wild Horse Sanctuary, and one of the region's premier golf courses. ⊠ *Hot Springs* ⊕ *www. hotsprings-sd.com.*

Keystone. Founded in the 1880s by prospectors searching for gold deposits, the small town of Keystone, 2 miles from Mount Rushmore, has an abundance of restaurants, shops, and attractions, from wax museums to miniature-golf courses to alpine slides. To serve the millions of visitors passing through the area, there are 700 hotel rooms—more than twice the town's number of permanent residents. ⊠ *Keystone* ⊕ *www. keystonechamber.com.*

Rapid City. Called the "City of Presidents" because of the life-size bronze statues of U.S. presidents that adorn virtually every downtown street corner, Rapid City is the largest urban center in a 350-mile radius. The city is the area's cultural, educational, medical, and economic hub, and a good base from which to explore the treasures of the state's southwestern corner, including Mount Rushmore (25 miles south) and Wind Cave National Park (50 miles south). ⊠ *Rapid City* ⊕ *www. visitrapidcity.com.*

Visitor Information Black Hills, Badlands & Lakes Association. ⊠ *1851 Discovery Circle, Rapid City* ☎ *605/355–3600* ⊕ *www.blackhillsbadlands.com.*

NEARBY ATTRACTIONS

CUSTER

FAMILY **Crazy Horse Memorial.** Designed to be the world's largest work of art, this tribute to the spirit of the North American Indian people depicts Crazy Horse, the legendary Lakota leader who helped defeat General Custer at Little Bighorn. A work in progress, thus far the warrior's head has been carved from the mountain, and the colossal head of his horse is beginning to emerge. Self-taught sculptor Korczak Ziolkowski started this memorial in 1948. After his death in 1982, his family carried on the project. Near the work site stands an exceptional orientation center, the Indian Museum of North America, Ziolkowski's home and workshop, and the Indian University of North America. ⊠ *12151 Ave. of the Chiefs, Crazy Horse Memorial* ✛ *Hwy. 385, 5 miles north of Custer* ☎ *605/673–4681* ⊕ *www.crazyhorsememorial.org* ⊡ *$10* ⊙ *May–Sept., daily 7 am–9 pm; Oct.–Apr., daily 8–5.*

FAMILY **Custer State Park.** This 71,000-acre park is considered the crown jewel of
Fodor'sChoice South Dakota's state park system. Elk, antelope, mountain goats, bighorn sheep, mountain lions, wild turkey, prairie dogs, and the second-largest (behind Yellowstone National Park) publicly owned herd of bison in the world roam this pristine landscape. Scenic drives roll past fingerlike granite spires and panoramic views (try the Needles Highway). Take the 18-mile Wildlife Loop Road to see prairies teeming with animals and some of the beautiful backdrops for countless Western films. ⊠ *13329 U.S. 16A, Custer* ✛ *4 miles east of Custer* ☎ *605/255– 4515* ⊕ *www.custerstatepark.info* ⊡ *From $15* ⊙ *24/7 year-round.*

Jewel Cave National Monument. Even though its more than 177 miles of surveyed passages make this cave the world's third largest (Kentucky's Mammoth Cave is the longest), Jewel Cave isn't renowned for its size.

Rather, it's the rare crystalline formations that abound in the cave's vast passages. Wander the dark passageways and you'll be rewarded with the sight of tiny crystal Christmas trees, hydromagnesite balloons that would pop if you touched them, and delicate calcite deposits dubbed "cave popcorn." Year-round, you can take ranger-led tours for a fee, from a simple half-hour walk to a lantern-light tour. Surface trails and facilities are free. ⊠ *11149 U.S. Hwy. 16, Custer ✛ 15 miles west of Custer* ☎ *605/673–2288* ⊕ *www.nps.gov/jeca* 🎫 *From $4* ☉ *Sept.–Apr., daily 8–4:30; May–Aug., daily 8–5:30.*

DEADWOOD

FAMILY **Adams Museum.** Between the massive stone-block post office and the old railroad depot, there are three floors of displays at the Adams Museum, including the region's first locomotive, photographs of the town's early days, and an exhibit featuring the largest gold nugget ever discovered in the Black Hills. ⊠ *54 Sherman St., Deadwood* ☎ *605/578–1714* ⊕ *www.deadwoodhistory.com* 🎫 *Free* ☉ *Late May–early Sept., Mon.–Sat. 9–7, Sun. noon–5; early Sept.–late May, Mon.–Sat. 10–4.*

FAMILY **Broken Boot Gold Mine.** You can pan for gold here, and even if you don't find any you'll leave with a souvenir stock certificate. Visitors may also take a short, guided tour through the mine. ⊠ *U.S. 14A, Deadwood* ☎ *605/578–9997* ⊕ *www.brokenbootgoldmine.com* 🎫 *Tour $5, gold panning $7* ☉ *May–Aug., daily 8–5:30.*

HOT SPRINGS

Black Hills Wild Horse Sanctuary. More than 600 wild mustangs inhabit this 11,000-acre preserve of rugged canyons, forests, and grasslands along the Cheyenne River. Take a guided tour or hike, and sign up for a chuck-wagon dinner. From Hot Springs, drive 14 miles south until you see signs off Route 71. Reservations are required. ⊠ *12165 Highland Rd. (Rte. 71), Hot Springs* ☎ *605/745–5955, 800/252–6652* ⊕ *www. wildmustangs.com* 🎫 *From $50* ☉ *Nov.–Apr., Mon.–Sat. 9–5; tours at 10 and 1; Apr.–Oct., daily 8–5.*

FAMILY **Mammoth Site.** While building a housing development in the 1970s, Fodor's Choice workers uncovered this sinkhole where giant mammoths came to drink, ★ got trapped, and died. To date, 61 fossilized woolly beasts have been discovered, and most can still be seen on-site. You can watch the excavation in progress and take guided tours. ⊠ *1800 W. Hwy. 18 Bypass, 15 miles south of Wind Cave National Park, Hot Springs* ☎ *605/745–6017* ⊕ *www.mammothsite.com* 🎫 *$10, with last guided tour at 4 daily* ☉ *May–Sept., daily 8–8; Oct., daily 9–5; Nov.–Apr., Mon.–Sat. 9–3:30, Sun. 11–3:30.*

KEYSTONE

FAMILY **Beautiful Rushmore Cave.** Stalagmites, stalactites, flowstone, ribbons, columns, helictites, and the "Big Room" are all part of the worthwhile tour into this cave. In 1876, miners found the opening to the cave while digging a flume into the mountainside to carry water to the gold mines below. The cave was opened to the public in 1927, just before the carving of Mount Rushmore began. The attraction also features the Soaring Eagle zipline, Gunslinger 7D interactive ride and Xpedition Adventure, a caving adventure tour. ⊠ *13622 Hwy. 40, Keystone* ☎ *605/255–4384*

In the fall, listen to elk bugling, a high-pitched, whistlelike sound the animals make as they mate.

⊕ *www.rushmorecave.com* ✉ *From $16* ☺ *June–Sept., daily 8–8; May and Oct., daily 9–5.*

Mount Rushmore. Abraham Lincoln was tall in real life—6 feet, 4 inches, though add a few more for his hat. But at one of the nation's most famous iconic sights, Honest Abe, along with presidents George Washington, Thomas Jefferson, and Theodore Roosevelt, towers over the Black Hills in a 60-foot-high likeness. The four images look especially spectacular at night, June through mid-September, when a lighting ceremony dramatically illuminates them.

Follow the Presidential Trail through the forest to gain excellent views of the colossal sculpture, or stroll the Avenue of Flags for a different perspective. Also on-site are an impressive museum, indoor theaters where films are shown, an outdoor amphitheater for live performances, an award-winning audio tour, and concession facilities. The nightly ranger program and lighting of the memorial is reportedly the most popular interpretive program in all of the national parks system.

Some of the attractions at Mount Rushmore include:

Avenue of the Flags: Running from the entrance of the memorial to the museum and amphitheater at the base of the mountain, the avenue represents each state, commonwealth, district, and territory of the United States.

Lincoln Borglum Museum: This giant granite-and-glass structure underneath the viewing platform has permanent exhibits on the carving of the mountain, its history, and its significance. There also are temporary exhibits, a bookstore, and an orientation film. Admission is free.

Building Mount Rushmore

Like most impressive undertakings, Mount Rushmore's path to realization was one of personalities and perseverance.

When Gutzon Borglum, a talented and patriotic sculptor, was invited to create a giant monument to Confederate soldiers in Georgia in 1915, he jumped at the chance. The son of Danish immigrants, Borglum was raised in California and trained in art in Paris, even studying under Auguste Rodin, who influenced his style. Georgia's Stone Mountain project was to be massive in scope—encompassing the rock face of an entire peak—and would give Borglum the opportunity to exercise his artistic vision on a grand scale.

But the relationship between the project backers and Borglum went sour, causing the sculptor to destroy his models and flee the state. South Dakota state officials had a vision for another mountain memorial, and Borglum was eager to jump on board.

His passion and flamboyant personality were well matched to the project, which involved carving legends of the Wild West on a gigantic scale. In time, Borglum convinced officials to think larger, and the idea of carving a monument to U.S. presidents was born.

On a massive granite cliff, at an elevation of 5,725 feet, Borglum began carving Mount Rushmore in 1927 with the help of some 400 assistants. In consultation with U.S. Senator Peter Norbeck and State Historian Doane Robinson, Borglum chose the four presidents to signify the birth, growth, preservation, and development of the nation. In 6½ years of carving over a 14-year period, the sculptor and his crew drilled and dynamited a masterpiece, the largest work of art on earth. Borglum died in March 1941, leaving his son, Lincoln, to complete the work only a few months later—in the wake of the gathering storm of World War II.

Presidential Trail: This easy hike along a boardwalk and down some stairs leads to the very base of the mountain. Although the trail is thickly forested, you'll have more than ample opportunity to look straight up the noses of the four giant heads. The trail is open year-round, so long as snow and/or ice don't present a safety hazard.

Sculptor's Studio: Built in 1939 as Gutzon Borglum's on-site workshop, this studio displays tools used by the mountain carvers, a model of the memorial, and a model depicting the unfinished Hall of Records. It's open May–September only; admission is free.

Youth Exploration Area: This new feature is on the Presidential Trail beneath the towering visage of George Washington. At this stone and wood structure, rangers present interactive programs for youngsters. ⊠ *Ave. of the Flags, Mount Rushmore* ☎ *605/574–2523* ⊕ *www.nps. gov/moru* ✉ *Free, but parking is $11 per vehicle* ☉ *Daily 5 am–9 pm.*

Mount Rushmore Information Center. Between the park entrance and the Avenue of Flags, the Mount Rushmore Information Center has a small exhibit of photographs detailing the carving of the presidents' faces. The information desk is staffed by rangers who can answer questions about

The colossal Mount Rushmore is one of the United States' most majestic monuments.

the area. A nearly identical building across from the information center houses restrooms, telephones, soda machines, and an award-winning audio tour by the nonprofit Mount Rushmore History Association. ⊠ *Ave. of the Flags, Keystone* ☎ *605/574–2523* ⊕ *www.nps.gov/moru* 🖅 *Free* ⊙ *Late-May–mid-Aug., daily 8 am–10 pm; mid-Aug.–Sept., daily 8 am–9 pm; Oct.–late-May, daily 8–5.*

RAPID CITY

FAMILY
Fodor's Choice
★

Bear Country U.S.A. Encounter black bear, elk, sheep, and wolves at this drive-through wildlife park, which has been entertaining guests for more than 40 years. There's also a walk-through wildlife center with red foxes, porcupines, badgers, bobcats, and lynx. The Babyland area features bear cubs and young otters. ⊠ *13820 S. U.S. 16, Rapid City* ☎ *605/343–2290* ⊕ *www.bearcountryusa.com* 🖅 *$16, with a maximum per vehicle of $60* ⊙ *Apr., daily 9–5; May, daily 8–6; June and July, daily 7:30–7; Aug., daily 8–6, Sept., daily 8–5; Oct., daily 9–4; Nov., daily 9–3.*

FAMILY
Black Hills Caverns. Amethysts, logomites, calcite crystals, and other specimens fill this cave, first discovered by gold-seekers in 1882. Half-hour and hour tours, as well as panning for gold, are available. ⊠ *2600 Cavern Rd., Rapid City* ☎ *605/343–0542, 800/837–9358* ⊕ *www. blackhillscaverns.com* 🖅 *From $12.75* ⊙ *May–mid-June and mid-Aug.–Sept., daily 8:30–5:30; mid-June–mid-Aug., daily 8–7.*

FAMILY
Reptile Gardens. In the valley between Rapid City and Mount Rushmore is western South Dakota's answer to a zoo. In addition to the world's largest private reptile collection, the site also has alligator wrestling, a raptor show, and giant tortoises. Enjoy more than 50,000 orchids,

tulips, banana trees on the grounds and in the giant dome. ✉ *8955 S. U.S. 16, Rapid City* ☎ *605/342–5873, 800/335–0275* ⊕ *www. reptilegardens.com* 🖆 *From 12.50; $17 in summer* ⊙ *Mid-Mar.–mid-May, daily 9–4; mid-May–Labor Day, daily 8–6; Labor Day–Nov., daily 9–4; Dec.–mid-Mar., daily 9–3.*

SPEARFISH

FAMILY **High Plains Western Heritage Center.** Focusing on a region now covered by five states—the Dakotas, Wyoming, Montana, and Nebraska—this center features artifacts such as a Deadwood-Spearfish stagecoach. Outdoor exhibits include a log cabin, a one-room schoolhouse, and, in summer, an entire farm set up with antique equipment. Often on the calendar are cowboy poetry, live music, and historical talks. ✉ *825 Heritage Dr., Spearfish* ☎ *605/642–9378* ⊕ *www.westernheritagecenter. com* 🖆 *$10* ⊙ *Daily 9–5.*

SPORTS AND THE OUTDOORS

The Black Hills are a haven for outdoor enthusiasts, and with good reason. The warmer temperatures of spring and summer make for excellent fishing, hiking, mountain climbing, mountain biking, camping, and horseback riding in the national forest. Autumn's cooler weather and changing colors bring out the leaf peepers, and the hunters aren't far behind. Snow can fall as early as October, but the white stuff really starts coming down in December and January, when snowmobilers and skiers (both downhill and cross-country) come out to play. The northern Black Hills, where there are two ski areas, generally receive the highest accumulations, and have seen up to 180 inches of annual snowfall.

FISHING

The Black Hills are filled with tiny mountain creeks, especially on the wetter western and northern slopes, that are ideal for fly-fishing. Rapid Creek, which flows down from the Central Hills into Pactola Reservoir and finally into Rapid City, is a favorite fishing venue for the city's anglers, both because of its regularly stocked population of trout and for its easy accessibility.

South Dakota Game, Fish, and Parks. Besides the local chambers of commerce, South Dakota Game, Fish, and Parks is your best bet for updated information on regional fishing locations and their conditions. ✉ *523 E. Capitol Ave., Pierre* ☎ *605/773–3485* ⊕ *gfp.sd.gov.*

HIKING AND BICYCLING

Mickelson Trail. Beginning in Deadwood and running the length of the Black Hills, the Mickelson Trail incorporates more than 100 converted railroad bridges, four tunnels, and 15 trailheads along its 108.8-mile-long course. Although the grade is seldom steep, parts of the trail are strenuous. A $3 day pass or $15 annual pass are available at self-service stations along the trail, some state park offices, and from the South Dakota Game, Fish & Parks. A portion of the trail is open for snowmobiling in winter. ✉ *Deadwood* ⊕ *gfp.sd.gov/state-parks/directory/ mickelson-trail.*

WATER SPORTS

Angostura Reservoir State Recreation Area. Water-based recreation is the main draw at this park 10 miles south of Hot Springs. Besides a marina, you'll find a floating convenience store, restaurant, campgrounds, and cabins. Boat rentals are available. ☒ *U.S. 385, off Rte. 79, 13157 N. Angostura Rd., Hot Springs* ☎ *605/745–6996, 800/364–8831* ⊕ *gfp. sd.gov/state-parks/directory/angostura* ☒ *$4 per person, $6 per vehicle; $30 per vehicle annually* ⊙ *Daily dawn–dusk.*

WINTER SPORTS

Heavy snowfalls and lovely views make the Black Hills prime cross-country skiing territory. Many trails are open to snowmobilers as well as skiers. Trade and travel magazines consistently rank the Black Hills among the top snowmobiling destinations in the country for two simple reasons: dramatic scenery and an abundance of snow.

Deer Mountain Ski Area. This resort has an enlarged beginner's area, a redesigned Zero Gravity tube park, skiing, and snowboarding. Its 6-acre terrain park is favored by snowboarders. **Facilities:** 60 trails; 450 acres; 650-foot vertical drop; 4 lifts. ☒ *11187 Deer Mt. Rd., Lead* ⊹ *3 miles south of Lead off U.S. 85* ☎ *605/580–1169* ⊕ *www.skimystic. com* ☒ *Lift ticket: $42; 2-hr tubing session: $25.*

Terry Peak Ski Area. Perched on the sides of a 7,076-foot mountain, Terry Peak claims the Black Hills' second-highest summit and high-speed quad lifts. The runs are challenging for novice and intermediate skiers and should also keep the experts entertained. From the top, on a clear day, you can see Wyoming, Montana, and North Dakota. **Facilities:** 26 trails; 450 acres; 1,100-foot vertical drop; 4 lifts. ☒ *21120 Stewart Slope Rd., Lead* ⊹ *2 miles south of Lead on U.S. 85* ☎ *800/456–0524, 605/584–2165* ⊕ *www.terrypeak.com* ☒ *Lift ticket: $53.*

Trailshead Lodge. Near the Wyoming border, this lodge has a small restaurant and bar, cabins, a gas station and garage, and dozens of brand-new snowmobiles for rent by the day. This is a favorite pit-stop for snowmobilers exploring the popular Black Hills' 400-mile trail network. ☒ *22075 U.S. 85 S, Lead* ⊹ *21 miles southwest of Lead on U.S. 85* ☎ *605/584–3464* ⊕ *www.trailsheadlodge.com.*

NIGHTLIFE AND PERFORMING ARTS

PERFORMING ARTS

Rushmore Plaza Civic Center Fine Arts Theater. This is the venue for a half-dozen touring Broadway shows and the Vucurevich Speaker Series, which has attracted prominent names such as the humorist Dave Barry, late astronomer Carl Sagan, and former Secretary of State Colin Powell. There's also an ice rink where the Rush hockey team plays in winter months. ☒ *444 Mt. Rushmore Rd. N, Rapid City* ☎ *800/468–6463, 605/394–4111* ⊕ *www.gotmine.com.*

NIGHTLIFE

Midnight Star. It doesn't offer live music, but the Midnight Star is owned by actor Kevin Costner and decorated throughout with props and costumes from his movies. The bar on the first floor is named for and modeled after the bar in the film *Silverado,* in which Costner starred. Wood accents, stained glass, and plush carpeting give the structure an elegant Victorian look and there's a sports bar, Diamond Lil's, on the second floor. Jakes, on the top floor, is among the region's finest restaurants. ✉ *677 Main St., Deadwood* ☎ *605/578–1555, 800/999–6482* ⊕ *www.themidnightstar.com.*

Fodor's Choice ★ **Old Style Saloon No. 10.** Billing itself as "the world's only museum with a bar," the Old Style Saloon No. 10 is where you want to come to drink, listen to music, and socialize. Thousands of artifacts, vintage photos, and a two-headed calf set the scene—plus the chair in which Wild Bill Hickok was supposedly shot. A reenactment of his murder takes place four times daily in summer. Upstairs, there's an exceptional restaurant, the Deadwood Social Club, with the state's premier wine and martini bar. ✉ *657 Main St., Deadwood* ☎ *605/578–3346* ⊕ *www.saloon10.com.*

Silverado. Sprawling over half a city block at the top of Main Street, and including the historic Franklin Hotel across the street, the Silverado is among Deadwood's largest gaming establishments. Although the wood paneling and brass accents around the bars recall Deadwood's Wild West past, the red carpets, velvet ropes, and bow-tie-clad staff give the place modern polish. ✉ *709 Main St., Deadwood* ☎ *605/578–1366, 800/584–7005* ⊕ *www.silveradofranklin.com.*

SHOPPING

Fodor's Choice ★ **Prairie Edge Trading Company and Galleries.** One of the world's top collections of Plains Indian artwork and crafts makes Prairie Edge Trading Company and Galleries seem more like a museum than a store. The collection ranges from books to stunning artwork representing the Lakota, Crow, Cheyenne, Shoshone, Arapaho, and Assiniboine tribes of the Great Plains. ✉ *6th and Main Sts., Rapid City* ☎ *605/342–3086* ⊕ *www.prairieedge.com.*

SCENIC DRIVES

Peter Norbeck National Scenic Byway. Although there are faster ways to get from Mount Rushmore to the southern Black Hills, this scenic drive in the Black Hills is a more stunning route. Take U.S. 16A south into Custer State Park, where bison, bighorn sheep, elk, antelope, and burros roam free. Then drive north on Highway 87 through the Needles, towering granite spires that rise above the forest. A short drive off the highway reaches 7,242-foot Harney Peak, the highest point in North America east of the Rockies. Highway 87 finally brings you to U.S. 16/U.S. 385, where you head south to the Crazy Horse Memorial. Because the scenic byway is a challenging drive (with one-lane tunnels and switchbacks) and because you'll likely want to stop a few times to admire the scenery, plan on spending two to three hours on this drive. Stretches of U.S. 16A and Highway 87 may close in winter. ✉ *Keystone.*

Spearfish Canyon Scenic Byway. The easiest way to get from Deadwood to Rapid City is east through Boulder Canyon on U.S. 14A. However, it's worth looping north and taking the long way around on this

20-mile scenic route past 1,000-foot limestone cliffs and some of the most breathtaking scenery in the region. Cascading waterfalls quench the thirst of quaking aspen, gnarled oaks, sweet-smelling spruce, and the ubiquitous ponderosa pine. The canyon is home to deer, mountain goats, porcupines, and mountain lions. Near its middle is the old sawmill town of Savoy, a jumping-off point for scenic hikes to Spearfish Falls and Roughlock Falls. In fall, changing leaves rival any found in New England. ⊠ *10619 Roughlock Falls Rd.* ⊕ *www.spearfishcanyon.com.*

WHERE TO EAT

IN THE PARK

PICNIC AREAS

Elk Mountain Campground Picnic Area. You don't have to be a camper to use this well-developed picnic spot, with more than 70 tables, fire pits, and restrooms. Some of the tables are on the prairie, others sit amid the pines. ⊠ *Wind Cave National Park* ✥ *½ mile north of visitor center.*

Wind Cave Picnic Area. On the edge of a prairie and grove of ponderosa, this is a peaceful, pretty place. Small and simple, it's equipped with 12 tables and a potable-water pump. ⊠ *Wind Cave National Park* ✥ *¼ mile north of visitor center* ⊕ *www.nps.gov/wica.*

OUTSIDE THE PARK

$$
STEAKHOUSE

✕ **Alpine Inn.** With its pastoral paintings, lacy tablecloths, and beer steins, the rustic Alpine Inn brings a version of old-world charm to the Old West. The lunchtime menu changes daily but always has selections of healthful sandwiches and salads—and no fried food. Filet mignon is the only item on the dinner menu, but it's one of the best steaks around. Weather permitting, lunch is served on the veranda overlooking Main Street. Hard liquor is not served. Arrive early, because they don't take reservations and this popular spot fills up fast. ⑤ *Average main: $13* ⊠ *133 Main St., Hill City* ☎ *605/574–2749* ⊕ *www.alpineinnhillcity. com* ⊟ *No credit cards* ⊘ *Closed Sun.* ⌂ *Reservations not accepted.*

$$
AMERICAN

✕ **Blue Bell Lodge and Resort.** Feast on fresh trout or buffalo, which you can have as a steak or a stew, in this rustic log building within the boundaries of Custer State Park. There's a kids' menu. On the property, hayrides and cookouts are part of the entertainment, and you can sign up for trail rides and overnight pack trips on old Indian trails with the nearby stable. ⑤ *Average main: $19* ⊠ *Custer State Park, 25453 S.D. 87, Custer* ☎ *605/255–4531, 800/658–3530* ⊕ *www.custerresorts.com/ blue-bell-lodge* ⊘ *Closed mid-Oct.–mid-May.*

$$
ITALIAN

✕ **Botticelli Ristorante Italiano.** With a wide selection of delectable veal and chicken dishes as well as creamy pastas and a palatable wine list, this Italian eatery provides a welcome respite from the traditional Midwestern meat and potatoes. The artwork and traditional Italian music in the background give the place a European air. ⑤ *Average main: $17* ⊠ *523 Main St., Rapid City* ☎ *605/348–0089* ⊘ *No lunch Sun.*

37

$ ✕**Carvers Cafe.** The only restaurant at the Mount Rushmore Memo-
AMERICAN rial affords commanding views of the memorial and the surrounding
ponderosa pine forest. It serves exceptional food at reasonable prices.
The menu includes pot roast, buffalo stew, and homemade rhubarb
pie. You can dine with the presidents for breakfast, lunch, and dinner. $ *Average main: $8* ✉ *Ave. of Flags, Keystone* ☎ *605/574–2515*
⊕ *www.mtrushmorenationalmemorial.com/dining/carvers-cafe* ☾ *No
dinner mid-Oct.–early Mar.*

$$$ ✕**Deadwood Legends Steakhouse at the Franklin Hotel.** In a place where
STEAKHOUSE legends aren't taken lightly, this new establishment in the lower level
of the historic Franklin Hotel has quickly made a name for itself, beck-
oning back locals who like its aged beef, moderate prices, and flair.
Opened in 2015, you'll find all the usual suspects on the menu—buffalo,
beef, and chicken—but each with a flavorful twist. Arrive early, and
have a cocktail in the lounge or the upstairs casino, because they don't
take reservations. $ *Average main: $22* ✉ *Franklin Hotel, 709 Main
St., Deadwood* ☎ *605/578–2241* ⊕ *www.silveradofranklin.com/food-
drink/legends-steakhouse* ☾ *No lunch* ⌂ *Reservations not accepted.*

$$ ✕**Deadwood Social Club.** On the second floor of historic Saloon No. 10,
ITALIAN this warm restaurant surrounds you with wood and old-time photo-
Fodor's Choice graphs of Deadwood. Light jazz and blues play over the sound system.
★ The decor is Western, but the food is northern Italian, a juxtaposition
that keeps patrons coming back. Try the wild boar bundles as an appetizer, paired with one of 96 martinis or a bottle from the largest wine
cellar in the state. The menu stretches from a Wellington to a walleye,
as well as creamy pasta dishes, buffalo, and melt-in-your-mouth rib-
eye steaks. The wine list has nearly 200 global selections. Reservations
are recommended. $ *Average main: $20* ✉ *657 Main St., Deadwood*
☎ *605/578–3346* ⊕ *www.saloon10.com.*

$$$ ✕**Jakes.** Owned by actor Kevin Costner, this restaurant is among South
ECLECTIC Dakota's classiest dining experiences. Cherrywood pillars inlaid with
etched glass, white-brick fireplaces, and a pianist add to the elegance
of the atrium dining room. Sample a cranberry walnut chicken salad,
Cajun seafood tortellini, roasted duck, or braised short ribs. $ *Average
main: $28* ✉ *677 Main St., upstairs in the Midnight Star, Deadwood*
☎ *605/578–1555* ⊕ *www.themidnightstar.com* ☾ *No lunch. Closed
Sun.–Tues.* ⌂ *Reservations essential.*

$ ✕**Laughing Water.** With windows facing the mountain sculpture, this airy
AMERICAN pine restaurant is noted for its fry bread and buffalo burgers. There's a
FAMILY soup-and-salad bar, but you'd do well to stick to the American Indian
offerings. Try the Indian taco or "buffaloski" (a Polish-style sausage
made with Dakota buffalo). A kids' menu is available. $ *Average main:
$10* ✉ *12151 Ave. of the Chiefs, Custer* ☎ *605/673–4681* ⊕ *www.
crazyhorsememorial.com* ☾ *Closed Nov.–Apr.*

$$ ✕**Woolly's Western Grill.** Run by a friendly couple, this place caters to
AMERICAN families with its modestly priced menu. It specializes in hand-cut steaks
FAMILY and prime-rib Philly. It's near the Mammoth Site and close to the exceptional Southern Hills Golf Course. $ *Average main: $15* ✉ *1648 Hwy.
18 Bypass, Hot Springs* ☎ *605/745–6414* ⊕ *www.woollys.com* ☾ *No
lunch.*

CLOSE UP

Best Campgrounds in Wind Cave

Camping is one of this region's strengths. While there is only one primitive campground within the park, there are countless campgrounds in the Black Hills. The public campgrounds in the national forest are accessible by road but otherwise secluded and undeveloped; private campgrounds typically have more amenities.

Elk Mountain Campground. If you prefer a relatively developed campsite and relative proximity to civilization, Elk Mountain is an excellent choice. You can experience the peaceful pine forests and wild creatures of the park without straying too far from the safety of the beaten path. ½ mile north of visitor center ☎ *605/745–4600.*

WHERE TO STAY

OUTSIDE THE PARK

$$$$
B&B/INN
Fodor'sChoice
★

🄷 **Audrie's Bed & Breakfast.** Victorian antiques and a hint of romance greet you at this out-of-the-way B&B, set in a thick woods 7 miles west of Rapid City. **Pros:** great antiques; terrific treats; inspiring isolation. **Cons:** fills up fast; cabins lack a/c and phones; no restaurant within walking distance. ⑤ *Rooms from: $205* ✉ *23029 Thunderhead Falls Rd., Rapid City* ☎ *605/342–7788* ⊕ *www.audriesbb.com* ⊟ *No credit cards* ⤳ *2 suites, 7 cottages and cabins, 1 vacation home* ❐ *Breakfast.*

$$$
B&B/INN

🄷 **Buffalo Rock Lodge B&B.** A native-rock fireplace surrounded by hefty logs adds to the rustic quality of this lodge. **Pros:** quiet location; exceptional furnishings. **Cons:** relatively pricey; drive to shopping and dining; no TVs. ⑤ *Rooms from: $155* ✉ *24524 Playhouse Rd., Keystone* ☎ *605/666–4781, 888/564–5634* ⊕ *www.buffalorock.net* ⤳ *3 rooms* ❐ *Breakfast.*

$
RESORT

🄷 **Deadwood Gulch Gaming Resort.** Pine-clad hills, a creek, and a deck from which to view the mountains are at your disposal at this family-style resort about a mile from downtown Deadwood. **Pros:** away from downtown bustle; spacious rooms; attentive staff. **Cons:** busy with bus tours. ⑤ *Rooms from: $99* ✉ *304 Cliff St., Deadwood* ☎ *605/578–1294, 800/695–1876* ⊕ *www.deadwoodgulch.com* ⤳ *87 rooms* ❐ *Breakfast.*

$
HOTEL

🄷 **Franklin Hotel.** Built in 1903, this imposing hotel has welcomed many famous guests, including John Wayne, Teddy Roosevelt, and Babe Ruth. **Pros:** at the top of Main Street; spacious rooms; historic. **Cons:** guest rooms need some attention. ⑤ *Rooms from: $89* ✉ *700 Main St., Deadwood* ☎ *605/578–2241, 800/688–1876* ⊕ *www.silveradoffranklin.com* ⤳ *81 rooms* ❐ *No meals.*

$$$
HOTEL

🄷 **K Bar S Lodge.** This contemporary lodge on 45 pine-clad acres feels as if it's stood here for a century. **Pros:** excellent staff; exceptional food; amid a wildlife preserve. **Cons:** quite a walk to dining options; pricey rates; often full. ⑤ *Rooms from: $167* ✉ *434 Old Hill City Rd.,*

37

Keystone ☎ *866/522–7724, 605/666–4545* ⊕ *www.kbarslodge.com* ↩ *96 rooms* ⦿ *Breakfast.*

$$$ 🏨 **Spearfish Canyon Lodge.** Midway between Spearfish and Deadwood,

RESORT this lodge-style hotel commands some of the best views in the Black Hills. **Pros:** wonderful location; snowmobile and bike rentals; as pretty as it gets. **Cons:** remote location; half-hour drive to restaurants; standard rooms. ⑤ *Rooms from: $152* ✉ *10619 Roughlock Falls Rd., Lead* ☎ *877/975–6343, 605/584–3435* ⊕ *www.spfcanyon.com* ↩ *54 rooms* ⦿ *No meals.*

$$ 🏨 **Sylvan Lake Resort.** This spacious stone-and-wood lodge in Custer

RESORT State Park affords fantastic views of pristine Sylvan Lake and Harney

FAMILY Peak, the highest point in the U.S. east of the Rockies. **Pros:** wonderful views; multitude of lodging options; alpine atmosphere. **Cons:** on a winding road; limited dining options; can be pricey. ⑤ *Rooms from: $149* ✉ *24572 S.D. 87, Custer* ☎ *605/574–2561, 800/658–3530* ⊕ *www.custerresorts.com* ⊗ *Closed Oct.–Mother's Day* ↩ *35 rooms, 31 cabins* ⦿ *No meals.*

YELLOWSTONE NATIONAL PARK

WELCOME TO YELLOWSTONE NATIONAL PARK

TOP REASONS TO GO

★ **Hot spots:** Thinner-than-normal crust depth and a huge magma chamber beneath the park explain Yellowstone's abundant geysers, steaming pools, hissing fumaroles, and bubbling mud pots.

★ **Bison:** They're just one of many species that roam freely here. Seemingly docile, the bison make your heart race if you catch them stampeding across Lamar Valley.

★ **Hiking:** Yellowstone has more than 1,000 miles of trails, along which you can summit a 10,000-foot peak, follow a trout-filled creek, or descend into the Grand Canyon of the Yellowstone.

★ **Yellowstone Lake:** Here you can fish, boat, kayak, stargaze, and bird-watch on black obsidian beaches—just don't stray too far into the frigid water.

★ **Canyon:** The Yellowstone River runs through the park, creating a deep yellow-tinged canyon with two impressive waterfalls.

1 **Grant Village/West Thumb.** Named for President Ulysses S. Grant, Grant Village is on the western edge of Yellowstone Lake.

2 **Old Faithful area.** Famous for its regularity and awesome power, Old Faithful erupts every 90 minutes or so. The geyser site is a full-service area with inns, restaurants, campsites, cabins, a visitor center, and general stores.

3 **Madison.** Here the Madison River is formed by the joining of the Gibbon and Firehole rivers. Anglers will find healthy stocks of brown and rainbow trout and mountain whitefish.

4 **Norris.** The Norris area is the hottest and most changeable part of Yellowstone National Park. There are campsites here and a small information center.

5 **Mammoth Hot Springs.** This full-service fortlike area has an inn, restaurants, campsites, a visitor center, and general stores.

6 **Tower-Roosevelt.** The least visited area of the park is the place to go for solitude, horseback riding, and animal sightings. A lodge, restaurant, and campsites are here.

7 **Canyon area.** The Yellowstone River runs through the canyon, exposing geothermally altered rock. Two massive waterfalls highlight "downtown" Yellowstone, where cars, services, and natural beauty all converge.

8 **Lake area.** The largest body of water within the park, Yellowstone Lake is believed to have once been 200 feet higher than it presently is. This is a full-service area with a hotel, lodge, restaurants, campsites, cabins, and general stores.

WYOMING

GETTING ORIENTED

At more than 2.2 million acres, Yellowstone National Park is considered one of America's most scenic and diverse national parks. The park has five entrances, each with its own attractions: the South has the Lewis River canyon; the East, Sylvan Pass; the West, the Madison River valley; the North, the beautiful Paradise Valley; and the Northeast, the spectacular Beartooth Pass.

38

KEY

👫	Ranger Station
⛺	Campground
🧺	Picnic Area
🍴	Restaurant
🏠	Lodge
🚶	Trailhead
🚻	Restrooms
⟫	Scenic Viewpoint
::::::	Walking/Hiking Trails

Updated by
Melynda
Harrison

A trip to Yellowstone has been a rich part of the American experience for five generations now. Though it's remote, we come—more than 3,000,000 strong—year after year. When we arrive, we gasp at the incomparable combination of natural beauty, rugged wilderness, majestic peaks, and abundant wildlife. Geysers, mud pots, fumaroles, and hot springs make this magma-filled pressure cooker of a park unlike any place else on Earth. If you're not here for the geysers, chances are that you've come to spot some of the teeming wildlife, from grazing bison to cruising trumpeter swans.

YELLOWSTONE PLANNER

WHEN TO GO

There are two major seasons in Yellowstone: summer (from May through October), the only time when most of the park's roads are open to cars; and winter (from mid-December through February), when over-snow travel—on snowmobiles, snow coaches, and skis—delivers a fraction of the number of summer visitors to a frigid, bucolic sanctuary. Except for services at park headquarters at Mammoth Hot Springs, the park closes from October to mid-December and from March to late April or early May.

You'll find big crowds from mid-July to mid-August. There are fewer people in the park the month or two before and after this peak season, but there are also fewer facilities open. There's also more rain, especially at lower elevations. Except for holiday weekends, there are few visitors in winter. Snow is possible year-round at high elevations.

AVG. HIGH/LOW TEMPS

Jan.	Feb.	Mar.	Apr.	May	June
30/10	33/12	42/17	49/28	60/32	71/41
July	Aug.	Sept.	Oct.	Nov.	Dec.
81/45	79/45	67/37	56/30	38/22	30/12

FESTIVALS AND EVENTS

FEBRUARY **Buffalo Bill Birthday Ball.** Hundreds of folks, some dressed in turn-of-the-20th-century attire, dance in Cody until the wee hours to celebrate the birthday of William F. Cody. The ball, held on a Saturday in late February, is at Cody Auditorium, which is dressed up as Wolfville Hall for the occasion. Tickets cost from $25 to $30 per person. Guests must be 21 or older. ⊠ *1240 Beck Ave., Cody* ☎ *307/527–5520* ⊕ *www.codykc.org/ball.html.*

JULY **Livingston Roundup Rodeo.** Since the 1920s, the small town of Livings-
FAMILY ton, Montana, has celebrated the Fourth of July with riding, roping, bull-dogging, and barrel racing at the Roundup Rodeo. Cowboys and cowgirls call this premier rodeo event Cowboy Christmas. The revelry includes a parade on July 2, and an art show all three days. ⊠ *Livingston* ☎ *406/222–3199* ⊕ *livingstonroundup.com.*

Cody Stampede Rodeo. The "Rodeo Capital of the World" has hosted the Stampede, one of the most important stops on the rodeo circuit, around July 4 since 1919. The main event takes place at Cody Rodeo Grounds, and there are nightly performances at the Cody Nite Rodeo. Ticket prices vary. ⊠ *421 W. Yellowstone Ave., Cody* ☎ *307/587–5155, 800/207–0744* ⊕ *www.codystampederodeo.com.*

PLANNING YOUR TIME

YELLOWSTONE IN ONE DAY

If you plan to spend just one full day in the park, your best approach would be to concentrate on one or two of the major areas, such as the two biggest attractions: the famous Old Faithful geyser and the Grand Canyon of the Yellowstone. En route between these attractions, you can see geothermal activity and most likely some wildlife.

Plan on at least two hours for Old Faithful, one of America's most iconic landmarks. Eruptions occur approximately 90 minutes apart, though they can be as close as 60 minutes apart. Check with the visitor center for predicted eruption times. Before and after an eruption you can explore the surrounding geyser basin and Old Faithful Inn. To the north of Old Faithful, make Grand Prismatic Spring in Midway Geyser Basin your can't-miss geothermal stop; farther north, near Madison, veer off the road to the west to do the short Firehole Canyon Drive to see the Firehole River cut a small canyon and waterfall (Firehole Falls).

If you're arriving from the east, start with sunrise at **Lake Butte, Fishing Bridge,** and the wildlife-rich **Hayden Valley** as you cross the park counterclockwise to **Old Faithful.** To try to see wolves or bears, call ahead

38

and ask if rangers will be stationed at roadside turnouts with spotting scopes. Alternatively, hike any trail in the park at least 2 miles. Remember that you're entering the domain of wild and sometimes dangerous animals, so be alert and don't hike alone.

If you're entering through the North or Northeast Entrance, begin at dawn looking for wolves and other animals in Lamar Valley, then head to **Tower-Roosevelt** and take a horseback ride into the surrounding forest. After your ride, continue west to **Mammoth Hot Springs,** where you can hike the **Lower Terrace Interpretive Trail** past Liberty Cap and other strange, brightly colored travertine formations. If you drive 1½ miles south of the visitor center you will reach the **Upper Terrace Drive** for close-ups of hot springs. In the late afternoon, drive south, keeping an eye out for wildlife as you go—you're almost certain to see elk, bison, and possibly a bear. Alternatively, from Tower-Roosevelt you can head south to go through **Canyon Village** to see the north or south rim of the **Grand Canyon of the Yellowstone** and its waterfalls, and then head west through Norris and Madison.

When you reach **Old Faithful,** you can place the famous geyser into context by walking the 1½-mile **Geyser Hill Loop.** Watch the next eruption from the deck of the **Old Faithful Inn.**

GETTING HERE AND AROUND
AIR TRAVEL
Yellowstone National Park is served by airports in nearby communities, including Cody, Wyoming, a one-hour drive east; Jackson, Wyoming, one hour south; Bozeman, Montana, 90 minutes north; and West Yellowstone, Montana, just outside the park's west gate, which has only summer service. The best places to rent cars in the region are at these airports.

BUS TRAVEL
There is no commercial bus service to Yellowstone.

CAR TRAVEL
Yellowstone is well away from the interstates, so drivers make their way here on two-lane highways that are long on miles and scenery. From Interstate 80, take U.S. 191 north from Rock Springs; it's about 177 miles to Jackson, then another 60 miles north to Yellowstone. From Interstate 90, head south at Livingston, Montana, 53 miles to Gardiner and the park's North Entrance. From Bozeman travel south 90 miles to West Yellowstone.

Yellowstone has five primary entrances. Many visitors arrive through the South Entrance, north of Grand Teton National Park and Jackson, Wyoming. Other entrances are the East Entrance, with a main point of origin in Cody, Wyoming; the West Entrance at West Yellowstone, Montana, and the North Entrance at Gardiner, Montana; and the Northeast Entrance at Cooke City, Montana, which can be reached from either Cody, Wyoming, via the Chief Joseph Scenic Highway, or from Red Lodge, Montana, over the Beartooth Pass.

Plants and Wildlife in Yellowstone

Eighty percent of Yellowstone is forest, and the great majority of it is lodgepole pine. Miles and miles of the "telephone pole" pines were lost in a 1988 fire that burned more than 35% of the park. The fire's heat created the ideal condition for the lodgepole pine's serotinous cones to release their seeds—which now provides a stark juxtaposition between 25-year-old and 100-year-old trees.

ASTONISHING SCENERY

Yellowstone's scenery astonishes at any time of day, though the play of light and shadow makes the visuals most appealing in early morning and late afternoon. That's exactly when you should be looking for wildlife, as most are active around dawn and dusk, moving out of the forest in search of food and water. May and June are the best months for seeing baby bison, moose, and other recent arrivals. Look for glacier lilies among the spring wildflowers and goldenrod amid the changing foliage of fall. Winter visitors see the park at its most magical, with steam billowing from geyser basins to wreath trees in ice, and elk foraging close to roads transformed into ski trails.

WHERE THE ANIMALS ROAM

Bison, elk, and coyotes populate virtually all areas; elk and bison particularly like river valleys and the geyser basins. Moose like the marshy areas along Yellowstone Lake and in the park's northeastern corner. Wolves are most common in the Lamar Valley and areas south of Mammoth; bears are most visible in the Pelican Valley–Fishing Bridge area, near Dunraven Pass, and near Mammoth. Watch for trumpeter swans along the Yellowstone River and for sandhill cranes near the Firehole River and in Madison Valley.

38

■TIP➔ The best way to keep your bearings in Yellowstone is to remember that the major roads form a figure eight, known as the Grand Loop, which all entrance roads feed into. It doesn't matter at which point you begin, as you can hit most of the major sights if you follow the entire route.

The 370 miles of public roads in the park used to be riddled with potholes and had narrow shoulders—a bit tight when a motor home was pulled over to the side to capture wildlife or scenery on film. But because of the park's efforts to upgrade its roads, most of them are now smooth, if still narrow. Roadwork is likely every summer in some portion of the park—check the *Yellowstone Today* newspaper or ask a ranger. On holiday weekends road construction usually halts, so there are no construction delays for travelers. Remember, snow is possible at any time of year in almost all areas of the park.

PARK ESSENTIALS

PARK FEES AND PERMITS

Entrance fees of $30 per vehicle, $25 per motorcycle, or $15 per visitor 16 and older entering by foot, bike, ski, and so on, gives you access for seven days. For $50, $40, and $20, respectively, you can get a pass to both Yellowstone and Grand Teton. An Interagency Pass costs $80.

Fishing permits (available at ranger stations, visitor centers, and Yellowstone general stores) are required if you want to take advantage of Yellowstone's abundant lakes and streams. Live bait is not allowed, and for all native species of fish, a catch-and-release policy stands. Anglers 16 and older must purchase an $18 three-day permit, a $25 seven-day permit, or a $40 season permit. Those under 16 need a free permit or must fish under the direct supervision of an adult with a permit. A state license is not needed to fish in Yellowstone National Park.

All camping outside designated campgrounds requires a backcountry permit. For trip dates between late May (Memorial Day) and September 10, the fee is $3 per person per night. The group fee is capped at $15 per night. Day-use horseback riding does not require a permit, but overnight trips with stock are $5 per person per night with no cap. All boats, motorized or nonmotorized, including float tubes, require a permit, which cost $20 (annual) or $10 (seven days) for motorized boats and $10 (annual) or $5 (seven days) for nonmotorized vessels. National Park Service rangers inspect all boats for aquatic invasive species before issuing a permit.

PARK HOURS
Depending on the weather, Yellowstone is generally open from late April through November and from mid-December to early March. In winter, only one road, going from the Northeast Entrance at Cooke City to the North Entrance at Gardiner, is open to wheeled vehicles; other roads are used by over-snow vehicles. The park is in the Mountain time zone. Yellowstone is open 24 hours a day, 365 days per year from the North Entrance at Gardiner, Montana, to Mammoth Hot Springs, and from Mammoth Hot Springs to the Northeast Entrance and the town of Cooke City (with no through-travel beyond Cooke City).

CELL-PHONE RECEPTION
A comprehensive cell-phone coverage plan is in process, but currently reception in the park is hit or miss and generally confined to developed areas such as Mammoth, Old Faithful, Canyon, and Grant Village. In general, don't count on having reception. Public telephones are near visitor centers and major park attractions. ■TIP➜ Try to use indoor phones rather than outdoor ones so your conversation doesn't distract you from being alert to wildlife that might approach you while you're on the phone.

EDUCATIONAL OFFERINGS
CLASSES AND SEMINARS
FAMILY **Yellowstone Association.** Learn about the park's ecology, geology, history, and wildlife from park experts, including well-known geologists, biologists, and photographers. Classes last from a few hours to a few days, and rates are reasonable. Some programs are designed specifically for young people and families. ✉ *308 W. Park St., Gardiner* ☎ *406/848–2400* ⊕ *www.yellowstoneassociation.org/experience.*

RANGER PROGRAMS
Yellowstone offers a busy schedule of guided hikes, talks, and campfire programs. For dates and times, check the park's *Yellowstone Today* newsletter, available at all entrances and visitor centers.

FAMILY **Daytime Walks and Talks.** Ranger-led programs are available during all seasons. Ranger walks are held at various locations throughout the summer. Winter programs are held at West Yellowstone, Old Faithful, and Mammoth. Check the website or park newspaper for information. ⊕ *www.nps.gov/yell/planyourvisit/rangerprog.htm.*

FAMILY **Evening Programs.** Gather around to hear tales about Yellowstone's fascinating history, with hourlong programs on topics ranging from the return of the bison to 19th-century photographers. Every major area hosts programs during the summer; check visitor centers or campground bulletin boards for updates. Winter programs are held at Mammoth and Old Faithful. ⊕ *www.nps.gov/yell/planyourvisit/rangerprog.htm* ☉ *June–Aug., nightly at 9 and 9:30.*

FAMILY **Junior Ranger Program.** Children ages five to 12 are eligible to earn patches and become Junior Rangers. Pick up the Junior Ranger booklet at any visitor center for $3 and start the entertaining self-guided curriculum, or download it for free online. Kids five and older can also participate in the Young Scientist Program. Purchase a self-guiding booklet for $5 at the Canyon or Old Faithful visitor center and solve a science mystery. ⊕ *www.nps.gov/yell/learn/kidsyouth.*

RESTAURANTS

When traveling in Yellowstone it's always a good idea to bring along a cooler—that way you can carry some snacks and lunch items for a picnic or break and not have to worry about making it to one of the more developed areas of the park, where all restaurants and cafeterias are managed by two competing companies (Xanterra and Delaware North). Generally you'll find burgers and sandwiches at cafeterias and full meals at restaurants. The entrée selection includes beef and chicken, game meats such as elk and bison, fish like salmon and trout, and there are kids-oriented offerings. At the several delis and general stores you can purchase picnic items, snacks, sandwiches, and desserts like fudge and ice cream. Considering the park's remoteness, the selection and quality are above average, but expect to pay more as well. Reservations are needed for dinner at the Old Faithful Inn, Lake Yellowstone Hotel, and Grant Village dining rooms; during the summer reservations are recommended for all dining rooms.

HOTELS

Park lodgings range from two magnificent old hotels to simple cabins to bland modern motels. Make reservations at least two months ahead for July and August for all lodgings. Old Faithful Snow Lodge and Mammoth Hot Springs Hotel are the only accommodations open in winter; rates are the same as in summer. Ask about the size of beds, bathrooms, thickness of walls, and room location when you book, especially in the older hotels, where accommodations vary and upgrades are ongoing. Telephones have been put in most rooms, but there are no TVs. There are no roll-away beds available.

Hotel reviews have been shortened. For full information, visit Fodors. com.

38

WHAT IT COSTS				
	$	$$	$$$	$$$$
Restaurants	under $13	$13–$20	$21–$30	over $30
Hotels	under $100	$100–$150	$151–$200	over $200

Restaurant prices are the average cost of a main course at dinner, or if dinner is not served, at lunch. Hotel prices are the lowest cost of a standard double in high season.

TOURS

FAMILY **Historic Yellow Bus Tours.** Tours on bright yellow buses from as far back as the 1930s, each known as a Historic Yellow Bus, tour Yellowstone on more than a dozen itineraries. Touring in these restored buses is an elegant way to learn about the park. If the weather is warm enough, your driver, who narrates the trip, will roll back the convertible top for you to bask under the sun. The tour lineup includes Evening Wildlife Encounters, Picture Perfect Photo Safari, and Wake Up to Wildlife, all longtime crowd-pleasers. Other tours, including some all-day ones that efficiently cover huge swaths of the park, are on newer buses. Tours depart from various locations, including the Old Faithful Inn, Mammoth Hotel, and Canyon Lodge in Canyon. ☎ 866/439–7375 ⊕ *www. yellowstonenationalparklodges.com* ✉ *From $50* ☉ *June–Sept.*

Yellowstone Alpen Guides Co. In summer this company conducts tours that might include day hiking in the backcountry or swimming in a thermally heated river, and there are photography safaris, kayaking excursions, and other diversions. Alpine Guides also leads ski trips and winter park tours, providing a quieter way than snowmobiling to sight buffalo herds, trophy-size bull elk, and moose. ⊠ *555 Yellowstone Ave., West Yellowstone* ☎ *406/646–9591, 800/858–3502* ⊕ *yellowstoneguides. com* ✉ *From $85.*

VISITOR INFORMATION

Park Contact Information Yellowstone National Park. ☎ 307/344–7381 ⊕ www.nps.gov/yell.

VISITOR CENTERS

FAMILY **Albright Visitor Center.** Bachelor quarters for U.S. Army cavalry officers from 1909 to 1918, the red-roof visitor center was totally renovated in 2015. In addition to picking up maps, information, advice, and permits inside the hefty stone structure, you can tour the museum, whose exhibits explain the park's history, flora, and fauna. Most kids love the extensive wildlife displays, especially the ones of bears and wolves. The center's hours are variable, so it's wise to verify them upon entering the park. ⊠ *Mammoth Hot Springs* ☎ *307/344–2263* ⊕ *www.nps. gov/yell/planyourvisit/visitorcenters.htm* ☉ *Late May–Sept., daily 8–7; Oct.–late May, daily 9–6.*

FAMILY **Canyon Visitor Center.** This gleaming visitor center contains elaborate interactive exhibits for adults and kids. The focus here is on volcanoes and earthquakes, but there are also exhibits about Native Americans and wildlife, including bison and wolves. As at all visitor centers, you can obtain advice, information, and backcountry camping permits. The adjacent bookstore is the best in the park, with hundreds of books on the park, its history, and related science. ⊠ *Canyon Village* ☎ *307/242–2550* ⊕ *www.nps.gov/yell/planyourvisit/visitorcenters.htm* ⊗ *Late May–early Sept., daily 8–8; Sept., daily 8–6; early Oct., daily 9–5.*

FAMILY **Fishing Bridge Visitor Center.** This distinctive stone-and-log building, built in 1931, is a National Historic Landmark. If you can't distinguish between a Clark's nut hatch and an ermine (one's a bird, the other a weasel), check out the exhibits here about the park's smaller wildlife. Step out the back door to find yourself on one of the beautiful black obsidian beaches of Yellowstone Lake. Adjacent is one of the park's larger amphitheaters. Ranger presentations take place here nightly in summer. The center's bookstore stocks books, guides, and other educational materials, but you can't buy coffee. ⊠ *East Entrance Rd., 1 mile from Grand Loop Rd.* ☎ *307/242–2450* ⊕ *www.nps.gov/yell/planyourvisit/visitorcenters.htm* ⊗ *Late May–late Sept., daily 8–7.*

Grant Village Visitor Center. Exhibits at each visitor center describe a small piece of Yellowstone's history—the ones here provide details about the 1988 fire that burned more than a third of the park's total acreage and forced multiple federal agencies to reevaluate their fire-control policies. Watch an informative video, and learn about the 25,000 firefighters from across the United States who battled the blaze. Bathrooms and a backcountry office are here. ⊠ *2 Grant Village Loop Rd., off U.S. 89/287, Grant Village* ☎ *307/242–2650* ⊕ *www.nps.gov/yell/planyourvisit/visitorcenters.htm* ⊗ *Late May–late Sept., daily 8–7.*

Madison Information Station. In this stone-and-timber National Historic Landmark, park rangers share the space with a store that sells books, maps, and learning aids. You might find spotting scopes set up for wildlife viewing out the rear window; if this is the case, look for eagles, swans, bison, and elk. Rangers will answer questions about the park, provide basic hiking information, and issue permits for backcountry camping and fishing. Rangers also staff the Junior Ranger Station for kids here. Picnic tables, toilets, and an amphitheater for summer-evening ranger programs are shared with the nearby campground. ⊠ *Grand Loop Rd. at West Entrance Rd.* ☎ *307/344–2876* ⊕ *www.nps.gov/yell/planyourvisit/visitorcenters.htm* ⊗ *Late May–late Sept., daily 9–6.*

Old Faithful Visitor Education Center. At this $27 million visitor center that's a park-system jewel, you can check out the interactive exhibits and children's area, read about the latest geyser-eruption predictions, and find out the schedules for ranger-led walks and talks. Backcountry and fishing permits are dispensed at the ranger station adjacent to the Old Faithful Snow Lodge. ⊠ *Old Faithful Bypass Rd.* ☎ *307/344–2751* ⊕ *www.nps.gov/yell/planyourvisit/visitorcenters.htm* ⊗ *Late May–Sept., daily 8–8; Oct. and Nov., daily 5–5; Dec.–late Apr., daily 9–6.*

West Thumb Information Station. This historic log cabin houses a bookstore and doubles as a warming hut in winter. There are restrooms in the parking area. In summer, check for informal ranger-led discussions beneath the old sequoia tree. ⊠ *Grand Loop Rd., western edge*

38

of Yellowstone Lake, West Thumb ☎ *307/344–2650* ⊕ *www.nps.gov/ yell/planyourvisit/visitorcenters.htm* ☉ *Late May–late Sept., daily 9–5.*

EXPLORING

SCENIC DRIVES

Firehole Canyon Drive. The 2-mile narrow asphalt road twists through a deep canyon and passes the 40-foot Firehole Falls. In summer look for a sign marking a pull-out and swimming hole. This is one of only two places in the park (Boiling River on the North Entrance Road is the other) where you can safely and legally swim in the thermally heated waters. Look carefully for osprey and other raptors. ⊹ *1 mile south of Madison junction, off Grand Loop Rd.*

Firehole Lake Drive. This one-way, 3-mile-long road takes you past Great Fountain Geyser, which shoots out jets of water reaching as high as 200 feet about twice a day. Rangers' predictions provide a two-hour window of opportunity. Should you witness an eruption, you'll see waves of water cascading down the terraces that form the geyser's edges. This road isn't open to over-snow vehicle traffic in winter, and it's hard to access by foot, snowshoes, or skis. ⊠ *Firehole Lake Dr., 8 miles north of Old Faithful, Old Faithful.*

Hayden Valley on Grand Loop Road. Bison, bears, coyotes, wolves, and birds of prey all call Hayden Valley home almost year-round. Once part of Yellowstone Lake, the broad valley now contains peaceful meadows, rolling hills, and the placid Yellowstone River. There are multiple turn-outs and picnic areas on the 16-mile drive, many with views of the river and valley. Ask a ranger about "Grizzly Overlook," an unofficial site where wildlife watchers, including NPS rangers with spotting scopes for the public to use, congregate in summer. North of Mud Volcano are 11 unsigned turnouts. Look for the telltale timber railings, and be prepared to get caught in a traffic-stopping "bison jam" along the way. ⊠ *Grand Loop Rd. between Canyon and Fishing Bridge.*

Fodor'sChoice **Northeast Entrance Road and Lamar Valley.** This 29-mile road has the rich-
★ est landscape diversity of the five entrance roads. Just after you enter the park, you cut between 10,928-foot Abiathar Peak and the 10,404-foot Barronette Peak. Lamar Valley is home to hundreds of bison, and the rugged peaks and ridges adjacent to it shelter some of Yellowstone's most famous wolf packs. (Wolves were reintroduced to the park in the mid-1990s.) This is the park's best place for wolf-watching, especially in the early morning and late evening. As you exit Lamar Valley, the road crosses the Yellowstone River before leading you to the rustic Roosevelt Lodge. ⊠ *From Northeast Entrance to junction with Grand Loop Rd..*

Northeastern Grand Loop. Commonly called Dunraven Pass, this 19-mile segment of Grand Loop Road climbs to nearly 9,000 feet as it passes some of the park's finest scenery, including views of backcountry hot springs and abundant wildflowers. Near Tower Falls, the road twists beneath a series of leaning basalt columns from 40 to 50 feet high.

Western Yellowstone

TO LIVINGSTON

Gardiner
North Entrance

MONTANA
WYOMING

Mammoth Hot Springs Terraces

Visitor Center

Fort Yellowstone

Undine Falls

Upper Terrace Drive
Bunsen Peak

Blacktail Deer Plateau

Sheepeater Cliff

Indian Creek

Porcelain Basin

Norris Geyser Basin

Back Basin

Norris

Canyon Village

Visitor Center

Steamboat Geyser

Virginia Cascade

Artist Point

Hayden Valley

West Yellowstone

West Entrance

20

Madison

Gibbon Falls

Firehole Canyon Drive
Firehole Falls

TO ASHTON

Central Plateau

Fountain Paint Pots

Lower Geyser Basin

Firehole Lake Drive

Grand Prismatic Spring
Fairy Falls

Great Fountain Geyser

Midway Geyser Basin

Biscuit Basin

Mystic Falls
Sapphire Pool

Black Sand Basin

Old Faithful
see detail map

Continental

Divide

Craig Pass

Yellowstone Lake

Lone Star Geyser

West Thumb Geyser Basin

Shoshone Lake

Grant Village

Visitor Center

191
287

89

Continental

Lewis Lake

Lewis Falls

Lewis Lake

Mount Sheridan

ID MT WY

191
287

0   5 mi
0   5 km

That behemoth to the east is 10,243-foot Mount Washburn. ⊠ *Between Canyon Junction and Tower Falls.*

Upper Terrace Drive. This popular 1½-mile drive at the top of the Mammoth Terraces will take you back into the woods, where you can see some impressive thermal features, among them White Elephant Back and Orange Spring Mound, that aren't visible from the main road. Park at the top of the Terraces for views of Fort Yellowstone and a short walk along the boardwalk to Canary Springs. RVs, buses, and trailers are not permitted along Upper Terrace Drive. ⊠ *Grand Loop Rd., 2 miles from Mammoth Hot Springs Hotel.*

HISTORIC SITES

OLD FAITHFUL

FAMILY

Fodor'sChoice

★

Old Faithful Inn. It's hard to imagine how any work could be accomplished with snow and ice blanketing the region, but this historic hotel was constructed over the course of a single winter. Open since 1904, this massive log structure is an attraction in its own right. Even if you don't spend a night at the Old Faithful Inn, walk through or take the free 45-minute guided tour to admire its massive open-beam lobby and rock fireplace. There are antique writing desks on the second-floor balcony. You can watch Old Faithful geyser from two second-floor outdoor decks. ⊠ *Old Faithful Bypass Rd., Old Faithful* ☎ *307/344–7311* ⊕ *www.nps.gov/yell/learn/historyculture/oldfaithfuldistrict.htm* ⊗ *May–mid-Oct.; tours daily, times vary.*

MAMMOTH HOT SPRINGS

Fort Yellowstone. The oldest buildings here served as Fort Yellowstone from 1891 to 1918, when the U.S. Army managed the park. The red-brick buildings cluster around an open area reminiscent of a frontier-era parade ground. Pick up a self-guided tour map of the area from the Albright Visitors Center on Officers Row, and start your walking tour there. ⊠ *Mammoth Hot Springs.*

LAKE AREA

Lake Yellowstone Hotel. Completed in 1891, this structure on the National Register of Historic Places is the oldest lodging in Yellowstone National Park. Casual daytime visitors can lounge in white wicker chairs in the sunroom and watch the waters of Yellowstone Lake through massive windows. Robert Reamer, the architect of the Old Faithful Inn, added a columned entrance in 1903 to enhance the original facade of the hotel, still aglow from its $28.5 million renovation in 2014. ⊠ *Lake Village Rd., 1 Grand Loop Rd., Lake Village* ☎ *307/344–7901* ⊕ *www.yellowstonenationalparklodges.com/lodging/summer-lodges/lake-yellowstone-hotel-cabins* ⊗ *Mid-May–early Oct.*

SCENIC STOPS

Along the park's main drive—the Grand Loop (also referred to as Yellowstone's Figure Eight)—are eight primary "communities," or developed areas. On the Western Yellowstone map are five of those communities—Grant Village, Old Faithful, Madison, Norris, and

Old Faithful Area

TO
FOUNTAIN POINT POTS,
GRAND PRISMATIC SPRING,
AND MADISON

BISCUIT BASIN

Morning Glory Pool
Fan, Mortar, and Spiteful Geysers

Chain Lakes
Riverside Geyser

Grotto Geyser

UPPER GEYSER BASIN

Comet Geyser
Splendid Geyser
Daisy Geyser
Giant Geyser
Oblong Geyser

Punch Bowl Spring
Round Spring
Chromatic Pool
Beauty Pool

Black Sand Pool
Turban Geyser
Grand Geyser
Solitary Geyser

Firehole River

Spasmodic Geyser
Sawmill Geyser
Liberty Pool
Aurum Geyser

Opalescent Pool
Crested Pool
Doublet Pool

Sunset Lake
Castle Geyser
Lion Group
Heart Spring
Geyser Hill Loop
Giantess Geyser
Anemone Geyser

Rainbow Pool
Plume Geyser
Beehive Geyser
Old Faithful Geyser

Emerald Pool
Cliff Geyser

GEYSER HILL

BLACK SAND BASIN

Iron Spring Creek

Grand Loop Rd.

Old Faithful Lodge & Cabins

Old Faithful Inn

Visitor Center

Backcountry Office, Ranger Station, Clinic

Old Faithful Snow Lodge

TO
WEST THUMB AND
YELLOWSTONE LAKE

Mammoth Hot Springs—with their respective sights. The Eastern Yellowstone map shows the remaining three—Tower-Roosevelt, Canyon, and Lake (for Yellowstone Lake area)—with their respective sights.

GRANT VILLAGE AND WEST THUMB

Along the western edge of Yellowstone Lake, called the West Thumb, Grant Village is the first community you encounter from the South Entrance. It has basic lodging and dining facilities.

FAMILY **West Thumb Geyser Basin.** The primary Yellowstone caldera was created by one volcanic eruption, while West Thumb came about as the result of a later eruption. This unique geyser basin is the only place to see active geothermal features in Yellowstone Lake. Two boardwalk loops are offered; take the longer one to see features like Fishing Cone, where fishermen used to drop their freshly caught fish straight into boiling water without ever taking it off the hook. This area is particularly popular with winter visitors, who take advantage of the nearby warming hut and a stroll around the geyser basin before continuing their trip via snow coach or snowmobile. ⊠ *Grand Loop Rd., 22 miles north of South Entrance, West Thumb.*

"This was a magical moment that I captured at West Thumb Geyser Basin—the sunset reflecting off the rain clouds, steam rising from the geyser basin, and an elk drinking." —photo by Paul Stoloff, Fodors.com member

OLD FAITHFUL

Fodor's Choice ★ The world's most famous geyser is the centerpiece of this area, which has extensive boardwalks through the Upper Geyser Basin and equally extensive visitor services, including several choices in lodging and dining, and a very fine visitor center. In winter you can dine and stay in this area and cross-country ski or snowshoe through the geyser basin.

Biscuit Basin. North of Old Faithful, this basin is also the trailhead for the Mystic Falls Trail. The namesake "biscuit" formations were reduced to crumbs when Sapphire Pool erupted after the 1959 Hebgen Lake earthquake. Now, Sapphire is a calm, beautiful blue pool again, but that could change at any moment. ⌧ *Grand Loop Rd., 3 miles north of Old Faithful, Old Faithful.*

Black Sand Basin. There are a dozen hot springs and geysers near the cloverleaf entrance from Grand Loop Road to Old Faithful. Emerald Pool is one of the prettiest. It's an easy walk, ski, or bike ride from the Old Faithful area to Black Sand Basin. ⌧ *Grand Loop Rd., north of Old Faithful, Old Faithful.*

FAMILY **Geyser Hill Loop.** Along the 1.3-mile Geyser Hill Loop boardwalk you will see active thermal features such as violent Giantess Geyser. Erupting only a few times each year, Giantess spouts from 100 to 250 feet in the air for five to eight minutes once or twice hourly for 12 to 43 hours. Nearby Doublet Pool's two adjacent springs have complex ledges and deep blue waters that are highly photogenic. Starting as a gentle pool, Anemone Geyser overflows, bubbles, and finally erupts 10 feet or more, every three to eight minutes. The loop boardwalk brings you close to the action, making it especially appealing to children intrigued by the basin's sights and sounds. To reach Geyser Hill, head counterclockwise around the Old Faithful boardwalk 0.3 mile from the visitor center, crossing the Firehole River and entering Upper Geyser Basin. ⊠ *Old Faithful, 0.3 mile from Old Faithful Visitor Center, Old Faithful.*

Fodor's Choice
★

Grand Prismatic Spring. You can reach Yellowstone's largest hot spring, 370 feet in diameter, by following the boardwalk. The spring, in the Midway Geyser Basin, is deep blue in color, with yellow and orange rings formed by bacteria that give it the effect of a prism. For a stunning perspective, look down on it from the Fairy Falls Trail. ⊠ *Midway Geyser Basin, off Grand Loop Rd..*

Great Fountain Geyser. Shooting water from 75 to 200 feet in the air every eight to 15 hours, this geyser is the most spectacular sight in Lower Geyser Basin. Check at the Old Faithful Visitor Center for predicted eruption times, which leave a window of opportunity of a couple of hours. Should the geyser spew while you're present, you'll see water waves cascading down the terraces that form its edges. ⊠ *Firehole Lake Dr., north of Old Faithful.*

Lower Geyser Basin. With its mighty blasts more than 150 feet high, the Great Fountain Geyser is this basin's superstar. Less impressive but more regular is White Dome Geyser, which shoots from a 20-foot-tall cone. You'll also find pink mud pots and blue pools at the basin's Fountain Paint Pots, a unique spot because visitors encounter all four of Yellowstone's hydrothermal features: fumaroles, mud pots, hot springs, and geysers. ⊠ *Grand Loop Rd., midway between Old Faithful and Madison.*

38

Midway Geyser Basin. Called "Hell's Half Acre" by writer Rudyard Kipling, Midway Geyser Basin is a more interesting stop than Lower Geyser Basin. Boardwalks wind their way to the Excelsior Geyser, which deposits 4,000 gallons of vivid blue water per minute into the Firehole River. Just above Excelsior is Yellowstone's largest hot spring, Grand Prismatic Spring. ⊠ *Grand Loop Rd., between Old Faithful and Madison.*

Morning Glory Pool. Shaped somewhat like a morning glory, this pool once was a deep blue, but the color is no longer as striking as before due to tourists dropping coins and other debris into the hole. To reach the pool, follow the boardwalk past Geyser Hill Loop and stately Castle Geyser, which has the biggest cone in Yellowstone. Morning Glory is the inspiration for popular children's author Jan Brett's story *Hedgie Blasts Off*, in which a hedgehog travels to another planet to unclog a geyser damaged by space tourists' debris. ⊠ *At the north end of Upper Geyser Basin at Old Faithful.*

FAMILY
Fodor's Choice
★

Old Faithful. Almost every visitor's itinerary includes the world's most famous geyser. Yellowstone's most predictable big geyser—although not its largest or most regular—sometimes shoots as high as 180 feet, but it averages 130 feet. The mysterious plumbing of Yellowstone has

A GOOD TOUR: OLD FAITHFUL AREA

Begin your tour at the impressive **Old Faithful Visitor Education Center**. Pick up the Old Faithful–area trail guide (50¢) and check a bulletin board with the latest predictions for six geyser eruptions.

THE MAIN ATTRACTION

Concentrate first on the main attraction: **Old Faithful** spouts from 130 to 180 feet high approximately every 94 minutes. You don't need to jockey for position on the boardwalk directly in front of the visitor center to enjoy the geyser. It's impressive from any angle on the boardwalk surrounding it. The view from the second-floor deck of the **Old Faithful Inn** is glorious, too. Speaking of that famous, century-old structure, check out its massive log-construction interior.

EXPLORING THE BASINS

At Old Faithful Village you're in the heart of the **Upper Geyser Basin**, the densest concentration of geysers on Earth, with about 140 geysers within a square mile. Once you've watched Old Faithful erupt, explore the larger basin with a hike around **Geyser Hill**, where you

may see wildlife as well as thermal features. Follow the trail north to the **Morning Glory Pool**, with its unique flower shape. Along this trail are Castle, Grand, and Riverside geysers. Return to the village and continue by car to **Black Sand Basin** or **Biscuit Basin**. At Biscuit Basin, follow the boardwalks to the trailhead for the Mystic Falls Trail, where you can get views of the Upper Geyser Basin.

PAINT POTS AND A SPRING

Take a break from geyser watching with a packed lunch at the Whiskey Flat picnic area. Afterward, continue your drive toward **Lower Geyser Basin**, with its colorful **Fountain Paint Pots**. Then, on the way back to Old Faithful, stop at **Midway Geyser Basin**, where steaming runoff from the colorful 370-foot **Grand Prismatic Spring** crashes continuously into the Firehole River.

RELAX AND CELEBRATE

Relax and celebrate your day's accomplishments with dinner (reservations required) at the Old Faithful Inn, or enjoy drinks on the second floor.

lengthened Old Faithful's cycle somewhat in recent years, to every 94 minutes or so. To find out when Old Faithful is likely to erupt, check at the visitor center or at any of the lodging properties in the area, or call the geyser prediction line at *307/344–2751*. You can view the eruption from a bench just yards away, from the dining room at the lodge cafeteria, or the second-floor deck of the Old Faithful Inn. The 1-mile hike to Observation Point yields yet another view—from above—of the geyser and its surrounding basin. ⊠ *Grand Loop Rd., southwest segment.*

Upper Geyser Basin. With Old Faithful as its central attraction, this mile-square basin contains about 140 different geysers—one-fifth of the known geysers in the world. It's an excellent place to spend a day or more exploring. You will find a complex system of boardwalks and trails—some of them used as bicycle trails—that take you to the basin's various attractions. ⊠ *Old Faithful.*

MADISON

The area around the junction of the West Entrance Road and the Lower Loop is a good place to take a break as you travel through the park, because you will almost always see bison grazing along the Madison River, and elk are often in the area, too. Limited visitor services are here, and there are no dining facilities.

Gibbon Falls. The water of this 84-foot fall on the Gibbon River rushes over the caldera rim. Driving east from Madison to Norris, you can see it on your right, but the angle is even better from the paved trail adjacent to the canyon's edge. ⊠ *Grand Loop Rd., 4 miles east of Madison.*

NORRIS

The area at the western junction of the Upper and Lower Loops has the most active geyser basin in the park. The underground plumbing occasionally reaches such high temperatures—the ground itself has heated up in areas to nearly 200°F—that a portion of the basin is periodically closed for safety reasons. There are limited visitor services: two museums, a bookstore, and a picnic area. ■TIP➔ **Ask rangers at the Norris Geyser Basin Museum when different geysers are expected to erupt and plan your walk accordingly.**

Back Basin. The trail through Back Basin is a 1½-mile loop guiding you past Steamboat Geyser. When it erupts fully (most recently in 2014), it's the world's largest geyser, climbing 400 feet above the basin. More often, Steamboat growls and spits, sending clouds of steam high above the basin. Kids will love the Puff 'n' Stuff Geyser and the mysterious cavelike Green Dragon Spring. Ask the rangers for an anticipated schedule of geyser eruptions—you might catch the Echinus Geyser, which erupts almost hourly. ⊠ *Grand Loop Rd., at Norris.*

FAMILY **Norris Geyser Basin.** From the Norris Ranger Station, choose Porcelain Basin, Back Basin, or both. These volatile thermal features are constantly changing, although you can expect to find a variety of geysers and springs here at any time. The area is accessible via an extensive system of boardwalks, some of them suitable for people with disabilities. The famous Steamboat Geyser is here. ⊠ *Grand Loop Rd. at Norris.*

Porcelain Basin. A ¾-mile partially boardwalked loop from Norris Geyser Basin Museum passes by this thermal area in the Norris basin's eastern portion. In this geothermal field of whitish geyserite stone, the earth bulges and belches from the underground pressure. You'll find bubbling pools, some milky white and others ringed in orange because of the minerals in the water, as well as small geysers such as the extremely active Whirligig. ⊠ *Grand Loop Rd.*

MAMMOTH HOT SPRINGS

This northern community within the park is known for its massive natural terraces, where mineral water flows continuously, building an ever-changing display. Water levels can fluctuate, though, so if it's late in a particularly dry summer, you won't see the terraces in all their glory. You will often see elk grazing here. In the park's early days, this was the site of Fort Yellowstone. The brick buildings constructed during that era are still used for various park activities.

38

FAMILY **Mammoth Hot Springs Terraces.** Multicolor travertine terraces formed by slowly escaping hot mineral water mark this unusual geological formation. You can explore the terraces via an elaborate network of boardwalks, the best of which is the Lower Terrace Interpretive Trail. If you head uphill from Liberty Cap, at the area's northern end, in an hour you'll pass bright and ornately terraced Minerva Spring. Along the way you might spot elk grazing nearby. Alternatively, you can drive up to the Lower Terrace Overlook on Upper Terrace Drive and take the boardwalks down past New Blue Springs to the Lower Terrace. This route, which also takes an hour, works especially well if you can park a second vehicle at the foot of Lower Terrace. There are many steps on the lower terrace boardwalks, so plan to take your time there. The boardwalk routes change as the terraces move and grow. A map and brochure at the boardwalk trailhead has a self-guided tour. ⊠ *Northwest corner of Grand Loop Rd.*

TOWER-ROOSEVELT

The northeastern region of Yellowstone is the least visited part of the park, making it a great place to explore without running into as many people. Packs of wolves may be spotted in the Lamar Valley.

Petrified Tree. A century of vandalism has forced park officials to surround this 45-million-year-old petrified redwood tree with high wrought-iron gates. Doing so has protected the geological landmark, but it has utterly ruined the experience of viewing it. ⊠ *Grand Loop Rd., 1 mile west of Tower-Roosevelt.*

FAMILY **Tower Fall.** This is one of the easiest waterfalls to see from the roadside; you can also view volcanic pinnacles here. Tower Creek plunges 132 feet at this waterfall to join the Yellowstone River. While a trail that used to go to the base of the falls has washed out, it will take trekkers down to the river. ⊠ *Grand Loop Rd., 2 miles south of Tower-Roosevelt* ⊕ *www.nps.gov/yell/planyourvisit/towerrplan.htm.*

CANYON

The Yellowstone River's source is in the Absaroka Mountains, in the park's southeastern corner. The river winds its way through the heart of the park, entering Yellowstone Lake, then heading northward under Fishing Ridge through Hayden Valley. When it cuts through the multicolor Grand Canyon of the Yellowstone, it creates one of the most spectacular gorges in the world, enticing visitors with its steep canyon walls and waterfalls. All types of visitor services are here, as well as many hiking opportunities.

Artist Point. An impressive view of the Lower Falls of the Yellowstone River can be had from Artist Point, which has two observation platforms, one accessible to wheelchairs. Rangers often give short talks on the lower platform; check the park newspaper for a schedule. The South Rim Trail goes past this point, and the nearby parking area is open year-round. ⊠ *South Rim Rd., east end* ⊕ *www.nps.gov/yell/planyourvisit/canyonplan.htm.*

Eastern Yellowstone

MONTANA
WYOMING

Cooke City
Silver Gate
Northeast Entrance

TO RED LODGE

◆ **Slough Creek**

Tower-Roosevelt

Pebble Creek ◆

Petrified Tree ◆
Roosevelt Lodge

Tower Fall

Lamar Valley ◆

212

Lamar Cache Creek

Northeastern Grand Loop

Mount Washburn ▲

Yellowstone River

Canyon Village
see detail map

Dunraven Pass

Grand Canyon of the Yellowstone ◆

R A N G E

◆ **Artist Point**

Grand Loop Road

Hayden Valley ◆

Pelican Valley

Sulphur Caldron

Mud Volcano

LeHardy Rapids ◆

Recreational Vehicle Park ◆

A B S A R O K A

Lake Yellowstone Hotel

Fishing Bridge

Visitor Center

Avalanche Peak ▲

TO CODY

Yellowstone Lake ◆

Sylvan Lake

14 16

20

East Entrance

Continental Divide

0   5 mi

0   5 km

Fodor's Choice
★

Grand Canyon of the Yellowstone. This stunning canyon is 23 miles long, but there is only one trail from rim to base. As a result, most visitors clog the north and south rims to see Upper and Lower Falls. Unless you're up for the strenuous six-hour hike called Seven Mile Hole, you have no choice but to join the crowds to see this natural wonder. The red-and-ochre canyon walls are topped by emerald-green forest. It's a feast of color. Keep an eye peeled for osprey, which nest in the canyon's spires and precarious trees. ⊠ *Canyon* ⊕ *www.nps.gov/yell/ planyourvisit/canyonplan.htm.*

Lookout Point. Midway on the North Rim Trail—also accessible via the one-way North Rim Drive—Lookout Point provides a view of the Grand Canyon of the Yellowstone. Follow the right-hand fork in the path to descend a steep trail, with an approximately 500-foot elevation change, for an eye-to-eye view of the falls from a half mile downstream. The best time to hike the trail is early morning, when sunlight reflects off the mist from the falls to create a rainbow. ⊠ *Off North Rim Dr.* ⊕ *www.nps.gov/yell/planyourvisit/canyonplan.htm.*

Upper Falls View. A spur road off Grand Loop Road south of Canyon accesses the western end of the North Rim Trail and takes you down a fairly steep portion for a view of Upper Falls from almost directly above.

✉ *Off Grand Loop Rd., ¾ miles south of Canyon ⊕ www.nps.gov/ yell/planyourvisit/canyonplan.htm.*

LAKE AREA

In the park's southeastern segment, the tranquillity of massive Yellowstone Lake sets the mood. Near Fishing Bridge you might see grizzly bears. They like to hunt for fish spawning or swimming near the lake's outlet to the Yellowstone River. Visitor information can be found at Lake Yellowstone Hotel, Fishing Bridge RV Park (for hard-sided vehicles only), and Bridge Bay Campground, with 432 sites the park's largest campground.

LeHardy Rapids. Witness one of nature's epic battles as cutthroat trout migrate upstream by catapult-

> ### CAUTION: A WILD PLACE
>
> As you explore the park keep this thought in mind: Yellowstone is not an amusement park. It is a wild place. The animals may seem docile or tame, but they are wild, and every year careless visitors are injured—sometimes even killed—when they venture too close. Particularly dangerous are female animals with their young, and bison, which can turn and charge in an instant. With bison, watch their tails: if standing up or crooked like a question mark, the animal is agitated.

ing themselves out of the water to get over and around obstacles in the Yellowstone River. The ¼-mile forested loop takes you to the river's edge. Look for waterfowl and bears, which feed on the trout. ✢ *3 miles north of Fishing Bridge.*

FAMILY **Mud Volcano.** Gasses hissing from vents underscore the volatile nature of this area's geothermal features. The ¾-mile round-trip Mud Volcano Interpretive Trail loops gently around seething, sulfuric mud pots with names such as Black Dragon's Cauldron and Sizzling Basin before making its way around Mud Volcano itself, a boiling pot of brown goo. ✉ *Grand Loop Rd., 10 miles south of Canyon, 4 miles north of Fishing Bridge.*

Sulphur Caldron. You can smell the sulfur before you even leave your vehicle to walk to the overlook of Sulphur Caldron, where hissing steam escapes from a moonscape-like surface as superheated bubbling mud. ✉ *Grand Loop Rd., 9½ miles south of Canyon, 4½ miles north of Fishing Bridge.*

FAMILY **Yellowstone Lake.** One of the world's largest alpine lakes, the 132-square-
Fodor's Choice mile Yellowstone Lake was formed when the glaciers that once covered
★ the region melted into a caldera—a crater formed by a volcano. The lake has 141 miles of shoreline, along which you will often see moose, elk, waterfowl, and other wildlife. In winter you can sometimes see otters and coyotes stepping gingerly onto the ice at the lake's edge. Many visitors head here for the excellent fishing—streams flowing into the lake provide an abundant supply of trout. ✉ *Intersection of East Entrance Rd. and Grand Loop Rd., between Fishing Bridge and Grant Village ⊕ www.nps.gov/yell/planyourvisit/explorefishingbridgelake.htm.*

Continued on page 841

38

YELLOWSTONE'S GEOTHERMAL WONDERS

Steaming, bubbling,
and erupting
throughout the day
like giant teapots.

Yellowstone's geothermal features are constantly putting on a show. The 10,000 hot springs, mud pots, and fumaroles, plus 300 or so active geysers within the park comprise more than half the entire world's thermal features. You'd need to search two or three other continents for as many geysers as you can see during a single afternoon around Old Faithful.

HEATING UP

Past eruptions of cataclysmic volcanoes brought about the steaming, vaporous landscape of Yellowstone today. The heat from the magma (molten rock) under the Yellowstone Caldera, an active volcano, continues to fuel the park's geyser basins, such as the Upper Geyser Basin, where more than 200 spouters cram into less than two square miles; and Norris, where water 1,000 feet below ground is 450° F. The complex underground plumbing in these geyser basins is affected by earthquakes and other subterranean hijinks that geologists are only beginning to understand. Some spouters spring to life, while others fall dormant with little or no warning.

HOT SPOT TIPS

■ **Stay on trails and boardwalks.** In some areas, like in Norris, water boils at temperatures of more than 200°. If you want to venture into the back country, where there are no boardwalks, consult a ranger first.

■ **Leave the area if you feel sick or dizzy.** You might be feeling this way due to overexposure to various thermal gases.

■ **These hot springs aren't for bathing.** The pH levels of some of these features are extremely acidic.

■ **They also aren't wishing wells.** In the past people threw hundreds of coins into the bright blue Morning Glory Pool. The coins clogged the pool's natural water vents, causing it to change to a sickly green color.

(left) Old Faithful. (above) Punch Bowl Spring.

HOW DO GEYSERS WORK?

A few main ingredients make geysers possible: abundant water, a heat source, a certain kind of plumbing system, and rock strong enough to withstand some serious pressure. The layout of any one geyser's underground plumbing may vary, but we know that below each vent is a system of fissures and chambers, with constrictions here and there that prevent hot water from rising to the surface. As the underground water heats up, these constrictions and the cooler surface water "cap" the whole system, keeping it from boiling over and ratcheting up the underground pressure. When a few steam bubbles eventually fight their way through the constrictions, the result is like uncapping a shaken-up soda bottle, when the released pressure causes the soda to spray.

FUN FACTS

■ A cone geyser (like Lone Star Geyser in Yellowstone's backcountry) has a spout-like formation around its vent, formed by silica particles deposited during eruptions.

■ A fountain geyser (like Daisy Geyser in the Old Faithful area) erupts from a vent submerged in a hot spring-like pool. Eruptions tend to be smaller and more sporadic.

■ Yellowstone's tallest geyser is Steamboat, in Norris, shooting up to 350 feet high.

■ When they erupt, geysers sometimes create rainbows amid their spray.

❶ RECHARGE STAGE

Groundwater accumulates in plumbing and is heated by the volcano. Some hot water flashes to steam and bubbles try to rise toward surface.

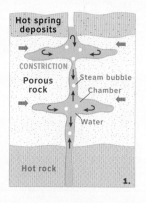

❷ PRELIMINARY ERUPTION STAGE

Pressure builds as steam bubbles clog at constriction. High pressure raises the boiling point, preventing superheated water from becoming steam.

❸ ERUPTION STAGE

Bubbles squeeze through constriction, displacing surface water and relieving pressure. Trapped water flashes to steam, forcing water out of the chambers and causing a chain reaction.

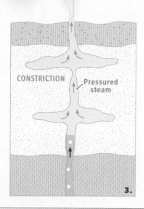

❹ RECOVERY STAGE

Eruption ends when the chambers are emptied or the temperature falls below boiling. Chambers begin to refill with ground water and the process begins again.

(left) Lone Star Geyser.

HOW DO HOT SPRINGS WORK?

Essentially, what keeps a hot spring from becoming a geyser is a lack of constriction in its underground plumbing. Like their more explosive cousins, hot springs consist of water that seeps into the earth, only to simmer its way back up through fissures after it's heated by hot volcanic rocks. Unlike in constricted geysers, water in a hot spring can circulate by convection. Rising hot water displaces cooling surface water, which then sinks underground to be heated and eventually rise again. Thus the whole mixture keeps itself at a gurgly equilibrium. As it rises, superheated water dissolves some subterranean minerals, depositing them at the surface to form the sculptural terraces that surround many hot springs.

The vivid colors that characterize hot springs and their terraces can be attributed alternately to minerals like sulfur and iron or to thermophiles. Thermophiles are microorganisms that thrive in extremely high temperatures. Blooming in thick bacterial mats, they convert light to energy, like plants, and their bright photosynthetic pigments help give hot springs their rainbow hues. Scientists suppose only a small percentage of Yellowstone's thermophiles have been identified. Still, these microbes have had a big impact on science. In 1965, a microorganism called Thermus aquaticus, or Taq, was discovered in the Lower Geyser Basin. From it, scientists extracted an enzyme that revolutionized molecular biology, ultimately making possible both DNA fingerprinting and the mapping of the human genome. NASA is among those performing research in the park today, studying thermophiles to gain insight on extraterrestrial life.

WHAT'S THAT SMELL?

Most people think hot springs smell like rotten eggs; some even say "burnt gunpowder" and "paper mill smokestack." Whatever similie you settle on, there's no question that hot springs and other thermal features stink to high heaven. Sulphur gases escaping from the volcano produce distinctive smells. Other gases are reduced to the stinky chemical hydrogen sulfide, which bubbles up to the surface. In high concentration, hydrogen sulfide can actually kill you, but the small amounts released by thermals can only kill your appetite. It's because hydrogen sulfide is often present in volcanic areas that we associate brimstone (or sulfur) with the underworld.

DID YOU KNOW?

Grand Prismatic Spring (pictured here) is the world's third-largest hot spring, at more than 370 feet across. The pool's vivid red and orange colors drizzle down its runoff channels, but from the boardwalk you can only glimpse a portion of these psychedelic tentacles. Thank the little guys: heat-loving microorganisms (bacteria and algae) tint the Grand Prismatic Spring with a rainbow of colors.

THE INNER WORKINGS OF HOT SPRINGS

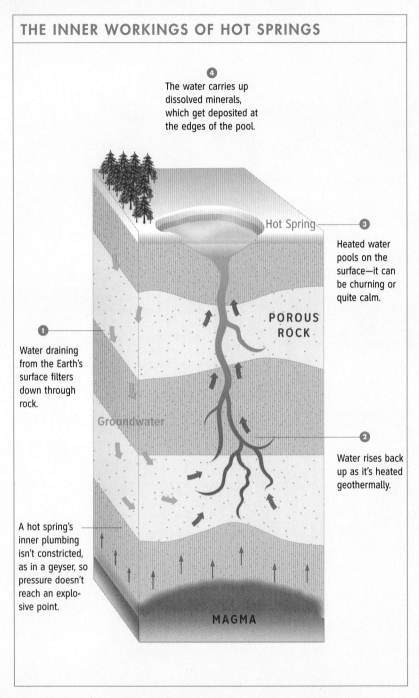

4 The water carries up dissolved minerals, which get deposited at the edges of the pool.

Hot Spring **3**

Heated water pools on the surface—it can be churning or quite calm.

POROUS ROCK

1 Water draining from the Earth's surface filters down through rock.

Groundwater

2 Water rises back up as it's heated geothermally.

A hot spring's inner plumbing isn't constricted, as in a geyser, so pressure doesn't reach an explosive point.

MAGMA

WHAT ARE FUMAROLES?

Take away the water from a hot spring and you're left with steam and other gas, forming a fumarole. Often called steam vents, these noisy thermals occur when available water boils away before reaching the surface. All that escapes the vent is heat, vapor, and the whisper-roar of a giant, menacing teakettle. Fumaroles are often found on high ground. The gases expelled from fumaroles might include carbon dioxide, sulfur dioxide, and hydrogen sulfide. Some hot spots, like Red Spouter in the Lower Geyser Basin, can exhibit different behaviors depending on the seasonal water table, so what's a fumarole today could be a hot spring in a few months.

FUN FACTS

■ The word fumarole comes from the Latin *fumus*, which means "smoke."

■ Fumaroles are also known as steam vents and solfataras, from *sulpha terra*, Latin for "land of sulfur."

■ Yellowstone's hottest fumarole is *Black Growler*, at Norris, which heats up to 280°F.

■ About 4,000 fumaroles are in Yellowstone.

Fumarole

WHAT ARE MUD POTS?

Mud pots in Lower Geyser Basin.

Might as well say it up front: mud pots are great because their thick, bursting bubbles can sound like a chorus of rude noises or "greetings from the interior." That's why the few places they're found in Yellowstone are usually surrounded by gaggles of giggling visitors with video cameras rolling. A mud pot is basically just a hot spring where the water table results in a bubbling broth of water and clay. The acid gases react with surface rocks, breaking them down into silica and clay. As gases escape from below, bubbles swell and pop, flinging mud chunks onto the banks to form gloppy clay mounds. The mud's thickness varies with rainfall through the seasons.

FUN FACTS

■ Mud pots have been nicknamed "paint pots" due to iron and other metals tinting the mud.

■ The biggest cluster of mud pots in the park is in Pocket Basin in Lower Geyser Basin.

■ Before it exploded in 1872, Mud Volcano was 30 feet tall by 30 feet wide.

PHOTOGRAPHY TIPS

■ Set your alarm clock: generally, the best light for shooting the geothermal features is early in the morning. You'll avoid the thickest crowds then, too. The runner-up time is the late afternoon.

■ Breezy days are good for photographing geysers, since the steam will be blown away from the jetting water. But avoid standing downwind or your view can be clouded with steam.

■ If you get water from a thermal feature on your lens, dry it off as quickly as possible, because the water has a high mineral content that can damage your lens.

Thermal pool in the Rabbit Creek Thermal Area.

SPORTS AND THE OUTDOORS

In winter, snowmobiling and cross-country skiing are the activities of choice. In summer, hiking, biking, and fishing are the best ways to get out and enjoy the park.

BOATING

Motorized boats are allowed only on Lewis Lake and Yellowstone Lake. Kayaking and canoeing is allowed on all lakes except Sylvan Lake, Eleanor Lake, Twin Lakes, and Beach Springs Lagoon. Most lakes are inaccessible by car, though, so accessing them requires long portages. Boating is not allowed on any river except the Lewis between Lewis Lake and Shoshone Lake, where nonmotorized boats are permitted.

You must purchase a seven-day, $5 permit for boats and floatables, or a $10 permit for motorized boats at Bridge Bay Ranger Station, South Entrance Ranger Station, Grant Village Backcountry Office, and Lewis Lake Ranger Station (at the campground). Nonmotorized permits are available at the Northeast Entrance; West Yellowstone Information Center; the backcountry offices at Mammoth, Old Faithful, and Canyon; Bechler Ranger Station; and locations where motorized permits are sold. Annual permits cost $20.

Boat permits issued in Grand Teton National Park are honored in Yellowstone, but owners must register their vessel in Yellowstone and obtain a no-charge Yellowstone validation sticker from a permit-issuing station.

TOURS AND OUTFITTERS

FAMILY **Bridge Bay Marina.** Watercraft, from rowboats to powerboats, are available for trips on Yellowstone Lake at Bridge Bay Marina. You also can rent 22- and 34-foot cabin cruisers with a guide. ⊠ *Grand Loop Rd., 2 miles south of Lake Village, Lake area* ☎ *307/344–7311* ⊕ *www. yellowstonenationalparklodges.com/things-to-do* ☑ *$90/hr for guided cruisers for fishing or sightseeing; $10/hr for rowboat; $50/hr for small boat with outboard motor* ☉ *June–early Sept., daily 8:30–8:30.*

Yellowstone Lake Scenic Cruises. This company takes visitors on one-hour cruises aboard the *Lake Queen II.* The vessel makes its way from Bridge Bay to Stevenson Island and back. Reservations are strongly recommended. ⊠ *Bridge Bay Marina, Lake area* ☎ *307/344–7311* ⊕ *www. yellowstonenationalparklodges.com/things-to-do* ☑ *$17* ☉ *Late May–mid-Sept., daily 8:30–8:30.*

FISHING

Fishing season begins in late May on the Saturday of Memorial Day weekend and ends in November. Native cutthroat trout are among the prize catches, but four other varieties—brown, brook, lake, and rainbow—along with grayling and mountain whitefish inhabit Yellowstone's waters. Popular sportfishing opportunities include the Gardner and Yellowstone rivers as well as Soda Butte Creek, but the top fishing area is Madison River.

38

Yellowstone fishing permits cost $18 for three days, $25 for seven days, and $40 for the season. Anglers ages 15 and younger must have a (no-fee) permit or fish under direct supervision of an adult with a permit. Permits are available at all ranger stations, visitor centers, and Yellowstone general stores.

FISHING CHARTERS

Xanterra Parks & Resorts. This park concessionaire operates two- to 12-hour guided Yellowstone Lake fishing charters for up to six passengers per boat. The fee includes gear. ⊠ *Grand Loop Rd., 2 miles south of Lake Village, Bridge Bay* ☎ *307/344–7311* ⊕ *www. yellowstonenationalparklodges.com/things-to-do* 🖃 *$90/hr* ⊙ *Mid-June–early Sept.*

HIKING

Your most memorable Yellowstone moments will likely take place along a park hiking trail. Encountering a gang of elk in the woods is unquestionably more exciting than watching them graze on the grasses of Mammoth Hot Springs Hotel. Hearing the creak of lodgepole pines on a breezy afternoon feels more authentic than listening to tourists chatter as you jockey for the best view of Old Faithful.

Even a one-day visitor to Yellowstone can—and should—get off the roads and into the "wilderness." Because the park is a wild place, however, even a half-mile walk on a trail puts you at the mercy of nature, so be sure to prepare yourself accordingly. As a guide on an Old Yellow Bus Tour said, "You don't have to fear the animals—just respect them."

■ **TIP→** Much of Yellowstone lies more than 7,500 feet above sea level. The most frequent incidents requiring medical attention are respiratory problems, not animal attacks. Be aware of your physical limitations—as well as those of young children or elderly companions.

HIKING TOURS

Yellowstone Association Institute. If you'd like a naturalist, a geologist, a wildlife specialist, or other park expert to accompany you on a hike, book one of the institute's daylong or multiday excursions, which include backcountry trips. ⊠ *308 W. Park St., Gardiner* ☎ *406/848–2400* ⊕ *www.yellowstoneassociation.org* 🖃 *From $150 per day.*

OLD FAITHFUL

EASY

Biscuit Basin Trail. This 2½-mile round-trip trail goes via a boardwalk across the Firehole River to colorful Sapphire Pool. *Easy.* ✛ *Trailhead: 3 miles north of Old Faithful Village off Grand Loop Rd.*

Fountain Paint Pots Nature Trail. Take the ½-mile loop boardwalk to see the fumaroles (steam vents), blue pools, pink mud pots, and mini-geysers in this thermal area. The trail is popular in summer and winter because it's right next to Grand Loop Road. *Easy.* ✛ *Trailhead: at Lower Geyser Basin, between Old Faithful and Madison.*

FAMILY **Old Faithful Geyser Loop.** The ¾-mile loop departs from Old Faithful's
Fodor'sChoice visitor center, circling the geyser's benches, filled nearly all day in sum-
★ mer with tourists. *Easy.* ✛ *Trailhead: at Old Faithful Village.*

MODERATE

Mystic Falls Trail. From the west end of Biscuit Basin boardwalk, this trail climbs gently for 1 mile through heavily burned forest to the lava-rock base of 70-foot Mystic Falls. It then switchbacks up Madison Plateau to a lookout with the park's least-crowded view of Old Faithful and the Upper Geyser Basin. *Moderate.* ✛ *Trailhead: 3 miles north of Old Faithful Village off Grand Loop Rd.*

MAMMOTH HOT SPRINGS

MODERATE

Bunsen Peak Trail. Past the entrance to Bunsen Peak Road, this moderately difficult trail is a 4-mile, three-hour round-trip that climbs 1,300 feet to Bunsen Peak for a panoramic view of Blacktail Plateau, Swan Lake Flats, the Gallatin Mountains, and the Yellowstone River valley. *Moderate.* ✛ *Trailhead: Grand Loop Rd., 1½ miles south of Mammoth Hot Springs.*

TOWER-ROOSEVELT

MODERATE

Fodor'sChoice ★ **Slough Creek Trail.** Starting at Slough Creek Campground, this trail climbs steeply along a historic wagon trail for the first 1½ miles before reaching expansive meadows and prime fishing spots, where moose are common and grizzlies occasionally wander. From this point the trail, now mostly level, meanders another 9½ miles to the park's northern boundary. Anglers absolutely rave about this trail. *Moderate.* ✛ *Trailhead: 7 miles east of Tower-Roosevelt off Northeast Entrance Rd.*

CANYON

MODERATE

Brink of the Lower Falls Trail. Especially scenic, this trail branches off of the North Rim Trail at the Brink of the Upper Falls parking area. You can also access it from the Brink of the Lower Falls parking area on the North Rim Drive. The steep ½-mile one-way trail switchbacks 600 feet down to within a few yards of the top of the Yellowstone River's 308-foot Lower Falls. *Moderate.* ✛ *Trailhead: 300 yards east of Grand Loop Rd. on entrance to North Rim Drive, 1 mile south of Canyon.*

North Rim Trail. Offering great views of the Grand Canyon of the Yellowstone, the 3-mile North Rim Trail runs from Inspiration Point to Chittenden Bridge. Particularly fetching is the ½-mile section of the North Rim Trail from the Brink of the Upper Falls parking area to Chittenden Bridge that hugs the rushing Yellowstone River as it approaches the canyon. This trail is paved and fully accessible between Lookout Point and Grand View. *Moderate.* ✛ *Trailhead: 1 mile south of Canyon.*

South Rim Trail. Partly paved and fairly flat, this 1¾-mile trail along the south rim of the Grand Canyon of the Yellowstone affords impressive views and photo opportunities of the canyon and falls of the Yellowstone River. It starts at Chittenden Bridge and ends at Artist Point. Beyond Artist Point, the trail gives way to a high plateau and high mountain meadows. Although popular with day hikers, this is technically backcountry. Prepare accordingly, make some noise, and carry bear spray. *Moderate.* ✛ *Trailhead: at Chittenden Bridge, off South Rim Dr.*

38

DIFFICULT

Uncle Tom's Trail. Accessed by the South Rim Drive, this spectacular and strenuous 700-step trail ½ mile east of Chittenden Bridge descends 500 feet from the parking area to the roaring base of the Lower Falls of the Yellowstone. Much of this walk is on steel sheeting, which can have a film of ice on early summer mornings or anytime in spring and fall. *Difficult.* ✛ *Trailhead: at South Rim Dr., 1 mile east of Chittenden Bridge, 3 miles south of Canyon.*

LAKE AREA

EASY

FAMILY **Storm Point Trail.** Well marked and mostly flat, this 1½-mile loop leaves the south side of the road for a perfect beginner's hike out to Yellowstone Lake, particularly with a setting sun. The trail rounds the western edge of Indian Pond, then passes moose habitat on its way to Yellowstone Lake's Storm Point, named for its frequent afternoon windstorms and crashing waves. Heading west along the shore, you're likely to hear the shrill chirping of yellow-bellied marmots, rodents that grow as long as 2 feet. Also look for ducks, pelicans, trumpeter swans, and bison. You will pass several small beaches kids can explore on warm summer mornings. *Easy.* ✛ *Trailhead: 3 miles east of Lake Junction on East Entrance Rd.*

DIFFICULT

Fodor'sChoice **Avalanche Peak Trail.** On a busy day in summer, maybe six parties will
★ fill out the trail register at the Avalanche Peak trailhead, so you won't have a lot of company on this hike. Starting across from a parking area on the East Entrance Road, the difficult 4-mile, four-hour round-trip climbs 2,150 feet to the peak's 10,566-foot summit, from which you'll see the rugged Absaroka Mountains running north and south. Look around the talus and tundra near the top of Avalanche Peak for alpine wildflowers and butterflies. Don't try this trail before late June or after early September—it may be covered in deep snow. Rangers discourage hikers from attempting this hike in September or October because of bear activity. *Difficult.* ✛ *Trailhead: 2 miles east of Sylvan Lake on north side of East Entrance Rd.*

HORSEBACK RIDING

Reservations are recommended for horseback riding in the park. Don't worry about experience, as rangers estimate 90% of riders have not been on a horse in at least 10 years.

Private stock can be brought into the park. Horses are not allowed in frontcountry campgrounds but are permitted in certain backcountry campsites. For information on planning a backcountry trip with stock, call the Backcountry Office (☎ *307/344–2160*).

TOURS AND OUTFITTERS

About 50 area outfitters lead horse-packing trips and trail rides into Yellowstone. Expect to pay from $250 to $400 per day for a backcountry trip, including meals, accommodations, and guides. A guide must accompany all horseback-riding trips.

CLOSE UP

Yellowstone in Winter

To see a spectacularly different Yellowstone than that experienced by 90% of its visitors, come in winter. Rocky outcroppings are smoothed over. Waterfalls are transformed into jagged sheets of ice.

CROWDLESS QUIET

The best reason for a visit to Yellowstone between December and March is the opportunity to experience the park without the crowds. The first thing that strikes you during this season is the quiet. The gargantuan snowpack—as many as 200 inches annually at low elevation—seems to muffle the sounds of bison foraging in the geyser basins and of hot springs simmering. Yet even in the depths of a deep freeze, the park is never totally still: the mud pots bubble, geysers shoot skyward, and wind rustles the snow-covered pine trees. Above these sounds, the cry of a hawk, the yip of a coyote, or even on rare occasions the howl of a wolf may pierce the air.

ANIMALS HEAD DOWN

Animals in Yellowstone head *down* when the thermometer falls. Herbivores like elk and bison head to the warmer, less snowy valleys to find vegetation; predators like wolves and cougars follow them. As a result, you're more likely to see these animals in the frontcountry in winter. The snow also makes it easier to pick out animal tracks.

SNOW PLAY

Snowmobiling is popular but also controversial (critics cite noise and pollution). At the time of this writing, guided trips with capped speed limits are offered in both Yellowstone and Grand Teton national parks. There are also the options of cross-country skiing and snowshoeing through geyser basins and along the canyon, both excellent ways to see the park. Dogsledding isn't permitted, but outfitters in Jackson lead trips in the nearby national forests.

—Brian Kevin, excerpted from Fodor's *Compass American Guides: Yellowstone and Grand Teton National Parks*

38

FAMILY **Xanterra Parks & Resorts.** The park concessionaire offers one-hour horseback rides at Mammoth, and one- and two-hour rides at Tower-Roosevelt and Canyon Village. You can also book an Old West Dinner Cookout that involves a ride. ⊠ *Mammoth Hot Springs, 1 Grand Loop Rd.* ☎ *307/344–7311, 866/439–7375* ⊕ *www.yellowstonenationalparklodges.com/things-to-do* ⊠ *From $45.*

Yellowstone Wilderness Outfitters. Exclusively dedicated to trips inside Yellowstone National Park, this company is owned by the musically inclined, multitalented Jett Hitt. Trips range from half- and full-day family rides to three- to six-day pack trips in every area of the park. Wildlife biologists and/or naturalists accompany the excursions. ⊠ *Yellowstone National Park* ☎ *406/223–3300* ⊕ *www.yellowstone.ws* ⊠ *From $125 for half-day trips.*

GOOD READS

The Yellowstone Story, by Aubrey L. Haines, is a classic.

Yellowstone: The Official Guide to Touring America's First National Park, published by Yellowstone Association, is a magazine-size, full-color, glossy, 80-page "yearbook."

Decade of the Wolf, by Douglas Smith and Gary Ferguson, is the most comprehensive and gripping account of the reintroduction of wolves into the park in the 1990s.

Yellowstone Trails, A Hiking Guide, by Mark C. Marschall, will help you navigate the shortest and longest trails in the park.

Lost In My Own Backyard, by Tim Cahill, is a hilarious account of one person's experience in the park.

Alston Chase's controversial *Playing God in Yellowstone* chronicles a century of government mismanagement.

SKIING, SNOWSHOEING, AND SNOWMOBILING

Yellowstone can be the coldest place in the continental United States in winter, with temperatures of −30°F not uncommon. Still, winter-sports enthusiasts flock here when the park opens for its winter season on the last week of December. Until early March, the roads teem with over-snow vehicles like snowmobiles and snow coaches, and trails bristle with cross-country skiers and snowshoers.

Snowmobiling is an exhilarating way to experience Yellowstone. It's also controversial: there's heated debate about the pollution and disruption to animal habitats. The number of riders per day is limited, and you must have a reservation, a guide, and a four-stroke engine, less polluting than the more common two-stroke variety. About a dozen companies have been authorized to lead snowmobile excursions. Prices vary, as do itineraries and inclusions: ask about insurance, guides, taxes, park entrance fees, clothing, helmets, and meals.

TOURS AND OUTFITTERS

Xanterra Parks & Resorts. At Mammoth Hot Springs Hotel and Old Faithful Snow Lodge, the park concessionaire rents skis, snowmobiles, and snowshoes. Ski rentals include skis, poles, and gaiters. Skier shuttles run from Mammoth Hotel to Indian Creek and from Old Faithful Snow Lodge to Fairy Falls and the Continental Divide Overlook. Lessons and guided tours, including day trips to the Grand Canyon of the Yellowstone, are also available. ⊠ *Mammoth Hot Springs, 1 Grand Loop Rd.* ☎ *307/344–7311, 866/439–7375, 307/344–5276* ⊕ *www. yellowstonenationalparklodges.com/things-to-do* ✉ *Ski rental $16/half day, $25/full day; snowshoes $12.50/half day, $22/full day.*

Yellowstone Association Institute. The institute's winter programs include daylong wildlife-watching excursions and multiday skiing and snowshoeing treks. ⊠ *308 W. Park St., Gardiner* ☎ *406/848–2400* ⊕ *www. yellowstoneassociation.org* ✉ *Call or check website for prices.*

WHAT'S NEARBY

Yellowstone National Park is a destination, not something to see as you pass through the area, and it covers a lot of ground. It's easily possible—and sometimes the most convenient strategy—to spend nearly your entire time within the park itself. That said, towns just outside the park contain numerous sights to see and outdoor activities, not to mention upscale resorts and destination restaurants. Below are some of the highlights of all these just outside the park.

NEARBY TOWNS

Because of its airport and its proximity to both Grand Teton and Yellowstone national parks, **Jackson,** the closest town to Yellowstone's South Entrance, is the region's busiest community in summer and has the widest selection of dining and lodging options. Meanwhile, the least-known gateway, the little town of **Dubois,** southeast of the park, is far from the madding crowds and a good place to stop on the way in or out of the park if you want to visit the National Bighorn Sheep Interpretive Center.

The most popular gateway from Montana, particularly in winter, is **West Yellowstone,** near the park's West Entrance. This is where the open plains of southwestern Montana and northeastern Idaho come together along the Madison River Valley. Affectionately known among winter recreationists as the "snowmobile capital of the world," this town of 1,000 is also a good place to go for fishing, horseback riding, and downhill skiing. Stop by the Grizzly & Wolf Discovery Center and the Yellowstone Historic Center to tap into the area's natural and cultural history.

As the only entrance to Yellowstone open the entire year, **Gardiner,** in Montana, is always bustling. The town's Roosevelt Arch has marked the park's North Entrance since 1903, when President Theodore Roosevelt dedicated it. The Yellowstone River slices through the town, population 800, beckoning fishermen and rafters. Its quaint stores and good restaurants attract shoppers and diners. North of Gardiner, along Interstate 90, is **Livingston,** a town of 7,500 known for its nostalgia-inducing historic district.

With both Yellowstone and the Absaroka-Beartooth Wilderness at its back door, the Montana village of **Cooke City,** at the park's Northeast Entrance, is a good place for hiking, horseback riding, mountain climbing, and other outdoor activities. Some 50 miles to the east of Cooke City and 60 miles southeast of Billings via U.S. 212 is the small resort town of **Red Lodge.** Nestled against the foot of the pine-draped Absaroka-Beartooth Wilderness and edged by the Limestone Palisades, Red Lodge attracts skiers, anglers, golfers, and horseback riders and has more options for dining and lodging than Cooke City. Driving along the Beartooth Scenic Byway between Red Lodge and Cooke City, you'll cross the southern tip of the Beartooth range, literally in the ramparts of the Rockies. From Cooke City, the drive into Yellowstone through the Lamar Valley is one of the prettiest routes in the park.

38

Named for Pony Express rider, army scout, and entertainer William F. "Buffalo Bill" Cody, the town of **Cody,** in Wyoming, sits near the park's East Entrance. It is a good base for hiking trips, horseback-riding excursions, and white-water rafting on the North Fork of the Shoshone or the Clarks Fork of the Yellowstone. It also is home to dude ranches and, in season, the nightly rodeo.

Visitor Information Cody Country Chamber of Commerce. ⊠ *836 Sheridan Ave., Cody* ☎ *307/587–2777, 307/587–2777, 800/393–2639* ⊕ *www.codychamber.org/visitcody.* **Cooke City Chamber of Commerce.** ⊠ *206 W. Main St.* ☎ *406/838–2495* ⊕ *www.cookecitychamber.org.* **Dubois Chamber of Commerce.** ⊠ *616 W. Ramshorn St., Dubois* ☎ *307/455–2556* ⊕ *www.duboiswyomingchamber.org.* **Gardiner Chamber of Commerce.** ⊠ *222 Park St., Gardiner* ☎ *406/848–7971* ⊕ *www.gardinerchamber.com.* **Jackson Hole Chamber of Commerce.** ⊠ *532 N. Cache St., Jackson* ☎ *307/733–3316, 307/733–3316* ⊕ *www.jacksonholechamber.com.* **Livingston Chamber of Commerce.** ⊠ *303 E. Park St., Livingston* ☎ *406/222–0850* ⊕ *www.livingstonchamber.com.* **Red Lodge Area Chamber of Commerce.** ⊠ *701 N. Broadway, Red Lodge* ☎ *406/446–1718, 888/281–0625* ⊕ *redlodgechamber.org.* **West Yellowstone Chamber of Commerce.** ⊠ *30 Yellowstone Ave., West Yellowstone* ☎ *406/646–7701* ⊕ *www.westyellowstonechamber.com.*

NEARBY ATTRACTIONS

CODY

Fodor's Choice ★ **Buffalo Bill Center of the West.** This sprawling "five-in-one" complex, sometimes called the Smithsonian of the West, contains the Buffalo Bill Museum, the Whitney Western Art Museum, the Plains Indian Museum, the Cody Firearms Museum, and the Draper Natural History Museum. All are well organized and mount superb exhibitions in their respective subject areas. The flagship Buffalo Bill Museum puts into context the life, era, and activities of its (and its town's) namesake, William F. "Buffalo Bill" Cody (1846–1917), whose numerous careers included guide, scout, actor, and entrepreneur. If you want to understand how the myth of the American West developed, this is the place to come. The other four museums—there's also a research library—are equally absorbing. Plan to spend at least four hours here—and to discover that this isn't enough time to take it all in. Luckily, your admission ticket is good for two consecutive days. ⊠ *720 Sheridan Ave., Cody* ☎ *307/587–4771* ⊕ *www.centerofthewest.org* ☞ *$19, good for 2 consecutive days* ⊗ *Mar., Apr. and Nov., daily 10–5; May–mid-Sept., daily 8–6; mid-Sept.–Oct., daily 8–5; Dec.–Feb., Thurs.–Sun. 10–5.*

WEST YELLOWSTONE

FAMILY **Grizzly and Wolf Discovery Center.** Home to eight grizzlies and three wolf packs, this facility provides an up-close look at Yellowstone's two most feared predators. In summer, birds of prey are also on display. The comprehensive Bears: Imagination and Reality exhibit compares myths about bears to what science has revealed about them. The grizzlies earn money toward their maintenance by helping to test bear-resistant products such as coolers and canisters. ⊠ *201 S. Canyon St., West Yellowstone*

☎ *406/646–7001, 800/257–2570* ⊕ *www.grizzlydiscoveryctr.org* ✉ *$11.50, good for 2 consecutive days* ⊗ *Daily 8:30 am–dusk.*

FAMILY **Yellowstone Historic Center.** West Yellowstone's 1909 Union Pacific Depot has been transformed into a museum dedicated to the modes of travel—from stagecoaches to planes—people employed to get to Yellowstone before World War II. Films provide insight on topics such as the fire that devastated Yellowstone in 1988 and the way earthquakes affect the area's hydrothermal features. ✉ *104 Yellowstone Ave., West Yellowstone* ☎ *406/646–1100* ⊕ *www.yellowstonehistoriccenter.org* ✉ *$6* ⊗ *Mid-May–mid-June and mid-Sept.–Oct., daily 9–6; mid-June–mid-Sept., daily 9–9.*

SHOPPING

Sunlight Sports. This 8,000-square-foot store that stocks major-brand products sells everything from camping gear to downhill and cross-country ski equipment. The staff is friendly and has extensive experience in most outdoor pursuits. ✉ *1131 Sheridan Ave., Cody* ☎ *307/587–9517* ⊕ *www.sunlightsports.com.*

WHERE TO EAT

IN THE PARK

$ ✕ **Bear Paw Deli.** You can grab a quick bite and not miss a geyser erup-
FAST FOOD tion at this snack shop in the Old Faithful Inn. Tasty salads and sand-wiches are available throughout the day, as is hand-dipped ice cream. If you're staying at the inn, fill up your water bottles at the soda fountain. Limited seating is available. ⑤ *Average main: $8* ✉ *Old Faithful Village, Old Faithful* ☎ *307/344–7311* ⊕ *www.yellowstonenationalparklodges.com/dining/old-faithful* ⊗ *Closed Mid-Oct.–early May* ⟜ *Reservations not accepted.*

$ ✕ **Canyon Lodge Cafeteria.** Grab a tray and get in line at this busy break-
AMERICAN fast, lunch, and dinner spot that serves country-fried steak, open-
FAMILY faced turkey sandwiches, and other traditional American fare. The pasta station's cannelloni, tortellini, and manicotti make the cafeteria a nice, inexpensive dinner option. There's a varied breakfast menu, too. ⑤ *Average main: $9* ✉ *Canyon Village* ☎ *307/344–7311* ⊕ *www.yellowstonenationalparklodges.com/dining/canyon-village* ⊗ *Closed Oct.–late May* ⟜ *Reservations not accepted.*

$ ✕ **Geyser Grill.** You're here for the geyser views, not the grub, of this
FAST FOOD busy grill near Old Faithful. Hamburgers, hot dogs, and chicken nuggets
FAMILY are the kids' menu highlights. For parents there are soups, salads, and burgers (meat and vegetarian) and other sandwiches. ⑤ *Average main: $7* ✉ *Snow Lodge at Old Faithful Village* ☎ *307/344–7311* ⊕ *www.yellowstonenationalparklodges.com/dining* ⊗ *Closed Nov.–mid-Dec. and mid-Mar.–mid-Apr.* ⟜ *Reservations not accepted.*

$$$ ✕ **Grant Village Dining Room.** The floor-to-ceiling windows of this
AMERICAN waterfront restaurant provide views of Yellowstone Lake through the thick stand of pines. The pine-beam ceilings, cedar-shake walls, and

38

contemporary decor lend the place a homey feel. Entrée choices at dinner range from pasta and trout to bison and elk meat loaf. Breakfast and lunch are also served. ⑤ *Average main: $21 ⊠ 1 Grand Loop Rd., 3 miles south of West Thumb Information Station, Grant Village* ☎ *307/344–7311, 866/439–7375* ⊕ *www.yellowstonenationalparklodges.com/dining* ⊙ *Closed Oct.–late May* ⚠ *Reservations essential.*

$ ✕ **Lake Lodge Cafeteria.** Much of the fare here may be standard cafeteria—roast turkey, pot roast, and the like—but the Yellowstone Lake views are awe-inspiring. The more upscale entrées might include trout amandine, prime rib, and poached salmon. There's a full breakfast menu. ⑤ *Average main: $10 ⊠ Lake Village Rd., 1 mile south of Fishing Bridge* ☎ *307/344–7311* ⊕ *www.yellowstonenationalparklodges.com/dining/lake-yellowstone* ⊙ *Closed Oct.–early June* ⚠ *Reservations not accepted.*

AMERICAN
FAMILY

$$$ ✕ **Lake Yellowstone Hotel Dining Room.** Opened in 1891, this double-colonnaded dining room off the lobby of the Lake Yellowstone Hotel is the park's most elegant dining spot. Arrive early and enjoy a beverage and the view in the airy Reamer Lounge, which debuted as a sunroom in 1928. The dinner menu includes such attractive starters as a charcuterie sampler with Montana cheeses. Lamb, bison, steak, duck, quail, and fish dishes are all served, and there's always at least one imaginative vegetarian entrée. Wines from California, Oregon, and Washington predominate on the wine list. Reservations are not needed for breakfast or lunch, but they are essential for dinner. Make them up to a year in advance with hotel reservations; otherwise, call a month ahead. ⑤ *Average main: $25 ⊠ Lake Village Rd., 1 mile south of Fishing Bridge, Lake Village* ☎ *307/344–7311, 866/439–7375* ⊕ *www.yellowstonenationalparklodges.com/dining/lake-yellowstone* ⊙ *Closed early Oct.–mid-May* ⚠ *Reservations essential.*

AMERICAN
Fodor's Choice
★

$$ ✕ **Mammoth Hotel Dining Room.** A wall of windows at the dining room overlooks an expanse of green that was once a military parade and drill field. While enjoying breakfast, lunch, or dinner you might catch a glimpse of elk grazing on the lawn. The art deco–style restaurant, decorated in shades of gray and white, has an airy feel. Montana beef, bison, and fish receive pride of place at dinner, which always includes at least one vegetarian entrée. The small-plate menu is right for those with lighter appetites. Dinner reservations are not taken in summer, but are essential in winter. ⑤ *Average main: $20 ⊠ Mammoth Hot Springs ✛ 5 miles south of North Entrance* ☎ *307/344–7311, 866/439–7375* ⊕ *www.yellowstonenationalparklodges.com/dining/mammoth-hot-springs* ⊙ *Closed mid-Oct.–mid-Dec. and mid-Mar.–mid-May* ⚠ *Reservations not accepted.*

AMERICAN

$ ✕ **Mammoth Terrace Grill.** Although the exterior looks rather elegant, this Mammoth Hot Springs restaurant serves simple fare. Expect dishes like biscuits and gravy for breakfast and hamburgers and vegetarian burgers for lunch and dinner. Take a break and wander the volcanic-rock Terraces outside before having some of the superb ice cream. ⑤ *Average main: $8 ⊠ Mammoth Hot Springs ✛ 5 miles south of North Entrance, west of Mammoth Hot Springs Hotel* ☎ *307/344–7311*

FAST FOOD

⊕ *www.yellowstonenationalparklodges.com/dining/mammoth-hot-springs* ⊙ *Closed late Sept.–mid-May.*

$$$
AMERICAN
Fodor'sChoice
★

╳ **Obsidian Dining Room.** From the wood-and-leather chairs etched with animal figures to the intricate lighting fixtures that resemble snow-capped trees, there's ample Western atmosphere at this smaller dining room inside the Old Faithful Snow Lodge. The huge windows give you a view of the Old Faithful area, and you can sometimes see the famous geyser as it erupts. This and the Mammoth Hot Springs Dining Room are the only places in the park where you can enjoy a full dinner in winter. The French onion soup will warm you up on a chilly afternoon; among the main courses, look for prime rib, elk, beef, and salmon. ⑤ *Average main: $23* ⊠ *Old Faithful Snow Lodge, south end of Old Faithful Village* 📞 *307/344–7311, 866/439–7375* ⊕ *www. yellowstonenationalparklodges.com/dining/old-faithful* ⊙ *Closed mid-Oct.–mid-Dec. and Mar.–early May. No lunch* ⚄ *Reservations not accepted.*

$$
AMERICAN

╳ **Old Faithful Inn Dining Room.** The Old Faithful Inn's original dining room—designed by Robert Reamer in 1903 and expanded by him in 1927—has lodgepole-pine walls and ceiling beams and a giant volcanic rock fireplace. Note the whimsical etched-glass panels that separate the dining room from the Bear Pit Lounge; the images of partying animals were commissioned by Reamer in 1933 to celebrate the end of Prohibition. The dinner buffet favors quantity over quality, so it's wiser to order grilled salmon, prime rib, bison rib eye, or other entrées, including a vegetarian one, off the à la carte menu. Save room for a signature dessert such as the Caldera, a chocolate-truffle torte with a molten middle. With 50 choices, the wine list here is the park's most extensive list. For breakfast, there's a buffet, and you can order individual entrées. ⑤ *Average main: $20* ⊠ *Old Faithful Village* ⚓ *Take first left off Old Faithful Bypass Rd.* 📞 *307/344–7311, 866/439–7375* ⊕ *www. yellowstonenationalparklodges.com/dining/old-faithful* ⊙ *Closed late Oct.–early May* ⚄ *Reservations essential.*

$
AMERICAN
FAMILY

╳ **Old Faithful Lodge Cafeteria.** This noisy eatery that serves kid-friendly fare like pizza and hamburgers has one redeeming value: it has some of the best views of Old Faithful, and while you eat you can watch it erupt. The cafeteria is not open for breakfast, but the snack shop just outside is, offering a small selection of baked goods and ice cream. ⑤ *Average main: $9* ⊠ *Yellowstone National Park* ⚓ *End of Old Faithful Bypass Rd.* 📞 *307/344–7311* ⊕ *www.yellowstonenationalparklodges.com/ dining/old-faithful* ⊙ *Closed mid-Sept.–mid-May* ⚄ *Reservations not accepted.*

$$
AMERICAN
FAMILY

╳ **Roosevelt Lodge Dining Room.** The menu at this log cabin in a pine forest includes appropriately rustic options like sirloin steak and barbecued ribs, but you can also order shrimp tacos or a burger and fries. Don't miss the killer cornbread muffins. For a real adventure, make a reservation for the Roosevelt Old West Dinner Cookout, which includes an hour-long trail ride or a stagecoach ride. ⑤ *Average main: $20* ⊠ *Grand Loop Rd. and Northeast Entrance Rd., Tower-Roosevelt* 📞 *307/344–7311* ⊕ *www.yellowstonenationalparklodges.com/dining/roosevelt-lodge* ⊙ *Closed early Sept.–early June* ⚄ *Reservations not accepted.*

38

PICNIC AREAS

The 49 picnic areas in the park range from secluded spots with a couple of tables to more popular stops with a dozen or more tables. Only nine areas—Snake River, Grant Village, Spring Creek, Nez Perce, Old Faithful East, Bridge Bay, Cascade Lake Trail, Norris Meadows, and Yellowstone River—have fire grates. Gas stoves only may be used in the other areas. None have running water, and all but a few have pit toilets. You can stock up your cooler at any of the park's general stores. It is also possible to purchase from some park restaurants box lunches that include drinks, snacks, sandwiches, and fruit, or vegetarian or cheese-and-crackers selections.

■TIP➜ Keep an eye out for wildlife. You never know when a herd of bison might decide to march through. If that happens, it's best to leave your food and move a safe distance away from them.

FAMILY **Firehole River.** The Firehole River rolls past this picnic area, and you might see elk grazing along the river's banks. There's one pit toilet here. ✉ *Grand Loop Rd., 3 miles south of Madison, Madison* ⊕ *www.nps. gov/yell/planyourvisit/picnic.htm.*

Gibbon Meadows. You are likely to see elk or buffalo along the Gibbon River from one of nine tables at this area, which has a wheelchair-accessible pit toilet. ✉ *Grand Loop Rd., 3 miles south of Norris* ⊕ *www. nps.gov/yell/planyourvisit/picnic.htm.*

Sedge Bay. On the northern end of this volcanic beach, look carefully for the large rock slabs pushed out of the lake bottom. Nearby trees offer shade and a table, or you can hop onto the level rocks for an ideal lakeside picnic. You may see bubbles rising from the clear water around the rocks—these indicate an active underwater thermal feature. The only company you may have here could be crickets, birds, and bison. ✉ *East Entrance Rd., 8 miles east of Fishing Bridge* ⊕ *www.nps.gov/ yell/planyourvisit/picnic.htm.*

OUTSIDE THE PARK

$$ ✕ **Beartooth Barbecue.** When you taste a rack of the hand-rubbed spare
BARBECUE ribs, pulled beef brisket, and zesty baked beans, you'll know why this place is a locals' favorite. In high season, go early in the day because it's so popular it sometimes sells out of ribs. Select from a dozen micro-brews crafted in Wyoming and Montana. ⑤ *Average main: $17* ✉ *111 Canyon St., West Yellowstone* ☎ *406/646–0227* ⌨ *Reservations not accepted.*

$$$ ✕ **Old Piney Dell.** This small hangout on the banks of Rock Creek has
AMERICAN good steaks and schnitzels, as well as daily pasta specials. Part of the
STEAKHOUSE Rock Creek Resort, the restaurant dates to the early 1940s. ⑤ *Average main: $25* ✉ *Rock Creek Resort, 6380 U.S. 212 S, Red Lodge* ☎ *406/446–1111* ⊕ *www.rockcreekresort.com* ☉ *Closed Mon. No lunch Tues.–Sat. No dinner Sun.* ⌨ *Reservations essential.*

$ ✕ **Running Bear Pancake House.** All the pies, muffins, and cinnamon rolls
AMERICAN are made on the premises at this eatery. There are a lot of choices, but
FAMILY trust the name and go for the buttermilk or buckwheat pancakes topped with blueberries, strawberries, peaches, coconut, walnuts, or chocolate

chips. There's also a basic lunch menu with sandwiches and salads and box lunches to go. $ *Average main: $7* ⊠ *538 Madison Ave., West Yellowstone* ☎ *406/646–7703* ⊕ *runningbearph.com* ⊗ *No dinner.*

$$ ✕ **Wild West Pizzeria and Saloon.** Aaron and Megan Hecht make superb
PIZZA pizzas with crispy crusts, flavorful sauces, and memorable frontier
FAMILY names. The Sitting Bull pie has pepperoni, sausage, salami, and Canadian bacon, and the Calamity Jane pleases diners with white sauce, mushrooms, artichoke hearts, minced garlic, and fresh tomatoes. There are also sandwiches and pasta dishes. The bar next door often hosts live music. $ *Average main: $16* ⊠ *14 Madison Ave., West Yellowstone* ☎ *406/646–4400* ⊕ *www.wildwestpizza.com.*

$$$ ✕ **Wyoming's Rib & Chop House.** This place can be packed in the summer
AMERICAN with cowboys and tourists enjoying succulent baby back ribs, and the steak, chicken, and seafood dishes are excellent, too. There are glutenfree options, but vegetarians need to make a special request ahead of a visit. The wine list is comprehensive. $ *Average main: $22* ⊠ *1367 Sheridan Ave., Cody* ☎ *307/527–7731* ⊕ *www.ribandchophouse.com.*

$$ ✕ **Yellowstone Mine.** Decorated with picks, shovels, and other min-
STEAKHOUSE ing equipment, this is a place for casual family-style dining. Townies
FAMILY come in for the steaks and seafood. Lunch and dinner are served yearround, and there's a breakfast buffet in summer. $ *Average main: $15* ⊠ *Best Western by Mammoth Hot Springs, 905 Scott St. W, Gardiner* ☎ *406/848–7336.*

WHERE TO STAY

38

IN THE PARK

CANYON

$$ 🏨 **Canyon Lodges.** The five Canyon Lodges—Hayden, Chittenden, Moran,
HOTEL Washburn and Rhyolite—were built in 2015. **Pros:** central location;
FAMILY new buildings constructed with sustainability in mind; pretty location. **Cons:** you'll likely want to drive to restaurants. $ *Rooms from: $122* ⊠ *North Rim Dr. and Grand Loop Rd., Canyon Village* ☎ *307/344–7311, 866/439–7375* ⊕ *www.yellowstonenationalparklodges.com/ lodging/summer-lodges/canyon-lodge-cabins* ⊗ *Closed late Sept.–late May* ⌁ *400 rooms* ⦿ *No meals.*

$$$ 🏨 **Canyon Western Cabins.** These recently renovated pine-frame cabins
HOTEL are arranged in clusters of four and six. **Pros:** can park close to your cabin; heart-of-the-park location; restaurants and a bar are nearby. **Cons:** busy area. $ *Rooms from: $194* ⊠ *North Rim Dr. and Grand Loop Rd., Canyon Village* ☎ *307/344–7311, 866/439–7375* ⊕ *www. yellowstonenationalparklodges.com/lodging/summer-lodges/canyon-lodge-cabins* ⊗ *Closed mid-Sept.–late May* ⌁ *100 cabins* ⦿ *No meals.*

$$ 🏨 **Dunraven Lodge.** This four-story lodge sits amid pine trees that
HOTEL edge the Grand Canyon of the Yellowstone. **Pros:** canyon location. **Cons:** far from dining and other services. $ *Rooms from: $122* ⊠ *1 Grand Loop Rd., at North Rim Dr., Canyon Village* ☎ *307/344–7311, 866/439–7375* ⊕ *www.yellowstonenationalparklodges.com/lodging/*

CLOSE UP

Best Campgrounds in Yellowstone

Yellowstone has a dozen frontcountry campgrounds scattered around the park, in addition to more than 200 backcountry sites. Most campgrounds have flush toilets; some have coin-operated showers and laundry facilities. The campgrounds run by Xanterra Parks & Resorts—Bridge Bay, Canyon, Fishing Bridge RV Park, Grant Village, and Madison—accept bookings in advance. The rest, operated by the National Park Service, are available on a first-come, first-served basis.

Bridge Bay. The park's largest campground, Bridge Bay rests in a wooded grove above Yellowstone Lake and adjacent to the park's major marina. Grand Loop Rd., 3 miles southwest of Lake Village ☎ 307/344-7311 ⊕ www.yellowstonenationalparklodges.com.

Canyon. A massive campground with 250-plus sites, Canyon Campground accommodates everyone from hiker/biker tent campers to large RVs. North Rim Dr., ¼ mile east of Grand Loop Rd., Canyon Village ☎ 307/344-7311 ⊕ www.yellowstonenationalparklodges.com.

Fishing Bridge RV Park. It's more of a parking lot than a campground, but RV services like tank filling/emptying and hookups are available. Grand Loop Rd., 3 miles southwest of Lake Village ☎ 307/344-7311 ⊕ www.yellowstonenationalparklodges.com.

Grant Village. The park's second-largest campground, Grant Village has some sites with great views of Yellowstone Lake. Some sites are wheelchair accessible. South Entrance Rd., Grant Village ☎ 307/344-7311 ⊕ www.yellowstonenationalparklodges.com.

Indian Creek. In a picturesque setting next to a creek, this campground is in the middle of a prime wildlife-viewing area. Grand Loop Rd., 8 miles south of Mammoth Hot Springs ☎ 307/344-2017.

Madison. The largest National Park Service–operated campground, where no advance reservations are accepted, Madison has eight loops and nearly 300 sites. Grand Loop Rd., Madison ☎ 307/344-7311 ⊕ www.yellowstonenationalparklodges.com.

Norris. Straddling the Gibbon River, this is a quiet, popular campground. A few of its "walk-in" sites are among the best in the park. Grand Loop Rd., Norris ☎ 307/344-2017.

Pebble Creek. Beneath multiple 10,000-foot peaks (Thunderer, Barronette Peak, and Mount Norris) the park's easternmost campground is set creekside in a forested canopy. Northeast Entrance Rd., 22 miles east of Tower-Roosevelt Junction ☎ 307/344-2017.

Slough Creek. Down the park's most rewarding 2 miles of dirt road, Slough Creek is a gem. Nearly every site is adjacent to the creek, which is prized by anglers. Northeast Entrance Rd., 10 miles east of Tower-Roosevelt Junction ☎ 307/344-2017.

Tower Falls. It's within hiking distance of the roaring waterfall, so this modest-size campground gets a lot of foot traffic. Grand Loop Rd., 3 miles southeast of Tower-Roosevelt ☎ 307/344-2017.

summer-lodges/canyon-lodge-cabins ⊘ *Closed mid-Sept.–early June* ⮐ *44 rooms* ⦿ *No meals.*

MAMMOTH HOT SPRINGS

$$
HOTEL

⛰ **Mammoth Hot Springs Hotel and Cabins.** The rooms at this 1936 lodge are smaller and simpler than those at the park's other historic hotels, but this one is less expensive and usually less crowded. **Pros:** great rates for a historic property; wake up to an elk bugling outside your window; cabins are among the park's nicest. **Cons:** many hotel rooms and cabins lack private bathrooms. ⑤ *Rooms from: $140* ✉ *U.S. 89, 2½ miles south of Montana border* ☎ *307/344–7311, 866/439–7375* ⊕ *www. yellowstonenationalparklodges.com/lodging/summer-lodges* ⊘ *Closed early Oct.–late Dec. and mid-Mar.–early May* ⮐ *97 rooms, 67 with bath; 2 suites; 115 cabins, 76 with bath* ⦿ *No meals.*

OLD FAITHFUL AREA

$$$
HOTEL
FAMILY
Fodor'sChoice
★

⛰ **Old Faithful Inn.** Easily earning its National Historic Landmark status, this lovely lodge has been a favorite of five generations of park visitors. **Pros:** a one-of-a-kind property; truly memorable rooms. **Cons:** thin walls; waves of tourists in the lobby; shared baths recall college dorm days. ⑤ *Rooms from: $200* ✉ *Old Faithful* ⊹ *1st left off Bypass Rd.* ☎ *307/ 344–7311, 866/439–7375* ⊕ *www.yellowstonenationalparklodges.com/ lodging/summer-lodges/old-faithful-inn* ⊘ *Closed mid-Oct.–early May* ⮐ *324 rooms, 246 with bath; 6 suites* ⦿ *No meals.*

$$
HOTEL

⛰ **Old Faithful Lodge Cabins.** There are no rooms inside the Old Faithful Lodge, but close to 100 cabins can be found at the village's northeastern end. **Pros:** good budget-friendly option; stone's throw from Old Faithful; services are within walking distance. **Cons:** some cabins lack private bathrooms; pretty basic. ⑤ *Rooms from: $140* ✉ *South end of Old Faithful Bypass Rd.* ☎ *307/344–7311, 866/439–7375* ⊕ *www.yellowstonenationalparklodges.com/lodging/summer-lodges/ old-faithful-lodge-cabins* ⊘ *Closed mid-Sept.–mid-May* ⮐ *96 cabins, 60 with bath* ⦿ *No meals.*

$$$$
HOTEL

⛰ **Old Faithful Snow Lodge.** This massive modern structure brings back the grand tradition of park lodges by making good use of heavy timber beams and wrought-iron accents in its distinctive facade. **Pros:** the park's most modern hotel; lobby is great for relaxing; open in winter. **Cons:** pricey, but you're paying for location. ⑤ *Rooms from: $240* ✉ *Far end of Old Faithful Bypass Rd., Old Faithful* ☎ *307/344–7311, 866/439–7375* ⊕ *www.yellowstonenationalparklodges.com/lodging/ summer-lodges/old-faithful-snow-lodge-cabins* ⊘ *Closed mid-Oct.– mid-Dec. and mid-Mar.–early May* ⮐ *100 rooms* ⦿ *No meals.*

$$$
HOTEL

⛰ **Old Faithful Snow Lodge Cabins.** Just yards from Old Faithful, many of these cabins sprang up after the 1988 fires. **Pros:** affordable; close to geyser. **Cons:** no amenities beyond the basics. ⑤ *Rooms from: $155* ✉ *Far end of Old Faithful Bypass Rd., Old Faithful* ☎ *307/344–7311, 866/439–7375* ⊕ *www.yellowstonenationalparklodges.com/lodging/ summer-lodges/old-faithful-snow-lodge-cabins* ⊘ *Closed mid-Oct.– early May* ⮐ *100 rooms* ⦿ *No meals.*

38

LAKE AREA

$$
HOTEL
FAMILY
☷ **Lake Lodge Cabins.** Just beyond the Lake Yellowstone Hotel lies one of the park's hidden treasures: Lake Lodge, built in 1920. **Pros:** the best porch at a Yellowstone lodge; great lobby; good for families. **Cons:** restaurant can get packed when motor coaches pull in. $ *Rooms from: $131* ✉ *Lake Village Rd., 1 mile south of Fishing Bridge, Lake Village* ☏ *307/ 344–7311, 866/439–7375* ⊕ *www.yellowstonenationalparklodges.com/ lodging/summer-lodges/lake-lodge-cabins* ⊗ *Closed mid-Sept.–early June* ⊃ *186 cabins* ⦿ *No meals.*

$$$$
HOTEL
☷ **Lake Yellowstone Hotel.** Dating from 1891, the park's oldest lodge maintains an air of refinement that Old Faithful Inn can't muster because of the constant rush of tour buses. **Pros:** relaxing atmosphere; the best views of any park lodging. **Cons:** the park's most expensive property; expensive restaurant; not particularly kid-friendly. $ *Rooms from: $373* ✉ *1 Grand Loop Rd., about 1 mile south of Fishing Bridge, Lake Village* ☏ *307/344–7311, 866/439–7375* ⊕ *www. yellowstonenationalparklodges.com* ⊗ *Closed early Oct.–mid-May* ⊃ *194 rooms* ⦿ *No meals.*

OUTSIDE THE PARK

$$$
HOTEL
☷ **The Cody.** This all-suites hotel incorporates Western themes into a thoroughly modern and eco-friendly property. **Pros:** shuttle to airport and downtown attractions; Continental breakfast included. **Cons:** luxury has its price. $ *Rooms from: $169* ✉ *232 W. Yellowstone Ave., Cody* ☏ *307/587–5915* ⊕ *www.thecody.com* ⊃ *90 suites* ⦿ *Breakfast.*

$$$
RESORT
☷ **Pahaska Tepee Resort.** Just 2 miles from Yellowstone's East Entrance, these cabins in a pine forest are a good base for destinations both inside and outside the park. **Pros:** historic property; on a scenic highway. **Cons:** few services between Cody and Fishing Bridge. $ *Rooms from: $179* ✉ *183 N. Fork Hwy., Cody* ☏ *307/527–7701, 800/628–7791* ⊕ *www. pahaska.com* ⊃ *43 cabins, 1 lodge* ⦿ *No meals.*

$$$
HOTEL
☷ **Pollard Hotel.** Guns have been banned in the hotel ever since Harry Longabaugh, aka the Sundance Kid, brandished one when he robbed a bank on the corner. **Pros:** full breakfast discounted; historical property. **Cons:** front-desk service can be erratic. $ *Rooms from: $165* ✉ *2 N. Broadway, Red Lodge* ☏ *406/446–0001, 800/765–5273, 406/446– 0002* ⊕ *www.thepollard.com* ⊃ *39 rooms, 11 suites* ⦿ *No meals.*

$$$$
HOTEL
FAMILY
☷ **Three Bear Lodge.** A towering stone fireplace and lots of natural wood greet guests in the lobby of the Three Bear Lodge. **Pros:** family-friendly feel; a block off the main drag; good-value rooms, especially in the off-season. **Cons:** no staff at front desk at night. $ *Rooms from: $239* ✉ *217 Yellowstone Ave., West Yellowstone* ☏ *406/646–7353, 800/646- 7353* ⊕ *www.threebearlodge.com* ⊃ *70* ⦿ *No meals.*

$$$
HOTEL
☷ **Yellowstone Village Inn and Suites.** Right in Gardiner across the street from the Yellowstone River, this hotel provides everything you need between day trips into Yellowstone. **Pros:** great location; homey feel. **Cons:** though not upscale this is one of Gardiner's best hotels. $ *Rooms from: $191* ✉ *1102 Scott St. W, Gardiner* ☏ *406/848–7417* ⊕ *www. yellowstonevinn.com* ⊃ *45 rooms* ⦿ *No meals.*

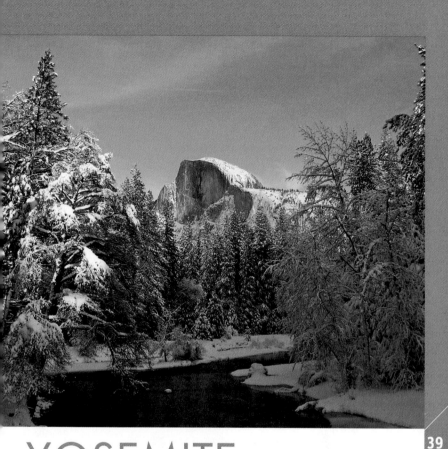

YOSEMITE
NATIONAL PARK

WELCOME TO YOSEMITE NATIONAL PARK

TOP REASONS TO GO

★ **Wet and wild:** An easy stroll brings you to the base of Lower Yosemite Fall, where roaring springtime waters make for misty lens caps and lasting memories.

★ **Tunnel vision:** Approaching Yosemite Valley, Wawona Road passes through a mountainside and emerges before one of the park's most heart-stopping vistas.

★ **Inhale the beauty:** Pause to smell the light, pristine air as you travel about the High Sierra's Tioga Pass and Tuolumne Meadows, where 10,000-foot granite peaks just might take your breath away.

★ **Walk away:** Leave the crowds behind—but do bring along a buddy—and take a hike somewhere along Yosemite's 800 miles of trails.

★ **Powder your nose:** Winter's hush floats into Yosemite on snowflakes. Lift your face to the sky and listen to the trees.

1 Yosemite Valley. At an elevation of 4,000 feet, in roughly the center of the park, beats Yosemite's heart. This is where you'll find the park's most famous sights and biggest crowds.

2 Wawona and Mariposa Grove. The park's southern tip holds Wawona, with its grand old hotel and pioneer history center, and the Mariposa Grove of Big Trees, filled with giant sequoias. These are closest to the south entrance, 35 miles (a one-hour drive) south of Yosemite Village.

3 Tuolumne Meadows. The highlight of east-central Yosemite is this wildflower-strewn valley with hiking trails, nestled among sharp, rocky peaks. It's a 1½-hour drive northeast of Yosemite Valley along Tioga Road (closed mid-October–late May).

4 Hetch Hetchy. The most remote, least visited part of Yosemite accessible by automobile, this glacial valley is dominated by a reservoir and veined with wilderness trails. It's near the park's western boundary, about a half-hour drive north of the Big Oak Flat entrance.

CALIFORNIA

GETTING ORIENTED

Yosemite is so large that you can think of it as five parks. Yosemite Valley, famous for waterfalls and cliffs, and Wawona, where the giant sequoias stand, are open all year. Hetch Hetchy, home of less-used backcountry trails, is most accessible from late spring through early fall. The subalpine high country, Tuolumne Meadows, is open for summer hiking and camping; in winter it's accessible via cross-country skis or snowshoes. Badger Pass Ski Area is open in winter only. Most visitors spend their time along the park's southwestern border, between Wawona and Big Oak Flat entrance; a bit farther east in Yosemite Valley and Badger Pass Ski Area; and along the east–west corridor of Tioga Road, which spans the park north of Yosemite Valley and bisects Tuolumne Meadows.

39

Tilden Lake

Stubblefield Canyon

Matterhorn Canyon

Return Creek

Pettit Peak
10,788 ft

Tuolumne River

TO
MONO LAKE

Tioga Rd.

Tioga Pass
Entrance

3 Tuolumne Meadows

Visitor Center

120   Cathedral Peak

Cathedral Range

Lyell Fork

**Yosemite
Valley 1**

Visitor Center
North Dome
Half Dome
Glacier Point

Merced River

Mount Lyell
13,114 ft

Clark Range

Sentinel Dome
er Pass
rea

Turner Ridge

Wawona   Wawona
Hotel

South
Entrance
Mariposa
Grove

41

KEY

🏠	Ranger Station
⛺	Campground
🌲	Picnic Area
🍴	Restaurant
🏨	Lodge
🥾	Trailhead
🚻	Restrooms
⚜	Scenic Viewpoint
⋯⋯	Walking/Hiking Trails

Updated by Cheryl Crabtree

By merely standing in Yosemite Valley and turning in a circle, you can see more natural wonders in a minute than you could in a full day pretty much anywhere else. Half Dome, Yosemite Falls, El Capitan, Bridalveil Fall, Sentinel Dome, the Merced River, white-flowering dogwood trees, maybe even bears ripping into the bark of fallen trees or sticking their snouts into beehives—it's all in Yosemite Valley.

In the mid-1800s, when tourists were arriving to the area, the valley's special geologic qualities and the giant sequoias of Mariposa Grove 30 miles to the south so impressed a group of influential Californians that they persuaded President Abraham Lincoln to grant those two areas to the state for protection. On October 1, 1890—thanks largely to lobbying efforts by naturalist John Muir and Robert Underwood Johnson, the editor of *Century Magazine*—Congress set aside 1,500 square miles for Yosemite National Park.

YOSEMITE PLANNER

WHEN TO GO

During extremely busy periods—such as July 4—you will experience delays at the entrance gates. For smaller crowds, visit midweek. Or come mid-April through Memorial Day or mid-September through October, when the park is a bit less busy and the days usually are sunny and clear.

Summer rainfall is rare. In winter, heavy snows occasionally cause road closures, and tire chains or four-wheel drive may be required on the roads that remain open. The road to Glacier Point beyond the turnoff for Badger Pass is closed after the first major snowfall; Tioga Road is closed from late October through May or mid-June. Mariposa Grove Road is typically closed for a shorter period in winter.

AVG. HIGH/LOW TEMPS.

Jan.	Feb.	Mar.	Apr.	May	June
48/29	53/30	55/32	61/36	69/43	78/49

July	Aug.	Sept.	Oct.	Nov.	Dec.
85/55	84/55	79/49	70/42	56/34	47/29

FESTIVALS AND EVENTS

JANUARY– FEBRUARY **Chefs' Holidays.** Celebrated chefs present cooking demonstrations and multicourse meals at The Ahwahnee hotel in Yosemite Village from mid-January to early February. Two-night packages are $318 to $448 per person, three-night packages $388 to $573 per person, and five-night packages $671 to $1,021 per person. Space is limited. ⊠ *Yosemite Village* ☎ *801/559–4870* ⊕ *www.yosemitepark.com/chefs.*

MAY **Fireman's Muster.** North of Sonora in the old mining town of Columbia, history springs to life at this festival of antique fire engines, with hose-spraying contests and a parade of the old pumpers. ⊠ *Columbia* ☎ *209/533–4479, 800/446–1333.*

Mother Lode Roundup Parade and Rodeo. On Mother's Day weekend, the town of Sonora celebrates its gold-mining, agricultural, and lumbering heritage with a parade, rodeo, entertainment, and food. ⊠ *Sonora* ☎ *209/532–7428, 800/446–1333* ⊕ *www.motherloderoundup.com.*

JULY **Mammoth Lakes Jazz Jubilee.** This festival, founded in 1989, features more than 20 different bands that play in a variety of venues, most with dance floors. ⊠ *Mammoth Lakes* ☎ *760/709–5299, 877/686–5299* ⊕ *www.mammothjazz.org.*

AUGUST **Bluesapalooza.** The first weekend of every August, Mammoth Lakes hosts a blues and beer festival—with an emphasis on the beer tasting. ⊠ *Mammoth Lakes* ☎ *888/992–7397* ⊕ *www.mammothbluesbrewsfest.com.*

39

OCTOBER **Sierra Art Trails.** The work of more than 100 artists is on display in studios and galleries throughout eastern Madera and Mariposa counties. Purchase the catalog of locations and hours at area shops. ☎ *559/658–8844.*

NOVEMBER– DECEMBER **Vintners' Holidays.** Some of California's most prestigious vintners hold two- and three-day midweek seminars in the Great Room of The Ahwahnee hotel in Yosemite Village. They culminate with an elegant—albeit pricey—banquet dinner. Arrive early for seats; book early for lodging and dining packages ($308–$1,021). ⊠ *Yosemite Village* ☎ *801/559–4870* ⊕ *www.yosemitepark.com.*

DECEMBER **Bracebridge Dinner.** Held at The Ahwahnee hotel in Yosemite Village every Christmas since 1928, this 17th-century-theme madrigal dinner is so popular that most seats are booked months in advance. Lodging packages start at $975, or $1,269 if you want to stay at The Ahwahnee. ⊠ *The Ahwahnee hotel, 1 Ahwahnee Dr., Yosemite Village* ☎ *801/559–4870* ⊕ *www.bracebridgedinners.com.*

PLANNING YOUR TIME
YOSEMITE IN ONE DAY

Begin at the **Valley Visitor Center,** where you can watch the documentary *Spirit of Yosemite* (which inexplicably shows no animals other than one deer). A minute's stroll from there is the **Indian village of the Ahwahnee,** which recalls American Indian life circa 1870. Take another 20 minutes to see the **Yosemite Museum.** Then, hop aboard the free shuttle to Yosemite Falls and hike the **Lower Yosemite Fall Trail** to the base of the falls. Then proceed via shuttle or a 20-minute walk to lunch at **Yosemite Lodge.**

Next choose one of three things: leisurely exploring **Curry Village**—perhaps going for a swim or ice-skating, shopping, renting a bike, or having a beer on the deck; checking out family-friendly **Happy Isles Nature Center** and the adjacent nature trail; or hiking up the **Mist Trail** to the Vernal Fall footbridge to admire the view.

Hop back on the shuttle, then disembark at **The Ahwahnee hotel.** Step into the Great Lounge, which has a magnificent fireplace and Indian artwork, and sneak a peek into the Dining Room, if you're up for a splurge. Get back on the shuttle, and head to **Yosemite Village,** where you can grab some food. Get back in your car and drive to the **El Capitan picnic area** and enjoy an outdoor evening meal. At this time of day, "El Cap" should be sun-splashed. (You will have gotten several good looks at world-famous **Half Dome** throughout the day.) Any sunlight left? If so, continue driving on around to see **Bridalveil Fall.**

GETTING HERE AND AROUND
AIR TRAVEL

The closest airport to the south and west entrances is Fresno Yosemite International Airport (FAT). Mammoth Yosemite Airport (MMH) is closest to the east entrance.

BUS TRAVEL

YARTS buses travel to Yosemite Valley along Highway 140 from Merced, Highway 41 from Fresno, and Highway 120 from Sonora, with scheduled stops at towns along the way. Once you're in Yosemite you can take advantage of the free shuttle buses, which operate on low emissions, have 21 stops, and run from 7 am to 10 pm year-round. Buses run about every 10 minutes in summer, a bit less frequently in winter. A separate (but also free) summer-only shuttle runs out to El Capitan. Also in summer, you can take the morning "hikers' bus" from Yosemite Valley to Tuolumne or pay to ride the bus up to Glacier Point. During the snow season, buses run regularly between Yosemite Valley and Badger Pass Ski Area.

CAR TRAVEL

Roughly 200 miles from San Francisco, 300 miles from Los Angeles, and 500 miles from Las Vegas, Yosemite takes a while to reach—and its many sites and attractions merit much more time than what rangers say is the average visit: four hours. Most people arrive via automobile or tour bus, but public transportation (courtesy of Amtrak and the regional YARTS bus system) also can get you to the valley efficiently.

Of the park's four entrances, Arch Rock is the closest to Yosemite Valley. The road that goes through it, Route 140 from Merced and

Mariposa, is a scenic western approach that snakes alongside the boulder-packed Merced River. Route 41, through Wawona, is the way to come from Los Angeles (or Fresno, if you've flown in and rented a car). Route 120, through Crane Flat, is the most direct route from San Francisco. The only way in from the east is Tioga Road, which may be the best route in terms of scenery—though due to snow accumulation it's open for a frustratingly short amount of time each year (typically early June through mid-October).

There are few gas stations within Yosemite (Crane Flat, Tuolumne Meadows, and Wawona; none in the valley), so fuel up before you reach the park. From late fall until early spring, the weather is especially unpredictable, and driving can be treacherous. You should carry chains.

PARK ESSENTIALS
PARK FEES AND PERMITS
The admission fee, valid for seven days, is $30 per vehicle ($25 November–March) or $15 per individual.

If you plan to camp in the backcountry or climb Half Dome, you must have a wilderness permit. Availability of permits depends upon trailhead quotas. It's best to make a reservation, especially if you will be visiting May through September. You can reserve two days to 26 weeks in advance by phone, mail, or fax (preferred method) (Box 545, Yosemite, CA 95389 ☎ 209/372–0740,📠 209/372–0739); you'll pay $5 per person plus $5 per reservation if and when your reservations are confirmed. You can download the reservation forms from ⊕ *www.nps.gov/yose/planyourvisit/upload/wildpermitform.pdf*. Without a reservation, you may still get a free permit on a first-come, first-served basis at wilderness permit offices at Big Oak Flat, Hetch Hetchy, Tuolumne Meadows, Wawona, the Wilderness Center in Yosemite Village, and Yosemite Valley in summer. From fall to spring, visit the Valley Visitor Center.

PARK HOURS
The park is open 24/7 year-round. All entrances are open at all hours, except for Hetch Hetchy entrance, which is open roughly dawn to dusk. Yosemite is in the Pacific time zone.

CELL-PHONE RECEPTION
Cell-phone reception is often just fine in the valley but hit or miss elsewhere in the park. There are public telephones at park entrance stations, visitor centers, all restaurants and lodging facilities in the park, gas stations, and in Yosemite Village.

EDUCATIONAL OFFERINGS
CLASSES AND SEMINARS
Art Classes. Professional artists conduct workshops in watercolor, etching, drawing, and other mediums. Bring your own materials or purchase the basics at the Yosemite Art Center, next to the Village Store. Children under 12 must be accompanied by an adult. The center also offers beginner art workshops and children's art and family craft programs ($5–$15 per person). ⊠ *Art Activity Center, Yosemite Village* ☎ *209/372–1442* ⊕ *www.yosemiteconservancy.org* 🔖 *$10* ⊙ *Early Apr.–Oct., Mon.–Sat. 10–2.*

Yosemite Outdoor Adventures. Naturalists, scientists, and park rangers lead multi-hour to multiday educational outings on topics from woodpeckers to fire management to pastel painting. Most sessions take place spring through fall, but a few focus on winter phenomena. ⊠ *Yosemite National Park* ☎ *209/379–2317* ⊕ *www.yosemiteconservancy.org* 🗎 *From $99.*

MUSEUMS

Nature Center at Happy Isles. Designed for children, this old-fashioned museum has dioramas with several stuffed animals, including a baby bear. A rotating selection of hands-on, kid-friendly exhibits teaches tykes and their parents about the park's ecosystem. Books, toys, T-shirts, and water bottles are stocked in the small gift shop. ⊠ *Yosemite National Park* ✛ *Off Southside Dr., about ¾ mile east of Curry Village* 🗎 *Free* ⊙ *May–Sept., daily 9:30–5.*

Yosemite Museum. This small museum consists of a permanent exhibit that focuses on the history of the area and the people who once lived here. An adjacent gallery promotes contemporary and historic Yosemite art in revolving gallery exhibits. A docent demonstrates traditional Native American basket-weaving techniques a few days a week. ⊠ *Yosemite Village* ☎ *209/372–0299* 🗎 *Free* ⊙ *Daily 9–5.*

RANGER PROGRAMS

Junior Ranger Program. Children ages seven to 13 can participate in the informal, self-guided Junior Ranger program. A park activity handbook (about $5) is available at the Valley Visitor Center, the Nature Center at Happy Isles, and the Wawona Visitor Center. Once kids complete the book, rangers present them with a badge and, in some cases, a certificate. ⊠ *Valley Visitor Center or the Nature Center at Happy Isles* ☎ *209/372–0299.*

Ranger-Led Programs. Rangers lead entertaining walks and give informative talks several times a day from spring to fall. The schedule is more limited in winter, but most days you can find a program somewhere in the park. In the evenings at Yosemite Lodge and Curry Village, lectures, slide shows, and documentary films present unique perspectives on Yosemite. On summer weekends, Camp Curry and Tuolumne Meadows Campground host sing-along campfire programs. Schedules and locations are posted on bulletin boards throughout the park as well as in the indispensable *Yosemite Guide*, which is distributed to visitors as they arrive at the park. ⊠ *Yosemite National Park* ⊕ *www.yosemitepark.com.*

RESTAURANTS

Yosemite National Park has a couple of moderately priced restaurants in lovely (which almost goes without saying) settings: the Mountain Room at Yosemite Lodge and Wawona Hotel's dining room. The Ahwahnee hotel provides one of the finest dining experiences in the country.

Otherwise, food service is geared toward satisfying the masses as efficiently as possible. Yosemite Lodge's food court is the valley's best lower-cost, hot-food option; Curry Village Pavilion's offerings are overpriced and usually fairly bland, but you can get decent pizzas on the adjacent outdoor deck. In Valley Village, the Village Grill whips up burgers and fries, Degnan's Deli has made-to-order sandwiches, and Loft Pizzeria has a chaletlike open dining area in which you can enjoy pizza, salads, and desserts.

The White Wolf Lodge and Tuolumne Meadows Lodge—both off Tioga Road and therefore guaranteed open only from early June through September—have small restaurants where meals are competently prepared. Tuolumne Meadows also has a grill, and the gift shop at Glacier Point sells premade sandwiches, snacks, and hot dogs. During the ski season you'll also find one at Badger Pass, off Glacier Point Road.

Delaware North Yosemite has been the official park concessioner for the last 15 years, operating nearly all restaurants, lodgings, activities, and services throughout the park. As of March 2016, Aramark will take over as official park concessioner, and changes in services may occur.

HOTELS

Indoor lodging options inside the park appear more expensive than initially seems warranted, but that premium pays off big-time in terms of the time you'll save—unless you are bunking within a few miles of a Yosemite entrance, you will face long commutes to the park when you stay outside its borders (though the Yosemite View Lodge, on Route 140, is within a reasonable half-hour's drive of Yosemite Valley).

Because of Yosemite National Park's immense popularity—not just with tourists from around the world but with Northern Californians who make weekend trips here—reservations are all but mandatory. Book up to one year ahead. ■TIP➔ If you're not set on a specific hotel or camp but just want to stay somewhere inside the park, call the main reservation number to check for availability and reserve (801/559-4884). Park lodgings have a seven-day cancellation policy, so you may be able to snag last-minute reservations.

Hotel reviews have been shortened. For full information, visit Fodors. com.

39

WHAT IT COSTS				
	$	$$	$$$	$$$$
Restaurants	under $13	$13–$20	$21–$30	over $30
Hotels	under $101	$101–$150	$151–$200	over $200

Restaurant prices are the average cost of a main course at dinner, or if dinner is not served, at lunch. Hotel prices are the lowest cost of a standard double room in high season.

TOURS

Fodor's Choice ★ **Ansel Adams Photo Walks.** Photography enthusiasts shouldn't miss these 90-minute guided camera walks offered four mornings (Monday, Tuesday, Thursday, and Saturday) each week by professional photographers. All are free, but participation is limited to 15 people. Meeting points vary, and advance reservations are essential. ⊠ *Yosemite National Park* ☎ *209/372–4413* ⊕ *www.anseladams.com* ✉ *Free.*

Glacier Point Tour. This four-hour trip takes you from Yosemite Valley to the Glacier Point vista, 3,214 feet above the valley floor. Some

Plants and Wildlife in Yosemite

Dense stands of incense cedar and Douglas fir—as well as ponderosa, Jeffrey, lodgepole, and sugar pines—cover much of the park, but the stellar standout, quite literally, is the *Sequoiadendron giganteum*, the giant sequoia. Sequoias grow only along the west slope of the Sierra Nevada between 4,500 and 7,000 feet in elevation. Starting from a seed the size of a rolled-oat flake, each of these ancient monuments assumes remarkable proportions in adulthood; you can see them in the Mariposa Grove of Big Trees. In late May the valley's dogwood trees bloom with white, starlike flowers. Wildflowers, such as black-eyed Susan, bull thistle, cow parsnip, lupine, and meadow goldenrod, peak in June in the valley and in July at higher elevations.

The most visible animals in the park—aside from the omnipresent western gray squirrels, which fearlessly attempt to steal your food at every campground and picnic site—are the mule deer. Though sightings of bighorn sheep are infrequent in the park itself, you can sometimes see them on the eastern side of the Sierra Crest, just off Route 120 in Lee Vining Canyon. You may also see the American black bear, which often has a brown, cinnamon, or blond coat. The Sierra Nevada is home to thousands of bears, and you should take all necessary precautions to keep yourself—and the bears—safe. Bears that acquire a taste for human food can become very aggressive and destructive and often must be destroyed by rangers, so store all your food and even scented toiletries in the bear lockers located at many campgrounds and trailheads, or use bear-resistant canisters if you'll be hiking in the backcountry.

Watch for the blue Steller's jay along trails, near public buildings, and in campgrounds, and look for golden eagles soaring over Tioga Road.

people buy a $25 one-way ticket and hike down. Shuttles depart from the Yosemite Lodge three times a day. ⊠ *Yosemite National Park* ☎ *209/372–4386* ⊕ *www.yosemitepark.com* ⊠ *From $41* ⊙ *June–Oct.* ⌖ *Reservations essential.*

Tuolumne Meadows Hikers Bus. For a full day's outing to the high country, opt for this ride up Tioga Road to Tuolumne Meadows. You'll stop at several overlooks, and you can connect with another shuttle at Tuolumne Lodge. This service is mostly for hikers and backpackers who want to reach high-country trailheads, but everyone is welcome. ⊠ *Yosemite National Park* ☎ *209/372–4386* ⊕ *www.yosemitepark.com* ⊠ *Free* ⊙ *July–Labor Day* ⌖ *Reservations essential.*

Valley Floor Tour. Take a two-hour tour of Yosemite Valley's highlights, complete with narration on the area's history, geology, and flora and fauna. Tours are either in trams or enclosed motor coaches, depending on weather conditions. Tours run year-round. ⊠ *Yosemite National Park* ☎ *209/372–1240* ⊕ *www.yosemitepark.com* ⊠ *From $25.*

Moonlight Tour. This after-dark version of the Valley Floor Tour takes place on moonlit nights, depending on weather conditions. ✉ *Yosemite National Park* ☎ *209/372–4386* ⊕ *www.yosemitepark.com.*

FAMILY **Wee Wild Ones.** Designed for kids under seven, this 45-minute program includes animal-theme games, songs, stories, and crafts. The event is held outdoors before the regular Yosemite Lodge or Curry Village evening programs in summer and fall; it moves to The Ahwahnee's big fireplace in winter and spring. All children must be accompanied by an adult. ✉ *Yosemite National Park* ☎ *209/372–1153* ⊕ *www.yosemitepark.com* ✲ *Free.*

VISITOR INFORMATION
Park Contact Information Yosemite National Park. ✉ *Yosemite National Park* ☎ *209/372–0200* ⊕ *www.nps.gov/yose.*

VISITOR CENTERS
Le Conte Memorial Lodge. This small but striking National Historic Landmark, with its granite walls and steeply pitched shingle roof, is Yosemite's first permanent public information center. Step inside to see the cathedral-like interior, which contains a library and environmental exhibits. To find out about evening programs, check the kiosk out front. ✉ *Southside Dr., about ½ mile west of Curry Village* ⊕ *vault.sierraclub. org/education/leconte* ⊗ *May–Sept., Wed.–Sun. 10–4.*

Valley Visitor Center. Learn about Yosemite Valley's geology, vegetation, and human inhabitants at this visitor center, which is also staffed with helpful rangers and contains a bookstore with a wide selection of books and maps. Two films, including one by Ken Burns, alternate on the half hour in the theater behind the visitor center. ✉ *Yosemite Village* ☎ *209/372–0200* ⊕ *www.nps.gov/yose* ⊗ *Late May–early Sept., daily 9–7; early Sept.–late May, daily 9–5.*

EXPLORING

39

SCENIC DRIVES

Tioga Road. Few mountain drives can compare with this 59-mile road, especially its eastern half between Lee Vining and Olmstead Point. As you climb 3,200 feet to the 9,945-foot summit of Tioga Pass (Yosemite's sole eastern entrance for cars), you'll encounter broad vistas of the granite-splotched High Sierra and its craggy but hearty trees and shrubs. Past the bustling scene at Tuolumne Meadows, you'll see picturesque Tenaya Lake and then Olmstead Point, where you'll get your first peek at Half Dome. Driving Tioga Road one-way takes approximately 1½ hours. Wildflowers bloom here in July and August. By November, the high-altitude road closes for the winter; it sometimes doesn't reopen until early June. ✉ *Yosemite National Park.*

HISTORIC SITES

The Ahwahnee. Gilbert Stanley Underwood, architect of the Grand Canyon Lodge, also designed The Ahwahnee hotel. Opened in 1927, it is generally considered his best work. You can stay here (for about $500 a night), or simply explore the first-floor shops and perhaps have breakfast or lunch in the bustling and beautiful Dining Room or more casual bar. The Great Lounge, 77 feet long with magnificent 24-foot-high ceilings and all manner of Indian artwork on display, beckons with big, comfortable chairs and relative calm. ⊠ *Ahwahnee Rd., about ¾ mile east of Yosemite Valley Visitor Center, Yosemite Village* ☎ *209/372–1489* ⊕ *www.yosemitepark.com.*

Indian Village of Ahwahnee. This solemn smattering of structures, accessed by a short loop trail behind the Yosemite Valley Visitor Center, is a look at what Native American life might have been like in the 1870s. One interpretive sign points out that the Miwok people referred to the 19th-century newcomers as "Yohemite" or "Yohometuk," which have been translated as meaning "some of them are killers." ⊠ *Northside Dr., Yosemite Village* ⊠ *Free* ⊙ *Daily sunrise–sunset.*

Pioneer Yosemite History Center. Some of Yosemite's first structures—those not occupied by Native Americans, that is—were relocated here in the 1950s and 1960s. You can spend a pleasurable and informative half-hour walking about them and reading the signs, perhaps springing for a self-guided-tour pamphlet (50¢) to further enhance the history lesson. Weekends and some weekdays in the summer, costumed docents conduct free blacksmithing and "wet-plate" photography demonstrations, and for a small fee you can take a stagecoach ride. ⊠ *Rte. 41, Wawona* ☎ *209/375–9531* ⊠ *Free* ⊙ *Bldg. interiors are open mid-June–Labor Day, Wed. 2–5, Thurs.–Sun. 10–1 and 2–5.*

Wawona Hotel. Imagine a white-bearded Mark Twain relaxing in a rocking chair on one of the broad verandas of one of the park's first lodges, a whitewashed series of two-story buildings from the Victorian era. Plop down in one of the dozens of white adirondack chairs on the sprawling lawn and look across the road at the area's only golf course, one of the few links in the world that does not employ fertilizers or other chemicals. The hotel, an excellent place for lunch, is closed December through March, though it opens for about two weeks around Christmas and New Year's. ⊠ *Rte. 41, Wawona* ☎ *209/375–1425* ⊕ *www. yosemitepark.com.*

SCENIC STOPS

El Capitan. Rising 3,593 feet—more than 350 stories—above the valley, El Capitan is the largest exposed-granite monolith in the world. Since 1958, people have been climbing its entire face, including the famous "nose." You can spot adventurers with your binoculars by scanning the smooth and nearly vertical cliff for specks of color. ✛ *Off Northside Dr., about 4 miles west of the Valley Visitor Center.*

Yosemite's Valley Floor

Half Dome 8,836 ft

KEY

🏠	Ranger Station
⛺	Campground
🏕	Picnic Area
🍴	Restaurant
🏨	Lodge
🚶	Trailhead
🚻	Restrooms
🌲	Scenic Viewpoint
····	Walking/Hiking Trails
---	John Muir Trail
····	Bicycle Path
	Valley Floor

Liberty Cap

Mist Trail

Nevada Fall

Emerald Pools

Vernal Fall

Footbridge

Clark Point

Mist Trail

John Muir Trail

Panorama Cliff

Grizzly Peak

Sierra Point

Illilouette Gorge

Happy Isles Bridge

Washington Column

Royal Arches

Royal Arch Cascade

bicycle path

Clarks Bridge

Upper Pines

North Pines

Nature Center at Happy Isles

Lower Pines

Road open only to bicycles and Shuttlebuses

Glacier Point 7,214 ft

Panorama Trail

CURRY VILLAGE

Curry Village Store

bicycle path

Housekeeping Camp

Le Conte Memorial Lodge

The Ahwahnee Hotel

Medical Clinic

Village Store

Auto Repair

Wilderness Office

P.O.

YOSEMITE VILLAGE

Indian Village of Ahwahnee

Yosemite Museum

Ansel Adams Gallery

Valley Visitor Center

Chapel

Moran Point

Union Point

Four Mile Trail

Glacier Point Road

Pohono Trail

Sentinel Rock

Sentinel Fall

Merced River

bicycle path

Yosemite Lodge

Yosemite Fall

0   1/2 mi

0   1/2 km

"This is us taking a break before conquering the top of Lembert Dome, while enjoying the beautiful view over Yosemite's high country." —photo by Rebalyn, Fodors.com member

Fodor's Choice
★
Glacier Point. If you lack the time, desire, or stamina to hike more than 3,200 feet up to Glacier Point from the Yosemite Valley floor, you can drive here—or take a bus from the valley—for a bird's-eye view. You are likely to encounter a lot of day-trippers on the short, paved trail that leads from the parking lot to the main overlook. Take a moment to veer off a few yards to the Geology Hut, which succinctly explains and illustrates what the valley looked like 10 million, 3 million, and 20,000 years ago. ✛ *Glacier Point Rd., 16 miles northeast of Rte. 41* ☎ *209/372–0200* ☺ *Late May–late Oct.*

Fodor's Choice
★
Half Dome. Visitors' eyes are continually drawn to this remarkable granite formation that tops out at more than 4,700 feet above the valley floor. Despite its name, the dome is actually about three-quarters intact. You can hike to the top of Half Dome on an 8.5-mile (one-way) trail whose last 400 feet must be ascended while holding onto a steel cable. Permits are required (and checked on the trail), and available only by lottery. Call *877/444–6777* or visit *www.recreation.gov* well in advance of your trip for details. Back down in the valley, see Half Dome reflected in the Merced River by heading to Sentinel Bridge just before sundown. The brilliant orange light on Half Dome is a stunning sight. ✉ *Yosemite National Park* ⊕ *www.nps.gov/yose/planyourvisit/halfdome.htm.*

Hetch Hetchy Reservoir. When Congress approved the O'Shaughnessy Dam in 1913, pragmatism triumphed over aestheticism. Some 2.5 million residents of the San Francisco Bay Area continue to get their water from this 117-billion-gallon reservoir. Although spirited efforts are being made to restore the Hetch Hetchy Valley to its former, pristine glory, three-quarters of San Francisco voters in 2012 ultimately opposed a measure to even consider draining the reservoir. Eight miles long, the reservoir is Yosemite's largest body of water, and one that can be seen up close from several trails. ⊠ *Hetch Hetchy Rd., about 15 miles north of the Big Oak Flat entrance station.*

High Country. The above-tree-line, high-alpine region east of the valley—a land of alpenglow and top-of-the-world vistas—is often missed by crowds who come to gawk at the more publicized splendors. Summer wildflowers, which usually pop up mid-July through August, carpet the meadows and mountainsides with pink, purple, blue, red, yellow, and orange. On foot or on horseback are the only ways to get here. For information on trails and backcountry permits, check with the visitor center. ⊠ *Yosemite National Park.*

Mariposa Grove of Big Trees. Of Yosemite's three sequoia groves—the others being Merced and Tuolumne, both near Crane Flat well to the north—Mariposa is by far the largest and easiest to walk around. Grizzly Giant, whose base measures 96 feet around, has been estimated to be one of the largest in the world. Perhaps more astoundingly, it's about 1,800 years old. Up the hill, you'll find more sequoias, a small museum, and fewer people. Summer weekends are usually crowded here.

Please note that due to major reconstruction the lower grove, which includes Grizzly Giant, Fallen Monarch, and the California Tunnel Tree, will be closed until summer 2017. The upper grove may be open intermittently during this time. Shuttle service from Wawona will not be available in 2016. Check the Yosemite website before visiting this area. ⊹ *Rte. 41, 2 miles north of the south entrance station* ⊕ *www.nps.gov/yose/planyourvisit/mariposagrove.htm.*

Sentinel Dome. The view from here is similar to that from Glacier Point, except you can't see the valley floor. A moderately steep 1.1-mile path climbs to the viewpoint from the parking lot. Topping out at an elevation of 8,122 feet, Sentinel is more than 900 feet higher than Glacier Point. ⊠ *Glacier Point Rd., off Rte. 41.*

Tuolumne Meadows. The largest subalpine meadow in the Sierra (at 8,600 feet) is a popular way station for backpack trips along the Pacific Crest and John Muir trails. The setting is not as dramatic as Yosemite Valley, 56 miles away, but the almost perfectly flat basin, about 2½ miles long, is intriguing, and in July it's resplendent with wildflowers. The most popular day hike is up Lembert Dome, atop which you'll have breathtaking views of the basin below. Keep in mind that Tioga Road rarely opens before June and usually closes by mid-October. ⊠ *Tioga Rd. (Rte. 120), about 8 miles west of the Tioga Pass entrance station.*

WATERFALLS

Yosemite's waterfalls are at their most spectacular in May and June. When the snow starts to melt (usually peaking in May), streaming snowmelt spills down to meet the Merced River. By summer's end, some falls, including the mighty Yosemite Falls, trickle or dry up. Their flow increases in late fall, and in winter they may be hung dramatically with ice. Even in drier months, the waterfalls can be breathtaking. If you choose to hike

GOOD READS

■ *The Photographer's Guide to Yosemite*, by Michael Frye, is an insider's guide to the park, with maps for shutterbugs looking to capture perfect images.

■ John Muir penned his observations of the park he long advocated for in *The Yosemite*.

■ *Yosemite and the High Sierra*, edited by Andrea G. Stillman and John Szarkowski, features beautiful reproductions of landmark photographs by Ansel Adams,

accompanied by excerpts from the photographer's journals written when Adams traveled in Yosemite National Park in the early 20th century.

■ An insightful collection of essays accompanies the museum-quality artworks in *Yosemite: Art of an American Icon*, by Amy Scott.

■ Perfect for budding botanists, *Sierra Nevada Wildflowers*, by Karen Wiese, identifies more than 230 kinds of flora growing in the Sierra Nevada region.

any of the trails to or up the falls, be sure to wear shoes with no-slip soles; the rocks can be extremely slick. Stay on trails at all times.

■TIP→ **Visit the park during a full moon and you can stroll without a flashlight and still make out the ribbons of falling water, as well as silhouettes of the giant granite monoliths.**

Bridalveil Fall. This 620-foot waterfall is often diverted dozens of feet one way or the other by the breeze. It is the first marvelous site you will see up-close when you drive into Yosemite Valley. ⊠ *Yosemite Valley, access from parking area off Wawona Rd.*

Nevada Fall. Climb Mist Trail from Happy Isles for an up-close view of this 594-foot cascading beauty. If you don't want to hike (the trail's final approach is quite taxing), you can see it—albeit distantly—from Glacier Point. Stay safely on the trail, as there have been fatalities in recent years after visitors have fallen and been swept away by the water. ⊠ *Yosemite Valley, access via Mist Trail from Nature Center at Happy Isles.*

Ribbon Fall. At 1,612 feet, this is the highest single fall in North America. It's also the first waterfall to dry up in summer; the rainwater and melted snow that create the slender fall evaporate quickly at this height. Look just west of El Capitan for the best view of the fall from the base of Bridalveil Fall. ⊠ *Yosemite Valley, west of El Capitan Meadow.*

Vernal Fall. Fern-covered black rocks frame this 317-foot fall, and rainbows play in the spray at its base. You can get a distant view from Glacier Point, or hike to see it close up. You'll get wet, but the view is worth it. ⊠ *Yosemite Valley, access via Mist Trail from Nature Center at Happy Isles.*

Fodor'sChoice ★ **Yosemite Falls.** Actually three falls, they together constitute the highest waterfall in North America and the fifth highest in the world. The water from the top descends a total of 2,425 feet, and when the falls run hard, you can hear them thunder across the valley. If they dry up—that sometimes happens in late summer—the valley seems naked without the wavering tower of spray. If you hike the mile-long loop trail (partially

paved) to the base of the Lower Falls in spring, prepare to get wet. You can get a good full-length view of the falls from the lawn of Yosemite Chapel, off Southside Drive. ⊠ *Yosemite Valley, access from Yosemite Lodge or trail parking area.*

SPORTS AND THE OUTDOORS

BICYCLING

One enjoyable way to see Yosemite Valley is to ride a bike beneath its lofty granite monoliths. The eastern valley has 12 miles of paved, flat bicycle paths across meadows and through woods, with bike racks at convenient stopping points. For a greater challenge but at no small risk, you can ride on 196 miles of paved park roads—but bicycles are not allowed on hiking trails or in the backcountry. Kids under 18 must wear a helmet.

TOURS AND OUTFITTERS

Yosemite bike rentals. You can arrange for rentals from Yosemite Lodge and Curry Village bike stands. Bikes with child trailers, baby-jogger strollers, and wheelchairs are also available. The cost for bikes is $12 per hour, or $34 a day. ⊠ *Yosemite Lodge or Curry Village* ☎ *209/372–4386* ⊕ *www.yosemitepark.com* ☉ *Apr.–Oct.*

BIRD-WATCHING

More than 250 bird species have been spotted in the park, including the sage sparrow, pygmy owl, blue grouse, and mountain bluebird. Park rangers lead free bird-watching walks in Yosemite Valley a few days each week in summer; check at a visitor center or information station for times and locations. Binoculars sometimes are available for loan.

TOURS

Birding seminars. The Yosemite Conservancy organizes day- and weekend-long seminars for beginner and intermediate birders, as well as bird walks a few times a week. They can also arrange private naturalist-led walks any time of year. ⊠ *Yosemite National Park* ☎ *209/379–2321* ⊕ *www.yosemiteconservancy.org* ✉ *From $99.*

FISHING

The waters in Yosemite are not stocked; trout, mostly brown and rainbow, live here but are not plentiful. Yosemite's fishing season begins on the last Saturday in April and ends on November 15. Some waterways are off-limits at certain times; be sure to inquire at the visitor center about regulations.

A California fishing license is required; in 2015 licenses ran $15.12 for one day, $23.50 for two days, and $47.01 for 10 days. Full-season licenses cost $45.93 for state residents and $126.36 for nonresidents. Buy your license in season at **Yosemite Mountain Shop in Curry Village** (☎ *209/372–1286*) or at the **Wawona Store** (☎ *209/375–6574*).

HIKING

TOURS AND OUTFITTERS

Wilderness Center. This facility provides free wilderness permits, which are required for overnight camping (advance reservations are available for $5 per person plus $5 per reservation and are highly recommended for popular trailheads in summer and on weekends). The staff here also provides maps and advice to hikers heading into the backcountry, and rents and sells bear-resistant canisters, which are required if you don't have your own. ⊠ *Between the Ansel Adams Gallery and the post office, Yosemite Village* ☏ *209/372–0308* ☉ *May–Oct., daily 8–5; permits at Valley Visitor's Center Nov.–Apr.*

Yosemite Mountaineering School and Guide Service. From April to November, you can learn to climb, hire a guide, or join a two-hour to full-day trek with Yosemite Mountaineering School. They also rent gear and lead backpacking and overnight excursions. Reservations are recommended. In winter, cross-country ski programs are available at Badger Pass. ⊠ *Yosemite Mountain Shop, Curry Village* ☏ *209/372–8344* ⊕ *yosemitemountaineering.com.*

EASY

FAMILY **"A Changing Yosemite" Interpretive Trail.** Take this 1-mile, wheelchair-accessible, looped path around Cook's Meadow to see and learn the basics about Yosemite Valley's past, present, and future. A self-guiding trail guide (available at a kiosk just outside the entrance) explains how to tell oaks, cedars, and pines apart; how fires help keep the forest floor healthy; and how pollution poses significant challenges to the park's inhabitants. *Easy.* ⊹ *Trailhead: across from the Valley Visitor Center.*

Fodor'sChoice **Yosemite Falls Trail.** Yosemite Falls is the highest waterfall in North America. The upper fall (1,430 feet), the middle cascades (675 feet), and the lower fall (320 feet) combine for a total of 2,425 feet, and when viewed from the valley appear as a single waterfall. The ¼-mile trail leads from the parking lot to the base of the falls. Upper Yosemite Fall Trail, a strenuous 7.2-mile round-trip climb rising 2,700 feet, takes you above the top of the falls. Lower trail: *Easy.* Upper trail: *Difficult.* ⊹ *Trailhead: off Camp 4, north of Northside Dr.*

39

MODERATE

Mist Trail. Except for Lower Yosemite Fall, more visitors take this trail (or portions of it) than any other in the park. The trek up to and back from Vernal Fall is 3 miles. Add another 4 miles total by continuing up to 594-foot Nevada Fall; the trail becomes quite steep and slippery in its final stages. The elevation gain to Vernal Fall is 1,000 feet, and to Nevada Fall an additional 1,000 feet. The Merced River tumbles down both falls on its way to a tranquil flow through the Valley. *Moderate.* ⊹ *Trailhead: at Happy Isles.*

Fodor'sChoice **Panorama Trail.** Few hikes come with the visual punch that this 8½-mile trail provides. It starts from Glacier Point and descends to Yosemite Valley. The star attraction is Half Dome, visible from many intriguing angles, but you also see three waterfalls up close and walk through a manzanita grove. If you take the last bus from the valley floor to Glacier

Point before starting your hike, you might run out of daylight before you finish. *Moderate.* ⊹ *Trailhead: at Glacier Point.*

DIFFICULT

Chilnualna Falls Trail. This Wawona-area trail runs 4 miles one-way to the top of the falls, then leads into the backcountry, connecting with miles of other trails. This is one of the park's most inspiring and secluded— albeit strenuous—trails. Past the tumbling cascade, and up through forests, you'll emerge before a panoramic vista at the top. *Difficult.* ⊠ *Wawona* ⊹ *Trailhead: at Chilnualna Falls Rd., off Rte. 41.*

Fodor's Choice ★ **John Muir Trail to Half Dome.** Ardent and courageous trekkers continue on from Nevada Fall to the top of Half Dome. Some hikers attempt this entire 10- to 12-hour, 16¾-mile round-trip trek in one day; if you're planning to do this, remember that the 4,800-foot elevation gain and the 8,842-foot altitude will cause shortness of breath. Another option is to hike to a campground in Little Yosemite Valley near the top of Nevada Fall the first day, then climb to the top of Half Dome and hike out the next day. Get your wilderness permit (required for a one-day hike to Half Dome, too) at least a month in advance. Be sure to wear hiking boots and bring gloves. The last pitch up the back of Half Dome is very steep—the only way to climb this sheer rock face is to pull yourself up using the steel cable handrails, which are in place only from late spring to early fall. Those who brave the ascent will be rewarded with an unbeatable view of Yosemite Valley below and the high country beyond. Only 300 hikers per day are allowed atop Half Dome, and they all must have permits, which are distributed by lottery, one in the spring before the season starts and another two days before the climb. Contact *www.recreation.gov* for details. *Difficult.* ⊹ *Trailhead: at Happy Isles* ⊕ *www.nps.gov/yose/planyourvisit/halfdome.htm.*

HORSEBACK RIDING

Reservations for guided trail rides must be made in advance at the hotel tour desks or by phone. Scenic trail rides range from two hours to a half day; four- and six-day High Sierra saddle trips are also available.

TOURS AND OUTFITTERS

Wawona Stables. Two-hour rides at these stables start at $65, and half-day rides are $88.50. Reservations are recommended. ⊠ *Rte. 41, Wawona* ☎ *209/375–6502* 💲 *From $65.*

RAFTING

Rafting is permitted only on designated areas of the Middle and South Forks of the Merced River. Check with the Valley Visitor Center for closures and other restrictions.

OUTFITTERS

Curry Village Recreation Center. The per-person rental fee ($31) at Curry Village Recreation Center covers the four- to six-person raft, two paddles, and life jackets, plus a return shuttle at the end of your trip. ⊠ *South side of Southside Dr., Curry Village* ☎ *209/372–4386* ⊕ *www.yosemitepark.com* 💲 *From $31* ⊙ *Late May–July.*

ROCK CLIMBING

The granite canyon walls of Yosemite Valley are world-renowned for rock climbing. El Capitan, with its 3,593-foot vertical face, is the most famous, but there are many other options here for all skill levels.

TOURS AND OUTFITTERS

Yosemite Mountaineering School and Guide Service. The one-day basic lesson at Yosemite Mountaineering School and Guide Service includes some bouldering and rappelling, and three or four 60-foot climbs. Climbers must be at least 10 years old and in reasonably good physical condition. Intermediate and advanced classes include instruction in first aid, anchor building, multi-pitch climbing, summer snow climbing, and big-wall climbing. There's a nordic program in the winter. ⊠ *Yosemite Mountain Shop, Curry Village* ☎ *209/372–8344* ⊕ *www. yosemitemountaineering.com* ☑ *From $148* ☉ *Apr.–Nov.*

SWIMMING

The pools at **Curry Village** (☎ *209/372–8324* ⊕ *www.yosemitepark.com*) and **Yosemite Lodge** (☎ *209/372–1250* ⊕ *www.yosemitepark.com*) are open to nonguests for $5, late May through early or mid-September. Additionally, several swimming holes with small sandy beaches can be found in midsummer along the Merced River at the eastern end of Yosemite Valley. Find gentle waters to swim; currents are often stronger than they appear, and temperatures are chilling. To conserve riparian habitats, step into the river at sandy beaches and other obvious entry points. ■TIP➔ **Do not attempt to swim above or near waterfalls or rapids; people have died trying.**

WINTER SPORTS

39

The beauty of Yosemite under a blanket of snow has long inspired poets and artists, as well as ordinary folks. Skiing and snowshoeing activities in the park center on Badger Pass Ski Area, California's oldest snow-sports resort, which is about 40 minutes away from the valley on Glacier Point Road. Here you can rent equipment, take a lesson, have lunch, join a guided excursion, and take the free shuttle back to the valley after a drink in the lounge.

ICE-SKATING

Curry Village Ice Rink. Winter visitors have skated at this outdoor rink for decades, and there's no mystery why: it's a kick to glide across the ice while soaking up views of Half Dome and Glacier Point. ⊠ *South side of Southside Dr., Curry Village* ☎ *209/372–8319* ☑ *$10.50 per session, $4 skate rental* ☉ *Mid-Nov.–early Mar., hrs vary.*

SKIING AND SNOWSHOEING

Badger Pass Ski Area. California's first ski resort has five lifts and 10 downhill runs, as well as 90 miles of groomed cross-country trails. Free shuttle buses from Yosemite Valley operate between December and the end of March, weather permitting. Lessons, backcountry guiding, and cross-country and snowshoeing tours are also available. You can rent downhill, telemark, and cross-country skis, plus snowshoes and snow-boards. **Facilities:** 10 trails; 90 acres; 800-foot vertical drop; 5 lifts. ⊠ *Yosemite National Park* ✛ *Badger Pass Rd., off Glacier Point Rd., 18 miles from Yosemite Valley* ☎ *209/372–8430* ⊕ *www.badgerpass. com* ⊠ *Lift ticket: from $48.50.*

Yosemite Cross-Country Ski School. The highlight of Yosemite's cross-country skiing center is a 21-mile loop from Badger Pass to Glacier Point. You can rent cross-country skis for $25 per day at the Cross-Country Ski School, which also rents snowshoes ($24 per day) and telemarking equipment ($29.50). ☎ *209/372–8444* ⊕ *www.badgerpass. com.*

Yosemite Mountaineering School. This branch of the Yosemite Mountaineering School, open at the Badger Pass Ski Area during ski season only, conducts snowshoeing, cross-country skiing, telemarking, and skate-skiing classes starting at $35.50. ⊠ *Badger Pass Ski Area* ☎ *209/372–8444* ⊕ *www.yosemitepark.com.*

Yosemite Ski School. The gentle slopes of Badger Pass make Yosemite Ski School an ideal spot for children and beginners to learn downhill skiing or snowboarding for as little as $47 for a group lesson. ☎ *209/372–8430* ⊕ *www.yosemitepark.com.*

NIGHTLIFE AND PERFORMING ARTS

Vintage Music of Yosemite. A pianist-singer performs four hours of live old-time music at the Wawona Hotel (call for schedule of performances). ⊠ *Wawona Hotel, Rte. 41, Wawona* ☎ *209/375–6556* ⊠ *Free* ☉ *Shows usually Tues.–Sat. at 5:30.*

Yosemite Theatre. Various theater and music programs are held throughout the year, and one of the best loved is Lee Stetson's portrayal of John Muir in *Conversation with a Tramp* and other Muir-theme shows. Purchase tickets in advance at the Conservancy Store at the Valley Visitor Center or the Tour and Activity Desk at Yosemite Lodge. Unsold seats are available at the door at performance time, 7 pm. ⊠ *Valley Visitor Center, Yosemite Village* ☎ *209/372–0299* ⊠ *$8.*

SHOPPING

Ahwahnee Gift Shop. This shop sells more upscale items, such as American Indian crafts, photographic prints, handmade ceramics, and elegant jewelry. For less expensive gift items, browse the small book selection, which includes writings by John Muir. ⊠ *The Ahwahnee hotel, Ahwahnee Rd.* ☎ *209/372–1409.*

Ansel Adams Gallery. Framed prints of the famed nature photographer's best works are on sale here, as are affordable posters. New works by contemporary artists are available, along with American Indian jewelry and handicrafts. The gallery's elegant camera shop conducts photography workshops, from free camera walks a few mornings a week to five-day workshops. ⊠ *Northside Dr., Yosemite Village* ☎ *209/372–4413* ☉ *Apr.–Oct., daily 9–6; Nov.–Mar., daily 10–5.*

Yosemite Mountain Shop. A comprehensive selection of camping, hiking, backpacking, and climbing equipment, along with experts who can answer all your questions, make this store a valuable resource for outdoors enthusiasts. This is the best place to ask about climbing conditions and restrictions around the park, as well as purchase almost any kind of clinbing gear. ⊠ *Curry Village* ☎ *209/372–8396.*

WHAT'S NEARBY

NEARBY TOWNS

Marking the southern end of the Sierra's gold-bearing mother lode, **Mariposa** is the last town before you enter Yosemite on Route 140. In addition to a fine mining museum, Mariposa has numerous shops, restaurants, and service stations. Motels and restaurants dot both sides of Route 41 as it cuts through the town of **Oakhurst,** a boomtown during the Gold Rush that is now an important regional refueling station in every sense of the word, including organic foods and a full range of lodging options. Oakhurst has a population of about 3,000 and sits 15 miles south of the park.

The tiny town of **Lee Vining,** near the park's eastern entrance, is home to the eerily beautiful, salty Mono Lake, where millions of migratory birds nest. Visit **Mammoth Lakes,** about 40 miles southeast of Yosemite's Tioga Pass entrance, for excellent skiing and snowboarding in winter, with fishing, mountain biking, hiking, and horseback riding in summer. Nine deep-blue lakes form the Mammoth Lakes Basin, and another hundred dot the surrounding countryside. Devils Postpile National Monument sits at the base of Mammoth Mountain.

Visitor Information Mammoth Lakes Tourism. ⊠ *2510 Main St., Mammoth Lakes* ☎ *760/934–2712, 888/466–2666* ⊕ *www.visitmammoth.com.* **Mono Lake Information Center and Bookstore.** ☎ *760/647–6595* ⊕ *www.leevining.com.* **Tuolumne County Visitors Bureau.** ⊠ *542 Stockton St., Sonora* ☎ *209/533–4420, 800/446–1333* ⊕ *yosemitegoldcountry.com.* **Yosemite/Mariposa County Tourism Bureau.** ⊠ *5158 Hwy. 140, Mariposa* ☎ *209/742–4567, 866/425–3366* ⊕ *www.yosemiteexperience.com.* **Yosemite Sierra Visitors Bureau.** ⊠ *40637 Hwy. 41, Oakhurst* ☎ *559/683–4636* ⊕ *www.yosemitethisyear.com.*

39

NEARBY ATTRACTIONS

Fodor's Choice ★ **Bodie Ghost Town.** The mining village of Rattlesnake Gulch, abandoned mine shafts, and the remains of a small Chinatown are among the sights at this fascinating ghost town. The town boomed from about 1878 to 1881, but by the late 1940s all its residents had departed. A state park was established here in 1962, with a mandate to preserve everything in a state of "arrested decay." Evidence of Bodie's wild past survives at an excellent museum, and you can tour an old stamp mill where ore was crushed into fine powder to extract gold and silver. Bodie lies 13 miles east of U.S. 395 off Highway 270. The last 3 miles are unpaved, and snow may close the highway from late fall through early spring. No food, drink, or lodging is available in Bodie. ⊠ *Bodie Rd., off Hwy. 270, Bodie* ☎ *760/647–6445* ⊕ *www.parks.ca.gov/bodie* ☞ *$5* ⊗ *Mid-Mar.–Oct., daily 9–6; Nov.–mid-Mar., daily 9–4.*

FAMILY **California State Mining and Mineral Museum.** A California State Park since 1999, the museum has displays on gold-rush history including a replica hard-rock mine shaft to walk through, a miniature stamp mill, and a 13-pound chunk of crystallized gold. ⊠ *5005 Fairground Rd., off Hwy. 49, Mariposa* ☎ *209/742–7625* ⊕ *www.parks.ca.gov* ☞ *$4* ⊗ *May–Sept., Thurs.–Sun. 10–5; Oct.–Apr., Thurs.–Sun. 10–4.*

Fodor's Choice ★ **Devils Postpile National Monument.** Volcanic and glacial forces sculpted this formation of smooth, vertical basalt columns. For a bird's-eye view, take the short, steep trail to the top of a 60-foot cliff. To see the monument's second scenic wonder, **Rainbow Falls,** hike 2 miles past Devils Postpile. A branch of the San Joaquin River plunges more than 100 feet over a lava ledge here. When the water hits the pool below, sunlight turns the resulting mist into a spray of color. From mid-June to early September, day-use visitors must ride the shuttle bus from the Mammoth Mountain Ski Area to the monument. ⊠ *Mammoth Lakes* ✛ *13 miles southwest of Mammoth Lakes off Minaret Rd. (Hwy. 203)* ☎ *760/934–2289, 760/872–1901 shuttle* ⊕ *www.nps.gov/depo* ☞ *$10 per vehicle (allowed when the shuttle isn't running, usually early Sept.–mid-Oct.), $7 per person shuttle* ⊗ *Park mid-June–mid-Oct.; shuttle mid-June–early Sept.*

Hot Creek Geologic Site. Forged by an ancient volcanic eruption, the Hot Creek Geologic Site is a landscape of boiling hot springs, fumaroles, and geysers about 10 miles southeast of the town of Mammoth Lakes. You can stroll along boardwalks through the canyon to view the steaming volcanic features. Fly-fishing for trout is popular upstream from the springs. ⊠ *Hot Creek Hatchery Rd. east of U.S. 395, Mammoth Lakes* ☎ *760/924–5500* ⊕ *www.fs.usda.gov/recarea/inyo/recarea/?recid=20414* ☞ *Free* ⊗ *Daily sunrise–sunset.*

Fodor's Choice ★ **Mono Lake.** Since the 1940s Los Angeles has diverted water from this lake, exposing striking towers of tufa, or calcium carbonate. Court victories by environmentalists have meant fewer diversions, and the lake is rising again. Although to see the lake from U.S. 395 is stunning, make time to visit South Tufa, whose parking lot is 5 miles east of U.S. 395 off Highway 120. There in summer you can join the naturalist-guided **South Tufa Walk,** which lasts about 90 minutes. The **Scenic Area Visitor**

BEST BETS FOR FAMILIES

■ **Bass Lake Recreation Area.** Rent a boat or splash around in the water.

■ **Bodie Ghost Town.** Wander through the once-bustling Gold Rush streets at this state historic park.

■ **Mammoth Mountain.** In winter, schuss through powder, then warm up with a hot chocolate.

■ **Yosemite Mountain Sugar Pine Railroad.** Listen to the vintage steam engine huff and puff as you ride into logging history on the narrow-gauge railroad.

Center, off U.S. 395, is a sensational stop for its interactive exhibits and sweeping Mono Lake views (closed in winter). In town at U.S. 395 and 3rd Street, the **Mono Lake Committee Information Center & Bookstore**, open from 9 to 5 daily, has more information about this beautiful area. ⊠ *Hwy. 120, east of Lee Vining, Lee Vining* ☎ *760/647–3044 visitor center, 760/647–6595 info center* ⊕ *www.monolake.org* ✉ *Free* ⊗ *Visitor center early Apr.–Nov., daily 8–5; hrs vary at other times.*

FAMILY **Yosemite Mountain Sugar Pine Railroad.** Travel back to a time when powerful steam locomotives hauled massive log trains through the Sierra. This 4-mile, narrow-gauge railroad excursion takes you near Yosemite's south gate. There's a moonlight special ($55), with dinner and entertainment, and you can pan for gold ($10) and visit the free museum. ⊠ *56001 Hwy. 41, 8 miles south of Yosemite, Fish Camp* ☎ *559/683–7273* ⊕ *www.ymsprr.com* ✉ *$22* ⊗ *May–Sept., daily; Apr. and Oct., weekends and selected weekdays.*

AREA ACTIVITIES

BOATING AND RAFTING

TOURS

Zephyr Whitewater Expeditions. This outfitter conducts half-day to three-day white-water trips on the Tuolumne, Merced, and American rivers for paddlers of all experience levels. ☎ *800/431–3636 reservations, 209/532–6249* ⊕ *www.zrafting.com* ✉ *From $109.*

SKIING

Mammoth Mountain. One of the nation's premier ski resorts, Mammoth Mountain offers more than 3,500 acres of skiable boulevards, canyons, and bowls. Ski season starts in November and can run through June. There's a ski school, cross-country trails, snowboarding, snowmobiling, and dogsledding. The resort has extensive lodging, dining, and shopping options. **Facilities:** 150 trails; 3,500 acres; 3,100-foot vertical drop; 28 lifts. ⊠ *Rte. 203, off U.S. 395, Mammoth Lakes* ☎ *800/626–6684* ⊕ *www.mammothmountain.com* ✉ *Lift ticket: $89.*

39

WHERE TO EAT

IN THE PARK

In addition to the dining options listed here, you'll find fast-food grills and cafeterias, plus temporary snack bars, hamburger stands, and pizza joints lining park roads in summer. Many dining facilities in the park are open summer only.

$$$$ ╳ **The Ahwahnee Dining Room.** Rave reviews about the dining room's
EUROPEAN appearance are fully justified—it features towering windows, a 34-foot-
Fodor'sChoice high ceiling with interlaced sugar-pine beams, and massive chandeliers.
★ Although many continue to applaud the food, others have reported that they sense a dip in the quality both in the service and what is being served. Diners must spend a lot of money here, so perhaps that inflates the expectations and amplifies the disappointments. In any event, the

lavish $49 Sunday brunch is a popular way to experience the grand room. Reservations are always advised, and the attire is "resort casual." For lighter lunch and dinner fare at more affordable prices, dine at the hotel bar. ⑤ *Average main: $39* ✉ *The Ahwahnee hotel, Ahwahnee Rd., about ¾ mile east of Yosemite Valley Visitor Center, Yosemite Village* ☎ *209/372–1489* ⊕ *www.yosemitepark.com* ⚑ *Reservations essential.*

$$
AMERICAN
✕ **Curry Village Pavilion.** This cafeteria-style eatery isn't as inexpensive or as good as it should be. Come early for breakfast or dinner (there's no lunch), as the food (which runs the gamut from roasted meats to pastas to burritos and beyond), gets worse as closing time nears. Alternatively, order a pizza from the stand on the deck, and take in the views of the valley's granite walls. ⑤ *Average main: $16* ✉ *Curry Village* ☎ *209/372–8303* ⊙ *Closed mid-Oct.–mid-Apr. No lunch.*

$
AMERICAN
✕ **Food Court at Yosemite Lodge.** Fast and convenient (if outdated), this food court serves simple fare, ranging from hamburgers and pizzas to pastas and roasted meats. At breakfast, you can get pancakes and eggs made any way you like. Salads are popular at lunch and dinner. There's also a selection of beer and wine. The coffee shop near the entrance keeps longer hours. ⑤ *Average main: $11* ✉ *Yosemite Lodge, about ¾ mile west of the visitor center, Yosemite Village* ☎ *209/372–1265* ⊕ *www.yosemitepark.com.*

$$$
AMERICAN
Fodor's Choice
★
✕ **Mountain Room.** Though good, the food becomes secondary when you see Yosemite Falls through this dining room's wall of windows—almost every table has a view. The chef makes a point of using locally sourced, organic ingredients whenever possible, so you can be assured of fresh vegetables to accompany the hearty main courses, such as steaks and seafood, as well as vegetarian and even vegan options. The Mountain Room Lounge, a few steps away in the Yosemite Lodge complex, has about 10 beers on tap. Weather permitting, take your drink out onto the small back patio. ⑤ *Average main: $28* ✉ *Yosemite Lodge, Northside Dr., about ¾ mile west of the visitor center, Yosemite Village* ☎ *209/372–1403* ⊕ *www.yosemitepark.com* ⊙ *No lunch.*

$
FAST FOOD
✕ **Tuolumne Meadows Grill.** Serving continuously throughout the day until 5 or 6 pm, this fast-food eatery cooks up basic breakfast, lunch, and snacks. It's possible that ice cream tastes better at this altitude. Stop in for a quick meal before exploring the meadows. ⑤ *Average main: $10* ✉ *Tioga Rd. (Rte. 120), 1½ miles east of Tuolumne Meadows Visitor Center* ☎ *209/372–8426* ⊙ *Closed Oct.–Memorial Day. No dinner.*

$$
AMERICAN
✕ **Tuolumne Meadows Lodge.** At the back of a small building that contains the lodge's front desk and small gift shop, this restaurant serves a menu of hearty American fare at breakfast and dinner. The decor is woodsy, with dark-wood walls, red-and-white-checkered tablecloths, and a handful of communal tables, which give it the feeling of an old-fashioned summer camp. The menu is small, often featuring a few meat and seafood dishes and one pasta or other special, including a vegetarian choice. If you have any dietary restrictions, let the front desk know in advance and the cooks will not let you down. Order box lunches from here for before hikes. ⑤ *Average main: $20* ✉ *Tioga Rd. (Rte. 120)* ☎ *209/372–8413* ⊕ *www.yosemitepark.com* ⊙ *Closed late Sept.–mid-June. No lunch* ⚑ *Reservations essential.*

$ ✕ **The Village Grill.** If a burger joint is what you've been missing, head
FAST FOOD to this bustling eatery in Yosemite Village that serves veggie, salmon,
and a few other burger varieties in addition to the usual beef patties.
Order at the counter by 5 pm, then take your tray out to the deck and
enjoy your meal under the trees. Degnan's Deli (open until 6 pm) and
Degnan's Loft pizzeria (summer only, open until 9 pm) are nearby.
⑤ *Average main: $12* ✉ *Yosemite Village* ✛ *100 yards east of Yosem-*
ite Valley Visitor Center ☎ *209/372–1207* ⊕ *www.yosemitepark.com*
⊘ *Closed Oct.–May. No dinner.*

$$$ ✕ **Wawona Hotel Dining Room.** Watch deer graze on the meadow while
AMERICAN you dine in the romantic, candlelit dining room of the whitewashed
Wawona Hotel, which dates from the late 1800s. The American-style
cuisine favors fresh ingredients and flavors; trout and flatiron steaks
are menu staples. There's also a brunch on some Sunday holidays, like
Mother's Day and Easter, and a barbecue on the lawn Saturday eve-
ning in summer. ⑤ *Average main: $28* ✉ *8308 Wawona Rd., Wawona*
☎ *209/375–1425* ⊘ *Closed most of Dec., Jan., Feb., and Mar.*

$$$ ✕ **White Wolf Lodge.** Those fueling up for a day on the trail or famished
AMERICAN after a high-country hike will appreciate the all-you-can-eat family-
style breakfasts and dinners in this tiny rustic dining room. Mashed
potatoes, big pots of curried vegetables, and heaps of pasta often grace
the tables in this cozy out-of-the-way place. Lunch is not served, but
box lunches can be ordered the night before. ⑤ *Average main: $24*
✉ *Yosemite National Park* ✛ *Tioga Rd. (Rte. 120), 25 miles west of*
Tuolumne Meadows and 15 miles east of Crane Flat ☎ *209/372–8416*
⊕ *www.yosemitepark.com* ⊘ *Closed mid-Sept.–mid-June. No lunch*
⌔ *Reservations essential.*

PICNIC AREAS

Considering how large the park is and how many visitors come here—
some 4 million people every year, most of them just for the day—it is
somewhat surprising that Yosemite has few formal picnic areas, though
in many places you can find a smooth rock to sit on and enjoy breathtaking views along with your lunch. The convenience stores all sell
picnic supplies, and prepackaged sandwiches and salads are widely
available. Those options can come in especially handy during the middle
of the day, when you might not want to spend precious daylight hours
in such a spectacular setting sitting in a restaurant for a formal meal.
None of the below options has drinking water available; most have
some type of toilet.

Cathedral Beach. You may have some solitude picnicking here, as this
spot usually has fewer people than picnic areas at the eastern end of the
valley. ✉ *Southside Dr. underneath spirelike Cathedral Rocks.*

Church Bowl. Tucked behind The Ahwahnee hotel, this picnic area nearly
abuts the granite walls below the Royal Arches. If you're walking from
the village with your supplies, this is the shortest trek to a picnic area.
✉ *Behind The Ahwahnee hotel, Yosemite Valley.*

El Capitan. Come here for great views that look straight up the giant
granite wall above. ✉ *Northside Dr., at western end of valley.*

39

Sentinel Beach. Usually crowded in season, this area is right alongside a running creek and the Merced River. ⊠ *Southside Dr., just south of Swinging Bridge.*

Swinging Bridge. This picnic area is just before the little wooden footbridge that crosses the Merced River, which babbles pleasantly by. ⊠ *Southside Dr., east of Sentinel Beach.*

OUTSIDE THE PARK

$$$$
EUROPEAN
Fodor'sChoice
★

✕ **Erna's Elderberry House.** Erna Kubin-Clanin, the grande dame of Château du Sureau, created this culinary oasis, stunning for its understated elegance, gorgeous setting, and impeccable service. Earth-tone walls and wood beams accent the dining room's high ceilings, and arched windows reflect the glow of candles. The seasonal prix-fixe dinner (5 courses $108, 4 courses $85) can be paired with superb wines, with each course delivered in perfect synchronicity by the elite waitstaff. Diners can also order à la carte. ⑤ *Average main: $48* ⊠ *Château du Sureau, 48688 Victoria La., off Hwy. 41, Oakhurst* ☎ *559/683–6800* ⊕ *www. elderberryhouse.com* ⊗ *No lunch Mon.–Sat.* ⌖ *Reservations essential.*

$$$
STEAKHOUSE
FAMILY

✕ **The Mogul.** Come here for straightforward steaks—top sirloin, New York, filet mignon, and porterhouse. The only catch is that the waiters cook them, and the results vary depending on their experience. But generally things go well, and kids love the experience. The knotty-pine walls lend a woodsy touch, and suggest Mammoth before all the development. There's an extensive salad bar—all you can eat, with hot bread included. ⑤ *Average main: $26* ⊠ *1528 Tavern Rd., off Old Mammoth Rd., Mammoth Lakes* ☎ *760/934–3039* ⊕ *www.themogul.com* ⊗ *No lunch.*

$$
AMERICAN

✕ **Tioga Gas Mart & Whoa Nelli Deli.** This might be the only gas station in the United States serving craft beers and lobster taquitos, but its appeal goes beyond novelty. Succulent fish tacos with mango salsa and barbecued ribs with a huckleberry glaze are among the many well-executed dishes. Order at the counter and grab a seat inside, or sit at one of the picnic tables on the lawn outside and take in the distant view of Mono Lake. ⑤ *Average main: $16* ⊠ *Hwy. 120 and U.S. 395, Lee Vining* ☎ *760/647–1088* ⊕ *www.whoanelliedeli.com* ⊗ *Closed early Nov.–late Apr.*

WHERE TO STAY

At press time, a trademark dispute with a former park concessioner may result in Yosemite National Park changing the names of several historic park lodges and properties, including the iconic Ahwahnee. This guide uses the historic names. Should the plan go through, the following changes will take place: Yosemite Lodge at the Falls will become Yosemite Valley Lodge, The Ahwahnee will become The Majestic Yosemite Hotel, Curry Village will become Half Dome Village, Wawona Hotel will become Big Trees Lodge, and Badger Pass Ski Area will become Yosemite Ski & Snowboard Area. For the latest information, visit the news section of the Yosemite National Park website: www.nps.gov/yose.

IN THE PARK

$$$$ 🛏 **The Ahwahnee.** A National His-
HOTEL toric Landmark, the hotel is con-
Fodor'sChoice structed of sugar-pine logs and
★ features Native American design
motifs; public spaces are enliv-
ened with art deco flourishes, Per-
sian rugs, and elaborate iron- and
woodwork. **Pros:** best lodge in
Yosemite; helpful concierge. **Cons:**
expensive rates; some reports that
service has slipped in recent years.
⑤ *Rooms from: $458* ✉ *Ahwahnee
Rd., about ¾ mile east of Yosemite Valley Visitor Center, Yosemite
Village* ☎ *801/559–4884* ⊕ *www.
yosemitepark.com* ☞ *95 lodge rooms, 6 suites, 24 cottage rooms* ⦿ *No
meals.*

LODGING TIP

Reserve your room or cabin in
Yosemite as far in advance as
possible. You can make a reservation up to a year before your
arrival (within minutes after the
reservation office makes a date
available, The Ahwahnee, Yosemite
Lodge, and Wawona Hotel often
sell out their weekends, holiday
periods, and all days between May
and September).

$$ 🛏 **Curry Village.** Opened in 1899 as a place for budget-conscious travel-
HOTEL ers, Curry Village has plain accommodations: standard motel rooms,
simple cabins with either private or shared baths, and tent cabins with
shared baths. **Pros:** close to many activities; family-friendly atmosphere.
Cons: not that economical after a recent price surge; can be crowded;
sometimes a bit noisy. ⑤ *Rooms from: $133* ✉ *South side of Southside
Dr.* ☎ *801/559–4884* ⊕ *www.yosemitepark.com* ☞ *18 rooms, 485 cab-
ins* ⦿ *No meals.*

$$$$ 🛏 **Redwoods in Yosemite.** This collection of more than 125 homes in the
RENTAL Wawona area is a great alternative to the overcrowded valley. **Pros:**
sense of privacy; peaceful setting; full kitchens. **Cons:** remote from the
valley; some have no TV. ⑤ *Rooms from: $219* ✉ *8038 Chilnualna Falls
Rd., off Rte. 41, Wawona* ☎ *209/375–6666 international, 844/266–
5133* ⊕ *www.redwoodsinyosemite.com* ☞ *130 units* ⦿ *No meals.*

$$ 🛏 **Wawona Hotel.** This 1879 National Historic Landmark at Yosemite's
HOTEL southern end is a Victorian-era mountain resort, with whitewashed
buildings, wraparound verandas, and pleasant, no-frills rooms deco-
rated with period pieces. **Pros:** lovely building; peaceful atmosphere.
Cons: few modern amenities, such as phones and TVs; an hour's drive
from Yosemite Valley. ⑤ *Rooms from: $148* ✉ *8308 Wawona Rd.,
Wawona* ☎ *801/559–4884* ⊕ *www.yosemitepark.com* ☾ *Closed Dec.–
Mar., except mid-Dec.–Jan. 2* ☞ *104 rooms, 50 with bath* ⦿ *Breakfast.*

$$ 🛏 **White Wolf Lodge.** Set in a subalpine meadow, the rustic accommoda-
HOTEL tions at White Wolf Lodge make it an excellent base camp for hiking
the backcountry. **Pros:** quiet location; near some of Yosemite's most
beautiful, less crowded hikes; good restaurant. **Cons:** far from the val-
ley. ⑤ *Rooms from: $138* ✉ *Yosemite National Park* ⊹ *Off Tioga Rd.
(Rte. 120), 25 miles west of Tuolumne Meadows and 15 miles east of
Crane Flat* ☎ *801/559–4884* ☾ *Closed mid-Sept.–mid-June* ☞ *24 tent
cabins, 4 cabins* ⦿ *No meals.*

$$$$ 🛏 **Yosemite Lodge at the Falls.** This 1915 lodge near Yosemite Falls is a
HOTEL collection of numerous two-story, glass-and-wood structures tucked

39

CAMPING IN BEAR COUNTRY

The national parks' campgrounds and some campgrounds outside the parks provide food-storage boxes that can keep bears from pilfering your edibles (portable canisters for backpackers can be rented in most park stores). It's imperative that you move all food, coolers, and items with a scent (including toiletries, toothpaste, chewing gum, and air fresheners) from your car (including the trunk) to the storage box at your campsite; day-trippers should lock food in bear boxes provided at parking lots. If you don't, a bear may break into your car by literally peeling off the door or ripping open the trunk, or ransack your tent. The familiar tactic of hanging your food from high tree limbs is not an effective deterrent, as bears easily can scale trees. In the southern Sierra, bear canisters are the only effective and proven method for preventing bears from getting human food.

beneath the trees. **Pros:** centrally located; dependably clean rooms; lots of tours leave from out front. **Cons:** can feel impersonal; appearance is a little dated; prices recently skyrocketed. ⑤ *Rooms from: $247* ⊠ *9006 Yosemite Lodge Dr., Yosemite Village* ☎ *801/559–4884* ⊕ *www.yosemitepark.com/yosemite-lodge.aspx* ⟿ *245 rooms* ⑩ *No meals.*

OUTSIDE THE PARK

$$
HOTEL
FAMILY

⛤ **Best Western Plus Yosemite Gateway Inn.** Perched on 11 hillside acres, Oakhurst's best motel has carefully tended landscaping and rooms with stylish contemporary furnishings and hand-painted murals of Yosemite. **Pros:** close to park's southern entrance; on-site restaurant; indoor and outdoor swimming pools; frequent deer and wildlife sightings. **Cons:** some rooms on the small side; Internet connection can be slow. ⑤ *Rooms from: $150* ⊠ *40530 Hwy. 41, Oakhurst* ☎ *800/545–5462, 559/683–2378* ⊕ *www.yosemitegatewayinn.com* ⟿ *133 rooms, 16 suites* ⑩ *No meals.*

$$$$
RESORT
Fodor's Choice
★

⛤ **Château du Sureau.** The inn here is straight out of a children's book: Every room is impeccably styled with European antiques, sumptuous fabrics, fresh-cut flowers, and oversize soaking tubs. **Pros:** luxurious; great views; sumptuous spa facility. **Cons:** expensive; cost might not seem worth it to guests not spa-oriented. ⑤ *Rooms from: $385* ⊠ *48688 Victoria La., Oakhurst* ☎ *559/683–6860* ⊕ *www.chateausureau.com* ⟿ *10 rooms, 1 villa* ⑩ *Breakfast.*

$$$$
RESORT
Fodor's Choice
★

⛤ **Double Eagle Resort and Spa.** Lofty pines tower over this very fine spa retreat on the June Lake Loop. **Pros:** pretty setting; spectacular indoor pool; 1½ miles from June Mountain Ski Area. **Cons:** expensive; remote. ⑤ *Rooms from: $249* ⊠ *5587 Hwy. 158, Box 736, June Lake* ☎ *760/648–7004* ⊕ *www.doubleeagle.com* ⟿ *17 2-bedroom cabins, 16 rooms, 1 3-bedroom house* ⑩ *No meals.*

$$$$
RESORT
FAMILY

⛤ **Evergreen Lodge.** The perfect blend of rustic charm and modern comfort, these cabins have sumptuous beds, comfy armchairs, pull-out sofas, and tree-stump end tables. **Pros:** romantic setting; friendly staff; lots of things to do. **Cons:** far from Yosemite Valley (though

Best Campgrounds in Yosemite

If you are going to concentrate solely on valley sites and activities, you should endeavor to stay in one of the "Pines" campgrounds, which are clustered near Curry Village and within an easy stroll from that busy complex's many facilities. For a more primitive and quiet experience, and to be near many backcountry hikes, try one of the Tioga Road campgrounds.

National Park Service Reservations Office. Reservations are required at many of Yosemite's campgrounds, especially in summer. You can book a site up to five months in advance, starting on the 15th of the month. Unless otherwise noted, book your site through the central National Park Service Reservations Office. If you don't have reservations when you arrive, many sites, especially those outside Yosemite Valley, are available on a first-come, first-served basis. ☎ 877/444–6777 reservations, 518/885–3639 international, 888/448–1474 customer service ⊕ www.recreation.gov ⊗ Daily 10–10.

Bridalveil Creek. This campground sits among lodgepole pines at 7,200 feet, above the valley on Glacier Point Road. From here, you can easily drive to Glacier Point's magnificent valley views. ⊠ From Rte. 41 in Wawona, go north to Glacier Point Rd. and turn right; entrance to campground is 25 miles ahead on right side.

Camp 4. Formerly known as Sunnyside Walk-In, and extremely popular with rock climbers, who don't mind that a total of six are assigned to each campsite, no matter how many are in your group, this is the only valley campground available on a first-come, first-served basis. ⊠ Base of Yosemite Falls Trail, just west of Yosemite Lodge on Northside Dr., Yosemite Village.

Housekeeping Camp. Composed of three concrete walls and covered with two layers of canvas, each unit has an open-ended fourth side that can be closed off with a heavy white canvas curtain. You can rent "bedpacks," consisting of blankets, sheets, and other comforts. ⊠ Southside Dr., ½ mile west of Curry Village.

Porcupine Flat. Sixteen miles west of Tuolumne Meadows, this campground sits at 8,100 feet. If you want to be in the high country, this is a good bet. ⊠ Rte. 120, 16 miles west of Tuolumne Meadows.

Tuolumne Meadows. In a wooded area at 8,600 feet, just south of its namesake meadow, this is one of the most spectacular and sought-after campgrounds in Yosemite. ⊠ Rte. 120, 46 miles east of Big Oak Flat entrance station.

Upper Pines. This is one of the valley's largest campgrounds and the closest one to the trailheads. Expect large crowds in the summer—and little privacy. ⊠ At east end of valley, near Curry Village.

Wawona. Near the Mariposa Grove, just downstream from a popular fishing spot, this year-round campground has larger, less densely packed sites than campgrounds in the valley. ⊠ Rte. 41, 1 mile north of Wawona.

White Wolf. Set in the beautiful high country at 8,000 feet, this is a prime spot for hikers from early July to mid-September. ⊠ Tioga Rd., 15 miles east of Big Oak Flat entrance.

39

close to Hetch Hetchy). $ *Rooms from: $250* ✉ *33160 Evergreen Rd., Groveland* ✛ *25 miles east of Groveland, 23 miles north of Yosemite Valley* ☎ *209/379–2606, 800/935–6343* ⊕ *www.evergreenlodge.com* ☽ *Closed Jan.–early Feb.* ⇆ *90 cabins* ⦿ *No meals.*

$$$ ⛺ **Homestead Cottages.** Set on 160 acres of rolling hills that once held
B&B/INN a Miwok village, these cottages (the largest sleeps six) have gas fireplaces, fully equipped kitchens, and queen-size beds. **Pros:** remote location; quiet setting; friendly owners. **Cons:** might be too quiet for some. $ *Rooms from: $184* ✉ *41110 Rd. 600, 2½ miles off Hwy. 49, Ahwahnee* ☎ *559/683–0495* ⊕ *www.homesteadcottages.com* ⇆ *6 cottages* ⦿ *Breakfast.*

$$$$ ⛺ **Narrow Gauge Inn.** The well-tended rooms at this family-owned prop-
B&B/INN erty have balconies with views of the surrounding woods and mountains. **Pros:** close to Yosemite's south entrance; nicely appointed rooms; wonderful balconies. **Cons:** rooms can be a bit dark; dining options are limited, especially for vegetarians. $ *Rooms from: $209* ✉ *48571 Hwy. 41, Fish Camp* ☎ *559/683–7720, 888/644–9050* ⊕ *www. narrowgaugeinn.com* ⇆ *26 rooms* ⦿ *Breakfast.*

$$$$ ⛺ **Rush Creek Lodge.** This sleek, nature-inspired complex occupies 20
RESORT acres on a wooded hillside and includes a pool and hot tubs, a restau-
FAMILY rant and tavern with indoor/outdoor seating, a guided recreation pro-
Fodor's Choice gram, an amphitheater, and a general store. **Pros:** close to Yosemite's Big
★ Oak Flat entrance; YARTS bus stops here and connects with Yosemite Valley and Sonora. **Cons:** no TVs; pricey in high season; remote setting. $ *Rooms from: $350* ✉ *34001 Hwy. 120, Groveland* ✛ *25 miles east of Groveland, 23 miles north of Yosemite Valley* ☎ *209/379–2373* ⊕ *www. rushcreeklodge.com* ⇆ *141 rooms, 2 suites* ⦿ *No meals.*

$$$ ⛺ **Tamarack Lodge Resort.** Tucked away on the edge of the John Muir
RESORT Wilderness Area, where cross-country ski trails loop through the woods, this 1924 lodge looks like something out of a snow globe. **Pros:** rustic but not run-down; tons of nearby outdoor activities. **Cons:** thin walls; some shared bathrooms. $ *Rooms from: $169* ✉ *Lake Mary Rd., off Rte. 203, Mammoth Lakes* ☎ *760/934–2442, 800/237–6879* ⊕ *www. tamaracklodge.com* ⇆ *11 rooms, 34 cabins* ⦿ *No meals.*

$$$$ ⛺ **Tenaya Lodge.** One of the region's largest hotels, Tenaya Lodge is ideal
RESORT for people who enjoy wilderness treks by day but prefer creature com-
FAMILY forts at night. **Pros:** rustic setting with modern comforts; exceptional
Fodor's Choice spa and exercise facility; close to Yosemite; activities for all ages. **Cons:**
★ so big it can seem impersonal; pricey during summer. $ *Rooms from: $295* ✉ *1122 Hwy. 41, Fish Camp* ☎ *559/683–6555, 888/514–2167* ⊕ *www.tenayalodge.com* ⇆ *282 rooms, 20 suites* ⦿ *No meals.*

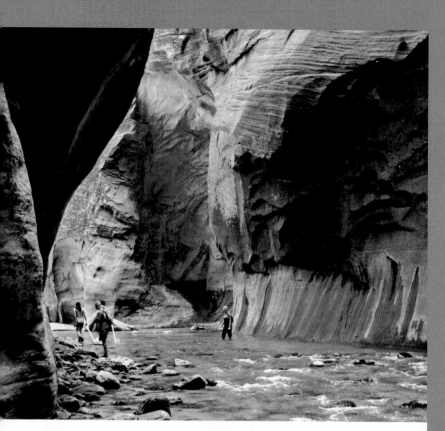

ZION NATIONAL PARK

WELCOME TO ZION NATIONAL PARK

TOP REASONS TO GO

★ **Eye candy:** Pick just about any trail in the park and it's all but guaranteed to culminate in an astounding viewpoint full of pink, orange, and crimson rock formations.

★ **Auto immunity:** From spring through autumn, cars are generally not allowed in Zion Canyon, allowing for a quiet and peaceful park.

★ **Botanical wonderland:** Zion Canyon is home to approximately 900 species of plants, more than anywhere else in Utah.

★ **Animal tracks:** Zion has expansive hinterlands where furry, scaly, and feathered residents are common. Hike long enough and you'll encounter deer, elk, rare lizards, birds of prey, and other zoological treats.

★ **Unforgettable canyoneering:** Zion's array of rugged slot canyons is the richest place on Earth for scrambling, rappelling, climbing, and descending.

1 **Zion Canyon.** This area defines Zion National Park for most people. Free shuttle buses are the only vehicles allowed during the crowded high season. The backcountry is accessible via the West Rim Trail and the Narrows, and 2,000-foot cliffs rise all around.

2 **The Narrows.** A quintessential slot canyon, this is one of the national park system's best hiking trails. Following the north fork of the Virgin River, there's something for everyone in the Narrows, whether you're a day-tripper or an overnight explorer.

3 Kolob Canyons. The northwestern corner of Zion is a secluded 30,000-acre wonderland that can be reached only via a special entrance. Don't miss the West Temple and the Kolob Arch, and keep looking up to spot Horse Ranch Mountain, the park's highest point.

4 Lava Point. Infrequently visited, this area has a primitive campground and two nearby reservoirs that offer the only significant fishing opportunities. Lava Point Overlook provides a view of Zion Canyon from the north.

UTAH

GETTING ORIENTED

The heart of Zion National Park is Zion Canyon, which follows the North Fork of the Virgin River for 6½ miles beneath cliffs that rise 2,000 feet from the river bottom. The Kolob area is considered by some to be superior in beauty, and because it's isolated from the rest of the park, you aren't likely to run into any crowds here. Both sections hint at the extensive backcountry beyond, open for those with the stamina, time, and the courage to go off the beaten path.

40

KEY	
🛉	Ranger Station
▲	Campground
🛱	Picnic Area
🍴	Restaurant
🏨	Lodge
🥾	Trailhead
🚻	Restrooms
❀	Scenic Viewpoint
⋯⋯	Walking/Hiking Trails

Lava Point
4 Lava Point Viewpoint
Upper Kolob Plateau
Kolob Plateau
Horse Pasture Plateau
West Rim Trail
Viewpoint
Left Fork
Right Fork
The Narrows
2 Orderville Canyon
Mountain of Mystery
Temple of Sinawava
Weeping Rock
Angels Landing
Great White Throne
Emerald Pools Trails
The Grotto
Zion Lodge
The Sentinel
Shuttle Bus (summer only)
East Entrance
Altar of Sacrifice
Court of the Patriachs
Canyon Junction
West Temple
Tunnel
Zion-Mount Carmel Hwy
Checkerboard Mesa
Zion Human History Museum
Visitor Center
Parunuweap Canyon
Rockville

Updated
by Mike
Weatherford

The walls of Zion Canyon soar more than 2,000 feet above the valley below, but it's the character, not the size, of the sandstone forms that defines the park's splendor. Throughout the park, fantastically colored bands of limestone, sandstone, and lava in the strata point to the distant past. Stripes and spots of greenery high in the cliff walls create a "hanging garden" effect, and invariably indicate the presence of water seepage or a spring. Erosion has left behind a collection of domes, fins, and blocky massifs bearing the names and likenesses of cathedrals and temples, prophets and angels.

Trails lead deep into side canyons and up narrow ledges to waterfalls, serene spring-fed pools, and shaded spots of solitude. So diverse is this place that 85% of Utah's flora and fauna species are found here. Some, like the tiny Zion snail, appear nowhere else in the world.

The Colorado River helped create the Grand Canyon, while the Virgin River—the Colorado's muddy progeny—carved Zion's features. Because of the park's unique topography, distant storms and spring runoff can transform a tranquil slot canyon into a sluice.

ZION PLANNER

WHEN TO GO

Zion is the most heavily visited national park in Utah, receiving 3 million visitors each year. Locals used to call the spring and fall the shoulder seasons because traffic would drop off from the highly visited summer months. Not so much anymore. These days the park is busy from April through October.

Summer in the park is hot and dry, punctuated by sudden cloudbursts that can create flash flooding and spectacular waterfalls. Expect afternoon thunderstorms between July and September. Whether the day starts out sunny or not, wear sunscreen and drink lots of water, even if you aren't exerting yourself or spending much time outside. The sun is very powerful at this elevation.

Winters are mild at lower desert elevations. You can expect to encounter winter driving conditions from November to mid-March, and although most park programs are suspended in winter, it is a wonderful and solitary time to see the canyons.

■ TIP➜ The temperature in Zion often exceeds 100°F in July and August.

AVG. HIGH/LOW TEMPS.

Jan.	Feb.	Mar.	Apr.	May	June
54/30	59/34	66/39	75/45	86/54	95/63

July	Aug.	Sept.	Oct.	Nov.	Dec.
100/70	99/68	91/61	79/48	64/37	54/30

FESTIVALS AND EVENTS

JANUARY **St. George Winter Bird Festival.** Bird-watchers gather in St. George every January to peep at more than 100 feathered species. After a Thursday-night kickoff event, join in two full days of field trips, exhibits, lectures, and activities. ⊠ *Tonaquint Park and Nature Center, 1851 S. Dixie Dr., St. George* ☎ *435/627–4506, 435/673–0996* ⊕ *www.sgcity.org/departments/recreation/birdfestival* ✉ *$10.*

SPRING **Hurricane Easter Car Show.** Classic cars from all over the region head to
FAMILY Hurricane every Easter weekend. Up to 10,000 people pack the Hurricane Community Center to see hot rods and munch hot dogs. ⊠ *Hurricane* ☎ *866/367–2817* ⊕ *eastercarshow.com* ✉ *$5.*

APRIL **Dixie Downs Horse Races.** The St. George Lions Club sponsors these quarter-horse races, a Hurricane tradition for nearly 50 years, on two consecutive Saturdays in April. ⊠ *Washington County Regional Park, 5500 W. 700 S, Hurricane* ☎ *435/673–3301* ⊕ *stgeorgelions.com.*

AUGUST **Western Legends Roundup.** For three days in late August, Kanab plays
FAMILY host to cowboy poets, musicians, and character actors from Old West TV series of yesteryear. A parade, tours to Western movie sites, a chuckwagon dinner, campfire entertainment, performances by Native American dancers, and a film festival draw enthusiasts from all over the country. ☎ *435/644–3444* ⊕ *westernlegendsroundup.com.*

SEPTEMBER **Dixie Roundup.** Dozens of professional rodeo cowboys from across the West take part in this three-day mid-September event held since the 1930s. Team roping, saddle-bronc riding, and bull riding are among the main attractions, along with the always entertaining mutton-busting competition for the kids and the rodeo parade. ⊠ *Sun Bowl Stadium, St. George* ☎ *435/703–4779* ⊕ *stgeorgelions.com* ✉ *$10.*

40

Plants and Wildlife in Zion

Zion National Park, on the Colorado Plateau and bordered by the Great Basin and Mojave Desert provinces, supports diverse flora and fauna.

MULTIPLE ENVIRONMENTS

More than 900 species of plants thrive in environments that range from desert to hanging garden to high plateau. On a visit you might encounter delicate ferns and mosses, hardy cacti and other desert plants, and many trees, grasses, and herbs. Poison ivy, in abundance here, is one species you'll want to avoid. If you're not sure how to recognize it, take a quick lesson from a ranger prior to your first hike so you don't wind up with an itchy souvenir.

WILDLIFE RETURNS

With car traffic having been almost completely replaced by a shuttle bus system from mid-March through October, wildlife has returned in force to the park. Even in high season you can spot mule deer wandering in shady glens, especially in early morning and near dusk. You'll also see scores of lizards and wild turkeys everywhere you go.

EXOTIC FAUNA

To observe the more exotic fauna, hit the hiking trails. Nearly 300 species of birds reside either full or part-time in the park, from tiny hummingbirds and chickadees to eagles and even pelicans. Ringtail cats (which are not cats but are similar to raccoons) prowl the park. Evening hikes may reveal foxes, but you're more likely to spot their tracks than the elusive animals themselves. All animals, from the smallest chipmunk to the biggest elk, should be given plenty of space, but only the extremely rare mountain lion or black bear poses a threat to humans.

READ ALL ABOUT IT

Brochures available at the Zion Canyon Visitor Center and downloadable (⊕ www.nps.gov/zion/planyourvisit/brochures.htm) have details about the park's birds, mammals, plants, and reptiles and amphibians.

PLANNING YOUR TIME

ZION IN ONE DAY

Begin your visit at the **Zion Canyon Visitor Center,** where outdoor exhibits inform you about the park's geology, wildlife, history, and trails. Get a taste of what's in store by viewing the far off Towers of the Virgin, then head to the **Court of the Patriarchs** viewpoint to take photos and walk the short path. Then take the shuttle (or your car, if it's off-season) to **Zion Lodge,** where you can hike a trail to one of the park's most beautiful spots, the **Emerald Pools.** The Lower Pool Trail is the second most popular walk at Zion; the trail branches off into Middle Pool and Upper Pool trails for those who are fit and have more time. Ride the next shuttle to the end of the road, where the paved, accessible **Riverside Walk,** Zion's most popular path, will deliver you to the gateway of the canyon's narrows.

Reboard the shuttle to return to the Zion Canyon Visitor Center to pick up your car (or continue driving off-season). Head out onto the beautiful **Zion–Mount Carmel Highway,** with its long, curving tunnels, keeping your camera at the ready for stops at viewpoints along the road. Once you reach the park's east entrance, turn around, and on your return trip stop to take the short hike up to **Canyon Overlook.** Now you're ready to rest your feet at a screening of *Zion Canyon: Treasure of the Gods* on the giant screen of the **Zion Canyon Theatre.** In the evening, you might want to attend a ranger program at one of the campground amphitheaters or at Zion Lodge. Or you can follow a relaxing dinner in **Springdale** with a stroll downtown.

GETTING HERE AND AROUND

AIR TRAVEL

The nearest commercial airport is 46 miles away in St. George, Utah. McCarran International Airport (LAS) in Las Vegas, Nevada, 170 miles away, is the nearest large airport. Salt Lake City's airport is 310 miles away.

CAR TRAVEL

Zion National Park lies east of Interstate 15 in southwestern Utah. From the interstate, head east on Highway 9. After 21 miles you'll reach Springdale, which abuts the main entrance.

From mid-March through October, you can drive into the park only if you have reservations at the Zion Lodge. Otherwise, you must park your car in Springdale or at the Zion Canyon Visitor Center and take the shuttle. There are no car restrictions from November to mid-March.

The Zion Canyon Visitor Center parking lot fills up quickly. You can avoid parking heartburn by leaving your car in Springdale and riding the shuttle to the park entrance. Shuttles are accessible for people with disabilities and have plenty of room for gear. Town shuttle stops are at Majestic View Lodge, Driftwood Lodge, Quality Inn, Bit & Spur Restaurant, Holiday Inn Express, Bumbleberry Inn, Zion Pizza & Noodle Co., Zion Canyon Clothing, Flanigan's Inn, and Zion Canyon Giant Screen Theatre. The average wait time is less than 15 minutes. Consult the print park guide or check online at ⊕ *www.nps.gov/zion/planyourvisit/shuttle-system.htm.*

PARK ESSENTIALS

40

PARK FEES AND PERMITS

Entrance to Zion National Park costs $30 per vehicle for a seven-day pass. People entering on foot or by bicycle pay $15 per person for a seven-day pass; those on motorcycle pay $25. Entrance to the Kolob Canyons section of the park costs $10. You'll receive credit for this fee if you later pay to enter Zion Canyon.

Permits are required for backcountry camping and overnight hikes. Depending on which parts of the trails you intend to explore, you'll need a special permit for the Narrows and Kolob Creek or the Subway slot canyon. Climbing and canyoneering parties need a permit before using technical equipment.

Zion National Park limits the total number of overnight and canyoneering permits issued per day and has a reservation system with most of the permits now issued in an online lottery to apportion them fairly. Permits to the Subway, Mystery Canyon, the Narrows through-hikes, and West Rim are in short supply during high season. The maximum size of a group hiking into the backcountry is 12 people. Permits cost $10 for one or two people; $15 for three to seven; and $20 for eight or more. Permits are available at the visitor centers.

PARK HOURS

The park, open daily year-round, 24 hours a day, is in the Mountain time zone.

CELL-PHONE RECEPTION

Cell-phone reception is good in Springdale but spotty in Zion Canyon. Public telephones can be found at South Campground, Watchman Campground, Zion Canyon Visitor Center, Zion Lodge, and Zion Human History Museum.

EDUCATIONAL OFFERINGS

CLASSES AND SEMINARS

Zion Canyon Field Institute. The Zion Natural History Association's educational arm conducts workshops about the park's natural and cultural history. Topics include edible plants, bat biology, river geology, photography, and bird-watching. Most workshops include a hike. For a glimpse of Zion's inner workings, volunteer to assist with one of the association's ongoing projects. ⊠ *Zion National Park* ☎ *435/772–3264, 800/635–3959* ⊕ *www.zionpark.org* ▢ *From $40.*

RANGER PROGRAMS

Evening Programs. Held each evening in campground amphitheaters and at Zion Lodge, these ranger-led talks cover geology, biology, and history. You might learn about coyote calls, the night sky, animal hideouts, or observing nature with all your senses. Slide shows and audience participation are often part of the proceedings. Check the park guide and visitor center for times, locations, and topics. ⊠ *Zion National Park* ☎ *435/772–3256* ⊕ *www.nps.gov/zion* ▢ *Free.*

Fodor'sChoice
★
Expert Talks. Informal lectures take place on the Zion Human History Museum patio. Past topics have included wildlife, geology, and the stories of early settlers. Talks usually last from 20 to 30 minutes, though some run longer. Park bulletin boards and publications have schedules. ⊠ *Zion National Park* ☎ *435/772–3256* ▢ *Free.*

FAMILY **Junior Ranger Program.** Educational activities aimed at younger visitors include the chance to earn a Junior Ranger badge. Kids do so by attending at least one nature program and completing the free Junior Ranger Handbook, available at visitor centers and elsewhere. The ranger-led programs cover topics such as plants, animals, geology, and archaeology through hands-on activities, games, and hikes. ⊠ *Zion National Park* ☎ *435/772–3256* ⊕ *www.nps.gov/zion/learn/kidsyouth* ▢ *Free.*

Ranger-Led Hikes. These guided hikes provide a overview of the park's geology and natural and other history. From an easy 1 mile to a moderate 2½ miles, the hikes have included a Riverside Ramble, a geological tour called Rock and Stroll, and a natural-history walk taking in the incredible vistas of Kolob Canyons. For locations and times, inquire at the visitor centers or check park bulletin boards. Wear sturdy footgear and bring a hat, sunglasses, sunscreen, and water. ⊠ *Zion National Park* ⊕ *www.nps.gov/zion/planyourvisit/ranger-led-activities.htm* ▢ *Free.*

FAMILY
Fodor's Choice
★

Ride with a Ranger Shuttle Tours. Twice a day, rangers conduct shuttle tours of points of interest along Zion Canyon Scenic Drive. In addition to learning about the canyon's geology, ecology, and history, you'll be treated to some great photo ops. The two-hour tours take place in the morning and evening and depart from the Zion Canyon Visitor Center. Seating is limited to eight people. Make reservations in person at the visitor center up to three days in advance. ⊠ *Zion Canyon Visitor Center* ☎ *435/772–3256* ⊕ *www.nps.gov/zion/planyourvisit/ranger-led-activities.htm* ⊠ *Free* ⊗ *May–Sept., daily at 9 and 6:30.*

RESTAURANTS

Only one full-service restaurant operates within the park, but there are numerous places just beyond it. Springdale is the best choice for family-friendly restaurants.

HOTELS

The Zion Lodge is rustic but clean and comfortable. Springdale has dozens of lodging options, from quaint bed-and-breakfasts to modest motels to chain hotels with riverside rooms. Panguitch and Hurricane have some good options for budget and last-minute travelers. *Hotel reviews have been shortened. For full information, visit Fodors.com.*

WHAT IT COSTS				
	$	$$	$$$	$$$$
Restaurants	under $13	$13–$20	$21–$30	over $30
Hotels	under $100	$100–$150	$151–$200	over $200

Restaurant prices are the average cost of a main course at dinner, or if dinner is not served, at lunch. Hotel prices are the lowest cost of a standard double room in high season.

VISITOR INFORMATION

Park Contact Information Zion National Park. ⊠ *Hwy. 9, Springdale* ☎ *435/772–3256* ⊕ *nps.gov/zion.*

VISITOR CENTERS

Kolob Canyons Visitor Center. Make this your first stop as you enter this remote section of the park. There are books and maps, a small gift shop, and clean restrooms here, and rangers are on hand to answer questions about Kolob Canyons exploration. ⊠ *3752 E. Kolob Canyon Rd., Exit 40 off I–15* ☎ *435/586–9548* ⊕ *www.nps.gov/zion* ⊗ *Late May–early Sept., daily 8–6; late Apr.–late May and early Sept.–mid-Oct., daily 8–5; mid-Oct.–late Apr., daily 8–4:30.*

Zion Canyon Visitor Center. Most of the information here is presented in an appealing outdoor exhibit next to a gurgling stream shaded by cottonwood trees. These displays introduce the area's geology, flora, and fauna. Inside, a large shop sells everything from field guides to souvenirs. Zion Canyon shuttle buses leave regularly from the center and make several stops along the canyon's beautiful scenic drive; ranger-guided shuttle tours depart twice a day. ⊠ *Zion Park Blvd. at south entrance, Springdale* ☎ *435/772–3256* ⊕ *www.nps.gov/zion* ⊗ *Late*

40

May–early Sept., daily 8–7:30; late Apr.–late May and early Sept.–mid-Oct., daily 8–6; mid-Oct.–late Apr., daily 8–5.

EXPLORING

SCENIC DRIVES

Zion Canyon's grandeur is best experienced on foot whenever possible, but there is something to be said for covering a lot of ground on wheels. Take the shuttle whenever possible. Driving is the only way to easily access Kolob Canyon, for example, and from November through March, driving your own vehicle is the only way to access the Zion Canyon Scenic Drive.

Kolob Canyons Road. The beauty starts modestly at the junction with Interstate 15, but as you move along this 5-mile road the red walls of the Kolob finger canyons rise suddenly and spectacularly out of the earth. With the crowds left behind at Zion Canyon, this drive offers the chance to take in incredible vistas at your leisure. Trails include the short but rugged Middle Fork of Taylor Creek Trail, which passes two 1930s homestead cabins, culminating 2¾ miles later in the Double Arch Alcove. During heavy snowfall Kolob Canyons Road may be closed. ⊠ *I–15, Exit 40.*

Kolob Terrace Road. This 22-mile road begins 14 miles west of Springdale at Virgin and winds north to Kolob Reservoir. The drive meanders in and out of the park boundaries, crossing several important trailheads, all the while overlooking the cliffs of North Creek. A popular day-use trail (permit required) leads past fossilized dinosaur tracks to the Subway, a stretch of the stream where the walls of the slot canyon close in so tightly as to form a near tunnel. Farther along the road you reach the Wildcat Canyon trailhead, which connects to the path overlooking the North Guardian Angel. The road terminates at the reservoir, beneath 8,933-foot Kolob Peak. This narrow, twisting road is not recommended for RVs. Because of limited winter plowing, the road is closed from December through April or May. ✛ *Drive begins at Hwy. 9 and Kolob Terrace Rd. in Virgin* ☉ *Closed Dec.–Apr. or May.*

Zion–Mount Carmel Highway and Tunnels. Two narrow tunnels as old as the park itself lie between the east entrance and Zion Canyon on this breathtaking 24-mile (round-trip) stretch of Highway 9. One was once the longest man-made tunnel in the world. As you travel the (1.1-mile) passage through solid rock, five arched portals along one side provide fleeting glimpses of cliffs and canyons. When you emerge you'll find that the landscape has changed dramatically. Large vehicles require traffic control and a $15 permit, available at the park entrance, and have restricted hours of travel. This includes nearly all RVs, trailers, dual-wheel trucks, and campers. The Canyon Overlook Trail starts from a parking area between the tunnels. ⊠ *Hwy. 9, 5 miles east of Canyon Junction.*

HISTORIC SITES

Zion Human History Museum. This quaint museum tells the park's story from the perspective of its human inhabitants, among them Ancestral Puebloans and early Mormon settlers. Permanent exhibits illustrate how humans have dealt with wildlife, plants, and natural forces. Temporary exhibits include finds from recent archaeological excavations. Don't miss the incredible view of Towers of the Virgin from the back patio. ⊠ *Zion Canyon Scenic Dr., ½ mile north of south entrance* ☎ *435/772–3256* ⊕ *www.nps.gov/zion/historyculture/zion-human-history-museum. htm* ⊒ *Free* ☉ *Mar.–Oct., usually daily 10–5 (sometimes longer in summer), but call or check park guide.*

Fodor's Choice ★   **Zion Lodge.** Architect Gilbert Stanley Underwood, responsible for many noteworthy national park lodges, designed the original Zion Lodge, which opened in the 1920s but was destroyed by fire four decades later. In 1990, it was restored to its original rustic style, in some cases down to the very paint color. Natural beauty is on display inside and out, from the lobby's rock columns and exposed wood to the cottonwoods shading the sprawling lawn. The main building includes a gift shop, a fine-dining restaurant, and a snack bar. The lodge has received numerous awards for its eco-friendly practices. Recent amenities include bike rentals, open-air narrated tram rides, and an electric-vehicle charging station. ⊠ *Zion Canyon Scenic Dr.* ☎ *435/772–7700.*

SCENIC STOPS

The park comprises two distinct sections, Zion Canyon and the Kolob Plateau and Canyons. Most people restrict their visit to the better-known Zion Canyon, but the Kolob area has much to offer and should not be missed if time allows. Though there's little evidence of Kolob's beauty from the entrance point off Interstate 15, once you negotiate the first switchback on the park road, you are hit with a vision of red-rock cliffs shooting out of the earth. As you climb in elevation, you are treated first to a journey through these canyons, then to a view into the chasm. ■ TIP→ Because you must exit the park to get from Zion Canyon to Kolob Canyon, it is not easy to explore both sections in one day.

40

Checkerboard Mesa. It's well worth stopping at the pull-out 1 mile west of Zion's east entrance to observe the distinctive waffle patterns on this huge white mound of sandstone. The stunning crosshatch effect visible today is the result of eons of freeze-and-thaw cycles that caused vertical fractures, combined with erosion that produced horizontal bedding planes. ⊠ *Zion–Mount Carmel Hwy..*

Court of the Patriarchs. This trio of peaks bears the names of, from left to right, Abraham, Isaac, and Jacob. Mount Moroni is the reddish peak on the far right that partially blocks the view of Jacob. Hike the trail that leaves from the Court of the Patriarchs Viewpoint, 1½ miles north of Canyon Junction, to get a much better view of the sandstone prophets; you may catch a glimpse of rock climbers camming their way up Isaac's sheer face. ⊠ *Zion Canyon Scenic Dr..*

Great White Throne. Dominating the Grotto picnic area near Zion Lodge, this massive Navajo sandstone peak juts 2,000 feet above the valley floor. The popular formation lies about 3 miles north of Canyon Junction. ⊠ *Zion Canyon Scenic Dr.*.

Fodor'sChoice   **The Narrows.** This sinuous 16-mile crack in the earth where the Virgin
   ★   River flows over gravel and boulders is one of the world's most stunning gorges. If you hike through it, you'll find yourself surrounded—sometimes nearly boxed in—by smooth walls stretching high into the heavens. Plan to get wet. ⊠ *Zion National Park* ✛ *Begins at Riverside Walk.*

Weeping Rock. Surface water from the rim of Echo Canyon spends several thousand years seeping down through the porous sandstone before exiting at this picturesque alcove 4½ miles north of Canyon Junction. A paved walkway climbs ¼ mile to this flowing rock face where wildflowers and delicate ferns grow. In fall, the maples and cottonwoods burst with color, and lizards point the way down the path, which is not suitable for wheelchairs. ⊠ *Zion Canyon Scenic Dr.*.

SPORTS AND THE OUTDOORS

Hiking is by far the most popular activity at Zion, with all sorts of trails leading to rewarding hinterland destinations: extreme slot canyons, gorgeous overlooks, verdant meadows, and dripping springs. Some sections of the Virgin River are ideal for canoeing (inner tubes are not allowed). In winter, hiking boots can be exchanged for snowshoes and cross-country skis, but check with a ranger to determine backcountry snow conditions.

BICYCLING

Zion National Park has something for every kind of biker. Mountain bikers can cake themselves with mud on the park's trails, and racers will find enough up and down to make their pulses race.

Zion has taken steps to become much more bicycle-friendly, including having bike racks at some of the facilities and on the shuttle buses themselves. If you are renting bikes by the hour from a Springdale outfitter, you can load your bike on the bus, have the shuttle take you to the last stop (Temple of Sinawava), and take an easy one-way pedal back to Springdale. ■ TIP➜ **When you're on the park road, shuttle buses and cars have the right of way. You're expected to pull off to the side and let them pass.**

Within the park proper, bicycles are allowed only on established park roads and the 3½-mile Pa'rus Trail, which winds along the Virgin River in Zion Canyon. You cannot walk or ride your bicycle through the Zion–Mount Carmel tunnels; the only way to get your bike past this stretch of the highway is to transport it by motor vehicle. ⊕ *www.nps. gov/zion/planyourvisit/bicycling.htm*

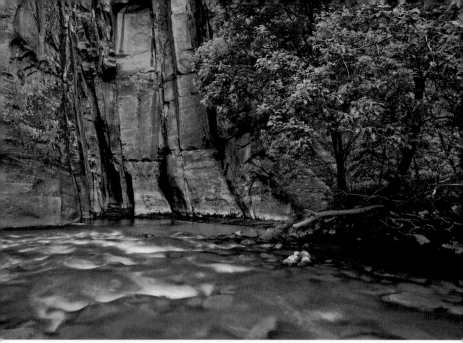

"There were great contrasts between the Narrows' red rock, green trees, and cool, clear water. This spot was an ideal swimming hole." —photo by Brad Campbell, Fodors.com member

TOURS AND OUTFITTERS

Bicycles Unlimited. A trusted southern Utah mountain-biking resource, this shop rents bikes and sells parts, accessories, and guidebooks. ⊠ *90 S. 100 E, St. George* ☎ *435/673–4492* ⊕ *bicyclesunlimited.com* ✉ *From $20 for 4 hrs* ☽ *Mon.–Sat. 9–6.*

Zion Cycles. This shop rents bikes by the hour or longer, sells parts, and has a full-time mechanic on duty. You can pick up trail and other advice from the staff here. ⊠ *868 Zion Park Blvd., Springdale* ☎ *435/772–0400* ⊕ *zioncycles.com* ✉ *From $45 for 4 hrs.*

BIRD-WATCHING

More than 200 bird species call Zion Canyon home, and scores more pass through the park on their annual migrations. Some species, such as the white-throated swift and ospreys, thrive in the towering cliff walls. Red-tailed and Cooper's hawks are abundant. Closer to the ground you'll doubtless see the bold Steller's jay and scrub jay rustling around the pinyon thickets. The wild turkey population has boomed in recent years; some of the flock might come your way looking for a handout. Five species of hummingbirds reside in the park, with the black-chinned variety being the most common. You might spot members of four transient species as well. Climb to the top of Angel's Landing and you might glimpse a bald eagle. Two of the park's rarest species are the Mexican spotted owl and the enormous California condor. ■TIP➔ Ask for the Zion Bird List brochure at the visitor center or download one. ⊕ *www.nps.gov/zion/learn/nature/birds.htm*

HIKING

The best way to experience Zion Canyon is to walk beneath, between and, if you can bear it (and have good balance!), along its towering cliffs. Trails vary, from paved and flat river strolls to precarious cliffside scrambles. Whether you're heading out for a day of rock hopping or an hour of meandering, pack and consume plenty of drinking water to counteract the effects of a high-altitude workout in the arid climate.

Keeping the sun at bay is a real challenge at Zion National Park. Put on sunscreen before you set out, and reapply at regular intervals. Because the park's hikes usually include uneven surfaces and elevation changes, wear sturdy shoes or hiking boots. Many veteran hikers carry good walking sticks, too, as they're invaluable along trails that ford or follow the Virgin River or its tributaries.

Zion is one of the most popular parks in the country, so it can be hard to envision just how alone you'll be on some of the less traveled trails. If you want to do a backcountry hike, make a reservation. Let park rangers know where you're going and when you plan to return.

■TIP➔ Park rangers warn hikers to remain on alert for flash floods; these walls of water can appear out of nowhere, even when the sky above you is clear. You can learn more about hiking safety and obtain a trail map at the visitor centers or online (⊕ *www.nps.gov/zion/ planyourvisit/hiking-in-zion.htm*).

EASY

FAMILY **Emerald Pools Trail.** Multiple waterfalls cascade (or drip, in dry weather) into algae-filled pools along this trail, about 3 miles north of Canyon Junction. The path leading to the lower pool is paved and appropriate for strollers and wheelchairs. If you've got any energy left, keep going past the lower pool. The ¼ mile from there to the middle pool becomes rocky and steep but offers increasingly scenic views. A less crowded and exceptionally enjoyable return route follows the Kayenta Trail, connecting to the Grotto Trail. Allow 50 minutes for the 1¼-mile round-trip hike to the lower pool, and an hour more each round-trip to the middle (2 miles) and upper pools (3 miles). *Lower, easy. Upper, moderate.* ✛ *Trailhead: at Zion Canyon Scenic Dr.*

FAMILY **Grotto Trail.** This flat trail takes you from Zion Lodge, about 3 miles north of Canyon Junction, to the Grotto picnic area, traveling for the most part along the park road. Allow 20 minutes or less for the walk along the ½-mile trail. If you are up for a longer hike and have two or three hours, connect with the Kayenta Trail after you cross the footbridge, and head for the Emerald Pools. You will begin gaining elevation, and it's a steady, steep climb to the pools, which you will begin to see after about 1 mile. *Easy.* ✛ *Trailhead: at Zion Canyon Scenic Dr.*

Pa'rus Trail. An approximately 2-mile, relatively flat paved walking and biking path, Pa'rus parallels and occasionally crosses the Virgin River. Starting at South Campground, ½ mile north of the south entrance, the walk proceeds north along the river to the beginning of Zion Canyon Scenic Drive. Along the way you'll take in great views of the Watchman, the Sentinel, the East and West temples, and Towers of the Virgin.

Leashed dogs are allowed on this trail. Wheelchair users may need assistance. *Easy. ✣ Trailhead: at Canyon Junction.*

FAMILY **Riverside Walk.** This 2-mile round-trip hike shadows the Virgin River. In spring, wildflowers bloom on the opposite canyon wall in lovely hanging gardens. The trail, which begins 6½ miles north of Canyon Junction at the end of Zion Canyon Scenic Drive, is the park's most visited trail, so be prepared for crowds in high season. Riverside Walk is paved and suitable for strollers and wheelchairs, though some wheelchair users may need assistance. Round-trip it takes about 90 minutes. At the end, the Narrows Trail begins. *Easy. ✣ Trailhead: at Temple of Sinawava shuttle stop, Zion Canyon Scenic Dr.*

MODERATE

FAMILY
Fodor'sChoice
★
Canyon Overlook Trail. The parking area just east of Zion–Mount Carmel tunnel leads to this popular trail, which is about 1 mile round-trip and takes about an hour to finish. From the overlook at the trail's end you can see the West and East temples, the Towers of the Virgin, the Streaked Wall, and other Zion Canyon cliffs and peaks. The elevation change is 160 feet. *Moderate. ✣ Trailhead: at Hwy. 9, east of Zion–Mount Carmel tunnel.*

Taylor Creek Trail. This trail in the Kolob Canyons area descends parallel to Taylor Creek, sometimes crossing it, sometimes shortcutting benches beside it. The historic Larsen Cabin precedes the entrance to the canyon of the Middle Fork, where the trail becomes rougher. After the old Fife Cabin, the canyon bends to the right into Double Arch Alcove, a large, colorful grotto with a high blind arch (or arch "embryo") towering above. To Double Arch it's 2¾ miles one-way—about four hours round-trip. The elevation change is 440 feet. *Moderate. ✣ Trailhead: at Kolob Canyons Rd., about 1½ miles east of Kolob Canyons Visitor Center.*

Watchman Trail. For a view of Springdale and a look at lower Zion Creek Canyon and the Towers of the Virgin, this strenuous hike begins on a service road east of Watchman Campground. Some springs seep out of the sandstone, nourishing the hanging gardens and attracting wildlife. There are a few sheer cliff edges, so supervise children carefully. Plan on two hours for this 3-mile round-trip hike that has a 380-foot elevation change. *Moderate. ✣ Trailhead: at Zion Canyon Visitor Center.*

DIFFICULT

Angels Landing Trail. As much a trial as a trail, this path beneath the Great White Throne is one of the park's most challenging hikes. Early on you'll work your way through Walter's Wiggles, a series of 21 switchbacks built out of sandstone blocks. From there you'll traverse sheer cliffs that have chains bolted into the rock face to serve as handrails in some (but not all) places. In spite of its hair-raising nature, this trail is popular. Allow 2½ hours round-trip if you stop at Scout's Lookout (2 miles), and four hours if you keep going to where the angels (and birds of prey) play. The trail is 5 miles round-trip and is not appropriate for children. *Difficult. ✣ Trailhead: at Zion Canyon Scenic Dr., about 4½ miles north of Canyon Junction.*

40

The vistas are stunning along Angels Landing Trail.

Fodor's Choice **Narrows Trail.** The hike on the Narrows Trail is a stunning and unique
★ nature experience, but it's no picnic. After leaving the paved ease of
the Gateway to the Narrows trail behind, the real fun begins. Rather
than following a trail or path, you walk on the riverbed itself. In places
you'll find a pebbly shingle or dry sandbar path, but when the walls of
the canyon close in, you'll be forced into the chilly waters of the Virgin
River, walking against the current—tack back and forth, don't fight it
head-on. A walking stick and shoes with good tread and ankle support
are highly recommended and will make hiking the riverbed much more
enjoyable. Be prepared to swim, as chest-deep holes may occur even
when water levels are low. Like any narrow desert canyon, this one is
famous for sudden flash flooding, even when skies are clear. Before hiking into the Narrows, check with park rangers about the likelihood of
flash floods. A day trip up the lower section of the Narrows is 6 miles
one-way to the turnaround point. Allow at least five hours round-trip.
Difficult. ✉ *Trailhead: at end of Riverside Walk.*

HORSEBACK RIDING

TOURS AND OUTFITTERS

FAMILY **Canyon Trail Rides.** Grab your hat and boots and see Zion Canyon the way
the pioneers did—on a horse or mule. Easygoing, one-hour and half-day
guided rides are available (minimum age 7 and 10 years, respectively).
The maximum weight allowed is 220 pounds. The friendly folks at Canyon, the only outfitter for trail rides inside the park, have been around
for years and know what they're doing. Reservations, recommended,

can be made online. ⊠ *Across from Zion Lodge* ☎ *435/679–8665* ⊕ *canyonrides.com* ✉ *From $40* ⊘ *Late Mar.–Oct.*

SWIMMING

Swimming is allowed in the Virgin River, but be careful of cold water, slippery rock bottoms, and the occasional flash floods when it rains. Swimming isn't permitted in the Emerald Pools. The use of inner tubes is prohibited within park boundaries, but some companies offer trips on a Virgin River tributary just outside the park.

WINTER SPORTS

Cross-country skiing and snowshoeing are best experienced in the park's higher elevations in winter, where snow stays on the ground longer. Inquire at the Zion Canyon Visitor Center for backcountry conditions. Snowmobiling is allowed only for residential access.

WHAT'S NEARBY

NEARBY TOWNS

Hotels, restaurants, and shops keep popping up in **Springdale**, population 529, on the southern boundary of Zion National Park, yet the town still manages to maintain its small-town charm—and oh, the view! There are many wonderful places to stay and eat, and if you take the time to stroll the main drag you can pick up souvenirs. A free shuttle carries you through town, or you can rent a bike.

If you have time to explore, there's always **Virgin, La Verkin,** and the ghost town of **Grafton,** which you might recognize from *Butch Cassidy and the Sundance Kid* and other films. Today there's only a stone school and a dusty cemetery. **Hurricane,** population about 14,000, has experienced much growth within the past decade and keeps sprouting new chain restaurants and lodgings. (Locals emphasize the first syllable, barely uttering the last.) There are historical sites, a world-class golf course, and the Hurricane Canal, dug by hand and used for 80 years to irrigate fields around town.

Heading east from Zion is **Mount Carmel Junction,** an intersection offering some funky small-town lodgings and the studio of American West artist Maynard Dixon.

Visitor Information Color Country Travel Region. ⊠ *St. George* ⊕ *utahtravelcenter.com/travelregions/colorcountry.htm.* **Kane County Office of Tourism.** ⊠ *78 S. 100 E, Kanab* ☎ *800/733–5263* ⊕ *www.visitsouthernutah.com.* **Zion Canyon Visitors Bureau.** ⊠ *118 Lion Blvd., Springdale* ☎ *888/518–7070* ⊕ *www.zionpark.com.*

40

NEARBY ATTRACTIONS

Coral Pink Sand Dunes State Park. Visitors to this sweeping expanse of pink sand enjoy a slice of nature produced by eroding sandstone. Funneled through a notch in the rock, wind picks up speed and carries grains of sand into the area. Once the wind slows down, the sand is deposited, creating this giant playground for dune buggies, ATVs, and dirt bikes. A small area is fenced off for walking, but the sound of wheeled toys is always with you. Children love to play in the sand, but check the surface temperature; it can become very hot. Off-road vehicles must have current registration. ⊠ *Coral Sand Dunes Rd./Hwy. 43, 12 miles west of U.S. 89, off Hancock Rd., Kanab* ☎ *435/648–2800* ⊕ *stateparks.utah. gov/parks/coral-pink* 🖾 *$8* ☉ *Daily sunrise–sunset.*

Maynard Dixon Living History Museum. Two miles north of Mount Carmel Junction, this was the final residence of the famous painter of Western life and landscapes. The property and log cabin structure are now maintained by the nonprofit Thunderbird Foundation for the Arts. Tours are self-guided or, from mid-March to mid-November, you can call ahead to arrange a docent tour. ⊠ *U.S. 89, mile marker 84, Mount Carmel* ☎ *435/648–2653* ⊕ *thunderbirdfoundation.com* 🖾 *$10; $20 for docent tour* ☉ *Daily 10–5, weather permitting.*

Snow Canyon State Park. Named not for winter weather but after a pair of pioneering Utahans named Snow, this gem of a state park is filled with natural wonders. Hiking trails lead to lava cones, sand dunes, cactus gardens, and high-contrast vistas. From the campground you can scramble up huge sandstone mounds and overlook the entire valley. Park staff lead occasional guided hikes. The park is about 10 miles northwest of St. George, and about an hour from Zion. ⊠ *1002 Snow Canyon Dr., Ivins* ☎ *435/628–2255* ⊕ *www.stateparks.utah.gov* 🖾 *$6 per vehicle* ☉ *Daily 6 am–10 pm.*

WHERE TO EAT

IN THE PARK

$
CAFÉ

✕ **Castle Dome Café & Snack Bar.** Next to the shuttle stop at Zion Lodge, this small fast-food restaurant is all about convenience. You can grab a banana, burger, smoothie, or salad to go, or while away an hour with ice cream on the shaded patio. This place gets busy during high season. ⑤ *Average main: $6* ⊠ *Zion Canyon Scenic Dr., 3¼ miles north of Canyon Junction* ☎ *435/772–7700* ⊕ *zionlodge.com.*

$$
AMERICAN

✕ **Red Rock Grill.** A monopoly on in-park fine dining has not made this restaurant at Zion Lodge complacent. The fare is solid American, with steaks, seafood, and Western specialties such as trout and bison meat loaf headlining the dinner menu. Photos of the area landscape adorn the walls of the spacious dining room, and the large patio has gorgeous views of the real thing. Salads, sandwiches, and hearty burgers are among the lunch highlights, and for breakfast you can partake of the plentiful buffet or order off the menu. Make a reservation for dinner,

40

especially during the summer. $ *Average main: $18* ⊠ *Zion Lodge, Zion Canyon Scenic Dr.* ☎ *435/772–7760* ⊕ *zionlodge.com/dining.*

PICNIC AREAS

FAMILY   **The Grotto.** Get your food to go at the Zion Lodge, take a short walk to this lunch retreat, and dine beneath a shady oak. The amenities include drinking water, picnic tables, and restrooms, but there are no fire grates. A trail from here leads to the Emerald Pools. ⊠ *Zion Canyon Scenic Dr..*

Kolob Canyons Viewpoint. Take in a shaded meal with a view at this picnic site 100 yards down the Timber Creek Trail, 5 miles from Kolob Canyons Visitor Center. ✛ *On Timber Creek Trail at end of Kolob Canyons Rd.*

FAMILY   **Zion Nature Center.** On your way to or from the Junior Ranger Program you can feed your kids at the center's picnic area. When the center is closed, use the restrooms in South Campground. ⊠ *Zion Canyon Scenic Dr.* ✛ *Near entrance to South Campground, ½ mile north of south entrance* ☎ *435/772–3256.*

OUTSIDE THE PARK

$ ✕ **Bear Paw Café.** The wait for weekend breakfast at this Western-theme
AMERICAN   diner is worth enduring for the Belgian waffles, French toast nearly
Fodor's Choice   two inches thick, and cherries-jubilee, spiced-apple, and other flavor-
★   ful crepes. For lunch there are panini, regular sandwiches—the Bear Paw Two-Story Club is a local favorite—and generous salads. Juices, smoothies, sodas, and specialty teas and coffee blends are all on the mile-long beverages list. Breakfast service starts at 7 am. Lunch is served until 3. $ *Average main: $9* ☎ *75 N. Main St., St. George* ☎ *435/634–0126* ⊕ *bearpawcafe.com* ⊘ *No dinner.*

$$ ✕ **Benja Thai and Sushi.** In St. George's charming Ancestor Square, you
THAI   can dine on exotic Thai soups, salads, and specialty dishes, and choose from an extensive sushi menu. The room's tapestries, intricate wood carvings, and lilting music give it warmth and tranquillity, and large windows provide views of the landscaped courtyard dotted with quaint historic buildings. $ *Average main: $14* ⊠ *2 W. St. George Blvd., St. George* ☎ *435/628–9538* ⊕ *benjathai.com* ⊘ *No lunch Sun.*

$$ ✕ **Bit & Spur.** This laid-back Springdale institution has been serving locals
SOUTHWESTERN   and tourists for more than 30 years. The well-rounded menu includes fresh fish and pasta dishes, but the emphasis is on creative Southwestern fare such as roasted-sweet-potato tamales and chile-rubbed rib-eye steak. Craft beers and the popular house-made sangria complement the zesty cuisine. With a fountain and shade trees, the outside dining area is a veritable oasis on warm days. $ *Average main: $20* ⊠ *1212 Zion Park Blvd., Springdale* ☎ *435/772–3498* ⊕ *www.bitandspur.com* ⊘ *No lunch.*

$ ✕ **Main Street Café.** This quaint locals' café pours one of the region's best
CAFÉ   cups of coffee, a fine prelude or follow-up to the salads, sandwiches, hearty omelets, homemade soups, and generous hamburgers on the menu. If you have the time, linger outside on the shaded outdoor patio and watch the hummingbirds. $ *Average main: $8* ⊠ *138 S. Main St., Hurricane* ☎ *435/635–9080* ▤ *No credit cards* ⊘ *Closed Sun.–Tues. No dinner.*

$$ ╳ **Spotted Dog Café & Pub.** This restaurant is more upscale than most in
ECLECTIC Springdale, but its staff makes patrons feel right at home even if they
saunter in wearing hiking shoes. The exposed wood beams and large
windows that frame the surrounding trees and rock cliffs set a Western
mood, with tablecloths and original artworks supplying a dash of refine-
ment. The varied menu might include pastas, lamb, wild-game meat
loaf, and rainbow trout. Some of the vegetables and herbs are grown
on-site. With smart selections in all price ranges and from key regions
throughout the world, the wine list is simultaneously sophisticated and
accessible. ⑤ *Average main: $20* ⊠ *Flanigan's Inn, 428 Zion Park Blvd.,
Springdale* ☎ *435/772–0700* ⊕ *www.flanigans.com/dining* ☉ *No lunch.*

$$$ ╳ **The Switchback Grille.** Known for its USDA prime steaks and seafood
AMERICAN flown in fresh daily, the high-ceilinged Switchback has walls of windows
framing stunning views. Like all good steak houses, it serves comforting sides such as roasted potatoes and sautéed mushrooms. Though not
uniformly impressive, the wine list has many worthy selections, as does
the associated liquor store next door. ⑤ *Average main: $25* ⊠ *Holiday
Inn Express, 1149 S. Zion Park Blvd., Springdale* ☎ *435/772–3700*
⊕ *switchbackgrille.com* ☉ *No lunch.*

$$ ╳ **Zion Pizza & Noodle Co.** Creative pizzas and a kick-back atmosphere
PIZZA make this a great place to replenish after a trek through the canyon.
FAMILY Meat lovers can dive into the Cholesterol Hiker pizza, topped with
pepperoni, Canadian bacon, and Italian sausage. More adventurous
types can opt for a Thai, barbecue chicken, or rosemary-garlic pie,
the latter with five different cheeses but no sauce. This house of "food
worship"—a former church; just look for the steeple—also serves pastas
and craft beers and offers dining in an outdoor beer garden. ⑤ *Aver-
age main: $16* ⊠ *868 Zion Park Blvd., Springdale* ☎ *435/772–3815*
⊕ *zionpizzanoodle.com* ☉ *No lunch. Closed Dec.–Feb.*

WHERE TO STAY

IN THE PARK

40

$$$$ 🛏 **Zion Lodge.** If location is your key concern, you'd be hard-pressed to
HOTEL improve on a stay at the historic Zion Lodge: the canyon's jaw-dropping
beauty surrounds you, access to trailheads is easy, and guests can drive
their cars in the park year-round. **Pros:** guests can drive their cars in the
park year-round; incredible views; bike rentals on-site. **Cons:** pathways
are dimly lit (bring a flashlight); Wi-Fi and cell reception can be spotty;
sells out months ahead for summer. ⑤ *Rooms from: $209* ⊠ *Zion
Canyon Scenic Dr.* ☎ *888/297–2757 reservations only, 435/772–7700*
⊕ *zionlodge.com* ⇌ *76 rooms, 6 suites, 40 cabins* ❏ *No meals.*

OUTSIDE THE PARK

$$$$ 🛏 **Cliffrose Lodge and Gardens.** The canyon views and acres of lush lawns
HOTEL and flowers at this riverside hotel make it more than a place to rest
your head, and you could throw a rock and hit Zion National Park's
south entrance. **Pros:** restaurant; beautiful grounds and views; many

Best Campgrounds in Zion

The two campgrounds within Zion National Park—South and Watchman—are family-friendly, convenient, and pleasant, but in high season they fill up fast. Outside Zion are the park-affiliated Lava Point campground and some private campgrounds.

South Campground. All the sites here are under big cottonwood trees that provide some relief from the summer sun. The campground operates on a first-come, first-served basis, and sites are usually filled before noon each day during high season. Hwy. 9, ½ mile north of south entrance ☎ *435/772–3256*.

Watchman Campground. This large campground on the Virgin River operates on a reservation system between April and October, but you do not get to choose your site. Access road off Zion Canyon Visitor Center parking lot ☎ *435/772–3256, 800/365–2267* ⊕ *www.recreation.gov.*

room types; close to park's south entrance. **Cons:** pricey for this area. ⑤ *Rooms from: $209* ✉ *281 Zion Park Blvd., Springdale* ☎ *435/772–3234, 888/567–6027* ⊕ *cliffroselodge.com* ⟿ *41 rooms, 12 suites, 3 villas* ¶◎¶ *Breakfast.*

$$$$
HOTEL
Fodor's Choice
★
🏨 **Desert Pearl Inn.** Offering spacious rooms with vaulted ceilings, oversize windows, sitting areas, and a pleasing contemporary decor, this riverside lodge is special. **Pros:** striking views; some rooms sleep six; rooms facing river have balconies or terraces. **Cons:** pricey for this type of accommodation. ⑤ *Rooms from: $229* ✉ *707 Zion Park Blvd., Springdale* ☎ *435/772–8888, 888/828–0898* ⊕ *desertpearl.com* ⟿ *72 rooms, 1 suite* ¶◎¶ *No meals.*

$$$
B&B/INN
🏨 **Flanigan's Inn.** A tranquil inn with canyon views, Flanigan's has big, comfortable accommodations, including two private villas, and suites that sleep six. **Pros:** wide array of spa services; a meditation maze on the hilltop; smoke-free; good restaurant. **Cons:** not all rooms have views; smaller property, so you need to book far ahead. ⑤ *Rooms from: $169* ✉ *428 Zion Park Blvd., Springdale* ☎ *435/772–3244, 800/765–7787* ⊕ *flanigans.com* ⟿ *29 rooms, 5 suites, 2 villas* ¶◎¶ *No meals.*

$$$
HOTEL
🏨 **Holiday Inn Express.** A recent addition to the Holiday Inn Express chain, this property has smartly renovated guest rooms, but what hasn't changed is a location with amazing views and the convenience of being on the park's shuttle route. **Pros:** on shuttle route; beautiful views; room rate includes breakfast. **Cons:** breakfast area fills up fast. ⑤ *Rooms from: $200* ✉ *1215 Zion Park Blvd., Springdale* ☎ *435/772–3200, 800/439–4745 reservations only* ⊕ *holidayinnexpress.com* ⟿ *117 rooms, 6 suites* ¶◎¶ *Breakfast.*

INDEX

PHOTO CREDITS

Loic Bernard/iStockphoto. 523, Justin Mair/Shutterstock. 524, Eric Foltz/iStockphoto. 533, Pixelite/ Shutterstock. 537, Greg Epperson/age fotostock. 538, pmphoto/Shutterstock. Chapter 25: Lassen Volcanic National Park: 541, Craig Lovell/Eagle Visions Photography/Alamy. 542 and 544, NPS. 549, Shyam Subramanyan, Fodors.com member. Chapter 26: Mesa Verde National Park: 557, Bryan Brazil/ Shutterstock. 558-59 and 560, NPS. 565, Kerrick James. 569, gary yim/Shutterstock. Chapter 27: Mount Rainier National Park: 579, chinana, Fodors.com member. 580, Washington State Tourism. 582, Cornforth Images/Alamy. 592-93, zschnepf/Shutterstock. Chapter 28: North Cascades National Park: 599, LoweStock / iStockphoto. 600, Washington State Tourism. 601, Don Geyer/Alamy. 602, Alan Kearney/age fotostock. Chapter 29: Olympic National Park: 617, Rita Bellanca, Fodors.com member. 618, 19 and 620, Washington State Tourism. 626, Lindsay Douglas/Shutterstock. 634, Super-Stock/age fotostock. Chapter 30: Petrified Forest National Park: 643, Kerrick James. 644, NPS. 646, Robert Harding Picture Library Ltd/Alamy. 650, Clara/Shutterstock. 653, Kerrick James. Chapter 31: Pinnacles National Park: 657, David Zaitz / Alamy. 658, Mike Brake | Dreamstime.com. 659, Konstantin Sutyagin | Dreamstime.com. 660, Christian Arballo/Flickr [CC BY-NC 2.0]. Chapter 32: Redwood National Park: 671, iStockphoto. 672, Michael Schweppe/wikipedia.org. 674, WellyWelly/Shutterstock. 688, Mike Norton/Shutterstock. Chapter 33: Rocky Mountain National Park: 691, Stock Connection Distribution/Alamy. 692, NPS. 694, Eric Wunrow/CTO. 705, Harold R. Stinnette Stock Photography/Alamy. Chapter 34: Saguaro National Park: 717, Johnny Stockshooter/age fotostock. 719 and 720, NPS. 726, Sasha Buzko/Shutterstock. Chapter 35: Sequoia and Kings Canyon National Parks: 735, Robert Holmes. 737, Greg Epperson/age fotostock. 738, Robert Holmes. 749, urosr/Shutterstock. 757, Robert Holmes. Chapter 36: Theodore Roosevelt National Park: 767, North Dakota Tourism. 768, Alan Majchrowicz/age fotostock. 770, Bruce Wendt/North Dakota Tourism. 776, Jim Parkin/ Shutterstock. Chapter 37: Wind Cave National Park: 783, 785, 786, 799 and 801, South Dakota Tourism. Chapter 38: Yellowstone National Park: 809, funtravlr, Fodors.com member. 810, Public Domain. 812, Mark Newman/age fotostock. 824, Paul Stoloff, Fodors. com member. 832-840, Jeff Vanuga. Chapter 39: Yosemite National Park: 857, Sarah P. Corley, Fodors.com member. 858, Yosemite Concession Services. 859 (top), Andy Z./Shutterstock. 859 (bottom), Greg Epperson/age fotostock. 860, Doug Lemke/Shutterstock. 870, Rebalyn, Fodors.com member. 873, Nathan Jaskowiak/Shutterstock. 884-85, Katrina Leigh/Shutterstock. Chapter 40: Zion National Park: 891, John Vaccarelli, Fodors.com member. 892 and 893, Public Domain. 894, True North Images/age fotostock. 903, Brad Campbell, Fodors.com member. 906, Geir Olav Lyngfjell/Shutterstock. 908, Kerrick James. About Our Writers: Shelly Arenas, Courtesy of Jannie Anderson. Lisa Church, Courtesy of Kelly Thornton. Andrew Collins, Courtesy of Fernando Nocedal. Cheryl Crabtree, Courtesy of Bryn Berg. Mara Levin, Courtesy of Shelley Shelton. All other photos courtesy of the writers.

NOTES

ABOUT OUR WRITERS

Sarah Amandolare is a Los Angeles–based freelance journalist whose work has appeared in the *Los Angeles Times,* the *New York Times* online, *BBC Travel,* and *Salon,* among others. For this edition, she updated the Joshua Tree chapter.

 Shelley Arenas grew up in eastern Washington and has lived in the Seattle area since college. She's been a regular contributor to *Fodor's Pacific Northwest* and other guidebooks for more than a decade; she's also co-authored a book about Seattle for families and writes for several regional publishers. She updated the Olympic, North Cascades, and Mount Rainier chapters this edition.

Lea Brayton is a writer from southwest Montana who focuses on ecological criticism and landscape studies in the West. A graduate of Montana State University, Lea holds degrees in writing and modern languages. She currently lives in Bozeman, where she writes outdoor-oriented pieces for *Outside Bozeman* magazine and maintains the website ⊕ *leabrayton. my-free.website.* Lea updated the Grand Teton chapter.

Whitney Bryen has been exploring Colorado since she moved there in 2010. She is the assistant editor and community reporter for *Colorado Hometown Weekly* and the east Boulder County reporter for the *Boulder Daily Camera* and *Longmont Times-Call.* Whitney is also a contributor to About.com's Colorado travel page and has written for Colorado Public Radio, the *Denver Post,* and the *Colorado Springs Independent,* among others. Whitney updated the Great Sand Dunes chapter.

 Lisa Church is a freelance writer and photographer based in Moab, Utah. She is also the editor of the *Times-Independent,* Moab's hometown newspaper for more than a century. With roots in the South and the Midwest, Church has made her home in Moab for the past 20 years. Her work has appeared in a variety of newspapers and magazines, including the *Salt Lake Tribune, High Country News,* and *Mother Jones.* Lisa updated the Arches and Canyonlands chapters.

Martha Schindler Connors is a freelance writer in Evergreen, Colorado, where she lives with her husband and two dogs. She enjoys hiking and skiing. She updated the Experience, Planning Your Visit, and Great Itineraries chapters.

 Andrew Collins, a former Fodor's editor, updated Lassen Volcanic, Redwood, and Crater Lake. A resident of Oregon, he has authored more than a dozen guidebooks, is editor in chief of *The Pearl* (about Portland's hip Pearl District), and produces the website ⊕ *GayTravel.About.com.* He also writes a syndicated monthly travel column; writes about restaurants, art, and design for *Four Seasons Magazine* and travel for *New Mexico Magazine*; teaches food writing and travel writing for Gotham Writers' Workshop; and has contributed to *Travel & Leisure, Sunset,* and dozens of other periodicals.

 Native Californian **Cheryl Crabtree**—who updated the Channel Islands, Sequoia and Kings Canyon, and Yosemite chapters—has worked as a freelance writer since 1987. Cheryl is the editor of *Montecito Magazine.* Her articles have appeared in many regional and national publications, including *US Airways Magazine* and *Santa Barbara Seasons,* and annual visitor magazines in

Santa Barbara, Ventura, and Pismo Beach. She also co-authors *The California Directory of Fine Wineries* books, Central Coast and Napa/Sonoma/Mendocino editions.

Lindsey Galloway lives in Boulder, Colorado, and frequently overeats at the many restaurants on Pearl Street. She contributes regularly to BBC Travel and AOL Travel, and founded TravelPretty.com to document her perils in packing. Lindsey updated the Rocky Mountain National Park chapter for this edition.

Long-time Fodor's writer **Thomas D. Griffith,** who's penned articles for such publications as the *Chicago Tribune, Denver Post, New Zealand Herald,* and *Rolling Stone India,* lives with his wife, Nyla, in Deadwood, South Dakota. He's written or co-authored more than 60 books, including *Fodor's Compass American Guides: South Dakota* and *American's Shrine of Democracy,* with a foreword by President Ronald Reagan. This edition, he updated the Badlands, Theodore Roosevelt, and Wind Cave chapters.

Melynda Harrison is a writer, naturalist, and social media manager. Her stories can be found in *High Country News, Backpacker Magazine, Big Sky Journal, Montana Quarterly, Women's Adventure, Montana Parent, Outside Bozeman, Great Falls Tribune, Carve,* and *Snowshoe Magazine.* Her company, YellowstoneTrips.com, specializes in vacation coaching and itinerary building for travel in and around Yellowstone National Park.

Aimee Heckel is a Colorado native who has been working at Colorado newspapers for 15 years. She is currently features writer at the *Boulder Daily Camera,* as well as the Colorado travel expert for About.com, a regular travel writer for *USA Today* 10Best.com, and a travel writer for ShopBlog. For this edition, she updated the Mesa Verde chapter.

Deb Hopewell lives, surfs, and cycles in Santa Cruz, California. Before embracing the life of a freelance writer, she was the travel editor at Yahoo for six years, and a longtime editor and columnist at the *San Jose Mercury News* before that. Her writing has appeared in *Travel+Leisure, Outside, Architectural Digest, Sunset magazine,* Yahoo, and Smarter Travel, among others. She updated the Death Valley and Pinnacles chapters.

 Kellee Katagi has lived in eight U.S. states, but Colorado is by far her favorite—not least because of the glorious scenery and the adventures to be had in its southwest region. A former managing editor of *SKI Magazine,* Katagi is now a freelance writer/editor specializing in travel, sports, fitness, health, and food. When not at her desk, she enjoys playing in the Colorado mountains with her husband and her three grade-school-age budding explorers (Shaelyn, David, and A.J.). Katagi updated the Black Canyon of the Gunnison chapter.

 Mara Levin divides her time between travel writing, traveling, and social work. A native of California, Mara now lives in Tucson, where the grass may not be greener, but the mountains, tranquillity, and slower pace of desert life have their own appeal. She contributed to the Grand Canyon and Saguaro chapters.

There is no place freelance writer **Debbie Olsen** would rather be than hiking a beautiful mountain trail. This Canadian-based Fodor's contributor is the mother of four children. Her travel adventures appear regularly in the *Calgary Herald,* the *Red Deer Advocate,* and other publications.

Marty Racine has been roaming the mountains, canyons, and deserts of the American Southwest for most of his life. His award-winning journalism career includes two decades of feature writing for the *Houston Chronicle* and seven years as editor of the *Ruidoso (NM) News*. Marty updated Big Bend, Carlsbad Caverns, and Guadalupe Mountains.

 A Phoenix-based freelance writer and editor, Elise Riley left her native Arizona to report for newspapers across the country. She quickly learned that no place had Mexican food like the Valley, and eventually found the way back to her favorite salsas and enchiladas. This edition, she contributed to the Grand Canyon, Petrified Forest, and Saguaro chapters.

When Stina Sieg was 9, she explored the U.S. for two years with her family in a colorful, converted school bus. She has been addicted to travel ever since. Based in Phoenix, she's now a writer, photographer, and radio reporter who's always on the hunt for quirky, heartfelt stories. Her work has appeared on NPR and in Fodor's guidebooks to Utah, and the Carolinas and Georgia.

 Michael Weatherford has been an entertainment reporter for the *Las Vegas Review-Journal* since about the time The Mirage opened. He is the author of *Cult Vegas—The Weirdest! The Wildest! The Swingin'est Town on Earth!* As a contrast to all that Las Vegas show business, he and his wife Joan, a freelance writer, like to explore the natural attractions of Nevada and southern Utah. He updated Bryce Canyon, Capital Reef, and Zion.